TECHNICAL ANALYSIS OF STOCKS & COMMODITIES™

VOLUME 10

Edited by Jack K. Hutson

D1360842

Technical Analysis, Inc., 3517 S.W. Alaska St., Seattle, WA 98126-2700 (206) 938-0570

SAN   661-5317   Technical Analysis, Inc., Seattle, WA 98146-0518

Library of Congress Cataloging in Publication Data
Main entry under title:
Hutson, Jack K., 1948-
Technical Analysis of STOCKS & COMMODITIES: Volume 10

   Includes bibliographies and indices.
   Contents: v.1. Profitable Trading Methods, v.2. Investment Techniques, v.3. Successful Speculation, v.4. Intelligent Trading, v.5. Trading Strategies, v.6. Market Timing, v.7. Volume 7, v.8. Volume 8, v.9. Volume 9, v. 10. Volume 10.
   1. Investments 2. Stocks 3. Stock exchange 4. Securities 5. Commodity Exchange 6. Futures 7. Speculation 8. Finance 9. Forecasting.

   1. Hutson, Jack K. 2. Title: Technical Analysis of Stocks & Commodities: Volume 10. 3. Title: Stocks & Commodities. 4. Technical Analysis, Inc.

   HG4521.T38   1992   332.63'2 86-50575

   ISBN 0-938773-00-3 (pbk. : v. 1)
   ISBN 0-938773-01-1 (pbk. : v. 2)
   ISBN 0-938773-02-X (pbk. : v. 3)
   ISBN 0-938773-03-8 (pbk. : v. 4)
   ISBN 0-938773-04-6 (pbk. : v. 5)
   ISBN 0-938773-05-4 (pbk. : v. 6)
   ISBN 0-938773-07-0 (pbk. : v. 7)
   ISBN 0-938773-08-9 (pbk. : v. 8)
   ISBN 0-938773-09-7 (pbk. : v. 9)
   ISBN 0-938773-11-9 (pbk. : v. 10)
   ISSN 0738-3355 Serial magazine
   ISSN 1060-328X Book volume series

 10 9   8   7   6   5   4   3   2   1

ISBN 0-938773-11-9

PREFACE

The contents of this book are derived from the pages of *Technical Analysis of Stocks & Commodities*, a magazine that documents and explains practical trading techniques for stocks, bonds, mutual funds, options and commodities. Listening to the news and your broker's advice without any real understanding of the underlying forces and signals from the market usually results in a long-term loss. The reasons behind this are simple: It is impossible for anyone to hear all the news; and your broker is primarily a salesman and will rarely have the time to analyze all the issues as well as sell. A successful trader's best adjunct to these classic techniques is to simply learn how to read the market.

The market is a mass psychology-driven animal that reacts to outside stimuli in a predictable manner. The purpose of this book is to teach you how to recognize some of these repetitive, predictable market patterns and to introduce you to several analytical techniques that speed up the process of eliminating bad trades.

Trading can be rewarding, frustrating and extremely exciting. At least 60% of all trading is done on the floor of the stock or commodity exchanges. The traders there are professionals. There is no middle man between them and the actual trade. They watch the news as avidly as you and I do, and they watch the market respond to that news. The information contained in this book starts you on your way to learning how to read the response to that news and to trade based on that response.

Since it is impossible for anyone to know all the news all the time, you can concentrate your efforts by studying the motion of the market. This is primarily associated with price and volume studies. These studies can often predict changes in the market and can likely indicate significant changes where you can buy or sell profitably simply by tagging along with the bulk of the professional traders. Without these tools, it is impossible for you to compete in a professional's game.

While names, addresses and telephone numbers referred to in this book may have changed since original publication of the magazine, the methods that describe how to trade the markets have proved to be useful year after year.

Jack K. Hutson
Seattle, Washington, U.S.A.
December 1992

Table of Contents

CHAPTER 1

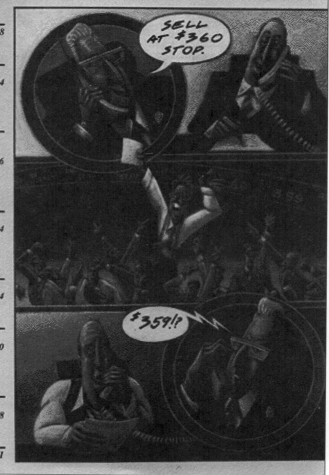

Slippage Costs Of A Large Technical Trader

If traders rely on technical trading systems, they need to know the size of slippage, which is the difference between estimated transaction costs and actual transaction costs. Authors Greer, Brorsen and Liu decided to use the trading record of a technically oriented money manager to determine slippage for the fund's transactions using 11 commodities and stop orders.

Slippage, which is the difference between estimated transaction costs and actual transaction costs with the difference usually composed of a price difference, occurs for stop† orders when prices move past the stop price before the order can be filled. Traders relying on technical trading systems need to know the size of slippage and how it varies across commodities when evaluating alternative technical trading systems, but this information, for one reason or another, has not been easily available in the past. So we used the trading record of a managed futures fund to determine slippage for the fund's transactions and thus thus provide previously unavailable information.

A study conducted recently by *Wall Street Journal* reporter Stanley Angrist discovered that slippage averaged $17 per contract for the 11 commodities covered here. From the results, it appears that slippage for a large technical trader may be higher than for the average trader. These large technical traders are often accused of causing sudden intraday price moves that cannot otherwise be explained. Comparing the slippage we discovered to that found in Angrist's study provides information about whether this fund trades when the market is moving quickly.

Traders relying on technical trading systems need to know the size of slippage and how it varies across commodities when evaluating alternative technical trading systems.

by Thomas V. Greer, B. Wade Brorsen and Shi-Miin Liu

SOURCES OF SLIPPAGE

Stop orders are instructions to the floor broker to execute the trade "at the market" if the futures contract trades at or through the specified price level of the order. The broker is ex-

†see Traders' Glossary for complete description

pected to fill the order at the best available price, but no guarantee or price limit comes with the order. Sell-stop orders always have a specified or trigger price that is below the last trade of the futures contract, while buy-stop orders always have a specified price above the last trade. Slippage can occur on stop orders once a trade occurs at the trigger price, at which point the order becomes a market order†. Even though this order is already on the floor in a "broker's deck†," in volatile markets it may not be possible for the broker to fill it at the target price. Since the market can move either way, slippage can be negative.

Many futures funds rely on technical trading models, which are usually trend-following. These funds may place stop orders for execution if market prices reach targets provided by the model. If several contracts are traded, it is less likely that all contracts will be purchased at the same price.

As a rule, stop orders should be executed at or near the specified price, since the broker holding them should be aware that a stop is about to be triggered. But trading by futures funds — and most other technical traders — is trend-following. Hence, if a buy stop is triggered, the market may move past the target before the order can be carried out. A study conducted in 1988 showed that different trading systems trade similarly and thus stop orders may be clustered together. Slippage may also occur when "gunning" or "gathering in" the stops, during which prices are driven down to where sell stop orders are presumed to exist. Stop orders then become market orders, adding liquidity to a thin market and giving floor traders a chance to profit.

DATA AND PROCEDURES

We used data from the trading records of a commodity fund that used a technical trading system in several commodity markets. The system was not continuously in the market, allowing for going long, short or neutral in the commodities traded. The fund used stop orders entered before daily trading opened for most of the trading period covered. The fund had assets of between $700,000 and $1.2 million. We examined records for 11 commodities traded between July 1984 and December 1986 — world sugar, coffee, pork bellies, soybean meal, heating oil, yen, Deutschemark, Treasury bills, copper, platinum and gold.

All market orders and limit orders were discarded. Generally, the commodities fund used market orders to roll contracts forward as they approached maturity and sometimes to get out of a losing position. Most of the trades were stop orders. Any transaction for which the target price was hit at or during the open was considered an interday gap. About a quarter of the trades occurred on the open. If the stop price was triggered on the open, that observation was deleted. The data used consisted of 297 trades. When the order was filled at multiple prices, a weighted average price (AP) was calculated. The target price was subtracted from the execution price for buys and the execution price was subtracted from the target for sells to determine slippage. The execution costs were multiplied by contract size (CS) to determine slippage in terms of

FIGURE 1

SLIPPAGE (LOSS) FOR STOP ORDERS Slippage in dollars per contract				
Commodity	**Mean**	**Min.**	**Max.**	**Stnd. dev.**
World sugar	$13.63	-$11.20	$200.20	$33.71
Coffee	$48.13	-$22.50	$168.75	$48.44
Pork bellies	$38.49	-$12.00	$168.00	$42.22
Soybean meal	$14.34	$0.00	$60.00	$21.46
Heating oil	$37.35	-$17.50	$109.39	$33.58
Yen	$18.53	-$12.50	$112.50	$28.86
Deutschemark	$18.06	$0.00	$162.50	$33.67
Treasury bills	$62.86	$0.00	$700.00	$139.51
Copper	$25.70	-$11.36	$62.50	$24.15
Platinum	$77.92	-$17.86	$280.00	$85.68
Gold	$65.80	$0.00	$410.00	$91.72
All	$38.16	-$22.50	$700.00	$69.15

Here are listed the 11 commodities studied, along with the mean, minimum and maximum slippage (loss) and the standard deviation.

dollars per contract (SLIP).

(1) SLIP = (AP - TARGET) x CS for buy order
(2) SLIP = (TARGET - AP) x CS for sell order

Regression models were used to explain slippage based on volatility, volume, size of order and market location. The study conducted by Angrist had no information on size of order and did no statistical tests of hypotheses. We gathered data from the

> **Slippage costs, which averaged $38.16 per contract, are presented in Figure 1. The largest slippage observed was $700 per contract for a Treasury bill trade.**

exchanges' statistical annuals on the price range on the day that transactions occurred (RANGE) and the volume for the contract on that day (VOLUME). A variable was created to measure the number of contracts traded, which was then divided by volume to show the size of the order relative to market activity (NCV). A dummy variable was created to show when the market was located in New York (NY) rather than Chicago. Thus, the model is:

(3) SLIP = a0 + a1 x RANGE + a2 x VOLUME +
       a3 x NY + a4 x NCV

The parameters were estimated using an algorithm, minimizing deviations around the median.

SOME RESULTS

Slippage costs, which averaged $38.16 per contract, are presented in Figure 1. The largest slippage observed was $700 per contract for a Treasury bill trade. Interestingly, academics shown these results found the slippage unacceptably high, while futures fund

FIGURE 2

Commodity	Contract size	Contract units	Minimum movement[1]	Avg size of order	Total number	Zero/neg. costs	Multiple executions[2]
World sugar	112,000 lbs	¢/lb	$11.20	9.5	44	22	15
Coffee	37,500 lbs	¢/lb.	$3.75	7.6	27	4	9
Pork bellies	38,000 lbs	¢/lb.	$9.50	18.1	27	0	8
Soybean meal	100 tons	$/ton	$10.00	21.8	11	7	1
Heating oil	42,000 gal.	$/gal.	$4.20	21.4	23	4	13
Yen	12.5 mil. yen	$/yen	$12.50	6.7	29	15	0
Deutschemark	125,000 marks	$/mark	$12.50	7.1	27	14	0
Treasury bills	$1 mil.	pts. of 100%	$25.00	5.2	35	25	0
Copper	25,000 lbs	¢/lb.	$12.50	24.6	26	5	14
Platinum	50 troy oz.	$/oz.	$5.00	16.1	27	4	12
Gold	100 troy oz.	$/oz.	$10.00	13.4	21	2	6
All				12.6	297	108	78

[1]Minimum price movement in dollars per contract (Commodity Trading Manual).
[2]Number of transactions that required trades at more than one price to complete execution of the order.

The individual contract specifications along with the data of the orders entered by the futures fund management are presented here.

managers shown the same results found the estimates relatively reasonable. Angrist's report pointed out that one trader received slippage averaging $3,850 per contract, which is considerably higher than the maximum of $700 per contract. Average slippage varied from $13.63 for world sugar to $77.92 for platinum.

Of 297 transactions studied, 108 had negative or zero slippage and 189 transactions had positive slippage (Figure 2). Gold had positive slippage for 90% of its transactions, while Treasury bills had positive slippage for only 29%. In 74% of all transactions, the entire order was executed at a single price. Most multiple transactions involved positive slippage, but some negative slippage also resulted.

The slippage is about double found by Angrist's study, which was to be expected because the fund is placing stops at the same level as other traders and the size of orders is also large. Edwin Lefèvre, in *Reminiscences of a Stock Trader*, argued a successful trading system should have higher execution costs, explaining, "It is surprising how many experienced traders ... who look incredulous when I tell them that when I buy stocks for a rise, I like to pay top prices, and when I sell, I must sell low or not at all." Thus, there is support for the belief that funds cause the market to move quickly intraday and can be said to increase intraday volatility.

Figure 3 shows the distribution of slippage in dollars per contract by commodity and is plotted by transaction, rather than by trade. Thus, minimums and maximums may differ from Figure 1. The mode† of most of the distributions is zero. The extreme slippage values resulted when the market moved quickly intraday, either due to new information or from a surge of orders from traders following a trend. For example, the $410.00 outlier† for gold occurred on July 31, 1986. *The Wall Street Journal* the next day reported that New York gold opened higher following the lead in London, where the activity in the market was so frenetic that five major London bullion houses needed nearly an hour to stabilize the price during morning trading.

The results of the median regressions are reported in Figure 4, suggesting that slippage size is most closely related to volatility. This is expected, since slippage is more likely to occur when prices are changing quickly. Median slippage is $10.00 a contract higher in New York markets than in Chicago markets. Slippage also increases with the size of the order relative to volume. Figure 4 reports parameter estimates from formula (equation) 3, explaining how to determine slippage in terms of dollars per contract (SLIP).

AND TO CONCLUDE

Slippage appears to be substantially higher for a technical trader than for the average trader. In general, slippage is higher than the execution costs of market orders found in previous studies. Slippage is substantially higher than the commission paid by large firms, all suggesting that firms should be more concerned about the fills they get than small differences in commission costs when choosing a broker. Since slippage for a futures fund is larger than it is for an average trader, this suggests that funds do indeed bunch orders together and may be responsible for increasing short-run volatility.

Technical trading systems and hedging strategies are sometimes developed and optimized without considering transaction costs, including brokerage commissions and slippage. Research suggests such costs can be significant, but they also vary across commodities. If stop orders are used, these added costs will have an adverse impact on expected results from such technical trading models. While such costs are usually small, the possibility of substantial slippage on a transaction still exists. Slippage increases as market volatility increases and as the size of order increases. Since slippage is correspondingly larger on large orders, commodity funds may find that slippage may be reduced by trading with several different systems and/or parameter sets. Lukac's study in 1988 showed that although different technical trading systems often did not signal trades on the same day, different trading systems do trade similarly and thus stop orders may be clustered together.

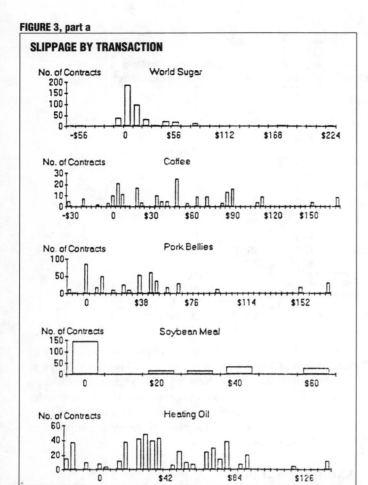

These histograms present the individual commodities' slippage in dollars per contract by transaction.

The question remains whether it might be better to watch the market and then use market orders or wait until after the initial run of stop orders has been filled and trade when the demand for liquidity is lower. In any case, the results certainly suggest that slippage will be larger for a large technical trader than it will be for the average trader.

Thomas Greer is a research assistant in the Department of Agricultural Economics at Purdue University. B. Wade Brorsen is an associate professor in the Department of Agricultural Economics at Oklahoma State University. Shi-Miin Liu is a post-doctoral researcher in the Department of Agricultural Economics at Purdue University.

REFERENCES

Angrist, Stanley W. [1991]. "Futures shock: Investors cope with slippage," *The Wall Street Journal,* April 30.

Commodity Trading Manual [1985]. Chicago Board of Trade.

Judge, George G., R. Carter Hill, William E. Griffiths, Helmut Lutkepohl and Tsoung-Chao Lee [1988]. *Introduction to the Theory and Practice of Econometrics,* John Wiley & Sons.

Lefèvre, Edwin [1980]. *Reminiscences of a Stock Operator,* Fraser Publishing, Burlington, VT.

Lukac, Louis P., B. Wade Brorsen and Scott H. Irwin [1988].

FIGURE 4

Estimated median regressions for slippage from futures trades of a managed futures fund[1]	
Explanatory variable	**dollars/contract**
Intercept	-2.77
	(-0.72)
Daily range	0.00678*
($/contract)	(6.89)
New York	10.571*
	(2.59)
Order size/volume	839.25*
	(4.24)
Volume	0.025
(1,000 contracts)	(0.13)

[1]The numbers in parentheses are approximate t-values and asterisks denote coefficients which are different from zero at a 5% significance level.

Slippage may be most closely related to volatility.

"Similarity of computer guided technical trading systems," *Journal of Futures Markets* 8.

The Wall Street Journal [1986]. August 1, p. 26, commodities page.

Chi Squared

Just how meaningful are statistics? Arthur Merrill explains how to find out.

by Arthur A. Merrill, C.M.T.

I f records show that market behavior exhibited more rises than declines at a certain time in the past, could it have been by chance? Yes. If a medicine produced cures more often than average, could it have been luck? If so, how meaningful *is* the record?

To determine how meaningful a particular statistic is, statisticians set up "confidence levels." If the result in question could have occurred by chance once in 20 repetitions, you can have 95% confidence that the result isn't just luck. This level is called "probably significant."

If the result in question could be expected by chance once in a hundred repetitions, you can have 99% confidence. This level is called "significant."

If the result in question could be expected by chance once in a thousand repetitions, you can have 99.9% confidence that the result wasn't a lucky record. This level is called "highly significant."

If your statistics are a simple two-way (yes/no, rises/declines, heads/tails, right/wrong), you can easily determine the confidence level with a simple statistical test — chi squared with Yates' correction, one degree of freedom.

The chi-squared formula can be seen in Figure 1. If the resulting chi squared is above 10.83, the confidence level is 99.9%. If the chi-squared result is above 6.64, the confidence level is 99%. If it is above 3.84, the level is 95%.

A sample calculation can be seen in Figure 2. If the expectation of the result seems to be about even, then the formula is simplified. The simplified formula is

CHRIS MILLS

FIGURE 1

CHI-SQUARED FORMULA
With Yates' correction, one degree of freedom

$$\chi^2 = (D - 0.5)^2 / E1 + (D - 0.5)^2 / E2$$

where:

$\chi2$ = chi square
D = O1 - E1 (If this is negative, reverse the sign; D must always be positive)
O1 = number of one outcome in the test
E1 = Expectation of this outcome
O2 = Number of the other outcome
E2 = Expectation of this outcome

If the resulting chi squared is above 10.83, the confidence level is 99.9%. If the result is above 6.64, the confidence level is 99%. If it is above 3.84, the level is 95%.

FIGURE 2

SAMPLE CALCULATION

Day	R	D	T	Er	Ed	χ^2
Mon	669	865	1,534	799	735	43.8
Tues	811	796	1,607	837	770	1.6
Wed	884	717	1,601	834	767	6.1
Thurs	845	743	1,588	827	761	0.7
Fri	912	670	1,582	824	758	19.3
t	4,212	3,791	7,912			
%	52.1	47.9	100.0			

R = Number of times the day was a rising day in the period 1952-83
D = Number of times it was a declining day
T = Total days
Er = Expected rising days
Ed = Expected declining days

Overall, there were more rising days than declining days, so the expectation isn't even money. Rising days were 52.1% of the total, so the expectation for rising days in each day of the week is 52.1% of the total for each day. Similarly, Ed = 47.9% of T.

For an example of the calculation of χ^2, using the data for Monday:

O1 = 669
E1 = 799
O2 = 865
E2 = 735
D = 669 - 799 = -130 (reverse the sign to make D positive)

$$\chi^2 = (130 - 0.5)^2 / 799 + (130 - 0.5)^2/735 = 43.8$$

This is a highly significant figure; confidence level is above 99.9%.

Market rises on Monday are not due to chance.

FIGURE 3

SIMPLIFIED FORMULA

If expectation seems to be even money (such as right/wrong), the formula is simplified:

$$\chi^2 = (C - 1)^2 / (O1 + O2)$$

where

$\chi2$ = chi-squared
C = O1 - O2 (if this is negative, reverse the sign; C must always be positive)
O1 = Number of one outcome in the test
O2 = Number of the other outcome

If the expectation of the result seems to be about even, then the formula is simplified.

in Figure 3.

I expect that you will find chi squared a useful tool. Using the formula in times of doubt will tend to keep you from leaping to a conclusion without an adequate foundation.

Arthur Merrill is a Chartered Market Technician and the author of many reports and books, including Behavior of Prices on Wall Street *and* Filtered Waves, Basic Theory.

Exponentially Smoothing The Daily Number Of Declines

MIKE CRESSY

This article presents an indicator that is the one-day rate of change of a triple exponential smoothing of the daily number of declines, an oscillator similar to TRIX (covered by Jack Hutson in the early years of STOCKS & COMMODITIES). Raff explains how the decline line, the number of stocks that have dropped in a given period (most often seen as a day), as the basis of this oscillator, could have warned of the impending stock market tumble in 1987.

The method looks good—but not good enough. It's deceptive: it works well enough, but in the period that Raff tried the method out on, it would have made only about 50% of a buy-and-hold strategy (although it would have shielded the user from violent declines in the period). He concludes that the method can be improved.

by Gilbert Raff

I found myself reading with piqued curiosity when in the May 1991 STOCKS & COMMODITIES John McGinley, the editor of the "Technical Trends" newsletter, was quoted as saying, "… the last 500 points of the crash of 1987 were, I think, uncallable. I held a contest in 1988 in which anyone who could produce an indicator that called the crash would get a free year's subscription to 'Technical Trends.'"

Always one to rise to a challenge, I found such an indicator and am happy to report it here for traders. (Please also see my article in the October STOCKS & COMMODITIES for a more long-term tool that predicted the 1987 stock market tumble.) Daily advances and declines on the New York Stock Exchange (NYSE) clearly provide much data about market internals and have been analyzed in many ways over the years. One particular example is in the form of the advance-decline line (Figure 1). Some analysts use trendline breaks in this line as an indication of changing direction, but in my experience, this is neither objective enough nor consistent enough to help the trader very much.

Further, daily advance and decline data tend to be very noisy — that is, the data have a great deal of random fluctuations (Figure 2). How, then, to use the data effectively?

HERE'S HOW

Jack Hutson described the triple exponential smoothing oscillator, a method that uses the one-day rate of change of a triple exponential moving average, in the early years of STOCKS & COMMODITIES. In MetaStock Professional, according to the manual, the TRIX indicator is (so there is no mistake about it):

The one-period percent change of an *x*-period exponential moving average of an *x*-period exponential moving average of an *x*-period exponential moving average of the closing price.

(See sidebar, "Triple exponentially smoothing a data series.")

I decided to apply this method to the daily advances and declines to see if a usable indicator could result. After some experimenting with the best number of days in the moving

> **I found that in the years 1981 through 1991, the indicator made 50% of the gains of a buy and hold strategy but was shielded from every violent decline during that period—a big plus.**

average, I found using 35 days in each average gave results that appeared to be useful. In examining the NYSE between 1981 and 1991, the declines are just a bit better getting in and out at the right time than either the advances or their crossover. When the 35-day TRIX of declines falls below zero, that is a signal to buy. When it crosses above zero, on the other hand, that is a signal to close a long trade. Because of the upward bias of the market, however, other indicators should be used in conjunction with this indicator to get useful short-sell signals.

To get back to the original challenge, how well did the indicator do in 1987, the year in question? If you check out Figure 3, it did very well indeed. Further, it did well in 1991 as well. Seem too good to be true?

Y our suspicions are absolutely correct. Both situations represented the start of strong trends in volatile markets. During flat markets, the indicator gave several false signals but rarely lost money and never very much (the largest loss in the 10-year period was 10 NYSE points). It was safe: When it said buy, you wouldn't have gone wrong. Many times, though, you would have been out of the market while some good upside progress ensued. I found that in the years 1981 through 1991, the indicator made 50% of the gains of a buy and hold strategy but was shielded from every violent decline during that period — a big plus. The advantage the indicator holds, therefore, is for the aggressive short-term trader who wants to go long

FIGURE 1

ADVANCE-DECLINE LINE VS. NYSE

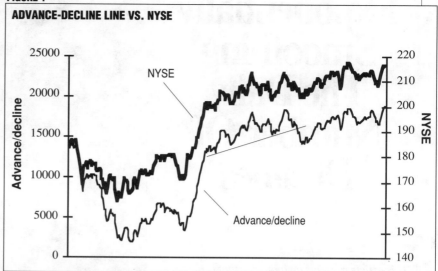

The advance/decline line is formed by using the net difference between each day's advances and declines, which is then added (if positive) or subtracted (if negative) to a running sum. Confirmation of new highs in the stock market by the advance-decline making new highs indicates broad market strength. Some technicians use trendline breaks as an indication of changing market direction.

FIGURE 2

DAILY VALUES OF ADVANCES AND DECLINES

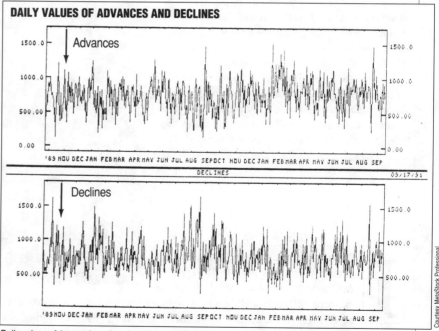

Daily values of the number of stocks advancing and stocks declining is very noisy, appearing to have a great deal of random fluctuations.

in an uptrending market with little risk of getting hurt in a market meltdown. In total, there were 30 buy signals in 10 years.

POSSIBILITIES

Can the TRIX declines be improved? Probably. Aside from combining it with other indicators, which is strongly recommended, it can be optimized by iterative testing — that is, hold all other variables constant and vary the first moving average by one day. Test the results over at least 10 years of NYSE data varying profitability, number of trades, the percent of successful trades and so forth. Then vary by one more day. After that, start the process over with the second moving average. To say this is tedious is certainly an understatement, since the number of potential combinations of the four variables, if we vary from, say, two to 60 days, is 60 to the fourth power — 1,296,000!

Obviously, this is a job for a computer. In the meantime, the TRIX declines (35-day) will keep you out of serious harm's way.

Gilbert Raff is president of Torsade Investments, Inc. He has traded equities and commodities since 1981. He trained in math and computer science at the Massachusetts Institute of Technology.

ADDITIONAL READING

Hartle, Thom [1991]. "John McGinley of Technical Trends," STOCKS & COMMODITIES, May.

Hutson, Jack K. [1983]. "Triple exponential smoothing oscillator: Good TRIX," *Technical Analysis of* STOCKS & COMMODITIES, Volume 1: July/August.

_____ [1984]. "Program enhancement: TRIX: Triple exponential smoothing oscillator," *Technical Analysis of* STOCKS & COMMODITIES, Volume 2: May/June.

MetaStock Professional. Equis International, P.O. Box 26743, Salt Lake City, UT 84126, (801) 974-5115.

Raff, Gilbert [1991]. "Trading the regression channel," STOCKS & COMMODITIES, October.

"Technical Trends," P.O. Box 792, Wilton, CT 06897, (203) 762-0229.

Warren, Anthony W. [1983]. "Optimizing TRIX: Further analysis of triple exponential smoothing," *Technical Analysis of* STOCKS & COMMODITIES, Volume 1: September/October 1983.

FIGURE 3

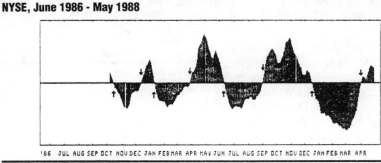

NYSE, June 1986 - May 1988

Smoothing the daily number of stocks declining with the 35-day TRIX produces the top chart. The rate of change of the number of stocks declining is negative whenever the oscillator drops below zero (the horizontal line), which is a positive indication for the market. If the oscillator is positive (above the horizontal line), then the rate of change of the number of stocks declining is positive, forewarning of a possible market decline.

FIGURE 4

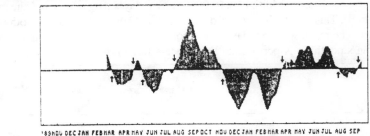

DECLINES AND THE 35-DAY TRIX
NYSE, October 19, 1989 - September 19, 1991

This indicator appears to perform best in markets where the trend is strong. During flat markets, the indicator has produced false signals.

Courtesy MetaStock Professional

TRIPLE EXPONENTIALLY SMOOTHING A DATA SERIES

One purpose of triple exponentially smoothing a data series is to remove meaningless fluctuations from the data while maintaining the correct appraisal of the direction of the trend. This is accomplished by smoothing the data three times with an exponentially smoothed moving average (EMA) using the same constant for the smoothing factor each time. The definition of an EMA is:

Exponential Moving Average —
The EMA for day D is calculated as: $EMA_D = \alpha\,PR_D + (1 - \alpha) \times EMA_{D-1}$, where PR is the price on day D and α (alpha) is a smoothing constant ($0<\alpha<1$). Alpha may be estimated as $2/(n+1)$, where n is the simple moving average length.

In the example of Figure 1, the number of stocks declining each day (column B) is smoothed three times (column C, D and E) using an EMA with an α estimated to approximate a 35-day simple moving average. The α is equal to 0.05556, which is determined by the formula $2/(n+1)$ where n =35. The smoothing process is simply three steps: Step 1) Subtract α from 1 and multiply the difference times yesterday's EMA (previous day in column C). Step 2) Multiply α (0.05556) by today's data (column B). This is today's adjusted data. Step 3) Add the two together. The result will be today's value for the EMA.

Triple smoothing is performing this process three times.

Once today's EMA (column C) is determined, then smooth today's EMA using the same α, which results in column D, then smooth this new EMA to complete the triple smoothing (column E).

The indicator Raff uses in his article is actually the one-day rate of change of the triple exponentially smoothed data. This is calculated by subtracting yesterday's triple-smoothed EMA from today's triple smoothed EMA and dividing the difference by yesterday's triple smoothed EMA. Finally, multiply this value by 100.

When first calculating an exponentially smoothed moving average, the previous day's EMA is the first day's data. If you start smoothing the data at another point, the final values can vary slightly from this example.

—Editor

SIDEBAR FIGURE 1

TRIPLE SMOOTHING USING EMA

	A Date	B #of declines	C 1st EMA	D 2nd EMA	E 3rd EMA	F Rate of change	G NYSE close
1	910903	955	955.00	955.00	955.00	0.0000	215.13
2	910904	1016	958.39	955.19	955.01	0.0011	213.95
3	910905	853	952.53	955.04	955.01	0.0002	213.47
4	910906	799	944.00	954.43	954.98	-0.0034	213.51
5	910909	803	936.17	953.41	954.89	-0.0091	213.14
6	910910	1181	949.77	953.21	954.80	-0.0098	211.00
7	910911	800	941.45	952.56	954.67	-0.0130	211.21
8	910912	604	922.70	950.90	954.46	-0.0220	212.42
9	910913	902	921.55	949.27	954.18	-0.0303	210.58
10	910916	704	909.46	947.06	953.78	-0.0415	211.65
11	910917	843	905.77	944.76	953.28	-0.0525	211.54
12	910918	700	894.34	941.96	952.65	-0.0660	212.23
13	910919	650	880.76	938.56	951.87	-0.0822	212.74
14	910920	653	=0.05556*B15+ (1-0.05556)*C14	0.05556*C15+ =(1-0.05556)*D14	=0.05556*D15+ (1-0.05556)*E14	=((E15-E14)/ E14)*100	212.98

Here, the number of stocks declining each day (column B) is smoothed three times (columns C, D and E) using an EMA with an α estimated to approximate a 35-day simple moving average.

The Gann Quarterly Chart

Longtime newsletter publisher Jerry Favors introduces a long-term indicator called the Gann quarterly chart, which will signal a turn up from bear market lows when the Dow Jones Industrial Average (DJIA) rallies above the high reached in the previous quarter during the trading day and not the high reached at the close of the trading day, which is more customary. Bear markets occur when the previous quarter's intraday low is breached. This technique requires careful monitoring of the intraday highs and lows of the previous quarter. Favors points out that W.D. Gann, who invented this particular technique, said that the upturns or downturns in this chart often signaled the onset of new bull or bear markets.

by Jerry Favors

The Gann quarterly chart, a long-term indicator, will signal a turn up from any bear market low when the Dow Jones Industrial Average (DJIA) rallies above the intraday high of the prior quarter. Until the DJIA falls below the intraday low of the previous quarter, the trend remains up. However, the trend turns down when the DJIA falls below the low of the previous quarter. Those quarters run the traditional schedule: January to March, April to June, July to September and October to December.

As each new quarter begins, for the Gann quarterly chart to be most effective it is necessary to keep track of the intraday high and low of the previous quarter. When prices rally above the prior quarter's high, they normally go significantly higher before a major top is reached. The converse is also true in that when prices fall below the intraday low of a previous quarter, they normally go significantly lower before a major bottom is reached. This technique is very effective. W.D. Gann stated that upturns or downturns in this chart often signaled the onset of new bull or bear markets.

Figure 1 shows every quarterly chart upturn or downturn since 1980. Notice that each upturn or downturn in the last 10 years led to what would be labeled a new bull or bear market. For

instance, the DJIA experienced a major low on March 27, 1980.

Second-quarter 1980 began on Tuesday, April 1. For the quarterly chart to signal a turn up, the DJIA in the second quarter needed to rally above the intraday high of the previous quarter. The intraday high of first-quarter 1980 was the 918.17 high seen on February 13. The DJIA failed to exceed that level by the end of second-quarter 1980, so the chart did not show a turn up.

THE THIRD QUARTER
Third-quarter 1980 began on Tuesday, July 1. For the chart to show a turn up in the third quarter, the DJIA had to rally above

FIGURE 1

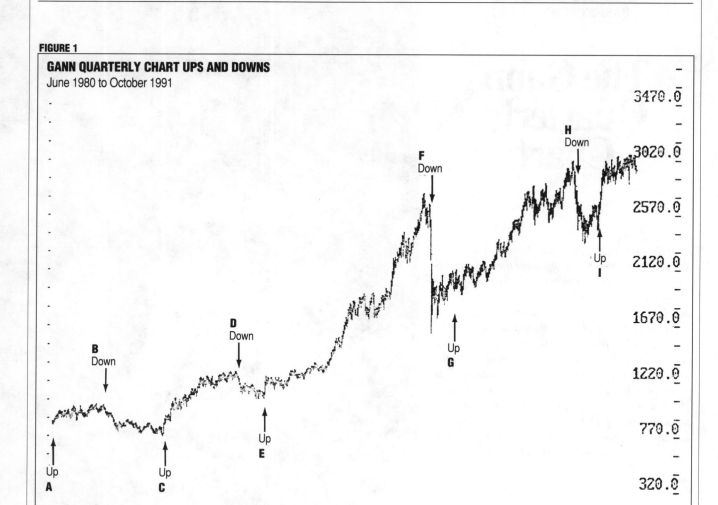

GANN QUARTERLY CHART UPS AND DOWNS
June 1980 to October 1991

Here is the weekly chart of the DJIA with the quarterly buy and sell signals placed. A buy signal occurs if the DJIA surpasses the previous quarterly intraday high. A sell signal occurs if the DJIA moves below the previous quarter's intraday low.

the intraday high of the second quarter, or the 896.33 intraday high of June 26, 1980. That occurred on July 7, 1980, at 896.34 intraday, and the quarterly chart turned up from there (point A on Figure 1). The bull market continued up 134 points more, or up 15%, to a bull market high of 1030 on April 27, 1981. The quarterly chart then turned down at 923.89 intraday on July 2, 1981 (point B). The bear market persisted, ultimately carrying prices down a further 154 points, or 17%, from the point at which the chart turned down.

The bear market bottomed on August 9, 1982, at 769 intraday. The quarterly chart then turned up on August 23, 1982, at 876.52 intraday (point C) in the DJIA. That leg of the bull market continued up a further 420 points, or 47.9%, from the point at which the quarterly chart turned up. The quarterly chart did not turn down during this time frame between August 23, 1982, to November 30, 1983. The quarterly chart then turned down on February 1, 1984, at 1209.33 intraday (point D). Here, too, a bear market followed, with prices continuing down 131 points, or a further

10.8%, after the signal was given. The quarterly chart turned up on August 3, 1984, at 1194.41 intraday. This confirmed that the next bull market leg up was under way.

> The DJIA continued down a further 283 points intraday, or 10.7%, before bottoming at 2344 on October 11, 1990.

In point of fact, the bull market continued higher by an additional 1,552 points, or up 129%, after the signal was given. Here again, the quarterly chart never *once* turned down throughout the entire 1984 to August 1987 bull market. The quarterly chart then turned down on October 15, 1987 (point F), at 2391.25 intraday. This was, of course, followed by the 1987 crash the following Monday.

FURTHER COLLAPSE
While the ensuing decline was brief in terms of time, the DJIA still collapsed a further 775 points, or down 32.4%, from the 2391.25 intraday level at which the quarterly chart turned down.

The quarterly chart then turned back up on April 12, 1988, at 2110.92 intraday (point G). Here again, the quarterly chart continued to point straight up from April 12, 1988, all the way up to the 3025 intraday high of July 17, 1990. The DJIA rallied 915 points, or up 43.3%, after the chart turned up—another very impressive signal. But ultimately the quarterly chart turned down on August 17, 1990 (point H), at 2627.69 intraday.

The DJIA continued down a further 283 points intraday, or 10.7%, before bottoming at 2344 on October 11, 1990. The quarterly chart turned up on January 18, 1991, at 2662.63 intraday. So far the DJIA has continued up 429 points, or up 16.1%, to a high of 3071 intraday in November 1991, as of this writing. Each up- or downturn in this entire 11-year period led to what most traders would label a bull or bear market. According to previous trends, the quarterly chart should turn down between October 1 and December 31, 1991, on any decline below 2836.31 *intraday* in the DJIA.

IN COMING MONTHS

Finally, it is normally true that the DJIA will reach a short-term high or low within one to three days after any up- or downturn in the quarterly chart. If 2836.31 intraday is broken, we should expect a short-term low within one to three days, and then an oversold rally attempt, which may last anywhere from a few days to a few weeks. Afterward, an even more severe decline to new lows should follow and most likely a major bear market.

Jerry Favors publishes "The Jerry Favors Analysis" newsletter, 7238 Durness Drive, Worthington, OH 43235, (614) 848-8177.

REFERENCES
Gann, W.D. [1942]. *How to Make Profits in Commodities*, Lambert-Gann Publishing Co.
_____ [1927]. *Tunnel Through the Air, or Looking Back from 1940*, Lambert-Gann Press.
Gartley, H.M. [1963]. *Profits in the Stock Market*, Lambert-Gann Publishing Co.

The Internal Dynamics of TRIN

by Jack Rusin

Consider four simplified trading days on the New York Stock Exchange:

Day 1: 1000 issues advance, 100 decline, with 1,000,000 shares up volume and 100,000 shares down volume. TRIN = (1000 / 100) / (1,000,000 / 100,000) = 10 / 10 = 1.00.

Day 2: 100 issues advance, 1000 issues decline, with 100,000 shares up volume and 1,000,000 shares down volume. TRIN = (100 / 1000) / (100,000 / 1,000,000) = 0.1 / 0.1 = 1.00.

Day 3: 1000 issues advance, 100 decline, with 1,000,000 shares up volume and 200,000 shares down volume. TRIN = (1000 / 100) / (1,000,000 / 200,000) = 10 / 5 = 2.00.

Day 4: 100 issues advance, 1000 decline, with 200,000 shares up volume and 1,000,000 shares down volume. TRIN = (100 / 1000) / (200,000 / 1,000,000) = 0.1 / 0.2 = 0.50. A TRIN below 1 is considered bullish.

The TRIN† (Figure 1) is a sophisticated yet simply calculated method of assessing relative volume flows. Conceptually, it is based on three ratios: the average declining volume, the average advancing volume, and a comparison between these two average volumes. It is an excellent way of measuring relative volume flows, but because of the mathematics of the index, it can yield counterintuitive results.

Most traders use a simpler method for assessing bullishness or bearishness, which may or may not be consistent with the TRIN figures. Rather than looking at daily and long-term moving averages of TRINs, those investors look at the daily and long-term net advances versus declines and whether the net volume is increasing. In fact, net advance-decline (Figure 2) considerations are central to technical analysis' conceptualizations of bullish and bearish.

Using these simpler, more common procedures, days 1 and 3 would be considered very bullish rather than neutral to bearish, the results obtained by TRIN analysis. Likewise, days two and four would be considered very bearish rather than neutral to bullish, the conclusion obtained by considering just the TRINs.

This is not to say one method is right and another wrong. Using TRIN is an excellent method of analysis, but it only goes so far. These examples illustrate substantial divergences not readily apparent when only the TRIN figures are used to represent the daily trading.

A MORE THOROUGH LOOK

To understand the cause of these divergences, a more thorough discussion of the TRIN is in order. Most often, TRIN is conceptualized as a comparison of the average daily up volume and the average daily down volume. If this is the case, TRIN as traditionally calculated is actually a comparison of the average daily down volume compared with the variable standard of the average daily up volume. If it were otherwise, a large TRIN would be bullish and a small one would be bearish.

These relationships are not immediately obvious from the way TRIN is traditionally calculated. With some simple algebraic transformations, however, the relationships become clear:

$$(1) \quad \text{TRIN} = (AI / DI) / (AV / DV)$$
$$(2) \qquad\qquad = (AI / DI) \times (DV / AV)$$
$$(3) \qquad\qquad = (DV / DI) \times (AI / AV)$$
$$(4) \qquad\qquad = (DV / DI) / (AV / AI)$$

where:
AI = Advancing issues
DI = Declining issues
AV = Advancing volume
DV = Declining volume

Thus, the daily TRIN is independent of the actual number of issues traded and of the actual net volume. In this way, TRINs can be meaningfully compared over a period of days, months or even years.

Further transformations suggest the cause of the potential divergence between the results obtained by TRIN analysis and by the simpler method of net advance-decline analysis:

†*See Traders' Glossary for complete description*

(2) Trin   = (AI / DI) x (DV / AV)
(5)   = (AI x DV) / (DI x AV)

 While it may not be immediately evident, the bullishness of Trin is directly related to the number of declining issues and inversely related to the number of advancing issues. Conversely, the bearishness of Trin is directly related to the number of advancing issues and inversely related to the number of declining issues.

This is diametrically opposed to what we get with the net advance-decline analysis. The more advancing issues, the more bullish the advance-decline reading is. Conversely, the more declining issues there are, the more bearish the A-D reading is.

> These four potential internal market dynamics lead to 13 potential Trins; five bullish, five bearish, three neutral.
> Of these 13, four are consistent with the internal market dynamics and nine are divergent.

With fractions, the larger the numerator, the greater the answer. Conversely, the larger the denominator, the smaller the answer. From Trin analysis, we know that a large number is regarded as bearish, while a small number is regarded as bullish.

With equation 5, it's possible to put the principles of mathematics together with the principles of Trin analysis to uncover the root of the divergence. In equation 5, everything above the slash is the numerator and everything below it the denominator. For simplicity's sake, only large values for the four variables will be considered. Obviously, the conclusions will be just the opposite for small values:

(1) *Advancing issues*: If we get a large numerator and thus a large Trin it is bearish.
(2) *Declining volume*: If we get a large numerator and thus a large Trin it is bearish.
(3) *Declining issues*: If we get a large denominator and thus a small Trin it is bullish.
(4) *Declining volume*: If we get a large denominator and thus a small Trin it is bullish.

How can Trin ever produce a result consistent with our more intuitive understanding of bullishness and bearishness? In point of fact, most Trins are more or less consistent with the net price change and the market's internal dynamics. To understand why, it is best to refer back to equation 1:

(1) Trin = (AI / DI) / (AV / DV)

The divergent aspect of Trin comes from the first half of the right-hand side of the equation. A large or small AI/DI ratio not modified by volume considerations will produce a divergent Trin. However, the Trin is a more complex and sophisticated measure than a simple advance-decline indicator is.

FIGURE 1

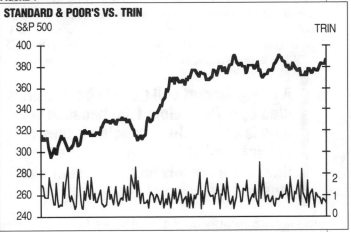

Plotting the one-day reading of Trin along with the S&P 500 provides an indication of the relative volume flows and extreme overbought readings below (0.80) and oversold readings (above 1.2).

FIGURE 2

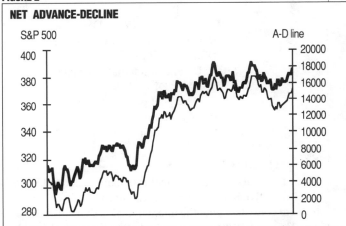

Many traders simply plot a cumulative sum of the daily advancing stocks minus the number of daily declining stocks to ascertain the underlying strength of the market.

With the Trin, the AI/DI part of the equation *is* modified by the relation between advancing and declining volume. The first part of the equation is divided by AV/DV, producing a result referring not just to the relationship between the advancing and declining issues, but between this relationship and the one between the advancing and declining volume.

In general, volume goes the way of the advance-decline ratio. When the market is advancing or declining sharply, usually the volume figures not only parallel the A-D figures but actually outdo them in the direction of the market move.

A sharply rising market will usually be accompanied by a Trin below 1.00 because volume is going into advancing issues vs. declining issues in greater proportion than there are advancing vs. declining stocks. If the AI/DI ratio is 2/1, volume can easily be coming into these shares at a rate of 3/1, for a theoretical Trin of 2/3 or 0.666 in this case.

Conversely, a sharply falling market usually produces a Trin above 1.00 because volume is going into declining issues vs.

advancing issues in greater proportion than the issues themselves are declining or advancing. If the AI/DI ratio is 1/2, volume can easily be coming into these shares at a rate of 1/3, producing a theoretical TRIN of 0.5/0.33, or 1.50 in this case.

While these two kinds of TRINs cover the majority of cases,

> **A rising market will usually be accompanied by a TRIN below 1.00 because volume is going into advancing issues vs. declining issues in greater proportion than there are advancing vs. declining stocks.**

they do not exhaust the range of possibilities. In these examples, the A-D and volume relationships were internally consistent and produced TRINs consistent with the internal dynamics of the market. It doesn't have to be this way. To start with, consider the four potential internal market dynamics (D):

D1: $AI \geq DI$; $AV \geq DV$
Result: Consistent internal dynamics
D2: $AI \geq DI$; $AV < DV$
Result: Divergent internal dynamics
D3: $AI < DI$; $AV \geq DV$
Result: Divergent internal dynamics
D4: $AI < DI$; $AV < DV$
Result: Consistent internal dynamics

MULTITUDINOUS TRINS

These four potential internal market dynamics lead to 13 potential TRINs; five bullish, five bearish, three neutral. Of these 13, four are consistent with the internal market dynamics and nine are divergent. Where the internal dynamics are themselves divergent, consistency is defined relative to simple advance-decline parameters. Where the advancing issues equal the declining issues, consistency is defined relative to the volume relationship.

D1: $AI \geq DI$; $AV \geq DV$
case 1: $AI = DI$; $AV = DV$; $AI / DI = AV / DV$
  $T = 1$; consistent TRIN
case 2: $AI > DI$; $AV > DV$; $AI / DI = AV / DV$
  $T = 1$; divergent TRIN
case 3: $AI > DI$; $AV > DV$; $AI / DI > AV / DV$
  $T > 1$; divergent TRIN
case 4: $AI > DI$; $AV > DV$; $AI / DV < AV / DV$
  $T < 1$; consistent TRIN
case 5: $AI = DI$; $AV > DV$; $AI / DV < AV / DV$
  $T < 1$; consistent TRIN
case 6: $AI > DI$; $AV = DV$; $AI / DV > AV / DV$
  $T > 1$; divergent TRIN

D2: $AI \geq DI$; $AV < DV$
case 1: $AI = DI$; $AV < DV$; $AI / DI > AV / DV$
  $T > 1$; divergent TRIN
case 2: $AI > DI$; $AV < DV$; $AI / DI > AV / DV$
  $T > 1$; divergent TRIN

D3: $AI < DI$; $AV \geq DV$
case 1: $AI < DI$; $AV = DV$; $AI / DI < AV / DV$
  $T < 1$; divergent TRIN
case 2: $AI < DI$; $AV > DV$; $AI / DI < AV / DV$
  $T < 1$; divergent TRIN

D4: $AI < DI$; $AV < DV$
case 1: $AI < DI$; $AV < DV$; $AI / DI > AV / DV$
  $T > 1$ consistent TRIN
case 2: $AI < DI$; $AV < DV$; $AI / DI < AV / DV$
  $T < 1$; divergent TRIN
case 3: $AI < DI$; $AV < DV$; $AI / DI = AV / DV$
  $T = 1$; divergent TRIN

For practical purposes, you will virtually never find a situation in which the advancing issues exactly equal the declining issues and the advancing volume exactly equals the declining volume. Ignoring this D1, case 1 possibility, the above chart simplifies to six situations.

D1, $T < 1$: internally consistent, externally consistent
D1, $T \geq 1$: internally consistent, externally divergent
D2, $T > 1$: internally divergent, externally divergent
D3, $T < 1$: internally divergent, externally divergent
D4, $T > 1$: internally consistent, externally consistent
D4, $T \leq 1$: internally consistent, externally divergent

From the above consolidated chart we can see that simply adding an internal dynamics classification number to TRIN considerably increases the amount of information we have about the market. Not all equal TRINs are created equally, and the analytical implications of each may vary depending on the internal dynamics that created them. This kind of internal dynamics classification is appropriate not only for daily TRINs but also for cumulative long-term issue/volume weighted moving averages described in "An issue/volume-weighted long-term Arms index."

However, while an internal dynamics classification number in conjunction with TRIN supplies significantly more information than TRIN alone, even this arrangement does not get to the heart of the problem. We have more information when we say that day 1 is D1:T1.00 while day 2 is D4:T1.00 (or, for simplicity, 1:1.00 and 4:1.00). We do not, however, have enough information yet.

Consider the possibility of a day 5:

Day 5: 800 issues advance, 400 decline, with 800,000 shares up volume and 400,000 shares down volume. TRIN equals 1.00, a neutral reading.

Comparing days 1 and 5 from a dynamics/TRIN perspective,

> **Comparing days 1 and 5 from a dynamics/TRIN perspective, we find that both are 1:1.00. While this gives us more information than simply saying that both TRINs are equal to 1.00, we certainly wouldn't say that these days were equivalent.**

we find that both are 1:1.00. While this gives us more information than simply saying that both TRINs are equal to 1.00, we certainly wouldn't say that these days were equivalent. Day 1 had an A-D ratio of 10 to 1, while day 5 had an advance-decline ratio of only 2 to 1.

At this point, you might be tempted to simply add the A-D ratio and be done with it. But the simple A-D ratio fails to take volume into consideration, and thus, we can considerably improve on this simple ratio if we can also factor volume into the equation.

Jack Rusin, P.O. Box 7016, Chicago, IL 60680-7016, is a private OEX options trader. He also writes a regular column, "Whither Goest Dow?" for ChiMe, the Chicago area Mensa newsletter.

FURTHER READING
Arms, Richard W., Jr. [1989]. *The Arms Index (TRIN),* Dow Jones-Irwin.
_____ [1991]. "Using the Arms index in intraday applications," STOCKS & COMMODITIES, April.
Rusin, Jack [1991]. "An issue/volume-weighted long-term Arms index," STOCKS & COMMODITIES, October. **TA**

Combining Sentiment Indicators For Timing Mutual Funds

Market sentiment can be useful in market timing, and mutual funds in particular. Here's a method in which a careful perusal of Investor's Intelligence, Market Vane *and* Barron's *can help you predict the best times to buy.*

by Joe Duarte

JOS PALMER

Market timing mutual fund purchases can be simplified by close observation of market sentiment. In his book *Winning on Wall Street*, technician Martin Zweig describes his use of sentiment indicators as predictors of future stock market direction. He describes two in detail: the 13-week moving average of the ratio of bulls/bulls + bears as provided by *Investor's Intelligence* (Figure 2), and the four-week moving average of bullish ads in *Barron's* (Figure 3).

Although the bullish ads indicator may be initially thought of as subjective, what's important is consistent interpretation on the part of the investor. I rate the ads as bullish or bearish, depending on how I feel after I read them, and I rate them the same way as they repeat in each issue. Any newsletter, company or mutual fund ad that touts its return I rate as bullish. If the word "short" or "put" is contained in the ad, I ignore the ad for the purpose of this oscillator, as I ignore neutral and negative ads.

I have added the Friday put/call ratio obtained in the Monday edition of *The Wall Street Journal* or *Investor's Business Daily*, the weekly Bullish Consensus numbers for Eurodollars, Treasury bonds and stock index futures, all found in *Barron's*, and whether the Standard & Poor's 500 is trading above its 20-day moving average to create a seven-indicator sentiment oscillator (Figures 3, 4, 5 and 6). A buy signal gives each indicator a value of 2 points. A sell signal is worth zero points.

Buy signals are as follow:
1. Bulls/bulls + bears 13-week average = <40%
2. Bullish *Barron's* ads four-week average = <7
3. Friday *Investor's Business Daily* put/call = >0.50
4. Bullish Consensus for each segment = <40%
5. S&P 500 above its 20-day moving average

Sell signals are as follow:
1. Bulls/bulls + bears 13-week average = >70%
2. Bullish *Barron's* ads four-week average = >15
3. Friday *Investor's Business Daily* put/call = <0.40
4. Bullish Consensus for each segment = >70%
5. S&P 500 below its 20-day moving average

> **Any newsletter, company or mutual fund ad that touts its return I rate as bullish.**

Seven indicators are involved. A total of 10 points gives a buy signal, while a reading of 4 gives a sell signal. I created the indicator in August 1988. Since then, it has given me 11 buy signals but no sell signals. The latest buy signal occurred July 19, 1991, correctly predicting the so-called summer rally. As of September 22, 1991, it was still on. Figure 1 illustrates the indicator's predictive success:

FIGURE 1

	S&P 500 in months			
Date	**1 mo.**	**3 mos.**	**6 mos.**	**1 year**
8/26/88	+3.54%	+2.9%	+10.8%	+32.59%
12/2/88	+1.29	+6.67	+19.76	+28.99
1/06/89	+5.47	+5.20	+14.56	+25.48
7/14/89	+3.38	+0.54*	+ 7.18	+10.68
12/8/89	+1.46	-3.08	+ 2.87	- 6.00
2/16/90	+2.76	+6.39	+ 0.00	+10.92
5/04/90	+8.60	+1.91	- 7.00	+12.53
11/2/90	+3.32	+10.00	+22.02	+25.48
1/18/91	+11.08	+16.92	+15.85	pending
6/14/91	-00.53	+00.34	pending	pending
7/19/91	+00.20	+1.99	pending	pending
Average	+ 2.68	+ 4.52	+ 9.56	+17.58

SUCCESS OF BUY SIGNALS MEASURED BY THE S&P 500

* Includes the market correction of October 1989

This table presents the percentage price changes over various periods after buy signals.

The S&P 500 has risen 91% of the time in the month following a buy signal, 91% of the time in the three months following, 75% of the time in the six months following and 86% in the year following. The indicator's ability to predict short and intermediate advances can be particularly useful in bear market rally-type scenarios as in May 1990. I trade mutual funds based on this configuration of well-proven indicators, which can be used in conjunction with the system described in the November 1991 STOCKS & COMMODITIES.

The oscillator has failed to give sell signals prior to significant market declines such as the October 1989 mini-crash, and market decline during the late summer and fall of 1990, but its record for predicting higher stock prices speaks for itself, as the market has recovered a large percentage of the time so far. Also, these declines, regardless of their dramatic nature, have been corrections in a long-term bull market, which started in the early 1980s.

In addition to following sentiment, I compare the S&P 500 to the broad market as represented by the Value Line Geometric Index. The charts of the S&P 500 and the Value Line illustrate how in 1990 the blue-chip laden S&P 500 outperformed the broadly based Value Line Geometric Index (Figure 7). The top line indicates the weekly closes of the S&P 500 and the middle line is the weekly closes of the Value Line Geometric Index. The bottom line reflects the difference in money flow to the S&P and the Value Line.

The upslope of the money flow line in 1990-91 illustrates the increased flow of capital into the S&P, suggesting that an index fund investing in S&P 500 stocks would have been a better investment than the average diversified stock fund during that period.

To calculate money flow on a weekly basis, subtract the closing price of the Value Line from that of the S&P 500 and plot a graph.

The sentiment oscillator is an excellent adjunct to this method and especially useful in short-term trading because of its excel-

FIGURE 2

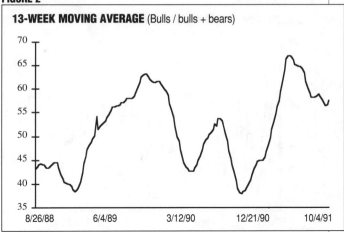

13-WEEK MOVING AVERAGE (Bulls / bulls + bears)

The 13-week moving average of the bulls/bulls + bears is plotted. Buy signals are flashed if the indicator is equal or less than 40%, while sell signals occur if the indicator is equal or greater than 70%.

FIGURE 3

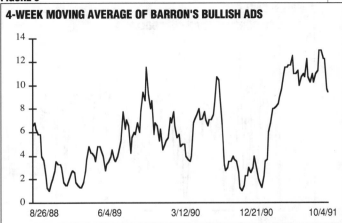

4-WEEK MOVING AVERAGE OF BARRON'S BULLISH ADS

The four-week moving average of the number of bullish advertisements found in Barron's is presented. This indicator is somewhat subjective. If the ad touts its return, then the ad is considered bullish. If the indicator declines to 7 or below, that is considered a buy signal. A sell indication occurs when the indicator moves to 15 or higher.

FIGURE 4

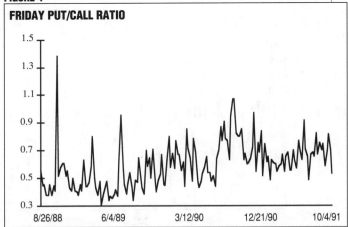

FRIDAY PUT/CALL RATIO

The put/call ratio is the volume of put options divided by the volume of call options found in Investor's Business Daily general market indicators. Only Friday's ratio is plotted. If the reading is equal or greater than 0.50, a buy signal is indicated, and if a reading is equal or less than 0.40, a sell is indicated.

FIGURE 5, PART A

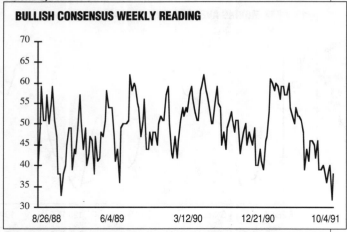

The weekly Bullish Consensus Index from Market Vane, found in Barron's, is a stock market sentiment indicator. Readings equal or below 40% indicate a buy opportunity, while readings equal or greater than 70% are sell signals.

FIGURE 5, PART B

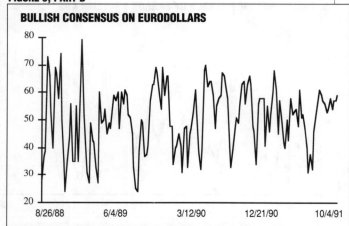

The Bullish Consensus index for the Eurodollar futures market from Market Vane indicates a buy if the index drops to or below 40% and a sell if the index reaches or surpasses 70%.

FIGURE 5, PART C

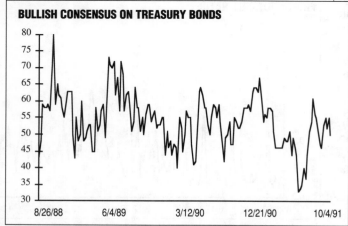

The Bullish Consensus index for the Treasury bond futures market from Market Vane indicates a buy if the index drops to or below 40% and a sell if the index reaches or surpasses 70%.

FIGURE 6

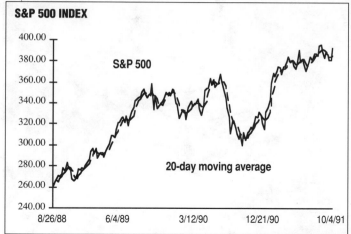

The S&P 500 is plotted along with the 20-day moving average. If the index declines below the moving average, a sell rating occurs, while a buy signal is indicated if the index is above the moving average.

FIGURE 7

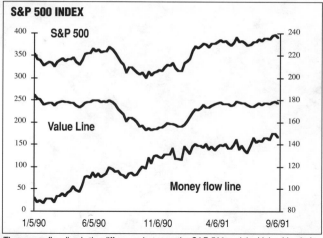

The money flow line is the difference between the S&P 500 and the Value Line index. The rising nature of the money flow line indicates that the S&P 500 is outperforming the broad market.

lent record of predicting the S&P 500 one month and three months after a buy signal. This tool is extremely useful for trading sector funds. By keeping mutual fund price data of a blue-chip fund and a small stock fund as well as several sector funds, the investor could easily have decided in which fund to invest.

To trade sector funds, just see which of the sector funds in your list responds best to the buy signals. In 1990 Fidelity Selects Biotechnology, Fidelity Selects Health Care, and Fidelity Selects Medical Delivery provided double-digit returns, while the S&P 500 and the other indices mostly languished.

In summary, an investor may profit from mutual funds by using the sentiment oscillator in combination with trend and momentum indicators to decide when to buy. By keeping daily or weekly price data of several mutual funds, including an S&P 500 index fund, a small stock fund and several sector funds, and by documenting whether money is flowing into larger or smaller stocks during the current market environment, the investor can

decide between blue-chip or smaller stock mutual funds. Sector funds are selected based on their response to the most recent sentiment oscillator buy signal.

Joe Duarte is an anesthesiologist and publishes a mutual fund newsletter, "The Wall Street Detective," PO Box 1623, Bowling Green, KY 42102-1623.

REFERENCES

Duarte, Joe [1991]. "Mutual funds as stock index proxies," STOCKS & COMMODITIES, November.

Zweig, Martin E. [1986]. *Martin Zweig's Winning on Wall Street*, Warner Books.

KRIEG BARRIE

Equivolume Using A Spreadsheet Program

Equivolume charting, which permits plotting price movements vs. volume instead of time, can be plotted by hand or with one of several charting programs, but a plain spreadsheet program on your personal computer can do the job and lets you add your own indicators. This author shows you how.

by James Leahy

quivolume charts, which were pioneered by Richard Arms, allow plotting price movements vs. volume instead of time as is usually done. The result of this graph is a rectangular box for each "point" plotted. The width of the box is represented relative to volume traded and the height of the box represents the high and low price range traded that period (Figure 1). Thus, when a stock price moves on high volume, the resulting box is wide. When the price moves on low volume, the box is narrow. This gives an indication of the ease of movement of the stock. A big price range on little volume means there is little resistance to price movements. Conversely, when the price moves little on heavy volume, there is a lot of resistance to price changes and could signal a turning point.

Several charting programs will plot Equivolume charts, but an ordinary spreadsheet and a personal computer can do the same for no additional cost. Using your own spreadsheet also allows you the flexibility of adding your own favorite oscillator to the Equivolume chart.

USING HIGH-LOW-CLOSE

Normally, stock prices are plotted on a spreadsheet using a high-low-close graph. This graph uses a vertical line to represent the high and low price range with a horizontal tick mark to represent the close. By using multiple entries per "point," the spreadsheet can create a box by using two vertical lines representing the sides and the close tick marks representing the top or bottom of the box. Some spreadsheets allow two tick marks per point, which normally represent opening and closing prices, allowing the box to be closed on top and bottom.

Since there are multiple entries per Equivolume "point," or box, it becomes tedious to enter these points manually. Therefore, using your spreadsheet's macro facility, you can automate the process so only three values need to be entered manually for each box. The following example illustrates how each box is formed. The spreadsheet used in this example is Quattro Pro version 1.0, but other popular spreadsheets have a similar function and work just as well.

FIGURE 1

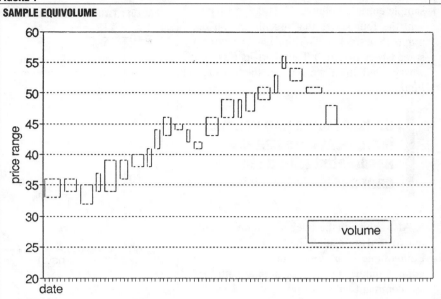

Equivolume charts use the price range for the vertical axis. The horizontal axis is the volume.

Before we plot the volume box, we need to pick an increment by which to calibrate the volume scale. This increment will vary from stock to stock, depending on the average daily volume for the stock. Stocks that have an average daily volume of 300,000 shares might use a volume increment of 75,000 or 100,000. The daily volume divided by the chosen volume increment determines the number of entries needed to form the base or top of the box and therefore determine the width. The stock with a 300,0000-share daily volume would end up with a box width of 3 or 4 points on a normal day's volume. A stock with a much lower daily volume would pick a lower volume increment. A stock with a higher average volume would pick a higher volume increment. It's best not to pick a volume increment that has less than 3 points per box width for an average day's volume.

The Quattro Pro spreadsheet program allows four entries for the high-low-close graph. The first two entries represent the lower and upper points, respectively, of the vertical line. The next two entries are normally used to represent the open and closing horizontal ticks. These four series are labeled LO, HI, UPPER and LOWER on the spreadsheet grid and can be plotted by Quattro's graphing facility. A daily spreadsheet entry for an Equivolume box consists of combinations of these four series. The left-hand side of the box is formed by the first HI, LO and UPPER entries. The base and top are formed by multiple UPPER and LOWER entries and the right-hand side is formed by the last LO, HI and LOWER entry. We enter one UPPER and LOWER row for each volume increment in the total volume. For example, if the volume is 30,000 shares and the volume increment is 10,000

we enter UPPER and LOWER values for two rows (the algorithm allows a closed box for a volume of less than or equal to the volume increment).

FROM THE BEGINNING

First, calculate the entries for a box manually. This example assumes a volume increment of 10,000 shares. Assume the stock had a daily low of 33 and a high of 36, trading 40,000 shares. The box is formed by entering the values in the appropriate column. The left side is formed by entering LO, HI and UPPER columns in the first row — 33, 36 and 36, respectively. We then subtract the volume increment, 10,000, from the total volume and enter values in the UPPER and LOWER columns. We repeat this process until the remaining volume is zero or less in the next row, and then enter the right side of the box by entering values in the LO, HI and LOWER columns. The resulting spreadsheet entries look like Figure 2:

FIGURE 2

SPREADSHEET ENTRIES			
LO	**HI**	**UPPER**	**LOWER**
33	36	36	
		36	33
		36	33
		36	33
33	36		33

By using a macro, we can automate this process and only enter values for low, high and daily volume. The date is entered for reference only and has no relevance in creating the Equivolume boxes. The cursor is left pointing to the low price entry and the macro is executed. Figure 1 in the sidebar represents the values that were generated by the macro for our sample entries. Columns G, H, I and J represent the four series that are plotted on the graph. (See sidebar, "Writing and executing a spreadsheet macro.") The chart in Figure 1 was plotted from the data in the sidebar's Figure 1.

> **Unusual price and volume increments are usually associated with a significant event.**

Also shown in the sidebar's Figure 1 is the macro used to calculate the numbers to plot the Equivolume chart given the low, high and volume inputs. The text beginning with "{;" are comments and are not executed by the macro. The table created is labeled "block." This reference offsets 0,0 into the table as the first row and column entry. The macro is called "Equi," as indicated by the label Equivolume.

The next macro listed entitled "Calcl" in the sidebar's Figure 1 is a subroutine called from the first macro. This macro implements the loop that fills in rows in the spreadsheet to create the top and bottom of the box. This subroutine loops until the volume calculation is zero or less. The volume number is moved to a temporary location for the calculation so as to not change the entered value. The macro keeps track of a row offset and uses this as an index to store the values to be plotted based on this value. When done, the updated index is stored in a temporary location for future reference when the next row of price and volume is entered.

VOLUME TIPS ON INSIDER TRADING

Unusual price and volume activity are usually associated with a significant event involving a company. Many times, this volume increases before the news is made public because those people who know or suspect a significant event is in the works buy or sell the stock long before others find out about it.

In applying this technique to trading stocks, consider the two-day Equivolume chart of Microsoft Corp. from October 5, 1990, to March 1, 1991. In Figure 3, I used a volume increment of one million shares. Notice that in both cases before a major move in

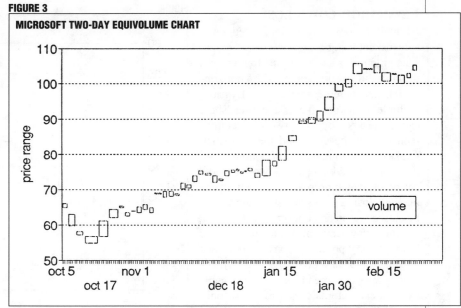

FIGURE 3

MICROSOFT TWO-DAY EQUIVOLUME CHART

This chart is a two-day Equivolume chart. The price and volume range encompass two trading days. Microsoft moved higher with good volume as indicated by the large boxes.

the price (in early October and mid-January), there was a large increase in the volume (wide boxes), accompanied by a large change in the stock price (tall boxes). This change in the normal pattern of the stock is easily determined on Equivolume charts. I have found that using short-term plot increments, either daily or every other day, results in the most accurate predictions of movements. Using weekly or larger increments tends to smooth out the volume and price jumps and makes them less apparent and useful. This is especially true of such volatile stocks as Microsoft.

James Leahy is an electrical engineer at a major computer manufacturer. He is a private investor and uses technical analysis and computer charting for trading in his personal account.

FURTHER READING

Hartle, Thom [1991]. "Arms on Arms," STOCKS & COMMODITIES, July.

_____ [1989]. "Trading T-bonds with Equivolume," *Technical Analysis of* STOCKS & COMMODITIES, Volume 7: September.

Quattro Pro. Borland International, 1700 Green Hills Road, Scotts Valley, CA 95066.

SIDEBAR FIGURE 1
PROGRAMMING

#	A	B	C	D	E	F	G	H	I	J	K	L	M	N	O	P	S
1	date	low	high	volume			lo	hi	upper	lower		0	vol_inc:	10000	upper_tick:	48	
2	1/1/91	33	36	40000			33	36	36		row->	75	price_inc	0.25	lower_tick:	45	
3	1/2/91	34	36	30000					36	33		3	equi:		{let lower_tick,@cellpointer("contents")}		{;initialize temporary location}
4	1/3/91	32	35	25000					36	33					{let index,0}		{;initialize index variable}
5	1/4/91	34	37	10000					36	33		-5000			{put block,column,row,@cellpointer("contents")}		{;store low entry}
6	1/5/91	34	39	25000			33	36		33					{r}		{;move cell pointer right one column}
7	1/6/91	36	39	20000			34	36	36						{let upper_tick,@cellpointer("contents")}		{;initialize temporary upper_tick}
8	1/7/91	38	40	25000					36	34					{put block,column+1,row,@cellpointer("contents")}		{;store hi entry}
9	1/8/91	38	41	10000					36	34					{r}		{;move cell pointer right one column}
10	1/9/91	41	44	9000			34	36		34					{let scratch,@cellpointer("contents")}		{;store a temporary copy of the volume}
11	1/10/91	43	46	14000			32	35	35						{calc1}		{; call the subroutine}
12	1/11/91	44	45	20000					35	32					{;put in the last entry to close the box}		
13	1/12/91	42	44	10000					35	32					{put block,column,row+index,lower_tick}		{; store lo entry for right side of box}
14	1/13/91	41	42	20000			32	35		32					{put block,column+1,row+index,upper_tick}		{; store hi entry for right side of box}
15	1/14/91	43	46	30000			34	37	37						{put block,column+3,row+index,lower_tick}		{;store upper tick for right side of box}
16	1/15/91	46	49	30000			34	37		34					{let row,row+index+1}		{;save row offset for next box plotted}
17	1/16/91	46	49	10000			34	39	39						{quit}		
18	1/17/91	47	50	20000					39	34							
19	1/18/91	49	51	30000					39	34							
20	1/19/91	50	53	10000			34	39		34							
21	1/20/91	54	56	10000			36	39	39								
22	1/21/91	52	54	30000					39	36							
23	1/22/91	50	51	40000			36	39	36								
24	1/23/91	45	48	25000			38	40	40								
25									40	38							
26									40	38							
27							38	40	38				calc1:		{ }		
28							38	41	41						{put block,column+2,row,upper_tick}		{;store upper tick}
29							38	41	38				loop:		{let scratch,scratch-vol_inc}		{;subtract volume increment}
30							41	44	44						{let index,index+1}		{;increment row offset value}
31							41	44	41						{if scratch<=0}{branch end}		{;test to see if done; branch if done}
32							43	46	46						{put block,column+2,row+index,upper_tick}		{;store another upper tick}
33									46	43					{put block,column+3,row+index,lower_tick}		{;store another lower tick}
34							43	46	43						{branch loop}		{;continue with loop}
35							44	45	45				end:		{return}		{;return to calling routine}
36									45	44							
37							44	45	44								
38							42	44	44								
39							42	44	42								
40							41	42	42								
41									42	41							
42							41	42	41								
43							43	46	46								
44									46	43							
45									46	43							
46							43	46	43								
47							46	49	49								
48									49	46							
49									49	46							
50							46	49	46								
51							46	49	49								
52							46	49	46								
53							47	50	50								
54									50	47							
55							47	50	47								
56							49	51	51								
57									51	49							
58									51	49							
59							49	51	49								
60							50	53	53								
61							50	53		50							
62							54	56	56								
63							54	56		54							
64							52	54	54								
65									54	52							
66									54	52							
67							52	54	52								
68							50	51	51								
69									51	50							
70									51	50							
71									51	50							
72							50	51	50								
73							45	48	48								
74									48	45							
75									48	45							
76							45	48	45								

WRITING AND EXECUTING A SPREADSHEET MACRO

A macro is a series of commands or keystrokes that can be stored for use for repeated operations. For all popular spreadsheets, macros can take on two different forms. One is a series of keystrokes that can be recorded as you enter them. This set of keystrokes can be saved in the spreadsheet and assigned a name for later reference. This kind of macro is useful for keystroke actions that are frequently performed, such as setting up a page layout for printing or entering repeated formulas or data. The second kind of macro is a series of commands that allow the user to perform calculations and make decisions as the macro executes. This kind of macro is similar to writing a program in a computer language, only in this case the language is the command set of the spreadsheet.

The macro used in creating the Equivolume chart is a command macro.

A command macro is more difficult to write because a precise syntax and grammar must be followed. Before writing a command macro, the writer must carefully design the algorithm and command flow, translate the algorithm into the allowable commands and then enter and debug the macro. This process is beyond the scope of this article but the comments in the Equivolume macro should explain the operation of the commands and the program flow. This sidebar explains the mechanics of writing and executing the Equivolume macro so the reader can tailor the macro to his or her particular application.

A macro is entered into spreadsheet cells as normal text. To differentiate a macro from ordinary cell entries, a special character is used to delimit the macro command. In the case of the Equivolume macro, the delimiters are the "brace" characters, { }. Text entered between these characters is interpreted by the spreadsheet program as a command to execute. When writing a macro, it is often necessary to reference cells where the source or destination of some calculation is located. Cells are labeled by a coordinate consisting of a row and column designation. The rows are referenced by numbers and the columns by letters.

However, the Equivolume macro does not reference cells by the row/column designation. Instead, it uses a label to reference cells. A label is text that has been defined in the spreadsheet to be associated with a particular cell location. The first label referenced in the Equivolume macro is referred to as a "lower_tick." This name is more meaningful when writing and debugging the macro than "cell O2," which is the actual location. To make the spreadsheet understand that it is supposed to use cell O2 whenever the phrase "lower_tick" is referenced, the label must be created in the spreadsheet and assigned the location O2. In Quattro, this is accomplished by pulling down the "Edit" menu, selecting "Names" and then "Create" in its dropdown menu. This causes a dialog box to appear where the label text can be entered (Figure 2). The user will then be prompted for the cell address to assign to the label.

This process is repeated until all labels have been defined. For all except the label "Block," one cell is referenced. For the label "Block," four columns and a thousand rows are referenced. (See Figure 4.) This label is associated with an array of cells. The first cell, F2, becomes row zero, column zero in the array. (Quattro assigns location 0,0 to the cell in the first column and first row in the array.)

This macro would work even if the labels weren't defined. It's possible to enter the actual cell location instead of the label. However, two disadvantages present themselves in doing this. First, the cell location reference makes it difficult to remember what the macro command was intended to do, and second, if rows or columns are later inserted in the spreadsheet, the cell location can move, causing the macro to reference the wrong cell. If labels are defined for the cell, the spreadsheet program will automatically update the label definition to point to the correct cell.

Once the macro is entered, all the labels defined and the data entered, the macro must be executed. To accomplish this in Quattro Pro, select the "Tools" pulldown menu (Figure 3), then the "Macro" selection, then the "Execute" selection. The spreadsheet will prompt for a cell block address. As the starting location of the macro has a label, the label can be entered in response to the prompt. An alternate method is to use the "hot key," ALT-F2. Likewise, this will prompt for the cell block address. Again, the label or the cell location for the first macro command can be entered.

Since the labels were defined for cell locations, we need a way to determine what cell is associated with the label. While this information is not normally needed once the macro is debugged, if the macro is copied to another spreadsheet or one of the constants must be updated, this information may be needed. One way to retrieve this information in Quattro Pro is to create a table of the labels and cell locations. This is done by selecting the "Edit" pulldown menu, then selecting "Names," then "Make Table" selection. The spreadsheet then prompts for a cell block location to insert the table. The entries shown in Figure 4 represent labels defined in Quattro and referenced in the macro.

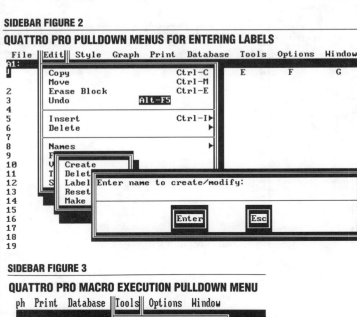

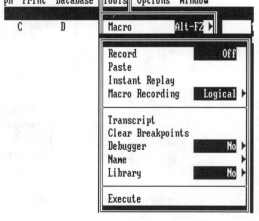

To execute the macro, select the "Tools" pulldown menu, then "Macro," then "Execute."

BLOCK	F2..I1001
CALC1	M29
COLUMN	K1
END	M37
EQUI	M3
INDEX	K3
LOOP	M31
LOWER_TICK	O2
PRICE_INC	M2
ROW	K2
SCRATCH	K5
UPPER_TICK	O1
VOL_INC	M1

The entries shown here represent labels defined in Quattro Pro and referenced in the macro.

Another easy way to identify the cell location is to enter the label text in the cell adjacent to the referenced cell. This provides an identification on the spreadsheet near the actual location of the macro.

NADIR KAINSERI

Using Futures And Options to Reshape Portfolio Risk

Portfolio management at its simplest is finding the highest possible return while limiting the risk involved. Because economic conditions constantly change, keeping to this goal requires moving assets in and out of the portfolio — a time-consuming and (worse) costly procedure. The goal can be reached without the tedious reshuffling, this writer says, if stock index futures and options are used.

Fraisse uses Standard & Poor's 500 index futures contracts as a tool with which to quickly increase a portfolio's exposure to market fluctuations if a money manager is bullish or decrease a portfolio's risk if a money manager is bearish.

by Jean-Olivier Fraisse, C.F.A.

imply, portfolio management consists of seeking out the highest possible return while simultaneously limiting investment risk. Changing economic conditions require periodic asset reshuffling, which is costly and time consuming. Futures and options offer a faster, cheaper and more effective way to redeploy assets or modify a portfolio risk profile. Since a portfolio beta† measures its systematic or market risk, to adjust portfolio risk, the portfolio's beta must be modified by introducing new assets or altering the weights of existing assets. If a portfolio manager

†See Traders' Glossary for complete description

is bullish on stocks, he or she can quickly increase the portfolio's stock exposure by purchasing stock index futures contracts such as the Standard & Poor's 500. If a portfolio manager is bearish, he or she can reduce the stock exposure by selling short stock index futures.

USING STOCK INDEX FUTURES

An S&P 500 futures contract is an agreement between seller and buyer to deliver and take delivery of, respectively, a portfolio of stocks represented by the S&P 500 stock price index at a specified future date. The delivery is a cash settlement of the difference between the original transaction price and the final price of the index when the contract is terminated. In practice, however, cash settlements occur in daily increments because futures positions are "marked to market†" until the contract is terminated as the contract trading price changes.

> **Buying a futures contract is equivalent to increasing a portfolio's market exposure by an amount equal to the contract's settlement value and reducing portfolio cash by an amount equal to initial and maintenance margin requirements.**

The price of an S&P futures contract is directly related to the price of the underlying S&P stock index. Since the S&P index has a beta of one, the beta of an S&P futures contract is also equal to one. A futures transaction may also have an impact on a portfolio's cash balance through margin requirements and final settlement. Cash balances are ignored when calculating a portfolio beta, since the beta of cash balances is equal to zero, but they must be included when calculating returns unless their yield is also equal to zero.

Buying a futures contract is equivalent to increasing a portfolio's market exposure by an amount equal to the contract's settlement value and reducing portfolio cash by an amount equal to initial and maintenance margin requirements. Conversely, selling a stock index futures contract will decrease stock exposure by the contract's settlement value and change cash amounts through payments received or made. At settlement, portfolio cash balances will reflect the full contract value. (See sidebar, "Modifying risk and return with S&P 500 futures," for details on the calculations for an increase in portfolio beta.)

Stock index futures also provide a convenient way to reshuffle portfolio assets quickly and are particularly helpful in separating market timing from stock selection, as they help increase market exposure before stocks to be purchased may be identified.

USING STOCK INDEX OPTIONS

Stock index futures options give the buyer the right — but not the obligation — to take a position in the underlying contract at any

MODIFYING RISK AND RETURN WITH S&P 500 FUTURES

Stock index futures modify risk by altering the portfolio beta and portfolio return by affecting cash balances. Take an example. A $10 million portfolio currently has a beta of 1.2. The manager wants to increase the beta to 1.4. How many S&P 500 contracts should he buy?

A portfolio beta is equal to the weighted average of individual assets' beta, each in proportion of their respective cost of total portfolio cost. Cash has a zero beta and so cash balances are ignored. Stock index futures have a beta of one. Consequently, the portfolio's beta is given by the formula:

$$A_p B_p = A_s B_s + A_f B_f$$

A_p and B_p are, respectively, the portfolio's cost and desired beta after the futures acquisition, A_s and B_s the current cost and beta prior to the acquisition, and A_f and B_f the futures' settlement value and beta (B_f equals one). Since the acquisition of the futures does not change the cost or nature of existing portfolio assets, excluding cash balances (which, if you recall, have a zero beta), A_p is equal to A_s.

Replacing all variables in the equation by their known values gives us:

$$\$10,000,000 \times 1.4 = \$10,000,000 \times 1.2 + A_f$$

Assuming that the S&P 500 futures is at 300, the value of one contract is 300 x $500, or $150,000. The number N_f of contracts to acquire to achieve the desired portfolio beta is then:

$$\$10,000,000 \times 0.2 = \$150,000 \times N_f$$
$$\text{or } N_f = 13.33$$

Thus, the purchase of 13 S&P 500 contracts would increase the portfolio beta to the desired level.

The purchase of stock index futures contracts may change the portfolio's cash balance if margin requirements are paid in cash. In addition, the total amount invested in stocks increased by the full settlement value of the futures contract. The impact of both must be taken into account when calculating the total portfolio return after the futures transaction. The rationale is the same to decrease a portfolio beta, except that futures would be sold rather than bought.

time before the option expires. Specifically, a call option gives the buyer the right to take a long position in the underlying contract, and a put option gives the buyer the right to take a short position in the underlying contract.

Since options are exercised only in the buyer's interest, their impact on portfolio risk is asymmetrical. A call buyer exercises his option only if the futures price exceeds the exercise price. Otherwise, the option simply expires and its sole impact on the portfolio is the cost of the option, the premium. When exercised, however, the call increases the portfolio beta and enhances the total return as if a futures contract had been bought. Similarly, a put is exercised only if the price of the stock index futures contract falls below the put exercise price, at which point it is equivalent to shorting the futures. When not exercised, its sole impact on the portfolio is the premium cost.

When futures and options contracts may be used to control a portfolio's systematic risk, options on individual stocks can help control unsystematic risk by increasing (that is, buying call options) or decreasing (that is, buying put options) exposure to price moves in an individual stock.

Jean-Olivier Fraisse, CFA, MBA, MS, is a consultant in international finance and a futures and options trader based in Washington, DC.

REFERENCES

Chicago Mercantile Exchange, *Using S&P 500 Stock Index Futures and Options*.

Fraisse, Jean-Olivier [1991]. "Assessing risk in an equity portfolio," STOCKS & COMMODITIES, December.

Harrington, Diana R. [1987]. *Modern Portfolio Theory, the Capital Asset Pricing Model & Arbitrage Pricing Theory: A User's Guide*, Prentice-Hall.

Maginn, John L., and Donald L. Tuttle [1990]. *Managing Investment Portfolio: A Dynamic Process*, Warren Gorham & Lamont.

Markowitz, H. [1952]. "Portfolio selection," *Journal of Finance*, March.

Sharpe, W.F. [1963]. "A simplified model of portfolio analysis," *Management Science*, January.

Futures According To Trend Tendency

Not all markets have the same tendency to trend. E. Michael Poulos uses his February 1991 STOCKS & COMMODITIES article, "Of trends and random walks," on the random walk index, which separates trends from random drifts by allowing for trend, as the basis of this article. He explains that the commodity futures you may for one reason or another assume trend strongly may not in fact. By using similar methods as previously, he produces a table of 28 commodities futures and debunks some futures assumptions — for instance, there is a school of thought that assumes that crude oil, gasoline and heating oil all show similar trending tendencies, whereas in truth crude oil and gasoline are near the top of the list, and heating oil, the poor country cousin, comes out only near the middle. Poulos goes into why.

by E. Michael Poulos

Which futures trend strongest? My February 1991 article, "Of trends and random walks," explained how the random walk index, which separates trends from random drifts by allowing for the direct measurement of trend, could be used toward this end. (See sidebar, "The random walk index.") By using a view of price-time history similar to the one used previously, we can determine how to rank various futures according to their inclination of trend. We attempted to maintain objectivity by not requiring the arbitrary choice of a predetermined fixed lookback interval (for example, the length of a moving average). Other attempted rankings of this kind are often questionable in result because they do not specially distinguish between random drifts and trends.

Some results may surprise you. For example, do you believe wheat trends stronger than corn? Or cattle trends stronger than hogs? Wrong. Cattle and wheat are the weakest of the 28 futures covered here. Corn, on the other hand, ranks near the top, sixth out of 28. Do you figure crude oil, gasoline and heating oil all show the same tendency to trend? Wrongo! Crude oil and gasoline are near the top of the list, while heating oil is well down toward the middle.

Some explanations are in order. The average channel height for yen (Figure 1) provides some. For the four-day channel length, for example, we start at Day 4 and look back for the highest high and the lowest low from Day 1 through Day 4. We record that high to low difference. We then repeat the above for Day 2 through Day 5, 3 through 6 and so on. We then average all these heights to get the average channel height figure for four-

day channels. This process is then repeated for each of the various channel length (that is, lookback intervals). The 2.29 ratio on the four-day row for yen is obtained by dividing the average four-day channel height by the average one-day channel height (141.7 divided by 62.0). For the sake of brevity, we show the average channel height only for yen, but the same procedure was used for all 28 futures (Figure 2).

As we indicated in "Of trends and random walks," these ratios follow, but tend to consistently exceed, the square root of the number of days. Notice that wheat, the weakest trender, barely manages to get beyond the square root figures (recall that 3 is the square root of 9, 4 is the square root of 16, and so forth).

Mathematician W. Feller showed that a "random walk" generated by tossing a coin (one step forward if heads, one step backward if tails) would show a displacement from the starting point, depending on the square root of the number of tosses.

The consistent move beyond the square root point

JOS PALMIERI

FIGURE 1

AVERAGE CHANNEL HEIGHT (YEN)

Channel length (days)	Square root of length	Avg. channel height (pts)	Ratio
1	1	62.0	1.00
4	2	141.7	2.29
9	3	224.9	3.63
16	4	310.8	5.01
25	5	403.3	6.50
36	6	502.6	8.11
49	7	605.2	9.76

The ratio of each average channel height to the average channel height for one day was greater than the square root of the length. This consistency indicates that the yen trends.

FIGURE 2

MARKETS RANKED BY TREND TENDENCY

Channel length (days)	Square root of length				Channel Height Ratio to One					
		Yen	Pound	Euro$	Cr. oil	U. gas	Corn	T-bill	S. meal	Beans
1	1	1.00	1.00	1.00	1.00	1.00	1.00	1.00	1.00	1.00
4	2	2.29	2.29	2.25	2.25	2.24	2.31	2.25	2.25	2.21
9	3	3.63	3.63	3.58	3.48	3.47	3.58	3.55	3.50	3.43
16	4	5.01	5.02	4.93	4.74	4.75	4.87	4.85	4.75	4.70
25	5	6.50	6.50	6.35	6.09	6.09	6.18	6.13	6.02	5.98
36	6	8.11	8.05	7.88	7.48	7.47	7.47	7.35	7.32	7.29
49	7	9.76	9.61	9.45	8.95	8.87	8.82	8.85	8.66	8.61
		D-mark	S. frnc	Can$	H. oil	S. oil	Coppr	Coffee	Belly	T-bond
1	1	1.00	1.00	1.00	1.00	1.00	1.00	1.00	1.00	1.00
4	2	2.25	2.22	2.21	2.23	2.19	2.18	2.18	2.18	2.15
9	3	3.47	3.44	3.46	3.45	3.39	3.40	3.40	3.38	3.28
16	4	4.66	4.63	4.74	4.65	4.64	4.63	4.61	4.61	4.43
25	5	5.93	5.89	6.16	5.93	5.90	5.86	5.83	5.82	5.62
36	6	7.25	7.23	7.30	7.21	7.15	7.12	7.11	6.99	6.89
49	7	8.63	8.64	8.57	8.48	8.45	8.44	8.41	8.22	8.12
		L. hogs	Cottn	Gold	Silver	Cocoa	SP500	NYSE	Sugar	L. catl	Wheat
1	1	1.00	1.00	1.00	1.00	1.00	1.00	1.00	1.00	1.00	1.00
4	2	2.14	2.17	2.18	2.15	2.18	2.28	2.15	2.12	2.14	2.15
9	3	3.31	3.30	3.32	3.31	3.34	3.26	3.27	3.20	3.28	3.25
16	4	4.79	4.44	4.45	4.44	4.49	4.37	4.37	4.31	4.36	4.33
25	5	5.73	5.61	5.60	5.57	5.61	5.50	5.50	5.43	5.43	5.39
36	6	6.88	6.82	6.78	6.78	6.77	6.68	6.66	6.59	6.52	6.41
49	7	8.07	8.09	7.99	8.05	7.93	7.92	7.86	7.74	7.63	7.40

January 1987 - June 1991 spliced nearby futures

The ratios shown above for yen and the S&P 500 are similar to those given in February, even though the histories differ: January 1975 through April 1990 for yen, and June 1982 through April 1990 for the S&P 500.

"There are times, Loretta, when I wish I had remained a teacher at the Harvard business school."

seen in all markets is evidence of trends. The yen clearly shows the strongest trending action, with its ratios well beyond the square roots, while wheat shows much less evidence of trends.

The price data used for this study were spliced nearby futures contracts. The splicing is such that the data file is always in the highest-volume nearby contract, with any price gap on rollover days shifted out by adjusting the new contract. The historical period was January 1987 to June 1991, four and a half years.

The rankings of the British pound and wheat were two of the biggest surprises, as far as I was concerned, so I thought it would be interesting to examine some of their charts. Figures 3 and 4 include the long-term random walk index (LRWI), a trend indicator. An LRWI of highs greater than 1.0 indicates a move beyond that expected for a random walk, and therefore an uptrend, while an LRWI of lows greater than 1.0 indicates a downtrend.

THE RANDOM WALK INDEX

The channel height ratio to one day figures given show a consistent excess beyond the square root column. This excess indicates the presence of trends and hints how to create a trend "yardstick." If no trends were present, the ratios would be expected to all fall exactly on the square roots, and thus an "expected random walk" over n days would be the square root of n multiplied by the average daily range (same as average one-day channel height).

We define the random walk index (RWI) as the ratio of an actual price move to the expected random walk. If the move is larger than a random walk (and therefore a trend), its index would be larger than 1.0.

To keep track of where today's high is relative to previous lows and where today's low is relative to previous highs, we need two indices:

$$RWI \text{ of high} = (H - Ln) / (Avg. \text{ rng.} \times \sqrt{n})$$

$$RWI \text{ of low} = (Hn - L) / (Avg. \text{ rng.} \times \sqrt{n})$$

where "Hn" and "Ln" are the high and low of n days ago and "avg rng" is the average daily range over the n days preceding today. In day-to-day use, these indices are calculated over a range of lookback lengths. Use the largest value returned for today's indicator. Thus, we let the market determine the lookback interval, rather than use a fixed arbitrary one as many current indicators do.

In addition, Figure 1 gives us a very important insight, showing the distribution of lookback lengths for the largest RWI (how many times did the largest RWI occur looking back two days, three days, four, five, six...?). Since the curve of

SIDEBAR FIGURE 1

NUMBER OF MAXIMUM INDEX OCCURRENCES
of occurrences lookback n for maximum RWI

x = S&P 500
• = T-bonds
o = Crude oil

No. of occurrences (y-axis): 100, 200, 300, 400, 500
Lookback n for maximum RWI (x-axis): 10, 20, 30, 40, 50

Figure 1 bends at a fairly sharp corner, the entire curve can be approximated by only two straight lines. This means that the markets, to a very good approximation, can be thought of as displaying two distinct personalities. The corner of Figure 1 is showing us where the dividing line between short- and long-term behavior is, between seven and eight days. We therefore calculate two RWIs, one for short term (two to seven days' lookback), and one for longer-term (eight days and up). The short-term one is a good overbought/oversold indicator and the long-term one is a very good trend indicator.

FIGURE 3

BRITISH POUND LWRI

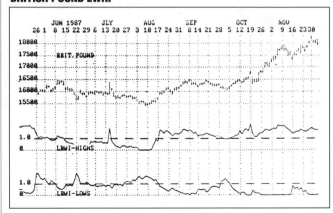
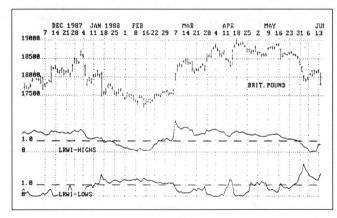
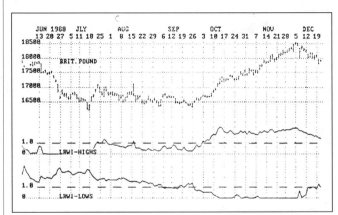
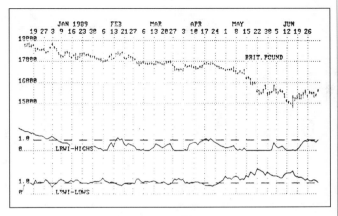
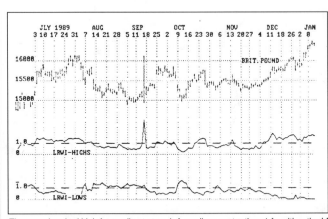
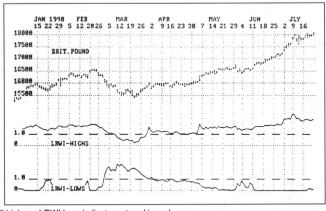

The pound ranked high for tending to trend. A reading greater than 1 for either the LRWI highs or LRWI lows indicates a trend is under way.

The charts show very clearly that the pound gets beyond the random walk boundary (with an index of 1.0) with greater strength and for more extended periods than wheat does.

If you're a trend-following futures trader, these rankings can help you answer one of your most important questions of which future to trade.

E. Michael Poulos, (516) 423-2413, writes software and works in the research and development of computer trading aids for Traders' Insight.

REFERENCES

Feller, W. [1968]. *An Introduction to Probability Theory and Its Applications,* Volume 1, John Wiley & Sons.

Poulos, E. Michael [1991]. "Of trends and random walks," STOCKS & COMMODITIES, February.

Stewart, Ian [1989]. *Game, Set and Math,* Blackwell Publishing.

Weaver, W. [1982]. *Lady Luck,* Dover Publishing. Does not refer specifically to random walk theory but does indicate that the standard deviation of the number of heads in a series of coin tosses varies as the square root of the number of tosses.

FIGURE 4

WHEAT LWRI

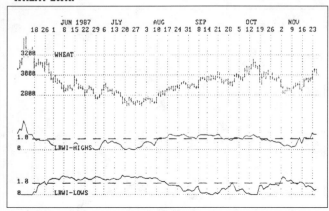

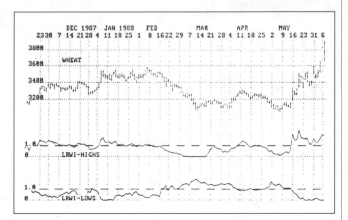

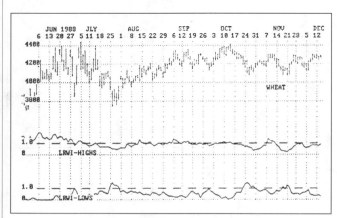

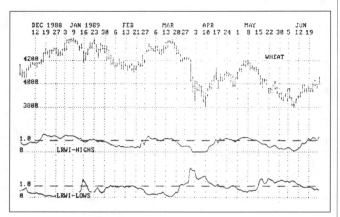

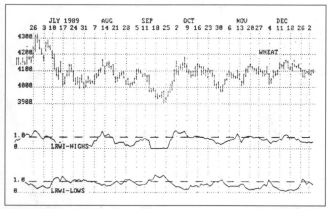

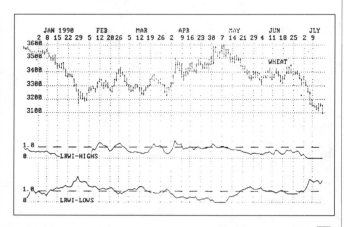

Wheat ranked last for trend tendency. Readings below 1 indicate a lack of a trend.

Testing Trading Rules Over Different Time Periods

by John Sweeney

After two Sundays of dinking around (Settlement, STOCKS & COMMODITIES, November and December 1991), I'd finally converted a chance idea to something with remotely promising prospects — something on the order of a three-to-one return on margin. I'd done that by emulating the basic ideas in four trading rules (Figure 1) plus two stops. As has been my experience, the stops were the most effective in improving the results and the stops were selected by the maximum adverse excursion (MAE) analysis (Figure 2) to cut off the big losers while allowing enough room for winners to be successful.

Many people look at Figure 2 and say, "Hey! We've got more losers than winners!" Right. That's normal. You want to look at the dollar income from that, as in Figure 3, because we know the test was profitable. This figure gives a better sense of whence the profits come. System Writer Plus accurately picked up two gap days when stops were ineffective, so we have an unusually high dollar loss on two trades, despite which our approach is profitable.

PROBLEMS ARISE

Even if profitable, the system raises questions. There are fewer than 30 trades, the magic number needed for reliability. Just one big winner earned a ton of money. What about other time periods? What about other tradeables? Couldn't the system be refined to be even more profitable by eliminating the losers?

To make the last first, refining things at this point is impossible. We're testing on too short a period to reliably sift through and spot problems in the logic. Better at this point to test on several other periods to find these problems, refine the system if possible and then retest on all the different periods. This iterative process, while tedious, usually highlights gaps in my trading concepts.

TESTING OTHER PERIODS

My first shot at how the system performed was with December 1986 Treasury bonds. Here (Figures 4, 5 and 6), the system with stops generated a $6,922 profit. Just to confirm the beneficial effects of stops, I ran the system on 1986 data without stops to produce a ($7,922) loss, then decided to keep the stops.

Incidentally, the work needed to rerun the entire system and get the results was two clicks to load in the new data and two clicks to invoke the system test — about 23 seconds on a slow

FIGURE 1

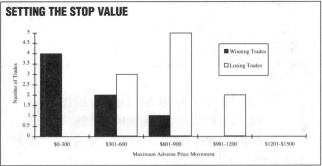

TRADING RULES

```
System: S&S w Stops.MDL
if (diff35 > trend35+.005 and diff35[1] < trend35[1]) then buy today at the
close;

exitlong tomorrow at entryprice - .7 stop;

if diff35 < trend35-.005 then exitlong today at the close;

if (diff35 < trend35-.005 and diff35[1] > trend35[1]) then sell today at the
close;

exitshort tomorrow at entryprice + .7 stop;

if diff35 > trend35+.005 then exitshort today at the close;
```

In the previous two Settlements, this logic was defined and tested successfully. I test it here on Treasury bond data in different periods. The [1] refers to yesterday's values.

FIGURE 2

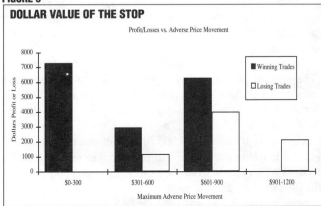

SETTING THE STOP VALUE

With a $700 stop, all the big losses and many of the middle-sized losses were cut off early.

FIGURE 3

DOLLAR VALUE OF THE STOP

The trades from Figure 2 generate sizable dollar profits, while the large dollar losses (over $700) are cut off, except for two trades where a gap prevented the stop from being fully effective.

Macintosh SE. This sort of productivity can remake your life!

My assessment of the 1986 results was that there were too many trades. I circled the areas of concern, vowing to come back to them later if other periods showed similar results. I also reviewed the graphics of the two indicators to see if these graphics were more accurate than those of 1989. There was a spare straight line visible in Figure 4 — I couldn't figure where that came from — and TREND35 still went way too high, as DIFF35 declined about the same time. The unreliability of the graphics made it tough to see if a key idea, skimming tops and bottoms of DIFF35 with TREND35 to define trend, worked.

Then I moved on to survey other years:

December	Wins	Losses	Profits	Figure
1986	5	19	$6,922	6
1987	7	16	16,580	7
1988	6	13	486	8
1989	7	10	9,282	
1990	5	17	5,091	9

Of course, this doesn't speak to total drawdown from a run of losses, but the stops controlled individual losses within my 2% of capital limit. Returns over a year run from 0 to 500% on margin, but clearly 1988 deserves close inspection. Figure 8 has highlighted the area that drew my attention.

This long sloping decline was perfect for trend profits. What

> ## No rule is going to be 100% effective in the market, so finding a few where the logic just didn't work isn't cause to change the logic.

happened? Checking the graphics of TREND35 and DIFF35, I found them still screwed up, so I went to the worksheet to check the trades on the chart against the actual numerical values of the indicators.

There were three buys (A, B and C) during the downtrend. (The upward-pointing arrow with a block on the bottom is a stop.) On inspection of the values of TREND35 and DIFF35, A and B turned out to be one-day anomalies in the relationship between the two time series. The anomalies were on the order of 0.003 and 0.016, after the 0.005 filter built into the logic.

Here is where people are tempted to adjust the filter and in System Writer Plus, it would be tempting to do so. You'd change the filter to a variable and then "optimize" its value so profits would be greater or there would be fewer losses. Don't do it. Filters should come from your trading logic, not a blind search for a value that works. Recall in the November Settlement that the value 0.005 was selected by inspection of the raw trading results with no stops. That inspection showed that nearly all one-day anomalies would be filtered out by the 0.005 value. Following Pareto's Law — 80% of re-

FIGURE 4

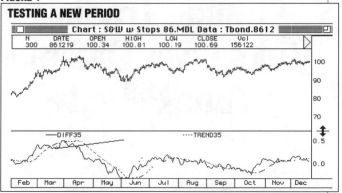

TESTING A NEW PERIOD

The system was originally developed on 1989 data. Shown here are the 1986 data and the indicators from which the system works. The graphic display of the two indicators is fouled up due to a bug in System Writer Plus Mac. The straight line is another bug. Graphics being fouled up means results must be checked manually.

FIGURE 5

1986 TRADING RESULTS

860327	99.00	120	860407	98.30	-765.00	4248.00	-765.00
860407	98.50	121	860408	99.72	-1284.00	-65.00	-1283.80
860612	92.00	198	860728	94.16	2091.50	8685.00	-65.00
860728	94.16	199	860729	94.86	-765.00	-65.00	-765.00
860729	95.62	202	860801	96.53	841.50	1466.30	-565.00
860801	96.53	207	860808	97.23	-765.00	1841.30	-765.00
860826	101.66	220	860827	100.88	-846.00	-65.00	-846.00
860827	100.31	221	860828	101.01	-765.00	-65.00	-765.00
860829	101.72	223	860902	101.02	-765.00	-65.00	-765.00
860902	99.72	233	860916	94.72	4935.00	6653.80	-65.00
860916	94.72	235	860918	94.02	-765.00	778.70	-765.00
860918	93.72	238	860923	94.42	-765.00	1653.80	-765.00
860925	95.66	240	860925	94.96	-765.00	-65.00	-765.00
860929	94.88	243	860930	95.58	-765.00	-65.00	-765.00
861022	95.59	278	861118	98.56	2903.50	3841.20	-65.00
861118	98.56	279	861119	99.26	-765.00	-65.00	-765.00
861119	99.84	281	861121	99.66	-252.50	310.20	-721.30
861121	99.66	282	861124	100.36	-765.00	-65.00	-765.00
861125	99.41	286	861201	99.41	-65.00	372.50	-502.50

#Wins	$Wins	#Loss	$Loss	#Trades	Net$	AvTrde	%Win
5	20082	19	-13160	24	6922	288	20.83

Trading the system on 1986 data shows a profit of about 2.8 times margin with only 21% of the trades being winners. Notice the large number of trades stopped at $765, which is the $700 stop plus slippage and commissions.

sults come from 20% of the effort — we should be happy with 80% effectiveness for our filters — which are really rules of thumb — because going for 100% (a single parameter hyperoptimized to 100% effectiveness) would create an exotic trading rule less robust in other periods than a rule that will

FIGURE 6

1986 TRADES

Inspecting the trades taken by the system to produce the results in Figure 5, I saw four areas of concern, areas with too many trades and suggestions of whipsaw. This also popped up elsewhere, so further evaluation will be necessary.

Courtesy SystemWriter Plus/Mac

FIGURE 7

1987 TRADES

N	DATE	OPEN	HIGH	LOW	CLOSE	Vol
81	870209	97.12	97.34	96.66	96.75	247910

Testing the system on 1987 yielded a solid profit, little whipsaw and good trend capture.

FIGURE 8

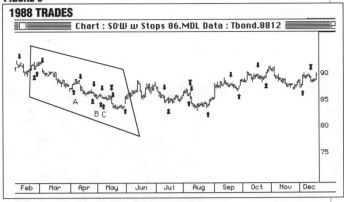

1988 TRADES

Trading looked good visually, but the year had a breakeven result. Alarming was the failure to fully capture the trend from February through June. This turned out to be explainable if not enjoyable.

FIGURE 9

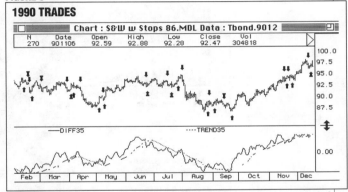

1990 TRADES

N	Date	Open	High	Low	Close	Vol
270	901106	92.59	92.88	92.28	92.47	304818

—DIFF35   ----TREND35

1990 had a solid profit, good trend capture and little whipsaw. Graphics for DIFF35 and TREND35 are still wrong. The results of these figures indicated the system was robust enough to work in a variety of trading environments.

transfer well to other periods because it truly does capture how a tradeable generally "behaves."

That preached, recall that 1986 also had a number of areas with too many trades. Finding this phenomenon in two different trading years means that one refinement will be to inspect all the trading years, merge the data and re-estimate the filter value based on all the experience.

A GOOD BUM BUY

Trade C was a genuine trade. The indicators flipped and signaled a buy — a signal that held for several days based on *current* price action, not price action at the tail end of the indicator's horizon. Chalk this one up to the trading concept and, again, refuse to optimize. No rule is going to be 100% effective in the market, so finding a few where the logic just didn't work isn't cause to change the logic. I chose to eat these losses as justified. Plus, the rest of the trades were well placed. Torturing the logic to eliminate two close calls and one bum trade might distort the good trades as well.

SUMMARY

In three Sundays' dinking around, I'd (1) defined a basic pair of indicators and tested them on a period that looked challenging because it had little violent action, (2) invoked MAE stops to change the basic profitability of the system from marginal to solidly positive in the three to one range vs. margin, and (3) tested the resulting system successfully on five other trading periods of similar length but differing activity levels.

The virtue of the system to date is its simplicity, which contributes, I believe, to its usefulness in a variety of time periods. It is also relatively safe, limiting losses well. It should be usable by the trader without undue amounts of time monitoring the market as it stands but there is still more work to be done.

Drawdowns from consecutive losses need to be investigated as well as pyramiding strategies and refining the filter value. Those come next.

The immediate idea of trying this on some other tradeable is a bad one. Recall that the system is built on the observed behavior of bond futures. Is there any reason it should relate to pork bellies or AT&T? Not at this point! Later, much later, I'll investigate twisting the concept into shape for something else, but for now, capitalizing on the bird in the hand is most important.

John Sweeney is the Technical Editor of STOCKS & COMMODITIES.

CHAPTER 2

THE TRADERS' MAGAZINE

FEBRUARY 1992

TECHNICAL ANALYSIS OF STOCKS & COMMODITIES

Using Bollinger Bands

Trading bands, which are lines plotted in and around the price structure to form an envelope, are the action of prices near the edges of the envelope that we are interested in. It's not the newest of ideas, but as John Bollinger of Bollinger Capital Management points out, it's one of the most powerful concepts available to the technically based investor, answering not whether absolute buy and sell signals are being given but whether prices are high or low on a relative basis. Trading bands can forewarn whether to buy or sell by using indicators to confirm price action. How do trading bands work? Bollinger, of Bollinger Bands fame, explains how.

MIKE CRESSY

Trading bands are one of the most powerful concepts available to the technically based investor, but they do not, as is commonly believed, give absolute buy and sell signals based on price touching the bands. What they do is answer the perennial question of whether prices are high or low on a relative basis. Armed with this information, an intelligent investor can make buy and sell decisions by using indicators to confirm price action.

But before we begin, we need a definition of what we are dealing with. Trading bands are lines plotted in and around the price structure to form an "envelope†." It is the action of prices near the edges of the envelope that we are par-

> **Asking the market what is happening is always a better approach than telling the market what to do.**

by John Bollinger

ticularly interested in. The earliest reference to trading bands I have come across in technical literature is in *The Profit Magic of Stock Transaction Timing;* author J.M. Hurst's approach involved the drawing of smoothed envelopes around price to aid in cycle identification. Figure 1 shows an example of this technique: Note in particular the use of different envelopes for cycles of differing lengths.

The next major development in the idea of trading bands came in the mid- to late 1970s, as the concept of shifting a moving average up and down by a certain number of points or a fixed percentage to obtain an envelope around price gained popularity, an approach that is still employed by many. A good example appears in Figure 2, where an envelope has been constructed around the Dow Jones Industrial Average (DJIA). The average used is a 21-day simple moving average. The bands are shifted up and down by 4%.

The procedure to create such a chart is straightforward. First, calculate and plot the desired average. Then calculate the upper band by multiplying the average by 1 plus the chosen percent (1 + 0.04 = 1.04). Next, calculate the lower band by multiplying the average by the difference between 1 and the chosen percent (1 - 0.04 = 0.96). Finally, plot the two bands. For the DJIA, the two most popular averages are the 20- and 21-day averages and the most popular percentages are in the 3.5 to 4.0 range.

CHAIKIN'S INNOVATION

The next major innovation came from Marc Chaikin of Bomar Securities, who, in attempting to find some way to have the market set the band widths rather than the intuitive or random-choice approach used before, suggested that the bands be constructed to contain a fixed percentage of the data over the past year. He stuck with the 21-day average and suggested that the bands ought to contain 85% of the data. Bomar bands were the result. Figure 3 depicts this powerful and still very useful approach. The width of the bands is different for the upper and lower bands. In a sustained bull move, the upper band width will expand and the lower band width will contract. The opposite holds true in a bear market. Not only does the total band width change across time, the displacement around the average changes as well.

BOLLINGER'S BRAINSTORM

Asking the market what is happening is always a better approach than telling the market what to do. In the late 1970s, while trading warrants and options and in the early 1980s, when index option trading started, I focused on volatility as the key variable. To volatility, then, I turned again to create my own approach to trading bands. I tested any number of volatility measures before selecting standard deviation as the method by which to set band width. I became especially interested in standard deviation because of its sensitivity to extreme deviations. As a result, Bollinger Bands are extremely quick to react to large moves in the market.

Bollinger Bands are plotted two standard deviations above and below a simple moving average. The data used to calculate the standard deviation are the same data as those used for the simple moving average. In essence, you are using moving standard deviations to plot bands around a moving average. The time frame for the calculations is such that it is descriptive of the intermediate-

FIGURE 1

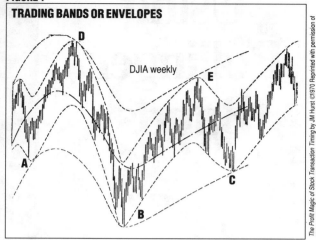

TRADING BANDS OR ENVELOPES

DJIA weekly

The Profit Magic of Stock Transaction Timing by JM Hurst ©1970 Reprinted with permission of Prentice Hall, a Division of Simon & Schuster, New Jersey

The trading bands or envelopes are first drawn by hand over the price series. An average width is determined by measuring the distance from the top and bottom of the bands.

FIGURE 2

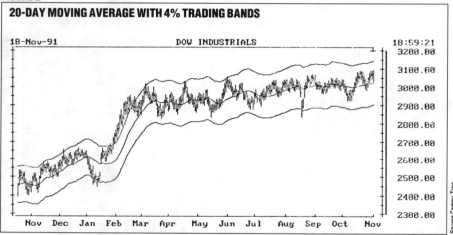

20-DAY MOVING AVERAGE WITH 4% TRADING BANDS

18-Nov-91   DOW INDUSTRIALS   18:59:21

3200.00
3100.00
3000.00
2900.00
2800.00
2700.00
2600.00
2500.00
2400.00
2300.00

Nov Dec Jan Feb Mar Apr May Jun Jul Aug Sep Oct Nov

Source Compu Trac

The concept emerged in the 1970s of shifting a moving average up and down by a certain number of points or a fixed percentage to obtain an envelope around price. Here, an envelope has been constructed around the Dow Jones Industrial Average (DJIA). The average used is a 21-day simple moving average. The bands are shifted up and down by 4%.

FIGURE 3

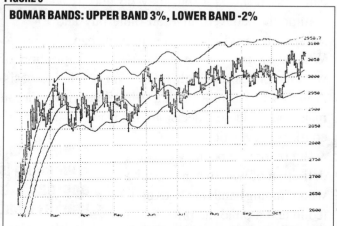

BOMAR BANDS: UPPER BAND 3%, LOWER BAND -2%

Source Bomar Securities

Marc Chaikin, to find some way to have the market set the band widths rather than the intuitive approach used before, suggested that the bands be constructed to contain a fixed percentage of the data over the past year. He stuck with the 21-day average and suggested that the bands ought to contain 85% of the data. Bomar bands were the result.

term trend. (See Figure 4 for a precise mathematical definition and the formula.)

Figure 5 again depicts the DJIA, this time with Bollinger Bands. Note the bands' responsiveness to changing market conditions. The width of the bands varies by more than three times from point A to point B; note that many reversals occur near the bands and that the average provides support and resistance in many cases.

There is great value in considering different measures of price. The typical price, (high + low + close) / 3, is one such measure that I have found to be useful. The weighted close, (high + low + close + close) / 4, is another. To maintain clarity, I will confine my discussion of trading bands to the use of closing prices for the construction of bands. My primary focus is on the intermediate term, but short- and long-term applications work just as well. Focusing on the intermediate trend gives one recourse to the short- and long-term arenas for reference, an invaluable concept.

For the stock market and individual stocks, a 20-day period is optimal for calculating Bollinger Bands. It is descriptive of the intermediate-term trend and has achieved wide acceptance. The short-term trend seems well served by the 10-day calculations and the long-term trend by 50-day calculations.

The average that is selected should be descriptive of the chosen time frame. This is almost always a different average length than the one that proves most useful for crossover buys and sells. The easiest way to identify the proper average is to choose one that provides support to the correction of the first move up off a bottom. If the average is penetrated by the correction, then the average is too short. If, in turn, the correction falls short of the average, then the average is too long. An average that is correctly chosen will provide support far more often than it is broken. (See Figure 6.)

Bollinger Bands can be applied to virtually any market or security. For all markets and issues, I would use a 20-day calculation period as a starting point and only stray from it when the circumstances compel me to do so. As you lengthen the number of periods involved, you need to increase the number of standard deviations employed. At 50 periods, two and a half standard deviations are a good selection, while at 10 periods one and a half do the job quite well.

In most cases, the nature of the periods is immaterial; all seem to respond to correctly specified Bollinger Bands. I have used them on monthly and quarterly data, and I know many traders apply them on an intraday basis.

ANSWERING THE QUESTIONS

Trading bands answer the question whether prices are high or low on a relative basis. The matter actually centers on the phrase "a relative basis." Trading bands do not give absolute buy and sell signals simply by

having been touched; rather, they provide a framework within which price may be related to indicators.

Some older work stated that deviation from a trend as measured by standard deviation from a moving average was used to determine extreme overbought and oversold states. But I recommend the use of trading bands as the generation of buy, sell and

> **Bollinger Bands can be applied to virtually any market or security. For all markets and issues, I would use a 20-day calculation period as a starting point and only stray from it when the circumstances compel me to do so.**

continuation signals through the comparison of an additional indicator to the action of price within the bands.

If price tags the upper band and indicator action confirms it, no sell signal is generated. On the other hand, if price tags the upper band and indicator action does not confirm (that is, it diverges), we have a sell signal. The first situation is not a sell signal; instead, it

FIGURE 5

BOLLINGER BANDS (20-DAY, TWO SIGMA) 11/18/91, DJIA

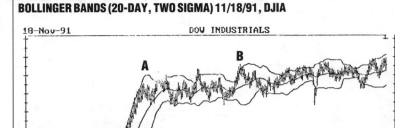

Here is the DJIA, this time with Bollinger Bands. Note the bands' responsiveness to changing market conditions. The width of the bands varies by more than three times from point A to point B; note also that many reversals occur near the bands and that the average provides support and resistance in many cases.

is a continuation signal if a buy signal was in effect.

It is also possible to generate signals from price action within the bands alone. A top (chart formation) formed outside the bands followed by a second top inside the bands constitutes a sell signal. There is no requirement for the second top's position relative to the first top, only relative to the bands. This often helps in spotting tops where the second push goes to a nominal new high. Of course, the converse is true for lows.

INTRODUCING %B AND BAND WIDTH

An indicator derived from Bollinger Bands that I call %b can be of great help, using the same formula that George Lane used for stochastics. The indicator %b tells us where we are within the bands. Unlike stochastics, which are bounded by 0 and 100, %b can assume negative values and values above 100 when prices are outside of the bands. At 100 we are at the upper band, at 0 we are at the lower band, above 100 we are above the upper bands and below 0 we are below the lower band. See Figure 7 for the exact formula.

Indicator %b lets us compare price action to indicator action. On a big push down, suppose we get to -20 for %b and 35 for relative strength index (RSI). On the next push down to slightly lower price levels (after a rally), %b only falls to 10, while RSI stops at 40. We get a buy signal caused by price action within the bands. (The first low came outside of the bands, while the second low was made inside the bands.) The buy signal is confirmed by RSI, as it did not make a new low, thus giving us a confirmed buy signal.

Trading bands and indicators are both good tools, but when they are combined, the resultant approach to the markets becomes powerful. Band width, another indicator derived from Bollinger Bands, may also interest traders. It is the width of the bands expressed as a percent of the moving average. When the bands narrow drastically, a sharp expansion in volatility usually occurs in the very near future. For example, a drop in band width below 2% for the Standard & Poor's 500 has led to some spectacular moves. The market most often starts off in the wrong direction after the bands tighten prior to really getting under way, of which January 1991 is a good example (Figure 9).

AVOIDING MULTIPLE COUNTS

A cardinal rule for the successful use of technical analysis requires avoiding multicolinearity† amid indicators. Multicolinearity is simply the multiple counting of the same information. The use of four different indicators all derived from the same series of closing prices to confirm each other is a perfect example.

So one indicator derived from closing prices, another from volume and the last from price range would provide a useful group of indicators. But combining RSI,

FIGURE 6

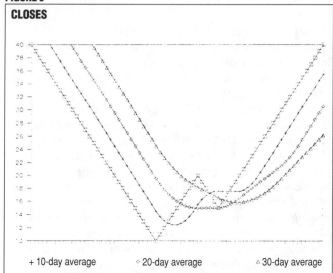

The easiest way to identify the proper average is to choose one that provides support to the correction of the first move up off a bottom. If the average is penetrated by the correction, then the average is too short. If, in turn, the correction falls short of the average, then the average is too long. An average that is currently chosen will provide support far more often than it is broken.

FIGURE 7

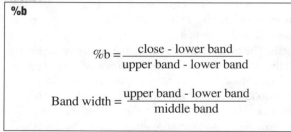

This indicator tells us where we are within the bands. Unlike stochastics, which are bounded by 0 and 100, %b can assume negative values and values above 100 when prices are outside of the bands. At 100 we are at the upper band, at 0 we are at the lower band, above 100 we are above the upper bands and below 0 we are below the lower band. Also shown is the formula for band width.

FIGURE 8

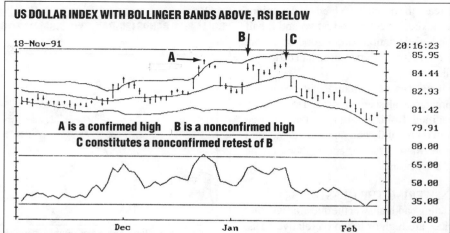

Selecting the relative strength index (RSI) as our confirming indicator, we can observe that at A, the dollar index moved above the upper band while the RSI made a new high (confirmation). At B, the dollar index edged close to the upper band while the RSI failed to confirm (divergence). C constitutes a nonconfirmed retest of B.

moving average convergence/divergence (MACD) and rate of change (assuming all were derived from closing prices and used similar time spans) would not. Here are, however, three indicators to use with bands to generate buys and sells without running into problems. Amid indicators derived from price alone, RSI is a good choice. Closing prices and volume combine to produce on-balance volume†, another good choice. Finally, price range and volume combine to produce money flow, again a good choice. None is too highly colinear and thus together combine for a good grouping of technical tools. Many others could have been chosen as well: MACD could be substituted for RSI, for example.

The Commodity Channel Index (CCI) was an early choice to use with the bands, but, as it turned out, it was a poor one, as it tends to be colinear with the bands themselves in certain time frames. The bottom line is to compare price action within the bands to the action of an indicator you know well. For confirmation of signals, you can then compare the action of another indicator, as long as it is not colinear with the first.

John Bollinger, CFA, CMT, PO Box 3358, Manhattan Beach, CA 90266, (310) 545-0610, is president and founder of Bollinger Capital Management and publishes the monthly "Capital Growth

FIGURE 9

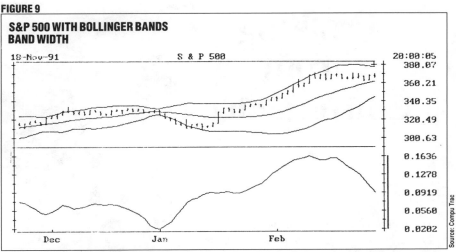

When the band width indicator falls, the implication is that volatility is declining. At some point, the volatility returns. A drop in the band width to below 2% for the S&P 500 has led to some spectacular moves (such as January).

Letter," a market letter for the average investor employing a technically driven asset allocation approach. He is also market analyst for CNBC/FNN.

FOR FURTHER READING

Hurst, J.M. [1970]. *The Profit Magic of Stock Transaction Timing,* Prentice-Hall.

Star, Barbara [1992]. "The Commodity Channel Index," STOCKS & COMMODITIES, February.

SIDEBAR FIGURE 1

CALCULATING BOLLINGER BANDS

	A	B	C	D	E	F	G	H	I	J
1	Date	High	Low	Close	Typical Price					
2	910924	3043.38	2995.97	2995.97	3011.77					
3	910925	3048.52	3004.92	3004.92	3019.45					
4	910926	3040.70	2996.87	2996.87	3011.48					
5	910927	3040.70	2989.49	2989.49	3006.56					
6	910930	3032.87	2982.78	2982.78	2999.48					
7	911001	3043.60	3002.46	3018.34	3021.47					
8	911002	3040.25	2992.40	3012.52	3015.06					
9	911003	3021.24	2972.50	2984.79	2992.84					
10	911004	3007.16	2956.17	2961.76	2975.03					
11	911007	2973.17	2926.21	2942.75	2947.38					
12	911008	2983.68	2927.77	2963.77	2958.41					
13	911009	2984.79	2925.54	2946.33	2952.22					
14	911010	2985.47	2930.23	2976.52	2964.07					
15	911011	3000.89	2957.51	2983.68	2980.69					
16	911014	3026.39	2975.85	3019.45	3007.23					
17	911015	3057.69	3000.22	3041.37	3033.09					
18	911016	3082.29	3016.10	3061.72	3053.37					
19	911017	3077.15	3027.06	3053.00	3052.40				Upper	Middle	Lower
20	911018	3089.45	3045.62	3077.15	3070.74	20 day Average	Standard Deviation	Bollinger Band	Bollinger Band	Bollinger Band
21	911021	3085.20	3042.49	3060.38	3062.69	3006.77	35.54	3077.85	3006.77	2935.70
22	911022	3084.53	3020.57	3039.80	3048.30	3008.60	36.67	3081.94	3008.60	2935.26
23	911023	3065.52	3015.21	3040.92	3040.55	3009.65	37.26	3084.18	3009.65	2935.12
24	911024	3047.63	2991.73	3016.32	3018.56	3010.01	37.31	3084.63	3010.01	2935.38
25	911025	3034.44	2983.01	3004.92	3007.46	3010.05	37.31	3084.67	3010.05	2935.43
26	911028	3055.23	3001.57	3045.62	3034.14	3011.79	37.58	3086.95	3011.79	2936.62
27	911029	3077.82	3020.13	3061.94	3053.30	3013.38	38.62	3090.61	3013.38	2936.14
28	911030	3090.12	3038.24	3071.78	3066.71	3015.96	40.33	3096.63	3015.96	2935.29
29	911031	3091.01	3045.62	3069.10	3068.58	3019.75	41.52	3102.79	3019.75	2936.70
30	911101	3091.91	3031.75	3056.35	=(B30+C30+D30)/3	=AVERAGE(E11:E30)	=STDEVP(E11:E30)	=F30+(2*G30)	=F30	=F30-(2*G30)

CALCULATING BOLLINGER BANDS

An Excel spreadsheet is used to calculate Bollinger Bands for the DJIA. The actual formula for each cell is shown at the bottom of the column; the formula presented is specific for the location of that cell.

First, determine the typical price (column E), which is the high, low and close summed and divided by three. Then calculate the 20-day simple moving average (column F). Next, the standard deviation of the typical price over the 20-day period is calculated using the *population* formula in the spreadsheet (column G). The standard deviation of the population formula is used. The upper Bollinger Band is the 20-day moving average plus two times the standard deviation (column H). The middle band is the 20-day simple moving average (column I). The lower band is the 20-day simple moving average minus two times the standard deviation.

Profiting From Convergence

Here are three ways to capitalize on the property of convergence—the fact that futures prices and spot prices will necessarily come together at the futures expiration. The same concept can be applied to many markets, including various other financial futures contracts, as well as assorted hard commodities.

by Ira G. Kawaller

LIBOR (London interbank offered rate) futures contracts are recognized as Chicago Mercantile Exchange (CME) contracts that pertain to a $3 million one-month Eurodollar time deposit, and the Eurodollar futures contract refers to the contract with a $1 million face value, three-month Eurodollar deposit. The convention is unfortunate, as both contracts are used to lock in the offered rates of the respective terms to maturity. When LIBOR futures prices reflect interest rates substantially different from underlying spot (cash) market interest rates, attractive trades may be available, and they may persist for reasonably extended periods of time.

CONSIDER THIS

Consider the situation: On October 7, 1991, the spot price for the LIBOR on one-month Eurodollar deposits was 5-1/4%, which converts to an International Monetary Market (IMM) index price of 100.00-5.25, or 94.75. On the same date, the December futures settled at a price of 94.20. With neutral or bullish tendencies (expecting interest rates to stay the same or fall), these conditions were very attractive. Not only could a trader make money on a spot market move, but the basis† would further enhance profits by 55 basis points (94.75-94.20) per contract. Of course, the trader could make an incorrect assumption about interest rates and see them rise instead of fall; but even here, the error would be cushioned by a 55-basis-point safety net.

Operationally, you would want to buy futures when prices are (sufficiently) lower than spot prices and sell futures when prices are (sufficiently) higher, keeping in mind the fact that, despite an attractive basis, it is still a speculative trade with unbounded risk. Even a seemingly large, advantageous basis may be dwarfed by an unanticipated, adverse interest rate move.

An alternative to the futures trade involves long options; a basis favoring long futures would justify the purchase of calls,

†See Traders' Glossary for complete description

DIANE BOSTWICK

CONTRACT SPECS

Eurodollar time deposits: Since time deposits are not transferable, "delivery" is actually a cash settlement. The full contract value is not exchanged; rather, the long and short positions are simply marked to a price dictated by the cash market. More precisely, the settlement price of the futures is determined by an authoritative exchange poll on the final contract trading day. The cash market offered rate for three-month Eurodollar time deposits (LIBOR) is deducted from 100 to determine the final contract settlement price.

One-month LIBOR: Also cash settled, in the same way as the Eurodollar time deposit. The only difference is that the cash market for one-month Eurodollar time deposits is deducted from 100.

Trading ends at noon on the business day before a Chicago Mercantile Exchange (CME) holiday and on any U.S. bank holiday that the CME is open.

Only first six consecutive contract months, beginning with the current month, are listed at one time.

—*Chicago Mercantile Exchange*

CONTRACT SPECIFICATIONS

	3-month Eurodollar time deposits	1-month LIBOR futures
Symbol	ED	EM
Contract size	$1,000,000	$3,000,000
Contract months	March, June, September, December [16 contracts listed]	All 12 calendar months [16 contracts listed]
Minimum price change	0.01 = $25	0.01 = $25
Trading hours (Chicago)	7:20 am to 2:00 pm (last day 9:30 am)	7:20 am to 2:00 pm (last day 9:30 am)
Last day of trading	Second London business day immediately preceding the third Wednesday of the contact month	Second London business day immediately preceding the third Wednesday of the contract month
Delivery date	No delivery for ED futures. Final cash settlement follows last day of trading	Last day of trading—cash settled

FIGURE 1

SEPTEMBER FUTURES VS. 1-MONTH LIBOR

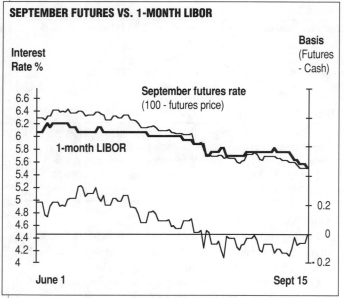

During some periods, convergence effects are of little importance, as is the case in Figure 1.

FIGURE 2

DECEMBER FUTURES VS. 1-MONTH LIBOR

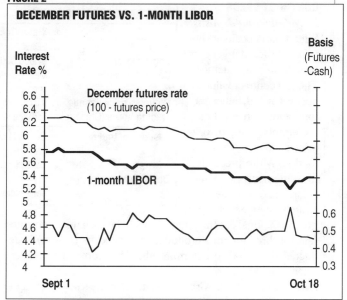

The basis for the December contract has been more than twice the basis for the September contract. But the basis must still converge to zero on expiration.

while a basis favoring short futures would justify buying puts. Select deep in-the-money† options, where the time value is small relative to the basis advantage, because this value works

> **Is there a *best* strategy? Unfortunately, it's not that easy. Each of the alternatives is capable of generating the greatest gain under some interest rate scenario.**

against long positions. As with the futures trade, a large unexpected interest rate move could result in losses; but with long options, the trader understands the maximum possible exposure.

ANOTHER POSSIBILITY

Finally, another possibility for the more adventurous — those willing to bear the prospect of unlimited risk for some bounded potential gain — is a trade involving the sale of options: selling puts when the basis favors the long futures position and selling calls when the basis favors short futures positions. These trades have both the futures basis *and* the time value of the options working advantageously. The choice of option strike should be a matter of discretion, reflecting the trade-off between the size of the potential gain (the option premium) and the breakeven

futures price. Keep in mind, however, that because time values tend to diminish as you move away from the at-the-money† strike price, selling options that are too deeply in-the-money† may reduce the magnitude of the attractive time value adjustment. Moreover, by selling a more expensive option, you necessarily reduce the probability of realizing a gain on the trade. (The moral? Don't get greedy.)

Is there a *best* strategy? Unfortunately, it's not that easy. Each of the alternatives is capable of generating the greatest gain under some interest rate scenario. Choosing among the alternatives, therefore, should reflect a "best guess" of where spot interest rates may be likely to go and a comparison of the results from the respective strategies. In the end, each trader must assess his or her own tolerance to bear risk relative to the rewards.

Ira Kawaller is the director of the New York office for the Chicago Mercantile Exchange. He served as an economist for the Federal Reserve Board and subsequently worked for AT&T and J. Aron Company Inc., a precious metals dealer and commodity trading firm. Currently, he serves on the board of directors of the National Option & Futures Society. He received a doctorate in economics from Purdue University.

"Technician's Technician" Martin Pring

Technician-writer-money manager: Martin Pring was described as the "technician's technician" by Barron's, *and his diverse background can certainly confirm that. Pring received his initial training with a Canadian investment dealer. His interest in technical analysis led him to join Storey, Boeckh in 1975, publisher of* The Bank Credit Analyst. *"The Pring Market Review" was introduced in 1984 as an extension of his interest in technical analysis. Along the way, he has lectured on and published a number of works on investing and technical analysis. He helped form investment counseling firm Pring-Turner Capital Group in 1988, dedicated to conservative asset allocation based on business cycle developments.* STOCKS & COMMODITIES *Editor Thom Hartle interviewed Pring via telephone on November 19, 1991, and asked him about, among other topics, his* KST *indicator and the market cycle model.*

"When you look at any mechanical trading system, you want to position yourself in the direction of the main trend."— Martin Pring

So how were you introduced to technical analyst?

I started off in the Canadian brokerage industry in 1969 and after a year's training, I got transferred to a one-man office about 120 miles north of Toronto in a town called Owen Sound. About then I found out that the firm's research was inadequate; I had learned a little bit about technical analysis by picking up a copy of Edwards & Magee [*Technical Analysis of Stock Trends*], and I decided that this would be my approach, I would use my own technical research to advise my clients. That's how I got started in technical analysis. About three years later, a good client friend gave me a copy of *The Bank*

Credit Analyst, which [at the time, in 1973-74] explained why interest rates were going up, why we had inflation, and so on and so forth. I thought it was brilliantly put together. The problem was, they had a paragraph on technical analysis that I did *not* think was well put together, and so I researched to find out what *The Bank Credit Analyst* had been doing on a technical basis previously. I found that they could have used technical analysis to their benefit if they had had a little better understanding of it.

So I suggested that I consult for them. About three months later they called me and said yes, and about two months after that, I was offered a chance to transfer to institutional sales with the same brokerage firm in Montreal, and since *The Bank Credit Analyst* was also based there, [I moved there]. I was again faced with the problem of not being able to market my research, so eventually I joined the staff of *Bank Credit Analyst*, where I was able to learn more about monetary and economic indicators and to further my knowledge of technical analysis.

Is that where you developed the approach based on a combination of monetary indicators and technical analysis?

That's correct. I began to get very interested in the bond market and I did some pioneering work on technical analysis of the bond market, because no one else at that time was doing it — this was in the early 1970s.

"No indicator is perfect, but some indicators work well most of the time. By combining a lot of them and taking the financial, economic and technical indicators, you get a much more accurate picture of the true environment. Your consensus indicator's going to give you a correct view of what the true environment is."

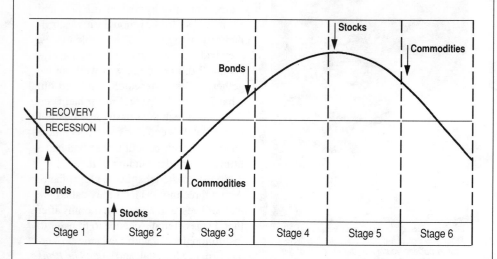

FIGURE 1

BUSINESS CYCLE AND SIX CYCLE STAGES

Six stages can be identified. First, interest rates peak; second, stocks join bonds in the bullish camp; three, bonds, stocks and commodities are all in uptrends. The latter three stages are the downside of the former three: interest rates begin to rise and bonds begin to drop, stocks follow suit and commodities are affected last of all.

You went off on your own ultimately, though.

There were a couple of steps to get to that. All the time I had been learning about technical analysis I was keeping a file on various approaches because I had read a number of books on technical analysis but I couldn't find a single comprehensive book that encompassed everything that I had picked up. Edwards & Magee is a great book as far as it goes, but it just covers chart patterns and so on. So eventually I decided I would write my own book, which I did — *Technical Analysis Explained.*

I also got involved in the commodity markets and decided I would like to do a little trading as well as work on *The Bank Credit Analyst* and the other publications. So I began to break away from *Bank Credit Analyst,* and eventually it led to the point where they were very kind and helped me start up my own publication, "The Pring Market Review." At that point, I went independent.

Along the way you've authored a number of books.

I did a book on how to forecast interest rates, and *International Investing Made Easy,* and then the commodities and futures handbook for McGraw-Hill.

And you're currently working on a new one?

Yes, for John Wiley called *The All-Seasons Investor,* which should be published in early 1992.

Is this book a summation of all your research about working with the various markets and the business cycle?

It *is* more of a fundamental book than a technical one, although there is a bit of technical analysis in there.

You're looking at the business cycle and the markets approach. Have you developed a philosophy about how these all work together?

If you look back over the past 150 or 200 years of the U.S. markets, you find in each business cycle a chronological series of events takes place: first bond prices bottom, then stocks and then commodities; then bonds peak, then stocks and then commodities. So this chronological sequence seems to repeat in virtually every cycle. In some cycles, things get a little out of order, but generally speaking, the chronological process continues. What's different in each cycle is that the lag between, say, the bottom in bonds and the bottom in stocks can vary, and they can vary from as little as a month to as long as a year or maybe even a year and a half.

And the magnitude, of course, of each market — rally and reaction — will be different in each succeeding cycle, because the characteristics of each business cycle differ.

Have you developed this into kind of a science at this point with your analysis?

What I try to do is split the business cycle down into stages (Figure 1) or seasons, just as in a calendar year; you can predict certain activities will be suitable for certain seasons — spring for planting crops, fall for harvesting and so on. You could do the same with the business cycle, because there are three markets and since you have three you in turn have three peaks and three troughs, which means you have six turning points. I split the business cycle into six stages instead of four seasons, and I can try and identify where those stages are and then determine how I should allocate the assets accordingly around the business cycle. That's really the function of the book — to explain how that takes place and how you can recognize those various stages. It's also the basis that we use in [money management firm] Pring-Turner Capital Group.

Did the 1980s go according to your expectations? How have the 1990s been going?

Reasonably well. Let me point out we talk about the business cycle as being four years from trough to trough; in the 1980s, we had a trough in 1982 and one in 1990 — a difference of eight years. But during those eight years, there was a growth recession, and U.S. economic activity slowed but did not go into a major recession. This has happened several times in the past. But you still get the same chronological sequence in the financial markets — the bonds/stocks/commodities relationship — during these four-year growth recessions.

The leads and the lags can really vary, though.

That's right. That, of course, is the trick. It's easy to look back and say, well, stocks peaked here, bonds topped back there, and so on; it's being able to find out where the leads and lags are in each cycle that's the tricky part.

You consider business cycle analysis to be more on the fundamental side, but do you bring in your technical analysis training to help identify when these turns are occurring?

Absolutely. I think the knowledge that this sequence tends to repeat can be quite helpful in pinpointing where you are in the cycle. For example, if you can identify a peak in stocks by using technical analysis, then what you would do is also look and see what bonds were doing. If, for example, bonds were in a bear market, defined as the [Shearson Lehman] bond index being below its 12-month moving average, say, and you can see that the commodity index was above its 12-month moving average, then you'd have a fix in the sense that bonds declining and commodities rallying would be consistent with a peak in stock prices. And this would go on through the cycle. So you can use the other two markets as a fix or confirmation for where you are.

What are some of the other technical indicators that you use to assist you in recognizing these turns?

I use a number of momentum indicators — rates of change, smoothed rates of change — that help. I also have models or barometers that are consensus indicators for the various markets. For example, the inflation barometer, which measures commodity prices, has 10 different indicators, some of which are fundamental — economic, rather — while some are financial and others are technical. I combine these, and when we get more than 50% of the indicators agreeing, which means six out of the 10 are, say, bullish, that gives me a bullish signal for commodities. I do the same thing for stocks and bonds, and from that point of view I can establish when the environment is bullish or bearish for a specific market, and that can help me identify which stage we're at.

Does your barometer take these indicators and just give them, say, a plus or minus rating and then tabulate the ratings?

That's right. We recognize that no indicator is perfect, but there are some indicators that work well most of the time. So by combining a lot of them and taking the financial, economic and technical indicators, you get a much more accurate picture of the true environment. Your consensus indicator's going to give you a correct view of what the true environment is.

By consensus, you mean the total summation of your indicators.

When, say, you have 10 indicators and six vote to be bearish or bullish, that gives me a majority, and I know that things have turned. It's very important when design these indicators to make sure they do reflect the environment; it's too easy to go back and backtest these things and make it fit exactly the historical peaks and troughs. But we're interested in the future, so we have to give some leeway when designing these things so they're not as accurate as they could be maybe, because we want them to reflect the environment for the *future*, rather than for the *past*.

What are some of your favorite indicators that, say, make up the commodity inflation indicator?

Technically, I look at the *Journal of Commerce* and CRB spot raw material index. I could take the CRB Composite, but that includes a lot of agricultural commodities that can be weather-driven, so I take a 12-month moving average. I've found that to be the most reliable of all long-term moving averages and of most markets; they fail from time to time, but on balance they seem to be the most reliable. And then I take things like the diffusion index of the number of commodities in the *Journal of Commerce* index —that's 18 commodities.

And then on the economic side, I consider such things as capacity utilization to be important; I use technical indicators like momentum and moving averages in my economic analysis because economic indicators move in trends, just like stocks and bonds. Because we recognize that there is a sequence of events, I incorporate into the barometers other markets such as the stock market; for example, if it goes bullish, that event normally will precede

a bottom in commodities prices, so if the stock market moves above its 12-month moving average, and here I use the Standard & Poor's Composite, that's actually a positive for the commodity index. Even though rallying stocks themselves are not an indication of inflationary pressures, they *are* a necessary ingredient before we get to the inflationary part of the cycle.

You've done a lot of work with momentum and rate of change analysis. What have you found is the most reliable use of, say, rate of change? Would you expect a high, strong rate of change at the early part of a cycle?

Normally, yes. Most people look at the overbought situation as a bearish condition, but in my opinion, at the beginning of a bull market, an extremely overbought condition indicates a very strong market; it's like a young person can run a mile very fast, whereas an older person takes a lot longer or can't run the mile at all. The strength of the momentum indicates the vibrancy and enthusiasm at the beginning of the bull market.

So if your business cycle analysis indicated that it was likely that the stock market was setting up for a bull run and you saw a very strong overbought reading early in the cycle, you'd have further confirmation that the analysis was on target?

That's correct. I've used that in conjunction with extremely high volume off the bottom, strong breadth and strong momentum. All these technical indicators would be used as confirmation. I don't like to have technical and fundamental positions contradicting each other, though. The fundamentals really help to alert me when the technical indicators are likely to be more reliable. We all know that any technical indicator can fail. If the fundamentals are in place, then the chances of the technical indicators failing are much less. Consequently, the technical indicators are principally used for timing.

One of the indicators that you've developed is the KST. Could you tell us about that?

I recognized some time ago through reading other people's work that price at any one point is determined by the interaction of a number of different time cycles. When we look at a simple rate of change or even a moving average, we're really just measuring one particular time cycle that's monitored by that particular indicator. So I designed a rate of change indicator that combined several different smoothed rates of change into one indicator and then weighted them according to their time span. That way, I was able to get a much more reliable indication of the underlying trend and momentum.

How do you calculate the KST?

The idea is that normally you take a long-term rate of change and smooth it, but the problem is that it tends to reverse direction well after the market has. So the idea of the KST is to combine the shorter-term and the longer-term indicators so that you still get the cyclicality and the smoothness, but it turns at a quicker pace.

I've also developed the KST for intermediate and shorter trends, and so if I arrange the chart in such a way that you have the market at the top and the short term underneath followed by the intermediate and the long term, you can get an idea of where you might be in the overall cycle (see sidebar, "Calculating a rate of change oscillator"). The long term will give you the perspective of whether the market is approaching a bear market low or a bull market high, and from that you can see whether you're in an intermediate rally within a bull market or a bear market, so it gives you some objective idea where you might be in the cycle.

When you refer to cycle, what kind are you talking about?

I'm talking about a primary bull or bear market cycle.

Have you developed a model along those lines, too?

I have. The model is the arrangement of the short-, intermediate- and long-term trends, and I can do this for any financial series. Some series it works with extremely well; those series are tied closely into the business cycle, such as gold or stocks or bonds, but as with all momentum series, it fails in certain conditions; for example, the linear uptrend bull market that we had in Japan during the 1980s. No momentum indicator was going to work in that kind of environment, because it's going to turn down prematurely. Similarly, in situations such as the Hong Kong market decline after the Tianenmen Square incident, no long-term indicator can pick those very short, quick durations. So there are some limitations, but if we assume that the market is going to revolve on an approximate four-year basis between trough and trough, then it works reasonably well.

> **When you look at any mechanical trading system, one of the important things you want to do is position yourself in the direction of the main trend.**

When you say "market," are you being generic as far as all markets are concerned or just the U.S. markets?

All markets. Certainly all stock markets.

For a four-year cycle?

Commodity markets, currencies, most of them seem to respond reasonably well, some better than others.

Can you tell us about your market cycle model?

The market cycle model is really an arrangement whereby we recognize there is a primary trend, an intermediate trend and a short trend. A market cycle model is just the arrangement of a chart with those three trends.

How do you apply your market cycle model to trading? What do you use to tell when you get an intermediate correction against a primary trend?

When you look at any mechanical trading system, one of the important things you want to do is position yourself in the direction of the main trend. That's where the KST market cycle model is very helpful, because it'll give you a good indication of both the direction and maturity.

And when you look at the short-term rallies or the short-term buy signals, in a cycle, you see that the magnitude almost invariably goes in the direction of the trend. So if you're in the early stages of a bull market and you get a short-term buy signal, then you should be going long rather than short and vice versa.

What about risk analysis? People are really interested in how they can place stop losses and stay involved, but at the same time try to manage their risks. Have you done much research on that?

I've done a lot of research in terms of trying to identify bullish or bearish environments for markets, and obviously a lot of that's tied up in the barometers. But there are a number of techniques that anyone can apply. For example, I've found that if you look at the stock market, if the S&P is above its 12-month moving average and the yield on commercial paper is below its 12-month moving average (Figure 2), this often corresponds with a very powerful upmove in the stock market. I call it my 120% indicator, because it seems to work almost invariably and give you excellent results.

For another, if you see that the bond market is above its 12-month moving average and industrial commodity prices are below their 12-month moving averages, this almost invariably gives you profits in the bond market and vice versa. If bonds are falling and commodities are in a long-term uptrend, this is usually when to stay away from bonds (Figure 3).

So you view risk management as correctly analyzing the environment and then trade with that trend.

That's correct. And obviously in the stock market, you look at things like yields — when the stock market is yielding less than 3% on the 24-month holding period, this has usually presented losses, whereas if the stock market's yielding 5% or 6% over the same period, this has usually been a profitable time to own stocks.

So valuation is also important in looking at these broad market indicators.

That's right.

Thank you for your time, Martin. Good luck with your new book.

FIGURE 2

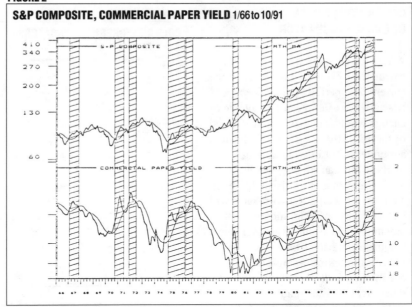

S&P COMPOSITE, COMMERCIAL PAPER YIELD 1/66 to 10/91

Shaded areas indicate bullish periods — that is, S&P is above its 12-month moving average, commercial paper yield (inversely plotted) is above its moving average.

FIGURE 3

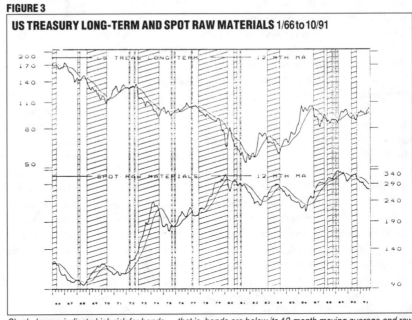

US TREASURY LONG-TERM AND SPOT RAW MATERIALS 1/66 to 10/91

Shaded areas indicate high risk for bonds — that is, bonds are below its 12-month moving average and raw materials are above its 12-month moving average.

REFERENCES

"Bank Credit Analyst," Box 238, Chazy, NY 12921, (514) 398-0653.

Edwards, Robert D., and John Magee [1966]. *Technical Analysis of Stock Trends*, John Magee Inc.

"Pring Market Review," International Institute for Economic Research, Inc., PO Box 329, Washington Depot, CT 06794.

Pring, Martin J. [1980]. *Technical Analysis Explained*, McGraw-Hill, first edition. Third edition was published in 1991 (includes candlestick techniques).

_____ [1981]. *How to Forecast Interest Rates*, and *International Investing Made Easy*, McGraw-Hill.

_____ [1985]. *McGraw-Hill Handbook of Commodities and Futures*.

_____ [1992]. *The All-Seasons Investor*, John Wiley & Sons.

TA

CALCULATING A RATE OF CHANGE OSCILLATOR

A rate of change oscillator (ROC) is calculated by dividing the price in the current time period by the price *n* periods ago. For example, a 10-day rate of change would be today's price divided by the price 10 days ago. ROC indicators are quite useful in wide trading range markets but can give misleading signals if a strong trend is in force. In addition, a specific ROC oscillator will reflect only one cycle. Incorrect interpretations will occur if another cycle length is dominant. Combining various ROC oscillators into a single indicator is one method with which to improve the reliability of this technique.

The KST indicator is the combination or sum of four smoothed rate of change oscillators, each individual oscillator weighted in rough approximation to its time span. A short-term KST indicator could be constructed by selecting four different values for the ROC such as 10, 15, 20 and 30. Each individual ROC is determined by dividing today's price by the price 10 days ago for the 10-day ROC, today's price by the price 15 days ago for the 15-day ROC, today's price by the price 20 days ago for the 20-day ROC and, finally, today's price 30 days ago for the 30-day ROC.

The next step is to smooth the ROC values. This can be accomplished by the use of a simple moving average or an exponentially smoothed moving average. For the short-term KST, smooth each rate of change value with a 10-day

GOLD AND THREE KST INDICATORS

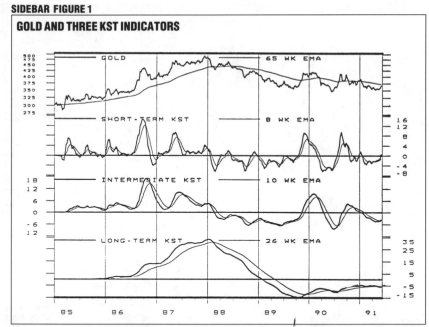

The gold market is presented with the short-term, intermediate-term and long-term KST oscillators. Each oscillator is smoothed with an exponentially smoothed moving average to signal trend changes.

simple moving average, except the 30-day ROC, in which case the ROC should be smoothed by a 15-day simple moving average.

After calculating the smoothed 10-day ROC, the smoothed 15-day ROC, the smoothed 20-day ROC and the smoothed 30-day ROC, the next step is to weight each ROC for summing. Multiply the smoothed 10-day ROC by 1, the smoothed 15-day ROC by 2, the smoothed 20-day ROC by 3 and the smoothed 30-day ROC by 4. Sum these values and divide by 10 (which is the sum of the weights: 1+2+3+4). This is an example of a short-term KST.

The KST indicator is often used with a

short-term moving average as a cross-over method to signal changes in trend. For example, calculate a 15-day simple moving average of the short-term KST. If the KST crosses below the moving average when the KST is at a high value, a sell signal is flashed.

The KST indicator can be calculated over any cycle length to generate indicators for various length trends. An intermediate-trend indicator could use a 10-week, 13-week, 15-week and 20-week ROC as the basis for the KST indicator. A long-term trend indicator could use a nine-month, 12-month, 18-month and a 24-month ROC as the basis for the indicator (see sidebar Figure 1).

BRAD WALKER

A Wyckoff Approach To Futures

by Craig F. Schroeder

The Wyckoff approach, which has been a standard for decades, is as valid for futures as it is for stocks, but even students of the technique appear to be unaware of its extended uses. Most technicians know that Wyckoff analysis stresses volume and price, and as there is always uncertainty about the level of volume on current and previous days for futures, it seems logical to conclude that Wyckoff and futures are not compatible. This may seem logical, but it's wrong. According to Schroeder, Wyckoff is not simply about price and volume; it is concerned with three laws — supply and demand, cause and effect, and effort and result — because these three laws apply to all interactions. Schroeder explains.

Many students of the Wyckoff method do not associate Wyckoff analysis with futures trading — unfortunate, but not difficult to understand how such a mistake can be made. Anyone familiar with the teachings of Richard Wyckoff knows that stocks and stock market action exclusively are used as examples of principles. The lack of examples from the futures market naturally leads to the erroneous conclusion that the principle cannot be applied to futures. Most technicians also know that Wyckoff analysis stresses the study of volume and its relation to price. As there is always uncertainty about the level of volume on both current and previous days, it is logical to conclude that Wyckoff and futures do not mix. Although these conclusions may seem logical, they are not correct.

Wyckoff analysis is not just about stocks and the stock market. It is not even just about price and volume relationships, even though they are the primary focus. Wyckoff is about three basic laws: supply and demand; cause and effect; effort vs. result. These three laws apply to everything that people buy from, sell to or exchange with others.

IF/THEN FOR ALL

In the law of supply and demand, when the pool of buyers demands more product than is immediately available, the price of that commodity will rise until demand diminishes to the level of available supply. At the same time, the pool of sellers, seeing that prices are rising, will take steps to increase the available supply of a commodity. When available supply exceeds the demand, then prices will start to fall.

The law of cause and effect is closely related to the law of supply and demand and states that every price movement is the direct result of a previous price movement or combination of movements. The price markup phase results from the accumulation phase that precedes it and is proportional to that accumulation phase. Similarly, the price markdown phase is the result of the distribution phase that precedes it and is in proportion to the distribution phase.

The law of effort vs. result states that for every effort there should be a result and that the result should be in direct relation to the effort. When this is not the case, a change in direction may be expected. Wyckoff analysis equates effort with volume and result with price.

Futures contracts have a price and a volume, and therefore, this law applies to futures just as it does to stocks. It is true that futures volume is not as readily available as it is with stocks or the stock market, but that does not alter the relationship. There is still a result (price) and an effort (volume). Price moves as a result of the effort being applied in the form of competing bids and efforts in an organized marketplace.

THE CONCEPTS REMAIN THE SAME

Using the Wyckoff approach is as valid in the futures market as it is in stocks. The concepts are the same. The differences that exist are the result of the highly leveraged nature of the trading vehicle and the limited availability of some key data. In futures trading, the highly leveraged nature of the vehicle can make excessive diversification a curse. Extreme leverage means that results come more quickly than with less leveraged or unleveraged vehicles. This is true whether the results are good or bad. Therefore, the windows of opportunity for both entering and exiting positions are smaller, and they open and shut more quickly.

Thus, the trader must be more alert. Diversification divides the trader's attention into smaller pieces. If the trader is trying to watch all the futures markets, his attention is fragmented into very small pieces, so countless opportunities are missed and many of those that are not are either poorly entered or poorly exited or both. Limiting diversification can help avoid this. The trader should follow no more than six markets on a regular basis and in selecting those, markets that are thinly traded — especially those that do not fit comfortably into a group of related futures — should be avoided.

> **Diversification divides the trader's attention into smaller pieces. If the trader is trying to watch all the futures markets, his attention is fragmented into very small pieces, so countless opportunities are missed. Limiting diversification can help avoid this.**

The Wyckoff method suggests that study begin with the general market, move to industry groups and end up with individual issues. With futures, this process can begin with the Commodity Research Bureau (CRB) index (Figure 1), which includes most commodities but not the currencies or interest rate futures. However, some sectors of the futures market periodically tend to trade counter to other sectors. Despite this, all sectors can provide worthwhile opportunities, and this is an important difference between futures and stocks. In stocks, Wyckoff dictates that those issues that are trading against the trend of the general market be avoided.

Since individual sectors of the futures market are more independent, a distinct benefit exists in the indexing of related contracts. Five sectors of the futures market appear to be best for this approach — interest rates, currencies, precious metals, grains and livestock. Figure 2 shows an index of interest rate futures.

The contracts used in this index are bonds, 10-year notes and five-year notes. Defined thus, the index provides a view of interest rate instruments overall but is aimed more directly at intermediate- and longer-term maturities. The definition could be broadened to include the two-year note future and Treasury bill futures. These additions would redirect the primary focus of the index to a shorter maturity. Another valid approach would be to leave the definition narrow with only three components, but to use the three shortest maturities. The effect would be to retain the sensitivity that comes with a narrower definition but to direct the primary focus at the short-term maturity end of the yield curve.

Indexing of related contracts provides two important benefits. One, it gives the trader a broad overview of each sector for a minimum amount of effort. With practice, the trader can determine at a glance which sectors are worthy of a closer look. Two, indexing also provides the basis for relative strength and weakness comparisons, which is an essential part of the Wyckoff method. The best comparisons to make are index to index and between the components of an index. The trading technique is the same as it is in the stock market. Look for relative strength for buy candidates during market reactions and commodities that show relative weakness on rallies for sell candidates.

Whether or not indexing is used, the Wyckoff futures trader is still faced with the problem of volume. He needs to gather as much information as possible. Although the need for information varies depending on what the price is doing, it is a good idea to get in the habit of collecting the same set of figures on a daily basis. Doing so can help avoid some errors in judgment.

he daily publications provide volume from the trading session two days ago, plus an estimated volume figure for yesterday. While it is true that more timely presentation would be better, the actual volume for a particular session is very important even two days after the fact by providing the basis for confirming the conclusion made about that day's action. With Wyckoff analysis, the conclusions made about the action on a particular day are built on those from the prior day or days. The ability to confirm those previous conclusions will help improve the quality of current conclusions. Without this confirmation, it is possible that the analysis will stray farther from the truth, resulting in more numerous and costly trading errors.

The estimates of the previous day's volume tend to miss the actual numbers by a wide margin regularly. However, they are important in Wyckoff analysis for developing a conclusion about the character of the previous day's action. The price spread, net change and relative level of volume for a day combine to make a statement about that day's action. These statements are an essential element in determining what action, if any, needs to be taken. Increasing or decreasing volume together with widening or narrowing price spread and expanding or contracting net progress indicates whether demand or supply is in control and whether that control is increasing or decreasing. The result is either a positive or negative statement, or an unclear statement. Where each statement is made relative to previous action determines what, if any, action needs to be taken from a trading standpoint.

Many traders with access to quotation devices or market monitoring systems intraday have access to the tick volume figures. Tick volume is activity. It measures the number of trades rather than contracts in a trade. A trade may present one contract or one thousand. Therefore, any attempt to relate tick volume to actual volume must be approached cautiously.

VOLUME, VOLUME, VOLUME

From a Wyckoff standpoint, relative volume, particularly when it is combined with price spread and net change, is as important as actual volume. An increase or decrease in the level of activity (tick volume) from one day to the next will usually reflect an increase or decrease in the level of volume from one day to the next. Thus, it is possible to arrive at a conclusion about the character and significance of a day's action before acquiring the actual volume during the next session. Keep in mind that this relationship is not absolute; as always, exceptions do exist. Therefore, it is always necessary to retrieve the actual volume as it becomes available to provide additional confirmation. Also, volume characteristics tend to change over time. Comparing the

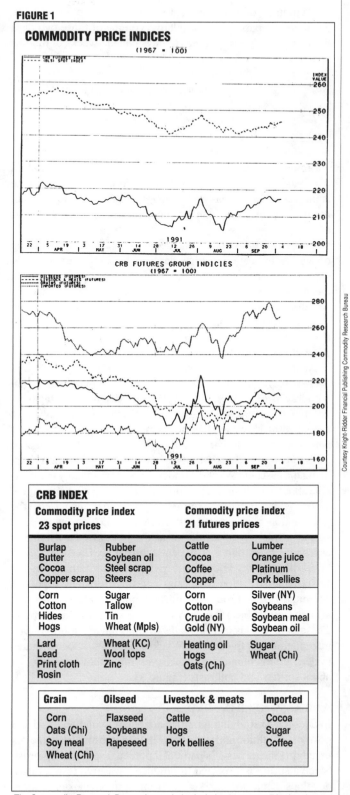

FIGURE 1

The Commodity Research Bureau futures index includes 21 commodities but does not include currencies or interest rate futures.

CRB INDEX

Commodity price index 23 spot prices		Commodity price index 21 futures prices	
Burlap	Rubber	Cattle	Lumber
Butter	Soybean oil	Cocoa	Orange juice
Cocoa	Steel scrap	Coffee	Platinum
Copper scrap	Steers	Copper	Pork bellies
Corn	Sugar	Corn	Silver (NY)
Cotton	Tallow	Cotton	Soybeans
Hides	Tin	Crude oil	Soybean meal
Hogs	Wheat (Mpls)	Gold (NY)	Soybean oil
Lard	Wheat (KC)	Heating oil	Sugar
Lead	Wool tops	Hogs	Wheat (Chi)
Print cloth	Zinc	Oats (Chi)	
Rosin			

Grain	Oilseed	Livestock & meats	Imported
Corn	Flaxseed	Cattle	Cocoa
Oats (Chi)	Soybeans	Hogs	Sugar
Soy meal	Rapeseed	Pork bellies	Coffee
Wheat (Chi)			

tick volumes of two consecutive days will provide a more accurate comparison of the relative volume of those two days than comparing tick volumes of days that are weeks or months apart.

Although volume is absolutely essential to Wyckoff analysis, sometimes volume is not necessary for a conclusion. Narrowing price spread and decreasing net change at the top of a rally is a negative indication; this is true whether the volume is larger or smaller. Narrowing price spread and decreasing net change at the bottom of a reaction is a positive indication; this is true whether volume is increasing or decreasing. Although these conclusions do not require volume, they can be more informative if volume is added.

Narrowing price spread and decreasing net change at the top of a rally indicates whether demand is being withdrawn or supply is being met. Both are negative indications, but the meeting of supply is viewed as being more negative than the withdrawal of demand. The level of volume indicates which process is most likely taking place. Increasing volume is equated to the meeting of supply, while decreasing volume is equated to the withdrawal of demand.

At the bottom of a reaction, narrowing price spread and decreasing volume indicate either the meeting of demand or the withdrawal of supply. Here again, the determining factor is volume. It enhances the degree of bearishness or bullishness of the situation. However, it is the character of the price spread and net change at the top of the rally or bottom of a decline that in truth indicates the desirability of establishing a position. That being the case, the Wyckoff trader can feel reasonably comfortable about establishing a position without knowing the volume.

The Wyckoff trader's confidence level can be increased if the price action is compared with past action. Narrowing price spread at the top of a rally or at the bottom of a decline is especially important if it is penetrating a previous key level. Wyckoff students know these positions as variations of the broader classification of springs and upthrust; they represent attempts to break through established support and resistance that are unusually subject to failure due to a lack of demand or supply. These conclusions can be made without having solid volume information. For this reason, Wyckoff students who are futures traders are encouraged to learn everything they possibly can about springs and upthrusts (Figure 3).

AND ALSO KEEP IN MIND

In addition to studying the price action and volume, trend and position, condition and potential (Figure 4) are important factors in judging the merits of a particular potential spring or upthrust. Since a spring is expected to produce a positive result, that it develops while the market is in an uptrend makes it more interesting to the Wyckoff trader. If the market is also positioned at the bottom of the uptrend channel when the spring develops (Figure 5), it is even more interesting to the Wyckoff trader. Trend and position are also important when an upthrust develops. The upthrust by itself is of interest to the Wyckoff trader, but

FIGURE 2

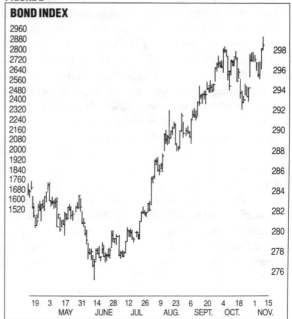

The bond index is formed by adding together the nearby price of the Treasury bond, 10-year Treasury note and five-year T-note contract prices.

the upthrust that develops in an established downtrend is more interesting and those that develop with the market positioned near the top of the downtrend channel are more interesting still.

Everyone likes a market that is in a well-defined uptrend or downtrend, especially when a position in harmony with the trend is in place. Most of the time, however, the futures trader will be looking at markets that are in trading ranges. This should not be viewed as a negative situation. As a result of the highly leveraged nature of futures trading, trading range activity can actually lead to more opportunities. Since the primary thrust of the action is horizontal, the trader can justify trading both spring and upthrust positions without having to worry about violating the Wyckoff method by being positioned counter to the trend.

During trading range activity, it is likely that only one spring or upthrust position will exist. In some cases, there will be one or both. However, repeated springs or upthrusts will be seldom seen. That being the case, how is it possible for trading ranges to produce more trading opportunities?

A trading range has three distinct parts. It begins with a stopping action that breaks the previous up- or downtrend and defines the trading range, which in turn is completed with an ending action. This provides a clue about the timing and direction of the departure from the trading range. The spring and upthrust belong in this category.

Between the stopping action and the ending action, there is the testing process, which may last for days, weeks or months. During this time, the price moves up and down within the trading range, testing the strength of the support and resistance. Each test that does not result in a penetration of the support or resistance level adds to the strength of that level and adds to the potential that will fuel the move that eventually leaves the trading range.

Each rally from the bottom of a trading range or reaction from the top of a trading range is a potential trading opportunity. The Wyckoff student selects his entry points from among these by first analyzing the character of the price action and the volume action as far as it is known — action that indicates the meeting of supply or withdrawal of demand at the top of a rally, which represents an opportunity on the short side, or action that indicates the meeting of demand or withdrawal of supply at the bottom of a reaction, which represents an opportunity on the long side. Opportunities on either side are confirmed by divergent action between price and volume and by the development of clearly overbought or oversold conditions.

IS TIMING ALL?

It is a commonly held belief, especially among futures traders, that timing is all. Wyckoff students are taught that although timing is important in achieving success, it is not everything. Good money management is as important as good timing. These money management guidelines given from a Wyckoff perspective should aid in futures trading:

FIGURE 3, PART A

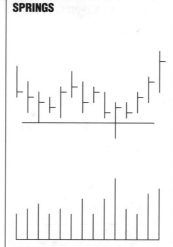

SPRINGS

A spring occurs when the price action carries the market below a previous support point. During the decline to new lows, the weak-hand traders are forced to liquidate to the strong hands that bid the price back up to above the previous support point. The volume is very good, indicating that large traders (good demand) have entered the market to assume new positions from the weak hands.

FIGURE 3, PART B

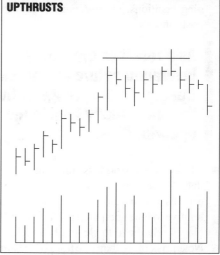

UPTHRUSTS

An upthrust occurs when the market fails to stay above a previous supply or resistance level. Typically, the news that pushes prices higher is quite favorable but viewed as an opportunity to unload positions held by large traders to the late buyers. The failed attempt to hold the new highs attracts supply, as indicated by the increased volume.

FIGURE 4

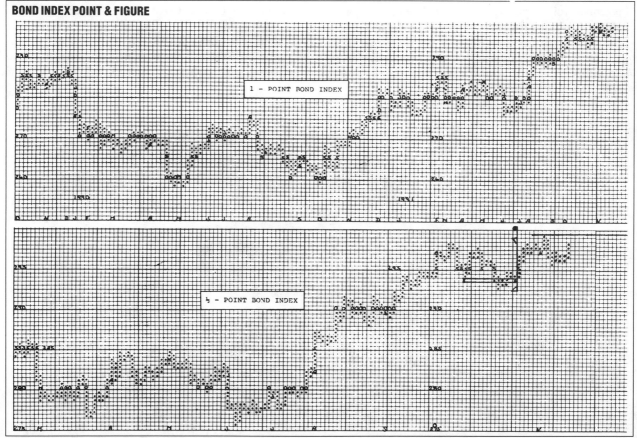

BOND INDEX POINT & FIGURE

The Wyckoff method uses point & figure charts to determine potential for a move in the market. Counting sideways along a horizontal trading range produces an objective; adding this count to the top or bottom of the trading range is the objective for the market once the price movement has exceeded the boundaries of the trading range.

- When establishing commitments, build winning positions. Do *not* average into losing positions.

> **As a result of the highly leveraged nature of futures trading, trading range activity can actually lead to more opportunities.**

- Always use a stop-loss order and be sure that the stop is set when the position is established. In addition to placing a stop relative to the anticipated profit, it should be placed relative to the level of capital.
- Never risk more than one third of the anticipated profit.
- Never risk more than 10% on any one trade.
- Never meet a margin call. If you get a margin call, one of two things is happening. The position held is too large for the capital, or the position itself is wrong. Either way, increasing the exposure to risk is more likely to make a bad situation worse.
- Finally, close out positions when profit adjectives are reached. No position has unlimited profit potential. The best estimate of potential profit is the one made just before the position is established. When it has been realized, it is time to get out.

Craig F. Schroeder is Educational Director of the Stock Market Institute in Phoenix, AZ. He has also served as technical advisor to several regional brokerage firms.

FIGURE 5

SPRING AT SUPPORT LINE

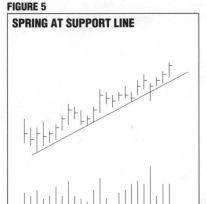

If the price movement temporarily breaks the uptrend line, only to uncover demand at a previous support level, the uptrend can be expected to continue.

FIGURE 6

WITHDRAWAL OF SUPPLY

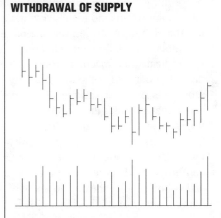

The shortening of the daily ranges along with contracting volume indicates that the lower prices are producing a withdrawal of supply, which is a bullish indication.

FOR FURTHER READING

Hutson, Jack K. [1986-87]. Wyckoff series, *Technical Analysis of* STOCKS & COMMODITIES, Volumes 4-5.

Schroeder, Craig F. [1991]. "Wyckoff: Relative strength and weakness," *Technical Analysis of* STOCKS & COMMODITIES, Volume 9: January.

_____ [1991]. "Wyckoff: Identifying opportunities," *Technical Analysis of* STOCKS & COMMODITIES, Volume 9: March.

_____ [1991]. "Wyckoff: Buying and selling tests," *Technical Analysis of* STOCKS & COMMODITIES, Volume 9: April.

_____ [1991]. "Wyckoff: timing your commitments," *Technical Analysis of* STOCKS & COMMODITIES, Volume 9: June.

The Commodity Channel Index

A technical analytical standard that's often misunderstood, the Commodity Channel Index, which was developed by technician/programmer Donald Lambert more than a decade ago, offers a broad range of trading options to use alone or with other indicators.

Lambert, during the course of his research, noticed that many commodities displayed cyclic patterns that reminded him of sine waves and formulated the theory based on that observation. The index, which author Barbara Star explains does not calculate cycle lengths, instead helps to determine when a cycle trend is in force; she goes on to explain how the Commodity Channel Index can be and has been used, along with enlightening commentary from inventor Donald Lambert himself.

by Barbara Star, Ph.D.

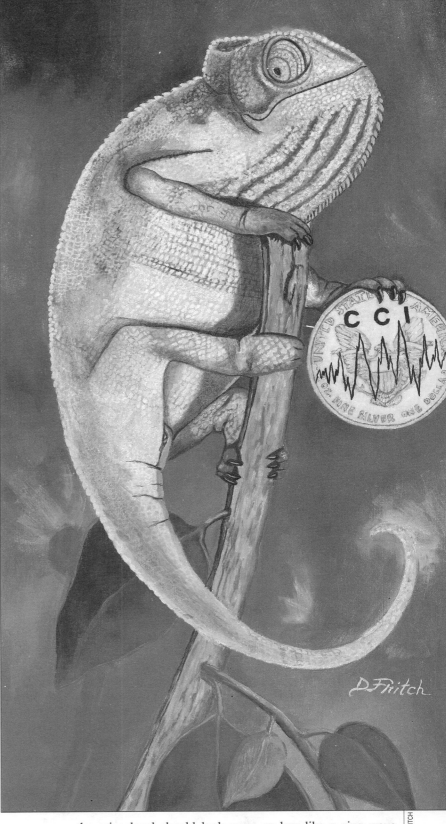

T he Commodity Channel Index (CCI), which was developed by Donald Lambert in 1980, started out as a programming experiment. At that time, personal computers were not yet widely used by individual traders; most calculations were done by hand. Lambert's work involved programming the TI-59, a hand-held calculator. "I wanted to develop something that could be used by traders," he told me, "but also something that showed the value of using hand-held calculators, which were becoming more affordable. So I developed the CCI mostly as a programming exercise because its calculations would be too difficult, time-consuming and prone to error if done by hand." Later, with the introduction of technical analysis software, the CCI became a standard inclusion, albeit somewhat misunderstood, among the indicators provided in computer trading packages.

In conducting his research, Lambert had noticed that many commodities displayed cyclic price patterns reminiscent of a sine wave. "I came up with the idea that as you approached a top, the price level should look more or less like a sine wave approaching its peak," he explained. "I related the CCI to that." According to his theory, a perfectly cyclic commodity would exhibit a relationship between price variability and where it is on the curve.

Of course, perfect cycles don't exist. A commodity with a dominant 22-day cycle from low to low, for example, rarely moves up for 11 days and and then down for another 11 days to make its low. If it did, there would be no need for the CCI or any other indicator; you could simply predict a change in trend every 11 days.

Although the CCI does not calculate cycle lengths, it does help determine when a cycle trend is in force. With technical analysis software, the CCI is usually displayed as an oscillator with lines at +100, zero and -100. The space between +100 and -100 should confine 70-80% of the random price fluctuations. However, once the CCI breaches either the +100 or -100 line, it is a signal that a commodity may have begun to trend.

CONSTRUCTING THE CCI

Fortunately for the nonmathematically inclined, the calculations for the CCI are built into most software programs and can be accessed with the touch of a key. The calculations are based on the four steps and figures shown in the sidebar, "Calculating the CCI."

As explained by Lambert, the indicator is based on a simple moving average of the "typical" price — that is, the high + low + close divided by 3. The moving average fluctuates up and down more or less as price does, depending on how today's price compares with the price data that are dropped out. It differs from many other indicators in the third step, which is the calculation of a mean deviation rather than a standard deviation. The mean deviation provides an average of the price deviations from the current price moving average; it is another way to show how much spread or variability exists. The mean deviation is multiplied by 0.015, which serves both to define the +/-100 channel range and also to encompass the majority of random price movement within that range. That number is then divided into the difference between today's "typical" price and today's simple moving average. The end result is the CCI number, which can be either positive or negative. When the CCI number is positive, it has moved above the zero line toward +100, and when it is negative, it has moved below the zero line toward -100.

Unlike some other indicators, the numeric value of a given CCI time unit remains constant, no matter how much price data are being viewed. If you use a 14-unit CCI, its numeric value for a particular day will be the same, no matter how many days of price come before or after. That can be very valuable when testing a trading system because it makes adding price data possible without worrying that the past CCI numeric value has changed in any way.

CHOOSING A TIME FRAME

As with a stochastic or momentum indicator, the CCI requires the selection of a time period or unit number. Too small a number could result in whipsaws, while too large a number would miss a large portion of the price move. The recommended number is between five and 25. Because the CCI concept was paired with cycles, Lambert's original article in STOCKS & COMMODITIES suggested a CCI unit that is less than one-third the cycle length of the commodity. For instance, a CCI unit of seven, eight or nine might be selected for use with a commodity that displays a 28-day cycle.

My use of the CCI, which is not tied to cycles, suggests that the

> **Unfortunately, as Figure 1 illustrates, many times the trader is left in the unenviable position of entering a market just as prices abruptly swing in the opposite direction.**

choice of a CCI time unit should be governed by the purpose for which it is being used. For example, when looking for bullish or bearish price divergences to time entry or exit moves, I sometimes find a nine-unit CCI more applicable than a 14- or 20-unit CCI. But when attempting to determine if a price trend is still in force, a 28-unit CCI may be more appropriate.

TRADING WITH THE CCI

Originally, Lambert conceived of the CCI as a breakout indicator. "Basically," he explained, "when you broke out of the + or -100 range you entered the market, and when you came back into

FIGURE 1

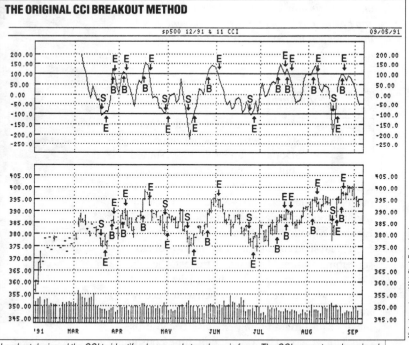

THE ORIGINAL CCI BREAKOUT METHOD

Lambert designed the CCI to identify when a cycle trend was in force. The CCI generates a buy signal when the indicator breaks above the +100 line and a sell signal when the CCI breaks the -100 line. First, it is necessary to determine a cycle length. For the December 1991 S&P 500, that was done by counting the number of days between the major lows. The day of the low is day #1; the last day of the cycle count includes the day of the next major low (which means that the last day of a cycle will become day #1 of the next cycle). There were three major lows during this time period — March to May (38 days), May to June (32 days), and June to August (35 days). The average length (add 38+32+35 and divide by 3) was 35 days. Lambert recommended selecting a CCI unit less than one-third of the cycle length. An 11-unit CCI satisfies that criterion. Cycle analysts recommend reviewing at least six cycles. Each buy (B) and sell (S) signal is followed by an exit (E) signal.

the boundaries you exited the market, because the breakout was finished. That's what I liked about it. It didn't keep you in the market all the time, the way so many systems do."

Figure 1 illustrates the breakout method with the December 1991 Standard & Poor's 500. In this time frame, the S&P exhibited a 32-38 day range from low to low, which averaged a 35-day cycle. In keeping with the original suggestion to use a CCI length that is less than one-third the cycle length, an 11-unit CCI was chosen. From March through August, this CCI produced eight buy signals and five sell signals. (See sidebar, "Profitability of breakout and oscillator methods with S&P 500.")

Unfortunately, as Figure 1 also illustrates, many times the trader is left in the unenviable position of entering a market just as prices abruptly swing in the opposite direction. Another problem with using the CCI as originally designed is that the commodity has made a substantial move before a buy or sell signal is generated. Traders do not like to miss that much of a price move before jumping aboard. These problems led traders to experiment with other ways to trade with the CCI:

■ *Oscillator.* _____

Many people use the CCI as an overbought/oversold momentum oscillator the way they would use a stochastics indicator. This method calls for buying when the CCI crosses above the -100 line and selling when it crosses the +100 line to the downside. It works well when price is in a trading range. It produced some highly profitable trades on the S&P 500 while prices fluctuated between 375 and 400 for many months in 1991 (Figure 2). No attempt was made to link the CCI unit to a cycle length; the 14-unit CCI happens to be the default setting on my technical analysis software. Of the 10 signals generated, each identified a change in trend and most resulted in a trip from oversold to overbought territory or vice versa. Placing a stop-loss a few points above or below the price of the day that an entry signal flashed would have prevented any major losses.

But when used as an oscillator, the CCI shares with other oscillators the tendency to produce premature buy or sell signals during periods when the market begins to trend. An example of this occurred during the upmove on the S&P from the end of June to the end of August. Most of the following methods are variations of using the CCI as an oscillator:

■ *Crossover.* _____

Some traders prefer dual CCI time units, buying or selling when the shorter unit crosses over the longer one (Figure 3). To try this method, choose a CCI

FIGURE 2

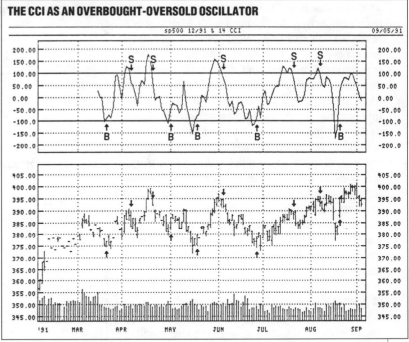

THE CCI AS AN OVERBOUGHT-OVERSOLD OSCILLATOR

As an oscillator, buy when the CCI crosses above the -100 line and sell when it crosses below the +100 line. From March through September 1991, the S&P 500 traded between 375 and 400. Of the five buy signals generated by the 14-unit CCI, three resulted in winning trades. The last buy signal led to a rise on the indicator up to 99.37 and not to +100, so it could not be included as a winning trade. Three of the five sell signals took the indicator from overbought to oversold. However, only two of those would have been profitable, which suggests taking those signals that are in the direction of the underlying trend.

FIGURE 3

THE CROSSOVER METHOD WITH MARCH 1992 SUGAR

The crossover method uses two CCI units, one being half the length of the other that generate buy and sell signals when the shorter unit crosses the longer CCI line above or below the 100 lines. Here's a variation of that method that views the first crossover above or below the 100 line as a warning (W) of a possible change in trend. A buy (B) or sell (S) signal is generated at the next crossover of the +/-100 line when one or both CCI units are above or below the 100 lines after the warning. Because this method still uses the CCI as an oscillator, it will produce better results in trading markets than in trending markets.

length for the intermediate term and overlay that on a CCI unit that is half that length to obtain a shorter-term perspective. In Figure 3 with March sugar, seven and 14 CCI units were selected. However, since people differ in their conception of what constitutes short–term and intermediate-term parameters, experiment with several CCI units such as five and 10, six and 12, 10 and 20, 14 and 28 until you find one that matches your personal comfort level.

As a variation, I often treat the crossover as a warning rather than a buy or sell signal. As shown in Figure 3, when the seven-unit CCI crosses the 14 unit it acts as an early warning system, foretelling an impending price reversal. To me, this signals a need to adjust stop-loss points to protect profits. The 14-unit CCI provides an intermediate range perspective that prevents a premature exit if price continues its trend. Sometimes I add a 28-unit CCI for an even longer view of trend.

■ Multiple nesting.

Another way to use multiple CCI units is to overlay two or even three CCI time units, buying or selling when all the units nest, or turn, at the same time above or below the 100 lines (Figure 4). Both a 14- and 21-unit CCI were overlaid and used in conjunction with the December 1991 live cattle contract. The arrows show that both indicators formed a valley (nested) below the -100 line in August and both nested again in September, forming a peak above the +100 line. Notice at point X that this method prevented a possible early exit from the trade in late August-early September when the 14-unit CCI moved toward the -100 line, but the 21-unit CCI maintained an upward bias. It also correctly identified the direction of the subsequent price move after cattle traded in a narrow range from 76 to 77 during September and October.

■ Divergence.

Using the CCI to detect divergences on either daily or weekly price charts is a favorite among traders. Divergence means that the indicator is going in one direction while price is either going in the opposite direction or moving in a sideways channel. In Figure 5, the CCI recorded several price divergences on the Swiss franc, which called the bottom in June and also the major corrections on its subsequent upmove. A word of caution, however; as Figure 5 also demonstrates, sometimes price continues its trend, producing two, three or more CCI divergences before prices actually top or bottom. This suggests the need for careful stop-loss placement to keep potential losses small in case price fails to move in the anticipated direction.

FIGURE 4

NESTING CCI UNITS WITH DECEMBER 1991 LIVE CATTLE

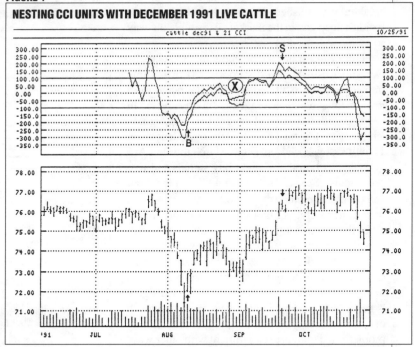

Instead of crossing over, the two CCI units simultaneously form a peak above the +100 line or a valley below the -100 line. In this case, both 14- and 21-unit CCIs were used, which seems to work well in most markets. To change the CCI units, divide the shorter one by 2. Add that result to the chosen unit to obtain the longer unit. For example, if you prefer a 10-unit CCI, divide 10 by 2 = 5. 10 + 5 = 15. You would then use both 10 and 15 CCI units.

FIGURE 5

DIVERGENCE ON THE COMMODITY CHANNEL INDEX

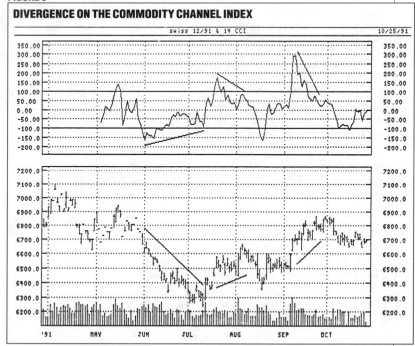

As the December 1991 Swiss franc continued its steep descent in June, the CCI showed positive or bullish divergence as it moved from below the -100 line up toward zero. When price reversed trend in July the CCI initially confirmed the upmove but then showed negative or bearish divergence as price continued to make a higher high at the 66.50 level in early August. This divergence signaled a rapid downmove to the 63.50 level before price was able to rally again. As price reached its September high at the 68.75 level, the CCI was moving down toward the +100 line, registering bearish divergence. Because currencies tend to trend, the CCI may show several divergences before prices actually bottom or peak.

■ *Zero line.*

According to an article in the March 1990 "Technical Traders Bulletin," research conducted using a 90-week CCI unit to test the NYSE Composite produced better results when buy or sell signals were taken at the zero line rather than waiting for price to cross the +/-100 line, as Lambert originally advocated. However, a 90-week CCI requires a minimum of 900 days of price data before the first calculation can be plotted. While this may be possible using data from continuous contracts, most traders base their indicators on much smaller amounts of data. With fewer data and a shorter CCI unit, trading each time the CCI indicator crosses the zero line can be hazardous to your wealth. Even a cursory glance at these figures would reveal that such trades are subject to numerous whipsaws.

But using the zero line to gauge support and resistance zones is quite another matter — and it is also a technique that can enhance the quality of trading. For example, despite the upward bias of the CCI in Figure 5, it was unable to penetrate the zero line in June. During the price correction from the middle to the end of July, the zero line provided support. Penetrating the zero line to the upside in August produced a move of more than 350 points on the Swiss franc in September.

FIGURE 6

MAGELLAN FUND AND COMMODITY CHANNEL INDEX

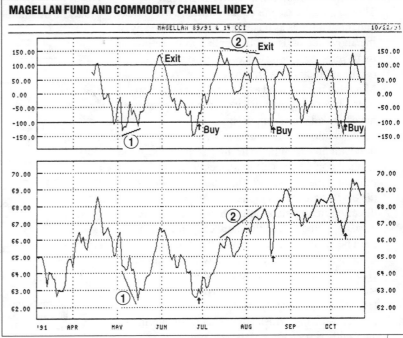

The bullish divergence (#1) in May preceded a 3.5-point upmove before the CCI crossed above the +100 line. The bearish divergence in July and August (#2) warned of the sharp move down into the August lows, which took the CCI below the -100 line. Buying each time the CCI dipped below the -100 line would have worked well toward building profits. The October highs suggest either taking profits or keeping a vigilant eye for another divergence similar to #1 or #2. Astute readers will spot divergences other than those highlighted in this chart, including the one made in late August when price made a new high at 69 that was not confirmed by a new high on the CCI. The divergences I trust most are those that take the indicator into the channel toward zero and then down to or below the -100 line (#1) or above the +100 line (#2) once again.

VERSATILITY BEYOND COMMODITIES

The versatile CCI seems equally at home with stocks and mutual funds as it is with commodities. Any of the above methods can be applied to these investment vehicles. For instance, Figure 6 combines the oscillator method with divergences to Fidelity's Magellan mutual fund and shows that entries in the oversold area and exits in the overbought area would have yielded consistent profits.

In addition, some traders advocate a two-step trend trading method. The first step of the trend method applies the CCI to a weekly chart to determine intermediate trend. Once the weekly exceeds the +/-100 area and begins to turn in the opposite direction, it signals a trend change. In the second step, apply the CCI to the daily chart for a shorter-term perspective. Trade only in the direction of the weekly intermediate trend. The weekly and daily charts of IBM (Figure 7) indicate how profitable this simple, and relatively conservative, method can be. However, even weekly indicators can diverge from price, producing a misleading change in intermediate trend, as seen toward the end of the chart.

Even though no indicator is perfect, the CCI offers a variety of trading options that can be used alone or with other indicators. It remains only for the trader to adapt the technique to his or her own trading style.

Barbara Star, Ph.D. (818) 712-9020, is a university professor and is currently writing a book on candlestick analysis of stocks and commodities. For information concerning the construction of the CCI, contact Donald Lambert, a software programmer of trading systems for individual investors, at (213) 658-6284.

REFERENCES

Kaufman, Perry J. [1987]. *The New Commodity Trading Systems and Methods*, John Wiley & Sons (referred to here as the "cycle channel index").

Lambert, Donald [1983]. "Commodity channel index: Tool for trading cyclic trends," *Technical Analysis of* STOCKS & COMMODITIES, Volume 1: July/August.

LeBeau, Charles [1990]. "Commodity channel index," *Technical Traders Bulletin*, Volume 2, No. 3, March.

Murphy, John J. [1986]. *Technical Analysis of the Futures Markets*, New York Institute of Finance.

FIGURE 7

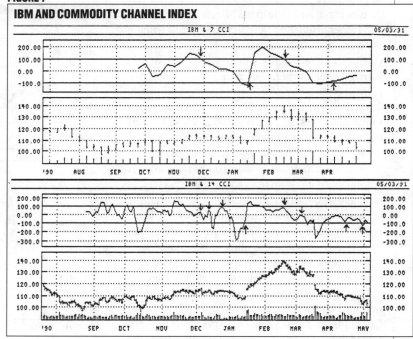

IBM AND COMMODITY CHANNEL INDEX

The trend method applies the CCI to both weekly and daily charts. Here, a seven-unit CCI helps determine the intermediate trend. The weekly CCI generates a change in trend as soon as it crosses the +/-100 lines and moves in the opposite direction, as shown by the arrows. Once the weekly trend has changed, wait for the daily CCI indicator to make a high, low or divergence in the direction of the weekly trend before trading the daily. Notice how waiting for the weekly trend to change prevented an early exit or premature sell in the January-February time frame. Sometimes the weekly indicator may also diverge from price the way it did in April, giving a false change in trend.

PROFITABILITY OF BREAKOUT AND OSCILLATOR METHODS WITH S&P 500

These figures compare the original breakout method and the oscillator method for profitability on the December 1991 S&P 500 contract from March to September using an 11-unit CCI. Buy/sell entries and exits were made on the open of the day after the signal. To keep the comparison more equitable, trades taken on the oscillator could not be exited until another signal was generated. No stops were used, although in real life prudent traders would probably set stop/loss points to limit any losses. The results show the number of points (not dollar amount) each trade either gained or lost.

SIDEBAR FIGURE 1

TRADE	SIGNAL	NEXT DAY OPEN	PTS PROFIT	PTS LOSS
1	Sell	374.90		
	Exit	376.65		1.75
2	Buy	386.10		
	Exit	382.05		4.05
3	Buy	389.00		
	Exit	388.00		1.00
4	Buy	394.90		
	Exit	389.70		5.20
5	Sell	383.00		
	Exit	388.30		5.30
6	Sell	375.00		
	Exit	378.70		3.70
7	Buy	388.70		
	Exit	394.50	5.80	
8	Sell	377.95		
	Exit	379.00		1.05
9	Buy	385.95		
	Exit	386.50	0.55	
10	Buy	390.40		
	Exit	389.00		1.40
11	Buy	394.60		
	Exit	393.45		1.15
12	Sell	382.70		
	Exit	395.80		13.10
13	Buy	397.70		
	Exit	397.00		0.70
	Total		6.35	38.40
	Net Total Points		(32.05)	
	Net Dollar Amount		$(16,025)	

Table title: **BREAKOUT METHOD WITH 11-UNIT CCI**

SIDEBAR FIGURE 3

TRADE	SIGNAL	NEXT DAY OPEN	PTS PROFIT	PTS LOSS
1	Sell	382.00		
	Exit	376.65	5.35	
2	Buy	376.65		
	Exit	382.05	5.40	
3	Sell	382.05		
	Exit	388.00		5.95
4	Sell	388.00		
	Exit	389.70		1.70
5	Sell	389.70		
	Exit	383.00	6.70	
6	Buy	383.00		
	Exit	378.70		4.30
7	Buy	378.70		
	Exit	394.50	15.80	
8	Sell	394.50		
	Exit	379.00	15.50	
9	Buy	379.00		
	Exit	386.50	7.50	
10	Sell	386.50		
	Exit	389.00		2.50
11	Sell	389.00		
	Exit	393.45		4.45
12	Sell	393.45		
	Exit	395.80		2.35
13	Buy	395.80		
	Exit	397.00	1.2	
	Total		57.45	21.25
	Net Total Points		+ 36.20	
	Net Dollar Amount		$ 18,100	

Table title: **OSCILLATOR METHOD WITH 11-UNIT CCI**

SIDEBAR FIGURE 2

S&P 500 12/91, 11 CCI

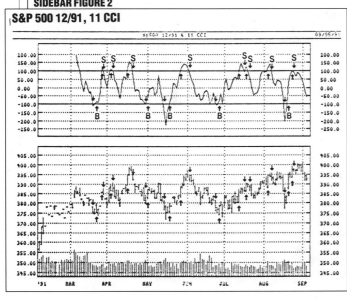

SIDEBAR FIGURE 4

S&P 500 12/91, 11 CCI

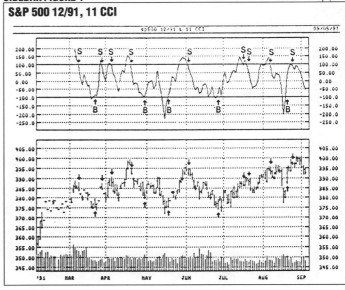

CALCULATING AN 11-PERIOD CCI

The commodity channel index (CCI) can be calculated using any lookback period chosen by the trader. The Excel spreadsheet (sidebar Figure 1) is an 11-period CCI for the Dow Jones Industrial Average. The first step is to calculate the daily typical price. This is the high, low and close added together and divided by three. This step is performed in column E. The formula for cell E2 is:

$$=(B2+C2+D2)/3$$

The second step is to calculate an 11-day simple moving average of the typical price. This is done in column F. The formula for cell F12 is:

$$=AVERAGE(E2:E12)$$

The next step is to determine the 11-day mean deviation. Take the absolute value of the difference between today's moving average and each of the last 11 days' typical prices. These values are the deviations. Sum these values and divide by 11. This calculated in column G. The formula for cell G12 is:

$$=(ABS(E12-F12)+ABS(E11-F12)+ABS(E10-F12)+ABS(E9-F12)+ABS(E8-F12)+ABS(E7-F12)+ABS(E6-F12)+ABS(E5-F12)+ABS(E4-F12)+ABS(E3-F12)+ABS(E2-F12))/11$$

The CCI, a ratio, is calculated in column H. The numerator is the difference between today's typical price and today's moving average. The denominator is today's mean deviation multiplied by the constant 0.015. The formula for cell H12 is:

$$=(E12-F12)/(0.015*G12)$$

—Editor

	A	B	C	D	E	F	G	H
1	Date	High	Low	Close	Typical Price	11 period	11 period	CCI
2	930104	3319.21	3298.68	3309.22	3309.04	Moving	Mean	
3	930105	3338.12	3279.23	3307.87	3308.41	Average	Deviation	
4	930106	3330.29	3276.53	3305.16	3303.99			
5	930107	3313.26	3260.85	3268.96	3281.02			
6	930108	3280.31	3221.68	3251.67	3251.22			
7	930111	3262.75	3250.05	3262.75	3258.52			
8	930112	3268.15	3239.51	3264.64	3257.43			
9	930113	3269.50	3243.83	3263.56	3258.96			
10	930114	3279.22	3251.13	3267.88	3266.08			
11	930115	3285.17	3258.15	3271.12	3271.48			
12	930118	3296.52	3244.65	3274.91	3272.03	3276.20	17.76	-15.66
13	930119	3283.28	3254.37	3255.99	3264.55	3272.15	13.99	-36.24
14	930120	3278.96	3231.41	3241.95	3250.77	3266.91	11.07	-97.23
15	930121	3269.77	3219.25	3253.02	3247.35	3261.76	8.42	-114.10
16	930122	3292.74	3225.74	3256.81	3258.43	3259.71	6.42	-13.30
17	930125	3324.89	3243.84	3292.20	3286.98	3262.96	8.42	190.18
18	930126	3331.91	3272.47	3298.95	3301.11	3266.83	11.68	195.58
19	930127	3318.67	3260.05	3291.39	3290.04	3269.80	13.21	102.16
20	930128	3327.86	3270.58	3306.25	3301.56	3273.67	15.46	120.31
21	930129	3331.10	3287.06	3310.03	3309.40	3277.61	18.37	115.35
22	930201	3332.45	3308.40	3332.18	3324.34	3282.41	21.63	129.26
23	930202	3355.68	3300.30	3328.67	3328.22	3287.52	23.55	115.19
24	930203	3397.83	3322.73	3373.79	3364.78	3296.63	27.20	167.02
25	930304	3441.33	3367.03	3416.74	3408.37	3310.96	33.07	196.38
26	930205	3443.21	3410.79	3442.14	3432.05	3327.75	40.44	171.94
27	930208	3472.94	3408.91	3437.54	3439.80	3344.24	48.73	130.72
28	930209	3436.46	3407.82	3414.58	3419.62	3356.30	51.48	82.01
29	930210	3423.76	3406.47	3406.47	3412.23	3366.40	50.92	60.01

SIDEBAR FIGURE 1: EXCEL SPREADSHEET. *This Excel spreadsheet calculates an 11-period CCI for the Dow Jones Industrial Average.*

The Lindsay A-D Indicator

The advance-decline line is handy for picking market tops, but lead time is a recurring problem, you say? Favors suggests this variation as an alternative to overcome that bothersome predicament.

by Jerry Favors

Most students of technical analysis are familiar with the advance-decline line†. To construct one, you simply begin with some base number and if today's advances exceed declines for the day, you add the number of net advances (advances minus declines) to that base number. If declines exceed advances for the day, you subtract the number of net declines (declines minus advances) from that base number. This same process is repeated each day and is then plotted along with a chart of the Dow Jones Industrial Average (DJIA). The theory is that if the DJIA moves to a new high but the advance/decline line does not, you have negative divergence and a potential top. Contrary to popular opinion, the regular A-D line is not especially reliable at identifying important market bottoms. While the A-D line does have an impressive record at market tops, the question of lead time remains a nagging problem.

LEAD TIME EXAMPLE

Prior to the July 1990 top, the A-D line peaked on August 8, 1989. The DJIA did not see its final high until July 17, 1990, 11 months later. This question of lead time remains a bothersome deficiency for the daily A-D line. Technician George Lindsay used the advance-decline data differently, in order to derive short-term buy or sell signals. Each day you will plot the difference between the advances and declines for the day. For instance, if there are 1,000 advances and 600 declines, your plot for that day is +400. If there are 900 declines and 400 advances, your plot for the day becomes -500. A sell signal from this indicator requires a "triple zigzag pattern," as illustrated in Figure 1.

Notice in Figure 1 you have three higher peaks in the DJIA on three lower peaks in the net advances. A sell signal requires three lower peaks before a signal can be given. A buy signal is given when the DJIA reaches a

†*See Traders' Glossary for complete description*

JIM FRISINO

bottom, then rallies, then falls to a new low. The A-D indicator, however, actually bottoms at point A, rallies to point B, then falls to a higher low at point C, showing positive divergence.

SELL SIGNALS FOR A-D

Figure 2 shows a sell signal for the A-D indicator during May and June 1990. Let's just examine the first signal. The DJIA rallied to a high of 2801 on May 11, 1990. That same day, there were 1,282 advances and 339 declines, showing 943 net advances for the day (1282 - 339 = 943). This represents point A on the chart. The DJIA pulled back and then rallied to a closing high of 2870 on May 29, 1990 (point B). However, on May 29 there were only 673 net advances for the day, versus 943 on May 11. Here, you have a higher close on a lower net

> While the A-D line does have an impressive record at market tops, the question of lead time remains a nagging problem.

A-D peak. Now, one more DJIA peak is needed on a still-lower peak in the number of net advances, which occurred on June 4, 1990, when the DJIA closed at 2935 on 628 net advances.

The DJIA fell 92 points to a closing low of 2842 on June 26, 1990. The DJIA then rallied to a new closing high of 2969 on July 12, 1990, but that day there were only 442 net advances, giving a repeat sell signal. The DJIA peaked two days later at 2999.75 on a closing basis and then began a major decline of 634 points on a closing basis. As you can see from Figure 3, this technique has been very accurate at catching short-term tops or bottoms and when combined with other tools can greatly increase the accuracy of your market timing.

Finally, for a signal to be truly valid via this technique the DJIA should reach a new hourly high or low the same day as the new closing high or low on each of the three peaks at a top or two troughs for a bottom. By this we mean new hourly and closing highs for that swing, not necessarily new bull or bear market highs or lows.

Jerry Favors publishes "The Jerry Favors Analysis" newsletter, 7238 Durness Drive, Worthington, OH 43235, (800) 231-4820.

FIGURE 1

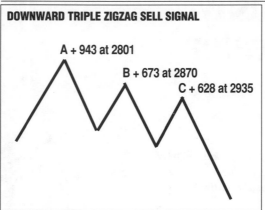

DOWNWARD TRIPLE ZIGZAG SELL SIGNAL

A + 943 at 2801
B + 673 at 2870
C + 628 at 2935

Short-term top signals occur when the net daily advances minus declines produce a series of three lower peaks, while the DJIA attain three higher peaks.

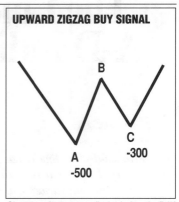

UPWARD ZIGZAG BUY SIGNAL

B
C
-300
A
-500

Short-term bottoms are flashed when the DJIA produces a series of two lower lows, while the net advances minus declines make a series of two higher lows.

FIGURE 2

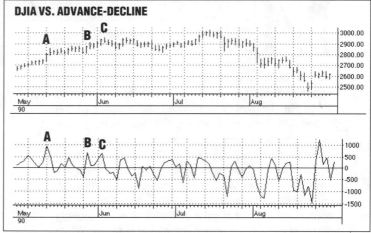

DJIA VS. ADVANCE-DECLINE

On May 11 (A), the DJIA rallied to 2801 while advances minus declines net a gain of +943. At B, the DJIA reached 2870 and the indicator touched +673. On June 4, the DJIA climbed to 2935 while the indicator lagged with a reading of +628 (C), thus creating a short-term sell signal.

FIGURE 3

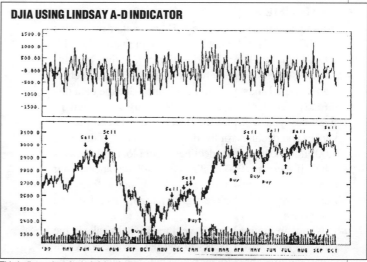

DJIA USING LINDSAY A-D INDICATOR

This indicator is quite helpful at forewarning short-term tops and bottoms. The indicator can complement other short-term timing tools.

JOE KRESOJE

Closing Tick

by Arthur A. Merrill, C.M.T.

Buyers' market or sellers' market? Counting the upticks and downticks can give you a clue, Merrill says.

Are buyers reaching for stock? Do they have to bid a price higher than the last price given (an uptick)? Or do sellers have to accept a lower price to get rid of their stock (a downtick)? A count of the upticks and downticks should indicate whether it's a buyers' or sellers' market.

The closing tick is reported each day in the financial press. It shows, for various markets, the number of stocks whose last change in price was an increase less the number the last change of which was a

decrease. How well does this statistic forecast the price movement on the following day? I asked my computer to check it out, using a database of the last 417 trading days on the New York Stock Exchange (NYSE).

If the upticks exceeded the downticks (a positive closing tick), how much of a difference is required to favor rising prices the following day? Take a look at Figure 1. For an example of the use of this chart, if upticks exceeded downticks by more than 750, the Standard & Poor's 500 index rose an average of 1.1% the following day.

My conclusion from Figure 1: The chances of a rising day seem mildly probable if the closing tick is positive but less

than 700. If the closing tick is more than 700, I'd rate it highly probable.

Look at Figure 2 for negative closing ticks. Here, zero is at the top of the chart, since the average price change is negative. My conclusion: Negative closing ticks are mildy bearish until they get lower than -450. If they are below that, I'd rate it a strong bearish sign.

Arthur Merrill is a Chartered Market Technician and the author of many reports and books, including Behavior of Prices on Wall Street *and* Filtered Waves, Basic Theory.

FIGURE 1

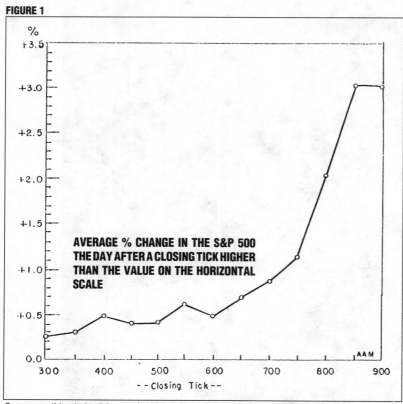

AVERAGE % CHANGE IN THE S&P 500 THE DAY AFTER A CLOSING TICK HIGHER THAN THE VALUE ON THE HORIZONTAL SCALE

On average, if the closing tick exceeds 300, the chances of a stock market rally the next day is mildly probable. If the closing tick is more than 700, then the indication of a rally the next day is stronger.

FIGURE 2

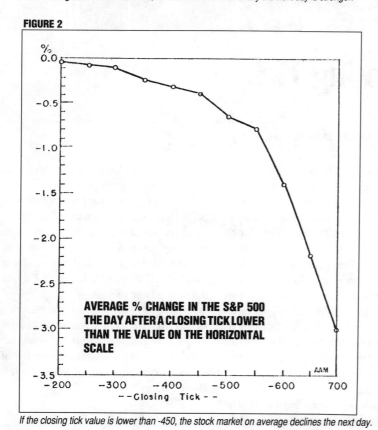

AVERAGE % CHANGE IN THE S&P 500 THE DAY AFTER A CLOSING TICK LOWER THAN THE VALUE ON THE HORIZONTAL SCALE

If the closing tick value is lower than -450, the stock market on average declines the next day.

MARY EMMONS

A Low-Risk, High-Potential Return Option Strategy

Can call options be used as a substitute for purchasing stocks? Covered calls—selling a call on stock being held—is one low-risk strategy, but profits can be limited on an up move. Another low-risk strategy, the long call plus cash equivalent, attempts to preserve capital while combining safety and potentially high profit. Jean-Olivier Fraisse explains how.

by Jean-Olivier Fraisse, C.F.A.

O ptions trading is not for the faint of heart. Beyond technical skills, it requires intuition and just plain luck. Some option strategies, however, are no riskier than stock ownership. A well-known low-risk strategy is covered call writing, which consists of selling a call on stock currently held. It works well in stable or declining markets, but it limits profits on an up move, which can be costly in the long run. A second low-risk strategy, the long call plus cash equivalent, strives to preserve capital while combining the safety of a fixed-interest income and the potentially high rewards of stock ownership. This low-risk strategy is most attractive when interest rates are relatively high. It does not work as well when short-term rates are low, as was the case at year-end 1991. It is up to the reader to decide whether the strategy remains attractive for his or her own circumstances.

STRATEGY: BUY CALL, INVEST CASH

The market outlook appears bullish and you are of the opinion that stock XYZ is currently undervalued at a price of $100 per share. In your view, XYZ should trade at a higher price with good prospects for a significant move in the near future. You are considering the purchase of one hundred shares of XYZ stock for an investment of $10,000 plus commissions (commissions are ignored from here on for the sake of simplicity).

> **Overall, the proposed option strategy is well worth looking into as an alternative to stock ownership with a short-term horizon.**

Instead of buying the stock outright, consider investing your $10,000 in a money market fund or Treasury bills yielding some 5% per annum. Simultaneously, purchase a six-month XYZ call with an exercise price of $105. The cost is the option premium plus commission (say, $5 per share, or $500 in total). Why an exercise price of $105? The closer the exercise price to the current stock price, the closer the call is to being at-the-money and the more expensive the premium. However, an option that is close to being at-the-money is more sensitive to stock price variations — its delta† is higher — than an option deeply out of the money. The tradeoff between delta and premium depends on how much you can afford for the option and on your assessment of how volatile the price of XYZ stock is.

OUTCOME: LOW RISK, HIGH POTENTIAL

If, at the end of the six-month period, XYZ trades at $115 per share, the profit on owning 100 shares would amount to $1,500. The call buyer would have gained $500, since the call is now 10 points in the money ($1,000 profit on the call less the $500 premium paid); in addition, the call buyer would have received a $250 interest on the money market instrument.

If, instead of going up, XYZ shares went down to $80, the loss for owning the stock would be $2,000. The call buyer would have lost only the $500 call premium and the option would expire worthless. However, the $500 loss would have been partly compensated by the $250 interest income on the Treasury bill, so the start-up capital is substantially unaffected.

As shown in Figures 1 and 2, the call buyer participates in most up moves in XYZ stock price while suffering little in down

moves. On the other hand, the call buyer will not receive any dividend payments during the call holding period, although such payments would probably amount to less than the interest received on the Treasury bill. Overall, the proposed option strategy is well worth looking into as an alternative to stock ownership with a short-term horizon.

The same strategy can also be applied to the market at large by buying a call option on a broad-based stock index, such as the Standard & Poor's 500 or 100. It is yet another way to cash in on expected rising stock prices. It can also be adapted to a bearish market outlook by buying a put and investing into a short-term fixed-income instrument instead of selling short the corresponding stock.

Jean-Olivier Fraisse, CFA, CMT, is a consultant in international finance and an options trader based in Washington, DC.

FURTHER READING
Fraisse, Jean-Olivier [1991]. "Assessing risk in an equity portfolio," STOCKS & COMMODITIES, December.
_____ [1992]. "Using futures and options to reshape portfolio risk," STOCKS & COMMODITIES, January.

FIGURE 1

STOCK OWNERSHIP AND THE LONG CALL

Stock Price	Investment	Stock Value	Profit (Loss)	Investment	Money market	Call Value	Profit (Loss)
65	10000	6500	-3500	10500	10250	0	-250
70	10000	7000	-3000	10500	10250	0	-250
75	10000	7500	-2500	10500	10250	0	-250
80	10000	8000	-2000	10500	10250	0	-250
85	10000	8500	-1500	10500	10250	0	-250
90	10000	9000	-1000	10500	10250	0	-250
95	10000	9500	-500	10500	10250	0	-250
100	10000	10000	0	10500	10250	0	-250
105	10000	10500	500	10500	10250	0	-250
110	10000	11000	1000	10500	10250	500	250
115	10000	11500	1500	10500	10250	1000	750
120	10000	12000	2000	10500	10250	1500	1250
125	10000	12500	2500	10500	10250	2000	1750
130	10000	13000	3000	10500	10250	2500	2250

Owning the stock shares outright provides the highest potential return with commensurate risk. Buying the call while investing the original balance in a money market instrument offers the potential of returns with a limited risk of the cost of the option offset by the interest from the money market instrument.

FIGURE 2

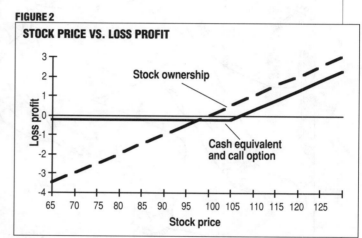

The profit and loss potential based on the price of the stock is presented here. If the stock falls in value, the stock owner suffers. The call option owner realizes a loss of the premium for the call but gains from the interest of the money market instrument.

Intermarket Analysis And The Deutschemark

MIKE HORSWILL

Richard Forest, a two-time Traders' Challenge winner, becomes a STOCKS & COMMODITIES author with this monograph on how intermarket analysis—that is, analyzing elements across more than one market and across countries to predict the outcome of seemingly disparate elements — can be used to trade the Deutschemark or other currencies. Forest points out that the U.S. dollar and the Deutschemark are interrelated and the dollar and interest rates are interrelated, and thus, by watching interest rates the behavior of the Deutschemark and the dollar may be predicted. He goes on to write that an analytical indicator called a dual moving average crossover (DMAC) works well to predict when currencies change trends because that indicator is most accurate in long-lasting trends instead of brief fluctuations.

by Richard Forest

I ntermarket analysis, a method by which a trader may compare pricing elements of two markets that are related or inversely related to one another, can be applied to straightforward technical analysis to successfully trade the Deutschemark or other currencies. One of the elements in question can be a direct influence on the other correlative element: For example, the behavior of the Deutschemark is closely linked to the U.S. dollar. In turn, the value of the U.S. dollar is closely linked to interest rate behavior. By monitoring interest rates, therefore, traders can make predictions about the price trend behavior of the U.S. dollar and the Deutschemark.

In general, a currency with high interest rates will attract large amounts of money due to the high return on investment for lenders and investors. On the other hand, falling interest rates are bearish for a currency, as investors will shy away from it and instead gravitate toward investment possibilities with higher rates of return. Thus, falling interest rates in the United States and increasing interest rates in Germany will decrease the value of the U.S. dollar but increase the value of the Deutschemark.

MONITORING PRICE TRENDS

Deutschemark price trends can be monitored by drawing an intermarket correlation with the U.S. long-term bond yield. Figure 1 is a correlative plot of the Deutschemark's price per $1,000 U.S. and the U.S. long-term bond yield. The chart is inversely proportional to the Deutschemark's value. The mark is plotted in this manner so that a rise in the bond yield correlates with a rise in the mark per U.S. dollar.

Technical analysis can be used in conjunction with intermarket analysis to predict trend continuation and reversals along with the correlation of the bond yield and the value of the Deutschemark. For example, sloping trendlines or support lines can be used to predict trend continuation. From March to July 1991, the mark per U.S. dollar performed according to the sloping support line seen in Figure 1. In July, the U.S. long-term bond

FIGURE 1

CORRELATIVE PLOT
Mark vs. $1,000 U.S. and U.S. long-term bond yield

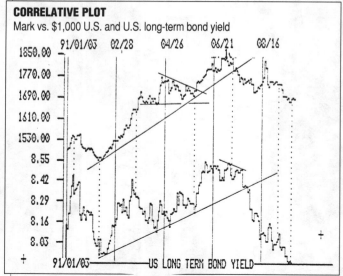

Here is a correlative plot of the Deutschemark's price per $1,000 U.S. and the U.S. long-term bond yield. The chart is inversely proportional to the Deutschemark's value. The mark is plotted in this way so that a rise in the bond yield correlates with a rise in the mark per U.S. dollar.

yield peaked as well as the mark per U.S. dollar value. Shortly thereafter, the mark per U.S. dollar value fell below the sloping support line, flashing a trend reversal. At that time, the upward

> ### The 10-day RSI curve indicated a trend reversal as early as June 21 before the DMAC flashed the trend reversal (Figures 2, 3 and 4).

trend for the U.S. dollar ended and the mark's value started to increase. The value of the mark is likely to remain bullish for a while until the U.S. bond yield starts to increase again.

FIGURE 2

DEUTSCHEMARK PER $1,000 U.S. AS OF 9/21/91
Short-term 10-day moving average vs. long-term 40-day moving average

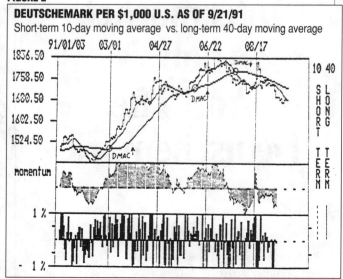

Because interest rates or bond yields are influenced by long-lasting economic cycles, the use of short-term and long-term moving averages work well in predicting trend continuation or reversals.

Because interest rates or bond yields are influenced by long-lasting economic cycles, the use of short-term and long-term moving averages work well in predicting trend continuation or reversals. By using a dual moving average crossover (DMAC)† traders could have predicted an increase in the U.S. dollar that occurred prior to March 1991 (Figures 2 and 3). In addition, this upward cycle started after the 10-day relative strength index (RSI) curve emerged from a period of oversold conditions (Figure 4).

DEVELOPING PATTERNS
From late February to mid-March, a sharp increase in the yield

FIGURE 3

U.S. LONG-TERM BOND YIELD USING DMAC
Short-term vs. long-term moving averages

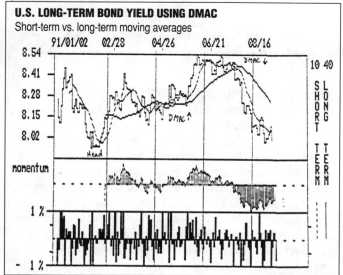

An increase in the U.S. dollar that occurred prior to March 1991 was also predicted by the formation of the yield head bottom. The 10-day RSI curve predicted a trend reversal as early as June 21 before the DMAC flashed the trend reversal.

FIGURE 4

DEUTSCHEMARK PER $1,000 U.S. AS OF 9/21/91
10-day RSI curve emerges from oversold conditions

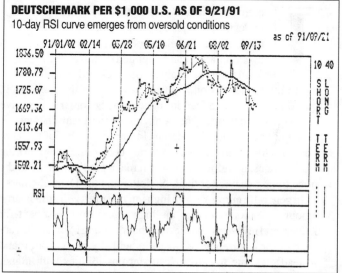

This upward cycle started after the 10-day relative strength index (RSI) curve emerged from a period of oversold conditions.

and the mark per U.S. dollar occurred, and from late March to early May a sideways pattern developed for the bond yield, slowing the rise in the value of the mark per U.S. dollar. During late May, the 10-day moving average crossed above the 40-day moving average, confirming the rally for the dollar. By July, however, the long-term bond yield and the U.S. dollar both peaked while the Deutschemark bottomed. In late July, German banks announced that their interest rates were likely to increase, and the U.S. long-term bond yield reacted by decreasing, creating another crossover of the short and long moving averages; and the beginning of a trend reversal flashed for the Deutschemark. The 10-day RSI curve indicated a trend reversal as early as June 21 before the DMAC flashed the trend reversal (Figures 2, 3 and 4). For now, a bullish trend appears to be under way for the Deutschemark, based on the recent downward slope of the long-term moving average of the mark per U.S. dollar and the falling U.S. long-term bond yield. A bottom formation for the yield will be the next formation to look for, at which time the mark's bullish trend should slow down.

Interest rates do not move at random but rather in long-lasting trends controlled by economic cycles that are themselves long lasting. This is why dual moving average crossovers work well for predicting currency trend reversals. Intermarket analysis or correlation is a tool that traders should make use of to predict the movement of the Deutschemark as well as other currencies.

Richard Forest, a two-time STOCKS & COMMODITIES *Traders' Challenge winner, is a petroleum geologist with an interest in developing software for the analysis of market movements. He lives in Calgary, Alberta, Canada.*

FOR ADDITIONAL READING

Murphy, John J. [1991]. "An interview with John Murphy," STOCKS & COMMODITIES, June.

Developing An Edge

by John Sweeney

Once you've developed something with an edge on the market, it's only natural to want to exploit it mercilessly, making hay while the sun shineth, so to speak. The simplest way I know to do this is to add more positions to your basic direction, buying dips when long, selling rallies when short. In my last three Settlements, I've battered one harebrained idea into reasonably profitable shape so that it gives us good trend selections and gets me out in a timely manner. However, there's more.

Once we're in a good trade (which we know via the maximum adverse excursion [MAE] statistics), we may as well add stocks or commodities, but in some rational formulation. How much, we ask, of a dip is enough to trigger additional entries?

Two things to think of immediately here: (1) We define the prospects for an additional good trade not by pyramiding (which is using the profits on early contracts for margin on additional contract) but by having the cash to buy more on a completely independent basis; and (2) we define a good trade in this mode just as we define a good trade in the original mode — exit and entry rules together with measurements of the worst price moves against the position.

Along this line, Figure 1 shows the trades from the basic trading system developed to date, together with a 10-day simple moving average. Take it from past work (Settlement, April and May 1991) that averages, because of their lag behavior, efficiently skim along the tops and bottoms of price ranges. You can eyeball this "efficiency" or you could test for it quantitatively. To speed things up and avoid the arguments of optimization, I'm simply specifying a value range I've used for years: eight to 10 days.

A BEHOLD! BUG?

It would be great at this point to add a trading rule and simply have N-Tech's Behold! trading system do the trades and report the results. Unfortunately, once I add logic that passes the programming test built into Behold!, no new trades showed up. I put in a call to N-Tech for help and moved on to test the new trades manually. (Later, N-Tech called back to let me know that they had disabled the pyramiding capability of the logic analysis of the system.)

Jumping ahead, Figure 5 shows a table for the 1989 results of add-on trades. The trading rule was "if already long, buy at the 10-day simple moving average price if the low of the day was less than the 10-day simple moving average. If already short, sell at the 10-day simple moving average price if the high of the day was more than the 10-day simple moving average. Exit all trades

FIGURE 1

10-DAY SIMPLE MOVING AVERAGE

In 1989, the system developed over the last three months traded for a $9,282 profit at the points shown. The 10-day simple moving average has been added to suggest points of additional entry.

FIGURE 2

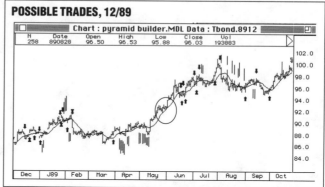

POSSIBLE TRADES, 12/89

The basic trades indicated by arrows are augmented by additional trades in the same direction (indicated by simple lines). These trades add additional positions when prices touch the 10-day simple moving average. The circled area looks as though it qualifies, but prices missed the target by a tick or so.

when the underlying system stops out or reverses."

Note that this table isn't very long. In fact, it's only about an eighth of the number of trades that could have been made, as shown by the plethora of lines on Figure 2. Looking at the net column, you'll see what are known as profits. In fact, after the first 13 trades, I stopped keeping track. The rate of return calculations would have been meaningless because the profits were so huge. If you tie into a good trend and keep trading it, you'll make money with little risk. Even not-so-sharp trends as in August 1989 could make money.

The results for the 1989 data are certainly pleasant, but things like that don't come along often, and who can pull the trigger that many times? I'd argue you could if you could be reasonably assured that every new trade, treated independently, had limited

FIGURE 3

TRADES VS. MAE

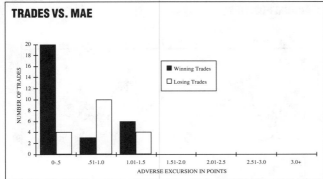

Add-on trades in this experiment had a very high probability of being winners. Here, the number of winners is almost twice the number of losers — but the MAE distributions of winners and losers are not distinct.

FIGURE 4

PROFIT OR LOSS, ADD-ON TRADES, 1989 T-BONDS

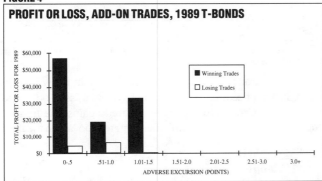

Given the high probability of a win when doing add-ons, it's not surprising that the dollar value of the wins far exceeds the losses, at least in this test case.

FIGURE 5

	ENTRY	Price	EXIT PX	EXIT DT	NET	Cumulative	MAE
\multicolumn{8}{l}{GAINS AND LOSSES FROM AN ADD-ON STRATEGY}

	ENTRY	Price	EXIT PX	EXIT DT	NET	Cumulative	MAE
1	95	-87.78	90.56	110	2780	2780	0
2	96	-88.16	90.56	110	2400	5180	0
3	113	90.38	-90.62	116	-240	4940	-0.4
4	114	90.5	-90.62	116	-120	4820	-0.28
5	115	90.72	-90.62	116	100	4920	-0.06
6	117	-90.625	89.9	120	-725	4195	-0.725
7	118	-90.675	89.9	120	-775	3420	-0.775
8	159	-88.431	94.97	209	6539	9959	-0.551
9	160	-88.38	94.97	209	6590	16549	-0.5
10	161	-88.31	94.97	209	6660	23209	-0.43
11	162	-88.31	94.97	209	6660	29869	-0.43
12	163	-87.97	94.97	209	7000	36869	-0.09
13	164	-88.62	94.97	209	6350	43219	-0.74
14	175	-89.51	94.97	209	5460	48679	-1.39
15	176	-89.509	94.97	209	5461	54140	-1.389
16	177	-89.527	94.97	209	5443	59583	-1.407
17	178	-89.22	94.97	209	5750	65333	-1.1
18	179	-89.178	94.97	209	5792	71125	-1.058
19	180	-89.44	94.97	209	5530	76655	-1.32
20	181	-88.56	94.97	209	6410	83065	-0.44
21	182	-88.28	94.97	209	6690	89755	-0.16
22	183	-88.66	94.97	209	6310	96065	-0.54
23	225	97.75	-98.45	237	-700	95365	-0.7
24	226	97.62	-98.45	237	-830	94535	-0.83
25	227	97.52	-98.45	237	-930	93605	-0.93
26	231	97.42	-98.45	237	-1030	92575	-1.03
27	233	97.241	-98.45	237	-1209	91366	-1.209
28	234	97.209	-98.45	237	-1241	90125	-1.241
29	235	97.41	-98.45	237	-1040	89085	-1.04
30	236	98.31	-98.45	237	-140	88945	-0.14
31	242	99.53	-97.03	262	2500	91445	0
32	247	98.484	-97.03	262	1454	92899	0
33	251	97.188	-97.03	262	158	93057	-0.252
34	253	96.969	-97.03	262	-61	92996	-0.151
35	256	96.59	-97.03	262	-440	92556	-0.53
36	257	96.5	-97.03	262	-530	92026	-0.53
37	258	96.528	-97.03	262	-502	91524	-0.502
38	260	96.434	-97.03	262	-596	90928	-0.596
39	261	96.391	-97.03	262	-639	90289	-0.639
40	269	-97.041	97.5	271	459	90748	-0.321
41	270	-97.119	97.5	271	381	91129	-0.399
42	272	97.31	-96.06	282	1250	92379	-0.28
43	273	97.313	-96.06	282	1253	93632	0
44	274	97.269	-96.06	282	1209	94841	0
45	291	-97.634	99.19	300	1556	96397	0
46	294	-98.219	99.19	300	971	97368	-0.279
47	295	-98.636	99.19	300	554	97922	0

Gains and losses from an add-on trading strategy. 1989 showed spectacularly positive results.

potential for loss. That is, each trade's loss could be limited to less than 2% of capital and the probability of loss to less than 67%, achieved by measuring how badly these add-on trades go against you.

Figures 3 and 4 show the MAE for December 1989 Treasury bonds, our experimental vehicle. The first significant difference from the results of the underlying trading rules is that there are more winners than losers. In fact, the "normal" ratio of one-third winners to two-thirds losers or draws is just about reversed. However, I also see a big problem.

rom Figure 3 we can see no sharp distinction between the adverse price movements of losing trades and winning trades. The first temptation might be to cut off all trades at 0.5 of a full point (16 ticks) and throw away the gains from the trades with losses up to 1.5 points. Looking at Figure 4, you realize you'd be throwing away winning trades worth over $55,000, turning them into losses.

Since neither winning nor losing trades showed an MAE exceeding 1.5 points, you might also ask whether you could live with losses of that size for profits of such high probability. You'd be tempted to say "Yes!" — but there's a trap here.

If you inspect Figure 5's net column, you can see that most of the losing add-on trades had an MAE equal to the amount of the loss on the trade. Those trades were — and, with any luck, generally will be — exited when the underlying position was closed out, indicating that the risk of the trade was controlled by the underlying position (since no stop was used) and the original trading rules.

For more temptation, the size of the losses may be manageable, at least in this experiment, though it did exceed the size of the losses ($700) specified for the underlying position and thus the 2% of capital requirement.

Don't buy it! The MAE chart is telling you that there is no

discernible difference in the behavior of the losing trades and winning trades. The add-on strategy doesn't have the ability to pick well. The profits are probably just a single, very favorable experience. Thus, whether to keep the add-ons depends on additional testing to see if this behavior is consistent.

> **Many opportunities I thought I saw visually were missed because the underlying system missed one good, long trend. Other trades actually entered against the trend as depicted by the average.**

SUSPICIONS CONFIRMED

I used 1986 to test my suspicions on. Figure 6 shows an almost perfect situation for the rule I'm following: Add positions as the prices skim the average. Circles mark opportunities acquired visually. This is what is known as a "target-rich" environment! If this strategy is going to work anywhere, it ought to work here.

It doesn't.

I'll spare you the full-blown table of results, but the strategy resulted in a $32,000 loss. Figure 7, parts a through d, show typical add-on entries, always made in the direction of the

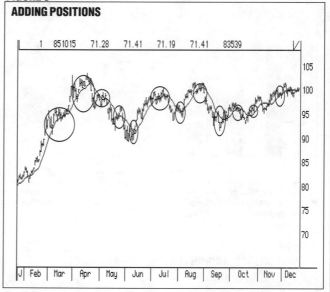

FIGURE 6

ADDING POSITIONS

The circles are from visually inspecting the chart for adding positions as the price skims the moving average.

underlying trade. Many opportunities I thought I saw visually were missed because the underlying system missed one good, long trend. Other trades actually entered against the trend as depicted by the average. Still others entered too late in the trend

FIGURE 7, PART A

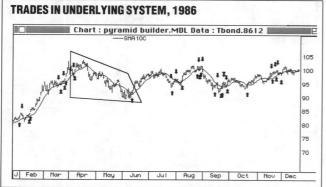

Trades taken by the underlying system in 1986. These are not the add-on trades. One long trend was missed by the underlying system.

FIGURE 7, PART C

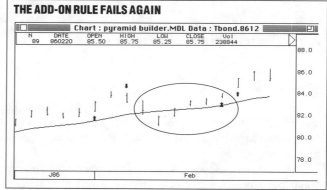

These trades both typify the failure of the add-on rule: entering in the direction of the underlying system but against the actual trend as indicated by the direction of movement of the average.

FIGURE 7, PART B

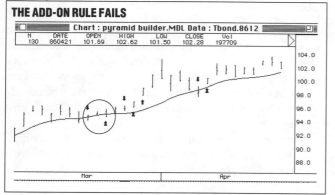

FIGURE 7, PART D

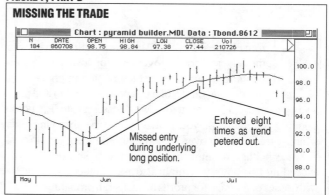

Here the opportunity to get with the underlying trade was present but muffed.

to make money.

The idea of adding on trades using a second indicator (in this case, the 10-day simple moving average) is not always a winner. I tried the system on other years' data with similarly spotty results. The MAE distributions were right: this add-on rule cannot distinguish a good trade from a bad one. This is also a good example of why you should treat add-on or pyramid trades as separate trading decisions subject to an evaluation independent of the evaluation of the underlying trading rules.

SUMMARY

I'm not going to give up on add-on trades. They are generally lucrative, but this particular add-on rule cannot be used. The next step in developing this trading system will be to look at other add-on rules.

John Sweeney is Technical Editor for STOCKS & COMMODITIES *magazine.*

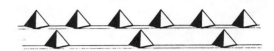

ADD-ONS VS. PYRAMIDING

Add-ons are trades adding to an existing directional position with full capitalization for each new trade. Pyramiding is adding trades to a directional position financed by profits from the original directional position. For add-ons, you must have the capital for the trades before you even take the first position. To pyramid, you must hope the original trade stays right, because if it turns around, you can quickly lose *all* your positions. With pyramiding, your break-even point on your original trade rises as you buy (sell) at higher and higher (lower and lower) prices. With add-ons, each additional position has its own break-even and stop point and is financed accordingly.

"To simplify our tax system, we've decided to deal directly with companies and eliminate the middle man--namely you, the worker."

CHAPTER 3

THE TRADERS' MAGAZINE

MARCH 1992

TECHNICAL ANALYSIS OF STOCKS & COMMODITIES™

Selecting Stocks For A Portfolio

As redundant as it may sound, following the stock market is in reality following a market of stocks. And surveying a market of stocks can present a challenge. The brothers Stewart, using time series analysis, here present a ranking method to design portfolios. It was this method that they used to select five stocks to build one portfolio for each year since 1967. We show here their results.

The first law of the jungle is the survival of the fittest, no matter how the jungle is defined. In the economic jungle, companies take the place of animals, and investors need to be keen observers of which ones are fittest to win their own battle of investment survival. To choose the fittest companies for inclusion in a portfolio, we conducted a study and determined that only three sets of data have to be statistically analyzed:

- The annual dividend
- The reported earnings
- The total market value of the outstanding shares

The study's goal was to locate companies with above-average growth, identify consistent performance among liquid securities and build low-risk portfolios.

In the economic jungle, companies take the place of animals, and investors need to be keen observers of which ones are fittest to win their own battle of investment survival.

by Donald Stewart and Kenneth Stewart

The first screen developed for the study was to determine the compound growth rate of earnings and dividends. For companies to qualify for the portfolio, they needed a 10% growth rate for both earnings and dividends. The growth analysis used six data points to cover five years of annual performance. The average annual percentage growth rate was determined by using least-squares fitting to the log of the data. The growth rate is the slope of the fitted line to the data. (See sidebar, "Determining growth rate.")

The second screen developed and used for the study measured the

BRAD WALKER

stability of earnings and dividend growth rates. Consistency in the rate of growth of earnings and dividends implies that the stock is less likely to shock investors with a surprise earnings announcement. We required a 90% reliability in the growth rates of the companies in order to be included in the portfolios built. Statisticians will recognize this measure as the r^2 of the growth rate regression. In calculating portfolio performance, we rolled over any merged and acquired companies into the successor stock. If the company went private, the proceeds were reinvested in the highest-rated stock not in the portfolio at the time of the acquisition. All the analysis begins and ends March 31; the first year for which we could construct portfolios was 1967.

Our model was based on an annual history of all companies on the New York Stock Exchange (NYSE). The data were constructed from the Standard & Poor's Daily Price Record for the NYSE, which was first published in 1962; it was the beginning of computerized data on the stock exchange. The earnings were those recorded by the pricing services at the time of the original report, and the companies had no chance to rewrite the original earnings reported in *The Wall Street Journal*. This is important, because it reflects what investors knew and when they knew it. In addition, the database contains all companies that merged or went bankrupt.

If companies passed the first two criteria screens, they were then ranked by total market value (the current price of the stock times shares outstanding). The companies with the highest market values are correlated with low market risk. Ranking stocks by market value produces stable lists on an annual basis, which are ideal for selecting vehicles that can be held for the long term. In Figure 1 are some examples of listing companies by their total market value in 1966 and 1990.

The top down approach to building portfolios has the added advantage of purchasing the strongest companies at the end of an economic boom and buying the smallest companies at the bottom of the cycle.

SPREADING THE RISK

The portfolios we constructed contain only five securities each. Most investors tend to be overdiversified, limiting the ability for a profitable idea to have a significant impact on returns. It is also important to ensure that the prospects for each company are not contingent on the occurrence of the same set of events; otherwise, the circumstances that would cause failure to one company would bring failure to all. Conveniently, the five stock portfolios contained different industries each year; 1970 was the only exception, when three of the five stocks were in the drug industry.

STOCKS FOR THE SMALL INVESTOR

We used our model to build a $2,000 portfolio that is typical for starting an investment retirement account (IRA) today. The returns for the top five stock portfolio since 1967 can be seen in Figure 2.

MEASURING THE RETURNS

Figure 3 lists portfolios that were formed each year using the same screening process. For example, in 1967 the stocks selected were MMM, GTE, SUO, KO and MRK. The numbers listed after each stock is the compounded rate of return since the stock was listed in the portfolio for that year. The next column is the portfolio's compound rate of return since that year, and finally the index fund's rate of return. The returns for all five stock model portfolios and an index fund include capital gains and dividends. This table presents a "what-if" scenario for the performance of a portfolio selected in each year, using the two screens to select from a list of stocks that are ranked by their prospective market value.

ASSESSING RISK AND LIQUIDITY

The stocks are listed in Figure 4, along with the number of years a particular stock was selected for a portfolio. The beta† is the percent change in the stock for every 1% change in the market based on the last 52 weeks of trading. The liquidity ratio is the dollar volume required to move the stock by 1%, expressed as a ratio to the market liquidity.

The average beta in the S&P 500 is 1.15, but due to the covariance† of the portfolio, the net beta is 1.00. Therefore, the model stocks have 6.5% less risk than the market itself does. The liquidity of these stocks is massive, taking more than $50 million to move the average stock by only 1%. Large investors can buy and sell in these markets.

FIGURE 1

DOMESTIC COMPANIES	
1966 Stock symbol	**($ in millions)**
T	$29,804
GM	26,809
IBM	18,176
XON	15,891
GE	9,972
TX	9,931
EK	9,888
DD	9,550
S	8,652
F	5,606
1990 Stock symbol	**($ in millions)**
IBM	$60,990
GE	57,747
XON	57,656
T	45,183
MO	36,768
BMY	27,974
GM	27,786
MRK	27,481
AN	27,471
WMT	26,742

T, American Telephone & Telegraph; AN, Amoco; BMY, Bristol-Myers Squibb; DD, Dupont; EK, Eastman Kodak; XON, Exxon; F, Ford; GE, General Electric; GM, General Motors; IBM, International Business Machines; MRK, Merck; MO, Philip Morris; S, Sears; TX, Texaco; WMT, Wal-Mart Stores

FIGURE 2

1967 MODEL PORTFOLIO
3/31/67 to 3/31/91

Stock	Shares	Price	Cost	Value	Beta
MMM	4	92.25	369.00	2820.64	1.13
GTE	7	51.375	359.63	2933.14	0.81
SUO	6	66.00	396.00	10819.12	0.56
KO	3	103.25	309.75	7993.10	1.23
MRK	4	81.50	399.35	10669.43	0.91
Gross			1833.73	35235.43	
Commissions			125.00	125.00	
Net			1958.73	35110.43	
Profit				33151.70	
Annual %				70.5	
Compound %				12.5	
Average Beta				0.928	

MMM, Minnesota Mining & Manufacturing; GTE, GTE Corp.; SUO, Shell Oil Corp.; KO, Coca-Cola

†See Traders' Glossary for complete description

SUMMARY

Based on the data gathered and analyzed, the biggest (market value), fastest (growth rate) and strongest (consistency) creatures of the economic jungle survive and prosper the way they do in the natural jungle. Of all, the biggest

> **Perhaps the largest species of the economic jungle are dinosaurs, destined to die out from sheer size.**

and best are experts at defending turf and expanding territory. Many small creatures in the jungle reproduce frequently and grow rapidly, but they also tend to have short life spans. Oftentimes they are food for larger creatures. Very few of the little creatures are elephants or tigers in vitro; these creatures are small and are meant to remain that way. On the other hand, considering what we know about the dinosaurs, the largest creatures to have ever walked this earth, perhaps the largest species of the economic jungle are investment dinosaurs, dominant now but destined to die out from

FIGURE 3

Year											Top 5 model	Sim. index fund
67	MMM	9	GTE	9	SUO	15	KO	15	MRK	15	11.42	9.79
68	GTE	11	KO	14	PRD	-1	MRK	15	BMY	13	12.55	10.10
69	GO	12	XRX	2	KO	14	GTE	11	MRK	16	12.42	9.85
70	XRX	2	MMM	9	AHP	12	WLA	11	BMY	15	11.22	10.83
71	IBM	7	XRX	1	ITT	5	AHP	12	MRK	16	10.56	10.58
72	XRX	-1	JNJ	11	KM	6	WLA	11	MO	22	14.30	10.62
73	JNJ	11	KM	5	MO	20	BDK	-3	GIS	16	13.68	10.83
74	JNJ	13	KM	7	MO	23	ITT	11	AEP	11	15.61	12.42
75	MO	25	BRY	17	RAL	13	BAX	8	BDK	-3	16.73	13.78
76	CCI	4	MO	26	EMR	12	CL	12	BRY	17	17.24	12.88
77	SLB	11	AHP	15	JNJ	20	CCI	6	MO	28	19.09	13.91
78	IBM	11	SLB	11	AHP	17	JNJ	21	MO	29	19.77	15.61
79	IBM	9	SLB	8	MO	30	AHP	7	JNJ	22	21.95	15.32
80	T	19	SLB	4	JNJ	24	MO	33	UNP	9	21.83	16.21
81	T	19	SLB	1	ARC	15	MMM	15	UNP	3	12.50	14.23
82	T	19	SLB	6	ARC	20	JNJ	23	PG	21	18.94	18.11
83	SLB	7	JNJ	22	MO	35	AHP	16	UCL	9	20.86	14.27
84	HWP	5	MO	39	AHP	16	TXO	-1	ABT	27	22.19	16.36
85	MO	38	AHP	15	HWP	7	ABT	26	CWE	14	22.54	16.13
86	MO	39	ABT	19	MCD	11	DNB	1	BUD	19	20.64	12.65
87	MO	37	WMT	28	ABT	14	MCD	8	DNB	-4	19.49	10.99
88	MO	48	WMT	40	ABT	29	BUD	20	PFE	28	33.96	17.40
89	MO	54	WMT	54	ABT	34	BUD	24	MCD	17	37.44	17.36
90	MO	74	WMT	63	AIG	3	ABT	47	BUD	41	45.55	15.31

1967-91 COMPOUND RATE FO RETURN

FIGURE 4

TOP FIVE MODEL MARKET FACTORS

Symbol	Years	Beta	Liq. Ratio	Stock
ABT	7	0.75	1.69	Abbott Labs
AEP	1	0.37	0.54	Amer Elec Power
AHP	8	0.80	1.61	Amer Home Prod
AIG	1	1.19	1.19	Amer Intl Group
ARC	2	0.62	2.27	Atlantic Richfield
BAX	1	1.26	0.60	Baxter Intl
BDK	2	1.73	0.17	Black & Decker
BMY	2	0.95	4.14	Brist.-Myers Squibb
BRY	2	0.90	3.70	Beatrice Foods
BUD	4	1.04	0.67	Anheuser-Busch
CCI	2	1.80	0.50	Citicorp
CL	1	1.21	0.63	Colgate-Palmolive
CWE	1	0.50	1.65	Commonwealth Edison
DNB	2	0.50	0.62	Dun & Bradstreet
EMR	1	0.94	0.58	Emerson Electric
GIS	1	1.40	0.73	General Mills
GO	1	0.85	2.07	Gulf Oil
GTE	3	0.81	1.64	GTE Corp
HWP	2	1.96	0.88	Hewlett-Packard
IBM	3	1.23	0.78	Intl Business Machines
ITT	2	1.72	0.70	ITT Corp
JNJ	9	1.12	2.50	Johnson & Johnson
KM	3	1.58	0.95	K mart Corp
KO	3	1.23	2.54	Coca-Cola

FIGURE 4 (cont'd)

Symbol	Years	Beta	Liq. Ratio	Stock
MCD	3	1.11	1.29	McDonald's Corp
MMM	3	1.13	2.15	Minnesota Mining
MO	17	1.11	6.56	Philip Morris
MRK	4	0.91	3.86	Merck & Co
PFE	1	1.56	1.97	Pfizer Inc
PG	1	1.17	2.13	Procter & Gamble
PRD	1	0.59	0.14	Polaroid Corp
RAL	1	1.07	0.52	Ralston Purina
SLB	7	1.17	1.57	Schlumberger Ltd
SUO	1	0.95	5.68	Shell Oil
T	3	0.68	5.82	AT&T
TXO	1	1.25	1.29	Texas Oil & Gas
UCL	1	0.97	0.53	Unocal Corp
UNP	2	0.86	0.62	Union Pacific
WLA	2	0.82	1.75	Warner-Lambert
WMT	4	1.38	3.70	Wal-Mart
XRX	4	1.39	0.56	Xerox
Weighted Avg.		1.08	2.69	

sheer size, while the economic mice survive. All investors and traders can do is invest cautiously, using the data set forth here and keeping in mind that only the fittest survive.

Donald Stewart is president of Stewart Asset Management, a Carefree, AZ, portfolio advisory firm. Kenneth Stewart is editor and publisher of "CODA Smartline." The analysis was originally developed for Stewart Asset Management.

DETERMINING GROWTH RATE

One method for determining a growth rate is to fit a regression line using the least-squares method to the data. Figure 1 is a graph of the annual dividends for Merck & Company with a regression line drawn. This straight line is calculated to fit the data with the least amount of error. The formula for this line is :

$$Y = a + bX$$

The letter Y is the dividends and the letter X represents time. The letter a is the Y intercept when X equals zero and the letter b is the slope of the line. The slope of the line is the rate of change of the line. The formula that statisticians use to estimate the slope of the regression line is:

$$b = \frac{\sum XY - n\overline{XY}}{\sum X^2 - n\overline{X}^2}$$

SIDEBAR FIGURE 1

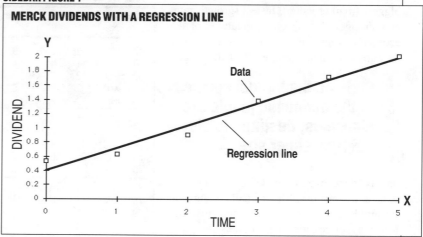

MERCK DIVIDENDS WITH A REGRESSION LINE

This chart is the reported dividends for Merck with a regression line drawn using the least-squares method.

If the data are converted to a logarithmic format, then the converted data will be on a percentage change basis. The rate of change will now represent the growth rate of the data.

The following table presents the calculation of determining the rate of growth of Merck & Co.'s dividends per share. The data are converted to natural logarithms, so that percentage changes in the data are measured.

n	Time	Dividends	Natural Log				
1	0	0.533	-0.6292	0	0.3959	0.0000
2	1	0.633	-0.4573	1	0.2091	-0.4573
3	2	0.899	-0.1065	4	0.0113	-0.2129
4	3	1.380	0.3221	9	0.1037	0.9663
5	4	1.720	0.5423	16	0.2941	2.1693
6	5	2.020	0.7031	25	0.4943	3.5155
	15		0.3745	55	1.5086	5.9808
	$=\sum X$		$=\sum Y$	$=\sum X^2$	$=\sum Y^2$	$=\sum XY$

n=6

$$\overline{X} = \frac{SX}{n} = 15/6 = 2.5$$

$$\overline{Y} = \frac{SY}{n} = 0.3745/6 = 0.0624$$

To calculate the growth rate b we substitute in the numbers for the symbols.

$$b = \frac{\sum XY - n\overline{XY}}{\sum X^2 - n\overline{X}^2}$$

$$b = \frac{5.9808 - 6\,(2.5)(0.0624)}{55 - 6(2.5)^2}$$

$$b = 0.2883$$

Remember that we converted the actual reported dividends to their natural logarithms to determine percentage changes. The value b — or slope of this regression line — needs to be converted back from this logarithmic format. We take the antilog of 0.2883, which is accomplished by raising the constant e to the power 0.2883, which results in 1.33. This step is on most calculators. Now subtract 1 and multiply by 100. The answer is 33% for the five-year growth rate. We subtracted 1 because the number returned was $1 + r$, where r is the five-year growth rate. Consider if last year's dividend was $1 and the rate of growth is 20%, then you would multiply $1 by 1.20 to determine that this year's dividend should be $1.20.

The steps for determining the growth rate of earnings per share is identical unless you are considering earnings during the present year as earnings are announced on a quarterly basis. Therefore, the first 5 points of data are fiscal year earnings, while the latest data may be only the first quarter of the present year. To compensate, we adjust the value of the time to represent what quarter the present earnings represent. If the first quarter is used, then the time values (the X variables) will be listed as "0, 1, 2, 3, 4, 4.25" instead of "0, 1, 2, 3, 4, 5." If the earnings represent the current first and second quarters' values, the X variables will be listed as "0, 1, 2, 3, 4, 4.50."

To determine the consistency of the dividend growth rate, the r^2 of the regression line is used. The r^2 is called the coefficient of determination and is an index that measures the degree that the dividends growth represents an exponential curve. An exponential curve represents consistent growth on a percentage basis. The best value would be 100 and the worst value zero. The coefficient of determination value is found by squaring the correlation coefficient. The formula is:

$$r = \frac{\sum XY - n\overline{XY}}{\sqrt{\left(\sum X^2 - n\overline{X}^2\right)\left(\sum Y^2 - n\overline{Y}^2\right)}}$$

Substituting the data, we find:

$$r = \frac{5.9808 - 6(2.5)(0.0624)}{\sqrt{\left(55 - 6\left(2.5\right)^2\right)\left(1.5086 - 6\left(0.0624\right)^2\right)}}$$

$r = 0.9895$
Now we will square r:
$r^2 = (0.9895)^2 = 0.9791$

Multiplying by 100 gives 97.91% reliability of dividend growth rate for Merck. The percentage change has been very consistent. To calculate earnings per share reliability, you must substitute in the natural logarithms of the fiscal year earnings for the Y variable. —*Editor*

Gail Dudack Of S.G. Warburg

"I'm a great believer in the idea that supply and demand works, and that's what the charts tell you."—Gail Dudack

S.G. Warburg senior vice president, head of market strategy and technical analyst Gail Dudack, C.M.T., is no newcomer to technical analysis or the world of Wall Street; she began her career at Pershing & Co. (now a division of Donaldson, Lufkin & Jenrette) in the early 1970s, eventually writing a weekly market strategy letter for Pershing before she joined international brokerage firm Warburg in 1987, where she writes both weekly and monthly strategy letters. In the meantime, she has served, among other capacities, on the Market Technicians Association board of governors and two terms as the MTA's president, and until recently was also on the board of directors for the New York Society of Security Analysts. She can also be seen as a regular panelist on the popular Wall Street Week *television show. Dudack spoke with* STOCKS & COMMODI- TIES *Editor Thom Hartle via a telephone interview on December 27, 1991, about, among other topics, the global markets, the indicators she uses, the use of flow of funds and general methodology.*

So I understand you started in the business as a fundamental analyst.

Well, I started as a fundamental analyst's assistant at Pershing & Co. back in the early 1970s in what was considered the training slot to become a junior analyst and eventually a full-fledged analyst, but while I was there I started studying technical analysis at night at the New York Institute of Finance and developed an interest in that "other" kind of analysis. About six to 12 months after I started at Pershing, our technician, who I think was called a "statistician" in those days, left,

and I asked for the job. Not that I got it directly, but since I was the only person who knew how to update those charts, I was allowed — *allowed!* — to update his charts after work. So I kept his charts up — a beautiful combination of breadth and market indices charts, which I still have today — for about six months and was eventually given an opportunity to be a technician.

During that time, how did you begin to see the value of technical analysis?

Well, I was just doing a lot of what we would call "bottoms-up," looking at individual stock patterns. Since Pershing was a retail organization, I was also looking at thousands and thousands of charts for the retail salesmen. It didn't take long to see that there was a lot of value in those charts, that stocks would break out and start an uptrend. So I got hooked on technical analysis after being in the business for really less than a year. Clearly, chart patterns showed you a lot about how people felt about companies before the news was ever out, and I'm a great believer in the

idea that supply and demand works, and that's what the charts tell you.

You said "bottoms-up"; do you have a bottoms-up approach and a top-down approach?

I am pretty eclectic; I will look and do anything and everything, but the system that I typically use to start with is the top-down, and I begin with a very long-term view of the market. For that study, I use the flow of funds analysis. The action of stocks is based on supply and demand and psychology, and there's no better way to get a feel for the very long-term view of supply and demand than the flow of funds work.

I start with that for the very long-term view and then I refine it with breadth and sentiment and some shorter-term liquidity on a top-down approach to the market. But there are times when you can go through all that and still not have a clear picture, because very often you will have indicators that are neutral, or indicators that are positive and negative, and it ends up being a wash.

† See Trader's Glossary for complete description

So when all else fails—

When all else fails, I go to the bottoms-up and look at what stocks are doing. There's usually a message there. I try to do that all the time, but I find that the time that bottoms-up really is best is when everything else looks neutral.

Let's start with the flow of funds you mentioned. What exactly are you measuring at that point when you look at flow of funds?

To me, flow of funds is looking at where money is invested, by all the different investing sectors, and looking at their stock, bond and cash ratios. For the flow of funds work, you can get most of the data from the Federal Reserve or through the Investment Company Institute, which is an organization of mutual funds.

So you're looking at —

I look to see what the total assets are in both the private and public institutions, what their stock/bond breakdown is, and of course, their cash, but I look to see how much equity they have in their portfolios, and look to see if that's historically high or low.

You're looking for extremes in equity ownership?

That's the first step. I do that for institutions, for foreign investors, for insurance companies, the mutual fund industry, which is small but a good sample of the public, and last but far from least, the households sector, because the households sector is by far the largest financial assets holder. Unfortunately, the numbers you receive from the Fed on this category is a derivative number. There is no research performed to get this number. It's derived after all the other parts have been figured out. It's not a good number, but it tells you a lot about the trend.

So I look at all those factors to see how much money is committed to equities, and whether they're overowned or underowned. That tells you a lot about the big picture.

The big picture you refer to is the long-term trend. You've looked at this going back how many years?

Back to the mid-1940s. We're looking at the postwar history. When you take that approach you have to make some mental adjustments. For example, institutions were not a big part of the pie in the 1940s; they never really grew up until the 1960s, so you have to account for that.

But we were talking about households, so let's take a look at them. Households hit a peak of equity ownership in 1968 (Figure 1), when 33.5% of their financial assets were in equities, and that was the beginning of the major top in the equity market. At the same time, foreigners also hit a historical high in equity ownership (Figure 2), with a very similar 33.6% of financial assets in U.S. stocks. Mutual funds peaked in 1970 (Figure 3). Between 1968 and 1972, which was the eventual top, each of those sectors went to historical levels of equity ownership, which told us one thing: the potential demand for stock was clearly decreasing, and at some point these sectors would become potential sellers; in other words, the supply of stock would increase. January 1973 was a major top, resulting in a 45% decline in the DJIA. Ownership patterns began to reverse in 1978 and most sectors got underowned by 1982, which to me was the end of the bear cycle. So we went from overownership in the late 1960s to early 1970s to underownership about 10 to 12 years later.

Where do you see us now?

Right now it's a mixed picture. The institutional sector, which is broken up between private and public pension funds, are what I would call fairly owned in equity. Private pension funds (Figure 4), which have been continuously adding to their equity base, now have 60% of their portfolios in equities. That's pretty close to their historical highs of 67%. So I have considered them zero players in the marketplace for the past few years. In fact, we have to see where and what might turn them from on-balance buyers to sellers.

Those are the private funds, right? Now what about the public funds?

The public pension funds, on the other hand, are probably the most interesting to analyze as well as the most difficult because up until the late 1960s, they could not hold more than 5% or 10% of their portfolios in equities. Those restrictions have slowly been relaxed, although a number of different states still restrict their public employee pension fund assets in terms of their exposure to equities. Currently, they have almost 40% of their assets in equities (Figure 5); it's hard to know what would be considered a peak, but I'm using a benchmark of about 50% to be the peak for public pension fund assets in equities, so we're getting close. So I think the pension sector as a total universe is fairly owned in equities.

So what's next? What about insurance, institutional …

The insurance group is not a major player, although they have huge assets and about 10.6% of their assets in equities (Figure 6). Recently, the range has been somewhere between 10 and 13%, but they're not big common stock players.

As for the institutional sector, it does not create a bullish picture for the market. But when we look at the remaining groups —the foreign, the mutual fund, the household—we find just the reverse. At the end of 1990, the household and foreign sectors had gotten close to creating a new all-time low ownership of U.S equities. They are potentially much bigger than the U.S. institutions, which I think surprises people. The institutions always have to be players in the stock market, but on balance it's the buying from foreigners and the public that has created market trends.

With households so underexposed in equities, I don't think that you can view the big bull market cycle, which I view as having started back in 1982, as anywhere near over, at least until you see the household sector more exposed to equities.

What do you see for the 1990s at this point?

At the beginning of the decade, equities will be the key form of investment; with low inflation, tangibles will not be the investment that they were in the 1970s and 1980s. I see long-term interest rates coming down, so bonds will become more like they were in the 1950s with much smaller real returns. You're going to find companies in a slow-growth economy that will be able to give you a steady 10% return on your money; this is really where people should be invested in the 1990s, yet households are still really very under-exposed to equities. I think there's quite a bit of bull market ahead of us when we look at the flow of funds.

In your flow of funds work, what about this record supply of stock offerings we've seen this year?

This was a concern, so we went back to our historical tables to see exactly how this could affect the stock market. Two things came to mind: First, we were running at a record level of new equity offerings the first half of this year. I asked myself whether we shouldn't relate this number to the outstanding supply of stock. Should we make a relationship between the two? The last time we had record offerings of stock, we had a lower stock base. So I compared the new stock offerings to the stock outstanding using the Wilshire 5000 index as a proxy. We found that the level was high in absolute terms, but on a percentage basis we were not at a record (Figure 7).

When was the record?

The all-time record level of stock offerings was in 1986, and if you recall, that was not a major market top; it was a flat, sideways market. So what was the big deal?

When we related stock offerings to the supply of outstanding stock, we found that the absolute peak on a percentage basis happened in 1983, which *was* a market top, if you recall, for a lot of technology stocks, which was the flood of new offerings at that time. When we compared stock offerings to stock outstanding, we found that we were not at an extreme; and I did not view that as a major problem.

But then again, if you're having this kind of stock supply after years of seeing the stock supply contract, don't you need new sources of demand for that stock?

Makes sense to me.

Right. So we went back to our flow of funds work, looking for historical average of equity ownership for each of the different sectors: the household, foreign, the institutional sectors; what would it take to get us there? What would they have to buy or sell in terms of dollar value

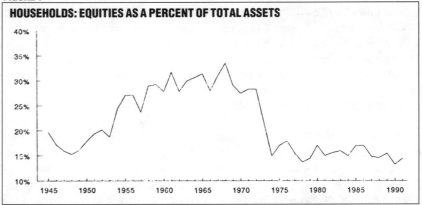

FIGURE 1

HOUSEHOLDS: EQUITIES AS A PERCENT OF TOTAL ASSETS

The peak of equity ownership for households reached a high of 33.5% in 1968, which was the beginning of a major top in the equity market.

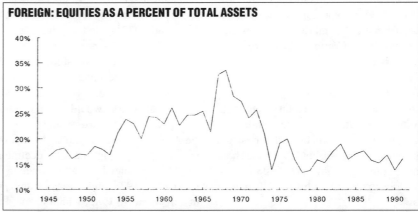

FIGURE 2

FOREIGN: EQUITIES AS A PERCENT OF TOTAL ASSETS

The peak of equity ownership by foreign nationals also occurred in 1968, with 33.6% of their financial assets.

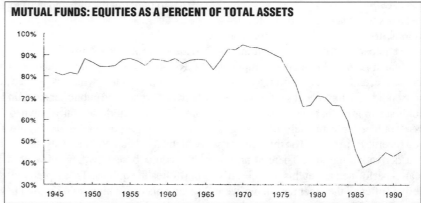

FIGURE 3

MUTUAL FUNDS: EQUITIES AS A PERCENT OF TOTAL ASSETS

The percentage of equity ownership by mutual funds (money market funds, equities, fixed income and balanced) peaked in 1970.

stock to reach an average equity ownership level? We looked at those averages, and they seem to make a lot of sense; this is important in this kind of work. The household sector shown in Figure 8 would have to have 21% of their assets in equities, and I felt that was a sensible number in an environment where long-term interest rates were falling and real interest rates

were going to their historical average of around 300-350 basis points.

So again, this was a table I was creating for potential demand for stock in an environment that I saw was changing.

And insurance—

Insurance companies would have slightly less than 10% of their assets in

FIGURE 4

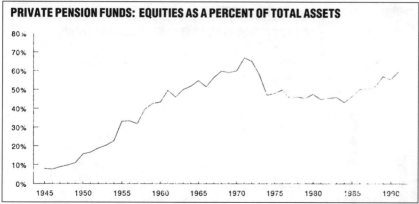

PRIVATE PENSION FUNDS: EQUITIES AS A PERCENT OF TOTAL ASSETS

Private pension funds currently have 60% of their portfolios in equities, close to the high of 67% reached in 1970.

FIGURE 5

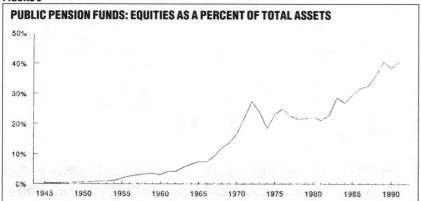

PUBLIC PENSION FUNDS: EQUITIES AS A PERCENT OF TOTAL ASSETS

Public pension funds were limited to the percentage of the portfolios that could be invested in equities. Since the restrictions have been removed, the percentage has grown to near 40%.

FIGURE 6

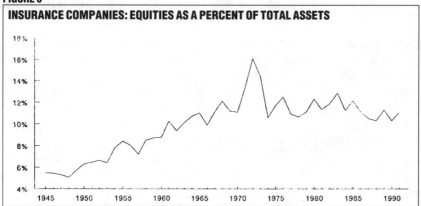

INSURANCE COMPANIES: EQUITIES AS A PERCENT OF TOTAL ASSETS

The insurance group has recently had a range of 10% to 13% commitment to equities.

equities, and in my table they were therefore net sellers — $13.5 billion in equities. Public institutions, which continue to be underweighted in equities, would be small buyers, but private pension funds, with their 60% holdings of equities, would end up being net sellers of stock of more than $76 billion.

Yet the mutual funds, household and foreigners who were underowned in equi-ties certainly outdid all those institutional sellers. We still ended up in our table with potential future demand for stocks — at $1.3 trillion. We redid our table again to strip out any possible double accounting by the Federal Reserve Board for mutual funds, pension fund assets or noncorporate equity and still found potential demand to be $1.1 trillion. Those numbers made sense in an environment where long-term interest rates were on the decline and headed down toward 350 basis points real return.

So new issues are not a problem?

No, I didn't see this new issuance of equities as a big problem, because I saw that the potential demand for equities to be much greater than people expect. In fact, we saw in the first 10 months of 1991 that through the mutual fund industry, the public has been a net buyer of about $36 billion of equities.

That's a nice bit of change.

And that's just the tip of the iceberg, because the household sector with $14.5 trillion in financial assets is at very low equity ownership levels. So we see the potential demand from the household sec-tor, either through the mutual fund indus-try or directly, of about a trillion dollars. That way overshadows the public and private pension funds that combine to have a little over $2 trillion in assets.

For those who are looking to get in-volved, what are some of the indicators you use to time transactions?

For timing I go back to my breadth and sentiment indicators, and other things like Dow theory. The classic Dow theory is looking at the Dow Jones industrial and transportation averages and making sure they confirm one another. I found in my market study that one of the best indica-tors, although it has a very long lead time, is the Dow Jones Utility Average (Figure 9). It tends to lead the industrials or the stock market by quite a few months, but it always gives you the right side of the fence to be on. So I've been watching the utility average very closely, and it's been performing quite well. There's been a hiccup with the Columbia Gas bankruptcy recently [June 1991], so I've added to my collection a look at the Standard & Poor's Electric Utility index (Figure 10), which has been going to all-time record highs in the past few months. I think the utility average is telling us that the environment for equities is pretty good; that is, this utility index is acting very well.

Do you measure its performance by just the index to a moving average or just

FIGURE 7

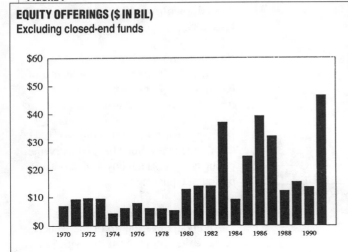

EQUITY OFFERINGS ($ IN BIL)
Excluding closed-end funds

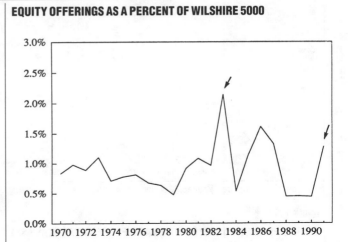

EQUITY OFFERINGS AS A PERCENT OF WILSHIRE 5000

Comparing new offerings to the stock outstanding using the Wilshire 5000 as a proxy indicates that the current level of stock offerings is below the peak that occurred in 1983.

higher highs and higher lows?

I'm really just looking at the major trend. I'm looking for confirmation from the Dow Jones Utility Average to see the utility average get above 221 and stay there. Utility's all-time record high was 236 back in January 1990. That was one of the few whipsaws that the utility average had, when the utility stocks became the place to be for a two- or three-week period. Utility stocks took off at the end of the year just as the economy was really showing signs of weakness. But I don't really use that high because I view that particular high as being a whipsaw.

You mentioned Dow theory. Do you use the utility average then as a confirmation of what you're also reading in the industrials and the transportation movements?

Yes, I look at the industrials and transports too. The important thing in technical work is to look at your technical indicators and be aware of the changes in the environment. You have to understand the reasoning behind Dow theory for it to work for you; if the industrial sector of the economy is doing well, those goods must be transported so the transport stocks should be doing well. If not, there's something wrong.

So the best thing you can do is to keep an eye on them.

Yes. But the transportation average,

over the past couple of decades, has been affected by energy prices — the price of oil moves transportation stocks, so I tend to keep to the basic theme of Dow theory when I'm looking at the way the industrial and the transports work. Dow theory lost a bit of its relevance when our Gross Domestic Product (GDP) became more than 50% service oriented. So perhaps the

transportation of goods is not as relevant as it was when Charles Dow formulated his theory.

> **Sentiment is very important. The problem is there aren't many really good sentiment indicators any more. There used to be a lot in terms of odd lots, short interest, specialist numbers, investor's intelligence and bull/bear numbers, but I find few are really giving us good signals.**

You mentioned breadth and sentiment. What are some of your indicators for those?

I keep things pretty simple. I look at a whole lot of things, but I look at a few

FIGURE 8

FUTURE DEMAND FOR STOCK ($ IN BIL)					
	Fin'l assets	1st-Qtr % equity	1945-90 avg. % equity	Historic high % equity	Potential demand for equities
Household	$14,580.5	14.4%	21.4%	33.5%	$1,020.6
Insurance	1,923.5	10.6	9.9	16.1	(13.5)
Foreign	1,650.5	15.3	20.2	33.6	80.9
Private Pension Funds	1,231.8	60.0	53.8 (a)	67.0	(76.4)
Public Pension Funds	801.1	39.9	53.8 (a)	40.8	111.4
Mutual Funds	660.5	46.1	77.4	94.8	206.7
Total	$20,847.9				$1,329.7

Source: "Flow of Funds," April 5, 1991, S.G. Warburg estimates
(a) Private pension fund equity investments were restricted until 1948, and public pension funds were restricted through 1970. This historical average percentage reflects the equity assets of private pension funds from 1970 to 1991 (i.e., in an unregulated environment).

The household sector has an estimated potential demand of $1 trillion for equities.

favorites. One is a simple daily cumulative advance-decline line and I look at the last 12 months for confirmation in the A-D line with movements in the market averages. That rarely leads you wrong. It's very simple and very good.

That was very important in 1991, because basic trendlines are in place and they've never been broken (Figure 11). So there's another confirmation that what we're seeing on the down side has been just modest corrections to a much larger bull market, which we also got confirmation for in our flow of funds work.

And you also look at breadth?

Another one of my favorite indicators is a breadth oscillator. This one is the 25-day net of advancing and declining issues (Figure 12). This is old-fashioned by some standards, but I use the 25-day net because it goes to great extremes and it tends to do those extremes at key points in the cycle, and because it tends to have a longer-term cycle within it. At the beginning of a major cycle, this breadth oscillator will go to extreme breadth readings on the high side and stay overbought for long periods.

As the bull market ages and matures, you will never see those kinds of breadth readings again. You will continue to see less extreme readings until finally you find new highs in the DJIA with this indicator unable to register a breadth overbought reading. That tells me we're at the end of a cycle.

So I look at the 25-day net oscillator because it isn't contained between, say, zero and 100 — it has extreme readings and those are important; it can stay overbought for weeks or months and that's important to me because that's very bullish. It's one of my favorite indicators because not only does it tell you it is not the time to buy because the market is overbought, but it will also tell you it may not be the optimal time to buy, but it's still a bull market.

Is sentiment important to you?

Very important, because I try very hard to get a grasp of what the potential supply and demand for equities might be, but you and I know that you can have a lot of cash on the sidelines for a long, long time but it takes a change in the sentiment to turn that cash into a demand for equities.

So sentiment is very important. The problem is there aren't many really good sentiment indicators any more. There used to be a lot in terms of odd lots, short interest, specialist numbers, investor's intelligence and bull/bear numbers, but I find few are really giving us good signals. But a couple are still my favorites and have done well. One is the simple specialist shorts as a percentage of total shorts (Figure 13); that very recently gave us a buy signal on the market, and it's been pretty good in terms of giving you buy and sell points. It doesn't really tell you the degree of move you can expect, but it does give good signals.

Is there anything else that you find can give you good signals?

Another one that we've had a lot of success with is what we now call the Dudack speculative index — I say that with a chuckle because I don't really like indicators named after people, but the original title of this one, "OTC-NYSE volume 200-day differential with a 13-day moving average," really was too intimidating! So I changed it to just speculative index (Figure 14). All this evolved because I was looking for a substitute for the old speculation index, which is a simple measure of American Stock Exchange (ASE) volume to New York Stock Exchange (NYSE) volume, and that had worked very well back in the 1960s and 1970s. But the ASE started to lose its following, as companies basically stayed on NASDAQ rather than following the previous path of over-the-counter to ASE and then graduating to the NYSE. We knew we had to create something that compared NASDAQ volume with NYSE volume.

I would think that would have been a real challenge.

Well, the problem with that relationship was that NASDAQ volume continued to grow, so you certainly couldn't do a straight relationship. What we basically do is detrend the relationship between over-the-counter to NYSE volume and look for extremes, and we found that was a pretty good indicator; when NASDAQ volume was at a relatively high level to NYSE volume — a sign of speculation — it was a market peak or an approaching market peak, and conversely, there was virtually no speculation in the over-the-counter market. It was also a good buying opportunity.

So we've had some good luck with that. That gave us a brief but accurate sell signal just before the market sold off recently. It's fallen very quickly and it looks like it could give us a buy signal very soon.

What about global markets? Do you accept the notion of the link among all the international markets becoming stronger and stronger?

FIGURE 9

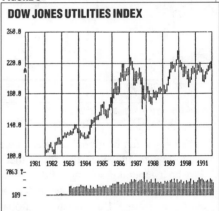

The Dow Jones Utility Average (DJUA) can be used as an indication of the environment for stocks. The recent uptrend is a favorable indication.

FIGURE 10

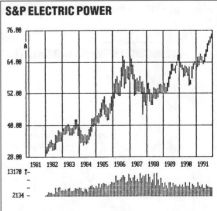

The Dow Jones Utility Average experienced a dramatic drop in June 1991; consequently, the S&P Utilities Electrical Power index was used to confirm the recent gains by the DJUA.

FIGURE 11

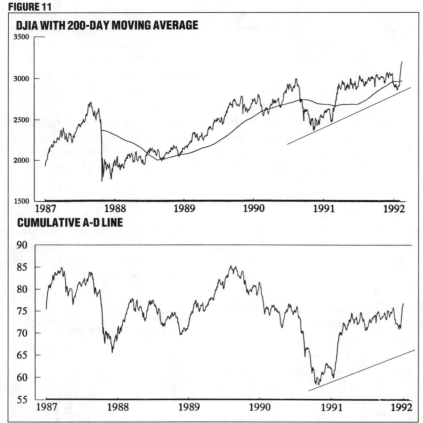

DJIA WITH 200-DAY MOVING AVERAGE

CUMULATIVE A-D LINE

Following the cumulative advance-decline line to confirm the trend of the market averages will alert the trader to changes in the trend. The trendlines from 1991 are still intact, which is a positive indication.

I'm a *big* fan of global markets. One has to realize, however, that while there may be a general global uptrend in equities, different markets may be under- or over-performing. But we are a global economy, and therefore we have global stock market trends.

It's also important to try to understand the relationship between different markets and their potential impact on one another. Whenever I come up with my market forecast, I always ask myself two questions: What could go right? What could go wrong? Or what would be the best thing that could happen, what could be the worst? I've been watching the Japanese market closely. It's pretty well known that there's a key support level around 19000 in the Japanese stock market and that the Japanese market and the banking sector are very closely tied. There's also a trendline that is now around 22500; if that trendline and the key support level were taken out, that would have a negative impact for the Japanese market, and that would reverberate around the world.

Have you seen any examples of that recently?

[The year 1991] was a very strange year in terms of global trends because you saw markets in very diverse patterns. There have been very strong markets — Hong Kong being one of the key ones — and then there's been the very weak ones — I just mentioned Japan. When you pull them all together, though, the basic trend is still one of a fairly bullish global stock market.

What about risk? How do you try to determine risk on a trade? Say you selected a stock and bought it or shorted it. What are some of the key things you might look at?

When I look at individual stocks — this is where the charts are so helpful — it's really easier in many ways because you're talking about one company and one set of supply and demand factors. When you buy a stock, you should have some kind of target in mind. If it's been a breakout from a base pattern — and my favorite stock patterns are bases and breakouts — it's easy to get your price objectives. Once you hit that price objective, basically you should sell the stock.

I add fundamentals to the chart patterns, but the way I add fundamentals is by asking what has happened to the company today that makes it much better than when I initially bought it. Unless there's something dramatic happening, I basically view the stock as being fully priced and it should be a sell. Along the way there will be trendlines and support levels. Those trendlines should be in place before you buy the stock, and right below the trendlines and support levels I place a stop-loss order.

How do you set price objectives?

Primarily, if I'm doing charts, I set price objectives off the pattern from basic point and figure charts, which I think are the best way to create price objectives. When you have a base pattern, it's a pretty

FIGURE 12

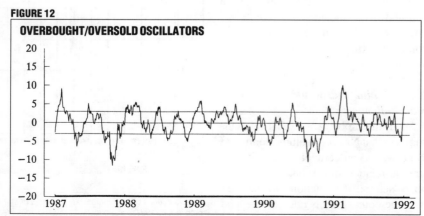

OVERBOUGHT/OVERSOLD OSCILLATORS

This oscillator is calculated by summing the last 25 days' difference between advancing stocks and declining stocks. The recent declines by this indicator held at levels that indicated the market is still in an uptrend.

FIGURE 13

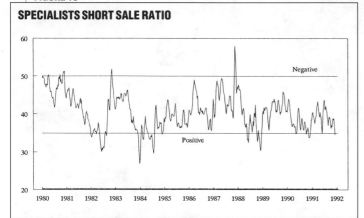

SPECIALISTS SHORT SALE RATIO

This indicator is calculated by tracking the ratio of specialist shorts to total shorts. Recently, a buy signal was generated.

FIGURE 14

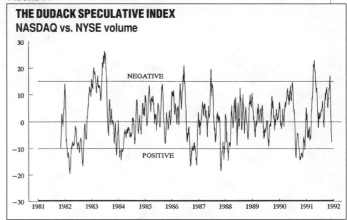

THE DUDACK SPECULATIVE INDEX
NASDAQ vs. NYSE volume

This indicator is a ratio smoothed with a 13-day moving average. The numerator is the difference between the daily NASDAQ volume and its 200-day moving average (MA), the denominator the difference between the daily NYSE volume and its 200-day MA.

simple technique for counting the base to see what your price objective might be. If it's a stock that's at new all-time highs in a simple uptrend, it's a bit more difficult but in that regard I let my profits run until the trendline is broken. Again, I would place a stop-loss and keep moving my stop-losses higher as the trendline moves up.

You also like to use some group analysis in your timing, don't you?

Yes, I do. I start off with a lot of top-down work and then I look at a lot of industries. In that regard I'm basically looking at price momentum, and I look again for changes. I use the Mansfield Chart Service, and I like to find stocks that have underperformed the market for several months on a seven-week basis; that is, their momentum on a seven-week basis has just been at the bottom of the pack. And when I see some dramatic change, and very often on a one-week basis they might rise to the top 20, that's my signal that something has changed here and that very often means that those groups will outperform the market over the intermediate term.

Sounds good, but is there a "but" in there somewhere?

The problem with this in the past year is I'm not finding really good signals in my group work. And when that happens I go to individual stock charts. And when I look at individual stock charts over the past year, in almost every single S&P

group, there are stocks that have done well and you would have made money, and there are stocks that have done poorly and you would have lost money.

Doesn't sound promising.

This has not been a group-oriented market. We always talk about group leadership — the strength or the weakness of the group leadership — but there's not been a lot of talk about that recently; it's very much of a stock-oriented market.

Why?

We're seeing this very diverse performance by stocks within an industry sector because we are in a very slow growth environment; in fact, we can only hope the economy is growing. If it is growing, it's probably not by much — we're talking about 2-3% GDP growth in 1991 or 1992, and who knows, maybe 1993. Companies are going to have to be flexible and efficient, not to mention aware of the value-consciousness of the customer base.

You really want to be with innovators, low-cost producers, strong management, and people who can never rest on their laurels, even if they are the low-cost producer, but continue to be willing to cut margins to put pressure on their competitors. These will be the survivors; these companies will grow because they're going to beat out their competition.

But that would go for any group, wouldn't it?

That's why there are winners and los-

ers in almost every industry group, because you really want to be buying strong management. For our analysts, I've put together strong charts and weak charts, trying to come up with the cohesive story in the winners and losers and figure out what the dividing line is. And to no one's surprise, it's the quality of the management.

So again, the charts told me something was different this time around, and a little detective work pulls together some of the fundamentals.

That covers everything I wanted to ask, Gail. Thank you. Did you have anything else you'd like to add or talk about?

That's all for me. Thank *you.*

REFERENCES

Investment Company Institute, 1600 M Street NW, Suite 600, Washington, DC 20036.

Mansfield Chart Service, 2973 Kennedy Boulevard, Jersey City, NJ 07306, (201) 795-0629.

S.G. Warburg, 767 Seventh Avenue, New York, NY 10019, (212) 459-7000.

NADIR KIANSERSI

Market Prediction
Through Fractal Geometry

Few have heard of fractal geometry and fewer still know how to use it. But it is a powerful tool with which to analyze nonlinear systems and is the main alternative for analyzing systems that defy development of predictive nonlinear equations. Krynicki presents a method by which to search for fractal patterns.

by Victor E. Krynicki, Ph.D.

ince its inception, technical analysis has been dominated by linear and/or statistical smoothing, averaging and estimation techniques. These techniques come in a vast array of forms: linear regression, quadratic regression, multiple correlation, oscillators, periodic regression, cycle estimation, moving averages, weighted moving averages, percentage retracement targets, projected price lines and angles, to name only a few. With specific reference to stock index analysis, these techniques have been applied to the values of the stock index itself, to advances-declines, to up volume/down volume, to new highs/new lows, and to a vast array of combinations or alternatives to these variables.

LINEAR, NONLINEAR

Market indices can be modeled as the output of a nonlinear dynamic system. Dynamics is the study of motion in the broadest sense of the term; thus, "motion" refers to events such as the oscillations of a pendulum, fluctuations in an animal population's density, appearance of chemical products in a reaction vessel, fluid convection in a box system, fluctuations in outbreaks of disease, changes in economic data such as monetary aggregates, and behavior of market indices.

On the other hand, "nonlinear" dynamic systems do not have a straightforward proportional relationship between variables. In a nonlinear system, small changes in one variable can have a nonproportionally large impact on other variables and the behavior of the system as a whole. Much recent work in nonlinear systems has focused on chaos. "Chaos" can be defined in a variety of ways, but overall, the term refers to a deterministic dynamic system that settles or dissipates into a bounded area. Within this area, the system's behavior appears to be random even though deterministic equations are present.

In a linear system, theoretically there is a single solution to each input, with "noise" or variability around this single value. In a nonlinear chaotic system, there is no single solution for each input, but rather an area of solutions, which reveals a complex patterning or structuring of solution values that is fractal (self-similar on many different scales of examination).

Nonlinear dynamic systems can be approached in two complementary ways. For systems with continuous output over time, differential equations can be developed to model the system and, theoretically, to predict future values of output. Attempts at developing nonlinear equations to model stock indices to date have not been very successful.

FRACTAL GEOMETRY

A complementary method of studying nonlinear dynamic systems is through fractal geometry. A fractal is a form or object that resembles itself across scales of measurement. As previously indicated, the mathematical solutions of the equations that govern many nonlinear dynamical systems are often fractal in form. Fractal forms can also be generated by equations such as those that produce the "Mandelbrot† set": in the graphic solution to this set of equations, a "gingerbread figure cutout" repeats endlessly along the boundary area.

Most objects in nature and dynamic systems are fractal: clouds, trees, waves, coastlines, hydrodynamic flows, microscopic surfaces, mountains, and crystal structures are all examples. Stock indices are also fractal in that they show

similar patterns across different time scales (hours, days, weeks, months and so forth).

Fractal forms can be analyzed, broken down and rebuilt through a comprehensive set of rules and principles, which taken together is referred to as the discipline of fractal geometry. Fractal geometry differs markedly from the linear or Euclidean geometry widely taught. Euclidean geometry studies idealized forms and shapes: straight lines, parallel lines, triangles and squares. Ideal forms can be used to approximate natural forms, but in truth they are not really adequate to fully describe any form.

As examples of the shortcomings of Euclidean geometry, consider this: a mountain range on the horizon can be approximated by a series of overlapping triangles; a tree can be approxi-

> **Fractal geometric techniques offer an alternative way of analyzing a complex system. In fractal geometry, the roughness or jagged edges are not considered "noise"; rather, they are considered to be an essential quality of the system.**

mated as a triangle on top of a straight line; waves on the ocean can be approximated as a series of curves or sinusoidal waves. The characteristics of these geometrical forms are well known mathematically, which serves as the rationale for using them to approximate natural forms.

Similarly, statistical techniques generally utilize approximations to straight lines and curves to make predictions. In linear regression, the approximation is to a straight line, and the "roughness" of the stock index in relation is considered "noise": the roughness is considered to be variability not accounted for by the straight line. Multiple regression takes this further by utilizing several variables, but the overall concept is the same. A moving average with bands around it is also conceptually similar; the moving average is the most probable trend path for the index, with the bands serving as the upper and lower limits for the "noise."

In a February 1991 STOCKS & COMMODITIES article, E. Michael Poulos presented a series of examples of the shortcomings of moving averages, stochastics and other indicators using fixed time frames for analysis (three days, five days, nine days and so on). Very different price patterns can still have the same five-day and eight-day moving averages, the same raw %K stochastic value, and so forth.

Spectral analysis, which is based on the model of a cycle embedded in noise, is in some ways a more powerful alternative technique. If data can be approximated this way, spectral analysis can discover the frequency of signals buried in noise. Moreover, data that appear unrelated to cycles can be analyzed through spectral techniques; a square wave can be approximated as the sum of odd, higher harmonics of a sine wave. Despite this flexibility, spectral analysis may not be able to handle all aspects of market index behavior. Nonlinear systems/chaotic systems are notorious for presenting constantly changing patterns such as movement toward a point, cyclic repetition, intermittent repetition and very complicated but bounded patterns known as strange attractors; the model of a cycle embedded in noise does not address adequately all these possibilities.

F ractal geometric techniques offer an alternative way of analyzing a complex system. In fractal geometry, the roughness or jagged edges are not considered "noise"; rather, they are considered to be an essential quality of the system. The roughness of the output of the system is a window into the dynamics of the system and is an indispensable tool for understanding the system. A variety of fractal geometric techniques have been developed to define and analyze different aspects of this "roughness."

Statistics and/or statistical approaches can be integrated into fractal geometry; the subfield is called fractal statistics. Statistical approaches can be used to help define the "roughness" of the fractal form, to rescale the fractal roughness (that is, perform a z-scale transformation), to perform sampling operations, and to perform other related operations. In using statistics, however, the point is not to approximate the form by a straight line, curve or cycle. Instead, statistics are used to define and study the roughness quantitatively, not to remove it by smoothing or treating it as "noise." Several new approaches offer an alternative to linear/statistical smoothing and trend estimation analysis.

A MUSICAL INTERLUDE

Suppose you were presented with the problem of discovering how the music of Bach differed from that of Mozart, and how in turn their music differed from that of a modern composer such as Stockhausen. How would you do so? It would not be surprising if many of the techniques used to analyze stock indices were used for this task —moving averages (of sound frequency or amplitude), linear channels of rising/falling frequency or amplitude, multiple regression techniques, factor analysis of frequency and amplitude measures, spectral analysis of sound frequencies, and so forth.

Two articles by Kenneth Hsu and Andreas Hsu have shown how questions like these can be answered through fractal geometry. The initial article demonstrated that the difference between successive frequencies

$$f(n+1) - f(n)$$

in musical compositions is fractal; the "fractal geometry" of Bach differs from Mozart and both differ from Stockhausen.

In the article "Self-similarity of the '1/f noise' called music," Hsu and Hsu show how complex structures such as musical

FIGURE 1

			Diff. between		
Day	Hour	No. of advances	successive hours	Expected difference	Rescaled difference
1	1	699			
1	2	836	137	50	87
1	3	844	8	0	8
1	4	612	-232	-10	-222
1	5	804	192	0	192
1	6	774	-30	20	-50
1	7	808	34	-20	54
2	1	546	-262	-50	-212
2	2	531	-15	50	-65
2	3	461	-70	0	-70
2	4	576	115	-10	125
2	5	529	-47	0	-47
2	6	282	-247	20	-267
2	7	432	150	-20	170
3	1	616	184	-50	234
3	2	660	44	50	-6
3	3	540	-120	0	-120
3	4	695	155	-10	165
3	5	701	6	0	6
3	6	646	-55	20	-75
3	7	797	151	-20	171
4	1	526	-271	-50	-221
4	2	827	301	50	251
4	3	785	-42	0	-42
4	4	761	-24	-10	-14
4	5	896	135	0	135
4	6	741	-155	20	-175
4	7	814	73	-20	93
5	1	479	-335	-50	-285
5	2	550	71	50	21
5	3	365	-185	0	-185
5	4	412	47	-10	57
5	5	369	-43	0	-43
5	6	369	0	20	-20
5	7	350	-19	-20	1

Initial steps of the affine transformation of hourly advances: rescaling of advances.

compositions can be analyzed down to their building blocks through fractal geometric techniques. Again, the variable of study is the difference between successive frequencies; this is rescaled in relation to a standard (60 Hz). The number of notes (or the time dimension) is scaled differently — by 1/2 and powers of 1/2. In fractal geometry, this process is known as a "contractive affine transformation"†: a transformation in which different scaling ratios are applied to the X and Y dimensions, and the X dimension in turn is contracted through scaling by 1/2 and powers of 1/2.

The fractal templates (basic note patterns) used by Bach were revealed through the use of a series of affine transformations. The techniques used to discover these basic building blocks of Bach's music are simple and more accurate in terms of pattern recognition compared with other statistical approaches. Now, having discovered these templates, modern composers can imitate Bach and write Bach-like compositions by using new and different combinations of his building-block templates.

APPLYING THEORY TO THE MARKET

If digitized classical music can be analyzed to reveal basic

† see Trader's Glossary for complete description

component patterns, why can't stock indices be similarly analyzed? For example, use the number of advancing stocks as the measure, as advances and declines are analyzed by many market technicians. Figure 1 presents simulated data for each hour (10 a.m. through 4 p.m.) of five trading days. The number of advances at each hour can be seen, as well as the difference between successive hourly values: $(n + 1) - (n)$.

Assume that research has shown that, on average, the difference between hour 1 minus hour 7 (of the previous day) is -50 advances; on average, the difference between hour 2 minus hour 1 is +50 advances; and so on. The differences seen in Figure 1 are rescaled with these values, presented in the column "Expected difference." This adjusts or rescales the "roughness" of each hourly value but does not smooth or average this roughness. Thus, the final column of Figure 1 presents the rescaled difference between hourly advances.

> Poulos as well as others have shown that there is short-term persistence in the market; sampling only serves to reduce intercorrelated data points.

Figure 2 begins where Figure 1 leaves off. The rescaled difference between hourly advances can be seen, with the rescaling of the time axis now carried out. Assume that research has shown that there are three critical time periods during the day: morning (hours 1 and 2), midday (hours 3, 4 and 5), and late afternoon (hours 6 and 7). Rather than average the values in each time period, one could randomly choose a value to represent each time period. Poulos as well as others have shown that there is short-term persistence in the market; thus, sampling only serves to reduce the number of intercorrelated data points. Carrying out this procedure results in the final column in Figure 2 ("Final data set").

The data in Figures 1 and 2 are also graphically shown in Figures 3 and 4. Figure 3 presents the raw data of advances by

FIGURE 2

RESCALING TIME

Day	Hour	Rescaled difference between successive hours	Random sample or each time block	Final data set
1	1			
1	2	87	Select	87
1	3	8	Not selected	
1	4	-222	Select	-222
1	5	192	Not selected	
1	6	-50	Select	-50
1	7	54	Not selected	
2	1	-212	Select	-212
2	2	-65	Not selected	
2	3	-70	Select	-70
2	4	125	Not selected	
2	5	-47	Not selected	
2	6	-267	Not selected	
2	7	170	Select	170
3	1	234	Select	234
3	2	-6	Not selected	
3	3	-120	Not selected	
3	4	165	Select	165
3	5	6	Not selected	
3	6	-75	Select	-75
3	7	171	Not selected	
4	1	-221	Not selected	
4	2	251	Select	251
4	3	-42	Select	-42
4	4	-14	Not selected	
4	5	135	Not Selected	
4	6	-175	Select	-175
4	7	93	Not selected	
5	1	-285	Not selected	
5	2	21	Selected	21
5	3	-185	Not selected	
5	4	57	Select	57
5	5	-43	Not selected	
5	6	-126	Not selected	
5	7	1	Select	1

Concluding steps of the affine transformation of hourly advances; rescaling of time by blocking of time into morning, midday and late afternoon, and random sampling to choose one value within each time block.

hour and the hour-to-hour difference between successive advance values. Figure 4 presents the rescaled difference between successive advance values and the ending affine transformation composed of the rescaled differences between successive advance values and rescaled time. Simulated stock index data are presented in Figure 4; in working with real data, one would search for fractal patterns related to tops and bottoms in the index.

Another contractive affine transformation could be performed at this point on the already transformed data of Figures 2 and 4, resulting in a related pair or even a series of affine transformations; one does not have to limit oneself to performing a single contractive affine transformation.

FRACTAL TEMPLATES

I have performed a series of contractive affine transformations on a different variable: the difference between successive hourly values of the DJIA. If the DJIA hour 1 value is 2990 and the DJIA hour 2 value is 3000, the successive difference value is +10 points. Further, to model the market as a two-control system (buyers vs. sellers), I have performed separate transformational analyses on the sequences of up hours and down hours. There is no "correct" set of affine transformations to apply to stock index data, so a variety of transforma-

FIGURE 3

INITIAL STEPS: AFFINE TRANSFORMATION

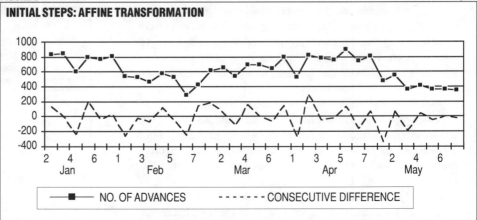

Initial steps of an affine transformation of number of advances per trading hour (simulated data). The number of advances by hour is seen, as well as the consecutive difference between advances during each trading hour.

FIGURE 4

SIMULATED FRACTAL PATTERNS DERIVED FROM SUCCESSIVE ADVANCES

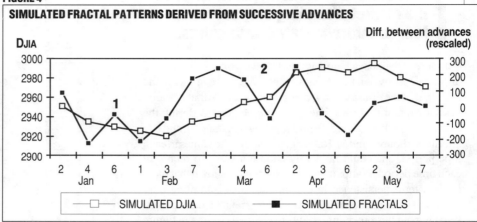

The consecutive difference between advances during each trading hour is rescaled, and time is rescaled by sampling 3 points per trading day. The result is plotted against simulated DJIA data. At point 1, a W-shaped fractal pattern is seen before a short-term bottom; at point 2, an M-shaped fractal pattern is seen before a short-term top.

tions must be explored to find those that yield reliable patterns.

Once potential fractal patterns are detected through series of affine transformations, one must search for the reappearance of these patterns over the database to verify that they are not random events. The next step is, of course, to try to use these templates for prediction.

O ur linear logic would expect to find that templates or patterns predict market moves in a simplistic, Morse-codelike logic along the following lines: Fractal Pattern 1 = strong upmove; Fractal 2 = moderate upmove; Fractal 3 = weak upmove; Fractal 4 = strong downmove; and so forth.

This is far from the actual case. Having used fractal geometry to analyze the nonlinear system into pattern templates, one is faced with a second nonlinear puzzle. Consider a two-component (two-control) biological system such as wolves and rabbits. Suppose that a "typical" pattern in this system is for one wolf to eat five rabbits; this event is a template. What can we predict next? This question can only be answered by referring to previous-state patterns of the wolf/rabbit system. If the previous-state pattern was "rabbits die off, only six remain," the loss of five would lead to extinction; but if the previous-state pattern was "rabbits rise to 1000, one wolf remains," then the logical prediction would be very different.

Similarly, the patterns discovered through fractal geometry generally have no fixed predictive meaning; instead, they are like the words of a nonlinear language. Similar to deciphering the meaning of a sentence, previous templates (like words) modify, qualify and determine the predictive meaning of each successive template.

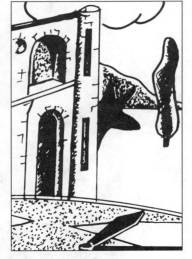

Ultimately, to reliably predict the market, one needs to not only detect the building blocks or patterns of the nonlinear system but also to untangle the nonlinear meaning of the multiple interactions between successive patterns. The task is a difficult one, but the potential rewards are equally enormous.

Victor E. Krynicki, Ph.D., Nonlinear Futures Timing Service, 27 Finish Line Rd., Bahama, NC 27503, (919) 477-3911, is a psychologist and neuroscientist who has studied systems such as the dynamics of eye movements in REM sleep.

REFERENCES

Barnsley, Michael [1988]. *Fractals Everywhere*, Academic Press.

Feder, Jens [1988]. *Fractals*, Plenum Press.

Hsu, Kenneth J., and Andreas J. Hsu [1990]. "Fractal geometry of music," *Proceedings of the National Academy of Sciences, USA*, Volume 87.

_____ [1991]. "Self-similarity of the '1/f noise' called music," *Proceedings of the National Academy of Sciences, USA*, Volume 88.

Krynicki, Victor E. [1991]. "Nonlinearity, chaos theory and the DJIA," *Technical Analysis of* STOCKS & COMMODITIES, Volume 9: September.

Peters, Edgar E. [1989]. "Fractal structure in the capital markets," *Financial Analysts Journal*, July/August.

_____ [1991]. "A chaotic attractor for the S&P 500," *Financial Analysts Journal*, March/April.

Poulos, E. Michael [1991]. "Of trends and random walks," *Technical Analysis of* STOCKS & COMMODITIES, Volume 9: February.

Adapting Moving Averages To Market Volatility

If a market is active, it has volatility: that cannot be avoided. And because the market is continuously changing, an indicator that attempts to predict market activity must itself adapt and change. How? Tushar Chande presents a dynamic—not static—indicators: a variable-length moving average, which adapts to the volatility in question by exponentially smoothing data based on standard deviation.

by Tushar S. Chande, Ph.D.

Technicians can be trend followers or contrarians. Trend followers use price-based indicators, such as moving averages, while contrarians prefer oscillators such as overbought-oversold indicators. But the market never does quite the same thing twice, and so no indicator works all the time. The market is dynamic, adjusting rapidly to information: a continuous tug of war between greed and fear, fact and fiction. Technical indicators, on the other hand, are static, mechanically applying the same formula to the relevant data. What is needed is a combination, dynamic indicators that will automatically adapt to the changing nature of markets, a new class of dynamic indicators that combine exponential moving averages with other technical indicators to adapt automatically to changing price behavior. What is needed is an exponential moving average with a continuously variable smoothing index that adjusts rapidly to changes in price behavior. The smoothing index can be tied to any market variable. It is the continuous, not discrete, changes in the smoothing index that increases the sensitivity of these moving averages to changes in price behavior. These new dynamic exponential averages can be referred to a variable index dynamic average (VIDYA).

Let us first examine exponential moving averages and how they can be modified to obtain VIDYA, and in turn compare VIDYA with conventional indicators to illustrate its dynamism. Then we will combine dynamic averages to derive other indicators and then illustrate their effectiveness.

CHRIS ROBERTSON

BUT FIRST, THE BACKGROUND

Exponential moving averages give greater weight to more recent data. An exponential moving average may be defined as:

$$(1) \quad E_d = t \times C_d + (1\text{-}t) \times E_{d\text{-}1}$$

where E_d is the new value of the moving average
$E_{d\text{-}1}$ is the previous value
C_d is the new data value
t is the smoothing constant of the average

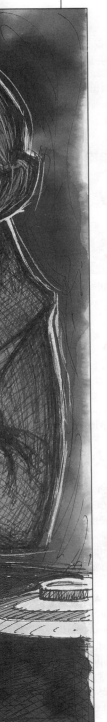

The smoothing constant t of the average may be referred to as the smoothing index of the moving average, so it no longer has to be visualized as a numerical constant. Implicitly, t must be less than 1 for the term (1-t) to be positive. As the smoothing index t increases, the new value has a greater proportion of the most recent data and the exponential average moves more rapidly. Conversely, as t decreases, more weight is given to the previous value, giving a heavily smoothed average that changes quite slowly. Thus, a larger value of t makes the exponential moving average more sensitive to new data; a smaller index t makes it less sensitive.

George Arrington in the June 1991 STOCKS & COMMODITIES discussed a variable-length simple moving average in which the number of days changed by discrete integers. The length is increased or decreased by an integral number of days based on the magnitude of price changes. He argued that this approach does not work well with exponential moving averages. A closer look at the smoothing constant t suggests that it could be a continuous variable (index), thus allowing the use of fractional time periods. For example, we can write t as

$$(2)\ t = k \times V$$

where k is a numerical constant such as 0.15 and V is a dimensionless market-related variable, such as a ratio of the standard deviation of the market's closing prices over two different periods.

The smoothing constant is simply a mechanism for incrementing the old value of the moving average to a new value, and a fractional value of t less than 1 prevents instability. Varying the smoothing index corresponds to taking larger or smaller portions of the latest data to update the moving average.

Any indicator may be used to connect the index t to the nature of the market's price changes. For example, the midpoint oscillator, %M, may be used as a measure of the market and inserted as V in equation 2. By design, the moving average will move faster as prices approach an overbought or oversold condition. Alternately, market momentum indicators (say, the 26-week price rate of change) may be used so that changes occur more quickly as prices change rapidly, slowing down as prices stabilize. This ability to quicken or slow down gives these variable-index exponential averages their dynamism.

DEFINING VIDYA AND RAVI

Specifically, I constructed a variable-index dynamic moving average (VIDYA) connecting the smoothing index to the market's volatility as follows:

$$VIDYA_d = \left(k\, \frac{\sigma_n}{\sigma_{ref}} C_d \right) + \left(1 - \left(k\, \frac{\sigma_n}{\sigma_{ref}} \right) \right) VIDYA_{d-1}$$

Here, the subscripts d and d-1 denote the new and old time

period, C is the closing price at the end of period d, σ (sigma) is the standard deviation of the market's prices over the past n periods, σ is a reference standard deviation of the market over some period of time longer than n, and k is a numerical constant. The reference standard deviation could also be an arbitrary value to obtain the desired degree of smoothing.

From an investor's viewpoint, a "long" VIDYA can be defined with $k = 0.078$, corresponding roughly to a 25-week exponential moving average. A 13-week standard deviation is used to adapt to market volatility. A reference standard deviation of 6 is used, which represents a 10-year average for weekly Standard & Poor's 500 data. More precisely, the long VIDYA is given by

$$(4)\ VIDYA^L_d = 0.078 \times \sigma_{13}\,/\,6 \times C_d + (1 - 0.078 \times \sigma_{13}\,/\,6) \times VIDYA^L_{d-1}$$

A "short" dynamic average is also defined with $k = 0.15$, roughly equal to a 12-week exponential moving average. The standard deviation of closing prices is calculated over 10 weeks. The value of the reference standard deviation is set at 4.

$$(5)\ VIDYA^S_d = 0.15 \times \sigma_{10}\,/\,4 \times C_d + (1 - 0.15 \times \sigma_{10}\,/\,4) \times VIDYA^S_{d-1}$$

To clarify the dynamism of these averages, I tabulated the 13-week standard deviation of the S&P 500 weekly close during three market periods. Also shown is the effective smoothing index using equation 4. Then I estimated the effective length of the equivalent simple moving average using the well-known formula for the smoothing constant of an exponential moving average (2/(n+1)), where n is the length of the equivalent simple moving average.

DYNAMISM OF VIDYA			
Weekly period	13-wk stand. dev. ($\sigma 13$)	Effective smoothing index 0.078 x σ_{13}/6 (k)	Effective length of VIDYA^L (weeks) (2-k)/k
9/11-12/4/87	36.83	0.479	3.18
6/22-9/14/90	18.38	0.239	7.37
4/19-7/12/91	4.83	0.063	30.75

The dynamic range of VIDYA^L is about a factor of 10 (i.e., 30.75 3.18), since it adjusts all the way from a rather long to a very short moving average based on market volatility. As market volatility increases, the effective length decreases. Even greater dynamic range is possible, as long as the factor (1-t) is positive. Clearly, VIDYA^L is superbly responsive to the market. VIDYA^S also exhibits a similar dynamism.

Now, we define the rapid adaptive variance indicator (RAVI), defined as

$$(6)\ RAVI_d = VIDYA^S_d - VIDYA^L_d$$

where the long and short dynamic averages are as defined in equations 4 and 5.

FIGURE 1

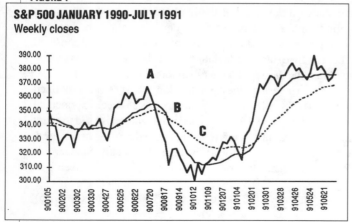

S&P 500 JANUARY 1990-JULY 1991
Weekly closes

The S&P 500 weekly closes (A) are plotted along with both the long variable index dynamic moving average (B) and with the equivalent exponential moving average (C). Note how quickly the indexed moving average responds to the decline by the S&P 500 in August 1990.

FIGURE 2

S&P 500 JANUARY 1990-JULY 1991
Weekly closes

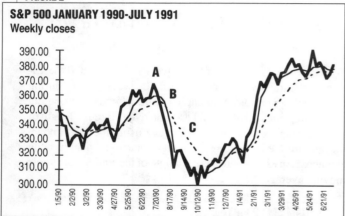

The S&P 500 weekly closes (A) are plotted along with both the short variable index dynamic moving average (B) and with the equivalent exponential moving average (C). The short version of the indexed moving average follows the market closely.

FIGURE 3

S&P 500 JANUARY 1990-JULY 1991
Weekly closes

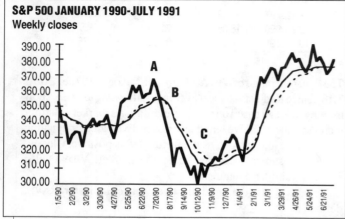

The S&P 500 weekly closes (A) are plotted this time with the long variable index dynamic moving average (B) and with the short exponential moving average (C). The long version of the indexed moving average still follows the market more closely than a short exponential moving average.

OTHER TRADING STRATEGIES

All trading strategies based on moving averages can be implemented using VIDYA. For example, RAVI is a two-average crossover indicator. A buy signal is generated when RAVI turns positive from a negative value. Similarly, a sell signal occurs when RAVI turns negative from a positive value.

> ▌ **I used weekly S&P 500 data to illustrate the smoothing characteristics using a VIDYA^L and VIDYA^S, representing heavy and light smoothing, respectively.**

RAVI can be combined with its moving average to simulate a moving average convergence/divergence (MACD)† strategy. Due to its sensitivity, this more responsive or TurboMACD can be defined as follows:

$$(7)\ \mathrm{TMACD}_d = \mathrm{RAVI}_d - (0.2 \times \mathrm{RAVI}_d + 0.8 \times \mathrm{RAVI}_{d-1})$$

where the second term represents the trigger line, an exponential moving average with a smoothing constant of 0.2. A buy signal is produced when TurboMACD changes from negative to positive values, and a sell signal occurs when it goes from positive to negative values.

BACK TESTING RESULTS

The results of back testing can be divided into two parts: first, the smoothing characteristics of VIDYA, and second, long trades using RAVI and TMACD. Now let us use moving average crossovers and MACD for comparison.

I used weekly S&P 500 data to illustrate the smoothing characteristics using a VIDYA^L and VIDYA^S, representing heavy and light smoothing, respectively. Figure 1 covers a market period from January 1990 to July 1991 and compares VIDYA^L to the equivalent exponential moving average with a smoothing constant of 0.078. Note how the variable index dynamic average adjusts rapidly to the drop in August 1990. In contrast, an exponential moving average barely responds to the rapid price changes. VIDYA^L takes small steps when the market trades in a narrow range and takes large ones when the market makes big moves in any direction. Observe how VIDYA^L responded near the market bottom in September-October 1990, while rising rapidly and leveling out in May 1991 when the market entered a trading range.

The lightly smoothed VIDYA^S follows the market even more closely, as shown in Figure 2. It also flattens as the market trading range narrows, as in June-July 1990. Clearly, it can be used as a trigger line in market trading systems. Even though the equivalent exponential moving average with a smoothing constant of 0.15 responds quickly to price changes, VIDYA^S responds with even greater agility.

An even better picture of VIDYA's responsiveness to price changes can be seen in Figure 3, which compares the smoothing

†See Traders' Glossary for complete description

behavior of VIDYA^L with a short exponential moving average with a smoothing constant of 0.15. The long dynamic average is more sensitive to rapid changes than even the short exponential average and tracks price changes more powerfully.

T he responsiveness of VIDYA and its vulnerability to instabilities was severely tested during the severe market correction of October 1987 (Figure 4). The narrowing of the variance between the two dynamic averages signaled a possible market top in September, confirmed in early November as the two averages crossed over. The lightly smoothed VIDYA^S tracks the market tightly and the heavily smoothed VIDYA^L responds rapidly as well. In comparison, the equivalent long exponential average glances over the extreme price changes. Note the slight instability caused by the market volatility when the short average dipped below the market low in early December.

The quantitative results are now easier to interpret, as we have a good feel for the smoothing behavior of these dynamic averages. Now look at RAVI. A buy is signaled when RAVI turns positive from negative territory and a sell occurs when RAVI goes negative from positive ground, which is the same as the short VIDYA crosses over or under the long VIDYA (Figure 5).

The results of long trades using RAVI over a test period of January 1980 to July 1991 are in Figure 6. The total point gain is approximately 207 points (with one open trade) using this strategy. If trade 9 were closed on July 12, 1991, the gain would be approximately 265 S&P 500 points. For comparison, the same moving average crossover strategy using the equivalent exponential moving averages with smoothing constants of 0.15 and 0.078 (same as the k values for VIDYA^S and VIDYA^L) produced a gain of just 122 S&P 500 points with five long trades (see Figure 7). If the currently open trade for the exponential averages were closed on July 12, 1991, the gain would be 159 S&P 500 points.

The MACD indicator is composed of the difference between

FIGURE 4

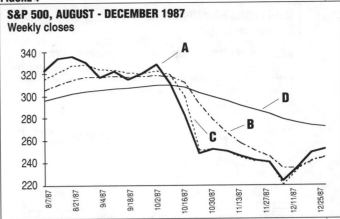

S&P 500, AUGUST - DECEMBER 1987
Weekly closes

The S&P 500 weekly closes (A) are plotted this time with the long (B) and short (C) variable index dynamic moving average and with the equivalent long exponential moving average (D). The narrowing of the difference between the two indexed moving averages indicates a possible trend reversal.

FIGURE 5

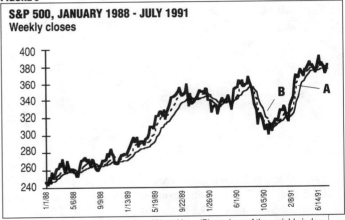

S&P 500, JANUARY 1988 - JULY 1991
Weekly closes

Using the difference between the short (A) and long (B) versions of the variable index dynamic moving average produces the rapid adaptive variance indicator, creating a crossover method for trading signals.

FIGURE 6

RAVI - LONG POSITIONS ONLY 5/30/80 to 7/12/91				
DATE	TRADE	S&P500	GAIN/LOSS POINTS	TOTAL POINTS
5/30/80	BUY	111.24		
9/11/81	SELL	121.61	10.37	10.37
9/30/82	BUY	120.97		
3/9/84	SELL	154.35	33.38	43.75
8/17/84	BUY	164.14		
9/26/86	SELL	232.33	68.19	11.94
10/31/86	BUY	243.98		
10/16/87	SELL	282.70	38.72	150.66
12/18/87	BUY	249.16		
12/25/87	SELL	252.02	2.86	153.52
1/1/88	BUY	247.08		
1/8/88	SELL	243.40	-3.68	149.84
1/15/88	BUY	252.06		
1/26/90	SELL	325.80	73.74	223.58
5/11/90	BUY	352.00		
8/10/90	SELL	335.52	-16.48	207.10
11/30/90	BUY	322.22		
7/12/90	SELL **	380.25	58.03	265.13

Total long trades:	9	Biggest loss:	-16.48
Profitable longs:	7 (78%)	Average gain:	29.45
Biggest gain:	73.74	Total gain:	265.13

** Trade closed for completeness; no sell signal from this model on 7/12/90

The results of long positions only are presented. The sell signal on July 12, 1991, is the open profit on that date.

two exponential moving averages with smoothing constants of 0.15 and 0.077. A moving average of the difference with a smoothing constant of 0.2 is used as a trigger line. I tested the profitability of MACD over the same test period using MetaStock software. The MACD indicator produced 20 trades and a gain of 205 S&P 500 points (Figure 8). Currently, there are no open trades with MACD, since it issued a sell signal on May 17, 1991. Trades with TurboMACD over the same period are summarized

in Figure 9. In total, there were 25 long trades, with a gain of approximately 218 points in all.

 comparison of each of the four methods discussed is found in Figure 10. Clearly, RAVI beat both the simple crossover of exponential averages and MACD over the past 11 years. RAVI produced more trades than did the simple crossover model but less than half as many as did the MACD. A look at the detailed trades shows that TMACD signaled key turning points two to three weeks before MACD. Its greater sensitivity produced more trades, which is a key limitation of the MACD approach from an investor's perspective. RAVI can also be used as an overbought-oversold indicator, since its values peak at over +10 or -10.

TO SUMMARIZE

Overall, the back testing results show that VIDYA tracks the market (as measured by the S&P 500 index) better than exponential moving averages do using a fixed smoothing constant. Trading strategies based on VIDYA seem to perform better than those based on exponential moving averages, as summarized in Figure 5.

> **In sum, this new class of variable index dynamic moving averages — VIDYA — adapts moving averages to the changing nature of markets.**

A single formulation tracks market changes well despite the increased volatility of recent years. VIDYA serves as a variable-length exponential moving average, taking a greater "bite" out of the most recent data as market volatility increases. Like all moving averages, VIDYA also lags the market, since it is derived from past data — probably its biggest limitation.

In sum, this new class of variable index dynamic moving averages — VIDYA — adapts moving averages to the changing

FIGURE 7

PRICE OSCILLATOR (LONG POSITIONS ONLY) S&P 500, Formula A 6/27/80 to 7/12/91			
Total long trades	: 5	Total short trades	: 0
Profitable longs	: 3 (60.0%)	Profitable shorts	: 0 (0.0%)
Total buy stops	: 0	Total sell stops	: 0
Biggest gain	: 84.080	Biggest loss	: -40.490
Successive gains	: 1	Successive losses	: 1
Total gain/loss	: 122.170	Average gain/loss	: 24.434
Total gain/loss ($)	: 1,004.77	Total gain/loss (%)	: 100.48

Using only long positions in a crossover trading strategy based on the equivalent short and long exponential moving averages produced a gain of 122.17 points in the S&P 500. If the current open trade had been closed on July 12, 1991, the total gain would have been 159 points.

FIGURE 8

S&P 500, MACD (9-unit moving average of indicator) 6/27/80 to 7/12/91			
Total long trades	: 20	Total short trades	: 0
Profitable longs	: 11 (55.0%)	Profitable shorts	: 0 (0.0%)
Total buy stops	: 0	Total sell stops	: 0
Biggest gain	: 70.760	Biggest loss	: -15.230
Successive gains	: 1	Successive losses	: 1
Total gain/loss	: 204.560	Average gain/loss	: 10.228
Total gain/loss ($)	: 1,344.96	Total gain/loss (%)	: 134.50

Testing the standard moving average convergence/divergence indicator for long positions resulted in the above. The MACD uses the difference between a 26- and 12-day exponential moving average and a nine-day exponential moving average of the MACD line for the signal line. Crossovers of the MACD line and the signal line generate the buy and sell signals.

FIGURE 9

TURBO MACD - LONG POSITIONS ONLY
5/30/80-7/12/91

DATE	TRADE	S&P500	GAIN/LOSS POINTS	TOTAL POINTS
5/30/80	BUY	111.24		
1/16/81	SELL	134.77	23.53	23.53
11/27/81	BUY	125.09		
1/15/82	SELL	116.33	-8.76	14.77
4/16/82	BUY	116.81		
6/18/82	SELL	107.28	-9.53	5.24
8/20/82	BUY	113.02		
12/10/82	SELL	139.57	26.55	31.79
1/14/83	BUY	146.65		
6/17/83	SELL	169.13	22.48	54.27
3/8/84	BUY	162.35		
11/30/84	SELL	163.58	1.23	55.5
1/18/85	BUY	171.32		
3/22/85	SELL	179.04	7.72	63.22
5/17/85	BUY	187.42		
8/2/85	SELL	191.48	4.06	67.28
11/8/85	BUY	193.72		
1/17/86	SELL	208.43	14.71	81.99
2/21/86	BUY	224.62		
4/11/86	SELL	235.97	11.35	93.34
6/27/86	BUY	249.6		
7/11/86	SELL	242.22	-7.38	85.96
8/29/86	BUY	252.93		
9/12/86	SELL	230.67	-22.26	63.7
10/31/86	BUY	243.98		
3/13/87	SELL	289.89	45.91	109.61
6/19/87	BUY	306.97		
9/4/87	SELL	316.7	9.73	119.34
11/20/87	BUY	242		
12/4/87	SELL	223.92	-18.08	101.26
12/11/87	BUY	235.32		
4/15/88	SELL	259.77	24.45	125.71
6/10/88	BUY	271.26		
7/22/88	SELL	263.5	-7.76	117.95
9/30/88	BUY	271.91		
11/18/88	SELL	266.47	-5.44	112.51
12/23/88	BUY	277.87		
3/3/89	SELL	291.18	13.31	125.82
4/14/89	BUY	301.36		
6/16/89	SELL	321.35	19.99	145.81
7/28/89	BUY	342.15		
9/15/89	SELL	345.06	2.91	148.72
12/8/89	BUY	348.69		
1/12/90	SELL	339.93	-8.76	139.96
3/16/90	BUY	341.91		
4/27/90	SELL	329.11	-12.8	127.16
5/4/90	BUY	338.39		
7/13/90	SELL	367.31	28.92	156.08
10/5/90	BUY	311.5		
3/15/91	SELL	373.59	62.09	218.17

Total long trades:	25		Biggest loss:	-22.96
Profitable longs:	16 (64%)		Average gain:	8.73
Biggest gain:	62.09		Total gain:	218.17

Testing the moving average crossover method produced these results.

FIGURE 10

COMPARISON OF TRADING RESULTS

	EXP MA * CROSSOVER	MACD	RAVI *	TURBO MACD
Total long trades:	6	20	9	25
Profitable longs:	4 (67%)	11 (55%)	7 (78%)	16 (64%)
Biggest gain:	84.08	70.76	73.74	62.09
Biggest loss:	-40.49	-15.23	-16.48	-22.96
Average gain:	26.56	10.23	29.45	8.73
Total gain:	159.37	204.56	265.13	218.17

NOTES:
* Assumes last open trade closed on 7/12/91; no sell signal from these models
at 7/12/91

Comparing the four different methods highlights the strengths of using moving averages that respond to changes in the market volatility.

nature of markets. Any dimensionless market variable can be used to link these averages to the market. The figures provided illustrate well the responsiveness of these averages to market changes. Common trading strategies for moving averages can be implemented using VIDYA, demonstrated with RAVI and TurboMACD. VIDYA is also well suited for setting stops, as it closely tracks the market. VIDYA should be a formidable and dynamic addition to the trader's arsenal.

Tushar Chande holds a doctorate in engineering from the University of Illinois and a master's degree in business administration from the University of Pittsburgh.

FIGURE 11

APPENDIX: LOTUS SPREADSHEET FORMULAS

APPENDIX: LOTUS SPREADSHEET FORMULAS

				F	G	H	I	J	K	L
CLOSE				S&P500 weekly close	EXP MA LONG	EXP MA SHORT	VIDYA LONG	VIDYA SHORT	RAVI (J-I)	TRADE INDICATOR
YR	MO	DT								
80	1	4		106.52	106.52	106.52	106.52	106.52	0.00	
80	1	11		109.92	106.79	107.03	106.79	107.03	0.27	
80	1	18		111:07	107.12	107.64	107.12	107.64	2.05	
80	1	25		113.61	107.63	108.53	107.63	108.53	3.91	
80	2	1		115.12	108.21	109.52	108.21	109.52	5.06	
80	2	8		117.95	108.97	110.78	108.97	110.78	6.59	
80	2	15		115.41	109.47	111.48	109.47	111.48	6.69	
80	2	22		115.04	109.91	112.01	109.91	112.01	6.23	
80	2	29		113.66	110.20	112.26	112.01	112.26	4.50	
80	3	7		106.51	109.91	111.40	109.04	111.47	5.56	0
80	3	14		105.43	109.56	110.50	107.60	110.60	5.07	0

```
G19: 0.078*F19+(1-0.078)*G18
H19: 0.15*F19+0.85*H18
I19: 0.077*@STD(F7..F19)/6*F19+(1-0.077*@STD(F7..F19)/6)*I18
J19: 0.15*@STD(F10..F19)/4*F19+(1-0.15*@STD(F10..F19)/4)*J18
K19: [W7] +J19-I19
L19: (F0) [W4] @IF(K19/K18<0,1,0)
```

The basic formulas for each column are presented in a Lotus spreadsheet. Column F is the weekly close for the S&P 500, while column G is the exponential moving average using a 0.078 smoothing constant. Column H is the EMA using a 0.15 smoothing constant, and column I is the Lotus formula for the long VIDYA. STD is the standard deviation formula in Lotus for the cell range stated within the parenthesis. Column J is the short version formula. Column K is the difference between column J and I.

REFERENCES

Arrington, George R. [1991]. "Building a variable-length moving average," *Technical Analysis of* STOCKS & COMMODITIES, Volume 9: June.

Chande, Tushar S. [1991]. "The midpoint oscillator," *Technical Analysis of* STOCKS & COMMODITIES: Volume 9: September.

Pindyck, Robert S., and Daniel L. Rubinfeld [1981]. *Econometric Models and Economic Forecasts*, McGraw-Hill Inc.

Modeling The Stock Market

The price/earnings ratio works perfectly well — for stocks. But, Paul Holliday points out, it doesn't work for stock indices such as the DJIA or the Standard & Poor's 500, where the effective interest rate works much better. To prove it, he's come up with a market model based on the theory that price is in proportion to earnings divided by interest rate and proceeds to demonstrate its use.

by Paul T. Holliday

The price/earnings ratio has been highly regarded as an indicator of whether the market is over- or underpriced. But closer analysis reveals that for stock indices, the price/earnings (P/E) ratio does not perform as advertised. Rather, the effective interest rate is the key to determining if the stock market is fairly priced.

To illustrate, I developed a model of the market based on the premise that price is proportional to earnings divided by interest rate. (See sidebar, "Math model formulas.") The Standard & Poor's Composite Index (S&P 500) is used because it is a broad representation of the market. The earnings in the model equation are the average of the yearly earnings a year ahead of the price. Figure 1 shows the S&P 500 earnings and the average represented by the straight line on the semi-log grid. The model gives a closer match to the actual price when average earnings are used in place of the actual earnings, indicating that the price of the index is not dependent on the quarter-to-quarter variation of earnings.

The interest rate in the model combines short- and long-term rates plus the inflation rate and is referred to as the effective interest rate pertinent to the stock market. An additional correction factor, amounting to a few percent, is added to account for changes in dividend yield.

The comparison of the model with the S&P 500 index for the past 35 years is shown in Figure 2. The mean error is 0.01% and the variance is 10.6%.

Now compare the Dow Jones Industrial Average (DJIA) to the S&P 500. Figure 3 shows the yearly earnings of the two indices, and it is evident that the DJIA earnings are almost exactly 10 times the S&P 500 earnings for 1935 to 1975; one would also expect the DJIA price to be 10 times the S&P 500 price.

THE FIVE-YEAR PICTURE

The price ratio, as well as the earnings ratio and the dividend ratio, are plotted as five-year moving averages in Figure 4. The price ratio is around 12 from 1935 to 1958, amounting to a

FIGURE 1

S&P 500 YEARLY EARNINGS

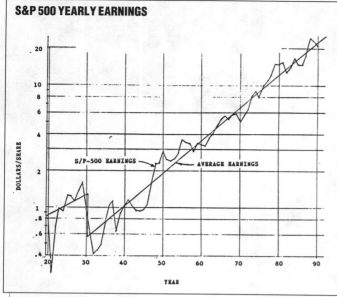

The yearly earnings are compared with the average earnings for the S&P 500.

premium of 20% to 30% over the S&P 500 for the same earnings. Figure 4 indicates that the premium starts to erode in 1958, while the earnings do not begin to deteriorate until 1975. The slide in the price ratio corresponds to the decline in the dividend ratio, which also starts to decline in 1958.

> ## The effective interest rate is the key to determining if the stock market is fairly priced.

The DJIA does not respond proportionally to changes in earnings. Therefore, to model the DJIA accurately, the average earnings used for the S&P 500 must be multiplied by 10 and used for the DJIA model, which also contains a correction factor representing the change in dividend rate between the DJIA and the S&P 500. The resulting model price is compared with the actual price in Figure 5 from 1967, with a mean error of 2.5% and a variance of 12.3%.

Figures 1 and 5 indicate that the model closely matches both the S&P 500 and the DJIA. The model uses average earnings, disproving the contention that index price changes are due to earnings change. To further illustrate, Figure 6 shows the DJIA P/E together with the nominal value from the model divided by the earnings. If the DJIA reflected changes in earnings, then the drop in DJIA earnings in 1983-84 would be evinced by lower prices and the P/E would not be over 100, as it was in that period.

Also, since the model matches the P/E of the DJIA, it is clear that changes in P/E are due primarily to the interest rate and inflation factors in the effective interest rate used in the model.

LEAST-SQUARES FIT

Finally, because the model is based on a least-squares fit to the

FIGURE 2

COMPARISON OF S&P 500 WITH THE MODEL

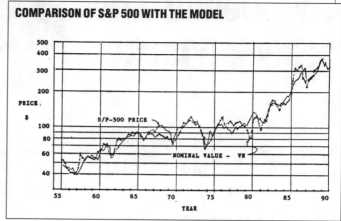

Presented is a comparison of the mathematical model (nominal value) and the S&P 500 for the past 35 years. The mean error is 0.01% and the variance, 10.6%

FIGURE 3

DJIA EARNINGS COMPARED WITH S&P 500

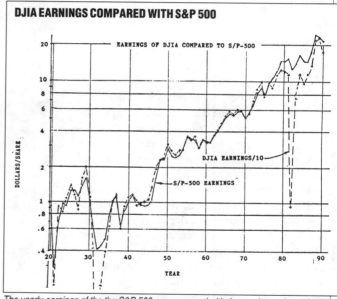

The yearly earnings of the the S&P 500 are compared with the yearly earnings of the DJIA divided by 10. The earnings relationship are obviously a factor of 10 and therefore the price relationship should also be a factor of 10. In 1982, the earnings for the DJIA fell dramatically.

FIGURE 4

DJIA RATIO TO S&P 500

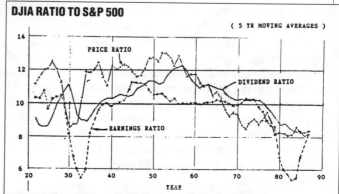

The price ratio of the DJIA to the S&P 500 began to erode in 1958, followed by the dividend ratio and the earnings ratio.

MATH MODEL FORMULAS

My mathematical model of the stock market is based on fundamental economic parameters and has been modified slightly from the model described in the article "Determining stock value from price and earnings." The Standard & Poor's 500 is used to represent the market as a whole. The premise is that stock index prices are proportional to earnings divided by interest rate:

$$\text{S\&P 500} = \frac{\text{Earnings}}{\text{Effective interest rate}}$$

The earnings in the model are the average earnings one year, or four quarters, ahead of the price of the S&P 500 and is expressed using the least-squares method by the following equation:

$$EA4 = 0.087546 \times (1.062992)^{\wedge}(T + 1)$$

$$T = \text{Year} + \text{Quarter}/4 - 1900$$

The interest rate in the model is a composite of short-term rates, long-term rates and the inflation rate. It is the interest rate that influences the stock market and is denoted as (RE), the effective interest rate.

$$RE = (\text{T-bill} / 100)^{\wedge}(EX \times XP)$$

$$EX = 0.92169 + 0.05502 \times (\text{T-bill minus T-bond}) + 0.02346 \times (\text{T-bill minus CPIC})$$

$$XP = 0.355493 + 0.0085054 \times (T - 1)$$

T-bill = 3-month T-bill rate in %

T-bond = 30-year T-bond rate in %

CPIC = Year to year change in consumer price index in %

For the S&P 500, an additional minor correction factor, KY, is used to compensate for dividend rate changes.

$$KY = 0.790426 + 0.0565 \times (\text{yield in \%})$$

The final equation for the S&P 500 is then:

$$VN (\text{S\&P 500}) = EA4/(RE \times KY)$$

The result of the model is construed as the nominal value of the index and, therefore, is designated as VN.

The model for the DJIA uses the same average earnings of the S&P 500 multiplied by 10. The yield correction factor differs slightly for the DJIA.

$$KY (\text{DJIA}) = 0.84650 + 0.04146 \times (\text{yield of DJIA in \%})$$

An additional correction factor is needed to compensate for the difference in yields between the DJIA and the S&P 500.

$$KD = 0.885 + 0.00325 \times (DR) \qquad DR < 3$$

$$= 0.800 + 0.03067 \times (DR) \qquad 3 < DR < 14$$

$$= 1.175 + 0.00325 * (DR) \qquad 14 < DR$$

$$DR = \text{Dividend ratio} = (\text{DJIA div}/10 \times \text{S\&P 500 Div} - 1) \times 100$$

The model for the DJIA is then:

$$VN (\text{DJIA}) = 10 \times EA4 \times KD / (RE \times KY (\text{DJIA}))$$

real data, the model's results may be interpreted as the nominal value of the index. As such, the nominal value, in relation to the actual price, gives a better indication than the P/E of whether the market is over- or undervalued.

If the P/E does not provide the required information, can the nominal value be used instead? It can. Figure 7 shows a weekly calculation of the nominal value compared with the DJIA price for the past two and a half years. In 1989 and the first part of 1990, the model indicates an undervalued DJIA by about 15%. The second half of 1990 was about equal to the nominal value. In 1991, the DJIA ran ahead of the nominal value by about 10% to 15% — large enough for concern but too small for panic. In the last four months of 1991, the nominal value grew and exceeded the DJIA, confirming a buy situation.

Since the driving factor in the model is the effective interest rate, it would be instructive to plot the reciprocal of this interest rate. According to the equation outlined in "Math model formulas," the reciprocal of the effective interest rate is proportional to the price/earnings ratio in which the earnings are the average earnings a year ahead of the price, a parameter that is also plotted in Figure 7 with trendlines to show that, indeed, the market is attuned to changes in this parameter.

Paul T. Holliday, 41580 Avenida Barca, Temecula, CA 92591, (714) 699-1449, is a retired engineer and has been involved with the analysis of the stock market since 1985.

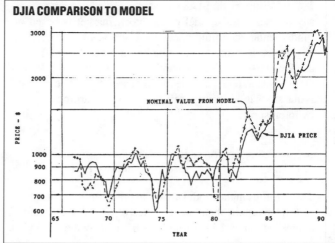

FIGURE 5

DJIA COMPARISON TO MODEL

The nominal value model is adjusted by multiplying the earnings by 10 plus a correction factor representing the changes in the dividend rates to model the DJIA. The model has a mean error of 2.5% and a variance of 12.3%.

ADDITIONAL READING

Holliday, Paul T. [1990]. "Determining stock value from price and earnings," *Technical Analysis of* STOCKS & COMMODITIES, Volume 8: May.

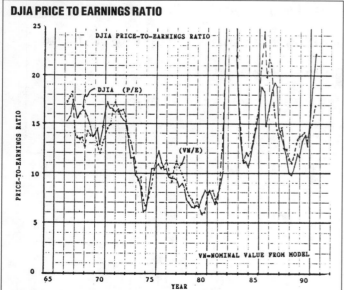

FIGURE 6

DJIA PRICE TO EARNINGS RATIO

In 1983, the earnings for the DJIA dropped sharply, creating a price/earnings ratio of over 100.

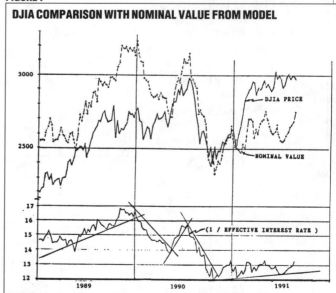

FIGURE 7

DJIA COMPARISON WITH NOMINAL VALUE FROM MODEL

Changes in the trend of the effective interest rate coincide with changes in the market.

The Presidential Election Cycle

It's an election year again. What does history say about them? This famous technician tells you that what you've heard about Presidential election years may very well be true.

by Arthur A. Merrill, C.M.T.

An election year is in progress. What are the prospects for the markets? We've been told that traditionally, politicians try to do everything they can to make the years with Presidential elections scheduled good ones in the market to put voters in a positive frame of mind. Does history confirm this truism?

To check this out, I asked my computer to calculate the percent changes in the Dow Jones Industrial Average (DJIA) every month since 1898. Then I averaged these changes in each month of the four-year Presidential cycle. We started on the December 1 after a Presidential election and then cumulated the percent changes up through the next Presidential election year. Figure 1 shows the results.

THE SECOND TAKES OFF

After a rise at the beginning of the cycle, nothing exciting seems to happen through most of year two in the Presidential term. However, beginning with the Santa Claus rally in the second year, the market, on average, takes off. It tends to level off in the following autumn and winter and so on through spring.

Beginning in June of the election year, however, the market takes off once more

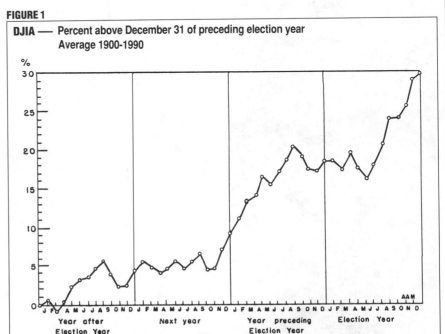

FIGURE 1

DJIA — **Percent above December 31 of preceding election year**
Average 1900-1990

During an election year, the market on average starts to advance in June.

and continues up through the election and the January following the election. After a pause, the market keeps going up through August of the year following the election. (See the left-hand end of Figure 1.)

Of course, these are average figures. But based on history, the prospects are favorable indeed!

Arthur Merrill is a Chartered Market Technician and the author of many reports and books, including Behavior of Prices on Wall Street *and* Filtered Waves, Basic Theory.

ADDITIONAL READING

Hannula, Hans [1991]. "The seasonal cycle," *Technical Analysis of* STOCKS & COMMODITIES, Volume 9: November.

Kaeppel, Jay [1990]. "January barometer: Myth and reality," *Technical Analysis of* STOCKS & COMMODITIES, Volume 8: July.

Kargenian, Bob [1990]. "'Tis the season," *Technical Analysis of* STOCKS & COMMODITIES, Volume 8: July.

Merrill, Arthur A. [1991]. "Summer rally: Fact or fiction?" *Technical Analysis of* STOCKS & COMMODITIES, Volume 9: July.

Warwick, Ben [1991]. "The end-of-the-month effect," *Technical Analysis of* STOCKS & COMMODITIES, Volume 9: June.

MARK MOLNAR

Candlesticks And The Method Of 3

Various uses of the number three, a number of importance in Japanese culture as well as Western culture, can be seen prominently throughout candlestick technique and particularly in the form of "Sakata's five methods." The five methods, though more than 200 years old, can be used in current-day trading with little modification, as Wagner and Matheny show.

by Gary S. Wagner and Bradley L. Matheny

In previous articles, we wrote about using artificial intelligence and pattern recognition to analyze candlestick charts and the importance of properly identifying two and three candle patterns. However, a particular method of candlestick analysis has rarely been discussed except as an aside, and yet this method is one of the most important candlestick teachings. Various patterns with different meanings comprise the Japanese candlestick technique. Before signals can be identified properly, therefore, both single-candle and multicandle patterns must be identified and analyzed in relation to each another.

THREE AGAINST FOUR

According to Seiki Shimizu in *The Japanese Chart of Charts*, the Japanese believe that the number three has a "divine power that lives within it"; many candlestick patterns are based on the number. However, the number four is considered bad luck. One Japanese pronunciation of the number is the same as the word "death" (*shi*). However, the Japanese culture is not the only one that classifies data by threes; Western technical analysis itself uses three fairly often. It can be found in many examples of technical analysis. For example, it can be found in:

- **Trend directions**
  1) Up
  2) Down
  3) Sideways

- **Trend classifications**
  1) Major
  2) Intermediate
  3) Minor

- **Triangle types**
  1) Symmetrical
  2) Ascending
  3) Descending

- **Primary information sources**
  1) Price
  2) Volume
  3) Open interest

Japanese candlestick technical analysis is based in most part on the works of Sokyu Honma and his "Sakata's five methods," a grouping of patterns based on three and named after Sakata city, where he was born. Sakata's five methods present the following pattern groups based on the number three:

Three Gaps (*Sanku*)

What Western technical analysis refers to as gaps are known as windows in candlesticks, either "open" or "closed." In candlestick analysis, gaps refer to spaces between the bodies of candles from one cycle to the next. The three-gap pattern group signals exhaustion or weakness of a current trend and is composed of three black or three white candles that gap away from each other.

Figure 1 is a daily October 1991 live cattle chart. After dropping almost 7 cents, a bullish black three-gap pattern formed on August 8, 1991, with an inverted hammer as the flagship candle (Figure 2). A bearish white three-gap pattern formed in the U.S. dollar on April 22, 1991, with a white star as the flagship candle (Figure 3). After a long rise from the low 80-cent level, this pattern signaled the exhaustion of the trend.

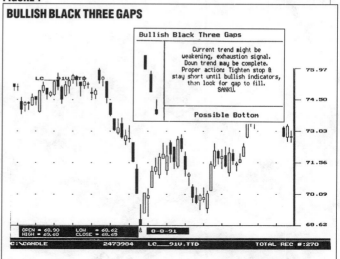

FIGURE 1

BULLISH BLACK THREE GAPS

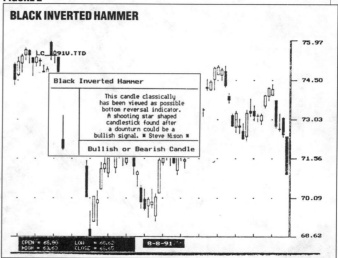

FIGURE 2

BLACK INVERTED HAMMER

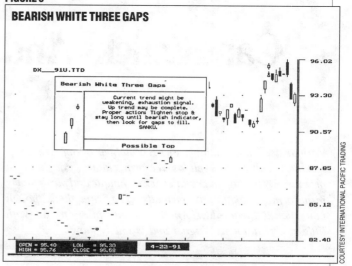

FIGURE 3

BEARISH WHITE THREE GAPS

COURTESY INTERNATIONAL PACIFIC TRADING

FIGURE 4

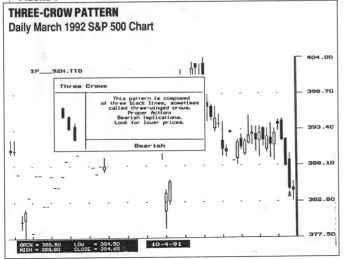

THREE-CROW PATTERN
Daily March 1992 S&P 500 Chart

FIGURE 5

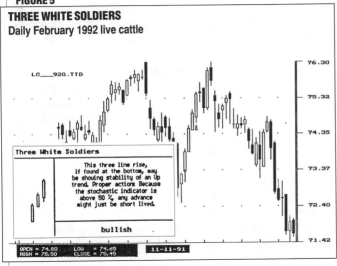

THREE WHITE SOLDIERS
Daily February 1992 live cattle

FIGURE 6

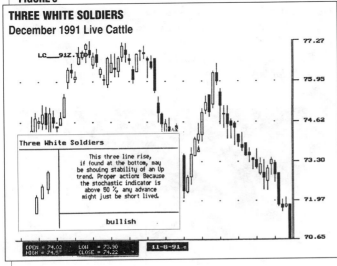

THREE WHITE SOLDIERS
December 1991 Live Cattle

Three Parallel Lines (*Sanpei*)

The opposite of three gaps, the three parallel lines can signal the continuation of trend. They are composed of three black or white candles that do not gap away from each other.

Parallel patterns are more common than three-gap patterns. Although traditionally these patterns are interpreted as continuation patterns, if found early in a trend move, they show strong momentum for the trend. In addition, these patterns may indicate a weakening market trend. Figure 4, an example of the three-crow pattern that indicates the continuation of a bearish trend, is a daily March 1992 Standard & Poor's 500 chart. On October 4, 1991, a three-crow pattern formed, showing that the bearish market tendency still prevailed. Figures 5 and 6, daily February 1992 live cattle charts, show examples of a three white-soldier pattern that was formed on November 11, 1991, indicating the continuation of the bullish trend.

Three Rivers (*Sansen*)

Perhaps the pattern group that Western candlestick technicians write about the most is the three-river group, composed of the three-river morning and evening stars, the southern cross and the "three-river bottom." "Three rivers" refers to a battle in Japanese history that was fought over a province with three rivers. The eventual victor won by conquering all sides of the river banks, thus controlling the rivers.

Figure 7 is a daily January 1992 platinum chart and shows a three-river morning black doji star pattern that was formed on November 11, 1991, indicating a support level and bottom in platinum. A three-river evening black doji star pattern can be seen in Figure 8, which shows a daily March 1992 Canadian dollar chart.

Three Mountains (*Sanzan*)

This group of patterns is analogous to the Western head and shoulders formation. The name refers to the belief that prices rise and fall in a series of three steps or levels (Figure 9).

Three Method (*Sanpo*)

This method refers to a trading philosophy that dictates when to be in and out of the market. The three states of activity of trading — the three methods — are buying, selling or resting.

In essence, this method refers to differing trading theories. Sokyu Honma tried to achieve a balance of when to enter and exit a market and when not to trade at all by using this method. He used many factors pertaining to nature and the seasons in considering market timing. In his time (the 18th century), the regional rice markets in Japan could be disastrously affected by adverse weather conditions and many other natural phenomena.

SAKATA'S STRATEGIES

Honma's methods are divided into "Sakata's strategies" and the "market's sanmi no den," which is basically a set of rules or guidelines that Honma followed. The methods are as follows:

FIGURE 7

THREE-RIVER MORNING BLACK DOJI STAR
Daily January 1992 platinum

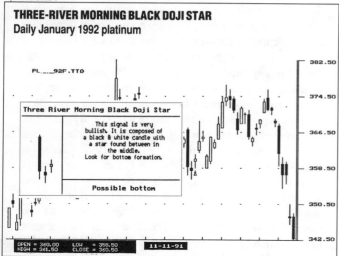

FIGURE 8

THREE-RIVER EVENING BLACK DOJI STAR
Daily March 1992 Canadian dollar

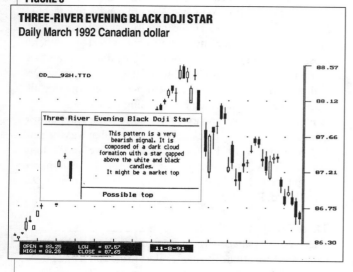

FIGURE 9

THREE MOUNTAINS

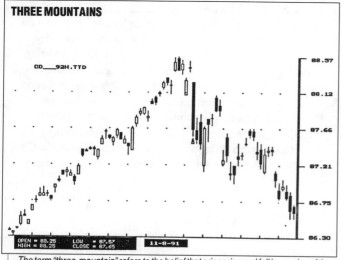

The term "three-mountain" refers to the belief that prices rise and fall in a series of three steps or levels.

- Use past price history when thinking about entering or exiting the market, and do so without being greedy.
- Always try to sell at the top and buy at the bottom.
- Increase one's positions after a rise of 100 bags from the bottom or a fall of 100 bags from the top. Honma traded rice, so this statement refers to his scaling in and out of the rice market.
- If one's forecasts are incorrect, one should try to catch the error as soon as possible, liquidate one's positions and stay on the sidelines for 40 to 50 days.
- Liquidate 70% to 80% of one's profitable positions. One should liquidate the remainder and change directions once the price has reached its ceiling or bottom.

These methods are considered "Sakata's strategies." The rules of the trade and their execution are an integral part of Sakata's five methods; Honma used these strategies with all the other candlestick signals in deciding when to trade. Honma used these methods to predict future market movements but never skipped over any of the other essential candle indicators.

A LITTLE KNOW-HOW IS DANGEROUS

These principles of candlestick charting are some of the most important in the technique. These examples demonstrate how Sakata's five methods can be applied to current-day trading. A group of patterns created more than two centuries ago can still be used to predict possible trend movements and reversals in the present day.

But the trader who wishes to try out candlesticks should be forewarned. There is more to the candlestick technique than simply Sakata's five methods. Understanding only a portion of anything can be dangerous, and the candlestick technique is no exception. Sokyu Honma gained his wealth by knowing when to get in and out of a market, and when not to trade at all.

Gary S. Wagner, CTA, and Bradley L. Matheny are currently developing technical market analysis software for International Pacific Trading Co. Together, they co-developed the Candlestick Forecaster, a candlestick-interpretation program based on artificial intelligence.

The TRIN-5

Whether you know it as the trading index (TRIN) or the Arms index, this particular indicator has inspired variations ranging from an issue/volume-weighted long-term index to this, a short-term trading indicator based on a five-day sum of TRIN. Newsletter publisher Jerry Favors explains.

by Jerry Favors

Most traders are familiar with the trading index (TRIN), which was originally devised by Richard Arms. (For obvious reasons, it is also referred to as the Arms index.) Its premise is simple enough: in order to compute the trading index each day, divide the ratio of advancing issues to the number of declining issues by the ratio of advancing volume to declining volume. The data necessary to compute TRIN can be found every day in *The Wall Street Journal*, or you can call your broker and get the closing TRIN reading for the day. If you have access to cable television, CNBC shows the closing TRIN reading on its tape at the end of each trading day.

VARIATIONS ON A THEME

Most analysts use a 10-day moving average of TRIN as an indicator. The 10-day TRIN reaches oversold when it rises above 1.00, while it reaches overbought when it falls below 0.80. The 10-day TRIN has a very impressive record at market bottoms but is not nearly as accurate at market tops. My favorite method of using TRIN data is based on a version from W.G. Bretz's *Juncture Recognition in the Stock Market*. In the book, Bretz recommends using a five-day moving sum of the daily TRIN numbers, which we have dubbed the TRIN-5. To compute the TRIN-5, simply add the closing trading index reading for the last five days: that is the TRIN-5. Do *not* divide this number by 5. The TRIN-5 reaches overbought territory when it falls below 4.00 and reaches oversold when it rises above 6.00. Readings below 4.00 tend to occur near market tops, while readings above 6.00 occur near market bottoms.

TRIN-5 appears to be as effective or better than the 10-day trading index at market bottoms, and it is far more effective at

HORSWILL

MIKE HORSWILL

market tops. Figure 1 shows the TRIN-5 from April 1990 to October 7, 1991, marking a down arrow above each extreme TRIN-5 reading above 6.00 and an up arrow below the day of each extreme TRIN-5 reading below 4.00. As can be seen from Figure 1, this technique has been very accurate at catching short-term tops or bottoms, often marking the high or low to the exact day. When the TRIN-5 reaches an extreme below 4.00 and then turns up, you are normally within one to four days of at least a short-term top. Traders may wish to research this technique as far back as possible to verify its effectiveness.

Jerry Favors publishes "The Jerry Favors Analysis" newsletter, 7238 Durness Drive, Worthington, OH 43235, (614) 848-8177.

FURTHER READING

Arms, Richard W., Jr. [1989]. *The Arms Index (TRIN)*, Dow Jones-Irwin.

_____ [1991]. "Using the Arms index in intraday applications," *Technical Analysis of* STOCKS & COMMODITIES, Volume 9: April.

_____ [1991]. "Cross your Arms," *Technical Analysis of* STOCKS & COMMODITIES, Volume 9: May.

Bretz, W.G. [1972]. *Juncture Recognition in the Stock Market*, Vantage Press.

Hartle, Thom [1991]. "Arms on Arms," *Technical Analysis of* STOCKS & COMMODITIES, Volume 9: July.

Rusin, Jack [1991]. "The issue/volume-weighted long-term Arms index," *Technical Analysis of* STOCKS & COMMODITIES, Volume 9: October.

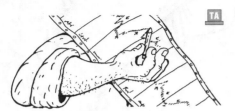

FIGURE 1

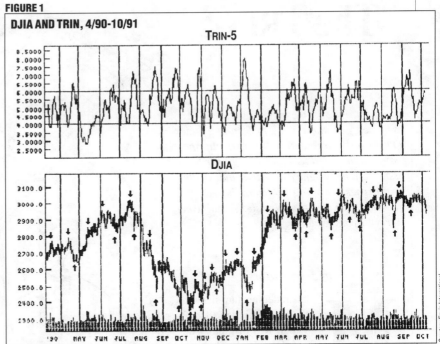

TRIN-5 appears to be as effective or better than the 10-day trading index at market bottoms, and it is far more effective at market tops. Here is the TRIN-5 from April 1990 to October 7, 1991, marking a down arrow above each extreme TRIN-5 reading above 6.00 and an up arrow below the day of each extreme TRIN-5 reading below 4.00. This technique has been very accurate at catching short-term tops or bottoms.

CHRISTINE MORRISON

The 4% Model: Using The Value Line Composite

Looking for an indicator that doesn't predict huge booms or busts, but tells you what the safest course of action is? Here it is. For this model, all you need is the Value Line Index. It's simple, but it works. Here's how.

by Bob Kargenian, C.M.T.

Originally, the 4% model was developed by Ned Davis of Ned Davis Research fame as a method with which to follow the trend of the stock market. Simply, a buy signal is given when the weekly close of the Value Line Index rises 4% or more from any weekly close; a sell signal is given when the weekly close drops 4% or more from any weekly peak. For example, if the lowest weekly close was 175, then to generate a buy signal the index would have to close at 182 or better on a weekly basis. As long as the weekly close does not decline by 4% or more, the buy signal stays in effect. One example of a sell signal would be if the Value Line rose to 225, then it would have to decline to 216 to generate a sell signal. Again, the indicator is giving a sell signal until there is a rally of 4% or greater off a weekly low. This indicator is always in the market, and consequently, the indicator is subject to giving false signals if the broad market enters into a trading range. However, this indicator will catch a strong trend.

PRESENT, PAST, FUTURE

The 4% model was originally tested going back to 1966 and was presented in Martin Zweig's *Winning on Wall Street*. Figure 1 presents the results of this indicator from 1980 to the most recent sell on November 22, 1991.

Interestingly, the entire gain in the index since 1985 has taken place since November 1990, when the index revisited the 1985 levels, illustrating the poor relative performance of the broad market and the secondary stocks during the past six years. The strength of the past year may signal that the trend is reversing.

Bob Kargenian, a Chartered Market Technician and first vice president with Prudential Securities, can be reached at 2390 E. Orangewood Ave., Suite 100, Anaheim, CA 92806, (714) 385-3717.

The opinions expressed in this article are solely that of Mr. Kargenian and in no way represent the opinions of any organization with which he is affiliated.

FIGURE 1

	REALIZED POINTS			
Date	Buy	Sell	Realized profit	% profit
4/11/80	110.22			
11/7/80		142.47	29.26	32.25
11/14/80	148.25			0
12/12/80		137.39	-7.33	-10.86
12/26/80	144.28			0
7/10/80		151.41	4.94	7.13
10/2/81	132.79			0
1/15/82		131.8	-0.75	-0.99
4/2/82	127.77			0
5/28/82		124.88	-2.26	-2.89
8/20/82	121.32			0
7/29/83		199.38	64.34	78.06
9/23/83	202.56			0
10/21/83		194.1	-4.18	-8.46
11/25/83	197.3			0
2/3/84		188.67	-4.37	-8.63
8/3/84	177.3			0
11/30/84		175.78	-0.86	-1.52
1/11/85	181.08			0
5/3/85		191.14	5.56	10.06
6/7/85	199.01			0
8/16/85		197.72	-0.65	-1.29
11/8/85	199.79			0
7/18/86		230.13	15.19	30.34
8/22/86	235.05			0
9/12/86		219.88	-6.45	-15.17
10/31/86	230.44			0
4/16/87		260.76	13.16	30.32
6/12/87	267.88			0
9/18/87		275.57	2.87	7.69
12/18/87	201.95			0
5/20/88		222.39	10.12	20.44
6/10/88	235.57			0
8/12/88		229.86	-2.42	-5.71
10/7/88	236.83			0
11/11/88		227.16	-4.08	-9.67
1/6/89	236.07			0
10/13/89		263.93	11.80	27.86
3/16/90	246.23			0
4/27/90		232.04	-5.76	-14.19
5/11/90	241.59			0
7/27/90		238.64	-1.22	-2.95
11/30/90	191.55			0
6/28/91		234.36	22.35	42.81
8/23/91	244.21			0
11/22/91		234.26	-4.07	-9.95
		135.18	194.68	-3.00

This table represents the trades generated by buying the Value Line Geometric Average if the weekly close is equal to or greater than 4% from the lowest weekly close. Sell signals occur if the weekly Value Line closes with a 4% decline or more from the highest weekly close.

ADDITIONAL READING

Hartle, Thom [1991]. "Tim Hayes: Running with the trend," *Technical Analysis of* STOCKS & COMMODITIES, Volume 9: August.

Zweig, Martin [1986]. *Winning on Wall Street*, Warner Books, Inc.

[TA]

FIGURE 2

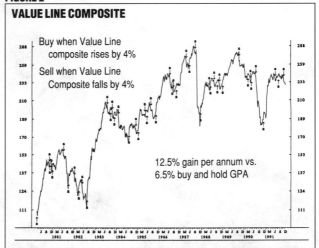

VALUE LINE COMPOSITE

Buy when Value Line composite rises by 4%

Sell when Value Line Composite falls by 4%

12.5% gain per annum vs. 6.5% buy and hold GPA

The Value Line Composite is plotted along with the buy and sell arrows.

FIGURE 3

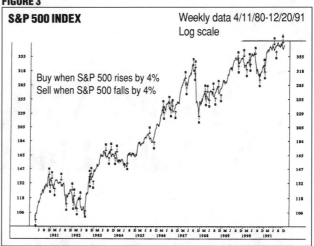

S&P 500 INDEX — Weekly data 4/11/80-12/20/91 Log scale

Buy when S&P 500 rises by 4%
Sell when S&P 500 falls by 4%

The same approach is presented but using the S&P 500 as the market index.

FIGURE 4

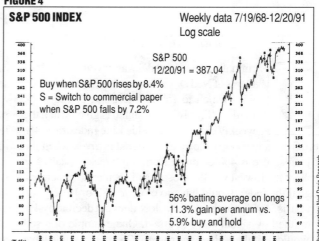

S&P 500 INDEX — Weekly data 7/19/68-12/20/91 Log scale

S&P 500 12/20/91 = 387.04

Buy when S&P 500 rises by 8.4%
S = Switch to commercial paper when S&P 500 falls by 7.2%

56% batting average on longs
11.3% gain per annum vs.
5.9% buy and hold

All charts courtesy Ned Davis Research

Expanding the percentage reversal to 8.4% for a buy signal and the sell signal based on a 7.2% decline produced a 56% batting average on the long positions. The sell signals required a shift to holding commercial paper during a declining stock market. This combined buy and sell strategy realized an 11.3% gain per annum since 1969.

KREIG BARRIE

Trading Currency Mutual Funds

Want to broaden your investment horizon? Using subjects covered in his previous STOCKS & COMMODITIES articles in November 1991 and January 1992, Joe Duarte explains how by combining a simple index/moving average with an oscillator, trading foreign currencies and foreign currency mutual funds can help you protect your mutual fund portfolio profits with a simple oscillator called the 10 minus 4 formula.

by Joe Duarte

I introduced the concept of mutual funds as stock index proxies in the November 1991 and January 1992 issues of STOCKS & COMMODITIES. By tracking several mutual funds and evaluating their individual responses to buy or sell signals given by slightly modified technical indicators of trends, momentum, and market sentiment, I showed how a mutual fund investor could participate in significant advances in the stock market and stay out or reduce exposure during significant declines. With that background, let's see how a mutual fund trader or investor can

FIGURE 1

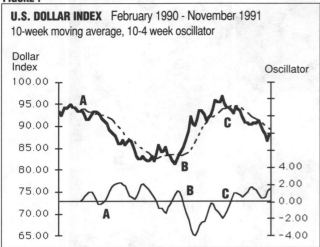

U.S. DOLLAR INDEX February 1990 - November 1991
10-week moving average, 10-4 week oscillator

In the U.S. Dollar Index since February 1990, the index maintained two identifiable trends while remaining in a broad trading range. The break below the 10-week moving average (point A) was confirmed by the oscillator breaking above the zero line; the dollar index remained below its 10-week moving average for the next eight months before bottoming out in November 1990. The 10 minus 4 oscillator remained above the zero line throughout most of that period, correctly confirming the downward trend. When the trend reversed (point B), the oscillator moved below the zero line, confirming the trend change.

FIGURE 2

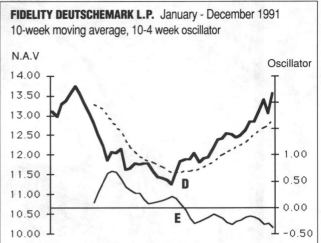

FIDELITY DEUTSCHEMARK L.P. January - December 1991
10-week moving average, 10-4 week oscillator

Invested in Fidelity Deutschemark L.P. from January to December 1991 are Dmark futures, forward contracts and/or money market instruments denominated in Dmarks. By charting Fidelity Deutschemark L.P. and its two sister funds, Yen L.P. and Sterling L.P., mutual fund investors or traders have three possible venues in which to participate in the profitable currency markets. Point D marks the break above the 10-week moving average of the Dmark fund in July 1991. Point E shows the confirmation by the oscillator.

broaden his/her investment horizon and enhance and protect overall mutual fund portfolio profits without the direct use of futures and options.

Because most open-ended mutual funds offer stocks or bonds as underlying assets, traders and investors can invest in low-yielding money market instruments or Treasury bills during bear markets in stocks and bonds. While short-term liquid securities can provide safety and protect capital during times of market uncertainty and volatility, other investment vehicles may also provide the mutual fund investor or trader an opportunity to profit from the market's uncertainty and volatility. These objectives can be fulfilled by allocating capital into currency funds based on technical analysis of simple trend indicators.

SIMPLE COMBINATIONS

A simple method of analyzing trends is to combine an index and a moving average. To track the relationship of the U.S. dollar to the major world currencies, I chart the U.S. Dollar Index as reported in *Barron's* Vital Signs section; to smooth out the intermediate trend of weeks to months, I calculate the 10-week moving average. A downtrend in the U.S. dollar should occur at the same time as an uptrend in at least some of the world's other currencies. When the index breaks above or below the 10-week moving average, it signals a possible trend change in the dollar, the world's cur-

rencies and often in other financial markets.

To evaluate further the authenticity of the trend change and to minimize whipsaws, I calculate a simple oscillator, which I call the 10 minus 4 formula. To calculate the oscillator, subtract the four-week moving average of the U.S. Dollar Index from its 10-week moving average. Next, chart the numbers along with the dollar index. When the oscillator breaks above or below the zero line in conjunction with a break above or below the dollar index's 10-week moving average, a trend change is confirmed.

A U.S. Dollar Index break above the 10-week moving average confirmed by a crossing through the zero line on the 10 minus 4 oscillator is a sell signal for the foreign currencies; a confirmed break below is a buy signal.

SOME PARTICULARS

As long as the oscillator remains on the same side of the zero line, the signal remains in effect. If the U.S. Dollar Index drifts toward the moving average and the oscillator remains on the same side of the zero line, usually that is an indication that a retracement in a continuing trend is occurring. At this point, further shares of the currency fund or funds may be added to a position.

Figure 1 charts the U.S. Dollar Index since February 1990. During this period, the index maintained two distinct, separate and easily identifiable trends while remaining in a broad trading range. The break below the 10-week moving average (point A) was confirmed by the oscillator breaking above the zero line; the U.S. Dollar Index remained below its 10-week moving

> **In July 1991, the Deutschemark L.P. showed the best response, while the Yen L.P.'s response was the weakest and the Sterling L.P.'s response was somewhere in between.**

average for eight months before bottoming out in November 1990. The 10 minus 4 oscillator remained above the zero line throughout most of that period, correctly confirming the downward trend. When the trend reversed (point B), the oscillator moved below the zero line, confirming the trend change.

When the dollar index broke down again in July 1991 (point C), the oscillator reconfirmed the trend change. Figure 2 charts Fidelity Deutschemark L.P. from January to December 1991. This mutual fund invests in Deutschemark futures, forward contracts and/or money market instruments denominated in Deutschemarks. By charting Fidelity Deutschemark L.P. and its two sister funds, Yen L.P. and Sterling L.P., mutual fund investors or traders have three possible avenues in which to participate in the profitable currency markets. Investors can maximize profits and decide on asset allocation by evaluating which fund responds best to the technical condition of the currency markets. In July 1991, the Deutschemark L.P. showed the best response, while the Yen L.P.'s response was the weakest and the Sterling L.P.'s response was somewhere in between.

The oscillator for the individual mutual funds is calculated in the same way as for the dollar index, and the buy and sell signals are interpreted in the same way. Point D in

Figure 2 marks the break above the 10-week moving average of the Deutschemark fund in July 1991, coinciding with the dollar index breaking below its 10-week moving average. Point E shows the confirmation by the fund's 10 minus 4 oscillator. The dips back to the 10-week moving average proved to be additional buying opportunities as the oscillator remained below the zero line, indicating the trend was intact.

In Essence

By combining a simple index/moving average blend with a simple oscillator, a mutual fund investor can enhance his or her profits by using currency mutual funds. This indicator performed well during the stock market break of November 15, 1991, as the Deutschemark fund continued its upward trend. By buying into the Dmark fund in July, investors could have improved the performance of the cash portion of their portfolios as well as providing themselves with relatively cheap portfolio insurance if they were unpleasantly surprised by the stock market during the November correction.

The currency markets often reflect the political perceptions of an extremely large pool of sometimes fickle money, and so these mutual funds can prove to be quite volatile. By using the 10 minus 4 oscillator to confirm trend direction, investors can avoid being whipsawed in a volatile market.

Joe Duarte publishes a mutual fund newsletter, "The Wall Street Detective: A Guide to Mutual Fund Investing," PO Box 1623, Bowling Green, KY 42102-1623.

References

Duarte, Joe [1991]. "Mutual funds as stock index proxies," *Technical Analysis of* Stocks & Commodities, Volume 9: November.

_____ [1992]. "Combining sentiment indicators for timing mutual funds," Stocks & Commodities, January.

Shifting To Another Dimension

by John Sweeney

I have spent the last several months tweaking a simple trading system to provide good profits with minimal drawdowns. The underlying idea ("Settlement," November 1991 through February 1992) isn't too complicated, and it is summarized in Figure 1. Last month, I tried to exploit the underlying system by adding on trades to the underlying positions with a separate, simple rule: Add positions when the trending price retraces to the simple average following it (Figure 2).

This logic failed, though it was spectacularly successful in some test periods. Its maximum adverse excursion (MAE) distributions showed no distinction between winning and losing trades, even in the winning test periods, which forced me to reject the strategy for this system.

TRENDS TAKE TIME

It's tough to ignore that the underlying system completely missed several good trends in different testing periods. I don't propose to "fix" that, because we'd then be back at ground zero with a whole new system to validate. Instead, I point out only that one of the ways we visually identify a trend is the consistency of price change over time. In other words, one of the ways we know we're in a good trade is that we're still in it a few days after we get started. The good ones keep going and the bad ones are usually stopped out immediately or in a few days.

After all, within the trade's horizon it can only go for us, against us or stay roughly neutral. The 30-40% success rates so common in trading systems are a reflection of that. Our task, then, is to stay with the good ones and reject the bad ones.

Just to give you an idea of how this looks, look at Figure 3. This relatively straight line is partly a result of the simple fact that it takes time for prices to change. I've found that the slope of the line changes with the tradeable and its units of denomination.

Another way to look at this is in Figure 4, which is the "typical" P&L performance of trades in 1989 by day in the trade. Of the losing trades, all but one were cut off after four trading days or less, many in just one or two days. Only one losing trade lasted longer than four trading days and that went for seven trading days.

In contrast, winning trades all lasted longer than four days. The shortest lasted nine days and the longest went 55 days. It is

FIGURE 1

TRADING RULES

```
▭════════ System: S&S w Stops.MDL ═══════▭
if (diff35 > trend35+.005 and diff35[1] < trend35[1]) then buy today at the
close;

exitlong tomorrow at entryprice - .7 stop;

if diff35 < trend35-.005 then exitlong today at the close;

if (diff35 < trend35-.005 and diff35[1] > trend35[1]) then sell today at the
close;

exitshort tomorrow at entryprice + .7 stop;

if diff35 > trend35+.005 then exitshort today at the close;
```

The "diff 35" is the one-day change in the 35-day simple moving average. The "trend 35" is the 17-day simple moving average of the "diff 35."

FIGURE 2

TREASURY BONDS

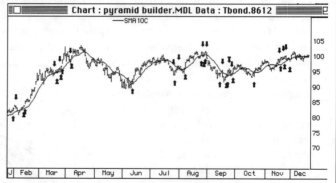

The basic system, validated previously, trades at the arrows shown. The 10-day simple moving average was used to add positions — an idea that failed in last month's article.

FIGURE 3

WINNING TRADES VS. LOSING TRADES

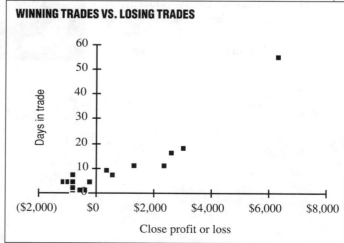

Winning trades simply last longer than losing trades, suggesting a rule for adding positions to them: wait a few days before doing so.

anecdotal and circumstantial, but this behavior is typical of trend-following systems with efficient stops. But it also suggests a way to add trades to the underlying trade.

OH, YEAH

The true problem with this concept is that there is no sense of whether we are buying cheap or selling high. This is the third of three basics every system should have ("Settlement," January 1991), so in violating the basics I need to be extra cautious in evaluating the results. Can buying or selling blindly without relation to value be profitable? Sounds unlikely.

BACK TO ADDING ON

The sample from 1989 is small, but it does suggest that after four days, if you're still in the trade, you have a high probability (around 90%) of being in a winner. After seven days, for all we know, the probability could be higher yet. Why not add to the position after four days?

A naive rule might be that if I'm still in a trade after four days, I'll enter on the open with an additional trade in the same direction. Exit will be with the underlying trade or an MAE stop, if one can be determined. The obvious risk is that, after four days, you're not getting in at the price that made the underlying trade a winner. This add-on trading must be treated as a completely independent trading strategy and evaluated for its own risk/reward characteristics.

Fortunately for this particular system, this isn't too tedious to evaluate. While I didn't have time to do a complete evaluation before my deadlines, I was able to evaluate it for 1986, 1987 and 1989, and the results look promising.

Twenty-four trades without stops showed profits of about $18,000 on a single contract basis, after $100 for commissions and slippage. Figure 5 shows a very nice pair of MAE distributions, with the winners showing very little adverse movement and the losers marked adverse movement.

If I convert the frequency chart into dollars as in Figure 6, the distinction is even more dramatic: It looks as though we could cut off losses in these trades at 32 points (about $1,000) and eliminate virtually all the dollar loss from the losing trades.

FIGURE 4

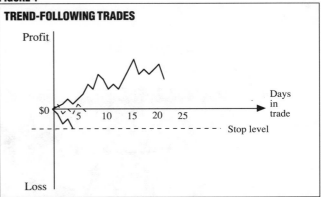

Naturally, trend-following trades can go for you, against you or go nowhere. With efficient stops, you cut off the losers quickly and look to ride the long-lasting winners.

MORE WORK

You've thought by now of three or so variants of this idea and probably want to test it over much more data. That's what a little dinking around on Sunday afternoons will get you: more work. At any rate, the process for these add-on trades is the same as for the underlying trades. They are capitalized separately and evaluated with the same sort of attention to adverse movement so you and I can efficiently cut off losses and ride the winners.

Believe it or don't, this system is not fully defined and I'm not referring to just doing more testing of the underlying and add-on rules. There is also the possibility of reversing direction when wrong. This needs to be analyzed and capitalized separately, but it is made possible by the edge the underlying system gives, an edge that must be exploited completely if we want to make money.

We don't spend enough energy making sure our indicators are capturing the behavior of our quarry nonjudgmentally. After all, it's unrealistic to think we are going to control the market by creating an indicator. No — we just want one that reliably tracks the market, abstracts from the noise and reports the repetitive.

John Sweeney is Technical Editor of STOCKS & COMMODITIES.

FIGURE 5

ADD-ON TREASURY BOND TRADES

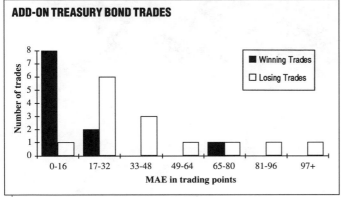

An unlikely add-on rule (entering four days after the initial entry) turns out to have a well-defined MAE distribution for both winners and losers — a key result if we are to trade the rule.

FIGURE 6

CLOSED P&L FOR ADD-ON T-BOND TRADES VS. MAE

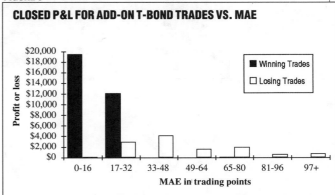

When the results of the add-on are converted to dollars, the distinction between losing and winning trades is spectacular. It appears we can cut off virtually all losses at 32 trading points.

CHAPTER 4

THE TRADERS' MAGAZINE

APRIL 1992

TECHNICAL ANALYSIS OF STOCKS & COMMODITIES™

Money Management Using Simulation And Chaos

Here's how to determine your trading system's minimum capital requirements and discover how market exposure should be modified to maximize profits without increasing risk. Bob Pelletier explains.

Any successful trading system must offer good timing signals, but timing alone does not guarantee profitable results. While good timing *is* essential, the addition of key money management techniques fashioned through mathematical manipulation can mean the difference between moderate success and the accumulation of true wealth. To succeed in the markets, a trader must use a combination of good timing, knowledge of required capital and optimal investment levels before entering each trade.

Techniques for timing market entry and exit points are as varied as trader personality and attitude. It suffices to say that trades should be based on a timing system that has demonstrated a positive mathematical expectation. Often, trading systems show immense profits on paper that are not reflected when real dollars are involved. As a result, traders have found themselves asking, "How can I be losing money with such a profitable system?" The discrepancy between hindsight analysis and real-time trading results has plagued technicians for years; the reason for it usually involves favorable actual experience that cannot be sustained or excessive process control in simulated trading. Process control in a trading system is explained by the number of parameters or rules

> **Once the profits have been tallied, I degrade them to correct for sample size, reducing total profit by a set factor depending on the number of reported trades.**

> ◼
> *by Bob Pelletier*

used in developing the system, and excessive process control can produce misleading results. For my purposes, a parameter is any quantifiable rule or control mechanism that is consistently applied to timing. I assume that each parameter has been exhaustively tested to verify optimal settings. Excessive process control is the introduction of too many parameters in a trading system relative to the number of simulated (or actual) trades.

A man asked me once why he was losing money trading a publicly offered system that showed great simulated profits in historical testing. Cursory analysis revealed the system had been highly optimized for each market. About a dozen parameters had been fitted to the historical data to enhance the simulated past performance. His software had come pre-optimized and, in fact, the developer regularly supplied him with new parameter settings. These were intended to keep his system finely tuned for profits.

Extensive optimization of this kind is common in off-the-shelf investment software and is gaining popularity among investors designing their own systems. Unfortunately, it can lead to inflated profit projections. Without an enormous sample base, an 11- or 12-parameter system exercises excessive control over the trading process, leaving little freedom to produce profits beyond the period on which the simulation was performed. If the system developer were to set more constants drawn through a reduction in the number of parameters, there might be a greater chance of future success. In essence, if two systems performing simulated trading generated the same profit in the same number of trades, the one with the fewer parameters would have the highest mathematical expectation for success and should produce greater profits (or smaller losses) in actual trading.

ON MATHEMATICAL EXPECTATION

To determine if a system has a positive mathematical expectation, try studying the profits and losses (either real or simulated) that the system has produced. This list of profits and losses should be as long as possible to supply an adequate sample size for analysis.

Once the profits have been tallied, I degrade† them to correct for sample size, reducing total profit by a set factor depending on the number of reported trades. When many trades are analyzed, the profit reduction is small. However, if the sample includes only a few trades, profit is reduced substantially. This adjustment compensates for exaggerated profits that can result from too small a sample size.

A profit degradation for each parameter is also included in this calculation. The parameter count represents the extent to which the system developer has introduced process control. This degradation helps compensate for developer bias. Typical degradation can be accomplished by use of an equation of the form:

$$DP = P \times N^{-(Q+1)/(N-1)}$$

where:
DP = degraded profit
P = raw profit
N = the number of profits and losses
Q = the quantity of parameters used to control the process

Q = 0 when an actual trading record is analyzed

For inflating the losses (IL), substitute L (a losing trade) for P (a winning trade) and change the exponent to be positive:

$$IL = L \times N^{+(Q+1)/(N-1)}$$

The objective can be accomplished in other ways, but this equation fulfills the general requirement of removing bias introduced by hindsight analysis.

Performance degradation is not generally practiced by system developers, perhaps because it is difficult to estimate and defend. But artificial results derived by hindsight simulated experience are even harder to defend, because the rules are assigned after the fact.

> ## To succeed in the markets, a trader must use a combination of good timing, knowledge of required capital and optimal investment levels before entering each trade.

If the trading system still shows a profit after degrading for sample size and parameter count, I consider it to have a positive mathematical expectation that may be repeated. Such a trading system may be evaluated further to solve for capital requirements and other money management needs.

The basic concept can be applied to some degree without a specialized program. Simply being aware of the amount of control a timing system applies to the trading process and limiting the number of control-producing parameters can improve system design.

A Monte Carlo simulation is an artificial problem-solving methodology that requires generating random numbers. In this application, I would use uniform random numbers that lie between zero and one and are defined such that any interval has the same likelihood of occurrence as any other interval of the same size. The random numbers are then applied to a model that identifies the subject of the simulation. The model in this simulation consists of the string of profits and losses that identify the system studied and all other relevant information that pertains to the subject. If you had a string of 100 profits and losses and the first random number produced was 0.564, then the 57th listing in the string of profits and losses would be listed as a selected trade. If the next random number generated was 0.316, then the next listing would be the 32nd from your table of profits and losses.

In my work, I go beyond the task of confirming that a system has a positive mathematical expectation; I determine the required capital stake with the Monte Carlo simulation, allowing me to experiment extensively through random sampling. Monte Carlo simulations can be used to evaluate any identifiable model for which procedural rules are known. We know only two things about simulated trading experience for sure: One is the quantity of experience identified through profits and losses; and the other is the number of ways that process control has been imposed as identified through the parameter count. When these factors are combined with market-based procedural restraints such as margin, commissions and slippage, we have sufficient input for a thorough analysis with the Monte Carlo simulation technique.

Complex problems that cannot be expressed easily in closed equation form are often candidates for study by random sampling. When applied to trading system evaluation, the technique draws trade results randomly from the list of profits and losses and allows the trader to evaluate the probability of reaching a profit goal using a predetermined amount of starting capital. A running tally is kept of the successful and unsuccessful attempts to reach the stated goal during the simulation. The process is repeated thousands of times for each capital level. When completed, the probability of reaching the goal at each capital level is determined within the boundaries of sampling error. Calculate the probability of remaining solvent by dividing the number of successful times of reaching the profit goals by the number of successes plus failures.

With Monte Carlo simulations, the trading record takes on a unique distributional form that precisely explains the nature of trading performance. With these results, a table and a graphic image of capital stake requirements versus the probability of reaching a given goal can easily be produced. You may find that a 99.99% chance of winning would require so much capital that a 4% passbook savings account would make better use of your money. On the other hand, you may be surprised at how much better off you could be by simply investing in stocks or commodities. Monte Carlo simulations can help you make those decisions.

This sort of analysis can help traders make informed decisions about the usefulness of a system and about the chances of success with the capital at hand. It also allows them to validate a system before accepting market risk.

Traders with a profitable timing system who set appropriate goals and allocate sufficient capital should do well over time. They could double or triple overall performance if they would take the process a step farther and become money managers.

When is it appropriate to increase or decrease the number of contracts traded on a given position? A well-timed trade in the right direction is twice as profitable if two contracts are traded instead of one. By the same token, perhaps four, five, 10 or more contracts should be traded on more promising positions. There may be a flaw in this reasoning, but later on I'll discuss a method that will isolate these promising opportunities. The main problem with doubling up contracts is that risk rises with increased investment. Another problem is that before a trade is completed, it is impossible to know exactly how successful the position will be.

I have found through recent work with simulation analysis that there are indeed ways to improve profits dramatically by selecting the proper level of investment exposure for each trade. This can be performed in either of two ways: the first based on the trader's individual performance and the second based on inherent economic factors affecting the market. Both can complement and support the overall money management result.

ON SYSTEM-BASED ALLOCATION

Calculating optimal levels of investment exposure for unique trading systems is a complicated problem and has not been easy to solve. This breakthrough in the area of money management is significant because it can guide investors toward success without increasing risk.

This analytical method is not a pyramiding process that increases risk without regard to the level of potential gains. It is a sophisticated procedure that allocates market exposure based on levels of profit that have been achieved while simultaneously decreasing the probability of losing your capital.

> **Artificial results derived by hindsight simulation experience are hard to defend, because the rules are assigned after the fact.**

This method requires a positive expectation timing system, as measured by a representative sample of profits and losses with a known level of parameter control. In the same manner as before, individual trade-by-trade profits are degraded to compensate for user control and sample size. I then use a recursive Monte Carlo simulation model on either actual or simulated trading results. As you may have noted, these initial steps are the same as those for evaluating a trading system and calculating required capital.

From here, I can select any level of capital stake as a starting point for money management analysis and use it as a base to compute the appropriate time to increase or decrease the number of shares or contracts invested based on the accumulation of profits or losses. Levels of market exposure are changed as marginal profit goals are realized without increasing market risk. This very significant addition, achieved only through simulation, can be used to form a true money management tool.

ON MAXIMIZING WEALTH

Figure 1 shows how a trader can maximize wealth in the fewest number of trades. (A trade is defined here as one round-trip market transaction of variable market exposure financed out of accumulated reserves with single-step changes in the number of contracts invested.) Minimizing the number of trades is equivalent to minimizing the required time to reach a goal, and hence, return on investment is maximized.

Figure 1 shows a two-window screen image of an exercise for a given capital stake. The system analyzed shows a 95% chance of returning a profit at the highest capital stake level. This would be the case with any system that reaches this point of analysis. Whenever you have a system with a positive mathematical expectation, some level of capital investment will eventually produce this high percentage. The trader selects the percentage chance of success, depending on how much money is risked as the capital stake. Don't be impressed by a relatively high 95% probability of success without considering what is required to achieve this success rate; be impressed only with a high probability of success coupled with a very low capital funding requirement. The example shown in Figure 1 was produced by a program I developed that requires the user to choose a capital stake from a full spectrum of possibilities. The trader simply selects an affordable level for his or her own finances.

The trading system analyzed uses a simple channel-breakout rule for trade timing. The profits and losses were brought current based on the few parameters I introduced in their original form 10 years ago. The uppermost curve in the top display gives the expected (average) probability of survival over a range of target goals. The second curve of the top display is the 95% confidence level based on the expected number of trials required to reach different points approaching the user's arbitrary goal.

The bottom curve in the top chart is simply the dollar earnings in the account and refers to the right-hand scale. This curve is based on the multiple-contract exposure suggested in the lower chart. The earnings for single-contract trading are not shown on the chart, but the lower chart shows the number of trades required in either case. From this, the reader can conclude that it would take perhaps four times longer to achieve the same result with single-contract trading.

The rules for determining when to modify contract exposure are based on single-contract changes in the contract count as profits are earned. The Monte Carlo simulation, although very complex in this event, evaluated these single-step changes in contract exposure throughout the simulation. Two events are monitored as profits are accumulated: The overall wealth in the trading account must improve when market exposure is increased; and the probability of remaining solvent as a result of increasing market exposure must also improve.

These charts can be illuminating in a variety of ways. For example, as the trader clears $50,000 in profits on a $44,000 investment, he or she should move from six-contract to seven-contract trading. After $200,000 in profits, the trader should move from 10-contract trading to 11-contract trading. The trader can also infer from these charts that in single-contract trading, approximately 1200 trades would have produced $450,000 in profits. Only 260 trades would be required to log nearly the same profit using the money manage-

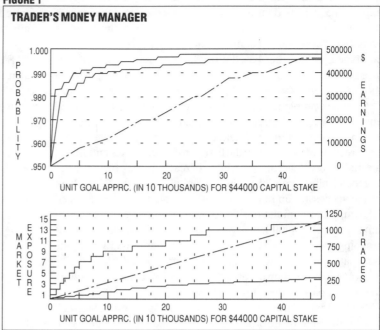

FIGURE 1

TRADER'S MONEY MANAGER

UNIT GOAL APPRC. (IN 10 THOUSANDS) FOR $44000 CAPITAL STAKE

UNIT GOAL APPRC. (IN 10 THOUSANDS) FOR $44000 CAPITAL STAKE

A system with a positive mathematical expectation of success will produce a high percentage with a large capital stake. The top line in the top chart is the expected (average) probability of survival for a range of target goals. The second line is the 95% confidence level. The third line refers to the right-hand scale and reflects the dollar earnings in the account. The bottom window also has three curves. The dotted line shows the number of trades required to achieve the same profits based on a point estimate for single-contract trading. The stop-function plot indicates when to add to or subtract from market exposure as a function of the state of the trader's wealth accumulation as defined by the horizontal axis. The solid line shows how the number of trades in multiple-contract trading increases over time as a function of trading performance.

ment mode when market exposure is periodically increased. In this example, profits are produced nearly four times faster when account earnings are used to shorten the time necessary to reach the $450,000 goal.

An interesting point can also be inferred from the figures in that even with an increase in market exposure in multiple contract trading, the probability of not going broke increases well beyond 99%. The point at which the lowest level of success begins is based on the level of capital selected from a capital analysis computation that precedes the money management exercise.

Of course, this example applies to the unique trading system I analyzed for demonstration purposes. Each system introduced through either a simulated or actual trading record will produce a different result.

ON CHAOS AS A MANAGEMENT TOOL

Another way to determine how many contracts or lots of stock to trade that can supplement these methods involves the study of long-term market data consisting of daily prices. This process applies some technical analysis techniques that will uncover the underlying chaos.

I liken this particular application of technical analysis to a sculptor chiseling away at a block of stone. The sculptor removes nonessential fragments to reveal his subject concealed inside. The technician applies his electronic chisel (his computer) to remove components of market data. Instead of lifelike figures, the technician's goal is to uncover trends, cycles, seasonals and such.

> **Every market has a characteristic cyclical signature. We have chosen the cyclical component for live hogs because it is easy to explain and is fundamental to the characteristics of hog production.**

Unfortunately, this process may delete the most valuable information. There is a money management technique that uses the residual price data cast aside in typical technical analysis. Search for trends, cycles and seasonal tendencies, but then cut them away. All that should remain is the underlying chaos. Although it may not be pretty, this chaos or residual price data can point the way.

When studying a market, the analyst can expose certain components in price data that are primarily useful in market timing. Every time series contains four elements loosely defined as trend, cycle, seasonal tendencies and irregular patterns; we should methodically isolate each of the first three components and remove them from the data, with the objective to remove all components except the irregular patterns, which represent chaos. The valuable chaos component can identify market posture and help determine the appropriate investment size. I have just begun to work on software that will automate these techniques, so the illustrations shown here must by necessity be hypothetical. The tools used lie in the realm of time series forecasting and estimation. Other related areas of interest could include differential filters, autoregressive integrated moving averages and more.

ON TIME SERIES

Suppose we have a time series of live-hog price data. I have chosen the classic hog market because it fulfills several nicely behaved characteristics: It follows a definite longer-term trend; it has a unique seasonal pattern; and it assumes a very explainable cycle. Like all markets, live hogs conform to the typical patterns of irregularity when other known components are removed. Figure 2 is a hypothetical chart for raw live-hog data over a typical period.

The first step to expose chaos is to remove the trend component from the hog market (Figure 2) by subtracting a fitted trend component from the raw data through a regression technique. I use a simple linear regression applying least squares. Variations such

FIGURE 2

RAW DATA, HOG MARKET

Simulated raw data of the hog market are shown here.

FIGURE 3

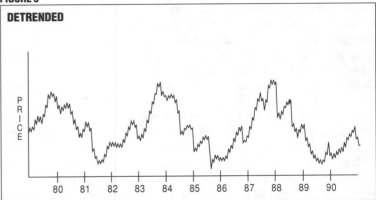

DETRENDED

Remove the trend component of the simulated data by subtracting a fitted trend component from the data through a regression technique. A simple linear regression applying least-squares method is used.

as fitting a Gompertz logistics function are possible, but simple measures that can be easily modified and manipulated are preferable. Getting too fancy on models tends to consume too great an amount of freedom for the process and unnecessarily inflate parameter counts. The result of detrending is a flattened time series (Figure 3). Figure 3 holds the residual cyclical, seasonal and irregular components of the hog market.

I did not use real data in my example because I wanted to spend my time illustrating a concept. It would have taken longer for me to make the same points with real data, as I have not yet completed the software that will automate the process.

Every market has a characteristic cyclical signature. We have chosen the cyclical component for live hogs because it is easy to explain and is fundamental to the characteristics of hog production. There is a four-year cycle for hogs that is related to the production elements of pig crop size, rate of slaughter and price. The price in one period affects the size of the farmer's pig crop in the next period. This, in turn, determines the number of pigs slaughtered. The number slaughtered affects the price, which influences the size of the next crop, and so on. The lag between price in one period and pig crop in the next and between pig crop in one period and slaughter in the next determines the length of the cycle. This is usually one year, making a complete hog cycle last four years. (See Figure 4.)

> **Time series contain four elements defined as trend, cycle, seasonal tendencies and irregular patterns; remove the first three components from the data to reveal the irregular patterns, which represent chaos.**

I use a centered moving average correction based on the two-year half-cycle period to first expose and then remove price cycle patterns. The detrending process exposes the longer-term cycles in the data. A point-by-point division of the detrended data by the moving half-cycle-period average will remove the cyclic effects. Figure 5 shows live-hog data without trend or cycles. The chart shows the remaining components of seasonal tendencies and irregular patterns.

Once the cycles have been removed, the analyst should take the final step of deseasonalization. Data deseasonalization is a complex procedure that may be accomplished in many ways. My technique involves creating an index for each trading day of the entire history by dividing every price by a centered 251-day moving average. There are approximately 251 trading days in one year. I then average all the indices for the 251 trading days over all like days for the entire history. This will produce an overall index for each trading day. Each day's detrended and decyclized price is then divided by the index value to arrive at the deseasonalized (irregular) time series. This step would build seasonal relationships and set the stage so that we can cut the seasonal forces away. The resulting chart will look something like Figure 6.

Figure 6 shows the market chaos (in units of the residual price standard deviations) that has been separated from the mass of other market forces that concealed it. As you can see, we have reduced the flattened-out irregulars into an amplified chaos diagram measured in standard deviations over time.

The chaos levels, shown as standard deviation readings, σ, reflect the tendency of prices to fluctuate from their historical norm (0σ). Positive sigma readings imply an overpriced product and negative readings imply an underpriced product. Economics tells us that with the known forces of trend, cycle and seasonal tendencies removed, prices tend to return to normal levels. Therefore, the market that is over- or underpriced is the most likely to experience a reversal. The trader should use the full price series to follow the market, using a proven timing tool to select

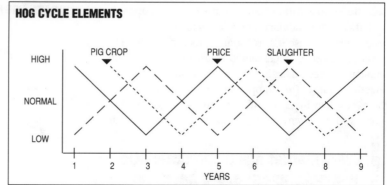

FIGURE 4

HOG CYCLE ELEMENTS

An ideal complete cycle in the hog market would last four years.

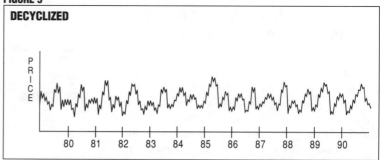

FIGURE 5

DECYCLIZED

A point by point division of the detrended data by the moving average half-cycle-period average would remove the cyclic effects.

trades. This chart tells us nothing about what or when to trade, only the appropriate amount of exposure when a trade is executed.

The quantity of contracts to trade is arbitrarily set proportionately to the number of standard deviations, as this relationship is necessary to spread risk. You wouldn't want to use the alternative measurement to standard deviation, which is probability, to allocate contract exposure, because the buy/sell quantities would not be correctly weighted. The trader should select a contract count he can afford to fund with margin funds and reserve capital at the zero σ level. Then set the 3- or 4σ level to be a single contract on both the buy side and the sell side, and fill in proportionate integral variations between. The resulting risk exposure table would then be appropriate for the trader's own situation.

The chaos level indicates how much market exposure is appropriate for the given trade and signals how many contracts or 100-share lots to buy or sell based on the magnitude of the readings. When the sigma readings are very high or very low, respective sell and buy signals generated by market timing tools are considered to be the safest. It may be appropriate to increase the number of contracts traded at these times. Conversely, signals that coincide with levels at the opposite extreme are risky. The number of contracts traded at these times should be minimal.

In this example, if the chaos level is at +3σ when a sell signal develops, the trader would sell eight contracts. If a signal to buy occurs at the +1σ level, four contracts should be purchased. The number of contracts in the buy and sell columns tend to be arbitrary. They represent proportionate levels of risk based on the tendency of the market to return to the norm of zero σ.

This market-oriented technique for determining the appropriate size of one's base investment should improve results to a noticeable degree because it uses natural market forces to amplify profits. The level of market exposure suggested is inversely proportional to historical levels of inherent risk.

ON SUMMATION

Either of these two new methods of determining trade exposure can double or triple the profits from a good timing system. When combined, these methods will further amplify profits. With a little effort, the application of simulation and sculpting techniques can turn any trader into a money manager.

Bob Pelletier is president of Commodity Systems, Inc. (CSI) in Boca Raton, FL. He trained as a mathematician, statistical analyst and estimation theorist and worked in radar and sonar system development for several years at General Electric before becoming a full-time trading advisor in 1974. The ideas presented here are incorporated in Commodity Systems, Inc.'s Trading System Performance Evaluator, the Trader's Money Manager and the forthcoming Unfair Advantage software.

Sabrina Carle, editor of the CSI News Journal, *contributed to this article, portions of which have appeared in the* News Journal.

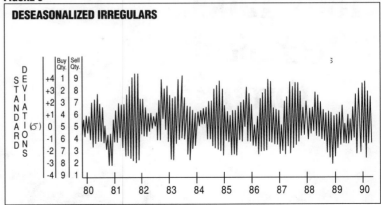

FIGURE 6

Each day's detrended and and decyclized price is then divided by an index value to arrive at the deseasonalized (irregular) time series.

REFERENCES

Commodity Systems, Inc., 200 West Palmetto Park Rd., Boca Raton, FL 33432, (407) 392-8663 or (800) 327-0175.

Harlow, Arthur A. [1962]. "Factors affecting the price and supply of hogs," *Technical Bulletin* #1274, U.S. Department of Agriculture, Washington, DC.

Pelletier, Robert C. *CSI News Journal*, December 1991, January 1992, February 1992, Commodity Systems, Inc.

_____ [1991]. "Trading System Performance Evaluator Manual," Commodity Systems, Inc.

_____ [1992]. "Trader's Money Manager Manual," Commodity Systems, Inc.

Tony Tabell: Technical Torch

Tony Tabell has carried the family tradition of technical analysis through the years, given to him from his father, technician Edmund Tabell, and his great uncle, Richard D. Wyckoff, long before most professional investors even recognized it as a legitimate technique. STOCKS & COMMODITIES Editor Thom Hartle interviewed Tabell in a telephone interview on January 24, 1992, asking him to recount some of his experiences as a second-generation technician. Practicing technical analysis since 1954, Tabell speaks about his impressions of the historical stock market as he sees it in five eras beginning with the early 1900s; his emphasis, in true Wyckoff tradition, on point and figure charting; the changes he's made in his own pool of indicators through the years, as well as the changes he's seen evolve in the markets' patterns themselves; his strict definition of the technician's role; and finally, his reading suggestions for beginning technicians.

"The advent of market globalization is another case of things changing and yet remaining the same; as long as markets are dominated by human emotions, you will get technical patterns behaving the same way they always have."
—Tony Tabell

Tony, you're probably one of the few second-generation technicians around today. What was it like, growing up around technical analysis?

There are a few of us second-generation technicians but not too many. My dad, Ed Tabell, was one of those who kept technical analysis alive at a rather difficult time, along with others such as Ken Ward and Ralph Rotnem. They kept the technical torch burning through the 1930s until the market recovered in the 1940s and 1950s and technical analysis became respectable again. Technical analysis was

just beginning to be considered for use by institutions when I arrived on the scene in 1954 and began working with my father. When he passed away in 1965, I took over his institutional research operation at Walston & Co.

But you weren't there that much longer, though —

I stayed there for five more years. Then some 21 years ago, in 1970, three of us — Mat Delafield, Ash Harvey and I — decided that we were tired of commuting, and we all wanted to start a new and

smaller firm, so we located that firm in Princeton where the three of us lived, and that's where we've been ever since.

With that much background, you're probably quite a student of market history. Am I right?

Being a student of market history is part of technical analysis; after all, what we're doing when we look at a chart, when we look at a computer study, whatever it is we do, we are looking at market history, on the assumption that a certain chart pattern, a certain level on an indica-

† *See Trader's Glossary for complete description*

tor, a certain behavior of an indicator, has done something in the past and may do something in the future. So in a sense all of technical analysis is market history. We have a reasonably extensive computerized databank we can draw on. For example, we have the entire history of the Dow Jones Industrial Average (DJIA) on a daily basis back to 1897. I don't think we've begun to exhaust the possibilities.

Do you see similarities in today's markets compared with what you can see in the early part of market history, in the early 1900s?

Yes and no. As you go back, you can divide markets into eras; one era lasted through the early part of the century up through the end of World War I. It was a rather slow period of growth, but with wide swings. Of course, there's another period that encompassed most of the 1920s in which stocks got out of line with all sense of valuation on the upside and shortly thereafter got equally out of line on the downside in 1932, so that's a second era. A third era of rather impressive growth ran from post-World War II through the mid-1960s; that's an era I'm used to, obviously, because that's when I started dealing with the stock market.

So then the fourth era—

The fourth era was the flat trading range we had with the repeated top at 1000 plus or minus a few points on the DJIA that lasted from the middle 1960s through the early 1980s. And then, of course, from 1982 you have the current era, which we can date now to 1992, where we appear to have gone in for another period of rather fast growth (Figure 1).

So basically, five eras of market history.

You can demonstrate this easily in many ways. The market behaved very differently in the 1920s than it does today. All you had to do was put a filter† on the market and look at the number of wide swings that you had then; this is something that may be coming back but certainly not to the degree that we saw in the 1920s. These different eras all have their own characteristics; the market remains the same in many ways, but it also changes,

and that's one of the things the technician has to do, recognize the changes.

One difference today is we have derivative products, compared to, say, in the 1920s, when they had real, extreme volatility. Can you see comparisons from the volatility?

We haven't reached the level of volatility that we had in the 1920s. We may wind up going in that direction, however. The game in the 1920s was very different — it was buying the cash market on 10% margin. In many ways the effect is the same and in many ways the mentality of the people trading the market is the same. But the techniques we use and they used in the 1920s are *very* different.

Derivatives have made a big difference.

Derivative products changed the market in a number of ways. One obvious example is October 1987. I'm not blaming October 1987 on derivatives; you can't do that. What characterized a difference in the market between the 1920s and today is that in October 1987 we had a decline of that enormous magnitude but we recovered very, very quickly. We had August through October 1987, which was only three months, and we had a drop that was almost equivalent to that of 1929; in fact, for two days it was a greater drop than anything that happened in 1929.

But only for two days.

Exactly. The amazing thing is that this had no effect outside the stock market; we went along in an economy that continued to grow despite the correction of enormous proportions, and eventually, the stock market recovered. We did not have the effect of the stock market disaster of 1929, of course. Here is a basic difference — we may have periods like 1987 that simply come along in the normal course of events but where they don't have any particularly long-lasting importance.

The exchange responded with rules to handle some of these problems, much the way it did in the 1920s.

All kinds of technical trading problems should be addressed; just like back in the 1920s, you had the short sale rule, the uptick rule. Incidentally, if you look back

at the history of the uptick rule, it was first proposed by the stock exchange itself, not, as popularly thought, by the government. This was a very small technical change but it improved the behavior of the markets and it prevented the possibility of a bear raid†.

Bear raids were common during the time Richard Wyckoff was developing his approach to the markets, weren't they? You have quite a bit of background in the Wyckoff approach to the markets.

It runs in the family. Richard Wyckoff was my mother's uncle, and he employed my father in *The Magazine of Wall Street* in the late 1920s. It was from Wyckoff that my father first learned about point and figure charting and carried it on; he started with charting when he entered the securities business himself back in 1932. So there is that historical relationship. And I still have Wyckoff's daughter's copy of his course in my library at home.

Then it makes a lot of sense that point and figure charting is important to you.

Yes. Point and figure charting is an old-fashioned technique but one that is still useful. Basically, the history of stock prices is the history of information, and information can be expressed in any number of ways. The conventional way of expressing information is the traditional bar chart with the high, low, close and the volume down at the bottom, the sort of thing that everyone looks at. I have nothing against that particular kind of charting, nor against Japanese candlesticks, which are still a further refinement of that method. I just happen to think that if you had to pick one tool with which to look at the market of individual stocks, I would prefer to look at it with point and figure than with any other.

Why?

Point and figure charts are time independent. Don't misunderstand me; time *is* very important. After all, the name of the game is time-weighted rate of return. But the fact is that significant market events from a technical point of view can take place over a short time horizon or a very long time horizon. If you compare the charts on the average stock and the average derivative product or the average future, for example, you'll find that the futures will often build patterns in a few days that take stocks months or years to form. However, the rules for interpreting these things remain the same *because* of time independence.

You mentioned patterns. What do you look for in a pattern?

The same sort of thing a bar chartist does. I look for accumulation or distribution areas; tops or bases, short for sideways trading ranges in which a given stock has held for a long time. Then I look for a downside or upside breakout from that range, confirming that something new has happened, that a price that has contained the stock for a fairly significant amount of trading has now been broken and the stock is on its way to a new price level.

So you look for major objectives based on point and figure charts?

I do. That's one of the major advantages of point and figure charting. You have something called a count, by which you can count horizontally across a given congestion area and reach an upside or downside target. One example would be Wal-Mart, which adjusted for the two-for-one split the latter part of 1990 and 1991 and held a flat range of 25 on the downside and 31 on the upside (Figure 2). A breakout from that range indicated a price of 52; it got to 51 before stalling earlier this year. After that, it formed a new base that had an upside objective of 58 and, of course, it's gotten up to 59. Recently, the stock has formed what *may* be a top that, if 54 is broken, might indicate a minor correction to 50. So we had the ability to take these counts also as we went along. That's something the point and figure chart gives you that a bar chart does not.

> **It was from Wyckoff that my father first learned about point and figure charting, and he carried it on when he entered the securities business himself in 1932.**

Speaking of price objectives, when a stock reaches an objective, do you like to take partial profits?

In my view, the phrase "taking profits" is one that should *never* be used by a technician. That's a trading strategy, and trading is not technical work; technical work is a servant of the trader or investor. We don't identify stocks as being buys or being sells; we certainly may verbally, but we don't do it in writing.

How do you identify stocks, then?

We rank them from one through five based on technical criteria. Trading strategy is as much a matter of psychology as it is of anything else. We stay away from it.

On the subject of technical criteria. What are some of the points that make up your ranking? Can you give me some examples?

One of the most important is the point and figure pattern. We have a fairly complex computer algorithm that we've developed over the years that measures 12 different aspects of a given point and figure chart and synthesizes them together

FIGURE 1

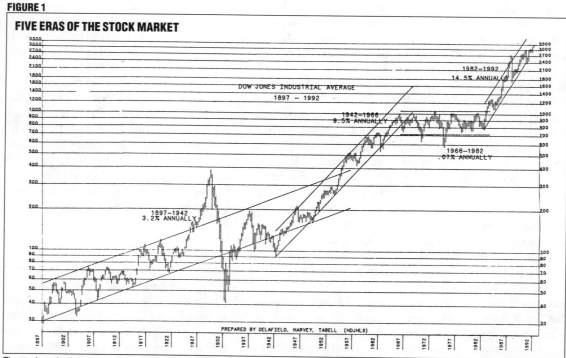

The stock market has experienced a number of growth periods. The first was a period of 3.2% annual growth during 1897 to 1942, which began with a slow period of growth and ended with both an excessive degree of overevaluation and underevaluation. Then the stock market advanced 9.5% annually from 1942 to 1966. However, only a 0.07% annual growth rate occurred from 1966 to 1982. From 1982 to early 1992 — the present time — the stock market has advanced 14.5% annualized.

FIGURE 2

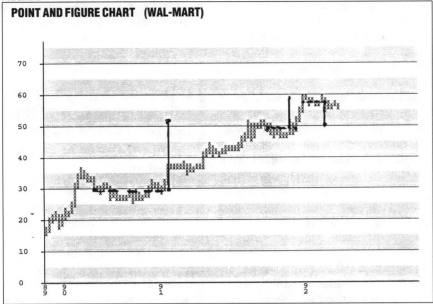

POINT AND FIGURE CHART   (WAL-MART)

A point and figure chart is a filter of price action. This chart requires a movement of at least one full point in the stock before the chart is updated; the Xs signify both advances and declines. Other styles of point and figure charts may use Xs for advances and Os for declines. Once a stock enters a trading range, the upper and lower boundaries of the range identify important support and resistance levels. A breakout indicates the expectations for the stock have changed. An objective for the price of the chart can be calculated by counting the number of columns during the trading range. An upside objective is determined by adding the number of columns to the breakout point. A down objective can be calculated by subtracting the number of columns from the breakdown point.

and winds up ranking each stock between one and five. Although the algorithm for producing the rating is computerized, it is the result of human analysis of the charts.

So you break it down.

We have a staff of five who look at the charts on all those stocks that, in our view, have exhibited significant technical action that particular week. These are the products of a computer system that screens 5,000 issues and comes up with anything from a couple of hundred to a thousand stocks on a given week that have done something technically significant. We then actively look at the chart and feed in the parameters on which the ranking is based.

You said 12 different aspects. What would you be looking for?

I'm looking for a significantly higher upside objective; a stock that is close to support; at the downside risk, if any. We look each week for unusual volume or activity in a stock; we consider group action; we consider relative strength. All these get fed into the equation.

You mentioned volume. Was volume important to Wyckoff? Do you use the same type of analysis?

> **The phrase "taking profits" should never be used by a technician. That's a trading strategy, and trading is not technical work; technical work is a servant of the trader or investor.**

No, we do not do a great deal of volume work. Wyckoff in his course mentioned volume occasionally, but actually, his favorite method of charting was point and figure, which doesn't have any volume in it at all!

Besides point and figure, do you have some other indicators you use of note?

We've tried to keep up a whole host of indicators, and they're all the standard ones. The indicators are all based on market statistics, and we have the mechanical ability to draw charts both on paper and on

a computer terminal or a personal computer, applying whatever you want to these particular data aspects.

And so you're always looking at —

We're always looking at standard things like breadth indicators and oscillators, and we'll change the indicators we're examining at any given point in time.

Any reason in particular?

There are some indicators that work very well for a short period of time and then cease to work; we try to vary them. Long-term relative strength has been important in recent markets — the leadership of Wal-Mart stores would be an example; the leadership that was established some years ago has remained. So long-term relative action has been quite important to look for in this market — there were times back in the 1960s that this wasn't the case.

What was different then that you couldn't count on relative strength?

You *could* count on relative strength, but you didn't have the super-cyclical movement of stocks that you have now, where major moves will encompass two or three or four cycles. Interestingly, you did have this back in the 1950s; the names were different, and you wouldn't believe some of them now —

Like who?

Names like Dow Chemical, International Paper, IBM. Then, you had upmoves that encompassed two- or three-cycle bull markets. You're beginning to see that again today, but whether that's a permanent change, I don't know. I think we need more evidence.

Some indicators will fall out of favor, you said. What are some that you don't really pay attention to now?

If you go 'way back, there was a fairly widely used indicator that was developed by Alan Silver in the 1940s, and what it did was to try to break volume down into upside and downside volume, and of course you didn't have Quotrons in those days. You had to express volume based on the number of stocks advancing and the number of stocks declining.

And when you did this consistently?

When you did this consistently, in all the major tops in the 1930s and 1940s and early to middle 1950s, there was consistent behavior in which total volume on a smoothed basis would dry up, caused entirely by a decline in upside volume; downside volume prior to the actual top didn't move up very much. The downside volume built up as the market moved down. But this sort of action — a peak in volume caused by a peak in upside volume — was characteristic of just about every major market top from the 1930s through the mid-1950s.

And then —

And all of a sudden, it stopped working. It still doesn't work now. I haven't the slightest idea why. The trouble is it's now coincident rather than leading, so your usefulness approaches zero. These days, by the time you've had a noticeable peak in upside volume, you're probably as close to being at a low as you're going to get. And we have no idea why. This is the kind of thing that makes life interesting for technicians.

What is a leading indicator you like today?

Breadth. I think it's still a valid leading indicator. You still have breadth confirming peaks in the current market, or at least according to the conventional interpretation. That leads you, for the time being, at least, to be positive about the market.

What do you think about the current focus on the globalization of markets? Do you follow the foreign markets too?

Like everyone else, we're beginning to look at foreign markets, and we now have the Nikkei and the FTSE and all the rest in our databank, and we chart them with some regularity. The advent of the globalization of foreign markets is another case of things changing and yet remaining the same. As far as we've been able to ascertain, the overseas markets act just like U.S. markets, and they do so because their actions are determined by human beings — and I don't think human emotions are a national characteristic.

Emotions do transcend national boundaries.

An example is in Japan in the past two years, you've seen a bear market that was almost classic and followed all the technical rules and shouldn't have been particularly surprising. As long as markets are

dominated by human emotions, and sometimes by the less attractive human emotions such as greed and fear, you will get technical patterns behaving the way they always have.

> **If you had to pick one tool with which to look at the market, I would prefer to look at it with a point and figure chart.**

Do you have any favorite books that you think people new to technical analysis would benefit from?

There are a few that I like very much: John Murphy's book, *Technical Analysis of the Futures Market*. Some of the points he raises and some of the indicators he discusses are valid for my market. Another one I like because it's an example of rigorous testing and exploration of indicators is Colby and Meyers's *Encyclopedia of Technical Market Indicators*. What Bob Colby and Tom Meyers do is look at about 50 widely followed indicators and then rigorously test each one to see if it is applicable and how profitable it really is. It is straightforward without a lot of witch-

FIGURE 3

BOND AND STOCK MARKET BOTTOMS, 1953-90

Bond bottoms	Stock bottoms	Days lead
Jun 16, 1953	Sept 14, 1953	63
Aug 15, 1957	Oct 22, 1957	47
Jan 28, 1960	Oct 25, 1960	188
July 2, 1970	May 26, 1970	-27
Sept 20, 1974	Apr 21, 1980	30
Oct 1, 1981		
Feb 9, 1982	Aug 12, 1982	
July 2, 1984	July 24, 1984	15
Oct 20, 1987	Oct 19, 1987	-1
Mar 29, 1989	Oct 11, 1990	390

Bull and bear market swings were identified by using a 10% filter to bond yield data. The bond bottoms appear to lead the stock market. However, the major all-time low for bonds (when yields reached 15%), October 1, 1981, did not appear to tie into a stock market bottom.

FIGURE 4

BOND AND STOCK MARKET TOPS, 1954-90

Bond top	DJIA	Days lead	Stock top	DJIA	%Chg
Oct 27, 1954	355.73	681	Jan 12, 1957	520.77	+46
June 17, 1958	478.97	879	Dec 13, 1961	734.91	+53
Mar 27, 1963	684.73	724	Feb 9, 1966	995.15	+45
Feb 16, 1971	890.06	685	Nov 1, 1973	948.53	+7
Jan 5, 1977	978.06	424	Sept 11, 1978	907.54	-7
June 17, 1980 Nov 30, 1981	879.27	216	April 27, 1981	1024.05	+16
May 11, 1983	1219.72	55	Nov 29, 1983	1287.20	+5
Jan 22, 1987	2145.67	149	Aug 25, 1987	2722.42	+27
Feb 3, 1988	1924.57	799	July 17, 1990	2909.75	+55

Bond market tops were identified using a 10% filter. The lead time between bond market tops and stock market tops indicate that the stock market typically continues well after bonds stop rallying.

Having access to a significant database provides Tony Tabell with the opportunity to study market history. Recently, he researched the relationships between bond and stock market bottoms and tops.

doctoring in it and I like that. Then, of course, you have classics such as Magee and Edwards. Another is Alexander Wheelan's book, *Study Helps in Point and Figure Technique*, which is kind of an old-time bible around here.

Tony, is there anything that you think would be important to add?

I think we've covered most of the bases.

In that case, thank you for your time.

REFERENCES

Colby, R.W., and T.A. Meyers [1988]. *The Encyclopedia of Technical Market Indicators*, Dow Jones-Irwin.

Delafield, Harvey, Tabell, Inc. 5 Vaughn Drive, CN 5209, Princeton, NJ 08543-5209.

Edwards, Robert D., and John Magee [1966]. *Technical Analysis of Stock Trends*, John Magee Inc.

Murphy, John J. [1986]. *Technical Analysis of the Futures Markets*, New York Institute of Finance.

Wheelan, Alexander [1989]. *Study Helps in Point and Figure Technique*. Fraser Publishing Co., Burlington, VT.

> **As long as markets are dominated by human emotions, you will get technical patterns behaving the way they always have.**

Closing Arms

The Arms index has been verified, deified, and even modified, certainly within the pages of STOCKS & COMMODITIES. Now the index is examined again, this time by noted veteran technician Arthur Merrill, to find out whether the daily closing Arms index is helpful in pointing the probable direction of the market on the following day.

by Arthur A. Merrill, C.M.T.

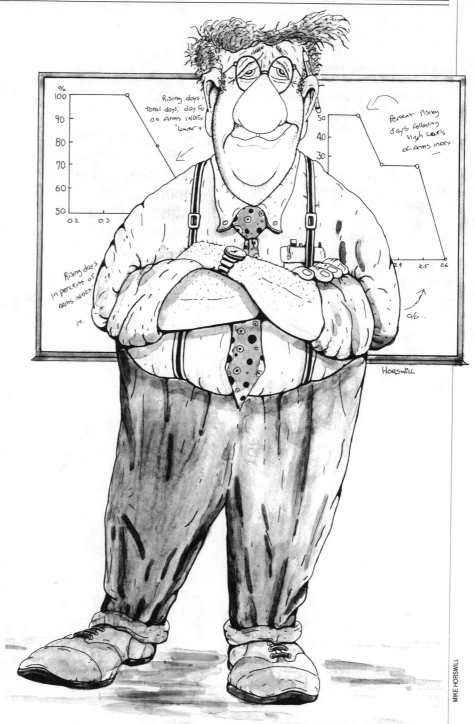

The index originally known as TRIN, or the short-term trading index, is now properly labeled the Arms index. (I may have been the first to suggest this change.) The index's usefulness and versatility has been discussed in several issues of STOCKS & COMMODITIES. Here, I'll address whether the daily closing Arms index is helpful in pointing the probable direction of the market on the following day. To appreciate the meaning of the index, which is defined in the Traders' Glossary, I modified it to the following formula, which gives the same answer. The numerator is: Total volume declining stocks divided by number of declining stocks. The denominator is: Total volume rising stocks divided by number of rising stocks. This modification of the formula shows the index as the average volume of declining stocks divided by the average volume of rising stocks. High figures are bearish; low figures are bullish. This is intuitively contradictory. Richard Arms told me that if he had to do it over again, he'd invert the formula to make high figures bullish.

In any case, I asked my computer to review a data bank of 435 trading days and report what happened to the Dow Jones Industrial Average (DJIA) on those days after various levels of the closing Arms index.

Note Figure 1. The average percent change in the DJIA is charted for the day following various low levels of the Arms index. For example, if the Arms index were 0.4 or lower, the DJIA averaged a rise of 0.46% on the following day. An index figure less than 0.4 appears to be a usefully bullish number. Above 0.4, the indications are noncommittal. The bad news is that only four of the 435 trading days were that low.

Note Figure 2. This chart shows the average percent change following high levels of the Arms index. For example, if the index closed higher than 2.4, the DJIA dropped an average of 0.21% on the following day. More bad news: Only three of the 435 trading days had an index reading above 2.4.

Note Figure 3. This chart reports the number of rising days as a percent of total days, on the day following low levels of the Arms index. If the Arms index was 0.4 or lower, the DJIA rose 75% of the time on the following day.

Note Figure 4. This chart reports the

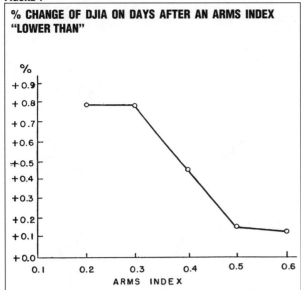

FIGURE 1

% CHANGE OF DJIA ON DAYS AFTER AN ARMS INDEX "LOWER THAN"

The average percent change in the DJIA is charted for the day following various low levels of the Arms index. It appears that an index figure below 0.4 seems to be a usefully bullish number.

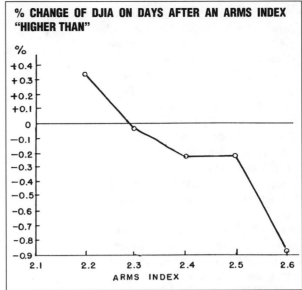

FIGURE 2

% CHANGE OF DJIA ON DAYS AFTER AN ARMS INDEX "HIGHER THAN"

Here's the average percent change in the DJIA following high levels of the Arms index. If the Arms index closed higher than 2.4, the DJIA dropped an average of 0.21%.

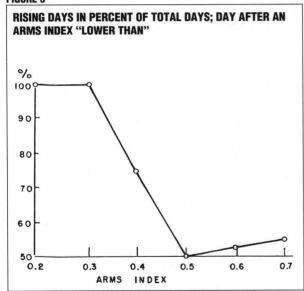

FIGURE 3

RISING DAYS IN PERCENT OF TOTAL DAYS; DAY AFTER AN ARMS INDEX "LOWER THAN"

Here's the number of rising days as a percent of the total days, on the day following low levels of the Arms index. The DJIA rose 75% of the time following a closing value of the Arms index of 0.4.

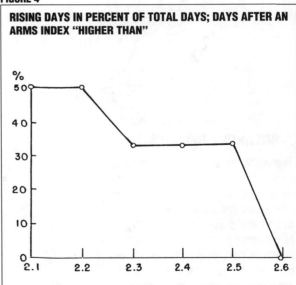

FIGURE 4

RISING DAYS IN PERCENT OF TOTAL DAYS; DAYS AFTER AN ARMS INDEX "HIGHER THAN"

The percentage of days the DJIA rose after a closing value of the Arms index dropped if the index was at 2.3 or higher.

percent of rising days following high levels of the Arms index. It appears that the index must be 2.3 or higher to give a bearish signal.

My conclusion? The simple daily closing Arms index seems to be useful in forecasting the direction of the market of the following day only at very high (above 2.3) or very low (below 0.4) levels. This occurs only rarely. For

The simple daily closing Arms index seems to be useful in forecasting only at very high (above 2.3) or very low (below 0.4) levels.

real usefulness, you have to look beyond the simple closing figure, as described in the reference section following.

Arthur Merrill is a Chartered Market Technician and the author of many reports and books, including Behavior of Prices on Wall Street *and* Filtered Waves, Basic Theory.

ADDITIONAL READING

Arms, Richard W., Jr. [1991]. "Using the Arms index in intraday applications," *Technical Analysis of* STOCKS & COMMODITIES, Volume 9: April.

_____ [1991]. "Cross your Arms," *Technical Analysis of* STOCKS & COMMODITIES, Volume 9: May.

Hartle, Thom [1991]. "Arms on Arms," *Technical Analysis of* STOCKS & COMMODITIES, Volume 9: July.

Merrill, Arthur A. [1989]. "Volume indices," *Technical Analysis of* STOCKS & COMMODITIES, Volume 7: September.

Rusin, Jack [1991]. "The issue/volume weighted long-term Arms index," *Technical Analysis of* STOCKS & COMMODITIES, Volume 9: October.

_____ [1992]. "The internal dynamics of TRIN," STOCKS & COMMODITIES, January.

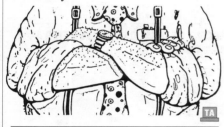

BREAKOUT RELIABILITY

The reliability of a breakout from a trading range as a signal for an impending trend is significantly improved if prices are still beyond the range after a number of days (e.g., 5). Other types of confirmation can also be used — minimum percent penetration, given number of thrust days, and so on. Although waiting for a confirmation following breakouts will lead to worse fills on some valid signals, it will help avoid many "false" signals. The net balance of this tradeoff will depend upon the confirmation condition used and must be evaluated by the individual trader. The key point, however, is that the trader should experiment with different confirmation conditions, rather than blindly following all breakouts.

—Jack D. Schwager
A Complete Guide to the Futures Markets

DIANA FRITCH

Blending Time Frames

The stock market has worlds within worlds, if you think about it — time frames within time frames, all interlinked and interdependent. The problem is, if you look at too small a time frame, you could find yourself drowning in minutiae, and if you look at too large a time frame, you could find yourself missing signals of opportunity. There must be a way to equitably look at situations both large and small without getting bogged down. Linda Satterfield has a few suggestions.

by Linda Satterfield

F or many traders, monitoring intraday charts can be an exciting experience. It's an upgrade into a fascinating world of easily accessible knowledge. Before computers, the world of intraday activity could only be laboriously perceived by keeping charts by hand. Now, with the touch of a button or two, a trader can zoom into a one-minute bar chart or back off to the larger perspective of a monthly chart. If the label and prices are removed and the scale adjusted, it is impossible to tell which time frame is on the screen. Such a wealth of information can be overwhelming and quite likely to result in a paralyzing situation for the unprepared trader. Which time frame is best for routine trading? Where are the best signals? Is it better to day trade or stay a month? Is it possible to suffer from time frame myopia? Is it better to act now or wait for the five-minute chart to go overbought? These are only a few examples of what could turn out to be difficult and uniquely personal questions. Trial and error can be an expensive learning experience in a fast-moving market.

By understanding the framework of the market, some of those choices can be simplified and understood better. Here are some guidelines for integrating the different time frames into a cohesive market overview, with an example of the dynamics of the relationships.

> ## What might be a small splash on the monthly chart could become a tsunami on the five-minute chart.

Each time frame is inextricably related to the pattern in another. For example, a bearish double top on a five-minute chart can be part of a triangle pattern on a 60-minute chart, which in turn can be part of a topping pattern on a daily chart, which again, in turn, can be the right shoulder of an inverted head and shoulders pattern on a weekly chart, which (yes, again) could be a prelude to the third wave explosion on the monthly chart. The action at one level will have implications on the others. What might be a small splash on the monthly chart could become a tsunami on the five-minute chart.

Some time frame observations can help the confused trader determine what is important and what is not:

- The same patterns and series of patterns occur on all time frames, from one-minute to yearly charts.
- The larger the time frame in which the pattern occurs, the greater the expected move, both time and price, from the pattern identified.
- The pattern in progress on the largest time frame dictates the amount of movement expected in a smaller time frame.
- A given move begins in the smallest time frame and ends on the largest time frame relevant to the dominant pattern.

STOCK INDICES, NOVEMBER-DECEMBER 1991

On November 14, 1991, an Elliott five-wave decline on a three-minute bar chart of the New York Composite Index (Figure 1) suggested the possibility that a much larger move could develop. The position of the market indices was precarious; the market had been edging its way higher in a nine-month trading range. A number of technical indicators were flashing negative divergences along with ringing overbought signals. Markets in that position may pull back and consolidate (at least) or push upward in a power drive that wipes out the divergences and remains overbought for weeks. Typically, a major move may be ex-

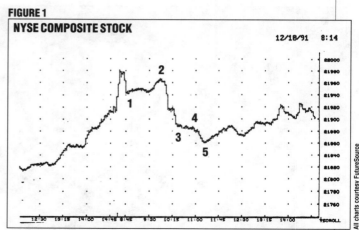

FIGURE 1

NYSE COMPOSITE STOCK

All trends have a beginning at the smallest of scales. On this three-minute bar chart, an Elliott five-wave decline was the first indication of a possible downtrend beginning.

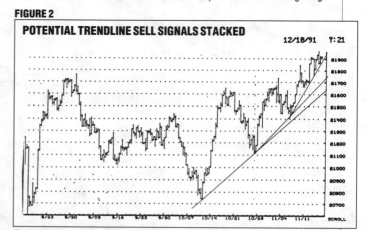

FIGURE 2

POTENTIAL TRENDLINE SELL SIGNALS STACKED

Each trendline drawn had an increasing angle of ascent. An accelerating market is often vulnerable to a swift retracement.

pected after such a lengthy period of consolidation.

The first indication that the index was beginning to move in the new direction could be noted on the three-minute bar chart — normally a time frame too small for anyone other than day traders, but the message was clear for anyone who understood the implications. On November 14, in the first three trading hours of the day, the market did five clear waves down in a dramatic intraday demonstration of weakness. It then spent the rest of the day in a labored crawl back to a 50% to 60% retracement. Was that weakness meaningful, and if so, how far would the weakness extend?

Isolated and alone, the day's pattern was a non-event — choppy for a day trader. Within the context of the larger time frames, it was an ominous position for the market to display such momentum to the downside. That three-hour burst of selling and the subsequent meager rally suggested that the trickle downward could become a waterfall if sell signals were triggered on the larger time frames. Each time frame was conveying the vulnerability of the market's position. The 180-minute bar chart shows it best (Figure 2).

The 15-minute bar chart confirmed the likelihood of a top with "three spikes to a high," a common prelude to a reversal

FIGURE 3

FIGURE 3

THREE SPIKES TO A HIGH

12/18/91   9:28

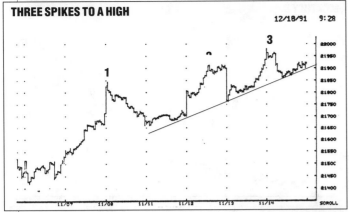

Classic chart analysis indicates that after three price rallies, a market should reverse its trend.

FIGURE 4

FIVE WAVES DOWN

12/18/91   7:27

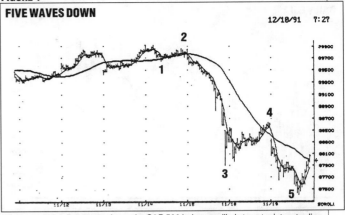

After completing five waves down, the S&P 500 index was likely to enter into a trading range.

FIGURE 5

MARKET CONTINUES LOWER, BUT STRENGTH IS SEEN

12/11/91   17:50

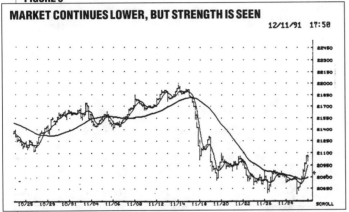

The stock market still continued lower, but signs of strength were indicated by the swift rally.

FIGURE 6

SIDEWAYS CONSOLIDATION FORMS

12/11/91   18:05

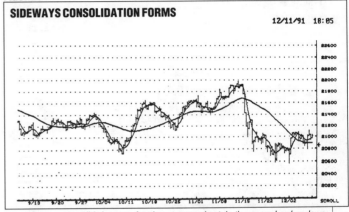

The sideways consolidation was forming at approximately the same level as lows established in early October.

(Figure 3).

On every chart from the monthly down to the smallest scale, potential sell signals were stacked under the market like dominoes; simply falling through the previous day's low would begin a cascade through a series of trendlines, moving averages and support levels that could have dramatic repercussions. Which level would hold? Where would the price level be perceived as a bargain and demand emerge? And for how long?

The next morning, the market confirmed more weakness early by easily penetrating the previous day's low, the short-term trendlines and moving averages. Then the market fell through immediate daily trendlines, giving traditional sell signals in each time frame out to the daily chart. As that was the largest time frame that gave the sell signals, the move could be expected to be completed eventually on the level of the daily chart. This five-wave pattern on the 15-minute December Standard & Poor's chart shows the low could have been in as early as November 19 (Figure 4).

That rally was only temporary, however. New lows continued to be made for two more weeks as the bottoming process continued on successively larger scales (Figures 5 and 6). By December 2, most indices had reached the lower end of the nine-month trading range on the daily, weekly and monthly charts. The Dow Jones Industrial Average (DJIA) continued down to test the lower extremes of that range on December 11. A bottom of unknown magnitude was finally completed on the weakest daily chart (Figure 7).

As the final low was made on December 11, the larger-scale charts showed no sell signals. The monthly chart with its dominant uptrend pattern dictated the amount of movement in smaller time frames and only showed more consolidation (Figure 8). The pattern on the weekly chart suggested that a buy signal could emerge, as the market had once again retested and confirmed the breakout point. The traditional buy signal was given when the price moved back above the pivot† area delineated by the December 6th high of 2958 (Figure 9).

After the downmove was completed within the appropriate time frames, the larger-scale charts prepared the trader for the next big move, the resumption of the uptrend — or, at least, a retest of the upper boundaries. Again, the smaller-scale charts gave significant clues to the trader who was alert to the potential

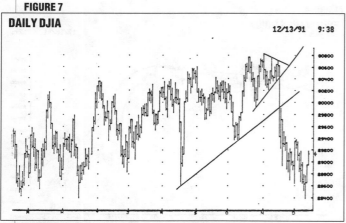

FIGURE 7

DAILY DJIA　　　　　　　　　　　12/13/91　9:38

Violation of the support trendlines produced a quick decline to the lower side of the trading range. Demand for stock was appearing at the lower end of the trading range.

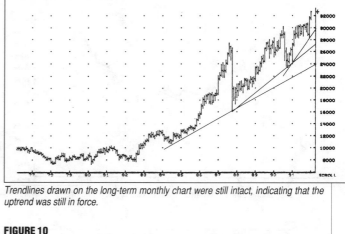

FIGURE 8

MONTHLY DJIA　　　　　　　　　1/19/92　11:08

Trendlines drawn on the long-term monthly chart were still intact, indicating that the uptrend was still in force.

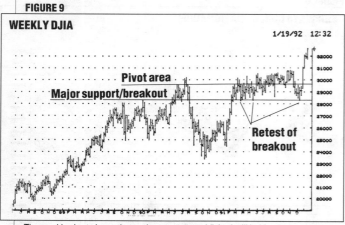

FIGURE 9

WEEKLY DJIA　　　　　　　　　　1/19/92　12:32

The weekly chart shows that major support established still held.

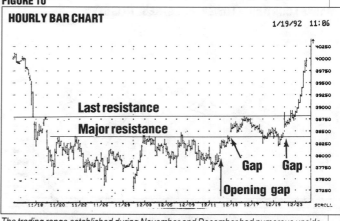

FIGURE 10

HOURLY BAR CHART　　　　　　　1/19/92　11:06

The trading range established during November and December had numerous upside gaps as the right side was being formed. This was a sign of strength in the market.

shown on the larger scales. The 60-minute chart in Figure 10 shows a flood of buying building behind a dam of resistance. The dam began to crack as resistance levels were penetrated days before the explosion began to the upside. The gaps added visual emphasis to the growing demand. The series of higher highs, higher lows, gaps and broken resistance levels again warned of the impending move.

IN PERSPECTIVE

Smaller time frames are not the ultimate answer to the question of market direction. Used alone, there is a real danger of getting lost in minutiae. Placed within the perspective of larger patterns, they aid in timing and judging the extent and magnitude of a coming move. As each stage of market history unfolds, the patterns on the smaller-scale charts are woven inexorably into the larger patterns, offering significant information to the patient trader who is willing to consider how time frames can be blended together.

Linda Satterfield, a financial advisor with Prudential Securities in Dallas, TX, has been involved with the futures industry since 1971 as a broker/trader/analyst. She is also co-leader of the Dallas-Fort Worth Traders' Group and a member of the Market Technicians Association. She can be reached at Prudential Securities, 2400 Renaissance Tower, 1201 Elm St., Dallas TX 75270 (214) 761-5175.

1991 Cycles

If you've always suspected that contracts have definite personalities, you would have your suspicions confirmed this way. Here's an overview of various cycles that appeared in some futures markets during 1991, the way only John Ehlers could explain it.

by John F. Ehlers

I n years past I have reported on the cyclic character of various commodity contracts, concluding that tradeable cycles were present from 15% to 30% of the time and that some contracts tend to have definite cyclic personalities. These conclusions were reached by making spectral estimates on a daily basis and then gathering and displaying the results in a histogram over the full year. The histogram allowed observation of how many times a 12-day cycle occurred, for example. This approach still makes the spectral estimate on a daily basis, but the display has been changed to view the continuity of the cycle content. This display shows the tradeable cycles, multiple simultaneous cycles and even failure of cyclic activity. The display allows you to pick entry points even when the market is in the trend mode by knowing the position of the superimposed cyclic extremes.

BUT FIRST, A LITTLE THEORY

Imagine a white light shining at a prism. The prism separates the white light, allowing the component colors or wavelengths to be seen. Sir Isaac Newton invented the word "spectrum" to describe the separation into components. Any band of wavelengths can have a spectrum, even the cycle lengths that appear in the market. The spectral estimates in Figures 1 through 12 were made using the MESA algorithm. MESA computations are the functional equivalent of applying the price data to a bank of filters, which spans cycle periods from eight to 50 days, with each filter in the bank only allowing its tuned cycle length to pass. The amplitudes of the filter outputs are sensed, and these amplitudes are compared to form the spectrum display. Figure 1 shows a theoretical 20-day sinewave cycle. The spectrum window in the upper left-hand corner of the bar chart shows that the 20-day cycle is the only cycle present.

The new color-coded display is the equivalent of a contour plot of the spectrum and is located below the bar chart. The color-coded spectral sequence is plotted directly below the price bar for each day so the spectrum and price are synchronized. The scale of the spectral contour plot ranges from 0 to 50 days, in harmony with the span of the spectrum filter bank. Spectral

FIGURE 1

THEORETICAL 20-DAY SINEWAVE CYCLE

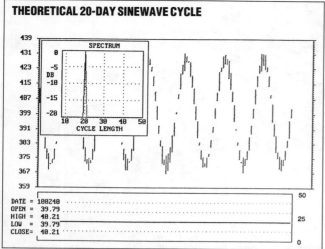

The solid line is positioned at the 20-day cycle length (right-hand scale of the chart), as this is the only cycle present.

FIGURE 2

THEORETICAL PRICE FUNCTION

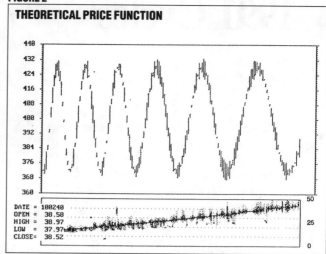

The cycle length is increasing in the simulated price data, indicated by the rising line. The line is becoming fuzzy because the cycle length is expanding slowly. You can observe the accuracy of the cycle estimate by counting the number of bars between the successive lowest lows or highest highs.

FIGURE 3

FREQUENCY CHANGES

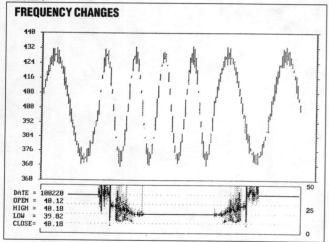

A slowly varying cycle will cause the spectral display to become fuzzy, while a sudden sharp change in the cycle frequency is accompanied by a decrease in resolution. Cyclical analysis is invalid for approximately half a cycle period at each transition.

FIGURE 4

US BONDS

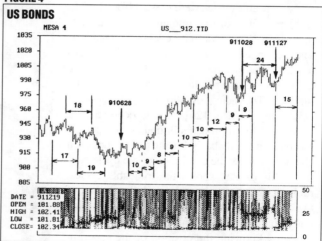

The 20-day cycle ended on June 28 and was replaced by a combination of a long cycle (greater than 50 days) and a shorter cycle (eight to 12 days). This can be observed by the combination of the yellow line along the bottom of the chart, with the yellow appearing along the top of the chart.

component amplitudes are displayed relative to the largest component on a decibel scale. Since decibels are logarithmic ratios, the smaller components have negative values. For example, a power ratio of 1/2 equals -3 dB, a power ratio of 1/10 equals -10 dB, and a power ratio of 1/100 equals -20 dB. Spectral amplitudes in the range between 0 and -5 decibels are yellow, between -5 and -10 dB are red, between -10 and -15 dB cyan, and between -15 and -20 dB are blue. The colors were selected to translate to decreasing print density when printed in black and white. The spectral contour plot of Figure 1 is not very interesting because the only cycle present is the pure 20-day cycle.

Figure 2 is a slightly more interesting display because the theoretical price function has a slowly increasing period as time increases. The spectral contour now becomes "fuzzier" because the data are not completely stationary over the measured period.

Nonetheless, the changing frequency is easy to recognize. The accuracy of the spectral estimate can be checked by counting bars between successive lowest lows (or highest highs). One big difference measuring from a price extreme is that MESA makes continuous measurements and does not rely on discrete points along the cycle.

If a slowly varying cycle period causes the spectral display to be fuzzy, what happens when the frequency changes sharply? The answer can be found in Figure 3, where the theoretical price cycle period switches instantly from 40 days to 20 days and then back to 40 days again four cycles later. Simply, cyclic analysis is invalid for approximately half a cycle period at each transition. Cycle analysis is invalid because the data are not stationary over the analysis period. In the transition zone, a mixture of 20-day cycle data and 40-day cycle data is used for the analysis. All

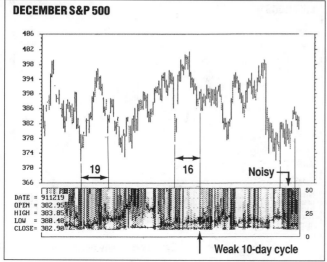

FIGURE 5

DECEMBER S&P 500

19   16   Noisy

DATE = 911219
OPEN = 382.95
HIGH = 383.85
LOW = 380.40
CLOSE= 382.90

Weak 10-day cycle

The stronger cycle varied from 16 to 30 days over the year for the S&P 500 December futures contract. During the latter part of the year, a multitude of cycles was present.

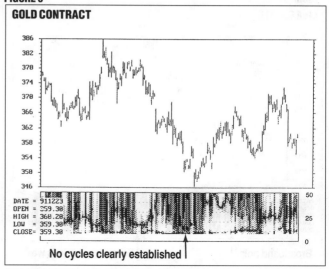

FIGURE 6

GOLD CONTRACT

DATE = 911223
OPEN = 359.30
HIGH = 360.20
LOW = 359.30
CLOSE= 359.30

No cycles clearly established

Gold did not show any clearly established cycles present.

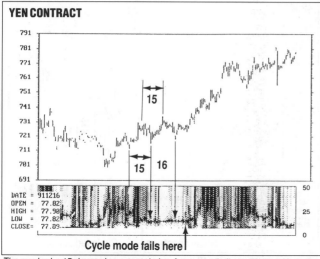

FIGURE 7

YEN CONTRACT

15

15   16

DATE = 911216
OPEN = 77.82
HIGH = 77.90
LOW = 77.82
CLOSE= 77.09

Cycle mode fails here

The yen had a 15-day cycle present during August, as indicated by the single line. However, this appearance of the cycle did not last very long.

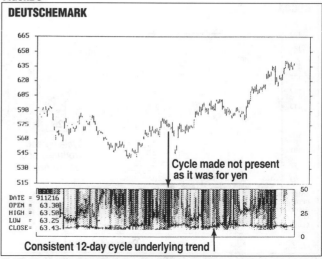

FIGURE 8

DEUTSCHEMARK

Cycle made not present as it was for yen

DATE = 911216
OPEN = 63.30
HIGH = 63.50
LOW = 63.25
CLOSE= 63.43

Consistent 12-day cycle underlying trend

The Deutschemark did not have the same cycle during August that the yen had. There was a fairly consistent 12-day cycle underlying the trend.

cycle analysis algorithms require stationary data. One major difference between fast Fourier transforms (FFTs) and MESA is that FFTs require a much longer datastream for the analysis. As a result, market data are seldom stationary long enough for a valid FFT analysis. The shift in cycle length can be recognized by a relatively rapid change in the cycle length of the spectral estimate, accompanied by a decrease in resolution (increased fuzziness) in the contour width.

Now, understanding the display and some constraints of cycle analysis, we can look back at 1991 from a cycles perspective for several commodity contracts.

REAL-WORLD CYCLE EXAMPLES
All the real-world cycle examples use the December contract, ending at respective termination dates. Each chart has a span of

about eight months, so the left-hand side of each chart is the beginning of April and the beginning of August is approximately at the center of the chart.

The U.S. Treasury bond contract is one of my favorites to trade on the basis of cycles. Traditionally, bonds seem to have a 10- to 12-day cycle personality. The spectral contour of bonds in Figure 4 confirms the previous observations. The eight- to 12-day cycle was present for most of the year, starting about June 28, 1991. Prior to the onset of the short cycles, the dominant cycle length slowly increased from about 16 to 20 days over a two-month period. Excellent predictions of the turning points resulted, as shown, knowing the dominant cycle length and the last occurrence of the lowest low or highest high. The MESA program is more subtle in providing the predictions by displaying the phase of the dominant cycle as well as the computed

FIGURE 9

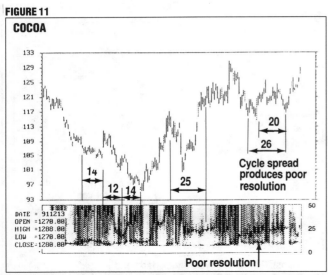

FIGURE 10

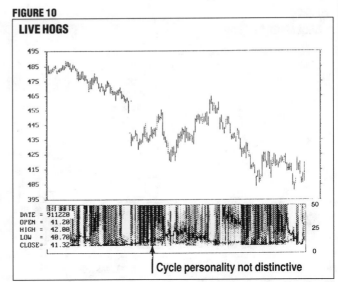

Live cattle rarely has a distinctive cycle. Broadband noise dominates the display.

The live hog contract does not appear to have any cyclical personality of less than 50 days.

FIGURE 11

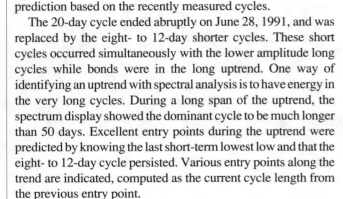

FIGURE 12

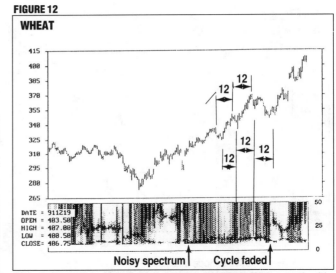

Cocoa had a 12- to 14-day cycle in April through July, but when the trend turned up the cycle length approximately doubled.

Wheat had a relatively strong 12-day cyclic component over the last four months of the uptrend.

prediction based on the recently measured cycles.

The 20-day cycle ended abruptly on June 28, 1991, and was replaced by the eight- to 12-day shorter cycles. These short cycles occurred simultaneously with the lower amplitude long cycles while bonds were in the long uptrend. One way of identifying an uptrend with spectral analysis is to have energy in the very long cycles. During a long span of the uptrend, the spectrum display showed the dominant cycle to be much longer than 50 days. Excellent entry points during the uptrend were predicted by knowing the last short-term lowest low and that the eight- to 12-day cycle persisted. Various entry points along the trend are indicated, computed as the current cycle length from the previous entry point.

The uptrend was arrested when a relatively strong 24-day cycle appeared on October 25, 1991. The 24-day cycle coexisted

with the nine-day cycle for a while. The 24-day cycle also gave some good predictive entries: for example, between October 25 and November 27, 1991, as shown. After November 27, 1991, the 24-day cycle almost disappeared and the length of the

Traditionally, bonds seem to have a 10- to 12-day cycle personality.

vestigial remains decreased rapidly. Simultaneously, the length of the 10-day cycle increased to about 15 days. The two cycle lengths almost appear to coalesce to form a single solid dominant cycle. In any case, the dominant cycle length at the end of the contract is approximately 15 days after the previous cyclic low, implying that it is time to go long by measuring from the last lowest low. To do this you must roll over to the March 1992 contract. As it turned out, this was immediately prior to the Fed action and a long position would have turned out to be profitable.

Figure 5 displays the December Standard & Poor's 500 contract. The S&P 500 has a cyclic personality clearly different from Treasury bonds. The stronger cycle varied from 16 to 30 days over the year. Although the 10-day cycle was present much of the time, its amplitude was relatively small. One of the more striking aspects of the S&P 500 cyclic contour is that high energy is spread across the spectrum for the last 13 days. One definition

> **Wheat, shown in Figure 12, had a relatively strong 12-day cyclic component over the last four months during the uptrend.**

of noise is having energy at all frequencies. Therefore, the cyclic analysis is noisy for the last 13 days and so we can glean no predictive insight on the basis of cycle analysis. The situation was similar but less severe in July when the major turning point was reached.

Figure 6 suggests that gold contracts were difficult to trade on the basis of cycles during the year. The dominant cycle length seemed to be constantly in transition, so that the data were rarely stationary.

Figure 7 shows that the 15-day cycle for the yen contract in August 1991 gave some excellent buy and sell signals by referencing previous lowest lows and highest highs. In contrast, curiously, the Deutschemark, shown in Figure 8, would have been nearly impossible to trade on the basis of cycles during the same time span. The Deutschemark also had a consistent 12-day cycle that could have provided excellent entry points along the trend. It is possible the actions of all contracts in a group, such as currencies, do not necessarily behave in a correlated way.

On the other hand, the meat group is difficult to trade on the basis of cycles. Figure 9 shows the cycles pertaining to live cattle. A distinctive cycle appears to occur only rarely, and broad-band noise dominates the spectral contour display. From the cycle perspective, live hogs, shown in Figure 10, is even worse. A cyclic personality doesn't seem to exist.

Cocoa, shown in Figure 11, appears to have a schizophrenic cyclic personality. In April through July, during the downtrend, the cocoa contract had a relatively consistent 12- to 14-day cycle. The consistent cycle enabled profitable short selling between the successive highest highs. When the trend turned up, the cycle length approximately doubled. The doubled cycle length was relatively noisy and faded to a very noisy spectrum. Over the last several months, the longer cycle was discernable but its exact cycle length was poorly defined.

Wheat, shown in Figure 12, had a relatively strong 12-day cyclic component over the last four months during the uptrend. Knowing the 12-day cycle existed, a trader could find and enter a good trend-following long position by counting from the last lowest low. The 12-day cycle faded in December, so the best strategy would have been to stand aside at that point unless you already had a long position and could let your profits run.

CONCLUSION

The measured 1991 cycle action and personalities are consistent with measurements made in previous years. The newest contribution to technical analysis is viewing cycle activity in a contour plot in synchronous time with the bar chart, allowing us to view the broad picture at a glance. We can then see the occurrence of a single, well-defined cycle; two cycles being present simultaneously; or when to make the best entry when the market is in a trend mode.

John Ehlers, Box 1801, Goleta, CA 93116, (805) 969-6478, is an electrical engineer working in electronic research and development and has been a private trader since 1978. He is a pioneer in introducing maximum entropy spectrum analysis to technical trading through his MESA computer program.

FURTHER READING

Ehlers, John F. [1989]. "Cyclic personalities," *Technical Analysis of* STOCKS & COMMODITIES, Volume 7: April.
_____ [1990]. "1989 cycles," *Technical Analysis of* STOCKS & COMMODITIES, Volume 8: June.
_____ [1991]. "Computing cyclic entries," *Technical Analysis of* STOCKS & COMMODITIES, Volume 9: July.

Developing Neural Network Forecasters For Trading

Neural networks, for many, still exist only in the realm of theory, without having real, practical, everyday uses — yet. But neural network applications need not be confined solely to theory and simulation for trading purposes. Ambitious traders can build neural nets for themselves. There are pitfalls along the way, but Jeffrey Owen Katz explains what they are and how to avoid them.

by Jeffrey Owen Katz, Ph.D.

JIM FRISINO

For many traders, neural networks exist only as fantasy, surrounded by an aura of mystery, unknown and unexplainable. For some, the term "neural networks" is more or less a recognized one, but the words do not mean much. A few traders have purchased neural network toolkits, thinking they can immediately begin to develop their own neural trading systems, but they have not been particularly successful. Let's shed some light on neural networks themselves by looking at a successful neural network forecaster and then seeing how to develop and train neural net forecasters.

The concept of neural network forecasting systems interests traders because neural nets appear to possess the potential to fulfill trading fantasies. The neural network that produced the output in Figure 1 signaled four out of five tradeable bottoms in the Standard & Poor's 500, almost as if it were a "perfect" oversold/not-oversold oscillator; this is especially impressive, considering the data depicted were collected almost a year after the network had last been trained†. The network applied what it had previously learned to the new data and then produced forecasts that would have allowed a trader to enter long positions with excellent timing in most instances.

In addition, neural networks compel the interest of traders for a number of other reasons. First, neural nets can cope with "fuzzy" patterns (those easily recognized by eye but difficult to define using precise rules — for example, the head and shoulders formation) and deal with probability estimates in uncertain situations; second, neural nets are able to integrate large amounts of information without becoming stifled by detail; third, neural nets can "learn" from experience (the design of such systems is not dependent on having an already-expert trader on whom to base the rules of an "expert system"); fourth, neural nets may be retrained and thereby adapt to changing market behavior; and finally, under the correct circumstances, neural nets, with proper training, would be able to recognize almost any pattern that might exist in any market.

†See Traders' Glossary for complete description

WHAT'S A NEURAL NET?

In a broad sense, a neural network can be considered to be a kind of heuristic pattern recognizer. (Those with a mathematical background may wish to view a neural network as "smoothly" mapping an n-dimensional to an m-dimensional space; in Figure 1, from a 25-dimensional space of historical price data to a one-dimensional space of a numeric indicator.) At a more concrete level, a neural net is an interconnected array of simulated neurons that are arranged in layers and attempts to mimic or reproduce the method in which the human brain differentiates and classifies events.

> ## A properly constructed neural network would be able to recognize almost any pattern that might exist in any market.

Figure 2 depicts the structure of a typical three-layer, feedforward† neural network that contains three "input" or first-layer neurons, four neurons in the second layer, and one output neuron. Input data enter neurons in the first layer. Summation takes place, the "transfer function" (which defines how a neuron responds to varying levels of stimulation at its inputs) is applied and the neural outputs are then "fed" via interconnections that vary in strength (as specified by interconnection weights) to neurons in the second layer (sometimes called the "middle" or "hidden" layer). The neurons in the middle layer respond according to their transfer functions and the neural outputs are again passed through interconnections to the third (or "output") layer. Summation again takes place, and the transfer function is applied again to obtain the output(s) from the neural network. Neural networks involving more than three layers follow the same basic design.

As a rule, the process of training a neural net is handled by a neural network training toolkit and involves repeated adjustments to the interconnection weights. In the networks referred to here, these adjustments are generally made using the "backpropagation learning algorithm," a method for adjusting the knowledge (in the form of "weights" between the layers) inherent in the network to improve the match between the network's output and the prediction target. A new neural network is usually initialized with a random set of weights; training then begins. The network engages in a kind of "hypothesis testing" in which it "guesses" on the basis of the data just received and the theories, or "constructs," about the market that it has thus far formed. If the forecast is wrong, the learning

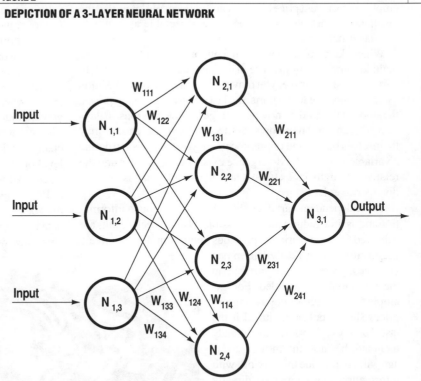

FIGURE 1

CLOSING PRICES AND NEURAL OUTPUTS FOR THE S&P 500 CASH INDEX
11/1/91 to 12/30/91

415.14

375.22

SIGNALS

40.00

NEURAL UP OUTPUTS (SIGNAL THRESHOLD = 0.40)

This chart presents the output values of a neural network trained to detect bottoms in the S&P 500. Values above 40.00 indicate a rally is due.

FIGURE 2

DEPICTION OF A 3-LAYER NEURAL NETWORK

Neurons are described as $N_{i,j}$, where i = the layer and j = the placement of the neuron in the layer. Weights are described as $W_{i,j,k}$, where i = the pair of layers, j = the source neuron, and k = the destination neuron.

algorithm adjusts the weights in such a way as to make the network's output better agree with the target. Training then moves on to the next "fact," which consists of input data for the network and a target against which the network's output can be compared. Training continues as additional facts are fed to the network and corrections made to the weights. This process is repeated as long as the network trains. As training proceeds, the correspondence between the network's outputs and the targets usually improves, and so the quality of the forecasts increases. Finally, there comes a point when additional training yields little improvement in the results. Training is terminated at this point and the network examined to evaluate its performance on the data on which it was trained, as well as on data it has never seen before (the latter to determine whether the network can generalize what it has learned to new situations). If the training is judged to have been successful and the neural network is producing accurate forecasts, then it can be used for trading.

A PRACTICAL FORECASTER

One of the first and most important tasks in developing a neural network trading system is selecting independent variables (the market or indicator variables upon which the system's forecasts are to be based) and deciding how they will be preprocessed into numeric inputs for the network. In the example earlier, simplicity was maintained by selecting the last 26 days of closing prices as independent variables. To preprocess the data, we computed differences between successive closing prices to remove the absolute level of the market and reduce colinearity† while emphasizing recent price behavior and pattern. We knew that the resultant 25 variables would be more acceptable as inputs to first-layer neurons.

When developing your own network, you may want to include some of your favorite market indicators as independent variables. For example, you may wish to include odd-lot shorts as a percentage of total shorts, the last 25 days of closing prices, the slope of the 50-day moving average and the previous 10 days of new highs and new lows. Some variables you choose may themselves be derived or preprocessed; you may wish to define a variable that is 1 if a divergence exists between price and the relative strength index (RSI), and a variable that is 0 if no divergence exists.

The independent variables should contain as much information and as little redundancy as possible. Usually, best results are achieved if each variable provides unique and predictively useful information. Easily determined variables, given the other variables in the set, should be avoided. For example, a 10-day moving average of prices should not be included if the last 10 days of prices are already included, because the moving average will not provide the network with information that cannot be directly extracted from the price data.

After having assembled a list of variables, how they will be preprocessed into appropriate network inputs must be decided. As with the selection of independent variables, designing a preprocessing system in-

cludes many considerations, for example, scaling. Neurons prefer inputs that vary between 0 and 1 and those fill that range fairly well. For example, a neuron will not do well with an input that is almost always 0.8, with occasional values of 0.5, 0.6, 0.7 or 0.9 and only one instance of 0.0 and 1.0. In most cases, preprocessing the data should produce variables with a good spread of values that are within the limits of the neuron's input characteristics.

> **Selecting the right input variables is crucial in that some variables have high predictive utility while others contribute little to a network's ability to forecast.**

Emphasizing the information in the independent variables relevant to the patterns to be detected and the predictions to be made should also be taken into consideration. A network should not be fed the closing prices directly, since this would emphasize the overall market level rather than the pattern of the prices presented. With stocks, this problem is more obvious: Some stocks sell for $5 per share while others sell for $20, but the selling price per se has little to do with whether the stock is about to move; what *does* matter is how prices have behaved over a period of time prior to the event. Feeding the prices themselves to the network would use up the ranges of the input neurons with the price level of the stocks ($5 versus $20), rather than with information pertinent to the price pattern or "shape" (for example, whether a chart of the recent past shows an inverted head and shoulders). This is why the data used by the network in Figure 1 were preprocessed the way they were; by using price changes rather than the prices themselves, we removed absolute level or "bias" and emphasized information relevant to recent market activity.

Preprocessing can also be used to reduce the colinearity that may be present in the chosen variables. Using the closing price data as an example, over a span of years today's closing price correlates well with yesterday's closing price because of the large, long-term swings in the market. However, the differences between today's and yesterday's closing prices show a much lower correlation. The goal of preprocessing is to emphasize to the network the kind of useful information contained in the variables; it should aim to deemphasize the kind of information that merely obscures, minimize redundancy and maintain reasonable scaling and distribution to keep the input neurons "happy."

Choosing the right independent variables and an appropriate model for preprocessing or transforming them into actual inputs to the neural network can make or break the results. Selecting the right input variables is crucial in that some variables have high predictive utility while others contribute little to a network's ability to forecast. Variables may be selected by a range of techniques: from the intuitive selection of variables that "work" for the individual trader to the statistical selection of variables based upon their effectiveness as predictors on historical data. Also, consider the selection of variables based on hypotheses regarding fundamental economic relationships (for example, interest rates as a variable in the prediction of the Standard & Poor's). Likewise, preprocessing decisions may be made on the basis of experience, statistics and/or actual trial and error — and plenty of trial and error should be planned for when developing a neural forecasting system.

S electing an effective target or "dependent" variable — that is, what you are trying to predict — is as crucial as selecting input variables. Simply, certain factors are more predictable than others. For example, given the particular input data and network configuration being used, it is easier to forecast whether a given day was a bottom than to forecast how much the Standard & Poor's will rise from today to tomorrow. Similarly, depending on the market, certain time frames may be easier to predict than others; better predictions of change in price over one month might be obtained than change in price over one day. Maximum predictability also depends on the market, input variables and preprocessing. The implied compromise here is that a target variable should be useful for trading *and* predictable.

In the final analysis, trial and error is the only way to determine the best combination of input and target variable(s).

CHOOSING A NETWORK CONFIGURATION

Once independent variables have been selected, the method of preprocessing into numeric inputs to the network has been defined and the target variable has been determined, the neural network itself should be considered. What should be used as the combination of neurons and connections that will receive as input the preprocessing results of the independent variables? Which will produce as output the forecast or hypothesis regarding the target for each fact? To be considered when specifying the network are the number of hidden layers and neurons in each hidden layer. The number of neurons in the input layer is not an issue because it is determined by the number of outputs from the preprocessing stage. Likewise, the number of output neurons has already been decided by the number of targets to be predicted — often one, sometimes more. What remains is deciding on the number of middle layers and number of neurons they contain.

In almost all cases, a three- or four-layer network (that is, a network with one or two hidden layers) will perform well; exceeding four layers is rarely a benefit and will add to the training time. In general, the layer that immediately follows the input layer will have between one-third the number of input neurons to perhaps two or three times the number of input neurons, depending on the problem. In a four-layer network, the layer that immediately precedes the output neuron generally has markedly fewer neurons than the preceding hidden layer and between three and 10 times the number of output neurons. These numbers may vary, depending on the forecasting problem and several other considerations that will be discussed later.

TRAINING AND EVALUATING THE SYSTEM

An actual example of the training and preliminary evaluation of a neural network will help clarify any questions, including

FIGURE 3

TRAINING STATISTICS FOR A NEURAL NETWORK

Run	TotFacts	Good	Bad	BadOutputs	TotalBad	Learn	Tolerance	AvgError	RMSError	StdDev	3:02:38	R2:R01	Bad:R01
1	2431	1472	959	959	959	.900	.200	0.2011	0.2575	0.1608	0:01:21	0.0000	959
10	24310	1535	896	896	9089	.900	.200	0.1867	0.2378	0.1473	0:13:26	0.0336	896
20	48620	1579	852	852	17876	.900	.200	0.1763	0.2248	0.1394	0:26:48	0.1362	852
30	72930	1576	855	855	26336	.900	.200	0.1701	0.2143	0.1303	0:39:59	0.2154	855
40	97240	1629	802	802	34623	.900	.200	0.1638	0.2028	0.1196	0:53:04	0.2970	802
50	121550	1668	763	763	42423	.900	.200	0.1587	0.1947	0.1129	1:05:52	0.3518	763
60	145860	1711	720	720	49819	.900	.200	0.1550	0.1884	0.1071	1:18:24	0.3934	720
70	170170	1742	689	689	56966	.900	.200	0.1524	0.1849	0.1047	1:30:47	0.4158	689
80	194480	1755	676	676	63870	.900	.200	0.1483	0.1800	0.1021	1:43:02	0.4459	676
90	218790	1767	664	664	70573	.900	.200	0.1476	0.1791	0.1014	1:55:10	0.4517	664
100	243100	1780	651	651	77063	.900	.200	0.1453	0.1761	0.0995	2:08:08	0.4699	651
110	267410	1828	603	603	83349	.900	.200	0.1403	0.1698	0.0956	2:20:02	0.5072	603
120	291720	1843	588	588	89321	.900	.200	0.1396	0.1681	0.0937	2:31:43	0.5170	588
130	316030	1846	585	585	95214	.900	.200	0.1396	0.1667	0.0911	2:43:21	0.5251	585
140	340340	1865	566	566	100916	.900	.200	0.1370	0.1636	0.0894	2:54:51	0.5426	566
150	364650	1907	524	524	106249	.900	.200	0.1326	0.1586	0.0871	3:06:06	0.5699	524
160	388960	1933	498	498	111483	.900	.200	0.1314	0.1564	0.0848	3:17:57	0.5819	498
170	413270	1923	508	508	116520	.900	.200	0.1329	0.1580	0.0854	3:29:02	0.5734	508
180	437580	1958	473	473	121439	.900	.200	0.1315	0.1557	0.0833	3:40:03	0.5856	473
183	444873	1967	464	464	122869	.900	.200	0.1309	0.1548	0.0826	3:43:41	0.5905	464

This table represents the output (every 10th run through the training fact set is shown) of a neural network. The steady rise of the value in the r-squared column indicates that the network is training properly.

statistics that show how the neural network performs and improves with each training run.

Figure 3 was generated in the course of training a neural network using the BrainMaker system. The columns refer to the following (left to right): "Run," the number of the run through the training set; "TotFacts," the number of facts on which the network has thus far trained; "Good," the number of correct forecasts; "Bad," the number of facts on which the network failed; "Bad Outputs," same as "Bad"; "Total Bad," a cumulative version of "Bad"; "Learn," the learning rate used in the training session; "Tolerance," the amount of deviation permitted before a prediction is considered "Bad"; "AvgError," the mean error of prediction in the run; "RMS Error," the "root mean square" error (another kind of average); "Std Dev," the "standard deviation" of the errors; "3:02:38," the time training was started and the amount of time the network has been training; "R2:R01," the "squared multiple correlation" (discussed below); "Bad:R01," same as "Bad."

Two items need to be assessed in training a neural network: First, how well is the training itself proceeding — are there problems with convergence, for example? Second, how well is the system as a whole (input variables, preprocessing, network and target variables) performing — once trained, is its forecasting accuracy sufficient for good trading? Both must be simultaneously evaluated because if the network is not training properly — for example, if the training algorithm fails to converge properly — then evaluating system performance is no longer meaningful, as it is not being evaluated with a properly trained network.

There is a variety of criteria to measure network performance and predictive accuracy, several of which are implemented in the training software we have used. Of these, in many cases we prefer r-squared, the squared multiple correlation, a generalization from linear regression analysis. (For a further discussion of this correlation statistic and the formula for r, see "Explaining r," elsewhere.) This statistic is the closest to what the back-propagation learning algorithm attempts to maximize and is a good measure in that it makes use of all the data and provides an estimate of how much of the variability in the target can be "explained" by the forecast. It is also a useful statistic for estimating confidence intervals or expected deviations around the predictions.

In evaluating whether the network is training properly, see whether the r-squared increases with every run through the network. It may not always increase with each run, but the overall trend should be decidedly up, with the numbers rising steeply at first, then rising more slowly as the network comes closer to final training before eventually reaching a plateau. The aim is to determine whether the training process is converging. Of greatest concern is whether, given its inputs, the training process is arriving

at a network that best forecasts the target rather than whether the result is of immediate usefulness for trading. The typical network, when all goes smoothly, will take anywhere from 50 to hundreds of runs through the training set before it is fully trained; the number of runs depends on the complexity of the particular problem.

Figure 3 is an example of a smoothly converging training process. The r-squared shows a steady rise until it plateaus at around 0.59. If, however, the r-squared had risen to a value such as 0.30 and then dropped to 0.05, climbed back to 0.15 and then dropped back to 0.05 again, we would have concluded that the

> **If you plan to experiment, be aware that the development of a neural trading system involves a lot of trial and error.**

training process had gone haywire — that is, the training algorithm was not converging. This can occur for a variety of reasons, some of which we will discuss later.

Assuming the network has converged and a stable plateau been achieved in the r-squared values as well as in the other measures of performance (for example, number of correct forecasts), it is time to evaluate the overall behavior of the system. The system should provide accurate predictions or, at least, predictions with enough accuracy to help achieve profitable trading.

To measure the quality of the predictions generated by the system, again we prefer r-squared and the bigger the better, although 1.0 — which signifies perfect predictions — would suggest severe memorization problems or some other equally serious complication. As a rule, values of r-squared above 0.60 are excellent; values from the high 0.40s to the mid-0.50s are very good; values in the high 0.30s to the mid-0.40s are fairly good; values in the low 0.30s are possibly useful; while values in the low teens or single digits have little relevance to the trader. The network used to produce the forecasts in Figure 1 had an r-squared in the training set of around 0.65; the correlation between the forecasts and the targets was better than 0.80, a sizable correlation that suggests the predictions are useful for

trading. In evaluating total trading system performance, other measures almost certainly will be handy in addition to r-squared—for example, maximum adverse excursion, total profitability, smoothness of equity growth and so forth.

At this stage, the system should also be tested on "fresh" data, data not contained in the training set. The r-squared (and any other measures of predictive accuracy being used) should be computed on fresh, out-of-sample data. This will reveal whether the system can generalize from its experience with past data to new situations. A system that cannot do this may be overfitted and would be useless for trading. As seen in Figure 1, our system has continued to perform reasonably well on data collected almost a year after the end of the training period.

ADVICE ON SYSTEM DESIGN

If you plan to experiment, be aware that the development of a neural trading system involves trial and error, especially before you acquire the knowledge that comes from experience. We will attempt to summarize certain basic requirements in terms of tools and knowledge, certain rules of thumb for system design, and certain problems that can cause a system to fail.

Tools and knowledge requirements: Unless you plan to take long vacations while your networks train, you will need a fast computer — for example, a 486 system, or perhaps even an Intel i860. Training a network is a time-consuming process that a fast system will make less painful.

Some knowledge of a programming language, or skill with spreadsheet macros, will be helpful for preprocessing and analyzing the data. Setting aside the time to become familiar with the mathematics of iterative solutions (convergence and methods involving steepest descent) is also advisable. With such knowledge, one should be able to recognize when the training software fails to converge and be able to diagnose why and what to do about it. Studying linear regression will also help: Neural networks are, in some sense, an extension of multivariate linear regression into the non-linear realm, and many of the problems encountered in multiple regression, like excessive colinearity and overfitting, also arise in neural system design.

Rules of thumb for system design: A fortunate result of our years of experience with neural networks are several rules of thumb that may be helpful for newcomers to the field:

- **Separating the networks.** Better results may be attained when attempting to predict market turning points by separating the networks — for example, developing one network for forecasting tops and another for forecasting bottoms, rather than one network for forecasting both. This separation also allows certain kinds of fact selection to occur in the preprocessing stage. Each network could be programmed to generate forecasts only for facts where uncertainty exists. For the bottom-detecting network (see Figure 1), we already know that if the market has been rising for the past several days, today cannot be a bottom; therefore, why waste the network's capacity and burden it with data for which we already have the answer? Instead, the network should be focused on those instances where the market has been declining and where one is uncertain as to whether today is a turning point (a bottom), or just one point in a continuing decline. This rule is not a hard and fast one; in some situations, it makes better sense to use a network with multiple outputs to solve forecasting problems.

- **Choosing an appropriate number of hidden layers.** In many instances, a three-layer network (which includes one hidden layer) is all that is needed. Under other circumstances, however, a four-layer network can yield better results with fewer neurons and interconnections. Often, a four-layer network is a better choice when some form of interaction must be analyzed, such as when considering both price and volume history in individual stocks; the network should be able to perceive interactions between the two, such as the tendency for volume to rise or fall with increases in price. Trial and error testing is advisable, as in most areas of neural systems design.

- **Choosing the correct number of neurons in the hidden layers.** In general, the smallest number of neurons consistent with good forecasts is the best. If there are too many neurons, the network may memorize the facts in the training set and provide perfect forecasts but not generalize its learning to fresh data. This is the neural network version of overoptimization. Unlike traditional systems, overfitting through memorization by a neural network may not yield incorrect signals and losing trades on fresh data; it may simply fail to give any signals at all. If, on the other hand, there are too few neurons, the network may generalize well but yield predictions that are insufficiently accurate to be useful.

As a rule, in a three-layer network, an optimal number of neurons is frequently between one-half and three times the number of input layer neurons; of course, this is a broad range but can be narrowed for specific types of input data. With more experience, more correct assessments of the necessary number of neurons for specific situations can be made. Another reason to try to keep the number of neurons relatively small is that smaller networks train faster and, therefore, allow more time to engage in the trial and error necessary to develop a good neural system.

In a four-layer network, the first hidden layer will normally have many more neurons than the second hidden layer. Again, the layer immediately following the input layer will have somewhere between one-half and three times the number of input neurons, whereas the layer following it (immediately preceding the output neurons) will have a much smaller number, often between three and 10 times the number of output neurons, depending on the problem.

- **Choosing the number of facts on which to train the network.** In general, the more facts the better. Too few and the network will memorize them but be unable to generalize to fresh data. Too many will produce a stable, reliable network, but it will take a long time to train. Using large numbers of facts, if possible, is best. The complexity of the network must also be considered. A large network with many neurons and interconnections,

	A	B	C	D	E	F	G	H	I	J
1	Date	Bonds	CRB	Bonds X CRB	Bonds Sqred	CRB Sqred	Averge Bonds	Average CRB	Sum (Bonds X CRB)	Sum (bonds) sqr
2	910102	95.875	218.46	20944.85	9192.02	47724.77				
3	910103	96.250	218.03	20985.39	9264.06	47537.08				
4	910104	95.343	218.10	20794.31	9090.29	47567.61				
5	910107	94.218	221.67	20885.30	8877.03	49137.59				
6	910108	93.687	219.65	20578.35	8777.25	48246.12				
7	910109	92.750	220.46	20447.67	8602.56	48602.61				
8	910110	93.656	220.60	20660.51	8771.45	48664.36				
9	910111	93.625	220.09	20605.93	8765.64	48439.61				
10	910114	93.062	221.25	20589.97	8660.54	48951.56				
11	910115	93.062	221.60	20622.54	8660.54	49106.56	94.15	219.99	207114.81	88661.37
12				=B12*C12	=B12^2	=C12^2	=AVERAGE(B3:B12)	=AVERAGE(C3:C12)	=SUM(D3:D12)	=SUM(E3:E12)

	K	L	M	N
1	Sum (CRB) sqr	Numerator	Denominator	r
2				
3				
4				
5				
6				
7				
8				
9				
10				
11	483977.88	-12.87	15.57	-0.83
12	=SUM(F3:F12)	=I12-10*G12*H12	=SQRT((J12-10*(G12)^2)*(K12-10*(H12)^2))	=L12/M12

The formula for r is :

$$ r = \frac{\sum XY - n\overline{XY}}{\sqrt{\left(\sum X^2 - n\overline{X}^2\right)\left(\sum Y^2 - n\overline{Y}^2\right)}} $$

in which n = number of observations
X = One variable
Y = Another variable
$\overline{X}$ = The mean or average of X
$\overline{Y}$ = The mean or average of Y

EXPLAINING r

Correlation analysis measures the degree of relationship between two variables. The correlation coefficient r is one popular statistical index for this purpose. The values for r range between +1 to -1; a +1 reading indicates that the two variables are perfectly correlated, while a -1 reading indicates a perfect inverse relationship. An r of 0 indicates that the two variables have no correlation. The correlation coefficient r measures the relationship between two variables that are believed to be linear. For instance, a straight line is used to describe the relationship if the two variables were plotted on a graph using an X and Y axis. Sometimes, two variables will have a relationship that is described by a line that curves. The use of the formula for r is restricted to relationships that are linear.

The correlation coefficient measures only the degree of association between two variables. It is important to remember that r is *not* a measure of cause and effect. A large positive r does not mean that if one variable is large, this causes the other variable to be large.

In our example, we are using the closing price for bond futures as the X variable and the closing price of the Commodity Research Bureau for the Y variable. Our observation period is n = 10. This is very small, due to space limitations.
—*Editor*

processing a large number of input variables, will require a large number of training facts; a very small network, processing only a few inputs, will require fewer facts to train adequately. As a rule, the number of facts should be at least two or more times the number of interconnections between neurons.

• **Avoiding overoptimization.** Basically, neural networks are pattern recognizers that form templates or constructs of observed patterns and, therefore, "learn" a variety of patterns that recur in the data fed to them. As a network is trained, it builds up these templates, and it continuously correlates them with incoming data. A properly trained network will build up templates that have a high potential for properly classifying future events; the templates will represent generalizations or abstractions. When a neural network is overoptimized — for example, through the use of too many neurons or too few training facts — the templates built up may not be in the form of generalizations or prototypes but instead be in the form of specific memories. This is what happens when "memorization" sets in; the network memorizes specific historical instances for which it can produce "predictions," but fails to generalize its knowledge to recurrent patterns that can be found in new data. As implied earlier, the secret to avoiding overoptimization (memorization) is to use as simple a network as will provide the desired results and to train it on as many facts as possible, given the constraints of data and time.

DIAGNOSING PROBLEMS

Convergence problems and training tools: Developers who fail to test and evaluate training tools properly may end up blaming themselves for faulty variable selection, preprocessing design or target selection when the problem is really a failure of the

training tool to converge properly during training. At least one of the commercially available neural network training toolkits we have used fails to converge properly when training four-layer networks and in certain other situations unless special adjustments are made. Before you blame yourself, check your training tools. We have already outlined some symptoms for diagnosing convergence problems — for example, if the r-squared rises to a substantial level such as 0.40 and then traces back into the teens or single digits (showing a loss of previous learning), the training software may be to blame. Sometimes there are ways around the problem. For example, reducing the learning rate and smoothing coefficient may allow proper training and convergence, but it will be at the expense of training speed; the fact set will have to be run many more times when training the network, but at least the network will eventually converge properly. If you encounter such a problem, the best thing to do is to notify the developer of the training toolkit.

Suspiciously high correlations: If a trained network has an r-squared over 0.90, become vaguely suspicious; if it is more than 0.95, be *very* suspicious. Reasons for such high correlations may range from something as simple as having a target that is directly and mathematically dependent on the input variables to such factors as a training set too small for the complexity of the network being trained, leading to extreme memorization. In practice, predictions as good as those implied by such high levels of r-squared hardly ever occur in real markets over extended periods of time.

If a network trains properly, in the sense that the r-squared slowly rises and achieves a plateau (implying proper convergence) but the forecasts are not all that good — the highest r-squared achieved, for example, is in the low teens or single digits — the problem may be with the independent variables (they may have little predictive utility for the target), the preprocessing (does it emphasize to the network the information contained in the input variables that is useful and relevant to the forecasting problem at hand?), the network itself (are there a sufficient number of middle-layer neurons, or are two middle layers perhaps needed to achieve the desired results?), or the choice of target (can it realistically be predicted, given the knowledge contained in the input variables that have been selected?). Systematic investigation should lead to better results.

"We join Bob Reemer and Mona Bittle in this limited partnership, with prenuptial agreements and the option to dissolve said partnership in the event that …"

No generalizability: Failure of the network to generalize may be due to several common problems, including memorization and (occasionally) changes in the markets over time. For instance, if a network was trained on the Standard & Poor's from 1965 to 1973 and then tested on data from 1983 onward, the results may be exceedingly poor, even though the system is essentially sound. Why? Because in this case, the market changed. Prior to 1973, there were no listed options or program trading; listed options were introduced in 1973, and program trading accounted for a large proportion of volume in the 1980s. The market that the neural network would be looking at in 1992 is a very different one than the market on which it had been

trained. Another consideration: It is possible that as neural networks become widely used by traders, they will affect the markets to which they are applied, altering price behavior to a great enough extent so as to make those networks responsible for their own demise! Of course, different, more sophisticated networks may be able to learn the market behavior produced by the more primitive networks and so forth. You get the idea.

IN CONCLUSION

As markets get more and more competitive, technologies like neural networks become more attractive because not only do neural networks, when appropriately used, yield remarkably accurate forecasts for the trader, but they are also adaptable; they may also be retrained as the markets undergo change.

Jeffrey Owen Katz's interest in the market began as a trader and researcher at a time prior to the ready availability of data services and the computational capabilities of current computer systems. His research on neural networks began in the mid-1980s, when he applied such technology to biomedical diagnostic electronics. In 1988, he applied his expertise in neural technology to the challenge of forecasting the markets; in early 1989, his company, Scientific Consultant Services, Inc., released The Predictor software series, which included a neural network system for forecasting the S&P/OEX, the latest generation of which is NexTurn.

Donna McCormick assisted in the writing of this article.

Trading Planetary Eclipses

Stock market lore has long been filled with claims that planetary motion affects stock and commodity prices. As most market students who pursue this topic find out, however, many rules and explanations of what causes tops and bottoms in markets contradict each other about which planets are important and what could cause these effects. There are relationships, but they differ from what one might find in the literature of financial astrology. Hans Hannula explains.

by Hans Hannula, Ph.D., C.T.A.

n financial astrology, the angles formed between two planets as viewed from the Earth have either bullish or bearish implications for the market. In astrological jargon, these angles are called aspects. The angles are measured from a line drawn from the Earth to the sun.

When a planet is aligned with the sun, it is said to be in geocentric (Earth-based) conjunction, or at zero degrees. If the planet is between the Earth and the sun, it is called an "inferior" conjunction. When a planet is positioned so that the Earth is directly between it and the sun, it is said to be in geocentric opposition, or at 180 degrees. Similarly, if the planet is at 90 degrees to the Earth-sun line, the planets are said to be square. Squares are supposedly bearish. Conjunctions and oppositions are supposedly positive.

But this interpretation is not universally accepted. David Williams, author of *Financial Astrology*, uses an aspect-scoring system in which he attributes bullish or bearish influences to each aspect according to which two planets are involved. For example, he considers the conjunction of Mercury and Earth positive, but that of Mars and Earth negative. Even with this difficulty, however, financial astrologers have used aspect rule-based systems to predict stock movements with enough success that they are still widely followed.

Personal computers have spawned renewed interest in using this approach for trading. First, compute the time of each aspect between each pair of planets and measure the change in market price some time later. If prices are up or down over some threshold, say 70% of the cases, record the aspect as bullish or bearish. If it is under the threshold, consider it insignificant. This gives a scoring table for the aspects. Second, on some periodic basis, such as daily, weekly, monthly, seasonal, or full moon, compute the aspects. If a majority is bullish, expect prices to rise. If a majority is bearish, expect prices to fall.

> My theory is that as planets move around the sun, they cause tidal forces, affecting the energy given off by the sun in the form of radiation, solar flares and so on. This energy then flows toward the Earth, where it in turn affects our electromagnetic field.

Many variations on this financial astrology theme are possible. The aspects can be weighted, assigning positive and negative numbers, using something like the average percentage movement for the value. Williams does so in his "solar ingress method," in which he computes, scores and totals the aspects at the start of each season, using his own weighting and aspect scoring tables.

Do such systems really work? After checking out many such systems, I can say that they may catch the timing of turns but not necessarily the direction. A daily plot of the William index can be seen in Figure 1 versus the Standard & Poor's 500. To make this computation:

1. Look in an ephemeris† to find the geocentric positions of the planets.
2. Compute the aspect between each pair of planets and the moon.
3. For each aspect within three degrees of one of the angles 0, 60, 90, 120 or 180 degrees, assign an aspect score as follows:

   0 degrees : +10 for all planetary pairs, except use -10 for any aspect involving Saturn or Mars, and the pairs Moon/Uranus, Sun/Neptune, Uranus/Neptune, and any planet with Pluto *except* Venus/Pluto.

   60 degrees: +4
   90 degrees: -4
   120 degrees: +6
   180 degrees: -8
4. Add each day's aspect total to a running index. A negative score is effectively a subtraction and a positive score is an addition.

FIGURE 1

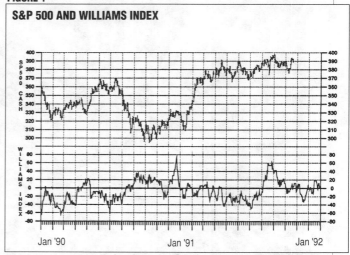

S&P 500 AND WILLIAMS INDEX

The Williams index scores and totals the aspects of the planets and plots the value as a running sum. This index may catch the timing of a turn but not necessarily the direction.

FIGURE 2

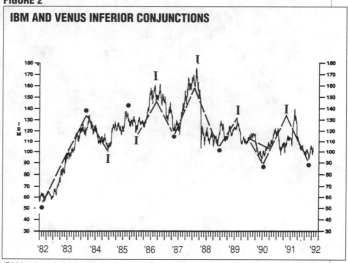

IBM AND VENUS INFERIOR CONJUNCTIONS

IBM is plotted along with the times of the planetary eclipses occurring due to Venus moving between the Earth and the sun. The dots represent the time of the eclipse and the Is represent the 1/3 to 1/2 time period between the eclipses. Figures 2 and 3 are drawn using the basic approach given in "Trading the seasonal cycle."

There are times when the Williams index moves in the same direction as price and times when it moves opposite (Figure 1). For example, the Williams index moved opposite the market from July until October 1990, but it moved with the market from July to September 1991, when it gave excellent results. In addition, turns in this indicator do have some correlation with market turns.

A CLOSER LOOK
While this sort of study looked promising, I decided to study a smaller piece of the problem. Since I examined solar eclipses in the December 1991 STOCKS & COMMODITIES and developed a theory of how they work on the markets, I decided to study the actions of Mercury and Venus. Essentially, my theory is that as planets move around the sun, they cause tidal forces that swirl

†See Traders' Glossary for complete description

the gases, affecting the energy given off by the sun in the form of radiation, solar flares, mass ejections and so on. This energy then flows toward the Earth, where it in turn affects our electromagnetic field. Evidence suggests these changes in the electromagnetic field affect human physiology and psychology. These effects then show up in trading.

Using this model of cause and effect, I related solar and lunar eclipses to market action. That study showed a significant effect due to solar eclipses, with the effects due to the moon interrupting the energy flow between the sun and the Earth. I reasoned that Mercury and Venus could also interrupt this energy flow. They both revolve between the Earth and the sun and potentially disrupt the flow of energy as the solar wind carries it from the sun to the Earth. Theoretically, these planetary "eclipses" would be natural cycles that would be very easy to explain. It seemed worth investigating.

Figures 2 and 3 shows a study with the effects of these two planetary eclipses on IBM. In a statistical study of these events,

> **During the attempted coup in the USSR, stock prices dropped and then rebounded as the coup attempt was aborted. Traders who were aware of the planetary eclipse during the attempted coup were able to anticipate price volatility during the event.**

in which I examined the correlation of these points to IBM's highs and lows in a given period, I found that 77% of the time the Mercury eclipse marked a significant market high or low, while Venus did the same 83% of the time. In order to see how planetary eclipses may be used in trading, try these steps:

1. Find the time of occurrence of the natural phenomenon. These particular geocentric inferior conjunctions will be found in *The Farmer's Almanac* and the *Astronomical Almanac*, and on certain calendars such as the "Wonders of the Universe" calendar.
2. Mark these points on your chart with dots, placed above for a high and below for a low.
3. Look for possible inversions one-half and one-third the way between the dots. Mark these with the letter I.
4. Sketch the cycle with a dotted line.

In Figure 2, IBM appears to have a good correlation with the Venus eclipses. Recently, it has been making lows near these dates and highs midway between them. In Figure 3, IBM also appears to correlate with the Mercury eclipses, but not as well. Traders who wish to apply this to their own trading should complement it with other techniques, using cycle work to

FIGURE 3

FIGURE 3

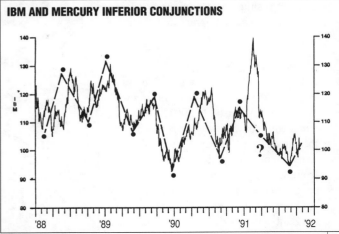

IBM AND MERCURY INFERIOR CONJUNCTIONS

IBM is plotted with the times of the planetary eclipses occurring due to Mercury moving between the Earth and the sun. The dots represent the time of the eclipse.

FIGURE 4

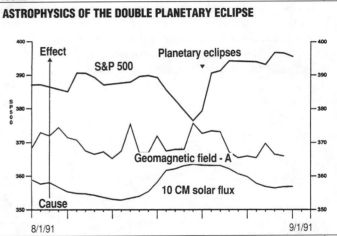

ASTROPHYSICS OF THE DOUBLE PLANETARY ECLIPSE

On August 21, Mercury and Venus came between the Earth and the sun. The energy from the sun, measured by the 10-centimeter solar flux, increased sharply.

FIGURE 5

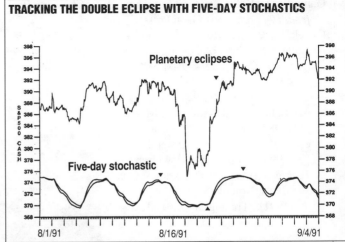

TRACKING THE DOUBLE ECLIPSE WITH FIVE-DAY STOCHASTICS

During volatile time periods, trading can be timed with the five-day stochastics indicator. This indicator indicated a sell on August 14, a buy on August 21 and a sell on August 23.

identify when a trend change could take place and using other techniques, such as trendlines, to identify entry and exit positions.

WORKING IN UNISON

Recent events gives an excellent example of these two cycles working together. On August 21, 1991, Mercury and Venus came between the Earth and the sun on the same day. Figure 4 shows what happened physically. The energy from the sun, measured here by the 10-centimeter solar flux, increased sharply. As Mercury and Venus passed between the Earth and sun, the geomagnetic field rose sharply, then fell. It was during this period that the attempted coup in what was then the Soviet Union occurred. As everyone who tried to trade during the attempted coup found out, stock prices dropped sharply and then rebounded as the situation stabilized and the coup attempt was aborted. Traders who were aware of the planetary eclipse were able to anticipate price volatility during this event.

It was even possible to use one of several standard technical indicators to successfully trade both sides of this double plan-

etary eclipse. One of the indicators I use for short-term trading is a five-day stochastic with 15-minute intraday data, which I have found useful for trading eclipse events (Figure 5). This system gave a sell on August 14, a buy on August 21 and a sell on August 23 — pertinent periods during the entire affair.

CYCLES IN COMBINATIONS

Careful study of natural cycles, of which there are many, can identify possible turning points in a stock or commodity. Traders who are aware of these cycles can profitably use them as aids in their trading. Like the solar eclipses, the planetary "eclipses" by Mercury and Venus have been shown to be important physical events for traders to be aware of. But natural cycles should not be used in isolation; they work best when complemented by standard technical analysis and good money management procedures. Used in combination, these tools can increase one's batting average in trading.

Hans Hannula is an engineer, programmer and trader with more than 25 years' experience.

ADDITIONAL READING

Astronomical Almanac [1990]. U.S. Government Printing Office.

Blizzard, J. B. [1986-90]. *Lunar Newsletter*, Boulder, CO.

Bradley, Donald [1982]. *Stock Market Prediction*, Llewellyn Publications.

Danby, J. M. A. [1962]. *Fundamentals of Celestial Mechanics*, Wilman-Bell.

Gann, W.D. [1927]. *Tunnel Through the Air, or Looking Back from 1940*, Lambert-Gann Press.

Gleick, J. [1987]. *Chaos, Making A New Science*, Viking Press.

Hannula, Hans [1991]. "Trading the seasonal cycle," *Technical Analysis of* STOCKS & COMMODITIES, Volume 9: November.

_____ [1987]. "In search of the cause of cycles," *Technical Analysis of* STOCKS & COMMODITIES, Volume 5: March.

_____ [1987]. "In search of the cause of the crash of 1987," *Cycles*, December.

_____ [1990]. "Making money with chaos," *Technical Analysis of* STOCKS & COMMODITIES, Volume 8: September.

_____ [1991]. "Trading the seasonal cycle,"

Technical Analysis of STOCKS & COMMODITIES, Volume 9: November.

_____ [1991]. "Trading the eclipse cycle," *Technical Analysis of* STOCKS & COMMODITIES, Volume 9: December.

Landscheidt, T. [1988]. "Multidisciplinary forecast of stock prices," *Cycle Proceedings*, May.

_____ [1989]. "Predictable cycles in geomagnetic activity and ozone levels," *Cycles*, September/October.

McCormac, B.M., ed. [1983]. *Weather and Climate Responses to Solar Variations*, Colorado Associated University Press.

Old Farmer's Almanac [1990]. Yankee Publishing.

Pugh, B.H. [1928]. *Science and Secrets of Wheat Trading*, six volumes.

Shirley, J.H. [1988]. "When the sun goes backward," *Cycles*, May/June.

Thompson, L.M. [1988]. "The 18.6 year and 9.3 year lunar cycles," *Cycles*, December.

Williams, David [1982]. *Financial Astrology*, American Federation of Astrologers, Tempe, AZ.

"Wonders of the Universe" calendar, published by the Hansen Planetarium (1-801-538-2242).

Measuring An Indicator's Forecasting Ability

Indicators are used to forecast a market. Traders have their favorite indicators. How can a trader determine whether an indicator leads the market? How can we tell whether one indicator is superior to another? Arrington explains how to measure a technical indicator's ability to forecast prices.

by George R. Arrington

Many traders use a variety of technical indicators to forecast changes in the prices of stocks and commodities, including such diverse indicators as stochastics, relative strength, on-balance volume, sentiment index, weather pat-terns, candlestick patterns, the Arms index and several pattern recognition techniques such as wave and cycle theories. In addition, many traders have one or two indicators of their own devising. A good indicator leads changes, and its signal is helpful when forming a trading strategy. Different technical indicators are useful at different times and in different markets.

With all the varied technical indicators we have available, how do we evaluate whether and how much an indicator leads the market? How do we compare one indicator to another? And how do we determine how much confidence we can put into a particular indicator? A personal computer and spreadsheet software with the ability to run simple regressions can help us find out.

FIGURE 1

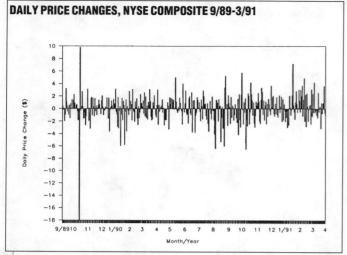

DAILY PRICE CHANGES, NYSE COMPOSITE 9/89-3/91

Here are the daily price changes in the NYSE Composite Index (first deferred) between September 1989 and March 1991.

FIGURE 2

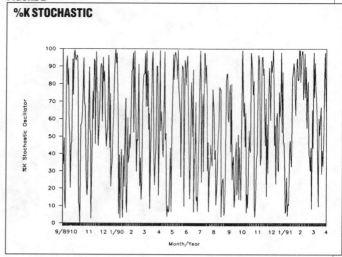

%K STOCHASTIC

The %K stochastic for the NYSE Composite fluctuated between 0 and 100, thereby indicating whether the market was oversold, overbought or somewhere in between.

Regression analysis is a powerful statistical technique that shows the relationship between two variables (one dependent, one independent). It can be used to assess the forecasting ability of a particular indicator (the independent variable) by measuring the strength of the relationship between the indicator and subsequent values in the variable being forecast (the dependent variable). Regression analysis can tell us whether the independent variable leads the dependent variable; if so, the length of the lead; and how much confidence we can have in the relationship.

INITIAL STEPS

First, choose the variable that you want to forecast (the dependent variable). For illustrative purposes, I've chosen daily changes in the NYSE Composite Index, which is composed of all the common stocks listed on the New York Stock Exchange (NYSE).

Next, select an indicator (the independent variable). I've selected the %K stochastic†, one of the most popular technical indicators. The %K stochastic oscillates between 0 and 100, thereby giving an indication of whether the market is oversold, overbought or somewhere in between. In theory, low %K values imply an oversold market (a buy signal), which should be followed by price increases; high %K values signal an overbought market (a sell signal), which should be followed by price decreases. In this example, we will evaluate the extent to which the %K stochastic leads changes in the NYSE Composite Index. Of course, the variables themselves are not important; only the procedure is.

Using a spreadsheet program such as Lotus 1-2-3, enter data for the variables in column form. Column A is the date, for reference purposes only. Column B is the daily change in the closing price of the NYSE Composite Index (first deferred contract). Column C is the daily %K stochastic calculated from price data over the previous five days. In this example, I used daily data between September 1989 and March 1991 (approxi-

mately 400 observations). Figure 1 illustrates the daily change in closing prices of the Composite Index. Figure 2 illustrates the daily %K stochastic during the same time period, while Figure 3 illustrates the layout of the spreadsheet.

RUNNING REGRESSIONS

Now run a regression between Column C and Column B. In Lotus 1-2-3, the command is /Data Regression. In this first regression, the X-range contains the data for the independent variable (%K), or Column C. The Y-range contains the data for the dependent variable (price changes), or Column B. The X-range and the Y-range must always have the same number of

> **R-squared values on regressions with lagged indicators provide a measure of how well the indicator "predicts" price changes.**

observations (rows) and should begin and end on the same row. After selecting an output range where the output is to be printed, select "Go." The regression's output is printed in the output range (Figure 4). The output will be interpreted later. Note this first regression was run using data observed for the two variables on the same date (no lag).

To run a regression where the %K indicator leads price changes by one day, the process is similar. First, set up a new column of data (lagged %K in Column D) so that each day's data reflect the %K of the prior day. Thus, each row contains that day's price change and the previous day's %K stochastic (Figure 3). In Lotus 1-2-3, Column D can be created by copying Column C and entering the data in Column D beginning on the next row. Second, reset the regression parameters. In Lotus 1-2-3, the command is /Data Regression Reset. Quit and return to the ready mode before completing the next regression. Third, begin a new

†See Traders' Glossary for complete description

regression — in Lotus 1-2-3, /Data Regression — and set the new X- and Y-ranges for the regression. The X-range (independent variable) should contain the data for the lagged indicator (%K) in Column D. When defining the X-range, do not include data from the other columns. The Y-range (dependent variable in Column B) must be reset so that it reflects *the same rows as the X-range* in Column D. (The X-range and the Y-range must start and stop on the same row.) After selecting an output range, select "Go." The regression's output will be printed in the output range (Figure 5). This regression measures the relationship between price changes and the prior day's %K indicator — that is, it measures how well the %K stochastic leads price changes by one day.

This procedure is then repeated for regressions where the %K indicator leads price changes by two, three, four or more days. For each regression, create a new column of data on the spreadsheet so there are longer lags between the indicator and the variable being forecast. Run simple regressions using each independent variable separately and print the regression output for later analysis.

T he output for each regression will contain a measurement called r-squared†, which is a measure of how well the independent variable (in this case, %K) in a simple linear equation explains changes in the dependent variable (price changes). The value of r-squared will be between 0 (indicating a poor fit) and 1 (indicating a perfect fit).

R-squared values on regressions with lagged indicators also provide an objective measure of how well the indicator (%K) predicts the dependent variable (price changes). R-squared also provides a standard basis by which to compare one indicator with another. For example, we see in Figure 4 that r-squared is 0.376. On a scale of 0 to 1, this suggests that the %K is a moderately good indicator of price changes observed on the same day (no lag).

FIGURE 3

LOTUS 1-2-3 SPREADSHEET

	A	B	C	D	E	F
1						
2		Price	%K	%K	%K	%K
3	Date	Change	No Lag	Lag 1	Lag 2	Lag 3
4						
5	08-Sep-89	0.45	36.11			
6	11-Sep-89	-0.15	33.96	36.11		
7	12-Sep-89	0.10	49.35	33.96	36.11	
8	13-Sep-89	-1.95	12.86	49.35	33.96	36.11
9	14-Sep-89	-0.95	8.54	12.86	49.35	33.96
10	15-Sep-89	3.25	90.00	8.54	12.86	49.35
11	18-Sep-89	1.10	95.92	90.00	8.54	12.86
12	19-Sep-89	-0.45	79.44	95.92	90.00	8.54
13	20-Sep-89	0.50	88.79	79.44	95.92	90.00
14	21-Sep-89	-0.95	57.47	88.79	79.44	95.92
15	22-Sep-89	0.60	50.00	57.47	88.79	79.44
16	25-Sep-89	-1.50	20.29	50.00	57.47	88.79
17	26-Sep-89	0.85	44.93	20.29	50.00	57.47
18	27-Sep-89	-0.05	47.30	44.93	20.29	50.00

To facilitate the running of regressions, data for the variables are arrayed in column format.

FIGURE 4

REGRESSION OUTPUT (NO LAG)

```
      Regression Output:

Constant                  -2.58510
Std Err of Y Est          1.705781
R Squared                 0.375557
No. of Observations            393
Degrees of Freedom             391

X Coefficient(s)  0.045614
Std Err of Coef.  0.002974
```

X refers to the independent variable, or %K. Y refers to the dependent variable, or price change. In this regression, %K and price change are observed on the same day.

FIGURE 5

REGRESSION OUTPUT (ONE-DAY LAG)

```
      Regression Output:

Constant                   0.154198
Std Err of Y Est           2.160382
R Squared                  0.000836
No. of Observations             392
Degrees of Freedom              390

X Coefficient(s)  -0.00215
Std Err of Coef.   0.003767
```

X refers to the %K observed on the day prior to the price change. Y refers to the dependent variable, or price change. The low r-squared measurement suggests that %K is a poor indicator of the next day's price change.

In Figure 5, r-squared is 0.0008 when the %K indicator leads price changes by one day. The very low r-squared measurement in this regression indicates that there is little or no relationship. Similar findings can be observed when %K leads price changes for up to 10 days (Figure 6). Thus, we can conclude that while

FIGURE 6

R-SQUARED VALUES: NYSE COMPOSITE FORECASTS

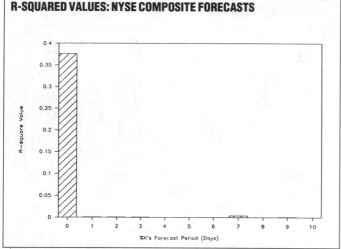

The r-squared values are summarized from regressions when the %K stochastic was used to forecast future price changes of the NYSE Composite Index. The low r-squared values indicate that the %K had no forecast power.

FIGURE 7

R-SQUARED VALUES: INDEX OF STOCK PRICE FORECASTS

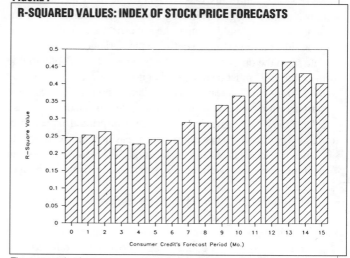

The r-squared values are summarized from regressions when the net change in consumer installment debt was used to forecast the subsequent index of stock prices. Consumer installment debt is a good leading indicator, with the strongest signal occurring when the r-squared value is at its highest (13 months).

%K is a fairly good coincident indicator, it has no value as a leading indicator of price changes.

For demonstrative purposes, Figure 7 depicts the r-squared values derived from a similar series of regressions between the net change in consumer installment debt (a leading indicator) and the subsequent index of stock prices (1967=100). These regressions covered monthly data between January 1967 and October 1987. The high r-squared values indicate that net changes in consumer installment debt lead the index of stock prices by several months; thus, net changes in consumer installment debt provide an early signal about future stock prices. The strongest signal occurs when the r-squared value is at its highest — in this example, at 13 months.

From the regression output (Figure 4), we are also able to graph the best-fitting line between the two variables by computing Y values with an equation in the form:

(1)   Y = constant + [X coefficient x X variable]
        or, substituting the values from Figure 4:

(2)   Price change = -2.5851 + [0.04561 x value of %K]

The equation describes how the independent variable (%K) can be used to make a forecast for the dependent variable (price changes). This relationship can be illustrated in graph form with Y on the vertical axis and X on the horizontal axis (Figure 8).

The regression output also provides an indication of how much confidence we can put into the findings. In Figure 4, the standard error of the coefficient (0.00297) in the regression analysis is the estimated standard deviation of the estimated coefficient of X. A small value of the standard error means that the estimated coefficient is a more precise estimate of the true coefficient. T-statistics provide an indication of how confident we can be in the regression's X coefficient and are calculated by dividing the X coefficient from the regression by the standard error of the coefficient.

> **Regression analysis is powerful, but it also has its limitations. It may not be appropriate if the relationship between the two variables is nonlinear or if the forecasting range exceeds the range of the underlying data.**

High t-statistics indicate a strong relationship between the variables, and we can be more confident that the true value of the X coefficient is not zero. If the X coefficient were zero, there would be no detectable relationship between the two variables, and therefore, no ability to forecast one from the other. If the t-statistic exceeds 1, for example, we can be 67% confident that the true X coefficient is not zero; if the t-statistic is greater than 1.98, we can be 95% confident; and if the t-statistic is greater than 2.62, we can be 99% confident. These t-statistic critical values are applicable if the number of observations in the regression is greater than 120. The critical values for other confidence intervals and for fewer observations can be found in most statistics texts.

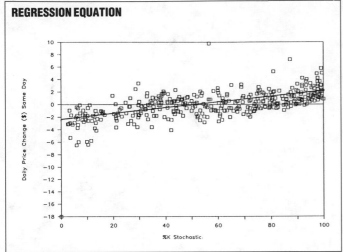

FIGURE 8

REGRESSION EQUATION

A simple regression equation generates a line that gives the best fit (least-squared deviations) between the independent variable (%K) on the x-axis and the dependent variable (price changes) on the y-axis.

The t-statistic in Figure 4 is 15.34 (0.045614/0.002974). Thus, we can be 99% confident that the %K stochastic can "predict" price changes on the same day — that is, we have a high level of confidence that %K is a coincident indicator. On the other hand, the t-statistic in Figure 5 (relationship with a one-day lag) is only 0.57 (0.00215/0.003767). This t-statistic is very low, and so we can have very little confidence that the %K indicator would be able to predict price changes for the following day. This suggests that the %K stochastic would be a poor indicator for forecasting price changes in the NYSE Composite Index, even for the next day.

> **Even the best technical indicators should be used with caution. Not all technical indicators are leading indicators; most leading indicators tend to be unreliable.**

MIGHT BE, MIGHT NOT

Regression analysis is a powerful tool, but it also has its limitations. For instance, it may not be appropriate if the actual relationship between the two variables is nonlinear or if the forecasting range (by extrapolation) exceeds the range of the underlying data. In addition, the relationship between the variables may change over time. Because of environmental changes, regressions over past data may not be relevant for the future.

Many technical indicators tend to be coincident indicators and by themselves have little ability to forecast future changes. If r-squared values are very low, other variables and more sophisticated analytical methods may provide better forecasts. These other approaches might include the use of multiple independent variables, methods to reduce serial correlation in the residuals, seasonal adjustments, transformations with logarithms, simultaneous equations, vector autoregression, simulations and moving average models. In the September 1991 STOCKS & COMMODITIES, two articles reflect different approaches: Thomas Lincoln illustrates a multiple regression forecasting model with an autoregressive moving average, while Victor Krynicki illustrates forecasting where relationships are nonlinear.

TO SUMMARIZE

Even the best technical indicators should be used with caution. Not all technical indicators are leading indicators; most leading indicators tend to be unreliable. Virtually all leading indicators provide some false signals; sometimes they give a signal too far in advance of the high or low, while sometimes they give little notice of the impending turning point. But because traders must make decisions that hinge on what they believe will happen in the future, there is no way to avoid making forecasts, explicit or implicit. The only question is how best to make them. Despite their limitations, leading indicators can be very useful signaling price changes. The astute trader should probably not rely on any single indicator but instead should look at several leading indicators, using one to check on another.

George R. Arrington has a doctorate in finance and economics. He works for the Federal Reserve System in New York City.

REFERENCES

Hartle, Thom [1990]. "Stochastics and long-term trends," *Technical Analysis of* STOCKS & COMMODITIES, Volume 8: January.

Krynicki, Victor E. [1991]. "Nonlinearity, chaos theory and the DJIA," *Technical Analysis of* STOCKS & COMMODITIES, Volume 9: September.

Lane, George [1984]. "Lane's stochastics," *Technical Analysis of* STOCKS & COMMODITIES, Volume 2: May/June.

Lincoln, Thomas [1991]. "Time series forecasting: ARMAX," *Technical Analysis of* STOCKS & COMMODITIES, Volume 9: September.

Lotus Development Corp., 55 Cambridge Parkway, Cambridge, MA 02142.

Pilloton, Roger [1991]. "Selecting and interpreting leading indicators," *Technical Analysis of* STOCKS & COMMODITIES, Volume 9: August.

On Composite Sentiment

Despite all the powerful technical tools available, even the savviest technicians are susceptible to emotion and on occasion succumb to psychological influences that prevent them from taking appropriate action, thus losing out on opportunity. Nevertheless, James Martin writes, how the market reacts is a fascinating subject. He continues his quest for more quantifiable measures for sentiment indicators.

by James P. Martin

In my first article in the June 1990 STOCKS & COMMODITIES, I showed a refinement of traditional call/put ratios that greatly enhanced their reliability. (See "Using option ratios," elsewhere.) My second in February 1991 delved further into the qualitative interpretation of the ratios and how they should be combined with sentiment surveys and the media. Numerous readers called me, hoping to find some magic mechanical signal that would tell them just when the market was about to turn. I explained that in my sentiment studies I have experimented with simple moving averages, exponential moving averages, envelopes, Bollinger Bands, rates of change and other methods I would be embarrassed to admit that I tried in public. While my studies have produced some general guidelines, I have yet to discover anything purely mechanical when trading off sentiment indicators.

The heart of the problem lies in determining when traders have truly put their money where their mouths are. Is an opinion survey reading at, say, one standard deviation coupled with a call/put ratio at plus two standard deviations a significant contrary opinion signal? Or is it merely a sign that a handful of savvy professionals have made sizable bets in the options market, thereby skewing the options ratios? Conversely, if sentiment surveys move sharply but option activity remains subdued, is it a sign that traders are already committed and are now merely "talking their own book"? Or will options traders be drawn in further before the market turns? This dilemma has led many

traders to dismiss sentiment indicators as being too subjective to be considered valuable timing tools.

The problem is further compounded in some markets by a shortage of data. There is a plethora of sentiment statistics for the equity markets, measuring both traders' opinions and their actions. For metals and fixed income, however, a number of different opinion surveys are available, but few timely indicators measuring investors' actions. Nevertheless, monitoring the actions of options speculators can be invaluable in measuring the mood of the markets.

THE COMPOSITE SENTIMENT INDEX

To address these concerns, I have created a composite sentiment index, which contains both "action" and "opinion" components. While the two correlate closely as a rule, they rarely deviate equally and usually do so a week or two apart. Viewed separately, this has often made me hesitant to act as I wait for the lagging component to catch up. When combined, however, the composite series inspires more confidence.

> **The volatility of the composite series will be fairly consistent over time and indicate when there is enough combined sentiment in the market to expect a turning point.**

I experimented extensively with various weights on the two different components, but after discovering that the two series displayed near-identical volatility, I settled on a simple 50/50 weighting. In the four markets I track — bonds, Eurodollars, gold and stocks — the two separate components exhibited this similar volatility. At various market turns one series may be more dominant than the other, but at other times the reverse will occur. The volatility of the composite series, however, will be more consistent over time and indicate when there is enough combined (action and opinion) sentiment in the market to expect a turning point.

COMPOSITE CONSTRUCTION

I construct the index on a weekly basis as of the Friday close. Sentiment readings on Fridays are the most significant, in my opinion. After all, daily closes are merely bookkeeping necessi-

FIGURE 1

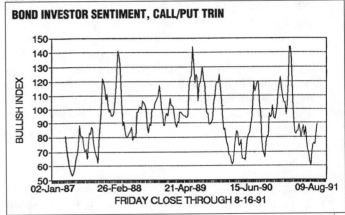

WEEKLY CLOSE OF THE TREASURY BOND FUTURES MARKET

The weekly close of the bond futures market has had numerous trends. The numbers plotted are synchronous with turns in the composite sentiment index plotted in Figure 4.

FIGURE 2

BOND INVESTOR SENTIMENT, CALL/PUT TRIN

This index is a ratio. The numerator is the daily bond futures call option volume divided by the call option open interest. The denominator is the daily put option volume divided by the put option open interest. A 20-day moving average is calculated of the ratio and plotted on Fridays.

FIGURE 3

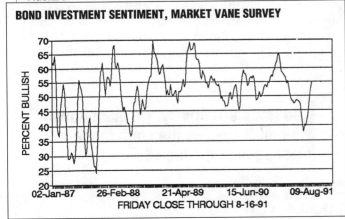

BOND INVESTMENT SENTIMENT, MARKET VANE SURVEY

A four-week moving average of the weekly Friday Market Vane survey. Extreme readings in this index can accompany changes in bond market trends.

FIGURE 4

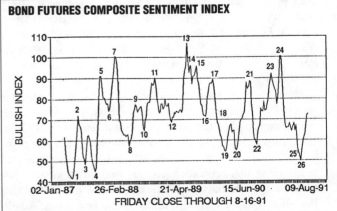

BOND FUTURES COMPOSITE SENTIMENT INDEX

This index is formed by adding Friday's closing value of the bond market's 20-day moving average of the call/put TRIN to the four-week moving average of the Market Vane survey and dividing by 2. The numbers on this chart are in sync with the numbers plotted on Figure 1, demonstrating changes in the indices' value can forewarn of changes in the bond market.

ties to tally wins and losses, and even this is becoming obscure in some markets as 24-hour trading becomes a reality. However, after a week of being bashed around and bombarded by the news media and the rumormongers, how traders feel and how they go home positioned on Fridays is very important. Experienced traders will also recall the old adage that major turning points often occur on Fridays and Mondays.

Figure 1 depicts a weekly chart of the spot bond contract using the bond futures market for illustration. Figure 2 shows the first component of the index — the 20-day option TRIN as of the Friday close (I use 20 market days to coincide with the four-week Market Vane). Figure 3 shows a four-week exponential moving average of the Friday Market Vane sentiment survey found in *Barron's*. Figure 4 exhibits the composite sentiment index, the simple average of the two separate series.

The most recent low in the bonds in June 1991 provides an excellent illustration of differences in market action and market opinion. The bonds bottomed on a closing basis on June 21, 1991, and retested that low to within 6/32 on July 5, 1991. The call/put TRIN on June 21 stood at 0.70. While this was relatively oversold, it had been lower in 1990 and 1987. Looking now at the Market Vane series individually, it stood at about 38 on June 21, which, although the lowest in three years, was still above the lows achieved in May 1988 and October 1987. Viewed separately, a trader might hesitate to consider buying, fearing perhaps a repeat of the 1987 experience where the crowd was right all through the September-October collapse, albeit for a few short weeks.

Examining now the composite index, on June 21, 1991, it stood at 54, lower than mid-1990 but still above the panic lows of October 1987. The composite sentiment index continued to fall until July 5, 1991, the date of the retest low in the bond contract. The composite sentiment index stood nearly two standard deviations from its five-year mean, only a fraction above one of the greatest panic bottoms in bond market history. The news media did its usual part to solidify the market's position. The June 10, 1991, *Wall Street Journal* had a headline stating, "Some Bond Players Remain Fearful of Inflation." The June 24th *WSJ* heralded, "Companies Rush To Sell New Bonds — Debt Binge Reflects Belief Rates Have Bottomed Out." This appeared on the Monday following the Friday, June 21st lowest intraday low.

The trader had to realize that the market was more bearish at present than at any time in the last five years, but at price levels considerably higher than comparable sentiment lows. The bond market arrived at this point after a relatively mild, seven-point, four-month correction, fed by the news media, which continued to assure us that economic recovery and inflation were just around the corner. Only if one was so bearish as to expect another 1987-like collapse was there reason *not* to buy bonds. Admittedly, this is hard to do; the media conditions us against it. It is its job to provide a rational explanation of the market's action for the public; but we tend to forget that the media is always a day late. Just about the time the crowd perceives the market to

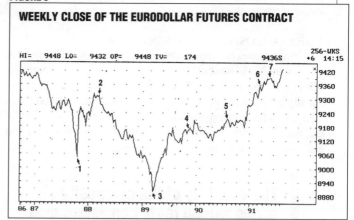

FIGURE 5

WEEKLY CLOSE OF THE EURODOLLAR FUTURES CONTRACT

The continuation chart of the Eurodollar contract is presented with numbers plotted that correspond with turns in the composite sentiment index for Eurodollars.

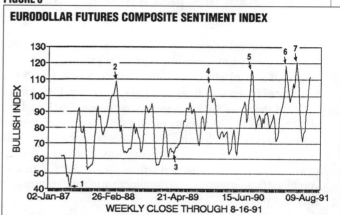

FIGURE 6

EURODOLLAR FUTURES COMPOSITE SENTIMENT INDEX

This index is formed by adding Friday's closing value of the Eurodollar market's 20-day moving average of the call/put TRIN to the four-week moving average of the Market Vane survey and dividing by 2. The numbers on this chart correspond with the numbers plotted on Figure 5. Points 5, 6 and 7 were extreme readings in the sentiment index that were followed by consolidation periods in the Eurodollar market.

possess the greatest risk is actually when it is at the point of the lowest risk. This may sound trite, but it is the basis for my search for a quantifiable measure of investor fear and greed. To trade effectively, we must have a tool to give us the confidence to act against the crowd if we desire to earn above-average returns.

> **To trade effectively, we must have a tool to give us the confidence to act against the crowd.**

LOOKING AT THE LONG TERM

By examining the long-term performance of the composite sentiment index, we can draw some general conclusions about using sentiment as a forecasting tool. I have numbered important peaks and troughs on the price chart and the composite chart to aid the discussion (Figures 1 and 4). The numbers on the bond price chart coincide with those on the chart of the composite sentiment index and the arrows show exactly where the corresponding sentiment peak/trough occurred. Note that over this four and a half year period, there have only been three clear-cut buy signals — 1987, 1990 and 1991. These periods were fraught with risk, as 1987 and 1990 were W-type bottoms† with a longer-term buy coming later on a lower low. This indicator was little help in catching the 1989 bull market, as it waffled in a trading range along with bond prices.

As can be seen here, the indicator appears to be valuable for catching the initial three- to four-point bounce off the bearish extreme, but beyond that, anything could happen. Most leveraged futures traders would be thrilled to catch such a move, but longer-term cash investors who act too early could be devastated if another washout the likes of 1987 were to occur. We all dream of buying the lows or selling the highs and building our positions, and this is the only technique I have discovered that can give a trader a high-probability chance of catching an important high or low. However, it still demands prudent risk control. Partial profits must be taken after the initial "rubber-band snap" and breakeven stops employed on position balances if one wishes to aim for a home run.

F or picking tops, the indicator worked beautifully in February 1988 and February 1991 but was weeks early in June 1989. This was one of those rare instances where the sheer momentum of the crowd pushed the market into a parabolic blowoff, finally peaking on August 1, 1989, some five points higher. (Stocks did the same in June through August 1987. Gold and crude oil behaved similarly during the invasion of Kuwait last August through September 1990, and bonds did it spectacularly in April 1986.) A mechanical trader would have needed some very deep pockets before being vindicated. The ideal selling opportunity in December 1989 came near a secondary high in the index, but it would have been difficult to sell on the basis of the composite sentiment index alone. Like bottoms, these sentiment highs mark a sudden, violent snapback but do not necessarily imply that the highest price high has been seen for the cycle.

Too frequently, I have seen analysts interpret a sentiment extreme as the terminal point of a market trend. The Eurodollar futures call/put ratio (not shown here) reached a remarkable three standard deviations last June 1991, pushing the composite sentiment index (Figures 5 and 6) to its all-time high. That was followed by a sharp 65 basis point washout over two weeks, quickly humbling the overzealous bulls, but six weeks later the market was at new highs! In addition, several stock market surveys maintained a strong bullish bias for the several years preceding the 1987 crash, but the market was interrupted only by several shallow, albeit

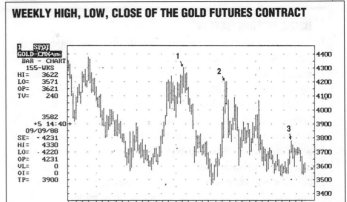

FIGURE 7

WEEKLY HIGH, LOW, CLOSE OF THE GOLD FUTURES CONTRACT

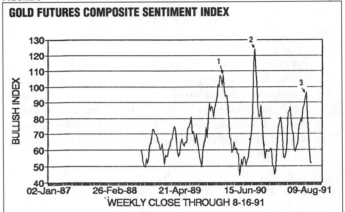

FIGURE 8

GOLD FUTURES COMPOSITE SENTIMENT INDEX

This index is formed by adding Friday's closing value of the gold market's 20-day moving average of the call/put TRIN to the four-week moving average of the Market Vane survey and dividing by 2. The numbers on this chart correspond with the numbers plotted on Figure 7. Points 1, 2 and 3 represent peaks in both the price of gold and the bullish sentiment.

sharp and quick corrections. Last spring, the equity composite sentiment index reached a two-standard-deviation extreme; thus far, the market has dissipated the bullishness by chopping sideways for several months, frustrating bulls and bears alike. After witnessing this behavior numerous times in several different markets over the past 15 years, I have reached the conclusion that sentiment extremes only tend to keep the public from earning above-average returns.

The majority of traders may still be right on the long-term secular trend, but when they look back on their performance, they find that because they succumbed to the influences of the crowd and the media (buying into the highs and panicking on news into the lows), they have only earned a mean return, or perhaps slightly below it after accounting for transaction costs. The media hype that accompanies highs and lows draws in (or shakes out) the masses, and the

USING OPTION RATIOS

To many traders and investors, the limited-risk aspect of the purchase of both call and put ratios is appealing. Many market followers believe that when the major activity is concentrated in either calls (bullish expectations) or puts (bearish expectations), extremes in crowd psychology will appear. An overabundance of optimism usually accompanies a market top, while market bottoms are typified by a preponderance of pessimism. The conventional method for gauging bullish and bearish sentiment in regard to options activity is to keep a ratio of the volume of call options traded compared with the volume of put options traded. Usually a 20-day moving average of this ratio is kept, as the day-to-day reading of this ratio can be very volatile.

$$\text{Call/put ratio} = \left(\frac{\text{Call volume}}{\text{Put volume}}\right)$$

For every buyer of an option, there is a seller (writer) of that option. It will be helpful then to note whether the volume activity is an indication of new buyers being met by new sellers or whether the volume actually represents traders who are liquidating positions. Combining open interest (the amount of outstanding contracts at the end of the trading session) with the call/put ratio of volume provides this additional information. This is called the call/put TRIN:

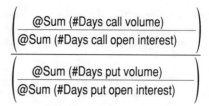

$$\text{Call/put TRIN} = \frac{\left(\dfrac{\text{Call volume}}{\text{Call open interest}}\right)}{\left(\dfrac{\text{Put volume}}{\text{Put open interest}}\right)}$$

When computing moving averages of the data, the following formula as it would appear in Lotus 1-2-3 code is used:

$$\frac{\left(\dfrac{\text{@Sum (\#Days call volume)}}{\text{@Sum (\#Days call open interest)}}\right)}{\left(\dfrac{\text{@Sum (\#Days put volume)}}{\text{@Sum (\#Days put open interest)}}\right)}$$

By summing the individual ranges and computing the ratios of the totals, high-activity days get a greater weighting, while quiet days get a lesser weighting.

—*Editor*

violent reactions that usually follow humble short-term speculators. Over the long run, the crowd will merely earn the average, and speculators will be net losers.

NO SENTIMENT ALONE

The ultimate intermediate and major turning points are usually accompanied by good sentiment signals. However, sentiment indicators alone cannot be the end-all by which to forecast the magnitude of a coming move. A three-standard-deviation reading versus a two-standard-deviation reading does not imply that

> The media hype that accompanies highs and lows draws in (or shakes out) the masses, and the violent reactions that usually follow humble short-term speculators.

the probable move will be significantly greater; it simply means the typical short-term snapback is all the more probable. If the larger deviation does precede a larger market move, it is merely coincidence. Other indicators would then have to be used to evaluate the magnitude and duration of the move. As of early October 1991, the bond futures rallied eight points virtually straight up before a meaningful correction, about double the average initial reaction. The composite sentiment index helps get you in the trade at a low-risk point; however, other tools and techniques are necessary to keep you in the trade if the market starts to trend.

Finally, the relative simplicity or complexity of the media theme driving a trending market should be considered. If the theme is easily identifiable and comprehensible by the general public, odds are greater that a less sophisticated speculative element is now involved in the market. The gold market is a prime example. Discuss the investment implications of a major war with novice investors and they will no doubt mention gold as a bullish beneficiary. But ask about gold's prospects in light of foreign exchange rate differentials, real versus nominal interest rates, central bank reserves and arcane political influences and a blank stare is likely to be the answer. Figures 7 and 8 show the gold market's response to the Kuwaiti invasion in August 1990. In this case, the unprecedented bullish high came within a few dollars of a gold peak, which was indeed a major high. Compare that action with the prior rally that began in mid-1989 and was influenced by interest rates, dollar weakness and inflation concerns. The complexity of these interacting forces kept speculators in check and allowed the rally to persist for some 22 weeks before reaching a high-risk condition.

SOME CONCLUDING REMARKS

I have examined investor sentiment indicators in a vacuum, but any experienced trader will warn never to rely solely on a single indicator. Every indicator is subject to occasional failure and the composite sentiment index is no exception. The real power of this tool can be realized when combined with other methods and

FIGURE 9

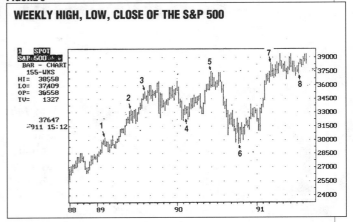

FIGURE 10

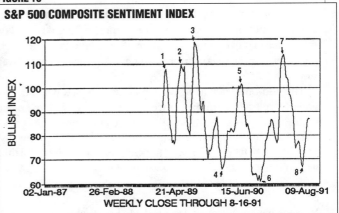

This index is formed by adding Friday's closing value of the OEX's 20-day moving average of the call/put TRIN to the four-week moving average of the Market Vane survey and dividing by 2. The numbers on this chart correspond with the numbers plotted on Figure 9. Extreme readings in the composite sentiment index warned of either extensive consolidations or market reversals of the S&P 500.

indicators; it provides that missing element to encourage one to take action on those instances when everything lines up perfectly but that little voice in your head keeps telling you you're crazy. Maybe you are. Maybe not. But using a sentiment indicator could give you that tie-breaker you need to proceed.

James P. Martin, (313) 473-2610, is a trader for Michigan National Bank. He has been trading since 1978.

REFERENCES

Hines, Ray [1989]. "Hines ratio," *Technical Analysis of* STOCKS & COMMODITIES, Volume 7: April.

Martin, James P. [1990]. "Option ratios for sentiment," *Technical Analysis of* STOCKS & COMMODITIES, Volume 8: June.

_____ [1991]. "Updating option ratios with market sentiment," *Technical Analysis of* STOCKS & COMMODITIES, Volume 9: February.

Noble, Grant [1989]. "The best trading indicator — the media," *Technical Analysis of* STOCKS & COMMODITIES, Volume 7: October.

Reversing Your Losses

by John Sweeney

Last month, Settlement closed with some incomplete work: the profit and loss charts for trades added onto the underlying system that was developed in the months prior. To finish the subject of evaluating add-on trades, I've completed those charts by trading the add-on system for the remaining years of data — 1991, 1990 and 1988. To recap, the underlying bond trading system trades solely off the 35-day simple moving average of closing bond prices in the December contract. The trend is determined by the 17-day average of the day-to-day difference in the moving average. When the one-day difference is greater than the trend, go long. When less, go short. Use a $700 stop.

The add-on idea was to wait three days to see whether the underlying trade went bad, since experience showed that most of the bad news came quickly. The idea was to enter in the same direction as the underlying trade on the opening of the fourth day and close when the underlying trade closes. The point of all this was to illustrate developing a system in gory detail.

So?

You can bet I was gratified to see the behavior pattern I'd found earlier holding up well in these widely varied years of bond trading. Figure 1 (comparable to Figure 5 last month) shows the distinct difference between the maximum adverse excursion (MAE) distribution of winning add-on trades and losing add-on trades, with the anomaly of two successful trades having adverse excursions greater than 65 trading points. This happens and, when it does, you must grit your teeth and give up these winners to have good loss control over the far greater number of losers with similar, or larger, MAE.

Figure 2 shows the same 49 trades' results in U.S. dollars and draws an even sharper distinction in the two distributions. If you were to cut off all trades with a stop at 33 points, you'd have suffered 18 stops being hit for $1,000 losses, lost on 13 other trades where the price didn't even go against you $1,000 and ended up netting $15,500 per contract.

This averages out to 100% to 150% on invested margin of $2,700 per contract, which is much lower than the underlying

system's 300% or so. Taken together (assuming this sample is indicative of future performance), well, you wouldn't take them together. An add-on trade is a separately capitalized risk-taking. Moreover, with 22 wins and 27 losses, this particular, unstopped add-on strategy would have generated $43,730 in wins, $22,888 in losses or about $21,000 net. This stems from the experience

> When you see trading as a long campaign with ups and downs, wins and losses, each trade with its peculiar tactical situation within an overall strategy, you'll get to know your adversary . . . .

that even losing trades with large adverse excursions tend not to become large dollar losers (Figure 2). Thus, this add-on strategy is low risk, as far as is known so far, justifying its lower return. You must have the grit to stare at some eye-popping drawdowns, though. Whether you use it or where or even if you "stop" it is up to you.

AN ADMITTED DIGRESSION

Before going off on another idea, I'd like to comment that so much discussion is related to the trading idea — the entry — that it distorts our understanding of trading. Trading is a process, not the "correct" entry. It's a constant evaluation of the situation, and many of the old adages try to capture this: limit losses, follow the trend, make money waiting, admit when you're wrong — don't

fight the market, and so forth and so on.

When you see trading as a long campaign with ups and downs, wins and losses, each trade with its peculiar tactical situation within an overall strategy, you'll get to know your adversary, respect it and apply a little judo, using the market's power to carry you where you want to go (preferably, the bank). The techniques being outlined here are the nitty-gritty pick-and-shovel work, nothing mind-

FIGURE 1

ADD-ON T-BOND TRADES
FREQUENCY OF TRADES BY MAE

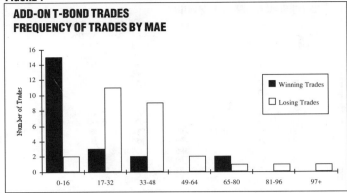

Trading the add-on system described last month for the additional years of 1988, 1990 and 1991 reinforced the findings that winning and losing trades differ markedly in their adverse price movement. To wit, winners generally don't go far bad.

FIGURE 2

CLOSED P&L FOR ADD-ON T-BOND TRADES VS. MAE

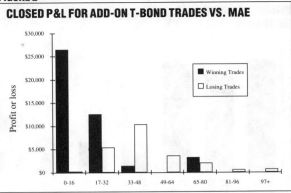

Converting Figure 1's results to dollars shows the even more remarkable differences in distributions. Winning trades reaped more than $35,000 with adverse excursions of only 32 trading points, while losers went as much as 97 points in the wrong direction.

boggling, that should be applicable to any trading concept. If applied, they put numbers to old adages, converting them to useful old adages.

I'd still like to bring up another trading idea. Remembering our underlying system had roughly a 30-35% success ratio, that suggests perhaps 30-35% of the trades would go against me. The remainder probably wouldn't do much of anything. How, then, to exploit the losers?

I made a suggestion in the January 1991 issue: reverse the bad trades at the stop-loss point. Figure 3 illustrates my point. Once a trade hits the MAE stop, there are only three choices within the original trading horizon: (1) It recovers somewhat but stays below the winning level (since we know it's most likely a loser); (2) it stays roughly even until the trade horizon is up (not shown on the figure); or (3) it continues in the "wrong" direction, at least from the original trade's point of view.

You know from looking at all the MAE charts I inflict on you that some trades go really, really bad. That's why I look for a reasonable point at which to place a stop. A point where the losses avoided and losses from the stop offset the wins given up by placing the stop is ideal. Figure 4 points out that had a stop been placed at 22 points, there was still money to be made (or recovered) by all the trades that went more than 22 points bad. We'd love to turn on a dime and have some trades go 67 or more points in our favor. This puts some objectivity to the old advice, "Admit when you're wrong."

Remembering this saying, I decided to try the now-notorious "underlying system" with a reversal feature added. Speaking of "added," these trades, too, must be separately capitalized. The underlying system is just a window that opens in front of you, allowing you entry to the market, in this case by losing! I want to establish the risk characteristics of these trades independently.

Just to whet your whistle, I enclose the results for 1986 in Figure 5. This is taken directly from my worksheet so it's a little rough, but the main message comes through in the P&L column. Reversing at the MAE point seems to be worth investigating, for two reasons. First, it generally generates a profit, and second, it

doesn't take long to do it.

Recall that the rule was to reverse at every MAE stop and exit at the end of the underlying trade. As a result, you get very quick trades with large excursions in the right direction. Only four trades took more than two days and many exited the same day as the close. The only trade that was a loss was one of those few underlying trades that would have been a winner had it not been cut short by a stop.

The MAE column takes some thought. We get into a limitation of our data in evaluating these trades. Because we don't know the time of the day the trades were reversed, we really don't know the MAE on that day. The figures here are conservative in that they use the high or low as the worst case. As a result, some of the MAEs are larger than the original stop. A trade's position would bounce down to the stop and then recover, though the close should be in the loss side. Also, there are some underlying trades that were really winners before they hit the stop. You can

FIGURE 3

TRADES AND MAE STOPS

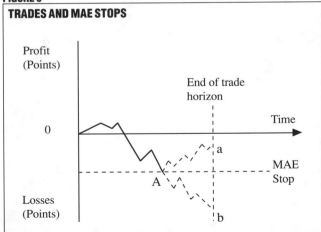

At point A, a trade having gone bad and hit the MAE stop, it may make sense to reverse and attempt to capture one of the big losers that the stop was meant to cut off (b). Risk on the second trade is limited to the 0 level, since if the trade went back over the 0 level within the trade horizon, it would be a winning trade in the first place — and experience indicates that trades hitting the MAE stop are not winning trades. Most likely, reversing at point A will yield a small loss (point a) or a large gain (b).

FIGURE 4

DECEMBER TREASURY BILLS
LOSING TRADES

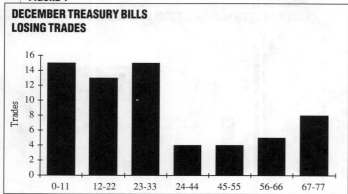

Losing trades should have a wide range of adverse price movement.

FIGURE 5

REVERSING AT MAE STOP POINT

Entry Date	Entry Price	Exit Date	Exit Price	Net P&L	MAE (Price)	MAE (Points)	Days in Trade
860213	-83.92	860214	85.47	$1,450	84.06	-4	
110	-95.54	114	99	$3,360	94.78	24	4
121	-99.72	122	101.69	$1,870	99.72	0	1
199	-94.86	199	95.62	$660	94.28	19	0
207	-97.23	215	101.59	$4,260	96.24	32	8
220	100.88	220	-100.31	$470	101.56	22	0
221	-101.01	222	101.72	$610	100.5	16	1
223	101.02	223	-99.72	$1,200	101.62	19	0
235	94.02	235	-93.72	$200	95.88	60	0
238	-94.42	239	95.66	$1,140	93.5	29	1
240	94.96	242	-94.88	($20)	96.28	42	2
243	-95.58	259	95.59	($90)	93.5	67	16
279	-99.26	279	99.84	$480	99	8	0
282	-100.36	286	99.41	($1,050)	98.75	52	4
286	-99.41	286	99.41	($100)	98.75	21	0

Net profit was $14,440. Reversing at the MAE stop point proved lucrative in 1986, but many more trades must be tested before statistical reliability can be established.

solve this with tick data or you can gain some comfort by inspecting the chart to estimate the likely action. Such inspection reassures me as far as 1986 goes: the likely action was strongly favorable, and I'd bet many of these large maximum adverse excursions are ephemeral.

Next? Expanding this test to all the other years' data and developing better MAE estimates.

John Sweeney is Technical Editor of STOCKS & COMMODITIES.

186 • *Technical Analysis of* STOCKS & COMMODITIES

CHAPTER 5

THE TRADERS' MAGAZINE

MAY 1992

TECHNICAL ANALYSIS OF STOCKS & COMMODITIES

Ranking The Currency Markets

MIKE CRESSY

The very idea of trading the currency markets can make the most seasoned traders shudder a little, but in truth, doing so could be lucrative when combined with a solid technical system. You can rank currencies by averaging the percentage rate of change over various periods. Combining the ranking table with your timing models will help with market timing, too. Tim Hayes, of Ned Davis Research, can fill you in on ranking the currency markets.

When currency markets come to mind, the risk-averse investor might cringe at the thought of wild short-term swings, an environment fit only for short-term futures traders. But for the institutional as well as novice investor, an intermediate-to long-term approach toward the currencies can be very rewarding when based on a proven technical system that effectively reduces risk while enhancing flexibility. While identifying the best currencies to invest in and the optimum junctures for action, an effective currency timing system can

> **Since currency trends tend to be long-lived, the investor needs to trade less and spend less on transactions.**

■

by Tim Hayes

add leverage and diversity to your portfolio and help the investor determine when to get into and out of foreign stocks, bonds and money market funds denominated in various foreign currencies.

By identifying the major trends and riding them for the intermediate term, the investor need not worry about a one- or two-day spike unless the spike marks the start of a trend change. The reduced risk of the longer-term approach is significant to those who prefer to seek consistent returns rather than risk big losses for big gains.

The risk posed by currency volatility is far less than it might seem, as is evident when looking at daily percent changes in the trade-weighted U.S. dollar. Although the first two weeks of 1992 included three days in which the dollar gained 1% and two days in which it fell 1%, relatively high volatility is normal for January (Figure 1). Generally, over the course of the year, the dollar is far less volatile than either the stock market or gold. While there have been 291 one-day dollar moves of at least 1% since 1978, there have been 802 one-day moves of at least 1% in the Dow Jones Industrial Average (DJIA) and 1106 such moves in gold, as indicated in Figure 2. When one-day moves of higher percentages are compared, the same order emerges, also showing that only the bond market is less volatile than the dollar.

Figure 3 looks at volatility somewhat differently, totaling all the gains of various percentages. Whereas gold has had 117 moves of 5% and the DJIA has had 84 such moves, the dollar has had 32. Since currency trends tend to be relatively long-lived, the investor needs to trade far less frequently and spend far less on transaction costs to stay in line with every dollar trend than would be the case in every gold or stock market trend.

WANTED: TIMING MODELS

But the relative lack of volatility doesn't mean that timing in the currency markets is any less important than it is in the stock market; in fact, it is *more* important. Although a very patient stock investor could eventually make money by simply buying and holding blue-chip stocks, that strategy wouldn't work very well with the currencies. At year-end 1991, the dollar stood close to its level at year-end 1970, down -1.7% per annum (compounded annually) during the 21-year period. Of eight major currencies, only three (the Swiss franc, yen and Deutschemark) would have returned more than 3% per annum to the buy-hold investor, and none would have returned more than 6% per annum. For healthy profits in the currency markets, it is essential to identify the intermediate-term turning points and get in line with the new trends as they get under way.

Of course, identifying the trend and getting in early is easier said than done. The prevailing trend may get lost in a long neutral trading range before resuming, or the trading range may itself be part of the reversing process. An approach based solely on chart reading can be hazardous. A more reliable and risk-averse approach is based on models that provide the bottom-line message of numerous technical indicators designed to generate buy and sell signals over a diversity of time frames.

In building a model, start off by using a computer to determine which indicators have worked best according to various criteria.

FIGURE 1

DAILY 1% MOVES IN TRADE-WEIGHTED DOLLAR BY MONTH (1/2/79-12/31/91)			
Month	**Up**	**Down**	**All**
January	17	12	29
February	8	10	18
March	14	11	25
April	11	17	28
May	15	8	23
June	13	15	28
July	12	14	26
August	12	19	31
September	13	16	29
October	7	9	16
November	5	11	16
December	5	12	17
Total	132	154	286

Reviewing January 1979 through December 1991 for daily 1% moves in the trade-weighted dollar indicates that there have been a total of 286 such moves.

FIGURE 2

COMPARING VOLATILITY (1/2/79-1/17/92)			
One-day moves exceeding (%)	**COMEX Gold**	**DJIA Trade-wghted Dollar**	**Dow 20 Bonds**
1	1106	802	291	50
2	441	163	26	2
3	197	41	2	0
4	89	16	1	0
5	39	6	0	0

Expanding the review period to include the first two weeks of January 1992 for daily 1% moves results in 291 such moves for the trade-weighted dollar, while the DJIA had 802 1% moves and COMEX gold had 1106 1% moves.

FIGURE 3

COMPARING VOLATILITY (1/2/79-1/17/92)			
All moves exceeding	**COMEX Gold**	**DJIA Trade-wghted Dollar**	**Dow 20 Bonds**
5%	117	84	32	15
10	39	16	9	7
15	19	9	4	5
20	11	6	4	1
25	7	2	1	1

Reviewing January 1979 to the first half of January 1992 for the number of price moves that exceeded various percentages highlights the relative low volatility of the dollar compared with other assets. For example, the dollar had 32 price moves exceeding 5%, while the DJIA had 84 moves.

Then select a group of those indicators to test further to determine which indicator combination would produce the most effective model. For instance, you might choose 12 indicators for further testing, determining that seven of them would work best together as a model. In this example, when four of the indicators signal to buy, the majority is bullish and so the model is on a buy signal. When four of the indicators signal to sell, on the other hand, the majority is bearish and so the indicator is on a sell signal.

Although the signal frequency of the individual indicators might range from as few as 12 to as many as 120 over the period tested, the signal frequency of the model will be consistent with the trading frequency desired by the user of the model. For the purpose of catching the intermediate-term swings, our models generate about three to five trades per year, so they typically have a record of 36 to 60 trades over 12 years. The differing number of signals produced by each model reflects their differing make-up.

While one currency model will rarely contain an indicator with the exact same formula as an indicator in another model, all our models contain the same *types* of technically based indicators, which fall into three general categories:

- *Moving average crossovers.* Buy signals are generated when the data cross above the moving average or do so by a specified percentage, and sell signals are generated when the data cross below the moving average or do so by a specified percentage. The moving averages can be simple moving averages, front-weighted moving averages (which weight the most recent data point) and exponential moving averages (which give the most weight to the most recent data point and decreasingly less weight to earlier data).

- *Moving average and momentum slopes.* Buy signals are flashed when the data or the moving average reverse upward or do so by a specified percentage, and sell signals are flashed when the data or the moving average reverse downward or do so by a specified percentage. The change needed for a buy or a sell is usually the same for the buy signals as it is for the sell signals. Slopes are also used with momentum (the data's moving rate of change), with buy signals generated by upward reversals and sell signals generated by downward reversals. While many indicators use the momentum of a moving average for generating signals, other indicators use the moving average of a momentum.

- *Relative strength indicators.* These methods above are also used to generate signals from a relative strength line produced by the currency's ratio to a currency composite.

A dissection of our seven-indicator Deutschemark model (Figure 4), for example, would reveal indicators that, for the most part, fit the following descriptions:

- *A 15- to 25-week simple moving average.* Signals are generated when the mark moves above the moving average (buy) or below the moving average (sell) by a specified percentage.

- *A five- to 15-week exponential moving average.* Signals are generated when the smoothing reverses upward (buy) or downward (sell).

- *A five- to nine-week front-weighted moving average.* Signals are generated when the moving average reverses by a specified percentage.

- *A 30- to 40-week momentum* of a three- to six-week exponential moving average, smoothed over 40 to 50 weeks with a simple moving average. Signals are generated by reversals in the final smoothing.

- *A 20- to 30-week front-weighted moving average* of a 25- to 35-week momentum. Signals are generated by reversals in the smoothing.

- *A two- to nine-week exponential moving average* of the D-mark relative to a currency composite (the Deutschemark's relative strength line). Signals are generated by specified reversals in the smoothing.

- *A 50- to 60-week simple moving average* of the 45- to 60-week momentum of the Deutschemark relative to a currency composite (the Deutschemark's relative strength line). Signals are generated by reversals in the smoothing.

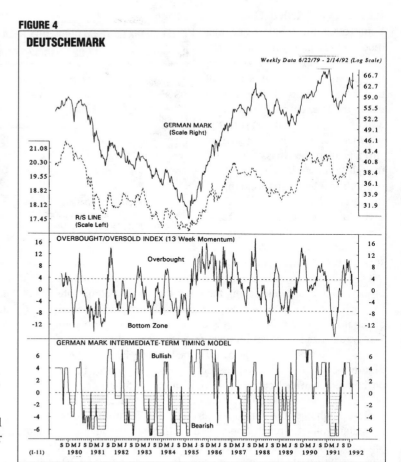

FIGURE 4

A timing model can be made up of a number of indicators falling into three categories: moving average crossovers, moving average and momentum slopes, and those techniques applied to the relative strength of the currency compared with a composite set of currencies. The model is a tally of the number of indicators that are bullish or bearish.

While a model will include indicators that generate signals with varying frequency, it will also include a variety of indicators that generate signals in different ways, through the methods described above. If, for example, a model were built entirely with long-term moving averages, it would be late most of the time. If it were built entirely with short-term moving averages, it would tend to whip-

> **An indicator diversity assures that any inaccurate signal will be offset by other readings.**

saw during trading ranges. And if it were built entirely with momentum, it would tend to be early. An indicator diversity, however, assures that any inaccurate signal will be offset by the other indicator readings, keeping the overall model reading correctly aligned with the prevailing trend.

What the models don't tell you is often an advantage as well. For example, they won't tell you about the temporary spikes. Since the models are updated once a week with weekly data, they keep you from getting caught up in a temporary move, engendering a more cool-headed, objective approach.

RELATIVE RANKINGS

Some other information that the models don't give you is information that could help you — which brings us to relative strength rankings. Since each timing model is based on the currency's price in dollars, it doesn't tell you directly whether, for instance, the yen is stronger than the Swiss franc, although you could draw a relative strength conclusion if, for example, the yen model were at +6 and the Swiss franc model were at +1. Relative strength rankings are a more direct and reliable vehicle for measuring strength among currencies.

FIGURE 5

INTERMEDIATE-TERM CURRENCY RELATIVE STRENGTH RANKINGS									
Currency	**1/17/92**	**1/10/92**	**1/3/92**	**12/27/91**	**12/20/91**	**12/13/91**	**12/6/91**	**11/29/91**	**11/22/91**
Yen	1	1	1	5	5	1	2	1	5
Swedish krona	2	2	2	1	1	2	1	5	2
US $	3	5	9	10	9	7	10	2	10
French franc	4	4	4	3	3	6	5	8	3
D-mark	5	3	3	2	2	3	3	7	1
Canadian $	6	7	8	8	8	5	6	3	9
Italian lira	7	6	5	4	4	4	4	6	4
UK pound	8	8	6	6	6	8	8	10	7
Swiss franc	9	9	7	7	7	9	7	9	6
Australian $	10	10	10	9	10	10	9	4	8

This table ranks currencies based on the average of the four, 12 and 56 weeks' rate of percentage change. For example, take the difference between Friday's closing price from the Friday four weeks ago. Divide by the difference by the closing price from four weeks ago. This is the four-week rate of change. Perform this same task for the 12- and 52-week intervals. Add together the four-week, 12-week and 52-week rates of change and divide by three.

Our relative strength rankings compare the technical strength of the various currencies using the same momentum composite for each currency. Calculating momentum is simple. Take the difference between this Friday's close and the close on four Fridays ago (for four-week momentum). Divide this difference by the close four weeks ago. The result is the four-week momentum. Figure 5 shows our intermediate-term rankings, which are based on the average of each currency's momentum over four, 12 and 56 weeks. By using momentum as the measure of comparison, it is irrelevant whether the currencies are priced in Deutschemarks, Canadian dollars, French francs, U.S. dollars or any other currency. No matter what your perspective and base currency, the rankings will issue the same message. If, for example, the 10-currency ranking shows the French franc at no. 4, the British pound at no. 6 and the U.S. dollar at no. 8, then the franc is rising faster than the pound versus the dollar and is therefore technically healthier than the pound. The pound is also technically healthier than the dollar in this example.

These rankings are helpful for cross-trading decisions, and they lend themselves to numerous strategies. One simple strategy is to maintain a two-currency position, switching between the 10 currencies so that you're always long the top-ranked currency and short the no. 10, bottom-ranked currency. Using the intermediate-term rankings since August 12, 1983, an investor would have gained 10.8% per annum by holding the top-ranked currency at all times. Also since then, the no. 10-ranked currency has fallen at a rate of -6.7% per annum, so shorting the bottom-ranked currency would have been profitable as well.

Another strategy is to maintain a six-currency portfolio, staying long the top three and short the bottom three. However, this strategy does have a pitfall. If the U.S. dollar is your base currency and the dollar is in a strong uptrend versus all the other currencies, the currencies ranked second and third could be dropping sharply in dollar terms. One of our clients gets around this by staying long the top three and short the bottom three unless the dollar is in the top two or the bottom two. If the dollar is ranked first, he will stay long the dollar and short the bottom three. If the dollar is no. 2, he will be long the dollar and the top-ranked currency and short the bottom three. The opposite would apply with the dollar in the bottom two positions.

USING RANKINGS WITH THE MODELS

These strategies lend themselves more to futures trading than the more risk-averse approach. So we prefer to use the rankings to confirm or lend caution to the messages from our timing models. For additional evidence, we also use

> **Perhaps the most useful external indicators are nominal and real interest rate differentials — the spreads between one country's interest rates and the same rates in a specific country or a country composite.**

short-term rankings, which are based on a short-term momentum composite. This is an average of the 10-day percentage rate of change and the 25-day percentage rate of change. To weight the indicator to the 10-day rate, the calculation is the 10-day rate multiplied by two and then this value added to the 25-day rate of change. Divide this sum by three. If, for instance, our Swedish krona model flashed a buy signal but with a reading of only +1 out of a possible +7, we may not feel comfortable about the longevity of the signal without the rankings confirming. In that case, we would maintain a neutral position until the evidence became more clearly bullish. If the krona subsequently rose to a high level in the short-term rankings and then the intermediate-term rankings along with an increasingly bullish model reading, we would quickly respond. But if the rankings refused to reflect improvement, we might return to a bearish position in anticipation of a new sell signal.

The most bullish situation, on the other hand, is when the model is on a solid buy signal along with a high intermediate-term ranking as well as a high short-term ranking. After a currency or market has been ranked no. 1 in both rankings, a decline in the short-term ranking without a subsequent decline in the intermediate-term ranking would reflect a corrective move, not warranting a change in position. For example, we wouldn't turn bearish on the yen based solely upon a big drop in the short-term ranking. Rather, we would need to see the intermediate-term ranking head downward alongside a drop in the intermediate-term model.

FINE TUNING WITH EXTERNALS

The relative strength rankings are used to fine tune the model readings, thus introducing some judgment into the objective and computer-driven, model-based approach. Fine tuning is also used with indicators that are external to the price action — in other words, not based on the price of the currency itself. These include

FIGURE 6

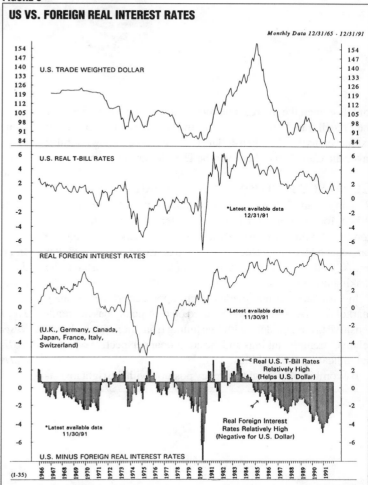

The bottom chart is the difference between U.S. real Treasury bill rates and real foreign interest rates. Comparing the bottom chart with the monthly trade-weighted dollar (top chart) illustrates that the dollar benefits from real U.S. T-bill rates being higher than real foreign interest rates.

economic, monetary and political conditions in the country of the currency in question, and the difference between those conditions and the conditions in either a particular trading partner or in a composite of countries.

Perhaps the most useful external indicators are nominal and real interest rate differentials — the spreads between one country's interest rates, before and after inflation, and the same rates in a specific country or a country composite. For the U.S. dollar, we look at such U.S. conditions as short-term interest rates, real (inflation-adjusted) short-term interest rates, the yield curve, the consumer price index and industrial production versus the same conditions in a country composite. Our real interest rate differential indicator is shown in Figure 6. We also consider trade balances, purchasing power parity and other long-term indicators.

The relative strength rankings are useful in addition when considering externals. Again, interest rates are useful in this regard. Rising interest rates typically benefit a currency; the country with the highest percentage rate of change for its interest rates should have a stronger currency. If, for example, French interest rates rank first, Canadian rates rank fifth and U.S. rates

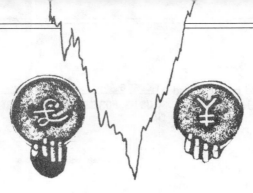

rank last, then the interest rate momentum is most beneficial for the French franc, especially versus the U.S. dollar and to a lesser extent versus the Canadian dollar. The rate momentum would also favor the Canadian dollar over the U.S. dollar in this example.

CURRENCY POSITIONS FOR LEVERAGE

Rankings can also be used in combination with one another. When, for example, our intermediate-term currency ranking is combined with our intermediate-term stock market ranking, we can see which foreign stock market looks strongest in U.S. dollar terms. With an effective currency ranking system, in fact, the ranking possibilities are endless.

In summary, an intermediate-term approach to the currency markets can be effective when based on technically based, trend-sensitive timing models, with fine tuning from momentum-based relative strength rankings and the additional perspective of external indicators and rankings.

By combining the right currency position with the right invest-ment vehicle — that is, the Japanese stock market, the German money market or the British bond market — the returns generated by the model-based approach can be exceptional. But would a single European currency render the system obsolete? Not at all. In fact, it would simplify the process. Whether the system is based on 10 currencies or three currencies, the core of the approach — the reliance on timing models — would be the same, using a variety of diverse technical indicators to issue a bottom-line reading on the trend's direction. The approach works effectively and reliably not only for timing the currency market but also for timing the U.S. stock market, foreign stock markets, gold, the bond market and just about any other tradable market.

Tim Hayes is the senior international strategist for Ned Davis Research, PO Box 1287, Nokomis, FL 34274-1287, (813) 484-6107, and writes the "Stock Market Strategy" and "International Currents" newsletters. **TA**

The Technical Song of Bernadette Murphy

"The investor is in conflict right now, because we've had the tremendous advance of consumer stocks throughout the 1980s. What we have is this battle: Should you be following capital goods? Or should you stay with growth stocks?"—Bernadette Murphy

Bernadette Murphy, C.M.T., of M. Kimelman & Co., who, like so many others, came to Wall Street out of curiosity but never intended to stay, is a longtime veteran of the markets. She has seen fads take the Street by storm and then promptly fade, and she's witnessed market peaks and crashes come and go. Indeed, you may have benefited from her expertise from her appearances on Wall $treet Week, where she's been a regular panelist for the past 12 years. She also appears weekly on CNBC/FNN and is a regular guest on Cable News Network. She's also no newcomer to technical analysis; in fact, she was the fifth president of the Market Technicians Association in the 1970s. STOCKS & COMMODITIES Editor Thom Hartle interviewed Bernadette Murphy via telephone on February 21, 1992, inquiring about, among other topics, what she witnessed at the conclusions of the bull and bear markets of the 1960s and the 1970s.

So tell us about the early days of your work in the market.

I started out at a conservative, primarily investment banking firm called Ladenburg Thalmann & Co. I was in the trading department. I hadn't really intended to make a career on Wall Street when I started out; I was curious about it, and I thought it would be an interesting learning experience.

But you stayed on, obviously.

Well, as with so many others, once you get into the business you find challenges daily, and you find you want to meet them. So I was clerking on the convertible bonds desk when the market crashed in May 1962, and chaos prevailed. I happened to notice during the hysteria that one of our clients, an insurance company in Toronto, had really anticipated a change in the direction of the market and for a number of months before had had scale orders in, which was the way transactions used to be entered. I was intrigued.

Resting orders?

They were limit price orders and, in this case, under the market, and they would buy a certain amount on the scale; you buy a certain amount at each price level and the firm was buying convertible

bonds that way, and so at the end of the market collapse, they had a bushel of convertible bonds that they had bought at substantially lower prices. It impressed me that they were so orderly in their approach to the market when everybody else threw securities out the window.

So I asked the insurance company's chief financial officer how he had done it. And he said, "Well, I sat down with Ed Tabell"—Edmund Tabell, Tony Tabell's dad—"and we went through the charts and we picked our targets and our price levels." I said, "I don't understand. *How* did you do that?" And he said, "It's technical analysis." And I said—I was young and naive—"What's technical analysis?"

The start of something big.

So he told me about it, and he mentioned some books. So on my own, I started to read the books and I began maintaining some charts. Now, in those days, technical analysis was not considered an acceptable discipline, not in a conservative firm. I had to keep my charts in the bottom drawer of my desk.

Like a bad habit you don't want to admit.

Then I started to take some courses at the New York Institute of Finance. There weren't as many opportunities to learn in those days as there are now, and I didn't have a mentor who was skilled in technical analysis; you'll find that many of the leaders of technical analysis today had the opportunity to work with somebody who practiced the craft. I didn't have that, but I did have exposure to the markets.

So you had practical market experience.

Working in the trading department, where you worked in this *huge* room where everybody was within shouting distance of each other, you realized there was a continuing flow of information back and forth between departments. I realized what happened in one market frequently influenced another. I was on the trading desk for equities and convertible bonds, and next to us was the corporate bond and equity desk and next to *those* traders were the municipal bond people. And in front of us all was the large teleregister board.

Now the teleregister was a *really* big board, and everytime there was a price change there'd be a *bang*! The Dow Jones news ticker bell would be forever ringing with news items. Then opposite that, orders would be coming in from Europe on the teletypes. From that time I was conscious of foreign influence in the market.

Did you start keeping charts on the flow of money into and out of the U.S. markets?

In the early 1970s, I started to maintain figures on the flow of money into and out of our markets by foreign investors.

As time went on, I became more and more interested in technical analysis, and in — I guess it was the early 1970s, I was with Shaw & Co. by then — I was calling on a client down in Philadelphia. They knew about my interest in technical analy-

sis, and the research director said: "This is our stock list. We'd like you to start monitoring it," using technical analysis.

Well, I was so flattered. I did, but I also knew I had to have a framework for the individual stocks because, let's face it, price action doesn't take place in a vacuum. So I started writing brief comments about the stock market.

Based on technical analysis?

Oh, everything was based on technical analysis. And at the time, I always tried to be a purist, because I felt that investors were interested in my expertise based on my training as a technician. There are so many fundamental analysts and economists around that I'm not sure they'd really need me for that. So I try to be as purely technical as I can, but of course, one's own philosophy and experience does come into play, and so once in a while I do make references to outside sources.

I don't think you can avoid it. So you began writing about the markets using technical analysis at that point?

Yes, and I started calling things correctly in 1972-73, when things were topping out — you know, forecasting the nifty 50. That caught the eye of some institutional clients, and I started to get phone calls and requests for more work in this area.

But you weren't actually a technician yet at that point, were you?

Exactly. So at that point, I went to my boss and said, "Do you mind if I started doing more of this work?" He was very obliging, and he said, sure, do what you want. So I began to build a business based on technical analysis, but at that time it was always with professionals — banks, insurance companies, money management firms, the pros of the business. I enjoyed that because their questions were challenging, and I felt working with this group made me a better technician because of the complexity of their questions.

That would have been in the 1970s, when technicians were beginning to be a little more accepted than previously—

Technicians benefited in the 1970s

because so many of them had anticipated the turn in the market, the major top in 1972-73, when you could not tell people the potential for Polaroid, for example, without confusing them.

What was going on with Polaroid?

You know, it was selling for something like 150; a technician could tell you it wasn't going to be 170, it was going to be more like 15, but nobody wanted to hear that. Technicians kept homing in on those points and so when the terrible decline in 1973-74 took place, technicians gained more credibility.

For historical reference, do you recall what some of the key indications were at that time for the upcoming decline in equities?

Well, I was monitoring the nifty 50 — remember we had had this tremendous narrowing of leadership in the market in the late 1960s, so that breadth had topped out years before. We got our first big decline in the 1970 market — there was a severe decline in the 1970s that was tied to currencies; the U.S. closed its gold window, the dollar was no longer convertible into gold — but then we got to the 1972-73 rally.

What happened at that point?

The theory then was that always after a war — in this case, Viet Nam — when you take that particular stimulation out of the economy, there is a stock market reaction because you have taken that stimulus out — that demand for corporate products, industrial, military, what have you. So there tends to be a reaction, one you can actually see in the price pattern. It was extraordinary how major stock after stock began sagging. Because breadth had narrowed, market averages were going to new highs, and major stocks were languishing. So these major bearish price patterns were forming. They were not accumulation patterns; it was almost a simplistic pattern that you could see, just top after top in what had been the key leadership in the market.

These were classic technical patterns that you can find in, say, Edwards and Magee?

Yes, but they were *huge*! And prices began dropping toward the lower parts of the trading ranges, and then they broke down.

From there, it was just a matter of projecting different levels of support and what the potential was, whether they would hold those levels. The tops were so great, you knew the chances of individual issues to hold those support levels were probably minimal.

By observing all the individual stocks, you could sense that the tide was turning.

You could. There were other indications, but to me, as a classical technician, that was just undeniable. When in doubt, you always go back to your individual stock chart. You could just not miss it there.

What was the bottom like in 1974?

You know what was interesting, interest rates peaked in I think it was July 1974, and of course the market continued downward. In August, many property and casualty insurance companies, because of tremendous demands due to natural disasters — I believe it was hurricanes — had to liquidate. They helped set the low in the market in August that year. The calls on their reserves were too great at that point. That was only part of the chaos at that time.

Interest rates plunged, I imagine.

Interest rates had already begun to decline by August, but the market just kept selling off and then on October 4 we hit the low; we bounced off that, and we rallied 100 points — a substantial rally — and then in December that year, we came back and set the final low in the market. So we had set a low, tested it, and then the market began to move on with explosive numbers; so many days had more than 70% of the issues traded on the upside. It was very exciting going into 1975.

So the bottom was built on a combination of a climactic selloff followed by large demand, indicated by large volume on the upside?

Yes, volume on the upside and issue demand. Today, we use the ratios —

advancing to declining issues and advancing to declining volume — I think Ned Davis and Marty Zweig may have done the research on that originally. I used to look at the percentages, and whenever I got an up market of more than 70% of the issues advancing, I know I have something really special.

> **At the low point in the market, you want to know that you have an accommodative Federal Reserve and bond market environment.**

So coming out of the bottom, you really like seeing the large upside volume?

The surge in volume and breadth. But we're also looking at what happened in the bond market and in the interest rate environment, because that's always very important at a turning point in the market. At the low point in the market, you want to know that you have an accommodative Federal Reserve and bond market environment. You look for that. So that's important as well at a turning point. Once the economy gets going, you would have a strong stock market but not necessarily a strong bond market, because the demand for money increases as the economy turns, so you're going to have friction. You will not necessarily have the bond market confirming the stock market all the time, as we've had in recent years.

You've been through major tops and bottoms in the stock market. But for the day-to-day work, what do you typically do to develop your conclusions about the stock market?

Well, we start off with the market diary and we do a lot of rate-of-change work. There's a group of short-term indicators that I like to follow every day — like the high-low differential (Figure 1), the daily ticks — I use 10-day, 21-day moving averages, 15 most active (Figure 2), blocks, and on the Arms Index, I use the 10-day (Figure 3), 21-day, 40-day, and 55-day. I like to use 10-day advance/declines, a 10-day cumulative advance/decline, which

is a very good indicator. I also keep the on-balance volume (Figure 4).

You mentioned rate-of-change. What do you do with that?

On the rate-of-change, what I do on the market indices, including the DJIA, the Standard & Poor's 500, the New York Composite, Wilson 5000, Russell 1000, 2000 and 3000, is use the annual rate-of-change, and then the rate-of-change of rate-of-change, and finally, the rate of change of *that* — which we refer to as acceleration.

What is it that you're looking for specifically, anyway?

I'm looking for patterns and divergences. We had a big up market yesterday, but it took place with declining acceleration.

Measured by?

By the annual rate-of-change. Now that's one way. Say my acceleration had reached its highest point on January 23, 1992, and at that point I had had an advance of 47% on my second rate-of-change. It's down to 4%. That would signal to me that this trend can't change. Or I could use a moving average. Sometimes I'll use a 10-day moving average of that. But it shows me a pattern of declining momentum. What I also use is the differential between moving averages, the difference between 20-day and 40-day moving averages for short-term calls.

What moving averages do you use on the stock indices?

I always keep my eye on the 40-day moving average, and where the market is and whether it's a percentage above or below that 40-day moving average. That comes out of the exposure to commodities. If we're above or below it, it gives me a sense of the trend or a change in it.

Again on rate-of-change you said an annual change, so you're talking about a 12-month rate-of-change?

That's right.

So a loss of momentum is a short-term negative indication?

It's a caution. I don't totally weight any

FIGURE 1

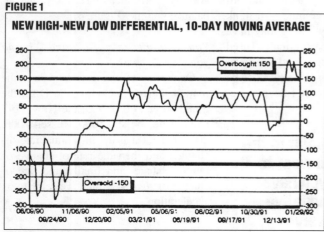

Among many of the short-term indicators that Bernadette Murphy follows is the 10-day moving average of the new high-new low differential. Overbought readings occur at above the +150 level and oversold readings are below the -150 level.

FIGURE 2

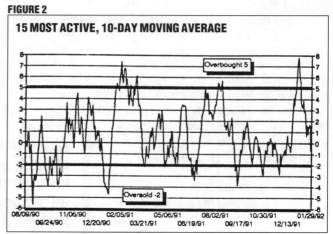

The 10-day moving average of the 15 most active stocks is another favorite indicator.

one thing. Also, not everything works together. We like to *think* it does, but it doesn't, really. I'm looking for pattern or confirmation and divergence. If I have divergence between price and my measurements, then it gives me a signal that I have to be more attentive. If my momentum figures are confirming price, then I tend to relax; I've got the trend in hand.

Do you do much group analysis?

Yes. On the group work, what I've been relying on is Telescan every week, which gives me the S&P 500, and also the Investors Daily groups. Telescan also creates its own Daily Graphs group work. We print those out every week, and I go through each group and I use primarily the relative strength index (RSI) on that. If I have a question, I'll turn to stochastics, and I'll also use moving average convergence/divergence (MACD).

Do you use the standard parameters that are typical in most computer packages, such as the 14-period RSI?

What we use is 15-period and five years of data, which can be a little confusing. It probably should be two years, but I'm more comfortable with five years. I think my clients prefer that. It just gives me equal periods, that's all. I use the standard parameters on the MACD, too.

If you see a group that begins to give all positive indications, do you go in and look at the original groups for stocks that

seem to be leading?

Yes. I use Mansfield charts. I can also do that on the Telescan system. I can't take the computer home with me, and so lots of times I just grab my charts and I'll start going through them and looking at the Mansfields for the price to be above the 10-week and 30-week moving averages. I want to find out if I'm getting a positive relative strength reading. And I can do that almost anywhere — on the train, say, to and from home.

Let's say you've selected a stock that meets all your buy indications and you buy it. How do you identify your risk points to determine that it's not a good trade?

I use point and figure from Market Charts for my price projections. If the price isn't holding, if it's advanced and all of a sudden it's going through a 10-week moving average, that makes me cautious. But I don't really take action unless it breaks the 30-week moving average.

And it declines below the 10- and the 30-week?

Right. Then I know I've really got a clunker there, because usually, if that happens, then you get into declining relative strength as well.

So you would just stop your risk and take yourself out of the position?

That would be for a trading account.

Now there are investment accounts for which I would stay with the stock. In this organization, most of our clients are long-term investors. So we will also then be checking out the fundamentals. If it's a minor pattern, I wouldn't be concerned. If I'm getting significant evidence of large distribution, though, then I would be concerned that there's really something wrong with the fundamentals, and we go back to check the company. Other factors come in at that point.

But some people think they like to trade a market; you have to be careful, because a lot of people, individuals particularly, don't have high tolerance for risk in the stock market. And if you're moving them in and out of stocks, they become uncomfortable.

Earlier, you mentioned reading. Do you have any favorite books that are applicable to technical analysis?

I love John J. Murphy's *Technical Analysis of the Futures Market* and his new book, *Intermarket Technical Analysis*. When in doubt I'll reach for those. I also like the *Encyclopedia of Technical Market Indicators* by Colby and Meyers, and *Technical Analysis Explained* by Marty Pring. I've got other various works that I use, but those are my handy reference books.

Based on your experience of what you saw for the top that occurred in the early 1970s, how do you feel about the market

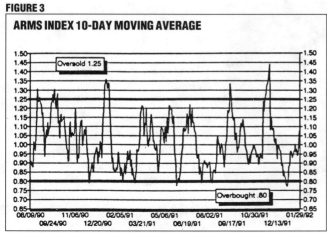

FIGURE 3

ARMS INDEX 10-DAY MOVING AVERAGE

Using a 10-day moving average of the Arms index is an additional favorite indicator. Overbought levels are 0.80 and oversold is above 1.25.

FIGURE 4

ON-BALANCE VOLUME

The on-balance volume index, which is a running total of volume based on the direction of the closing price of the NYSE. If the market closes higher than the volume of shares, the trades are added to the total. The volume is subtracted for down closes. This indicator is used to confirm the direction of the price trend.

---

in general right now?

The investor is in conflict right now, because we've had the tremendous advance of consumer stocks throughout the 1980s, what I consider growth stocks. We keep seeing these major bases in capital goods, and so what we have right now is this battle: Should you be following capital goods, is the economy really in a turn? Or should you stay with growth stocks?

So what do you say?

I think we're going to end up with a mix, because from what I'm seeing there are still growth stocks, like Procter and Gamble, that haven't done anything in a year and a half, had a breakout and have pulled back. But P&G hasn't formed a major top—to my eye, it hasn't, anyway, because of the breakout. Perhaps if P&G does not continue its breakout trend, *then* I could be concerned that maybe a big top is forming in this stock, but I don't have that yet, whereas we have had the early recognition in some of the industrial stocks.

And...

Not only that, I've seen good moves in stocks that also have a global exposure, like Emerson Electric. And if you take a look at auto stocks, the bases that formed here, the question is if they will support higher levels. These are evolving. We maintain a ratio of capital goods to consumer goods.

Capital goods are your recommenda-

tion, then?

Logic says capital good stocks are the area to be in right now, because at some point — I don't know when — we're going to be getting a turn in the economy (Figure 5). What we're seeing is the real price movement in what you call the softer cyclicals, like the airlines and department stores, and some industrials.

So where are we now?

Nowhere! We don't have the confirmation, but we see the potential for change here in the marketplace, which could be very exciting. But we need more time. But as a technician, I see value in capital goods because that area's been out of favor for so long. But ultimately, I think we will end up with a mix of growth as well as industrials.

Did you have anything that you'd like to talk some more about?

Just one thing. I think nowadays we do have to be conscious of what's happening in other markets. We can't monitor all the world markets, but we monitor the FTSE, the German Dax and the Nikkei Dow daily. These are critical because of the way money flows around the world. We also follow the Canadian exchanges. The flows are much faster now and you have to keep in touch with what's happening. Right now, we have major concerns in Tokyo, as to whether the Nikkei is going to hold above its 1990 low, and if not, what will be the implications? Will this be

a factor in our market?

What's interesting is that we have had a tremendous flow of U.S. domestic managers investing in Japan since third-quarter 1988. If that market comes under pressure, what's going to happen there? Will they withdraw from that market if the yen weakens? Will they compensate by selling stocks? We don't know. It's one of the dramas we're facing right now.

What are some of the other dramas going on right now?

Currencies. You have to watch currencies. What's happening with the dollar is very important right now. In 1987, we had a tremendous inflow of foreign funds into our market because we had a strong currency. In the summer to fall of that year, we ended up in a battle royale with Germany over interest rates and we threatened to depress the dollar.

As a result, the foreign non-U.S investor began to withdraw from our markets, and it added to an already serious situation in our market. That's *my* theory. I saw only one article on that subject in *Barron's* a year or two after 1987. I could not understand why nobody had looked at that before then, because it was so clear we were in a currency war with Germany.

Everyone wanted to blame the derivative traders for the 1987 stock market fall.

Derivative traders may have added to the downside of the market at that time but they didn't create the trend, they only

"If we get a strong rally in the dollar, it will eventually be harder to compete in the foreign markets for industrial businesses. Yet it will attract another source of demand for U.S. stocks and bonds."

we have a trend here that is going to last a while longer. I don't think it's going to be over in a year.

Thank you for talking with me, Bernadette.

REFERENCES

Colby, R.W., and T.A. Meyers [1988]. *The Encyclopedia of Technical Market Indicators*, Dow Jones-Irwin.

Edwards, Robert D., and John Magee [1966]. *Technical Analysis of Stock Trends*, John Magee Inc.

Mansfield Chart Service, 2973 Kennedy Boulevard, Jersey City, NJ 07306, (201) 795-0629.

Market Charts Inc. 10 Hanover Square, 20th floor, New York, NY 10005, (212) 509-0944.

Murphy, John J. [1986]. *Technical Analysis of the Futures Markets*, New York Institute of Finance.

_____ [1991]. *Intermarket Technical Analysis,* John Wiley & Sons.

Pring, Martin J. [1985]. *Technical Analysis Explained,* McGraw-Hill Book Co.

Telescan Analyzer. 2900 Wilcrest, Houston, TX 77042, (713) 952-1060.

exaggerated it.

How would you interpret the movement of the dollar and its relationship to the stock market?

I follow the dollar because I know that if it's strong, our market tends to be more attractive to foreign investors because they have the opportunity to make a play to profit from the currency. If the dollar is stronger relative to their currency, then they will benefit from riding a dollar rally as well as a stock rally. It also influences industry groups.

So then if we got an extreme move in the dollar…

If we get an extreme move in the dollar, it would eventually make a negative impact on some of our industrial companies that export, but it takes more than a short-term move in the dollar for that to happen. So you have to be sensitive. If we get a strong rally in the dollar, it will eventually be harder to compete in the foreign markets for industrial businesses. Yet it will attract another source of demand for U.S. stocks and bonds.

Is there anything we missed?

Just to mention the importance of the small-capitalization stocks. They've had a tremendous move, so when a market corrects itself, that situation's going to correct too. But I always refer back to

1977, when the Dow Jones Industrial Average (DJIA) went down all year and everybody made a lot of money in small-capitalization stocks. That can happen again. It strikes me that the move that's taken place in small-capitalization stocks recently is more than just a flash in the pan. There's a theory that there is a seven-year cycle in small caps, but I'm not sure about that. It so happened last time that it was seven years and once small caps began their move it lasted seven years, but

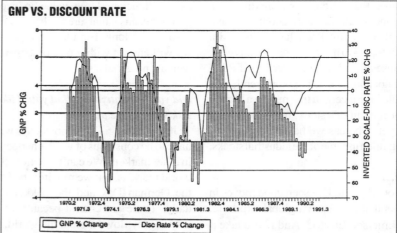

FIGURE 5

GNP VS. DISCOUNT RATE

Most technicians will look at other indicators to understand the background for a market. Here, the percent change in the Gross National Product is compared to the percent change in the discount rate (plotted inversely) with a six-month lag. The change in the discount rate shows a strong correlation to the change in the economy.

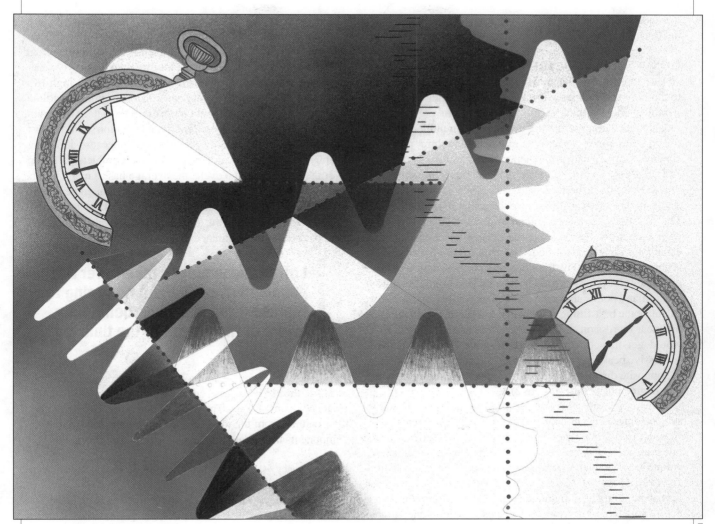

Optimum Detrending

Look at any price chart, and you'll find that markets move up and down even while in a trend. Removing the trend can help identify short-term turning points. Frequent STOCKS & COMMODITIES contributor John Ehlers presents different techniques for detrending prices and his optimized detrending method as well.

by John F. Ehlers

We want to detrend data because we want to remove the longer-term variations so short-term turning points are easier to discern, enabling us to better pinpoint the best entry and exit points for short-term trades. Since the goal of detrending is separation of time variables, it is logical that we can optimize the calculation for our approach to the market. Short-term and long-term variations are synonymous with high-frequency and low-frequency components, respectively. This is important because optimization is accomplished using modern digital filter theory. Using filters, we can readily separate the desired frequency components and discard the undesired frequency components. Short term and long term are relative to trading style. A 26-week cycle used by a stock trader is long term for a commodity trader using daily data, for example. Similarly, an intraday trader considers anything longer than several hours to be long term. The optimization we derive considers daily data, but the principles can be expanded for any trading situation.

Before we optimize detrending, let us review conventional

detrending techniques for their comparative strengths and weaknesses.

CONVENTIONAL DETRENDING

At least three different detrending techniques can be commonly found: First, calculating the best-fitting straight line as the trendline and subtracting the trendline from the raw data; second, calculating a moving average as a trendline and subtracting that trendline from the raw data; and third, taking the difference of two data points separated in time.

The easiest way to calculate the best-fitting trendline is to draw a straight line between successive highest highs or lowest lows and then translate this line to the center of the data spread. The best-fitting straight line can also be calculated by linear regression, often desirable because nearby successive maxima cannot be clearly identified. But this calculation can have accuracy problems. The trendline of a perfect sine wave taken over one full cycle is exactly horizontal because the sine wave has as many points above zero as it does below zero. When we calculate the best-fitting straight line to a single sine wave cycle by linear regression, we get the result as seen in Figure 1. We would get the correct result if we took the span between successive peaks or valleys and would get the incorrect slope in the opposite direction if we took the span over the cycle with a 180-degree phase shift (Figure 2).

Linear regression calculations for the trendline are therefore subject to errors, depending on the phase of the cycle forming the short-term variation. The error can be reduced by performing the linear regression calculation over several cycles, but this has a unique set of problems because market data are seldom stationary over a span of several cycles. After all, if cycles were persistent, all traders could recognize their existence and trade them. This fact guarantees that cycles must ebb and flow as traders exploit the cycles when they recognize them. The net result is that the linear regression calculation of trendlines is flawed because the correct span of time is ambiguous. There is perhaps a better way.

The second way to calculate a trendline is to compute a moving average. The moving average smoothes the data, removing the short-term variations. In a sense, the moving average is a low-pass filter that allows the low-frequency (slowly varying) components to be retained but attenuates the high-frequency (faster-varying) components. The resulting trendline has only the low-frequency components of the data. The length of the moving average for the trendline calculation should be just the period of the dominant cycle in the data because a moving average of this length removes this cycle completely. Taken over the full period of a cycle, the average has as many points above zero as it does below zero so the full cycle average is zero, regardless of the starting phase angle of the full cycle average. Frequencies higher than the dominant cycle are also attenuated but not necessarily eliminated.

> **I often use averages taken over the dominant cycle without centering to represent the trendline, being fully aware of the impact of the time lag.**

The moving average method of generating the trendline adapts to the current market conditions and attenuates the high-frequency components. The data are detrended by subtracting the trendline from the total data to remove the low-frequency components in the detrended result. In equation form, this is:

$$HighFrequency = (HighFrequency + LowFrequency) - LowFrequency$$

This approach has a problem in that the moving average necessarily has a lag relative to the original price, which can be compensated for by centering the moving average value in the span over which it was calculated. Centering the moving average, while helpful for historical analysis, doesn't help with real trading because there is no trendline for the last half cycle if the

FIGURE 1

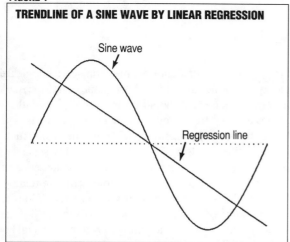

TRENDLINE OF A SINE WAVE BY LINEAR REGRESSION

Sine wave

Regression line

Calculating the best-fitting straight line to a sine wave using linear regression produces this trendline. The trend appears to be down because the peak was first and the trough second.

FIGURE 2

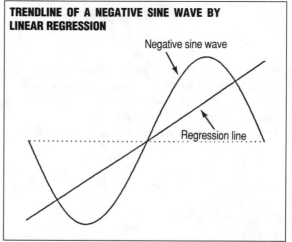

TRENDLINE OF A NEGATIVE SINE WAVE BY LINEAR REGRESSION

Negative sine wave

Regression line

The slope of the trendline is up if the sine wave is shifted 180 degrees.

moving average value is centered. I often use averages taken over the dominant cycle without centering to represent the trendline, being fully aware of the impact of the time lag.

NOW TRY THIS

The third way to detrend data is to take the difference of two data points separated in time. Figure 3 shows a sine wave superimposed on a trend and the resulting detrended sine wave when the difference is taken between successive samples. (This would be successive days, using daily data.) Note that the trend is not only eliminated but the detrended sine wave leads the original sine wave by 90 degrees; that is, the detrended sine wave is a momentum function. When the original sine wave is near its peak or valley, the rate of change is near zero. On the other hand, when the original sine wave is near the midpoint, the rate of change is maximum both in the positive and negative direction. The phase lead of the momentum function has some fascinating possibilities for the generation of "anticipate functions." In the real world, the high-frequency components are enhanced so much that the detrended data can appear to be "noisy" and intermediate-term turning points are lost. This problem can be alleviated by widening the spread between the data points. The noisiness can be reduced by smoothing (low-pass filtering), but the smoothing introduces a time lag that can eliminate the phase lead of the momentum function.

T he mathematical equivalent of smoothing is to separate the differencing points in time. The trending price with the samples taken exactly a half cycle apart (lettered pairs) can be seen in Figure 4. The difference between points A at the midpoint of the cycle is the value of the trend slope. The difference between points B is the same trend slope value plus the peak-to-peak swing of the sine wave. The resulting detrended sine wave has a constant offset from zero equal to the trend slope. Although the slope of the detrended sine wave is zero, the offset can introduce problems for further analysis. For one, the slope isn't exactly constant in the real world; a slowly varying trendline appears as a low frequency in the detrended price, and we have not fully attained our goal of eliminating the low-frequency components.

Another problem that arises from separating the differencing points is that the high-frequency components are also not eliminated. Consider Figure 5, where a frequency and its third harmonic are overlaid. The difference between the peak and valley is the same for both sine waves, so the conclusion is that extraneous high-frequency components are not attenuated by the differencing. Of the three conventional detrending methods, differencing has the most potential for optimization. Little can be done to change either method for computing the trendline, but more complex differences can be combined with low-pass filtering to optimize the detrending calculation.

OPTIMUM DETRENDING

The basic idea of optimum detrending is to take the difference of one group of data points from another group. Weighting

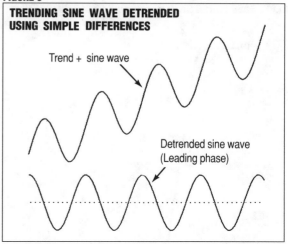

FIGURE 3

TRENDING SINE WAVE DETRENDED USING SIMPLE DIFFERENCES

Trend + sine wave

Detrended sine wave (Leading phase)

The top chart is a sine wave superimposed on a trend. The bottom chart is the detrended sine wave when the difference between successive samples is taken.

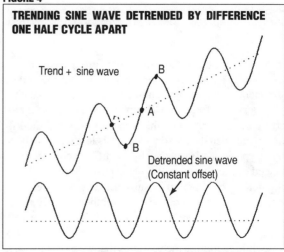

FIGURE 4

TRENDING SINE WAVE DETRENDED BY DIFFERENCE ONE HALF CYCLE APART

Trend + sine wave

B
A
B

Detrended sine wave (Constant offset)

A sine wave superimposed upon a trend is smoothed by taking samples a half cycle apart. The difference between the two As is the slope of the trend. The difference between the two Bs is the same trend slope plus the peak-to-peak swing of the sine wave .

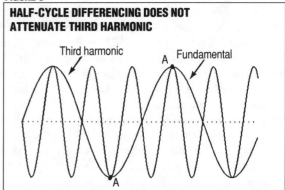

FIGURE 5

HALF-CYCLE DIFFERENCING DOES NOT ATTENUATE THIRD HARMONIC

Third harmonic   A   Fundamental

A

Two sine waves are overlaid. The second sine wave is the third harmonic of the first. The difference between the peak and valley is the same for both sine waves, and consequently, the extraneous high-frequency components are not attenuated by differencing.

FIGURE 6

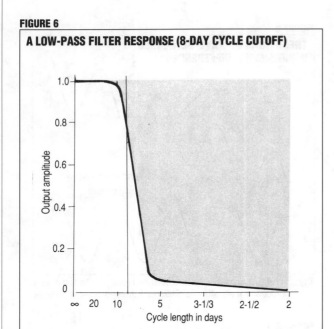

A low-pass filter with an eight-day cycle cutoff will have little if any effect on cycles greater than eight days. Cycles shorter than eight days are blocked from passing.

FIGURE 7

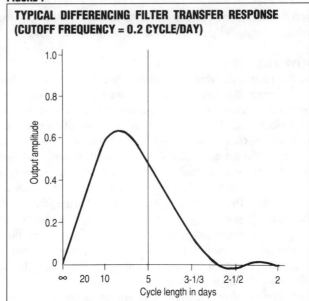

An optimized detrender (differencing filter) using a cutoff frequency of 0.2 cycles per day will eliminate low-frequency trending components while attenuating the very high frequency, often noisy, components.

factors are given to each data point in both groups, with the result being similar to a low-pass filter. This eliminates the undesired high-frequency components. The difference function itself eliminates the very low-frequency components. The constant offset caused by the separation of the data groups is minimal if the separation between the two data groups is less than a half cycle. Finally, the phase lead produced by the differencing momentum is balanced by the phase lag of the low-pass filter, with the result that the detrended function is substantially in phase with the original price function. For the more mathematically inclined, R.W. Hamming describes differencing filters in detail in *Digital Filters*.

Meanwhile, sampling theory states that we must have at least two samples of the highest frequencies we wish to analyze. There is no restriction on the lower frequencies or the maximum number of samples per cycle. Using daily data, our sampling rate is once per day. Therefore, the shortest cycle we can analyze is a two-day cycle, one having a frequency of 0.5 cycles per day. Frequency is the reciprocal of the cycle period. For example, the frequency of an eight-day cycle is 0.125 cycles per day. Figure 6 shows the transfer response of an ideal low-pass filter. Frequencies below 0.125 cycles per day (longer than an eight-day cycle) are allowed to pass through the filter with very little, if any, attenuation. However, frequencies above 0.125 cycles per day are blocked from passing. Experience suggests that cycles having periods ranging between eight and 32 days are useful for trading with daily data. Weekly data can be used to trade longer cycles, enabling the same filtering theory to be used without modification for cycle lengths varying from eight weeks to 32 weeks. Similarly, intraday traders can use the theory unmodified to trade cycles between eight hours and 32 hours using hourly data.

Figure 7 is the transfer response of a typical optimized detrender (differencing filter). Zero frequency is just a constant value in the original price data. This constant value is completely eliminated when the difference between two balanced groups of data points is taken. The amplitude of the transfer response increases almost linearly as the input data frequency increases because of the imbalance of the value between the two weighted groups of data. The transfer response increases until a *cutoff* frequency, a frequency we can select, is reached. I choose the cutoff frequency to be the dominant cycle present in the data. Above the cutoff frequency, the weighted data values perform as a low-pass filter, attenuating the higher-frequency components in the data.

The optimized detrender differencing filter fully accomplishes our goals. It eliminates the very low frequency trending components. It attenuates the very high frequency, often noisy, components. Those frequency components that pass through the differencing filter are just those that have the tradable short-term variations that we wanted to isolate. By careful selection of the filter parameters, the detrended data will be almost exactly in phase with its unfiltered counterpart.

DESIGN PARTICULARS

The filter cutoff frequency, F_c, should be the reciprocal of the dominant cycle period to be traded. The number of data points in each group, N, is the integer number of points in a half cycle of the dominant cycle, so $N=8$ for a 16-day dominant cycle. I round downward, so $N=7$ for a 15-day dominant cycle.

The formula B for calculating the weighting factors is a function of k and is written $B(k)$. The weighting factors, $B(k)$, are symmetrical relative to the center point; k is the counting number, starting from the center. The weighting factor of the

FIGURE 8

TREASURY BOND TRENDING PERIOD

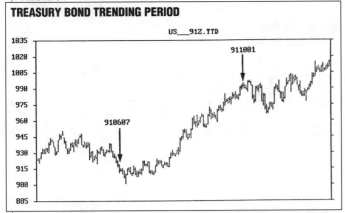

The December T-bond futures contract had a clear uptrend from June to October 1991.

FIGURE 9

OPTIMUM DETRENDED SIGNAL

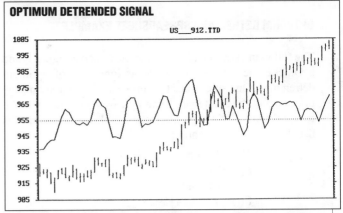

The optimum detrended signal using a 10-day cycle is overlaid on the chart of the bond contract. The detrended signal is in close sync with the cyclic component of the market.

center point is always zero. The filter weighting factors are calculated as:

$$B(k) = \left(\frac{\sin\left(2\pi k F_c\right)}{k^2} - \frac{\left(2\pi F_c\right)\cos\left(2\pi k F_c\right)}{k} \right) \frac{\sin\left(\frac{\pi k}{N}\right)}{\frac{\pi k}{N}}$$

where   SIN and COS functions are computed in radians
             $\pi = 3.1415926$
             F_c = cutoff frequency
             N = INT(DominantCycle/2)
             k = counting number

The last data point in the group, Bn, is always zero. The $B(k)$ to the right of center (the most recent data points) have positive values and the $B(k)$ to the left of center (more distant data points) have negative values. The difference filter output is calculated by multiplying each successive data point by its associated weighting factor, $B(k)$. All the weighted data points are summed to get the detrended value.

Due to symmetry, it is easiest to calculate the $B(k)$ weighting factors relative to the center of the filter. However, for traders, the most significant data point is the most recent data. I locate the last $B(k)$ having a finite value as the multiplier for the most recent data point and map the $B(k)$ weighting values backward. (See sidebar, "Optimum detrending spreadsheet example.") When we do this, the filter output is skewed from the center of the filter.

This is approximately what we desire, because the leading property of the momentum function just about compensates for the skew-induced lag. As a result, the optimum detrended price is just about in phase with the short-term price variation in the unfiltered data.

PROOF IS IN THE PUDDING
One of the best ways to demonstrate the benefits of optimum detrending is with an example using data. Figure 8 indicates that December 1991 Treasury bonds had a decided uptrend between June 7, 1991, and October 1, 1991 (yymmdd format). This range is expanded to the full span of Figures 9 through 11 to show the detrended signals better. The detrended signals in Figures 9 though 11 are displayed using a normalized amplitude (equal scales) and are superimposed on the bar chart data for visual correlation. Further, during the time span of interest, Treasury bonds had a nominal 10-day dominant cycle.

Since the nominal dominant cycle was 10 days, the cutoff frequency was selected to be 0.1 cycles per day and N was selected to be 5 for the calculation of the $B(k)$ filter weighting factors to compute the optimum detrended signal. The optimum detrended signal is shown on the bar chart in Figure 9. It was computed using the average of the high and low for each day as the price data. Note that the detrended signal is almost perfectly in sync with the cyclic component of the price. It would have been very profitable to make a long entry or increase your long position at each lowest turning point of the detrended signal. While you also could have traded short at each highest turning point, it may not be a good idea to trade against a strong trend.

OPTIMUM DETRENDING SPREADSHEET EXAMPLE

The following is a spreadsheet example (sidebar Figure 1) and a QuickBasic source code (sidebar Figure 2) of optimum detrending. Our spreadsheet example is for detrending the price data of the bond market example used in Figure 9 of the text of the article. Our spreadsheet example uses the variables listed in the text of the article:

$$N = 10/2 = 5$$
$$F_C = 0.1$$
$$k \text{ ranges from -4 to +4}$$
$$PI() = \pi \cong 3.1415926$$

The weighting factors are set to be symmetrical about the center point, which is zero. The counter k only ranges from -4 to +4, even though the nominal cycle in our example is 10 days because if $k = 5$ or -5 then $B(k) = 0$ because $\sin(\pi)/\pi = 0$. An additional weighting factor of 0 is unnecessary because the steps to detrending require the sum of the products of the weighting factors and the data. Obviously multiplying by 0 results in a 0 and does not contribute to the smoothing of the data.

In the Excel spreadsheet, column D lists the values for k (for notational purposes) that are used in column E to calculate the weighting factors. The formula for cell E2 using a k of -4 :

= ((SIN (2 * PI() * -4 * 0.1) / 16) - (2 * PI() * 0.1) * COS (2 * PI() * -4 * 0. 1) / -4) * (SIN (PI()*-4 / 5)) / (PI()*-4 / 5)

The next cell, E3, uses the same formula, except the k is now -3 instead of -4. The final weighting factor uses $k = 4$. Notice the symmetry in cells E2 through E10; note the cells above the zero figure (E2 through E5) with the values having a

SIDEBAR FIGURE 1
FORMULA OUTPUT

	A	B	C	D	E
1	Date	Today's Avg Px	Detrended	k	B(k)
2	910523	93.938		-4	-0.038
3	910524	93.750		-3	-0.086
4	910528	94.015		-2	-0.106
5	910529	94.141		-1	-0.074
6	910530	94.344		0	0.000
7	910531	94.343		1	0.074
8	910603	93.750		2	0.106
9	910604	93.563		3	0.086
10	910605	93.250	-0.056	4	0.038
11	910606	92.859	-0.206		
12	910607	92.359	-0.348		
13	910610	92.266	-0.438		
14	910611	92.141	-0.463		
15	910612	91.844	-0.438		
16	910613	91.422	-0.399		
17	910614	92.078	-0.338		

This spreadsheet shows the output of the formulas for optimum detrending of the bond market. Column E is the weighting factors used to smooth and difference the price data in column B. Column C is detrended data.

negative sign and a positive sign in the cells (E7 through E10) below zero. This change in the sign of the weighting factor produces the differencing between two groups of data.

Column C represents the detrended data. The original price data (column B) is multiplied by the weighting factors and then summed. Because there are nine weighting factors, there will be nine days of data to smooth and difference. The formula for cell C10 is:

=$E$10*B10+$E$9*B9+$E$8*B8+$E$7*B7+$E$6*B6+$E$5*B5+$E$4*B4+$E$3*B3+$E$2*B2

The $ before the column and row numbers fix that cell to be a constant when the formula is copied to another cell. For cell C11, the first term of the formula will be:
$E$10*B11+$E$9*B10+ … $E2$B3.

A plot of column C should match the optimum detrended line shown in Figure 9 of the article.—*Editor*

SIDEBAR FIGURE 2
SOURCE CODE

```
'BASIC code for optimum detrending

Pi = 3.14159
TwoPi = 2 * Pi
FOR D = FR + 50 TO LR
  DominantCycle(D) = 10                    'this usually varies day to day
  Wc = TwoPi / DominantCycle(D)
  SyntheticPrice!(D) = 0
  Q = INT(DominantCycle(D))                'rounds cycle length to integer
  FOR I = 0 TO Q - 1
    K = (Q / 2 - I - 1)                    'makes K symmetrical about center
    IF K = 0 THEN GOTO SkipMid
    B = (SIN(K * Wc) / (K * K) - (Wc / K) * COS(K * Wc)) * (SIN(TwoPi * K / Q) / (TwoPi * K / Q))
    SyntheticPrice(D) = SyntheticPrice(D) + B * (HI(D - I) + LO(D - I))
SkipMid:
  NEXT
NEXT
```

This is the source code listing for optimum detrending.

FIGURE 10

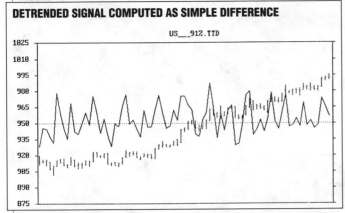

DETRENDED SIGNAL COMPUTED AS SIMPLE DIFFERENCE

The detrended signal is computed as a simple difference of price. The high-frequency components are accentuated, which makes identifying real turning points and noise difficult.

FIGURE 11

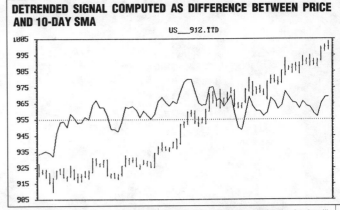

DETRENDED SIGNAL COMPUTED AS DIFFERENCE BETWEEN PRICE AND 10-DAY SMA

Plotting the difference between a 10-day SMA and the price on a day-by-day basis still has high-frequency content (jaggedness) complicating the task of identifying real turning points.

But these points can be used to reassess the value of your stop.

Figure 10 shows the detrended signal computed as a simple difference (momentum) of the price. As we predicted, the turning point of the detrended signal often precedes the price turning point. The problem is that the high-frequency components have been accentuated to the point that it is difficult to discern the difference between the real turning points and the noise.

The detrended signal of Figure 11 is found by computing the 10-day simple moving average (SMA) and subtracting the SMA from the price on a day-by-day basis. The moving average is not centered because if it were, we would have no quantitative way to find the detrended signal for the last five days. As a result, the moving average lag causes the detrended signal to have a constant offset from the center line. Also note that the detrended signal has much more high-frequency content (jaggedness) in comparison to the optimum detrended signal in Figure 9.

The benefits of using an optimum detrended signal are clear. More important, by knowing the mechanism of computing the optimized detrended signal, you can adapt the procedure in an intelligent way to improve your trading. You can use a cutoff frequency higher than the dominant cycle in the data. This will produce a leading signal, but at the cost of increased high-frequency components producing potential false alarms. Since you recognize the trade-off, you can best fit the procedures to your trading style.

SUMMARY

An optimum detrending filter rejects the slowly varying trend, or low-frequency, components and the high-frequency noise-like data components. The resulting output emphasizes the cycle we desire to trade, making turning points more discernible.

The sample basis of the signal can be hourly, daily, weekly, and so forth with equal validity. All you need to know is the length of the dominant cycle to be traded. The dominant cycle can be determined by measuring the distance between successive lowest lows or highest highs by using a cycle finder in the popular toolbox computer programs or by directly measuring

the dominant cycle in a more sophisticated program such as MESA. Knowing the dominant cycle, optimum detrending is mechanical, computing the weighting factors and summing the product of the weighting factors and the data points.

John Ehlers, Box 1801, Goleta, CA 93116, (805) 969-6478, is an electrical engineer working in electronic research and development and has been a private trader since 1978. He is a pioneer in introducing maximum entropy spectrum analysis to technical trading through his MESA computer program.

REFERENCES

Ehlers, John F. [1992]. "1991 cycles," STOCKS & COMMODITIES, April.

_____ [1989]. "Leading indicators with momentum," *Technical Analysis of* STOCKS & COMMODITIES, Volume 7: September.

Hamming, R.W. [1989]. *Digital Filters*, 3d ed., Prentice-Hall.

Kaufman, Perry J. [1987]. *The New Commodity Trading Systems and Methods*, John Wiley & Sons.

Murphy, John J. [1986]. *Technical Analysis of the Futures Markets*, New York Institute of Finance.

MARK MOLNAR

The Link Between Bonds
And Commodities

Like a set of tumbling dominoes, intermarket analysis is based on the theory that one instrument affected will in turn affect another. Technical pioneer John Murphy, best known for his trailblazing work in technical analysis and intermarket analysis, explains how that interrelationship between bonds and commodities works.

by John J. Murphy

Intermarket analysis adds another layer to the work of the technician by considering activity in related markets. Whereas traditional technical analysis treats each market separately, intermarket technical analysis suggests that important directional clues can be obtained in one market by studying what is happening in related markets. The stock market and the U.S. dollar, for example, are influenced by the direction of interest rates. The direction of interest rates, in turn, is influenced by the direction of commodity prices, and so on.

FIGURE 1

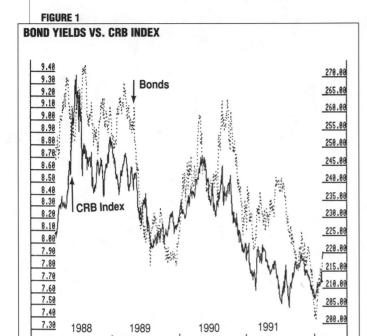

BOND YIELDS VS. CRB INDEX

Bond yields and the CRB Index generally trended in the same direction from mid-1988 to early 1992.

FIGURE 2

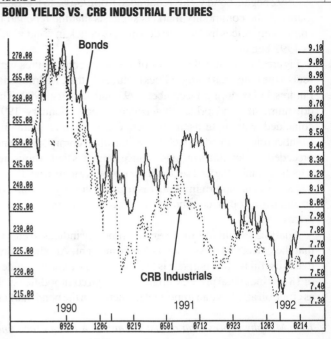

BOND YIELDS VS. CRB INDUSTRIAL FUTURES

A strong visual correlation can be seen between bond yields and the CRB Industrial Futures Index (copper, cotton, crude oil, lumber, platinum, silver) from mid-1990 to early 1992.

Commodity prices and bond prices usually trend in opposite directions; bond *yields* trend in the same direction as commodities. Thus, commodities and bonds should be viewed together. Analysis of either sector is incomplete without analysis of the other. Figure 1 shows the Commodity Research Bureau (CRB) Futures Price Index, a basket of 21 commodities, and bond yields generally trended in the same direction from 1988 to February 1992. At year-end 1991, the drop in bond yields to new lows was not confirmed by the CRB Index, which held above its mid-1991 trough; that divergence was followed by a rebound in both measures.

> **Analysts should follow several commodity indices to ensure that the correct inflation message is being sent. Another index that is useful for this purpose is the Journal of Commerce Index of 18 raw industrial prices.**

INDUSTRIAL AND AGRICULTURAL

Since the CRB Index includes many agricultural commodities, industrial commodity prices should be tracked as well. Figure 2 shows the strong correlation between bond yields and the CRB Industrial Futures Index from mid-1990 to early 1992. (That commodity sub-index includes copper, cotton, crude oil, lumber, platinum and silver.) Figure 2 shows bond yields and industrial commodities peaking in unison in 1990, rebounding together during the first half of 1991, falling together during the

FIGURE 3

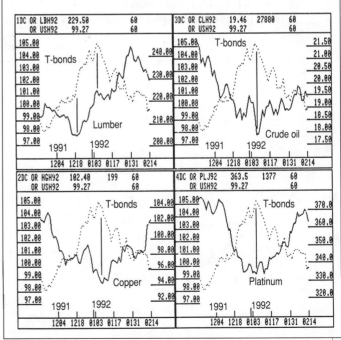

DOWNTURNS AND UPTURNS

The downturn in Treasury bond futures in January 1992 coincided with upturns in copper, crude oil and platinum. Lumber, which usually leads other commodities, was the first to turn up.

second half of 1991, and rebounding as one into February 1992. As 1992 began, bond yields rebounded from 7.40% to 8.00%. A glance at the commodity markets suggests that the rebound in commodity prices had a lot to do with the uptick in bond yields as 1992 began.

Figure 3 compares the prices of Treasury bond futures with four of the industrial commodities included in the CRB Industrial Futures Index during December 1991 and January 1992. The downturn in bond prices that began in early January 1992 coincided with upturns in copper, crude oil and platinum. Lumber prices turned up well before the other commodities and preceded the downturn in bonds. Since lumber is tied to housing, which is usually the first sector of the economy to turn up during a recession, an upturn in lumber is usually an early warning of an upturn in other commodities and of a downturn in bond prices.

Analysts should follow several commodity indices to ensure that the correct inflation message is being sent. Another index that is useful for this purpose is the *Journal of Commerce* Index of 18 raw industrial prices. Certain individual commodities such as crude oil also have an important influence on the bond market.

John Murphy is president of JJM Technical Advisors Inc., and publishes the monthly "Futures Trends and Intermarket Analysis." He is also the technical analyst for CNBC/FNN.

REFERENCES

JJM Technical Advisors Inc., 297-101 Kinderkamack Road, Suite 148, Oradell, NJ 07649.

Murphy, John [1986]. *Technical Analysis of the Futures Markets*, New York Institute of Finance.

_____ [1991]. *Intermarket Technical Analysis*, John Wiley & Sons.

UNDERSTANDING STANDARD MATHEMATICAL SYMBOLS

It is inevitable that today's technician will encounter steps to calculating an indicator that uses standard mathematical symbols that appear to be beyond simple arithmetic. In reality, these symbols are simply shorthand notation for no more than basic arithmetic. The following is a guide and interpretation to mathematical symbols commonly seen in STOCKS & COMMODITIES.

By convention, the first few lowercase letters of the Roman alphabet (a, b, c) are used to denote constant terms or coefficients. A constant is simply a value that does not change. For example, if a formula states that $a = 1.5$, then whenever you see the a in the formula you know that you can substitute 1.5. A coefficient is a factor in a product. If you see bx in a formula, then you know that the variable x is multiplied by the coefficient b. Variables are typically denoted by the last few letters of the Roman alphabet (x, y and z). A variable can be any observed value such as today's closing price of the stock market. Statistics will use capital letters of the alphabet (X, Y and Z) as variables.

A subscript is used with the variable to define a list of differing values from the same set of values. A set of values could be the last month's daily closing prices of a stock. The daily closing price of a stock could be assigned the variables $x_1, x_2, x_3, x_4, x_5, \ldots x_i$ for each individual day. The notation for the subscript value is identified by the letter i. Sometimes, a formula will instruct to use a specific quantity of observed values — for example, the last five days' closing prices. The notation for the number of variables is the letter n. In the previous example, therefore, $n = 5$.

A formula may require you to add together a series of variables — that is, the last five days' closing prices. The formula could be stated as $x_1 + x_2 + x_3 + x_4 + x_5$. Instead of this lengthy style, the Greek letter Σ (epsilon) is used, meaning "to sum." If a specific number of variables is to be summed, the notation includes a counter, n.

$$\sum_{i=1}^{n=5} x_i$$

Here, the letter i indicates to start with the first x (number 1) and the letter $n = 5$ indicates to count up to a total of five x's and to sum the x's. In simple English, the instructions are to add $x_1 + x_2 + x_3 + x_4 + x_5$ together.

A number of technical indicators and statistical formulas use an average of the observations or variables in the calculations. Another name for the average is the mean. The mean is identified by a line over the variable such as $\bar{x}$. The steps to calculate the average or mean of a series of prices is to first decide on the number of periods to be averaged — for example, a five-day average. Sum the five days' prices and then divide by 5. The following is the formula for a five-day average:

$$\bar{x} = \frac{1}{n} \sum_{i=1}^{n=5} x_i$$

In the above example, the variable x_i represents a single day's closing price. This variable could represent something other than one set value. A variable could be something more complicated. Let's say you wanted to calculate the difference between two values x_i and y_i and then square this difference and finally sum a series of these squared differences. Our set of values are $x_1 = 12, x_2 = 22, x_3 = 25$ and $y_1 = 10, y_2 = 15, y_3 = 20$. The formula to do this would look like this:

$$\sum_{i=1}^{n=3} \left(x_i - y_i \right)^2$$

Here, we will subtract the first y from the first x ($12 - 10$), which equals 2; the next step is to square 2, which equals 4. The next step is to subtract the second y from the second x ($22 - 15$), which equals 7; squaring 7 equals 49. The last difference is subtracting the third y from the third x ($25 - 20$), which equals 5; squaring 5 equals 25. The last step is to sum the squared differences ($4 + 49 + 25$), which equals 78.

While some of the formulas may appear to be complicated, the notation is usually just a shortcut to present a series of steps that involves no more than simple arithmetic.

—Editor

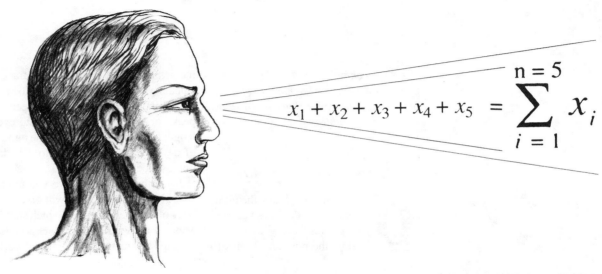

$$x_1 + x_2 + x_3 + x_4 + x_5 = \sum_{i=1}^{n=5} x_i$$

MIKE HORSWILL

The Elapsed Time Calculator

Veteran technician Arthur Merrill explains how to derive the number of days, actual or calendar, between two dates using a simple table and some elementary steps.

by Arthur A. Merrill, C.M.T.

o you need to know the number of calendar days between two dates? Do you need to know the number of days to

the expiration of a futures contract to calculate fair value? Do you need to know the number of calendar days between two peaks or two troughs to estimate cycle length? Do you need to know the number of days between two dates to calculate interest due?

If so, this table will give you the answer. It's easy. The table will give you a "day of the year" number, which starts at March 1 to avoid some problems caused by leap year changes. Here's how it works:

FIGURE 1

ELAPSED TIME CALCULATOR												
Day of Month	**Day**		**of**			**the**		**Year**				
	Mar	**Apr**	**May**	**June**	**July**	**Aug**	**Sep**	**Oct**	**Nov**	**Dec**	**Jan**	**Feb**
1	1	32	62	93	123	154	185	215	246	276	307	338
2	2	33	63	94	124	155	186	216	247	277	308	339
3	3	34	64	95	125	156	187	217	248	278	309	340
4	4	35	65	96	126	157	188	218	249	279	310	341
5	5	36	66	97	127	158	189	219	250	280	311	342
6	6	37	67	98	128	159	190	220	251	281	312	343
7	7	38	68	99	129	160	191	221	252	282	313	344
8	8	39	69	100	130	161	192	222	253	283	314	345
9	9	40	70	101	131	162	193	223	254	284	315	346
10	10	41	71	102	132	163	194	224	255	285	316	347
11	11	42	72	103	133	164	195	225	256	286	317	348
12	12	43	73	104	134	165	196	226	257	287	318	349
13	13	44	74	105	135	166	197	227	258	288	319	350
14	14	45	75	106	136	167	198	228	259	289	320	351
15	15	46	76	107	137	168	199	229	260	290	321	352
16	16	47	77	108	138	169	200	230	261	291	322	353
17	17	48	78	109	139	170	201	231	262	292	323	354
18	18	49	79	110	140	171	202	232	263	293	324	355
19	19	50	80	111	141	172	203	233	264	294	325	356
20	20	51	81	112	142	173	204	234	265	295	326	357
21	21	52	82	113	143	174	205	235	266	296	327	358
22	22	53	83	114	144	175	206	236	267	297	328	359
23	23	54	84	115	145	176	207	237	268	298	329	360
24	24	55	85	116	146	177	208	238	269	299	330	361
25	25	56	86	117	147	178	209	239	270	300	331	362
26	26	57	87	118	148	179	210	240	271	301	332	363
27	27	58	88	119	149	180	211	241	272	302	333	364
28	28	59	89	120	150	181	212	242	273	303	334	365
29	29	60	90	121	151	182	213	243	274	304	335	366
30	30	61	91	122	152	183	214	244	275	305	336	
31	31		92		153	184		245		306	337	

This reference table will allow you to determine the number of days between two dates, the expiration of a futures contract to calculate fair value, between two peaks or two troughs to estimate cycle length and the number of days between two dates to calculate interest due. It's simple!

1 Put down the "day of the year" for your second date — this is the ending date of the span you are measuring.
2 Add 365 for each February 28 passed over. For a leap year, use 366.
3 Subtract "day of the year" for the first date; this is the date at the beginning of the span.
4 The result is the number of days between the two dates.

For example, what is the number of days between May 3, 1992, and June 17, 1993?

Step 1	109
Step 2	Add 365
Step 3	Subtract 64
Step 4	The result is 410 days between the two dates.

It's easy!

Arthur Merrill is a Chartered Market Technician and the author of many reports and books, including Behavior of Prices on Wall Street *and* Filtered Waves, Basic Theory.

Trading With The True Strength Index

The true strength index, which was introduced late last year in these pages, may be considered to be a cross between a relative strength indicator and a moving average convergence/divergence indicator with many of the desirable properties from each. Creator William Blau, who introduced the indicator to S&C readers last year, explains how to trade with the index.

by William Blau

T he true strength index introduced in STOCKS & COMMODITIES November 1991 was discussed as a smooth momentum indicator stripped of high-frequency noise useful for expressing the direction of market trends, the amount of movement of the market and highlighting market turning points. Figure 1 depicts a section of a price chart showing the daily close (with the open, high and low of the price bars omitted). Momentum is defined as the close minus the close of an earlier period. The daily momentum is today's close minus yesterday's close; for example, the one-day momentum is

$$Mtm = close_{today} - close_{yesterday}$$

When the close's value increases from one day to the next, the slope of the close curve is positive; momentum is increasing from one day to the next.

On the other hand, if price falls from one day to the next (like C in Figure 1), the price change exhibits a negative slope (that is, it is going down) and has a one-day momentum that is a negative number. Momentum describes price changes in magnitude and direction. In Figure 1, for example, the price valley at the earliest time shown begins with zero momentum. As time passes, the one-day momentum becomes positive and gets larger when prices rally sharply and then as the peak at D gets closer, the rally slows down with decreasing momentum. At the peak itself, the momentum is zero. Immediately past the peak,

the momentum changes sign to indicate prices have passed a turning point on their way down. Momentum possesses many characteristics necessary for investing and trading in that it expresses the direction of the market and the amount of the movement of the market, and it also highlights market turning points. The formula for the true strength index is given by:

$$TRSI_{y,z} = 100 \frac{E_z(E_y(Mtm))}{E_z(E_y(|Mtm|))}$$

In the numerator, an exponential moving average (EMA) of the one-day momentum of the close is made for y-days. This result is subjected to a second EMA for z-days. In effect, the numerator performs double smoothing of the momentum. The denominator, however, performs double smoothing on the absolute value or magnitude of the momentum; its sole purpose is to normalize the true strength formula so that the numbers are bounded and easy to handle across a variety of price conditions. (See sidebar, "Calculating TrSI.")

Figure 2 shows the true strength index of the close for double smoothing of 25 and 13 days, respectively. (Notation employed on charts is TrSI (close,25,13), where the first numeric represents the first smoothing and the second numeric represents the second smoothing.) The true strength index is seen as relatively

Does double smoothing of momentum via the true strength index lead to new possibilities in trading systems? Let's explore.

smooth (not as choppy as the close curve). Peaks and valleys of the index track those of the close with little or no measurable lag. The true strength index appears to be confined between plus and minus 100, no matter what the variation in price (this is the normalization provided by the denominator). Two parallel *basis* lines are placed at levels where they serve as thresholds to indicate historic overbought and oversold price conditions. A signal line may be employed to select turning points via crossover of the true strength index over its EMA. The signal line in Figure 2 results from a seven-day EMA of the true strength index line.

Like its predecessor, the relative strength index (RSI), the true strength index also shows divergences between it and the close curve from which it is derived, often signifying a coming change of price direction. Support and resistance often become evident on the true strength index prior to price. Similarly, trendlines appear on the true strength index chart corresponding to those on the price chart. The true strength index also provides noise cleaning with low lag by virtue of its double smoothing.

A PROXY FOR PRICE?

What is the underlying mechanism that permits us to use moving average momentum as a stand-in for price? Why do price and moving average momentum diverge? Can we control divergences? What is the effect of double smoothing on trending? Is it possible to perform moving average trending in the domain of the true strength index more "efficiently" than in the price domain? Does double smoothing of momentum via the true strength index lead to new possibilities in trading systems? Let's explore the possibilities.

Mathematically, it can be shown that moving average momentum is a *valid representation of price* (except for scaling) *if* the window of the moving average is allowed to increase without limit. Moving average momentum is defined by the true strength

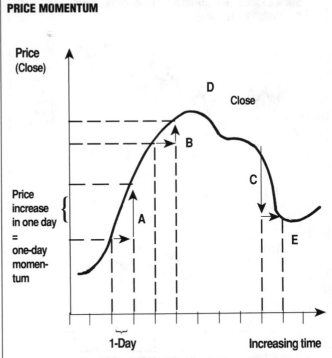

FIGURE 1

PRICE MOMENTUM

A and B have positive momentum (rising prices, or upward slope of price curve)
C has negative momentum (decreasing price, or downward slope of price curve)
D and E are turning points with zero momentum
B has less momentum than A (rising at a slower rate)

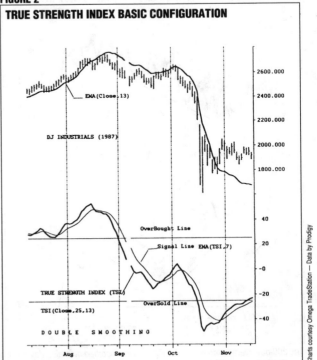

FIGURE 2

TRUE STRENGTH INDEX BASIC CONFIGURATION

The true strength index has maximum/minimum values of +100/-100 showing overbought/oversold price regions. The signal line is a moving average of the true strength index. Turning points are highlighted by true strength index crossovers.

FIGURE 3

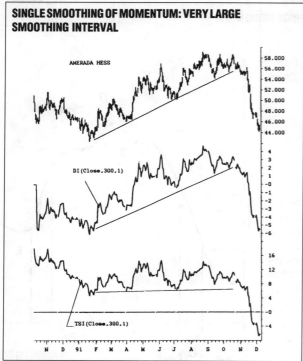

**SINGLE SMOOTHING OF MOMENTUM: VERY LARGE
SMOOTHING INTERVAL**

*A large 300-day moving average of momentum, DI (close,300,1), produces a
curve that is a good approximation of price shape. The true strength index is
"normalized" momentum and is an amplitude-compressed version of momentum
showing divergences not otherwise present.*

FIGURE 4

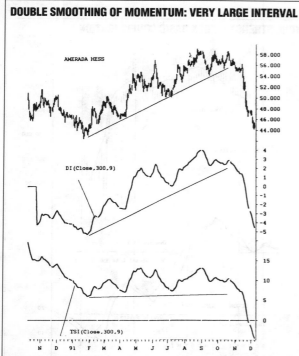

DOUBLE SMOOTHING OF MOMENTUM: VERY LARGE INTERVAL

*The 300-day average momentum of Figure 3 is smoothed by a nine-day EMA,
resulting in a noise-free curve with low lag, similar to a nine-day EMA of the close.*

index numerator, which I call the divergence indicator (DI):

$$DI_{y,z} = E_z(E_y(Mtm))$$

which is defined for y, z days' double smoothing. Single
smoothing is defined for z-days when y = 1.

Figure 3 is a high-low-close bar graph of Amerada Hess with
subgraphs of the divergence indicator and true strength index.
Single smoothing (exponential moving average) of momentum
is displayed for a moving window of 300 days. The divergence
indicator appears to be an excellent replica of the price curve.
There are no divergences between price and the large window
moving average; the shapes of the curves track each other well.
The true strength index plotted on the graph does not track in the
same manner due to the scale compression resulting from
amplitude normalization (the denominator in the true strength
index formula). However, the position of turning points and
secondary maxima and minima are preserved. Scale changes
produce changes in the relative size of peaks and valleys, giving
birth to divergences between the true strength index and the price
curve — for example, mid-April to early June. In addition, note
that the trendline appearing on the price curve is preserved in
both the divergence indicator and true strength index subgraphs.
In the latter, the scale compression of the true strength index has
changed the slope of the trendline.

Figure 4 introduces double smoothing to the 300-day moving
average. In this example, the second smoothing is for nine days.
The shapes of the respective curves are preserved with rapidly
fluctuating noise removed and with low lag of turning points.
Both the 300-day DI and true strength index can be viewed as
being reasonably smooth replicas of the price curve. See Figure
5 for a magnified section of Figure 4, with the DI closely tracking
the exponential moving average (EMA) of the close. The true
strength index also tracks the EMA of the close with the added
feature of a down divergence.

T he next step in our iteration is to reduce the large
moving average from 300 days to 100 days while
maintaining the second smoothing of nine days, as
can be seen in Figure 6. The DI and true strength
index now appear to be shaped approximately the same, although their respective amplitude scales are different. Both
exhibit the same trending and divergence characteristics. In this
sense, the true strength index with its desirable normalization is
thus justified, permitting many price curves to be compared on
the same numeric scale (see also Figure 2).

TRADING AND DOUBLE SMOOTHING
As a consequence of double smoothing, the true strength index
appears to have many characteristics suitable for trading found
also in the moving average convergence/divergence (MACD)
indicator. The true strength index is very smooth and is usually
more timely than moving averages taken directly on price. A
timely trend of price can be obtained by selecting the two

smoothing intervals. Divergence between the true strength index and price usually signals a price reversal, although the amount of movement in the new direction is not specified. The index has overbought and oversold regions that flag imminent price reversals based on prior price performance.

To demonstrate the index as a component of a trading system, look at Genentec in Figure 7. (However, this example is not a complete trading system, nor should it be construed as such.) The trend is defined by a true strength index with double-smoothing values of 100 and 20 days, respectively. A true strength index uptrend results from mid-August to mid-November. The aim, of course, is to buy low and sell high. In this example, the bottom curve will give us an entry time to buy; the sell signal, however, is late, occurring in the second week of November, well past the price peak. To alleviate this situation, a fast oscillator is used for entry/exit purposes with the "slow" trending true strength index. The oscillator selected in this example is a "fast" version of the true strength index, having double smoothings of 20 and six days, respectively (the middle graph of Figure 7). The indicator component of the trading system consists of a fast true strength index for entry/exit with a slow index trend. Three possible buy entries in the direction of the slow index uptrend can be seen. A down divergence appears in the overbought region of the fast index (note the overbought basis line at +40). The sell exit signal immediately follows the divergence and is timely, occurring at the peak.

Pretty much the same results for Genentec can be obtained in Figure 8 with a slightly different method. Again, a fast index with 20 and six days of double smoothing is employed. The trend is obtained by taking a 20-day EMA of the fast true strength index. Another example can be seen in Figure 9 for the Dow Jones Industrial Average (DJIA), using the fast/slow true strength index method. Timeliness of entry and exit points is crucial.

The fast oscillator selected for entry/exit may be a particular favorite, such as the slow stochastic %D or the MACD. You may also employ a fast version of the Ds_stochastic (double-smoothed stochastic) indicator. These are useful in that they are all mutually competitive in regard to timeliness (low lag) and are relatively smooth indicators. Timeliness is present in J. Welles Wilder's RSI and Donald Lambert's Commodity Channel Index (CCI) but at the expense of (usually) jittery noiselike fluctuations.

CONCLUDING REMARKS

The true strength index provides avenues for a variety of trading systems, limited only by the trader's imagination. It permits trending; it maps price onto a numeric scale for absolute comparison of price with historic price; it is, more or less, invariant in its usefulness with any particular security, whether hourly, daily, weekly or monthly data; for example, double true strength index smoothing of 25 and 13 days produces substantially similar results in trending. I suggest the following double smoothing parameters: fast-TRSI using a double-exponential smoothing of 20 and six days; slow-TRSI using a double-exponential smoothing of 40 and 20 days; and the slower-TRSI

FIGURE 5

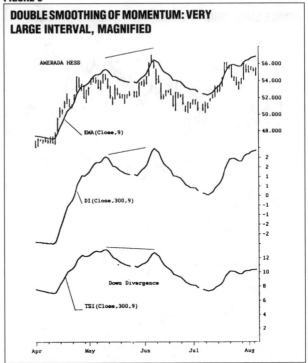

DOUBLE SMOOTHING OF MOMENTUM: VERY LARGE INTERVAL, MAGNIFIED

Here's a magnified view of Figure 4.

using a double exponential smoothing of 80 and 40 days. These are *suggested* numbers and are not appropriate for everyone. The numbers are a trade-off, which is different for each individual. Lag, as usual, is the unseen enemy.

William Blau, (407) 368-9095, is an independent futures trader.

REFERENCES

Appel, Gerald [1985]. *The Moving Average Convergence-Divergence Trading Method,* Advanced Version, Scientific Investment Systems.

Blau, William [1991]. "True strength index," *Technical Analysis of* STOCKS & COMMODITIES, Volume 9: November.

_____ [1991]. "Double-smoothed stochastics," *Technical Analysis of* STOCKS & COMMODITIES, Volume 9: January.

Lambert, Donald R. [1983]. "Commodity Channel Index: Tool for trading cyclic trends," *Technical Analysis of* STOCKS & COMMODITIES, Volume 1: Chapter 5.

Lane, George C. [1984]. "Lane's stochastics," *Technical Analysis of* STOCKS & COMMODITIES, Volume 2: Chapter 3.

Wilder, J. Welles [1978]. *New Concepts in Technical Trading Systems,* Trend Research.

FIGURE 6

DOUBLE SMOOTHING OF MOMENTUM: SMALLER INTERVAL

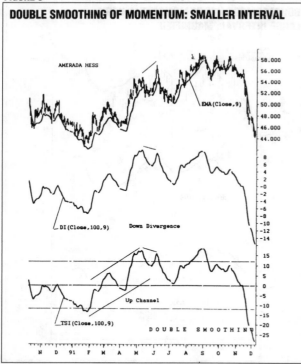

A reduction in smoothing interval to 100 days and nine days produces a divergence in the DI momentum where it did not exist before. Except for scaling, the DI and true strength index appear almost identical.

FIGURE 7

TRADING: FAST AND SLOW TRUE STRENGTH INDEX

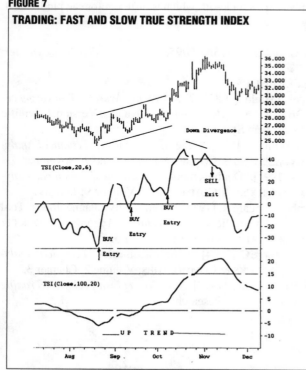

As a component of a trading system, a slow TRSI (close,100,20) defines a trend. A fast TRSI (close,20,6) selects entry/exit points. Smoothness of the true strength index, divergence property and overbought/oversold scale all aid in timely trading.

FIGURE 8

TRUE STRENGTH INDEX TRADING EXAMPLE

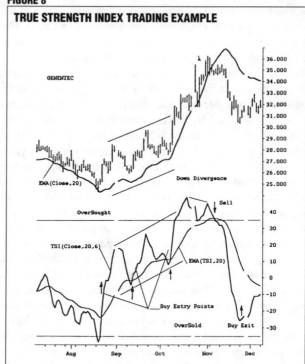

A fast TRSI (close,20,6) defines entry and exit points. Moving average of true strength index defines the trend.

FIGURE 9

TRUE STRENGTH INDEX TRADING EXAMPLE: DJIA

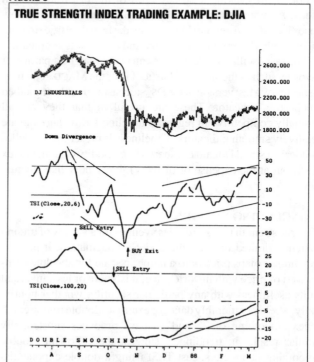

Here's another trading example, this time using the DJIA.

CALCULATING TrSI

Calculating the true strength index requires an introduction to exponentially smoothed moving averages (EMA):

Exponential Moving Average—The EMA for day D is calculated as: $EMA_D = \alpha PR_D + (1-\alpha)EMA_{D-1}$ where PR is the price on day D and α (alpha) is a smoothing constant ($0<\alpha<1$). Alpha may be estimated as $2/(n+1)$, where n is the simple moving average length.

The one-day changes in price are smoothed using an EMA for calculating the TrSI. Momentum (Column C) is the net change in price for today from yesterday. Column D is the absolute value of the one-day change in price. The first smoothing is a 14-day exponentially smoothed moving average. The constant for the smoothing is $2/(14+1) = 0.1333$. First, the constant is subtracted from 1, with the result multiplied by yesterday's EMA value. Then the constant is multiplied by the change in price today and then added to the new EMA value. The result is listed in Column E. The next step toward calculating TrSI is to smooth the 14-day EMA smoothed value with a three-day EMA (Column F). The three-day EMA uses a new constant $2/(3+1) = 0.50$. The steps to the smoothing are the same, except the 14-day EMA values are being smoothed—hence, the term double smoothing. This result is the numerator for the TrSI. The numerator is also used as the standalone directional indicator. The denominator is calculated by smoothing the absolute value of the momentum (Column D) with, first, the 14-day EMA (this result is shown in Column G). The results of this smoothing is smoothed a second time with a three-day EMA (Column H). The final calculation to TrSI is to divide Column F by Column H. Each cell's formula is shown at the bottom of each column.

—Editor

A	B	C	D	E	F	G	H	I
Date	Close	Momentum	Absolute Value (Mtm)	14-day EMA of (Mtm)	3-day EMA of (14-day EMA of (Mtm))	14-day EMA of Absolute(Mtm)	3-day EMA of (14-day EMA of (Abs Mtm))	TrSI
910121	335.75	-0.9	0.9	-0.90	-0.90	0.9	0.9	-1.00
910122	332.55	-3.2	3.2	-1.21	-1.05	1.21	1.05	-1.00
910123	334.15	1.6	1.6	-0.83	-0.94	1.26	1.16	-0.82
910124	339.60	5.45	5.45	0.00	-0.47	1.82	1.49	-0.32
910125	340.75	1.15	1.15	0.16	-0.16	1.73	1.61	-0.10
910128	339.55	-1.2	1.2	-0.02	-0.09	1.66	1.63	-0.05
910129	339.60	0.05	0.05	-0.01	-0.05	1.44	1.54	-0.03
910130	345.20	5.6	5.6	0.73	0.34	2.00	1.77	0.19
910131	347.60	2.4	2.4	0.96	0.65	2.05	1.91	0.34
910201	346.20	-1.4	1.4	0.64	0.65	1.96	1.94	0.33
910204	351.70	=B12-B11	=ABS * (B12-B11)	=0.1333*(C12) + (1-.1333)*E11	=0.5*(E12) + (1-.5)*F11	=0.1333*(D12) + (1-.1333)*G11	=0.5*(G12) + (1-.5)*H11	=F12/H12

DIANE BOSTWICK

Forecasting Tomorrow's Trading Day

Using linear regression as a crystal ball for forecasting the market? After all, if you were to be able to determine tomorrow's high, low and close for trend changes and placement of stop points, it would simplify your life immeasurably. Can it work? Tushar Chande explains how it can be done.

by Tushar S. Chande, Ph.D.

ouldn't you trade better if you could "see" the future? A simple linear regression can provide an objective forecast for the next day's high, low and close. These ingredients are essential for a trading game plan, which can help you trade more mechanically and less emotionally. Best of all, a regression forecast oscillator, %F, gives early warning of

impending trend changes. The linear regression method is well known for finding a "best-fit" straight line for a given set of data. The output of the regression are the slope (*m*) and constant (*c*) of the equation

$$(1) \quad Y = mX + c$$

Here, *m* and *c* are derived from a known set of values of the independent variable X and dependent variable Y. The relative strength of the linear relationship between X and Y is measured by the coefficient of determination r^2, which is the ratio of the variation explained by the regression line to the total variation in Y. Here is a table to help interpret the values of r^2, which range from 0 to 1:

Range	Trend interpretation
$0.0 \le r^2 < 0.1$	None
$0.1 \le r^2 < 0.3$	Weak
$0.3 \le r^2 < 0.6$	Moderate
$0.6 \le r^2 < 1.0$	Strong

The coining of the term "regression" can be attributed to Sir Francis Galton, who observed in the late 1800s that tall fathers appeared to have as a rule short sons, while short fathers appeared to have as a rule tall sons. Galton suggested that the heights of the sons "regressed" or reverted to the average. Technician Arthur Merrill also had a good explanation in a recent issue of STOCKS & COMMODITIES, and Patrick Lafferty recently wrote on an application of multiple regression to gold trading. Virtually all introductory books on statistics have a detailed discussion of the linear regression method.

Successful professional traders emphasize the importance of having a trading plan. A trading game plan, much like that of a football team, clearly defines specific actions under different conditions. The linear regression method is very useful in developing a forecast for the next trading day's high, low and close based on the last five trading sessions. The method is general and broad-based enough so that it can be used with stocks, indices or commodities. The forecast is the basis of my trading plan: I can define what I should do if the market rises above the forecast high, falls below the forecast low or stays within the forecast range. This way, I can avoid being emotional and trade as mechanically as possible by having a plan to rely on.

FORECASTING WITH LINEAR REGRESSION

I like to use at least 10 days of data and develop a forecast for the high, low and close. The five-day regression is a good choice for short-term trading. You can use any length of regression you like. Here are the calculations with the daily close in a spreadsheet format:

1 Perform a linear regression with the first five days of data to obtain the slope m and constant c such that

X Value	Daily Close
1	Day 1
2	Day 2
...	...
5	Day 5

2 Forecast the next day's close with the slope m and constant c from step 1:

(2) Forecast close (Day 6) = $6m + c$

3 Record m, c and r^2 on the same line as Day 5. Record the forecast from step 2 one day ahead, with Day 6. Note when we are using five days' data, the first forecast is for Day 6.

4 Step the calculation ahead one day such that

X Value	Daily Close
1	Day 2
2	Day 3
...	...
5	Day 6

5 Record m, c and r^2 as in step 3.

6 Calculate the regression forecast oscillator, %F, as

$$(3) \quad \%F = \left(\frac{Y - Y_{Forecast}}{Y} \right) 100$$

where Y is the close for Day 6 and Y(Forecast) is the forecast for Day 6 from step 2 (from Day 5).

7 Record the oscillator on the same line as Day 6.

8 Step the calculations ahead one day at a time until the most recent day.

Technically, we can use the linear regression to develop a point forecast (single value) for the next day (as in step 2) or a range (interval) of values with a certain confidence level. The interval widens, greater the variation in the data and greater the desired confidence level.

I use the forecast oscillator, %F, to determine if my forecast is above or below the actual market data. Since

$$\%F = \left(\frac{Y - Y_{Forecast}}{Y} \right) 100$$

where Y can be any market variable for stocks, indices or commodities, %F measures the percent deviation of the actual value from its forecast. In a trading market, %F changes its sign before a significant trend change. In trending markets, %F tends to change sign early in the trend. I interpret %F in the context of the r^2 of the regression. A low value of r^2 plus a change in sign of %F is a good signal of a change in trend. Market extremes and periodicity can also be observed on the %F charts.

DEVELOPING A TRADING PLAN

You can use the forecasts to develop a specific trading plan to suit your trading style. I use the forecasts in several ways.

Forecasts as stops. I use the high and the low as action points. If the market exceeds the forecast high, it wants to go up. To trade with the trend, I put a buy stop a few ticks above the high. If the market falls below the forecast low, it wants to go down. Hence, I set a sell stop a few ticks below the forecast low. If you want to trade against the trend, sell short near the forecast high and buy near the forecast low.

Forecasts as intraday range scale. The forecasts provide a scale for evaluating the trading day. The market can stay within the

FIGURE 1

FORECAST AND ACTUAL S&P 100 FOR 1/20/92

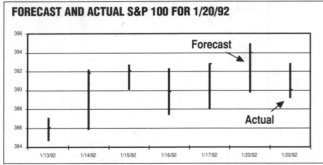

The actual trading day was below the forecast high, low and close for January 20. The forecast trading range provided a template for the day prior to the actual day's range.

expected range or go outside. On a down day, the intraday high is well below the forecast high and may be below the forecast close. On an up day, the market stays well above the forecast low and often above the forecast close.

General rules for trading with forecasts. Here are some general rules:

* Use the forecasts only if r^2 is greater than 0.1. Higher the value of r^2, the greater the confidence in the forecasts.
* A trend change is imminent when r^2 falls below 0.1. Prepare to close longs.
* A trend is in place if r^2 is greater than 0.6. As a trend follower, you could wait for this value to be exceeded before opening positions. This would keep you out of short-term fluctuations.
* An early warning of a trend change is provided by a zero-crossing of %F, the forecast oscillator. Prepare to tighten stops and look for changes in slope and coefficient of determination for confirmation.
* A change in trend is confirmed by a change in slope of the regression. Open positions in direction of trend change. To trade against the trend, look for peaks in slope and strength of the linear trend.
* The trend will usually change in the direction of %F.
* Always be prepared for a market move against the forecast. Use stops!

A SAMPLE TRADING PLAN

I have developed a forecast for the high, low and close for January 20, 1992, from the previous five trading days, seen in Figure 1. The market was making new highs the previous week. Was a downward movement imminent? Let's look at the data from Friday, January 17, 1992:

	Forecast 1/20/92	Actual 1/20/92	r^2	Slope ——1/17/92——	%F
High	394.89	392.83	0.56	1.16	-0.44
Low	389.87	389.30	0.41	0.85	-0.55
Close	393.99	390.06	0.45	1.15	-0.14

The market was trending moderately ($0.4 <= r^2 < 0.6$), but the

FIGURE 2

S&P 100 DAILY CLOSE WITH FORECAST

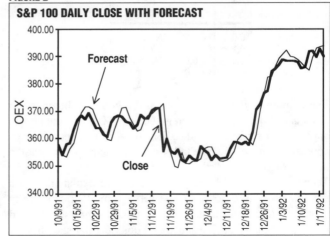

Forecasting tomorrow's closing price and comparing the actual close with the expected close can provide insight into changes in the trend.

FIGURE 3

OEX CLOSE: 5-DAY REGRESSION R-SQUARED VALUES

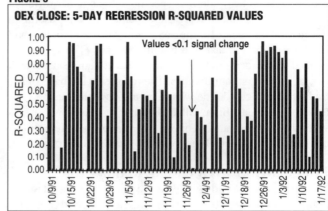

When the r squared values drop below 0.1, a change in the direction of the trend is indicated.

FIGURE 4

OEX CLOSE FORECAST OSCILLATOR

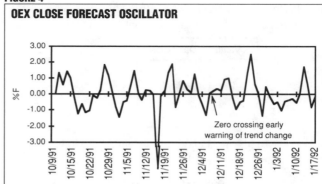

The %F oscillator is the percent difference between the forecast price and the actual price. The crossing of the zero line is an early warning of a change in the trend.

forecast oscillator %F was negative for high, low and close, warning of a possible change in trend. The relatively small slope of the regression for the high meant the market was meeting resistance. The slope of the regression for the close had turned down from the high values during the recent strong uptrend. The

FIGURE 5

%F FORECAST OSCILLATOR FOR S&P 100 INDEX

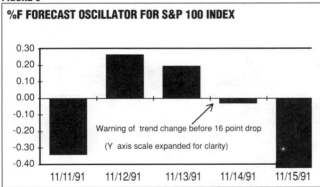

The %F oscillator shown during the middle of November crossed zero, indicating a new trend downward was beginning.

FIGURE 6

WHEAT (CASH) WITH FIVE-DAY REGRESSION FORECAST

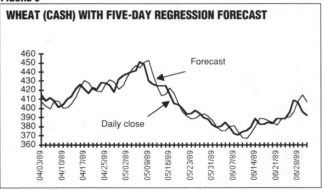

Other markets can be approached using the forecasting technique. The wheat market is presented with the forecast close and the actual close.

forecast, however, called for a strong close near the highs of the day, but that seemed doubtful, given the low slopes in a moderating trend. The plan was to watch for a change in trend. If the market opened weak, a bearish strategy was called for. For example, I would consider buying the Standard & Poor's 100 Index OEX January 390 puts, or selling short the S&P 500 March futures contract.

> **The high daily volume of OEX index options traded makes the S&P 100 index an interesting application of the regression forecast approach.**

The market opened at the Friday close and weakness was evident at the open, as the S&P 500 futures opened lower. It was clear in early trading that the trend would be down, as the market traded well below the forecast high and close. Clearly, the forecast range provided a good scale, since it reinforced the concept that the market was weaker than the trend of the prior five days. A bearish stance would have been profitable.

THE NATURE OF REGRESSION FORECASTS

The high daily volume of OEX index options traded makes the S&P 100 index an interesting application of the regression forecast approach. I have examined a time period from early October 1991 to mid-January 1992. The OEX close and its forecast are in Figure 2; the r^2 values in Figure 3; %F in Figure 4, and Figure 5 has %F around the mid-November plunge.

everal observations can be made from the OEX analysis. First, the forecast lags the OEX in an uptrend or in a downtrend. Second, the close and the forecast cross over several days before a trend change. This crossover can be seen as a zero crossing in the %F chart. Significant trend changes are preceded by trendless periods with values of r^2 near zero. Strong trends are accompanied by high values of r^2 and regression slope. These observations support the general rules of interpretation noted above. As

FIGURE 7

WHEAT (CASH) WITH FIVE-DAY REGRESSION R-SQUARED

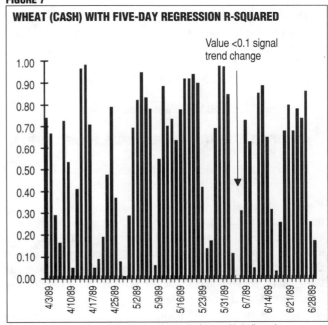

When the r squared drops below 0.1, a change in the trend is indicated.

FIGURE 8

WHEAT (CASH) FIVE-DAY FORECAST OSCILLATOR

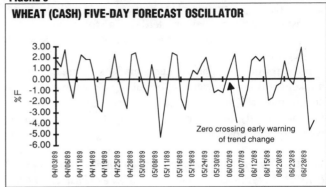

The %F oscillator crosses zero, forewarning of changes in the trend.

SETTING UP AN EXCEL SPREADSHEET

Following is an example of setting up an Excel spreadsheet for creating a forecast using a five-day linear regression for tomorrow's close. Sidebar Figure 1, Column A, lists the dates and Column D lists the closing prices (the Y variables) used for the forecasted close. Cells E1 through E5 are the constants used for the X variables. An Excel spreadsheet has built-in formulas to calculate the estimated coefficients m and c of a linear regression and the r-squared value. For example, the formula in cell E8 is:

$$=\text{INDEX}(\text{LINEST}(D4:D8,\$E\$1:\$E\$5),2)$$

This formula is calculating coefficient c, which is our constant based on the last five days' data. Cell F8 returns the value of the slope m:

$$=\text{INDEX}(\text{LINEST}(D4:D8,\$E\$1:\$E\$5),1)$$

The formula for cell G8 returns the r-squared:

$$=\text{INDEX}(\text{LINEST}(D4:D8,\$E\$1:\$E\$5,\text{TRUE},\text{TRUE}),3)$$

The key is the last value showed in the formula before the final parenthesis, as this instructs the spreadsheet to either return c, m, or r-squared.

Once you have the first set of coefficients, you can forecast tomorrow's close. This is performed in cell H9:

$$=E8 +F8*6$$

Finally, the formula for the forecast oscillator is listed in I9:
$$=(D9\text{-}H9)/D9*100$$

—*Editor*

SIDEBAR FIGURE 1

	A	B	C	D	E	F	G	H	I
1	DATE	hi	lo	OEX CLOSE	1.00				
2					2.00				
3					3.00				
4	10/2/91	366.05	363.31	364.22	4.00				
5	10/3/91	364.22	360.60	360.62	5.00				
6	10/4/91	361.50	357.34	357.34	Constant	SLOPE	R-Squared	FORECAST	FORECAST
7	10/7/91	358.11	355.81	356.25					OSCILLATOR
8	10/8/91	358.46	356.28	357.73	364.44	-1.74	0.72		
9	10/9/91	357.73	353.59	354.05	361.02	-1.28	0.71	354.03	0.01
10	10/10/91	358.22	353.28	358.08	356.91	-0.07	0.00	353.37	1.31
11	10/11/91	358.65	356.88	358.50	355.47	0.49	0.18	356.47	0.57
12	10/14/91	363.52	358.35	363.51	353.57	1.60	0.56	358.38	1.41
13	10/15/91	367.65	362.71	366.81	350.91	3.09	0.96	363.18	0.99
14	10/16/91	368.94	365.53	368.46	354.35	2.91	0.95	369.47	-0.28

Column A lists the dates and D lists the closing prices used in the forecasted close. Cells E1 through E5 are the constants used for the X variables.

Figure 5 shows, %F provided a timely warning of an impending trend change just before the OEX fell 15.68 points.

I have included data for wheat (cash) from 1989 to indicate the use of this approach with commodities. The market showed significant trends during this period with good periodicity, as shown in Figures 6, 7 and 8. The %F zero crossings were timely indicators of trend change. Features observed with OEX charts are also seen here; note in particular how %F can be used to identify extremes in the market from Figures 8 and 4.

Simple linear regression yields forecasts of the high, low and close for stocks, indices or commodities. These forecasts can be used to develop a trading plan. You can trade with the trend, against the trend, intraday or interday. The forecast oscillator, %F, provides early warning of trend changes taken together with the regression slope and coefficient of determination. This approach works best in trending markets or trading range markets; it is only moderately useful in volatile markets with choppy price action. These objective forecasts will let you trade less emotionally and more mechanically. Profits will look up when you can look ahead.

Tushar Chande holds a doctorate in engineering from the University of Illinois and a master's degree in business administration from the University of Pittsburgh.

REFERENCES

Lafferty, Patrick [1991]. "A regression-based oscillator," *Technical Analysis of* STOCKS & COMMODITIES, Volume 9: September.

Merrill, Arthur [1991]. "Fitting a trendline by least squares," *Technical Analysis of* STOCKS & COMMODITIES, Volume 9: December.

Pfaffenberger, Roger, and James Patterson [1987]. *Statistical Methods for Business and Economics,* Irwin.

Using Probability Stops In Trading

Does controlling losses by using predetermined stop-loss points help? To find out, Nauzer Balsara selected randomly moving average crossover systems and ascertained the best stop-loss points to use. Then he tested the system over different data. We present his results.

by Nauzer Balsara, Ph.D.

The goal of risk management is conserving capital — getting out of a trade without incurring too much of an unrealized loss. The question here is how much is too much? An unrealized loss arises during the life of a trade, representing the difference between the current price and the entry price. An equity reduction or drawdown during the life of a trade results from a reduction in the unrealized profit or, conversely, an increase in the unrealized loss on a trade.

When confronted with an equity drawdown on an active trade, a trader must choose between two conflicting actions: liquidating the trade in an attempt to conserve capital, or continuing with the hope of recouping losses on the drawdown. An unrealized loss might possibly be recouped by continuing with the trade instead of being converted into a realized loss on liquidation. However, if the trade continues to deteriorate, the unrealized loss *could* multiply. The aim is to be aware of equity drawdowns while simultaneously minimizing the probability of erroneously short-circuiting a trade.

FIXED-PARAMETER TRADING SYSTEMS

Fixed-parameter mechanical trading systems hold one of two key parameters constant: the time period over which historical data are analyzed, as in the case of trend-following systems; or the magnitude of the price reversal, as in the case of price breakout systems. While prices have a tendency to trend every so often, these trends do not recur with any regularity. Moreover, the magnitude of the price move in a trend varies over time, and no two trends are exactly alike.

While the existence of trends cannot be denied, there *is* a randomness to their magnitude and periodicity. This randomness is the weakness in fixed-parameter mechanical trading systems, since it is virtually impossible for such systems to consistently capture trends in a timely fashion. Ideally, a trader would want to use a flexible parameter mechanical system,

which adjusts its parameters in response to changes in market conditions instead of expecting the market to operate within a fixed set of rules. In the absence of such a system, however, a trader would have to make the best use of the available fixed-parameter systems. Under such circumstances, it would be advisable to analyze the unrealized loss patterns on profitable trades generated by a given fixed-parameter system with a view to defining probability stops.

UNREALIZED LOSS, PROFITABLE TRADES

A trader *could* analyze the maximum unrealized loss or equity drawdown suffered during each profitable trade over a historical time period, with a view toward identifying distinctive patterns. If a detectable pattern occurs, it could be used to formulate appropriate drawdown cutoff rules for future trades. The assumption is that the larger the unrealized loss, the less likely that

FIGURE 1

UNREALIZED LOSS DRAWDOWNS ON EURODOLLARS DURING 1990-91 USING STOPS, BASED ON 1988-89 DATA

	Without stops		Using drawdown stops	
	Winners	**Losers**	**Winners**	**Losers**
Six- and 27-day crossover				
Drawdown				
0 - 5	3	1	3	1
6 - 15	2	0	2	0
16 - 20	0	3	0	11
≥ 21	2	6	0	0
Total Trades	7	10	5	12
Profit/(Loss) without stops	$2250			
Profit/(Loss) using 18-tick stop	$(425)			
Nine- and 33-day crossover				
Drawdown				
0 - 4	1	0	1	0
5 - 12	3	0	3	0
13 - 24	1	3	1	3
≥ 25	2	5	0	7
Total Trades	7	8	5	10
Profit/(Loss) without stops	$550			
Profit/(Loss) using 25-tick stop	$(2550)			
12- and 39-day crossover				
Drawdown				
0 - 6	5	0	5	0
7 - 18	0	1	0	1
19 - 24	1	2	1	4
≥ 25	0	2	0	0
Total Trades	6	5	6	5
Profit/(Loss) without stops	$6000			
Profit/(Loss) using 22-tick stop	$6050			
15- and 45-day crossover				
Drawdown				
0 - 8	2	0	2	0
9 - 16	1	0	1	0
17 - 24	1	1	0	6
≥ 25	1	3	0	0
Total Trades	5	4	3	6
Profit/(Loss) without stops	$250			
Profit/(Loss) using 19-tick stop	$425			

All the testing was based on only the closing prices, and each of the parameters of the moving average crossover systems were randomly selected. The stop-loss points were selected based on testing from January 1988 to December 1989. The tables present the results of testing from January 1990 to November 1991 using the same moving average crossover systems and stop-loss points. Most losing trades in the Eurodollar market were cutoff by the stop-loss rules.

FIGURE 2

UNREALIZED LOSS DRAWDOWNS ON SWISS FRANCS DURING 1990-91 USING STOPS, BASED ON 1988-89 DATA

	Without stops		Using drawdown stops	
	Winners	**Losers**	**Winners**	**Losers**
Six- and 27-day crossover				
Drawdown				
0 - 20	5	0	5	0
21 - 40	2	0	2	0
41 - 80	3	2	2	14
≥ 81	1	10	0	0
Total Trades	11	12	9	14
Profit/(Loss) without stops	$15,112			
Profit/(Loss) using 57-tick stop	$20,238			
Nine- and 33-day crossover				
Drawdown				
0 - 20	5	0	5	0
21 - 40	2	1	2	1
41 - 80	1	1	1	1
81 - 140	1	2	1	8
≥ 141	0	6	0	0
Total Trades	9	10	9	10
Profit/(Loss) without stops	$15,688			
Profit/(Loss) using 120-tick stop	$19,287			
12- and 39-day crossover				
Drawdown				
0 - 30	5	0	5	0
31 - 60	2	1	0	12
61 - 90	0	0	0	0
≥ 91	3	6	0	0
Total Trades	10	7	5	12
Profit/(Loss) without stops	$19,738			
Profit/(Loss) using 53-tick stop	$ 8500			
15- and 45-day crossover				
Drawdown				
0 - 40	3	0	3	0
41 - 80	1	1	0	6
81 - 160	1	0	0	0
≥ 161	0	3	0	0
Total Trades	5	4	3	6
Profit/(Loss) without stops	$26,813			
Profit/(Loss) using 45-tick stop	$27,938			

Testing the Swiss francs showed that a number of losing trades without stops would have been cut off by the use of stops.

the loss will be recouped and the trade will end profitably. If 90% of all profitable trades have an unrealized loss value less than $500, a drawdown stop may be set at $500, because only 10% of all profitable trades suffer an unrealized loss greater than $500, mitigating the odds of prematurely stopping out of a profitable trade.

In Figures 1 through 5, we examine the unrealized loss patterns on profitable trades across five commodities between January 1988 and December 1989, using four randomly selected pairs of dual moving-average crossover rules. The commodities studied are Eurodollars, Swiss francs, Standard & Poor's 500 index futures, live cattle and crude oil. The optimal unrealized loss level is set equal to the maximum unrealized loss registered on 90% of all winning trades. These drawdown cutoff rules are then applied to data for the period of January 1990 to November 1991, and a comparison effected against the conventional no-stop moving average rule for the same period.

A dual moving average crossover system generates a buy signal when the shorter of two moving averages exceeds the longer one; a sell signal is generated when the shorter moving

FIGURE 3

UNREALIZED LOSS DRAWDOWNS ON S&P 500 INDEX FUTURES DURING 1990-91 USING STOPS, BASED ON 1988-89 DATA				
	Without stops		**Using drawdown stops**	
	Winners	**Losers**	**Winners**	**Losers**
Six- and 27-day crossover				
Drawdown				
0 - 50	5	0	5	0
51 - 100	1	2	1	2
101 - 150	1	2	0	16
≥ 151	1	12	0	0
Total Trades	8	16	6	18
Profit/(Loss) without stops	$(3050)			
Profit/(Loss) using 130-tick (or 6.50 index point) stop	$5175			
Nine- and 33-day crossover				
Drawdown				
0 - 50	3	0	3	0
51 - 100	1	3	1	3
101 - 150	2	0	2	0
151 - 200	1	3	1	12
≥ 201	0	9	0	0
Total Trades	7	15	7	15
Profit/(Loss) without stops	$(31,650)			
Profit/(Loss) using 192-tick (or 9.60 index point) stop	$(9225)			
12- and 39-day crossover				
Drawdown				
0 - 50	4	0	4	0
51 - 100	1	0	1	0
101 - 150	0	3	0	13
151 - 200	1	1	0	0
≥ 201	0	8	0	0
Total Trades	6	12	5	13
Profit/(Loss) without stops	$(17,100)			
Profit/(Loss) using 115-tick (or 5.75 index point) stop	$7475			
15- and 45-day crossover				
Drawdown				
0 - 60	1	0	1	0
61 - 125	1	2	1	2
126 - 188	1	2	1	10
189 - 250	0	3	0	0
≥ 251	0	5	0	0
Total Trades	3	12	3	12
Profit/(Loss) without stops	$(43,600)			
Profit/(Loss) using 167-tick (or 8.35 index points) stop	$(13,125)			

The moving average crossover technique produced losses, while the use of stops helped mitigate the losses.

average falls below the longer moving average. Once stopped out of a trade, the system stays neutral until a reversal signal is generated. Therefore, the total number of trades generated for each commodity is unaffected by the stop rule, although the mix between winners and losers could change.

DRAWDOWN CUTOFF RULES

The results are summarized in Figures 1 through 5. In the no-stop case, as the unrealized loss or trade equity drawdown increases, the number of profitable trades declines sharply, both in absolute numbers and as a percentage of total trades. The larger the unrealized loss, the smaller the probability of the trade ending up as a winner. Consequently, as the unrealized loss increases, losing trades outnumber winning trades. It is significant that this conclusion holds across each of the five commodities and each of the four crossover rules, supporting the hypothesis that unrealized loss cutoff rules could help short-circuit losing trades without prematurely liquidating profitable trades.

I n the case of live cattle and the S&P 500 index, each of the four pairs of moving average rules under review generates a loss. The introduction of a drawdown-based probability stop helps mitigate the loss, and this is true for both commodities across each of the four crossover rules. In some cases, the loss observed in trading a given rule without stops is converted into a profit upon the introduction of stops.

The conclusion is not as clear-cut when the moving average crossover rule is profitable. At times, the imposition of drawdown stops results in higher profits. In some cases, however, the introduction of stops leads to a profit reduction, or even a small loss. Clearly, drawdown stops are not directly geared to maximizing the profits generated by a fixed-parameter mechanical system.

CONCLUSION

A drawdown-based probability stop acts as a circuit-breaker, short-circuiting a trade when it gets out of control. The chief contribution of these stop rules is in the area of capital conservation, by not requiring a trader to agonize over unconscionably large equity drawdowns during the life of a trade. While drawdown cutoff rules are not guaranteed to improve the profitability of a fixed-parameter mechanical trading system, they may pleasantly surprise a trader.

Nauzer J. Balsara, Ph.D., is a Commodities Trading Advisor and an associate professor of finance at Northeastern Illinois University, Chicago, IL. He is actively involved in futures and options trading.

FURTHER READING

Balsara, Nauzer J. [1992]. *Money Management Strategies for Futures Traders*, John Wiley & Sons.

FIGURE 4

ANALYSIS OF UNREALIZED LOSS DRAWDOWNS ON LIVE CATTLE DURING 1990-91 USING STOPS, BASED ON 1988-89 DATA

	Without stops		Using drawdown stops	
	Winners	Losers	Winners	Losers
Six- and 27-day crossover				
Drawdown				
0 - 45	4	0	4	0
46 - 902	2	2	2	21
91 - 135	1	2	0	0
≥ 136	2	14	0	0
Total Trades	9	18	6	21
Profit/(Loss) without stops	$(7536)			
Profit/(Loss) using 85-tick stop	$(2776)			
Nine- and 33-day crossover				
Drawdown				
0 - 51	6	0	6	0
52 - 102	3	1	3	1
103 - 153	0	0	0	11
≥ 154	0	11	0	0
Total Trades	9	12	9	12
Profit/(Loss) without stops	$(4512)			
Profit/(Loss) using 115-tick stop	$1484			
12- and 39-day crossover				
Drawdown				
0 - 63	3	0	3	0
64 - 126	1	1	1	1
127 - 189	0	2	0	12
≥ 190	0	10	0	0
Total Trades	4	13	4	13
Profit/(Loss) without stops	$(9232)			
Profit/(Loss) using 162-tick stop	$(3756)			
15- and 45-day crossover				
Drawdown				
0 - 75	2	0	2	0
76 - 150	1	1	1	1
151 - 225	0	1	0	1
226 - 300	0	3	0	10
≥ 301	0	7	0	0
Total Trades	3	12	3	12
Profit/(Loss) without stops	$(9416)			
Profit/(Loss) using 249-tick stop	$(6220)			

The stop-loss rules helped reduce the losses produced by using a trend-following method in live cattle futures.

FIGURE 5

ANALYSIS OF UNREALIZED LOSS DRAWDOWNS ON CRUDE OIL DURING 1990-91 USING STOPS, BASED ON 1988-89 DATA

	Without stops		Using drawdown stops	
	Winners	Losers	Winners	Losers
Six- and 27-day crossover				
Drawdown				
0 - 102	10	4	9	12
103 - 204	0	4	0	0
≥ 205	1	2	0	0
Total Trades	11	10	9	12
Profit/(Loss) without stops	$11,030			
Profit/(Loss) using 61-tick stop	$15,950			
Nine- and 33-day crossover				
Drawdown				
0 - 132	11	3	5	13
133 - 264	0	1	0	0
≥ 265	1	2	0	0
Total Trades	12	6	5	13
Profit/(Loss) without stops	$10,450			
Profit/(Loss) using 35-tick stop	$(2610)			
12- and 39-day crossover				
Drawdown				
0 - 65	8	3	8	10
66 - 130	0	2	0	0
≥ 131	2	3	0	0
Total Trades	10	8	8	10
Profit/(Loss) without stops	$27,870			
Profit/(Loss) using 54-tick stop	$29,340			
15- and 45-day crossover				
Drawdown				
0 - 27	4	0	4	0
28 - 54	2	0	2	4
55 - 81	0	0	0	0
≥ 82	1	3	0	0
Total Trades	7	3	6	4
Profit/(Loss) without stops	$24,690			
Profit/(Loss) using 43-tick stop	$16,540			

Sometimes the use of stops can help reduce losses, while at other times a trade may recover to be a winner.

JOS PALMIERI

Computer Data Conversion

Computers talk to each other all *the time — except when* you *get involved. A familiar feeling? Ever have data you'd love to have on your system, except the data aren't compatible with your setup and you end up having to input everything all by hand? Well, you're not alone. Fear not, for Hans Hannula explains the whys and wherefores and how to convert that data to your needs.*

by Hans Hannula, Ph.D., C.T.A.

ot long ago, one of the major problems a technical analyst had was *getting* data. This usually meant hours at the library, scrolling through microfiche of back newspapers. Thanks to the computer age, that problem has disappeared.

Stock and commodities data of all sorts are now readily available. The shortage problem has now been replaced by another problem — data in abundance that cannot be used by your analysis programs. Back to square one.

The advent of the personal computer has given individuals the freedom to choose. But when it comes to data formats, that freedom has resulted in a Tower of Babel. There are dozens of data vendors and software suppliers that use different data formats. For all the hype, there is *no* standard data format. If you buy software from CompuTrac, it uses that company's format and cannot necessarily use your CSI data, for example. So your ability to profit from your own technical analysis will be restricted by your ability to convert your data from one format to another. If you can convert the data effectively, you can take advantage of any newly available technical analysis programs.

COMPUTER PRIMER

Let's start with some computer basics. First, I'll assume that you are using an IBM-PC clone and MS-DOS 5.0. I'll assume you know the bare minimum about using your computer. You probably know that data are somehow stored in files on your hard or floppy disk. And you probably know that you can locate the files with the MS-DOS directory command, DIR. I also assume that you know that there are two kinds of files, some that contain data and some that contain programs. The program files are those with a .EXE extension. Data files can be named anything. They are read and processed by a particular program, which must assume that the data are formatted in a certain way in the data file. For example, a charting program might assume that the data are in a format of YYMMDD H L C, for year_month_day, high, low, close. Programs can only read and process data arranged exactly as expected.

There are two different ways to store data in a computer — binary or ASCII. First let's talk about bits, bytes and binary. The most fundamental item of data a computer stores is called a *bit*. It can have only two values, 0 and 1. Physically, these values are stored on a disk as a positive or negative magnetic flux spot, much like the north and south poles of a magnet. In the electronics of the computer, the circuits use a voltage to represent a one or a zero. Typically, this is five volts for a one and zero volts for a zero. At the lowest level, the computer works by moving these information bits around and doing logic operations on them to perform the higher-level operations such as add, multiply, store, and so on.

To represent larger numbers, bits are arranged into *bytes*. Bytes are usually eight bits. Each of these bits can take on the two values of zero or one, so there are

$$2 \times 2 \times 2 \times 2 \times 2 \times 2 \times 2 \times 2 = 2^8 = 256$$

possible ways to set the bits.

This byte can represent one of 256 choices of numbers, computer instructions or whatever you choose. For more choices, bytes are combined into words. Typical patterns are two bytes, or 16-bit words, and four bytes, or 32-bit words. These permit 65,536 or 4,294,967,296 choices. One byte would have a hard time representing all the values that the Dow Jones Industrial Average (DJIA) can take on, but a 16-bit word could if we dropped the decimal fractions.

These bit patterns can represent a number system. If the bits are treated as columns of digits, each of which can take on the value of 0 or 1, one can have a binary number system. This is what computers use to add, subtract, count, and so on. Eight bits can represent the positive numbers from 0 to 255, or the numbers from -127 to 128, including zero. To do positive and negative numbers, one of the bits is used as a plus or minus sign. In 16 bits, numbers from +32768 to -32767 can be represented. This could handle the DJIA, but not the Nikkei. There are other formats, including various types of floating point numbers, but that's beyond what we need here. For now, just remember that binary is the way computers "naturally" store data.

In contrast, humans aren't binary. We use alphabets using considerably more than two letters, all manner of numbers and a variety of punctuation marks and special symbols. To represent all these, ASCII was invented. ASCII stands for "American Standard for Computer Information Interchange." This standard, now used by practically all computers, describes the bit patterns used to represent letters, numbers, punctuation and special control characters inside the computer.

In eight bits, 128 patterns could specify the standard ASCII

> There is a final important reason to use ASCII files: They are easily examined visually. For example, if you suspect one of your data files is not all there, you can easily print it to the screen with the MS-DOS "type" command or print it on your printer with the "copy" command.

character set, with the other 128 being available for special use by the computer's programs. The ASCII character set contains all the upper and lower case letters, numbers, punctuation and some standard control characters, such as carriage return and linefeed. ASCII files do not use the 128 special code patterns but restrict themselves to the 128 codes in the ASCII standard. Consequently, they are easily processed. For example, if you send an ASCII file to a regular printer, it will print out so you can see it. All such printers would, for example, recognize the bit pattern "01000001" as the letter "A." If you move ASCII files to any other computer, it can use them without any special software. So ASCII is the most portable, basic and universal way to store computer data.

Such flexibility *does* have a price. It takes more memory or disk space to store data in ASCII than in the computer's binary code. For example, to store the numbers from 0 to 65535 takes only two bytes in binary, but five, one for each digit, in ASCII. So why store data in ASCII? Because it is easy to edit and process. Every computer system has at least one and usually more text editing programs that can edit any ASCII file. These are used for editing the programs that run the computer, such as MS-DOS's "config.sys" and "autoexec.bat" files. So wherever you take your ASCII data, you can update it, display it and print it without special programs. Further, when programs read in data to be processed, they usually expect it to be in ASCII format and for numbers to be presented just as they would be printed. This makes for greater human efficiency.

There is a final important reason to use ASCII files: They are easily examined visually. For example, if you suspect one of your data files is not all there, you can easily print it to the screen with the MS-DOS "type" command or print it on your printer with the "copy" command. These benefits often make ASCII files worth their storage inefficiency.

Many, and perhaps even most, technical analysis programs store their data in binary, for storage efficiency. However, when this is done, programmers are free to use the binary bit patterns any way they want. So the data you may own or eventually acquire can be in any number of formats, and your software may use only one particular format. With several programs, you may need your data in several formats. So what do you do?

A CONVERSION TOOLKIT

There is no one way to attack data conversion. What you must do is assemble a toolkit and then attack each case as it comes up. To be successful, you will need:

1 A data editor
2 A directory manager
3 A standard format converter
4 A programmable format converter

For each data format, you need some means to enter, modify and update the data. This program is called an editor. Each data provider can usually supply a data editor for that data format. For ASCII data, the MS-DOS 5.0 EDIT program is sufficient. Every technician using an MS-DOS machine should know how to use this editor, because it is the basic tool used to configure and manage MS-DOS. It is fully described in the MS-DOS manual and is very easy to use.

A directory manager is used to organize your data files into groups. For many binary formats, such as those from Technical Tools, and for ASCII data files, this directory manager is MS-DOS

itself. With it, you can create, copy, move and erase data files. For some other formats, such as the CompuTrac and the CSI formats, you need a data manager for that particular format, because they use a special file called QMASTER to record which data are in which data file. For this reason, you must always move QMASTER and the related data files together when moving this information around. In essence, these formats duplicate what MS-DOS has done in its file system, which is understandable, because both CompuTrac and CSI began before MS-DOS was around.

A standard format converter is a program that can read and write data in a variety of formats. Basically, it is a format X to format Y converter. The one you choose should include ASCII as one of the formats available. One such product is Quote Butler from Technical Tools.

No matter what other tools you have, you will always need some custom programming capability to manage all data problems. This can be any programming language, such as BASIC, or C, supported by a compiler. Those are probably overkill except for the most ambitious technican. For average mortals, there exists a marvelously simple-to-use programming language named AWK (for Aho, Weinberger and Kernighan, the Bell Labs creators). This language was specifically designed for use by non-programmers to format ASCII files.

Ramona sulked — for Monty was preoccupied with investments: should he,
for instance, dispose of natural gas and move into pork bellies?

You can find a few details about each of these tools toward the end. I've also included some examples of how to use these tools to solve your data conversion problems in "Samples of use." Each problem is typical of the data conversion needs of active traders. Each problem can be solved with the proper application of a few basic tools. A little money and study time spent on these tools will pay you good returns for many years.

IN CONCLUSION

Data conversion is a necessary evil. It can be challenging, but if one understands the tools and the formats, a way to do the required job can usually be found. In the future, programs will not need to know how data are stored, as they will be using an object model of data, in which data are sent a request message and sends back the reply in the format requested. Such software exists today in academic and some commercial settings, but it will take years to filter down to personal computers. There is no substitute for learning a bit more about your data, acquiring some tools and digging in. Who knows? You just might make all that computer hardware, technical analysis software and data pay for themselves!

Hans Hannula publishes the Market AstroPhysics newsletter. He is an engineer, programmer and trader with more than 25 years' experience. He can be reached at (303) 452-5566.

SUGGESTED TOOLS

Quote Butler. Technical Tools, 334 State Street, Suite 202, Los

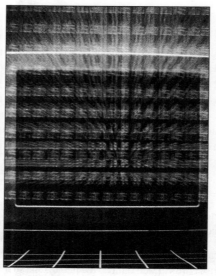

Altos, CA 94022 (415) 948-6124.
Price: $199 list
This program converts data to and from various formats, including ASCII, CompuTrac, Metastock, and CSI. The program runs on MS-DOS. It is entirely menu-driven and can use a mouse but does not require one. The manual is well-written and clear. Operation was very easy and straightforward. Customer support was very good.

AWK. Mortice Kern Systems Inc., 43 Bridgeport Rd., East Waterloo, Ontario Canada, N2J 2J4 (519) 884-2251.
Price: $99 list, $66 street
MKS AWK is a versatile first language and a sophisticated data retrieval and report generation tool. AWK is an easy-to-learn language, clearly described in a 45-page tutorial. The manual is an excellent language manual and is especially suited for non-programmers. AWK is used worldwide in UNIX systems as the "super-glue" that holds all the other software together.

EDIT. Part of MS-DOS 5.0 upgrade. Microsoft Corporation, One Microsoft Way, Redmond, WA 98052-6399.
Price: $100 list, $64 street
MS-DOS 5.0 upgrade enhances PC systems by providing more memory for applications and better memory management. It also provides a number of improved utilities, the most significant of which is EDIT. EDIT is a simple-to-use, what-you-see-is-what-you-get screen-based text editor. The 18-page chapter in the MS-DOS manual explains usage. This is the editor that should have been in DOS 1.0. ▣

SAMPLES OF USE

Problem 1

You have CompuTrac data, and you want to use GannTrader 2 with CSI format input.

This problem is easy, thanks to Technical Tool's Quote Butler, which is a general purpose data conversion program. It inputs, converts and exports data in the following formats:

> ★ CSI; CompuTrac 5; Lotus 1-2-3; Symphony; comma, tab or field-delimited ASCII; Technical Tools; Future Source; Market Research Language; DollarLink; Chartwolf bar; Gauss; Signal DBC; Master Chartist; DynaTrack; CodeWorks tick; Dow Jones; Indexia; AIQ Expert; Coast Investments; ComStock Tickers; Futures Market Analyst; Ensign; Metastock 5 and Metastock 7.

To handle this problem, start Quote Butler, and follow the menus to select your input format and file name and your output format and file name. As long as your data formats are one of those that Quote Butler handles, your conversion problems are handled easily.

Problem 2

Suppose you got your start in computerized analysis with the free STOCKS & COMMODITIES magazine Access, Plot, and EXport (APEX) software. This set of programs allows you to collect data from Warner Computer, do various technical analysis on and plot the data. This software stores data in a binary format. Fortunately, it will also allow you to export data in ASCII comma delimited, ASCII space delimited, Lotus WKS spreadsheet, DIF spreadsheet and CompuTrac formats. You now want to use the data with a trading system that can accept ASCII, CSI or TechTools format data, such as the Trading System Toolkit (TSTK).

There *are* a couple of options. You could export the data in CompuTrac format and then use Quote Butler to convert to TechTools format. That approach would make sense if you were switching over to use TechTools for all your data collection. Or you could export in ASCII and convert the APEX ASCII output to the .HLC ASCII format required by the TSTK. This format requires a space-separated line of month day year (with19xx or 20xx) volume high low close. For example, a line might look like:

> 12 31 1989 12345 2945.62 2935.12 2940.33

To get started, we run the APEX software, select Export, select ASCII delimited data, choose the TRNE21 data file and do the export to an ASCII file, called TRNE21.asc. This file would look like this:

YYMMDD	OPEN	HIGH	LOW	CLOSE	VOL	O I
880104	87.563	89.5	87.125	88.313	2555680	273704
880105	88.469	89.719	88.406	88.938	3278060	280677
880106	89.156	89.344	88.031	88.125	2776270	284352
880107	87.813	88.375	87.406	88.219	3233760	286742
880108	88.375	88.563	86.281	86.313	3296280	293372

We can look at these data by using the MS-DOS "type" command, or we can print it by entering

```
copy trne21.asc lpt1:
```

which will send the file to the printer. Also, we can edit this data using the MS-DOS editor by entering

```
edit trne21.asc
```

So we now have the data in a format easily handled by MS-DOS tools. But we aren't done. We still can't use the data with the TSTK program. It is not in the format required. The needed information is present but there is an extra header line and the date is all packed together, and we don't need the open interest. Are we stuck? No. This is what AWK was made for. AWK reads a line from a file, treats each string of characters separated by spaces as a field named $1, $2, $3, and so on and then executes every line of your AWK program on that line of the file. ASCII to ASCII conversions are trivial using the print and substring commands. To convert the APEX input format above to the needed .HLC format, the AWK program is

```
{ print substr($1,3,2) " " substr($1,5,2) " 19"
substr($1,1,2) " " $6 " " $2 " " $3 " " $4 }
```

The function substr($1,3,2) reads two characters from field 1, starting at character 3. AWK will take this one line program and execute it on each line of our trne21.asc file. This works for all except the first line, which we simply want to skip. AWK has a special command, BEGIN, which can be used to specify certain actions to be done before processing the input file. In this case, adding a line

```
BEGIN { getline }
```

to our AWK conversion program will remove the header line. So the whole conversion program is:

```
BEGIN { getline }

{ print substr($1,3,2) " " substr($1,5,2) " 19"
substr($1,1,2) " " $6 " " $2 " " $3 " " $4 }
```

To create this AWK program, we would use the MS-DOS EDIT program and just type in the two lines, and save the file, perhaps with a file name such as apex2tst.awk. Then to run this conversion program, we would enter

```
awk871 -f apex2tst.awk <trne21.asc >trne21.hlc
```

This will run the AWK language interpreter, awk871. It will read in your AWK program from file apex2tst.awk. This program will input your data from file trne21.asc and write the converted data to trne21.hlc. The resulting data will look like

```
01 05 1988 3278060 89.719 88.406 88.938
```

as required. This example is a template for most non-standard conversion problems. I've given enough details to show what needs to be done and what tools to use. With this, you should be able to handle any problem.

Problem 3

Suppose your data source does not have the 90-day Treasury bill rate. You have a CompuServe login and can download the data. You want to use the data in Master Chartist. You use your CompuServe Professional Connection program to capture your data in a file that looks like this:

```
               US TREASURY BILL YIELDS
91-DAY BILLS Cusip: 195              Exchange: Z
Ticker: USTBA

   Date                  Close Bid ——————
1 03 92                     3.810
1 06 92                     3.760
1 07 92                     3.790
1 08 92                     3.770
1 09 92                     3.840
1 10 92                     3.900
1 13 92                     3.900
Prices Available: 6 29 79 through 1 13 92
```

This file can be converted with a combination of AWK or the

MS-DOS EDIT program and Quote Butler. If you only have a few lines, as in this case, you can use EDIT to delete the non-data lines and convert the others to :

```
920103,3.810
920106,3.760
920107,3.790
920892,3.770
920109,3.840
920110,3.900
920113,3.900
```

This file can then be converted to Master Chartist format with Quote Butler. Note that Quote Butler needs the date in yymmdd format, but CompuServe has it in MM DD YY format. Editing a few lines to convert this format is okay, but for more than a few, AWK is the tool to use. Quote Butler also needs the file to end with a .PRN file extension. Also, it is most convenient if we have the data in a comma-separated ASCII format.

This conversion turned out to be a bit tricky, but I made it work by first converting my ASCII file to a TechTools .TDD file and then converting that to a Master Chartist file. The Master Chartist file is ASCII, so it can be printed. For this example, it looked like this:

```
01/03/92 0.000 0.000 0.000 3.750 0

01/06/92 0.000 0.000 0.000 3.750 0

01/07/92 0.000 0.000 0.000 3.750 0

01/09/92 0.000 0.000 0.000 3.875 0

01/10/92 0.000 0.000 0.000 3.875 0

01/13/92 0.000 0.000 0.000 3.875 0
```

Calculating Relative Strength Of Stocks

Heavy on consumer stocks? You may want to rethink your strategy and make some adjustments to your portfolio. Robert Hand addresses the shift of leadership early this year from consumer stocks to technology stocks, and how relative strength can identify emerging trends.

by Robert L. Hand Jr.

CHRISTINE MORRISON

Bear markets come in two forms, the more visible form when all stocks decline below previous lows several times for a total drop from the highs of more than 15%. The less visible form of bear market is often referred to as a sector rotation and is less visible because the changes cannot be easily quoted in television news. Sector rotation occurs when there is a change in leadership of an industry group. The stocks of the old leaders, consumers, are falling in value while the stocks of the new leaders, technology, are rising in value. Sometimes, a function of a bear market is to effect such a change in leadership, but recently this sector rotation has taken effect even though the Standard & Poor's 500 is reaching new highs (Figure 1). You'd miss this sector change completely if you didn't use relative strength analysis.

FIGURE 1

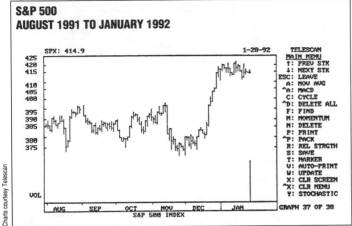

The stock market has continued its trend by making new highs in January 1992.

FIGURE 2

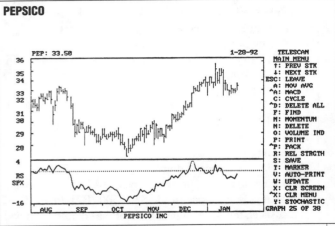

The relative strength line (lower chart) has turned downward, indicating that this stock is beginning to lag the broad market.

FIGURE 3

KELLOGG

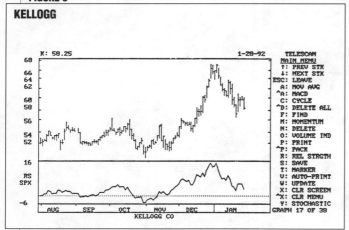

The declining relative strength line evinces that the stock market is outperforming this particular stock.

FIGURE 4

APPLE COMPUTER

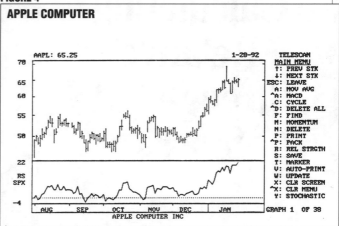

The relative strength line is making higher highs and higher lows here. An uptrending relative strength line is a sign of a strong stock.

RELATIVE STRENGTH MOVES

Relative strength determines how much an individual stock has moved relative to the market as a whole, so it detects underperformance. The formula used to measure this (see sidebar, "Calculating relative strength") is:

$$\frac{\frac{A2}{B2} - \frac{A1}{B1}}{\frac{A1}{B1}}$$

A1 = Beginning price of stock A, A2 = Ending price of stock A
B1 = Beginning price of stock B, B2 = Ending price of stock B

When relative strength is rising, the stock is overperforming, and it is underperforming during periods of falling relative strength.

The charts show how the current sector rotation out of consumer stocks into technology stocks is emerging just now. Using Telescan software, you can produce two charts in one, the top chart showing the last six months' stock price and the bottom chart showing the stock's relative strength compared with the

> **Relative strength determines how much an individual stock has moved relative to the market, so it detects underperformance.**

S&P 500. Consumer stocks such as Pepsico (Figure 2), Kellogg (Figure 3), Ralston Purina, General Mills, Johnson & Johnson and Quaker Oats are, for the first time in many years, showing a decline in relative strength, starting at the end of December 1991. However, stocks such as Apple Computer (Figure 4), Storage

CALCULATING RELATIVE STRENGTH

Calculating relative strength performance in a spreadsheet is easy. Our example, sidebar Figure 1, uses the closing price of Pepsico (column A) versus the closing price for the S&P 500 (column B). Any two items can be compared. The formula for relative strength is today's closing price for Pepsico (A3) divided by today's closing price of the S&P 500 (B3) minus the beginning closing price of Pepsico (A2) divided by the beginning closing price for the S&P 500 (B2). This difference is divided by the the beginning closing price of Pepsico (A2) divided by the beginning closing price of the S&P 500 (B2). In an Excel spreadsheet, the dollar sign in front of the column letter and row number indicate that the values are constant. In our

SIDEBAR FIGURE 1

	A	B	C	D
1	Pepsico	S&P	Relative Strength	Date
2	25.937	359.54		900702
3	26.250	360.16	=((A3/B3)-($A$2/$B$2))/($A$2/$B$2)	900703
4	25.906	355.68	=((A4/B4)-($A$2/$B$2))/($A$2/$B$2)	900705
5	26.625	358.42	0.0297	900706
6	26.281	359.52	0.0133	900709
7	26.187	356.49	0.0183	900710
8	26.656	361.23	0.0229	900711
9	26.656	365.44	0.0111	900712
10	27.031	367.31	0.0201	900713

example, the A2 and B2 are kept constant while each new day's closing prices are used in the formula.

—Editor

FIGURE 5

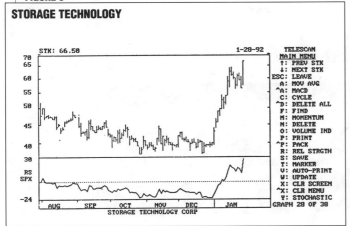

GRAPH 28 OF 38

The dramatic uptrend by Storage Technology is confirmed by the rising relative strength line.

Technology (Figure 5), Hewlett Packard, Intel, Motorola and Sun Microsystems emerged at the same time as superior performers.

This change has a precedent. We saw it in 1981 with oil stocks such as Amoco, which fell in relative strength after outperforming from 1977 to 1981. At the time, common perception was that the fall was simply a pullback and oil prices would eventually rise again, causing oil stocks to reach for new highs. It didn't

happen. Relative strength alerted the investor to the situation first. The new leaders were the consumer nondurable stocks, such as Ralston Purina, which had poor relative strength in the 1970s but achieved superior relative strength in 1981. We didn't find out until 1983 exactly why: Consumer stocks experienced earnings explosions in a lower oil price and lower inflation economy. Investors who were able to identify this change and switched to Ralston Purina from Amoco realized a gain of two and a half times more than if they had not adapted.

Your question at this point may be, Why change *now*? In January 1992, when the Dow Jones Industrial Average rose from 3100 to 3220, why did Quaker Oats fall from 74 to 67, Johnson & Johnson 112 to 102, General Mills 72 to 69, Ralston 57 to 54 and Kellogg 66 to 55? One underlying fundamental reason behind this change is that consumer spending is tapped out and technology stocks are the beneficiaries of newfound economic growth. If earnings growth follows up superior stock performance, these could be the new leaders. Take a look.

Robert Hand is an investment executive with 11 years' experience in New Orleans.

"You're turning me down? You'll be sorry when I tell Mom!"

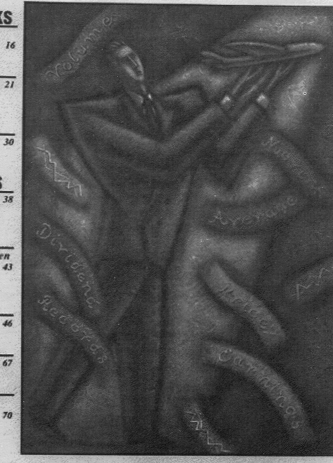

CHAPTER 6

THE TRADERS' MAGAZINE

JUNE 1992

TECHNICAL ANALYSIS OF STOCKS & COMMODITIES

Stock Selection

How does a veteran technician like Arthur Merrill select stocks for investment? He explains that it's not the simplest of methods and it does require research and work, but the results, he notes, are worth it—his growth stock index started at 874 in 1965, at the level that the DJIA was back then; when the DJIA reached 3169 recently, Merrill's index hit 15,149!

I have been asked how I pick stocks for investment. I have a definite preference for growth stocks — stocks that have been delivering a consistent and rapid growth in earnings per share (EPS). This preference limits me to specific parameters. It rules out turnaround situations, which can be profitable. It rules out stocks that are bargains because of temporary poor performance. However, adhering to the policy appears to outperform the Dow Jones Industrial Average (DJIA) handsomely over the years. I started a price index of a group of growing companies back in 1965, when the DJIA was at 874. I started my growth stock index at the same figure. When the DJIA reached 3169 recently, my growth stock

> **I have been asked how I pick stocks for investment. I have a definite preference for growth stocks — stocks that have been delivering a consistent and rapid growth in earnings per share (EPS).**

by Arthur A. Merrill, C.M.T.

index had achieved a level of 15,149!

I check the earnings record of each potential stock over the past five years. If there has been a decrease in any year, the stock is deleted from the list of potentials. I check the earnings quarterly over the last two years; if the EPS in any quarter is lower than in the same quarter of the preceding year, the stock is again deleted from my list. A regression line is then fitted to the earnings per share, and the most

FIGURE 1

RAPID GROWTH RATINGS: ALL NYSE LISTED								
Fundamental factors								
	P/E	P/E rank (1)	Capitali-zation (2)	Growth rate (3)	Recent growth trend (4)	Recent div. increases (5)	Ratio P/E to growth rate (6)	Fundamental rank
KO	33	-	++	--	++	++	--	23
FNM	12	++	++	+	-	++	++	4
CMH	20	+	-	--	+	-	-	31

Technical factors								
	Moving avg. relativity (7)	MW wave patterns (8)	Insiders (9)	On-balance volume (10)	Relative strength (11)	Institutions holding (12)	Institutions buying,selling (13)	Technical rank	Total rank
KO	++	++	0	--	+	+	0	8	9
FNM	++	++	0	+	+	++	0	3	4
CMH	++	++	-	++	+	-	--	12	28

For ranking, no. 1 is top score, no. 2 is second, and so forth.

rapid are pulled out for me to study further.

I use another limitation, that the stock must be listed on the New York Stock Exchange (NYSE). This rules out some fine over-the-counter stocks for me. However, I find there are plenty of qualifying stocks on the Big Board, and these are perhaps more closely watched and audited. I watch the earnings of hundreds that meet my standards and select 30 to 50 for further study.

RATING FROM ANGLES

The next step is to walk around each stock and rate it from several angles. Six are fundamental; seven are technical (Figure 1).

The fundamental factors are:

1. *Price/earnings rank:* The stocks with the highest P/E — most expensive — are rated with a double minus (- -); the lowest P/E get a double plus (+ +). The stocks in between are rated plus (+) or minus (-), depending on their position in the rank.

2. *Capitalization:* Stock price is multiplied by the number of shares outstanding to get an estimate of capitalization. Since large companies tend to be more stable, I give ratings from a + + for the largest company down to - - for the smallest.

3. *Growth rate:* Average growth rates are calculated from the slope of a least-squares regression fitted to the logarithms of the earnings per share. A + + is given to the highest; a - - the lowest and a + or - to the stocks in between. A - - is not a bad rating, since all the stocks in the list have rapid growth rates.

4. *Recent earnings trend:* Is the growth rate accelerating, or is it slowing down? The deviation of the most recent EPS from the fitted trendline is noted. The percent deviation is rated from a + + for the most positive down to - - for the most negative deviation.

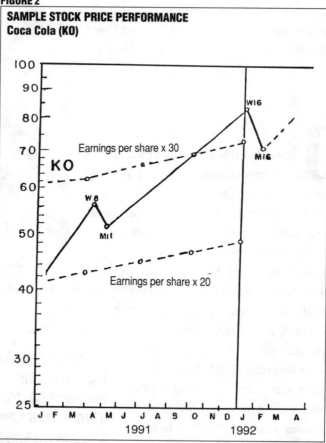

FIGURE 2

SAMPLE STOCK PRICE PERFORMANCE
Coca Cola (KO)

In these sample stock charts, all swings of less than 10% are filtered out. The vertical scale is logarithmic so charts are comparable.

FIGURE 3

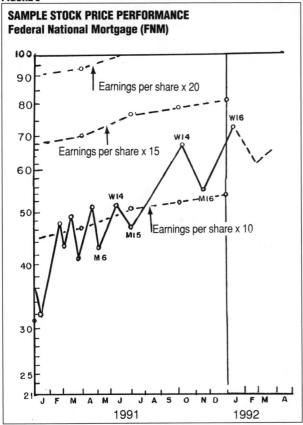

SAMPLE STOCK PRICE PERFORMANCE
Federal National Mortgage (FNM)

Dashed lines are earnings per share multiplied by 10, 15 or 20. To judge expensiveness, check the position of the price relative to P/E ratios (the dashed lines). To compare growth rates, note the slope of the dashed lines.

FIGURE 4

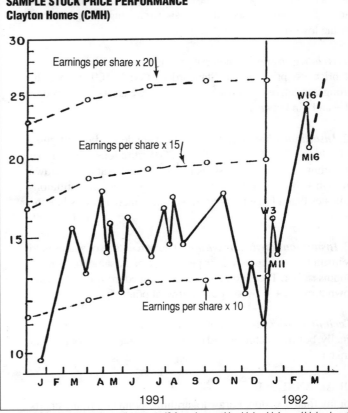

SAMPLE STOCK PRICE PERFORMANCE
Clayton Homes (CMH)

Note the trend. Are prices zigzagging upward? Are prices making higher highs and higher lows? Applying Merrill's rating system, both fundamental and technical, can help in evaluating a stock.

5. ***Dividend record:*** Stock splits and stock dividends aren't counted; only cash dividends are noted. The ratings are:

Three or more increases in the last three years:	++
Two increases	+
One increase	0
No dividends paid	-
Dividend decreased	—

6. ***P/E growth:*** Rapid growth stocks should deserve a higher P/E than those with a lower rate of growth. To rate P/E adjusted for growth, I use a simple ratio of P/E to the growth rate. The top 25% of the ratios are rated - -, the next -, the next +, and the lowest 25% is rated + +.

•***Fundamental rank:*** The plus and minus ratings are totaled for each stock in the list, and the totals are ranked. The top score has a rank of one, the next two, and so forth. Because of duplications, some ranks are skipped.

The technical factors are:

7. ***Moving average relativity:*** Michael Zahorchak used moving averages of various lengths to determine the trends of stocks. With

his help, I fitted his guidance rules into a rating scale. I compare current prices (C) with exponential equivalents of five- and 19-week averages:

Highest	C	5	C	5	19	19
Central	5	C	19	19	C	5
Lowest	19	19	5	C	5	C
Rating	++	+	+	-	-	—

8. ***M and W wave patterns:*** Price changes of less than 10% are filtered out, and the resultant swings are classified and rated.

9. ***Insider rating:*** I use the rating calculated and published by the Institute for Econometric Research. My rating scale reflects theirs.

For their rating of 9 or 10, I assign + +

7 or 8	+
5 or 6	0
3 or 4	-
0, 1 or 2	—

10. *On-balance volume:* I compare volume on the last five rising days with the volume on the last five declining days and rank the ratios. The ratios are scored from + + for the highest down to - - for the lowest.

11. *Relative strength:* I compare current price with a regression of price vs. price of the Standard & Poor's 500 index. The strongest relative strength is rated + +, the weakest - -, with scores of + and - in between.

12. *Institutions holding:* These ratings are derived from figures collected by S&P from more than 2,000 institutions. The number of institutions holding the stock is rated from + + at the top down through +, 0, to - - at the bottom. A large number of institutions indicates that a large number of well-informed analysts like the stock.

13. *Institutions buying or selling?* The percentage of shares held by institutions is expressed as a percentage of the same figure three months earlier. These comparisons are ranked from + + at the top down through +, 0, -, to - - at the lowest point.

•*Technical rank:* The technical factors are totaled and ranked. Finally, both the technical and fundamental factors are totaled and ranked.

FINAL ANALYSIS

For my final decision, I draw logarithmic point and figure charts and select for purchase those with prices that are zigzagging upward, with a P/E that doesn't seem excessive.

All this takes a bit of work, but the resultant stocks do quite well. Whenever a stock falters and reports earnings per share in a quarter lower than in the same quarter of the preceding year, I bite the bullet, sell and pay the capital gains tax. The result is a portfolio completely free of deadwood and packed with healthy, growing companies.

Arthur Merrill of Merrill Analysis, Inc., Elm #3325, 3300 Darby Road, Haverford, PA 19041, is a Chartered Market Technician and the author of many reports and books, including Behavior of Prices on Wall Street *and* Filtered Waves, Basic Theory.

REFERENCES

Institute for Econometric Research, 3271 North Federal Highway, Fort Lauderdale, FL 33306.

Market Technicians Association [1982]. *MTA Newsletter*, August.

Merrill Analysis, Inc., Elm #3325, 3300 Darby Road, Haverford, PA 19041.

Merrill, Arthur A. [1988]. "Computing curved trendlines," *Technical Analysis of* STOCKS & COMMODITIES, Volume 6: July.

_____ [1991]. "Merrill MW waves," *Technical Analysis of* STOCKS & COMMODITIES, Volume 9: November.

Zahorchak, Michael [1977]. *The Art of Low-Risk Investing*, Van Nostrand Reinhold.

TA

Global Analyst Mitzi Wilson Carletti

"I think investors should be looking outside the U.S. for investments for two reasons: to reduce risk by diversification and to increase long-term returns."—Mitzi Wilson Carletti

Senior research analyst Mitzi Wilson Carletti joined Frank Russell Company as a research analyst in 1988 from Merrill Lynch. Carletti researches, monitors and evaluates international money managers as well as assisting client executives and other research staff to develop client strategy recommendations. In addition, she oversees and is responsible for non-U.S. derivative and global tactical asset allocation research. STOCKS & COMMODITIES Editor Thom Hartle spoke with Carletti on March 27, 1992, via telephone interview, on topics ranging from non-U.S. markets to the ups and downs of the Japanese markets.

I'd like to start with your background. How did you get started in the business?

Well, from 1979 to 1981, I was an associate in the stock lending department of Merrill Lynch, Pierce, Fenner & Smith's San Francisco office, where I was also the liaison between the firm's New York office and the Pacific Coast depository. Later, I was responsible for order control on the options floor of the Pacific Stock Exchange. I then became a financial consultant with Merrill Lynch's Seattle office from 1981 to 1988. I came to Frank Russell Company in 1988.

Do you focus on some specific non-U.S. markets?

I focus on managers based in the U.K. and continental Europe. I'm also responsible for researching global tactical asset allocation managers and non-U.S. derivative products.

Do you think investors should be looking outside the U.S. for investments today?

Yes, for two reasons: to reduce risk by diversification and to increase long-term returns (Figure 1). There are three basic assumptions on which we base this recommendation: the first is that the low correlation between the U.S. and non-U.S. markets will continue. The second reason is that less mature economies are expected to grow at a faster rate than the U.S. Third and finally, two thirds of the world's gross national product is produced outside the U.S. (Figure 2), and world industries are no longer dominated by U.S. companies. We can take the top four producers in the world — say, in chemical or food companies — and the U.S. companies only make up maybe two of the top four firms in each of those categories. The others are overseas. It's not dominated by just one country outside the U.S., either.

What would be some different ways for people to invest outside the U.S.?

You can either buy stocks outright such as American depository receipts or in a mutual fund.

† See Trader's Glossary for complete description

Are there advantages to investing in funds versus individual stocks for the average investor?

One reason to invest in a mutual fund versus individual stocks is that you are only getting a small sampling of a market if you buy one or two stocks, so you could miss a market move altogether. Outside the U.S., the number of variables that an investor needs to consider increases dramatically. It is much more than just market or specific risk; the financials of one company may not be comparable to another company due to accounting differences between countries. You also have to take into consideration the possibility of liquidity problems and settlement differences, so it can be difficult to move in and out of stocks in the way you may have been used to in the U.S. market.

Are there other things to consider when investing outside the U.S.?

As I said earlier, there are a number of variables to consider when investing outside the U.S. Besides just deciding which stock to buy, an investor needs to consider the political and economic environment of individual countries and even what direction currencies may move. These issues are very difficult to address as an individual investor, so you can see that it is exponentially more difficult to identify the "right" stock.

Like the old needle in a haystack. You have to choose the right country first, right?

No, not necessarily. The country decision is just one of the factors that one needs to be aware of. Many successful money managers are stock driven; in other words, what countries or sectors they invest in are driven primarily by the decision of what stocks look attractive to them. Other equally successful managers' portfolios are constructed from a more macroeconomic perspective. The point is, none of these decisions are made without considering all these variables to some degree.

It sounds like quite a challenge.

Well, as you can see, it's very difficult for the individual investor to make choices when there are so many factors to con-

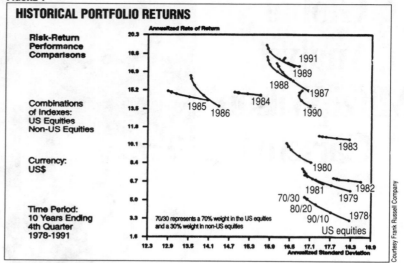

FIGURE 1

HISTORICAL PORTFOLIO RETURNS

Risk-Return Performance Comparisons

Combinations of Indexes:
US Equities
Non-US Equities

Currency:
US$

Time Period:
10 Years Ending
4th Quarter
1978-1991

70/30 represents a 70% weight in the US equities and a 30% weight in non-US equities

Courtesy Frank Russell Company

Historical portfolio returns (based in dollars) have increased, while the risk has been reduced by diversifying into non-U.S. equities.

sider.

And that's why you recommend looking at mutual funds instead?

That's right. I would look at a mutual fund, because you're hiring the expertise of people who are aware of and have taken into consideration all the different variables I've talked about.

The managers are better suited to handle the risks than investors. They can at least estimate the risk involved in their decisions.

Yes. The managers should have the experience and the access to data to at least make well-informed decisions. In addition to hiring the expertise necessary, you are also buying diversification rather than buying just one or two stocks; you can gain exposure to 50 or 100 different companies with the same amount of money.

Are there different kinds of non-U.S. mutual funds out there? I see country funds and I also see other funds that are more globally oriented.

Oh, yes. There are a number of ways to gain exposure to non-U.S. markets; you aren't limited to investing in just one country or region, or globally, for that matter. You can decide what best meets your investment objective. For example, an in-

vestor may not feel comfortable buying stocks globally but think that there is some merit to Europe 1992. A European fund would meet their needs. Another investor may not feel comfortable making those decisions about country and currency calls and would rather leave that to a professional. In that case, putting their money with a manager that invests globally would better suit their needs.

Are there differences in cost between buying, say, a regional versus a global fund?

There can be some differences in cost. It all depends on the manager.

Do you mostly look at performance of the managers when you're trying to determine what manager to use?

No. We look at four different things — we refer to them as the "four Ps": people, process, portfolio and performance. When we talk about people, our goal is to identify managers with experienced investment professionals, what kind of leadership the firm has, the continuity of the investment professionals, the environment they are working in and whether it's conducive to keeping an investment team intact.

What do you mean by experience?

Their educational background and prior

"Our goal is to identify managers with experienced investment professionals, what kind of leadership the firm has, the continuity of the investment professionals, the environment they are working in and whether it's conducive to keeping an investment team intact." Carletti with assistant Terry Pettit.

work experience — does it relate to their responsibilities, is it sufficient to warrant the level of responsibility, and so forth.

And the second?

The second "P," process, is developing an understanding of the important factors that drive a manager's process. For example, where does the manager place its emphasis? Is it in asset allocation/country moves, sector bets or stock selection? What are the criteria for buys and sells? What sort of resources do they have available to support the process and the growth of assets? What kind of valuation methods do they use?

And the third "P"?

The third "P" is portfolio, which means we focus on analyzing the source of the managers' return. Did it come from asset allocation? Currency/country allocation? Sector/industry weights or stock selection? We are continually monitoring investment managers through a variety of tools available to us.

Are you talking about their bottom line performance?

That's right. This gets back to process — we want to see if the manager did indeed add value and where. It's very important to know how the portfolio was constructed.

You could probably also compare just

the performance of the manager to an index, right?

Right. Which brings us to the fourth "P," performance. But you need to look at returns in two ways, depending on your objective. How a fund performed relative to an appropriate benchmark is important — but so are return patterns over time. An investor may not be willing to accept a manager with high volatility in returns. Someone may be more comfortable with a fund that generates average returns relative to other similar managers year after year, rather than a fund that is the best performer one year and the worst the next. It's important to look at returns over a period of time. For example, you may find that a fund with the best three-year record is being carried by one good year.

Are there any other points you'd like to make?

Yes. One of the problems with looking at returns outside the U.S. market is the lack of data. The historical data only goes back about 10 years, which is short relative to the U.S. market. It makes it not only difficult to compare managers, but it's also very difficult to identify a market cycle and make assumptions of how different managers may perform in different market environments. Basically, you don't have the luxury that you have in the U.S. market. That's one thing investors looking to international markets may find frustrating — the lack of data.

Do active managers tend to look like the underlying indices?

It varies. Some more closely resemble the underlying indices—country weights, capitalization size and so forth — than others. Japan has made up a large part of cap weighted indices since the mid-1980s. Because the Japanese market advanced to such high levels and reversed in late 1989, the Japanese market has had a major impact on index returns as a result. A lot of active managers were not willing to make that kind of a bet in one market. The average investment manager that underweighted Japan relative to the index went through a period of underperformance when that market was soaring but began outperforming the index when that market started moving

FIGURE 2

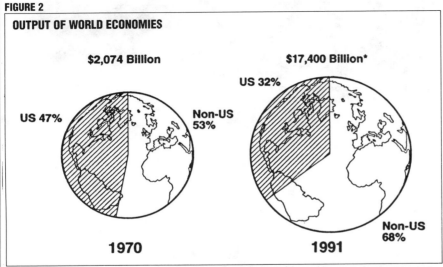

OUTPUT OF WORLD ECONOMIES

$2,074 Billion

US 47%   Non-US 53%

1970

$17,400 Billion*

US 32%

Non-US 68%

1991

Today, the U.S. makes up a smaller percentage of the measured output of the world's economies than it has in the past.

downward.

So Japan really swamped returns?

Yes. It's basically been a bet on Japan relative to the indices. Some investors tired of underperforming the index, so they decided to index their non-U.S. exposure in the late 1980s — just in time to see a reversal in that market.

Anything else?

I guess it gets back to setting your objectives and sticking with it. You need to allow for a reasonable time horizon in which to evaluate your investment and not try to chase the best-performing markets or stocks. How you want to go about investing outside the U.S. market is a personal choice — just make sure it's an informed decision.

The non-U.S. market is a challenging arena. Can we expect considerably more growth there?

We certainly believe so!

Thanks for taking time to talk with me, Mitzi.

Anytime, Thom.

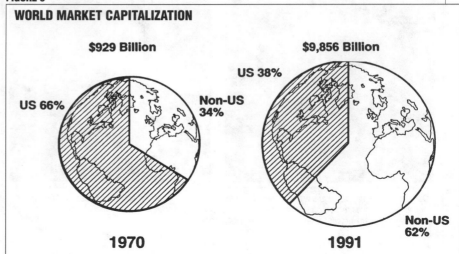

FIGURE 3

The total world market capitalization has less of a contribution from the U.S. today than there was 20 years ago.

"Set your objectives and stick with them. You need to allow for a reasonable time horizon in which to evaluate your investment and not try to chase the best-performing markets or stocks."

The Financial Volume Index Expanded For The 1990s

The financial volume index, which was first introduced by Patrick Cifaldi in the pages of STOCKS & COMMODITIES in 1989, takes on and uses the study of volume, surprisingly underutilized in technical analysis. The index combines futures contracts, the Dow Jones Utility Index and the Dow 20 Bond Index, and here, Cifaldi examines its uses for the current decade.

by Patrick Cifaldi, C.M.T.

I n the study of technical analysis, price data are the information most often used in research. Often underplayed is the study of volume, either by itself or in tandem with price analysis. Most often, volume is used to confirm that a price move is being supported by sufficient power to continue the movement. If volume is not sufficient (usually measured on a relative basis), then a warning that a change in trend is likely may be signaled. Volume is the gas that runs the engine of the investment. The more volume, the more gas — or potential for a move.

VOLUME STUDY

Of course, volume is not a new study. L.M. Lowry was one of the most famous masters of volume studies. His work laid the groundwork for those who followed. The most famous and flamboyant of the volume studies masters is Joseph Granville. His never-ending vigilance in continuing volume research has always been both inspiring and impressive.

I initiated the research that led to the development of the financial volume index (FVI) in summer 1987. I was employed by a regional bank as a government Treasury bill trader at the time, and I was leery of the equity markets' technical condition. In my own trading account, I had sold all my equities in July that year and tried shorting the market several times. Nothing seemed to work, as the equities were having an inverse reaction to a rise in rates. This type of configuration *can* occur, but with many of the technical indicators that I was following being in extremely overbought areas, I could not understand what was pushing the

equities up and could not begin to guess when the bubble was going to burst.

All this was happening around me, and it woke me up one night and asked, "Wouldn't it be fun to compare the volume techniques of Joe Granville to the recent modification that Marc Chaikin" — better known as the creator of Bomar trading bands† —"developed?"

Soon after, I hired a programmer to help design a testing program. I tested both Granville's and Chaikin's techniques on the Treasury bond futures markets from 1977 to spring 1983. The results were interesting, showing that both techniques had some very powerful results when used with a trading discipline. So what was I going to do with the results?

JOS PALMIERI

I had a tool and a technique, but I still needed an instrument to trade or at least to measure against such an index. Granville uses the Dow Jones Industrial Average (DJIA) to measure his volume research, but I wanted to work with the interest rate market, and there was no index for measuring volume of bond trades. There *was* one market that recorded volume — the futures market. The Dow Utilities and the 20 Dow bonds also recorded volume.

> **The basic premise in the analysis is when the FVI moves, it should be confirmed by a corresponding move in the volume signals.**

THE FVI

I called the index that I developed the financial volume index (FVI). I included markets that would represent the long and short end of the yield curve and two (the Dow Utilities and the Dow bonds) that would also represent credit risk. Over the years, credit risk in the municipal market has always been an important subject because creditworthiness can vary from one municipality to the next, and the Dow bonds have taken on the appearance of a pseudo-equity with the concerns of junk bond performance.

The FVI measures a cross-section of interest-sensitive investments in both price moves and the corresponding analysis of the volume. Classic chart analysis can be performed on the index, as it would with any price chart. This index allows what the analysis of most individual fixed investments cannot do: the analysis of volume.

To avoid a problem with convergence in the futures markets, I average the front two months of price data and continually roll forward as a contract approaches expiration. I also weighted the prices to compensate for the difference in raw data levels and volatility. The FVI (Figures 1 and 3) was originally and still is made up of and weighted with the following investments:

> 50% of the Dow Jones Utility Index
> 100% of the Dow Jones 20 Bond Index
>
> plus an average of the front two contracts of:
>
> 200% of the CBT Treasury bond futures
> 200% of the CBT Treasury note futures (10-year)
> 100% of the IMM Treasury bill futures
> 100% of the IMM Eurodollars futures
> 100% of the CBT municipal futures
> 100% of the CBT Treasury note future (five-year)

I then use Granville's techniques in monitoring the on-balance volume for each market. Each entity's price and volume readings are recorded and charted. The daily tally of price and volume signals can be charted to show how the index has performed. I then assign a +1 to each bullish short-term or long-term signal. Conversely, I apply a -1 to each bearish signal. A market may be between readings and if it is, it is assigned a zero.

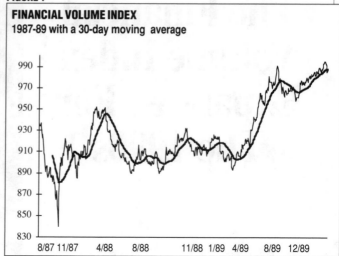

FIGURE 1

FINANCIAL VOLUME INDEX
1987-89 with a 30-day moving average

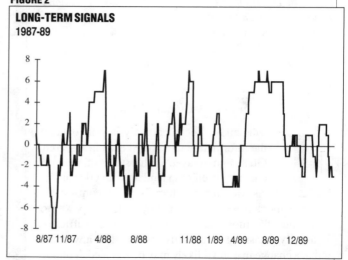

FIGURE 2

LONG-TERM SIGNALS
1987-89

In January 1988, the financial volume index formed a double top while the long-term indicator diverged drastically. In April 1989, the financial volume index fell below the March lows, but the long-term indicator did not. The subsequent move above the 30-day moving average signaled an upward trend in the financial markets.

I then keep a continuous accounting of the total readings (Figures 3 and 4).

LOOK THESE WAYS

I have developed several ways of looking at the index and its various components. The index from August 1987 to the present with a 30-day moving average overlaid is presented in Figures 1 through 4. Below each price chart is the corresponding continuous reading of the long-term signals.

The basic premise in the analysis is when the FVI moves, it should be confirmed by a corresponding move in the volume signals. The long-term-indicator alone has produced excellent results, but when used with other tools such as the 30-day moving average, confirmations of the signals become more reliable.

An example of how the indicator has worked can be found in

FIGURE 3

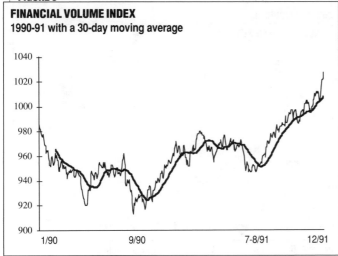

FINANCIAL VOLUME INDEX
1990-91 with a 30-day moving average

FIGURE 4

LONG-TERM SIGNALS
1990-91

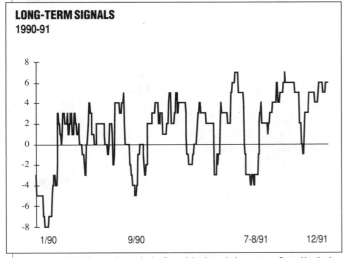

In January 1990, the weakness in the financial volume index was confirmed by the low long-term indicator readings. There was a premature sell signal in late 1991 by the long-term indicator that was quickly reversed.

January 1988, when the indicator did not confirm the double top in price, followed by a negative crossover of prices through the 30-day moving average, which precedes a drop in price and a rally in rates. In April 1989, when the long-term indicator did not confirm the new low in the FVI, a warning was signaled and when the index crossed over the 30-day moving average, a rally in prices and a drop in rates occurred.

I n August 1989, the long-term indicator held at a high level as the indicator started to break down through the 30-day moving average, suggesting that there was still some underlying strength in the index. By the time the long-term indicator started to break down, the price returned above the moving average. The sell signal finally occurred in January 1990 when both indicators were in agreement. The opposite set-up occurred soon afterward; in late February 1990 the indicator started to rise and in late May the bullish signal was confirmed when prices crossed above the 30-day moving average. These are examples of how the confirmation of the two indicators can prevent whipsaw.

In the closing paragraphs of my April 1991 article, I wrote: "After the August collapse, the volume indicator quickly returned to the pre-August selloff levels, indicating that prices should at least return to the trading channel that confined yields during the summer." I was happy that the analysis was on target.

As 1991 drew to a close, the long-term indicator gave a sell signal, which was confirmed by a negative crossing of the FVI through the 30-day moving average. This signal was quickly reversed and not too soon, as the federal government cut the discount rate and sent the FVI climbing.

LOOKING FORWARD

What 1992 holds in store seems to be at least a consolidation of rates, as the price of the FVI has outpaced its 30-day moving average by a substantial pace. The long-term indicator is having trouble moving to new highs. This pattern does not hold well for a continuation in a drop in rates and should it continue, more

THE VOLUME INDEX AND ON-BALANCE VOLUME

The volume index is a sum of each financial index's current on-balance volume (OBV) reading. On-balance volume is an indicator based on each day's change and the accompanying volume. If a market closes on a positive note for the day, then the volume for that day is added to a running total. If a market closes on the negative side, on the other hand, the volume for that day is subtracted from the running total. Each day's value of the OBV is plotted. The indicator is useful as a leading and confirmation tool to interpret the trend of a market. In Figure 1, the OBV for the bond futures contract is making a series of higher highs and higher lows (A, B, C). This movement by the indicator is viewed as a positive confirmation of the trend. If the indicator begins to make a series of lower lows and lower highs, however, then the reading is negative.

The volume index is the total of positive, neutral and negative readings of each of the financial indices that make up the financial volume index. A bullish breakout reading is given a +1 reading and a bearish breakdown is given a -1. The

SIDEBAR FIGURE 1

MARCH BOND FUTURES

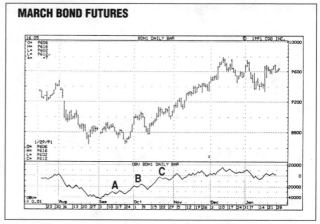

Points A, B and C on the on-balance volume index are flashing a bullish signal.

range of the indicator index is from +8 to -8. The tally is then charted and compared to the financial index.   —*Editor*

downside and then consolidation should be expected.

Volume studies should have more value in the future as new inflows of funds are recorded, confirming that the basic trend is still in place.

Patrick Cifaldi, CMT, was previously a government securities trader, wrote an international technical market letter and has been a speaker at CompuTrac and Market Technician seminars. He is currently quoted by Reuter and is a private consultant. He can be reached at 4201 North Lake Drive, Shorewood, WI 53211 (414) 963-1773.

REFERENCES

Granville, Joseph. "Granville Market Letter," (800) 874-0977.
Chaikin, Marc. C/o Bomar Securities, (212) 785-1160.
CompuTrac Inc. (800) 535-7990.
Cifaldi, Patrick [1991]. "Financial volume index and volume analysis," *Technical Analysis of* STOCKS & COMMODITIES, Volume 9: April.
_____ [1989]. "Financial volume index," *Technical Analysis of* STOCKS & COMMODITIES, Volume 7: August.

Chaos Theory And Neural Network Analysis

Do markets have memory? In this new theory by Edgar Peters, an offshoot of chaos theory, John Kean explains, markets can be regarded as nonlinear dynamic systems, and neural networks can be used to analyze and gauge behavioral patterns in price change data useful in prediction.

by John Kean

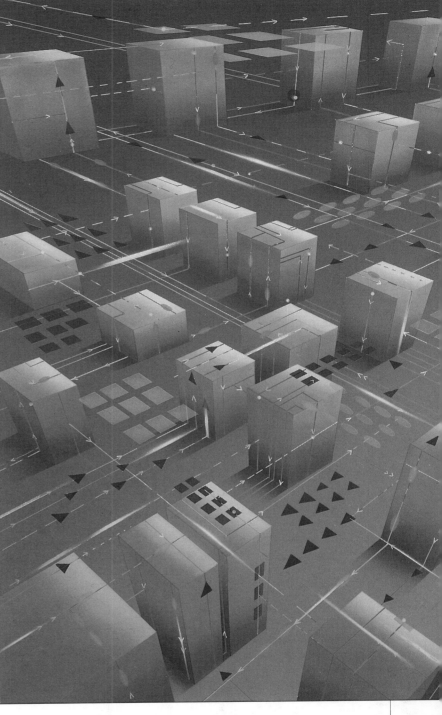

I t's convenient that, at a time when the behavioral natures of commodity and financial markets are being rethought, a new technique for examining the data has appeared. Chaos theory, in its infancy, challenges the statistically based conventional view of markets as unforecastable series of random events. A recently published work by Edgar Peters presents evidence that markets do have memory, which results in price change trends, compared with reversion to a mean. To the extent that markets are indeed chaotic, they are best thought of as nonlinear dynamic systems — complicated and difficult to deal with using normal analytical methods. Neural networking is a powerful new method of dealing with data that can provide a test of whether market prices are in any way prophetic, and so whether the conventional view of markets holds.

SELF-TAUGHT INTELLIGENCE

Neural networks are an advanced type of artificial intelligence in which the system teaches itself to solve problems. The internal methods by which the system performs its self-teaching had their origins in the ongoing studies of animal and human intelligence. The process involves furnishing the program with a paired series of input data that leads up to an output event, which in turn would be used to form a prediction. The neural network program then takes the series of inputs, computes its own outputs and compares them to the actual outputs. In the process of trying to get as many of the computed outputs within the given tolerance limits of the actual outputs, the neural program modifies connection strengths amid the neurons that make up the network and thus trains itself. A succession of runs is made through the data until the level of accuracy that is desired is reached. At that point, the "trained" network is ready to be applied to real-world situations.

To demonstrate how neural network analysis differs from other forms of analysis and other forms of computer programming, here's a simple example. In marked contrast to other computer programs, neural networks are the proverbial blank slate; they don't even come equipped with the facility to perform simple arithmetic. They have to be taught to do so. In an actual test run, two series of integers from 0 to 10 were randomly generated; these served as inputs. The two series were added together to form the output. Of the data, 80% was used for the neural program to train on to learn how to add. The other 20% was withheld as test cases to check to see if the training results were valid. The tolerances used were such that if a computed output were within plus or minus 10%, it was counted as correct (that is, the computed output of 5 + 5 would be counted as acceptable if it fell within the range of 9 to 11).

On the first run through the data, less than half the computed output in both the test and training cases fell in the acceptable range. But the program learned fast in the next 20 runs, rising to a level of about 90% correct. The program then went through 30 more runs before it learned enough to get all the training and test case-computed outputs to fall within the tolerance limits.

Obviously, the forte of neural network analysis lies outside of mundane math. The method has shown its greatest strength in application to messy nonlinear problems, such as those involving pattern recognition and modeling. Neural networks have been successfully applied to such challenges as speech and handwritten character recognition, medical diagnosis, flight control and even identifying and matching specific propeller sounds to specific ships.

PATTERNS IN PRICE

If the method has been successful in finding recognizable patterns in such natural and manmade phenomena, it should be a good test to determine if patterns occur in the price changes of financial markets. The Standard & Poor's 500, a much-studied index, was used in the following work.

Data for 233 weeks extending from March 18, 1987, to August 28, 1991, were used for training the neural network. Within those 233 weeks, 20%, or 47 weeks, were randomly selected and withheld to be used as untrained-on test cases. An additional 26 weeks, extending from September 4, 1991, to February 26, 1992, were used to demonstrate how well the resulting trained network was able to predict stock price changes past the training and testing time period. The data were set up so that 10 consecutive weeks of price changes were the basis by which to predict the ensuing week's variation, amounting to a pure test of the predictive capacity of price changes.

> **Neural networks have been successfully applied to such challenges as speech and handwritten character recognition, medical diagnosis, flight control and even identifying and matching specific propeller sounds to specific ships.**

The percentage of neural network outputs that fell within the tolerances for the training and testing runs is shown on an accompanying graph. Through most of the 100 runs, the training runs were getting a substantially higher percentage of correct outputs than the testing runs (Figure 1), implying that some of the associations of the trained networks were being form-fitted to the trained data rather than being true basic relationships that would persist outside the set of known data. However, between runs 87 and 92, the gap between training and testing disappear, indicating these runs were homing in on true behavioral relationships.

 un 88 was selected as the best, and the results of its output are shown with the other three graphs. Figure 2 compares the predicted change for the coming week compared with the actual change for some of

FIGURE 1

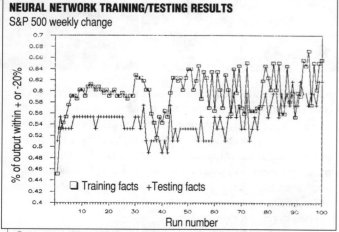

NEURAL NETWORK TRAINING/TESTING RESULTS
S&P 500 weekly change

Between runs 87 and 92, the gap between training and testing disappears, indicating these runs are homing in on true behavioral relationships.

FIGURE 2

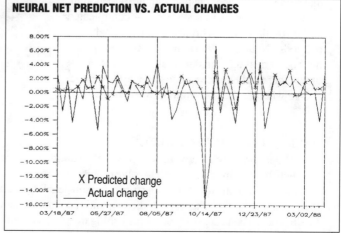

NEURAL NET PREDICTION VS. ACTUAL CHANGES

On average, the neural output tended to slightly overestimate the coming week's price change in the S&P 500.

FIGURE 3

NEURAL NET TRADING VS. S&P INDEX

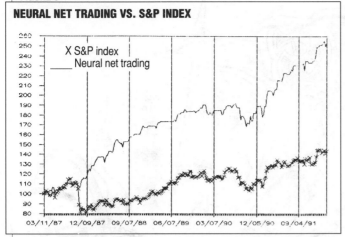

X S&P index
Neural net trading

03/11/87 12/09/87 09/07/88 06/07/89 03/07/90 12/05/90 09/04/91

The graph shows the results of weekly trading based on the predictive neural output compared with the Standard & Poor's 500 index. The graph covers the training period from March 18, 1987, to August 28, 1992, plus the ensuing 26 weeks, which was totally excluded from neural analysis.

FIGURE 4

RESULTS PAST TRAINING INTERVAL

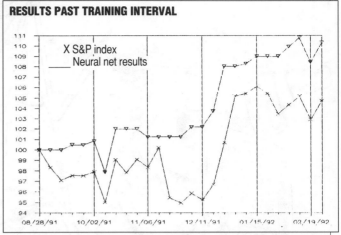

X S&P index
Neural net results

08/28/91 10/02/91 11/06/91 12/11/91 01/15/92 02/19/92

The trading results indicate that the neural network found behavioral patterns in the price change data useful in prediction. Not only were the results superior to the training and testing period, but they continued thus when the network for run 88 was used to predict past August 28, 1991. Predictive ability was poorest during the period immediately after Iraq's invasion of Kuwait, perhaps because of the element of the unknown involved.

the training and testing period. On average, the neural output tended to slightly overestimate the coming week's price change in stocks. The last two graphs show the results of weekly trading based on the predictive neural output compared with the Standard & Poor's 500 index (Figure 3). The graphs cover the training period from March 18, 1987, to August 28, 1992, plus the ensuing 26 weeks, which were excluded from neural analysis.

The trading results indicate that the neural network found behavioral patterns in the price change data useful in prediction. Not only were the results superior within the training and testing period, but they continued thus when the network for run 88 was used to predict past August 28, 1991 (Figure 4). Predictive ability was poorest during the period immediately after Iraq's invasion of Kuwait, perhaps because of the element of the unknown involved.

PRICES IN MEMORY

The exact method by which neural networks make their predictions is contained in a labyrinth of associations between the layers of neurons making up the network and is largely indeci-

pherable. That the test described above succeeded, however, indicates that predictive information does exist within stock index price variations and supports the concept in chaos theory that stock prices do have memory.

John Kean is a systems analyst who has been investing and trading for more than 10 years. He can be reached at PO Box 26,463, Colorado Springs, CO 80936, (719) 282-2027.

REFERENCES AND RELATED READING

Krynicki, Victor E. [1991]. "Nonlinearity, chaos theory and the DJIA," *Technical Analysis of* STOCKS & COMMODITIES, Volume 9: September.

Mendelsohn, Lou [1991]. "The basics of developing a neural trading system," *Technical Analysis of* STOCKS & COMMODITIES, Volume 9: June

Peters, Edgar E. [1991]. *Chaos and Order in the Capital Markets,* John Wiley & Sons.

Shih, Yin Lung [1991]. "Neural nets in technical analysis," *Technical Analysis of* STOCKS & COMMODITIES, Volume 9: February.

MIKE HORSWILL

The Link Between Bonds And Stocks

Intermarket analysis is based on the premise that all markets are linked. Last month, technical trailblazer John J. Murphy explored the inverse interrelationship between commodity and bond prices; this month, he examines the relationship between bonds and stocks and how bond prices can be used as a leading indicator for stocks. Take a look.

by John J. Murphy

Bonds and stocks usually trend in the same direction. However, it's not as simple as that. At important turning points, bond prices usually turn *ahead* of stocks. At bottoms, bond prices usually turn up before stocks. At tops, bond prices usually turn down before stocks. Viewed in that fashion, bond prices can be used as a leading indicator for stock prices.

The tendency for bond prices to turn ahead of stocks also explains the apparent "decoupling" that often occurs when bonds and stocks trend in different directions. What may appear to some to be a "decoupling" is an early warning to others who are aware of the interrelationship between the two. A dramatic example of that phenomenon occurred in 1987, when bonds plunged during April (coinciding with a strong upturn in commodity prices), four months before the August peak in stocks. During mid-1991, bonds turned up six months before stocks. Figures 1 through 3 compare bonds futures with the Standard & Poor's 500 index over three timespans beginning shortly after the 1987 crash.

COMPARING FIGURES

Figure 1 compares those two markets from late 1987 to March 1992. A strong visual correlation can be seen between bond prices and stocks during those five years. The bond rally during fourth-quarter 1987 led the stock market higher after that year's crash. Later, the double top in bonds in late 1989 contributed to weakness in stocks entering 1990. During the summer of 1990, a new high by the S&P 500 was unconfirmed by the bond market, paving the way for the plunge in both markets during the late summer. Both markets turned higher that autumn.

> **The tendency for bond prices to turn ahead of stocks also explains the apparent "decoupling" that often occurs when bonds and stocks trend in different directions.**

Figure 2 covers the two years from 1990 to March 1992 and shows bonds leading stocks higher during September and October 1990. The bond peak in February 1991 coincided with the onset of a 10-month trading range in stocks. The upturn in bonds during the summer of 1991 set the stage for the explosive breakout in stocks in December. The catalyst for that bullish breakout in stocks was the one-point discount rate cut by the Federal Reserve Board on December 20, 1991. The Fed's action pushed bond prices to a four-year high and stock prices to a new record.

Figure 3 shows bond futures leading stocks higher and then lower from late October 1991 to early March 1992. The downturn in bond prices as 1992 began (coinciding with a rebound in commodity prices) can be seen pulling stock prices lower. These charts suggest that the bond market has a strong impact on stocks and can be a useful tool in stock market analysis. It's also important to follow utility stocks (especially electrical utilities), which usually trend in the same direction as the bond market and also act as a leading indicator for stocks. Utility

FIGURE 1

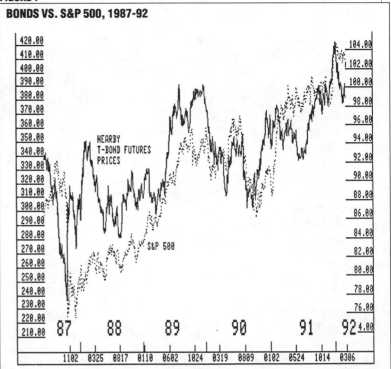

BONDS VS. S&P 500, 1987-92

Bond futures and the S&P 500 index generally trended in the same direction from late 1987 through the first two months of 1992. Bonds turned before stocks at the 1987 bottom, the 1989 top and the 1990 bottom.

FIGURE 2

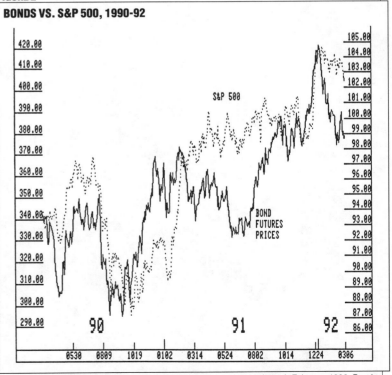

BONDS VS. S&P 500, 1990-92

Bond futures can be seen influencing the S&P 500 from mid-1990 through February 1992. Bonds turned up a month before stocks in September 1990. The bond peak in February 1991 began a 10-month trading range in stocks. The mid-1991 upturn in bonds preceded the stock market breakout by six months.

stocks plunged along with bond prices during the first two months of 1992.

John Murphy is president of JJM Technical Advisors Inc. and publishes the monthly "Futures Trends and Intermarket Analysis." He is also the technical analyst for CNBC/FNN.

REFERENCES

JJM Technical Advisors Inc., 297-101 Kinderkamack Rd., Suite 148, Oradell, NJ 07649.

Murphy, John J. [1986]. *Technical Analysis of the Futures Markets*, New York Institute of Finance.

_____ [1991]. *Intermarket Technical Analysis*, John Wiley & Sons.

_____ [1992]. "The link between bonds and commodities," STOCKS & COMMODITIES, May.

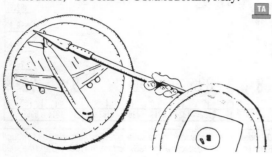

FIGURE 3

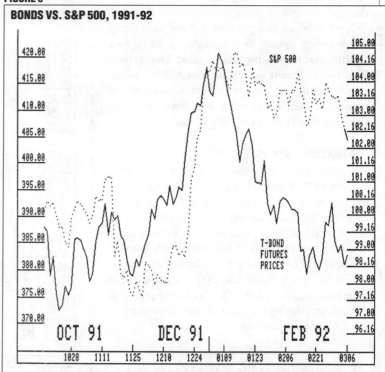

Bond futures can be seen leading the S&P 500 higher at the end of 1991 and then lower during the first two months of 1992.

CHRISTINE MORRISON

Trading Bond Funds

Bond funds have become popular investment vehicles for in-come-oriented investors. The bond market, however, is often much more responsive to news events, especially in times of high government deficits and international markets, than the stock market is. Therefore volatility is often present and can be extreme. As a result, technical intermarket analysis can be a useful tool in trading the bond market. Joe Duarte explains.

by Joe Duarte

T raders and investors must have an excellent knowledge of the underlying conditions that affect this market. It is virtually impossible to anticipate news events and how financial and commodity markets will react to them. By using key indicators that reflect the expectations and the sentiment of influential market participants, individual investors and traders can enhance bond fund returns by timing aggressive zero-coupon bond funds. I use the Benham Target 2020 fund as a proxy for the U.S.

30-year Treasury bond.

Because markets often trade based on the expectations and perceptions of the participants, I use indicators that reflect the views of large interests, such as international corporations, smart speculators and large institutions. These indicators meet those criteria.

GREAT EXPECTATIONS?

The average maturity in days of money market fund portfolios reveals the expectations of a very large group of well-informed interest rate watchers, short-term money managers. Their knowledge of the short-term domestic and international debt obligations market, both government and corporate, is reflected in the length of maturity of their portfolio. When they expect higher interest rates, they decrease the length of the maturities to escape holding low-yielding assets for prolonged periods and vice versa. This indicator is reported weekly in *Barron's*, *Investor's Business Daily* and *The Wall Street Journal*.

> **Because markets often trade based on the perceptions of the participants, I use indicators that reflect the views of large interests, such as international corporations, smart speculators and large institutions.**

Figure 1 displays the significant increase in the duration of money market fund maturities that began in December 1990 as the Federal Reserve began lowering interest rates. The trendline highlights support at the 52-day area: note how the retracement of the maturities during the period correlates to the sideways action of the Treasury-bill yield in Figure 2. The right side of Figure 1, which depicts the period beginning in January 1992, illustrates the money market mutual fund managers' response to expectations of a possible economic recovery and subsequent higher interest rates, leading them to shorten their maturities.

Figure 2 also illustrates the correlation between the trend in the length of money market mutual fund maturities and short-term interest rates as measured by the 90-day U.S Treasury bill rate. The year-long decrease in the 90-day T-bill yield stalled along with the decrease in money market mutual fund maturities in January 1992.

THE CURRENCY MARKETS

Currency values are often influenced by a country's interest rate environment and political situation. Currency rates often respond to longer-term interest rates. By charting the U.S. Dollar Index, investors can indirectly measure the current interest rate expectations of currency traders. This is a very large pool of money, and the perceptions of currency traders can lead to dramatic moves in other markets. An increase in the value of the U.S. Dollar Index is often related to the currency market's expectation of rising longer-term interest

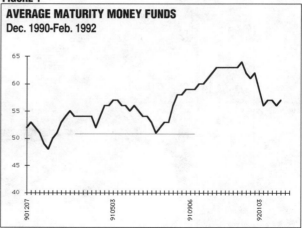

FIGURE 1

AVERAGE MATURITY MONEY FUNDS
Dec. 1990-Feb. 1992

Note the significant increase in the duration of money market fund maturities that began in December 1990 as the Federal Reserve began lowering interest rates.

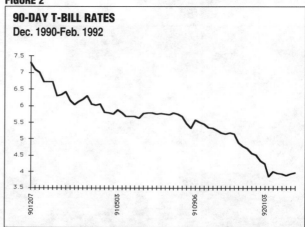

FIGURE 2

90-DAY T-BILL RATES
Dec. 1990-Feb. 1992

There is a correlation between the trend in the length of money market mutual fund maturities and short-term interest rates as measured by the 90-day U.S Treasury bill rate. The year-long decrease in the 90-day T-bill yield stalled along with the decrease in money market mutual fund maturities in January 1992.

rates in the U.S., and vice versa.

Figures 3 and 4 illustrate those expectations during this period. As short-term interest rates declined (Figure 2), the U.S. Dollar Index continued to rise. However, the top in the dollar index occurred very near the top in the 30-year bond yield, illustrating the correlation between the two markets. Furthermore, as the right side of the chart indicates, the decline of the dollar index reversed as the 30-year bond yield began to creep upward.

In my December S&C 1991 article, I described a stock mutual fund trading oscillator based almost entirely on sentiment measures. Sentiment measures quantify expectations. The Treasury bond Bullish Consensus, as reported in *Barron's*, is often a leading indicator of significant rallies and tops in the bond market.

Sentiment does have an impact on markets. Excessive optimism (which is usually, but not always, defined as 70% bullish sentiment) often precedes a top. But this is not a great predictor

FIGURE 3

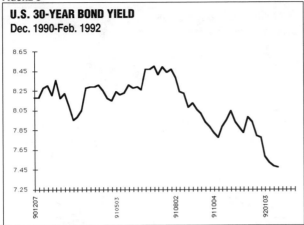

U.S. 30-YEAR BOND YIELD
Dec. 1990-Feb. 1992

As short-term interest rates declined (Figure 2), the dollar index continued to rise. But the top occurred near the high in the 30-year bond yield, illustrating the correlation between the two.

FIGURE 4

U.S. DOLLAR INDEX
Dec. 1990-Feb. 1992

The falling bond yields were confirmed by the weakening dollar.

FIGURE 5

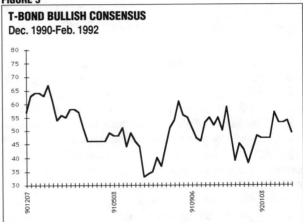

T-BOND BULLISH CONSENSUS
Dec. 1990-Feb. 1992

The actual sentiment top occurred on January 11, 1991, at 67% Bulls, but December had 60%-plus readings, revealing high bond market expectations, setting the stage for the increase in yield (decline in prices) seen in the middle portion of Figure 4, which in turn set the stage for the increased pessimism in June and July 1992 from which an impressive rally arose. The coming rally in the bond market was confirmed by the top in the U.S. Dollar Index during the same period, as illustrated in Figure 3.

of bond yields for the long term because of the volatile nature of the bond market. Excessive pessimism, indicated by less than 43% bullish sentiment, usually signals a bottom. The pessimism figures (such as in the top half of the table below) have performed better as predictors of higher bond prices as reflected by lower yields.

Extreme optimism (70% bulls) in the Bullish Consensus figures has only been registered three times since 1988 (bottom half of the table below).

U.S. 30-year bond yield in response to high levels of market pessimism, measured by T-bond Bullish Consensus

Date	% Bulls	Yield	Yield in 3 mos.	6 mos.	1 year
8/26/88	43%	9.44	9.20	9.15	8.18
1/13/89	43	8.89	8.83	8.21	8.16
2/23/90	40	8.55	8.58	9.11	8.05
4/27/90	41	9.02	8.47	8.77	8.21
8/24/90	42	9.15	8.44	8.05	8.13
6/14/91	33	8.47	7.96	7.79	pending
11/8/91	39	7.80	7.75	pending	pending
% correct			86%	83%	100%

U.S. 30-year bond yield in response to low levels of market pessimism, measured by T-bond Bullish Consensus

Date	% Bulls	Yield	Yield in 3 mos.	6 mos.	1 year
10/21/88	80%	8.89	8.89	8.98	7.98
5/26/89	73	8.61	8.18	7.87	8.63
7/14/89	72	8.09	8.03	8.16	8.46

It is an accepted rule of thumb that extreme sentiment usually signals that a market is near a trend reversal. Nevertheless, the 80-plus percentage accuracy of this indicator in predicting important bottoms in the bond market is impressive.

Figure 5 charts the weekly T-bond Bullish Consensus beginning in December 1990. The actual sentiment top occurred on January 11, 1991, at 67% Bulls, but December had 60%-plus

readings, revealing high bond market expectations, at least for the intermediate term. In fact, that burst in optimism set the stage for the increase in yield (decline in prices) seen in the middle portion of Figure 4, which in turn set the stage for the increased pessimism in June and July from which an impressive rally arose. The coming rally in the bond market was confirmed by the top in the U.S. Dollar Index during the same period, as illustrated in Figure 3.

Figure 6 charts the response of the Benham Target 2020 zero-coupon bond fund. The 30-year maturity of the bonds contained in this portfolio makes it an ideal proxy for the 30-year U.S. Treasury bond. Because zero-coupon bonds pay a single dividend at maturity, this fund exaggerates the moves of the underlying bond market. This built-in volatility and pseudo-leverage makes the Benham Target series ideal for bond market timing.

By calculating my ten minus four formula oscillator, which is simply defined as the difference between the 10-week moving

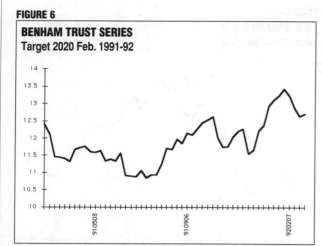

FIGURE 6

BENHAM TRUST SERIES
Target 2020 Feb. 1991-92

The 30-year maturity of the bonds contained in the Benham Target 2020 makes it an ideal proxy for the 30-year U.S. Treasury bond. Because zero-coupon bonds pay a single dividend at maturity, this fund exaggerates the moves of the underlying bond market. This built-in volatility and pseudo-leverage makes the Benham Target series ideal for bond market timing.

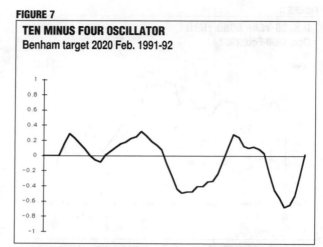

FIGURE 7

TEN MINUS FOUR OSCILLATOR
Benham target 2020 Feb. 1991-92

Figure 7 shows the ten minus four formula for the Benham Target 2020 fund. Note how direction changes in the oscillator correlate to price reversals in the fund. The overall price trend of the fund matches that of the bond market.

average and the four-week moving average, a trader could further confirm the trend. The volatility of this fund led me to modify the interpretation of the oscillator's signals. For this fund, I usually begin buying or selling when the oscillator changes direction instead of waiting for it to cross the zero line. Figure 7 shows the ten minus four formula for the Benham Target 2020 fund. Note how direction changes in the oscillator correlate to price reversals in the fund. The overall price trend of the fund matches that of the bond market.

Bond market timing is still another available avenue to mutual fund investors and traders. By reading underlying conditions, finding an appropriate trading vehicle and applying trend confirmation techniques in combination with intermarket analysis, mutual fund traders and investors can enhance their short- and intermediate-term mutual fund portfolio profits.

Joe Duarte publishes a mutual fund newsletter, "The Wall Street Detective," PO Box 1623, Bowling Green, KY 42102-1623.

REFERENCES

Duarte, Joe [1992]. "Trading currency mutual funds," STOCKS & COMMODITIES, March.
_____ [1992]. "Combining sentiment indicators for timing mutual funds," STOCKS & COMMODITIES, January.
_____ [1991]. "Mutual funds as stock index proxies," *Technical Analysis of* STOCKS & COMMODITIES, Volume 9: November.
IBC/Donoghue's Money Fund Report. 290 Eliot St., Ashland, MA 01721.
Benham Group. 1665 Charleston Rd., Mountain View, CA 94043.

TA

The Basics Of Managing Money

A trader can score that one big win, but it's all for naught if he can't hold onto his profits. Money management is the step both before and after trading, the study of risk and reward and how best to utilize investment capital — and keep it. Here's an excerpt from The Elements of Successful Trading, *scheduled for release in June 1992 from New York Institute of Finance.*

by Robert P. Rotella

Money management is the evaluation of risk and reward in a trade or portfolio and determining the most efficient use of investment capital. Money management is the study of risk and return; we are trying to get the best return for the money we risk. Money management involves these steps:

1. Determining the different kinds of risk in any trade.
2. Deciding how much risk to take on a trade.
3. Assessing the amount of return on a trade for a given level of risk.
4. Deciding whether to accept the return and risk.
5. Implementing the entire process.

This process can be a lot of work, but it is also worth the effort.

Money management is important to trading successfully, yet most traders do not understand it. Money management is important to success for practical reasons. How much money should be risked on a trade? If a trader risks too much money, then there is always a fair chance of losing all the capital in one disastrous trade or a series of losing trades. On the other hand, if the trader risks too small an amount of money, then the capital will be underutilized and the trader will not achieve as high a return as may be possible. There is not much sense in trading commodities and obtaining returns equivalent to Treasury bills because the risk is so much greater but the return is not.

PRESERVING CAPITAL

Every trader must realize that preserving capital is of paramount consideration and a fundamental principle of money management. Futures trading is notorious for high leverage, which can yield fast profits — and losses. *Any* trading strategy, no matter how well thought out and seemingly profitable, may ultimately lose money. Every trader must determine the appropriate amount of capital to risk for each trade. Above all, you must always place the preservation of mind, body and capital above all else when trading.

EQUITY JOURNEY

Money management is in reality an equity journey where you start with initial capital at point A and end with final capital at point Z. The profits are the high points of the journey and the losses are the low points, as shown in Figure 1. The easiest and quickest trip is a straight line from A to Z, but every trip has ups and downs. If the deviation from the path is too great then the journey can end abruptly at the point of no return, with the loss of all capital.

One critical difference exists between the ups and downs. There is virtually no limit to how long the journey may be heading up, but there is always a limit to how far down one may go. The journey will end quickly if too much capital is lost. Equity increases of 50%, 100%, 1,000%, 10,000% and higher are possible, but any equity drop of 100% will immediately and abruptly end the journey. This is why the trader must always be concerned about losses and the preservation of capital.

The different paths that are possible is the essence of money management. It is also one of the most important but least-asked questions in trading. Most travelers along the equity journey believe the route is dependent on picking the right trading method, but in fact the route is independent of trading method. Both technicians and fundamentalists have successfully traversed the same road. The path is affected by two critical factors: risk and reward.

RISK AND REWARD

The relationship of risk and reward is integral to trading. Every trade should be evaluated by measuring the inherent risk and associated reward. A portfolio of investments is measured by the amount of reward for a given level of risk. Money management attempts to determine the best risk and reward potential for a trade as well as a portfolio of investments. Traders are not evaluated for their knowledge of technical or fundamental analysis but on their money management skills and trading performance — how much is gained versus how much is lost.

Technical and fundamental analyses provide the means to evaluate various types of risk and reward in any trade. For example, a head and shoulders pattern may provide indications of the risk and reward in a trade. Using fundamental analysis, the cost of production yields clues as to how low prices may drop and substitute goods help to determine how high prices might rise. Portfolio theory is one aspect of money management that deals with the risk and reward in combining investments. It is helpful in determining "efficient portfolios" — portfolios that yield the highest return for a given level of risk.

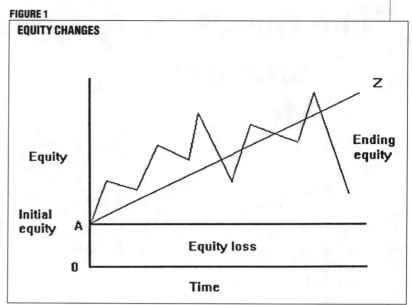

FIGURE 1

EQUITY CHANGES

Money management is really a study in how equity changes from point A to Z. Is the path linear or jagged?

Most people do not understand the significance of risk and reward, which contributes greatly to poor trading results. Most investors think more about reward but are less knowledgeable about or concerned with risk. A balanced understanding of both is essential to trade successfully. Combining risk and reward is the ultimate measure of any trade or trader. One of the few useful and relevant trading axioms is one that deals with risk and reward: "It's not just how much you make in trading but also how much you lose!"

> **Any trading strategy, no matter how well thought out and seemingly profitable, may ultimately lose money.**

DEFINING RISK AND REWARD

How would you define risk and reward in trading? Which is riskier and which entails more reward, buying a Standard & Poor's 500 stock index future contract or buying a lottery ticket?

What *is* risk? When most of us think of risk, we probably consider the amount of loss. If we have $10,000, then this becomes our risk capital and it is considered the amount that we may lose trading. What are the chances of losing the entire $10,000? It depends on the investment. The amount and chances of loss may differ when investing in Treasury bills versus futures, but the rewards may differ, too. Using magnitude and probability of loss may be considered the amount and chance of a loss or adverse event.

There is one other important consideration when we think of risk. We usually invest in a variety of assets or the same ones over an extended time, so we must also be concerned about a series of losses occurring. Therefore risk may be defined as the amount and probability of an adverse or series of adverse events occurring. This is an important reference frame for determining trading risk.

The definition of risk may be slightly altered and applied to the definition of reward. When thinking of reward, we must not only consider the amount but also the chance of receiving it. Reward is the amount and probability of a favorable or series of favorable events occurring.

What is a good measure of risk and reward? Normally, reward is easier to measure, but risk is another story. Common sense and good judgment are just as valuable as any complex equation or valuation model. To consider the question of measuring risk and reward, meet Lucky and Sharky.

MEASURING RISK

Lucky and Sharky are both trying to make money. Lucky buys a $1 lottery ticket that has a chance of winning $10 million. Sharky decides to buy an S&P 500 futures contract at 400 instead of buying a lottery ticket. He places two orders — one to sell if the market goes to 398 and the other to sell if it goes to 402. With this strategy, Sharky will either gain $1,000 if the market moves to 402 or lose $1,000 if the market drops to 398 (ignoring slippage and commissions). Which strategy is riskier?

To answer that question, we need to take two separate steps to measure risk. The first step is to determine actual possible loss. Lucky is risking $1 and Sharky is risking $1,000. Clearly, Sharky is risking more than Lucky on an absolute basis.

But there is more to this problem. The second step in measuring risk involves evaluating the chance or probability of the loss occurring. The probability of loss for Lucky is at least 99.99%. The probability of loss for Sharky is approximately 50% if random markets are assumed. If nonrandom markets are assumed and Sharky is a good trader, then the probability of loss may be less. Therefore, if the probability of loss is viewed as the criterion for measuring risk, then Sharky's risk is clearly less than Lucky's. The probability of loss is an important consideration in assessing risk and therefore essential in making a more informed trading decision.

As for which strategy is riskier, we have a tie. If the total amount lost is the primary criterion, then Sharky's trade is riskier. If the chance of loss occurring is the primary criterion, then Lucky's lottery ticket is riskier. Although we now understand the problem better, it is still difficult to say which strategy is more risky.

One other consideration has not been discussed. What if Lucky and Sharky risk the same amount? Since Sharky is risking $1,000, what if Lucky buys $1,000 worth of lottery tickets? Now Lucky and Sharky are risking the same amount, but the probability of loss has not changed much. In this situation, Lucky's chance of losing is still close to 100%, but now he will lose $1,000. Sharky's chance of losing $1,000 has not changed and is still 50%. If we multiply the total amount at risk with the chance of losing it, we will arrive at an amount both may expect to lose:

- For Lucky, this is $1,000 x 0.999, which is almost $1,000

- For Sharky, this is $1,000 x 0.5, which is $500

Using these comparisons, Lucky's strategy is much riskier both in terms of the total amount lost and the chance of losing it.

We have not definitively answered which strategy is riskier if Lucky only buys one ticket. In addition, one might object that Lucky's reward should be taken into account because it is so much greater than Sharky's.

REWARD IS HARDER TO REALIZE

Now for reward. Reward is a concept that most of us are probably more familiar with than risk, since it is the foremost reason most of us trade. It is also much easier to understand but unfortunately often harder to realize.

> What is a good measure of risk and reward? Normally, reward is easier to measure, but risk is another story. Common sense and good judgment are just as valuable as any complex equation or valuation model.

With Lucky and Sharky, Lucky's risk was definitely $1 but his reward *might* be $10 million. Sharky's risk was definitely $1,000 but his reward *might* be $1,000. Lucky and Sharky will always be at risk as long as they keep playing, but neither may ever attain *any* reward. There is an important distinction with risk and reward: Risk is always present, whereas reward is possible but by no means assured. This has significant implications in developing a trading strategy.

Why not discuss the reward side of the market opening in our favor, say, or slippage occurring and getting a better fill than expected? That scenario can and does happen, but the ramifications of reward differ from those of a loss. Profits are always desired in trading, but we must usually be more concerned about losses because when losses become too severe they may bankrupt us, taking us out of the game. Trading profits, no matter how great, will allow us to play one more day, but no one has ever been ruined by making great profits. Losses, not profits, is what the trader must always guard against. Risk, not reward, is the ruin of most traders.

USING EXPECTED OUTCOME

The risk and reward of any trade must always be considered when evaluating a trade. Individuals focused only on reward may end up ruined by risk. Individuals concerned only about risk would never invest in anything, because there is always the chance of losing money, no matter what the investment. Not investing is, ironically, a form of speculation because the investor has chosen to keep capital in the form of cash. There is no way of getting around it; we always take on risk, no matter what we do.

Now that we have looked at different kinds and ways to measure risk and reward, the next step is to combine risk and reward to see how they relate to each other. One of the simplest ways to look at risk and reward is by calculating the expected outcome of an event. In trading, the expected outcome is important because we must not only focus on simply how much might be made or lost but also what the combined chances of profit and loss are together. The expected outcome of an event is the sum of the chances of each element of the event occurring and may be calculated thus:

$$\text{Expected outcome} = \sum (w_i p_i)$$

where i = period when event happens
w_i = chance of event i occurring
p_i = event i

The expected outcome is easy to calculate, so let's look at an example. If we expect to make $100 on 50% of our trades and lose $50 on the other 50%, what is the expected outcome after two trades?

$$\text{Expected outcome} = (100)(0.5) + (100)(0.5) + (-50)(0.5) + (-50)(0.5) = 50$$

After two trades, we can expect to make $50 because half the time we will make $100 and half the time we will lose $50. On average, we can expect to make $25 (50 divided by 2) per trade.

Remember Sharky and Lucky? They are still playing, so now we can see what the chances of winning and losing are and the amounts that each might make below:

	Chance of wins	Chance of losses	Potential profit	Potential loss
Lucky	0.0000001	0.9999999	10,000,000	1
Sharky	0.5	0.5	1,000	1,000

Using the equation, the expected outcome is:

$$\text{Expected outcome}_{Lucky} = (0.0000001)(10,000,000) + (0.9999999)(-1) \cong 0$$

$$\text{Expected outcome}_{Sharky} = (0.5)(1,000) + (0.5)(-1,000) = 0$$

The expected outcome for both is zero, so neither can expect to profit over the long run.

You may have noticed that we used the expected outcome equation in a previous calculation. We determined the risk of loss for Lucky and Sharky by multiplying the amount of loss by the chance of loss. We arrived at an expected loss or expected outcome of loss for both. Now we look at the expected outcome for both risk and reward.

What if Sharky is a good trader? Then he will have a much better chance of making money, and in fact, his expected outcome will be positive. The same cannot be said for Lucky. The expected outcome addresses the original objection of not including the reward in the analysis. Expected outcome provides an indication of whether a strategy will be profitable in the future. Every trader must develop a trading method that will yield a positive expected outcome. Anyone developing a method with a negative expected outcome will eventually go broke.

The question of who is riskier, Lucky or Sharky, will be answered in a later article.

Expected outcome is helpful in looking at all the possibilities of a trading event and determining whether a trader could make or lose money. But remember the key word: *expected*. The *expected* outcome is what we hope to achieve over time, assuming our input variables and assumptions are correct. It is *not* what we are due or will always realize.

Robert P. Rotella is a Commodity Trading Advisor and an independent futures trader. He trades for his own account and institutional clients and is a member of the Coffee, Sugar, and Cocoa Exchange.

Used with permission. *The Elements of Successful Trading: Developing Your Comprehensive Strategy through Psychology, Money Management, and Trading Methods*, Robert P. Rotella, New York Institute of Finance.

FURTHER READING

Rotella, Robert [1992]. *The Elements of Successful Trading*, New York Institute of Finance.

The Mass Index

Range oscillation, not often covered by students of technical analysis, delves into repetitive market patterns during which the daily trading range narrows and widens. Examining this pattern, Donald Dorsey explains, allows the technician to forecast market reversals that other indicators may miss. Dorsey proposes the use of range oscillators in his mass index.

by Donald Dorsey

Range oscillation is one of the least explored areas of technical analysis. Typically, markets tend to repeat a pattern in which the average daily range (that is, the difference between the high and low) oscillates from narrow to wide and back again. Oftentimes, this pattern will predict critical market reversals, while traditional technical indicators may miss them. The mass index is designed to identify important changes in daily ranges; in fact, the mass index has proved its ability to measure range oscillation patterns and depict market turns with precision. (See sidebar, "The mass index and moving average formulas.")

The most important pattern in range oscillation analysis is the reversal bulge, a gradual but definite increase of the average daily range that indicates the market is near a turning point. Little is known about range oscillation patterns because they can be difficult or even impossible to spot on an ordinary graph, but with the use of a smoothed graph, an ideal reversal bulge can be clearly seen (Figure 1). The overall action of the market is unimportant to the pattern. Whether the bulge occurs while the market is tracing out a wide trading range or while the market is rocketing forward at increasing momentum, the result is the same.

To quantify range oscillation patterns, the mass index sums up an exponentially smoothed average of daily ranges over a period of 25 days to see if the range is widening or narrowing. Values above 25 indicate a widening range, while those below 25 indicate a narrowing range. Because the reversal bulge involves a temporary widening of the daily range, it can be confirmed by an increase in the mass index to 27 or above and

CHRIS ROBERTSON

its subsequent decline back through 26.5. Once the mass index drops down through 26.5, an imminent reversal can be expected.

> **Indicators such as the mass index can bring a sense of order to the market. With continued study, perhaps range oscillation patterns will someday be a part of every investor's vocabulary.**

DIRECTIONAL QUANTIFICATION

To quantify direction, a fast moving average (MA1) and a slow moving average (MA2) are maintained (see sidebar). As usual,

FIGURE 1

REVERSAL BULGE   S&P 500

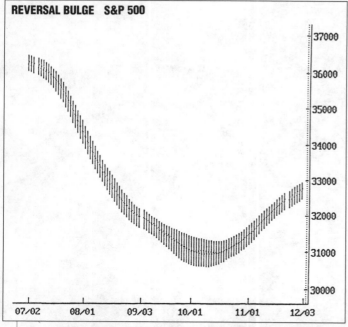

Reversal bulges, gradual but definite increases of the average daily ranges that indicate the market is about to turn, can be difficult or near impossible to identify, but a smoothed graph can be useful to do so.

if MA1 is greater than MA2, that indicates the most recent direction is up and vice versa. Since the reversal bulge warns of an impending direction change, the opposite direction should be taken as defined by MA1 and MA2 when the mass index comes down through 26.5. For example, suppose the mass index recently reached a high of 27.3 and just crossed below 26.5. If MA1 is greater than MA2, the market can be expected to drop in

FIGURE 2

SIGNALING TURNS
April gold

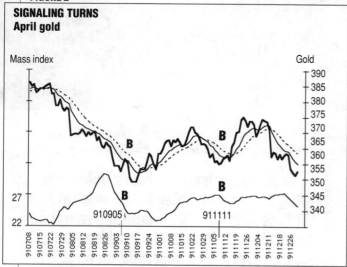

The closing price along with the exponentially smoothed moving averages are presented along with the mass index. The mass index moved above 27 and dropped below 26.5 on September 5, indicating the market was close to reversing the downtrend. An additional buy signal occurred on November 11. Because this technique warns of trend reversals, it is important to use stop-loss orders in case the trend fails to reverse.

THE MASS INDEX AND MOVING AVERAGE FORMULAS

The mass index is a 25-day moving sum of a ratio of two moving averages. The numerator of the ratio is the exponentially smoothed moving average of the daily ranges. The denominator is the numerator smoothed a second time. When the value of the daily ranges begins to increase, the numerator will increase faster than the denominator and the ratio will become larger than 1. The 25-day moving sum will then become larger than 25. If the moving sum reaches 27, then falls below 26.5, a reversal signal is indicated.

Equation (1)

$$\text{Mass index} = \sum_{n=1}^{25} \frac{R_n}{L_n}$$

where:

$R_n = 0.8\,(R_{n-1}) + 0.2\,(\text{Range})$
$L_n = 0.8\,(L_{n-1}) + 0.2\,(R_n)$
Range = Today's high - low
R_{n-1} = Yesterday's R_n
L_{n-1} = Yesterday's L_n

Two moving averages of the daily closes are maintained. The first is an exponentially smoothed moving average of the daily close. The second moving average is the first moving average smoothed a second time.

Equation (2)

$$MA1 = 0.8\,(MA1_{n-1}) + 0.2\,(\text{Close}_n)$$

Equation (3)

$$MA2 = 0.8\,(MA2_{n-1}) + 0.2\,(MA1_n)$$

where:

MA1 = Fast moving average
MA2 = Slow moving average

To calculate the first value of an exponential moving average (EMA), substitute yesterday's close for MA1$_{n-1}$; then begin the smoothing process using Equation 2 above. For more on this, see "Understanding exponential moving averages" on page 277 of this book.

Once the mass index reaches 27 and reverses back below 26.5, a reversal in the price is indicated. The trade is placed against the direction of the two moving averages. As with all trading techniques, a stop-loss order should be placed with the new position.

—*Editor*

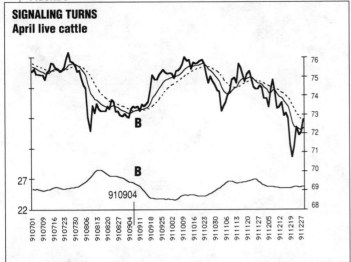

FIGURE 3

SIGNALING TURNS
April live cattle

910904

The mass index moved above 27 and back below 26.5 on September 4, indicating a trend reversal.

the near to moderate future. In a recent test of the mass index, an arbitrary period of 15 days was chosen as an exit point. Results showed that on the 15th day following entry, 80% of all mass index signals would have been profitable. Similar results were also obtained for 10- and 20-day periods. In addition, note how the mass index often gives signals in Figures 2 and 3 while the market was still making new closing highs or lows. This feature not only leads to good price entry, it can predict market weakness at a time when close-based indicators may be forecasting continued market strength.

The reversal bulge is only one of many patterns typical of range oscillation analysis, and a great deal of work remains to be done to identify and explain the various formations. The analysis can often seem baffling and contradictory. Indicators such as the mass index can bring a sense of order to the market. With continued study, perhaps range oscillation patterns will someday be a part of every investor's vocabulary.

Donald Dorsey trades commodities and develops trading systems. He holds degrees in physics, mathematics and chemistry.

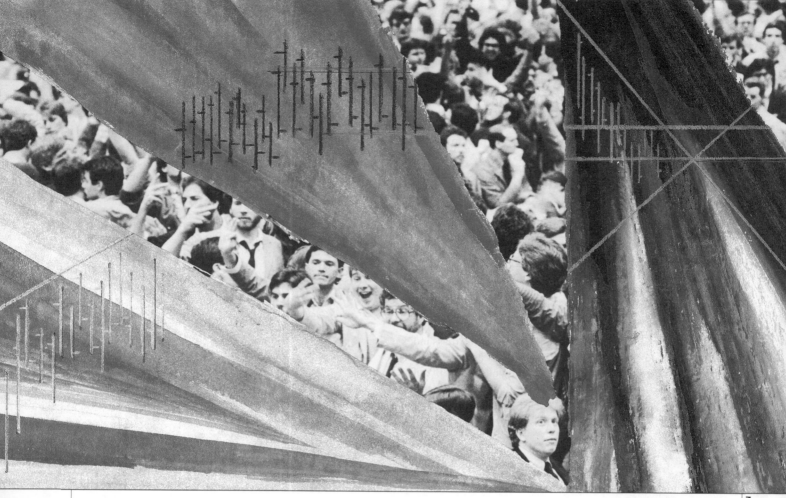

CHRISTINE MORRISON

The Gann Method

W.D. Gann's trading methodologies are not always easy to define or to analyze, which is a pity, since they can be applied to everyday trading principles across many different markets when interpreted correctly. John Blasic simplifies Gann's techniques in this article into terms more easily understood, sketching a brief background of the essential elements and how the applications can be applied within your trading strategy.

by John J. Blasic

D. Gann firmly believed that knowledge is the foundation of all successful analysis. He constantly stressed that a novice should learn from the experts first hand and apply this knowledge daily. He viewed the future as simply being a repetition of a consensus of opinion of the past. Once a game plan has been developed, it is important to adhere to it and take advantage of the opportunities as they are presented. Knowledge and patience is the first phase of the game plan and stop-loss orders are the second phase. "You cannot get something good for nothing. You must pay with time, money or knowledge for success," he stressed. Gann considered this the key, and the only key, to becoming successful. Many of Gann's rules for trading are still followed daily. They have withstood the test of time by holding up in different market environments. (See "Gann's 28 trading rules.")

While Gann was successful with methodologies, he also researched the human element of trading and how the elements influenced different investors in different markets. He observed a vast array of methods that took into account factors that caused investors to buy at the top and sell at the bottom. Gann developed other rules to allow traders to take advantage of anticipated market movements through entry and exit points. This let traders "never to trade on hope and fear, but enabled them to know why the trade is being made," because anything else wasted not only time but also money. The human element has been, and always will be, the greatest weakness. The stock market is driven by human energy, and the habits and methods of individuals in the market will always be the driving force in the market. This allows the investor to buy and sell on solid ground rather than buying hope, which is another form of gambling. Do the opposite of what the general public is doing. Act when others are tiring. Investors should use their time to study human nature to anticipate when the crowd will throw in the towel.

GANN'S 50% RETRACEMENT RULE

Using trading rules such as Gann's 50% retracement rule is an art, not a science. Part of that art involves judging when to apply them most effectively. The object is not to predict the moves from the top or bottom, but rather to recognize and take advantage of them. Let the charts tell you what to do. "Trade with the trend" is an axiom that must be adhered to because it reflects market psychology at the point in the market when many of the less experienced players close out their positions. Look for solid evidence that the trend has changed before trying to pick points.

> **Once prices close outside the retracement zone, look for a possible trend change after the initial support/resistance levels are tested.**

Experience shows that the majority of price reactions will terminate in the 45-50% price range, which is why it becomes necessary to stagger orders so they are filled within this range. The professional market makers won't dabble over a quarter of a point, so there is no reason for the individual investor to do so. Remember that the market will never act to please you.

When, in doing your homework, you find there are a number of reversal points in the market, it is advisable to average these points. Occasionally, the market will fail to reach this average 50% retracement level. This may cause a number of 50% retracements to fall short. In fact, most intermediate retracements will occur within larger ones before a more complete pattern develops. The simplified method of equilibrium that only takes a few minutes to apply is described as follows:

1. In bull moves, determine the low price before the previous move occurred.
2. Determine the most recent high before the correction took place.
3. Subtract the low price from the high before the correction occurred.
4. Take the sum from step 3 and multiply by 50% to arrive at the corrective number.
5. Subtract the corrective number from the high to determine where support will come into play and another reaction will occur.

FIGURE 1

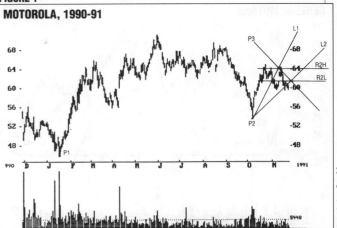

Motorola demonstrates how Gann angles are used to project price advances. Here, P2 is defined as the low point within the upward move to draw the 45-degree and 63-degree angles. P3 is used to find the intersection and clearly define the retracement zone high and low.

FIGURE 2

The S&P 500 provides numerous examples of the strict adherence to Gann's retracement zones, defining both zones from the single pivot point in January labeled P1-1. P1-2 is defined by the low on June 22, 1991, as 370.65 while the high was established on August 28, 1991, at 396.64. The 50% level of this move falls at 383.50, while 63% is defined at 380.00. The October lows closed within the 63% retracement zone for two days before bouncing and resuming the move. The longer-term move has the first retracement zone lows defined on June 25, 1991, while the longer-term retracement is defined by the lows set in January.

When using the 50% retracement rule, note that it can be expanded to include retracements of 63%, 75% and 100%. Stop orders should be placed at the 66% level on a close-only basis in case it's not a minor trend reaction but rather a trend reversal. This exposes approximately 16% of your capital, since your original order was placed at the 50% retracement zone. This is one of the best ways to remove yourself psychologically from the market, ensuring locking in larger profits through the movement of the stop point once it has withstood the tests.

Gann also researched the definition of time to determine when trending prices would react within a specific time frame; this method was held as one of the most important elements of

FIGURE 3

GENERAL MOTORS

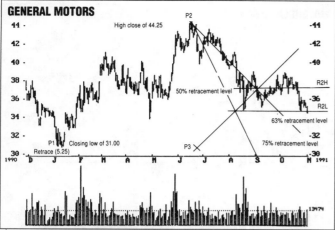

This figure defines some of Gann's critical rules. The low in January of $31.00 subtracted from the high in June of $44.25 results in $13.25. Taking 50% of this move to determine the retracement zone gives the high of $37.625; then the retracement zone low is determined by taking 63%, which results in $35.905. These zones can also shown using the angles from the pivot point of P2 defined as the June high. These rules are also seen from the intermediate-term move from January through May.

FIGURE 4

CIRCUIT CITY

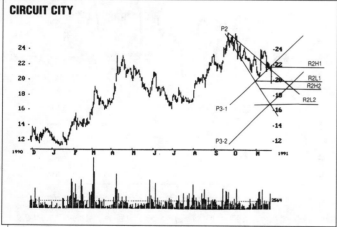

CC is used to demonstrate the use of more than one pivot point to show the shorter-term price objective as well as the longer-term price objective obtained from the retracement zones.

GANN'S 28 TRADING RULES

1. Never risk more than 10% of your trading capital in a single trade.
2. Always use stop-loss orders.
3. Never overtrade.
4. Never let a profit run into a loss.
5. Don't enter a trade if you are unsure of the trend. *Never* buck the trend.
6. When in doubt, get out, and don't get in when in doubt.
7. Only trade active markets.
8. Distribute your risk equally among different markets.
9. Never limit your orders. Trade at the market.
10. Don't close trades without a good reason.
11. Extra monies from successful trades should be placed in a separate account.
12. Never trade to scalp a profit.
13. Never average a loss.
14. Never get out of the market because you have lost patience or get in because you are anxious from waiting.
15. Avoid taking small profits and large losses.
16. Never cancel a stop loss after you have placed the trade.
17. Avoid getting in and out of the market too often.
18. Be willing to make money from both sides of the market.
19. Never buy or sell just because the price is low or high.
20. Pyramiding† should be accomplished once it has crossed resistance levels and broken zones of distribution.
21. Pyramid issues that have a strong trend.
22. Never hedge a losing position.
23. Never change your position without a good reason.
24. Avoid trading after long periods of success or failure.
25. Don't try to guess tops or bottoms.
26. Don't follow a blind man's advice.
27. Reduce trading after the first loss; never increase.
28. Avoid getting in wrong and out wrong; or getting in right and out wrong. This is making a double mistake.

trading. Gann broke each trading year down into many smaller and more manageable periods. Each had significant importance, as they were based on mathematical relationships that determined tops and bottoms. Gann supported three time periods that held the most significance:

- Anniversary dates of major tops and bottoms.
- Seven months after a major top or bottom for a minor reaction.
- The length for a reaction to occur in a normal market is 10 to 14 days. If this period is exceeded, the next reaction should be expected after 28 to 30 days.

In general, time is a universally accepted measurement across all markets so reactions can be spotted in a number of different markets. When studying time periods, take note when a reaction exceeds the greatest number of days of a previous reaction and consider that the main trend has changed. From this point, all rallies should be used to establish new positions in the direction of the new trend. Large advances and declines always come after long solid base formations or narrowly defined trading ranges. Watch for tops and bottoms to occur at 49 days (seven weeks) or 45 days, because this is one-eighth of a year, and then 90-98 days and 120-135 days. Gann emphasized anniversary dates of previous moves of one, two, or three years. If an advance or decline reaches a point it hasn't touched for months or years, it shows that there is a hard driving power in that direction that is the opposite or reverse of a power move.

FIGURE 5

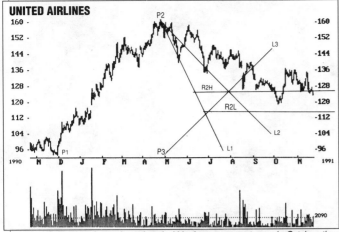

UNITED AIRLINES

UAL demonstrates how prices closed within the retracement zone in October, then appeared to change direction by closing outside the zone. Later, closes reentered the retracement zone. A secondary test is not unusual.

fter determining the "when" aspect of his model, Gann went further to define "how much." This emphasizes specific price levels rather than actual dates. Prices are divided into ranges because they are utilized as percentages and applied as reference points to previous price trends. Each offers different degrees or levels of support and resistance, which are known more specifically as retracements.

Gann's research led him to define retracements as a price reversal from the direction of the current price before it resumed its previous move. This included what he referred to as the balancing point, which occurred most often and offered the strongest level of support and resistance. The balancing point is the basis for the 50% retracement rule, since the division of the previous ranges of fluctuation fall into two equal parts. Therefore, one-half becomes the most important point for resistance at tops or bottoms. The initial sustained price move, either up or down, will react 50% of the initial price trend before resuming its move. If it continues on up past this level, prices should continue to the 62-1/2% or 5/8 level before another reaction occurs.

Other significant percentages include 75%, 100% and to a slightly lesser degree the 63% retracement. Gann clearly stated that if a move is following what he called a base angle and then changes, a trend change has occurred and will begin to follow another angle. This forms the foundation for the last and possibly the foremost relationship he developed between price and time, the Gann angles.

RETRACEMENTS AND GEOMETRIC ANGLES

Gann angles can be written in the expression as price versus time, established by putting units of time along the X axis and units of price along the Y axis. With these lines, the trader will be able to determine the price level where reactions will occur; unique because the angles allow specific details to be exploited by individual markets. While geometric angles will not always be constant across all market conditions, they are used in coordination with the 50% retracement rule to determine price-only movements with greater success.

Retracement zones are quite simply plotted by determining where P1, P2 and P3 currently lie. P1 (Figure 1) is located and determined to be the significant high/low point, P2 is the next significant high/low point and is chosen as the point where prices will react to the 50% retracement level. Then P3 is located from coordinates derived from P1 and P2. Lines are then drawn from P2 at 23 1/2 degrees, 45 degrees and 63 degrees, and are labeled L1 and L2, respectively. A L3 line is drawn from P3 at a 45-degree angle in the opposite direction, so that L3 intersects with both L1 and L2.

The objective in determining these intersections will ultimately allow the upper and lower limits of the retracement zone to be defined. The retracement zone defines where prices are anticipated to reach and fluctuate within this price channel before resuming the current move. Once prices close outside the retracement zone, look for a possible trend change after the initial support/resistance levels are tested. Keep in mind that the retracements are applied to both upward and downward moves.

A change in trend can be seen from Figure 3, demonstrating how the force behind General Motors' (GM) downward move is close to establishing a new trend. The Standard & Poor's 500 provides numerous examples of the strict adherence to Gann's retracement zones.

All traders should abide by some strict discipline, whether or not it is derived from Gann's trading rules. This discipline should be top priority on every trader's list. Experience is still the best teacher; be willing to learn from your trading mistakes. This will enable you to fine-tune the rules that are so vital to trading successes.

John J. Blasic is a New Jersey-based registered investment adviser. His specialties include portfolio management and market strategies using a blend of technical and fundamental analysis. **TA**

Price: The Ultimate Indicator?

What does it take to make consistent profits trading commodities? Roger Altman theorizes that like support and resistance levels in stock charts, historical floor and ceiling prices in commodities can be used to gauge relative cheapness and richness of prices and whether a price decline or increase is likely.

by Roger Altman

D espite the use of an array of sophisticated and esoteric indicators, most commodity newsletter trade recommendations lose money. According to *Commodity Trader's Consumer Report*, which tracks the performance of 26 commodity newsletter writers, the average return for 1989 was -14.9%, -5.4% for 1990 and -27.7% for 1991. In fact, only three of 26 newsletter writers made more than 10% for their subscribers last year. Since the vast majority of these newsletter writers are trend followers, just what *does* it take to make consistent profits trading commodities?

ECONOMICS 101

A basic course in economics can tell you that a relationship exists between supply and demand. If farmers reap a bumper crop, oversupply swamps demand and prices plummet. Conversely, when drought or insects decimate crops, demand overpowers limited supply and prices rise dramatically. So how can traders use this fundamental economic truism to decide when to buy and sell? The answer is simple. You simply wait until prices reach such historic extremes that commodity producers as well as consumers are forced to make significant adjustments to future production and consumption. Very low prices tend to diminish future supply because marginal producers begin to lose money and cease operation. As prices continue to decline, future supply begins to dry up and consumers switch to a less expensive commodity, increasing demand, so that ultimately, prices stop

DIANA FRITCH

declining and begin to rise. In other words, with each price decline to new extremes, the probability of a price rise increases.

Very high prices, on the other hand, tend to generate increasing supplies and reduce demand, which will result in lower prices in the long run. Even a drought in the United States could still result in greater supplies because other grain-producing regions around the world could increase production.

FIGURE 1, Part A

OPTIMUM FLOOR, CEILING & TRIGGER PRICES OF LONG & SHORT TRADES			
Commodity		1st half of database	2nd half of database
Soybeans	Buy at	525	525
	Sell at	830	900
	Short at	900	900
	Cover at	525	525
Copper	Buy at	57.5	57.5
	Sell at	138	138
	Short at	138	138
	Cover at	57.5	129
Heating Oil	Buy at	40	37
	Sell at	108	105
	Short at	104	100
	Cover at	68	49
Corn	Buy at	225	225
	Sell at	319	301
	Short at	335	335
	Cover at	255	225
Soybean meal	Buy at	120	120
	Sell at	305	315
	Short at	290	290
	Cover at	134	120

FIGURE 1, Part B

OPTIMUM FLOOR, CEILING & TRIGGER PRICES OF LONG & SHORT TRADES			
Commodity		1st half of database	2nd half of database
Soybean Oil	Buy at	15.5	15.5
	Sell at	32.5	34.0
	Short at	45.6	33.8
	Cover at	15.5	15.5
Wheat	Buy at	250	250
	Sell at	444	408
	Short at	445	445
	Cover at	432	300
Cotton	Buy at	52	52
	Sell at	88.5	80
	Short at	84	84
	Cover at	75	58
Pork bellies	Buy at	30.25	30.25
	Sell at	56.00	55.50
	Short at	90.00	90.00
	Cover at	32.00	43.00
Hogs	Buy at	33	40
	Sell at	58	64
	Short at	62	62
	Cover at	39	47

Here are two sets of floor and ceiling prices selected from long-term monthly futures charts. The first set was obtained from the first half of each database and the second was obtained from the second half of each database.

COMMODITY FLOOR AND CEILING PRICES

By far the easiest way to anticipate the likely floor or ceiling price is to look at very long-term (20 years or more) monthly futures charts of commodity prices. Incidentally, floor and ceiling prices refer to tangible† commodities only. This strategy should not be applied to currencies, interest rates or the stock market.

> **Very high prices tend to generate increasing supplies and reduce demand, which will result in lower prices in the long run.**

For trading strategy, Figure 1 shows two sets of floor and ceiling prices selected from long-term monthly futures charts. The first set was obtained from the first half of each database and the second was obtained from the second half of each database. To avoid being accused of curve fitting, I then programmed my computer to make buy and sell deci-

FIGURE 2

GAIN AND DRAWDOWN, 1975-91									
Year	75	76	77	78	79	80	81	82	83
% gain on 3.33 initial margin	69.11	66.53	44.05	19.68	59.46	49.67	48.89	45.22	49.63
Maximum % drawdown during the year	8.22	13.08	16.65	12.86	7.36	8.61	11.29	7.74	8.68
Maximum % drawdown from initial equity	0	0	16.65	1.23	6.73	3.86	11.29	1.86	0
Year	84	85	86	87	88	89	90	91(10 mo.)	
% gain on 3.33 initial margin	28.83	9.85	22.79	61.58	28.09	36.09	38.54	5.47	
Maximum % drawdown during the year	11.37	10.75	7.69	5.91	6.36	7.24	8.16	7.02	
Maximum % drawdown from initial equity	0.41	10.75	5.91	0	6.36	7.24	8.16	7.02	

Here are the results of trading corn, wheat, soybeans, soybean oil, soybean meal, copper, bellies, hogs, cotton and heating oil between 1974 through October 1991. Annual return on 3.33 times margin is excellent and drawdown is very low.

†See Traders' Glossary for complete description

sions in the first half of the database from optimized floor, profit target and ceiling prices obtained from the second half of the database. It was also programmed to make buy and sell decisions in the second half of the database from optimized floor, profit target, and ceiling prices obtained from the first half of the database. How does one arrive at the profit target figure? A futures contract was purchased when prices fell to the floor price and liquidated when prices reached the profit target. A short sale was initiated when prices rose to the ceiling price and subsequently covered† at its respective profit target. Since most positions were held for a very long time, actual contract prices were used so rollovers reflected real futures spread differences and carrying charges. Slippage and commission were set at $68 per round turn.

Figure 2 gives the combined results of trading corn, wheat, soybeans, soybean oil, soybean meal, copper, bellies, hogs, cotton and heating oil between 1974 through October 1991. Not all databases started in 1974;

the heating oil database, for example, started in 1980. As can be seen, annual return on using 3.33 times margin is excellent and drawdown is very low.

TO CONCLUDE

Trading commodities using trend-following methods may be much more difficult than commonly appreciated. Perhaps successful trading depends more on common sense and doing nothing most of the time. If you reflect on your own experience as a consumer, you can understand how sensible it is to wait until you can buy something at bargain basement prices and sell it when it is dear. If you follow this simple rule and practice sound money management, you will be successful trading commodities.

Roger Altman, (908) 359-4672, is the developer of Supply/Demand Trader, software designed to help the scale trader increase profits while minimizing drawdown.

The Basics Of Moving Averages

Moving averages are one of the most common technical tools that technicians, both veteran and novice, may take advantage of. But for those novices, the concept may be somewhat confusing. What is a moving average, anyway? And what about all those variations — linear, stepweighted, exponential, even triangular? George Arrington explains the basics of the moving averages. And for those veteran traders out there, it never hurts to brush up on those basics.

by George R. Arrington, Ph.D.

The first maxim a trader learns is to "buy low and sell high." The trick, however, is to identify when the lows and highs occur and to act before others in the market. Trading profits go to those who are both correct and early. Trading losses go to virtually everyone else.

A moving average† is probably the most common tool used by technicians to identify market trends. A moving average eliminates minor fluctuations in prices and helps identify any underlying trend (Figure 1). Moving averages may be constructed in a variety of ways. The most frequently used are the simple†, linear and exponential† moving averages (see "Moving average calculations"), but others such as triangular† and step-weighted moving averages are also used by traders.

The biggest difficulty in constructing a moving average is building one that is sensitive enough to signal when a new trend has begun (or when an old trend has ended), yet insensitive enough to ignore short-term random price movements (or "data noise"†). If the moving average is too sensitive, random noise can give false signals and generate unnecessary trades (whipsaws) and excessive commissions. There are several basic methods of applying data filters to data to segregate short-term

random price movements from the underlying trend.

DATA FILTERS

1. Length. The most common approach to filtering price data is to adjust the length of the moving average. The sensitivity† of the moving average decreases as the number of observations in the average increases (and vice versa). While longer moving averages give fewer false signals, they have the disadvantage of providing later signals. Thus, there is a trade-off between sensitivity and timeliness of the signal. In general, a shorter moving average works better when prices are in a sideways (trendless) trading range, and a longer average works better once prices begin to trend†.

2. Closing price/range. When using a single moving average, a change in the direction of the average may signal a buy or sell. One common filter is to require that prices close beyond the moving average. Some technicians impose a stronger filter and require that the entire day's price range clear the moving average.

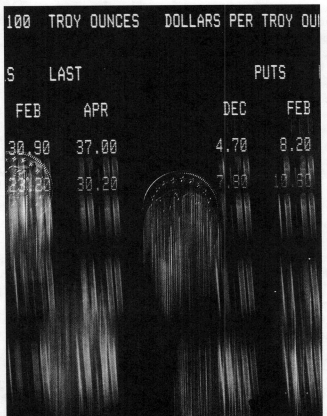

3. Price penetration. Another method of trading is to require that the closing price extend beyond the moving average by a specified amount. The penetration criterion can be expressed as either a dollar amount or in percentage terms. Larger filters provide more protection against whipsaws, but they also result in later buy and sell signals.

4. Confirmation. An independent confirmation signal can be another useful noise filter. Some traders require that the moving average signal be confirmed by some additional evidence that a change may be occurring. This provides a stronger buy/sell signal and reduces whipsaws in a sideways trading range. Typical confirmation filters include a penetration of support/resistance levels on point and figure charts, a weekly channel breakout, momentum oscillators, stochastics

JOS PALMIERI

†*See Traders' Glossary for complete description*

and large changes in volume or open interest (Figure 2). The problem with confirmation filters: the more the trader relies on them, the less important the original moving average signal becomes.

5. Time. Time filters can also be employed to impose a one- to three-day waiting period before taking action. False signals often reverse themselves within a day or two, while genuine trends usually do not. Requiring the signal to remain in effect for an additional day or two will reduce whipsaws from false signals. The disadvantage is later entry on a good signal.

6. Envelopes. Another popular filter is the use of "percentage envelopes" or "volatility bands." Essentially, this filter

> **Moving averages are trend-following by nature and work well when markets are in a trending period. Shorter moving averages give trend signals earlier in the move but also generate more false signals.**

uses parallel lines that are plotted at certain percentage points above and below the moving average line (Figure 3). For example, the envelopes might be a 40-day moving average plus or minus 1.5%, or a 20-day average plus or minus 3%.

The percentage envelope filter requires that closing prices be above the upper envelope line before a buy signal is given. No action is taken if prices are in the "buffer zone" between the upper envelope and the moving average, but the moving average line becomes the stop-out (or liquidation) point. A sell-short signal requires a close below the bottom envelope line, and a close back above the moving average line is needed before the short position is covered. An advantage of this filter is that a buffer zone exists where no positions are taken, so the trader is not always in the market.

7. "High-low" bands. A particular envelope filter arises from "high-low" bands, which are two separate moving averages constructed from the daily highs and lows instead of the daily close. The closing price must be above the higher average to generate a buy signal; the lower line is used as the stop-out point. A sell-short signal is given if the closing price is beneath the lower line, and the upper line becomes the point to cover the short position. Envelope filters in general reduce the number of crossings and eliminate some false signals.

8. Multiple averages. Finally, traders can design data filters by working with more than one moving average. Longer averages work well as long as the underlying price trend continues, but shorter averages do a better job of indicating trend changes.

FIGURE 1

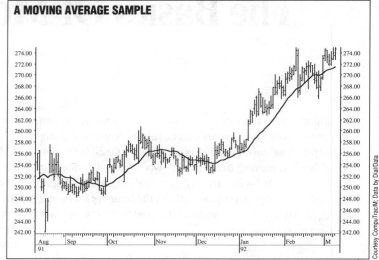

A moving average smoothes data and shows the underlying trend.

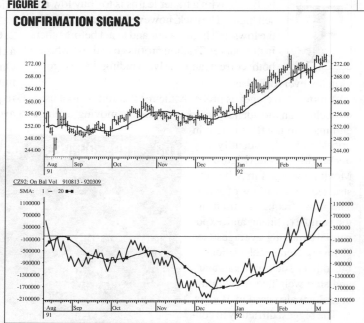

Here, trend changes are confirmed by an on-balance volume line with its own 20-day moving average.

Many technicians use two or more averages to generate signals.

With the popular double-crossover method, for example, a short-term moving average of prices over three to 14 days (the "leading" average) is plotted against a longer-term moving average of 20-200 days (the "lagging" average). When the leading average "crosses over" the lagging average, the trend of the market has changed and this is often viewed as a signal to buy or sell. For example, if prices start declining, the leading average will fall below the lagging average, and this will be a signal to sell (Figure 4). This technique lags the market more than a single moving average does but produces fewer whipsaws.

MOVING AVERAGE CALCULATIONS

The formulas below use this standard notation:

t = time indicator (1 for first period; 2 for second period and so forth)

P_t = Price at time t

n = number of observations in the average

The simple moving average is calculated by summing up all the prices to be included in the average and then dividing that sum by the number of observations. Thus,

$$SMA = \frac{\sum_{t=1}^{n} P_t}{n}$$

The linear weighted moving average (LMA) assigns weights to the price series so that the more recent prices have larger weights. The oldest price is assigned a weight of 1; the second oldest price is assigned a weight of 2. This process continues until the most price is assigned a weight that is equal to the number of observations in the average. The LMA is obtained by dividing the sum of the weighted observations by the sum of the weights. Thus,

$$LMA = \frac{\sum_{t=1}^{n} P_t \, t}{\sum_{t=1}^{n} t}$$

For a five-day LMA,

$$LMA = \frac{(1P_1 + 2P_2 + 3P_3 + 4P_4 + 5P_5)}{(1+2+3+4+5)}$$

The exponential moving average assigns weights in a manner similar to the LMA. The most recent price is assigned a weight, α calculated (approximated) as $2/n + 1$ where n is the simple moving average length. Instead of calculating weights for all previous prices, however, it simply takes the previous day's EMA and multiplies it by (1 - weight). Thus,

$$EMA_t = \left(a P_t\right) + \left(\left(1 - a\right) EMA_{t-1}\right)$$

For a five-day EMA,

$$EMA_t = \left(0.333 P_t\right) + \left(\left(0.667\right) EMA_{t-1}\right)$$

—Editor

FIGURE 3

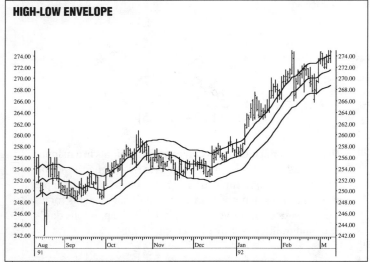

HIGH-LOW ENVELOPE

A price envelope can reduce the number of trades and whipsaws.

FIGURE 4

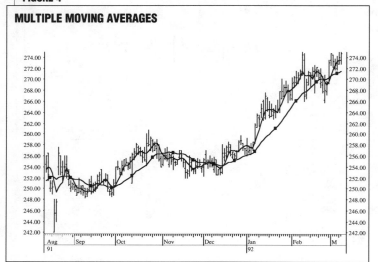

MULTIPLE MOVING AVERAGES

Multiple moving averages smooth data differently and give buy/sell signals. Buy signals are the five-day crossing above the 20-day moving avefrage. Sell signals are the five-day crossing below the 20-day moving average.

The area between two moving averages can also be used to identify a "neutral" (or no trading) zone. A buy signal would require a close above both averages. A sell-short signal would require a close below both averages. All positions would be canceled if prices closed in the neutral zone between the averages. Besides reducing whipsaws, this approach has the advantage of keeping the trader out of the market at times.

A SHORT REVIEW

Moving averages are trend-following by nature and work well when markets are in a trending period. Shorter moving averages give trend signals earlier in the move but also generate more false signals. Even under ideal circumstances in which a market trend exists and data filters are employed, there is still a trade-off between sensitivity and the timing of the signal.

Moving averages perform relatively poorly when markets trade sideways, and sideways markets occur anywhere from a third to half of the time. When markets are choppy and trade sideways in narrow ranges, it is difficult to consistently "buy low and sell high." Trading schemes that are sensitive enough to generate early signals also tend to be sensitive to short-term random price movements (or noise) and thereby generate trade whipsaws. Even in the worst-case scenario where there is no underlying trend, data filters can be useful in reducing the number of false signals attributable to random price movements.

George R. Arrington holds a Ph.D. in finance and economics. He works in New York City for the Federal Reserve System.

FOR FURTHER READING

Glazier, Jason S. [1990]. "Moving average myths," *Technical Analysis of* STOCKS & COMMODITIES, Volume 8: November.

Evans, Richard L. [1991]. "Support and resistance," *Technical Analysis of* STOCKS & COMMODITIES, Volume 9: September.

Johnston, A. Bruce [1990]. "Finding cycles in time series data," *Technical Analysis of* STOCKS & COMMODITIES, Volume 8: August.

Kosar, John J. [1991]. "Support and resistance levels," *Technical Analysis of* STOCKS & COMMODITIES, Volume 9: January.

McGuiness, Charles J. [1990]. "How to calculate moving averages," *Technical Analysis of* STOCKS & COMMODITIES, Volume 8: April.

Murphy, John J. [1986]. *Technical Analysis of the Futures Markets,* New York Institute of Finance (Prentice-Hall).

Payne, J.S. [1989]. "A better way to smooth data," *Technical Analysis of* STOCKS & COMMODITIES, Volume 7: October.

Identifying Trading Opportunities

One of the most important aspects of any trade is timing the entry. Perhaps surprisingly, daily and weekly analysis can be instrumental in planning an entry for long-term trades. Here's an overview on how to use daily and weekly technical analysis to identify trading opportunities that may only come up once a year. S&C Editor Thom Hartle outlines a complete approach to trading, incorporating basic charting and trendline plotting, the stochastics oscillator and momentum studies.

by Thom Hartle

Over the years, my trading style has evolved out of necessity. What could possibly cause anyone to alter his or her trading approach? Losses, of course! It's easy to avoid losses — don't trade. But that approach is too extreme for me, and it doesn't meet my other goals. Thus, the challenge for me is to identify situations that offer the best opportunity for making money with the least amount of risk.

My early reading of the literature of technical analysis revealed that the trading concept stressed most often was trend following. The literature was — and is — full of charts showing beautiful trends with simple moving averages plotted over the prices. It looked easy until I faced the problem of getting on board the trend. First, there was the possibility that the trend had been in force for some time and a consolidation or reversal of the trend could occur. Second, there was another possibility. The market could stay in a trading range for some time. If that happened, each position taken with each false trend indication would result in an equity drawdown†.

Moreover, simply acting on trading signals didn't work for me; I needed additional filters to reduce the number of false trades. The technique that helped me the most had very little to do with trend following — a return to basic chart analysis. I decided to outline my methodology for approaching a trade using basic chart analysis and additional trading techniques applied to the bond market.

WEEKLY ANALYSIS, CONTINUOUSLY

Figure 1 is a continuous weekly bar chart of the bond futures market. Bonds traded above 105-00 in January 1992. The 105-00 level was a critical resistance level, because this same price level was hit in April 1986 and represented the end of a bull market. In January, market participants focused on this price level because of its historical — 1986 — significance. The subsequent price decline reflects that profit taking by longs† found very

few buyers. The price markdown was rather swift. Note that the price moved all the way to the lower side of the trend channel plotted in Figure 1.

The market turned up in late March at two key levels of support. The first level, approximately 97-16, was established in late October 1991. The second key support level is represented by the upward trendline drawn along the September 1990 and June 1991 lows. Simple observation of Figure 1 indicates that the trend is up in the bond market. Higher highs are followed by higher lows, and the price action is confined to an upward sloping parallel channel. Based on this elementary analysis of the weekly chart, these price tests (that is, when prices touch a previously established support line) and price advances from key support levels represent the best opportunity for establishing a long position with the trend of the bond market.

The first step, then, in identifying situations with the least risk is to study the weekly charts and determine price levels that have established importance. Importance can be based on previous major reversals or major trendlines.

STOCHASTICS OSCILLATOR

Technical analysis has responded to the difficulty of identifying price trends and changes in price direction with the development of technical indicators. A number of these indicators modify, smooth or adjust price activity to be normalized (viewed on a scale of zero to 100). The goal is to create a clear graphic or tabular (for computer testing) representation of changes in the trend. One of my favorite indicators of changes in price direction

FIGURE 1

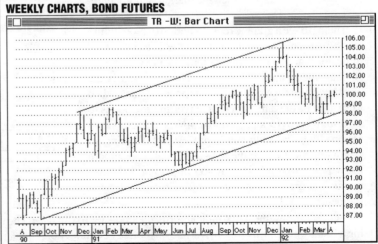

A weekly chart of the bond futures market indicates that the trend is up. If the long-term support line is broken, the trend will be down.

†*See Traders' Glossary for complete description*

is the slow version of the 14-bar stochastics applied to the weekly bar chart (Figure 2).

The stochastics oscillator measures the relationship of the closing price to a predetermined trading range and is then smoothed. At the bottom half of Figure 2, the low values observed on the stochastics chart in March 1992 indicate that the market was at a very oversold level based on previous oversold levels (June and September 1990). The crossover of the %D by the %K in late March confirms the positive price performance observed on the bar chart in Figure 1.

> **If I had to sum up my method for identifying the best low-risk trading opportunities, it would boil down to this: Start with the weekly charts and identify major support or resistance and major trendlines.**

This indicator does not forecast changes in market direction; it simply helps to identify when a turn has occurred. Because it is useful for confirming trend changes, I use the weekly stochastics oscillator in my second step to identify a good trading opportunity.

MOMENTUM CHANGES

Another good technique for identifying changes in trend is observing changes in momentum. The trend of the market cannot change without a change in the momentum. Evidence of a momentum change can be found by studying a bar chart. If the market is making lower lows and lower highs, then the momentum is down. If the price is the same today as it was approximately three weeks ago, then the market's momentum is flat.

It helps to see a graphic representation of momentum to confirm our observations from the bar chart. One indicator that displays momentum is called TRIX (see sidebar titled "Indicator TRIX"). This indicator is the one-day difference of the triple exponential smoothed logarithm of the daily prices. Converting the prices to logarithms provides percentage price changes. Triple exponential smoothing is a process for filtering or removing cycles from the data. The goal is to smooth the data without introducing too much lag. What remains is a graphic representation of the direction of momentum.

Figure 3 shows the TRIX indicator (using alpha approximating a 21-day moving average) overlaid on the daily continuation chart of the bond contract. Note that the rally beginning in the middle of March is confirmed by an upturn in the TRIX indicator. The momentum has turned up, which is a positive indication.

FIGURE 2

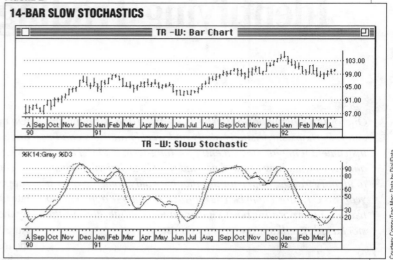

The 14-bar slow version of the stochastics oscillator can help identify overbought and oversold levels on the weekly chart. The signals do not occur very often.

FIGURE 3

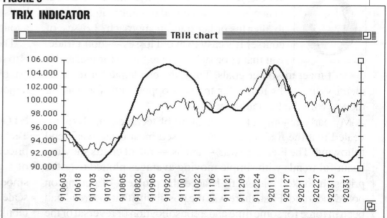

The TRIX indicator is the one-day difference of the triple exponential smoothed log of the prices. This indicator is used to determine changes in momentum.

FIGURE 4

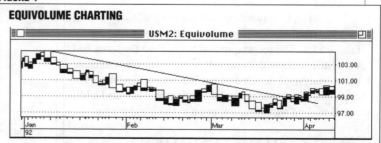

Equivolume charts use the daily volume for the horizontal axis. The black portion is the close for the day. The move above the down trendline is a positive indication.

The third step in identifying a good trading opportunity, then, is determining the momentum of the market.

DAILY ANALYSIS WITH EQUIVOLUME

For daily analysis, we can use a unique form of charting known

INDICATOR TRIX

The indicator TRIX is an oscillator designed to indicate changes in momentum and a filter of random market noise. The process is the triple exponential smoothing of the log of price. The indicator is the one-day difference of the smoothed data. TRIX is simple to set up in a spreadsheet. Column C (sidebar Figure 1) is the log of the price, and Column D is the first smoothing of the log of the price.

	A	B	C	D	E	F	G
1	Date	Close	Log	1st smooth	2nd smooth	3rd smooth	1 day diff
2	900102	98.062	=LN(B2)	=C2	=D2	=E2	
3	900103	97.500	=LN(B3)	=((C3-D2)*$K$3)+D2	=((D3-E2)*$K$3)+E2	=((E3-F2)*$K$3)+F2	=(F3-F2)*10000
4	900104	97.531	=LN(B4)	=((C4-D3)*$K$3)+D3	=((D4-E3)*$K$3)+E3	=((E4-F3)*$K$3)+F3	=(F4-F3)*10000
5	900105	97.250	4.577	4.584	4.585	4.586	-.229
6	900108	97.000	4.575	4.583	4.585	4.586	-.391
7	900109	97.000	4.575	4.582	4.585	4.585	-.585
8	900110	97.031	4.575	4.582	4.585	4.585	-.795
9	900111	97.000	4.575	4.581	4.584	4.585	-1.015
10	900112	96.343	4.568	4.580	4.584	4.585	-1.286
11	900115	95.968	4.564	4.578	4.583	4.585	-1.620
12	900116	95.687	4.561	4.577	4.583	4.585	-2.012
13	900117	95.718	4.561	4.575	4.582	4.585	-2.435
14	900118	94.812	4.552	4.573	4.581	4.584	-2.942

Column E smoothes Column D, and Column F is the third and final smoothing. Column G is the one-day difference between each day's output of the third smoothing. The one-day difference is multiplied by 10,000 for easier use. This day-to-day change (one-day momentum) is the TRIX indicator. Momentum can be considered to be up when the indicator is increasing, while momentum can be considered to be down when the indicator is falling.

The algorithm used in Columns D, E and F has a smoothing constant that is referred to as alpha in triple exponential smoothing. The alpha in the cell formula is represented by $K$3. Using the $ keeps this cell fixed when copying the formulas in the spreadsheet. The formula in cell K3 is:

$$=2/(K2+1)$$

This formula calculates the alpha that approximates a simple moving average in which the value placed in cell K2 is the simple moving average length. In "Identifying Trading Opportunities" (Figure 3) and this example (sidebar Figure 1), the value in cell K2 is 21 and the output of cell K3 is 0.090909. The spreadsheet is set up in this manner to permit adjusting the alpha, and thus the sensitivity of the TRIX indicator.

Varying the number of days (cell K2) allows adjustment of the indicator, and through trial and error, the indicator can be modified to fit with the time horizon desired for trading. Triple exponential smoothing is a filter of cycles, and so cycles of less than the number of days selected will be filtered out. This indicator presents the direction of momentum in a graphic fashion. Trades that are in concert with momentum should be initiated.

---

as Equivolume charting (Figure 4), a technique introduced by Richard Arms. Equivolume charts use the daily volume for the scale of the horizontal axis. The vertical scale is the price. What is produced is a chart that displays the daily volume and daily price range as a box. The larger boxes indicate active days, while the small boxes indicate inactive days. In Figure 4, the top of the black half of each box indicates the close for the day. A day that closes at the high would be all black, while a day that closes at the low would be all white.

The value of Equivolume charts is in the combination of volume and price movement. The large boxes indicate heavy volume. Large white boxes with very little black would be bearish, since there is much more selling on down days. Large black boxes with little white indicates that the volume is accompanying price rallies, which is a positive indication.

The application of trendlines on Equivolume charts can also be useful. Looking still at Figure 4, note that the market moved above the downward trendline drawn along the highs from January to early March. The price found support in mid-February at approximately 97-16 and again in late March at the same price level. This indication of demand at 97-16 and the move above the downward trendline are positive short-term indications.

FIGURE 5

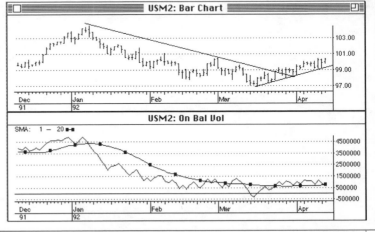

The daily bar chart shows that the bond market has moved into an uptrend. The lower chart is the on-balance volume line along with its 20-day moving average. The inability of the OBV line to lead the 20-day moving average higher is not a positive indication.

ANOTHER MEASURE OF VOLUME

In Figure 5, the daily bar chart has broken its downward trendline and the market has stayed above the upward trendline drawn along the lows of late March and early April. Both of these technical signs are positive short-term indications. However, not everything is perfect. The bottom chart in Figure 5 is the on-balance volume (OBV) line, a technical indicator introduced by Joe Granville. This indicator is the running sum of the daily volume. Days with positive closing prices have the volume added, while days with negative closes have their volume subtracted. A 20-day moving average of the OBV line helps indicate the trend of the volume.

In January, the OBV line moved below its 20-day moving average, indicating that volume was down. Recently, the OBV line and its 20-day moving average have only been moving sideways. This lack of increasing upside volume during the price rally indicates that there may be trouble ahead. If the OBV line begins to increase, then this indicator supports the other positive indicators.

The fourth step involves identifying short-term trading signals that will coincide with the technical message from the weekly charts. Then place your stop loss at the price level that indicates the analysis is incorrect. For example, if the upward trendline in Figure 1 were violated, then the major uptrend would be broken.

It should be noted that four significant changes in the technical picture all occurred approximately within a week of each other: the advance from major weekly support, the buy signal based on the stochastics oscillator, the momentum change indicated by the TRIX indicator and the break of downward trendlines on the daily bar charts. Prior to these changes in the technical indicators, the direction of the bond market was down, but the risk of a trend change was high.

Avoiding risk, keeping losses small and waiting for the best opportunity brings us to the final step: patience. You must have the patience to wait for the trades that offer the highest chance for success.

If I had to sum up my method for identifying the best low-risk trading opportunities, it would boil down to this: Start with the weekly charts and identify major support or resistance and major trendlines. Wait until the market has reached these levels to initiate trades. The price action at historically significant levels will provide information about the direction of the market.

Remember that *everyone* is looking at the same price levels. The successful traders simply act according to their trading rules. Use an indicator that will confirm changes in direction of the price and the momentum. Apply simple techniques such as trendlines on the daily charts for short-term signals. Place your stops at the price level that would indicate that your analysis is *wrong*. Above all, *wait* for these opportunities.

REFERENCES

Hartle, Thom [1991]. "Stochastics," *Technical Analysis of* STOCKS & COMMODITIES, Volume 9: March.

Hutson, Jack K. [1983]. "Triple exponential smoothing oscillator: Good TRIX," *Technical Analysis of* STOCKS & COMMODITIES, Volume 1: July/August.

Reversing For Dollars

by John Sweeney

arebrained ideas being a plentiful item in my daydreams, the idea that I mentioned in April's Settlement that I implement an automatic reversing trade at my maximum adverse excursion (MAE) stop point had less than a 2% chance of survival after analysis. I tested it anyway. (To spare your digging out old issues, this idea is explained in Figure 1.)

BUT FIRST, A SYNOPSIS

Anyone who dropped in on this Settlement without having read the last five must be wondering what in the world I'm talking about. Briefly, I defined a basic, underlying trading rule in the November 1991 Settlement with no more than a casual observation from a chart. That turned out to be profitable. Next, I showed how to measure the system's behavior to put in stops at the right place (December). Then I tested the system (January) successfully on five years of data. Emboldened, I next tried to define an add-on trade — a separately capitalized trading opportunity triggered by the underlying trade, only to fail (February). I had better luck in March and April finding a viable add-on strategy. In April, the whole reversing discussion began, culminating here.

1986-91 RESULTS

This strategy proved effective — but not for the reasons I described in Figure 1. The final results show a profit of about $18,000 on a single contract basis, with $100 for commissions and slippage figured in. There were 37 wins and 20 losses, a very comfortable statistic indicating that the MAE point was indeed a nifty reversal point. Average win was just over $800 and average loss about $550, also a comfortable ratio.

However, some extraordinary drawdowns showed up in Figure 4, the maximum adverse excursion chart for this approach. Keep in mind my caveat in April that MAE figures shown here are likely to be overdrawn because I don't have access to intraday data. MAEs shown here are likely to be overstated. Even so, it's upsetting to see so many large adverse excursions.

Had my insight, as described in Figure 1, been correct, the adverse excursions should generally had been small, the size of the MAE stop. I didn't think far enough ahead: what can and does happen is that during the trade's time horizon, the price can oscillate back above the break-even line and then back into losing status. Had you stood pat after hitting the MAE stop, there

FIGURE 1

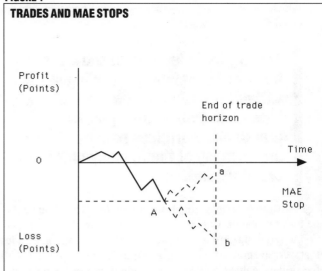

TRADES AND MAE STOPS

At point A, a trade having gone bad and hit the MAE stop, it may make sense to reverse and attempt to capture one of the big losers that the stop was meant to cut off (b). Risk on the second trade is limited to the 0 level, since if the trade went back over the 0 level within the trade horizon, it would be a winning trade in the first place — and experience indicates that trades hitting the MAE stop are not winning trades. Most likely, reversing at point A will yield a small point (point a) or a large gain (b).

FIGURE 2

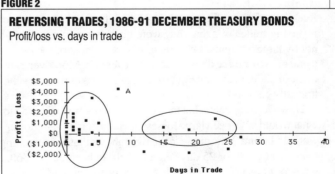

REVERSING TRADES, 1986-91 DECEMBER TREASURY BONDS
Profit/loss vs. days in trade

It turns out that reversing trades have two nifty characteristics: they are usually profitable and they take profits very quickly, usually within two days.

FIGURE 3

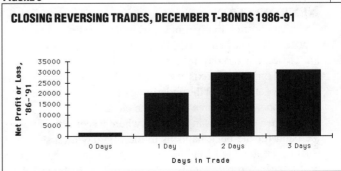

CLOSING REVERSING TRADES, DECEMBER T-BONDS 1986-91

Here's an unusual message: be patient. Don't take profits on a reversing trade on day one but wait for the second or third day. Net profits rise substantially by waiting.

would be occasions where the trade would go back into the black — which would be an "adverse" excursion had you actually reversed at the MAE stop (Figure 5).

> **The original idea was to show the basics of developing a trading system without focusing on the trading "idea." In truth, trading ideas are practically worthless because there are so many of them, many untried or unfounded.**

From a trade management standpoint, this doesn't appear to be a big problem. Losses can be cut off anywhere above 32 points, retaining most of the winners while dropping some trades that were eventual losers anyway. Figure 6 dramatizes that with the dollars gained and lost from winning and losing trades compared with the adverse excursion suffered to gain those wins. The distinct difference in the two distributions indicates we have a very viable trading strategy: admitting you're wrong, turning around and going with the market. Again, we've put numbers to an old trading adage — "The trend is your friend."

TIME, TIME, TIME

Recalling 1986's figures, it appeared that a key virtue of reversing trades was that they were quickly profitable, though not by large amounts. Looking at Figure 2, most of the money came in two or three days, an attractive feature. Moreover, most of these trades are winners, something that makes them psychologically easy to handle.

However, it appears that the original idea — reversing to turn what would have been large losses into large winners — doesn't work. In Figure 2, the circle to the right shows that even winning trades that go 20 or 25 days aren't likely to become big dollar winners. Only point A remotely tempts me to wait 10 days to see if the reversal would work out. Moreover, once I go beyond 10 days, there's probably just as much chance of getting a loser as there would be a winner and I'd have no way to tell which is which.

NEXT QUESTION

The next question in my mind is what's the optimal amount of time to anticipate being in these reversing trades. Many, indeed, are closed out the day they are entered — see all the trades clustered on on the Y axis at zero days? What if the trades were closed, not at the end of the underlying trade horizon, but naively at zero, one, two or three days at the close?

The answer appears in Figure 3, where it seems that most of the bang for the buck happens in the first day after the trade. Closing on the day of the trade (that is, 0 days) is marginally profitable but probably statistically unreliable. By the end of one additional day, a solid profit has been built up and after two days, overall profitability improves another 50%. However, after that, incremental gains are marginal. The rule would appear to be:

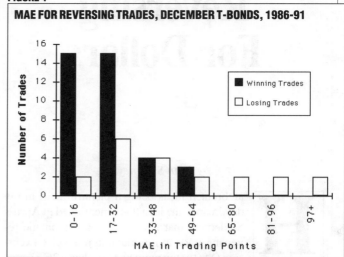

FIGURE 4

MAE FOR REVERSING TRADES, DECEMBER T-BONDS, 1986-91

Reversing trades on Treasury bond futures show an excellent distinction between the behavior of winning trades and that of losing trades. Stops could be put in at 32, 48 or 64 points.

Reverse at the MAE stop but expect to terminate at the close of the next day or the day after, your choice.

The win percentage is:

	Wins	Losses
Closing on day of entry	54%	46%
Closing next day	61	39
Closing at 2 days	69	31
Closing at 3 days	69	31

Needless to say, these likelihoods are much easier to live with on a day-to-day basis than the usual 30% true winners and the rest losers and nail-biters. In this respect, reversing trades are much niftier than the underlying system — remember *that* one?

SUMMARY

The original idea was to show the basics of developing a trading system without focusing on the trading "idea." In truth, trading

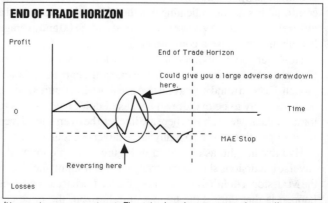

FIGURE 5

END OF TRADE HORIZON

It turns out you can — contrary to Figure 1 — have large moves against you if you reverse at the MAE stop. Here's one scenario where reversing at the MAE stop could suffer before eventually breaking even at the end of the trade horizon.

FIGURE 6

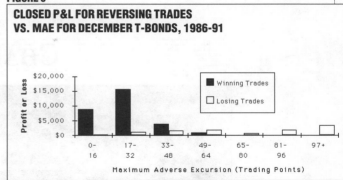

**CLOSED P&L FOR REVERSING TRADES
VS. MAE FOR DECEMBER T-BONDS, 1986-91**

Converting Figure 4's results to dollars shows a very sharp distinction between the overall profitability and adverse price movement of winning reversing trades and losing reversing trades.

ideas are practically worthless because there are so many of them, many untried or unfounded. However, the process of creating a trading strategy — or "discipline," as I call it — is priceless.

John Sweeney is STOCKS & COMMODITIES' Technical Editor.

FURTHER READING

Sweeney, John [1992]. "Reversing your losses," STOCKS & COMMODITIES, April.

CHAPTER 7

THE TRADERS' MAGAZINE

JULY 1992

TECHNICAL ANALYSIS OF STOCKS & COMMODITIES

JUNE YEN: BAR CHART

Technically Trading The Yen With Money Management

Any good trading methodology includes selecting the best indicators for a tradeable and applying money management techniques to hold on to profits. In the April 1990 STOCKS & COMMODITIES, 34 indicators were tested for profitability. Here, Timothy Krehbiel, Thomas Drinka and Gisele Hamm take the indicator that was found to be most profitable and combine it with different money management techniques to statistically test for profitability. First, the indicator and money management strategy was optimized over one year's worth of data. Then the strategy was tested for the following quarter. Next, the simulator moved everything up one quarter and repeated the process. The goal of the study was to determine if money management strategies could enhance the profitability of optimized trading strategies.

Speculators and commercial hedgers who trade currency futures often use technical analysis to determine trading signals. Previously, we reported on the profitability of 34 technical indicators used to simu-

late trading of the International Money Market (IMM) yen futures contract; some of these indicators exploited price trends, while others exploited price volatility.

This time, we report on the results of a second study that builds on the results of the speculation study only. For this study, we selected the technical indicator that appeared to be the most profitable in the previous study and used it with various money management strategies to assess the impact of these strategies on profitability.

by Timothy L. Krehbiel, Thomas P. Drinka, Gisele F. Hamm

DIANA FRITCH

THE INDICATOR OF CHOICE

The indicator found to be most profitable in our previous study was a moving average crossover method. Three simple moving averages (short, intermediate and long) are used to define buy and sell signals. This system is not always in the market; open positions are offset and the trading system is out of the market until the next signal. The three simple moving average offset indicator works thus:

1) A long (or short) position is taken when the short moving average is greater (or less) than the intermediate moving average and the intermediate moving average is greater (or less) than the long moving average.
2) A position is offset following a subsequent crossover of the short and intermediate moving averages.

> **Six money management strategies produced significantly positive quarterly net returns when applied with the three simple moving average offset indicator.**

DETAILS

First of all, optimization was conducted on a year's worth of data using the nearby contracts. The simulator chose the parameter combination that produced the greatest profits through the year, a process called *in-sample optimization*. These parameters were then used to trade the next quarter to produce one observation of quarterly net return, which is known as *out-of-sample testing*. The in-sample data were moved forward one quarter and the simulator was used to re-optimize and a new parameter set determined. These parameters were used to trade out-of-sample in the next quarter to produce the second observation of quarterly net return. In this fashion, quarterly net returns were generated from March 2, 1978, to September 1, 1987.

The trading of the IMM yen futures contract was optimized and simulated by using the following procedure. The short moving average was incremented in two-day steps from a two-day to a 24-day moving average; the intermediate moving average was incremented in four-day steps from a four-day to a 40-day moving average; and the long moving average was incremented in six-day steps from a six-day to an 84-day moving average. A total of 1,680 parameter sets were tested. Unless otherwise specified, trades were made at the open of the trading day following a trading signal; for rollovers, open positions were liquidated at the close of the first trading day of the expiration month.

Nine trading strategies involving stops and entry-exit methods were tested. A 10th strategy — the benchmark strategy — involved trading yen futures without money management.

STOPS

Four strategies involving stops were analyzed:

Entry stop: An entry stop minimizes loss. On assuming a

market position, the maximum loss — say, x points — that will be risked on the trade is determined. If the market moves against the position by x points from the entry price, the stop is activated and the position offset.

To determine the usefulness of such a strategy, the 1,680 moving average short/intermediate/long parameter combinations were re-optimized with the stop incremented from five points to 70 points in five-point steps (in dollar terms, the stop was incremented by $62.50 steps from $62.50 to $875); thus, 23,520 parameter sets were tested in total (Figure 1).

TESTING INDICATORS FOR PROFITABILITY

In our first study of 34 indicators, MicroVest's BackTrak was used to simulate optimization using three strategies: speculation, hedging for a commercial holding a long position in the cash yen market and hedging for a commercial holding a short position in the cash yen market. Simulated quarterly net returns were screened using tests for serial correlation† and nonnormality before applying standard statistical procedures. Simulated quarterly net returns that did not meet the statistical criteria necessary for standard t-tests were eliminated; simulated quarterly net returns must be drawn from a normal distribution, and simulated quarterly net returns in adjacent quarters must not be correlated with one another for the t-test methodology to be valid. Of the 34 indicators that were simulated, a total of 16 survived these statistical procedures when traded speculatively; five survived when traded for short hedges; and one survived when traded for long hedges.

†See Traders' Glossary for complete description

Trailing stop: A trailing stop is designed to both limit loss and protect profit. If, on one hand, the market initially moves against the trader's position by *x* points from entry, the stop is activated and the position is offset; in this case, a trailing stop is identical to an entry stop.

If, on the other hand, the market initially moves in favor of the position, the stop is re-positioned *x* points from the settlement price; if the settlement price continues to move in favor of the trader's position, the stop is repositioned each day *x* points from the most favorable settlement price and at some point could be positioned at a price that will guarantee a profit. If the market turns against the position, the stop remains positioned *x* points from the most favorable settlement price and is activated when the market moves *x* points from the most favorable settlement price.

Profit stop: A profit stop is designed to protect profit. This stop is activated when the market moves in favor of the position by *x* points from the entry price.

Entry stop and profit stop (combined): While an entry stop is designed to minimize loss, a profit stop is designed to protect profit. The basic 1,680 moving-average parameter combinations were reoptimized by simultaneously incrementing the entry stop from 10 points to 230 points by 10-point steps, and the profit stop from 10 points to 250 points by 10-point steps.

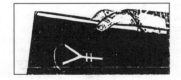

ENTRY-EXIT METHODS

Five strategies involving entry-exit methods were analyzed:

Today's close: To trade the daily close, the settlement price required for a technical indicator to generate a trading signal must be anticipated. If such a price *is* anticipated, the broker would have to be instructed during the trading session to trade before the close. If the market appears to be overbought (or oversold), it may be advantageous to sell (or buy) on the close before selling (or buying) pressure drives the price down (or up) on the next trading day's open. One disadvantage of this method is the effort required to implement it.

Tomorrow's open (favorable): A trader using this entry-exit method may be able to avoid trading on false signals. Following a trading signal during the session, one would wait for the market to show some strength (or weakness) before buying (or selling). The trader would attempt to determine whether the market agrees with the analysis before taking a position.

Tomorrow's open (unfavorable): This entry-exit method may allow a trader to enhance profit by extracting a few extra

T-TEST RETURNS

For each of the 10 trading strategies, Figure 2 presents the mean quarterly net returns, the standard deviation† of these returns, the results of the t-test, the autocorrelation coefficient (the column titled Auto contains the estimated values of the correlation coefficient between adjacent returns), and the value of the Shapiro-Wilkes statistic (the column titled S-W). The Shapiro-Wilkes test statistic is bounded between 0 and 1, with small values cause for rejection of the null hypothesis†; the distribution of the Shapiro-Wilkes test statistic is right-skewed and, thus, even relatively large values can lead to rejection. The seven trading strategies in Figure 2 that are marked with a single asterisk are characterized by statistical significance at the 5% level.

Six money management strategies produced significantly positive quarterly net returns when applied with the three simple offset indicator. While producing significant positive returns, the profit stop and tomorrow's open (favorable) entry-exit strategies produced smaller quarterly net returns on average than did the benchmark. None of the significantly profitable money management strategies showed any signs of autocorrelation. The simultaneous use of the entry and profit stops produced the largest mean quarterly net returns of any of the strategies tested in this study.

A difference-in-means test† was performed to determine if the money management strategies produced quarterly net returns markedly different from the quarterly net returns of the benchmark. Tests for difference in the mean quarterly net returns did not reject the null hypothesis of no difference in mean quarterly net returns at the 5% confidence level when comparing returns of the significantly profitable money management strategies with benchmark returns. However, the entry stop with the profit stop produced quarterly net returns that were significantly greater than the benchmark at the 6.5% confidence level.

Test results indicate that net trading returns from applying the three simple offset indicator to the IMM yen contract can be improved by incorporating money management. In particular, the entry and profit stops used with one another produced mean quarterly net returns that were significantly greater (at the 6.5% confidence level) than the returns of the benchmark indicator.

points from the market. Following a signal, the trader would trade during the next trading session if the price moves from the open against the direction of the trading signal. Thus, one would wait for the market to show some strength (or weakness) before selling (or buying). This strategy should only be used with a reliable indicator.

Today's close (favorable and unfavorable): These two techniques are analogous to the favorable and unfavorable methods for tomorrow's open. One advantage of these methods is that the trader knows — before the open of the next trading session — the price to be traded during the trading session (that is, the close plus or minus the optimal number of points), and the broker can be instructed accordingly before the open.

COMMISSIONS AND MARGINS

The quarterly net returns reflect the trading of one contract; a transaction cost of $47.50 per turn was used, amounting to a $10 brokerage fee plus three ticks' slippage. In addition, the appropriate 90-day Treasury bill rate was used to reduce returns by the interest cost of maintaining a $3,500 margin; no credit for interest earned was applied on equity in excess of exchange minimum margin. As a result, these procedures resulted in an unrealistically high transaction cost.

CONCLUSIONS

For each of the 10 trading strategies, Figure 2 presents the mean quarterly net returns, the standard deviation of these returns, the results of the t-test, the autocorrelation coefficient and the value of the Shapiro-Wilkes statistic. (See sidebar, "T-test returns.") Six money management strategies produced significantly positive quarterly net returns when applied with the three simple moving average offset indicator. While producing significant positive returns, the profit stop and tomorrow's open (favorable) entry-exit strategies produced smaller quarterly net returns on average than did the benchmark. The simultaneous use of the entry and profit stops produced the largest mean quarterly net returns of any strategy tested in this study.

Test results indicate that net trading returns from applying the three simple offset indicator to the IMM yen contract can be improved by incorporating money management. In particular, the entry and profit stops used with one another produced mean quarterly net returns that were significantly greater (at the 6.5% confidence level) than the returns of the benchmark indicator.

Timothy L. Krehbiel is an assistant professor at Oklahoma State University. Thomas P. Drinka and Gisele F. Hamm are professor and graduate assistant, respectively, at Western Illinois University. BackTrak is available from MicroVest (309-837-4512).

FURTHER READING

Drinka, Thomas P., Timothy L. Krehbiel and Stephen Ptasienski [1990]. "Technically trading the yen," *Technical Analysis of* STOCKS & COMMODITIES, Volume 8: April.

FIGURE 2

QUARTERLY NET RETURNS, SIMULATED SPECULATIVE POSITIONS
1978-87 IMM Yen Futures

Trading strategy	Dollars		T-statistic	Auto	S - W
	Mean	Standard deviation			
No money management	1,358.55	2484.24	3.19 *	0.04	0.96
Stops					
Entry	1,620.02	2,321.31	4.07 *	(0.05)	0.98
Trailing from close	589.34	1,847.41	1.86	0.05	0.94
Profit	1,023.72	1,410.12	4.23 *	(0.07)	0.98
Entry & Profit	2,199.66	2,091.64	6.13 *	0.04	0.96
Entry-exit method					
Today's close	1,712.08	2,478.97	4.03 *	(0.01)	0.98
Favorable move from tomorrow's open	1,009.34	2,809.76	2.09 *	(0.18)	0.96
Unfavorable move from tomorrow's open	663.66	2,612.90	1.48	(0.09)	0.99
Favorable move from today's close	1,447.66	2,559.99	3.30 *	(0.25)	0.98
Unfavorable move from today's close	697.10	2846.82	1.43	(0.07)	0.97

* Statistical significance at the 0.05 level.

For each of the 10 trading strategies, here are the mean quarterly net returns, the standard deviations, the results of the t-test, the autocorrelation coefficient and the value of the Shapiro-Wilkes statistic. The seven trading strategies that are marked with a single asterisk are characterized by statistical significance at the 5% level. The benchmark (that is, no money management) strategy and all the money management strategies had positive average quarterly net returns. Notice that the standard deviation of each strategy is large, indicating a wide range of quarterly returns. The question whether the mean (average) quarterly return is influenced by the range of returns — that is, whether the true mean (from a much larger population of data) is actually zero or possibly negative — arises. The t-statistic addresses this question. The values in this column with the asterisk indicate that the chances were less than five in 100 that the true mean quarterly returns are zero. The Auto column (autocorrelation) is a measure of the strength of the relationship between adjacent quarters. Values close to zero indicate that the quarterly returns are independent. The S-W (for the Shapiro-Wilkes test) column is a statistical test indicating that the likelihood of the net returns were drawn from a normal distribution. High values (close to 1) increases our confidence in the reliability of the t-test.

Elizabeth Marbach of Rodman & Renshaw

Elizabeth Marbach, first vice president and broker/analyst in the financial futures group for Rodman & Renshaw, started out in the early 1980s down in the Treasury bill trading pit on the Chicago Mercantile Exchange floor before eventually moving off the exchange floor. STOCKS & COMMODITIES Editor Thom Hartle interviewed Marbach on April 20, 1992, on topics ranging from the Eurodollar market to the dangers of pyramiding.

"Eurodollars have outpaced other markets because banks have changed the way that they operate. So much more of the world floats now—which is to say that the interest rates that banks lend at are reset throughout the life of the loan."— Elizabeth Marbach

So how did you get started in the business?

Well, I started out in the government bond department at Continental Illinois in the late 1970s, where I sold cash governments, money markets and munis. Then I got into the futures market in 1981 down on the floor of the Chicago Mercantile Exchange in the Treasury bill pit. Treasury bill futures, if you'll recall, preceded Eurodollar futures and Standard & Poor's futures markets. Eventually, I moved off the floor, working with customers as a broker and as an analyst for eight years at Drexel Burnham Lambert and the last two years at Rodman & Renshaw.

What are some of the big differences in financial futures between today and when you first worked on the floor, considering how much financial futures have changed over the years?

Well, we're talking about more than 10 years ago. At that time you had people who were just getting into financial futures. There was a difference in terms of

who traded the markets. Some knew the cash markets, while others knew the futures markets. With some exceptions, there weren't many who understood both. Different traders followed their own set of guidelines for their own markets. Futures traders watched more for either the technicals or the underlying specifics of the contracts—for example, futures traders would follow the cash and carry for the bond contract. The bottom line was that two distinct groups were trading these instruments, converging at the time of delivery.

At that time, the futures markets were the only places to hedge interest rate risk, weren't they?

Yes. You didn't have the over-the-counter derivative products that we have now, which financial institutions and corporations use to transfer interest rate risk. Basically, back in those days you had the T-bill market, the bond market at the Board of Trade, and Ginnie Maes, which

were still active at that time. These futures contracts were the only readily available vehicle to hedge risk. Since then, the Ginnie Mae contract has ceased to trade, but the Eurodollar futures market has thrived since its debut.

Why have Eurodollars outpaced other markets?

Eurodollars are popular because, basically, banks have changed the way that they operate. So much more of the world floats now — which is to say that the interest rates that banks lend at are reset throughout the life of the loan. When people go in to borrow money now, the interest rate may float to a six-month LIBOR or a three-month LIBOR. With the Eurodollar contract converging to the three-month LIBOR rate on the day the contract expires, banks have the opportunity to hedge their interest rate risk in the futures market.

So banks and corporations can use Eu-

FIGURE 1

EURODOLLAR FUTURES VS. T-BOND FUTURES

The ratio of the average daily volume per month-end open interest for T-bond futures and Eurodollar futures illustrate that the Eurodollar futures daily volume is a lower percentage of open interest when compared with the T-bond volume and open interest figures.

FIGURE 2

CBOT TREASURY BOND FUTURES

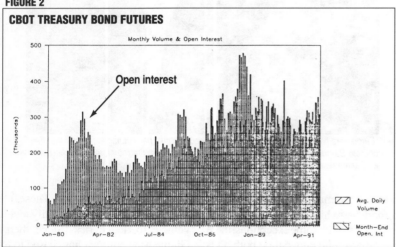

The T-bond open interest peaked in late 1988. Typical average daily volume has grown to approximately the same levels as open interest.

FIGURE 3

EURODOLLAR FUTURES

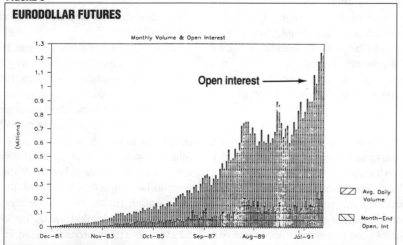

The open interest for Eurodollar futures has grown to more than a million contracts. This reflects the use of Eurodollar futures as a prominent tool used by hedgers for long-term horizons.

rodollar futures for managing their balance sheets.

That's right, you have a much more interdependent market by having a mechanism for a hedge. Both the end-user and the banks themselves are not necessarily taking the risks that they took when they had enormous mismatched books. Euros have continued to grow because the marketplace itself has continued to become more sophisticated.

But the Treasury bond futures market hasn't?

Oh, the Treasury bond market has kept up. But there is a difference. These futures tend to serve the needs of hedgers on a much more temporary basis. Let me give you an example. T-bond futures could be used by, as an example, the lead manager of a corporate issue to be announced. Just the other day, we had a break —kind of a quick break, a 10-tick break in five-year note futures, and it wasn't explained at the time but it turned out the underwriters of the Kingdom of Norway issue were hedging when the European market was closing.

On any given day, you may have someone who does a hedge using the T-bond, T-note or five-year note contract, and that person hedges up for whatever reason until he or she gets the other side of the trade done. In contrast, the Eurodollar contracts are put on in a series of hedges called strips†. For example, a two- or four-year strip of Eurodollar contracts may be bought or sold and kept until each contract expires.

Is that why the open interest in T-bonds hasn't kept up with the volume?

Good question. I went back and looked because, in my opinion, the markets have changed so much over the last 10 or 12 years that I just wanted to check that my perception wasn't wrong. Back in 1981, bond futures had about an average daily volume somewhere around 59,000 contracts. That's the average daily volume. The open interest by that time was around 240,000 contracts. So around 24% or 25% of the open interest is in volume (Figure 1). By 1985, the average daily volume had increased to about 160,000 contracts. By 1991, particularly toward

"The markets will sometimes tread water for three days, waiting for economic releases."

the end of the year, the daily volume was averaging 253,000 contracts, but the open interest at the end of 1991 was just over 315,000 contracts (Figure 2). Well, if you're trading 250,000 contracts a day on that open interest, obviously, the dynamics have changed since 1981.

On the other hand, it is very different compared with Eurodollars because their open interest figures are very much in excess of their volume; the open interest continues to grow. There is more than a million in open interest on Eurodollar futures (Figure 3).

That is quite a change. What's the bond market being used for, then?

People using bond futures as well as T-note and five-year note futures as a hedge may be using them for short-term protection. Someone may want to have some protection in place into the unemployment report two days from now, as an example. To the hedger, the temporary position in the futures market helps avoid a sudden adverse price move that could hurt their current position.

Because Euros aren't a temporary hedging vehicle.

Right. Literally, a depository institution will put on a trade, such as a two-year strip, and hold it for two years.

And the interest rate swap† market probably has a lot to do with that?

Yes, indeed.

What other changes have you seen over the years with the growth of the financial futures markets?

Remember what I was saying about the two different types of users in the market back in the 1980s? Now the cash traders know all about futures and pretty much vice versa and you have integrated markets. You have a whole generation of traders, particularly in the primary dealerships, that know how to use futures. They can rely on futures. They need the liquidity of futures. A case in point on that is what happened this week with our catastrophe in Chicago, when the futures markets were closed due to the flood. *(Editor's note: During the week of April 13, 1992, much of Chicago's business district was shut down for several days when a breach in the retaining wall of the Chicago River caused the basements of older buildings in the area to flood. The leak caused river water to flood old freight tunnels under downtown Chicago.)* The bond futures in particular had an entire session when nothing was traded, after which trading hours were abbreviated for two days. Market participants and observers became very aware how futures and cash markets work together.

How so?

My clients mentioned to me, and some newswires mentioned it too, that there are just a lot of people who are used to having the liquidity of the futures pit to rely on, so they maybe make a little more tentative or wider bid-ask spread when they're making a market in government securities when the Board of Trade isn't open. That's one of the things you saw a lot in the early days—I could name you a primary dealer or two that didn't even use futures in the early 1980s, and it was something that people were just getting into. Also, now the end-user is much more familiar with the contracts and how they work and is just much more knowledgeable of how

the whole market mechanism works.

Can you think of any other changes?

Oh, the rise of these trading accounts. Now, the trade is beginning to call these accounts managed futures and there's a whole argument on managed futures being called an asset class. That discussion aside, these funds do have an impact on trading.

These managed futures accounts are now one of the growth areas of the futures markets. The basic idea is these trading advisors are given a specific amount of money for a specific period, usually six months to a year. So the investors don't have a vested interest necessarily in what they're trading; they just want to get a return. More and more of these managed futures accounts are coming into the market, and a lot of them are technically driven, so on any given day they can make an impact on the market.

How do they do that?

From my experience, and I've really watched these kind of funds now for about 10 years, both at Drexel and Rodman, they have such an impact because so many of them trade based on the close. This accounts for why you may or may not get the requisite follow-through price action that a lot of people like in a move.

For a next-day follow-through?

You got it. It doesn't mean they won't be right in the long run and most of them have very deep pockets, but so many are based on how a market closes, whether it's a combination of moving averages or a breakout to new highs or new lows. On any given day, market participants can begin to anticipate what those market orders are going to be for the close, and that can affect in particular those last 40 minutes of trading.

So someone keeping technical indicators should have an idea of what price levels other traders are going to react to going into the last hour of trading?

Definitely.

Globalization is another popular topic. What changes have you seen in the futures markets due to globalization?

"If you expect a quick price move and you get it, take it."

Whenever you see articles where everyone's bemoaning the dwindling U.S. market share, the reason mostly is all these other markets coming on stream. It is very healthy; for example, the German Bund contract and the Eurosterling market are developing. Now, various markets can determine reactions to certain events, to see, say, how London is reacting to markets that are trading in Japan. I fully expect that trend to continue.

Let's go back to what goes on in the pits. Sometimes, the person on the street thinks the traders in the pit have an unfair advantage. Do you think people off the floor are overreacting and blaming market volatility on how the pits work?

Another good question. I started off covering accounts from the floor and then made the transition in the mid-1980s to work off the floor. At one time, there may have been some advantage to being near the pit and on the floor, and obviously there is still *some* advantage, or you wouldn't have the prices of seats as high as they are.

But things have changed dramatically in the way the markets will sometimes tread water for three days, waiting for economic releases. The news comes out, the market goes into a fast market† and market participants off the floor have as much of an advantage as those on the floor. One reason the market goes into these critical vacuums when we don't get a good bid or offer is because traders in the pits don't have any better idea than anyone else where anything should be priced.

The market has to regain its composure.
That's right.

What should individuals who are just starting to trade do?

Well, traders have to decide what their time horizon is for any given trade. Most traders who have successfully traded the futures market have had game plans, both an entry point and an exit point for a profitable trade and an exit point for a unprofitable trade. That sounds easy, but once the market is open and it's reacting to various news, it's very easy for someone to get emotional about the market. Someone I worked with in my early years said something that I have really grown to appreciate: You do best if you do your thinking before or after the market closes. Whether you rely on technical or fundamental factors, you should have your game plan in mind so that once the markets are open, all you're doing is executing that plan.

Do novice traders tend to make plans and ignore them or do they make one at all?

It is very difficult to follow a plan. Some of the most disastrous trades have occurred when traders just can't believe a market is doing something and they have to either react to the new direction or sit through a lot of pain. In the process, even if in the end those traders are vindicated because the market comes back, not only have they spent a lot of emotional energy, they have missed other trading opportunities.

It just comes back to having a game plan and sticking to it. The first rule is: *Don't break the rules.* Whatever rules you've set out for yourself, you need to stick to them, particularly as a new trader.

What are some of your rules?

Well, take, for example, a trading rule that a day trader might use. Say he is looking to buy the market and the market opened at a key support level and held above the opening range, trading above it for, say, 10 or 15 minutes, at that point what he should do is buy and place a stop-loss order five ticks below the opening range (Figure 4) for this trade.

The premise is that the market took the overnight news, adjusted to it and opened near a level that a day trader was looking to buy and held support. I've seen this work a lot in the currency markets. If the market reverses direction and the opening range gives way, the trader avoided a situation in which he has to make a painful decision because the stop loss is already in the market.

FIGURE 4

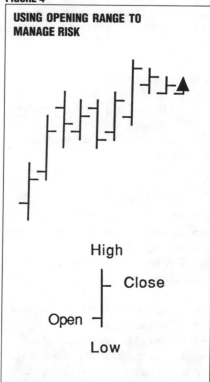

USING OPENING RANGE TO MANAGE RISK

High
Close
Open
Low

One strategy for placing stop-loss orders is to use the opening range as a level to manage your risk. In this example, the market is in an uptrend defined by higher daily highs and higher daily lows. Today, the market opened at the lows for the last two days. The market is trading up from the opening (up arrow) and so buy the market based on the positive price action and place your stop loss just below the opening range.

What about longer-term trading?

One rule would be if you're more of a position trader, you can use a crossover of an intermediate- and a long-term moving average. Again, if the moving averages cross over, then you will take the signal. Knowing that, you can identify the trend based on the moving averages and you will only have trades that are with the trend that gives you a set of rules to follow. Another suggestion: If a trader is not going to use price stops based on a technical level or price level, then an appropriate stop loss based on how much money to risk should be determined. For example, to risk half a point to try to make three points, well, that makes *some* sense.

Any other observations?

From working with traders and hedgers for years, I've noticed that human nature is such that everyone has at first the tendency to think that *every* trade will be *the* home run trade. But my advice is this: If you were expecting a quick price move and you get the move, *take it.* Then look for the next trade. The tendency is to think that this trade might become one of the bigger moves and a trader will change his plan by altering his objective.

I'm not suggesting that traders want to be getting in and out of the market constantly and not stick with well-established trends. But some of the most successful traders I've seen over the years have had objectives in mind, and when the market reached those objectives, they've tended to pare down their positions. They are not always going for the home run.

"The person on the street thinks the traders in the pits have an unfair advantage. At one time, there may have been some advantage to being near the pit and on the floor, and obviously there is still some advantage, but things have changed dramatically since then."

In short, be cautious about pyramiding†.

Right. It's human nature: as a position starts to really work for you, you began to add more and before you know it, you —

Fall in love with it.

Yes. Then all of a sudden, the market is at your objective and you've got a huge position; if anything adverse happens you have a bigger *emotional* problem because you've ended up with your biggest position. This is just common sense.

To wrap up, do you have any favorite books?

Well, sure. For technical analysis, John Murphy's *Technical Analysis of the Futures Markets* is much easier to read, particularly for anyone starting out, than Edwards and Magee's *Technical Analysis of Stock Trends* is. That, and just keeping up with articles as they're published. Whatever you look at, you do have to keep it simple.

Thanks for your time, Elizabeth.

You're welcome.

The Damping Index

Variety is the spice of life — except when you're trying to optimize a trading system. This new indicator identifies those places on the price graph where highs and lows are getting closer and closer together, and when used in conjunction with buy rules and sell rules, it can be used to create a computerized trading system. Longtime S&C contributor Curtis McKallip demonstrates.

by Curtis McKallip Jr.

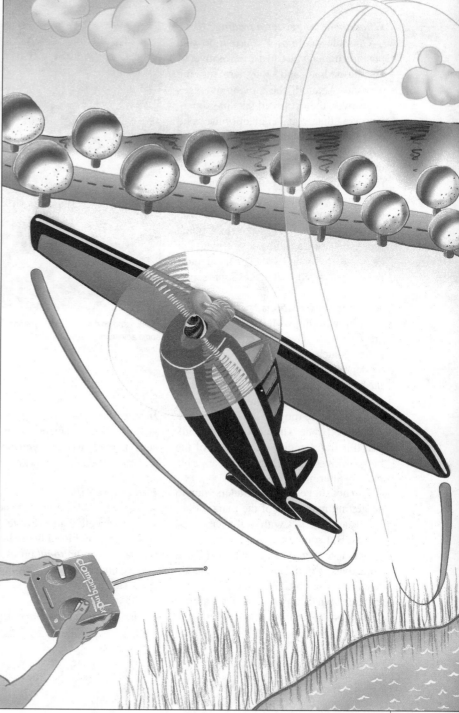

NADIR KIANSERSI

W hy is it so difficult to optimize a trading system for different markets? One reason may be that most technical indicators are not easily related to classic economic theory. Designing a trading system becomes not unlike designing an airplane without understanding aerodynamics. You might come up with a design that flies better than another, but not knowing why it does so makes it difficult to translate that success into other designs.

You can relate price patterns to supply and demand curves, even though you may not have all the necessary fundamental data. Those curves are still active; they don't depend on data for their existence. Rather, they are the stuff that markets are made of because they depict human behavior.

When a news event is reported, particularly an unexpected one, the price reacts and then settles down in a zigzag pattern (Figure 1). The price versus quantity chart is known as a cobweb chart because of its appearance. Normally, the equilibrium price of a tradeable occurs at the point where the supply and demand curves cross. When a reported news event forces the price up without shifting either curve, that causes the market to supply more of the product than it needs (or less if the price is forced lower). Since the demand is not sufficient to account for all these products, the price drops below equilibrium, which in turn causes producers to cut back on production, producing less than necessary. When the supply drops, the price goes back up.

This cycle continues until the price eventually reaches equilibrium or another news event is reported that instigates the same set of actions into motion. The cycle length of the zigzag price pattern created by this process is related to the production time of the commodity. Originally, the theory was developed for agricultural products with one- to four-year crop cycles. For our purposes, however, the cycle length can be as short as a few minutes for the supply time of floor traders. In other words, the cobweb process is a naturally recurring market process.

News events come out more or less at random so the zigzags may overlap, which is why sometimes it is difficult to make sense out of why the price fails to react to news announcements; it may still be reacting to what happened yesterday.

If the news event also starts a trend, however, it makes sense to identify these patterns because they can mark the beginning of trends. Thus, to be a trend follower, find these patterns to get on a trend. To this end, I have created a new technical indicator, which I call the damping index. It identifies those areas on the price graph where the highs and lows are getting closer and closer together. Used in conjunction with buy and stop rules, the damping index can be used to create a computerized trading system.

DEFINING DAMPING

Damping behavior is similar but not identical to such classic chart formations as triangles and pennants. Damping behavior can be much more sinuous in character than triangles or pennants, as these latter formations are limited to predefined geometric shapes. For trading purposes, damping patterns have an

> **Designing a trading system can be like designing an airplane without understanding aerodynamics. Not knowing why something flies better makes it difficult to translate that success into better designs.**

advantage over triangles in that the trader does not have to wait for a breakout the way one does to trade with conventional triangles, so the trader can get into a market sooner and set stops closer. Some examples of damping behavior can be seen in Figure 2. The damping index also differs from volatility in that volatility can expand or contract without creating such a pattern.

The formula for the damping index is as follows:

Damping index =

$$\frac{\text{Average high of bar}_{-1} \text{ to bar}_{-5} - \text{average low of bar}_{-1} \text{ to bar}_{-5}}{\text{Average high of bar}_{-6} \text{ to bar}_{-10} - \text{average low of bar}_{-6} \text{ to bar}_{-10}}$$

The length of the averages can be adjusted, but overall these values generally give favorable results. This index typically varies from a low of about 0.5 to a high of 2 or 3. Any value less than 1 is a strong indication that valid damping behavior has been detected.

USING THE DAMPING INDEX

Adding a few buy and sell rules to this formula makes a trading system. If the denominator is not zero, a buy is indicated if the index is less than 1, the close of today is greater than the average high of the preceding two bars and the average low of the last three bars is greater than the average high of the four bars starting

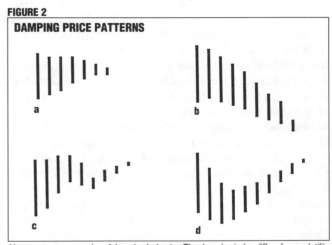

FIGURE 1

COBWEB CHART

DAMPING PRICE PATTERN

When a news event is reported, the price reacts and then settles down in a zigzag pattern.

FIGURE 2

DAMPING PRICE PATTERNS

Here are some examples of damping behavior. The damping index differs from volatility in that volatility can expand or contract without creating such a pattern.

FIGURE 3

DAMPING INDEX

Crude Oil 15 min bars

Expanding

Damping

Here is how the damping index behaves on an intraday chart, coupled with a trading system that buys when prices move higher after damping has been detected.

Chart courtesy TradeStation

10 bars ago. The latter condition ensures that the market is in an uptrend. A protective stop is set at the lowest low of the last four bars. Long trades are exited when the price moves below the lowest low of the last four bars.

A sell is indicated if the index is less than 1, the close of today is less than the average low of the last two bars and the average high of the last three bars is less than the average low of four bars starting 10 bars ago. A protective stop is set at the highest high of the last four bars. Shorts are exited when the price moves above the highest high of the last four bars.

Figure 3 indicates how the damping index behaves on an intraday chart. It has been coupled with a trading system that buys when prices move higher after damping has been detected. Several trades are shown in Figure 4. Trade 1 was set up by a sinuous damping pattern and turned out to be a very good trade, netting about $600 a contract over three days. Note how tight and well defined this pattern was and how it signaled a trade before the actual breakout. The trade was exited when the price fell below the low of the last four days. Trade 2 was a sell signal. It probably would not have been taken because the market had already moved down markedly by that point. This was also the case for the buy in Trade 3. It was a poorly defined pattern, with a very loose set of highs and lows. These examples evince how this system can be used to keep watch for advantageous trades but also allow for operator interpretation before the trade is actually taken.

Figure 5 shows how the index looks on a weekly chart of the yen. A simple computerized trading system based on this index is shown on the price graph. The index did well at catching major moves in the yen over a 14-year period; its excellent record can be seen in Figure 6. The actual trading rules used are listed in Figure 7.

Of course, the damping index does not perform this well in all markets. But it *does* allow a trader to connect trading signals to supply and demand curves and economic theory — something few other indicators can claim. In turn, this should help traders develop systems in a logical and theoretically sound manner.

Curtis McKallip Jr. is a long-time investor and market theorist currently residing in Austin, TX. His interests include computer programming, ecology and music.

FURTHER READING

McKallip, John Curtis [1991]. *Visualizing Economics: The Art of Investing Without Statistics*, Fresh Ink.

FIGURE 4

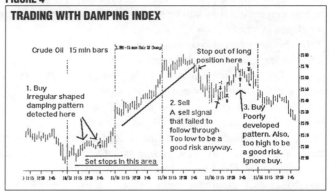

TRADING WITH DAMPING INDEX

Here is a close-up of the trades in Figure 3. These examples show how this system can be used to keep watch for good trades but also how operator interpretation before the trade is actually taken.

FIGURE 5

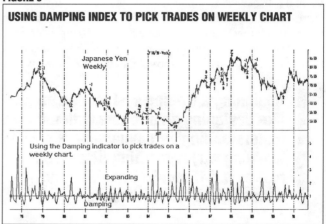

USING DAMPING INDEX TO PICK TRADES ON WEEKLY CHART

Here is how the index looks on a weekly chart of the yen. The index did well at catching major moves in the yen over a 14-year period.

FIGURE 6

TRADING RESULTS			
Performance summary: All trades			
Total net profit	$85,225	Open position P/L	$9,200
Gross profit	99,937	Gross loss	(14,712.50)
Total of trades	14	Percent profitable	57%
Winning trades	8	Losing trades	6
Largest winning trade	$ 28,200	Largest losing trade	$ (5,425)
Average winning trade	12,492.19	Average losing trade	(2,452.08)
Ratio avg. win/avg. loss	5.09	Avg. trade (win/lose)	6,087
Max. consec. winners	4	Max. consec. losers	3
Avg. bars in winners	52	Avg. bars in losers	11
Max. intrad. drawdown	$(7187.50)		
Profit factor	6.79	Max contracts held	1
Account size required	10,187.50	Return on account	837%

The excellent record of the index can be seen here.

FIGURE 7

SYSTEM DAMPING

```
inputs: lenday(4), thresh(1),bout(2);

    value1 = (@average(high,lenday)[1] - @average(low,lenday)[1]);
    value2 = (@average(high,lenday)[6]-@average(low,lenday)[6]);
    if value2 > 0 then value1 = value1 / value2;

    if  close > @average(high,bout)[1] and
     value1 <=thresh and
    @average(low,3)[1]  > @average(high,4)[10] then

    begin
     if @marketposition = -1 then exitshort("xs") @currentcontracts
     contracts at market;

     buy("newlg") 1 contract at market;
    value4 = @lowest(low,4)[1];
    end;
    if @marketposition = 1 then exitlong("protsell") @currentcontracts

    contracts at value4 stop;

    if  close < @average(low,bout)[1] and
     value1 <= thresh and
```

```
@average(high,3)[1] < @average(low,4)[10] then

begin
if @marketposition = 1 then exitlong("xl") @currentcontracts
   contracts at market;

 sell("newsht") 1 contract at market;
value5 = @highest(high,4)[1];
end;
if @marketposition = -1 then exitshort("protbuy") @currentcontracts

contracts at value5 stop;
```

Here are the rules for trading the damping index in TradeStation.

EXPERTS AND EGOS

The few people I have known over the years who have been successful making money in stocks were decisive, decision-making individuals without huge egos.

—William J. O'Neil
How to Make Money in Stocks

The CRB Index/Bond Ratio

Veteran technician John J. Murphy, whose trailblazing work on technical analysis and intermarket analysis are classics of the field, has delved into how bonds and commodities are inter-related and then how bonds and stocks influence each other. Now, he introduces the CRB index/ bond ratio as another example of how these three market sectors interact, allowing us to determine the relative strength between bonds and commodities.

by John J. Murphy

I n my last two articles, I examined first the inverse relationship between the Commodity Research Bureau (CRB) Index and bond prices and then the tendency for bond prices to act as a leading indicator for the stock market. Another way to combine these three sectors is to compare the CRB Index/Treasury bond ratio to equities. The CRB Index/bond ratio simply divides the CRB Index by Treasury bond futures prices:

$$\frac{\text{CRB Index}}{\text{Treasury bond futures}}$$

When the ratio is rising, commodity prices are outperforming the bond market and inflation pressures are rising. When the ratio is falling, bond prices are outperforming commodity prices and inflation pressures are falling. From an asset allocation standpoint, a rising ratio line also suggests that commodities should be emphasized over bonds. When the ratio is falling, bonds are favored over commodities.

INFLATION MEASURE
Since the CRB Index/bond ratio helps measure inflation, it should have some impact on the stock

JIM FRISINO

market, and it does. A rising ratio generally has a negative effect on the stock market, while a falling ratio usually has a positive impact. The use of a ratio line also permits trendline and breakout analysis to identify turns. Figure 1 compares the Standard & Poor's 500 cash index (upper chart) to the CRB Index/Treasury bond futures ratio (bottom chart) from mid-1987 through mid-April 1992.

As can be seen from Figure 1, the two lines generally trend in opposite directions. Arrows 1, 3, 4 and 6 mark important peaks in the CRB/bond ratio, which coincide with upturns in the S&P 500. The most noteworthy bullish stock signals occurred at the end of 1987 and autumn 1990. (A rising ratio preceded the 1987 stock market crash.) Arrows 2 and 5 mark upturns in the ratio line. The upturn in the ratio in the spring of 1988 had only a modest negative impact on stocks, while the upturn in late 1989 had a much more bearish impact on the S&P 500.

> ## The CRB Index/bond ratio allows us to gauge the relative strength between bonds and commodities and provides us with a useful stock market indicator.

Figure 2 compares the same two charts from mid-1989 to April 1992. Arrow 1 shows the upside breakout in the CRB/bond ratio in January 1990, which coincided with a downturn in stocks. Note the double top in the ratio that formed between April and September 1990. The decline from the first peak coincided with an upturn in equities. However, the completion of the second peak toward the end of 1990 coincided with a major rally in the S&P 500 (arrow 2). A rebound in the ratio in the spring of 1992 halted at its down trendline, helping to support stocks.

Figure 3 shows the period from November 1991 to mid-April 1992. A falling ratio in late 1991 supported a stock rally to new highs. An upturn in the ratio in early January coincided with the onset of a stock market correction as inflation fears resulted from a rally in commodities and a downturn in bond prices. The ratio broke its up trendline in early April, which was followed shortly by the S&P 500 rising above its 13-week down trendline. The CRB Index/bond ratio allows us to gauge the relative strength between bonds and commodities and provides us with a useful stock market indicator. The CRB/bond ratio is just another example of how closely these three market sectors are linked.

John Murphy is president of JJM Technical Advisors Inc. and publishes the monthly "Futures Trends and Intermarket Analysis." He is also the technical analyst for CNBC.

REFERENCES
Forest, Richard [1992]. "Intermarket analysis and the Deutschemark," STOCKS & COMMODITIES, February.

FIGURE 1

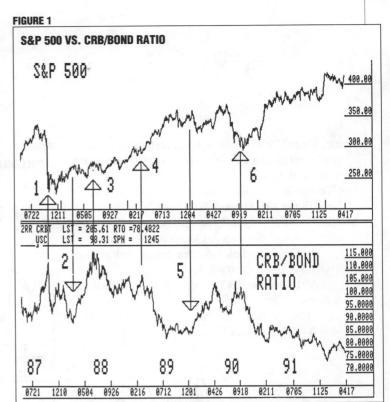

The S&P 500 trended in the opposite direction of the CRB index/bond ratio the past five years. Downturns in the ratio (arrows 1, 3, 4 and 6) coincided with stock market rallies. Ratio troughs (2 and 5) were negative for stocks.

FIGURE 2

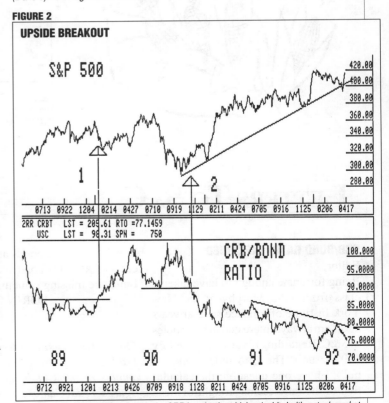

Arrow 1 marks an upside breakout in the CRB/bond ratio, which coincided with a stock market peak in early 1990. The double top in the ratio in late 1990 helped launch a major stock market rally.

Hartle, Thom [1991]. "John J. Murphy: Intermarket analyst," *Technical Analysis of* STOCKS & COMMODITIES, Volume 9: June.

JJM Technical Advisors Inc., 297-101 Kinderkamack Road, Suite 148, Oradell, NJ 07649.

Murphy, John J. [1992]. "The link between bonds and commodities," STOCKS & COMMODITIES, May.

_____ [1992]. "The link between bonds and stocks," STOCKS & COMMODITIES, June.

_____ [1991]. *Intermarket Technical Analysis*, John Wiley & Sons.

_____ [1986]. *Technical Analysis of the Futures Markets*, New York Institute of Finance.

FIGURE 3

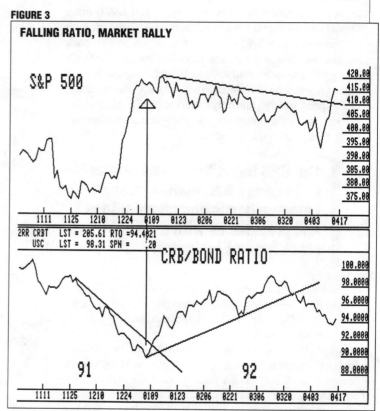

The CRB/bond ratio turned up in early January 1992, creating some downward pressure on the S&P 500. A falling ratio in early April helped launch a stock market rally.

LETTERS TO S&C

CRB/BOND RATIO EXPLAINED

Editor,

Being fortunate enough to have taken a class from John Murphy at the New York Institute of Finance several years ago, I am always interested in his articles in S&C. Regarding his article in the July 1992 issue ("The CRB index/bond ratio"), I have one question: the calculation of the ratio seems straightforward, but the results shown in the accompanying figures have me confused. If the CRB is 205.61 and the bonds are 98-31, how can the CRB index/bond ratio be 77.1459? I must be missing something.

LORIN CHEVALIER
New York, NY

The article used Knight-Ridder's TradeCenter software to produce examples of the CRB/bond ratio for the figures. TradeCenter adjusts the ratio to have a starting point at 100 so that the user can compare this ratio to other market ratios for ranking purposes.

The formula for adjusting the ratio to start with a value of 100 is:

$$100 - \left(\left(\frac{CRB_{Day1}}{Bonds_{Day1}} - \frac{CRB_{Today}}{Bonds_{Today}} \right) 100 \right)$$

—Editor

MARK MOLNAR

System Optimization Techniques

What is system optimization and is it good or bad? It's a little of both, system designers will tell you. David Nicol explains the whys and wherefores.

by David S. Nicol

ystem optimization is a controversial subject among market analysts, but it is also misunderstood by analysts and traders. So what *is* system optimization? When designing a technical trading system, the designer must use a mathematical

formula or algorithm of some kind to produce trading signals. This is usually referred to as an indicator and can be as simple as a single moving average or as complex as a fast Fourier transform. Whatever the indicator may be, all indicators have one characteristic in common: they all contain one or more parameters. A parameter can be set to one of several possible numeric values, the value of which can greatly alter the behavior and performance of the indicator. Because parameters exist in every indicator, the system designer must set each parameter to *some* value. For each system designer, the dilemma is what value to assign each parameter. That is where optimization occurs. Optimization is the process of choosing the best parameter values for the indicator. So what do we mean by "best parameter value"?

FINDING THE BEST VALUE

One approach to finding the best parameter value is to backtest the indicator with a range of parameter values and simply choose which parameter value produced the most profitable trading signals. This approach has several problems. First, how far back should the testing go? Should the parameters be changed during the test run? If so, when and how? The way that the system designer handles these questions will greatly affect the validity and utility of the optimization process.

However, those systems that are optimized without the benefit of hindsight experimentation because of the fear of curve-fitting are not properly optimized because no effort has been made to verify the validity of their parameters. This process is simply choosing parameters randomly. This is the dart-board method to optimization, because money is risked based on parameters that could have been chosen by the toss of a dart.

Both methods of parameter selection are inadequate to set parameter values properly. The backtesting method, if taken to extremes, would result in a different parameter set for each day and trading rules that would be specific and usable only in the past. For example, say that on May 11, 1985, the June live hog contract had a high of 55.35 and a low of 54.075. The most extreme form of optimization would include the rule "On May 11, 1985, buy hogs at 54.075 and sell at 55.35." This rule would produce the greatest possible profit from the day's trading activity, but it would also be completely useless as a predictive rule. Thus, if the main consideration in a backtest is past profitability, the results of such a test may not provide us with anything usable for the future.

On the other end of the optimization spectrum, the dart-board method is just as bad because the parameters are picked randomly. Because the parameter values greatly affect the trading signals and these parameters have been picked randomly, the trading system is a random system. A coin could be flipped to determine trades and obtain similar long-term results. The only way the system would not be random is if the designer had subjectively optimized the parameter values inadvertently.

The way to determine the best parameter values for an indicator is to observe the past behavior of a market and determine why the market behaved as it did. If a market does not

FIGURE 1

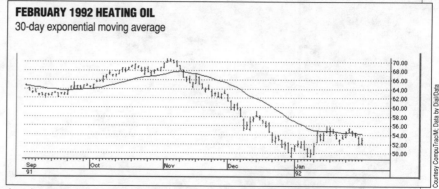

FEBRUARY 1992 HEATING OIL
30-day exponential moving average

A moving average is typically used as a trend-following indicator. Buying when the market is above the moving average and selling when the market is below the moving average is effective as long as the market is in a consistent trend.

FIGURE 2

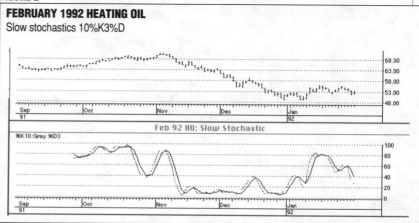

FEBRUARY 1992 HEATING OIL
Slow stochastics 10%K3%D

A stochastics indicator is an oscillator that indicates to buy when the indicator is below 20 and sell when the indicator is above 80. This indicator is more effective in trading range markets and is not effective if the market is in a consistent trend.

FIGURE 3

MAY 1989 WHEAT
30-day exponential moving average

A market may display a cyclical nature for a period of time. Here, the wheat market has a regular cycle during October, November and December. Using a longer-term trend-following indicator during these times would be costly.

have a consistent and repeating phenomenon, then future behavior cannot be predicted. While it is possible to make money reacting to market behavior, it is much more rewarding to predict market behavior. Before demonstrating how this is possible, first let me describe various types of market behavior.

MARKET BEHAVIOR

The first type of market behavior is *linear motion*, or the change of prices along a linear slope. This type of market behavior results in trend-following indicators, such as moving averages and volatility breakout systems, per-

> **Because parameters exist in every indicator, the system designer must set each parameter to some value. For each system designer, the dilemma is what value to assign each parameter. That is where optimization occurs.**

forming well. Trending markets can cause contrarian indicators, including the commodity channel index (CCI), the relative strength index (RSI), the moving average convergence/divergence (MACD), stochastics and other oscillators, to fail miserably. A very recent example of linear market motion can be seen in Figure 1 in the February 1992 heating oil contract. The moving average price penetration method — the trend-following method that has been around for decades — performed very well under these market conditions. On the other hand, Figure 2 shows that the stochastic oscillator crossover method, a contrarian technique, failed miserably during the same period.

The second type of market behavior is *periodic motion*, or cycles. This behavior results in the failure of trend-following indicators and the success of contrarian indicators. Figure 3 shows a fairly good example of periodic motion in the May 1989 wheat contract. The same trend-following indicator used in Figure 1 gets decimated when applied to a cyclical market. Figure 4 shows how the contrarian method, again using the stochastic oscillator, performed well during this cyclical period.

The third type of market behavior is *random motion*. This causes all technical indicators to fail but enables probability systems such as martingale-based† rules to succeed. Random market behavior can be observed in the October 1988 live hog contract in Figure 5. The trend-following indicators get confused with this type of market behavior. Figure 6 indicates the same confusion in the contrarian indicator.

No one single technical approach will succeed in more than

FIGURE 4

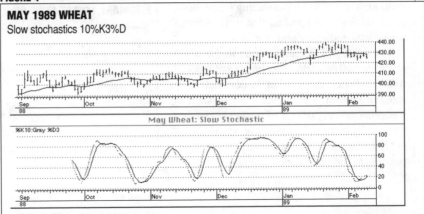

MAY 1989 WHEAT
Slow stochastics 10%K3%D

A stochastics indicator is appropriate for a market that displays a cyclical nature of trading range for a period of time.

FIGURE 5

OCTOBER 1988 HOGS
30-day exponential moving average

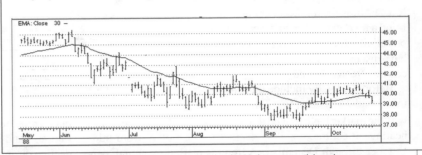

Here's what the October 1988 hog contract would do using the 30-day exponential moving average.

FIGURE 6

OCTOBER 1988 HOGS
Slow stochastics 10%K3%D

A market may appear to be almost random. Consequently, both trend-following and trading range indicators may fail.

one of these three market behaviors. To compound the problem, actual market activity consists of these three behaviors combined. When linear motion dominates its activity, the market is referred to as being in a trend, but a trend is never without some wavelike (periodic) fluctuations and some random price jumps.

†See Traders' Glossary for complete description

When the market is dominated by periodic motion, it is said to be in a trading range, but it never stays within a perfect sine wave shape of consistent frequency and amplitude.

There are always aberrations in the wave shape caused by underlying linear and random motion. When the market is dominated by random motion, fundamental factors such as trader uncertainty or lack of market leadership are usually blamed, but even during the apparent chaos, underlying linear and periodic components to the price action remain.

Because a real market is a mixture of these three market behaviors and because most technical indicators will work only while a market is exhibiting a strong tendency to one of the three market behaviors, it becomes imperative to forecast how the market is going to behave. If I find a market that has had a consistent linear or periodic motion at a particular time, then I have discovered a repeating phenomenon that can be effectively traded.

Before I actually include this phenomenon into a trading system, first I must understand why the market has behaved this way. For example, the February heating oil contract exhibits distinct linear motion from mid-October through December. A trend is caused by actual, perceived or anticipated changes in the supply or demand of a commodity. Because demand for heating oil can be anticipated to increase in fall and winter, common perception is that the price of heating oil should rise under normal conditions. Because of this perception, many traders take long positions in mid- to late autumn in anticipation of increased demand.

Eventually, the actual supply/demand situation becomes apparent through government and industry reports, causing either an increase in buying or a sharp selloff. Thus, we have a trend virtually every year because of popular market perception and because of a reliable seasonal occurrence called winter. I call this phenomenon *seasonal volatility*. Note, however, that this is not the same as seasonal trades or the seasonal index offered by some companies. A seasonal trade is a prediction of the market direction at a particular time of year.

I have found few examples of true seasonal trades, and the heating oil example is not one. In fact, if you examine the February heating oil market between mid-October and December back 10 or 12 years, there are not more uptrends than downtrends

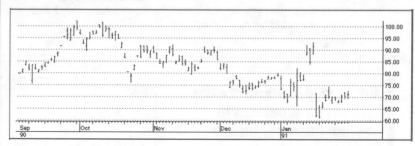

FIGURE 7
FEBRUARY 1991 HEATING OIL

FIGURE 8
FEBRUARY 1988 HEATING OIL

The heating oil contract is thought to rise from mid-October to December due to the increased demands for heating oil in the winter. However, these charts indicate that the market may actually fall during early winter.

but there are many more trends than periodic or random markets. Figures 7 and 8 indicate that the February heating oil contract can decline during this period. Although there appear to be one or two trends virtually every year at that time of year, the lack of a consistent uptrend indicates the lack of a true seasonal trade and the presence of seasonal volatility.

SEASONAL VOLATILITY
The heating oil contract example clearly shows how a market's behavior can be predicted. Note that this is not the only instance of seasonal volatility. I have found several other instances of both seasonal volatility and seasonal periodicity, which is a repeating phenomenon of cyclical market behavior. Many markets exhibit some form of cyclicality or repetition and therefore predictable behavior, and the study of these phenomena is the means by which the system designer can predict market action.

If a market exhibited any patterns or cycles, then it would be useful to study the market's past behavior and to base a system on anticipating the market's past behavior. If the markets are indeed random, then studying the past would still be useful because you would know, at least, that the market is random. With this knowledge, you could either avoid the market or trade it effectively with a probability system. In either case, it is inconsistent to shy away from historical backtesting but believe that the markets contain cyclical events.

Each market has its own fundamentals that ultimately control market behavior. How would it be possible for a market affected by the hog slaughter to have the same behavior as a market influenced by interest rates? Although technicians are reluctant to admit it, the markets are controlled by actual, perceived and anticipated fundamental factors. Technical analysis is simply the most efficient way for most individual traders to analyze and trade markets. The logical course of action is to make a trading system as specific to a market or group of markets as possible to take advantage of the unique fundamentals of the market or markets.

> **Although technicians are reluctant to admit it, the markets are controlled by actual, perceived and anticipated fundamental factors.**

SEPARATE BUT EQUAL

Each contract month of a commodity is actually a separate market. The July corn contract is not influenced by the same fundamentals as December corn, and so they are separate markets that may require separate trading systems. Likewise, February hogs are influenced by different fundamentals than are October hogs and so they too are separate markets. Figure 9 shows the average profit, drawdown and percentage of winning trades when a price oscillator is tuned to various cycle lengths and tested on both February and October hogs. The oscillators were tuned to 20, 30, 40 and 50 days' cycle length by setting the moving averages to one quarter and one half these values. For example, the price oscillator tuned to the 20-day cycle calculates the difference between a five- and a 10-day moving average of the price. Five and 10 is one quarter and one half of 20, after all. A simple moving average of the oscillator, set to a quarter of the cycle length, was used as a trigger line for crossover signals.

In effect, this test measured the extent of periodicity in the contract month in the final three months preceding the contract expiration month. The tests were performed on data from 1986-90. The February contract showed a high degree of profitability when a cyclical indicator was applied. On the other hand, the October contract shows very poor performance when tested in

FIGURE 9

CONTRACT	CYCLE	PROFIT	DRAWDOWN	% WINS
February hogs	20	$ 240	$ 943	44.8
	30	221	925	44.6
	40	1,260	192	80.0
	50	828	381	69.8
October hogs	20	$ 63	$1,158	43.0
	30	(949)	1,530	41.6
	40	(549)	1,437	40.0
	50	87	843	30.4

the same manner. How would it be possible for February hogs to be very cyclical and October hogs to be very noncyclical or random if they were not influenced by different fundamentals? If they are actually controlled by different fundamentals, are they not separate markets? And if they are, would it not be best to study their fundamentals to determine why they behave the way they do?

And if this study were to produce an apparent example of seasonal volatility or seasonal periodicity, would it not be best to design a trading system to anticipate this behavior? This is why different trading systems are often required to trade different contract months of the same commodity.

A trading system that updates its parameters regularly is not properly optimized. Why would the system require a change in parameters if the system were not reacting to recent market behavior? While several reactive techniques *are* profitable, constant reoptimization does more for improving a system's advertising appeal through inflated historical results than actually improving profitability. Also, user flexibility is not an appropriate optimization technique. While flexibility is desirable in a charting and analysis program, it is not in a trading system.

Systems that allow the user to choose a mode or other variable are actually two or more different systems within one system. By including different modes, the designer has ensured that at least one mode will always perform well. But the user has no way to determine beforehand which mode will perform well.

IN SUMMATION

Determining the best parameter values for a trading system involves observing the past behavior of a commodity contract and determining what, if any, repeating phenomena occur. If a repeating phenomenon is observed, it should be understood why it occurred or as much as is possible. A technical system or indicator should then be developed and its parameters set to anticipate the recurrence of the observed phenomenon. Ideally,

the indicator should be flexible enough to allow some amount of unanticipated market behavior without significantly degrading the indicator's utility.

If you are expecting a trend, the indicator that you are using should be able to handle a significant amount of periodic and/or random price action without significantly degrading its performance. Ideally, the indicator used should either be very simple, to accommodate unanticipated change, or highly complex, to adjust for all market behavior that deviates from the anticipated behavior. Next, the capital requirements of the system must be established if actual trading is to occur, accomplished by extensive historical testing and subjective interpolation of best- and worst-case scenarios, based upon the designer's understanding of the anticipated market behavior.

Once the capital requirements of the system are known, it is imperative to determine the money management technique. A successful system should respond to the trader's success with increasing numbers of contracts traded, but in an orderly and controlled fashion with an eye to the limits of market liquidity.

Finally, the system for each commodity contract traded should be integrated with each of the other commodity contracts so that no conflict occurs in account fund allocation. The properly optimized system must take into account real trading dilemmas such as when to stop trading February hogs and to begin trading April hogs. No element of trading, including order placement and money management, should be left to chance, or the system is likely to fail. But when the system is properly optimized, profitable results are possible.

David Nicol of Exponential Trading Technology in Logan, UT, is a former commodity broker and has been active in trading and analyzing futures markets behavior since 1988. The ideas presented are incorporated into Exponential Trading Technology's Oracle Trading System software.

Back to Basics With Quantitative Analysis

Ever notice how we seem to want to do things the hard way? Anthony Macek, publisher of the "Just the Facts" newsletter, has, and he's proposed a solution to simplify our lives using quantitative analysis. Here, Macek uses a technique of combining momentum and trend data to rate the condition of the market. Take a look.

by Anthony J. Macek

Developing an infatuation with complex formulas and intricate analyses can cause us to lose sight of what we are striving to attain. If we are not careful, we can find ourselves afflicted with paralysis by overanalysis. Many persuasive ar-

guments exist for examining our world in a less complex fashion. In doing so, the larger picture becomes clearer, and phenomena previously overlooked, such as trend and momentum, become more evident.

Simply stated, trend is defined as the tendency of a phenomenon to continue in its current path or direction. In essence, it measures the internal dynamics of a particular area under study. Momentum, a measure of price change over a series of prices, is directly related to the trend in that it relies on the same criteria. Because momentum is an indicator that gauges the strength of the trend, however, it is slower to react to new data and is therefore considered to be a longer-term indicator.

Examining trend and momentum can be simple or complex. In my experience, after years of number crunching using various computer models, employing countless variations of exponential and other weighted moving averages, using measures of relative strength, oscillators, stochastics, and so forth, I discovered that there was no great statistical advantage to using more complex means of measuring various phenomena. That is not to say that the use of more complex methods of analysis does not produce superior results; but the slight statistical advantage gained using more complicated methods would have to be evaluated in relation to the time spent in the process. Choosing a less elaborate method may not only be more time effective, but it may also be more than adequate to achieve the ultimate goal: more timely and better-informed investment decisions.

> **Numerous studies have been performed regarding the relationship between trend and momentum based on their mutual dependence on the same circumstances. However, very little work has been devoted to combining the two phenomena into one meaningful indicator. Quantitative analysis achieves just that.**

Simple or "arithmetic" moving averages can be used to monitor both trend and momentum, with the added bonus of requiring only rudimentary math skills. An arithmetic moving average is simply the average of a series of values over a certain period. In my case, a short-term arithmetic moving average is used to monitor the trend of whatever I am studying. If the data are reported weekly, I find a moving average of five weeks to be very effective. If monthly data are compiled, then a three-month moving average does the job.

Momentum can be measured by monitoring the internal dynamics of the trend. Again, I use an arithmetic moving average, this time of the trend itself. If a five-week moving average is used to determine the trend, then a 10-week moving average of the trend is generally used to monitor the momentum. If a three-month moving average is used to determine the trend, then a six-month moving average of the trend is used to determine the momentum.

Numerous studies have been performed regarding the relationship between trend and momentum based on their mutual dependence on the same circumstances. However, very little work has been devoted to combining the two phenomena into one meaningful indicator. Quantitative analysis achieves just that. By combining the data given by both trend and momentum, the current condition of a particular index, market segment or whatever it is you wish to examine can be evaluated quickly and simply.

HOW IT WORKS

To use quantitative analysis, first evaluate the status of both the trend and momentum separately. In Figure 1, the graph display-

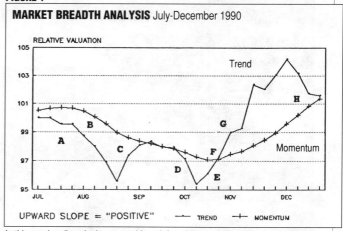

FIGURE 1

MARKET BREADTH ANALYSIS July-December 1990

UPWARD SLOPE = "POSITIVE"   —⊢— TREND   —+— MOMENTUM

In this graph, a line sloping upward from left to right would be viewed as favorable.

FIGURE 2

DETERMINING THE Q FACTOR			
MOMENTUM	**TREND**	**"Q"**	**EVALUATION**
+	+	1	Very positive
+	0	2	Positive
+	-	3	Fairly positive
0	+	4	Fairly positive
0	0	5	Neutral
0	-	6	Fairly negative
-	+	7	Fairly negative
-	0	8	Negative
-	-	9	Very negative

A number is assigned based on the intersection between the trend and the momentum, with 1 indicating a positive condition in which both the trend and momentum are healthy.

ing market breadth, a line sloping upward from left to right would be viewed as favorable. When a large number of stocks are participating in an upward move, such as here, it is considered a healthy condition. The market condition is then given a designation, with a plus (+) representing a positive condition and a minus (-) denoting a negative situation (Figure 2). A zero is a neutral state.

Finally, a number is assigned based on the intersection between the trend and the momentum (Figure 2), with the number 1 indicating a positive condition in which both the trend and momentum are healthy. Each sequentially higher number displays a progressively weaker market condition ending with the number 9, which indicates a very negative market evaluation. The number 5 indicates that neither the trend nor the momentum is displaying much direction, a condition generally seen at market turning points.

In this technique of quantitative analysis, or Q, more weight is given to the momentum rather than the trend to emphasize longer-term analysis and to eliminate frequent whipsaws. In addition, the position of the trendline with respect to the momen-

FIGURE 3

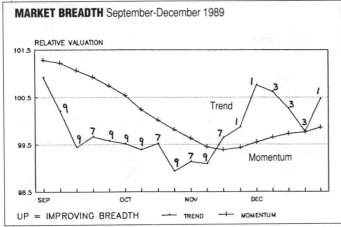

MARKET BREADTH September-December 1989

UP = IMPROVING BREADTH   —•— TREND   —+— MOMENTUM

Turning back to fall 1989, quantitative analysis revealed an extreme weakness in market breadth several weeks prior to the minicrash that occurred on October 13, 1989. Later, the recovery was shown by Q as well.

FIGURE 4

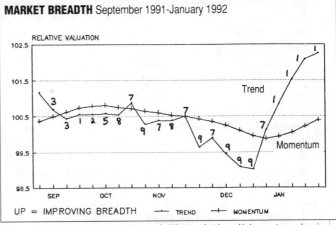

MARKET BREADTH September 1991-January 1992

UP = IMPROVING BREADTH   —•— TREND   —+— MOMENTUM

More recently, quantitative analysis revealed that market breadth began to weaken in October 1991, several weeks before the market turbulence seen in mid-November. The Q evaluation remained unhealthy until the market rally later in December.

FIGURE 5

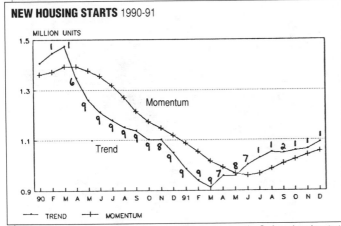

NEW HOUSING STARTS 1990-91

—•— TREND   —+— MOMENTUM

Displaying quantitative analysis in an economic application, the Q of new housing starts began to deteriorate in spring 1990 as the recession started to take hold. The recovery in housing was seen with an improving Q in summer 1991.

FIGURE 6

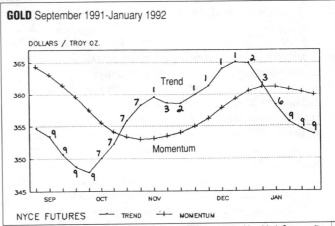

GOLD September 1991-January 1992

NYCE FUTURES   —•— TREND   —+— MOMENTUM

Precious metals can also be tracked by Q analysis, as seen in the New York Commodity Exchange futures price of gold. A rally that began in October 1991 gradually weakened, with gold eventually losing its luster late in December.

FIGURE 7

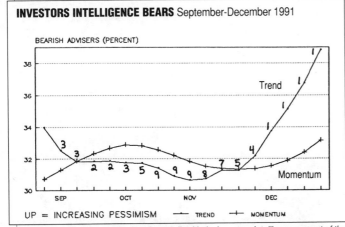

INVESTORS INTELLIGENCE BEARS September-December 1991

UP = INCREASING PESSIMISM   —•— TREND   —+— MOMENTUM

Sentiment can be monitored by Q as well, with the Investors Intelligence report of the number of bearish advisors used as a contrary indicator. According to Q, too much optimism existed in the market in October 1991. After the market dropped in November, pessimism returned and soon after that, the market rallied.

FIGURE 8

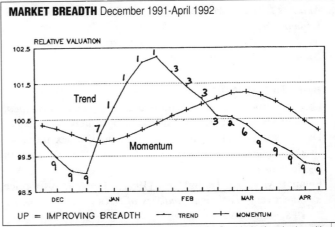

MARKET BREADTH December 1991-April 1992

UP = IMPROVING BREADTH   —•— TREND   —+— MOMENTUM

The strength of the market rally in December 1991, as the Q analysis of market breadth revealed, began to weaken in late January 1992. Market breadth turned very negative in March.

tum line is insignificant, with the slope of the respective lines being the only determinant for quantitative evaluation..

Referring again to Figure 1, note that at position A the momentum was generally flat while the more sensitive trend had turned down, giving a Q rating of 6, or fairly negative. As the bear market of 1990 drew near, market breadth continued to weaken until at point B both the trend and momentum were down, with a very negative Q rating of 9.

At C the trend turned up, but with the momentum decidedly down, a Q of 7 was assigned. Then, at point D, the rally failed, with a very negative Q rating of 9 again the result. At point E, the more sensitive trend once again turned up. Momentum, although showing signs of strength, was still down, giving a Q of 7. At F, the momentum strengthened, showing a stronger rally than it did at point C. With momentum flat and trend rising, a Q of 4, fairly positive, was the result. The strength of the market breadth continued. At point G both the trend and momentum were strong, giving a Q of 1, a very positive analysis. The Q factor correctly evaluated relative health as the market gained strength after the bear market eased.

Several weeks later, the market weakened somewhat with the trend turning down. At point H, however, the momentum was still strong, as a Q of 3, a positive situation, indicated. This underlying strength carried well into the next year, remaining positive throughout the February 1991 rally.

Additional examples of using quantitative analysis to monitor the behavior of various market phenomena are shown in Figures 3 to 7. In some cases, quantitative analysis may appear to suggest advantageous entry and/or exit points. But I am not implying that Q analysis could be used exclusively for the purpose of market timing; a more prudent application would be to use Q analysis with other recognized methods of market examination to help determine when to commit funds or protect assets.

To be effective, a systematic study of phenomena, market or otherwise, need not be overly complex. Instead, try more basic techniques of analysis. Your investment decisions may become more timely and profitable as you learn to filter out data noise and concentrate on the factors that really matter.

Anthony J. Macek, Madison Avenue Publishing, P.O. Box 188, Endicott, NY 13761-0188, is the editor of "Just the Facts/Just the Fax" newsletter and is currently writing a book on less complex methods of market analysis.

FURTHER READING

Creel, Clifford [1991]. "Trend exhaustion index," *Technical Analysis of* STOCKS & COMMODITIES, Volume 9: January.

Duarte, Joe [1991]. "Mutual funds as stock index proxies," *Technical Analysis of* STOCKS & COMMODITIES, Volume 9: November.

Flynn, E.M.S., and Thom Hartle [1991]. "Guidelines for price objectives," *Technical Analysis of* STOCKS & COMMODITIES, Volume 9: November.

Poulos, E. Michael [1991]. "Of trends and random walks," *Technical Analysis of* STOCKS & COMMODITIES, Volume 9: February.

[TA]

Stocks According To Trend Tendency

Many times, a question asked of STOCKS & COMMODITIES readers will more than likely find an answer — and more than an answer, further questions. Such was the article that E. Michael Poulos presented early in 1991, when he showed how assumed trend tendencies ain't necessarily so. Here, Stuart Meibuhr answers one of those corollary questions. If certain futures contracts show decided trend tendencies, can the same be said about certain stocks or indices?

by Stuart Meibuhr

T he question that E. Michael Poulos asked in the January 1992 STOCKS & COMMODITIES was "Which futures trend the most?" In turn, that question triggered a corollary question, "Which stocks or stock indices trend the most?" Poulos's methodology involved measuring the difference between the highest high and the lowest low for seven channel lengths (days) from 1 to 49. The range was averaged to arrive at an average channel height for one-, two-, four-, nine-, 16-, 25-, 36- and 49-day channels. Each average was divided by the average for the one-day channel to arrive at a ratio.

Applying the same methodology to several market indices and seven stocks provided some enlightening information. A spreadsheet program was used for the calculations on data transferred from a charting program. Only those securities with histories dating to back before 1985 were used. Data for any holidays were eliminated before the trend calculations. All calculations were performed on data dating from January 2, 1985, to January 31, 1992, a period of seven years and one month.

SIX SELECT

For each security, I analyzed six different time periods, which consisted of the entire data set; the first year; the first two years; the last year; the last two years; and one year selected from the middle. This ensured that the ratios were independent of the selected time periods. This turned out not to be completely true. For example, the data in Figure 1 for the OEX are shown for these six different time periods.

Although some variations amounted to almost 10% between the smallest and the largest ratio for any given time period, the trends from the shortest to the longest time period remained the same. Consequently, the ratios for only the entire seven years and one month of data are reported here for the other studied securities. These results for five stock market indices and seven stocks can be seen in Figure 2.

The indices and the stocks are ranked separately in descending order of their ratios. The data for the S&P 500 represent only six years and seven months and differs significantly from those reported by Poulos. The data here were for the S&P 500, whereas Poulos's data represented spliced future contracts and the time periods covered were different. The trending tendency of indices appears to increase with the increasing number of securities that make up that index. Unfortunately, that does not explain why the Major Market Index (MMI) (Figure 3) showed a greater trending tendency than did the Dow Jones Industrial Average (DJIA) (Figure 4), the tendency of which was extraordinarily low. The DJIA values were consistently below the square root point, which, according to mathematician W. Feller, evinces a lack of trends. All other indices showed strong trending characteristics, with the over-the-counter (NASDAQ) showing the strongest trending action (Figure 5).

All seven stocks showed good trending behavior, with Eli Lilly & Co. (LLY) having the biggest numbers and Xerox (X) ranking last for trending tendency. Other companies and symbols are : General Motors (GM), IBM, Merrill Lynch (MER), National Medical Enterprises (NME) and Texaco (TX).

TRADING IMPLICATIONS

If options are the tradeable, then it is imperative to follow the index on which the options are based and *not* the DJIA, because the DJIA tends not to trend. The same conclusion can be drawn about stocks; the short-term trader would prefer to deal in options on stocks that have high trending behavior. Overall, with this methodology, the trader can ascertain the trending behavior of any security before expending time and capital on a trade.

FIGURE 1

RATIOS FOR THE OEX

Size of DB	1-d	4-d	9-d	16-d	25-d	36-d	49-d
All	1.00	2.22	3.43	4.64	5.89	7.10	8.25
First year	1.00	2.23	3.42	4.59	5.74	6.94	7.96
First two years	1.00	2.23	3.42	4.65	5.87	7.05	8.03
Last year	1.00	2.10	3.20	4.42	5.75	6.77	7.55
Last two years	1.00	2.17	3.33	4.50	5.75	6.88	7.89
Middle one year	1.00	2.19	3.36	4.57	5.86	7.05	8.17

For each security and index, six different time periods were analyzed.

FIGURE 2

DATA FOR 7 YEARS AND A MONTH

Channel length (days)	Square root of length	7 yrs, 1 month from January 1, 1965										
		Channel height ratio to one										
		OTC	SPX	OEX	MMI	DJIA	LLY	NME	IBM	MER	TX	GM	X
1-d	1	1.00	1.00	1.00	1.00	1.00	1.00	1.00	1.00	1.00	1.00	1.00	1.00
4-d	2	2.70	2.34	2.22	2.18	1.86	2.38	2.31	2.25	2.28	2.26	2.25	2.26
9-d	3	4.68	3.67	3.43	3.35	2.73	3.79	3.62	3.52	3.58	3.50	3.45	3.45
16-d	4	6.84	5.03	4.64	4.52	3.59	5.20	4.98	4.85	4.91	4.78	4.64	4.63
25-d	5	9.13	6.43	5.89	5.72	4.48	6.64	6.32	6.22	6.21	6.04	5.85	5.84
36-d	6	11.48	7.80	7.10	6.91	5.36	8.05	7.71	7.58	7.43	7.22	7.10	7.00
49-d	7	13.84	9.10	8.25	8.03	6.19	9.41	9.07	8.86	8.63	8.34	8.33	8.06

An indication of trend tendency is if the ratio of the average channel height to the averge daily range is larger than the square root of the channel length. The NASDAQ index showed the greatest tendency to trend, while Xerox ranked the least.

FIGURE 3

MAJOR MARKET INDEX

The Major Market Index when compared to the DJIA has a greater tendency to trend, even though there are fewer stocks in the MMI.

FIGURE 4

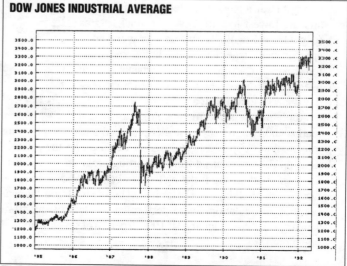

DOW JONES INDUSTRIAL AVERAGE

The DJIA showed less tendency to trend than the Major Market Index did.

Stuart Meibuhr trades stocks and options for his own account. He has lectured and taught on computerized investment topics for the past 10 years.

ADDITIONAL READING
Poulos, E. Michael [1992]. "Futures according to trend tendency," STOCKS & COMMODITIES, January.

FIGURE 5

NASDAQ INDEX

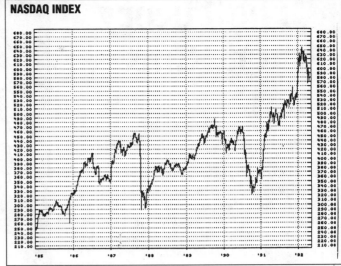

The NASDAQ index demonstrated the highest degree of trending tendency.

The Theory Of Runs

Are you the kind of trader who assumes that everything will go your way, only to be hit with a string of disastrous losses? Or are you the kind of trader who assumes that the worst scenario is the most likely one, only to find that you could have done a lot better with a much less fatalistic attitude? What are the chances of a series of bad trades occurring, anyway? In an excerpt from his Elements of Successful Trading, *published by the New York Institute of Finance, Robert P. Rotella explains the theory of runs.*

by Robert P. Rotella

What are the chances of a series of bad trades occurring? Some traders ignore the possibility that they could get hit with one. Many others answer the question fatalistically with Murphy's Law — "Anything that can go wrong will go wrong." Although this is a pessimistic way of viewing the problem, it's probably a good start, especially when it comes to trading. Let us look at what the possibilities are of any series of events occurring.

First, we need to know what the possibility of one event is to determine the chance of a series of the same events. If a coin is flipped, the chance of a tail or head appearing is one in two, or 50%. What are the chances of flipping *two* tails in a row? The probability of a series of events happening is the product of the probability of each independent event occurring. The equation to determine the chances of a series of independent events occurring is:

Chance of a series of events occurring $= (p)^n$

where

p = probability of the event happening

n = number of times the event occurs

What are the chances of getting heads to occur three times in a row when flipping a coin? The chance of a head coming up is one in two in any one flip. Therefore, using the equation, the chance of heads coming up three times in a row is:

Chance of a series of events:

$$= (1/2)^3$$
$$= (1/2)(1/2)(1/2)$$
$$= 1/8$$

Thus, there is a one in eight chance of heads coming up three times in a row in a series of coin flips. We could also say that the event had a 12.5% chance of occurring (that is, $1/8 = 0.125$). Figure 1 presents the matrix of possibilities, each having a chance of one in eight.

If heads came up three times in a row, what are the chances of a head again appearing on the next flip? The answer is still one in two, no matter how many times heads or tails have come up before, because the flipping of a coin is an independent event. An independent event is one that is not affected by any other event. The coin itself has no memory of what has occurred before. What are the chances, then, of flipping a head four times in a row? Using the equation, the chance is $(1/2)^4 = 1/16$, or a one in 16 chance of heads occurring four times in a row.

APPLICATIONS TO TRADING

The theory of runs has useful trading applications to determine the chance of a series of winning or losing trades. Some traders, however, seem to be more concerned with the chances of a series of profitable trades occurring than they are of the inverse. Profitable trades are always welcome, but those will not put the trader out of business or deplete the trader's funds. Instead, we should be aware of what the chances are for a series of losing trades in a row. This stems from the fact that too many losses will ultimately bankrupt the investor. Certainly, this is one reason why many traders are forced to stop trading, but there is another reason. More often, traders become so psychologically battered from a series of losing trades that they no longer want to or are able to trade.

We can use the equation in a trading example. Say that Joe has devised a trading system that yields approximately 50% winning and 50% losing trades. What are the chances of having five losing trades in a row? Using the theory of runs:

Chance of five losing trades in a row:
$$= (1/2)^5$$
$$= (1/2)(1/2)(1/2)(1/2)(1/2)$$
$$= 1/32$$

There is a one in 32 chance, or almost a 3% chance of getting five losing trades in a row. Pretty remote chance — or is it? Remember, this is an estimate and by no means a guarantee. Joe the trader could have 10 losing trades in a row for a variety of reasons. In addition, if he trades often, then the one in 32 chance becomes very possible because the frequency of trading is great. If he makes 100 or more trades, there is a reasonable chance that he could get five losing trades in a row.

If Joe has $10,000 and risks $2,000 on each trade, then there is a one in 32 chance of losing the entire $10,000. If he does not want to take this kind of risk, he can reduce his risk on each trade to an amount he is comfortable with. If he only risks 10% on a trade, or $1,000, then what are his chances of losing the entire $10,000? If he risked 10% of his capital each time, or $1,000, a series of 10 losing trades in a row would exhaust his capital:

Chance of 10 losing trades in a row $= (1/2)^{10}$
                                        $= 1/1024$

So the chances are approximately one in 1000 of losing all his capital. This is better than before but may still be on the high side. Because there is a real chance of 10 losing trades in a row occurring, more experienced traders tend to risk less than 4% on any one trade. The theory of runs is one way of measuring the chances of a series of runs going against you or with you. We are generally more concerned with the chances of a series of losing runs. This will help you to determine the proper amount of capital to risk for any one trade or series of trades. The theory of runs is a theoretical way of viewing a series of bad trades occurring.

LIMITATIONS WITH THE THEORY

There are some constraints with the theory of runs that should be understood before applying it to trading:

■ *Independent events* — The chance of a series of two or more events occurring assumes that the events are independent. *The coin has no memory*. Some trades are independent of each other, but other trades are dependent or have some relationship to each other. For example, markets that are highly correlated may not yield trades that are independent of each other. Similar trades in the Standard & Poor's 500 and New York Stock Exchange (NYSE) futures will probably both prove profitable or unprofitable because both markets are highly related. Trading the NYSE and coffee futures contract would be a better example of relatively unrelated markets and independent events.

> The theory of runs is a good start in determining the chance of a series of losses occurring. In general, it is always safer to estimate conservatively, partly due to the limitations.

If some markets are highly related, does this imply the theory of runs is not applicable? No. The theory of runs must be used with caution when evaluating risk, as any other trading measurement should. If markets are somewhat related, then there is a greater chance of having a larger string of losses. However, the theory of runs is still a helpful guide.

■ *Probability of a losing trade* — The chances of heads or tails coming up in a coin flip is one in two. Although we may have a fair approximation, we can never be certain of the chances of a losing trade in the future. Markets and traders go through various phases that will affect the percentage of losing trades. The percentage of losing trades may be very high one month but quite low in another and may appear to go beyond mere chance on occasion. The chance of a losing trade is a function of the trader, method and market and is not always precisely known the way the outcome of a series of coin tosses can be.

■ *Amount of loss* — We can strictly regulate the amount of risk and loss incurred on any trade, but we can never guarantee the amount we might lose due to risk beyond our control. Markets may race beyond our protective stops or open limit against us and so we may not get filled at our intended price.

These limitations do not mitigate the usefulness of the theory of runs. Traders should understand the benefits and liabilities of using the theory of runs in helping to develop a trading plan. The theory of runs is a good start in determining the chance of a series of losses occurring. In general, it is always safer to estimate conservatively, partly due to the limitations. For example, if there is a 20% chance of five losing trades in a row occurring using the theory of runs, there may actually be a 30% or 40% chance, depending on the limitations. The experience of the trader can go a long way in dealing with these limitations.

Let's take the example of Lucky and Sharky, who are both trying to make money. Assume Lucky buys a $1 lottery ticket that has a one in 10 million chance of winning $10 million. Sharky opts to buy an S&P 500 futures contract and will either make $1,000 profit or $1,000 loss on the trade. If the market drops $2 ($1,000), he will get stopped out and lose $1,000. If the market rallies $2, he will make $1,000. Assuming the market is random and there is no slippage or commissions, the expected outcome for each strategy is zero. Which of their strategies is riskier, looking at risk in terms of maximum drawdown and the theory of runs? What should the maximum drawdown of Lucky and Sharky be? Part of the answer will depend on how much money each risks, how often Lucky buys a lottery ticket and how often Sharky makes a trade. Assume they both risk $100,000 in a 10-year period. Recall the chances of loss for both:

The chance of loss for Lucky = 0.9999999
The chance of loss for Sharky = 0.5

What are Lucky's chances of sustaining a $100,000 drawdown in a series of $1 bets placed 100,000 separate times? Using the theory of runs, the chances of losing the entire $100,000 are:

$$\text{Chance of Lucky losing } \$100,000 = (0.9999999)^{100,000}$$
$$= \text{approximately } 1$$

Thus, there is a very good possibility that Lucky's drawdown will be $100,000, resulting in his losing all his capital.

In contrast, what are Sharky's chances of sustaining a $100,000 drawdown in a series of $1,000 losses? Since Sharky must lose $1,000 in 100 trades to lose $100,000, then he must have 100 losing trades in a row. Using the theory of runs, the chances of losing the $100,000 are:

Chance of Sharky losing $100,000 = $(0.5)^{100}$ = a very small number but close to 0

Therefore, the chances of Sharky sustaining a $100,000 drawdown are very small. It could happen if Sharky trades frequently, but it does not really matter. Sharky's theoretical drawdown will always be lower because of the theory of runs. Lucky may win three lotteries in a row, but this will not affect the subsequent drawdown calculation.

Although the original question concerned risk, what is the reward for either Lucky or Sharky? If you recall, the expected outcome for both players was zero, so the reward is zero for both and neither may expect to make money over the long run.

Is either strategy better than the other? A subtle but salient difference exists between the two strategies, even though the expected outcome is zero for each. Lucky's chance of losing all his capital is much greater because his drawdowns will be larger, so there is a better chance he will eventually have to stop playing. Sharky's chances of losing all his capital are small because the drawdowns are lower, so he can continue playing virtually forever. While neither may expect to make money, Sharky can at least expect to continue playing indefinitely, whereas Lucky is likelier to get blown out of the game.

The risk is much greater for Lucky than for Sharky because the chance of a large drawdown is greater. Since the reward is the same, which strategy would you choose? If neither can win in the long run, then why should either try? The odds are always against the lottery player and can be against the futures trader as well. However, the futures trader may be able to change the odds in his favor. The same cannot be said for the lottery player. Poor Lucky will always be unlucky.

CONCLUSION

Maximum drawdown and reward provide some indications of risk and reward in trading. However, many other simple and elaborate formulas can analyze trading performance. There are limitations with any measurement, including those just presented.

Maximum drawdown is a practical or real-time way of looking at risk. The theory of runs is a theoretical way of looking at risk. The combination gives us a powerful theoretical and practical way of evaluating risk in trading.

Reward is usually much easier to define and measure than risk because most investors view reward in the same way, but each investor has a different perspective about risk. Maximum drawdown, variance of returns, chances of a severe loss and other indicators are all ways to measure risk. However, every trader must understand drawdown because sooner or later every trader will experience drawdown.

Performance measurements are helpful in assessing the amount of risk and reward of a trader or trading system. The investor must always realize that behind every performance number is a trader. In addition, the money management philosophy of the trader should be analyzed when making any decision about trading.

Robert P. Rotella is a Commodity Trading Advisor and an independent futures trader. He trades for his own account and institutional clients and is a member of the Coffee, Sugar and Cocoa Exchange.

Used with permission. *The Elements of Successful Trading: Developing Your Comprehensive Strategy through Psychology, Money Management, and Trading Methods*, Robert P. Rotella, New York Institute of Finance.

Stock Splits: Boon Or Bust?

Even the most sophisticated market participants are tempted to buy a stock that has been announced to split two for one. They, of all investors, should know better, because not all stock splits turn out to be positive events. So how often are they positive for three to six months after? Michael Sheimo, best known for books such as Dow Theory Redux *and* Stock Market Rules, *explores the question.*

by Michael D. Sheimo

MARAL SASSOUNI

S ay that XYZ Corp. has just announced a two-for-one stock split to take effect in two months. Is it time to sell what you hold, buy more or do nothing? How *do* stock splits generally effect the price movement of individual stocks? What reasonably sound decisions can be based solely on the announcement of a stock split?

As investors we tend to be more buyers than sellers. This leads to the buying bias of the stock market. The fact is that most of the time we want to buy stock and are hesitant to sell; as buyers we often look for any possible excuse to buy. The excuse might be general — say, a Santa Claus rally — or it might be more specific, such as a company that has just announced a two-for-one stock split. That a stock will split is a drawing point, as stockbrokers are aware, and they will often mention the number of times a stock has split in the past five years.

Although the number of splits in the past five years can provide a useful historical reference, the split information by itself isn't much of a recommendation.

NEUTRAL STOCK SPLITS

Since we have observed other stock splits, we know that the effect is neutral on the stock's financial status. A split does nothing to increase the financial strength of a company. In a two for one split, everything will now be divided by two; earnings, dividends and price. The financial data will be adjusted according to the conditions of the split. The stock price will be about half what it was prior to the split, and if we owned 100 shares before the split, we would now own 200 shares. That's all a two for one split does.

Many investors think that stock splits are nearly always positive events, as can be observed in the price rise during the weeks following a stock-split announcement. A common misconception is that the price is rising so rapidly that the company wants to split the stock to keep the price low enough for individual investors. Companies are seldom so generous, although sometimes they appear to split the stock in an attempt to support a falling price. Nearly half the stock splits that occurred in 1987 occurred after the October crash, most likely attempts to rally support for those falling prices.

> As investors we tend to be more buyers than sellers. This leads to the buying bias of the stock market. Most of the time we want to buy stock and are hesitant to sell; as buyers we often look for any excuse to buy.

The information presented looks at a four-year period from April 1987 to April 1991. The study was conducted by observing graphs of price trends of split stocks. Both exchange-traded and over-the-counter stocks were observed for price changes three months previous, then three months and six months after the split. Prices of the stocks at these periods were compared with the prices at the time of the actual splits. Prices were then tabulated as being either higher or lower than at the time of the split. If a price was neither, it was tabulated as being lower, since it shows no gain. The following shows the number of stock splits included in the study.

EXCHANGE-TRADED STOCK SPLITS				
1987*	1988	1989*	1990*	1991
164	87	132	95	13
OVER-THE-COUNTER STOCK SPLITS				
1987*	1988	1989*	1990*	1991
94	48	68	56	10
TOTAL NUMBERS OF STOCK SPLITS				
1987*	1988	1989*	1990*	1991
258	135	200	151	23

*Years with a severe correction or bear market.

There appears to be a larger number of stock splits in years that had severe corrections or bear markets. Severe corrections are defined as the Dow Jones Industrial Average (DJIA) being down 150 points or more. A bear market is defined as being when the DJIA drops 20% or more. The single-session correction of October 1987 is reckoned as a bear market. The severe correction in October 1989 was a little more than 190 points, and the bear market of 1990 was slightly more than a 20% drop.

The price trend data and split information for this study was taken from the 1991 Standard & Poor's Trendline *Current Market Perspectives* (April edition) and the *OTC Chart Manual* (March-April edition).

A look at exchange-traded stock three months prior to the split contains few surprises. We expect to and do for the most part see

FIGURE 1

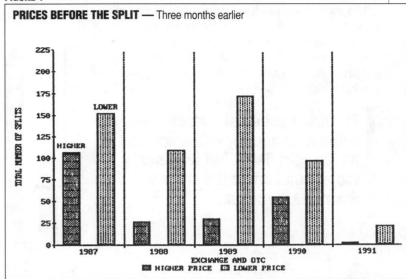

PRICES BEFORE THE SPLIT — Three months earlier

As can be seen, most years show the stock price at a level lower than three months prior to the split.

FIGURE 2

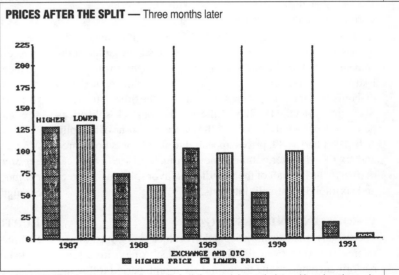

PRICES AFTER THE SPLIT — Three months later

In 1988 and 1989, prices appeared to favor splits both three and six months later, although not by much.

the stock price is lower than it will be at the split. The lower price before the split clearly delineates the attraction that is often created by the announcement of a split.

Surprisingly, the OTC stocks in 1987 were about 50/50 for the presplit price being lower three months before the split actually occurs; the gap narrows again in 1990. The phenomenon occurs in both over-the-counter and exchange-traded stocks. Since both years had bear markets, part of this can be attributed to the price declines in the latter part of both years.

DECIPHERABLE PATTERNS

The usual pattern for stock splits goes something like this: The split is announced, whereupon the stock price begins to rally just as the market drops significantly, thereby causing a price decline in the newly split stock.

It is easy to see stock prices rising before a split actually occurs; in fact, it is the most common event. As can be seen in Figure 1, most years show the stock price at a lower level three months prior to the split. The price rise shown here reflects the investors' positive opinion of splits.

> **The price action of a stock that splits is frequently not dependent on the split itself, but on other factors that make the stock a desirable purchase.**

A price increase after a split is announced is so common that some splits may be announced specifically to firm up a stock's price after a decline. This is supported by simply observing a graph of stock prices and also by the fact that down years or years with sharp price corrections tend to have more stock splits.

Of the splits that occurred in 1987, nearly half were after the market peak near the end of August, suggesting that the splits were activated for the purpose of bringing support to the prices. Examining what happened three months after the split shows that only half the prices were higher than at the time of the split. Six months after the 1987 splits, the majority of stock-split prices had dropped to levels lower than they were at the time of the split.

In 1988 and 1989, prices appeared to favor splits both three and six months later, although not by much. In 1990, the bear market in the last half of the year did not favor splits in the three- and six-month post-split intervals.

UNIQUE AND INTERESTING

Each year is unique in the price action of stock splits, but the most interesting point from the data is the lack of positive price performance during the three- and six-month period following the splits.

Clearly, not all stock splits have a positive impact on prices for the three- and six-month periods after the stock split. Price performance six months after a split is more likely to be influenced by other factors such as earnings, acquisitions, reorganizations, market performance and economic changes. This lack of positive price performance is contrary to what many individual investors think, that nearly all stock splits have a positive impact on the stock price in the short-term period after the split.

The price action of a stock that splits is frequently not dependent on the split itself, but on other factors that make the stock a desirable purchase. Some reliability can be assumed in the historical performance of an individual stock after previous splits, but future performance, of course, can never be guaranteed.

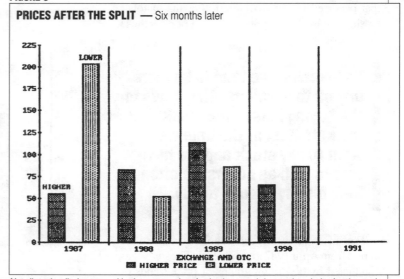

FIGURE 3

PRICES AFTER THE SPLIT — Six months later

Not all stock splits have a positive impact on prices for the three- and six-month periods after the stock split. Price performance six months after a split is more likely to be influenced by other factors such as earnings, acquisitions, reorganizations, market performance and economic changes.

IN ALL

The most reliable consistency appears to be the rise in price before the split goes into effect. The tendency of a split announcement to spur buying activity suggests that the only contemplated actions, based purely on the stock split, should be to hold and observe or to sell the stock into this new price strength. Any other actions are most often highly speculative.

Michael D. Sheimo has been an investor, stockbroker and registered options principal in the Minneapolis area. He has just completed a book on stock selection for John Wiley and Sons, Strength of Four Stock Selection, *due out later this year.*

FURTHER READING

Sheimo, Michael D. [1989]. *Dow Theory Redux*, Probus Publishing.
_____ [1990]. *Stock Market Rules*, Probus Publishing.

Returning To The Basics

by John Sweeney

Since November last year, I've gone through exploiting the trend-related activities — trading the underlying trend, adding trades to the trend trades and reversing trades when wrong about the trend — but there's the other half of trading that some would say is going on 80% of the time: trading-range trading.

Recall that the original system was a trend-following system but inevitably, there were times when no trend was apparent. Thus, the first clue to a trading range is being out of the market when using the underlying system.

Another clue to look for is flat behavior in the trend indicator, in this case Sma35C (Figure 1), which is the simple 35-day moving average of the closing prices. Segment A is a flat area in the 35-day average with very high and very low values. At B, we know prices leaped upward and are being replaced with much lower prices at A, so the average must move downward; hence, it is not a trading range.

By the end of period 2, old prices seem stable and about at the level of the new prices. If they don't move, we could be in for a nontrending period. By the end of 3, I've got a range in place, so I sell the market short, hoping for another trip to the low side.

It doesn't work. Depending on the stops for the short, I'm stopped out in late April or early May or reversed at E, when the breakout of the range from the D to C comes. By then, the trending indicator is clearly on the move and we're no longer in a possible trading range.

At F, we have a typical setup. Old prices are about the level of new ones and a high and low have potentially set in. I go long, hoping for a return to the high side of the 35-day average — with the results you see in Figure 1.

Day to day, you wonder what mode you're in. These happen to be good times for solid, simple rules. Figure 2 shows another typical situation, almost an ideal situation. At A, the short average, 10 days, declines due to a sharp down day, creating the possibility of trading ranges around the 10- and the 35-day averages. Expecting the price to fall as far below the average as it had gone above it, we'd expect prices to go to point B, which was, in fact, exceeded the next day before rebounding. Next, I'd hope for a short sale back into the range at point C, but prices didn't quite get to my target.

With prices falling away from the upper side of the initial trading range, I'd start thinking of support at the bottom side of the initial range (B) and, in addition, predicting the bottom of the 35-day trading range (D). The day after C, the market penetrated the 10- and 35-day averages. The equidistant parallel line below the 35-day average was line D at 97.5, which turned out to be an incredibly accurate guess.

FIGURE 1

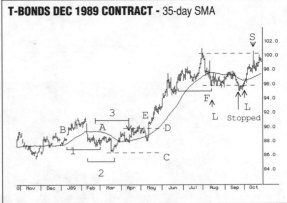

T-BONDS DEC 1989 CONTRACT - 35-day SMA

Here, a trading range is defined by its time period — here, 35 days — and price range about the defining average, also 35 days.

FIGURE 2

T-BONDS DEC 1991 CONTRACT - 35-day SMA

Elaborating on Figure 1, A starts the trading range; C, D and E trade into the range, F stops out of the range and G reverses the strategy into a trending mode.

D is more than a guess. Looking at the 35-day history, unless the price goes up from that point, the 35-day average must begin to fall, the event of which, in concert with the fall of the 10-day average, puts me back into the trending mode. Thus, going long at D could be stopped and reversed to enter a trend trade. It could also be successful to the other side of the trading range, at which point it would be (1) reversed or (2) reversed, then stopped and reversed long to go with a trend. Either way, I've captured the trading range, paid a small price in the reversing process and gotten aboard any developing trend. As it actually worked out, I went short at E, was stopped and reversed at F, whipsawed short the next day and then reversed long at G to enter the trend.

This is nifty if the market settles into a trading rang, but ranges don't stick around long enough for us to use a 35-day time horizon, especially in futures. Stocks tend to form more ranges so they're more vulnerable to that. I need something that's more proactive — like the 10-day average — and I also need something I can teach to a machine.

My purpose here is to discuss trading a trading range. Next month, I'll tackle teaching the computer to do the same.

John Sweeney is STOCKS & COMMODITIES' Technical Editor.

CHAPTER 8

THE TRADERS' MAGAZINE

AUGUST 1992

TECHNICAL ANALYSIS OF **STOCKS &** **COMMODITIES**™

Rate of Change

Respected and well-known technician and author Martin Pring debuts as a STOCKS & COMMODITIES author, writing about the rate of change oscillator, a simple method of figuring advances or declines in a given period.

The rate of change (ROC) is perhaps the simplest form of oscillator or momentum to understand and calculate. It measures the speed of an advance or decline over a specific time span and is calculated by dividing today's level by a level *n* periods ago and multiplying the result by 100. For example, an annualized (or 12-month) ROC is calculated by dividing the price in January 1992 by that of January 1991. Take the difference between the indicator and the 100 level and plot the result as a positive or negative number, using a reference line of 0. In this case, 101 is plotted as +1, 102 as +2, 98 as -2 and so on. The result is plotted as a positive or negative figure in a continuous oscillating series. If the price is identical in both periods, the ROC is plotted at zero. The longer the time span under consideration, the greater the significance of the trend being measured. Consequently, movements in a 10-day ROC are far less meaningful than those calculated over 12-month or 24-month time spans.

WARNING IN ADVANCE
Using ROC helps explain some cyclical movements in markets, often

Using ROC helps explain some cyclical movements in markets, often giving advance warning of a reversal in the prevailing trend.

by Martin J. Pring

giving advance warning of a reversal in the prevailing trend. This indicator comes into its own during light trading-range markets, but like any other oscillator, the ROC gives misleading signals when a sustained or linear trend is under way.

ROC indicators are usually plotted as raw data, as can be seen in Figure 1. The problem here is that the price movements are jagged and often result in misleading signals. A useful alternative is to smooth the oscillator with a moving average. Whipsaw signals still occur, but far less often. The indications of a trend reversal in the indicator are also more reliable. In general, the further the smoothed rate of change is from the equilibrium (or zero) level, the more reliable the signal.

In addition, another problem arises in that a specific time frame used in the ROC calculation reflects only one cycle. If that particular cycle is not operating or is dominated by another or a combination of cycles, that specific ROC indicator is of little value.

THREE IN TIME

Figure 2 shows three momentum indicators calculated for different time spans — six-month, 12-month and 24-month rate of change oscillators. Both the six-month and the 12-month ROC is smoothed by a six-month moving average, while the 24-month ROC is smoothed by a nine-month moving average. The six-month series is usually the first to turn, followed by the 12- and 24-month indicators. The six-month ROC is much more sensitive to prices and on most occasions and is therefore more timely; at other times, it turns long before the data series itself, giving an unduly premature signal. Prices on the six-month indicator are not always reflected in the longer-term 12- or 24-month momentum series because markets experience different cyclical phenomena simultaneously.

The six-month series explains virtually every intermediate-trend price movement, but the longer-term 24-month indicator only reflects the major market trends. Several characteristics can be observed from these relationships:

■ The smoothed 24-month ROC sets the background for the major move.

■ The strongest price trends usually occur when all three curves move simultaneously in the same direction (for example, 1973-74, early 1975, late 1977, late 1982 and so forth).

■ If the 24-month ROC peaks out when either the six- and/or 12-month series are rising, the selloff is normally mild because the cycles are conflicting. A classic example occurred in early 1982, when the 24-month ROC indicator was falling but the six-month series had already turned up.

FIGURE 1

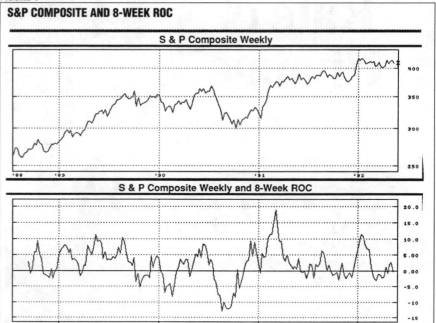

ROC indicators are usually plotted as raw data, as can be seen in Figure 1. The problem with this is that the price movements are jagged and often result in misleading signals. A useful alternative is to smooth the oscillator with a moving average. Whipsaw signals still occur, but far less often.

FIGURE 2

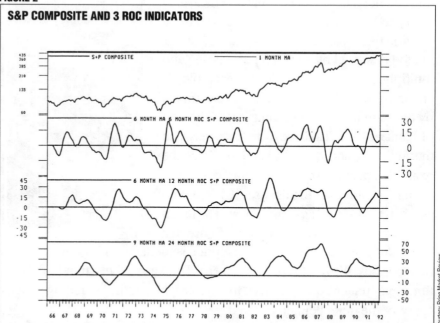

Figure 2 shows three momentum indicators calculated for different time spans — six-month, 12-month and 24-month rate of change oscillator. Both the six-month and the 12-month ROC is smoothed by a six-month moving average, while the 24-month is smoothed by a nine-month moving average.

■ When the 24-month indicator is in a rising mode but the six- and nine-month indicators peak out, the implied decline is usually mild. An example of such occurred in 1971 when a decline was signaled by the peaking action of the six- and 12-month indicators, but the 24-month indicator was only just crossing above its zero reference line, indicating that the bull market was in a relatively early stage. Ensuing reaction proved to be an intermediate decline within a bull market. Another example occurred in 1976 when the 24-month momentum made a strong upturn, but the 12- and six-month ROCs were falling sharply. The result was a distributional top.

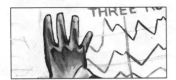

The same principle can be applied to daily and weekly data. Figure 3, for example, shows the daily close for the Standard & Poor's 500 between January and July 1990. Note how the April low appears to be associated with a bottom in all three indicators.

The market did not respond in a negative way to the May peak in the 10-day indicator because the 15- and 30-day oscillators were still rising; the result was a standoff. The S&P responded with a modest rally. When the 15-day ratio peaked, the market experienced its final runup.

Later, in mid-June, all three indicators peaked and the S&P experienced a sharper sell-off.

After that, note how the July top was associated with a top in all three momentum indicators once again when the market experienced a very sharp decline. These examples clearly indicate that the strength and sustainability of a market trend is determined by the simultaneous interreaction of a number of different cycles, far more than could be shown here.

COMPLEX YET SATISFACTORY

It is a complex process to plot and follow indicators reflecting many different time spans, though it is possible to come up with a satisfactory compromise. This alternative involves the construction of one single indicator that combines four different ROC series and weights them according to the length of their time span. Next time, I will demonstrate how this can be achieved, as well as outline the strengths and weaknesses of this interesting approach.

Martin Pring is the author of a number of books, publishes "The Pring Market Review" and is a principal of the investment counseling firm Pring-Turner Capital Group.

FURTHER READING

"Pring Market Review," International Institute for Economic Research, Inc., PO Box 329, Washington Depot, CT 06794.
Pring, Martin J. [1991]. *Technical Analysis Explained*, McGraw-Hill, 3d ed.
_____ [1981]. *How to Forecast Interest Rates*, McGraw-Hill.
_____ [1981]. *International Investing Made Easy*, McGraw-Hill.
_____ [1985]. *McGraw-Hill Handbook of Commodities and Futures*, McGraw-Hill.

FIGURE 3

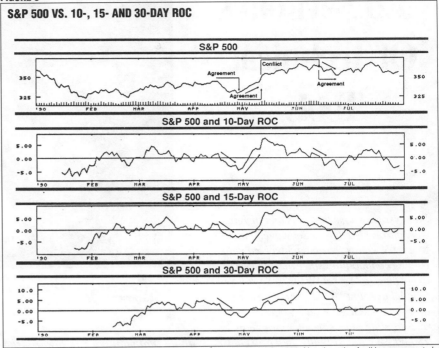

Figure 3 shows the daily close for the S&P 500 between January and July 1990. Note how the April low appears to be associated with a bottom in all three indicators.

FIGURE 4

CALCULATING RATE OF CHANGE IN A SPREADSHEET

	A	B	C	D
1	Date	S&P 500	10 day ROC	5 day Average
2	920317	409.58		
3	920318	409.15		
4	920319	409.80		
5	920320	411.25		
6	923023	409.91		
7	920324	408.88		
8	920325	407.52		
9	920326	407.86		
10	920327	403.50		
11	920330	403.00	-1.6065	
12	920331	403.69	-1.3345	
13	920401	404.23	-1.3592	
14	920402	400.50	-2.6140	
15	920403	401.55	-2.0395	-1.7907
16	920406	405.59	-0.8046	-1.6304
17	920407	398.06	-2.3214	-1.8277
18	920408	394.50	-3.2756	-2.2110
19	920409	400.64	-0.7088	-1.8300
20	920410	404.29	0.3201	-1.3581
21	920413	406.08	0.5920	-1.0787
22	920414	412.39	2.0187	-0.2107
23	920415	416.28	3.9401	1.2324
24	920416	416.04	=((B24/B15)*100)-100	=AVERAGE(C20:C24)

Calculating a rate of change in a spreadsheet is very simple. Here, the 10-day rate of change is calculated in column C and the five-day moving average of the 10-day rate of change is calculated in column D.

Ed Seykota Of Technical Tools

"The biggest secret about success is that there isn't any big secret about it, or if there is, then it's a secret from me, too. The idea of searching for some secret for trading success misses the point."
— Ed Seykota

Ed Seykota, whose thoughts and insights were chronicled in Jack Schwager's book Market Wizards, *has been involved with trading commodities since the late 1960s. According to Market Wizards, Seykota's "model account" — an actual customer account — started with $5,000 in 1972 and to date has earned more than a 250,000% gain. Recently, in a new challenge, he purchased data and software vendor Technical Tools. STOCKS & COMMODITIES Editor Thom Hartle interviewed Seykota in a series of written correspondence that took place over several months ending in May 1992, during which Hartle posed a number of questions relevant to all traders, including any secrets to trading successfully. Not too surprisingly, the answer to that was the same answer as for any endeavor — persistence and commitment!*

How did you get started in technical analysis? What was your first trade?

The first trade I remember, I was about five years old in Portland, OR. My father gave me a gold-colored medallion, a sales promotion trinket. I traded it to a neighbor kid for five magnifying lenses. I felt as though I had participated in a rite of passage. I started early to get interested in technical analysis, too. By the time I was nine, I had a bedroom filled with old radios, test equipment and oscilloscopes. I liked to generate and display wave forms. Later, when I was 13, my father showed me how to buy stocks. He explained that I should buy when the price broke out of the top of a box and to sell when it broke out of the bottom. And that's how I got started.

With all that pointing you toward trading, was it inevitable that you would end up in it?

Actually, no. At the Massachusetts Institute of Technology (MIT), I studied servo theory, which is about self-controlling mechanisms such as thermostats, governors and chemical process controllers. Professor Jay Forrester showed me how to apply servo theory to economic modeling. His feedback dynamics approach required careful observation and deep thought about how things work.

So how did you get introduced to technical analysis?

About the time I graduated from MIT, I read an article by technician Richard Donchian that intrigued me. He demonstrated how a diversified simple five- and 20-day moving average crossover system made a respectable rate of return. That idea — the idea of an automatic mechani-

cal moneymaking machine — fascinated me. So I bought some block time at a local computer service, spent my evenings punching up cards from *The Wall Street Journal* and began to reproduce Donchian's results. I tried varying the parameter sets and found that other combinations also worked. I noticed that

> **Through the years I have gained tremendous insight, perspective, skills, inspiration and strength from books. A short list of some of my favorite books about the markets would have to include *Extraordinary Popular Delusions* by Charles McKay and *Reminiscences of a Stock Operator* by Edwin LeFevre.**

longer-term smoothing worked pretty well, while transaction costs seemed to chop up shorter-term systems.

And then what did you do?

In the early 1970s, I went to work for a wire house. I would go in on weekends to use the IBM 360/65 accounting mainframe to run tests. I punched cards and ran batch jobs in FORTRAN 4. I managed to test four types of systems on about 50 different parameter sets on eight commodities going back a decade. It took me half a year. To show you how much computers have changed the way we do

† See Trader's Glossary for complete description

things, these days it might take one weekend on a PC.

So what did you do with that information?

Well, eventually, the management of the wire house packaged a product around my research. The problem was, my boss was unable to follow the system and *his* boss was more interested in souping up the system to generate more commissions. I told them their best move was to make money for their customers. No sale! Not only that, my boss reneged on his handshake that they would give me 10% of the commissions generated from the system. I got disgusted with them all and left.

So at age 23, I went out on my own with about a half-dozen accounts in the $10,000-25,000 range. A few years later, I checked back with the boys at the wire house. They had hundreds of sales agents raising money for their souped-up rewrite of my system. I had more money under management than they did, and mine came from internal growth of my original accounts. I felt exonerated and glad I had escaped from a system based so heavily on commissions.

And since then?

I still test systems and think about the markets. I still collect data. I still manage money.

What is the secret to your success? What do you consider to be good mental skills for successful trading?

The biggest secret about success is that there isn't any big secret about it, or if there is, then it's a secret from me, too. The idea of searching for some secret for trading success misses the point. It's like golf. Some golfers play to spend time outdoors. They hang out with their cronies, become one with nature, study the greens, reconnect with their muscles, drop into focused concentration and, incidentally, pick up a birdie or two. For others, it's an exercise in finding some new Holy Grail putter. Different strokes for different folks!

In that case, what can an individual do to become a successful trader?

The "doing" part of trading is simple. You just pick up the phone and place orders. The "being" part is a bit more subtle. It's like being an athlete. It's commitment and mission. To the committed, a world of support appears. All manner of unforeseen assistance materializes to support and propel the committed to meet grand destiny.

Should a person focus his or her time on developing mechanical or non-mechanical (judgmental) methods?

Judgmental systems are inherently mechanical. Gut traders trade according to set rules of attitude, approach and personality. But I also feel that mechanical systems are inherently judgmental. System traders typically use judgment for the enormously important tasks of rolling forward, changing bet size and adding or deleting instruments.

The point is, no real conflict exists between judgment and mechanical trading. A conscious trader is aware of money management algorithms, trading systems and the need for supportive relationships. He maintains his knowledge of broad and local economic trends and remains aware of his feelings. He is also aware of how his own personality works and creates a workable ecology between himself and the world around him.

If you don't use a mechanical trading system, have you built a set of rules to trade by? What are they?

I have many rules and some higher laws. Some of the rules are: Trade with the long-term trend. Cut your losses. Let your profits ride. Bet as much as you can handle and no more.

What do you mean by "higher laws"?

I feel that higher laws and rules govern much of my trading. There is a higher law that commitment and service favor performance. There is a higher law that greed and selfishness impede it. I feel I am in tune with these laws when things just seem to click. Other times I feel out of sync, as if I'm pushing a dull mower through tall wet grass. Next to these higher laws, trading rules seem rather insignificant.

Are price moves random? Is there any basis for trends? What makes prices move?

I feel the "aha!" process lies at the heart of price change. For instance, consider the series: OTTFFSSE. What is the next letter? This puzzle creates tension — *until* you see the first letters of the ordinal numbers — one, two. "Aha!" you say. A lot happens during an "aha." The puzzle dies and the tension dissipates.

A societal "aha!" drives price. Read the newspapers and the news magazines during a major move. At first, no one gets why the move is happening. There's a lot of confusion. Part of the move's way up, some people get it. At the end, *everybody* gets it. The tension is resolved and the move ends.

Aha. I'll have to think about that. Can you tell us how you set stop-loss points?

Before I enter a trade, I set stops at a point at which the chart sours.

What about starting capital? How much money should a person have before starting to trade?

Good money management is equity invariant. I'd ask a trader who thinks he needs a certain amount before he can trade exactly what amount he would need to *stop* trading.

What are some of your favorite books that people should consider reading?

Through the years I have gained tremendous insight, perspective, skills, inspiration and strength from books. A short list of some of my favorite books about the markets would have to include *Extraordinary Popular Delusions* by Charles McKay; *Reminiscences of a Stock Operator* by Edwin LeFevre; and *The Crowd* by Gustare Le Bon.

Successful trading can be thought of as a business. Your new focus is running Technical Tools. Can you draw some comparisons between trading and running a business?

Yes. I find a lot of similarities between trading and business. In trading, I have learned to ride the long-term trend, cut losses and manage money. In the case of Technical Tools, our customers, suppli-

"The 'doing' part of trading is simple. You just pick up the phone and place orders. The 'being' part is a bit more subtle. It's like being an athlete. It's commitment and mission."

ers, competition and trade publications such as STOCKS & COMMODITIES indicate the long-term trend and help point to where we should be heading as a company in this industry. When I hire someone, it is usually on a trial basis until a strong "trend" of productivity sets in. Cutting losses in business has to do with discontinuing unprofitable products. Firing, also like cutting losses, is tough on the emotions and vital to the eventual success of all involved. Managing money means spending less than we make as well as not betting the ranch on just one idea. I find that the principles of sound trading have close analogs in running a business.

As Technical Tools develops, I envision it as part of an enterprise in which trading and business converge. Lately, I have been beating the drum to call together a trading tribe, a kind of support group that borrows from tribal traditions as a means of cultivating group participation. Readers can write me in care of Technical Tools if they are interested in finding out more about this.

Running a business like a tribe sounds pretty unique. Thank you for your time, Ed.

You're welcome.

REFERENCES

Le Bon, Gustare [1960]. *The Crowd,* Viking, New York.

LeFevre, Edwin [1923]. *Reminiscences of a Stock Operator*, American Research Council, New York; also, Books of Wall Street, Burlington, VT, 1980.

McKay, Charles [1932]. *Extraordinary Popular Delusions and the Madness of Crowds*, L.C. Page, London.

Technical Tools, 334 State St., Los Altos, CA 94022, fax (415) 948-5697, BBS number (415) 949-1538.

DONCHIAN'S TRADING GUIDES

Richard D. Donchian, a well-respected Wall Street technician who began his career in 1930, initially compiled these guides in 1934 after suffering losses in 1929. He later dug them up again while working for Hayden Stone (now Shearson Lehman Brothers) and reviewed them in the firm's July 3, 1974, "Trend Timing" commodity letter. In that publication, Donchian noted which points he felt remained the most important: *General* 1, 2, 3, 4 and 5 and *Technical* 1, 4, 5 and 9.

Donchian's General Guides

1. Beware of acting immediately on widespread public opinion. Even if it is correct, it will usually delay the move.

2. From a period of dullness and inactivity, watch for and prepare to follow a move in the direction in which volume increases.

3. Limit losses and ride profits, irrespective of all other rules.

4. Light commitments are advisable when a market position is not certain. Clearly defined moves are signaled frequently enough to make life interesting, and concentration on these moves to the virtual exclusion of others will prevent unprofitable whipsawing.

5. Seldom take a position in the direction of an immediately preceding three-day move. Wait for a one-day reversal.

6. Judicious use of stop orders is a valuable aid to profitable trading. Stops may be used to protect profits, limit losses and take positions from certain formations such as triangular foci. Stop orders are apt to be more valuable and less treacherous if used in proper relation to the chart formation.

7. In a market in which upswings are likely to equal or exceed downswings, a heavier position should be taken for the upswings for percentage reasons; a decline from 50 to 25 will net only 50% profit, whereas an advance from 25 to 50 will net 100%.

8 In taking a position, price orders are allowable. In closing a position, use "market" orders.

9 Buy strong-acting, strong-background commodities and sell weak ones subject to all other rules.

10 Moves in which rails lead or participate strongly are usually worth following more than moves in which rails lag.

11 A study of the capitalization of a company, the degree of activity of an issue and whether the issue is a lethargic truck horse like Consolidated Edison or a spirited, volatile race horse like Case Threshing Machine is fully as important as a study of statistical reports.

Donchian's Technical Guides

1 A move followed by a sideways range often precedes another move of almost equal extent in the same direction of the original move. Generally, when the second move from the sideways range has run its course, a countermove approaching the sideways range may be expected (Figure 1).

2 Reversal or resistance to a move is likely to be encountered on reaching levels at which the commodity has fluctuated for a considerable length of time within a narrow range in the past or on approaching previous highs or lows.

3 Watch for good buying or selling opportunities when trendlines are approached, especially on medium or dull volume. Be sure such a line has not been adhered to or hit too frequently.

4 Watch for "crawling along" or repeated bumping of minor or major trendlines and prepare to see such trendlines broken (Figure 2).

5 Breaking of minor trendlines counter to the major trend gives most other important position-taking signals. Positions can be taken or reversed on stops at such places (Figure 3).

6 Triangles of either slope may mean either accumulation or distribution depending on other considerations, although triangles are usually broken on the flat side.

FIGURE 1

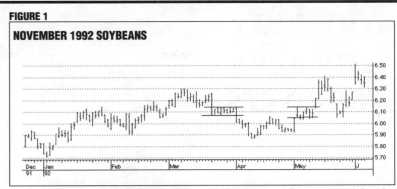

NOVEMBER 1992 SOYBEANS

Sideways price action may be followed by a resumption of the prior trend. Prices may travel about the same distance as before the sideways trading range and then move back toward the trading range.

FIGURE 2

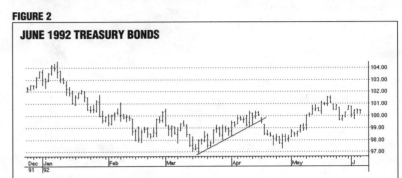

JUNE 1992 TREASURY BONDS

Trendlines are typically broken where the market is repeatedly touching them.

FIGURE 3

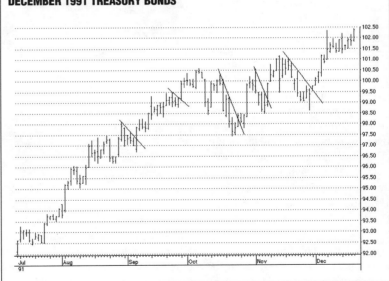

DECEMBER 1991 TREASURY BONDS

Draw minor trendlines along minor trends that are counter to the major trend. In this example, the major upward trend resumed when the minor downtrend lines were broken.

7 Watch for volume climax, especially after a long move.

8 Don't count on gaps being closed unless you can distinguish among breakaway gaps, normal gaps and exhaustion gaps.

9 During a move, take or increase positions in the direction of the move at the market the morning following any one-day reversal, however slight the reversal may be, especially if volume declines on the reversal.

Moving Average Crossovers

Are moving average crossovers more effective than other indicators? More specifically, how about moving average crossovers applied to the Dow Jones Industrial Average? S&C contributor Arthur Merrill decided to research the question using weekly data for the last 24 years, checking out crossovers with a four-week exponential moving average and with 13-, 26- and 52-week exponential averages. Here are his results.

by Arthur A. Merrill, CMT

O ne of the earliest technical tools, as easy to figure with pens and paper as well as with computer later on, was a price chart and a moving average with a simple set of instructions: When the red line crosses over the blue line, *buy!*

I have wondered just how good the Dow Jones Industrial Average (DJIA) crossovers were in forecasting the future of the DJIA itself. When the DJIA is above its 26-week average, what are the prospects for the future? Would it be better to watch the four-week average compared with the 26-week? How about the other possible crossovers?

Intrigued, I decided to put the question to my computer, and the results are in Figures 2 through 6. I wanted to look at the weekly data bank for the last 24 years, and I decided to divide the 24-year period into two 12-year tests. The first would cover 1968 through 1979. The results for this period are the left-hand bar in each pair. The second period covered the years from 1980 through 1991. These results are reported in the right-hand bar of each pair.

JOS PALMIERI

I asked the computer to check out crossovers of the current price with the four-week, the 13-week, the 26-week and the 52-week exponential moving averages. (See sidebar, "Exponential moving averages.") These are marked as C/4, C/13, C/26 and C/52 on the figures. I then asked the computer to check out other possibilities. For example, 13/26 checks the 13-week compared with the 26-week average.

Note that the test includes all weeks in the test period, not just the week of the actual crossover. The entire period after a bullish crossover was considered bullish until a bearish crossover occurred, when the stance was changed to bearish. With this interpretation, we get enough data points to check significance.

YES OR NO?

Then I asked the computer to look into the future one week. Was the DJIA higher or lower? The results can be seen in Figure 2. What about four weeks later (Figure 3)? What about 13 weeks (Figure 4)? What about 26 weeks (Figure 5)? Or even 52 weeks (Figure 6)?

The computer looked at each week in the test periods. If the short-term average was higher than the longer-term average and the DJIA was higher at the later date,

EXPONENTIAL MOVING AVERAGES

Defining exponentially smoothed moving averages — which, for most traders, would be a series of closing prices — is simply another form of a moving average. An exponentially smoothed moving average utilizes a smoothing constant (α) that approximates the number of days for a simple moving average. This constant is multiplied times the difference between today's closing price and yesterday's moving average value. This new value is then added to yesterday's moving average value (Figure 1):

$$EMA_{today} = EMA_{yesterday} + \alpha \left(P_{today} - EMA_{yesterday} \right)$$

SIDEBAR FIGURE 1

EXPONENTIALLY SMOOTHED MOVING AVERAGE

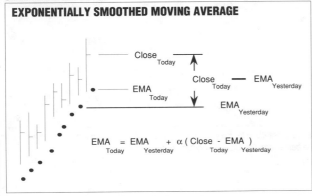

$$EMA_{Today} = EMA_{Yesterday} + \alpha (Close_{Today} - EMA_{Yesterday})$$

The actual formula that is mathematically reduced for a geometrically (exponentially) weighted moving average is:

Exponential Moving Average—The EMA for day D is calculated as: $EMA_D = \alpha PR_D + (1-\alpha)EMA_{D-1}$ where PR is the price on day D and α (alpha) is a smoothing constant (0–1). Alpha may be estimated as $2/(n+1)$, where *n* is the simple moving average length.

The α constant approximates for a simple moving average. Its value is determined by the formula $2/(n + 1)$ where *n* is the number of days for a simple moving average. An approximation for a 10-day moving average would use an $\alpha = 2/(10+1) = 0.18$.

—*Editor*

REFERENCES

Granger, C.W.J., and Paul Newbold [1986]. *Forecasting Economic Time Series*, second edition, Academic Press, Inc.

Hutson, Jack K. [1984]. "Filter price data: moving averages vs. exponential moving averages," *Technical Analysis of* STOCKS & COMMODITIES, Volume 2: May/June.

†See Traders' Glossary for complete description

FIGURE 1

CHART KEY
Left-hand bar: 1968-79 Right-hand bar: 1980-91
PS = Probably significant (95% level) S = Significant (99% level) HS = Highly significant (99.9% level)
C/4: Current price is above or below its four-week exponential average 4/13: Four-week exponential average is above or below the 13-week exponential average

the call was rated successful. If the DJIA was lower, it was called unsuccessful. In addition, if the short-term average was below the longer term and the DJIA was lower at the later date, the call was rated successful. If the DJIA was higher, it was rated unsuccessful. The percent of the weeks that were successful are charted in the bars in Figures 2 through 6.

> **When the DJIA is above its 26-week average, what are the prospects for the future? Is it better to watch the four-week average compared with the 26-week?**

For example, look at the first pair of bars in the upper left-hand corner of Figure 2. When the DJIA was above its four-week average, it was successful in calling the direction of the market in the following week only 51.5% of the time in the first test period, and 50.6% of the time in the second. This is almost even money, and it certainly was no help!

The next job assigned to the computer was a check of significance. Did the results differ significantly from pure chance? To find out, I used the chi-squared† test. If the result could have occurred by chance once in 20 repetitions of the test, the result was referred to as probably significant (Ps). If the result could have occurred by chance once in 100 repetitions, it was referred to as being significant (S). If the result could have occurred once in 1,000 times, it was considered to be highly significant (Hs).

After inspecting the charts, the first

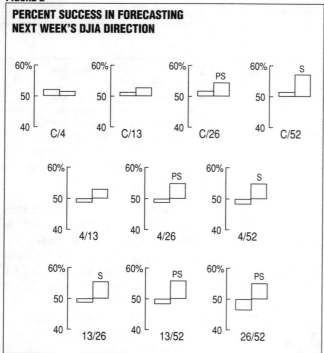

FIGURE 2

PERCENT SUCCESS IN FORECASTING NEXT WEEK'S DJIA DIRECTION

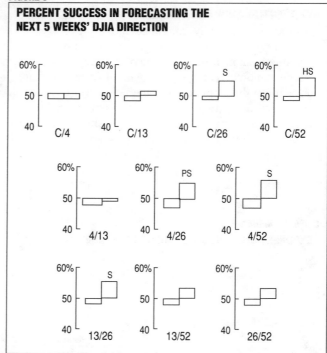

FIGURE 3

PERCENT SUCCESS IN FORECASTING THE NEXT 5 WEEKS' DJIA DIRECTION

The percent of the weeks that were successful are charted in Figures 2 through 6. Here, when the DJIA was above its four-week average, it was successful in calling the direction of the market in the following week only 51.5% of the time in the first test period and 50.6% of the time in the second, almost even money.

Here, the results in forecasting five weeks ahead were better but still not enthusiastic. The best score was C/52 (highly significant, 57.5%).

impression garnered is the poor record reported for the first 12 years (the left-hand bar of each pair). The only significant deviation from chance is in Figure 6, when the forecasts were significantly incorrect. This isn't necessarily bad; the incorrect forecasts merely signaled a reversal of trend at the later date. However, the difference in the two 12-year periods isn't reassuring. Some indicators decline in effectiveness through the years; perhaps these moving average relationships have improved their effectiveness in recent years. The second 12 years certainly reported some significantly successful results.

LESS THAN ENTHUSIASTIC?

For the test results, consider Figure 2. The success in calling the DJIA one week ahead is certainly far from enthusiastic. The three best were C/52 (56.4%), 4/52 (55.6%) and 13/26 (55.5%).

In Figure 3, the results in forecasting five weeks ahead were better but still not enthusiastic. The best score was C/52 (highly significant, 57.5%).

In Figure 4, the crossovers put in the best performance of all the time periods. Two of the crossovers were more than 60% (4/52: 61.5% and 13/26: 62.3%). The odds here are six to four. Several of the reports were highly significant, but below the 60% level.

Figure 5 shows the success in calling the DJIA in the following six months. Several of the crossovers were highly significant but slightly below the 60% level. The best were C/26 (59.0%), C/52 (59.2%) and 13/26 (59.0%). Close behind were 4/13 (58.0%), 4/52 (58.3%) and 26/52 (58.2%).

The forecasts one year ahead (Figure 6) lean toward the negative, forecasting a change in trend. The longest-term averages gave highly significant forecasts in the first 12-year period (13/52: 42.8% and 26/52: 42.5%). For a continuation of the trend in the same direction, the very short term (C/4: 56.7%) reported the best performance.

THE MOST USEFUL

Overall, which averages were the most useful? If we skip the one-year forecast and consider the average performance in

forecasting one week, five weeks, 13 and 26 weeks ahead, the best average score was reported by the longer-term 13/26.

The conclusions I determined from this study were:

1) The relative position of moving averages can give significant opinions of the future.

2) The odds for success aren't high; they rarely exceed six to four.

3) The results reported by the first 12-year period don't confirm the second.

My overall conclusion? I'll watch these moving average relationships but I won't give them too much weight, because of conclusions 2 and 3.

Arthur Merrill of Merrill Analysis, Inc., Elm #3325, 3300 Darby Rd., Haverford, PA 19041, is a Chartered Market Technician and the author of many reports and books, including Behavior of Prices on Wall Street *and* Filtered Waves, Basic Theory.

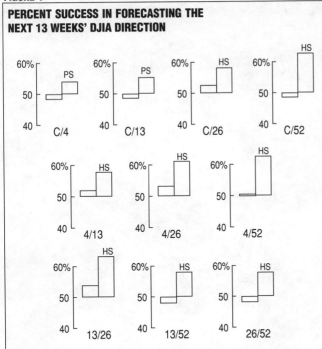

FIGURE 4

PERCENT SUCCESS IN FORECASTING THE NEXT 13 WEEKS' DJIA DIRECTION

Here, the crossovers put in the best performance of all the time periods. Two of the crossovers were more than 60% (4/52: 61.5% and 13/26: 62.3%). The odds here are six to four. Several of the reports were highly significant, but below the 60% level.

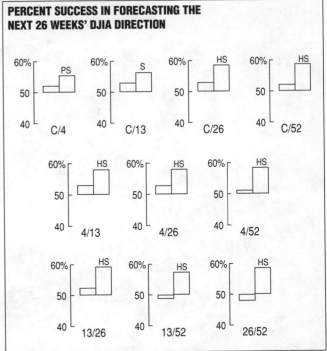

FIGURE 5

PERCENT SUCCESS IN FORECASTING THE NEXT 26 WEEKS' DJIA DIRECTION

Several crossovers were highly significant but slightly below the 60% level. The best were C/26 (59.0%), C/52 (59.2%) and 13/26 (59.0%). Close behind were 4/13 (58.0%), 4/52 (58.3%) and 26/52 (58.2%).

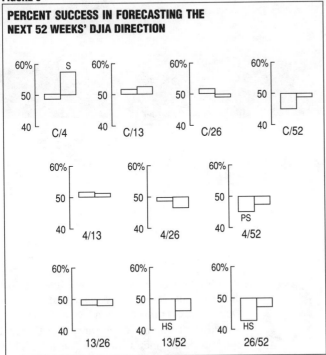

FIGURE 6

PERCENT SUCCESS IN FORECASTING THE NEXT 52 WEEKS' DJIA DIRECTION

The forecasts one year ahead lean toward the negative, forecasting a change in trend. The longest-term averages gave highly significant forecasts in the first 12-year period (13/52: 42.8% and 26/52: 42.5%). For a continuation of the trend in the same direction, the very short term (C/4: 56.7%) reported the best performance.

MIKE CRESSY

Utilities And Bonds

Of all the interrelationships between markets, one that has been taken for granted for decades is the relationship between the Dow Jones Industrial Average and the Dow Jones Transportation Average. John Murphy, veteran technician and leading proponent of intermarket analysis, points out that the third Dow Jones average, the Dow Jones Utility Average, can be used for forecasting purposes for stocks as well as bonds. Murphy explains.

by John J. Murphy

O ne of the basic premises of the Dow theory is that the Dow Jones Industrial Average (DJIA) and the Dow Jones Transportation Average (DJTA) should always trend in the same direction and confirm each other's moves. The third Dow Jones average, the Dow Jones Utility Average (DJUA), also has valuable predictive qualities not only for stocks but for bonds as well. The utilities usually act as a leading indicator for the stock market at tops and bottoms. This tendency for the utility stocks to lead the rest of the stock market is based on their strong ties to the bond market.

FIGURE 1

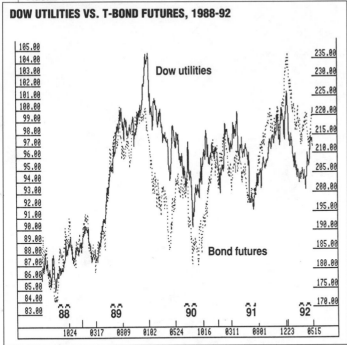

DOW UTILITIES VS. T-BOND FUTURES, 1988-92

The strong tendency for the Dow Utilities (solid line) and Treasury bond futures (dotted line) to peak and trough together is seen from 1988 to spring 1992.

FIGURE 2

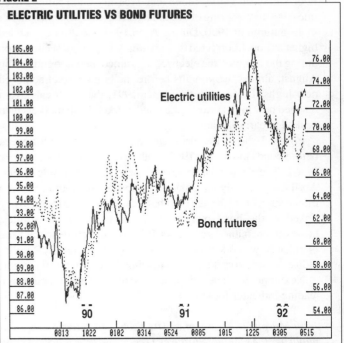

ELECTRIC UTILITIES VS BOND FUTURES

The S&P Electrical Utility Index (solid line) and Treasury bonds (dotted line) are seen trending together from mid-1990 to May 1992. The electricals led bonds higher in late 1990 and throughout 1992. Both peaked in early 1992.

Courtesy Knight-Ridder TradeCenter

My article in June showed how the bond market usually acts as a leading indicator for stocks. This time, I will try to establish the link between the utilities and the bond market and then show how certain utilities often act as a leading indicator for bonds.

Figure 1 compares the DJUA with bond futures from 1988 to May 1992. A strong visual correlation can be seen between the two markets and their tendency to peak and trough together. Note the simultaneous bottoms in 1988, the peaks in late 1989, the bottoms in 1990 and 1991 and the concurrent peaks in early 1992.

> **After a modest correction during the summer, the electricals resumed their uptrend during August, almost two months before the bond market achieved new highs.**

LINKS AND INFLUENCES

The utilities are linked to bonds because they are influenced by the direction of long-term interest rates. However, the Dow utilities also include natural gas stocks, which are influenced more by the direction of natural gas prices than they are by interest rates. Electrical utilities, on the other hand, are more of an interest-sensitive play. Electric utilities not only track the bond market more closely than the broader utility averages but often lead the bond market.

Figure 2 shows the strong correlation between the Standard &

FIGURE 3

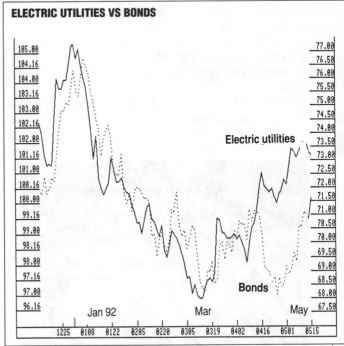

ELECTRIC UTILITIES VS BONDS

Electrical utilities (solid line) turned down a week before bonds (dotted line) in January 1992 and broke out to the upside in mid-April, one month before bonds.

Poor's Electric Utility Index and Treasury bond futures from mid-1990 to the spring of 1992. The electricals led bonds higher in the autumn of 1990. During April 1991, the utilities trended higher as bonds corrected downward. After a modest correction during the summer, the electricals resumed their uptrend during August, almost two months before the bond market achieved new highs. During fourth-quarter 1991, the electricals again reached new highs prior to the bond market. Both markets then peaked in early January 1992.

Figure 3 shows the electricals turning down about a week before bonds in January 1992. Both markets hit bottom in early March. The electricals, however, broke out to the upside in mid-April and correctly anticipated the upside breakout in bonds a month later. Of all the utilities, the electricals are the most closely linked to the bond market. Three of the 15 Dow utilities, however, are natural gas stocks. It's wise, therefore, to track the broader New York Stock Exchange (NYSE) and S&P utility indices as well to get a correct reading on this important sector.

Next time, I will deal with how the utilities also function as a leading indicator for stocks.

John Murphy is president of JJM Technical Advisors Inc. and publishes the monthly "Futures Trends and Intermarket Analysis." He is also the technical analyst for CNBC.

REFERENCES

JJM Technical Advisors Inc., 297-101 Kinderkamack Road, Suite 148, Oradell, NJ 07649.

Murphy, John J. [1992]. "The link between bonds and stocks," STOCKS & COMMODITIES, June.

_____ [1992]. "The link between bonds and commodities," STOCKS & COMMODITIES, May.

_____ [1991]. *Intermarket Technical Analysis*, John Wiley & Sons.

_____ [1986]. *Technical Analysis of the Futures Markets*, New York Institute of Finance.

TA

JIMFRISINO

Detecting Seasonality

Seasonal or cyclical patterns, whether real or only imagined, have been a popular topic among traders for years. Lewis Carl Mokrasch, continuing research published originally in his article in April 1991, presents this time a generalized method for detecting seasonal patterns. However, Mokrasch warns, there are certain caveats that the trader should be aware of, and he notes that the trader should take a good long look at the data involved for significant patterns before risking capital on so-called seasonal trades. Here's how to figure it out.

by Lewis Carl Mokrasch, Ph.D.

Generally, investors sincerely want to believe that there is something inherently predictable *and* profitable about their preferred media of investment. Some advisors would have us believe that they can inform us reliably about future price movements in stocks, bonds and commodities based on historical price movement. *The Stock Trader's Almanac* has

FIGURE 1

S&P 500 INDEX AVERAGE BY MONTH

Years 1961-1990	Jan	Feb	March	April	May	June	July	Aug	Sept	Oct	Nov	Dec
Average	131.35	132.13	133.93	134.31	134.27	135.69	136.04	136.32	135.88	135.2	134.96	136.46
Std. Dev.	74.45	74.43	77.49	75.41	75.89	80.14	81.17	81.2	79.14	76.25	74.28	76.53
p=	0.33	0.34	0.36	0.37	0.37	0.36	0.36	0.35	0.36	0.37	0.37	0.35

The first row lists the average monthly prices for each month in the years from 1961 to 1990. The standard deviations are relatively large due to the upward trend in prices. The high p values (greater than 0.05) indicate that no price average for any month is significantly different from any other month.

hundreds of intriguing suggestions on how the market will even behave on a certain hour on a certain day. Other advisory material tells us to buy January heating oil futures in July and sell them in December or to buy gold stocks in October and sell in February.

If there *were* such discernible patterns, every trader would try to exploit them. Then the patterns would vanish, because an overwhelming number of traders would be taking advantage of them. Indeed, a contrarian approach to those markets would seem to be a wiser choice.

If it seems unwise to simple-mindedly take the word of some sage, how can we find seasonal trends by simply examining some historical data? If the average price of a tradeable in one period differs *significantly* from its price in another period, it is at that point that a seasonal difference is worth talking about.

But first a definition of "seasonality," or cyclicality, as it is used here is in order. A cyclic pattern in any phenomenon need not be based on a 12-month pattern, but in this study, a 12-month pattern is the basis. Some stocks, on the other hand, tend to follow a nine- or 10-month pattern.

In "Studying 10-year stock price patterns," I wrote about the decennial pattern of stock index values, which is a form of seasonality. Here, presenting a generalized method for detecting seasonal patterns is my goal. My interest is in stocks, but the basic methodology is applicable to any financial instrument and to cycles of any length.

METHODS, SOURCES, RESULTS

The Standard & Poor's 500 average monthly prices were taken from S&P's "Security price index record." The formulas and other methods used to get the *p* values are essentially the same

as in "Studying 10-year stock price patterns." Again, the conventional criterion of significance is a *p* value of 0.05 or less. In economic literature, a *p* value of 0.10 is sometimes accepted as a significant value. The spreadsheet formulas appear in the sidebar "Describing a spreadsheet program."

> ## If the average price of a tradeable in one period differs significantly from its price in another period, then a seasonal difference is worth talking about.

Figure 1 represents the results of analyzing a 30-year matrix of the monthly prices of the S&P 500 index. Obviously, there is an upward trend in the index. Because this trend causes an upward bias to the prices for each month, the standard deviations are relatively large. No price average for any month differs significantly from that of any other. Nevertheless, this table is invaluable in considering some seasonal strategies.

If the index were detrended, for instance, the standard deviations for each month's average should be much smaller. The most rigorous way to eliminate the effect of the trend on the data would be to derive the linear regression formula expressing the S&P index (or the logarithm of the index) as a function of the number of months from the first item of information. Most of the more sophisticated spreadsheet programs can make this calculation if a two-column matrix is used. Next, one would calculate the idealized or interpolated price for each month. Finally, the real price would be divided by (or subtracted from) the idealized price for each period and the result would be a new matrix.

FIGURE 2

S&P 500 INDEX DETRENDED

Years 1961-1990	Jan	Feb	March	April	May	June	July	Aug	Sept	Oct	Nov	Dec
Average:	98.13	98.66	99.51	100.26	100	99.98	100.02	100.2	100.33	100.41	100.81	101.68
Std. Dev.	7.48	5.59	5.95	4.51	3.83	5.69	4.2	4.66	5.57	5.77	6.49	7.65
p=	0.12	0.14	0.29	0.31	0.38	0.37	0.37	0.33	0.31	0.3	0.24	0.15

For each calendar year, a 12-month average was calculated. Each month's average index was divided by the 12-month average for the same year and expressed as a percentage. The first row of Figure 2 is the monthly average of the detrended data. The January data are lower than the December data due to the upward trend in prices. The p values are still above the significant level.

FIGURE 3

Years	Jan	Feb	March	April	May	June	July	Aug	Sept	Oct	Nov	Dec
S&P 500 INDEX MONTH-TO-MONTH PERCENTAGE AVERAGE CHANGE												
1961-1990												
Average:	2.21	0.74	0.88	0.87	-0.16	0.02	0.08	0.25	0.15	0.14	0.44	0.83
Std. Dev.	5.21	3.68	3.03	2.91	3.68	3.59	2.36	4.2	4.03	3.5	4.13	3.32
p=	0.08	0.32	0.25	0.26	0.18	0.22	0.18	0.3	0.27	0.25	0.35	0.28

The month-to-month change expressed as a percentage of the previous month's data is presented. The first row is the average of these percentage changes by month. The difference between the two consecutive months of December and January has a p value of 0.08, which is nearly significant.

There is a simpler method to detrend the data, the results of which are shown in Figure 2. For each calendar year, I calculated the average 12-month index. Each month's average index was divided by the 12-month average for the same year and expressed as a percentage. The January data are mostly less than 100 and the December data are mostly greater than 100 because the secular upward trend† is still observed, although the index change is much smaller than the change for the 30-year period used. The standard deviation of each month's data is much smaller than that for the data not corrected for the trend.

The p values for all comparisons with the year average index value are above the significant level. If the December data were compared only with the January data of the same calendar year, there would be a spuriously significant difference between these two data due to the residual trend. But there is no other seasonal pattern detectable.

The trend in the data can also be reduced by focusing on the month-to-month change in the index. Of course, the overall trend will express itself in an excess of positive changes over negative changes. Figure 3 presents the average month-to-month percentage change.

In Figure 3, there is an overall 0.55% increase in the index from one month to the next. The difference between the two consecutive months of December to January has a p value of 0.08. It would be significant if 0.05 were the significance criterion. May has the only negative value, but it is insignificant.

THE TRADERS' CHOICE

The method of choice for those who believe in seasonal trends is to assemble tables of numbers and then add up each column, which is the method favored in the *Stock Trader's Almanac*. On close examination, sure enough, one column gives the highest total, while another column gives the lowest.

By itself, such a comparison is meaningless. Without the calculation of the averages and the standard deviations, no comparison of such numbers really says

anything about the possible patterns in the data. If the columns of a table of random single-digit numbers were added, there would certainly be one column that added up to a greater total than the others. Another column would sum to the smallest total. However, the average for each column would be very close to 4.5. The differences between the averages in 68% of the cases would be well within the standard deviation for the whole set.

One advisory service recommends being in stocks between the beginning of November and the end of April and in Treasury bills the rest of the year. This would have been good advice for those periods in 1962-63, 1970-71, 1982-83, 1985-86 and 1988-89; even the interval in 1987-88 would have been good. Of course, entering the market one month too soon in the 1987-88 interval would have meant disaster. With the upward trend that does exist, both the November to April interval and the April to November interval should show favorable market actions. Indeed, in 18 of the 30 years, the November index was higher than the April index of the same year. This would support the contrarian's view of the November to April ploy.

On the other hand, the November to April advice would have been poor for the periods in 1968-69, 1972-73, 1973-74 and 1981-82, among others.

TO EACH HIS OWN

The methodology presented here is not meant simply to discredit bad advice about favorable periods for investing; I found no evidence for the so-called summer rally or the November to April stock swing. Some traders are also skeptical about such patterns and use these myths as a contrarian tactic.

The methodology expressed in this spreadsheet program shown here is applicable to any price or index that may be seasonal. Seasonal patterns *do* exist and *can* be found. This methodology was developed to *find* favorable price/time patterns.

One other point is worth considering about patterns: Patterns, although genuine, may have a

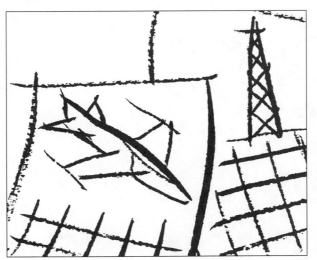

DESCRIBING A SPREADSHEET PROGRAM

Column A lists titles

Matrix 1, cells B4 to M34:

Column N is the average for each row in matrix 1.

Column O is the standard deviation for the data in each row of matrix 1.

Column P is the data count for each row in matrix 1.

Cells Q4 to Q9 are the coefficients in the normal curve approximation formula.

Cells R4 to R9 are the numerical values of the coefficients:

R4: C_0= 0.7070735

R5: C_1= 0.1411281

R6: C_2= 0.08864028

R7: C_3= 0.02743349

R8: C_4= -0.00039446

R9: C_5= 0.00328975

Row 36 contains the averages for each column in matrix 1.

Row 37 contains the standard deviations for each column in matrix 1.

Row 38 contains the data counts for each column in matrix 1.

Cell N36 is the overall average for the data in matrix 1.

Cell O37 is the standard deviation for the data in matrix 1.

Cell P38 is the data count for the data in matrix 1.

Row 40 contains the T values for the columns in matrix 1 based on the data in rows 36 to 38.

T=absolute value of (column average minus matrix average) divided by square root of ((standard deviation for column)squared /data count for column + (standard deviation of matrix)squared /data count of matrix). For example, that is, the formula for B41:

=ABS(B36-N36)/SQRT(O37^2/P38+B37^2/B38)

Row 41 contains the p values based upon the data in row 40 and the coefficients in cells R4 to R9.

p=0.5/(1+C1*(T value+C0)+C2*(T value+C0)^2+C3*(T value+C0)^3+C4*(T value+C0)^4+C5*(T value+C0)^5)^2.

For example, the formula for cell B41:

=0.5/(1+R5*(B40+R4)+R6*(B40+R4)^2+R7*(B40+R4)^3+R8*(B40+R4)^4+R9*(B40+R4)^5)^2

Matrix 2 (cells B46 to M75) contains the month average prices as a percentage of the year's average price.

B46: (100*B5/N5)

. . . .

M75: (100*M34/N34)

Row 77 contains the averages of the columns in matrix 2.

Row 78 contains the standard deviations for the columns in matrix 2.

Row 79 contains the data count for the columns in matrix 2.

Cell N77 is the average of data in matrix 2.

Cell O78 is the standard deviation of data in matrix 2.

Cell P79 is the data count of matrix 2.

Row 81 contains the T values based on data in rows 77, 78 and 79, using the formula defined for row 40.

Row 82 contains the p values calculated from the T values in row 81, using the formula defined in row 41 and the coefficients in cells R4 to R9.

Matrix 3 (cells B86 to M115) contains the month-to-month change in prices expressed as a percentage of the previous month's datum. *Note*: the formula in cell B86 contains the index price for December 1960.

Row 117 contains the averages of the columns in matrix 3.

Row 118 contains the standard deviations of the data in the columns of matrix 3.

Row 119 contains the data count for the columns of matrix 3.

Cell N117 is the data average for matrix 3.

Cell O118 is the standard deviation for data in matrix 3.

Cell P119 is the data count for matrix 3.

Row 121 contains the T values based upon the data in rows 117, 118 and 119, using the formula defined for row 40.

Row 122 contains the p values based upon the T values in row 121, using the formula defined in row 41 and the coefficients in cells R4 to R9.

finite life-span. Authentic patterns may not be stable over long periods. I would recommend collecting at least 10 years (or other data column length) of data to ascertain the validation of a pattern in question. Three or five years may give you an important clue to the pattern's "half-life," so to speak, but the spreadsheet program is likely to reject the presence of a pattern for such a small set of numbers. To look for patterns in weekly sets of data instead of monthly sets would require a data matrix four times wider than those used here.

As an example, in the early 1980s, I detected a profitable pattern in the prices of the Japan Fund. Seizing the opportunity, I bought the mutual fund in July-August and then sold it in February-March. Unfortunately, the security went to an open-end capitalization and has never been the same since.

Further, not all cycles are matched to 52 weeks or 12 months. The work of the Foundation for the Study of Cycles has characterized stock market cycles of many odd time intervals. In my experience, Fourier analysis of the data sets either provides too much information about cycle lengths or misses significant cycles altogether. In any case, Fourier analysis could be a useful guide for selecting the width of the matrices for analysis by the accompanying spreadsheet program. Otherwise, the "move" function of most spreadsheet programs can be used to reshape the data matrix until either significant patterns appear or we give up.

NORMALIZING UPWARD

Nikolai Kondratiev may have been the first to apply an exponential regression equation to normalize upward trending economic series. I was uncomfortable about the procedure used on the detrending method used to produce Figure 2. But after spending time with various regression equations for the S&P prices from January 1961 to December 1990, I concluded that the comparison of monthly data with the annual average was, in fact, the best that could be done. This is similar to the use of splines† — the linear interpolation between to adjacent points on a curve —for the interpolation between data points where the exact regression equation is unknown. Both linear and exponential relations for the index as a function of time did not give reasonable interpo-

lated values for the index for the 1965-85 period. Between 1965 and 1980, the S&P remained in a comparatively narrow range. Beginning in the early 1980s, the increase in the index was much faster than previously. The result was that a new matrix of trend-corrected prices gave much higher variances than comparing the actual prices to the annual mean. The p values for the comparisons were all larger than those in Figure 2.

IN ESSENCE

Data in a spreadsheet relating price and time can be analyzed for significant temporal patterns. It is important to calculate the means of the data columns and their standard deviations, *not* the column totals. By using statistical tests for significance, we can judge whether apparent patterns are trustworthy or potentially profitable. Those interested in having the spreadsheet listed in "Describing a spreadsheet program" may send me a self-addressed, stamped envelope and a 5 1/4-inch disk.

Lewis Carl Mokrasch, 324 Horace Mann Ave., Winston-Salem, NC 27104-3229, has been active in the market for about 35 years and has offered a private advisory service for the last 20.

REFERENCES

Anonymous [1991]. "Summer swoon? Another twist on Wall Street," *Barron's*, June 17, page 55.

Foundation for the Study of Cycles, 3333 Michelson Dr., Irvine, CA 92715.

Hirsch, Yale [1990]. *Stock Trader's Almanac*, Hirsch Organization, Old Tappan, NJ.

Mokrasch, Lewis Carl [1991]. "Studying 10-year stock price patterns," *Technical Analysis of* STOCKS & COMMODITIES, Volume 9: April.

Sease, D.R. [1991]. "Time to rally 'round the barbecue?" *Wall Street Journal*, May 28, page C1.

"Security price index record" [1990]. Standard & Poor's Corp., New York.

Wilson, L.I. [1964]. *Catalog of Cycles: Part I, Economics*, Hawthorne Books.

The Gann Quarterly Revisited

The Gann quarterly chart, a trend-following indicator like other range breakout techniques, was previously described by Jerry Favors in the January STOCKS & COMMODITIES. Most trend-following indicators give less than satisfactory results in the absence of a strong trend, and Reif, whose research on the indicator goes back a number of years, concludes that the Gann quarterly chart is no exception. Take a look.

by David C. Reif

The Gann quarterly chart is a long-term indicator that I began following 15 years ago. In doing so, I have put together a collection of charts that provides valuable insight into the profitability of this indicator's signals since the sell signal on October 3, 1929, when the underlying research originated. To refresh your memory, the Gann quarterly chart will signal a turn up from any low when the Dow Jones Industrial Average (DJIA) trades above the prior quarter's intraday high. (A quarter is traditionally counted as being January to March, April to June, July to September and October to December.) The signal remains up until the DJIA trades below the low of the prior quarter. With this technique, it is imperative to keep track of the intraday highs and lows made each quarter because it is quite possible for the chart to make more than one turn in any given quarter. For example, the chart turned twice in fourth-quarter 1991, a situation I will discuss next.

Now let us examine the price movements of the DJIA (Figure 1) going into fourth-quarter 1991. At the end of September 1991, the quarterly chart was up and had been so since January 18, 1991. The third-quarter intraday high was 3068.60, while the third-quarter intraday low was 2836.30. On November 1, 1991, the DJIA made a new intraday high for the fourth quarter at 3092.00. The average then reversed and penetrated the third-quarter low of 2836.30 on December 11, 1991, so turning the

chart down and giving a sell signal. The moment the chart turned down, you had to know at what price would turn the chart back up, which you could proceed to find out in the following manner. In this case, the high of the third quarter had been exceeded in November, so the November high was the price to use as the price for the rest of December and the first quarter of 1992. As it turned out, the market penetrated the November high of 3092.00 on December 26, 1991, reversing the chart and sending it back up. In this case, the chart had turned down and made its low on the same day. Any trader shorting the market on this sell

FIGURE 1

DJIA, APRIL 1991 TO MAY 1992

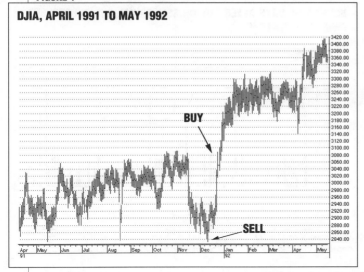

BUY

SELL

A penetration of the previous quarter's intraday extreme high or low price provides the signal for this trend-following indicator. On December 11, 1991, the DJIA traded below the previous quarter's low, which turned the indicator negative. However, the market quickly reversed, producing a 9% loss.

signal was unpleasantly subjected to a sharp 9.03% loss in only 15 trading days.

SWING AND A MISS

I have studied the details of every swing of the DJIA going back to October 1928. A close examination of the results depicted for the last 62 years is enlightening. As related by Jerry Favors in January, the Gann quarterly chart has been extremely effective as a long-term indicator for the last 10 years. (See Figure 2.) Unfortunately, the results for the previous 52 years are not as encouraging. Just look at Figure 3. A cumulative gain of 198.14% is the entire cumulative profit made by trading only the

> ## In this technique, it is imperative to keep track of the intraday highs and lows made each quarter because it is quite possible for the chart to make more than one turn in any quarter.

long signals of this chart from April 1, 1930, to March 17, 1980, representing only 3.885% per year over 51 years. The most illuminating statistic is the cumulative loss shown in Figure 4, a loss of 27.68% on *all* short trades made from October 3, 1929, to March 17, 1980. When you consider these figures do not include commissions, slippage or long or short pay dividends, the results are notably dismal.

Since the up signal on August 3, 1982, the record is far better, as both the long and short side trades made net cumulative profits.

A quick scan of Figures 3 and 4 will also provide some insight in that it shows numerous long periods or consecutive losses

FIGURE 2

% CUMULATIVE PROFIT OF ALL TRADES

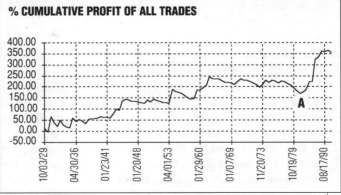

Since 1980 (A), this indicator has been profitable.

FIGURE 3

% CUMULATIVE PROFIT OF LONG TRADES

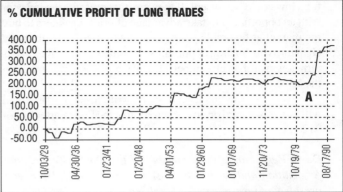

The cumulative profits were only 198% for buy signals from April 1, 1930, to March 17, 1980 (A).

FIGURE 4

% CUMULATIVE PROFIT OF SHORT TRADES

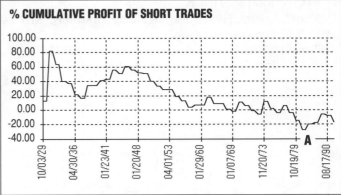

The cumulative profits for only the sell signals was a negative 27.68% as of March 17, 1980 (A).

(drawdowns), both on the long and short sides.

Another statistic to take note of is the number of signals that made a high or low within 30 days of the date of the signal. There are 93 completed signals recorded (Figure 5) and 28 (or 30%) of them made a swing high or low within 30 days of the signal. Of the rest, 22 or 23.7% of the cases made a low or high within 15 calendar days and 10 or 10.8% of the cases made a high or low within two calendar days of the signal (Figure 6).

The most conclusive evidence of this method's failure is the cumulative net short side loss of -16.77% over a period of 62 years on 47 sell signals.

ALL IN ALL

Despite this method's success over the last 10 years, it appears to be far inferior to and far less effective than other simple methods that are available to the long-term investor. Simple use of the signals generated by a crossing of the 39-week moving average does a much better job with less drawdown.

However, researching this indicator *does* provide a good record of all the significant highs and lows and some statistics that can be generated from them. For example, because a large number of lows (14 of 47 sell signals) are made within 15 days after the chart gives a sell signal, I use this information to study my other indicators very carefully to see whether the conditions for a low could be present. If they are, that presents the investor with an opportunity to take advantage of price weakness to buy the market at favorable prices long before the Gann quarterly chart turns up. Such an opportunity presented itself on the chart's turn downward on December 11, 1991, as the low was made on the same day.

In April 1992, as this article is being written, the chart is up and will turn downward on any penetration of the first quarter low of 3120.00.

David Reif is an affiliate member of the Market Technicians Association and sat for the CMT II exam in May. He is vice president of investments for Stifel, Nicolaus in Tulsa, OK.

REFERENCES

Favors, Jerry [1992]. "The Gann quarterly chart," STOCKS & COMMODITIES, January.

Merrill, Arthur A. [1992]. "Moving average crossovers," STOCKS & COMMODITIES, August.

Pierce, Phyllis, ed. [1986]. *The Dow Jones Averages 1885-1985*, Dow Jones-Irwin.

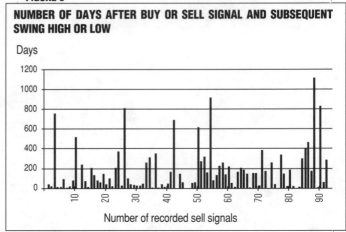

FIGURE 5

NUMBER OF DAYS AFTER BUY OR SELL SIGNAL AND SUBSEQUENT SWING HIGH OR LOW

There have been a total of 93 signals recorded. The number of days after a buy or sell signal was recorded that the market continued in the same direction ranged from zero to 1117.

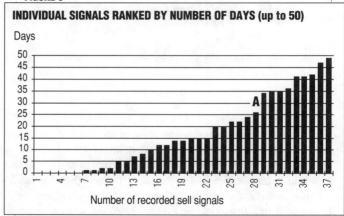

FIGURE 6

INDIVIDUAL SIGNALS RANKED BY NUMBER OF DAYS (up to 50)

Of the 93 recorded signals, 37 reached their swing high or low between zero and 49 days. Twenty-eight (point A) or 30% of the signals made a swing high or low within 30 days of the signal. Six signals were reversed on the same day.

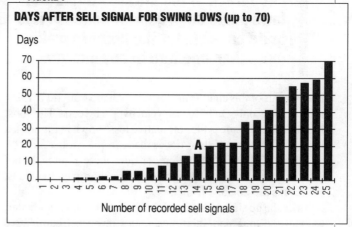

FIGURE 7

DAYS AFTER SELL SIGNAL FOR SWING LOWS (up to 70)

There was a total of 47 sell signals. The number of days following the down signal for the final low ranged from zero to 747. Fourteen of the signals (A) had their lows within 15 days of the signal.

Market Thrust

An abundance of articles and letters concerning the Arms index, or the trading index (TRIN), during the past year was one proof of its popularity. The articles were concerned with both the uses and limitations of the Arms index. The two major problems with the Arms index, as characterized in the articles and letters, arose in constructing a long-term Arms index and with using the index in mixed markets. STOCKS & COMMODITIES contributor Tushar Chande proposes a way to measure market thrust and overcome the limitations of the Arms index.

by Tushar S. Chande

Richard Arms invented his Arms index, or the trading index (TRIN), to indicate when abnormally high volume was going into advancing or declining stocks. He defined it as:

$$(1) \qquad \text{Arms index} = \frac{\left(\dfrac{AI}{DI}\right)}{\left(\dfrac{AV}{DV}\right)}$$

where: AI = # Advancing issues
AV = Advancing volume
DI = # Declining issues
DV = Declining volume

A reading of 1.00 is neutral; a value greater than 1.0 indicates more volume per declining issue, while a value below 1.0 shows more volume per advancing issue. Broad buying forces values below 1, while widespread selling sends the index soaring above 1. A 10-day simple moving average (SMA-10) is usually used to smooth daily data. Oversold market conditions occur when SMA-10 rises above 1.20. Conversely, the market is overbought when SMA-10 falls below 0.80.

INDEX LIMITATIONS

Jack Rusin examined the limitations of the Arms index in two recent articles. In October 1990 he looked at the problems in calculating a long-term (21-day or 55-day) Arms index. Rusin explained that if two days are the opposite of each other, then a simple average of the Arms index can be misleading. He recommended using an issue/volume-weighted long-term Arms index (LTAI):

$$(2) \qquad \text{LTAI} = \frac{(\text{Sum of AI}) / (\text{Sum of DI})}{(\text{Sum of AV}) / (\text{Sum of DV})}$$

Look at Figure 1, below.

FIGURE 1

LONG-TERM ARMS INDEX

Day	AI	AV	DI	DV	Arms index	Avg. Arms index	LTAI
1	10	100	10	200	2.0		
2	10	200	10	100	0.5	1.25	
Sum	**20**	**300**	**20**	**300**			1.0

BOBSCHUCHMAN

Even though the two days together represent a neutral market by LTAI calculations, a simple moving average suggests the market was oversold. The issue/volume-weighted long-term Arms index has greater intuitive appeal, at least to Rusin.

In his later article on the internal dynamics of the Arms index, Rusin examined the limitations of the Arms index in detail. He found that on days when the market is mixed, the three ratios in the index obscure the true nature of volume flows into advancing and declining issues. He identifies four classes of market dynamics where:

D1: AI>=DI; AV>=DV; consistent internal dynamics
D2: AI>=DI; AV<DV; divergent internal dynamics
D3: AI<DI; AV>=DV; divergent internal dynamics
D4: AI<DI; AV<DV; consistent internal dynamics

When the volume follows AI or DI, internal behavior is consistent. If DI is greater than AI, DV should be greater than AV for internal consistency. Within each class, Rusin identified various cases based on the exact nature of the AI/DI and AV/DV relationship (Figure 2).

FIGURE 2

CLASSIFICATION OF ARMS INDEX COMBINATIONS				
Class	Case	Relationship of		Arms
		AI to DI AV to DV	AI/DI to AV/DV	index
D1	1	= =	=	1
	2 *	> >	=	1
	3 *	> >	>	>1
	4	> >	<	<1
	5	= >	<	<1
	6 *	> =	>	>1
D2	1 *	= <	>	>1
	2 *	> <	>	>1
D3	1 *	< =	<	<1
	2 *	< >	<	<1
D4	1	< <	>	>1
	2 *	< <	<	<1
	3 *	< <	=	1

Cases with divergent Arms index.

Rusin argued that adding an internal dynamic number to the Arms index would increase its information content. But even this does not get to the heart of the problem. An investor could have two days with an identical Arms index and an internal dynamic number and yet have one day with an AI/DI ratio of 10 to one, while the other has just a two to one AI/DI ratio. Thus, the Arms index only goes so far. Rusin offers no solution. Here are two possible answers:

TRY TROS

One way to solve this dilemma is to look at the net difference in average advancing and declining volume, normalizing the difference by the sum of the average volumes to define a trading oscillator (TROS):

$$(3) \qquad TROS = \frac{(AV/AI - DV/DI)}{(AV/AI + DV/DI)}$$

$$= \frac{(1 - Arms\ index)}{(1 + Arms\ index)}$$

This formulation has several advantages. First, TROS can have positive or negative values, instantly showing the balance of relative volume flows. The Arms index, however, is positive for all values. Second, TROS is symmetrically bounded by +1 and -1, with 0 being the neutral value. The Arms index is bounded by 0 below 1 but is unbounded above 1. Hence, the scales are different for bullish and bearish days. A 10-day moving average or five-day daily sum may be used to smooth the data or observe extremes.

A simple check shows that the Arms index must equal or be less than 0.33 for TROS to exceed 0.5, a relatively rare occurrence. Similarly, the Arms index must equal or exceed 3 for TROS to be less than or equal to -0.5, also a rare occurrence. Thus, ±0.5 may be used as overbought/oversold values of TROS.

To illustrate the Arms index and TROS, I will use the hypothetical data from the January 1992 article.

FIGURE 3

COMPARING THE ARMS INDEX AND TROS					
Day	Advancing issues	Advancing volume	Declining issues	Declining volume	Arms index TROS
1	1000	1,000,000	100	100,000	1 0.0
2	100	100,000	1000	1,000,000	1 0.0
3	1000	1,000,000	100	200,000	2 (0.33)
4	100	200,000	1000	1,000,000	0.5 0.33
5	800	800,000	400	400,000	1 0.0

This formulation resolves half of Rusin's dilemma. When the average volume in declining and advancing issues is equal, both the Arms index and TROS are neutral. But unlike the Arms index, on successive days such as those in Figure 1, TROS gives results consistent with the LTAI. Though Days 3 and 4 are opposites, the sum of TROS over the two days is zero. However, TROS does not reveal how volume was overwhelmingly into advancing or declining issues on Days 3 and 4. My other formulation following resolves the dilemma more clearly.

MARKET THRUST AND THRUST OSCILLATOR

A better way to look at market action is to look at the product of the number of shares advancing or declining and the volume into those shares. Hence, market thrust (MT):

$$(4) \qquad MT = \frac{\left((AI)(AV) - (DI)(DV)\right)}{1,000,000}$$

I divide the thrust by 1,000,000 to give reasonably small numbers for convenience and simplicity. You could choose any other scaling constant. The daily number may be used to spot large moves in one direction. MT is cumulated to identify underlying trends. Alternately, MT may be smoothed with moving averages for trading purposes. Note that if Av=Dv=1, then MT reduces to the usual AI-DI line except for the scaling constant. Thus, the A-D line may be considered a special case of MT, where we assume equal volume flow into AI and DI, and the scaling constant equals the volume into AI or DI.

Now let us define thrust oscillator (TO) to compare relative volume flows:

(5)
$$TO = \frac{(AI)(AV) - (DI)(DV)}{(AI)(AV) + (DI)(DV)}$$

Note that the multiplication by 100 is optional, so that TO varies between +1 and -1 or +100 and -100. Values above ±0.5 may be used as overbought/oversold limits. In strongly trending markets, TO stays above 0.5 (or below -0.5) for several days. A quick check will show that the ratio (AI)(AV)/(DI)(DV) must equal or exceed 3 for TO to equal or exceed 0.5. Thus, values beyond ±0.5 are relatively rare.

This MT definition has many advantages. First, it can be subdivided into upthrust (AI)(AV) and downdraft (DI)(DV), so that a strong up day or down day is clearly identified. With the Arms index, as shown in Figure 2, a strong one-sided up or down action is sometimes obscured by neutral readings. Second, it shows the net balance between bullish and bearish activity on a given day, using the relative volume flows. Third, it captures the various possibilities identified by Rusin — it presents consistent information. TO shows normalized relative volume flows and may be used as an overbought/oversold indicator.

There is another significant advantage. MT and TO can be averaged without introducing the errors found in the Arms index. Thus, they lend themselves naturally to calculating long-term moving averages.

As is clear from the definition, in the special case of equal advancing and declining volumes TO reduces to a variation of the A/D line, where

(6)
$$TO = \frac{(AI - DI)}{(AI + DI)}$$

if Av = Dv. Equation 7 shows how TO may be considered a volume-weighted A/D ratio variation, because

(7)
$$TO = \frac{AI\left(\frac{AV}{DV}\right) - DI}{AI\left(\frac{AV}{DV}\right) + DI}$$

"Remember, Hagedorn, you no longer work for the private sector. In the public sector, the customer is never right."

Now examine the behavior of MT using Rusin's data and some other simulated data. Figure 4 shows my calculations; data for Day 1 through 5 are from Rusin's January 1992 article. I made up the rest to represent every item in Figure 2.

In Figure 4, though the Arms index specifies that Days 1 and 2 are neutral, MT clearly shows the dominant trend of each day with TO near its extremes as well. Day 3 is also a strong up day but has somewhat greater down volume than does Day 1. The Arms index flags it as a bearish day even though advances led declines by 900 stocks. MT assigns it a value of 980, indicating that Day 3 was almost as strong as Day 1. Day 4 is a reversal of Day 3. MT reads -980 and To -0.96, capturing the reversal. But the Arms index calls Day 4 an overbought day with strong bullish demand. The index says Day 5 is neutral; MT indicates it is firmly on the upside.

Day 12 contrasts the Arms index and MT. The Arms index calls it strongly bearish, while MT calls it a dead heat. Days 15 and 16 are about equally bearish, with a net thrust of -300 and -330, but the Arms index calls Day 16 moderately bullish. Day 17 finds MT strongly bearish, while the Arms index is neutral at 1.0. The cumulative MT resembles the cumulative advance-decline line in Figure 1, which shows how MT provides interpretations consistent with the A-D line.

RUNNING ON MT

The product of (AI)(AV) and (DI)(DV) shows the thrust up or down. Using the product eliminates confusion caused by comparing average volumes in advancing and declining shares. Each of Rusin's cases can be clearly distinguished. MT also gives consistent results with long-term moving averages. Thus, MT and thrust oscillator TO are solid alternatives to the Arms index.

Tushar Chande holds a doctorate in engineering from the University of Illinois and a master's degree in business administration from the University of Pittsburgh.

FIGURE 4

SIMULATED MARKET DATA TO COMPARE ARMS INDEX, MT AND TO									
Day	**AI**	**AV**	**DI**	**DV**	**D**	**Case**	**Arms index**	**MT**	**TO**
1	1000	1,000,000	100	100,000	D1	2	1.0	990	0.98
2	100	100,000	1000	1,000,000	D4	3	1.0	(990)	(0.98)
3	1000	1,000,000	100	200,000	D1	3	2.0	980	0.96
4	100	200,000	1000	1,000,000	D4	2	0.50	(980)	(0.96)
5	800	800,000	400	400,000	D1	2	1.0	480	0.60
6	600	600,000	600	600,000	D1	1	1.0	0	0.0
7	800	700,000	400	500,000	D1	3	1.43	360	0.47
8	800	900,000	400	300,000	D1	4	0.67	600	0.71
9	600	700,000	600	500,000	D1	5	0.71	120	0.17
10	675	600,000	525	600,000	D1	6	1.29	90	0.13
11	600	550,000	600	650,000	D2	1	1.18	(60)	(0.08)
12	700	500,000	500	700,000	D2	2	1.96	0	0.0
13	475	600,000	725	600,000	D3	1	0.66	(150)	(0.21)
14	575	775,000	625	425,000	D3	2	0.50	180	0.25
15	550	400,000	650	800,000	D4	1	1.69	(300)	(0.41)
16	400	525,000	800	675,000	D4	2	0.64	(330)	(0.44)
17	400	400,000	800	800,000	D4	3	1.00	(480)	(0.60)

REFERENCES

Arms, Richard W., Jr. [1989]. *The Arms Index: An Introduction to the Volume Analysis of Stock and Bond Markets*, Dow Jones-Irwin.

_____ [1991]. "Using the Arms index in intraday applications," *Technical Analysis of* STOCKS & COMMODITIES, Volume 9: April.

_____ [1991]. "Cross your Arms," *Technical Analysis of* STOCKS & COMMODITIES, Volume 9: May.

Favors, Jerry [1992]. "The TRIN-5," STOCKS & COMMODITIES, March.

Rusin, Jack [1991]. "An issue/volume-weighted long-term Arms index," *Technical Analysis of* STOCKS & COMMODITIES, Volume 9: October.

_____ [1992]. "The internal dynamics of TRIN," STOCKS & COMMODITIES, January.

Avoiding Bull And Bear Traps

Bull and bear traps are gap openings that are reversed the same day and that can cost a trader dearly. S&C contributor Nauzer Balsara presents his method of analyzing market history to calculate the proper placement of stops to avoid being caught in such traps.

by Nauzer J. Balsara, Ph.D.

A bull or bear trap occurs when a market does an about-face after an extremely bullish or bearish opening, leaving a trader who entered a position at the opening price with a possible loss at the end of the day. Bullish expectations are reinforced by a sharply higher or "gap-up" opening, just as bearish expectations are reinforced by a sharply lower or "gap-down" opening. A bull trap occurs as a result of prices retreating from a sharply higher or gap-up opening; the pullback occurs during the same trading session that witnessed the strong opening, belying hints of a major rally. A bear trap occurs as a result of prices recovering from a sharply lower or gap-down opening; the retracement occurs during the same trading session that witnessed the depressed opening, confounding expectations of an outright collapse.

BULL AND BEAR TRAP EXAMPLES

An illustration of a bull trap is provided by price action on December 3, 1991, in July 1992 Chicago wheat futures (Figure 1). On December 2, 1991, July wheat settled at 324.75 cents a bushel. A trader, noticing a strong uptrend in the July wheat chart, might not hesitate buying wheat futures at the gap-up opening price of 340.00 cents on December 3. However, instead of prices moving higher, they worked their way down to a low of 328.50 cents, bridging much of the 15-cent gap on the opening before settling at 330.50 cents.

Although the settlement price of 330.50 cents is 5.75 cents higher than the preceding day, this offers little or no consolation

to the harried trader who has bought wheat at the opening price of 340.00 cents. At the close, the bull trap results in an unrealized loss of 9.50 cents, or $475 per contract!

The December 1990 crude oil contract (Figure 2) provides a good example of a bear trap. After topping out at $30.00 a barrel on Thursday, August 23, 1990, prices retreated to $29.22 the following day. On Monday, August 27, we had a limit-down move to $27.22. A depressed opening at $26.05 on Tuesday, August 28, confirmed the bearish mood of the market and might have tempted many an unsuspecting trader to short December crude at the opening.

However, contrary to expectations, prices recovered soon

after the opening to reach a high of $26.98, thereby filling much of the gap caused by the depressed opening. Although the settlement price of $26.84 represented a slight drop from the preceding day's close, it was still a good $0.79 above the opening price of $26.05! This bear trap would translate into an unrealized loss of $790 per contract for a trader who went short at the opening.

> **Because a bull or bear trap develops as a result of entering the market at or soon after the opening, a stop-loss order should be set with reference to the opening price.**

AVOIDING BULL AND BEAR TRAPS

Because a bull or bear trap develops as a result of entering the market at or soon after the opening on any given day, a stop-loss order should be set with reference to the opening price. When prices are trending upward, the opening price for any given period lies near the low end of the day's range and the settlement price lies above the opening price. Consequently, we observe a narrow spread between the opening price and the period low when prices are trending upward.

Conversely, when prices are trending downward, the opening price lies near the high end of the day's trading range and the settlement price lies below the opening price. As a result, we observe a narrow spread between the period high and the opening price when prices are trending downward. In some cases, we find the opening price to be exactly equal to the high of a down day or the low of an up day, leading to a zero spread.

To determine proper stop placement, we first analyze the location of the opening price in relation to the high and low ends of the daily (or weekly) trading range over a historical time period. For our analysis, an up period, either day or week, is defined as a trading period at the end of which the settlement period is higher than the opening price. Similarly, a down period is defined as a trading period at the end of which the settlement price is lower than the opening price.

Using this definition of up and down periods, we analyze the percentile† distribution of the spread between the opening price and the low (high) for up (down) periods. A 10-percentile value of, say, 25 ticks implies that the distance between the opening price and the low (high) is less than or equal to 25 ticks in 10% of the sample under review. Similarly,

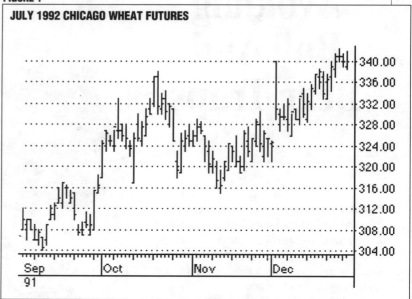

FIGURE 1

JULY 1992 CHICAGO WHEAT FUTURES

Courtesy CompuTrac/M; Data by Dial/Data

Here's an example of a bull trap. On December 2, 1991, July wheat settled at 324.75 cents a bushel. A trader, noticing a strong uptrend in the July wheat chart, might not hesitate buying wheat futures at the gap-up opening price of 340.00 cents on December 3. However, instead of prices moving higher, they worked their way down to a low of 328.50 cents, bridging much of the 15-cent gap on the opening before settling at 330.50 cents.

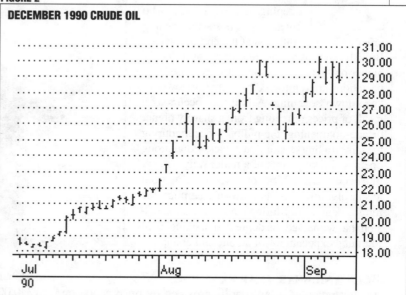

FIGURE 2

DECEMBER 1990 CRUDE OIL

The December 1990 crude oil contract provides a good example of a bear trap. After topping out at $30.00 a barrel on August 23, 1990, prices retreated to $29.22 the following day. On Monday, August 27, we had a limit-down move to $27.22. A depressed opening at $26.05 on Tuesday, August 28, confirmed the bearish mood of the market and might have tempted many an unsuspecting trader to short December crude at the opening. However, prices recovered after the opening to reach a high of $26.98, thereby filling much of the gap caused by the depressed opening. Although the settlement price of $26.84 represented a slight drop from the preceding day's close, it was still a good $0.79 above the opening price of $26.05! This bear trap would translate into an unrealized loss of $790 per contract for a trader who went short at the opening.

a 90-percentile value of, say, 60 ticks signifies that the distance between the opening price and the low (high) is less than or equal to 60 ticks in 90% of the cases under review. Figures 3 and 4 tabulate the percentage distribution of the spread for wheat and crude oil, respectively, for both up and down periods based on data from January 1987 to December 1991.

The information given in Figures 3 and 4 could be used by a trader who has a definite opinion about the future direction of the market, who observes a gap opening in the direction he believes the market is headed and who wishes to participate in the rally without getting snared in a costly bull or bear trap. For example, our wheat trader who enters a long position in July 1992 wheat at a gap-up opening of 340.00 cents on December 3, 1991, would want to set a sell stop-loss order *n* ticks below the opening price.

Conversely, a trader who enters a short position in December 1990 crude oil at the gap-down opening of $26.05 on August 28 would want to set a buy stop-loss order *n* ticks above the opening price of that day.

The value of *n* is based on the information given in Figures 3 and 4 and on the percentile value of the spread between the opening and the low (or high) the trader is most comfortable with. The tighter the stop, the lower the dollar value of the loss upon getting stopped out; however, the risk of getting stopped erroneously is greater. A conservative approach would be to set a stop based on the 90-percentile value of the distance in ticks between the open and the high for an anticipated move downward in crude oil, or between the open and the low for an anticipated move upward in wheat.

According to Figure 3, the distance between the open and the low for wheat is equal to 2.50 cents for 90% of the up days studied. Therefore, our trader would be advised to set his sell-stop 2.50 cents below the opening price of 340.00 cents, or 337.50 cents. The rationale is that there is only a one in 10 chance of prices falling below 337.50 cents and then recovering enough to settle at a price higher than the opening.

Similarly, Figure 4 shows that there is a 29-tick spread between the high and the open for down days in crude oil. Consequently, our trader would want to set his buy-stop 29 ticks above the opening price of $26.05, or $26.34. Once again, there

is only a 0.10 probability of prices rising above $26.34 and then retreating to settle at a price lower than the opening price.

CONCLUSION

The trauma arising out of bull and bear traps is not inevitable and can be avoided by means of an appropriate stop-loss order. A logical approach to setting stops is to study the spread between the opening price and the low (high) for up (down) periods over a sample period. A comparative study of spreads for 1980-87 and 1987-91 shows that the distributions of the spreads are highly consistent, boding well for setting probability stops based on historical analysis of spreads.

Nauzer J. Balsara, Ph.D., is a Commodities Trading Advisor and an associate professor of finance at Northeastern Illinois University, Chicago, IL. He is actively involved in futures and options trading.

FIGURE 3

ANALYSIS OF OPENING PRICES FOR CHICAGO WHEAT FUTURES

Analysis for up periods

Percent of total cases	Difference in cents between the open (O) and the low (L)	
	Daily data (O-L) in cents	Weekly data (O-L) in cents
10%	0	0.25
20	0	0.75
30	0.25	1.00
40	0.50	1.25
50	0.75	1.75
60	1.00	2.50
70	1.25	3.50
80	1.50	4.25
90	2.50	5.75

Analysis for down periods

Percent of total cases	Difference in cents between the high (H) and the open (O)	
	Daily data (H-O) in cents	Weekly data (H-O) in cents
10%	0.25	0.50
20	0.50	1.00
30	0.50	1.50
40	0.75	2.00
50	1.00	2.75
60	1.25	3.50
70	1.50	5.25
80	2.00	6.00
90	3.00	8.00

Based on price data from January 1987 through December 1991. Minimum price fluctuation of 0.25 cents per bushel is equivalent to $12.50 per contract.

In Figure 3, the distance between the open and the low for wheat is equal to 2.50 cents for 90% of the up days studied. Therefore, our trader would be advised to set his sell-stop 2.50 cents below the opening price of 340.00 cents, or 337.50 cents. The rationale is that there is only a one in 10 chance of prices falling below 337.50 cents and then recovering enough to stay above the open.

FIGURE 4

ANALYSIS OF OPENING PRICES FOR CRUDE OIL FUTURES

Analysis for up periods

Percent of total cases	Difference in ticks between the open (O) and the low (L)	
	Daily data (O-L) in ticks	Weekly data (O -L) in ticks
10 %	0	0
20	1	3
30	3	6
40	5	11
50	7	17
60	9	24
70	12	32
80	16	45
90	28	80

Analysis for down periods

Percent of total cases	Difference in ticks between the high (H) and the open (O)	
	Daily data (H-O) in ticks	Weekly data H -O) in ticks
10%	2	4
20	4	7
30	6	10
40	7	15
50	9	19
60	10	26
70	15	35
80	19	46
90	29	73

Based on price data from January 1987 through December 1991. Minimum price fluctuation of one tick, or $0.01 per barrel, is equivalent to $10.00 per contract.

Figure 4 shows that there is a 29-tick spread between the high and the open for 90% of the down days in crude oil. Therefore, the trader would be advised to set his buy-stop 29 ticks above the opening price of $26.05.

Understanding Exponential Moving Averages

Do you ever find yourself thinking that maybe you ought to try using the exponential moving average but find yourself intimidated into paralysis? Don't be. Let Raymond Rothschild be your guide into a not-so-alarming technique.

by Raymond Rothschild

Moving averages in general have been extensively analyzed by many investigators — all except the exponential moving average. The objective in technical analysis is to use *every* tool available, and that includes exponential moving averages. But first to review the formula for the simple moving average: in an *n*-day simple moving average, the prices of the previous *n* days are added and the sum is divided by *n*. For example, if *n* were equal to 10, we would add the prices of the prior 10 days and then divide this value by 10 to obtain the moving average for the current day. As we continue along to successive days, it is not really necessary to always add *n* days

of data. All we really have to do is drop off the first day's price, add the current day's price to our sum and then divide by *n*.

That is the simple moving average. Other forms exist, one of which is the exponentially smoothed moving average. This particular moving average has a recursive† form that makes it easier to use than the simple moving average. The recursive form refers to the fact that the exponential average for the current day is determined by the value of the previous day, defined thus:

$$(1) \qquad E_2 = E_1 + a\,(P_2 - E_1)$$

where:

   E_2 = New exponential average
   E_1 = Prior exponential average
   P_2 = Current price
   a = smoothing constant, often represented by α (alpha)
in the formula for an exponential moving average.

We begin the process by setting the average for the first day equal to the price for that day. As we go on, each day's E_1 is equal

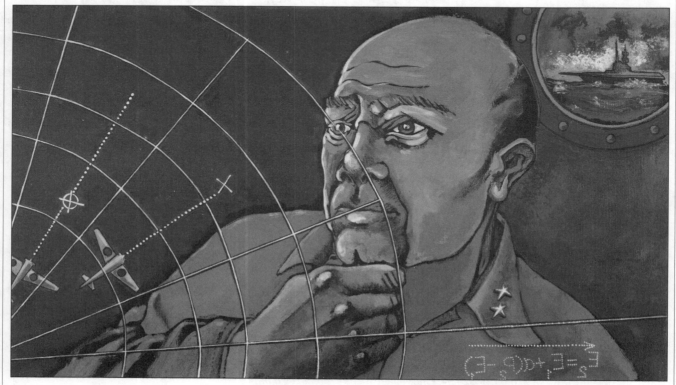

DIANE BOSTWICK

EXPANDING THE AVERAGE

To expand the exponential moving average, it is convenient to rearrange equation (1) as:

$$(2) \qquad E_2 = aP_2 + (1-a)\, E_1$$

Start by setting the average for the first day equal to the price for that day. Thereafter, we know each prior day's average, and hence, we can calculate the exponential average for the current day. Continuing in this fashion, we get:

$$(3) \qquad E_i = a\, [P_i + (1-a)\, P_{i-1} + (1-a)^2\, P_{i-2} + \ldots + (1-a)^{n-1} P_{i-n+1}]$$

at point i after repeated application. Consider a weighted moving average of the form:

(4)

$$E_t = \frac{P_t + (1-a)P_{t-1} + (1-a)^2 P_{t-2} + \ldots + (1-a)^{n-1} P_{t-n+1}}{1 + (1-a) + (1-a)^2 + \ldots + (1+a)^{n-1}}$$

The denominator is a geometric series the sum of which is:

$$S = [(1-a)^n - 1]\,/\,(1-a-1)$$

If $0 < a < 1$ and n becomes very large, then $S = 1/a$ or:

$$(5) \qquad E_t = a\, [P_t + (1-a)\, P_{t-1} + (1-a)^2 P_{t-2} + \ldots + (1-a)^{n-1} P_{t-n+1}]$$

Thus, we see that a moving average formed by a process such as equation (1) or equation (2) results in a weighted moving average similar to equation (4) or equation (5). Equation (4) represents a front-weighted average because the most recent price is given a greater weight than past prices.

To answer the question "How many days must elapse before the exponential average comes close to its long-time value?" it is first necessary to define:

$$a = 2/(s+1)$$

The coefficient of the last term in equation (5) becomes:

$$(6) \qquad (1-a)^{n-1} = \left[\frac{s-1}{s+1}\right]^{n-1}$$

The last term will become small when its coefficient becomes small — say, approximately 0.1. But $e^{-2} = 0.135$ (where e is the base of natural logarithms). Because we are dealing with approximations, there is nothing particularly compelling about the use of 0.1; we could use 0.135 in its place. Thus, it is convenient to set:

$$(7) \qquad \left[\frac{s-1}{s+1}\right]^{n-1} = e^{-2}$$

Taking the log of both sides to the base e, we get:

$$(8) \qquad (n-1)\,[Ln\,(s-1) - Ln(s+1)] = -2$$

But $[Ln\,(s-1) - Ln(s+1)]$ approaches $-2/s$ when s is very large. Replacing the logarithmic difference in equation (8) by its approximate equivalent, we get:

$$(n-1)(-2/s) = -2$$

Dividing both sides by -2:

$$\frac{n-1}{s} = 1$$

Hence, $s = n-1$. Thus, if a is selected in accordance with $a = 2/(s+1)$ and s is large, then:

$$a = 2/(n-1+1) = 2/n$$

$$(9) \qquad n = 2/a$$

Therefore, this is the solution for the minimum number of days (or intervals) required before the exponential average approaches its long-time value.

Remember that approximations were employed in the derivation and choosing a larger value of n will result in smaller errors. For most practical purposes, however, this is a suitable value of n to start the plot of the exponential average.

---

to the previous day's E_2.

Clearly, the initial points are in error because their values would be different if we had started a long time ago. Is there a minimum number of days we should use to reduce the subsequent errors to insignificance? This aspect is discussed in the sidebar "Expanding the average."

Sometimes examining a pseudo condition can be revealing. Consider a stock that starts with a price of one and increases each day by one, until on day 40 a price of 40 is reached. A summary is presented in spreadsheet form in Figure 1, in which two conditions can be seen: $a = 0.200$ and $a = 0.100$. A graph of the

To begin the calculations for the exponential moving average, we set the first day's average equal to the price for that day. As we proceed, yesterday's average will be smoothed by the constant "alpha" to calculate today's average.

TIME DELAY OF LINEAR EXPONENTIAL AVERAGES

Figure 2 indicates that if the price goes up linearly, after a while the exponential moving average will also be a straight line that is parallel to the original. For this to occur, there must be a constant separation between the lines. Let's designate the separation as "B." This situation is pictured in Figure 2. Recalling equation (1):

(1) $E_2 = E_1 + a(P_2 - E_1)$ or

(10) $E_2 - E_1 = a(P_2 - E_1)$

Referring to Figure 2, we see that at any given time:

(11) $P_2 = E_2 + B$

Substituting the value for P_2 into equation (10), we get:

(12) $E_2 - E_1 = a(E_2 - E_1 + B)$

Since P_2 represents a straight line, it can be expressed as:

(13) $P_2 = mt$

Substituting the value for P_2 into equation (11), we get:

(14) $E_2 = mt - B$

But E_1 is the value of E_2 one day earlier, or

(15) $E_1 = m(t - 1) - B$

Subtract (15) from (14) to get:

(16) $E_2 - E_1 = m$

Substituting into equation (12), we get:

(17) $m = a(m + B)$

Solving for B:

(18) $B = m[(1-a)/a]$

Substituting for B in equation (14):

(19) $E_2 = mt - m[(1-a)/a]$

Factoring m:

(20) $E_2 = m[t - (1-a)/a]$

The time delay is:

(21) $T = (1-a)/a$

To summarize, when P_2 is a straight-line relationship, then after a while the exponential average (E_2) will also assume a straight-line relationship parallel to the original line but shifted to the right by T units.

Let us suppose that $a = 2/(n+1)$. Substituting into equation (21), we get:

$$T = \frac{1-2/(n+1)}{2/(n+1)} = \frac{n-1}{2}$$

But this is similar to the time delay in an n-day simple moving average. We also know that the simple moving average of a straight line is also a straight line parallel to the original line. Thus, we can say that if the n of a simple moving average is determined by the relationship $a = 2/(n+1)$, then it is somewhat like an exponential average, the smoothing factor of which is a.

Obviously, not all curves resulting from an exponential average are identical to the curves from a simple moving average. Nevertheless, an exponential average with a smoothing constant of a is often likened to a simple moving average of n days where n is determined from $a = 2/(n+1)$.

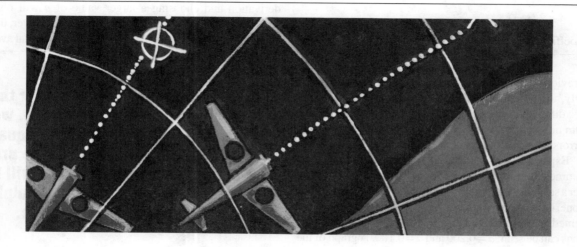

data is presented in Figure 2. The final exponential moving average for both $a = 0.200$ and $a = 0.100$ are straight lines, parallel to the original. These curves become fairly close to their final shape at $n = 2/a$ ($2/0.2 = 10$ for $a = 0.2$ and $2/0.1 = 20$ for $a = 0.1$), corroborating the derivation presented in the sidebar "Expanding the average"; namely, that $n = 2/a$.

STRAIGHT-LINE PARALLEL

In Figure 2, after a period of time the exponential average of a straight line assumes the shape of a straight line that is parallel to the original but shifted over. The amount of the shift is referred to as the "time delay."

The derivation for the time delay is shown in the sidebar "Time delay of linear exponential averages." The derivation indicates that the time delay is $(1-a)/a$. Referring to Figure 2, for $a = 0.2$, the calculated delay is $(1-0.2)/0.2 = 4$. The observed delay is very close to 4. For $a = 0.1$, the calculated delay is $(1-0.1)/0.1 = 9$. The observed delay is 8.9 — close enough. If closer accuracy is required, we need more points.

Exponential moving averages were studied in great length during World War II in conjunction with navigational systems for military aircraft and missiles. An assessment of the past—position of the projectile was used to predict the anticipated course or collision point. It should be readily apparent how such studies soon made their way into the technical analysis of stocks and commodities. In addition, many methods effectively employ exponential moving averages, and notable among these are the relative strength index, average directional movement index and moving average convergence/divergence.

Raymond Rothschild is a retired electrical engineer. He lives in Miami Beach, FL.

REFERENCES

Eshback, Ovid W. [1952]. *Handbook of Engineering Fundamentals,* John Wiley & Sons.

Glazier, Jason S. [1990]. "Moving average myths," *Technical Analysis of* STOCKS & COMMODITIES, Volume 8: November.

Hartle, Thom [1991]. "Moving average convergence/divergence (MACD)," *Technical Analysis of* STOCKS & COMMODITIES, Volume 9: March.

Kaufman, Perry J. [1987]. *The New Commodity Trading Systems and Methods,* John Wiley & Sons.

Wilder, J. Welles [1978]. *New Concepts in Technical Trading Systems*, Trend Research.

FIGURE 1

CALCULATING AN EMA

	A	B	C	D	E	F	G	H
1	1			1				1
2	2	1.0000	0.2000	1.2000		1.0000	0.1000	1.1000
3	3	1.8000	0.3600	1.5600		1.9000	0.1900	1.2900
4	4	2.4400	0.4880	2.0480		2.7100	0.2710	1.5610
5	5	2.9520	0.5904	2.6384		3.4390	0.3439	1.9049
6	6	3.3616	0.6723	3.3107		4.0951	0.4095	2.3144
7	7	3.6893	0.7379	4.0486		4.6856	0.4686	2.7830
8	8	3.9514	0.7903	4.8389		5.2170	0.5217	3.3047
9	9	4.1611	0.8322	5.6711		5.6953	0.5695	3.8742
10	10	=A10-D9	=0.2*(A10-D9)	=D9+0.2*(A10-D9)		=A10-H9	=0.1*(A10-H9)	=H9+0.1*(A10-H9)

Begin the process of calculating an exponentially smoothed moving average by setting the first day's value of the EMA to the closing price for that day. From that point on, we are smoothing the data. Column D is an EMA with an alpha of 0.2 and column H is an EMA with an alpha of 0.1.

FIGURE 2

PLOTTING A FIXED RISING PRICE

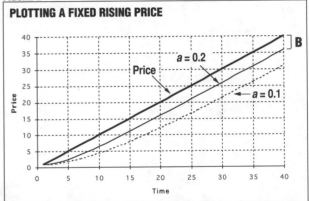

Plotting a fixed rising price of one point per day along with an EMA using an alpha of 0.2 and 0.1 indicates that the EMA plot is parallel to the original with a time delay of $T = (1 - a)/a$. That is, today's EMA value (using $a = 0.2$) is approximate to the price four days ago ($4 = (1 - 0.2/0.2)$, using $a = 0.2$).

FIGURE 3

DECEMBER 1992 CORN
SMA vs. EMA

The top chart presents a simple 10-day moving average, while the bottom chart uses an exponentially smoothed moving average with an alpha of 0.18, which approximates a 10-day simple moving average. Note the general similarity between the two different moving averages. However, the exponentially smoothed moving average reacted quicker to the downturn in early March.

Courtesy CompuTrac/M; Data by Dial/Data

MIKE HORSWILL

Filtering Trades With A Moving Average Slope

Moving averages are attractive because they simply and reliably execute the "cut your losses and let your profits run" strategy. Moving averages also have drawbacks, however, in that they discard much of the information that the market offers. A simple moving average represents simple quantified information — either prices are above it or below it. Can additional information, in this case the slope of the moving average, be put to use to improve trading performance? Adam White of the Technical Traders Bulletin *shows you how.*

by Adam White

Despite the theories to the contrary, a simple filter device can eliminate the losing trades of a simple moving average reversal system. Although other, more valuable applications of the moving average slope are bound to exist, keeping matters simple will, with any luck, be a more suitable introduction of the main idea.

Since moving averages tend to be smooth, short subsections approximate straight lines. Measuring the slope of a straight line is fairly straightforward—simply calculating the line's standard deviation does the trick. When the slope of a short line is low, the vertical distance between the two endpoints is small, and as the slope increases, the vertical difference between the endpoints increases. As a result, the standard deviation of a short subsection of a moving average is low when its slope is low and in turn high when its slope is high.

THE TREND ANALYSIS INDICATOR

I have devised the trend analysis indicator (TAI) based on this calculation. In essence, it is simply the standard deviation of the last x bars of a y-bar moving average. Thus, the TAI is a simple trend indicator — when prices trend with authority, the slope of the moving average increases, and when prices meander in a trendless range, the slope of the moving average decreases. Note that the characteristics and uses of this simple indicator are similar to the far more complex average directional index† (ADX).

Using MetaStock Professional 3.0, the syntax of a TAI that consists of an eight-bar lookback of a 21-bar moving average is std(mov(c,21,s),8). (See sidebar, "Spreadsheet trend analysis indicator.") The TAI is a flexible indicator because simply adjusting the two variables — the moving average length and the lookback period — allows different market characteristics to be studied. Adjusting the moving average period controls the indicator's cycle speed while adjusting the lookback period controls its smoothness.

Figure 1 illustrates the 21/8 TAI; note how the indicator falls during congestion and rises as a strong trend unfolds.

A MOVING AVERAGE TEST

New indicators are of little use if they cannot help realize an actual trading advantage. We designed a test to see if the TAI could filter out the lower-quality trades generated by a simple moving average reversal system. The test used 1,440 recent daily price bars of the Standard & Poor's 500, ignoring, for the sake of clarity, both commission and interest. For a standard of comparison, an unfiltered 26-bar moving average was tested in the traditional fashion (buy on a crossover above the 26-day moving average and sell on a crossover below the 26-day moving average). Here are the results:

Unfiltered	S&P
Trades (W-L)	22-76
Win-loss percent	22.4%
Win-loss ratio	2.3:1
$W-$L	537-807

The results look familiar for this type of strategy: a low win/loss percent but a healthy win/loss ratio. However, a buy and hold approach over this time period would have rewarded an investor with a respectable profit, while the trading strategy generated 98 trades to realize a -6.8% annual return.

DESIGNING THE FILTER

The purpose of the filter is to pinpoint market conditions where

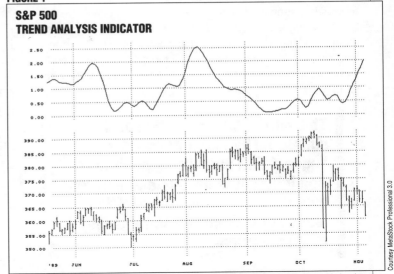

Courtesy MetaStock Professional 3.0

FIGURE 1

S&P 500
TREND ANALYSIS INDICATOR

The top chart is the eight-day standard deviation of the 21-day simple moving average. Notice that the indicator rises as the market stays in a trend.

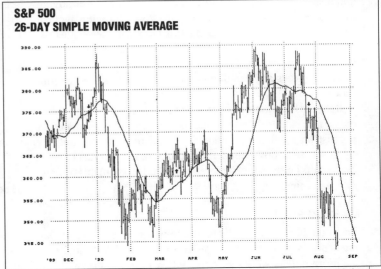

FIGURE 2

S&P 500
26-DAY SIMPLE MOVING AVERAGE

Using optimized parameters for the crossover of two trend analysis indicators and a 26-day simple moving average of the closing price delayed trades and reduced the number of losing trades.

moving averages do not excel. A trend indicator is an excellent candidate for such situations because trendless markets are more likely to make the short-lived thrusts that make moving average trading so difficult.

The challenge involved in applying the TAI or any other trend indicator is having the computer be able to consistently equate indicator signals to actual trend conditions. Even very careful and detailed language can still accidentally permit unintended consequences to be introduced into the process. To eliminate or at least reduce these glitches without sacrificing the simplicity of the original system is the technician's biggest challenge. As statisticians Robert Goodrich and Eric Stellwagen said: "... For forecasting, simple is better unless there is sound evidence that a more complex approach will yield returns in forecasting accuracy. Complex models provide a better fit to the historical data but are often poorer forecasting tools." While these comments are about forecasting models and not system testing per se, they are still relevant.

> **This particular application of the simple TAI indicator does indeed suggest that harnessing the information inherent in the slope of a moving average can improve the performance of a simple trend-following reversal system.**

After much experimenting to address these concerns, the following set of rules were agreed on: Construct two TAIs — a fast TAI that is a four-bar lookback on a 38-bar moving average, and a slow TAI that is a 10-bar lookback on the same moving average. Permit a trade signaled by the 26-bar moving average crossover of prices only when the fast TAI is a higher value than the slower TAI. Another way of expressing this is to execute a trade when the fast TAI crosses above the slow TAI, making sure to buy if prices are trending up and sell if prices are trending down.

It should be noted and emphasized here that these numbers are *optimized* values. These particular values were used not to suggest an ideal for all conditions and markets but only to suggest a more powerful demonstration of the central concept. The results below should, therefore, be judged with this optimization in mind.

TEST RESULTS

The filter that was tested did indeed improve results by eliminating a surprising 92% of all trades, mostly losers. While 36.5% of the profit dollars were sacrificed, 98% of the loss dollars were avoided.

Filtered	S&P
Trades	4-2
Win-loss percent	66.6%
Win-loss ratio	10.5:1
$W-$L	341-16

This filter's logic is straightforward: If the more recent slope of the moving average is greater than the slope of a longer period, which includes data from the more distant past, then the market is beginning to move with authority in a strong trend. Furthermore, since the fast TAI is likelier to be greater than the slow TAI when the slow TAI is low, and since only a mature trendless market can produce a low slow TAI, trades are thus more likely

SPREADSHEET TREND ANALYSIS INDICATOR

	A	B	C	D
1	Date	S&P	21 Moving	8 day
2	920401	404.23	Average	Standard
3	920402	400.50		Deviation
4	920403	401.55		
5	920406	405.59		
6	920407	398.06		
7	920408	394.50		
8	920409	400.64		
9	920410	404.29		
10	920413	406.08		
11	920414	412.39		
12	920415	416.28		
13	920416	416.05		
14	920420	410.16		
15	920421	410.26		
16	920422	409.81		
17	920423	411.60		
18	920424	409.02		
19	920427	408.45		
20	920428	409.11		
21	920429	412.02		
22	920430	414.95	407.41	
23	920501	412.53	407.80	
24	920504	416.91	408.58	
25	920505	416.84	409.31	
26	920506	416.79	409.84	
27	920507	415.85	410.69	
28	920508	416.05	411.72	
29	920511	418.49	412.57	1.72
30	920512	416.29	413.14	1.79
31	920513	416.45	=AVERAGE(B11:B31)	=STDEVP(C24:C31)

Most spreadsheets have a formula for the standard deviation. Column A is the date, column B is the closing price, column C is the 21-day moving average and column D is the standard deviation of the eight recent simple moving average values.

to occur at the end of a trendless market. And if we can further assume that major trends follow major trendless periods, this is an excellent opportunity to take a trend-following position. Figure 2 demonstrates a few trades. The 26-bar moving average is included for reference. Although trades are a little later than the ideal unfiltered trades, most of the trades that would have been executed during choppy markets were strategically avoided.

This particular application of the simple TAI indicator does indeed suggest that harnessing the information inherent in the slope of a moving average can improve the performance of a simple trend-following reversal system.

Adam White, (612) 379-2613, 725 Tyler St. NE, Minneapolis, MN 55413, is the editor of the Technical Traders Bulletin, *a monthly newsletter for traders and technicians.*

Trading Back Into A Range

by John Sweeney

Last month in Settlement, I wrote briefly about some simple ideas for defining nontrending periods. Although exotic approaches *are* possible, simple things are easier to teach to computer packages. The program I've been using here for testing, Behold!, has a great worksheet capability and many sophisticated functions, so virtually anything can be defined mathematically. The problem with this software occurs when defining trading rules beyond entry and exit. Reversals and add-on trades are tougher if not impossible to program. When trading a range, you want to reverse if price breaks out from the range and starts trending. But given Behold!'s limitation, I won't be able to show you that here. Instead, I'll just focus on evaluating a simple trading range model.

Since I can't show you an example of a trading range breakout with this system, the results I am going to present here are pretty pared down. I generally find that working a narrow range of prices is not terribly profitable by itself but it does prevent losses from trying to trade a range with a trend-following system. Since preventing losses is the first rule of investing, learning to identify and work a range is vital. Also, as outlined in Settlement last month, proper range trading should set you up for a good entry into a trade should a trend begin to develop.

TEACHING THE COMPUTER

Teaching a machine to trade a particular system is a vast subject. The trading system that I've been using as a basis for my work in previous Settlement articles relies on 10- and 35-day moving averages and a regression trendline slope of 10 days. From there, I use the change in price over that period (the slope) to indicate a lack of trend and then trade back into the range. (Remember, I'm leaving reversing into the trend until later.) The trading rules for this system that I'm using to trade Treasury bond futures are illustrated in Figure 3. Simply put, when the 10-day slope is flat and the price is within, say, a point away from the 10-day average, I trade back toward the 10-day average.

Figure 1, which is a Behold! trading analysis graph, shows the trades back into trading ranges for arbitrary values of the trading range ("trdgrng" of +/- 0.07 in Figure 3) of the trendline slope (abbreviated as "TLS") and

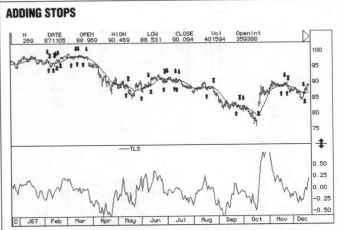

FIGURE 1

TRADING ANALYSIS GRAPH

Typical unstopped trading signals generated by the rules in Figure 3 cluster around the nontrending portions of 1987's bond prices.

FIGURE 2

ADDING STOPS

Adding stops based on maximum adverse excursion cuts losses on the same set of trades, increasing profits.

FIGURE 3

TRENDLINE SLOPE

```
IF TLS > (0- trdgrng) AND TLS < trdgrng and Close > SMA10C - ntryrng and Close < SMA10C THEN
buy today on the close;

IF TLS > (0-trdgrng) AND TLS < trdgrng and Close < SMA10C + ntryrng and Close > SMA10C THEN
sell today on the close;
```

The first rule reads: If the trendline slope (TLS) is greater than an arbitrary negative value ("trdgrng" or trading range) and less than a positive value (that is, it's within a narrow range about zero, which would be perfectly flat), and the close is within the entry range ("ntryrng") below the 10-day average (SMA10C), then buy. A flat TLS above the average within the entry range would produce a sell signal.

the entry range ("ntryrng" of 0.75 or 24 ticks) about the 10-day simple average (SMA10C) (see Figure 3 for trading rules). Here is an example of how the system would carry out these rules given the following criteria: "If the slope is between plus or minus 0.02 and the close is within 24 ticks of the simple 10-day average, enter in the direction of the 10-day average." No stops were used.

Without judging the profitability of the trades, I was happy that the computer was able to enter during the flat periods. While it didn't pick up the same trading ranges that my eye selected, it probably did a better job! It certainly found some flat spots I had overlooked.

With no stops or reversing rules, the trades washed about even over the years 1986-90. However, analysis of the nature of the losses showed a sharp difference between the behavior of winning trades and losing trades. Figure 4 is a nicely defined maximum adverse excursion (MAE) graph, with a sharp distinction between the distributions of wins and losses. However, two profitable trades have very large MAEs and will become losses once we have our stops in place.

Another tricky characteristic of this system: the average win is around $900, while the average loss in any given year ranges

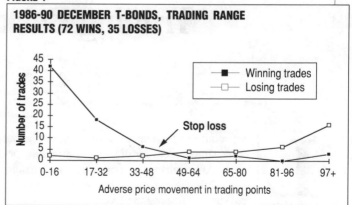

FIGURE 4

1986-90 DECEMBER T-BONDS, TRADING RANGE RESULTS (72 WINS, 35 LOSSES)

Testing a simple trading range system generated results with a high percentage of wins and a sharp distinction in the distribution of adverse price movements for winning vs. losing trades. This makes the setting of efficient stops possible.

> **Setting stops to cure the system's inherent flaws, I sought to take advantage of the high percentage of wins. I focused on the area of one to one and a half full points (32 to 48 trading points).**

"Proceed with the Emory deal, Hankins. The omens are all good."

FIGURE 5

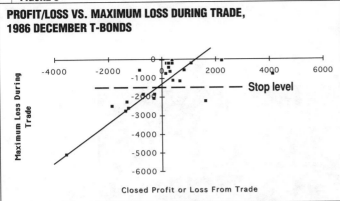

PROFIT/LOSS VS. MAXIMUM LOSS DURING TRADE, 1986 DECEMBER T-BONDS

Plotted here are 29 trades. This chart shows the same stop cutoff as Figure 4 (around $1,500) and also points out that the system has very small winning trades, even though it has lots of them — a typical trading range result.

from $1,400 to $2,700! These figures indicate why trading ranges are so difficult to exploit. Figure 5 shows 1986, the worst year of trading into the trading range. It's easy to see from this graph that good trades just don't go very far to the downside, in this case perhaps $1,500 to the bad side. On the other hand, with range trading, good trades don't go very far *your* way, either!

Setting stops to cure the system's inherent flaws, I sought to take advantage of the high percentage of wins. I focused on the area of one to one-and-a-half full points (32 to 48 trading points). Keep in mind our rule that this loss has to be less than 2% of trading capital, meaning you'd have to have $1,500 / 0.02 = $75,000 to trade conservatively with a 48-tick stop.

Results of this system were ambiguous. Though profits jumped 33%, they still were not statistically significant, averaging about 51% of $2,700 margin annually. CSI's Trader's Money Manager, a profitability-testing program that I reviewed for this issue, gave the range-trading system no chance at all of being profitable on a standalone basis. Of course, if the alternative is to go into trading ranges with a trend-following system, this result might be acceptable, but I also need to estimate the size of the losses from reversing out of the range and into a trend. Finally, though it's not time to merge the rules for both the trend-following and trading range systems, when I do I'll compare trading without a trading range phase and trading with it.

ELABORATIONS

Virtually anyone who follows this discussion is to likely have a question that begins with: "Why didn't you try…?" Well, I leave that to *you*! There are variations I've thought about, but the technique for analyzing them shouldn't vary much. Define an entry and exit rule, measure the profitability and adverse price movements, define stops and capital requirements and see if the return is adequate.

One more thing. The questions of how flat is flat (that is, which values should be used for the trendline slope) and how far from the average we should define the trading range raise the temptation to optimize. For now, I'll only say that both these values vary with volatility and appear to me to be characteristic of individual tradeables — which means a lot of research peripheral to these articles. For now, I'll just select some arbitrary values and develop the range strategy to show the technique of trading the range and reversing for trend. You can develop specifics for your tradeable with those guidelines.

Now that there exists the germ of a trading range rule, I need to define what would constitute a reversal *out* of the range. I will do this by defining the amount of movement beyond the range using MAE stops — which I just did; it appears to be around $1,500 for this particular system. This is the same logic as reversing a trend-following trade when wrong; the MAE stop is a good point of reference not only for exiting but for going the other direction. Once I can determine the size of losses resulting from reversing out of the range and into a trend, I can estimate the total profitability of range trading.

John Sweeney is Technical Editor of STOCKS & COMMODITIES.

REFERENCES

Behold! Investor's Technical Services, Inc. P.O. Box 164075, Austin, TX 78716-4075, (512) 327-8666.

Sweeney, John [1990]. "A program to Behold!" *Technical Analysis of* STOCKS & COMMODITIES, Volume 8.

_____ [1992]. "Returning to the basics," STOCKS & COMMODITIES, July.

Trader's Money Manager. Commodity Systems, Inc. (CSI), 200 W. Palmetto Park Rd., Boca Raton, FL 33432, (407) 392-8663.

CHAPTER 9

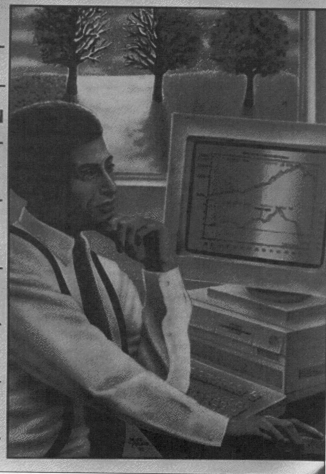

THE TRADERS' MAGAZINE

SEPTEMBER 1992

TECHNICAL ANALYSIS OF STOCKS & COMMODITIES

Summed Rate Of Change (KST)

In the August STOCKS & COMMODITIES, noted technician Martin Pring presented smoothed rate of change indicators as a method to identify both the trend and reversals of trend in the markets. He pointed out that different rate of change measurements could lag important market turns due to the presence of different time cycles. Here, Pring presents his method of combining various rate of change indicators for enhanced trend and reversal of trend identification.

Previously, I pointed out that price trends in financial markets are influenced by the interaction of many different time cycles. Figure 1 shows several smoothed rates of change (ROC)†, each reflecting a different cycle. Major market turning points usually occur when all three indicators reverse direction simultaneously. Similarly, trading range markets have a habit of occurring when they are in conflict. These three indicators do not reflect every cycle, but they do give a more revealing picture than simply using one indicator on its own.

Movements of the nine-month moving average of the 24-month rate of change in the bottom panel of Figure 1 closely monitor the primary bull and bear swings of the

Generally, the summed ROC indicator has been quite reliable, but as with any technical approach it is not perfect.

by Martin J. Pring

market itself. Signals of trend reversals are often given well after the fact, however, because it is slow to reverse direction. One way around this is to combine four smoothed rates of change into one indicator, weighting each one in rough proportion to its time span. (See sidebar, "The KST.") This enables the longer-term smoothed momentum to turn faster but keeps whipsaw signals to a minimum. Because such an indicator also includes several rates of change cover-

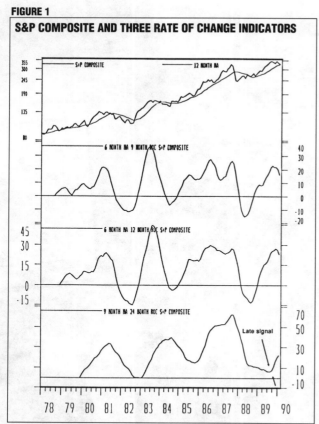

FIGURE 1

S&P COMPOSITE AND THREE RATE OF CHANGE INDICATORS

Three smoothed rate of change indicators are presented below the S&P 500 composite index. The nine-month moving average of the 24-month rate of change closely follows the primary bull and bear market swings but can lag important market turns as it did in late 1989.

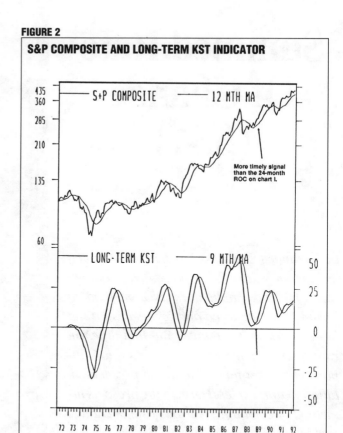

FIGURE 2

S&P COMPOSITE AND LONG-TERM KST INDICATOR

The KST indicator is a weighted summed rate of change oscillator that is designed to identify meaningful turns. Various smoothed rate of change indicators can be combined to form different measurements of cycles. The long-term KST is shown above. Notice that the long-term KST crossed above its nine-month moving average much sooner than the 24-month ROC shown in Figure 1.

ing different time spans, it also reflects the interaction of several time cycles.

ROC FOR THE USA

Figure 2 shows a summed ROC for the U.S. stock market using this concept. The momentum series has been constructed from smoothed nine-, 12-, 18- and 24-month rates of change. In this calculation, the first three periods are smoothed with a six-month moving average and the 24-month time span with a nine-month moving average. The resulting series are then weighted in proportion to their respective time spans, so that the 24-month ROC has a far larger weighting (4) than its nine-month counterpart (1).

Direction reversals of the indicator signal most of the major movements in the stock market on a *relatively* timely basis yet do not suffer much from whipsaw activity. For example, the smoothed 24-month rate of change in Figure 1 only reverses direction in late 1989, almost at the 1989 high. On the other hand, the summed rate of change began to turn up almost a year earlier.

Periods of accumulation and distribution occur when the summed ROC and its moving average change direction. Three levels of signals can be observed. The first is triggered when the indicator itself changes direction, the second when it crosses its moving average and the third when the moving average also

reverses direction. In most cases, the moving average crossover offers the best combination of timely signals with a minimum of whipsaws.

Generally, the summed ROC indicator has been quite reliable, but as with any technical approach it is not perfect. For instance, during a period of prolonged uptrend (as occurred for Japanese equities in the 1980s), this approach will produce false or very premature signals (Figure 3).

In addition, because the summed ROC moves fairly slowly, it is unable to respond to random events. One example that comes to mind is the effect on the Hong Kong market of the 1989 Tiananmen Square massacre. Another was the abrupt change in Federal Reserve policy that occurred in 1981, when interest rates literally reversed their primary downtrend on a dime.

Fortunately, the vast majority of market movements operate around the business cycle and so the summed rate of change concept does give us a reasonably accurate view of the situation, which is why I call this indicator the "Know Sure Thing" (KST) — most of the time it is reliable, but it's also important to "know" that it's not a sure thing.

FIGURE 3

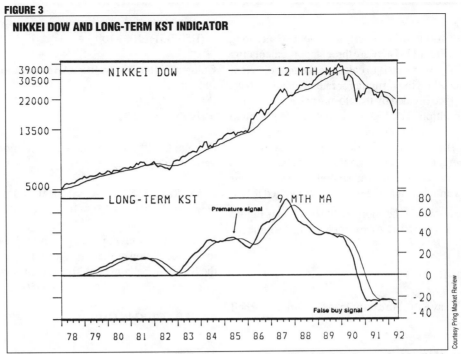

NIKKEI DOW AND LONG-TERM KST INDICATOR

As with any technical indicator, the KST is not infallible. If there is a prolonged trend, the indicator may give false signals of a trend reversal.

FIGURE 4

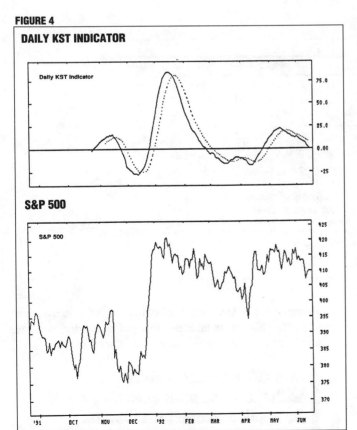

DAILY KST INDICATOR

S&P 500

The KST can be tailored for any time frame. Here, the daily KST is presented with the S&P 500. The daily KST indicator should be used as a complement to additional technical indicators.

FIGURE 5

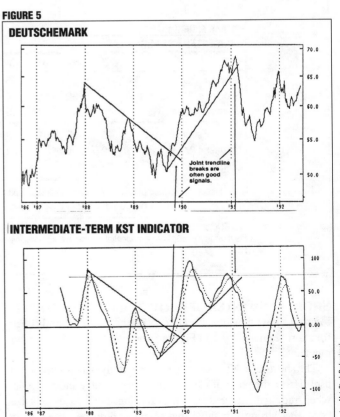

DEUTSCHEMARK

Joint trendline breaks are often good signals.

INTERMEDIATE-TERM KST INDICATOR

One method of using the KST is to apply trendline analysis to the indicator. Here, the intermediate KST has trendlines drawn upon it along with trendlines drawn on the Deutschemark. Joint trendline breaks are often reliable signals.

THE KST

The suggested KST formulas for short, intermediate and long term can be found in Figure 1. There are three steps to calculating the KST indicator. The first step is to calculate the four different rates of change. Recalling the formula for rate of change (ROC) is today's closing price divided by the closing price n days ago. This result is then multiplied by 100. Then subtract 100 to obtain a rate of change index that uses zero as the center point. The second step is to smooth each individual ROC with either a simple moving average or an exponential moving average. The third step is to multiply each of the four smoothed ROCs by their respective weights and then sum the weighted smoothed ROCs.

A spreadsheet example of the short-term daily KST is Figure 2. Column C is the 10-day ROC. An example of the formula for cell C50 is:

=((B50/B41)*100)-100

Column D is the 15-day ROC. An example of the formula for cell D50 is:

=((B50/B36)*100)-100

Column E is the 20-day ROC. An example of the formula for cell E50 is :

=((B50/B31)*100)-100

Column F is the 30-day ROC. An example of the formula for cell F50 is:

=((B50/B21)*100)-100

Column G is the sum of the weighted moving averages of the various ROCs:

=((AVERAGE(C41:C50))+(2*AVERAGE(D41:D50))+(3*AVERAGE (E41:E50))+(4*AVERAGE(F36:F50)))

Note that each moving average is multiplied by its weight prior to the calculation of the sum. An additional moving average of the KST is in column H. A five-day moving average is used as a crossover. The formula for cell H50 is:

=AVERAGE(G46:G50)

The KST indicator can use the parameters listed in Figure 1, or the users can try different values to fine tune the KST to their particular markets.

SIDEBAR FIGURE 1

SUGGESTED KST FORMULAS												
	ROC	MA	Wt	ROC	MA	Wt	ROC	MA	Wt	ROC	MA	Wt
Short-term (D)	10	10	1	15	10	2	20	10	3	30	15	4
Short-term (W)	3	3E	1	4	4E	2	6	6E	3	10	8E	4
Intermediate-term (W)	10	10	1	13	13	2	15	15	3	20	20	4
Intermediate-term (W)	10	10E	1	13	13E	2	15	15E	3	20	20E	4
Long-term (M)	9	6	1	12	6	2	18	6	3	24	9	4
Long-term (W)	39	26E	1	52	26E	2	78	26E	3	104	39E	4

It is possible to program all KST formulas into MetaStock and the CompuTrac SNAP module.
(D) Based on daily data. (W) Based on weekly data. (M) Based on monthly data. (E) EMA.

The ROC column is the rate of change, the MA column is the moving average value, and E after the moving average value indicates that the moving average is an exponential moving average. Multiply each smoothed ROC by its weight prior to summing the four smoothed ROCs.

SHORT- AND INTERMEDIATE-TERM INDICATORS

Figure 4 shows that the same concept can be applied to daily charts for short-term swings and Figure 5 for intermediate price movements.

The short-term KST constructed from daily data is particularly useful from the point of view of *filtering* out entry and exit points when trading the futures markets. Filtering should be emphasized because I strongly believe that trades should be based on the condition of more than one indicator. In this respect, when the KST reverses its prevailing trend is a signal to see what the other indicators are showing. It is also important to ensure that KST signals are confirmed by some kind of trend reversal in the price series itself. This could take the form of a moving average crossover or trendline violation as well as other forms.

> **The KST can also be interpreted with the same principles that would be applied to other oscillators.**

The KST can also be interpreted with the same principles that would be applied to other oscillators. Divergences, overbought

SPREADSHEET FOR THE SHORT-TERM DAILY KST

	A	B	C	D	E	F	G	H
1	Date	S&P500						
2	8/12/91	388.02						
3	8/13/91	389.62						
4	8/14/91	389.90						
5	8/15/91	389.33						
6	8/16/91	385.58						
7	8/19/91	376.47						
8	8/20/91	379.43						
9	8/21/91	390.59						
10	8/22/91	391.33	10 ROC					
11	8/23/91	394.17	1.58					
12	8/26/91	393.85	1.09					
13	8/27/91	393.06	0.81					
14	8/28/91	396.64	1.88					
15	8/29/91	396.47	2.82	15 ROC				
16	8/30/91	395.43	5.04	1.91				
17	9/3/91	392.15	3.35	0.65				
18	9/4/91	389.97	-0.16	0.02				
19	9/5/91	389.14	-0.56	-0.05				
20	9/6/91	389.10	-1.29	0.91	20 ROC			
21	9/9/91	388.57	-1.34	3.21	0.14			
22	9/10/91	384.56	-2.16	1.35	-1.30			
23	9/11/91	385.09	-2.91	-1.41	-1.23			
24	9/12/91	387.34	-2.30	-1.02	-0.51			
25	9/13/91	383.59	-2.99	-2.68	-0.52			
26	9/16/91	385.78	-1.62	-2.05	2.47			
27	9/17/91	385.50	-1.15	-1.92	1.60			
28	9/18/91	386.94	-0.57	-2.45	-0.93			
29	9/19/91	387.56	-0.40	-2.25	-0.96			
30	9/20/91	387.92	-0.17	-1.90	-1.59	30 ROC		
31	9/23/91	385.92	0.35	-1.59	-2.01	-0.54		
32	9/24/91	387.71	0.68	-0.58	-1.36	-0.49		
33	9/25/91	386.88	-0.12	-0.58	-2.46	-0.77		
34	9/26/91	386.49	0.76	-0.67	-2.52	-0.73		
35	9/27/91	385.90	0.03	-0.69	-2.41	0.08		
36	9/30/91	387.86	0.61	0.86	-1.09	3.03		
37	10/1/91	389.20	0.58	1.07	-0.20	2.57		
38	10/2/91	388.26	0.18	0.24	-0.23	-0.60		
39	10/3/91	384.47	-0.89	0.23	-1.19	-1.75		
40	10/4/91	381.24	-1.21	-1.18	-1.89	-3.28		
41	10/7/91	379.50	-2.12	-1.56	-1.32	-3.64		
42	10/8/91	380.67	-1.61	-1.62	-1.15	-3.15		
43	10/9/91	376.80	-2.51	-2.78	-2.72	-5.00		
44	10/10/91	380.55	-1.39	-1.90	-0.79	-4.02	KST	
45	10/11/91	381.45	-1.65	-1.16	-1.12	-3.54	-11.89	
46	10/14/91	386.47	-0.70	-0.32	0.25	-1.45	-12.09	
47	10/15/91	391.01	0.71	1.07	1.05	0.27	-11.50	
48	10/16/91	392.80	2.17	1.63	1.35	0.94	-10.10	5 day MA
49	10/17/91	391.92	2.80	1.56	1.03	0.72	-8.41	-10.80
50	10/18/91	392.50	3.43	1.20	1.71	1.01	-6.14	-9.65

The KST can easily be calculated on any spreadsheet.

and oversold conditions, trendline violations and price pattern analysis are as relevant to the KST as to rate of change, relative strength index (RSI) and moving average convergence/divergence (MACD), as well as others. Trendline violations of the KST do not occur very often, but when they do, they have the effect of strongly reinforcing the KST moving average crossover signals. Figure 5 demonstrates this quite clearly.

ALTERNATIVES

The formulas set out in the sidebar "The KST" are not the last word on the subject; someone who wanted to optimize the time frames, moving averages and weightings could come up with statistically superior results. Even though they are offered here as a starting point for additional experimentation, we should bear in mind that there is no Holy Grail. Substituting the impossible objective of statistical perfection for sound and reasoned analysis is certain to lead to trouble.

Next, we will see how all the long-, intermediate- and short-term KSTs can be arranged on one chart to understand not only the interaction of these three important trends but also to evaluate the current position of the market in relation to the primary trend.

Martin Pring is the author of a number of books, publishes "The Pring Market Review" and is a principal of the investment counseling firm Pring-Turner Capital Group.

REFERENCES

"Explaining the KST," videotape and booklet, International Institute for Economic Research Inc., PO Box 329, Washington Depot, CT 06794.

Pring, Martin J. [1992]. "Rate of change," STOCKS & COMMODITIES, August.

_____ [1992]. *The All-Season Investor,* John Wiley & Sons.

_____ [1992]. *Investment Psychology Explained,* John Wiley & Sons (publication due date October 1992).

_____ [1991]. *Technical Analysis Explained,* McGraw-Hill Book Co.

"Pring Market Review," International Institute for Economic Research Inc., PO Box 329, Washington Depot, CT 06794.

Real Life: Shearson's Jeffrey Weiss

MICHAEL MELLA

"I kept wheeling and dealing and things were great until 1973-74, when I experienced what was at that point the most devastating bear market in many, many decades." — Jeffrey Weiss

"I realized that if we were in a bear market the way we were in 1973-74, no matter what I purchased, the chances were that I was going to lose money. So I began to look less at specific stocks but instead incorporate these specific stock analyses into market segments and then the market as a whole."

Some people get a start on their careers early, but Jeffrey Weiss, a Chartered Market Technician and a first vice president with Shearson Lehman, began earlier than most, at age 13. The technical analysis risk management approach (TARMA) he pioneered was developed from his own trading experiences, including the disastrous 1973-74 bear market. His opinions have been widely solicited and he has been a guest on such well-known financial and investment shows as "Wall $treet Week," CNBC's "Inside Opinion" and "Business View" and CNN's "Business Morning" and "Moneyline." He is frequently quoted in the print media as well. STOCKS & COMMODITIES Editor Thom Hartle interviewed Weiss via telephone on June 23, 1992, covering topics ranging from trading perspectives to the philosophy behind TARMA.

How did you get started following the markets and with technical analysis?

Well, it all began when my sixth-grade mathematics teacher gave me and the other pupils in the class 50,000 hypothetical dollars each to invest in the stock market and I managed to make quite a bit of paper money — so to speak. Around that time was my 13th birthday and my dad gave me $400 to do the real thing. I doubled my money over the next year and my fascination with the stock market was born. It all seemed too easy, though, and it led me down—

A garden path?

It led me down a *false* path, you might say. It was that easy to double my money in one year, in Mattel Toy, from 1968 to

1969. I made 100% and sold the stock at the equivalent of $160 per share. But I learned my *real* lesson in the market after I had piled up some profits, purchased a bicycle with my profits from Mattel and began peddling after school every day up to the Shearson Hammill —that's what our firm was called back then — brokerage office in the late 1960s. I kept on wheeling and dealing, and things were great until 1973-74, when I experienced what was at that point the most devastating bear market in many, many decades. Out of that I was able to transform a financial loss into a real-life gain, the

essence of which was a discipline to help me cope with capital preservation and not just capital appreciation. That's called TARMA, or technical analysis risk management approach, which is what I'm known for today at Shearson Lehman Brothers.

> I began trying, first of all, to gauge what the key elements of bull and bear markets are, because no matter what stock you buy it's the market you're in that will probably dictate how successful you are in any specific stock purchase.

What did you do after suffering this string of losses?

I did something that I don't see done enough today. I dwelled on my losses. I forgot about the times I made a profit because I didn't learn too much from those times, but I consistently analyzed my losses in depth. And I realized that if we were in a bear market the way we were in 1973-74, no matter what I purchased, the chances were that I was going to lose money. So I began to look less at specific stocks but instead incorporate these specific stock analyses into market segments and then the market as a whole. And I also learned about the uses of a stop order and that capital preservation should always precede capital appreciation in any sound, comprehensive investment discipline.

What stages did you go through? Did you read books? What did you study?

I read books! The best book I could ever recommend for someone to read on the stock market is *Reminiscences of a Stock Operator* by Edwin LeFevre, which is still a big seller today, even 70 years or so after it was written, in the early 1920s. I began to study technical analysis when I was about 17 because my broker at the time was a technician and he alerted me to certain formations in the stock market that I had no idea existed. He helped me turn my attention not to the news about the market but to the market's response to the news, which is actually a technical phenomenon.

How did your perspective develop?

I began trying, first of all, to gauge what the key elements of bull and bear markets are, because no matter what stock you buy, it's the market you're in that will probably dictate how successful you are in any specific stock purchase.

Then I began looking at groups because I realized from my own experience that when I had a losing trade, it was often because the whole group was poor and not just the stock I was buying. So I began to broaden my scope and look at not only the stocks but the groups; not only the near-term trend but the longer-term trend within which the near-term trend exists, and other aspects of technical analysis. I began drawing trendlines, reading books on chart formations and really learning and absorbing, like a sponge, every bit of information I could.

You said key elements. What would be some examples of key elements?

Key elements of what I use in technical analysis are the 30-week moving average,

"If we purchase a stock in a bull market, we never want to put a lid on how high it might go under most circumstances. We only want to have a floor on how much we could lose."

"When you factor in money and all the other emotional issues involved when investing in the markets today as well as throughout history, what very often seems like a straightforward decision becomes more difficult."

MICHAEL MELLA

trendline analysis — which would include uptrend lines, downtrend lines and internal trendlines — as well as the 50% retracement rule, which I find to be of remarkable benefit to me in doing market analysis. I also spend time looking at groups as well as specifically at stocks and doing some work on market cycles and even more on chart-pattern recognition. This involves getting to know the dozen or so major patterns that can develop in the market and the variations thereof and analyze them on a short-term, intermediate-term or longer-term basis.

Expand on TARMA, if you would.

TARMA — the technical analysis risk management approach — involves always knowing our downside when we purchase a stock. If we purchase a stock in a bull market, we never want to put a lid on how high it might go under most circumstances. We only want to have a floor on how much we could lose. I try to speak in nontechnical terms about technical analysis and make it extremely understandable, taking a technical subject and breaking it down into its nontechnical components. That's the key element of

what I do, which gives it a lot more appeal than is normally associated with technical analysis.

How about some examples?

Well, for instance, when I speak about letting your profits run and cutting your losses, I talk about never putting a lid on how good something could get in your life but always having a floor on the downside. When people continue to buy stocks as they are going lower and are averaging down a losing position, a losing trade, and compounding their losses, I equate this in life to being in a steadily deteriorating relationship. When I speak about a stock retracing up to half of its gains, that's also really a recipe of life, trying to take two steps forward in life for every step back. But when you factor in money and all the other emotional issues involved when investing in the markets today as well as throughout history, what very often seems like a straightforward decision becomes more difficult.

How do you manage the emotional side of the decision?

We realized that the stock market always goes to extremes. As one famous stock trader always said, "The cheap get cheaper, and the dear get dearer." In a bull market, however dear a stock gets is not going to hurt us, so we just continue to raise our stop order to protect ourselves on the downside. In a bear market, the cheap are going to get cheaper, and what looks like a bargain often turns out to be just the opposite because the market goes to extremes due to emotions.

So a person just needs to accept the emotional issue at face value and then try not to deal with it then?

You have to deal with it, but what it involves really is the saying "The trend is your friend." We never want to fight the prevailing primary market trend if we're investors in the stock market. We *do* pay some attention to the sentiment side of the market. To me, though, it's more important what the market is saying about itself through its underlying technical indicators than just simply what other participants are saying about the market. So I use sentiment as an adjunct to comprehensive market analysis but certainly not as a substitute. I do think that contrary opinion analysis is a bit more difficult today.

Do you have a grass-roots feel?

Yes. Probably one of the big benefits is that we do have a great grass-roots feel. But we really don't use that to make investment decisions. Today, so many people are trying to go against the consensus that they're almost forming a new consensus. So when people say that they want to be contrary to the majority, they often have so much company that they're forming their *own* majority.

So contrary isn't so contrary anymore.

That's why contrary opinion analysis has gotten cloudier these days than it's been before. What I try to do with the stock market is in some ways similar to what John Madden does with a football play on television. I try to dissect the stock market, breaking it up into its component parts and looking beneath the surface. This helps to tell me if a seemingly healthy market is going through internal problems or a seemingly sick market is starting to act better than many realize. I think

that's the case today.

You look for subtle changes, so looking at the markets today, what would be some examples of some subtle changes?

A very important change that's taken place since early April is the visible relative strength from the Dow Jones Utility Average (Figure 1). Let's review some history of this indicator (Figure 2). Note the surge on the weekly chart to new second-half 1990 highs during the crisis in the Middle East and prior to the broader market's early 1991 surge.

Then, following the failed coup in the former USSR during August 1991, the DJUA sprinted ahead better than 10% while the DJIA moved sideways (Figure 3). This relative strength helped pave the way for the market's sharp ascent in late 1991. So far at the present time, the utility average is unchanged in June 1992 after the April-May rally versus some sizable setbacks in many other averages.

One more point: the DJUA is one of the best relative performers among the popular market indices since early April — a bullish indication for the general market. The utilities average is an important leading indicator despite the fact that the lead times often vary. They're also a very good indicator of interest rates because they're such heavy borrowers.

What else do you follow?

I look at the weekly advance-decline line (Figure 4) on the New York Stock Exchange, which has been making new highs regularly over the past year. And I want to emphasize that it's the weekly

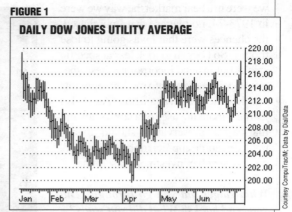

FIGURE 1

DAILY DOW JONES UTILITY AVERAGE

Since April the Dow Jones Utility Average has been advancing, a bullish indication for the broader markets.

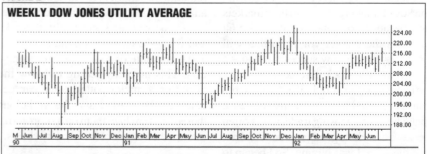

FIGURE 2

WEEKLY DOW JONES UTILITY AVERAGE

The Dow Jones Utility Average has been holding above its long-term support line.

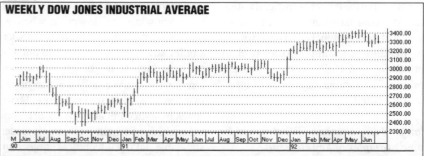

FIGURE 3

WEEKLY DOW JONES INDUSTRIAL AVERAGE

The Dow Jones Utility Average moved higher from the middle of 1991, while the Dow Jones Industrial Average moved sideways until late 1991.

breadth of the stock market as measured by a stock's net change from week to week that has called this market's long-term trend.

Weekly instead of daily?

The weekly line is a far better long-term market gauge than the daily advance-decline line, which measures the cumulative total of advancing minus declining issues, the net change, day to day. If you look at the daily advance-decline line over a period of many years, you would see that it peaked in 1956 — and I hate to tell you where the DJIA was back in 1956. So as a short-term indicator, the daily advance-decline line does have some merit, but on a longer-term basis, it's the weekly action of the broad market that's called the market's tune. And this is something that is not stressed nearly enough, even in technical circles!

Why do you feel that the weekly advance-decline line is that much better than the daily advance-decline?

It removes the downward day-to-day bias of the advance-decline figures. By looking at the market's net change for the week, it gives a truer reflection of the market's trend because the daily advance-decline line has a severe downward bias, which does not, in my opinion, make it useful as a long-term indicator.

The utilities and weekly advance-decline line are two of your indicators. Do you have any others?

I examine the bond market. I think the chart of the Dow Jones 20 Bond Average (Figure 5) looks awfully good technically, and I also think that this is one area of the market that will go higher over time. It has a splendid overall technical pattern.

Patterns. Do you have any favorite patterns that you look for?

I like to use internal trendlines a lot. I find them to be of immense help. You'll see more of them in my publication, "Technical Snapshots." Then, of course, I use a lot of the classic technical patterns, but I also put a lot of stock in the 50% retracement principle. In fact, your readers might be interested to know that from

FIGURE 4

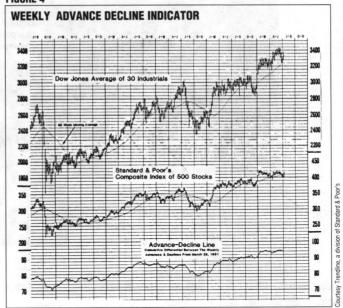

The weekly advance-decline line has recently moved to new highs, which is a bullish indication.

FIGURE 5

The Dow Jones 20 Bond Average has broken its long-term downtrend line in 1986 and had an additional breakout of its consolidation in late 1990.

the crash of 1987 to the high before the Iraqi invasion of Kuwait (July 1990) — that would be from 1738 to 2999 on the DJIA — the DJIA bottomed in October 1990 at 2365 on a closing basis. This was almost a picture-perfect 50% midpoint retracement of that major upmove.

If a stock had had a sustained advance and then had a 50% correction, what would you look for to tell you to go ahead and repurchase it?

First, I would look for the stock to hold. On a longer-term basis, if the stock were to have a very good rally over, say, a six-month period or more, I'd look for it to stabilize in and around the 50% area, provided there was a market reaction that was severe enough to take stocks there.

Second, I never hang my hat on one indicator. I'd want to look for a long-term uptrend line, a long-term moving average, any other technical formation that would enhance and complement the 50%

"If you want to see what a stock looks like, look at the group, not just the specific stock or company. Very often in the market, as in life, the apple doesn't fall far from the tree. A stock is often only as good as the group it's in."

"I don't buy a stock if I deem it to have a lot more than 13-17% of intermediate-term risk in it from where I'm buying it to where I would be stopped out."

rule. In other words, what I do is look at where the moving average is, where the major uptrend lines are, where the 50% retracement is, how the stock is doing within its group picture and how is the stock acting versus the market. I'll ask what type of market we are in. And as I plug in the answers to those questions and plug in the respective numbers, the more numbers that occur in a cluster, the more technical significance I assign to that level.

Comparing a stock to its group. So you like relative strength analysis, then?

Only partially! It's really not so much relative strength, but what I like to call this is the "family" concept. The way I relate it to life is this. If someone wants to see what a family member is going to look like years from now, they might want to look at their mom or dad. If you want to see what a stock looks like, look at the group, not just the specific stock or company. That's very important. I call that the family concept because very often in the market, as in life, the apple doesn't fall far from the tree. A stock is often only as good as the group it's in.

How do you measure risk in a stock?

Basically, I don't buy a stock if I deem it to have a lot more than, say, 13-17% of intermediate-term risk in it from where I'm buying it to where I would be stopped out. I also use point and figure charts, which I believe to be of tremendous help in my work. I don't use volume as much

as others do in analyzing the market.

What is it that you like about point and figure charting?

Point and figure charts interest me because they don't even incorporate volume, and they are still one of the most accurate types of charts available today. I like point and figure charts because they show me clusters of distribution and accumulation. In addition, I like the 45-degree angle that I can view on the Chartcraft point and figure charts because stocks, over time, seem to be able to rise and fall for fairly long periods of time at 45-degree angles. So I also look at the angle at which a stock is rising or falling.

Do you have any last-minute closing comments?

Yes, I have several! I would strongly suggest that if any of your readers haven't read *Reminiscences of a Stock Operator* by Edwin Lefevre that they consider doing so. It's a wonderful and enjoyable book on the stock market, and many top Wall Street professionals have credited this book with putting them on a sounder stock market path than they otherwise would be without having read it.

Anything else?

I'd like to leave you with this comment: The reason I dwell so much on the capital preservation side of the equation is because I lived through 1973-74 and learned at a very young age the damage

that a bear market can do. I might also add that it took 662 weeks for the DJIA to rise from its 1974 low to its 1987 high. It took the market slightly more than 1% of this time, approximately eight weeks, to surrender 50% of these gains during the September/October 1987 market slide. Which is like saying the market surrendered approximately 50% of a 13-year gain in less than 2% of the time.

That's why I suggest that market participants know their downside, trying to make as much money as they can on the way up but not take extreme risks on the way down. I always talk about preventive market medicine, about stopping a small financial cut before it becomes a large financial hemorrhage. The stock market is not a business to learn by trial and error because it is too expensive a lesson. That's the reason I have a list of 13 market rules that can potentially help investors (see sidebar, "Thirteen investment tenets that could improve your investment performance").

Excellent advice, Jeff. Thank you for your time.

FURTHER READING

Jiler, William L. [1990]. *How Charts Can Help You in the Stock Market*, Fraser Publishing. Originally published in 1962.

LeFevre, Edwin [1980]. *Reminiscences of a Stock Operator*, Fraser Publishing. Originally published in 1923.

THIRTEEN INVESTMENT TENETS THAT COULD IMPROVE YOUR INVESTMENT PERFORMANCE

1 Capital preservation should precede capital appreciation.

2 Don't shun a stock just because its price may be higher than you want to spend. One is far better off buying a higher-priced issue that rises in value than owning a lower-priced issue that declines in price.

3 Don't be afraid to take losses, but do everything possible to keep them manageable.

4 Never place a lid on how much money you can make, but always have a floor on how much you can lose.

5 Don't fight the prevailing market trend.

6 A stock often proves to be only as good as the group it is in.

7 Keep in mind that in a primary downtrend, many support levels are usually broken, and support often proves to be just a weigh station prior to lower prices.

8 Be aware that in a primary uptrend, numerous resistance levels are often overcome, and resistance is just a temporary hurdle en route to higher quotes.

9 Be flexible and disciplined at all times.

10 Once you have decided to sell a stock, you are usually better off doing so "at the market." Although you may get that extra eighth or quarter of a point nine times out of 10, the one time you don't *could* prove costly.

11 Don't purchase a stock solely because it has declined sharply in price. Successful "bottom fishing" is a difficult task at best.

12 The stock market discounts.

13 Consider the use of a risk management discipline to address market risk.

—*Jeffrey Weiss*

Four Common Errors In Testing Trading Systems

MIKE HORSWILL

The author of The Technical Analysis Course *debuts as a* STOCKS & COMMODITIES *writer with this article, in which Thomas Meyers explains that yes, trading systems should be tested, but these mistakes in systems testing can make the difference between the accurate assessment of a system's profitability and a distorted picture that didn't take into account certain inevitable factors. Meyers shows you how to fine tune your testing techniques so that these problems can't cost you all your trading capital when you go to trade in real time.*

by Thomas A. Meyers

A trading system is a set of rules that can be used to generate specific buy and sell signals. For example, a simple trading system can be based on a moving average crossover. You buy when prices rise from below to above the moving average line and sell when prices drop from above to below the moving average line. For short positions, you do just the opposite. You sell short when prices decline from above to below the moving average line and cover the short sale when prices move from below to above the moving average line.

More complex trading systems can be developed using multiple moving averages, oscillators, stochastics, relative strength index, moving average convergence/divergence (MACD) or numerous other technical analysis techniques, either by themselves or in combination. A variety of price and time filters can also be used to enhance the reliability of signals and stop-loss rules can be incorporated to control losses.

Regardless of the simplicity or complexity of a trading system, it is *always* a good idea to test it before actually investing money. Fortunately, this task has become much easier with the advent of relatively inexpensive personal computers. Rather than having to paper trade for lengthy periods of time to test a trading system, now you can use technical analysis software to access vast databases of historical stock and commodity market prices. In a matter of minutes, you can evaluate a particular trading strategy and determine how successful it would have been during a past time period.

In theory, if a trading system is successful when applied to historical data, it will generate profits under real market conditions. In reality, it doesn't always turn out that way, primarily due to incorrect assumptions being made during the testing phase.

Four mistakes are frequently made when testing trading

systems. Each can contribute to a distorted view of the true profitability of a particular trading system. They are:

TRANSACTION COSTS

Perhaps the most common error made when testing trading systems relates to transaction costs: Either no or an unrealistically low amount is factored in for commissions and slippage.

Figure 1 illustrates the effect that transaction costs can have on trade results. In this example, a total profit of $6,000 was registered on 30 trades prior to deducting transaction costs. Using per-trade transaction costs of $100, $200 and $300 results in a net profit of $3,000, zero and a net loss of $3,000.

Transaction costs can vary significantly depending on the market you are trading and how your trades are being executed (full-service broker, discount broker or on the trading floor), and that adds to the difficulty in defining what amount to use in testing trading systems. Nevertheless, the more realistic you can be, the more likely it is that real-time trading performance will approach test results.

TRADE EXECUTION PRICES

A second common mistake is the use of unrealistic buy and sell execution prices. Let's examine two hypothetical examples.

First, suppose your system calls for you to buy when you cross from below to above a moving average line of the Standard & Poor's 500 index futures contract. Furthermore, suppose your moving average is at 411.03 and that prices rise above that level. What do you use as your buy price? Do you use 411.03 (the crossover price)? It would be a mistake to do so, because S&P 500 futures only trade at 0.05 increments (thus, you could never have bought at 411.03) and you don't know you want to buy until *after* you cross above 411.03. In this example, 411.03 would be an unrealistic buy price to use; a higher price that would diminish the trade results is more appropriate.

nother trade execution price mistake relates to using the closing price for a given period. In many trading systems, buy and sell signals are generated when the closing price for a period (five minutes, day, week and so forth) is above or below a certain level. In these cases, often the closing price is incorrectly used in testing as the buy or sell price. Obviously, you could not have bought or sold at the closing price, since your signal to do so did not occur until the closing price was posted. In real time, therefore, you would have to execute your trade in the following period.

Using the closing price as opposed to the next period's opening price can greatly distort the true value of a trading system. For example, the opening, high, low and closing prices for the June 1992 S&P 500 index futures contract from March to May 1992 are plotted in Figure 2. Note the difference between the closing price and the next day's opening price.

On April 1, the S&P 500 index opened at 401.65, or 2.55 points lower than the 404.20 closing price on March 31. On

FIGURE 1

HYPOTHETICAL TEST RESULTS WITH VARIOUS TRANSACTION COST ASSUMPTIONS

Assumed transaction costs per trade (dollars)	Number of trades	Gross profit (dollars)	Total transaction costs (dollars)	Net profit/ loss (dollars)
0	30	$6,000	0	$6,000
$100	30	6,000	$3,000	3,000
200	30	6,000	6,000	0
300	30	6,000	9,000	(3,000)

Varying the total transaction cost to reflect commissions and slippage can dramatically affect the net profit of a trading system.

April 14, the S&P 500 index opened at 407.95, almost three points higher than the closing price of 405.10 on April 13. Throughout the three-month period from March to May, the average difference between the opening price and the previous day's closing price was 0.73. Out of the 63 trading days, the opening price was equal to the previous day's closing price on only one occasion. Obviously, using the more realistic opening prices as opposed to the closing prices can greatly change the overall test results.

These are only two of many examples of how improper trade execution prices can distort test results and, in most cases, overstate profit potential. Realistic trade execution prices must be used if you are going to have any chance of having real-time trading profits match your test results.

INTRAPERIOD TRADES

Intraperiod trades are often overlooked by those testing trading systems. Suppose you are testing a simple moving average

FIGURE 2

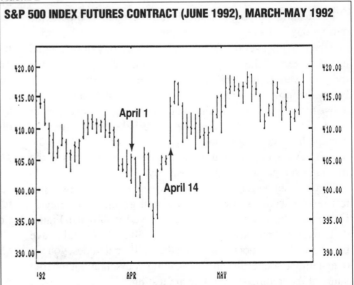

S&P 500 INDEX FUTURES CONTRACT (JUNE 1992), MARCH-MAY 1992

Identifying the correct price for initiating a position based on a signal from a trading system is important. Many times, the following day's opening price can vary greatly from the previous day's closing price. On April 1, the S&P 500 opened 2.55 points below the previous day's close. On April 14, the S&P opened close to 3 points above the previous day's close.

FIGURE 3

HYPOTHETICAL BUY SIGNAL

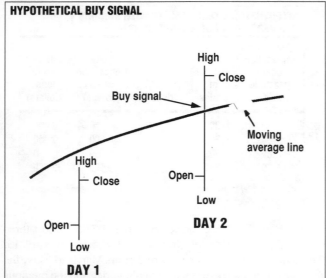

Basing a trade on the penetration of a simple moving average would have produced a buy signal on day 2.

FIGURE 4

POSSIBLE PRICE MOVEMENT ON DAY 2

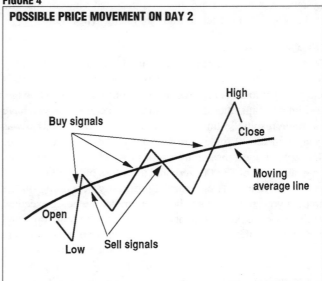

Basing a trade on the penetration of a simple moving average would have produced three buys and two sells on the same day if the market had traded intraday as above.

crossover system on a daily basis. A buy signal occurs when prices rise from below to above the moving average line; a sell signal is generated when prices decline from above to below the moving average line.

> **For testing purposes, compare the current day's closing price to the previous day's and the moving average to determine when a buy or sell signal has occurred.**

For testing purposes, using historical data, compare the current day's closing price to the previous day's closing price and the moving average to determine when a buy or sell signal has occurred. If the current day's closing price is above the moving average line and the previous day's closing price is below the moving average, you assume that you bought at just above the moving average line on the current day. On the other hand, if the current day's closing price is below the moving average line and the previous day's closing price is above the moving average, you assume that you sold at just below the moving average line on the current day.

Figure 3 shows a hypothetical buy signal. In this case, your test results would show one buy signal generated on day 2. However, what if during day 2 prices moved as shown in Figure 4? In reality, three buy signals and two sell signals would have been recorded. By not recognizing the additional trades, you are overstating trade results and misleading yourself about the true value of the trading system you are testing.

If you want to obtain realistic test results, you must include intraperiod trades, even though it makes historical testing more difficult and time consuming.

TIME PERIOD TESTED

Another frequent mistake made in testing trading systems is examining an insufficient time period. Most trading systems are trend following in nature. If you test them throughout a time period when prices are rising sharply, they will be very successful. Likewise, if you test them throughout a time period when prices are declining, they will show profitable performance. However, if you test them when prices are moving sideways, they will produce significant losses. To gain a true picture of the value of a trading system, it is important that you test it throughout a time period that includes all three types of price movement — up, down and sideways.

TO SUM

It is wise to test a trading system before applying it under real market conditions. If you want to make that testing meaningful, you must use assumptions that closely fit the real market trading environment. Otherwise, you will quickly discover that a trading system that looks good based on your historical testing is disappointing, and perhaps costly, in real-time trading.

Thomas A. Meyers is a recognized authority on technical analysis. He lives in New Jersey.

REFERENCES

Colby, Robert W., and Thomas A. Meyers [1988]. *The Encyclopedia of Technical Market Indicators*, Business One Irwin.
Meyers, Thomas A. [1989]. *The Technical Analysis Course*, Probus Publishing.

Utilities And Stocks

Last month, this technical trailblazer examined how utilities and bonds were interconnected. This month, John J. Murphy analyzes how utilities in turn affect stocks.

by John J. Murphy

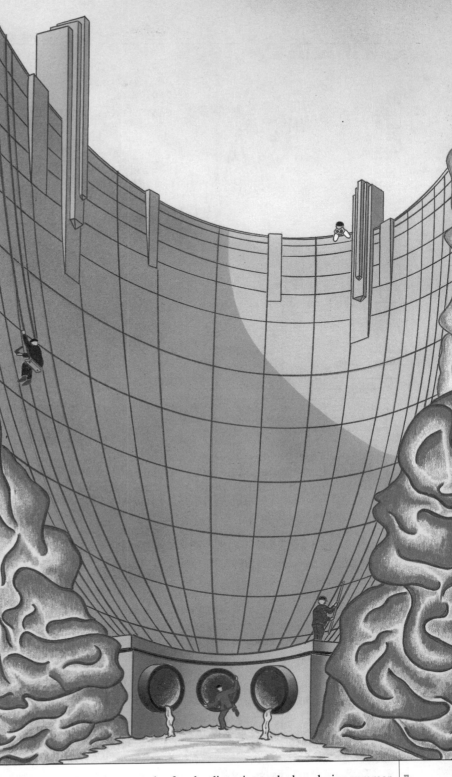

My article on utilities and bonds examined the close link between utility stocks and Treasury bond prices. Because bonds usually act as a leading indicator for stocks and because utilities are sensitive to interest rates, it should be no surprise that utilities also provide advance warning about the future direction of the stock market as a whole.

Figure 1 provides a five-year comparison of the Dow Jones Utility Average (solid line) and the Standard & Poor's 500 index (dotted line) from late 1987 to mid-June 1992. Visual comparison permits a couple of observations. First, both lines generally trend in the same direction. Usually, rising utilities are positive for stocks, while falling utilities are usually bearish. However, as is the case with bonds, utilities usually change direction before the rest of the market.

LEAD TIME SHORT AND LONG

Sometimes, the lead time can be quite short — from days to weeks — as was the case with the 1987 and the 1990 bottoms. At other times, the lead time can be several months (as was the case with the 1990 peak and the mid-1991 bottom). During 1990, the utilities peaked in January, six months before the S&P 500 peak that July. In 1987 (not shown), the utilities also peaked in January, seven months before the August stock market top. During the second half of 1991, the rising utilities had only a minimal upside impact on stocks until year-end, when stocks exploded to new highs.

Since the Dow Jones Utility Average (DJUA) of 15 stocks can be distorted by the inclusion of three natural gas stocks, which are influenced more by natural gas prices than interest rates, the electric utilities give a "purer" reading on interest rate expecta-

tions. An example of such a distortion took place during summer 1991, when a devastating drop in one natural gas stock pushed the DJUA to a new yearly low. Figure 2 compares the S&P Electric Utility Index to the S&P 500 from the late 1990 bottom to mid-June 1992. Note the much milder downward correction in the electric utilities during summer 1991.

Figure 2 also shows the strong tendency of the interest rate-sensitive electric utilities to lead turns in the broader market both

NADIR KIANSERI

FIGURE 1

DJUA VS. S&P 500, 1988-92

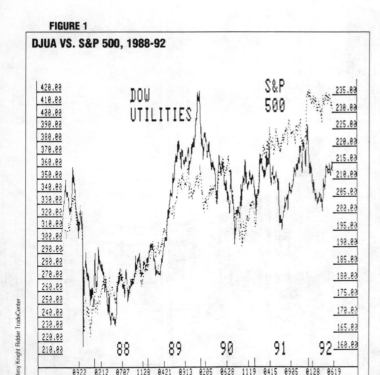

A comparison of the DJUA (solid line) and the S&P 500 Index (dotted line) from late 1987 to June 1992. The utilities usually change direction before the S&P 500 and are therefore a leading indicator for stocks.

FIGURE 2

S&P 500 VS. ELECTRIC UTILITIES, 1990-92

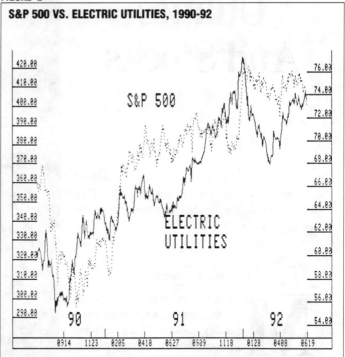

The S&P Electric Utilities (solid line) and the S&P 500 (dotted line) from the late 1990 bottom to June 1992. The electric utilities can be seen leading stocks at almost every turn over the past two years.

FIGURE 3

S&P 500 VS. ELECTRIC UTILITIES, 1991-92

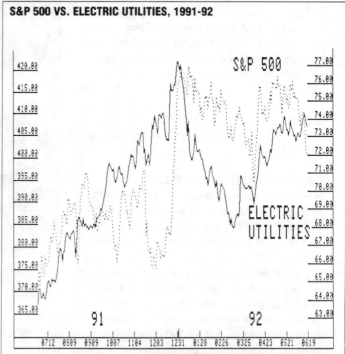

The S&P 500 Electric Utilities (solid line) and the S&P 500 (dotted line) from mid-1991 to June 1992. The utilities peaked a week before stocks in January 1992 and then troughed during March, a month before the S&P 500.

on the upside and the downside. Note the relatively short lead times at the 1990 bottom and the early 1992 top and the much longer lead time at the mid-1991 trough. The peak in the utilities in early 1991 caused the stock market rally to stall, as it did again in early 1992.

Figure 3 provides a closer view of the electric utilities and the S&P 500 from mid-1991 to mid-1992. After leading stocks higher during the second half of 1991, the electricals peaked a week before stocks did in January 1992. The electricals again displayed their leading tendencies by turning up during March 1992, a month before the S&P 500. Dow theorists who monitor the Dow Jones industrial and transportation averages would do well to include the DJUA in their analyses. It would also be a good idea to monitor the broader S&P and New York Stock Exchange utility averages.

John Murphy is president of JJM Technical Advisors Inc. and publishes the monthly "Futures Trends and Intermarket Analysis." He is also the technical analyst for CNBC.

REFERENCES

JJM Technical Advisors Inc., 297-101 Kinderkamack Road Ste. 148, Oradell, NJ 07649.

Murphy, John J. [1986]. *Technical Analysis of the Futures Markets*, New York Institute of Finance.

_____ [1991]. *Intermarket Technical Analysis*, John Wiley & Sons.

_____ [1992]. "Utilities and bonds," STOCKS & COMMODITIES, August.

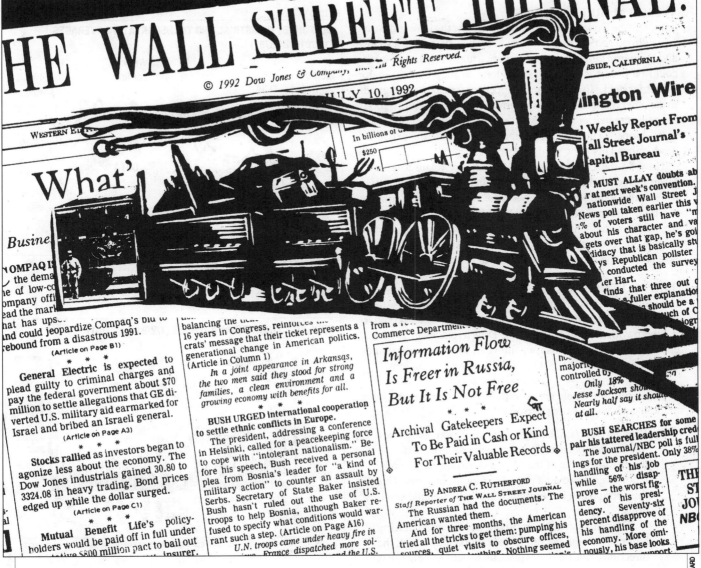

Is Dow Theory Sending Us A Warning?

Michael Sheimo, best known for books such as Dow Theory Redux *and* Stock Market Rules, *tackles the age-old question of whether the Dow theory is still valid — and if it is, is it really sending us a warning?*

by *Michael D. Sheimo*

After more than a hundred years, are the concepts of the Dow theory still useful in determining stock market strength? The Dow theory was arrived at by an evolutionary process over a period of several years. At the turn of the century, Charles Henry Dow discussed stock trading ideas in the newspaper he was both editor and publisher of, *The Wall Street Journal*. The discussions, which appeared in a section called "Review & Outlook," involved analyzing stock price movements each day, prices conveniently published in the *Journal*.

Concepts of what would eventually be called the Dow theory were presented after Dow's death in 1902 by managing editor William Hamilton, who succeeded Charles Dow. Hamilton's work occasionally had errors and false signals but was believed reliable by many *Journal* readers. Hamilton used the theory to correctly call the approaching bear market of 1929. Hamilton deserves credit for much of the development of the Dow theory.

WHICH MARKET INDICES

Although the Dow theory was created around the Dow industrial and railroad (now transportation) averages, both Charles Dow and William Hamilton believed that virtually any list of stocks could be used for the analysis as long as they contain major industrial stocks in one list and shippers or transporters of goods in the other list. Their logic was simple and basic. If more goods are being created and sold, it stands to reason that the goods have to be shipped. The increased shipping confirmed the expanded production. This logic holds true today.

How do the concepts in the Dow theory relate to today's faster-paced market? The market in Charles Dow's time might have traded a million shares in a year. Today, the stock market can trade 100 million shares and be judged a slow day. Clearly, the situation has changed, but is the Dow theory still valid despite these changes? It is valid if the signals can still be observed in the same way they could at the turn of the century.

THE MAIN CONCEPTS

Looking at three of the main concepts in the Dow theory — trend definition, trend confirmation and forming a line — and comparing them with the movement of the Dow averages in 1991 will enable us to see the effects for a full year. Then we can examine the first few months of 1992 and draw some conclusions.

Trend definition: There are essentially three trends to the stock market, each with its own personality.

- *Primary trend* is the longer-term direction of the stock market and specifically refers to the pattern created by the closing levels of the Dow industrial and transportation averages over a period of months or years. This time period can be shorter in unusually volatile situations.

  The primary trend is most often either an advancing bull market or a declining bear market, although the direction of the market is difficult to determine at times (see "Forming a line").
- *Secondary trend* is a shorter-term trend running in a direction contrary to the primary trend in the Dow industrial and transportation averages. It can last from a day or two to several weeks.
- *Tertiary trend* is the day-to-day changes of the market averages.

Trend confirmation: According to Dow theory, the industrial and transportation averages must confirm each other in direction for a strong market move or trend. When the industrial average trends up, the trend of the transportation average should also be up. The closer the two trends mirror each other, the greater the strength of the market move. Divergence in the trends when the Dow industrials are climbing and the transports are declining is a sign of market weakness and can often be an early signal of approaching change.

- *1991 market—primary trend up 800 points*: A graph of market closing levels for 1991 shows the Dow Jones

FIGURE 1

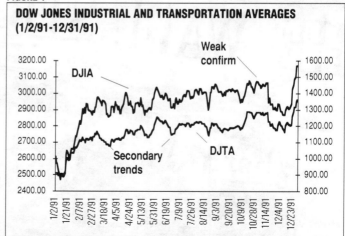

Both the DJIA and the DJTA extended their advances from the October 1990 lows, indicating the continuation of a bull market.

FIGURE 2

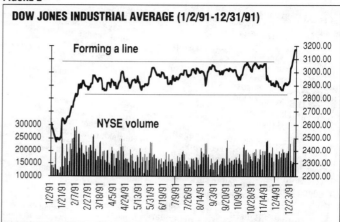

Volume surged in February 1991 and continued to increase on rallies and decrease on declines — a bullish indication.

Industrial Average moving up about 800 points, showing a continuation of the bull market that began in October 1990 (Figure 1).

In 1991 the 800-point move in the industrial average was not alone; the transportation average confirmed the climb by moving up more than 400 points, indicating the continuation of a bull market from October 1990. Note the first two quarters have strong confirmation and the last half of the third quarter shows a slightly weaker confirmation with the transports. Confirmation is evident, but it appears to be less enthusiastic than it was earlier in the year.

Confirmation returned in the fourth quarter, when the market encountered strong resistance approaching new territory at the 3100 level. The market didn't have strength enough to break through the resistance and so it corrected, dropping into a secondary downtrend. Toward the end of December, the averages established support and started another rally, this time breaking through the 3100 resistance level. The primary trend for 1991 was up, although many shorter-term secondary downtrends also appeared throughout the year.

Forming a line: Many times, the market fluctuates in a narrow range of about 5% on either side of an average level. The fluctuation indicates a period of stock accumulation and distribution, and it can be difficult to observe any direction to the trend. The movement appears to be quite flat, neither rising nor falling. Whether the market is bullish or bearish can be determined by watching volume during periods of sudden advances (breakouts) or sudden declines (corrections). The market is considered bullish if greater volume occurs during times of breakout on the upside and bearish if the larger volume appears on the corrections.

- *1991 forming a line.* Note the surge in volume during the strong rally in mid-February 1991 (Figure 2). During the rest of the year, the volume dropped on secondary trend declines and increased on rallies, a distinctly bullish tendency. Volume increased in the November-December secondary downtrend, but a fundamental economic change (the lowering of the Federal Reserve discount interest rate) created an ideal situation for the market to touch support and rally to new highs leading into 1992.
- *1992 current market and the Dow theory.* Now narrow the focus to the first six months of 1992 (Figure 3). What can the three main concepts of the Dow theory tell us?

> **Examination of the Dow averages on an hourly basis shows the impact of the institutions and the presence of Dow theory activity.**

- *Trend definition 1992.* The primary trend is still in an upward direction, with a 200-point increase in the first five months of 1992. Much of this increase came in April and May, while the market tended to be flat during the first three months.
- *Trend confirmation 1992.* Some serious divergence occurred in the latter part of January and again in March. It may even be fair to hypothesize that the correction of March-April was signaled by the lack of trend confirmation. In the second quarter, both averages appeared to establish some support and resume the upward climb.

But the overall picture of the first half of the year showed a lack of trend confirmation. The transportation average is not showing much of an increase (actually, it is down from mid-February), while the industrial average is rising on its own. Divergence here is a sign of weakness and could lead to a correction, a secondary downtrend or

FIGURE 3

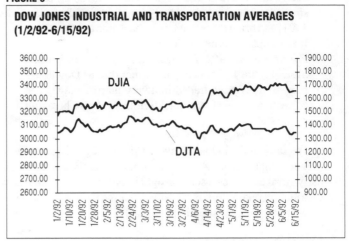

DOW JONES INDUSTRIAL AND TRANSPORTATION AVERAGES (1/2/92-6/15/92)

The overall picture of first-half 1992 showed a lack of trend confirmation. The late April-May rally by the DJIA made new highs, while the DJTA failed to do so.

FIGURE 4

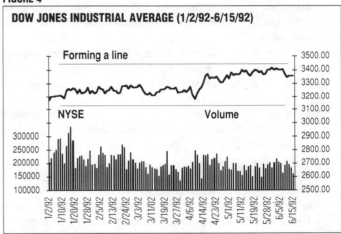

DOW JONES INDUSTRIAL AVERAGE (1/2/92-6/15/92)

The DJIA was forming a line during first-half 1992.

FIGURE 5

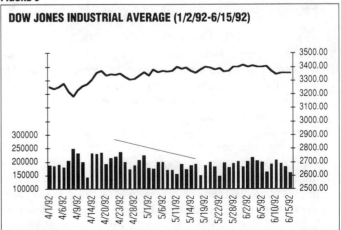

DOW JONES INDUSTRIAL AVERAGE (1/2/92-6/15/92)

The DJIA showed declining volume beginning in May, indicating a weakening situation.

even a turn in the primary trend. This is not an absolute; strength can reappear suddenly (as with the rally in late 1991) and bring the two averages back into confirmation. It is a time for some caution.

- *Forming a line 1992.* The market has again been forming a line (Figure 4). For nearly three months, the Dow Jones Industrial Average traded in a very narrow range. The correction in April was quickly followed by a breakout rally.

The rally of the industrial average in the second quarter was a significant breakout. A closer look at this and the correction in early April can give us some insight into this accumulation and distribution phase (Figure 5). Now examine the volume in each of the two changing situations.

DEFINITE WEAKNESS
The early April 1992 correction clearly showed a volume surge to 200 million shares in a day, illustrating weakness in the broader market (volume is for the entire New York Stock Exchange [NYSE]), but the industrials turned around and staged another rally. The rally drove the DJIA into new territory above 3300. Volume surged to more than 200 million shares and then settled back down to between 175 and 200 million shares. The obvious weakness signal in the volume decline that appeared throughout the rest of May gives some cause for concern. Beginning with May, there doesn't seem to be a day with much more than 200 million shares traded, but there could be cause for greater concern if volume were to show another decline to below 150 million shares a day.

WHAT ABOUT SECOND-HALF 1992?
The market of early June 1992 reached into new territory with a bull market primary trend, but weaknesses were starting to appear. The second half of 1992 is likely to see a decline in the market unless the indicators show strength developing. Greater strength will be seen in better trend confirmation by the transportation average and larger, increasing volume behind the rallies.

WHY DOES THE DOW THEORY WORK?
The Dow theory continues to work for three basic reasons. First, the theory has validity because the stocks appearing in the DJIA and DJTA are carefully selected to be representative of the market. Second, the theory works because of the attention that large institutional stock traders pay to it. Examination of the Dow averages on an hourly basis shows the impact of the institutions and the presence of Dow theory activity. Trend confirmation is common, obviously illustrating anticipation of the next market move. Third, the Dow theory works because market participants and observers *expect* it to work. One large stock trader might not be completely sold on the concept but keeps track because others follow the signals. This is also why the individual investor should have a basic understanding of the concepts of the Dow theory. The knowledge will be helpful in determining trend and looking for signals of strength or weakness.

THE SIGNALS ARE THERE
These are just a few of the main concepts of the Dow theory. They are as relevant today as they were more than a hundred years ago when Charles Dow first began formulating them in his column in *The Wall Street Journal.*

The Dow theory is composed of components that can be looked at individually or in combination. The theory was never intended to precisely predict but rather to indicate market direction and signals of weakness or strength. Charles Dow's successor, William Hamilton, often referred to the theory as a barometer, and commented that if it had been any more precise he would have called it a thermometer instead. In essence, that is the Dow theory: it is a barometer of the market because there is no soothsayer who can predict the future without a doubt. But a barometer can always tell you about the warning signs of the change in the weather.

Michael D. Sheimo has been an investor, stockbroker and registered options principal in the Minneapolis area. He has just completed a book on stock selection for John Wiley & Sons, Stock Investing to the Fourth Power, *due out later this year.*

FURTHER READING
Bowman, Melanie [1990]. "Dow theory," *Technical Analysis of* STOCKS & COMMODITIES, Volume 8: September.

Evans, Richard L. [1991]. "Dow theory confirmation and divergence," *Technical Analysis of* STOCKS & COMMODITIES, Volume 9: July.

Sheimo, Michael D. [1990]. *Stock Market Rules,* Probus Publishing.

_____ [1989]. *Dow Theory Redux,* Probus Publishing.

Sundquist, Carl [1991]. "The historical Dow," *Technical Analysis of* STOCKS & COMMODITIES, Volume 9: May.

DIANA FRITCH

Are There Persistent Cycles?

Most technical indicators use a fixed lookback length based on the idea that cycles are present in the price data. Should the same fixed lookback length be used for all markets? Are there persistent cycles present to justify the use of the same lookback length for evaluating the market? Mike Poulos searches through a number of markets for persistent cycles and offers his solutions.

by E. Michael Poulos

Most technical indicators either smooth (filter) or normalize (on a scale to 0 to 100) the tradeable price in an attempt to indicate the trend direction or a trend change. The vast majority of technical indicators use fixed lookback lengths (for example, 14 days for the relative strength index [RSI], 14 and 28 days for moving averages and so forth) in the formulas in constructing an indicator. The popular justification for these fixed lengths is the supposed existence of *persistent cycles*. For example, there is supposedly a 28-day cycle that justifies the use of 14 days (a half cycle) in the RSI oscillator when applied to all commodity markets. Common sense should alert you to question the existence of any persistent, or continuously present, cycle.

A problem arises regarding the use of indicators that are using the same lookback length over all time periods and all markets; these indicators are subject to providing misleading information because the indicators can be out of step with the markets. *Is there evidence of persistent cycles?* To answer, first let us look at close to 1,000 days of closing price data in eight different futures markets and two stocks for some evidence of persistent cycles by using correlation analysis.

CORRELATION ANALYSIS

Correlation analysis is a statistical index that tells us the degree to which two variables are related. The index has a range of +1 to -1. An indication of strong correlation would have a reading close to +1, while a negative correlation indication would have a reading of -1. A lack of correlation would have a reading near zero. In this case, we will look at price changes of the same instrument as our two variables. We are measuring the extent that today's price change is related to a previous day's price

> In fact, if you look at data over a long period, no evidence exists of any persistent cycle. Our evidence that repetitive cycles don't exist, therefore, casts severe doubt on the validity of using a technical indicator with the same lookback length over all periods of time.

change (up to 40 days ago). This measurement is called *autocorrelation*. Each instrument's prices were converted to "first differences" (that is, today's close minus yesterday's) before computing the correlations. We are measuring the correlation of each instrument's one-day price change to a previous one-day price change one day back, two days back and up to 40 days. If there are five-day cycles in the data, for example, then a large correlation would appear at five days back. Bear in mind that a reading of zero indicates a complete lack of correlation, while the maximum possible value of 1.0 indicates perfect correlation; thus, results approaching 1.0 would be considered high correlation. Figure 1 presents the histograms of the eight futures contracts and the two stocks. The standard error of estimate for all of these tabulations is approximately 0.03.

A correlation is considered significant if it is greater than three times the standard error. This occurred only rarely — for example, Standard & Poor's 500 at lag 2 and crude oil at lag 3. In those cases the correlation, although considered statistically significant, is so small that it cannot be used for prediction. Data for eight futures contracts and two stocks (Digital Equipment Corp. [DEC] and Teledyne [TDY]) are included. In fact, if you look at data over a long period, no evidence exists of any

AUTOCORRELATION

Each histogram is the autocorrelation based on a range of one to 40 days of closing price data. The values do not range very far from zero, which indicates that there is low autocorrelation in the price data.

AUTOCORRELATION

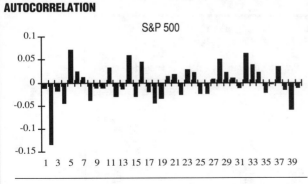

S&P 500

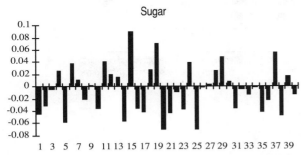

Sugar

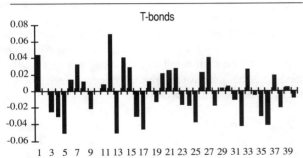

T-bonds

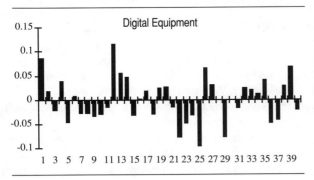

Digital Equipment

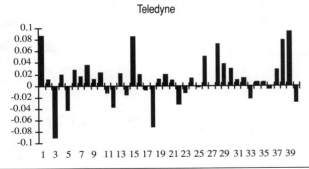

Teledyne

persistent cycle. Our evidence that repetitive cycles don't exist, therefore, casts severe doubt on the validity of using a technical indicator with the same lookback length over all periods of time. The lack of correlation denies the use of a consistent fixed lookback interval on the basis of a persistent short-term cycle (it should be noted that the validity of the use of seasonal cycles is confirmed by strong autocorrelation at 12 months' lag for some commodities).

DIFFERENT CYCLES, DIFFERENT TIMES

Some observers feel that different cycles can occur at different periods. My analysis cannot detect cycles that occur for a short time because the measurable effects would be washed out due to the data length; this research was oriented toward simply identifying persistent cycles.

If there is no basis for using a fixed length for an indicator, then the question arises of how to use variable lengths. I have described one such method in my previous STOCKS & COMMODITIES articles on the random walk index (RWI).

Mathematician W. Feller demonstrated that a random walk generated by tossing a coin (take one step forward if heads, one step backward if tails) would show a displacement from the starting point depending on the square root of the number of tosses. Thus, an "expected" random walk over n tosses would be the square root of n steps away from the start point.

To compare this concept to price movement, first define one step as one day's average price range (high minus low). We will call the number of tosses the number of lookback days. If markets were a consistent random walk, then we could generally expect that the price deviation of the market over n days would be the square root of n multiplied by the average daily range. Taking this concept one step further produces the idea that the ratio of today's price range to the range of prices over the last n days should be the square root of n. Look at Figure 2.

The channel length is the number of days' lookback. The average channel height is the highest price minus the lowest price in the lookback period. The ratio to one day column is the ratio of the average channel height for n days to that for one day. The averages were calculated over 1,121 days of data. As we indicated in an earlier article, "Of trends and random walks," these ratios follow but tend to consistently exceed the square root of the number of days. The channel height ratio to one day figures given show a consistent excess beyond the square root column, indicating the presence of trends and giving a hint on how to create a trend "yardstick." If no trends were present, the ratios would all fall exactly on the square roots.

DEFINING RANDOM WALK

The random walk index (RWI) is defined as the ratio of an actual price move to the expected random walk (see the "Random walk

FIGURE 2

PRICE AND TIME									
		YEN		**CRUDE OIL**		**SOYBEANS**		**S&P 500**	
Channel Length (days)	Square root of days	Avg Channel Height (pts.)	Ratio to 1 day	Avg Channel Height (pts.)	Ratio to 1 day	Avg Channel Height (pts.)	Ratio to 1 day	Avg Channel Height (pts.)	Ratio to 1 day
1	1	62.0	1.0	58.8	1.0	45.9	1.0	493.5	1.0
4	2	141.7	2.29	132.3	2.25	101.3	2.21	1056.5	2.14
9	3	224.9	3.63	204.8	3.48	157.3	3.43	1611	3.26
16	4	310.8	5.01	278.6	4.74	215.7	4.70	2156	4.37
25	5	403.3	6.50	358.0	6.09	274.7	5.98	2715	5.50
36	6	502.6	8.11	439.6	7.48	334.4	7.29	3299	6.68
49	7	605.2	9.76	526.4	8.95	395.4	8.61	3911	7.92

Note: All futures contracts 1/2/87-6/7/91 (1121 days)

The ratio to one day column is the ratio of the average range of the lookback lengths listed in the channel length (days) column to one day's average range (channel height). If the markets did not trend, then the ratio should approximate the square root of the days. Ratios greater than the square root are a measure of trendiness of the markets.

index spreadsheet" sidebar). If the move is larger than a random walk (and therefore a trend), its index would be larger than 1.0. To keep track of where today's high is relative to previous lows and where today's low is relative to previous highs, we need two indices:

$$\text{RWI of high} = (H-L_n)/(\text{Avg Rng})(\text{square root of } n)$$

$$\text{RWI of low} = (H_n-L)/(\text{Avg Rng})(\text{square root of } n)$$

where H_n and L_n are the high and low of n days ago and Avg Rng is the average daily true range† over n days preceding today. In day-to-day use, these indices are calculated over a range of lookback lengths to find the largest for use as today's indicator. Thus, we let the market determine the lookback interval, rather than use a fixed arbitrary one as so many current indicators do.

To research this concept further, I examined the distribution of lookback lengths for the largest RWI (how many times the largest RWI occur looking back two days, three days, four, five, six and so forth). The distribution curve obtained bends at a fairly sharp corner, enabling approximation by only two straight lines. Thus, the markets, to a very good approximation, can be thought of as displaying two distinct personalities! The curve's sharp corner shows that the dividing line between short- and long-term behavior lies between seven and eight days.

The RWI approach examines *all* the zigs and zags on your chart and finds which move, up to and including today, is most significant relative to a random drift. The length of time to look back is thus chosen in a rational way, depending on market price action. We let the market tell us what today's proper lookback interval is rather than use an arbitrary one, or one that depends on nonexistent repetitive cycles.

Mike Poulos, president of Traders' Insight Inc., researches personal computer trading aids. He can be reached at (516) 423-2413.

REFERENCES

Box, G.E.P., and G.M. Jenkins [1970]. *Time Series Analysis, Forecasting and Control,* Holden Day.

Feller, W. [1968]. *An Introduction to Probability Theory and Its Applications,* Volume 1, John Wiley & Sons.

Jenkins, G.M., and D.G. Watts [1968]. *Spectral Analysis and Its Applications,* Holden Day.

Poulos, E. Michael [1992]. "Futures according to trend tendency," STOCKS & COMMODITIES, January.

_____ [1991]. "Of trends and random walks," *Technical Analysis of* STOCKS & COMMODITIES, Volume 9: February.

Stewart, Ian [1989]. *Game, Set and Math,* Blackwell Publishing.

RANDOM WALK INDEX SPREADSHEET

Figure 1 is a bar chart with 10 days of simulated data; today's current high and low are plotted as if the market is still trading. The random walk index of the lows can measure if today's low price indicates that the market is trending or just in a random trading range. Figure 2 is an example of setting up an Excel spreadsheet for creating the random walk index for lows. This spreadsheet is set up with the most current day's data in the bottom row. Remember that the denominator for the index uses the average range of the lookback period multiplied by the square root of the number of the days of the lookback period. The average range uses the true range†, which is the greatest of two comparisons: today's high minus today's low or yesterday's close minus today's low. For cell F11 (true range), the formula is:

=MAX(B11-C11,D10-C11)

The true range is used because if there was a gap down today and today's range was very narrow, then the daily range would be appear to be small. The additional comparison of today's low to yesterday's close permits a clearer picture of the average daily range. For each day, the true range is calculated and listed in column F.

The formulas for the calculation of the RWI for the low is listed in the current row (row 11) for the current market prices. For cell G11, the formula is as follows:

=(B10-C11)/(AVERAGE(F9:F10)*SQRT(2))

This is the formula for comparing today's low to yesterday's

high divided by the product of the two days' average range multiplied by the square root of 2. For a three-day lookback, the formula is in cell H11 as follows:

=(B9-C11)/(AVERAGE(F8:F10)*SQRT(3))

Note that today's low is compared with the high two days ago and the average range is the last three days' average range. This process is carried out to a nine-day lookback (column N). Now, if any of the lookback lengths generate a value of greater than one, then the market is trending. Therefore, the largest value of the RWI formula for the series of lookback lengths from one through nine (cells G11 through N11) is listed in cell E11:

=MAX(G11:N11)

Because the largest RWI value is 1.25 — larger than 1 — we can conclude that today's low is an indication of a trend (Figure 1).

This series of formulas may be calculated for a lookback length as far as you want to go. Our example only goes to nine days. Poulos concludes that lookback lengths of longer than eight days are appropriate for longer-term indications of trends. For calculating the RWI of the highs, you would substitute today's high minus the low *n* days ago in the numerator of the formulas in cells G11 through N11.

—Thom Hartle, Editor

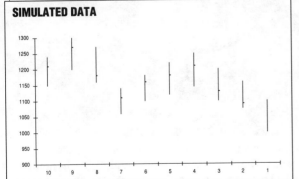

This chart of simulated data appears to be in a downtrend. Today's trading range (day 1) is plotted as if the market is still open.

SIDEBAR FIGURE 2
EXCEL SPREADSHEET FOR THE RANDOM WALK INDEX

	A	B	C	D	E	F	G	H	I	J	K	L	M	N
1	Day	High	Low	Close	RWI	TR	2	3	4	5	6	7	8	9
2	10	1240	1150	1210		90								
3	9	1300	1200	1270		100								
4	8	1270	1160	1180		110								
5	7	1140	1060	1110		120								
6	6	1180	1100	1160		80								
7	5	1220	1120	1180		100								
8	4	1250	1145	1210		105								
9	3	1200	1100	1130		110								
10	2	1160	1075	1090		85								
11	1	1100	1000		1.25	100	1.16	1.15	1.25	1.02	0.73	0.52	0.94	1.00

The calculation of the random walk index for lookback ranges of one through nine days (column G through N) is calculated in row 11. The largest value of the RWI is returned in cell E11.

†*See Traders' Glossary for definition*

Gann Weekly Swing Chart

Newsletter publisher Jerry Favors, no stranger to STOCKS & COMMODITIES, here presents another Gann method, this time the weekly swing chart as a timing tool with which to track individual stocks.

by Jerry Favors

One of the methods that W.D. Gann used to determine and trade the main trend of stocks and commodities was what are commonly referred to as swing charts. These swing charts cover varying degrees of time spans ranging from hourly charts to yearly charts. Each of the Gann swing charts turns up or down based on specific rules. The longer the time span covered by any swing chart, the stronger and more important are the signals given to me. For instance, a buy or sell signal from a weekly swing chart would be stronger and more important than a buy or sell signal from a daily swing chart but not as strong or as important as the signals from a monthly swing chart.

While many of Gann's other techniques and methods of trading have been explained in detail by others, one area that has not been examined or explained in depth is the use and interpretation of these swing charts. I utilize more than 20 different Gann swing charts on a daily basis, each turning up and down on differing sets of rules. I am often asked, "If you had to use only one swing chart in your day-to-day trading, which would you use?" This is always a difficult question to answer, because it has been my experience that each of the various swing charts tells you something different about the stock or index in question. The overall picture does not become clear until every signal from all the various charts has been gathered and summed. To skip even one of these swing charts is to risk missing or overlooking a potentially important piece of the puzzle. However, when I can choose only one chart, the Gann weekly swing chart is the one.

WEEKLY SWING CHART DETAILS

The weekly swing chart will turn up from any extreme low price

PETER STERN

when the stock in question rises above the highest price seen in the prior week. The chart will then continue higher to the highest price reached before the stock falls below the lowest price seen in any prior week, which then turns the chart down. Figure 1 is a weekly chart of House of Fabrics (HF) from April 30, 1991, to May 15, 1992. HF reached a high of 41-1/2 on October 30, 1991. Now walk through the process of constructing the weekly chart from that point. Prior to the 41-1/2 top on October 30, 1991, the weekly chart had pointed up from the 36-1/2 low on October 28, 1991. Here is the high, low and closing price for HF for the week of October 28, 1991, to November 15, 1991:

FIGURE 1

HOUSE OF FABRICS , APRIL 30, 1991, TO MAY 15, 1992

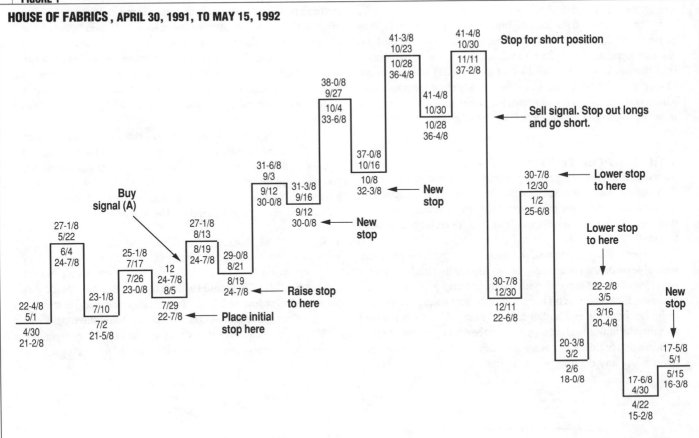

The weekly swing chart is a trend-following method designed to position the trader with the main trend.

Day	Date	High	Low	Close
Monday	10/28/91	38-3/4	36-1/2	38-3/4
Tuesday	10/29/91	39-3/8	38-1/2	39
Wednesday	10/30/91	41-1/2	39	40-5/8
Thursday	10/31/91	40-3/8	40	40-1/4
Friday	11/01/91	40-1/4	40	40-1/4
Monday	11/04/91	40	39-1/2	39-7/8
Tuesday	11/05/91	40	39-1/2	39-3/4
Wednesday	11/06/91	40	39-1/4	39-3/4
Thursday	11/07/91	40-1/8	39-1/2	39-1/2
Friday	11/08/91	39-1/2	39	39-1/8
Monday	11/11/91	38-7/8	37-1/4	37-5/8
Tuesday	11/12/91	38	37-1/2	38
Wednesday	11/13/91	39-1/2	37-3/4	39-1/2
Thursday	11/14/91	39-7/8	39-1/2	39-1/2
Friday	11/15/91	39-5/8	36-1/2	36-1/2

It is important to remember that the weekly chart will turn down from any high when the stock falls below the lowest price seen in any prior week. Beginning the week of November 4, any decline below the lowest price seen the week of October 28, 1991, would turn the chart down. The lowest price seen that week was 36-1/2, seen on October 28. Any decline below that level after November 1 would then turn the weekly chart down. The lowest price seen the week of November 4 to November 8 was 39-1/8, so the weekly chart did not turn down that week.

Beginning the next week, November 11 to November 15, the weekly swing chart would then turn down on any decline below the lowest price seen in the prior week of November 4 to November 8, or 39. HF fell below 39 on November 11, and the weekly chart turned down from that point. Once the chart turns down, draw a horizontal line representing the prior high and place that price high of 41-1/2 just above the bar along with the date of the high, October 30, 1991. Once the chart turns down it continues to point down to the lowest price reached before the stock rallies above the high of any prior week. For instance, after the chart turned down on November 11, HF would have had to exceed the highest price seen in a prior week (November 4 to November 8) of 40-1/8 to turn the weekly chart back up. Keep in mind this would have to occur the same week (November 11 to November 15) for the weekly chart to turn up on a move above 40-1/8. Note the highest price reached the week of November 11 to November 15 was 39-7/8, seen on Thursday, November 14. Therefore, the weekly chart did not turn up that week. The next week, or November 18 to November 22, HF would have to exceed the high of the prior week (39-7/8 seen on November 14) to turn the weekly chart back up.

In fact, HF failed to exceed the high of a prior week all the way down to the 22-3/4 low of December 11. The weekly chart did not turn up until December 30 when 29-1/4 (the highest price seen the week of December 23 to December 27) was exceeded. Once the stock reaches a low and the weekly chart turns up, draw a horizontal line across where that low would be and place under it the low price and the date that it was reached. We then turn our line back up.

UTILIZING THE TECHNIQUE

This describes the basic rules governing how the weekly chart turns up or down. Remember that it is always the highest or lowest price seen in the prior week that turns the weekly chart's direction. Now how do we actually utilize this technique in stock trading?

The overriding concern of the trader is the main trend of any tradeable he or she is trading. The weekly swing chart's purpose is to identify and keep you with the main trend, whether it is up or down. If the main trend is up, the stock will trace out a pattern of higher bottoms and higher tops, in that order. Keep in mind an uptrend is not higher tops and higher bottoms, but higher bottoms and higher tops, which are not synonymous. If the main trend is up, any decline below a prior swing chart bottom is a

signal of lower prices (at least short term) and a potential change in trend from up to down. If the main trend is down, the swing chart will trace out a pattern of lower tops and lower bottoms and in that order. When the trend is down, any rally above a prior swing chart high is a signal of higher prices, at least short term, and a potential change in trend. If the main trend is up, showing higher bottoms and higher tops, you will remain long in the stock in question and keep raising your stop to each higher swing-chart bottom.

The first time the stock falls below a prior swing chart bottom, you will sell long positions and go short, with a stop then placed just above the prior swing chart top. If the trend continues down, you will keep lowering your stop to just above each successively lower top. Now let's just walk through an example of what we mean by studying each signal on HF on Figure 1.

THE FIRST SIGNAL

The first signal to take action on this chart was at point A, when the prior swing high of 25-1/8 on July 17 was exceeded on August 6, 1991. We would then go long with a stop place just below the prior low of 22-7/8. If we had purchased HF the day the signal was given, the highest price we could have paid was 25-1/4, which was the high for the day. After the buy signal on August 6, HF continued up to a high of 27-1/8 on August 13, 1991.

GOOD OLD WHATSHISNAME

HF then pulled back to a low of 24-7/8 on August 19. The weekly chart actually turned down on August 19, when HF fell below the prior week's low of 25-3/4. Note that the 24-7/8 low of August 19 was above our prior stop of 22-3/4, so we remained long. After the August 19th low of 24-7/8, the weekly chart turned back up on August 21 when the prior week's high of 27-1/8 was exceeded. Since our rule is to always place our stop for long positions just under each prior weekly chart swing bottom, we will now raise our stop from 22-3/4 to 24-3/4 (just under the August 19th low). In this same manner, we will keep raising our stop to each higher bottom as indicated. Note that the chart would have put you long near 25-1/4 and would have kept you long all the way to the 41-1/2 high on October 30, 1991. You would then have been stopped out of your long positions on the break of the prior low at 36-1/2, which occurred on November 19, 1991. Since the rules state to reverse position anytime we are stopped out, we would not only sell long positions when HF fell below 36-1/2 but would also now go short with our stop just above the prior high of 41-1/2. We would keep lowering our stop to each lower top as indicated on Figure 1.

If we review our trades now from August 5, 1991, to May 15, 1992, we find that we would have gone long near 25-1/4 (on August 6) and stopped out near 36-1/2 on November 19, 1991. Even if we assume the worst possible execution price on November 19 we would still have sold long positions at 34-3/4. Therefore, we would have a worst-case gain near 9-3/8 point minus commissions. We would then go short on November 19 on the break at 36-1/2. Once again, if we assume a worst-case fill, we should have been short near 34-7/8 on November 191. As of this writing on May 15, 1992, so far HF has reached a low of 15-1/4 on April 22. That worst-case execution of 34-7/8 for our short sale would have shown a paper profit of 19-5/8 or 56% (not including commissions) at the 15-1/4 low. When using this technique, our goal is not just to go long or short when a signal is given and then just wait to be stopped out; rather, our goal is always to attempt to buy as near the low as possible and sell near the high. We will utilize other techniques to attempt to pinpoint the most probable area for an important top or bottom. The Gann charts are there to protect you if you are wrong. In each of the above cases, we would on a worst-case basis have been stopped out at nice profits.

ENCOURAGEMENT AND SUGGESTIONS

Those who would like to use the Gann weekly swing chart should research its behavior and signals on each of your stocks for at least one year (and preferably longer), as each stock will show its own special nuances. There are also times when every stock enters narrow trading ranges, and these will produce whipsaws for brief periods of time. Inevitably, the stock will snap back in line and provide excellent buy or sell signals with reasonably tight stops.

Jerry Favors publishes "The Jerry Favors Analysis" newsletter, 7238 Durness Drive, Worthington, OH 43235, (614) 848-8177.

REFERENCES

Favors, Jerry [1992]. "The Gann quarterly chart," STOCKS & COMMODITIES, January.

Gann, W.D. [1942]. *How to Make Profits in Commodities*, Lambert-Gann Publishing Co.

_____ [1927]. *Tunnel Through the Air, or Looking Back From 1940*, Lambert-Gann Press.

Gartley, H.M. [1963]. *Profits in the Stock Market*, Lambert-Gann Publishing Co.

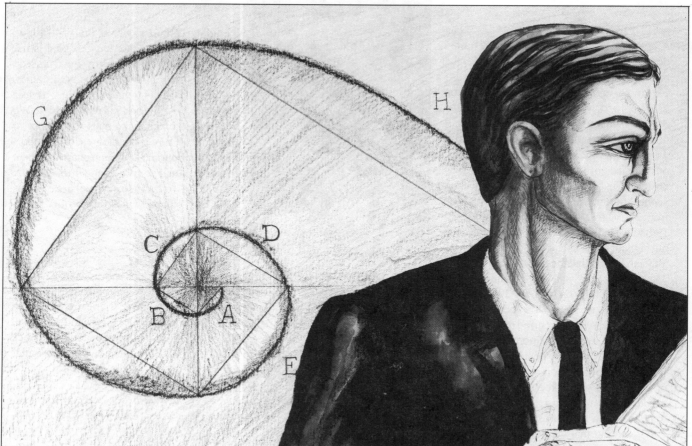

Forecasting Market Turns Using Static And Dynamic Cycles

Cycles are nothing new, either in technical analysis or trading and certainly not in nature. Nor are static and dynamic cycles anything new: anyone who's ever paid income taxes can tell you about static cycle dates — every April 15, come rain or shine or bankruptcy —and dynamic cycles, of course, are best characterized by the mention of Fibonacci ratios. Who hasn't heard of Fibonacci ratios by now, but to actually use them in predicting market turns? Here, software developers Brad Swancoat and Ed Kasanjian give novice and veteran technicians alike a few things to ponder over.

by Brad Swancoat and Ed Kasanjian

C ycles have long been used by technicians to forecast turns in the markets. However, the student of cycle analysis can become frustrated by the intermittent nature of regular rhythmic time cycles. The understanding and use of dynamic cycles will allow the technician to accurately forecast trend changes weeks, if not months, in advance.

Most of us are familiar with static cycles. Static cycles are characterized by a set interval between events (such as birthdays, full moons, income tax due dates). Dynamic cycles are just as predictable, but they do not have a fixed interval between events. Dynamic cycles are distinguished by a constant proportion. One such popular dynamic is the Fibonacci cycle. The numerical series (1, 1, 2, 3, 5, 8, 13, 21, 34, 55 ...) obviously is not made up

FIGURE 1

STATIC CYCLES VS. DYNAMIC CYCLES

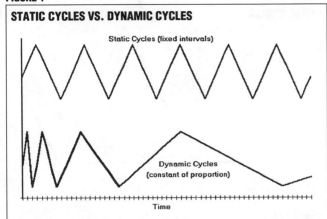

Static cycles will have fixed intervals between peaks, while dynamic cycles will have a constant proportion between peaks.

FIGURE 2

GOLDEN RATIO EXPRESSED AS A LOGARITHMIC SPIRAL

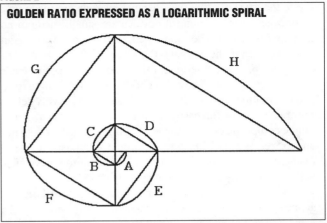

The logarithmic spiral is an example of an expanding form based on a constant of proportion. Each section is a 1.618 ratio to the previous section.

FIGURE 3

DYNAMIC RECTANGLES

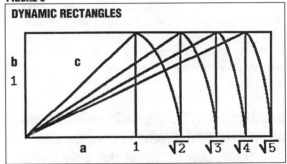

Dynamic rectangle ratios are based on the diagonal of the rectangle. For example, the diagonal of the 1 x 1 rectangle is used as the base for the next rectangle.

of equal intervals, but the proportion (ratio) between each number is a constant 1.618. The ratio of 1.618 is known as the "golden ratio" and is represented by the Greek letter phi (Φ). Figure 1 illustrates the two types of cycles.

The golden ratio can also be expressed as a logarithmic spiral. The relation between each section can be stated arithmetically as a ratio, because lines in continued proportion form a geometric progression. For example, in Figure 2,

A to B = Φ, B to C = Φ, C to D = Φ, D to E = Φ and so on.

Each section increases by proportions of 1.618. A geometric progression is nothing more than a constant of proportion. The sections of the Φ spiral can also be numerically expressed as follows:

A = Φ^1, B = Φ^2, C = Φ^3, D = Φ^4, and so on.

Each number in the progression is Φ raised to a successively higher exponent. The golden spiral, or Φ ratio, forms many shapes in nature, from snail shells to the cochlea of the inner ear to the mighty spiral galaxies of our universe.

These examples, however, are simplistic. Most occurrences of spiral patterns in nature and the universe contain a multitude of logarithmic spirals. Researchers and observers have identified the most common spirals (ratios) prevalent in nature *and* the financial markets. Figure 3 demonstrates the mathematical principle of multiple logarithmic ratios that constitute the architectural plan of nature.

DYNAMIC RECTANGLES

Here, the square and its diagonal form a series of root rectangles and ratios that are the primary building blocks for nature's designs. In Figure 3, we divide the 1 x 1 square by its diagonal, the length of which is the $\sqrt{2}$ because $a^2 + b^2 = c^2$ or $1^2 + 1^2 = 2$, to form the base for the next rectangle in the series. The 1 x $\sqrt{2}$ rectangle is divided by its diagonal, $\sqrt{3}$, and the process contin-

FIGURE 4

DYNAMIC PROGRESSION OF RATIOS IN FINANCIAL MARKETS

ϕ	$\sqrt{2}$	$\sqrt{3}$	$\sqrt{5}$
0.618	0.707 = $(\sqrt{2})^{-1}$	0.577 = $(\sqrt{3})^{-1}$	0.447 = $(\sqrt{5})^{-1}$
1.618	1.414 = $\sqrt{2}$	1.732 = $\sqrt{3}$	2.236 = $\sqrt{5}$
2.618	2.000 = $(\sqrt{2})^2$	3.000 = $(\sqrt{3})^2$	5.000 = $(\sqrt{5})^2$
4.236	2.828 = $(\sqrt{2})^3$	5.196 = $(\sqrt{3})^3$	11.180 = $(\sqrt{5})^3$

ues through $\sqrt{5}$. These roots and their ratios are the proportions found to be the dynamic cycles present in the financial markets. Thus, in addition to the static (fixed-interval) cycles, the markets are made up of dynamic cycles as well. The dynamic cycles include the Φ ratio (1.618) and the root ratios ($\sqrt{2}$, $\sqrt{3}$ and $\sqrt{5}$). Figure 4 lists the progression of ratios for the dynamic cycles. Figure 5 lists the progression of static ratios.

As you move down each column of Figure 4, the values increase by the ratio of Φ and the roots (that is, 0.618, 1.414, 1.732, 2.236).

FIGURE 5

STATIC RATIOS

0.250 = 1/4
0.333 = 1/3
0.500 = 1/2
0.667 = 2/3
0.750 = 3/4
1.000 = 1/1
1.250 = 1-1/4
1.333 = 1-1/3

Static ratios are whole numbers plus 1/4s and 1/3s or 1/4, 1/3, 1/2, 2/3, 3/4.

BASIC CYCLE THEORY

Cycle theory states that the financial markets are made up of composite cycles. Composite cycles are small, medium and large cycles, which, when combined, shape the price actions and reactions seen in the markets (Figure 6).

Figures 6, 7 and 8 represent three possible types of cycles found in the markets. They differ both in the cycle length (time) and in amplitude (price). Each individual cycle is easily defined for price and time forecasts. However, the market is a summation or composite of many cycles varying in length of both time and price. We can illustrate a simple composite cycle by mathematically combining each one of these three cycles together, producing a summation cycle (Figure 9).

When you consider the number of cycles present in the market at once, you can see why an understanding of dynamic cycles is necessary to cycle analysis. In reality, identifying trend changes, especially during the accumulation†, distribution† or consolidation† phase, is not always as clear cut as it is in theory. The price highs or lows do not always correspond with the cycle high or low. Noise† or incidental price spikes often cloud the technician's ability to properly quantify time and price cycles. For example, where is the first cycle low in Figure 9? Is it pivot point D or point E? Could it possibly even be point F? Working with dynamic ratios can help identify cycle highs and lows and find the important pivot points.

> **By calculating future data points from both static and dynamic cycles, the technician can forecast not only trend changes but also price swings, market retracements, extensions and support and resistance levels.**

MODEL OF A TYPICAL MARKET SECTION

Figure 10 represents a market section containing trend changes. The section is made up of both actions and reactions.

To project a trend change within a market segment using dynamic ratios, first identify the significant changes in trend (pivot points), going back at least 100 data points (whether hours, days, weeks or months).

Then calculate the time between each combination of pivot points. For example, in Figure 10, you would calculate the distance from:

A to B; A to C; A to D; A to E; A to F;
B to C; B to D; B to E; B to F;
C to D; C to E; C to F;
D to E; D to F;
E to F;

Next, multiply each time interval by the ratios in the dynamic spiral (that is, Φ, √2, √3, √5) and add the result to the end of that time interval. Mark where the result lands on the time line in the future. You must also multiply each time interval by the static ratios in Figure 5 and mark the results on the time line.

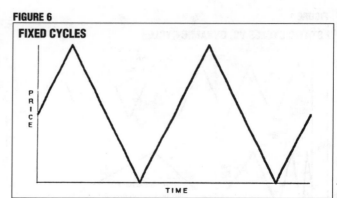

FIGURE 6

FIXED CYCLES

All three fixed cycles vary in cycle length and amplitude.

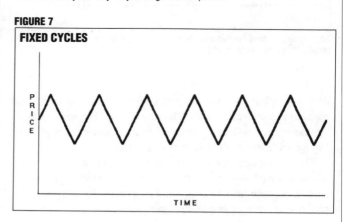

FIGURE 7

FIXED CYCLES

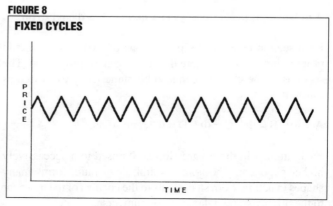

FIGURE 8

FIXED CYCLES

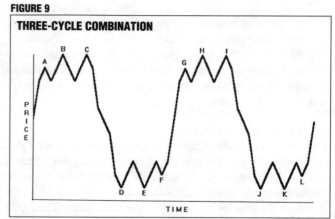

FIGURE 9

THREE-CYCLE COMBINATION

Combining all three cycles will produce this image.

As you begin to mark the time line with your projections, you will begin to notice certain periods where the results will cluster. These are the periods that are harmonically related to the previous trend changes and where future trend changes can be expected to occur. The higher the concentration of projected data points, the more confidence you can have in the forecasted trend change. It is also important to note the spirals from which the clustered projections originated. Our research has shown that multispiral clusters are more powerful. Multispiral clusters are clusters derived from different spirals, where some data points in the cluster are in proportion to previous pivot points by the Φ spiral, some by the √2 ratio, some by the static ratios and so on. Although the calculations are cumbersome, we have found after working with this method for years that the accuracy of the technique justifies the work.

JUNE 1992 TREASURY BOND CHART

Now look at the June 1992 Treasury bond chart (Figure 11) to see how trend changes occur at multispiral and static clusters of ratios from previous pivot points using dynamic ratios. For the sake of brevity, we have left out the √3 and √5 calculations.

Trend change E =

A to C x	1.414	(√2)
A to B x	4.236	(Φ)
C to D x	2.000	(static)
B to C x	2.618	(Φ)

Trend change F =

D to E x	0.707	(√2)
B to D x	1.618	(Φ)
A to C x	2.000	(static)

Trend change G =

B to E x	1.000	(static)
C to F x	0.618	(Φ)
B to F x	0.500	(static)
E to F x	2.000	(static)
D to E x	2.000	(static)

Trend change H =

F to G x	0.707	(√2)
C to E x	2.000	(static)
B to E x	1.414	(√2)
A to F x	0.707	(√2)
A to D x	2.500	(static)

Trend change I =

B to D x	4.236	(Φ)
A to E x	1.414	(√2)
B to G x	0.381	(Φ)
G to H x	0.707	(√2)

IN SUMMING UP

By calculating future data points from both static and dynamic cycles, the technician can forecast not only trend changes but also price swings, market retracements, extensions and support

FIGURE 10

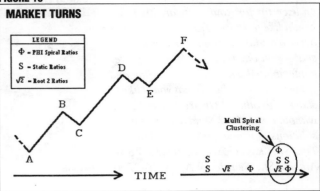

MARKET TURNS

LEGEND
Φ = PHI Spiral Ratios
S = Static Ratios
√2 = Root 2 Ratios

Look for important market turns to occur near time periods during which the ratios cluster.

FIGURE 11

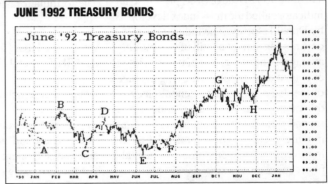

JUNE 1992 TREASURY BONDS

Prices may change direction at time periods that coincide with clusters of dynamic and static ratios.

and resistance levels. Although this explanation of the process has been somewhat simplified, the concept should allow the technician to perform further research into this method of cycle analysis.

Ed Kasanjian (Kasanjian Research, P.O. Box 4608, Blue Jay, CA 92317, 714-337-0816) and Brad Swancoat develop software and provide research to individuals and institutions. They have been trading and developing software for a combined total of 25 years. The ideas presented have been incorporated into the Nature's Pulse software.

REFERENCES

Hambidge, Jay [1920]. *Dynamic Symmetry*, Yale University Press, New York.

Lawlor, Robert [1982]. *Sacred Geometry*, Crossroads Publishing Co.

Gann, W.D. [1976]. *How to Make Money in Commodities*, Lambert-Gann Publishing.

Nature's Pulse. Kasanjian Research, PO Box 4608, Blue Jay, CA 92317, (714) 337-0816.

TRADERS' TIPS

METASTOCK PROFESSIONAL 3.0
Mass Index

The June 1992 issue of S&C presented an indicator called the mass index developed by Donald Dorsey. The indicator is a 25-day moving sum of a ratio of two moving averages. The numerator of the ratio is the exponentially smoothed moving average of the daily ranges. The denominator of the ratio is the numerator smoothed a second time using the same exponential moving average. The exponential moving averages use a smoothing factor (alpha) equivalent to a nine-day simple moving average. The formula is :

$$\text{Mass Index} = \sum_{n=1}^{25} \frac{R_n}{L_n}$$

where:
$R_n = 0.8(R_{n-1}) + 0.2(\text{Range})$
$L_n = 0.8(L_{n-1}) + 0.2(R_n)$
Range = Today's high - low
R_{n-1} = Yesterday's R_n
L_{n-1} = Yesterday's L_n

TEXACO WITH MASS INDEX

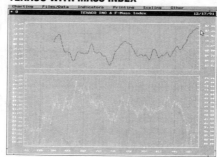

FIGURE 1. *The mass index reached 27 in late 1991.*

The formula for MetaStock Professional is :

sum(mov((HIGH-LOW),9,E)/mov(mov((HIGH-LOW),9,E),9,E),25)

Dorsey recommended that when the mass index increased to 27 and then declined to below 26.5, a trend reversal was indicated. The trend was identified by two nine-day exponential moving averages. The first moving average was of the closing price, while the second moving average smoothed the first moving average. The formula for MetaStock Professional for a nine-day exponential moving average is:

mov(CLOSE,9,E)

The second moving average is:

mov(mov(CLOSE,9,E),9,E)

When the mass index signals a reversal of trend (Figure 1), you would buy the market if the first moving average has a lower value than the second moving average. A sell is indicated if the first moving average has a higher value than the second moving average.

Damping index

The July 1992 issue of S&C presented an indicator called the damping index, developed by Curtis McKallip Jr. This indicator identifies those areas where the highs and lows are moving closer together. McKallip suggests that trends can begin after damping behavior has occurred.

The formula for the damping index is shown in Equation 1 below.

The formula for MetaStock Professional is presented in two different versions in Equations 2 and 3 below (they both produce the same values).

The index typically varies from 0.5 to 2 to three (Figure 2). Values less than 1 are a strong indication of valid damping behavior. As with most indicators, the parameters can be varied for different markets.

—Allan McNichol
Equis International

BOEING WITH DAMPING INDEX

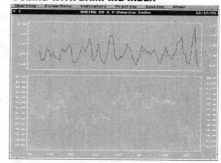

FIGURE 2 . *Minor trend reversals were accompanied by low damping index values.*

(1)

$$\frac{\text{Average high of bar}_{-1} \text{ to bar}_{-5} - \text{average low of bar}_{-1} \text{ to bar}_{-5}}{\text{Average high of bar}_{-6} \text{ to bar}_{-10} - \text{average low of bar}_{-6} \text{ to bar}_{-10}}$$

(2) ref(mov((HIGH-LOW),5,S),-1)/ref(mov((HIGH-LOW),5,S),-6)

The damping index 1 formula is a shortcut version of the formula shown in Equation 3 below.

(3) (ref(mov(HIGH,5,S),-1)-ref(mov(LOW,5,S),-1))/(ref(mov(HIGH,5,S),-6) -ref(mov(LOW,5,S),-6)

This damping index formula for MetaStock Professional 3.0 is simply a longer version of the formula in Equation 2 to make the math easier to follow.

Breaking Out Of The Trading Range

by John Sweeney

Some blessed day, after being mired in a trading range for two years, your market is going to finally go into a trend. You must be there when it does, not trading something else or, worse, ignoring it from the golf course. Ideally, you've been trading the range back and forth trying to avoid losing money and possibly even making a little. You've been selling the tops and buying the bottoms as best you can, waiting for a breakout. How can you tell if it's happened?

Graphically, as in Figure 1, you are waiting for a trade that hits your maximum adverse excursion (MAE) stop. To refresh your memory, MAE is the amount that winning trades go against you. Beyond that point, your expectation is that the trading range trade will be a loser. If it is, then mightn't it be a winner if reversed? When is a breakout far enough from the trading range to be legitimate? Answer: when experience shows that it's moved far enough to become a loser as a trading range trade.

Last month, when analyzing trades back into the range, I defined a simple test for nontrending behavior in Treasury bonds plus some simple rules for entry and exit. I also measured how far wrong these trades went and arrived at the conclusion that, for this tradeable — Treasury bond futures — and this trading rule,

$1,500 would have to be risked before reversing. This turned out to work fairly well in recent bond trading, but now I need to test a variety of data to see what happens when that $1,500 loss is taken and a reversing trade, with any luck into a trend, is entered.

MAXIMUM FAVORABLE EXCURSION

Before that can be done, a rationale must be constructed for exiting the reversing trade into the trend, assuming, as is likely, that your underlying trend trading system hasn't picked up the trend you're now in or would have entered it at a different level.

I can't depend on my underlying system to give me an exit — it might not even be in on this trend or mini-trend or whatever it is. What rationale could I use? How about: "Enough is enough"?

Many moons before I started trading, the Gotthelfs explored the idea of measuring the size of the advances from entry to tell when the win was likely to have run its course. Indeed, they even measured the likelihood of further winnings given a certain amount of winnings already, a more sophisticated measure than I'm about to use but one that you might keep in your idea file.

I propose that you measure how far your breakout trades go before taking a loss and label that the maximum favorable excursion. Naturally, you won't neglect to measure the adverse

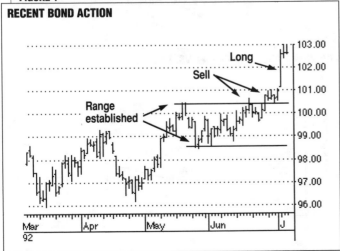

FIGURE 1

RECENT BOND ACTION

Recent bond action was a good example of exploiting a trading range and reversing the breakout.

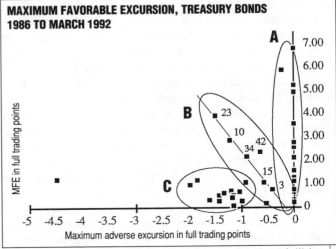

FIGURE 2

MAXIMUM FAVORABLE EXCURSION, TREASURY BONDS 1986 TO MARCH 1992

Breakout trades show three distinct behaviors: (1) they never go bad as at A, (2) they go bad as much as 1.5 points (B), or (3) they have a little favorable action but then go seriously wrong (C). Numbered trades match those of Figure 7.

excursion at the same time.

If I do this for December Treasury bonds for all of 1986 through March 1992 (43 trades) and plot the results, you get Figure 2. First, note that many of the breakout trades never go bad at all! Twenty of the 43 trades fell into this category. With

> **The breakout trades like other trades in this campaign, are to be a separately analyzed, separately capitalized trade. As a caution, relatively few trades are being found, even in six years of data.**

this consistent experience over six years, setting a very close stop at, say, 12 to 16 ticks (or even less) would capture the bulk of the big winners and cut out all the horrendous losers.

Behavioral group is tougher to deal with. Adverse excursion reaches as high as 1.5 points or $1,500 and, on the basis of this information, can't be distinguished from the adverse excursion of group C, which are flat losers.

Figure 3 brings our major indicators together. Here we can see that the most favorable moves (the maximum *favorable* excursion) generally occur with no adverse excursion at all. They are genuine breakouts: prices jump out of the trading range, move away from the trading range and the reversal point and stay away from them.

Moving down the MAE axis, I'd say the size of the adverse moves is not big, mostly below two points but that's huge to some folks. If you're willing to endure a move of 0.5 (16 ticks) against you, you can pick up some eventual winners, but I'd bet that if people had a chance to set a stop at the point of entry for a trade with no possibility of loss trade, they'd do it (transaction costs excepted).

The question remains: At which point do we close the trade, given that we've had no adverse movement at all, and that it's been in the black since entry?

As a first cut, look at the behavior of general Treasury bond maximum favorable excursion in Figure 4. Unsurprisingly, it advances steadily with time in the trade. If we delete all the Group C trades from Figure 2, the pattern (Figure 5) still holds: favorable excursion advances with time, as I'd expect from a genuine breakout into trending mode. Even when we delete the Group B trades (the ones where we're tempted to put up with adverse excursion of as much as 1.5 points to get an eventual win), Figure 6 shows that the trades with no adverse movement at all (the group A trades) advance regularly with time. The only question is when to take profits.

What about the group B trades, the ones that might be lucrative if we could dodge the drawdowns? Figure 7, whose trade numbers are key to those in Figure 2, shows that the Group B trades just don't advance that much and also don't advance in a timely manner. In other words, they aren't worth the trouble of going after them.

FIGURE 3

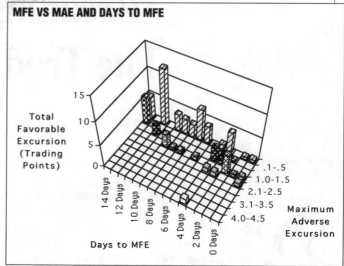

MFE VS MAE AND DAYS TO MFE

Here, favorable excursion — the price action moving our way — is clearly concentrated in trades with no adverse excursion at all, though there is one $5,000 winner that took 14 days and $500 adverse movement to mature.

FIGURE 4

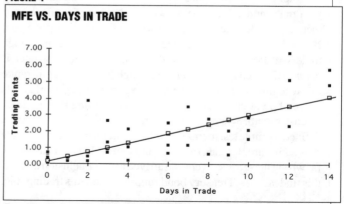

MFE VS. DAYS IN TRADE

Examining the favorable movement more closely, it's generally a consistent advance after breakout, which we'd expect of a good trend trade.

FIGURE 5

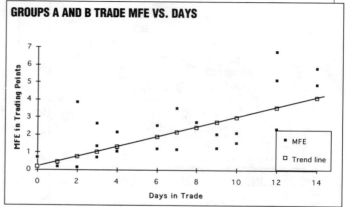

GROUPS A AND B TRADE MFE VS. DAYS

Dropping the Group C trades from Figure 2 shows that consistent advance is characteristic of the remaining trades. But are A and B trades alike?

FIGURE 6

GROUP A TRADE MFE VS. DAYS

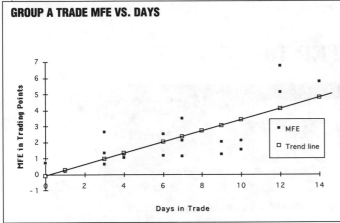

Group A trades do advance consistently, reinforcing the notion that they are true trend trades, and trades with few if any losses, except for commissions and slippage.

FIGURE 7

GROUP B TRADE MFE VS. DAYS

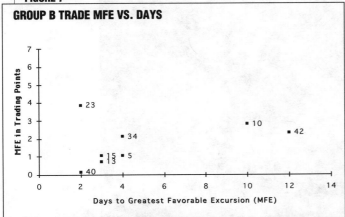

Group B trades are widely scattered and don't contain any big winners. Conclusion: they aren't worth the trouble of pursuit. Go with the no-loss Group A trades.

ARE WE RICH YET?

This roundabout exploration of the breakout trades may be diverting and graphically stunning, but did money appear at the end of it all? Well, how could we lose with a stop at our entry point, commissions and slippage aside? Totaling it all up, I get nearly $44,000 off these 22 trades. If I arbitrarily set the cutoff at $1,000 after three days, it's only $19,800, with no losses. Over six years that's not an astounding return on margin, but it is an extremely safe, somewhat profitable way to play this particular breakout.

OVERALL

The breakout trades, like other trades in this campaign, are to be a separately analyzed, separately capitalized trade. As a caution, relatively few trades are being found, even in six years of data. With just 40-odd trades, caution in generalizing about the behavior of the market is a good idea.

That aside, it turns out that a breakout strategy is viable for this particular trading range identification. The only problem is a gap past our stop so that entry at the MAE reversal point isn't possible. This happened once during this test period. It's unusual to find a breakout strategy — or any strategy — that allows you to set stops for absolutely no losses, but in this peculiar case, the evidence is there. More often, you'll have a loss point greater than zero for your breakout trade as for all the other trades demonstrated in this campaign. As a practical matter, you'd probably set your stop a couple of ticks below your entry.

You might think that after demonstrating the trending system, piling on the trending system, reversing the trending system, demonstrating the accompanying trading range system and reversing it, there'd be little left in defining a robust trading system. While we have, in 10 Settlement columns, covered the basics from dinking to elaboration, there are always the sophisticated points to any enterprise. I'll deal with those next.

John Sweeney is the Technical Editor for STOCKS & COMMODITIES.

CHAPTER 10

THE TRADERS' MAGAZINE

OCTOBER 1992

10-YEAR ANNIVERSARY

TECHNICAL ANALYSIS OF STOCKS & COMMODITIES

CHRIS ROBERTSON

Stocks Yield To Bonds

A stock's price may be considered a mechanism to adjust its dividend yield. In the short run, the dollar amount of the dividend is fixed, and so stock prices change to accommodate changes in bond yields. Lags occur because it takes time to convince participants that bond yields have changed meaningfully. Here's an example of quantitative intermarket analysis, analyzing the relationship of bond yields to stock dividends.

The general relationship between stocks and bonds is widely recognized. Stock dividends and interest rates play an important role in any fundamental analysis of stock valuations. An excellent intuitive explanation of the link between stocks and bonds was provided by John J. Murphy in the June 1992 issue of STOCKS & COMMODITIES, in which he noted that stock

by Tushar S. Chande

FIGURE 1

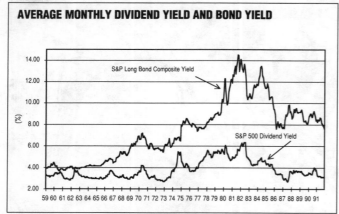

Stocks and bond yields typically move in the same direction, with the bond yields leading the way.

FIGURE 2

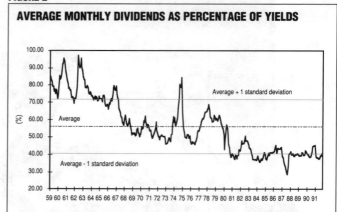

The ratio of stock dividends to bond yields has recently been trading in the 30-50% range.

and bond prices generally move in the same direction. At important turning points, however, bond prices usually turn ahead of stock prices.

Prices are inversely related to yield because the dollar amount of the interest paid on a bond is fixed. As prices increase, bond yields decrease. In the short run (many months or perhaps a few years), the dollar amount of the stock dividend is fixed because

> **A simple way to view the stocks-bonds relationship is to look at the ratio of stock dividends to bond yields.**

corporate managements typically change their dividend policy only once a year. Hence, price changes are needed to adjust a stock's dividend yield. In the long run, the dividend can be changed (cautiously increased or reluctantly decreased), thereby adjusting relative yield relationships without requiring large price changes.

In effect, the market is trying to maintain a ratio of stock dividends to bond yields that reflects expectations of relative risk. If stocks are perceived as being riskier than bonds, then investors demand a relatively higher stock dividend yield, lowering stock prices. Even if the perception of stock returns remains unchanged, a change in the perception of bond riskiness may increase bond yields. The adjustment of stock yields may occur quickly or slowly and proportionately or disproportionately to changes in bond yields. Since stock traders mostly trade stocks and bond traders mostly trade bonds, the two markets may go their own separate ways when observed on a daily basis. A rough parity is eventually re-established, often with dramatic price changes.

A simple way to view the stocks-bonds relationship is to look at the ratio of stock dividends to bond yields. In financial theory, the company is expected to exist forever — hence, given the "infinite" time horizon, it makes sense to compare stock dividends to the yield of bonds with maturities greater than 10 years. You could use the yield of the 30-year U.S. Treasury bonds or a

FIGURE 3

12-MONTH RATE OF CHANGE OF AVERAGE YIELDS

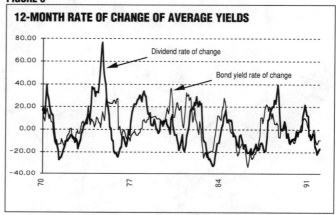

The rate of change in bond yields has often led a corresponding change in stock dividends.

composite of long bond yields, which measures interest rates on a variety of maturities greater than 10 years. The dividend yield of the Standard & Poor's 500 index can be used as a proxy for stock dividends. Standard & Poor's also publishes a composite bond yield series, data for which are available going back to the early part of the century. I will use it as a proxy for composite long bond yields.

OVERVIEW, YIELDS TO DIVIDENDS

A 32-year overview of the relationship of long bond yields to dividends on the S&P 500 index is shown in Figure 1. The year 1959 marked the first full year in recent history in which bond yields exceeded stock dividends, confirming Murphy's observation that in general stocks and bonds move in the same direction, with bonds turning before stocks at key turning points. Figure 2 shows the long-term changes in the ratio of stock dividends to bond yields, which now trades in the 30-50% range. The inflationary 1970s and the debt-ladened 1980s can be seen in Figure 3 by comparing the 12-month rate of change of average monthly long bond yields and stock dividends. The annual rates of change for

FIGURE 4

WEEKLY STOCK YIELDS VS. BONDS YIELDS 1987-92

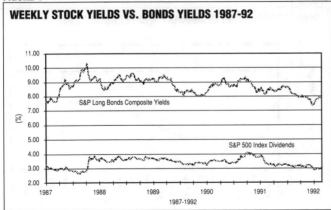

The last five years are presented for comparison.

FIGURE 5

STOCK DIVIDENDS AS A PERCENTAGE OF LONG BOND YIELDS

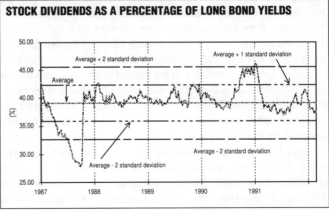

On average, the dividend yields have been 39.1% of the long bond yields for the last five years. An extreme was reached in late 1990, when the ratio rose to two standard deviations above the average.

stock dividends and long bond yields have generally tracked each other closely (Figure 3). Significant deviations represent good stock-buying opportunities. The dividend rate of change is positive when stock prices fall. Hence, high values occur near stock market bottoms, as in 1974 and 1989. Further, the rate of change in bond yields has often led a corresponding change in stock dividends, particularly in the 1980s.

A five-year overview of S&P 500 dividends and S&P Composite long bond yields is provided in Figure 4. The data in Figure 4 are replotted in Figure 5 with stock dividends expressed as a percent of composite long bond yields. On average, the dividend yield was 39.1% of long bond yields. I also plotted the plus or minus one and plus or minus two standard deviation regions about the average. Relative percentage changes in dividends have closely tracked relative percentage changes in long bond yields, which can be seen in

FIGURE 6

WEEKLY PERCENTAGE CHANGE IN DIVIDENDS/YIELDS SINCE 1989

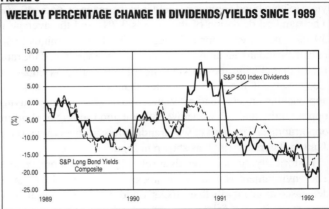

Relative percent changes in dividends have closely tracked bond yields.

Figure 6, using January 1989 as the reference for relative percentage changes in bond yields and dividends. Finally, Figure 7 shows the influence of relative percentage changes in bond yields on stock prices. This information is derived from Figure 6, which shows how stock dividends respond to changing bond yields.

From Figure 5, it is clear that the ratio of stock dividends to bond yields was unusually low in third-quarter 1987. Such divergences cannot be sustained forever, and in this case, the divergence was resolved with the resounding stock market crash in 1987, which restored the dividend/yield ratio to average levels.

In the last five years, good opportunities to buy stocks occurred when the ratio rose to one standard deviation above average. In particular, there was an excellent opportunity to buy stocks in late 1990 as the ratio rose to 45, two standard deviations above the average.

FIGURE 7

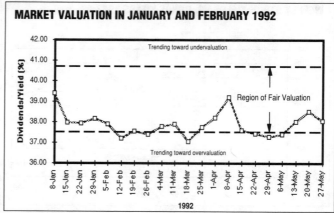

During early 1992, the market was trending toward overvaluation.

FAIR MARKET VALUE AND SUMMARY

The data in Figure 5 permit an objective estimate of fair market value. The market is fairly valued if the ratio of S&P 500 dividend yield to long bond composite yield is in the range of 37.5 - 40.7%. The standard deviation of the ratio is 3.2%, and the average is 39.1%. The fair valuation is the region 39.1% plus or minus 1.6%, or half a standard deviation on either side of the average. If the ratio is less than 37.5%, the market is trending toward overvaluation. Conversely, if the ratio is greater than 40.7%, the market is approaching undervaluation. Values above 42% are good buying opportunities and values below 36% are good selling or shorting opportunities. The market was trending toward overvaluation in January-February 1992, as shown in Figure 7.

Historically, stock dividends are closely related to bond yields. The environment is bullish for stocks when bond yields have decreased more rapidly than stocks' dividend yields on an annual percentage change basis and vice versa. In essence, stocks yield to bonds.

Tushar Chande, CTA, holds a doctorate in engineering from the University of Illinois and a master's degree in business administration from the University of Pittsburgh. He is a principal of Kroll, Chande & Co., 1 Todd Drive, Sands Point, NY 11050, (516) 627-0800.

REFERENCES

Standard & Poor's Statistical Service, Standard & Poor's Corp., 25 Broadway, New York, NY 10004.

Murphy, John J. [1992]. "The link between bonds and stocks," STOCKS & COMMODITIES, June.

First Citizen Of Technical Analysis: Arthur Merrill

By our reckoning, someone with, say, 10 years' worth of experience in the markets and trading has seen a great deal — until we remember that Arthur A. Merrill, currently of Merrill Analysis and Analysis Press and previously of Technical Trends, drew his first bar chart in 1930. His first, earliest calculations were made on slide rule, long before the pocket calculator or indeed the personal computer became a matter of course. Who else has had a chance to watch the markets evolve quite the way that Art Merrill has? Who else has experience quite like his to learn from? STOCKS & COMMODITIES Editor Thom Hartle interviewed Art Merrill on July 27, 1992, in a combination of telephone and correspondence, inquiring about, among other topics, today's markets compared with yesterday's and whether statistical analysis has ever steered him wrong.

"The earliest indicators that I really analyzed were chart formations in 1930. I tried point and figure for a while, but I found that line charts gave me more information, and they could be put on a logarithmic chart, which is better for price changes."—Arthur A. Merrill

So, Art, tell us about your early work with the stock market and technical analysis.

Well, I was first inspired by R.W. Schabacker's *Stock Market Theory and Practice*. It had many of the stock formations that were described in more detail 18 years later by Edwards and Magee.

I drew my first bar charts in 1930. The next year, Humphrey Neill's book *Tape Reading and Market Tactics* added fuel to the technical fire.

Did you keep everything by hand yourself?

Yes. All my data and calculations were made by hand, and I kept up my charts by hand.

I made the earliest calculations by slide rule. From the slide rule, I progressed through the manual calculator, then the electric calculator, then the pocket calculator — I think I bought the first commercial model; it was the size of a carton of cigarettes and cost $300 — then the programmable calculator with printer, then the computer, first with audiocassette storage, then diskette, and finally hard drive. It was quite a progression!

While I have never used it, I have an abacus now hanging behind my computer labeled "backup."

Did you develop a feel for what was happening in the markets?

It was more a visual impression than a feel. A line chart can tell you at a glance about the support and resistance levels and the trend direction.

Is that lost today with the reliance on computers?

Not necessarily. The computer is a helpful tool, but I don't make any decisions until I see the output in chart form.

What were some of the first indicators that you studied?

The earliest indicators that I really analyzed were chart formations from Schabacker's *Stock Market Theory* in 1930. The indicator was the stock's own price and volume expressed on a line chart. I tried point and figure for a while, but I found that line charts gave me more information, *and* they could be put on a logarithmic scale, which is better for price changes.

> For the overall market, though, I depend on the indicators that test out with good batting averages. Some of these are the advance-decline divergence oscillator, odd-lot shorts, public shorts, ratio of public to specialist shorts and large block transactions.

So despite modern technology, you still rely on old-fashioned "impression"?

Again, not necessarily. The computer is a helpful beast, but I don't let him give me a definite buy or sell mandate. Instead, I like to take his output in chart form and add some judgment before making a decision.

I now use log charts (see sidebar), using the point and figure idea to filter out minor moves, using a percentage filter. I described these in my article in your October 1991 issue.

How was using line charts preferable to point and figure?

Point and figure charting doesn't ex-

LOGARITHMIC POINT & FIGURE

The point and figure chart, which is built on a filtering technique, is an old favorite. In a one-point chart, moves of less than one point are filtered out; in a three-point chart, all moves of less than three points are filtered out. The idea is good, but this type of chart has several drawbacks. First, the chart makes the error of using points and not percentages. Points are a poor measure of importance in a stock chart. One point can be very important in a $10 stock but be a very minor move in a $100 stock.

Another limitation of the P&F chart is the use of arithmetic scale, which has a built-in distortion. A 5% move at the bottom of the chart may be completely hidden, while at the top of the chart it may look like a major move. On an arithmetic chart, a trend rising at a uniform 10% per week seems almost flat at the bottom but skyrockets at the top of the trendline. A straight trendline on an arithmetic scale actually has a decreasing rate of incline as you travel up the line. Another limitation of the point and figure chart is it ignores the aspect of time.

You can eliminate these limitations with three simple steps. First, set up your filter as a percentage, not in points. Ignore any reversals of less than your specified percent. Second, use a logarithmic scale for prices, Third, put time on the horizontal scale of prices (see sidebar Figure 1).

There is one more minor problem:

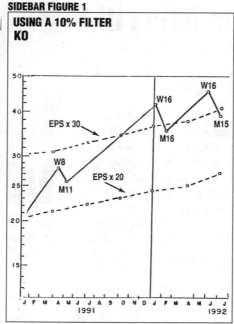

Any price moves of less than 10% are not recorded. The scale is logarithmic to reflect percentage change in price. The dotted lines are earnings per share for the last year multiplied by a constant. This way, the price of the stock can be judged as cheap (low P/E ratios) or rich (high P/E ratios).

You don't know the location of a turning point until after you have passed it. I correct for this by using a pencil line or a dotted line until the turning point has been established by a pullback of the specified percentage.

This style of charting provides two major benefits. First, trendlines are now valid and meaningful, and second, charts for different stocks or averages are comparable. You can compare a chart for a $100 stock with one for a $10 stock without worry of distortion.

press volume, and the arithmetic scale bothered me. A log chart provides better trends.

Do you have any favorite indicators that have been with you since the very beginning?

In individual stocks, I rely on the price log point and figure charts.

For the overall market, though, I depend on the indicators that test out with good batting averages. Some of these are the advance-decline divergence oscilla-

tor, odd-lot shorts, public shorts, ratio of public to specialist shorts and large block transactions.

When did you first want to test indicators?

I really began to get serious about it in 1981, with the calculation of weights for the various indicators based on their performance.

Why?

At any given time, some indicators are

bullish and some bearish. At the same time, some market technicians are bullish and some bearish. They are all looking at the same indicators, but they weight them differently, so coming up with different answers. I sometimes wonder if the bullish technicians tend to give weight to indicators that agree with their own bullish inclination; and whether bearish technicians believe the bearish indicators, since they agree with their bearishness.

Viewpoint is important, certainly.

That's why I got interested in checking relative accuracy from the performance record. The computer certainly helped out. I asked it to check an indicator's opinion every week for 10 years and then to check whether the market went in that direction the next week, in the next four weeks, 13 weeks, 26 weeks and a year after the forecast. I could then give the indicator a batting average for the various time periods.

This method was described in more detail in your May 1991 issue.

You base your analysis mostly on statistics; can statistical analysis ever steer you wrong?

Yes. The statisticians recognize two types of errors:

In error type one, the record shows that success isn't demonstrated significantly, but when you perform a longer test, the new test demonstrates significant success.

In error type two, the record reports significant success, when the longer-term testing shows no significance. An example of the type two error is the Super Bowl indicator [in which the outcome of the game predicts the outcome of the stock market]. I sometimes wonder if the astrology test reports aren't also type two.

So statistics aren't perfect. But they are certainly helpful.

Can you compare today's market to other periods in the market?

I'm very suspicious about these anecdotal comparisons. Conditions are always different in some respects; the differences may not be obvious, but they may be important. So straight comparisons are impossible.

ADVANCE-DECLINE DIVERGENCE OSCILLATOR (ADDO)

The most popular technique of noting divergence within the stock market is to compare the cumulative curve of the difference between advances and declines — the A-D line — with the plot of the Dow Jones Industrial Average (DJIA). Quantifying divergence is difficult because one curve is accumulation and one curve is price. The ADDO is designed to indicate when the DJIA is diverging from the A-D line.

First, the daily number of advances minus declines is calculated. This difference is divided by the daily number of unchanged stocks. This added refinement (originally suggested by Edmund Tabell) gives added emphasis when the market has real conviction. If the number of unchanged stocks is low, the denominator is low and the ratio becomes a relatively high figure. Keep a cumulative record of this ratio:

$$\Sigma\ ((A\text{-}D)/\text{Unchanged})$$

The daily figures are kept, but the ADDO uses the end-of-the-week figures only.

The second step is to establish a historical reference by comparing the cumulative adjusted A-D line to the weekly close of the DJIA. Calculate a regression line of the DJIA and the cumulative adjusted A-D line for the last year. The formula for the regression line will be:

Expected DJIA value =
$$A + B_1(\text{cumulative adjusted A-D})$$

A and B are the constants from the regression formula. This line will produce the average expected value of the DJIA for any current cumulative adjusted A-D line (see sidebar Figure 2). Then the actual level of the DJIA is compared to the expected value. ADDO is the percent difference:

$$\text{ADDO} = (100D/(A + BE))\text{-}100$$

where D= DJIA, E = cumulative adjusted A-D, and A and B are constants produced from the calculated regression line.

A value higher than 6% is bearish and a value below 1% is bullish. When the indicator is positive, the DJIA is higher than it should be and when the indicator is negative, the DJIA is lower than it should be. The most recent testing indicated that this indicator's best accuracy for forecasting the DJIA is 26 and 52 weeks out.

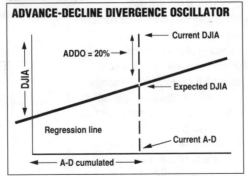

SIDEBAR FIGURE 2

ADVANCE-DECLINE DIVERGENCE OSCILLATOR

The regression line calculates where the DJIA should be in relation to the current cumulated advance-decline numbers. The ADDO indicator measures how far ahead or behind the A-D line the DJIA is.

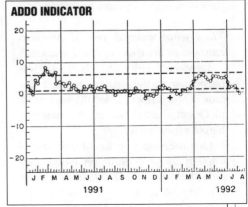

SIDEBAR FIGURE 3

ADDO INDICATOR

Currently, the indicator has been neutral.

ODD-LOT SHORTS

Short interest — the sale of a borrowed stock — is one of the most useful tools of the technician. Theoretically, the selling short of a stock is an indication of pessimism and therefore represents buying power on the sidelines as the short sale must be purchased at some point in the future. This series prior to the 1980s included small traders taking flyers†, while it now includes only specialist odd-lot trading. In fact, the shorting by the odd-lotter is not reported. Today, this indicator provides clues about how much program trading has occurred. Large traders get around the uptick rule by selling short in odd-lots with the specialist.

This index is calculated by dividing the average odd-lot short sales in the last five trading days by the average of odd-lot sales plus purchases in the same period. Recent testing of this indicator points out that the bearish calls are poor but the bullish calls are good for 13, 26 and 52 weeks ahead.

†See Traders' Glossary for definition

I don't know who said it, but I like the quote "Conditions are more like they are right now than they have ever been."

Then what warned you of previous changes in the trend of other markets?

I always got suspicious about what was happening in the markets when I saw crowds around the old Merrill Lynch kiosk in Grand Central Station or when my barber asked me for tips.

One measure I've found very useful through the years is the price/dividends ratio, the ratio of the DJIA to its dividends. It's the inverse of the yield on the DJIA. When it gets above 28, I rate it expensive and risky. This ratio corrects for inflation, since both the numerator and denominator are in dollars, and so the value of the dollar cancels out. It was described in the October 1988 S&C.

How's it doing?

I'm concerned about this indicator right now because it's been as high as 35, a dangerous level. It has been this high just once in the last 60 years, in 1987. It wasn't even this high in 1929.

You don't like to compare conditions, but you do study the history of other markets. Can you compare today's market with other bull markets that way?

I'm concerned about the age and amplitude of our current bull market. It started in October 1987 with the DJIA at 1712, and it hit its high so far in May this year with the DJIA at 3417.

That's quite a rise.

That's a rise of 99%. The DJIA has almost doubled since the low in 1987. I looked back at the 18 bull markets we've had since 1898 and found only seven that rose a higher percentage. Eleven of the 18 didn't reach our current 99%. Our current bull has risen more than the average bull; the chances for a continued rise are still there, but the probability is diminishing.

So what do you see?

When you look at the duration of the market, the view isn't good. Our May peak was 55 months after the 1987 low; that's more than four years. When you look at the 18 bull markets since 1898,

PUBLIC SHORTS AS A PERCENT OF TOTAL NYSE VOLUME

Weekly total short sales figures are a useful set of figures (published in *Barron's*) for gauging market moods. You can calculate the total exchange member figures by adding the specialist, floor trader and other member numbers. Deduct the member data from the total and you have a figure for the nonmembers — that is, the public. Express the short selling as a percentage of the total weekly volume. This reveals the size of the shorting, corrected for the volume. A bullish reading occurs when the indicator is greater than 1.8 and bearish reading occurs when the indicator is less than 1.16 (see sidebar Figure 4). Recent testing indicates this indicator has success in bullish calls in the 26-

SIDEBAR FIGURE 4

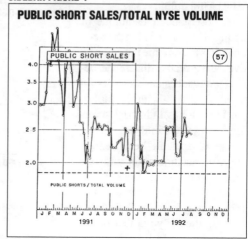

This indicator has remained in the bullish region (readings above 1.8).

and 52-week outlook, but its bearish calls are better for one, five, 13, 26 and 52 weeks out.

RATIO OF PUBLIC SHORTS TO SPECIALIST SHORTS

This idea was developed by John McGinley and Walter Deemer. The index is a ratio of the short sales by nonmembers (the public) to the short sales by the specialists. Data are available in *Barron's*. High values by the index imply that the public is more bearish than the professional, a positive indication. Bullish levels occur when the ratio is above 0.54, while bearish indications occur at readings below 0.35 (sidebar Figure 5). Recent testing indicates that smoothing the ratio with a four-week simple moving average can improve results. Recent testing shows that this indicator's bullish calls are successful in the one-, 13-, 26- and 52-week

SIDEBAR FIGURE 5

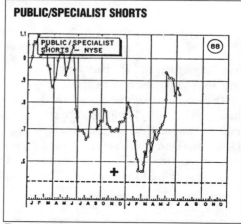

The public/NYSE short sales indicator has remained above the bullish 0.54 reading.

outlook and bearish calls are successful in the one-, five-, 13-, 26- and 52-week outlook.

LARGE BLOCK TRANSACTIONS

This indicator reveals the direction of the enthusiasm of the big operators. The source for the data is *Barron's*. The steps used to create the final indicator are:

1. Total the daily figures to produce weekly data. Create separate totals for upticks, downticks and unchanged for all trades over 50,000.

2. Smooth these three totals with a 14% exponential moving average, which are approximately equivalent to 13-week simple moving averages. To calculate these exponential moving averages, add 14% of each new statistic to 86% of the preceding average.

3. Calculate a ratio from the exponentials by subtracting the downtick average from the uptick average and dividing the difference by the unchanged average.

4. Calculate a 52-week moving average of the ratio.

5. Calculate the deviations of the current ratio to its 52-week moving average. You could use this as the indicator, if you wish.

6. For charting, I take one more step and put the deviations in *z*-scores by dividing the deviations by the standard deviation of the preceding 52 weeks. This step simplifies the interpretation of the chart. Approximately half the data will fall between +0.67 and -0.67. Approximately two thirds of the data points will be between +1.00 and -1.00; approximately 95% will be between +2.00 and -2.00. You can use these levels as benchmarks (see sidebar Figure 6).

Recent testing indicates that bullish calls occur with readings less than -0.98 and are good for the 26- and 52-week outlook. The bearish calls occur at the greater than +1.7 reading and are good for the one-, five-, 13-, 26- and 52-week outlook.

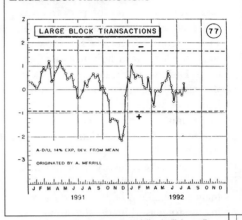

In late 1991, the indicator readings fell to bullish readings (below -0.98), while recent readings have been neutral.

---

only three were longer; 15 didn't last 55 months. So the probabilities, based on duration, don't favor continuation.

I'm 86 years old and not as spry as I was at 40. I think the market is also beginning to feel its age.

You have written 53 articles for STOCKS & COMMODITIES. Do you have any favorites?

That number is no longer any good. My article in your August issue makes it 54!

I'm especially enthusiastic about these articles:

"Advance-decline divergence as an oscillator" (September 1988)
"Price/dividends ratio" (October 1988)
"5% swings" (December 1988)
"Price resistance" (March 1990)
"Last four hour indicator" (April 1991)
"Testing method" (May 1991)
"Filtered waves" (June 1991)
"Log point and figure" (October 1991)
"MW waves" (November 1991)
"Election cycle" (March 1992)
"Stock selection" (June 1992)

You've seen S&C evolve in the past 10 years. What are some changes you have seen in this magazine over the years?

I can't be specific, but the magazine seems to improve and improve.

One test I have for magazine helpfulness is the number of articles that I clip out for future study and file. STOCKS & COMMODITIES passes this test enthusiastically.

Is there anything specific that we should emphasize? What would you like to see in our magazine?

Just keep on the same track.

What should a person who is just starting to invest do?

1. Subscribe to *Technical Analysis of* STOCKS & COMMODITIES magazine.

2. Read the background books, starting with Edwards and Magee.

3. Start watching the overall market and individual stocks, drawing handmade line charts, preferably on a log scale, to get a feel for what the market's doing.

How should they follow the broad market?

Well, the DJIA is a very poorly de-signed index, but it does a fair job of representation. It's readily available, and you can watch it hourly.

The advance-decline line can also give you a picture of the overall market.

What about building and managing portfolios?

Use opinion of market trend and expensiveness to set the percentage of the portfolio to be put in equities and the percentage in bonds. In the equity section, pick stocks that are increasing their earnings quarter by quarter, with prices that are zigzagging upward.

Finally, do you have any favorite books?

Yes, two by Art Merrill: *Behavior of Prices on Wall Street* and *Filtered Waves*.

Please forgive my modesty! My friends have written many fine books, but I hesitate to mention any, since I might skip a good one and lose a friend.

Thank you for your time, Art.

TESTING INDICATORS

I devised a method of testing indicators that gives me simple, understandable and useful measures of performance. The method gives me batting averages. First, accumulate a data file for each indicator, logging in the indicator's forecasts. I ask each indicator, each week in the past 10 years, whether it is bullish, bearish or on the fence. Each week I log in the digit "2" if the forecast in that week was bullish, "1" if bearish and "0" if on the fence.

To check the accuracy of the forecast, I then log in another file, the performance of the DJIA in the period following the forecast. I ignore the amount of change in the DJIA for simplicity. My performance log of the DJIA consists of a five-digit number inserted in each week following the forecasts. If the DJIA closed higher one week later, the digit "2" is the first digit of the five-digit number; if the DJIA closed lower, "1" would be used and finally a "0" for an unchanged close. The second digit reports performance in the following five weeks using the same criteria for the first week. Similarly, the third digit report changes in the 13th week; the fourth digit report changes in the 26th week and the final digit reports the direction of change in the 52nd week (sidebar Figure 7).

Next, I ask my computer to compare the forecast file with each digit in the benchmark file and tell me the number of agreements (successful forecasts) and disagreements, and then report a simple batting average. The successful plus the unsuccessful make up 100% of the batting average; the "on the fence" weeks are ignored.

Five batting averages are produced, one for each time period. Some indicators were more successful for the shorter time periods and some were successful for the longer term.

In the final step, the results are checked for significance by calculating a statistic with the name "chi squared with one degree of freedom, with the Yates correction." We are using a formula for chi squared based on an expected outcome that is either right or wrong:

$$X^2 = (|R-W|-1)^2 / (R+W)$$

where:

R = number of times right
W = number of times wrong

Then compare the values with sidebar Figure 8 to measure the significance of the outcome.

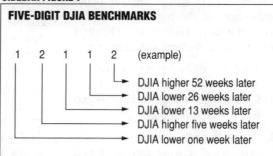

SIDEBAR FIGURE 9

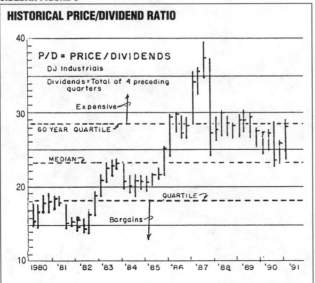

More than 60 years of data indicate that readings above $28.30 are expensive and readings below $18.10 are bargains.

SIDEBAR FIGURE 10

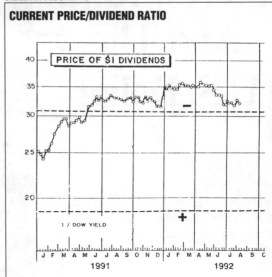

Currently, the P/D raio has reached 35 and has retreated slightly. The average peak of bull markets has been 31.

PRICE/DIVIDENDS RATIO

This indicator is a measure of expensiveness. It reports the current price of enough stock to yield $1 in dividends. It's the inverse of stock yield. You can calculate the ratio any time by dividing the DJIA by the total of the dividends in the preceding four quarters. These dividends are found in a table in *Barron's*. In the 60-year history of the ratio, I found 25% of the points above $28.30. The area above this level is labeled "expensive." The lowest quarter of the points fell below $18.10. This area is labeled "bargains" (see sidebar Figure 9). Currently, the price/dividend ratio has been as high as 35 (see sidebar Figure 10).

Note: Recent testing of these indicators was performed by Technical Trends. The test period ranged from 1978 to 1991.

FURTHER READING

Edwards, Robert D., and John Magee [1966]. *Technical Analysis of Stock Trends*, John Magee Inc.

Merrill, Arthur A. [1984]. *Behavior of Prices on Wall Street*, The Analysis Press.

_____ [1977]. *Filtered Waves, Basic Theory,* Technical Trends.

Merrill Analysis Inc., Elm 3325, 3300 Darby Rd., Haverford, PA 19041.

Neill, Humphrey [1931]. *Tape Reading and Market Tactics.* Now published by Fraser Publishing.

Schabacker, R.W. [1930]. *Stock Market Theory and Practice.* Now published by Fraser Publishing.

Technical Trends, PO Box 792, Wilton, CT 06897, (203) 762-0229.

Interest Rates And The U.S. Dollar

John Murphy, veteran technician and leading proponent of intermarket analysis, continues to delve into the interrelationships between markets, this time between interest rates and the U.S. dollar.

by John J. Murphy

P reviously, I have focused on intermarket linkages between commodities, bonds and stocks. The U.S. dollar also plays an important role in the intermarket chain. The dollar, for example, is affected by movements in interest rate futures. The dollar, in turn, influences the direction of other markets such as gold, the CRB index, bonds and ultimately the stock market. Here, I will examine the close relationship between the dollar and interest rate futures.

THE DOLLAR'S UPS AND DOWNS

The dollar is influenced by the direction of interest rates. During a period of economic strength, the Federal Reserve pushes interest rates higher, which in turn strengthens the dollar. In recent history, we have seen an extended period of Fed easing to stimulate a weak economy. When the Federal Reserve lowers interest rates, the dollar weakens. Shifts in Fed policy can be seen primarily in the direction of short-term rates, such as Treasury bills. Figure 1 shows the inverse relationship between Treasury bill futures and the U.S. Dollar Index from late 1987 to mid-1992.

The upturn in Treasury bill futures that began in early 1989 has had a decidedly bearish influence on the dollar. (Rising T-bill prices indicate that short-term rates are dropping.) Given the clear link between these two markets, a dollar trader should always keep an eye on what the T-bill market is doing. Because interest rates generally trend in the same direction, Treasury bond prices also have an impact on the dollar.

Figure 2 shows the inverse relationship between the dollar index and Treasury bond futures prices from mid-1990 to mid-

1992. The four vertical lines on the chart show the close coincidence of turns in both markets in opposite directions. Bond market peaks during first-quarter 1991 and January 1992 coincided with rebounds in the dollar. Upturns in bonds during fourth-quarter 1990, summer 1991 and spring 1992 coincided with downturns in the U.S. dollar.

Figure 3 provides a closer view of the inverse dollar/bond relationship in the eight months from December 1991 to mid-July 1992. The downturn in Treasury bond futures during January 1992 followed a full-point cut in the discount rate on

FIGURE 1

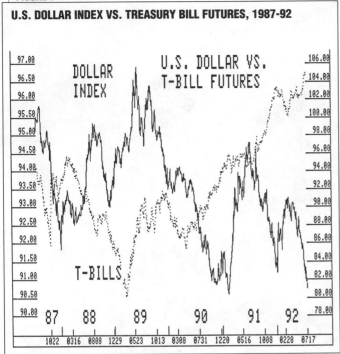

U.S. DOLLAR INDEX VS. TREASURY BILL FUTURES, 1987-92

The inverse relationship can be seen between the U.S. Dollar Index (solid line) and Treasury bill futures prices (dotted line) from late 1987 to mid-1992. Rising T-bill prices (falling short-term rates) are bearish for the dollar.

FIGURE 2

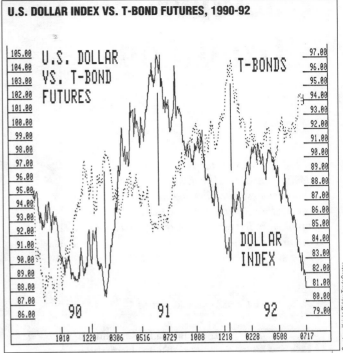

U.S. DOLLAR INDEX VS. T-BOND FUTURES, 1990-92

The inverse relationship can be seen between the dollar index (solid line) and Treasury bond futures prices (dotted line) from mid-1990 to mid-1992.

December 20. That aggressive easing move by the Fed raised hopes for a strong economic rebound, which pushed long-term bond yields higher. The resulting drop in bond prices supported a dollar rally. As the economic recovery stalled, raising expectations for more Fed easing, bonds turned back up in April, in turn pushing the dollar lower.

POLICY AND EXPECTATIONS

Although short-term rates are directly affected by the Fed, long-term bond yields have the dual influence of Fed policy and inflation expectations. As a result, a circular relationship between the dollar and bond prices exists. Rising bond prices hurt the dollar. The falling dollar, however, eventually reawakens inflationary expectations, which in time begin to hurt bonds. One of the first indications that the process has begun is a rally in the gold market, which leads us to the next subject — the relationship between the U.S. dollar and gold.

John Murphy is president of JJM Technical Advisors Inc. and publishes the monthly "Futures Trends and Intermarket Analysis." He is also the technical analyst for CNBC.

REFERENCES

JJM Technical Advisors Inc., 297-101 Kinderkamack Road Ste 148, Oradell, NJ 07649.

Murphy, John J. [1991]. *Intermarket Technical Analysis*, John Wiley & Sons.

_____ [1986]. *Technical Analysis of the Futures Markets*, New York Institute of Finance.

FIGURE 3

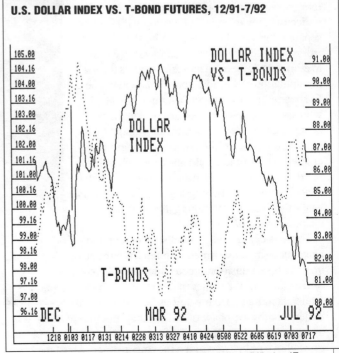

U.S. DOLLAR INDEX VS. T-BOND FUTURES, 12/91-7/92

A closer inspection of the inverse relationship of the dollar index (solid line) and Treasury bond futures prices (dotted line) from December 1991 to July 1992. The January setback in bonds supported a dollar rally, while the April bond rally helped push the dollar lower.

Phase Transitions

Here's a concept to visually compare an indicator's historical profitability over a variety of time frames, allowing the trader to identify those trading signals that have been historically profitable. Will it work for you? All you can do is read on and try.

by Christopher K. Smith

Market technicians use technical indicators to help clarify some aspect of market behavior. For example, the price moving average helps clarify the longer-term trend of the market while eliminating shorter-term noise. One problem that arises in using indicators, however, is that it is often difficult to separate the signal being given by the indicator from the noise. Traditionally, traders have sought to eliminate noise from indicator signals through manipulation of the indicator's parameter values. For example, if the moving average is producing whipsaw† signals, the parameter length is increased. Conversely, if the indicator's signals are lagging the market, the parameter length is decreased. The problem with this approach is that it is often difficult to determine which parameter values are best for trading a given market. This can be solved by searching for key indicator changes called *phase transitions*.

Phase is calculated as the distance of an indicator above or below a median point (often a zero point). Phase transitions occur when an indicator moves through the center of their value ranges. Understanding phase transitions begins with an understanding the phase of an indicator. For the simple moving average, phase may be defined as the distance of the closing price above or below a given moving average. Thus, the phase is positive when price is above the moving average and the phase is negative when price is below the moving average. Phase may be calculated for nearly any indicator. (See sidebar "Indicator phase" for a discussion of potential methods to calculate phase for a variety of indicators.) Searching for significant phase transitions in the market helps extract important signals from an indicator while ignoring the noise. Searching for phase transitions also helps clarify the overall state of the market by examining indicator action over a variety of time frames.

Indicator phase can be viewed over an entire range of parameter values with indicator phase diagrams. Figure 1 shows an indicator phase diagram of the Standard & Poor's 100 index as it appeared at the end of trading on December 2, 1991. The parameter values for the moving average are shown on the horizontal axis (x-axis) and the distance between the price and the moving average is shown on the vertical axis (y-axis). We can see from examining this chart that the OEX is above its moving average for the five- through 12-day moving average. For parameter values 14 through 70, the OEX index remains below its moving average.

> **For the simple moving average, phase may be defined as the distance of the closing price above or below a given moving average.**

DIAGRAMMING A PHASE

Indicator phase diagrams have several interesting properties. First, the selection of scaling values for the horizontal axis determines the time frames encompassed by the chart. In Figure 1, the x-axis ranges from 5 to 70, so the indicator's performance is diagrammed across 14 weeks. By scaling the x-axis logarithmically, a wide variety of time frames — from intraday to yearly — can be compressed into a single phase diagram.

Second, if we were trading this security based on a simple moving average crossover trading system, we would hold a long position when the graph was in positive territory for a given parameter value and go short whenever the graph fell in negative territory. Remember that the moving average crossover system signals a buy when the price moves above its moving average and a sell when the price moves below the moving average.

Now examine Figure 1 again. The moving average crossover system signals a buy where the indicator phase crosses the zero area (at the 13-day moving average), because the price has just closed above the 13-day moving average. Parameter values below 13 already suggest a long position and parameter values above 13 suggest a short position. This crossover of the price at the 13-day moving average is an example of a phase transition.

P hase transitions tend to move across the parameter space in a "wave" from lower to higher parameter values. If we were to view phase diagrams for several days in sequence like frames in a motion picture, this waving effect would be seen quite clearly. This waving pattern can be attributed to the smoothing effect of the moving averages, where the longer-term moving averages will produce more lag than the shorter-term ones. Short-term indicators, of course, issue reversing signals before their longer-term counterparts.

FIGURE 1

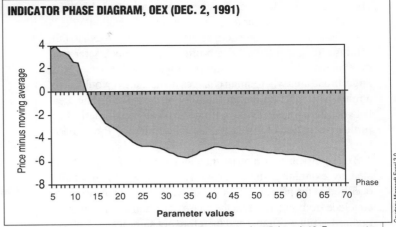

INDICATOR PHASE DIAGRAM, OEX (DEC. 2, 1991)

Courtesy Microsoft Excel 3.0

The S&P 100 closed above its moving average for parameter values 5 through 12. For parameter values 14 and above, the closing price remains below the moving average. A phase transition occurs at the 13-day moving average.

FIGURE 2

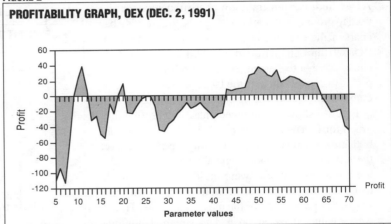

PROFITABILITY GRAPH, OEX (DEC. 2, 1991)

The profitability resulting from trading a moving average crossover system is erratic except for parameter values 48 through 65, where a broad area of profitability is found. Phase transitions that occur in areas of erratic profitability should not be considered significant.

Identifying phase transitions is not by itself a sufficient criterion for finding profitable trades. In fact, just about any stock will cross a moving average of some parameter value several times in one day, not to mention in one week or one month. We must be able to distinguish between phase transitions that are significant and those that are not.

To determine the significance of moving average crossovers, we can observe a particular parameter set's accuracy in producing profitable buy and sell signals. Technician Arthur Merrill would refer to this as the "batting average" of the indicator. Figure 2 shows the profitability of trading the parameters used in Figure 1 for the OEX using the moving average crossover system. Profitability was measured using APEX software. The software was configured to enter and exit the market on a price crossover duration of two days; that is, signals were generated when the price closed through the moving average for two days in a row.

Figure 2 shows two small areas of profitability below parameter values of 43. However, these parameter areas would not be wise choices for trades, as they represent an optimization "cliff." A small shift in the market could cause the trading system to fall off this cliff into an area of unprofitability. A much safer and more potentially profitable chart pattern to look for would be a large, broad area where small changes in the market would have a minimal impact on the profitability of the system. The area between the parameter values 48 and 65 meets these criteria. For further discussion of this issue, see John Ehlers's "Profit mapping."

The significance of a phase transition can therefore be evaluated by examining the profitability of transitions that have occurred in the past at similar parameter values. Thus, we may conclude from Figure 2 that the phase transition diagrammed in Figure 1 is not profitable and therefore not significant. A phase transition would have to occur somewhere between the 43-and 65-day parameters to issue a signal worth getting excited about.

TRANSITIONING FOR PROFITABILITY

A case study can illustrate how phase transitions can be used to produce entry and exit signals. Figure 3 is a bar chart of the over-the-counter stock Knowledgeware (KNOW) through first-quarter 1992. The left side of the chart, October to December 1991, finds the stock in a period of consolidation in the 10-12 area after a considerable decline from the mid-30s earlier in the year.

Figure 4 shows a combined phase and profitability graph for KNOW on October 15, 1992. In this graph, both indicator phase and profitability are combined on the vertical axis and parameter values are shown on the horizontal axis. Profits were divided by 10 to scale together with the phase. Profitability is based on a single-day penetration of the moving average. Trades were evaluated based on a data stream beginning January 17, 1990, and one-half point was deducted for each trade to simulate commissions and slippage.

O ctober 15, 1991, finds KNOW beginning to move up off its lows set earlier in the month. Figure 4 shows a phase transition occurring at the 13-day moving average. However, the profitability at this parameter point is about -7, showing that trading on this parameter would have resulted in a loss of about 70 points. This indicates that phase transitions at the 13-day moving average have not been profitable in past trading and therefore should not be considered significant. Buying is therefore postponed until a phase transition takes place in the upper 30s.

Figure 5 shows a phase/profit graph for KNOW on November 15, 1991. A phase transition occurs at the 38-day moving average, an area that shows a past profitability of about 12 points. Thus, a significant phase transition has occurred and a buy signal is issued

FIGURE 3

KNOWLEDGEWARE, INC.

Knowledgeware is shown with its 38-day moving average. A significant positive phase transition occurs on November 15 (see Figure 5) and a significant negative phase transition occurs on February 24 (see Figure 6) for a gross profit of about five points.

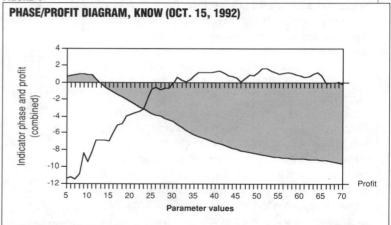

FIGURE 4

PHASE/PROFIT DIAGRAM, KNOW (OCT. 15, 1992)

Knowledgeware displays a phase transition at the 13-day moving average on October 15. This area corresponds to a region of extreme unprofitability, disqualifying it as a significant phase transition.

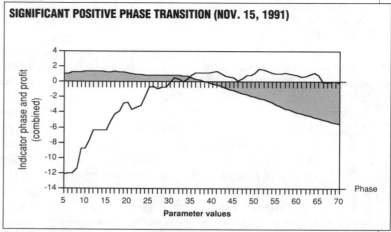

FIGURE 5

SIGNIFICANT POSITIVE PHASE TRANSITION (NOV. 15, 1991)

A significant positive phase transition occurs on November 15 as Knowledgeware closes above its 38-day moving average, well within an area of profitability.

for the next trading day, November 18, when KNOW is purchased for approximately 12.50 per share.

Knowledgeware continues to build a base throughout the middle of December. After a brief dip below the 38-day moving average (Figure 3), KNOW moves up smartly to the $19-per-share area into the first weeks of 1992. The indicator phase is positive at this point, with the stock moving up strongly above all its shorter-term moving averages.

By middle to late February, the rally begins to fade as Knowledgeware stock moves off its highs in the low 20s. Figure 6 is an example of a negative phase transition in progress, with the lower parameter values leading the way down, just as they led the way up during the rally. On February 24, 1992, KNOW closes below its 38-day moving average, well within a broad area of profitability. Because this negative phase transition fits the criteria for significance, we interpret it as a sell signal. The stock is sold the next trading day, February 25, 1992, for about 17.87 per share.

CLASSROOM LEARNING

The examples shown here are textbook cases of buy and sell signals as extracted from indicator phase diagrams. In the real world, phase transitions take on all shapes and forms. For example, one might argue that a significant phase transition occurred toward the end of December 1991, when KNOW dipped briefly below its 38-day moving average. However, when we diagram this phase transition (Figure 7), we see that it differs significantly from the classic negative phase transition shown in Figure 6.

Clearly, phase transition diagrams do not provide an all-encompassing solution to determining market entry and exit. However, they do provide a condensed picture of both long- and short-term market action. Think of each phase transition diagram as a momentary snapshot of an indicator, encompassing both long- and short-term market action. Perhaps the most significant application of phase transition diagrams is that they can readily be fed into neural networks, where computers can discover how their forms and sequences of forms relate to market changes.

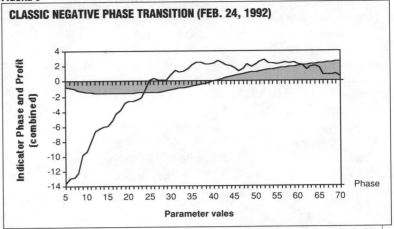

FIGURE 6

A significant negative phase transition occurs on February 24 as Knowledgeware closes below its 38-day moving average, well within an area of profitability. Note that the lower parameter values — that is, the shorter-term moving averages — lead the way down just as they led the way up during the rally.

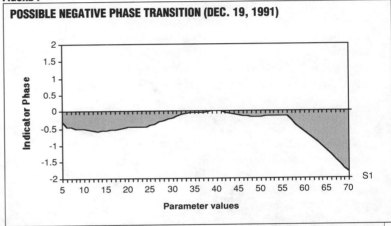

FIGURE 7

Knowledgeware closes slightly below its 38-day moving average on December 19. However, the form of this phase diagram differs significantly from the classic negative phase transition diagram shown in Figure 6.

Christopher K. Smith (Scarborough Manor, Scarborough, NY 10510) is a private trader involved in researching and implementing computer-assisted trading systems. He has a master's degree in computer science from Union College in Schenectady, NY.

INDICATOR PHASE

The phase of an indicator is defined as the distance of an indicator above or below a median value. For indicators that are plotted together with the price such as moving averages and on-balance volume, the phase is simply the difference between the price and the value of the indicator at a certain time period. Thus, phase may be calculated at time t with the formula:

$$phase(t) = price(t) - indicator(t)$$

Phase may also be expressed as a percentage value of the price above or below the indicator value at t with the formula:

$$phase(t) = (price(t) - indicator(t)) / indicator(t)$$

Phase may also be expressed in terms of standard deviations around an indicator. This method is used for Bollinger Bands, where envelope channels are drawn around a price moving average to a specific number of standard deviations. The indicator phase diagrams shown in Figures 1, 4, 5, 6 and 7 may be plotted using any of these methods described.

For indicators that oscillate between 0 and 100 (such as stochastics), phase may be calculated as the distance of the indicator value above or below the median value of 50. Thus, phase is calculated for time t as:

$$phase(t) = indicator(t) - 50$$

Phase will then assume values between -50 and +50. For other oscillators whose values are not restricted to a particular range, phase is simply the difference between the indicator value and its median over a given time period.

R. ALLEN BROWN

Identifying Trends With The KST Indicator

The direction of price is influenced by different time cycles. Important market turns occur when a number of these cycles are changing direction. The KST indicator is an oscillator designed to identify market turns based on the existence of these time cycles. Here, noted author Martin Pring presents the application of different-length KSTs to identify important market moves.

by Martin J. Pring

L ast time, I introduced the KST indicator, which is an oscillator that combines several smoothed rates of change and then weights them according to their time span. (See sidebar, "The KST indicator.") The concept behind the oscillator is that price trends are determined by the interaction of many different time cycles and that important trend reversals take place when a number of price trends are simultaneously changing direction. The KST cannot include all possible cycles and combinations, but it performs better than a simple momentum oscillator that can only reflect one cycle or combination of cycles. Different KSTs have been designed to reflect short-, intermediate- and long-term (primary) trends. The goal is to obtain an indicator to capture important market moves for a particular time frame while minimizing whipsaws. Buy and sell signals are triggered when a specific KST crosses its designated moving average, simple or exponential. However, the confirmation of a trend reversal in the actual price such as a moving average crossover or price pattern completion is also necessary.

THREE MAIN TRENDS

It is common knowledge that several trends operate in the market at any particular time, ranging from intraday and hourly trends to very long-term or secular ones developing over a 20- or 30-year period. For investment purposes, the most widely recognized are short-, intermediate- and long-term trends. Short-term trends (that is, those that range from two to four weeks) are usually monitored with daily prices, intermediate (six weeks to six months) with weekly, and long-term (one to three years) with monthly prices. Figure 1 reflects a hypothetical bell curve incorporating all three trends.

From both an investment and trading point of view, it is important to understand the direction and maturity of the main, or primary, trend. In the same way that a rising tide lifts all boats, short-term rallies in a bull market are much more profitable than when the market tide is retreating — that is, in a bear market. If you want proof, try comparing the results of short-term buy signals for mechanical trading systems in a bull and bear market environment. An indicator that can give you a reliable hint, not only of the direction but also the maturity of the primary trend, can be invaluable.

COMBINING THREE TRENDS

Ideally, it would be helpful to track the KST for monthly, weekly and daily data on the same chart, but plotting constraints make this onerous. It is possible, however, to simulate these three trends by using different time spans based on weekly data (shown for the Standard & Poor's Composite in Figure 2). These indicators differ from those presented in the September STOCKS & COMMODITIES in that they are smoothed by exponential moving averages rather than simple moving averages and use weekly closing prices. (See sidebar and use weekly formulas.) This arrangement, which is possible in the popular MetaStock Professional charting software, facilitates the identification of both the direction and maturity of the primary trend (shown at the bottom) as well as the interrelationship between the short and intermediate ones.

Reversals in trend are signaled sometime near when the KST and its moving average reverse direction. The best signals are given when the KST crosses above or below its exponential

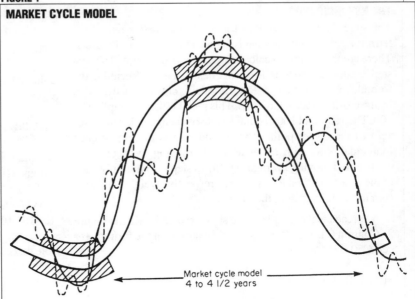

FIGURE 1

MARKET CYCLE MODEL

Market cycle model —
4 to 4 1/2 years

A hypothetical market is represented by an overlay of trends. The primary or long-term trend is the wide band. The intermediate trend is the solid line and the short-term trend is represented by the dashed line.

moving average (EMA). The KST gives a very good indication for the prevailing stage of the specific trend that it measures, but like any indicator it is far from perfect, especially in highly volatile markets or markets that fail to undergo a specific cyclic correction.

> **In the classic conceptual sense, a primary bull market consists of three intermediate uptrends and, in certain cases, a fourth.**

The best investments are made when the primary trend is in a rising mode but is not overextended, and the intermediate- and short-term market movements are bottoming out. In a sense, any investments made during the early and middle stages of a bull market are redeemed by the fact that the primary trend is rising, whereas investors have to be much more agile during a bear market to capitalize on the rising intermediate-term swings. During a primary bear market, shorting† is best accomplished when intermediate- and short-term trends are peaking out.

Bullish intermediate signals that met the two criteria — that is, the correct position on the long-term indicator and the moving average crossover by the intermediate-term one — occurred in mid-1984, late 1985, December 1986 and mid-1990. The first three all resulted in powerful rallies. The last one, in 1990, did not, primarily because the long-term indicator made its peak in early 1990.

Intermediate-term sell signals are less powerful when they occur against a backdrop of a rising primary trend KST. These signals occurred in 1985, early 1986 and early 1987.

THE KST INDICATOR

The suggested KST formulas for short, intermediate and long term for either daily or weekly data can be found in Figure 1. There are three steps to calculating the KST indicator. The first step is calculate the four different rates of change. Recalling the formula for rate of change (ROC) is today's closing price divided by the closing price n days ago. This result is then multiplied by 100. Then subtract 100 to obtain a rate of change index that uses zero as the center point. The second step is to smooth each individual ROC with either a simple moving average or an exponential moving average. The third step is to multiply each of the four smoothed ROCs by their respective weights and then sum the weighted smoothed ROCs.

A spreadsheet example of the short-term daily KST is Figure 2. Column C is the 10-day ROC. An example of the formula for cell C50 is:

=((B50/B41)*100)-100

Column D is the 15-day ROC. An example of the formula for cell D50 is:

=((B50/B36)*100)-100

Column E is the 20-day ROC. An example of the formula for cell E50 is :

=((B50/B31)*100)-100

Column F is the 30-day ROC. An example of the formula for cell F50 is:

=((B50/B21)*100)-100

Column G is the sum of the weighted moving averages of the various ROCs:

=((AVERAGE(C41:C50))+(2*AVERAGE(D41:D50))+(3*AVERAGE (E41:E50))+(4*AVERAGE(F36:F50)))

Note that each moving average is multiplied by its weight prior to the calculation of the sum. An additional moving average of the KST is in column H. A five-day moving average is used as a crossover. The formula for cell H50 is:

=AVERAGE(G46:G50)

The KST indicator can use the parameters listed in Figure 1, or the users can try different values to fine tune the KST to their particular markets.

SIDEBAR FIGURE 1

SUGGESTED KST FORMULAS

	ROC	MA	Wt	ROC	MA	Wt	ROC	MA	Wt	ROC	MA	Wt
Short-term (D)	10	10	1	15	10	2	20	10	3	30	15	4
Short-term (W)	3	3E	1	4	4E	2	6	6E	3	10	8E	4
Intermediate-term (W)	10	10	1	13	13	2	15	15	3	20	20	4
Intermediate-term (W)	10	10E	1	13	13E	2	15	15E	3	20	20E	4
Long-term (M)	9	6	1	12	6	2	18	6	3	24	9	4
Long-term (W)	39	26E	1	52	26E	2	78	26E	3	104	39E	4

It is possible to program all KST formulas into MetaStock and the CompuTrac SNAP module.
(D) Based on daily data. (W) Based on weekly data. (M) Based on monthly data. (E) EMA.

The ROC column is the rate of change, the MA column is the moving average value, and E after the moving average value indicates that the moving average is an exponential moving average. Multiply each smoothed ROC by its weight prior to summing the four smoothed ROCs.

SIDEBAR FIGURE 2

SPREADSHEET FOR THE SHORT-TERM DAILY KST

	A	B	C	D	E	F	G	H
1	Date	S&P500						
2	8/12/91	388.02						
3	8/13/91	389.62						
4	8/14/91	389.90						
5	8/15/91	389.33						
6	8/16/91	385.58						
7	8/19/91	376.47						
8	8/20/91	379.43						
9	8/21/91	390.59						
10	8/22/91	391.33	**10 ROC**					
11	8/23/91	394.17	1.58					
12	8/26/91	393.85	1.09					
13	8/27/91	393.06	0.81					
14	8/28/91	396.64	1.88					
15	8/29/91	396.47	2.82	**15 ROC**				
16	8/30/91	395.43	5.04	1.91				
17	9/3/91	392.15	3.35	0.65				
18	9/4/91	389.97	-0.16	0.02				
19	9/5/91	389.14	-0.56	-0.05				
20	9/6/91	389.10	-1.29	0.91	**20 ROC**			
21	9/9/91	388.57	-1.34	3.21	0.14			
22	9/10/91	384.56	-2.16	1.35	-1.30			
23	9/11/91	385.09	-2.91	-1.41	-1.23			
24	9/12/91	387.34	-2.30	-1.02	-0.51			
25	9/13/91	383.59	-2.99	-2.68	-0.52			
26	9/16/91	385.78	-1.62	-2.05	2.47			
27	9/17/91	385.50	-1.15	-1.92	1.60			
28	9/18/91	386.94	-0.57	-2.45	-0.93			
29	9/19/91	387.56	-0.40	-2.25	-0.96			
30	9/20/91	387.92	-0.17	-1.90	-1.59	**30 ROC**		
31	9/23/91	385.92	0.35	-1.59	-2.01	-0.54		
32	9/24/91	387.71	0.68	-0.58	-1.36	-0.49		
33	9/25/91	386.88	-0.12	-0.58	-2.46	-0.77		
34	9/26/91	386.49	0.76	-0.67	-2.52	-0.73		
35	9/27/91	385.90	0.03	-0.69	-2.41	0.08		
36	9/30/91	387.86	0.61	0.86	-1.09	3.03		
37	10/1/91	389.20	0.58	1.07	-0.20	2.57		
38	10/2/91	388.26	0.18	0.24	-0.23	-0.60		
39	10/3/91	384.47	-0.89	0.23	-1.19	-1.75		
40	10/4/91	381.24	-1.21	-1.18	-1.89	-3.28		
41	10/7/91	379.50	-2.12	-1.56	-1.32	-3.64		
42	10/8/91	380.67	-1.61	-1.62	-1.15	-3.15		
43	10/9/91	376.80	-2.51	-2.78	-2.72	-5.00		
44	10/10/91	380.55	-1.39	-1.90	-0.79	-4.02	**KST**	
45	10/11/91	381.45	-1.65	-1.16	-1.12	-3.54	-11.89	
46	10/14/91	386.47	-0.70	-0.32	0.25	-1.45	-12.09	
47	10/15/91	391.01	0.71	1.07	1.05	0.27	-11.50	
48	10/16/91	392.80	2.17	1.63	1.35	0.94	-10.10	**5 day MA**
49	10/17/91	391.92	2.80	1.56	1.03	0.72	-8.41	-10.80
50	10/18/91	392.50	3.43	1.20	1.71	1.01	-6.14	-9.65

The KST can easily be calculated on any spreadsheet.

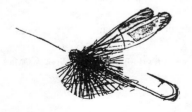

This arrangement is helpful from the viewpoint of trying to assess the maturity of a primary bull or bear market. In the classic conceptual sense, a primary bull market consists of three intermediate uptrends and, in certain cases, a fourth. During the 1984-87 period, there were in fact three rallies in the intermediate-term indicator.

D uring a bear market, the same conditions should hold in reverse — that is, three intermediate-term declines, but during the 1983, 1984 and 1987 periods, the primary declines were only accompanied by one downtrend. The position of the long-term indicator can also provide a valuable clue to the maturity of a primary trend. All things being equal, the farther it is from the equilibrium level, the more mature the trend.

The intermediate- and short-term momentum series can also flag positive and negative divergences and occasionally lend themselves to the construction of important trendlines. This is especially true of the more volatile short-term index. For example, it is possible to construct four downtrend lines in the 1983-89 period, each of which was followed by an important rally.

RESEARCH IS KEY

Obviously, it is not possible to ascertain when the long-term KST will reverse direction, but if it is in an overbought condition at a time when both the short- and intermediate-term series are also in a reversal mode, the odds of a long-term reversal are that much higher. If you can spot some trendline violations in these two shorter-term KSTs, so much the better. This KST arrangement works well for virtually all markets as well as individual stocks, currencies, commodities and so forth. As with any indicator, some entities work better than others, so the KST market cycle should not be blindly adopted for everything. Research is key: see if the KST market cycle has worked historically, and if the fit is good, the chances are better that it will operate in the future. Next, we will see how the KST market cycle model can be applied to relative strength analysis.

Martin J. Pring is the author of a number of books, publishes "The Pring Market Review" and is a principal of the investment counseling firm Pring-Turner Capital Group.

FIGURE 2

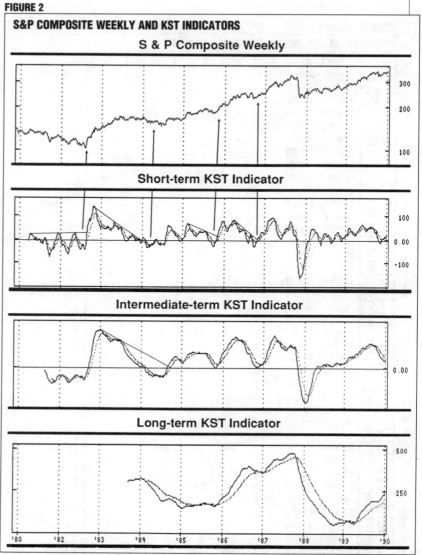

S&P COMPOSITE WEEKLY AND KST INDICATORS

The best opportunities occur when the primary trend is in a rising mode but is not overextended and the intermediate- and short-term trend KSTs are turning up. You can draw trendlines on the short-term KST to identify important turns. The short-term KST uses an 8-week simple moving average for the crossover, the intermediate-term uses a 10-week moving average and the long-term uses a 26-week moving average for the crossover.

REFERENCES

"Pring Market Review," International Institute for Economic Research, Inc., PO Box 329, Washington Depot, CT 06794.

Pring, Martin J. [1992]. *The All-Season Investor*, John Wiley & Sons.

_____ [1991]. *Technical Analysis Explained*, McGraw-Hill, 3d ed.

_____ [1981]. *How to Forecast Interest Rates*, McGraw-Hill.

_____ [1981]. *International Investing Made Easy*, McGraw-Hill.

_____ [1992]. "Summed rate of change," STOCKS & COMMODITIES, September.

_____ [1992]. "Rate of change," STOCKS & COMMODITIES, August.

A Gann Study Of A Bull Move In Wheat

Gann's methods have been studied for years and applied by many to trading stocks and commodities. Here, Richard Diaz of Refco, Inc., provides us with his Gann analysis of a bull market in wheat.

by Richard Diaz

FIGURE 1

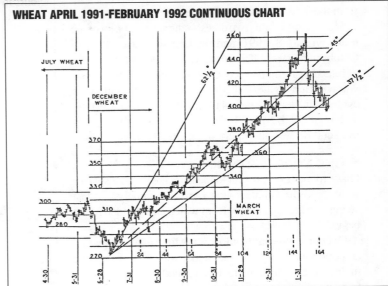

WHEAT APRIL 1991-FEBRUARY 1992 CONTINUOUS CHART

This daily continuation chart plots the relevant futures contract and adjusts the price scale when the switch is made to the next relevant contract.

FIGURE 2

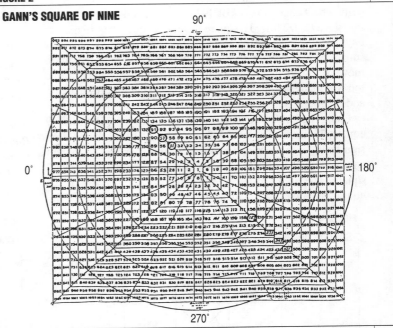

GANN'S SQUARE OF NINE

Important turning points in the wheat market for price and time fell on the 45- and 225-degree line.

Wheat futures rallied recently more than $1.88 to trade at the highest level since 1980. The move carried from the July 8, 1991, low made at 272-1/2 in the December 1991 contract to the high made at 463-1/4 on February 10, 1992, in the March 1992 contract. Several Gann factors were exceptionally helpful in calling the top price as well as its timing.

Figure 1 is a daily continuation chart that plots the relevant futures contract and adjusts the price scale when the switch is made from one contract to the next. Thus, on June 14, 1991, July wheat went out at 293 and the December contract settled at 310-1/4 on that day (I skip the September contract because I prefer to work on a longer run of contract). From that point on through November 15, 1991, the chart plots the price activity of the December 1991 contract. Adjusting the price scale allows a realistic appraisal of the continuous price movement.

Figure 2 is Gann's square of nine and is very useful in determining future time/price intervals that are significant to a given key high or low price. The low made on July 8, 1991, was 272-1/2, and this number can be found along the 225-degree line in the eighth cycle. The strongest points for resistance in both price and time are at the opposition points (180 degrees apart) and at the full-cycle points (a complete move of 360 degrees). Starting at 31, note the numbers along the 45-degree line (opposition) and along the 225-degree line, that is, 31, 43, 57, 73, 91, and so on. Figure 3 indicates where these numbers, taken as market days from the low of July 8, 1991, occurred.

The sharp break that occurred on August 19, 1991, was the result of the attempted coup in the former USSR. The low was made at 291-1/2 on the following day, which was 31 days from the start. The number 31 is on the 45-degree line in the square-of-nine chart. The next number along this line is 57, and 57 days from July 8, 1991, occurs on September 27, 1991. December wheat made a low on September 28 and two days later regained the 45-degree line up from the low. This line was not broken on a closing basis until the December wheat contract fell to 344-1/2 on November 12, 1991. On that day, the market was 91 days from July 8, 1991; 91 follows 57 along the 45-degree line in the square of nine chart. Note that the low made that day was only 1-1/2 cents from 343, which was one full cycle up from the 272-1/2 low.

Figure 3 highlights two dates — the starting point of the move on July 8, 1991, and the first significant high of October 25, 1991. This move carried 96-3/4 cents and unfolded in 79 market days. On the square of nine chart, you will find 96 along the 90-degree line; the following cycles of 90 degrees are at 411-1/2 (272-1/2 plus 139) and 462-1/2 (272-1/2 plus 190). We'll see shortly why 79 market days was an important time interval.

SWING YOUR PARTNER

I have found it very useful to measure the vertical span of what I call the counterswing move — namely, the last swing into the high or low from which an extended move begins.

Of course, one has to allow some time to ascertain that an important swing is in fact under way. Very often, the main swing conforming to the intermediate- or long-term trend will make important highs or lows at time and price intervals that are mathematically derived from the "counterswing move."

Allowing for the scale adjustment, this counterswing on the daily wheat chart consists of 49 boxes — in this case, 49 cents into the 272-1/2 low. To square this range thus takes 49 market days by 49 cents starting from the low price. Figure 4 has this square of 49 overlaid on the daily chart. Note how the entire move followed the 45-degree line up from the low and how the top was made against the 45-degree line in the fourth square up and the fourth square over in time.

Using the golden mean in Fibonacci theory, 1.618 times 49 equals 79 days. The move from July 8, 1991, to the first significant high made on October 25, 1991, covered 79 market days and, thus, was at the Fibonacci point in time in the second square. The area formed by the square of 49 is 2,401. If we double the area of that square to get the square with twice the

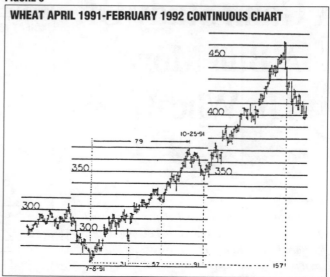

FIGURE 3

WHEAT APRIL 1991-FEBRUARY 1992 CONTINUOUS CHART

From the square of nine chart, the day counts are plotted. Notice that the countertrend moves ended 31, 57 and 91 days from the beginning of the bull market.

time/price area, we get a square with sides of 69.29. This means a square of 69-1/4 cents by 69-1/4 days. The top made at 463-1/4 occurred at the 2-3/4 point of this double square (2.75 times 69.29 = 190.56 plus 272-1/2 = 463) in price and at the 2.25 point of the square in time (2.25 times 69.29 = 155.9).

These measurements were derived from the square of the "counterswing move" into the low of July 8, 1991. They helped to reinforce the time/price points indicated by the square of nine chart. In all, properly utilized, Gann analysis appears to be useful for calling the timing and price activity of wheat futures.

Richard Diaz is a commodities analyst and the originator of Gann Scan, a daily commentary distributed globally to subscribers. For a sample, call (312) 930-3908. ◼TA

FIGURE 4

SQUARE OF 49

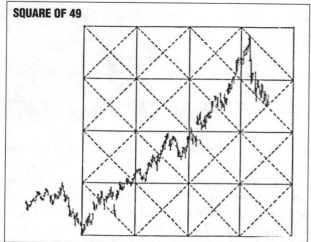

The last decline by December wheat was for 49 cents and ended on July 8, 1991. Squaring 49 cents by 49 days produces the square-of-49 chart. Notice that the wheat market peaked in the fourth square up and the fourth square over.

FIGURE 5

DOUBLE SQUARE

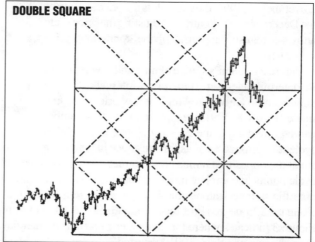

Doubling the square of 49 and taking the square root forms a double square with sides 69.25 cents by 69.25 days. The bull move ended with a price gain that was 2.75 times 69.25 cents.

Selecting The Best Futures Price Series For Computer Testing

One problem that traders studying commodity markets face is the fact that individual futures contracts have price characteristics that are not continuous with other contracts within the same market. Jack Schwager, author and director of futures research at Prudential Securities, has some suggestions on dealing with this problem.

by Jack Schwager

System traders who wish to test their ideas on futures prices face a major obstacle: the limited life span of futures contracts. In contrast to the equities market, where a given stock is represented by a single price series spanning the entire test period, in futures, each market is represented by a string of expiring contracts. Proposals for a solution to this problem have been the subject of many articles and much discussion. In the process, substantial confusion has been generated, as is evident by the use of identical terms to describe different types of price series. Even worse, a great deal of misinformation has circulated on this subject. My goal here is to attempt to set the facts straight.

Four basic types of price series can be used. Each has advantages and disadvantages.

ACTUAL CONTRACT SERIES

At a glance, the best apparent route might be to simply use the actual contract series. However, two major problems arise with this approach. First, if you test a system over a meaningful length of time, each market simulation requires a large number of individual price series. For example, a 15-year test run for a

typical market would require using approximately 60-90 individual contract price series. Moreover, using the individual contract series requires an algorithm for determining what action to take at the rollover points. As an example of a problem that may develop, it is quite possible for a given system to be long in the old contract and short in the new one or vice versa. These problems are hardly insurmountable, but they make the use of individual contract series somewhat unwieldy.

But the awkwardness involved in using a multitude of indi-

CHRISTIN TROSTLE

vidual contracts is not the main problem. The primary drawback in using individual contract series is the period of meaningful liquidity, which in most contracts is very short — much shorter than the already limited contract life spans. Examine a cross section of futures price charts depicting the price action in the one-year period prior to expiration. In most instances, the first half of the chart is filled with price gaps, reflecting the absence of significant trading in these contracts until they approach at least six months of expiration. In a number of markets, many contracts do not generate meaningful liquidity until the final four or five months of trading. This means that any technical system or method that requires looking back at more than four to five months of data — as would be true for the whole spectrum of longer-term approaches — cannot be applied to individual contract series. Thus, the use of individual contract series is not a viable alternative except for short-term system traders. It is not merely a matter of the approach being a difficult one; rather, it is impossible because the necessary data simply do not exist.

NEAREST FUTURES

The problems in using individual contract series has led to the construction of various linked price series, with the most common approach usually known as "nearest futures." This price series is constructed by taking each individual contract series until its expiration and then continuing with the next contract until its expiration, and so on. This approach may be useful for constructing long-term price charts for purposes of chart analysis, but it is worthless in providing a series that can be used in the computer testing of trading systems.

The problem in using the nearest futures series is that price gaps occur between expiring and new contracts — and quite frequently, these gaps can be very substantial. For example, assume that the July corn contract expires at $3.00 and that the next nearest contract — September — closes at $2.50 on the same day. Assume that on the next day, the September contract moves limit up from $2.50 to $2.62. A nearest futures price series will show the following closing levels on these two successive dates: $3.00, $2.62. So, the nearest futures contract would imply a 38-cent loss on a day during which longs would have enjoyed or shorts would have suffered a limit-up price gain of 12 cents. This example is by no means artificial. In fact, it would be simple to find a plethora of extreme situations in actual price histories. Moreover, even if the typical distortion at rollover is considerably less extreme, there is virtually always some distortion, and the cumulative effect of these errors would destroy the validity of any computer test.

Fortunately, few traders are unsophisticated enough to use the nearest futures type of price series for computer testing. The two other linked price series described here have become the approaches employed by most traders who want to use a single series for each market in computer testing.

CONSTANT-FORWARD (PERPETUAL) SERIES

The "constant-forward" or "perpetual" price series consists of quotes for prices a constant amount of time forward. A constant-forward series can be constructed from futures price data through interpolation.

For example, if we were calculating a 90-day constant-forward (or perpetual) series and the 90-day forward date fell exactly one-third of the way between the expirations of the nearest two contracts, the constant-forward price would be calculated as the sum of two-thirds of the nearest contract price and one-third of the subsequent contract price. As we moved forward in time, the nearer contract would be weighted less, but the weighing of the subsequent contract would increase proportionately. Eventually, the nearest contract would expire and drop out of the calculation, and the constant-forward price would be based on an interpolation between the subsequent two contracts.

The constant-forward price series eliminates the problem of huge price gaps at rollover points and is certainly a significant improvement over a nearest-futures price series. However, this

> **A linked futures price series can only accurately reflect either price *levels*, as does nearest futures, or price *moves*, as does continuous futures, but not both — much as a coin can either land on heads or tails but not both.**

type of series still has major drawbacks. First, it must be stressed that a constant-forward series cannot be literally traded, because the series does not correspond to any real contract. An even more serious deficiency of the constant-forward series is that it fails to reflect the effect of the evaporation of time that exists in actual futures contracts. This deficiency can lead to major distortions, particularly in carrying-charge markets.

To illustrate, consider a hypothetical situation in which spot gold prices remain stable at approximately $400 an ounce for a one-year period, while forward futures maintain a constant premium of 0.5% per month over the nearby contracts. Given these assumptions, futures would experience a steady downtrend, declining $24 an ounce ($2,400 per contract) over the one-year period (the equivalent of the cumulative carrying charge premiums). Note that the constant-forward series would fail to reflect this bear trend because it would register an approximate constant price. For example, a three-month constant-forward series would remain stable at approximately $406 an ounce — $400 + (3)(0.005)($400). Thus, the price pattern of a constant-forward series can deviate substantially from the pattern exhibited by the actual traded contracts — a highly undesirable feature.

CONTINUOUS PRICE SERIES

The "continuous" or "spread-adjusted" price series is constructed by adding the difference between the old and new contracts at the rollover point to the new contract series. For example, if, at the time of rollover between the June and August gold contracts, June closed at $405 and August at $410, the $5 difference would be subtracted from all August prices (plus or minus the cumulative adjustment factor carried over from prior rollovers). In effect, the construction of the continuous series can be thought of as the mathematical equivalent of taking a nearest futures chart, cutting out each individual contract series that makes up the chart and pasting the ends together (assuming a continuous series employing all contracts and using the same rollover dates as the nearest futures chart). Typically, it is convenient to shift the scale of the entire series by the cumulative adjustment factor, a step that will set the current price of the series equal to the price of the current contract without changing the shape of the series.

A linked futures price series can only accurately reflect either price *levels*, as does nearest futures, or price *moves*, as does continuous futures, but not both—much as a coin can either land on heads or tails but not both. The adjustment process used to construct continuous series means that past prices in a continuous series will not match the actual historical prices that prevailed at the time. The essential point: the continuous series is the only linked futures series that will exactly reflect price swings and hence equity fluctuations in an actual trading account. Consequently, it is the only linked series that can be used to generate accurate simulations in computer testing of trading systems.

Now this is an absolutely critical point! Mathematics is *not* a matter of opinion. There is only one right answer and many wrong answers. If a continuous futures price series is defined so that rollovers occur on dates consistent with rollovers in actual trading, results implied by using this series will precisely match results in actual trading (assuming, of course, accurate commission and slippage cost estimates). The continuous series will exactly parallel the fluctuations of a constantly held (that is, rolled-over) long position.

I have often seen comments or articles by industry "experts" arguing for the use of constant-forward (perpetual) series instead of continuous series to avoid distortions. This is *exactly* backward. This is not a matter of opinion; if you have any doubts, try matching up fluctuations in an actual trading account with those implied by constant-forward price series as I have defined here. You would soon be a believer.

There are, of course, drawbacks to the continuous futures type series. This series type may be the best solution to the linked series problem, but it is not a perfect answer. A perfect alternative simply does not exist. One potential drawback, which is a consequence of the fact that continuous futures only accurately reflect price swings and not levels, is that continuous futures cannot be used for any type of percentage calculations. (If a system requires the calculation of a percentage change figure, use continuous futures to calculate the nominal price change and nearest futures for the divisor.) In addition, some unavoidable arbitrari-

ness is involved in constructing a continuous series, as one must decide which contracts to use and on what dates the rollovers should occur. This is not really a problem, however, since these choices should merely mirror the contracts and rollover dates used in actual trading. Moreover, arbitrariness is involved in the use of any of the price series discussed.

hich price series would be most appropriate for chart analysis? To some extent, this is like asking which factor a consumer should consider before purchasing a new car, price or quality. The obvious answer is both, because each factor provides important information about a characteristic that is not measured by the other. In terms of price series, comparing nearest futures versus continuous futures, each series provides information that the other does not. Specifically, nearest futures provides accurate information about past price *levels* but not price *swings*, whereas continuous futures provide accurate information about past price swings but not price levels.

Consider Figure 1. What catastrophic event caused the instantaneous 40-cent collapse depicted by the nearest futures chart for cotton in 1986? Answer: absolutely nothing. This phantom price move reflected nothing more than a transition from the old-crop July contract to the new-crop October contract. (The wide price gap between the two contracts that year was due to a change in the government farm program, which drastically reduced the loan level, and in turn lowered the effective floor price, for the new crop.) In fact, cotton prices were actually in an uptrend during this particular contract transition!

Figure 2, which depicts the continuous futures price for the same market (and by definition eliminates price gaps at contract rollovers), illustrates the general uptrend in the cotton market during this period — an uptrend that actually began off a major low set in the previous year. Clearly, the susceptibility of nearest futures charts to distortions caused by wide gaps at rollovers can make it difficult to use nearest futures for chart analysis that focuses on price swings. On the other hand, the continuous futures chart achieves accuracy in depicting price swings by sacrificing accuracy in reflecting price levels. To accurately show the magnitude of past price swings, historical continuous futures prices can end up being far removed from the actual historical price levels. In fact, it is not even unusual for historical continuous futures prices to be negative (see Figure 3). Such "impossible" historical prices can have no relevance as guidelines to prospective support levels.

The fact that each type of price chart — nearest and continuous —

has certain significant intrinsic weaknesses argues for combining both chart types in a more complete analysis. Often, these two types of charts will provide entirely different price pictures. For example, consider the nearest futures chart for hog contracts depicted in Figure 4. Looking at this chart, it is tempting

> For long-term chart analysis, technicians might find it useful to supplement standard nearest futures charts with continuous futures charts, as these two representations can often provide very diverse information.

to conclude that hogs have essentially been in a wide-swinging trading range market for the entire 11-year period shown. Now go back and reexamine Figure 3, which is the continuous version of the same market. In this chart, it is evident that the hog market has witnessed a number of major trends — price movements that were completely hidden by the nearest futures chart (and would have been realized in actual trading). Without the benefit of the chart labels, it would be virtually impossible to recognize that Figures 3 and 4 depict the same market.

Despite the sometimes extraordinary contrast between the nearest and continuous futures charts, these price representations often yield similar conclusions. For example, the nearest futures chart for hogs (Figure 4) implies major support near the lower end of the broad trading range (approximately the 35-38 cent area). In the continuous futures chart, the combination of a major peak in 1988 and the low end of the 1990-92 trading range ·also implies major support in this same price zone. When both chart types provide similar conclusions, one can have greater confidence in the analysis. Technical analysts should at least experiment in using the continuous futures chart as a supplement to the conventional nearest futures chart to see whether such an addition would enhance the reliability of their analysis.

TO CONCLUDE

For long-term chart analysis, technicians might

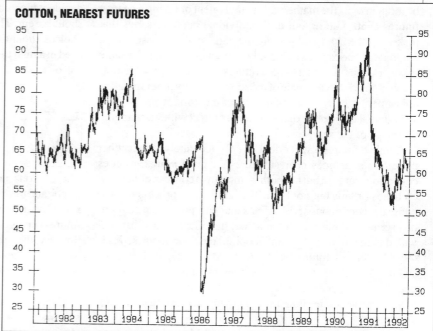

FIGURE 1

This chart implies that the cotton market tumbled 40 cents in 1986. In reality, the change in price is due to the difference between July (old crop) and October (new crop) at the time of the July expiration.

FIGURE 2

The continuous chart reflects the general uptrend that existed in 1986.

FIGURE 3

LIVE HOGS, CONTINUOUS FUTURES

The historical continuous chart will indicate price trends but not provide accurate price levels.

FIGURE 4

LIVE HOGS, NEAREST FUTURES

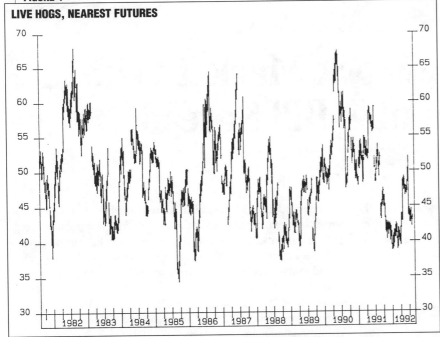

This chart will provide price levels but does not indicate the true market trends.

find it useful to supplement standard nearest futures charts with continuous futures charts, as these two representations can often provide very diverse information. For the purpose of computer testing of trading systems, only two types of valid price series are relevant: individual contract series and continuous futures series. Individual contract series are only a viable approach only if the methodologies employed do not require looking back more than four or five months, a restriction that rules out a vast number of technical approaches. In addition, the use of individual contract series is far clumsier. As a result, for most purposes, the continuous futures price series provides the best alternative. As long as one avoids using continuous prices for percentage calculations, this type of price series will yield accurate results — that is, results that parallel actual trading — as well as provide the efficiency of a single series per market. I strongly caution data users against using constant-forward type series in computer testing applications. If your goal is a price series that will accurately reflect futures trading, the constant-forward series will create distortions rather than avoid them.

Jack Schwager is the director of futures research at Prudential Securities, a CTA of Wizard Trading and an author whose latest book, The New Market Wizards, *is due out late this year from HarperCollins.*

Portions of this article appeared in the June/ July 1992 "MTA newsletter" published by the Market Technicians Association, Inc., 71 Broadway, 2nd Fl., New York, NY 10006, (212) 344-1266.

Timing The Stock Market With A Discount/T-Bill Spread

JIM BALKOVEK

Building on a February 1990 article by Jay Kaeppel, Formula Research editor Nelson Freeburg and engineer/investor Charles Skelley introduce a stock market timing model using the Fed discount rate and the 13-week Treasury bill rate spread.

by Nelson Freeburg and Charles Skelley

Tracking two well-known interest rates — the Federal Reserve discount rate and the 13-week Treasury bill rate — allows us to build a powerful stock market timing model, one that backtesting over the past 40 years shows could have consistently outperformed the Standard & Poor's 500. Properly manipulated, the spread between these two rates can give buy and

sell signals with 78% historical accuracy, produce only small losses when wrong and yield gains totaling 513 S&P points since 1953, far more than the rise in that index throughout its history.

In the February 1990 STOCKS & COMMODITIES, Jay Kaeppel introduced a trading method keyed to the Fed discount rate and the 13-week T-bill rate. More than 90% of the buy signals were accurate. In 35 years of testing — from 1953 to 1988 — total long-side profit was 312 S&P points, almost 40% more than the corresponding gain in the market. A $10,000 initial investment would have grown to $375,000. The appreciation works out to a compound annual return of 10.6% compared with a buy and hold gain of about 7% (excluding dividends and interest).

Kaeppel's procedure was as follows. Each week, take the Fed discount rate and subtract the yield on the three-month U.S. Treasury bill. (The data can be found in *The Wall Street Journal*,

FIGURE 1
S&P 500 1953-59

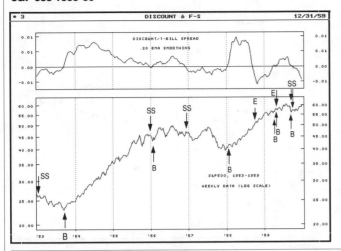

FIGURE 2
S&P 500 1960-69

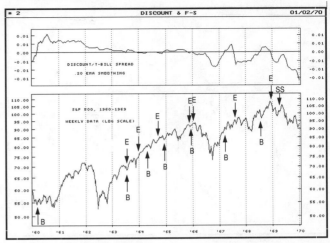

The upper chart is the smoothed discount rate - T-bill spread. When the indicator rises above zero, a buy (B) was indicated. When the indicator fell below zero, an exit long (E) was signaled. A sell short (SS) was flashed when the Fed raised the discount rate four times in a row and the indicator was below zero.

Investor's Business Daily or *Barron's*.) Then smooth the series with a 12.5% (15-week) exponential moving average (EMA):

CALCULATING THE 12.5% EXPONENTIAL MOVING AVERAGE

Spread = Discount rate - T-bill rate
$$\text{EMA}_{\text{This week}} = (\text{Spread} - \text{EMA}_{\text{Last week}})(0.125) + \text{EMA}_{\text{Last week}}$$

Calculations prepared with weekly data. To initialize the sequence, begin with a simple 15-week average of the spread.

You enter long when the smoothed spread turns positive and sell when the indicator turns negative.

The logic is clear. Treasury bill yields reflect the play of supply and demand in a competitive market, whereas the discount rate is administered by the Federal Reserve. When open market forces push T-bill yields below the discount rate, the upshot is greater liquidity throughout the monetary system and a bullish stimulus for stock prices. Conversely, when T-bill yields climb above the Fed's prescribed rate, the credit contraction that ensues is negative both for the economy and for stocks. Fed watchers routinely monitor this spread precisely because it hints when monetary authorities are apt to change the discount rate.

BUY-SIDE STRENGTH

While the track record of the Fed discount rate/T-bill spread is impressive, Kaeppel readily admits that this technique is more effective on the buy side than on the sell side. In contrast to the 90%-plus winning long trades, sell signals resulted in lower prices only 67% of the time. When we tested the method, bringing the results forward to July 1992, sell-side performance had slipped even further. Only 60% of the bearish signals could be called successful over the 40-year test period.

With most timing models, sell-side accuracy of 60% would be more than acceptable, especially in the case of the stock market, which has been in a broad uptrend for years. In an effort to realize this method's full potential, however, we went back to the historical record and introduced three minor changes. These simple adjustments improved an already capable method.

> **The performance is all the more striking in view of the underlying timing logic. Buy and sell signals derive solely from trends in short-term credit, a fundamentally distinct market.**

First, we increased the sensitivity of the calculations to allow for more timely entries and exits. While a broad range of values might serve just as well, we settled on a 20% EMA, the equivalent of a nine-week rather than a 15-week spread smoothing.

Second, in compiling the track record, we explicitly allowed for short sales. When conditions were found to be especially bearish, sell signals were treated as signals to enter short, not simply exit and stand aside.

Finally, and most important, we introduced a filter to tell us when conditions were particularly bearish. Here, the governing logic was an adaptation of the three steps and a stumble rule. When the Fed raised the discount rate four times in a row, the monetary climate was regarded as being highly negative. In such cases, a sell signal prompted not just an exit from a long trade but a reversal to the short side. Furthermore, if a sell signal was in effect and the "four-step" rule was subsequently activated, we went short at that time as well.

In all other cases, a sell signal prompted only the closing out of a long position. Rather than reverse and go short, we maintained a neutral stance and awaited the next signal. All trades used end-of-week closing prices.

FIGURE 3
S&P 500 1970-79

FIGURE 4
S&P 500 1980-92

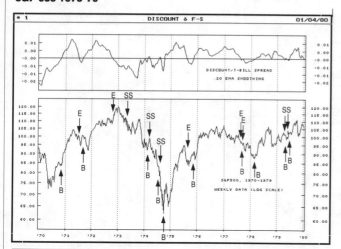

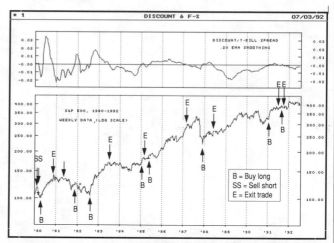

The effect of these enhancements can be seen in the historical record. In testing back to 1953, profits surged to 513 S&P points. Significantly, the index itself stood 100 points lower at the time this study was prepared.

Readers can look over Figures 1 through 4 and gain a concrete sense of how the model traded through the years. The staggering variety of market conditions would pose a challenge to any fixed set of trading tactics. While the charts do reveal clear lapses, on the whole this method has been notably effective in adapting to diverse market environments.

LIMITING LOSS

As for reliability, 36 out of 46 trades were profitable, a respectable 78% batting average. Among long entries, 26 of 32 trades were successful (81%), while 10 out of 14 short sales (71%) showed gains. Those with experience in mechanical trading systems will appreciate this pattern of consistent performance.

The findings are equally welcome from the perspective of money management. For all the splendid profit comparisons, this method excels in controlling risk. The largest loss was limited to 1.6% through four decades of testing. On just *one* occasion were there as many as three losing trades in a row in contrast to the longest streak of winning trades, considerably higher at 15.

With respect to drawdown, our treatment of that barometer of risk was conservative. Following the practice of System Writer Plus, we defined drawdown as the most severe dip in open equity measured from a peak in closed-out equity. These are the losses you would have had to trade through had you chosen the worst possible sequence of signals to act on.

Because drawdown is cumulative—it can go up but not down —the longer the period is under study, the greater the potential

exposure. Over the 40 years sampled here, one might expect drawdown to reach 10% or 15% of profit, not unusual for a mechanical trading method. Yet results show drawdown peaked at just 10.58 S&P points, scarcely 2% of profit at the time. This is a remarkable showing for a straightforward timing model tested against a database of such scope and breadth.

The complete performance data appear in the sidebar "Performance summary." The track record highlights long and short trades as well as the composite results when all entries are taken into account. Whatever the statistical focus, the conclusions are the same. This trading method operates aggressively on both sides of the market and disengages when the odds favor caution.

The performance is all the more striking in view of the underlying timing logic. Buy and sell signals derive solely from trends in short-term credit, a fundamentally distinct market. Unlike many conventional timing methods, the discount/T-bill spread is wholly independent of the very price trends it seeks to capture and exploit.

Nelson Freeburg, (901) 767-1956, is editor of Formula Research, a monthly report that develops and tests historically profitable trading systems. Charles Skelley is an engineer and investor who employs systematic timing methods to trade the stock market.

ADDITIONAL READING

Formula Research. 4990 Poplar Ave., Suite 210, Memphis, TN 38117.

Kaeppel, Jay [1990]. "Stock market timing with interest rates," *Technical Analysis of STOCKS & COMMODITIES*, Volume 8: February.

PERFORMANCE SUMMARY

```
/////////////////////////////////////////\\\\\\\\\\\\\\\\\\\\\\\\\\\\\\\\\\\\\\\\
Directory : F:\SWP                          Printed on   : 07/21/92 01:32pm
                         PERFORMANCE SUMMARY

Model Name      : 529                  Developer    :
Test Number     :      1 of       1
Notes :

Data            : 20%              00/00
Calc Dates      : 01/01/53 - 07/03/92

Num. Conv. P. Value  Comm  Slippage  Margin  Format  Drive:\Path\FileName
----------------------------------------------------------------------------
7000   2  $  0.010  $  0   $  0    $ 3,000  Ascii   D:\FORMRES\20%.PRN
```

```
//////////////////////// ALL TRADES - Test 1 \\\\\\\\\\\\\\\\\\\\\\\\\\\\\

Total net profit            $512.82
Gross profit                $533.28   Gross loss                  $-20.46

Total # of trades               46    Percent profitable             78%
Number winning trades           36    Number losing trades           10

Largest winning trade       $91.41    Largest losing trade        $-6.25
Average winning trade       $14.81    Average losing trade        $-2.05
Ratio avg win/avg loss        7.24    Avg trade (win & loss)      $11.15

Max consecutive winners         15    Max consecutive losers          3
Avg # bars in winners           37    Avg # bars in losers            5

Max closed-out drawdown     $-6.25    Max intra-day drawdown     $-10.58
Profit factor                26.06    Max # of contracts held         1
Account size required    $3,010.58    Return on account              17%
```

```
                   Highlights - All trades
   Description                  Date       Time     Amount
   ---------------------------------------------------------
   Largest Winning Trade        02/13/87    -    $     91.41
   Largest Losing Trade         09/20/91    -    $     -6.25
   Largest String of + Trades   07/26/74    -           15
   Largest String of - Trades   06/15/79    -            3
   Maximum Closed-Out Drawdown  09/20/91    -    $     -6.25
   Maximum Intra-Day Drawdown   09/13/91    -    $    -10.58
```

```
//////////////////////// LONG TRADES  - Test 1 \\\\\\\\\\\\\\\\\\\\\\\\\\\\\

Total net profit            $416.52
Gross profit                $433.61   Gross loss                  $-17.09

Total # of trades               32    Percent profitable             81%
Number winning trades           26    Number losing trades            6

Largest winning trade       $91.41    Largest losing trade        $-6.25
Average winning trade       $16.68    Average losing trade        $-2.85
Ratio avg win/avg loss        5.85    Avg trade (win & loss)      $13.02

Max consecutive winners         11    Max consecutive losers          1
Avg # bars in winners           40    Avg # bars in losers            7

Max closed-out drawdown     $-6.25    Max intra-day drawdown     $-10.58
Profit factor                25.37    Max # of contracts held         1
Account size required    $3,010.58    Return on account              13%
```

```
                   Highlights - Long trades
   Description                  Date       Time     Amount
   ---------------------------------------------------------
   Largest Winning Trade        02/13/87    -    $     91.41
   Largest Losing Trade         09/20/91    -    $     -6.25
   Largest String of + Trades   03/15/74    -           11
   Largest String of - Trades   09/20/91    -            1
   Maximum Closed-Out Drawdown  09/20/91    -    $     -6.25
   Maximum Intra-Day Drawdown   09/13/91    -    $    -10.58
```

```
//////////////////////// SHORT TRADES  - Test 1 \\\\\\\\\\\\\\\\\\\\\\\\\\\\\

Total net profit             $96.30
Gross profit                 $99.67   Gross loss                   $-3.37

Total # of trades               14    Percent profitable             71%
Number winning trades           10    Number losing trades            4

Largest winning trade       $18.52    Largest losing trade        $-1.87
Average winning trade        $9.97    Average losing trade        $-0.84
Ratio avg win/avg loss       11.83    Avg trade (win & loss)       $6.88

Max consecutive winners          5    Max consecutive losers          3
Avg # bars in winners           30    Avg # bars in losers            1

Max closed-out drawdown     $-2.73    Max intra-day drawdown      $-5.27
Profit factor                29.57    Max # of contracts held         1
Account size required    $3,005.27    Return on account               3%
```

```
                   Highlights - Short trades
   Description                  Date       Time     Amount
   ---------------------------------------------------------
   Largest Winning Trade        10/04/74    -    $     18.52
   Largest Losing Trade         06/15/79    -    $     -1.87
   Largest String of + Trades   10/04/74    -            5
   Largest String of - Trades   02/15/80    -            3
   Maximum Closed-Out Drawdown  02/15/80    -    $     -2.73
   Maximum Intra-Day Drawdown   02/08/80    -    $     -5.27
```

The performance summary as analyzed by System Writer Plus. Note that the margin listed ($3,000) is not the margin requirement for the S&P 500 futures contract.

A Guide To Pyramiding

Pyramiding, the process of adding to the number of contracts during the life of a trade, needs to be distinguished from the strategy of increasing or decreasing the trading size contingent on the outcome of a closed-out trade. Typically, pyramiding is undertaken with a view toward concentrating resources on a winning trade, but pyramids could also be used to average or dilute the entry price on a losing trade. Adding to a losing position is essentially a case of good money chasing after bad and so, in this article, Nauzer Balsara examines the concept of adding to profitable positions.

by Nauzer J. Balsara

C ritical to successful pyramiding is an appreciation of the concept of the effective exposure on a trade, which measures the dollar amount at risk at any point during the life of a trade. It is a function of the entry price, the current stop price and the number of contracts traded of the commodity in question. The effective exposure on a trade is defined as:

(a) for a short trade:

(current stop price - entry price)(number of contracts)

(b) for a long trade:

(entry price - current stop price)(number of contracts)

As long as a trade has not registered an unrealized profit, the effective exposure on a trade is positive and represents the maximum amount of capital at risk, assuming that prices do not gap through the stop price. A trade protected by a breakeven stop equal to the trade entry price has no effective exposure. For example, a trader who has purchased two futures contracts of June 1992 gold at $335 an ounce with a protective sell-stop at $330 is risking $5 an ounce, leading to an effective exposure of $500 per 100-ounce futures contract or $1,000 for two contracts.

If gold continues to rally, and the protective sell-stop is moved up to $335, our trader is assured a breakeven trade, disregarding gaps through the stop price.

NET EXPOSURE

Hypothetically, once the stop is moved past the breakeven level, the trade registers a locked-in, or assured, unrealized profit. The effective exposure now turns negative, indicating the trader's funds are no longer at risk. A negative exposure measures the locked-in unrealized profit on the trade. The trader might now wish to expose a part or all of his locked-in profits by adding to the number of contracts traded. Let p denote the fraction of assured unrealized profits to be reinvested into the trade. The value of p could vary from trade to trade. Whereas a p value of one suggests that 100% of assured unrealized profits are to be reinvested into the trade, a p value of zero implies that there will be no pyramiding. Therefore, the additional exposure on a profitable trade is defined as:

Additional exposure on profitable trade =
(p) (Assured profit per contract) (number of contracts)

The net exposure on a trade with assured unrealized profits is the sum of the effective exposure on the trade and the additional exposure resulting from reinvesting all or part of the assured unrealized profits. Therefore,

Net exposure = Effective exposure + additional exposure

Whereas the effective exposure on a profitable trade is necessarily negative, the additional exposure could be either zero or positive, leading to a zero or negative net exposure.

FACTORS INFLUENCING REINVESTMENT
A trader's willingness to expose unrealized profits is an important, albeit subjective, factor influencing the reinvestment fraction p. For our purposes here, let us assume that a trader has no qualms about reinvesting a fraction of his or her unrealized profits should conditions warrant such reinvestment. A continuation chart pattern (Figure 1) provides an opportune time for pyramiding a profitable trade, inasmuch as the continuation pattern provides a definitive clue as to the potential risk and reward on a breakout from the pattern. Symmetrical triangles, wedges and flags are the most commonly observed continuation patterns, all of which offer definite guidelines in regard to trade reward and risk.

For example, a breakout from a flag suggests that prices are likely to move a distance approximately equal to the length of the flagpole in the direction of the breakout. A logical place to set an exit stop would be just below the lowest point of a bull market flag formation and above the highest point of a bear market flag formation. Armed with this knowledge, the trader can now estimate the reward/risk ratio for the continuation pattern. There is a direct relationship between the reward/risk ratio and the reinvestment fraction p. The higher the reward/risk ratio, the stronger the case for a higher p value. Conversely, a reward/risk ratio close to 1 suggests extreme caution in plowing back assured unrealized trade profits.

COMPUTING INCREMENTAL CONTRACT SIZE
The incremental contract size is a function of the assured unrealized profits to be reinvested into the trade and the dollar amount at risk per contract. Specifically, the formula for computing the incremental contract size is:

FIGURE 1

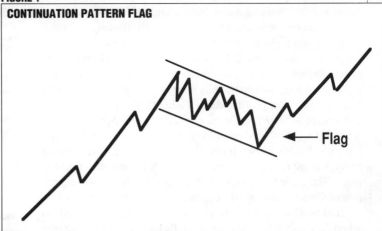

CONTINUATION PATTERN FLAG

— Flag

Continuation patterns are a period of consolidation during a trend. The flag pattern will have a downward slant with the line of resistance and the line of support being approximately parallel. Technicians expect the flag formation to mark the halfway point in the current trend.

$$\frac{(p) \text{ (assured unrealized profits) (number of contracts)}}{\text{permissible dollar risk per contract}}$$

Referring to the previous example, assume that gold is currently trading at $350 an ounce and the sell-stop is raised to $345 an ounce, leading to a permissible risk exposure of $500 per contract. Since two contracts of gold were purchased at $335 an ounce, we have an unrealized profit of $15 per ounce, of which $10 is locked in by the protective stop as an assured unrealized profit. This translates into an assured unrealized profit of $2,000 for two contracts.

> ## Pyramiding a futures trade is a means by which to enhance the leverage of an already leveraged trading vehicle.

If 25% of this amount or $500 is to be reinvested, the trader should buy one additional contract at $350 with a sell-stop for the entire position at $345. If p is set at 0.50 or $1,000, the trader should buy two additional contracts at $350. Finally, if the trader wishes to reinvest 100% of assured unrealized profits or $2,000, this would entail buying four additional contracts at $350 with a sell-stop for all six contracts set at $345.

When the number of contracts added to a position is less than the number of contracts currently traded, we have a conventional, scaled-down pyramid. Conversely, when the number of contracts added to a position exceeds the number of contracts currently traded, we have an inverted, scaled-up or leveraged pyramid. When the number of additional contracts is the same as the number of contracts currently traded, the formation is symmetrical as opposed to a pyramid.

IMPACT OF PYRAMIDING
The shape of the pyramid determines the sensitivity of overall

profits to changes in futures prices, as is evident from Figure 2. Assume that prices fluctuate from a high of $355 to a low of $345. With no profit reinvestment, the profit spread associated with these price fluctuations is $2,000. In the case of the scaled-down pyramid where 25% of assured unrealized profits are reinvested into the trade, we observe marginally higher profits at a price of $355 and marginally lower profits at a price of $345, leading to a wider profit spread of $3,000. The profit spread is maximized at $6,000 in the case of the leveraged pyramid case when 100% of assured unrealized profits are plowed back into the trade. Profits are maximized in the event of a favorable price move but are reduced to zero should prices retreat to the stop price. The scaled-up pyramid magnifies the double-edged nature of the leverage sword, suggesting that a 100% plowback of assured profits should be reserved for those special situations when the possibility of an exceptionally high reward justifies the risk.

CONCLUDING

Pyramiding a futures trade is a means by which to enhance the leverage of an already leveraged trading vehicle. Reinvesting a fraction of assured unrealized profits into the trade is a conservative approach to pyramiding, inasmuch as the trader is only risking a portion or all of the locked-in profits on the trade. In the worst-case scenario, if 100% of assured unrealized profits are plowed back into the trade, the trader risks losing this entire amount, ending up with a breakeven trade.

Nauzer Balsara, Ph.D., is a Commodities Trading Advisor and an associate professor of finance at Northeastern Illinois University, Chicago, IL. He is actively involved in futures and options trading.

REFERENCES

Balsara, Nauzer J. [1992]. "Avoiding bull and bear traps," STOCKS & COMMODITIES, August.

_____ [1992]. "Using profitability stops in trading," STOCKS & COMMODITIES, May.

_____ [1992]. *Money Management Strategies for Futures Traders,* John Wiley & Sons.

FIGURE 2

SENSITIVITY ANALYSIS OF PROFITS TO ALTERNATIVE PYRAMIDING STRATEGIES

Initial purchase of two contracts of June 1992 gold futures at $335
Current futures price: $350
Current stop-price: $345

Reinvestment fraction	0	0.25	0.50	1.00
Assured unrealized profits	$2,000	$2,000	$2,000	$2,000
Reinvested profits	0	$500	$1,000	$2,000
Number of additional contracts	0	1	2	4

Case (a): Prices move up to $355
Unrealized profits on:

Initial two contracts	$4,000	$4,000	$4,000	$4,000
Incremental contracts	0	$500	$1,000	$2,000
Total profit	**$4,000**	**$4,500**	**$5,000**	**$6,000**

Case (b): Prices move down to the stop-price of $345
Realized profit/(loss) on:

Initial two contracts	$2,000	$2,000	$2,000	$2,000
Incremental contracts	0	$(500)	$(1,000)	$(2,000)
Total profit	**$2,000**	**$1,500**	**$1,000**	**0**
Profit spread ((a) - (b))	$2,000	$3,000	$4,000	$6,000

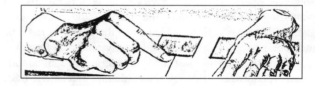

Seasonal Variations In A Semiconductor Stock

STAN SHAW

Do seasonal variations exist in the heavily traded and re-searched stock market? Good question. Recently, a securities analyst was quoted as saying that semiconductor stocks de-clined an average of 40% from their seasonal highs to their seasonal lows. Jack Karczewski presents this primer on the analytical procedure of investigating seasonal fluctuations in the stock market, using a semiconductor stock as an example.

by Jack Karczewski

Predictable seasonal variations in commodities are both well known and documented. Whether the same kind of patterns can be detected elsewhere, most notably in the stock market, remains to be seen, however. Thus, to analyze cyclical phenomena in stocks, I chose the ratio to moving average method to illustrate the seasonal tendency in a semiconductor stock. This method has been in existence for many years and preceded the advent of computers — *including* mainframes. It was the method that the U.S. Census Bureau used prior to the adoption of the current Census X-11 program. Now, of course, most

FIGURE 1

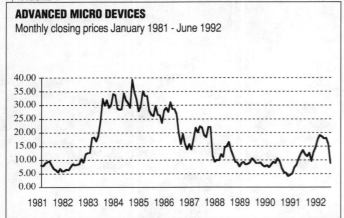

ADVANCED MICRO DEVICES
Monthly closing prices January 1981 - June 1992

The monthly closing prices indicate that the stock has had a number of trends, both up and down.

FIGURE 2

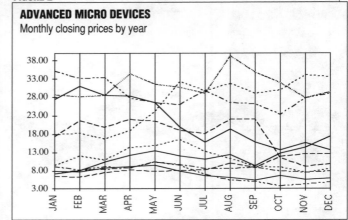

ADVANCED MICRO DEVICES
Monthly closing prices by year

Through visual inspection, there appears to be a slight downward bias in prices through the year.

traders with access to a personal computer and spreadsheet software such as Microsoft Excel can easily construct a seasonal index on literally any promising time series.

For the sake of simplicity, I chose only one stock in an industry rather than a basket of stocks or an index. I will show that a seasonal pattern exists in the stock selected, in this case Advanced Micro Devices (AMD), and also illustrate a method that might give a clue to using the seasonal variation to anticipate seasonal price moves.

I have presented the material in a way that illustrates the procedure and components for the construction of the seasonal index. Sophisticated programs that will construct these indices *are* available, but I am presenting a learning exercise in addition to a means of understanding the seasonal nature of a particular stock.

ANALYSIS OF TIME SERIES

Seasonal analysis can be applied to any regularly repetitive movement in a time series lasting a year or less. The variations occur because of climatic or economic activity or customs and other conditions. The analysis of trends is incomplete without at least a cursory examination to determine if a seasonal pattern exists. For example, most economic statistics (time series) released by government agencies are seasonally adjusted. These seasonal adjustments can and often do have a major impact on the market. The housing starts statistic reported monthly by the U.S. government is one example of the importance of seasonal adjustment; traditionally, February has the fewest actual starts recorded. Logically, to compare February with July, a month that is characterized by a large number of starts, the data must be annualized and seasonalized. Small changes in February actual starts can and do have a major impact on the seasonally adjusted number released by the U.S. Commerce Department.

In our analysis of AMD, I have chosen to investigate the seasonal pattern with quarterly data to illustrate all the calculations involved. Monthly data will be produced without calculations for those interested in seeing the final product in a monthly form, which is more useful for trading and investing purposes.

Look at Figure 1, which shows the monthly closing prices of AMD. Here, it is easy to observe the trend and a possible cyclical component of the price trends. Examining Figure 2, which is each year's worth of monthly closing prices, reveals a slight bias downward in prices as we scan the chart. Symbolically, the price can be represented as:

$$P=T*C*S*I$$

where:
P = Individual price in the time series
T = Trend component
C = Cyclical component
S = Seasonal component
I = Irregular component

The raw price includes all the variables that influence that current price in the time series. Dividing the original observations by the four-quarter moving average (MA) yields the following:

$$P/MA=(T*C*S*I)/(T*C)=S*I$$

If a seasonal component *does* exist, then these steps I present will aid us in identifying this seasonal influence.

RATIO TO MOVING AVERAGE

Twelve years' worth of quarterly data were selected to arrive at the quarterly seasonal index. The same time span was used in the determination of the monthly numbers but is not illustrated here. These steps are useful aids in determining whether a seasonal component exists:

1 The first step is to construct a four-quarter moving average of the quarterly closing prices. This smoothed price series contains the trend and cyclical components present in the original data. Why these data include the trend and the cyclical component is best understood by what they *don't* contain. They no longer contain the seasonal fluctuations because by definition the seasonal

FIGURE 3

ADVANCED MICRO DEVICES
Quarterly prices with a four-quarter moving average

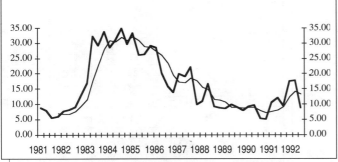

The four-quarter moving average will filter out the seasonal and irregular components of the price.

fluctuations average each other out over the course of a year and thus are filtered out by the moving average (Figure 3). Irregular movements also tend to cancel each other out over the course of a year.

> ## The analysis of trends is incomplete without at least a cursory examination to determine if a seasonal pattern exists.

2 Divide the original data for each quarter by the corresponding moving average (Figure 4). We are now left with the only seasonal and irregular components of the time series. The problem with the average at this point is centering the average opposite the appropriate time frame so the average is positioned properly. The data in the last column, the ratio to moving average, are two of the four quarters' moving totals divided by eight. These values are plotted in Figure 5.

3 Next, arrange the ratio to moving average figures in an array that groups similar elements, in this case by quarter

FIGURE 5

PERCENT OF MOVING AVERAGES

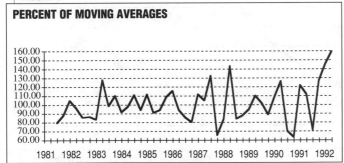

The quarterly ratio to the moving average is graphically presented.

(Figure 6). These quarterly columns will be averaged to eliminate the irregular movements and thus isolate the stable seasonal component. The method of calculating this mean is called "the modified mean" — that is, the ratio to moving average numbers after dropping the highest and lowest numbers (Figure 7).

4 Finally, adjust the four modified means to total 400 and therefore average out to 100 by multiplying the quarterly means by an adjustment factor. This adjustment factor is the ratio of 400 divided by the summed raw quarterly. For example, in Figure 5 the seasonal index is found by multiplying each quarterly mean by 400/404.62. This adjusts the quarterly means to average 100 each. The statistical measures are given to illustrate the effect of dropping the highs and lows. The final figures are then our seasonal indices for each quarter. This procedure was applied to monthly data as well, and the results are presented in Figures 8 and 9.

I have reproduced daily charts on AMD going back to early 1989. Without any further analysis, arrows were placed at the approximate seasonal highs and lows. The seasonal information indicates the time span of a month; the arrows are arbitrarily placed in those months and so no inference should be drawn as to the precise timing of this indicator. This information clearly indicates that seasonal information can be a useful aid in the timing of investment decisions where stocks indicate a strong seasonal pattern.

Figures 10 through 13 are charts with J. Welles Wilder's relative strength index (RSI)

FIGURE 4

ADVANCED MICRO DEVICES
Quarterly prices

DATE	PRICE	Four Quarter Moving Total	Two of a Four Quarter Moving Total	Moving Average	Ratio to Moving Average
03/81	8.75				
06/81	7.86				
09/81	5.41	27.90	54.54	6.82	79.35
12/81	5.88	26.65	53.56	6.69	87.76
03/82	7.50	26.91	57.29	7.16	104.74
06/82	8.13	30.38	67.44	8.43	96.39
09/82	8.88	37.06	83.37	10.42	85.16
12/82	12.56	46.31	116.75	14.59	86.07
03/83	16.75	70.44	161.00	20.12	83.23
06/83	32.25	90.56	202.19	25.27	127.61
09/83	29.00	111.63	235.00	29.38	98.72
12/83	33.63	123.38	245.25	30.66	109.68
03/84	28.50	121.88	249.50	31.19	91.38
06/84	30.75	127.63	251.13	31.39	97.96
09/84	34.75	123.50	251.88	31.48	110.37
12/84	29.50	128.38	252.00	31.50	93.65
03/85	33.38	123.63	238.75	29.84	111.83
06/85	26.00	115.13	229.75	28.72	90.53
09/85	26.25	114.63	224.38	28.05	93.59
12/85	29.00	109.75	213.50	26.69	108.67
03/86	28.50	103.75	197.00	24.63	115.74
06/86	20.00	93.25	171.25	21.41	93.43
09/86	15.75	78.00	147.38	18.42	85.50
12/86	13.75	69.38	137.75	17.22	79.85
03/87	19.88	68.38	143.00	17.88	111.19
06/87	19.00	74.63	145.38	18.17	104.56
09/87	22.00	70.75	132.63	16.58	132.70
12/87	9.88	61.88	121.25	15.16	65.15
03/88	11.00	59.38	106.00	13.25	83.02
06/88	16.50	46.63	92.00	11.50	143.48
09/88	9.25	45.38	88.25	11.03	83.85
12/88	8.63	42.88	79.00	9.88	87.34
03/89	8.50	36.13	72.00	9.00	94.44
06/89	9.75	35.88	71.00	8.88	109.86
09/89	9.00	35.13	70.88	8.86	101.59
12/89	7.88	35.75	71.25	8.91	88.42
03/90	9.13	35.50	67.13	8.39	108.75
06/90	9.50	31.63	60.25	7.53	126.14
09/90	5.13	28.63	58.63	7.33	69.94
12/90	4.88	30.00	62.50	7.81	62.40
03/91	10.50	32.50	69.25	8.66	121.30
06/91	12.00	36.75	86.13	10.77	111.47
09/91	9.38	49.38	106.00	13.25	70.75
12/91	17.50	56.63	110.00	13.75	127.27
03/92	17.75	53.38	97.38	12.17	145.83
06/92	8.75	44.00	44.00	5.50	159.09

First, calculate the four-quarter moving total (column 3), then add two of the moving totals together (column 4). This sum is divided by eight (column 5), which is the moving average. Divide the quarter's closing price by the moving average to determine the ratio to the moving average (column 6). The price of the stock is the average monthly price.

FIGURE 6

ADVANCED MICRO DEVICES
Seasonal index table unadjusted

	I	II	III	IV	Mean
1981			79.35	87.76	
1982	104.74	96.39	85.16	86.07	
1983	83.23	127.61	98.72	109.68	
1984	91.38	97.96	110.37	93.65	
1985	111.83	90.53	93.59	108.67	
1986	115.74	93.43	85.50	79.85	
1987	111.19	104.56	132.70	65.15	
1988	83.02	143.48	83.85	87.34	
1989	94.44	109.86	101.59	88.42	
1990	108.75	126.14	69.94	62.40	
1991	121.30	111.47	70.75	138.27	
1992	145.83	159.09			
Mean	106.50	114.59	91.96	91.57	404.62
Hi	145.83	159.09	132.70	138.27	
Lo	83.02	90.53	69.94	62.40	
SD	18.37	22.10	18.41	21.36	
SI	105.28	113.28	90.909	90.526	400

Arrange the data in an array that groups the data by quarter. The gray-celled areas are the high and low extremes. Multiply each quarterly mean by 400/404.62 to calculate the seasonal index (bottom row).

FIGURE 7

ADVANCED MICRO DEVICES
Seasonal index table adjusted

	I	II	III	IV	Mean
1981			79.35	87.76	
1982	104.74	96.39	85.16	86.07	
1983	83.23	127.61	98.72	109.68	
1984	91.38	97.96	110.37	93.65	
1985	111.83		93.59	108.67	
1986	115.74	93.43	85.50	79.85	
1987	111.19	104.56		65.15	
1988		143.48	83.85	87.34	
1989	94.44	109.86	101.59	88.42	
1990	108.75	126.14			
1991	121.30	111.47	70.75		
1992					
MM	104.73	112.32	89.88	89.62	396.55
Hi	121.30	143.48	110.37	109.68	
Lo	83.23	93.43	70.75	65.15	
SD	12.50	16.88	12.26	13.68	
SI	105.64	113.30	90.66	90.40	400.00

The modified means are determined by dropping the high and low values from each column. The seasonal index is calculated by multiplying the modified mean (MM) by 400/396.55.

added as a potential indicator to improve timing with this type of analysis. My conclusion is that this type of analysis and information gives additional depth and insight into the technical analysis of a particular vehicle. It is important to note that the seasonal index is an indicator that has predictive value during the year and not just on the seasonal highs and lows. The table can be used to determine if the stock is behaving according to its seasonal tendencies or deviating from them. The table, as the listing of indicator values, is a useful signpost to be used during the year. I have included individual charts for each of the years that were illustrated, so a closer inspection might reveal additional opportunities.

POSTULATIONS

This technique can be applied to stocks in industries that are very seasonal in nature and might also be mature industries, but admittedly, I have not investigated this theory far enough to determine if it is indeed correct or even worth pursuing. I might postulate that candidate industries would be personal computer manufacturers, retail companies, hard disk drive manufacturers and, obviously, the semiconductor industry. Companies with strong growth characteristics would not be candidates, since the trend component of the time series would have a tendency to overwhelm any cyclical and seasonal factors that are present. Overall, however, it is clear that seasonal variations exist; the challenge is to find out where.

Jack Karczewski is a Paine Webber broker residing in Scottsdale, AZ.

FIGURE 8

ADVANCED MICRO DEVICES
Monthly seasonal index table adjusted

	Jan	Feb	Mar	Apr	May	Jun	Jul	Aug	Sep	Oct	Nov	Dec
1981						109.05	93.96	87.83	78.54	97.11	84.13	86.28
1982	92.26		97.15	101.28			79.33	88.51	72.50	88.82	83.01	74.08
1983	96.01	89.07			95.07	120.19	107.41	111.00	97.53	97.78	109.94	109.05
1984	92.39	89.18	89.06	108.01	100.76	97.67	90.74	121.63	107.58	100.57	88.36	94.43
1985		111.41	114.57	96.87	92.14	91.50	106.23	95.62	95.35	84.82	102.06	109.52
1986	106.94			122.76	121.19	95.59		100.03	84.00	75.21	86.66	76.01
1987	95.64	116.52	105.53	119.76	119.83	108.22	107.74		77.94	64.35	70.17	
1988		96.32	93.04		130.20			103.31	86.63	87.76	76.68	92.72
1989	101.51	93.07	96.51	101.31	118.85	113.11	100.98	100.67	104.79	91.69	87.38	92.59
1990	87.33	103.06	118.86	118.56		135.71	100.07		70.69			
1991	85.40	90.70	110.47	119.03	120.17	98.00	84.56	89.12				
MEAN	94.68	98.67	103.15	110.95	112.28	107.67	96.78	99.75	88.62	89.08	86.95	89.43
HIGH	106.94	116.52	118.86	122.76	130.20	135.71	107.74	121.63	107.58	100.57	109.94	109.52
LOW	85.40	89.07	89.06	96.87	92.14	91.50	79.33	87.83	70.69	75.21	64.35	70.17
STD DEV	7.08	10.58	10.80	10.24	14.13	14.04	10.30	11.27	13.48	8.77	13.22	14.28
Sea Index	96.45	100.51	105.08	113.02	114.37	109.68	98.59	101.61	90.28	90.74	88.57	91.10

The same methods described for the quarterly seasonal index is presented on the monthly data.

FIGURE 9

ADVANCED MICRO DEVICES
Monthly seasonal index

The monthly seasonal index indicates a seasonal high in May and a seasonal low in November.

REFERENCES AND FURTHER READING

Arnold, James G. [1990]. "Four-year cycles," *Technical Analysis of* STOCKS & COMMODITIES, Volume 8: September.

Hamburg, Morris [1970]. *Statistical Analysis for Decision Making,* Harcourt Brace.

Hannula, Hans [1991]. "Trading the eclipse cycle," *Technical Analysis of* STOCKS & COMMODITIES, Volume 9: December.

_____ [1991]. "The seasonal cycle," *Technical Analysis of* STOCKS & COMMODITIES, Volume 9: November.

Kaeppel, Jay [1990]. "The January barometer: Myth and reality," *Technical Analysis of* STOCKS & COMMODITIES, Volume 8: July.

Kargenian, Bob [1990]. "'Tis the season," *Technical Analysis of* STOCKS & COMMODITIES, Volume 8: July.

Merrill, Arthur A. [1991]. "Summer rally: Fact or fiction?," *Technical Analysis of* STOCKS & COMMODITIES, Volume 9: July.

Mokrasch, Lewis Carl [1992]. "Detecting seasonality," STOCKS & COMMODITIES, August.

_____ [1991]. "Studying 10-year stock price patterns," *Technical Analysis of* STOCKS & COMMODITIES, Volume 9: April.

Warwick, Ben [1991]. "The end-of-the-month effect," *Technical Analysis of* STOCKS & COMMODITIES, Volume 9: June.

Wilder, J. Welles [1978]. *New Concepts in Technical Trading Systems,* Trend Research.

FIGURE 10
ADVANCED MICRO DEVICES
21-day relative strength index

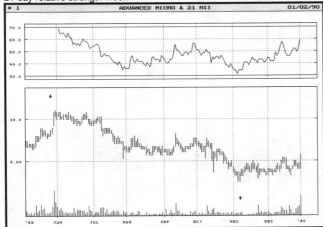

FIGURE 11
ADVANCED MICRO DEVICES
21-day relative strength index

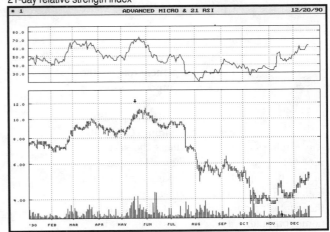

FIGURE 12
ADVANCED MICRO DEVICES
21-day relative strength index

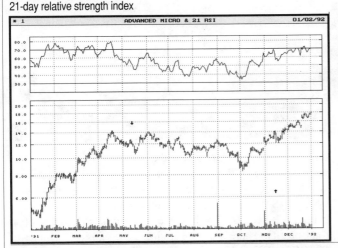

FIGURE 13
ADVANCED MICRO DEVICES
21-day relative strength index

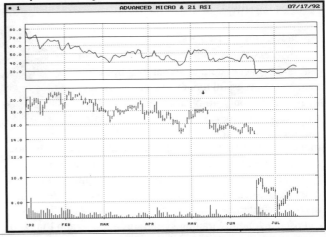

The charts begin in 1989 and conclude in June 1992. The down arrow indicates the projected seasonal high and the up arrow indicates the projected seasonal low. The 21-day RSI is used to indicate oversold (below 30) and overbought readings (above 70) situations.

Trading The Equity Curve

Technical analysis is typically applied to prices to determine the trend and changes in the trend. Now, if you will, consider applying the same concept to analyzing your equity curve to determine those times when your equity may not be trending in the preferred direction.

by Joe Luisi

Money management may be the single most important aspect in trading, but few traders spend the necessary time required for successful trading. Generally, it is a rule of thumb that traders should spend 30% of their time analyzing the markets and 70% of their time split between looking for low-risk, high-profit trades and money management. With the increasing popularity and availability of the home computer, trading systems promising huge rewards have burst on the scene, but not necessarily delivering. The novice trader may be led to believe that with the right system, he or she can beat the market and achieve great monetary success. The truth is quite the opposite.

SECRETS OF SUCCESS?

To be successful, a trader only needs a system that is 51% accurate and sometimes not even that. Most successful money managers use systems that are only 40-50% accurate, but they have very strict money management standards and their risk to reward ratio is very high. A money management plan is very important; even if a trader does not use a mechanical system to trade, an accurate record of trades executed should always be kept and equity plotted on a daily basis. Such records can give the trader a visual idea of how his or her trading is faring — trending up, down or flat.

I used a volatility trading system in Investograph Plus software on the Standard & Poor's 100 (OEX) from December 31, 1991, to May 20, 1992. The system uses an eight-day time frame and a 20% volatility breakout. I used $61 as a one-way commission, and to adjust for the OEX index, I used a $266 move per unit. Thus, every dollar move in the index equals $266. This was recommended by the software to approximate trading $1,000 worth of OEX options. The volatility system is a stop and reverse system† (SAR) that is always in the market. The initial starting capital was $10,000. The initial testing produced $20,616.66 in total profits. There were 68 trades, a winning percentage of 52.94% and $303.18 profit per trade. The highest account value was $20,616.66 and the lowest $9,853.98. The largest losing trade was -6.95.

Figure 1 shows the trades' equity together with a 10-day

†See Traders' Glossary for definition

simple moving average of the equity line. Overall, the system's results aren't bad, but they can be improved. We can apply a simple crossover technique to the 10-day moving average of the equity line to stop trading the system during those times when the equity is below the moving average. When the equity line

> **By constantly monitoring your equity, you can control your risk as well as preserve your hard-earned money.**

crosses above the moving average, we resume trading. One drawback is you will miss the profitable trade that brought the equity above the moving average in the first place. The equity fell below the moving average during the periods February 11-21, March 3 through April 7 and May 7-18. During such times, the trader should stop using real money to trade and trade hypothetically, still tracking the trades and updating the equity line to know when to resume trading (Figure 2). Figure 3 shows the new equity line, which is much smoother. But how were the results?

Our simple moving average crossover money management technique produced $23,217.37 in profits in half as many trades. Trades totaled 37 with 56.57% wins, while the highest account value was $23,217.37 and the lowest $9,853.98. The largest losing trade was -4.43 and the profit per trade was $627.49. Using this money management technique can provide a much smoother equity curve with less risk and a higher profit per trade. Plotting your equity with a moving average can give you an early warning sign that your system is not working or that you have hit a streak of losing trades. By stopping trading altogether, you can preserve your capital in case the system never returns to profitability.

ROUNDING OUT THE TECHNIQUE

A useful addition to this money manage-

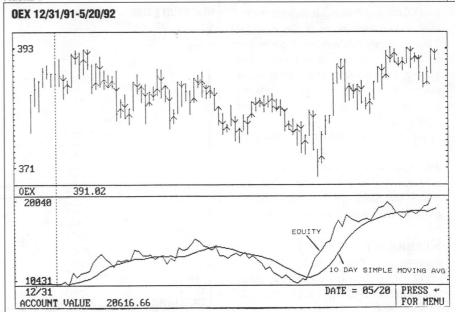

FIGURE 1

A volatility system uses an average of the true range over recent days. This particular case uses an eight-day average true range. Multiply the average true range by 20% and add it to the close for today's buy signal. Subtract the eight-day average true range multiplied by 20% from the close for today's sell signal. The bottom chart is the equity curve (with a 10-day moving average) of applying these trading rules to the OEX.

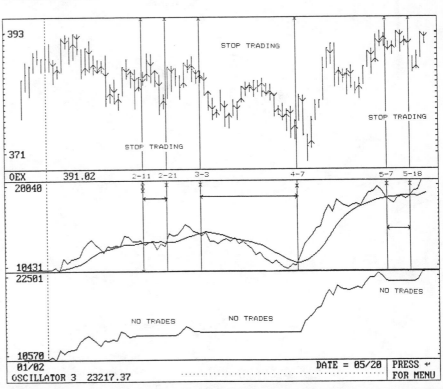

FIGURE 2

The equity fell below the moving average during the periods February 11-21, March 3 through April 7 and May 7-18. During such times, the trader should stop using real money to trade and trade hypothetically, still tracking the trades and updating the equity line to know when to resume trading.

ment technique would be to maintain several trading systems at the same time, allocating money between the systems. Then, if one system's equity drops below its moving average, stop trading that system and allocate more capital to the system that is trading above the moving average. By constantly monitoring your equity, you can control your risk as well as preserve your hard-earned money.

Joe Luisi, (410) 867-7424, is the director of research at the Rich Financial Group, which specializes in foreign exchange advisory and money management.

REFERENCE

Investograph Plus. Liberty Research, 1250 Capital of Texas Highway, Bldg 2 Suite 300, Austin, TX 78746, (512) 467-0887.

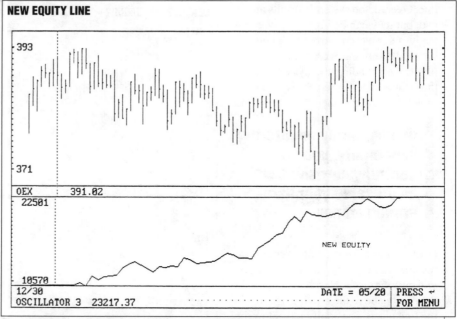

FIGURE 3

NEW EQUITY LINE

Figure 3 shows the new equity line, which is much smoother. But how were the results? Our simple moving average crossover money management technique produced $23,217.37 in profits in half as many trades.

■ MetaStock Professional 3.0 The Discount Rate/T-Bill Spread

(See Nelson Freeburg and Charles Skelley's article in this issue, "Timing the stock market with a discount/T-bill spread.")

The formula for the indicator is:

$$EMA_{This\ week} = (Spread - EMA_{Last\ week})\ (0.20) + EMA_{Last\ week}$$

where: Spread = Discount rate - T-bill rate

The rules are to buy whenever the smoothed spread is positive and exit longs when the smoothed spread is negative. Sell short signals occur when the Federal Reserve raises the discount rate four times in a row.

To duplicate the charts shown in Freeburg and Skelley's article, you need to have data on Treasury bill yields, the Fed discount rate and the Standard & Poor's 500. The first step is to create a composite security with the Federal discount rate as the first security and T-bill yields as the second security using subtraction as the operator. Load the composite security and plot the custom formula "mov(Close,9,e)." Use the indicator buffer [Ctrl-B] to save this indicator.

Next, load the equivalent time frame of the S&P 500. Use the indicator buffer to restore the smoothed discount rate/T-bill spread. If desired, a chart of the Fed discount rate can be plotted on the screen at the same time to look for four consecutive rate hikes as mentioned in the article.

—Allan McNichol, Equis International

■ Volume-Weighted RSI: Money Flow

The March 1989 STOCKS & COMMODITIES presented an article on modifying J. Welles Wilder's relative strength index by weighting the closing price with volume.

First, calculate today's average price:

$$Average\ price = \frac{High + Low + Close}{3}$$

If today's average price is greater than yesterday's average price, then money flow (as explained in the next step) is positive. If today's average price is less than yesterday's average price, then money flow is negative. Next, calculate money flow:

Money flow = (Volume)(Average price)

Over a selected time period (14 days is a good choice), positive money flow (PMF) is the sum of daily positive money flows. Negative money flow (NMF) is the sum of negative money flows. Next, calculate money ratio (MR):

Money ratio = (PMF)/(NMF)

Money flow index =

$$100 - \frac{100}{1 + Money\ ratio}$$

The following formulas are used for MetaStock Professional:

Formula #1   V*((H+L+C)/3)
Formula #2   IF((H+L+C)/3,>,REF((H+L +C)/3,-1),FML(#1),0)
Formula #3   IF((H+L+C)/3,<,REF((H+ L+C)/3,-1),FML(#1),0)
Formula #4   SUM(FML(#2),14)
Formula #5   SUM(FML(#3),14)
Formula #6   FML(#4)/FML(#5)
Formula #7   (100-(100/(1+FML(#6))))

After entering the above formulas, the MFI can be graphed by simply selecting formula 7. Please note that the actual formula numbers such as fml(#3) will probably need to be changed to match the particular locations you use in MetaStock Professional.

The MFI can be used as follows:
- Tops and bottoms are indicated when the MFI goes above 80 or drops below 20.
- Divergence between the MFI and the price are an indication of a price reversal.

—Editor

CHAPTER 11

THE TRADERS' MAGAZINE

NOVEMBER 1992

TECHNICAL ANALYSIS OF STOCKS & COMMODITIES

A Twist On The Arms Index

The Arms index, which was originally known as TRIN (for trading index), utilizes up and down volume and advancing and declining issues for calculation. The indicator, which aims to identify possible turning points in the stock market, has been studied keenly since its introduction. Here, Harley Wilbur presents a new version of this indicator, bruised and battered but still standing in the field of trading battle.

I have long been fascinated with the Arms index†, also known as the TRIN indicator. I was introduced to it in the early 1970s when it had the unwieldy name of "short-term trading index" and could be accessed intraday on brokers' quote machines. As a buy/sell indicator the Arms index worked well sometimes but failed miserably at other times.

One of the problems I have encountered in using the index is that the daily TRIN can be very erratic. Because of the way the index is calculated, the value 1.00 is theoretically neutral, and values below 0.30 are relatively rare. On the high side, however, it sometimes spikes above 2.4 or higher. On the occa-

sional days when the stock market drops swiftly, the index often assumes very large values, which in turn have a disproportionate influence on TRIN moving averages, making them erratic too. (Technician Arthur Merrill presented an interesting analysis of the significance of extreme daily values of the Arms index in the April 1992 STOCKS & COMMODITIES.)

In the late 1970s, I searched for a better way to smooth the TRIN's erratic tendencies. When construct-

> **As a buy/sell indicator the Arms index worked well sometimes but failed miserably at other times.**

■

by Harley D. Wilbur

†See Traders' Glossary for definition

BRAD WALKER

ing moving averages of the index, I would first calculate moving averages of the four TRIN components (advances, declines, up volume and down volume) and then calculate the Arms index itself from the four component moving averages. This reduced the influence of the occasional extreme days on the moving average.

Initial results from my then-new approach to calculating the Arms index were published in the fall 1983 issue of *Financial and Investment Software Review*. Peter Eliades, publisher of "Stock Market Cycles," adopted this new method of calculating the Arms index in his newsletter and called it the "open TRIN." It is now the name generally used in literature describing the technique of calculating the Arms index from the component averages.

A reading of 1.00 is theoretically the neutral value of the open TRIN; however, a bias exists because trading volume in stocks whose prices are increasing tends to be higher than the volume in declining stocks. This tendency has the overall effect of lowering Arms index values. Over the past four years (since July 1988), the mean value of the 10-day open TRIN has actually been about 0.89. Even when it is smoothed with moving averages, the TRIN still behaves in a fashion that makes it awkward to use for market timing. During bull markets, it can have very low values for weeks on end, and for this reason it is generally not useful as a sell signal. Index values above 1.00 are sometimes excellent oversold signals that mark favorable buying points, but in bear markets open TRIN may remain above 1.00 for long periods while prices continue to fall. At those times, buying on the first open TRIN move above 1.00 can be a costly mistake. The problem: the index is an indicator whose behavior characteristics depend on whether the market is in a bull or bear phase and how long it has been there.

Figure 1 shows the Standard & Poor's 500 index and the New York Stock Exchange (NYSE) 10-day open TRIN (hereafter called TRIN10) during summer and fall 1990, when the market declined following the Iraqi invasion of Kuwait. At the beginning of August, when the invasion began, the TRIN10 was coming off a peak around 1.15, which normally would have signaled an oversold situation and therefore a buying opportunity. However, the market continued to register more oversold readings in the following weeks as prices plummeted because of the uncertainties of war. Then in October, as prices finally found a bottom, the TRIN10 made one small tentative foray above 1.00 but otherwise gave no hint of a major buying opportunity. While we cannot expect technical indicators to anticipate unusual world events that affect markets or to always present clear directions at decision points, we could hope for something a little more illuminating than what appears in Figure 1.

BOLLINGER BANDS WITH ARMS INDEX

In the course of trying to make a better technical indicator out of the Arms index, I have been using the MetaStock Professional (Version 3.0) software to examine the TRIN10 in relation to its own volatility patterns, using the concept of Bollinger trading bands†. (Also, see "Weighted average TRIN10" sidebar for the spreadsheet version.) This approach seems to hold some promise. The calculation procedure is as follows:

Step 1. Calculate the TRIN10. The first step cannot be done in MetaStock without some complex data juggling. However, it is easily done with a spreadsheet or with a shareware program I use called Trendtek. After the calculation, I manually enter the TRIN10 value into MetaStock each day.

Step 2. Calculate 10-day, two-standard deviation Bollinger bands around TRIN10 and normalize the value of TRIN10 for each day with respect to the values of its Bollinger bands on that day. This step also provides an opportunity to correct the topsy-turvy nature of the Arms index. Thus, when TRIN10 is at its lower Bollinger band, the normalized value is set at 100, and when it is at its upper Bollinger band, the normalized value is zero. Values in between zero and 100 depend on where

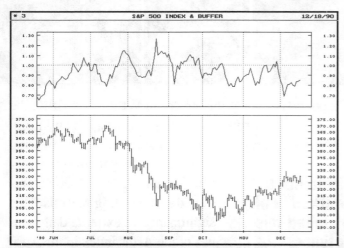

FIGURE 1: 10-DAY OPEN TRIN AND THE S&P 500 INDEX. *At times, the peaks and troughs in the 10-day open TRIN will coincide with market turns. Other times, an oversold reading is a precursor of lower prices to come, such as late July 1990.*

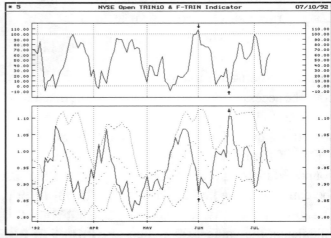

FIGURE 2: TRIN10 WITH 10-DAY BOLLINGER BANDS AND NORMALIZED TRIN10. *The arrows at the beginning of June 1992 denote a point where the TRIN10 declined outside its lower Bollinger band; thus, the normalized TRIN10 had a reading greater than 100. The other arrows in mid-June denote a point when TRIN10 rose above its upper band and so the normalized TRIN10 had a reading below zero.*

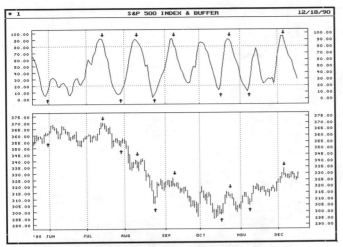

FIGURE 3: WEIGHTED AVERAGE TRIN10 AND S&P 500. *Instead of the erratic pattern of TRIN10, WTRIN10 oscillates smoothly between zero and 100. Inspection of the WTRIN10 pattern suggests a trading strategy: Buy when WTRIN10 has an uptick after falling below 20, hold until it goes above 80 and then sell after WTRIN10 turns down. The suggested trading rule is to buy on an uptick from below 20 and sell on a downtick from above 80. The buy and sell signals are presented on the day of the signals.*

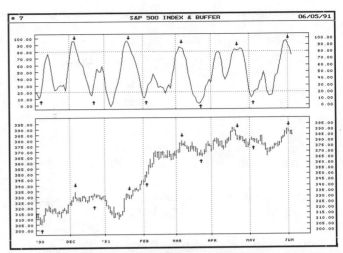

FIGURE 4: WEIGHTED AVERAGE TRIN10 AND S&P 500. *WTRIN10 sold out early in the January 1991 rally and called for buying back in at higher prices.*

TRIN10 is in relation to the two extremes. The normalized value can go below zero or above 100 at times when TRIN10 is outside its Bollinger bands. Step 2 can be done easily with the Bollinger band capability in MetaStock, but it isn't actually necessary unless you want a visual presentation of the TRIN10 with its Bollinger bands. With TRIN10 loaded in MetaStock as if it were a security, this formula will calculate the Bollinger bands about TRIN10 and normalize the value of TRIN10 with respect to the Bollinger bands:

Formula 1: (TRIN10 indicator normalized in 10-day bands)

$$100-100*((C-(mov(C,10,S)-2*std(C,10)))/4*std(C,10))$$

Step 3. Smooth the normalized TRIN10 value with a five-day weighted average. The MetaStock formula is:

Formula 2: (five-day weighted average of normalized value)

$$mov(fml(\#1),5,W)$$

With TRIN10 displayed on the screen, execute formula 2. The result, which I call WTRIN10, is then plotted in the indicator window. Figure 2 illustrates the process. The arrows at the beginning of June 1992 mark a point where TRIN10 declined outside its lower Bollinger band. The other arrows in mid-June denote a time of the other extreme, when TRIN10 rose above its upper band.

Figure 3, which covers the same period as Figure 1—summer and fall 1990—shows a plot of the WTRIN10. Instead of the somewhat erratic pattern of the TRIN10, the WTRIN10 oscillates

smoothly between zero and 100. (Its behavior during the June 1990 period is an exception discussed later.) Inspection of the WTRIN10 pattern in Figure 3 suggests a trading strategy: *Buy* when WTRIN10 has an uptick after falling below 20, *hold* until it goes above 80, and then *sell* on its first downtick. Implementation of the strategy is illustrated by the arrows in Figure 3.

> ## Using WTRIN10 with an essentially no-brain strategy gives good trading results sometimes and not so good at other times.

In testing this strategy, I assume that the trades are made on the day that WTRIN10 gives its signals. A glance at the arrows in Figure 3 shows that this assumption can be especially important on the buy side. (When the market is ready to move up, it moves quickly.) My experience has been that this is not an unrealistic assumption, but it does require the trader to be in touch with the intraday market when the WTRIN10 is in the below-20 buying zone. Assuming that the trading vehicle is the S&P 500 index (for example, a no-load index mutual fund) and that the trades are made at the close on the day of the signal, this strategy generated five trades during the seven-month period of May 18 to December 18, 1990, as follows:

Buy 5/31/90 at 361.23
Sell 7/16/90 at 368.95. Gain: 2.14%
Buy 7/30/90 at 355.55
Sell 8/10/90 at 335.52. Loss: 5.63%
Buy 8/24/90 at 311.51
Sell 9/11/90 at 321.04. Gain: 3.06%
Buy 10/17/90 at 298.76

WEIGHTED AVERAGE TRIN10

The steps for calculating WTRIN10 begin with the calculation of the open TRIN10 (column G). The 10-day moving average of the individual day's value of the number of advancing shares (column C), number of declining shares (column D), advancing volume (column E) and declining volume (column F) are used to calculate the open TRIN10. The formula for cell G20:

$$=(AVERAGE(C11:C20)/AVERAGE(D11:D20))/(AVERAGE(E11:E20)/AVERAGE(F11:F20))$$

Next, calculate the 10-day moving average of the open TRIN10. This moving average is part of the steps for the calculation of the Bollinger bands. The formula for cell H20:

$$=AVERAGE(G11:G20)$$

Next, determine the standard deviation of the open TRIN10 (note this is not the standard deviation of the moving average). Use the formula for the standard deviation of the population. The formula for cell I20:

$$=STDEVP(G11:G20)$$

The upper-band Bollinger band is the 10-day moving average of the open TRIN10 plus two standard deviations. The formula for cell J20 is:

$$=H20+(2*I20)$$

The lower Bollinger band is the 10-day moving average minus two times the standard deviation. The formula for cell K20 is:

$$=H20-(2*I20)$$

Normalizing the value of the open TRIN10 in relation to the Bollinger bands is cell L20:

$$=100*(J20-G20)/(J20-K20)$$

The last step is a five-day weighted moving average. Today's value is multiplied by five, yesterday's value is multiplied by four and so on. Sum the weighted values and divide by the sum of the weights; in this case, it is 15. The formula for cell M20:

$$=((5*L20)+(4*L19)+(3*L18)+(2*L17)+L16)/15$$

—*Editor*

	A	B	C	D	E	F	G	H	I	J	K	L	M
1	Date	S&P 500	ADV	DEC	ADV VOL	DEC VOL	Open	10 day MA	10 day	Upper	Lower	Normalize	5 day
2	8/6/90	334.43	255	1530	37362	192913	Trin	of	Standard	Bollinger	Bollinger		weighted
3	8/7/90	334.83	740	845	107628	96494	10	0pen	Deviation	Band	Band		moving
4	8/8/90	338.35	1015	601	128667	48593		TRIN	Population				average
5	8/9/90	339.94	837	695	82694	50424		10					
6	8/10/90	335.52	448	1043	33243	97822							
7	8/13/90	335.73	726	766	72217	38123							
8	8/14/90	339.39	852	640	66534	46296							
9	8/15/90	340.06	887	619	66483	53005							
10	8/16/90	332.39	330	1300	14936	116343							
11	8/17/90	327.83	310	1330	36504	160423	0.9518						
12	8/20/90	328.51	629	920	55155	55239	0.8883						
13	8/21/90	321.86	243	1441	15723	169229	0.9798						
14	8/22/90	316.55	360	1202	27474	127450	1.0963						
15	8/23/90	307.06	148	1645	9095	237040	1.2532						
16	8/24/90	311.51	956	649	133200	49434	1.0955						
17	8/27/90	321.44	1453	256	142446	12945	1.1163						
18	8/28/90	321.34	837	664	57206	53911	1.1379						
19	8/29/90	324.19	972	508	83966	33906	1.1102						
20	8/30/90	318.71	482	998	20777	83395	1.1236	1.0753	0.1005	1.2763	0.8743	37.9922	12.6641
21	8/31/90	322.56	885	595	66982	19848	1.0798	1.0881	0.0917	1.2715	0.9047	52.2555	27.5497
22	9/4/90	323.09	673	814	38601	37186	1.1061	1.1099	0.0631	1.2360	0.9837	51.4874	38.6957
23	9/5/90	324.39	953	571	71262	34855	1.0353	1.1154	0.0530	1.2215	1.0094	87.7730	58.5044
24	9/6/90	320.46	511	960	27701	82321	1.0173	1.1075	0.0606	1.2288	0.9863	87.1954	72.2690

SIDEBAR FIGURE 1: OPEN TRIN

Sell 10/24/90 at 312.60. Gain: 4.63%
Buy 11/8/90 at 307.61
Sell 12/6/90 at 329.07. Gain: 6.98%

This works out to a net trading gain of 11.19% for seven months, disregarding money market dividends received while out of equities. During the same period, a buy and hold strategy would have resulted in a loss of 9.27%, disregarding dividends received.

It looks like we may have something here, but, alas, it doesn't always work so well. A hint of the problems appears in WTRIN10 behavior in June 1990. After the May 31st buy signal, both WTRIN10 and prices remained in a holding pattern for the whole month. The Desert Storm rally that started in January 1991 provides another example of problems with WTRIN10. Figure 4 shows what happened using the same trading strategy during the seven-month period from November 1990 to June 1991, which covers part of the Desert Shield and Desert Storm period. For reference, Figure 4 starts with the last trade of Figure 3. The WTRIN10 trades were as follows:

Buy 11/8/90 at 307.61
Sell 12/6/90 at 329.07. Gain: 6.98%
Buy 12/21/90 at 331.75
Sell 1/22/91 at 328.31. Loss: 1.04%
Buy 2/5/91 at 351.26
Sell 3/6/91 at 376.17. Gain: 7.09%
Buy 3/21/91 at 366.58
Sell 4/22/91 at 380.95. Gain: 3.92%
Buy 5/3/91 at 380.80
Sell 6/3/91 at 388.06. Gain: 1.91%

This works out to a net trading gain of 20.07% for seven months, disregarding money market dividends received while out of equities. During the same period, a buy and hold strategy would have achieved a somewhat better (and problem-free) gain of 22.41%, disregarding any dividends received. The WTRIN10 strategy underperformed buy and hold only slightly but required holding a long position during the early January 1991 selloff, when investors were anticipating war and assuming it would be bad for stocks. This certainly would have been emotionally difficult to do. Then, WTRIN10 sold out at the first price hesitation after the rally started and called for buying back in at higher prices two weeks later — again, emotionally difficult.

THEN AND NOW

All very good, you may say, but what has this indicator done for us lately? Figure 5 shows its behavior in the recent period from November 1991 to June 1992, which includes the strong December 1991 rally. Here is a summary of the WTRIN10 trades:

Buy 11/22/91 at 376.14
Sell 12/16/91 at 384.46. Gain: 2.21%
Buy 1/14/92 at 420.44
Sell 2/27/92 at 413.86. Loss: 1.57%
Buy 3/12/92 at 403.89
Sell 3/24/92 at 408.88. Gain: 1.24%

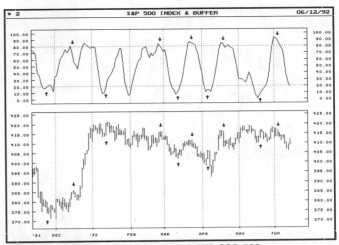

FIGURE 5: WEIGHTED AVERAGE TRIN10 AND S&P 500. *The results were mixed in 1992. The indicator caught some turns in the S&P 500 but missed the late 1991 rally.*

Buy 4/6/92 at 405.59
Sell 4/20/92 at 410.18. Gain: 1.13%
Buy 5/19/92 at 416.37
Sell 6/3/92 at 414.59. Loss: 0.43%

This works out to a net trading gain of 2.57% for seven months, disregarding money market dividends received while out of equities. During the same period, a buy and hold strategy would have achieved a gain of 3.28%, disregarding any dividends received. Again, WTRIN10 strategy underperformed a buy and hold strategy. Moreover, it handled the late December 1991 rally very poorly, missing most of it.

Using WTRIN10 with an essentially no-brain strategy gives good trading results sometimes and not so good at other times. There are many things that could be tried to improve the performance of WTRIN, and using a 10-day period for the open TRIN smoothing may not be the best one. Using 10 days for the Bollinger bands may not be the best, either. In addition, many different trading strategies might be used. All this offers rich fields for investigation and optimization, and I intend to continue working on it.

Analyzing this Arms index variation thus far reminds us of what technical analysts already know: Never rely on just one indicator, because it will inevitably have spells during which it misbehaves. However, I believe the WTRIN10 is a stock market indicator good enough to rate a place in the technician's arsenal.

Harley D. Wilbur is a retired naval officer, mathematician and amateur stock market technician. He can be reached at 9709 Elrod Road, Kensington, MD 20895, (301) 949-8131.

REFERENCES

Arms, Richard W. [1989]. *The Arms Index (TRIN)*, Dow Jones-Irwin.
_____ [1991]. "Cross your Arms," *Technical Analysis of STOCKS & COMMODITIES*, Volume 9: May.
Merrill, Arthur A. [1992]. "Closing Arms," STOCKS & COMMODITIES, April.

Frank Gretz of Shields & Company

> "I noticed that when I was buying stocks, they did very well when the market went up and they didn't do so well when the market went down. So it struck me that the overall trend of stock prices seemed to have a lot to do with my success in making money in the stock market."
>
> —Frank Gretz

> "It sounds kind of strange, but we all think we know our own opinions — but if you have to reassess your opinion and have to write it down once a week, it really helps you come to grips with what you're doing. This forces you to think about how firm your opinion is and whether you're on the right side of your positions."

Frank Gretz wears many hats for Shields & Company—technician, broker, money manager and market letter writer (not to mention appearing on CNBC in his capacity as a technical analyst) — but he also undertakes the challenge of managing his firm's trading account. Over time, he has developed a trading philosophy designed to keep his trading on an even keel and profitable. How does he do it? STOCKS & COMMODITIES Editor Thom Hartle conducted an interview with Gretz via telephone on August 20, 1992, asking, among other questions, what some of his trading methods are and details on his trading philosophy.

Frank, how did you get started in the business?

I got interested in the stock market while I was in college. I didn't know if I wanted to be a broker or an analyst or whatever, but I decided that the place to find out what the stock market was all about was New York City. I started at Merrill Lynch in 1967 and I joined the training program, which was fundamentally oriented.

What did you do?

Part of the training program was in portfolio analysis, which was reviewing stocks that the clients held on a fundamental basis. I was very interested in the market for my own money and I was doing some trading the way I had through college. I noticed that when I was buying stocks, they did very well when the market went up and they didn't do so well when the market went down. So it struck me — smart, right? — that the overall trend of stock prices seemed to have a lot to do with my success in making money in the stock market and was also largely responsible for my losing money in the stock market.

When was this?

Back in 1968, which was really a pretty good market for stocks, but nonetheless, I noticed that when stocks went down, so did mine. So I became interested in just what made the market trend. I was very fortunate because at Merrill Lynch, there was a guy named Bob Farrell heading the technical analysis department, which is now called the market analysis department.

So you transferred over?

I became kind of a trainee in that department. That was very good for me. I was there with Bob for about six years, and I have great respect for Bob Farrell. I learned a *lot* from Bob and from being exposed to the broad array of technical analysis that was offered in there. I stayed there for about six years and then I became an independent investment advisor, worked for myself literally, managing money and writing a market letter.

> **The important indicators to me are trend-following. An investor can look at indicators such as the New York Composite, Standard & Poor's 500 or the Dow Jones Industrial Average in relation to their respective 200-day moving averages.**

When did you start writing market letters?

I wrote my first market letter in October 1976. Surprising as it may seem, I'm *still* writing a market letter. I never expected to be in the market letter business this long, but I have. I've gone through many phases in writing market letters. There was one time when I thought I wanted to market a newsletter or sell the letter. But my background is analytical; I'm interested in analyzing the market, not selling market letters. But I have kept up the market letter because I found that it was helpful in making me sit down once a week and go over exactly what I think of the market.

It sounds kind of strange, but we all think we know our own opinions — but if you have to reassess your opinion and have to write it down once a week, it really helps you come to grips with what you're doing. This forces you to think about how firm your opinion is and whether you're on the right side of your positions. So I've been writing a market letter all this time.

When did you join Shields & Company?

I joined Shields & Company in 1985, here in New York. Shields is a brokerage firm and we manage about $700 million under the name of Capital Management Associates. My function is severalfold: First, I am a broker, I have clients that I advise and I manage clients' money. Second, I'm an analyst, a technical analyst, and I write a market letter for Shields & Company called "Equities Perspective." Third, I'm an advisor to the money management arm of Shields & Company. Another responsibility I have and enjoy *very* much is trading. I manage the firm's trading account.

Tell us about your trading style.

The most important point to start with is a very simple one: the direction of the market. Is the market going up or down? The important indicators to me are trend-following. An investor can look at indicators such as the New York Composite, Standard & Poor's 500 or the Dow Jones Industrial Average in relation to their respective 200-day moving averages. That is a bigger picture kind of look. That's not a bad definition of the market direction. If the market's above its 200-day moving average, that's a pretty good sign and I conclude that it's still okay to be positive on the stock market. So when an investment client comes to me, someone who wants to buy and own stock as an investor,

then you look for stocks. Then it's right to be long in the market, not either in cash or to short the market.

What about as a trader?

As a trader, the perspective is different because your time horizon is much more short-term oriented. Again, the key is figuring out which way the market's going, based on some parameter. I still look at simple moving averages, but instead of a 200-day moving average I use shorter-term moving averages. I think you can look at something even as simple as a 10-day moving average, which I use in my trading. You need something *objective* to keep you on the right side of the market.

So do you have to use more than one indicator?

I look at many different indicators like a lot of people do, but after a while you tend to get bogged down in indicators that don't pick up on market direction. For example, oscillators such as 10-day overbought and oversold or five-day or whatever. They tell you the market's oversold and should rally, but until the market crosses some kind of moving average, it hasn't rallied. It hasn't moved up.

I've learned to respect the fact that once you get a crossing of these short-term moving averages, the short-term trend has changed. I'm always impressed to see how many times a little short-term rally that I think is just nothing turns into more. Following short-term moving averages mechanically gets you on the right side automatically. You can complain about the whipsaws, but if you can find the right moving average to suit your trading, that gets you on the right side of the trend or at least is a mental alert. If the market's rallying, you don't want to be short; you can't be too negative as long as the index is above its moving average.

Sometimes, a lot of indicators get away from what the market is actually doing. I prefer a 200-day moving average from an investment standpoint and for trading I use a weighted 10-day moving average.

What do you trade using such a short-term indicator?

The New York Futures Exchange (NYFE) futures contract. I want to stress

that it doesn't matter what moving average it happens to be for the individual. It's important that you have *something* to judge the direction of the market. My own trading experience has been that if I had always adhered to that principle — that is, be long when the market's above its 10-day and the NYFE is above its 10-day moving average and vice versa — I'd be a lot happier today.

▌ Trading is a mental game.

But you follow more than one indicator, right?

I follow the usual array of momentum indicators or oscillators. These are useful in terms of telling you the overbought or oversold position of the market or whether you're likely to rally. But it's more along the lines of "Get ready to buy, get ready to short," versus going short or long when I see the trend has actually changed, and that's where the moving average indicator that I use comes in. Then I know the trend has changed. We all know the market can get oversold and stay oversold or get overbought and stay overbought, and if you move too soon, it can cost you money.

Do you look at sentiment indicators like the put/call ratio?

I look at sentiment indicators a great deal, but again they are similar to overbought and oversold indicators. It's nice to say there's a lot of put-buying or the market's due for a rally. That's important, but that's just another item of background data to me; until the market rallies, I don't act. In my market letter I'll point things out that I think can be useful information, such as there's a huge amount of put option buying. You can even point out that the market's never gone down when there's this much put-buying but that there's always a first time. So sentiment is what I really consider to be part of background information, but it's not something I act on. It's the kind of information that I consider to be part of the background.

Is the advance-decline line important to

you?

I pay a lot of attention to the advance-decline numbers. I look at the cumulative advance-decline numbers. It's no big secret, because most technical analysts pay attention to the A-D line. The trick with advance-decline numbers is that we get into periods where we get divergences in the market. Right now, you have divergence in the advance-decline line (Figure 1), which reached its peak on Valentine's Day, February 14. So you have about five or six months where that advance-decline line has failed to reach a higher high.

Meanwhile, the Dow Jones Industrial Average first reaches a higher high, the S&P and New York Composite reaches a higher high and you have this divergence in the advance-decline line versus these broader-based price averages. Historically, that is extremely negative. That's a very big warning that there's a problem ahead. Now, the problem with using this kind of data is it's a long-term divergence. Long-term divergences are negative, but by definition they're *long term*. It doesn't mean the market is going to go down *today*, but it's background information that one has to keep in mind to define where the market is in the cycle. So while I'm looking at short-term indicators from a trading standpoint, I'm also aware of what's going on in the overall market background.

How long can divergences exist?

People get excited over those divergences, but when they go on for five months or so, they decide that it doesn't really matter. For example, if the S&P ultimately makes a new high, then people are relieved. They conclude that this advance-decline divergence thing didn't mean a thing, so let's not worry about it. Well, of course, they *do* matter! And it's almost by the time people stop worrying about it is when they *should* be worrying about it. As a matter of fact, 1987 was the last time you had a divergence this long (Figure 2). In 1987 the advance-decline line made a high in March, about a five-month divergence between a peak in the advance-decline index and the market peak. Remember the DJIA's peak was in August. So it was a five-month divergence there as well. I'm not trying to

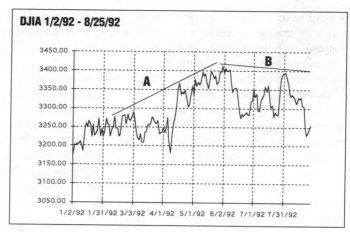

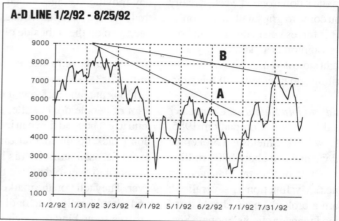

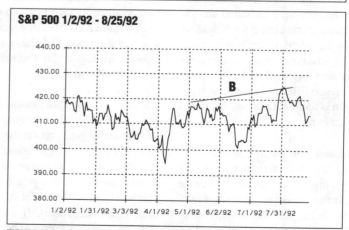

FIGURE 1: *The advance-decline line peaked in February, while the DJIA continued to new highs. This divergence (trendline A) is a longer-term negative indication. The S&P 500 moved to a new high in August, while the DJIA did not make a new high. This divergence (trendline B) is also not a healthy sign.*

suggest this is 1987 and we're about to have a 500-point decline. I am merely pointing out it is a historical background against which one has to be very careful.

Do you use advance-declines for short-term analysis?

I look for very short-term divergences in the advance-decline index. If you go back to 1987, for example, you had a pretty good rally going into the August peak in the industrial average, the advance-decline numbers acted reasonably well confirming the advance up to about a week or so before the DJIA peak in August. Just before the August peak, the advance-decline numbers turned terrible so that you had this series of negative divergences in the advance-decline index — the DJIA moving to higher highs and the advance-decline index failing to confirm those highs, on a day-to-day basis almost.

Now when you get into that kind of pattern, that's usually negative. When it happens against a background of an ongoing divergence in the advance-decline index, that can be extremely negative. This was the case in August 1987 and the same thing happened again in October 1987. So I pay a lot of attention to the background of this divergence analysis.

We're not in that same position now, I might add; the advance-decline numbers have acted pretty well and they have kept pace with the advance in not only the DJIA but on a short-term basis with the advance in the S&P and the New York Composite.

What about divergences between market averages?

Divergences of any type are not healthy. Look at what has happened recently with the S&P making a new high and the New York Composite finally breaking out. It's a problem when you've got the S&P or the NYSE breaking out but the DJIA's not. Divergences in the market of any sort are negative. Divergences send the message that all is not well. One example I can give you that this can indeed make a difference is November 1991 (Figure 3). If you take a look at the action of the S&P going into the November peak compared with the DJIA, the S&P went to a higher high in November but the DJIA did not go to a higher high in the November rally, and the DJIA subsequently suffered a 200-point decline.

Not all divergences lead to big declines. But my experience has been that very rarely do you have an important decline, a decline of much consequence, that is not preceded by a divergence.

Putting this analysis to work, how do you select stocks for a portfolio?

The key to my trading philosophy is to always be in sync with what the market's doing. If the market's going up, I don't care how bearish I am, I'm going to make myself get in sync with the market. Same

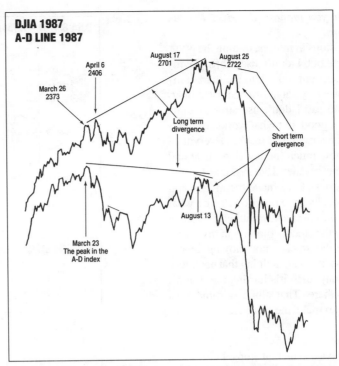

FIGURE 2: *A previous example of long-term divergence occurred when the advance-decline line peaked in March 1987, while the DJIA continued higher until August 1987. This was a long-term negative indication regarding the technical health of the market. There was a short-term negative divergence in October 1987.*

on the downside. I don't care how bullish I am, if the market starts going down, I'm going to start selling stocks to stay in sync with the market. As a technician there are always stocks that look good to me and stocks that look bad to me. I almost take a generic approach to selecting stocks. I'm looking for a group of stocks with good patterns to be long if I'm bullish, and I look for a group of stocks with technically weak patterns to be short when I'm negative.

What would be a good pattern?

I buy stocks that are in uptrends. I like stocks that are showing relative strength or stocks that are above their 30-week moving average. I look for stocks where the group action is positive. You can look at *Investor's Business Daily* and find stocks that are strong on a relative strength basis. I want to look for stocks that are above 80 on a relative strength basis. Those are the characteristics of stocks that I prefer to be long. I look at Mansfield charts for stocks that are above their 30-week moving average and stocks that are in strong groups, like energy stocks now or insurance stocks a month ago.

So you keep a current list of favorite stocks?

Yes. I pull out this list of stocks that I have, this reservoir of stocks, and if I want to get long in the market, I've got a list of stocks there that I like. If I am bearish on the market and I want to get short in the market, I've got another list of stocks that I think are acting badly. I adjust the portfolio in question to what I see the trend as doing and I'm probably always long something and always short something. It's rare that the market seems to be so one-sided, but I certainly adjust to what the market's doing. The portfolio I manage is short-term oriented, and it's margined. I have no qualms about being short speculative stocks or volatile stocks; I'm very diversified. I don't have any big positions.

If there's five stocks that I think have lousy patterns, I know that I'm not smart enough to know which one of those five is going to go down and which one isn't, and I'd rather just spread myself out and short all five or go long all five or 10 or whatever. I have small positions. I watch my positions every day, and I'm very quick to react to anything that goes against me.

How do you manage the risk? Do you use stops?

I use stops in futures, trading the NYFE contract, but I don't use stops on my equity account. I mark to the market my account every day. I'm almost embarrassed to say I don't use stops. I think stops are good, but what works for me is to mark everything to market. Everyday I know how much money I've made and how much money I've lost and I know which stocks have made me money and which stocks have not. I don't care what I've paid for a stock, what I care about is whether the stock's moving in my direction. If the stock's not moving in my direction, if it's not helping that net figure for the day, then it's hurting me. I don't need it there. That alone is sometimes enough to make me sell a stock.

Is that it?

I always use mental stops. I also use a kind of stop loss, what I may call a time stop. If I'm in a stock and I've been in it a few weeks, and the market's going up and the stock hasn't gone up with the market, then I'm wrong. I haven't lost money in the stock or in the position, but I'm still wrong. I've found that works very well many times, because when I hold a stock too long and I hold it because "it hasn't done anything wrong," sure enough, if I wait, it *will* do something wrong. There's a message there. If the market's going up, everything on my list is up but I've got something that's not, chances are there's a reason. I've just learned through experience.

It is helpful to keep an eye on things in terms of not just are they hurting you, but are they helping you. I may be long a stock that's acting great, but if I change my mind on the market I'll sell the stock anyway. It's not just a matter of reaching my objective; I'll adjust the portfolio, the whole nature or direction of the portfolio, toward my market opinion. I pay attention to changes in the market.

Do you think indicators change?

That's an important point. I think a big part of technical analysis is the analysis of change. It's not just looking at these indicators but observing how the indicators might be different over time. One ex-

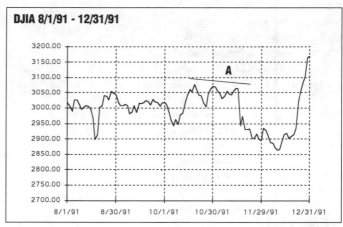

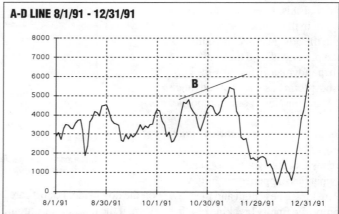

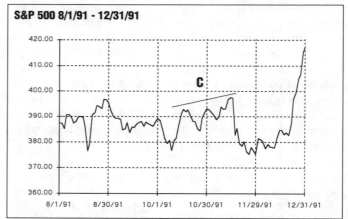

FIGURE 3: *In November 1991, the DJIA traced out a series of lower highs (A), while the advance-decline line moved higher (B) along with the S&P 500 (C). However, this divergence in November predicted a decline going into December.*

ample of always trying to look for a change in the market might be options expirations for the stock market. My research shows that the probability of the market being down the Monday after a Friday expiration is around 80%. It doesn't matter — or it hasn't so far — what the market did during the week of the Friday expiration.

Any examples?

Going into December 1991, the market had been down all but two of the 11 Mondays following the option expiration on Friday. But in December, after the expiration, the market was up more than 88 points. In the next five days, the market rallied an additional 150 points. As a technician and a trader, I'm always thinking in terms of probabilities. In turn, when

I'm looking for the market to do something that has a high probability of happening and when it does just the opposite, then I know there has been a change. This kind of change usually means something important. You need to react quickly to these kind of changes.

As a trader?

Right. One thing that I've learned over the years is the importance of developing the ability to react quickly to change. It's easy to say but difficult to do and seems to only come with experience. I know that you've heard it before, but I really believe that "a quick loss is the best loss." By the time a trader waits around to see if a trade is going to work out, it may be too late. If the trade is going against me, I just get out of the way and worry about the reasons later. I don't just sit there and hope. I've learned that if you have a big loss, it's hard to find the big winner. You just can't afford a big loss. You can take lots of little losses, survive in the game and be there for the good trades. We all make money in the stock market, but the real problem is avoiding having to give the money *back*. I've found that a quick reaction time has really helped me.

Another thing I do is mentally prepare before I start the day.

How, sketch out a game plan for what you expect from the market?

I may theorize what the market should do during the day. I think through the indicators that I follow, what the trend is, what price level would change the trend. No one knows exactly what the market is going to do, of course, but it's helpful to have *some* sort of plan. In turn, it's helpful to think about the possibility of being wrong. I come to work with a "what-if" strategy. That way, I consider different possibilities that can reduce the [unpleasant] surprise factor. That cuts down on my reaction time, which certainly helps my trading performance.

So have a game plan, don't be complacent and go with the flow?

Exactly! You have to be open-minded. Don't *be* your position. Are you bullish because you are long or are you long because you are bullish? Don't let your

"One thing that I've learned over the years is the importance of developing the ability to react quickly to change. It's easy to say but difficult to do and seems to only come with experience. By the time a trader waits around to see if a trade is going to work out, it may be too late."

"It is helpful to keep an eye on things in terms of not just are they hurting you, but are they helping you. I may be long a stock that's acting great, but if I change my mind on the market I'll sell the stock anyway. I'll adjust the whole nature or direction of the portfolio toward my market opinion. I pay attention to changes in the market."

position cloud your judgment about what the market may be doing right now. To function well on a short-term basis, you can't get locked into the opinion that you had last week. Longer-term investing shouldn't change on a day-to-day basis, but for short-term trading you have to be open-minded. Something else that I think helps in trading is the size of your position.

So you vary the size of your position? Why?

I find that when I have been trading well for three or four good days, for example, I should begin to trade smaller positions. I think this is due to the fact that I am a trend-follower and after three or more days of good trading, the market may begin to get choppy, and that can hurt me. Believe it or not, making money can affect you negatively. You may start thinking that you are better than you really are. Then you become vulnerable to losing your discipline. Now, some traders expand their trading when they're going hot at the moment and be active until they go cold. But for me, I start to trade smaller positions after a string of successes because that way I can keep my head screwed

on tight. Trading is a mental game.

How so?

There is an inherent contradiction to trading. First, you have to think you are pretty bright to tackle trading. It takes a big ego to think that you will have an edge over everyone else and make money. At the same time, you have to be very humble to be a successful trader. What a combination! But the reality is that you have to have tremendous self-confidence to accept the fact that you are going to be wrong at least sometimes. There is constant frustration and disappointment in trading. Trading is challenging work. You have to be able to put into perspective dealing with the losses and the successes. That takes a *lot* of self-confidence and humility.

Any concluding thoughts?

Good trading comes from experience, and experience comes from bad trading. You'll learn from losing money. Hopefully, you'll learn before you lose all your money.

I hope so! Thank you, Frank.

You're welcome!

Sentiment And Trendlines For Bond Fund Trading

The Hines ratio, a key sentiment indicator, is designed to help traders pinpoint emotional extremes in the bond market. Here, the Hines ratio is combined with Barron's *Bond Bullish Consensus, classic trendline and retracement analysis to help traders identify buying and selling points for the intermediate term.*

by Joe Duarte

The Hines ratio is a modified put/call ratio that refines traditional option ratio analysis by including the open interest figures in the equation. I use the options volume and open interest figures found in *Barron's* futures options section under the listing of "U.S. Bonds." These figures are the total volume traded and final open interest for the period covering Thursday to Thursday. The formula for the Hines index is:

$$\frac{\text{(Total put volume/Total put open interest)}}{\text{(Total call volume/Total call open interest)}}$$

The Hines ratio presents the options volume as a ratio of open interest. Including open interest is valuable because increased volume along with increased open interest indicates that new positions are being added. Extreme levels of option sentiment, both bullish or bearish, cause the Hines index to rise or fall to levels that often precede significant intermediate-term tops and bottoms in the bond market. For example, a Hines index buy signal usually but not always occurs when the index reaches numbers above 1.8. Measurements below but not necessarily at 0.65 usually signal intermediate-term weakness. The buy signals are much better at predicting higher bond prices than the sell signals are at predicting falling prices.

> **Of the three peaks in the Bullish Consensus during the June 1991 to January 1992 advance, only the first reached greater than 60%, and it proved to be quite early.**

I use *Barron's* Bond Bullish Consensus, which is published weekly, and the Hines index to confirm each other. The two indicators may give buy and sell signals anywhere from simultaneously to within a few weeks of each other, and I seldom act if they don't confirm each other, as disagreement between the two indicators often leads to trendless market periods of frustrating volatility. A Bond Bullish Consensus buy signal usually occurs at readings below 43%, while short-term sell signals usually occur at readings above 60%. Personal experience indicates that readings of less than 43% are about 80% accurate, while sell signals are somewhat more subjective.

FIGURE PERFORMANCE

Figure 1 summarizes the performance of the Hines index's buy signals back to May 4, 1990, when the bond market began what has been at least a two-year bull run, during which the yield has fallen from levels above 9% to current levels, which were less than 7.5% as of July 31, 1992. Higher bond prices lead to falling yields.

Figure 2 is the 30-year Treasury bond yield and Figure 3 shows the Hines ratio. As Figure 3 indicates, high readings are rare; there have been only four buy signals in a two-year period. I regard these as serious signals and usually begin my buying on the Monday after the confirmation of the signal by the Bullish Consensus, unless its buy signal has preceded the Hines signal. The Bullish Consensus polls bond traders and is therefore a volatile indicator, as can be seen from Figures 2 and 3. However, when these two indicators are combined, they are powerful predictors of the intermediate trend of the bond market.

Figure 4 is the Bond Bullish Consensus from May 4, 1990, to July 31, 1992. The "B" marks the intermediate-term buy signals

PERFORMANCE TABLES

HIGH READING OF HINES INDEX AS PREDICTOR OF INTERMEDIATE-TERM BULLISH U.S. 30-YEAR BOND PERFORMANCE

Date	Bond Hines	30-yr. yield	3 months	6 months	1 year
5/4/90	1.93	8.82	8.44	8.55	8.23
8/24/90	1.98	9.15	8.44	8.05	8.12
6/14/91	2.10	8.47	7.96	7.77	7.85
4/24/92	1.81	8.03	7.57		pending

ACTUAL PERFORMANCE OF HINES INDEX BUY AND SELL SIGNAL COMBINATIONS

Date	Hines ratio	Yield	Actual low yield for move
5/4/90	1.93 (Buy)	8.82%	
6/15/90	0.798 (Sell)	8.42	8.40 (6/29/90)
8/24/90	1.98 (Buy)	9.15	
2/8/91	0.585 (Sell)	7.95	7.95 (2/8/91)
6/14/91	2.10 (Buy)	8.47	
11/15/91	0.641 (Sell)	7.80	7.47 (1/10/92)
4/24/92	1.81 (Buy)	8.03	
7/31/92	0.682 (Sell)	7.46	pending

PERFORMANCE OF BOND BULLISH CONSENSUS BUY AND SELL SIGNALS

Date	Bullish consensus	Yield	Low yield for move
4/27/90	41% (Buy)	9.02%	
5/18/90	63 (Sell)	8.69	8.40 (6/29/90)
8/24/90	42 (Buy)	9.15	
12/14/90	63% (Sell)	8.18	7.95 (2/8/91)
6/14/91	33 (Buy)	8.47	
8/9/91	61 (Sell)	8.22	7.47 (1/10/92)
11/8/91	*39 (Buy)	7.87	
3/13/92	39 (Buy)	8.06	pending

*No sell signal was given. No confirmation from Hines index occurred.

FIGURE 1: *Here are the buy and sell signal for the Hines index and the Bullish Consensus with the subsequent changes in the long bond yield.*

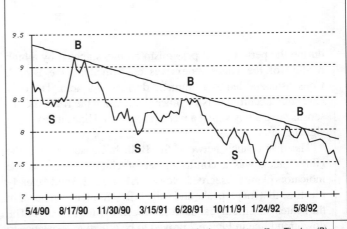

FIGURE 2: *The yield chart has remained below the long-term trendline. The buy (B) and sell (S) signals are based on sentiment extremes from the Hines index and the Bond Bullish Consensus index.*

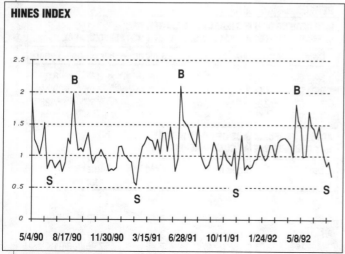

FIGURE 3: *The Hines index is a sentiment indicator based on option volume and option open interest. Low readings (below 0.65) often signal sells, while high readings (above 1.8) are buy signals.*

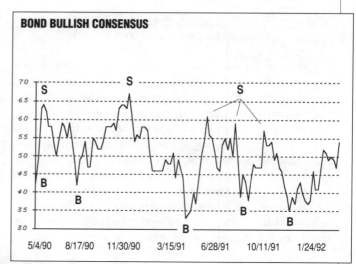

FIGURE 4: *The Bond Bullish Consensus typically signals sell (S) when the index reaches 60% and usually signals buy (B) when the index falls to 43%.*

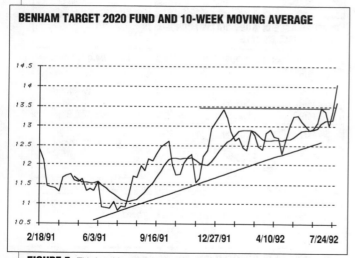

FIGURE 5: *This bond fund has held above the bullish long-term uptrend line.*

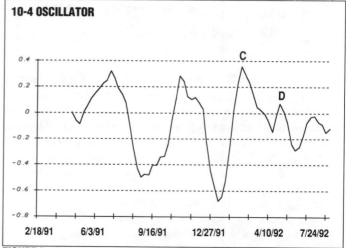

FIGURE 6: *The oscillator is the 10-week moving average minus the four-week moving average of the weekly closing price of the Benham Target 2020 fund. Changes in direction (C) are early warnings of a trend change. Crossing the zero line confirms the new trend (D).*

during the period. Each pessimism climax signaled by a high reading of the Hines index was confirmed by the Bullish Consensus and led to a dramatic decrease in yield. The only exception occurred in November 1991, when the Bullish Consensus gave a buy signal a week prior to the Hines index's sell signal.

The discrepancy between the Bullish Consensus and the Hines index was a confusing set of circumstances, as the indicators plainly disagreed. However, Figures 2, 3 and 4 clearly illustrate that major peaks and valleys in sentiment can occur in the context of a multiyear move, and such was the case here. The downtrend line in Figure 2 proved to be effective resistance to rising 30-year bond yields in each case. Simultaneously, the uptrend line for the Benham Target 2020 (Figure 5) proved to be effective support. As long as the Treasury yields (Figure 2)

remains below the trendline and the price of the bond fund (Figure 5) above its rising trendline, the long-term trend remains bullish and all intermediate-term trades must be placed within that context.

The "S" in Figures 2, 3 and 4 marks possible selling points. Of the three peaks in the Bullish Consensus (Figure 4) during the June 1991 to January 1992 advance, only the first reached greater than 60%, and it proved to be quite early. Trendline analysis was helpful in staying with the trade, as the peaks in optimism were unconfirmed by the Hines index (Figure 3), and the downtrend line on the yield chart remained intact.

A helpful hint for traders is the bond market's attraction to round yield numbers as trend reversal points. Traders should become more and more aware of increased optimism and pessimism as the 30-year bond reaches these round-number yield areas. Figure 1 shows this, as the four rallies were launched from bond yields very close to round numbers on each occasion.

RETRACING PERCENTAGE

Percentage retracement analysis is quite useful and easily incorporated into the system, as it was during the rally that began on June 14, 1991 (Figure 2). The yield on the date of the buy signal was 8.47. The rally reversed on January 10, 1992, at a yield of 7.47, a full point below the breakout. The next buy signal occurred on April 24, 1992, at a yield of 8.04%, almost exactly a 50% retracement of the yield, confirming that this was in fact the continuation of a longer-term bull market in bonds as the trendline suggested.

Figures 5 and 6 illustrate the performance of the Benham Target 2020 zero coupon bond fund and its companion indicator, the Ten Minus Four formula (abbreviated the 10-4 from here on), during the last two sentiment buy signals. The 10-4 is calculated by subtracting the arithmetic four-week moving average of the weekly closing price of the fund from the arithmetic 10-week moving average. Changes in the direction of the line are early warnings of intermediate-term trend changes and can be used as initial selling points (C). When the oscillator crosses the zero line, it confirms a trend change (point D). I prefer no-load zero coupon bonds as proxies for bond futures because of their volatility and built-in leverage at low cost.

Percentage retracement analysis of the Benham Target 2020 mutual fund during the same period as above illustrates similar behavior. The fund bottomed at $10.90 on June 17, three days after the buy signal, and it rallied until October 7, reaching a price of 12.62. It then retraced 50% of its gain to 11.76, where it held support before rallying again into January 1992.

Of importance is that even though the sentiment indicators gave conflicting signals, the mutual fund acted correctly within acceptable long- and intermediate-term technical parameters. As an intermediate-term trader, I stay with the trend as long as it remains in one direction.

CURRENTLY CAUTIOUS

The Hines index is currently reaching cautionary readings but the Bullish Consensus remains at somewhat subdued levels, and the trendline and 10-4 remain intact. Only by observing carefully will we be able to tell if this pattern and bull market will continue.

By identifying the long-term trend with trendlines and combining sentiment indicators with the 10-4 for the Benham Target 2020 for precise entry and exit points, a mutual fund trader will be able to participate in and profit from the bond market. This strategy is available at lower costs than directly trading futures contracts.

Joe Duarte, a frequent S&C contributor, publishes a mutual fund newsletter, "The Wall Street Detective," P.O. Box 679008-197, Dallas, TX 75367-9008.

REFERENCES

Duarte, Joe [1992]. "Trading bond funds," STOCKS & COMMODITIES, June.

Hines, Ray [1989]. "Hines ratio," *Technical Analysis of* STOCKS & COMMODITIES, Volume 7: April.

Kosar, John J. [1991]. "Support and resistance levels," *Technical Analysis of* STOCKS & COMMODITIES, Volume 9: January.

Gold And The U.S. Dollar

Last month, intermarket analyst and veteran technician John Murphy explored the relationship between interest rates and the U.S. dollar. This month, he progresses to the interrelationship between the U.S. dollar and gold.

by John J. Murphy

ast time, I showed that the U.S. dollar moves in the opposite direction of interest rate futures prices. At some point, however, the falling dollar will reawaken inflation pressures. One of the first hints of inflation — or disinflation — usu-ally comes from the gold market, due to the strong historical link between the gold market and the dollar.

Historically, the gold market trends in the opposite direction of the dollar. The inflationary 1970s saw gold soar above $800 while the dollar fell. The dollar turned higher in 1980 and rallied before peaking in 1985 while, concurrently, gold peaked in 1980 and dropped all the way down to $300 during the same five years that the dollar rallied. February 1985 marked the last major turn in both markets. That month, the dollar fell from its highest point in the 1980s, while gold rebounded from its lowest price for that decade.

In Figure 1, the gold market is compared to German Deut-schemark futures from that 1985 turning point. Utilizing a

FIGURE 1: *A strong positive correlation can be seen between gold (solid line) and the German mark (dotted line) since 1983, particularly at the 1985 bottom and the 1987 peak.*

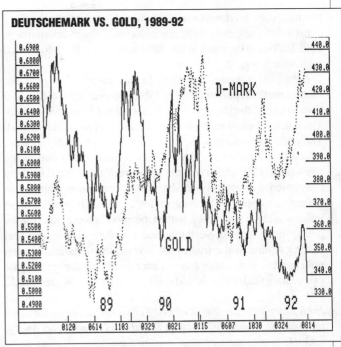

FIGURE 2: *Although gold (solid line) and the mark (dotted line) have trended in opposite directions since 1990, their peaks and troughs are still closely correlated.*

foreign currency has the same effect as comparing an inverted chart of the dollar to the gold market and makes visual comparison easier. If the dollar and gold trend in opposite directions, then the mark and gold should trend in the same direction. Figure 1 shows the remarkably close positive correlation between the mark and gold from 1983 to 1989. Both markets turned up in early 1985 as the dollar peaked, fell in late 1987 as the dollar rallied and then turned up together in 1989 as the dollar fell.

> **Even with the obvious deterioration in the positive relationship between gold and the mark since 1990, Figure 2 shows that the peaks and troughs in both markets are still closely correlated.**

A GOLDEN OPPORTUNITY?

The link between gold and the currencies has not been as strong since 1990. That period is examined more closely in Figure 2. Gold and the mark parted ways from early 1990 in that the mark strengthened while gold weakened. This relationship is consistent with a period of prolonged economic weakness characterized by falling U.S. interest rates, a weak dollar (that is, rising foreign currencies) and low U.S. inflation. Even with the obvious deterioration in the positive relationship between gold and the mark since 1990, Figure 2 shows that the peaks and troughs in both markets are still closely correlated. The late 1990 rally in

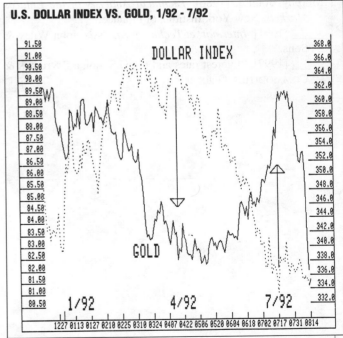

FIGURE 3: *The inverse relationship between gold (solid line) and the U.S. Dollar Index (dotted line) is visible during the first seven months of 1992. Central bank intervention to support the dollar during July coincided with the gold peak.*

the mark coincided with a gold rebound. Downturns in the mark in early 1991 and early 1992 coincided with sharp downturns in gold. Rallies in the mark in late 1991 and spring 1992 coincided with rallies in gold.

Figure 3 contrasts the U.S. Dollar Index with gold for intermarket comparison during 1992. Despite the weakness in both markets, the impact of the dollar on gold can still be seen. The dollar rebound early in the year coincided with a fall in gold. The dollar downturn in April contributed to the rally in gold, which lasted until mid-July. The gold rally ended during the week of July 20, which was the same week that central bankers intervened aggressively in the foreign exchange markets to defend the dollar. (The August 1992 gold collapse was also influenced by a sharp drop in the Commodity Research Bureau [CRB] index to a six-year low and a plunge in platinum and silver.) Although the traditional inverse relationship between gold and the U.S. dollar has not been as strong during the past two years, gold traders should still keep an eye on the greenback.

John Murphy is president of JJM Technical Advisors Inc. and publishes the monthly "Futures Trends and Intermarket Analysis." He is also the technical analyst for CNBC.

REFERENCES

JJM Technical Advisors Inc., 297-101 Kinderkamack Road Ste 148, Oradell, NJ 07649.

Murphy, John J. [1986]. *Technical Analysis of the Futures Markets*, New York Institute of Finance.

_____ [1991]. *Intermarket Technical Analysis*, John Wiley & Sons.

_____ [1992]. "Interest rates and the U.S. dollar," STOCKS & COMMODITIES, October.

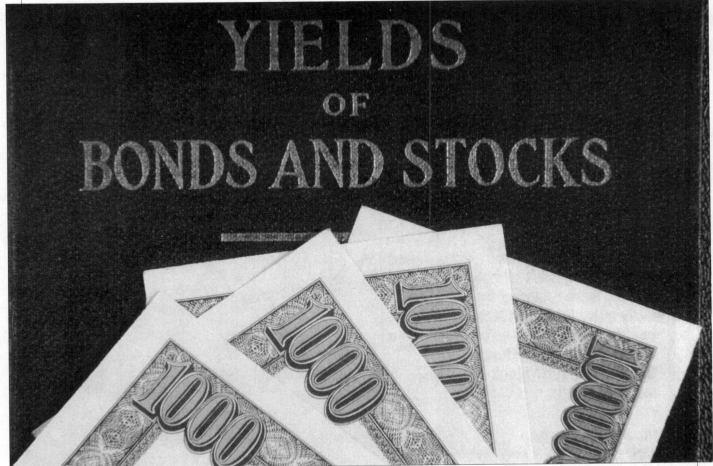

YIELDS OF BONDS AND STOCKS

JOS PALMIERI

Stocks, Interest Rates And The MACD

The notion that markets are interlinked is gaining widespread acceptance. However, the technique of timing trades in one market based on the price direction of another market still requires further fine tuning. Here, the moving average convergence/divergence (MACD) is presented as a method with which to identify the trend of interest rates that will in turn signal the coming trend in stocks.

---

by Kent Perkers

The importance of changes in interest rates and their impact on equity markets has long been recognized by astute fundamental and technical analysts. The ability of bond price trends to act as a leading indicator of equity market direction is extraordinary, as illustrated by Figure 1. Discovering when a change in the trend of interest rates has occurred is the challenge, one that the moving average convergence/divergence (MACD) can answer.

The MACD, which was developed by technician Gerald Appel, is an oscillator based on the difference between two exponentially smoothed moving averages of the closing prices. First, calculate the 26-week exponentially smoothed moving average (using a smoothing constant of 0.075) of the closing price. Second, calculate the 12-week exponentially smoothed moving average (using a smoothing constant of 0.15) of the closing price. The difference between the two moving averages is known as the MACD line. The method then smoothes the MACD line with a nine-week exponentially smoothed moving average (using a smoothing constant of 0.2). This line is called the signal line.

I use the MACD method by adjusting to take a longer-term view of the trends. To this end, I use a 66-week exponentially smoothed moving average (using a smoothing constant of 0.0299) of the closing price for the first EMA. Then I calculate the 33-week exponentially smoothed moving average (using a smoothing constant of 0.0589) of the closing price. Whenever the difference between the two EMAs crosses above zero, a buy signal is indicated. A sell signal occurs when the difference between the two EMAs is negative. I prefer to use a histogram to represent the values of the MACD line. (See sidebar, "An MACD variation.")

> **As shown at the upper portion of Figure 1, timely signals were provided for early entry into the 1982 bull market, as well as an early exit months before the October 1987 stock market tumble.**

CHANGES WHEN CROSSED

The lower portion of Figure 1 is a 14-year chart of the Dow Jones Industrials Bond Average (or the inverse of the interest rate trend for these debt issues). An MACD histogram reveals fundamental changes in interest rate trends when the zero line is crossed. An upward crossing of this line, for example, indicates that interest rates are establishing a trend toward lower yields.

The value of the MACD and the Dow Jones Industrials Bond Average is revealed when the crossover point is extended to the top half of Figure 1, which is the Dow Jones Industrial Average (DJIA). Not only were the major long opportunities identified but approaching bear markets were identified in plenty of time to take action as well. As bonds tend to lead equity markets both up and down, this simple trend-following indicator of bonds becomes a trend predictor for equities.

In addition, the apprehension associated with adjusting portfolios during stressful periods is eliminated by using this indicator. Two recent shakeouts (November-December 1991 and June 1992) brought the New York Stock Exchange (NYSE) Composite Index below its 40-week moving average, whether attributable to the market's overvaluation, concurrent

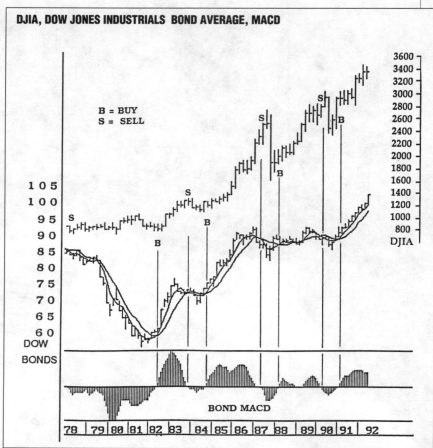

FIGURE 1: When the MACD histogram for the Dow Jones Industrials Bond Average turns positive, the falling interest rate environment has preceded a stock market rally. When the histogram turns negative, the stock market has become vulnerable to declines.

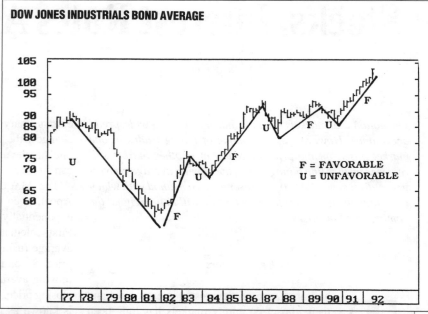

FIGURE 2: When the MACD has been positive (Figure 1), the rallying bond market has indicated a favorable period for stocks. When the MACD has been negative, the declining bond prices have been an unfavorable environment for stocks.

AN MACD VARIATION

The method used is a variation of the original moving average convergence/divergence (MACD) indicator. Longer-term exponentially smoothed moving averages (EMA) have been used in the calculation of the MACD. The new smoothing constants a are 0.0299 and 0.0589, which approximate a 66-week simple moving average and a 33-week simple moving average, respectively. Recalling that the formula for an EMA is:

$$E_2 = E_1 + a(P_2 - E_1)$$

where:
E_2 = Today's EMA
E_1 = Yesterday's EMA
P_2 = Today's price
a = smoothing constant

Sidebar Figure 1 is a spreadsheet example. Column D is a 66-week EMA and the formula for Cell D10 is:

$$=D9+0.0299*(C10-D9)$$

Column E is a 33-week EMA and the formula for Cell E10 is:

$$=E9+0.0589*(C10-E9)$$

	A	B	C	D	E	F
1	DATE	DJIA	D 20	66 week	33 week	DIFFERENCE
2			BONDS	EMA	EMA	
3	8/10/90	2716.58	90.79	90.79	90.79	0.00
4	8/17/90	2644.80	90.39	90.78	90.77	-0.01
5	8/24/90	2532.92	89.04	90.73	90.66	-0.06
6	8/31/90	2614.36	89.11	90.68	90.57	-0.10
7	9/7/90	2619.55	89.50	90.64	90.51	-0.13
8	9/14/90	2564.11	89.54	90.61	90.45	-0.16
9	9/21/90	2512.38	89.14	90.57	90.38	-0.19
10	9/28/90	2452.48	88.77	90.51	90.28	-0.23

SIDEBAR FIGURE 1: MACD. *The indicator is simply the difference between the 66-week EMA and the 33-week EMA.*

Column F is the difference between the two EMAs. The formula for cell F10 is:

$$=E10-D10$$

To start the EMA, you do not have a starting value for the previous one. Just start on day 2 and use the previous day's close for the first EMA.

—*Editor*

Note: We used the Dow Jones 20 Bond Average in this sidebar, while author Kent Perkers used only the Dow Jones 10 Industrial Bond Average. The Dow Jones 20 Bond Average is made up of the Dow Jones 10 Utility Bond Average and the Dow Jones 10 Industrial Bond Average.

declines in most world equity markets, falling advance/decline lines and so forth. These selloffs had no influence on and were not confirmed by the bond/equity indicator. Consequently, this buying opportunity could be seen more clearly without the distractions that affect investment decisions. (For comparison purposes, the 40-week moving average of the NYSE Composite was the standard used in *The Encyclopedia of Technical Market Indicators* for determining buy and sell signals.)

The results of this intermarket relationship broke the 1978-92 period into eight distinct intermediate equity climates (Figure 2). While some individual stocks can rise or fall almost independently of the market, identifying the general market trend is perhaps the single most important criterion for successful results with reduced risk. Shorter-term bond MACDs can be valuable for trading decisions, but this analysis begins with a study of longer trends.

ENTER AND EXIT
As shown at the upper portion of Figure 1, timely signals were provided for early entry into the 1982 bull market, as well as an early exit months before the October 1987 stock market tumble. An exit signal was provided well before Iraq's Saddam Hussein entered Kuwait, followed by a signal to reinvest before his troops were ejected. The backup in interest rates prior to the invasion left the market vulnerable to a selloff, according to this technical indicator. In fact, the initiation of hostilities set off a rapid market spike, which occurred during a "favorable" period when interest rates had already turned lower. The last buy signal, which made its appearance in late 1990 and continues today, has recently increased its momentum, despite some argument that we are in a bearish environment. While an objective methodology was the basis of Figure 1, Figure 2 is a subjective analysis that demonstrates a convincing ability in the bond price trends to identify generally favorable or unfavorable equity markets accurately.

Finally, Figure 3 quantifies the results in DJIA index percentage gains. Only four and a half round-trip signals have been given over 14 years, with no losing cycles. Modifying the indicator or riding out the 1987 bubble a little longer, for example, could have added to the 362.6% compounded return provided by this indicator since August 1982, assuming the investor did not overstay the party's end by even *one* day. A short-term version of this interest rate/equity market relationship also provides aggressive trading opportunities for those willing to monitor daily bond movements. But another benefit of this longer-term indicator is that being hyperactive in the markets or acutely aware of every tick in interest rates is of no advantage to an intermediate-term investor.

A GROWING DIVERGENCE
This interest rate/equity market indicator, a trend-following technique with bonds, is a predictive tool with equities. The recent breakout in bonds to a multiyear high should set back the date of the next bear market cycle, whenever that may occur. The importance of this recent bond breakout move was summed up in *Technical Analysis Explained* with the observation that

DJIA INDEX PERCENTAGE GAINS ON EACH ROUND-TRIP TRADE			
Signal	Date	DJIA	% Gain (Loss)
1978-81: Sell signal in progress			
Buy	8/12/82	843	
Sell	2/18/84	1,184	+40.5%
Buy	12/18/84	1,210	
Sell	7/17/87	2,493	+106.0%
Buy	5/26/88	2,047	
Sell	6/7/90	2,859	+39.7%
Buy	4/17/91	2,911	
Sell	interim recent value	3,330	+14.4%
Compounded 10-year gain: +362.6%			

FIGURE 3: *These trades would be the result if the DJIA were based on the MACD indicator applied to the Dow Jones Industrials Bond Average.*

"every cyclical stock market peak in this century was preceded by, or has coincided with, a peak in *both* the long and the short ends of the bond market" (emphasis mine). That peak will manifest itself as a growing divergence between declining bond prices and rising equities.

Kent Perkers is a money manager (registered investment advisor) and can be reached at (310) 839-2753.

REFERENCES

Colby, R.W., and T.A. Meyers [1988]. *The Encyclopedia of Technical Market Indicators*, Dow Jones-Irwin.
Pring, Martin J. [1991]. *Technical Analysis Explained,* McGraw-Hill Book Co., 3d edition.

Using Neural Nets For Intermarket Analysis

Changes in Treasury bill yields, Treasury bond yields, gold and the U.S. dollar affect the stock market in subtle but predictable ways. These are complex and challenging relationships to decipher—tasks well suited to the abilities of neural networks, because neural nets are designed to detect patterns in relationships. Here, systems analyst John Kean presents his work on utilizing a neural network for researching intermarket relationships.

by John Kean

Watching changes in market prices and interest rates may suggest that hidden somewhere in these seemingly chaotic fluctuations, useful patterns that are discernible may be used to predict price changes in the stock market. It's easy to speculate on such things, but how does one take an intuitive notion such as market interdependence, test it and perhaps turn it into a lucrative trading method?

One possible strategy would be to devise a computer program that through trial and error would produce a sequence of conditional statements. These statements could define certain intermarket conditions that, if satisfied, would signal the trader to be long, flat or short the stock market. For example, suppose that during the preceding week gold prices fell, the U.S. Dollar Index rose and Treasury bond and bill rates fell. Our computer program would signal that it might be profitable to be long in stocks the coming week.

Obviously, the potential for subtle variations in any set of conditions abound, making trial and error analysis arduous and limited. Neural networks, a form of artificial intelligence that is rapidly gaining recognition, is adept at handling this type of problem and gives superior results.

MARKET KNACK

The first step in testing such an idea depends on market knack and common sense. To begin with, it takes experiential judgment to decide on the optimum period during which to perform the analysis. It should include enough varying market conditions to allow the generation of rules that can cope with likely scenarios, rather than just what has happened most recently. But if the time period is too long, then the rules will be affected by outdated relationships and the trading results will suffer.

There is no way of establishing the "right" length of time over which to perform trading analyses; perhaps a good rule of thumb is to base your predictions on an analysis of 200 to 300 times the length over which you want to predict. If you want to cast a prediction for the coming week, base your rule generation analysis on 200 to 300 weeks of data. If you want to forecast an ensuing month, use at least 200 or 300 months.

Next, pick relevant inputs for your predictions. If you're trying to forecast weekly stock index changes, then monthly Consumer Price Index (CPI) inputs — which are posted two weeks after the fact and then continually revised — may not be the thing. But price and interest rate changes in other financial and commodity items just might be. It's important to narrow the number of inputs down and include only those that you are familiar with from study and experience and that have a relationship with the item to be predicted (in this case, the Standard & Poor's 500).

Choose inputs that are unique in their nature. Don't include Treasury bond rates and corporates, for example; they're too similar. Choose one or the other. Likewise, don't use both gold and platinum; gold is probably the better choice. If you include too many inputs, there will be a tendency to get curve-fitted results.

Curve fitting is probably the most dangerous snare a trader can walk into because it leads you to being overconfident of your trading system, causing costly mistakes. A curve-fitted trading system is typically generated by using numerous inputs of questionable relevance and then devising a lengthy, complicated set of conditions that maps into giving seemingly reasoned predictions. Unfortunately, the predictions are based on nuances or isolated occurrences within the analyzed data set, not genuine enduring relationships.

A smart analyst adds input series jealously. A second rule of the thumb is to keep the number of time periods analyzed at least 20 times the number of input series.

NEURAL NETWORKS

This all applies whether you're working up an analytical model "by hand" or by using an artificial intelligence innovation known as a neural network. Neural networks have been applied in such diverse areas as medical diagnosis, credit application rating, optical character recognition, weapons systems and (of course) securities trading in recent times. Evidence is mounting that this approach gives results superior to conventional methods of statistical analysis and pattern recognition.

The concept behind neural networks originated in studies of the brain and nervous system in the mid-1940s. Since then, neural nets have gone through periods of favor with researchers based on whatever the current perceptions of its promise and

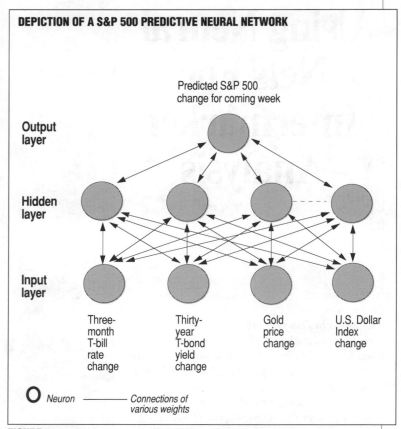

DEPICTION OF A S&P 500 PREDICTIVE NEURAL NETWORK

Predicted S&P 500 change for coming week

Output layer

Hidden layer

Input layer

Three-month T-bill rate change

Thirty-year T-bond yield change

Gold price change

U.S. Dollar Index change

O Neuron ——— Connections of various weights

FIGURE 1: Neural networks are made up of layers. The input layer for this model uses weekly changes. These input neurons are connected by "weighting" transform functions to the neurons in the hidden layer connected to the output layer. The arrows point in both directions, indicating that predictions beyond the user-determined tolerance limit from the correct answer result in the remodification of the connecting weights.

available hardware power were. It was only during the 1980s that there was a resurgence of interest in this field; now in the 1990s, neurals are very much a going concern.

There are many forms of neural nets, and the type discussed here is software that imitates the brain's learning process. In the brain, the basic learning unit is the neuron, of which there are

> **Instead of perfection, our neural net analysis aims to see if intermarket changes bear enough predictivity to beat the S&P 500 index *and* if it can avoid the sharp plunges in the market that could take a leveraged trader out of the game.**

many varieties. When neurons are activated, they interact with each other by releasing electrochemical packets across the synaptic gaps between them. The nature of the synapses and the gaps determines the internal activity level of the neurons. The learning process comes about through the modification of these connections between neurons.

Computer neural networks can be composed of three types of neuron layers: an input layer, one or more hidden layers, and an output layer. Each layer may have any number of neurons. Aping the brain, the neurons of each layer are connected to neurons of adjoining layers. Instead of a lot of complex biochemicals, neural network software uses transform functions to serve as the connectors. These functions involve matrix algebra and, in the BrainMaker neural net used here, include a variety of transfer functions that the user may choose. The transform functions establish the weights of the connections between neurons, analogous to the learning functions of the synapses and gaps in biological systems.

Figure 1 is a depiction of the neural net used to analyze intermarket predictivity for the S&P 500. At the input layer, there are four neurons that represent weekly changes in the three-month Treasury bill rate, the 30-year Treasury bond yield, the price change in gold and in the Federal Reserve's U.S. Dollar Index. These input neurons are connected by "weighting" transform functions to the neurons in the hidden layer, which in turn are connected to the output neuron. The connecting arrows point in both directions, indicating that as the BrainMaker neural software runs through its training examples, any predictions that are beyond the user-specified tolerance limit from the correct answer result in a remodification of the connecting weights back through the network (known as "back-propagation" in neural network terminology).

Our aim is to predict the change in the S&P 500 index for the coming week. It is important to note that financial market predictions are a different sort of problem than neural nets are usually used for, which leads to misconceptions among many neural net users. If we were trying to solve a problem involving a physical law like gravity, then we would be working with a unique and specific relationship (the law of gravity). All we would have to worry about was getting accurate, precise data and then let the neural net train to "converge," meaning that all training outputs would have to be within a given tolerance limit of the correct answer. The resulting trained network would then have deciphered the way the law of gravity behaves and could then take new inputs and presumably give good outputs (that is, predictions) every time.

PREDICTION AND PERFECTION

But in analyzing the financial markets, we are not dealing with the laws of nature; we're dealing with a market (the S&P 500) that changes in

price due to an unknown total number of factors. Our inputs don't encompass the universe of influences for the rise and fall of stock prices. Much of what determines stock index fluctuations evolves quickly due to participants' ever-changing focus. Even if a general "law" explaining weekly stock price changes existed, the required number of inputs would be enormous. Considering the limits of what we're doing, we shouldn't aim for perfection (which we don't need for trading profits, anyway).

> If the neural network connections were deciphering true causal relationships between the four inputs and the predicted output (next week's S&P 500 change), then the percentage of correct guesses in the training and testing cases should be about the same.

Instead of perfection, our neural net analysis aims to see if these intermarket changes bear enough predictivity to beat the S&P 500 index *and* if it can avoid the sharp plunges in the market that could take a leveraged trader out of the game. The neural net trained on weekly data spanning from December 31, 1986, to November 27, 1991, a period of 257 weeks. But the program did not get to see all 257 weeks during training; 20%, or 51 weeks, were withheld and used as testing cases during training. An additional 29 weeks, spanning December 4, 1991, to June 17, 1992, were excluded from the training and testing period to see how the final product fared past November 27, 1991.

TESTS AND BALANCES

As the neural program made its successive runs through the 206 training cases, it continually modified the connective weights, seeking to develop a network of relationships that would allow it to predict the coming week's S&P 500 change within the tolerance limits. During each pass through the training cases, the network's guesses were compared with the actual S&P 500 changes of the following week, and the number of good and bad guesses were saved at each run's end. Then the same network ran through the test cases. There was no right or wrong feedback and no modification of network connections; the purpose was purely to determine the number of right and wrong guesses that the current network made over this set of data not trained on and to save the numbers to a file.

If the neural network connections were deciphering true causal relationships between the four inputs

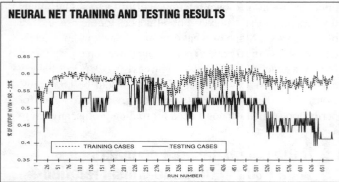

NEURAL NET TRAINING AND TESTING RESULTS

FIGURE 2: *Over 650 runs of training and testing were performed. Past run 280, the percentage correct of the test cases began to trend down, indicating the neural network was beginning to memorize nuances instead of discerning relationships.*

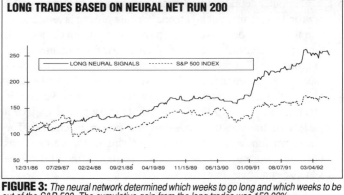

LONG TRADES BASED ON NEURAL NET RUN 200

FIGURE 3: *The neural network determined which weeks to go long and which weeks to be out of the S&P 500. The cumulative gain from the long trades was 152.02%.*

and the predicted output (next week's S&P 500 change), then the percentage of correct guesses in the training and testing cases should be about the same. If a network based a significant part of its guesses on memorized nuances that it was exposed to in the training data, then the results should degrade when it was used on the testing data. Figure 2 shows the percent right for this analysis recorded in more than 650 runs of training and testing. Between runs 180 and 280, many of the trained networks were about as effective on the test cases as they were on the trained cases. Past run 280, however, the percentage correct in the test cases trended downward, even as the trained cases gained or held steady in "correctness" — a good indication that past run 280, the neural program tended to memorize nuances rather than decipher relationships.

Another pitfall in neural net training is overusing the option to increase the number of hidden layers and hidden layer neurons. This increases the capacity of the network and often leads to higher percentages of correct training answers. The problem: this additional capacity often leads to memorization instead of genuine learning progress. In this analysis, only one hidden layer was used. However, the program did have the option of adding a neuron to the hidden layer every 10 runs, thus expanding the learning capacity of the network.

PERFORMANCE RESULTS
Having gone over how to develop a neural network trading

model, let's see how well it performed. From the training/testing relationships shown in Figure 2, the neural network generated in run 200 was selected for trading. The total intermarket input data file from December 31, 1986, through June 17, 1992, was analyzed by the network from run 200 and a prediction for each following week's S&P 500 change was made. This included all the weeks trained on and tested and then the last 29 weeks that followed the training/testing period — a thorough evaluation.

Overall, the trading results were very good. The cumulative results of this trading can be seen in Figures 3 and 4. The BrainMaker neural network predictions were used to decide whether to be long or short the S&P 500 index for the coming week. Over the total period, the S&P 500 index gained 66.11%, compared to the gain through long trading of 152.02%, and through short trading of 53.8%. Long and short trading combined resulted in a 287.61% gain. Most important, the cumulative returns showed no signs of degrading over the last 29 weeks, which were not included in the training of the network.

The long trades were successful 62.57% of the time and the short trades 51.14% of the time. The network didn't learn how to be infallible; it just learned to ferret out the best opportunities and to avoid the worst pitfalls. The maximum drawdown of the combined long and short trading was less than half that of the S&P 500 index. Much of this drawdown could be reduced by playing only the stronger signals for going long or short; in other words, by staying flat some weeks.

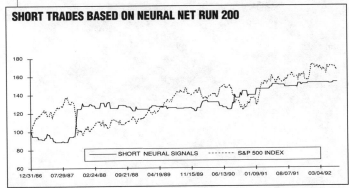

SHORT TRADES BASED ON NEURAL NET RUN 200

SHORT NEURAL SIGNALS ——— S&P 500 INDEX --------

FIGURE 4: *The weeks to be short the S&P 500 were selected by the neural network. The cumulative gains were 53.8%.*

theory is based on the theoretical workings of animal and human intelligence, and as such, it is subject to similar quirks and limits. A well-trained neural network is like an intuitive human expert who does superior work but can't quite explain how he does it. Nevertheless, there's little doubt that neural networks will have a major competitive impact trading the markets in the years ahead.

John Kean is a systems analyst and has been investing and trading for more than 10 years. He consults on applying neural nets to trading and investment and can be reached at (719) 282-2027 or P.O. Box 26463, Colorado Springs, CO 80932.

SOME CONCLUSIONS
The neural network is an excellent tool for deciphering patterns and relationships in market data. With the use of a neural net, intermarket factors can be instrumental in profitably predicting stock index changes. One drawback, however, is that due to the complex nature of neural networks, we cannot dissect them to see the relationships that led to the predictions. Neural network

ADDITIONAL READING AND REFERENCE
BrainMaker. California Scientific Software, 10024 Newtown Road, Nevada City, CA 95959, (800) 284-8112.

Fishman, Mark B., Dean S. Barr and Walter J. Loick [1991]. "Artificial intelligence and market analysis," *Technical Analysis of* STOCKS & COMMODITIES, Volume 9: March.

_____. "Using neural nets in market analysis," *Technical Analysis of* STOCKS & COMMODITIES, Volume 9: April.

Katz, Jeffrey Owen [1992]. "Developing neural network forecasters for trading," STOCKS & COMMODITIES, April.

Mendelsohn, Lou [1991]. "The basics of developing a neural trading system," *Technical Analysis of* STOCKS & COMMODITIES, Volume 9: June.

RICARDO SCOZZARI

KST And Relative Strength

In previous articles, technician and author Martin Pring has analyzed the KST indicator, an oscillator designed to identify market turns based on time cycles. This month, he explains how to use the KST in gauging the relative strength of stocks.

by Martin J. Pring

I n the September STOCKS & COMMODITIES, I introduced the KST, a momentum indicator constructed from a weighted summed rate of change. To recap, four different smoothed rates of change (ROC) are combined into one oscillator. This captures the under-

lying price movements of several different market cycles as reflected by the various ROC time spans. Trend reversals are signaled when the KST crosses above or below its moving average.

KST indicators can be constructed to monitor any type of market trend. By giving different weights to the different ROC components that make up the KST indicator, we can construct oscillators with different outlook lengths. One particularly practical use of the KST indicator is to stack three printouts of the oscillator, reflecting the short-, intermediate- and long-term trend, on top of each other (Figure 1). The long-term KST monitors the primary trend of the market (that is, price movements lasting for one, two or three years); its position gives us

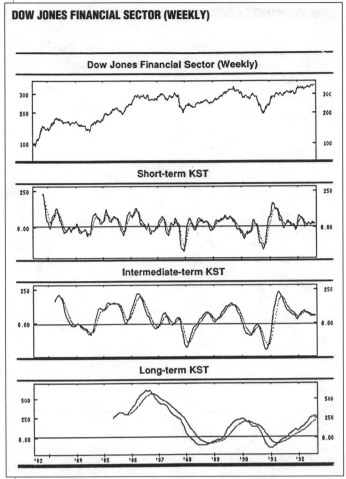

FIGURE 1: *The KST indicator is a summed weighted measure of rate of change. Varying the weights and the rates of change can produce indicators that measure rate of change for short-term, intermediate-term and long-term time horizons.*

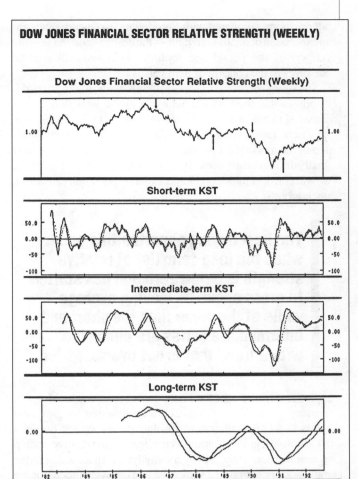

FIGURE 2: *Rates of change analysis can also be applied to a relative strength chart. The most reliable buying opportunities are when the long-term KST indicator is below zero and is turning up (up arrows). Negative indications occur when the long-term KST is above zero and turning down (down arrows).*

some perspective on the trend maturity. The intermediate- and short-term indicators are used more for timing purposes. For example, if a short-term buy is triggered when the long-term indicator rises just above the zero level, a bull market rally is indicated. On the other hand, a short-term buy signal that occurs when the long-term indicator is declining tells us that a bear market rally is underway. The difference is important, since the former is usually profitable and the latter deceptive, unreliable and unprofitable.

This arrangement of three KST oscillators into what I call the market cycle model not only helps the trader or investor position himself in the direction of the main trend but also gives some indication as to its maturity. For example, when a long-term KST is overextended on the upside and an intermediate sell signal is generated, the odds are fairly high that the implied intermediate correction will turn out to be the beginning of a major reversal formation or, more likely, the first downleg of a new bear market.

RELATIVE PRICING

Thus far, we have considered the KST indicator in terms of absolute price, but the analysis can be extended to relative pricing as well. Relative strength (RS) measures the relationship between two price series and should in no way be confused with the relative strength index (RSI), which compares the current price of a security to the past. Normally, an RS line compares a specific item such as a stock to a base to some market measure such as a stock index. The line is calculated by dividing the stock price by the market index value and the result is plotted as a continuous line. When the line is rising, the stock is outperforming the market; when it is in a decline, the market is outperforming the stock. A rising RS line does not tell us that the absolute or actual price of the stock is appreciating but only that it is outperforming the market. For example, the market may decline 20%, but the stock may lose only 10% of its value. Both are losers, but the stock's losses are less than those of the market.

Relative strength can also be used to compare two different price series. The gold/silver ratio, for example, is a relative strength relationship; so too is the "Ted spread," where Treasury bill prices are compared with Eurodollars. Even currencies are an expression of relative strength — the dollar versus the yen, the yen versus the pound and so forth. Here we will confine ourselves to the concept of item versus basket.

Since relative strength moves in trends like absolute prices do, it follows that the KST market cycle model approach can be extended to this area as well. In my analysis I take a top-down approach. This involves an examination of the long-term position of the market as a whole, followed by industry groups and finally the individual stocks included in the group. In this article, we will consider the second stage: isolating potentially attractive stock groups.

> **The best buying opportunities occur when the long-term KST of relative strength is below zero and has started to cross above its moving average, while at the same time the short and intermediate series are consistent with a trend that is not overextended.**

STOCK GROUP SELECTION

In many ways, the KST approach is more suited for analyzing trends in relative rather than absolute prices. As the business cycle unfolds, group rotation occurs, leaving the relative pricing system far more subject to cyclic rhythms than an actual index and stock price. Figure 2 shows the market cycle model for the relative strength of the Dow Jones financial sector. The series in the top panel is the RS itself, while the other three are the KST indicators. When the line is rising, the Dow Jones financial sector is outperforming the market, and vice versa.

The best buying opportunities occur when the long-term KST of relative strength is below zero and has started to cross above its moving average, while at the same time the short and intermediate series are consistent with a trend that is not overextended. It is also important to make sure that the RS itself has generated some kind of buy signal, such as an exponential moving average (EMA) crossover or a trendline break. In a similar vein, the probabilities do not favor situations in which the long-term KST is in an overextended reading far above zero. Such readings indicate that the trend of the superior RS is well advanced. The trend could well continue for some time, but the law of averages is against it. Far better would be to search for a group in which the long-term KST is depressed and turning up.

The best approach is to isolate those groups for which the market cycle model is in a positive mode, not only for the relative price but for the absolute price as well. The last up arrow in Figure 2 indicates a period when both aspects of the model were positive. Each instance is followed by superior results.

In any given situation, rotation occurs continually between the various industry groups in terms of relative strength. This can best be appreciated by comparing two groups that traditionally

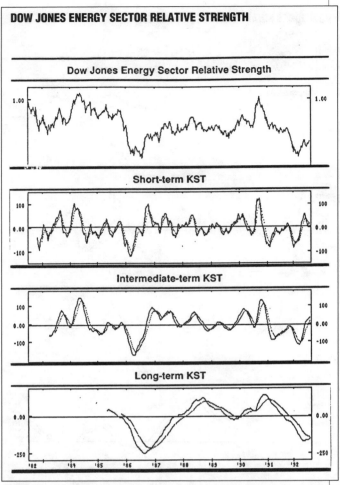

DOW JONES ENERGY SECTOR RELATIVE STRENGTH

FIGURE 3: *When a bull market in stocks begins to mature, the energy stocks tend to take over the leadership role. The long-term KST should begin to turn up, indicating better relative performance by the energy group.*

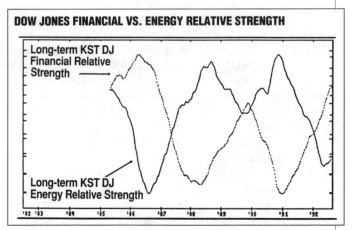

DOW JONES FINANCIAL VS. ENERGY RELATIVE STRENGTH

FIGURE 4: *Plotting the long-term KSTs for both the financial relative strength line and the energy relative strength line displays the rotation of these two stock groups. Strength in one group coincides with weakness in the other stock group.*

CALCULATING THE KST

The suggested parameters for short, intermediate and long term can be found in sidebar Figure 1. There are three steps to calculating the KST indicator. First, calculate the four different rates of change. Recalling the formula for rate of change (ROC) is today's closing price divided by the closing price n days ago. This result is then multiplied by 100. Then subtract 100 to obtain a rate of change index that uses zero as the center point. Second, smooth each ROC with either a simple or exponential moving average (EMA). Third, multiply each smoothed ROC by its prospective weight and sum the weighted smoothed ROCs.

The formula for an exponential moving average (EMA) requires the use of a smoothing constant (α) alpha. The constant used to smooth the data is found using the formula $2/(n+1)$. For example, for $n=3$, then $\alpha = 2/(3+1)=0.50$. The formula for the EMA is:

$$E_2 = E_1 + \alpha\,(P_2 - E_1)$$

where:
E$_2$ = New exponential average
E$_1$ = Prior exponential average
P$_2$ = Current price

Please note the first day's calculation does not have a prior exponential average. Consequently, you just use the first day's price and begin the smoothing process the next day. Figure 2 is a spreadsheet example of the short-term weekly KST using exponential moving averages for the smoothing. Column C is the three-week rate of change. The formula for cell C20 is:

$$=((B20/B18)*100)-100$$

The three-week rate of change is smoothed with a three-week EMA. The constant used to smooth the data is found using the formula $2/(n+1)$. For $n=3$, then, the constant equals $2/(3+1)=0.50$, and thus, the formula for cell D20 is:

$$=D19+0.5*(C20-D19)$$

Cell E20 is a four-week ROC:
$$=((B20/B17)*100)-100$$

Cell F20 is a four-week EMA:

$$=F19+0.4*(E20-F19)$$

Cell G20 is a six-week ROC:
$$=((B20/B15)*100)-100$$

Cell H20 is a six-week EMA:
$$=H19+0.29*(G20-H19)$$

Cell I20 is a 10-week ROC:
$$=((B20/B11)*100)-100$$

Cell J20 is an eight-week EMA:
$$=J19+0.22*(I20-J19)$$

Finally, cell K20 is the summed weighted smoothed ROCs. Each smoothed ROC is weighted according to sidebar Figure 1 and summed:

$$=D20+(2*F20)+(3*H20)+(4*J20)$$

—Editor

SUGGESTED KST FORMULAS

	ROC	MA	Wt	ROC	MA	Wt	ROC	MA	Wt	ROC	MA	Wt
Short-term (D)	10	10	1	15	10	2	20	10	3	30	15	4
Short-term (W)	3	3E	1	4	4E	2	6	6E	3	10	8E	4
Intermediate-term (W)	10	10	1	13	13	2	15	15	3	20	20	4
Intermediate-term (W)	10	10E	1	13	13E	2	15	15E	3	20	20E	4
Long-term (M)	9	6	1	12	6	2	18	6	3	24	9	4
Long-term (W)	39	26E	1	52	26E	2	78	26E	3	104	39E	4

It is possible to program all KST formulas into MetaStock and the CompuTrac SNAP module.
(D) Based on daily data. (W) Based on weekly data. (M) Based on monthly data. (E) EMA.

SIDEBAR FIGURE 1: *The ROC column is the rate of change. The MA column is the moving average value, and E after the moving average value indicates that the moving average is an exponential moving average. Multiply each smoothed ROC by its weight prior to summing the four smoothed ROCs.*

	A	B	C	D	E	F	G	H	I	J	K
1	Date	S&P 500	3 week	3 Week	4 Week	4 week	6 Week	6 week	10 Week	8 week	Summed
2	920103	419.34	ROC	EMA	ROC	EMA	ROC	EMA	ROC	EMA	Weighted
3	920110	415.10									ROC
4	920117	418.86	-0.11								
5	920124	415.48	0.09		-0.92						
6	920131	408.78	-2.41	-2.41	-1.52						
7	920207	411.09	-1.06	-1.73	-1.86		-1.97				
8	920214	412.48	0.91	-0.41	-0.72	-0.72	-0.63				
9	920221	411.46	0.09	-0.16	0.66	-0.17	-1.77				
10	920228	412.70	0.05	-0.05	0.39	0.05	-0.67				
11	920306	404.44	-1.71	-0.88	-1.95	-0.75	-1.06		-3.55		
12	920313	405.84	-1.66	-1.27	-1.37	-0.99	-1.28	-1.28	-2.23		
13	920320	411.30	1.70	0.21	-0.34	-0.73	-0.29	-0.99	-1.80		
14	920327	403.50	-0.58	-0.18	-0.23	-0.53	-1.93	-1.26	-2.88		
15	920403	401.55	-2.37	-1.28	-1.06	-0.74	-2.70	-1.68	-1.77		
16	920410	404.29	0.20	-0.54	-1.70	-1.13	-0.04	-1.20	-1.65		
17	920416	416.05	3.61	1.54	3.11	0.57	2.52	-0.13	0.87	0.87	
18	920424	409.02	1.17	1.35	1.86	1.08	-0.55	-0.25	-0.59	0.54	
19	920501	412.53	-0.85	0.25	2.04	1.47	2.24	0.47	-0.04	0.42	6.26
20	920508	416.05	1.72	0.99	0.00	0.88	3.61	1.38	2.87	0.96	10.71

SIDEBAR FIGURE 2: SPREADSHEET FOR SHORT-TERM WEEKLY KST. *Here, the KST is calculated using exponential moving averages.*

perform at different stages in the cycle. At the beginning of a bull market, interest-sensitive issues such as financials typically outperform the market. As the cycle matures, this leadership gives way to inflation-sensitive issues such as the energy sector (Figure 3). This rotation can be seen in Figure 4, which compares the long-term KST of relative strength for both series. Note that there is a tendency for them to move in opposite directions. For example, the KST for the financial series peaked in mid-1986 while the long-term KST energy relative strength was turning up. The reverse held true in late 1990. Since then, the financial issues have outperformed the rest of the market and energy has lagged. In late August, the energy RS looks as though it is trying to bottom but has not yet succeeded in crossing above its exponential moving average.

MARKET CYCLE MODEL

Relative KST analysis can not only be used for timing the purchase and sale of securities that make up industry groups, but also for ascertaining the prevailing stage of the market cycle. When the long-term KST for the relative strength of financials is bottoming, a new cycle is probably beginning, and when energy is reversing to the upside, it warns that the cycle is rapidly maturing.

So far in this series of articles we have barely tapped the surface of KST analysis. The concept is far from perfect, but it

does provide the analyst with a good long-term perspective of a specific market from which more informed short-term decisions can be made. Anyone searching for the Holy Grail is likely to be disappointed. Hamilton Boulton, founder of the "Bank Credit Analyst," put it this way: "The goal of imperfection in the investment world is likely to lead to greater profits than the pursuit of perfection."

Martin Pring is the author of a number of books, publishes "The Pring Market Review" and is a principal of the investment counseling firm Pring-Turner Capital Group.

FURTHER READING

"Pring Market Review," International Institute for Economic Research, Inc., PO Box 329, Washington Depot, CT 06794.

Pring, Martin J. [1991]. *Technical Analysis Explained,* McGraw-Hill.

_____ [1992]. "Identifying trends with the KST indicator," STOCKS & COMMODITIES, October.

_____ [1992]. "Summed rate of change," STOCKS & COMMODITIES, September.

_____ [1992]. "Rate of change," STOCKS & COMMODITIES, August.

_____ [1992]. "The KST," audiotape and booklet, International Institute for Economic Research, Inc.

CHRISTINE MORRISON

The Gann Quarterly Swing Chart And Trend Duration

The Gann quarterly swing chart — which is a trend-following indicator and not a trading system as presented in the August STOCKS & COMMODITIES — is best used as a complement with other analyses like most individual indicators. Here, Jerry Favors of "The Favors Analysis" newsletter delves into detail about what the indicator can and cannot do.

by Jerry Favors

The Gann quarterly chart is a tool that all readers can use with relative ease, but you must know the correct rules for its construction and interpretation. To begin, the quarterly swing chart will turn up from any extreme low when the Dow Jones Industrial Average (DJIA) rises above the highest intraday reading of the prior quarter. The chart will continue to point up to the highest price reached before the DJIA falls below the intraday low of a prior quarter. The swing chart is an indication of the trend direction, not a mechanical trading system. Nowhere in W.D. Gann's works does he state that the correct way to use this chart is to buy when it turns up or sell whenever it turns down. It is not up- or downturns in this chart themselves that generate buy or sell signals. Gann specifically stated: "Observe how many times after a prolonged advance (bull market) or decline (bear market) the first time prices break the bottom of a previous quarter it indicates a change in trend .... The first time the prices of one quarter exceed the high levels of the previous quarter, it nearly always indicates a change in trend and a bull market follows."

Upturns in the Gann quarterly chart represent a buy signal only if:

1 The main trend is up in an already established bull market.
2 An established bear market has lasted one of the standard time spans for a bear market and is near termination.

Likewise, a downturn in the Gann quarterly chart would represent a sell signal only if:

1 The main trend is down in a bear market and that bear market has not yet lasted one of the standard time spans for bear markets.

2 An established bull market has run one of the standard time spans for bull markets and is near a final high.

When the main trend is up (that is, a bull market) the downturns in the quarterly chart will tend to occur near the next important bottom. If the main trend is down (as in a bear market), upturns will tend to occur near the next important top.

> The chart is used to identify true bull and bear markets. No matter how severe the decline, if prices fail to fall below the intraday low of a prior year, the decline remains a correction in an ongoing bull market, and that bull market remains in force.

LOOKING BACK
Let me illustrate how the quarterly chart would have been properly used in the past 92 years. Figure 1 shows the Gann yearly chart, the only swing chart more important than the quarterly chart. The yearly chart will turn up when the DJIA

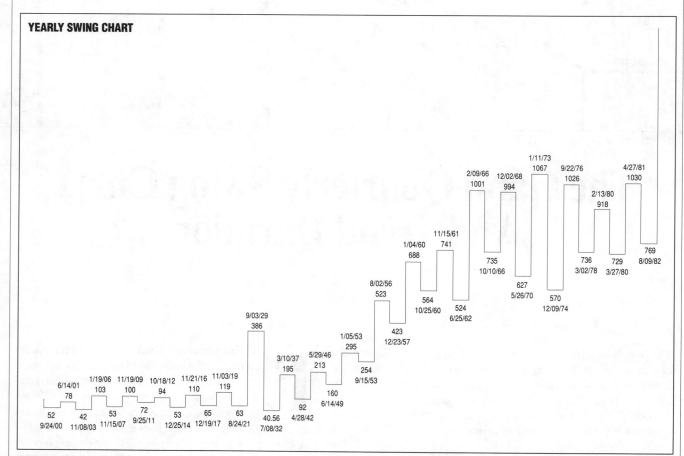

YEARLY SWING CHART

FIGURE 1: This chart turns up from any bottom when the highest intraday reading of a prior year is exceeded and turns down from any high when the intraday low of a prior year is broken.

BULL AND BEAR MARKET DURATIONS

BULL MARKET	TIME SPAN	BEAR MARKET	TIME SPAN
11/08/1903 to 1/19/1906	802 days	1/19/06 to 11/15/1907	665 days
11/15/07 to 11/19/09	734 days	11/19/09 to 9/25/11	675 days
9/25/11 to 10/08/12	379 days	10/08/12 to 12/25/14	798 days
12/25/14 to 11/21/16	697 days	11/21/16 to 12/19/17	393 days
12/19/17 to 11/03/19	684 days	11/03/19 to 8/24/21	660 days
8/24/21 to 9/03/29	2932 days (8 yrs & 1 month)	9/03/29 to 7/08/32	1039 days
7/08/32 to 3/10/37	1706 days (4 yrs, 119 days)	3/10//37 to 4/28/42	1875 days
4/28/42 to 5/29/46	1492 days (4 yrs, 32 days)	5/29/46 to 6/14/49	1112 days
6/14/49 to 1/05/53	1301 days (3 yrs, 206 days)	1/05/53 to 9/15/53	253 days
9/15/53 to 8/02/56	1052 days (2 yrs, 322 days)	8/02/56 to 12/23/57	508 days
12/23/57 to 1/04/60	742 days	1/04/60 to 10/25/60	295 days
10/25/60 to 11/15/61	386 days	11/15/61 to 6/25/62	222 days
6/25/62 to 2/09/66	1325 days (3 yrs, 230 days)	2/09/66 to 10/10/66	243 days
10/10/66 to 12/02/68	784 days	12/02/68 to 5/26/70	540 days
5/26/70 to 1/11/73	961 days	1/11/73 to 12/09/74	697 days
12/09/74 to 9/22/76	653 days	9/22/76 to 3/01/78	525 days
3/01/78 to 4/27/81	1153 days	4/27/81 to 8/09/82	469 days

FIGURE 2: *Here are the dates and day count of the bull and bear markets of the last 92 years.*

rallies above the intraday high of the prior year and continues up to the highest price reached until the DJIA falls below the lowest intraday reading of a prior year. For instance, for the yearly chart to turn down in 1992, the DJIA would have to fall below the lowest intraday reading seen in 1991 (which was the 2448.27 intraday low seen on January 14, 1991). Once again, buy and sell signals are not generated on every up- or downturn in the chart itself.

The chart is used to identify true bull and bear markets. No matter how severe the decline, if prices fail to fall below the intraday low of a prior year, the decline remains a correction in an ongoing bull market, and that bull market remains in force. Every bull and bear market in the DJIA for the last 92 years shows up on this chart without exception. While one might argue about what magnitude of decline constitutes a "true" bear market or just how long a true bear market will last, it is nevertheless true that every real bear market recorded in the past has seen prices fall below the intraday low of the prior year. Check the records of prior bull and bear markets and you will find every one shows up on the yearly chart. This chart can also be used to determine the very long-term trend of equity prices. The yearly chart is also used to identify the normal time spans (as well as the extremes) for bull and bear markets. Listed in Figure 2 is every true bull or bear market from 1900 to 1982, as well as how long they lasted.

Our goal with the table in Figure 2 is to establish the normal time spans for bull or bear markets as well as the extremes. What is immediately obvious is that the majority of bull markets during that period covered have each lasted near the norm of roughly two years (730 days). The bull markets of the last 100

years can be classified in the following time spans:

BULL MARKETS

Duration	Days
Short	379-396
Medium	520-820
Long	1,001-1,492
Superlong	1,706-2,932

The bear markets of the last 100 years have fallen into the following time spans:

BEAR MARKETS

Duration	Days
Short	222-253
Medium	384-697
Long	798-1,875

HEART OF THE CHART

Now we come to the heart of how the quarterly chart is used. We return to Gann's own rules: If after a prolonged advance (that is, a bull market) or decline (a bear market) the quarterly chart turns down, then a bear market is signaled. We do not begin looking for a true bull market top until that bull market has run one of the time spans noted for normal bull markets. For instance, if after a bear market bottom we get an advance that runs 150 days to the first important top, we would not be able to classify that movement as a true bull market because no true bull market has ever lasted only 150 days. The shortest true bull markets have lasted between 379 to 396 days. The same logic applies for bear markets. The sharp decline from February 13 to March 27, 1980, cannot be classified as a true bear market because no bear market in the past century has only lasted 43 days. A decline would have to last at least 222 days to qualify as a true bear market.

Now look at Figure 3. The bear market that began on January 4, 1960, ended on October 25 of that same year, lasting 295 days.

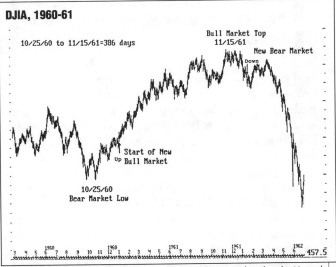

FIGURE 3: *The bull market began October 1960 and the quarterly swing chart turned up on January 1961 at 21. The DJIA peaked in November 1961.*

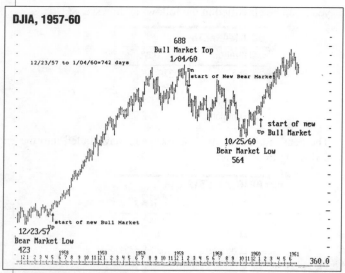

FIGURE 4: *The bull market began from the December 1957 bear market low of 423 and continued until January 1960.*

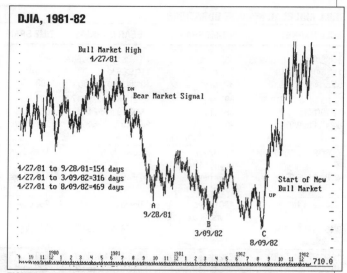

FIGURE 5: *The shortest length of time for a true bear market is 222 to 253 days, so a true bear market low should not appear until December 5, 1981 (4/27/81 + 222 days = 12/5/81).*

The quarterly chart turned up on January 4, 1961, at 621, indicating the onset of a new bull market. That bull market continued until November 15, 1961, lasting 386 days. Since short bull markets last from 379 to 396 days, we could not start looking for a true bull market top until at least 379 days had passed. If we add 379 days to the bear market low, we arrive at November 8, 1961, as the earliest any bull market could end. The DJIA peaked seven days later at 741. The quarterly chart then turned down on January 18, 1962, at 693 in the DJIA. This downturn heralded the onset of a new bear market, which saw prices collapse 29.28% over the next 222 days.

Figure 4 shows the bull market that began from the December

> # The long bull markets in history have essentially been composed of two or three separate bull markets separated by brief corrections, or "mini" bear markets.

23, 1957, bear market low of 423. Remember we cannot start looking for a true bull market high until prices have rallied for at least 379 days, which means no true bull market high could occur before January 6, 1959, at the earliest. If the quarterly chart had turned down from an extreme high reached after that date, we could then look for a possible bear market. In fact, the quarterly chart continued to point straight up all the way to the January 1960 bull market top. The bull market from December 1957 to January 1960 lasted 742 days, right in the normal time span (nearly two years) for medium bull markets (520 to 820 days). The first downturn in the quarterly chart after January 4, 1960, could now signal the onset of a new bear market. The quarterly chart turned down toward the end of January 1960 at 624.54 intraday. This signaled a new bear market, which saw the

DJIA fall 18% in 295 days.

Figure 5 shows the bull market high of April 27, 1981. Now follow the ensuing bear market from the quarterly chart signal that the bear market has ended. The shortest length of time for a true bear market is 222 to 253 days, and therefore, we could not start looking for a true bear market low until December 5, 1981 (4/27/81 + 222 days = 12/5/81). The first low at point A was the low on September 2, 1981. Prices surged from that point but no true bear market low was likely, because the decline to September 28, 1981, lasted only 154 days, and no bear market in the last century has lasted that short a time. Thus, even if the quarterly chart *had* turned up (which it did not) after the September 1981 low we would know that it was unlikely this upturn would have signaled that a new bull market was underway. The next important low was on March 9, 1982 (point B). The decline from April 1981 to March 1982 lasted 316 days. No bear market in the last century has lasted that particular time span, but because the bear market had been in force for such a long time we could have seen a bottom — if the quarterly chart had turned up from that point, which it did not. The final low came on August 9, 1982, at 769 in the DJIA, 469 days from the April 27, 1981, bull market high and right in the medium time span of 384 to 697 days that most bear markets have lasted. The quarterly chart turned up on August 23, 1982, at 876.5 intraday, trumpeting the onset of the greatest bull market in 63 years and the longest bull market in history.

LONG BULL MARKETS

The average bull market will run near two years, but there have been several long bull markets that lasted three to four years or more. The long bull markets in history have essentially been composed of two or three separate bull markets separated by brief corrections, or "mini" bear markets. In these instances, we see first a long rally phase that often runs the length of a short or medium bull market, followed by a sharp pullback or correction of intermediate-term significance, and then a third leg up or rally phase to final bull market highs. In these long bull market phases, often the first downturn in the quarterly chart does not mark the real onset of the bear market, but in most cases if the first downturn did not signal the onset of the bear market, the second one did.

Figure 6 shows the long bull market of July 1932 to March 1937, lasting four years and 119 days. The first rally phase of the bull market lasted from July 1932 to July 1933, or 375 days. Short bull markets historically have lasted 379 to 396 days, so it is possible a bull market high *could* have been seen on July 18, 1933; the quarterly chart did in fact turn down on October 19, 1933, but this did not signal a bear market, which was confirmed when the quarterly chart turned back up on January 16, 1934.

The DJIA reached a high of 111.93 on February 5, 1934, 577 days from the bear market low in July 1932. This was within the range of medium bull markets (520 to 820 days), and so the first quarterly chart downturn after February 1934 could have signaled a new bear market. The quarterly chart turned down on May 7, 1934, at 96.25. The DJIA tumbled 23.41% in 171 days to the double bottom low at 85.7 on September 17. The time of this decline did not fit with prior short bear markets, and note the Gann yearly chart did not turn down — that is, the decline in

1934 did not fall below the intraday low of 1933. So the decline in 1934 was still just a correction in an ongoing bull market.

W.D. Gann stated in *Truth of the Stock Tape* that the last leg of this bull market began on July 26, 1934. The quarterly chart turned back up on November 13, and when 111.93 was exceeded in May 1935, the second leg of the bull market was confirmed. The first rally phase lasted from July 1934 to April 1936, lasting 620 days. Since this was within the range of the medium bull markets of the past (520 to 820 days), this could have marked the end of the second leg of the bull market as well as the end of the entire bull market from July 8, 1934. The quarterly chart did turn down at the end of April 1936, but the chart turned back up 54 days later, and when the prior high of 163.07 was exceeded, it was clear that the bull market was still in force.

NEXT TIME

Often if after a bull market has lasted one of the required time spans and the first quarterly chart downturn does not signal the onset of a bear market, the very next downturn usually does. The second downturn after the July 1934 low came on April 8, 1937, when 179.3 intraday was broken, signaling the onset of a major bear market. The initial stage of the ensuing bear market saw the

"So the evil corporate raider thought: 'I know, I'll use a leveraged buyout to acquire a major stock position, drive up the undervalued shares — and then ...'"

FIGURE 6: *The quarterly chart turned down in May 1934 but the yearly swing chart did not, indicating that the 1934 decline was a bull market correction.*

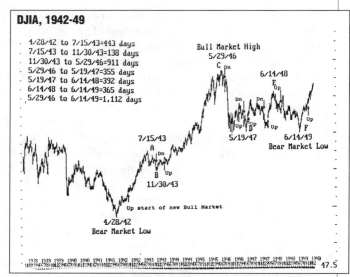

FIGURE 7: *No true bear market has lasted 138 days, so the July 1943 to November 1943 decline could not have marked a bear market low, only a correction.*

DJIA plummet 50% in the next 12 months. The yearly chart continued to point straight up from July 1932 to March 1937, lasting four years and 119 days. Every pullback in that time frame was just a correction in an ongoing bull market. Also, the rally phase from the double bottom low of September 1934 to the March 1937 top lasted 905 days, a time span that has occurred many times in the past.

Figure 7 shows the long bull market from 1942 to 1946. The first leg of this bull market ran from April 1942 to July 1943, lasting 443 days. No true bull market in the last 100 years has lasted that particular length of time, but nevertheless, this rally could have marked the top of a short bull market. The quarterly chart turned down and the total decline lasted 138 days. No true bear market has ever lasted that particular length of time, so the

decline from July 1943 to November 1943 could not have marked a bear market low, merely a correction.

The chart turned back up on March 13, 1943, and when the prior high of 146.41 intraday was exceeded, the third leg of the bull market was underway. The quarterly chart continued to point straight up until the bull market high of May 29, 1946. Note the third leg of the bull market lasted 911 days (near the same time span as the second leg from the September 1934 low to the March 1937 bull market high). The entire bull market lasted 1,492 days, or four years and 32 days. If you look at the yearly chart, you will see that the bull market continued to point up all the way from the April 1942 bear market low to the final bull market high of 213.36 on May 29, 1946, showing this was all one long bull market separated into three legs, or two bull markets separated by a brief correction.

After a long bull market of this duration, market observers should watch the quarterly chart carefully for the next downturn, which could now signal an end to the bull market and the onset of a new bear market. The quarterly chart turned down on July 23, 1946, and a long bear market began. The initial decline in that bear market saw the DJIA decline 24.9% in 154 days, bottoming on October 30, 1946, at 160.49.

A decline of 154 days was far too short to be a complete bear market, so we would not take any upturn in the quarterly chart seriously until the decline had lasted at least 222 days. The quarterly chart turned up and down several times in the next two years, but none of the declines in this time frame carried prices below the lows of October 1946. The DJIA reached a double bottom at 160.62 intraday on June 14, 1949, and a new closing low of 161.60 on the previous day (June 13), and the bear market ended there. The yearly chart (Figure 1) continued to point straight down from the May 1946 bull market high to the June 1949 bear

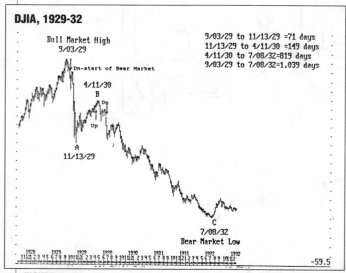

FIGURE 8: *The quarterly chart turned down on October 3, 1929, after the September 3rd high. The DJIA dropped 49.48% within 71 days, bottoming at 195 on November 13. Despite the severity of that first leg down, no true bear market will last 71 days, so the November 13th bottom could not have marked a bear market low.*

market low.

Finally, we will examine the historic bear market from 1929 to 1932, as can be seen in Figure 8. The quarterly chart turned down after the September 3, 1929, high on October 3, 1929. The DJIA plunged 49.48% within 71 days, bottoming at 195 on November 13, 1929. Despite the severity of that first leg down, no true bear market lasts only 71 days, so the November 13, 1929, bottom could not have marked a bear market low. The second leg of the bear market ran from November 13, 1929, to the secondary top on April 11, 1930. The quarterly chart turned up on April 1, 1930. But because the first leg down was only 71 days, we would not go long on the upturn in the quarterly chart on April 1.

The quarterly chart turned back down on June 12, 1930, and when prices fell below the prior bottom of 195.35 (seen on November 13, 1929), the chart signaled that the bear market was still in force and was now into its third leg down. The quarterly chart continued to point down all the way to the 40.56 bear market low of July 8, 1932. Not once in that entire two-year and one-month time frame did the quarterly chart signal that the bear market was over, so the use of this chart would have kept the investor short the entire time. The first time the quarterly chart turned back up was on August 25, 1932, which signaled the onset of one of the longest and strongest bull markets of the last 100 years.

SUMMING IT ALL UP

To summarize, Gann *at no time* stated that the proper use of the quarterly chart was to buy when the chart turns up, hold and then sell the next time the chart turns down. The quarterly chart is used to signal the end of a bull or bear market, but only when the required amount of time has elapsed. The chart is also used as a long-term trend indicator. To this end, one must remember that the main trend is up if a market is making higher bottoms and higher tops (in that order). The main trend will turn down when a market traces out a pattern of lower tops and lower bottoms (in that order).

Looking at Figure 9, it is clear that the main trend on the quarterly chart has been up ever since the March 1980 low, even though the current bull market actually began in 1982 (yearly chart). Since then, each bottom in the quarterly chart has been higher than the last and each top has been higher than the last. The first time the DJIA falls below the prior low of 2832.29 intraday, we will have a signal of a potential change in the long-term trend. However, the current bull market has been in force for nine years and 10 months, the longest in the 200-year record of equity prices I have studied. The only prior analogous period was the bull market from August 1921 to September 1929, which lasted eight years and one month.

If the analogies between the present bull market and that of the 1921-29 period persist, any decline below 3141.77 intraday in the DJIA should lead to a new bear market lasting at least three years. As I stated in my previous quarterly chart article, in most instances the DJIA will reach a short-term low within one to three days of any downturn in the quarterly chart and then rally anywhere from several days to several weeks. Thus, we do not

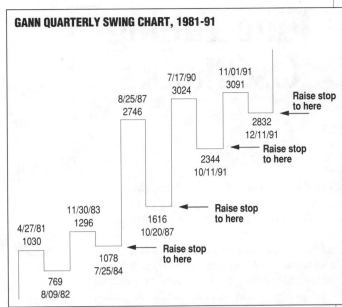

GANN QUARTERLY SWING CHART, 1981-91

FIGURE 9: *The main trend on the quarterly chart has been up since the March 1980 low.*

advise going short the day the chart turns down. After that rally, however, prices should then turn down in an even more powerful decline. The shortest bear market must run at least 222 days.

As of this writing, we cannot be sure that June 2, 1992, marked a final bull market high, but if so, we know that no bear market bottom could occur before January 10, 1993, at the earliest (that is, 6/2/92 + 222 days = 1/10/93). The quarterly chart can also be used in the same way on individual stocks and commodities, but you will need a long history spanning several decades to use it to its fullest potential.

Jerry Favors publishes "The Jerry Favors Analysis" newsletter, 7238 Durness Drive, Worthington, OH 43235, (614) 848-8177.

FURTHER READING

Favors, Jerry [1992]. "The Gann quarterly chart," STOCKS & COMMODITIES, January.

Gann, W.D. [1942]. *How to Make Profits in Commodities*, Lambert-Gann Publishing Co.

_____ [1927]. *Tunnel Through the Air, or Looking Back from 1940*, Lambert-Gann Press.

_____ [1923]. *Truth of the Stock Tape* and *Wall Street Selector*, W.D. Gann.

Fine Tuning Oscillators

The conventional wisdom in technical trading systems implies that for a trading system to be reliable, it should work across all markets and all time frames. Here are some potential reasons why it's difficult to find a single trading system that works all the time for all markets, and how optimized oscillators can be used to overcome these problems and build a sound trading plan.

by Ed Downs

I t is a given that each stock has its own unique collection of primary participants (buyers/sellers), its own appeal (industry) and its own market strength (shares outstanding). It is also a given that over time the personality of each issue gradually changes; the "go-go" stock of a decade ago becomes the staid holding of a pension fund today. This is why a single indicator cannot always be used over the long haul and why research shows that persistent cycles do not tend to be present in stock market data.

Figures 1 and 2 are charts of the stocks CSX Corp. and Cray Research (CYR). The charts cover the same time period and the price and volume levels for each stock happen to be about the same. But look how different their price action is. One tends to trend steadily, while the other is more volatile, exhibiting more cyclic price swings. It would be very difficult for any single trading system to profitably trade both of these stocks, at least during this time period.

A stock's personality exhibits itself by virtue of its volatility, periodicity, trendiness and volume accumulation/ distribution patterns. If we can find a way to measure a stock's personality by virtue of these attributes over past data, we should be able to identify likely market turning points by projecting those measurements into the immediate future, assuming the stock's personality doesn't change appreciably in that time.

CHARACTERIZING VOLATILITY

How do we characterize an issue's volatility? Simply measuring price change and rate of change over time is not good enough.

We must measure *the way* the prices move. Do they tend to move in smooth waves or in quick, jerky motions with lots of price gaps?

In my research, I have found that each of the classic oscillators tends to characterize different stocks' personality types. For cyclical stocks with well-defined channels, the stochastics† oscillator works quite well. The relative strength index (RSI) tends to characterize stocks that exhibit sudden reversals after long intermediate-term rallies or declines. The commodity channel index (CCI) works well on stocks whose price volatility tends to decrease at important turning points.

One reason that an oscillator may work better than another for a given stock is the way that oscillators are calculated. The

†*For definition, please see Traders' Glossary*

MIKE HORSWILL

relative strength index attempts to measure up versus down days in an *n*-day period. The stochastics oscillator measures relative position of the current close to the range of prices over the last *n* days. The commodity channel index is similar to the stochastic, but it takes into account the average difference in price over the lookback period, thereby adding a measurement of volatility.

The lookback period (the *n* in an *n*-day period) is an important ingredient in the calculation of each of these oscillators. Based on personal observations and that of other traders over the years, default lookback periods have been established as the values that work best on most markets. Figure 3 lists these values.

Figure 4 shows American Airlines (AA) plotted from January 1, 1991, to January 1, 1992, along with each of these indicators using their respective default values. My research team and I used MetaStock's System Tester to test each indicator for profitabil-

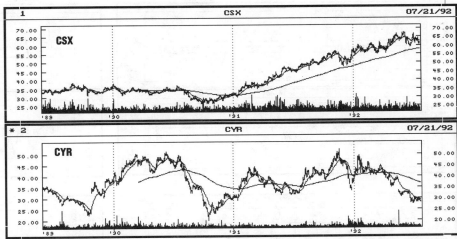

FIGURE 1: CSX. FIGURE 2: CRAY. *CSX is shown with 21-day and 200-day moving averages. CSX tends to trend steadily, so the moving average crossover signal in January 1991 would have proved quite profitable. For Cray Research, the 21- and 200-day moving average crossover signals produced losing trades because Cray tends to cycle up and down.*

> **A stock's personality exhibits itself by virtue of its volatility, periodicity, trendiness and volume accumulation/ distribution patterns.**

OSCILLATORS DEFAULT LOOKBACK PERIOD	
Oscillators	**Default lookback periods**
Relative strength index	14
Stochastic oscillator	5 to 9
Commodity channel index	12 to 14

FIGURE 3: *The lookback periods listed are the periods typically recommended for these popular indicators.*

ity, and we found that none of the indicators used with their default values was profitable: RSI generated a 3% loss, stochastics generated a 16% loss and CCI lost 17%. Also shown in Figure 4 is the Chaikin oscillator, which generated a 25% loss, and a 4% trading band using a 21-period default, which generated a 21% profit. Based on these results, the trading bands would have been the best tool to use for trading AA during this period.

L et me emphasize once again how important the lookback period used in the oscillator calculations is. We can find out which values would have generated the highest profit over a given time through the use of a computerized optimizer. The optimization process involves testing a range of values for the lookback period of each oscillator and determining how much profit would have been generated in each case. For the stochastic oscillator, we started with a five-day period and tested each value up to 25 days in increments of four days. This enabled us to test values commonly used for lookback periods: five days, nine days, 13 days, 17 days and 21 days. We used MetaStock's System Tester to perform and test the optimizations (see sidebar, "Oscillator trading systems defined"), but a technical analysis program with an optimizer will work.

We found that the optimized trading bands generated the highest profit for AA during this period at 21%. Chaikin was second at a profit of 15%, CCI was third at 13% and the stochastic oscillator finished at 12%. Results for the trading bands and the Chaikin oscillator will be discussed shortly.

CHARACTERIZING VOLUME ACCUMULATION/DISTRIBUTION

As with price, volume patterns tend to repeat in the short term for each individual stock. (For the examples used here, we defined the short term as being one year.) Technicians can avail themselves of several indicators that measure volume accumulation and distribution, of which on-balance volume† is certainly the best known. But this indicator is hard to interpret, because you must look for divergences between the price and the indicator. However, a good oscillator to use for measuring change in accumulation/distribution is the Chaikin oscillator†. When the oscillator turns down, it means that there is less accumulation than before. When it turns up, we have less distribution. Therefore, we use the peaks of the Chaikin oscillator to identify turning points.

The level at which the Chaikin oscillator peaks varies considerably from stock to stock, and we found these levels to be a more

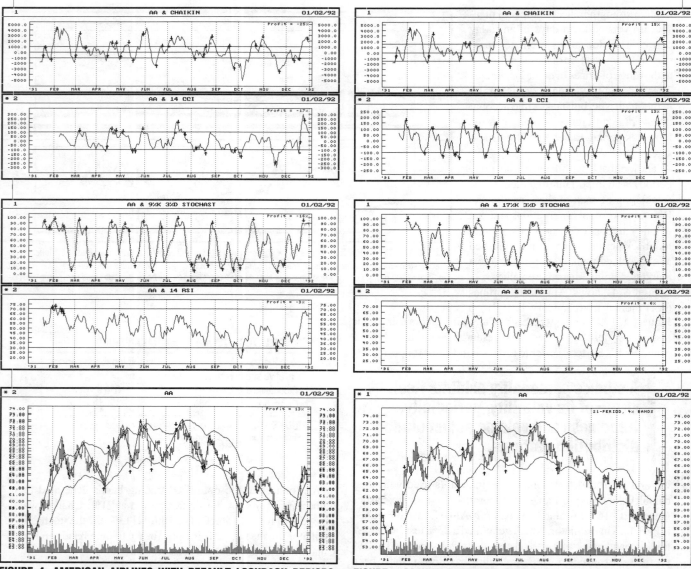

FIGURE 4: AMERICAN AIRLINES WITH DEFAULT LOOKBACK PERIODS. *American Airlines is shown with common trading indicators using their default lookback periods: a 14-period CCI, a nine-period stochastic oscillator, a 14-RSI, a 21-period 4% trading band and a 1,000-level Chaikin oscillator.*

FIGURE 5: AA WITH OPTIMIZED VALUES. *American Airlines is shown with trading indicators using their optimized values: an eight-period CCI, a 17-period stochastic, a 20-period RSI, a 13-period 4% trading band and a 1500-level Chaikin oscillator.*

meaningful characteristic of the oscillator than the particular lookback period used to calculate it. So we optimized the trading levels of the Chaikin oscillator (the horizontal lines in Figure 5) to the values that would have generated the highest profit had trades been taken on reversals (peaks) above or below these levels.

CHARACTERIZING THE TREND

The problem with most trend-following methods is that by the time you see the trend, it's well underway. Moving average crossover methods are particularly late. However, if you look at the trading bands in Figure 4, it's fairly easy to see when the trend turns. For example, the envelope's turning point on September 1 from an uptrend to a downtrend is fairly visible, since the upper band makes a lower peak at about this time.

Most traders use envelopes or trading bands to help illuminate overbought and oversold points. To find the best trading band for American Airlines in 1991, we will define a trading band system as follows: take long trades when the issue penetrates the bottom band and take short positions when it penetrates the upper band. Optimizing the trading band system for its moving average period and the percentage level above and below (to draw the bands), we arrive at the bands shown on the chart in Figure 5, plotted at 4% above and below a 13-day moving average.

Characterizing the trend is the last element in our quest to find a personality profile for AA. Over the one-year period, we found that, in order of profitability, the best trading systems to use for AA were:

1) 13-period 4% trading bands (21% profit)
2) 1500-level Chaikin oscillator (15%)
3) 8-period Cci (13%)
4) 17-period stochastics (12%)
5) 20-period relative strength index (6%)

In our forward test†, we will examine signals in the same order.

CUSTOMIZING OSCILLATORS

Quite a few articles have appeared in STOCKS & COMMODITIES over the years illustrating the dangers of using overoptimized trading systems. The more facets of a system you optimize, the more curve-fitted† the results become and the less reliable they are.

However, as long as we understand the limits of optimization, we can still use the information to improve our trading. For example, we determined that the best value to use for stochastics in 1991 for AA was 17 periods. Our hypothesis, then, is that 17 is a good value to use for the stochastic on AA in 1992, because the cycles that were present in 1991 are likely to continue to some extent in 1992. This does *not* imply that a trading system based on a 17-period stochastic will work as well in 1992 as it did in 1991 — just that it is likely to work better than the default value of 14 periods. The same can be said of our optimized values for RSI, CCI, the trading band and Chaikin trading levels.

TRADING WITH CUSTOM OSCILLATORS

To trade using individualized oscillators, two primary trading rules should be adhered to: 1) Enter at market turning points signaled by the oscillators, and 2) trade with the trend. We want as much confirming evidence as possible to enter any trade, and this is where some judgment comes into play. At point "A" in Figure 6, we have a Chaikin buy signal, a CCI buy signal, a stochastic buy signal and the trend was up. What more could we ask for? Since three oscillators are producing buy signals *with* the trend, we would have taken this signal and entered long the next day.

If we construct a table summarizing oscillator buy and sell recommendations at each time we had at least two of our optimized oscillators confirming, we come up with Figure 7. Using this table, we were able to identify two conservative, profitable trades. The fact that the price penetrates the trading bands at points A through F (Figure 6) lends weight to the decisions at those points. Note also that the buy signal between points G and H was ignored because the stock was experiencing a downtrend during this period.

One way to screen a large number of stocks for potential trades is to find the oscillator and lookback period that best characterize each stock and use that oscillator as your trading system. In our American Airlines example, the Chaikin trading system or the trading band system would have worked best. When an optimized oscillator produces a buy or sell signal, plot the other optimized oscillators and trading bands and examine

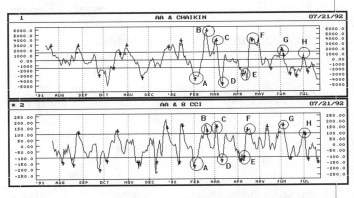

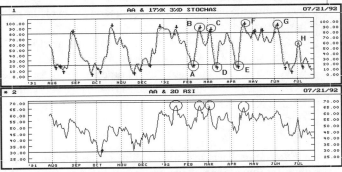

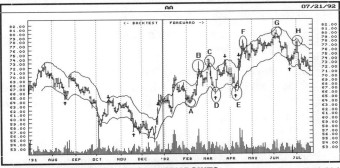

FIGURE 6: AA WITH OSCILLATOR ENTRY POINTS. *The previous six months (which were used in the back test) are shown for reference. All oscillator entry points with at least two signals are circled and labeled to correspond to Figure 7.*

the chart. Using this method, you should be able to find 10 or so stocks out of 100 that exhibit interesting signals on any given market day. Then compare the signals using a table such as the one in Figure 7 to decide which ones should be acted on, and use proper money management (such as placing stops) to manage each trade after placing it.

The primary principle of successful trading is to decrease risk as much as possible. Because stocks have their own personalities and stocks tend to exhibit the same personality in the near term as they did in the immediate past, optimizing oscillator periods to find custom-designed oscillators for each stock appears to be one way of finding low-risk entry points. Identifying the trend using optimized trading bands and placing trades in the direction of the trend provides an even greater level of risk reduction for each trade.

OSCILLATOR TRADING SYSTEMS DEFINED

 An oscillator is an indicator that moves back and forth between two limits. Most oscillators, such as stochastics, relative strength index and commodity channel index, are defined so that they range between 0 and 100 or -100 and +100.

Usually, an oscillator is interpreted by watching for crossovers; that is, when the indicator crosses a given level (such as 20 or 80 for stochastics), a buy or sell signal is generated. The problem with crossover systems is that they are usually late — by the time the indicator penetrates the trigger level, the price has already advanced 50% or more of its move.

To counteract the tendency of crossover systems to lag the market, we can use a peak or trough reversal system, which will generate a trading signal every time the oscillator passes its trigger level and reverses direction — that is, every time it forms a peak or trough above or below the trigger level. Long entry and exit rules for a peak reversal system can be defined as follows:

• *Enter long* when yesterday's value of the indicator is less than the buy trigger level and when the two-day moving average of the indicator is below the indicator.

• *Exit long* (close the trade) if the indicator drops back below the buy trigger level.

The exit rule is designed to simply cancel an existing open trade if the oscillator positions itself to generate another signal. We do this because we want to be alerted to as many *potential* trading signals as possible.

■ FOR METASTOCK USERS:
The long and short trading systems can be written in MetaStock Professional, version 3.0, as shown here:

    ENTER LONG: WHEN(REF(IND,-1),<,BL) AND
    WHEN(MOV(IND,2,s),<=,IND)

    EXIT LONG: WHEN(REF(IND,-1),>=,BL) AND WHEN
    (IND,<,BL)

    ENTER SHORT: WHEN(REF(IND,-1),>,SL) AND
    WHEN(MOV(IND,2,s),>=,IND)

    EXIT SHORT: WHEN(REF(IND,-1),<=,SL) AND
    WHEN(IND,>,SL)

In each trading system described below, you would replace IND, BL and SL with the given values to realize the individual trading system for each oscillator. Where OPT1 is used in the formulas, you must specify the range of optimization values. Consult the MetaStock manual.

All tests performed for this article used MetaStock version 3 with 1% entry/exit and commissions (2% total) to keep each trading system from overtrading. In addition, 100% trading capital was invested and positions were taken at the closing price on the day that the signal was generated. Entry signals appear as arrows on the charts and exit signals (as defined above) show up as equal signs.

■ CHAIKIN TRADING SYSTEM:
Accumulation/distribution (A/D) for a given day can be found by multiplying trading volume for the day by a percentage that represents the relative position of the closing price to the high or low. In this way, A/D measures whether a security had accumulation, which would occur if the closing price were closer to the high, or distribution, which would be the case if the closing price were closer to the low. The Chaikin oscillator represents the difference between the three-period and 10-period exponential moving average of the A/D values, which means it generates a peak when accumulation decreases or a trough when distribution decreases in this time frame.

In our Chaikin trading system, we did not optimize the periods used to calculate the oscillator because our research has found that the levels reached by the oscillator are much more significant. If the oscillator goes above the OPT1 level and then drops, a sell is signaled. If it goes below the negative OPT1 value and rises, then a buy signal is given. For some stocks, this level will be 1,000. For others, it will be 5,000 or more.

    Parameters for the Chaikin trading system:
    BL: OPT1   where OPT1 = 1000,1500,…,10000
    SL: -OPT1
    IND: co()

In MetaStock, the periods used to calculate the Chaikin oscillator are fixed at three and 10 for the two moving averages, which is why the Chaikin formula appears as co() with no parameters.

■ STOCHASTIC OSCILLATOR:
The stochastic oscillator, which varies between 0 and 100%, measures where a security's price closed relative to its trading range over the last *n* time periods. The most commonly used buy and sell levels for the stochastic oscillator are 20 and 80, respectively. In our optimized stochastic trading system, we optimized the period used to calculate the stochastic.

    Parameters for stochastic trading system:
    BL: +20
    SL: +80
    IND: stoch(OPT1,3), where OPT1 = 5,9,13,17,21,25

■ COMMODITY CHANNEL INDEX (CCI):
The CCI measures the rate at which the mean price is changing by comparing today's mean price with the average of the mean prices over the last *n* periods. This difference is then compared with the *average difference* over *n* periods, giving the CCI a unique measure of volatility. The CCI is

multiplied by a constant so that it will oscillate between -100 and 100. In our CCI trading system, we optimized the period used to calculate the indicator.

Parameters for the CCI trading system:
    BL: -100
    SL: +100
    IND: cci(OPT1) where OPT1 = 5,8,11,14,17,20,23

■ RELATIVE STRENGTH INDEX (RSI):

The relative strength index compares the number of up days with down days over the oscillator's period and expresses the value as a percentage between 0 to 100%. In our RSI trading system, we optimized the period used to calculate RSI.

Parameters for RSI trading system:
    BL: +30
    SL: +70
    IND: rsi(OPT1) where OPT1 = 8,11,14,17,20,23

AMERICAN AIRLINES								
Trade	A	B	C	D	E	F	G	H
Chaikin	Buy	Sell	Sell	Buy	Buy	Sell	Sell	-n-
CCI	Buy	Sell	Sell	Buy	Buy	Sell	Sell	Sell
Stochastic	Buy	Sell	Sell	Buy	Buy	Sell	Sell	-n-
RSI	-n-	Sell	Sell	-n-	-n-	Sell	-n-	-n-
Trend up	Up	Up	Up	Up	Up	Up	Down	
Action	Buy	Sell	None	Buy	None	Sell	None	Short

FIGURE 7: USING DIFFERENT OSCILLATORS

Ed Downs has a bachelor's degree in mechanical engineering and a master's degree in electrical engineering. He has extensive software background in computer-aided design. He has researched computerized trading systems since 1980 and is currently president of Nirvana Systems, Inc., which specializes in automated trading systems and utilities for MetaStock Professional and other software.

REFERENCES

Nirvana Systems, Inc., 3415 Greystone Dr., Suite 205, Austin, TX 78731, (512) 345-2545.

MetaStock Professional, EQUIS International Inc., P.O. Box 26743, Salt Lake City, UT 84126, (801) 974-5115 or (800) 882-3040.

Poulos, E. Michael [1992]. "Are there persistent cycles?" STOCKS & COMMODITIES, August.

Candlesticks As A Leading Indicator

Most technical indicators are coincident with the market — that is, the indicators do not forecast market turns but only turn if the market turns. Certain candlestick formations, on the other hand, can forecast market reversals. Consequently, combining candlestick formations with traditional technical indicators such as oscillators should lead to better trading performance.

by Gary S. Wagner and Bradley L. Matheny

Western technical analysis encompasses many different types of mathematical calculations, but many can best be described as lagging indicators. A lagging indicator can predict market moves only after a turning point, while a leading indicator can predict market moves before a turning point. Aside from Fibonacci retracement theory and possibly the moving average convergence/divergence (MACD) indicator, to our knowledge no other leading indicators exists besides candlestick technical analysis. This is why traders and market technicians are so interested in candlesticks.

VENERABLE PEDIGREE

The Japanese candlestick technique interprets price movement by isolating patterns to predict future price trends. It was developed nearly three centuries ago by a rice futures trader named Sokyu Honma. Using the techniques that Honma developed can provide insight into markets. The trader combined many factors to develop this trading technique. Over time, he developed an extensive group of patterns to accurately identify potential tops, bottoms, reversals and buy and sell signals. Today, Honma's work is being accepted as a technical tool for trading the markets and many traders are finding candlesticks to

be a valid trading method. Here's how this type of market analysis can provide market investors with insights available from candlestick charts.

SIDE BY SIDE

Traders who have used the candlestick technique found that certain candle formations, when found at specific points in a market, can indicate a reversal before the market turns. These candles and patterns, because of their shape and location, can provide specific data not available when the same market is

MARK MOLNAR

viewed with a standard bar chart. Figures 1 and 2 are the same market but seen through both candlestick and bar charts. The candlestick chart provides the viewer with many insights not obvious from the bar chart. Viewing the charts side by side, with some knowledge of Japanese technical analysis, one can easily see how much more information can be gleaned from the candlestick chart.

> **The strength or weakness of a candlestick pattern can be inferred by two factors: where the closing price is in relation to the opening price and the size of today's candle compared with the previous day's candles.**

LIST OF INGREDIENTS

What makes up a candlestick formation? The candle or pole line is defined as one complete cycle with an open, low, high and close. The thick part of the candle is known as the real body. The thin lines above and below the real body are the shadows and represent the high and low for that cycle. Candlesticks consist of the same price data that every other technical analysis tool uses; they simply appear in a different form. A white candle (empty) is created when the closing price is above the opening price for the cycle. Black candles (full) are just the opposite — the opening price must be above the closing price for the cycle. The strength or weakness of a candlestick pattern can be inferred by two factors: where the closing price is in relation to the opening price and the size of today's candle compared with the previous day's candles.

High and low prices are used in combination with the opening and closing prices to differentiate specific candle patterns. The three candle classes are white, black and doji, though many variations to these basic candle types exist. White and black candles have a similar construction, although they can have completely different meanings. Doji candles are formed when the open and close prices are equal or very close to being equal. They can be either black or white and almost any size. The doji candle is considered neutral unless it is found within a stronger multicycle pattern or at the top or bottom of a trend.

The doji candle is commonly found at strategic market turning points. Many of the strongest candle patterns incorporate one or more doji candles. Doji candles symbolize a clashing of heads between the bulls and the bears; both the bulls and the bears are trying to push the market, but neither can succeed. Dojis can signal major and minor reversal areas, known as support and resistance price levels, and can be interpreted more accurately during critical top and bottom formations. This candle is known as one of the most important candles and should always be watched for.

Bozu candles are considered the three strongest pole lines for either black or white candles. Bozu lines are formed when the trading cycle opens or closes on its high or low, indicating a

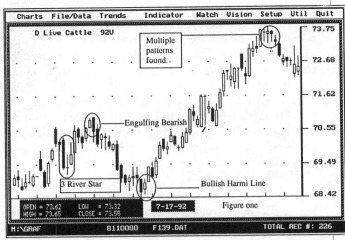

FIGURE 1: DECEMBER LIVE CATTLE. *Important candlestick patterns occur at turning points in the market.*

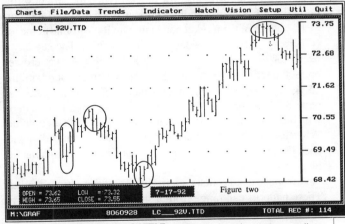

FIGURE 2: DECEMBER LIVE CATTLE. *Bar charts do not have as many patterns to rely on for identifying short-term reversals.*

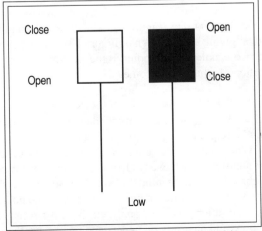

FIGURE 3: UMBRELLA LINES. *These candles have tight opening and closing ranges, with the lower shadow at least twice the length of the body.*

victory for the bulls or the bears. Bozu means "monk" or "priest" in Japanese, and because Japanese Buddhist monks are traditionally bald, we can see the correlation to the candle's shape. The three types of bozu candles are long opening bozu, long closing bozu and long marubozu lines. Opening bozu indicates that the opening price is the bald side of the candle. A closing bozu would indicate that the closing price is the bald side, while marubozu indicates that both sides of the candle are bald. The marubozu is of course the strongest bullish or bearish candle, representing a victory for the bulls or the bears. All bozu candles must exceed the average size of the candles in the chart.

T he forecasting ability of candlestick charting can be seen in a candle classification called umbrella lines, which can be either bullish or bearish, depending on where in a trend they appear. This formation can be recognized by its tight opening and closing ranges, with the lower shadow at least twice the length of the body (Figure 3). This candle is known as a hammer if it occurs at the bottom of the market or a hangman if it is found at the top (Figure 4). Figure 5 is a daily live cattle chart. The stochastic oscillator is overbought, but the %K line has not yet crossed under the %D line. In this instance, the hangman found on July 15, 1992, was the candle that resulted in an engulfing bearish pattern found the same day (Figure 6). The engulfing pattern, which is a strong reversal signal, is bearish during an uptrend. When used with other technical indicators and advanced candlestick pattern interpretation, the umbrella line can predict market reversals very well.

Advanced candlestick patterns incorporate multiple candles. These patterns can range from a simple two-day pattern or be composed of a pattern as complex as 30 to 60 days. The candlestick chart of the daily cash Standard & Poor's 500 in Figure 7 shows how a single candle can evolve into an advanced pattern. A hammer formed on June 22, 1992, was the first sign of a potential bottom (Figure 8). (A hammer only occurs in a downtrend and are known to be bullish; they are market signals at or near the bottom.) The hammer was followed by an inverted hammer the next day (Figure 9), which in turn engulfed the hammer, giving us a buy signal (Figure 10). The appearance of these two candles at this point in the market gave us a clear indication of what was to come.

READING CANDLESTICK CHARTS

Candlesticks are unlike any other indicator. Proper identification and interpretation of candlesticks is key to understanding them. When analyzing candlestick charts, the trader should be sure to analyze the last seven to 15 trading cycles for any patterns that confirm the current trend (or lack of it). Sometimes the best approach to interpreting candlesticks is to wait and not to trade at all; then, after you have analyzed the most recent candle formations and have a good understanding of what they might mean, you should look for other signs, such as confirmation, continuation and confluence patterns. This approach is called the three Cs of candlesticks.

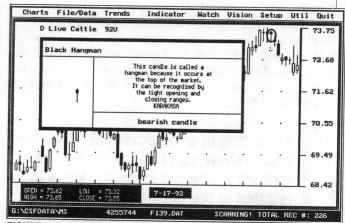

FIGURE 4: BLACK HANGMAN

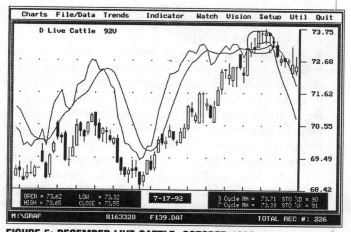

FIGURE 5: DECEMBER LIVE CATTLE, OCTOBER 1992. *The circled area represents an overbought condition based on the high stochastics readings. There is a negative candlestick pattern present.*

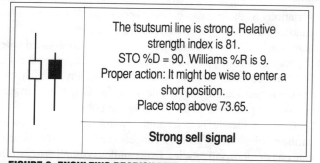

The tsutsumi line is strong. Relative strength index is 81. STO %D = 90. Williams %R is 9. Proper action: It might be wise to enter a short position. Place stop above 73.65.

Strong sell signal

FIGURE 6: ENGULFING BEARISH LINE

Confirmation: A candlestick pattern is confirmed if the pattern predicted the proper outcome. For example, a dark cloud pattern that predicted a sell would be confirmed if the next trading cycle produced a black candle with a lower high and a lower low, indicating the formation of a defined bearish trend, and thus showing confirmation.

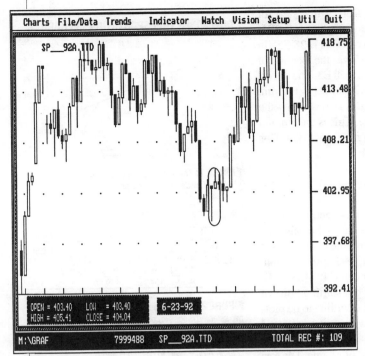

FIGURE 7: S&P 500. *The circled area is an advanced candlestick pattern.*

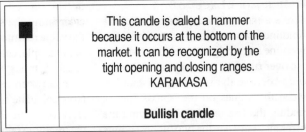

This candle is called a hammer because it occurs at the bottom of the market. It can be recognized by the tight opening and closing ranges. KARAKASA

Bullish candle

FIGURE 8: BLACK HAMMER

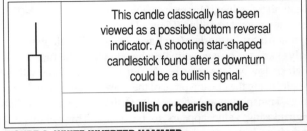

This candle classically has been viewed as a possible bottom reversal indicator. A shooting star-shaped candlestick found after a downturn could be a bullish signal.

Bullish or bearish candle

FIGURE 9: WHITE INVERTED HAMMER

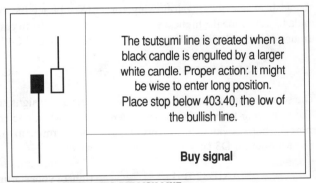

The tsutsumi line is created when a black candle is engulfed by a larger white candle. Proper action: It might be wise to enter long position. Place stop below 403.40, the low of the bullish line.

Buy signal

FIGURE 10: ENGULFING BULLISH LINE

Continuation: After receiving a confirmation pattern, look for a continuation pattern to appear. Continuation patterns occur when a trend has formed and a shorter candle pattern has predicted the price move. Or they can appear within other confirming patterns, and not necessarily as an extension of the original buy or sell signal.

Confluence: These patterns consist of a variety of other indicators, oscillators and candle patterns that all predict the same outcome. For example, you might find a hangman, a dark cloud and a bearish engulfing pattern along with bearish crossing stochastics all within the last five trading cycles — all bearish implications.

LEADING CANDLESTICKS

Candlestick charts contain many complex and beautiful formations that provide unique insight into future market events. They are a tool that more and more traders are adding to their arsenal. The candles and their advanced patterns, when properly identified, can actually act as leading indicators, providing information about a potential market move before or as it happens.

Gary S. Wagner, CTA, a registered commodity broker since 1984, and Bradley L. Matheny, a systems analyst who has been developing custom software applications for eight years, are currently developing technical market analysis software for International Pacific Trading Co. Together, they co-developed the Candlestick Forecaster, a candlestick-interpretation program based on artificial intelligence.

REFERENCES

Hartle, Thom [1991]. "Steve Nison on candlestick charting," *Technical Analysis of* STOCKS & COMMODITIES, Volume 9: March.

Kosar, John J. [1991]. "Support and resistance levels," *Technical Analysis of* STOCKS & COMMODITIES, Volume 9: January.

Nison, Steve [1991]. *Japanese Candlestick Charting Techniques*, Simon & Schuster.

Shimizu, Seiki [1986]. *The Japanese Chart of Charts*, Tokyo Futures Trading Publishing Co.

■ MICROSOFT EXCEL 3.0

Here's a method to calculate and plot a trendline from the data in a spreadsheet. A trendline is a straight line that is a plot of rise over run. The run calculation is easy to do because the run is equidistant between the values on the X-axis (time). Finding the rise requires identifying the difference between the two highest points (for a downward trendline) or the two lowest points (for an uptrend). Excel can locate these values. Our example will be for a downward trendline (Figure 1). The first step is to plot the data (such as a close-only chart) so you can estimate where the high or low values may be. In our example, using the closing price of the Dow Jones Transportation Average (DJTA), the high closing value appears to be near early June. In my spreadsheet, this is in the range of cells B35 to B53. Return to the spreadsheet and use the following formula for returning the highest value from a range of cells. The formula for cell D2 is:

$$=MAX(B35:B53)$$

The second peak is during early August. The following formula is used to determine the highest value during this range. The formula for D3 is:

$$=MAX(B82:B91)$$

In our spreadsheet example (Figure 2), we now have the two data values that are the difference in the rise for our trendline. The next step is calculating the run. In Excel, the Formula pulldown menu has a function called Find, which will locate the cell that has the high values for us. First, select the column with the values, which in our case is column B. Then select the Find function (Figure 3) from the Formula pulldown menu. You will have three choices: values, part, and column. Input the value from the maximum value found in cell D2 (Figure 3) — 1388.64 — and press return. Excel will then highlight the cell that contains 1388.64. In our example, Excel highlighted cell B48. Type

in "48" in cell E2. Repeat this step for calculating the second high point using the value returned in cell D3 (1328.75). In our example, cell B85 was the location of 1328.75. Input "85" in cell E3. The difference between cell E2 and E3 is the run. Now calculate rise over run, which is the slope of the trendline. This is the amount the trendline falls (or rises) each day. This formula is in cell E4:

$$=(D2-D3)/(E2-E3)$$

To calculate and plot this trendline, move to the first cell that contains the value the trendline will touch on the chart. This is cell B48 in our example (Figure 4). Input the values in B48 for cell C48 (1388.64). Think of this cell as your starting point of the trendline. For the trendline to be plotted to the left of this value, you will need to subtract the one-day change in the trendline from yesterday's value. The formula for cell C47 is:

$$=C48-\$E\$4$$

The dollar signs keep the E4 cell location fixed when you copy this formula. Copy this formula up to the top of your spreadsheet.

For the trendline to be plotted to the right of your starting point (cell C48), you will need to add the one-day change in the trendline from yesterday's value. The formula for cell C49 is:

$$=C48+\$E\$4$$

Copy this formula to the bottom of your spreadsheet (Figure 4).

Next, plot this column along with your closing prices. By extending your calculations for the trendline, you can calculate precise values of the trendline into the future. For example, you could find out what price in the future would break this trendline.

—Editor

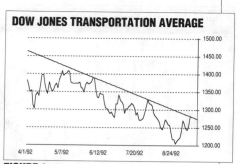

FIGURE 1: *The trendline was calculated in the spreadsheet and plotted with the closing price.*

SLOPE CALCULATION

	A	B	C	D	E
1	Date	DJT	Trendline	Rise	Run
2	4/1/92	1381.17	1463.10	1388.64	48
3	4/2/92	1366.59	1461.48	1328.75	85
4	4/3/92	1348.28	1459.86		-1.62

FIGURE 2: *Cells D2 and D3 are the highest values from two selected ranges in column B. Cells E2 and E3 are the row numbers from column B of the highest values from the selected ranges in column B. Note the dates listed in column A only apply to column B and C.*

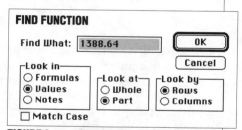

FIGURE 3: *The Find function found under the Formula menu will search for our first point, which was 1388.64. Excel will highlight the cell with this value.*

CALCULATING THE TRENDLINE

	A	B	C
45	6/3/92	1373.13	1393.50
46	6/4/92	1377.06	1391.88
47	6/5/92	1387.89	1390.26
48	6/8/92	1388.64	1388.64
49	6/9/92	1360.80	1387.02
50	6/10/92	1335.01	1385.40

FIGURE 4: *The trendline is calculated in column C. Our first point where the trendline crosses was 1388.64, which is located in cell B48. The values above 1388.64 are simply the previous day's value minus the slope (cell E4, Figure 2). Values below 1388.64 is the previous day's value plus the slope.*

CHAPTER 12

THE TRADERS' MAGAZINE

DECEMBER 1992

TECHNICAL ANALYSIS OF STOCKS & COMMODITIES™

'92   FEB   MAR

Multiple-Length Stochastics

Plotting different indicators together and combining their analyses is a popular analytical method for timing trades. But how about using one indicator and varying its parameters? Stuart Meibuhr takes stochastics and varies the length of the lookback for trades of different time frames.

The popular concept "if one is good, two are better" has often been used by technicians in the selection of indicators in the belief that combining the signals of different indicators is a more reliable strategy than following just one. But this idea has rarely been applied to the use of multiple-length indicators, with the exception of perhaps multiple-length moving averages. Few other indicators have been studied for their value as multiple-length trading tools. In a recent STOCKS & COMMODITIES article, Barbara Star showed that the crossover of the seven-day and the 14-day commodity channel index (CCI, short and intermediate term) could serve as an early warning system forewarning of impending price reversal for live cattle. Star sometimes also used the 28-day CCI (long term) and even suggested that the three CCI plots be overlaid, with buying or selling then occurring

when all the plots turn at the same time above or below the 100 level.

In contrast, Martin Pring used multiple-length rate of change (ROC) indicators on monthly and daily price data for the Standard & Poor's 500 index and other markets. He showed that when three ROC plots peak or bottom together, significant moves occur in the S&P 500. With monthly data, he used six-, 12- and 24-month ROC curves that were

> **One logical conclusion stemming from these charts was that a long-term stochastic could help the investor or trader remain on the correct side of the market.**

by Stuart Meibuhr

smoothed by six- and nine-month moving averages. For daily data, he used 10-, 15- and 30-day ROC curves.

Walter Bressert, in his book *The Power of Oscillator/Cycle Combinations*, calculated the relative strength index (RSI) indicator for different lengths using the Fibonacci series up to 21 on daily Treasury bond data. When all the RSI curves peaked above the 70 level at the same time, the T-bond price would also tend to make a significant peak. A similar situation existed for lows when the RSI curves bottomed below the 30 line.

These multiple-length indicators appear to reflect the importance of the interaction of several different time cycles. When these cycles are peaking (or bottoming), all the different length indicators are also peaking or bottoming, and so, a low-risk trading opportunity exists. How the trader takes advantage of that opportunity reflects the needs of the individual trader; securities, options (puts or calls), LEAPs (long-term equity appreciation securities) and futures are all valid trading vehicles. Traders select the vehicles that best meet their trading time frames for the best possible dollar gain per dollar invested. And so, it would behoove us to examine the benefits that can be gleaned from the use of multiple-length stochastic plots (see sidebar, "Calculating stochastics").

> In comparing the many charts, I realized that at certain times, many of the stochastics reached an extreme value simultaneously. That led me to overlay the stochastic plots.

SIMPLY STOCHASTICS

An article in the January 1990 S&C examined the use of a 14-bar stochastic on a monthly T-bond chart over a 12-year period. I was intrigued, so I charted the 14-bar stochastic on monthly data for both the Dow Jones Industrial Average (DJIA) and the OEX. Figure 1 shows the 14-bar stochastic for the DJIA and Figure 2 shows the same stochastic for the OEX. I then charted the 59-bar stochastic on weekly DJIA data, as there are about 59 weeks in 14 months. The weekly stochastic plot was more jagged, but the same times were identified by the extreme values. Moreover, the same time periods were identified by a 294-bar stochastic plotted on daily data (there are about 294 trading days in 14 months).

One logical conclusion stemming from these charts was that a long-term stochastic could help the investor or trader remain on the correct side of the market. A 294-bar stochastic slowed by 21 units crossed below the 80 level on Wednesday, October 14, before the severe market tumble on Black Monday, October 19, 1987! Figure 3 shows the daily OEX; the vertical marking connects the day of the stochastic crossover with the same day on the index.

How much shorter could the stochastic become before it no longer served as a useful trading tool? I experimented with various stochastic time periods, down to five. In comparing the charts, I realized that at certain times, many of the stochastics reached an

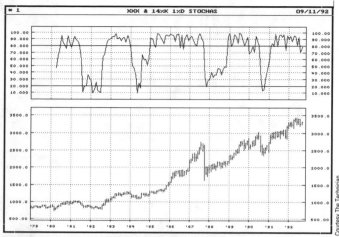

FIGURE 1: MONTHLY DOW JONES INDUSTRIAL AVERAGE, 14-BAR STOCHASTIC. *Values below 20 indicate buying opportunities. The stochastics indicator stayed above 80 during most of the bullish phases.*

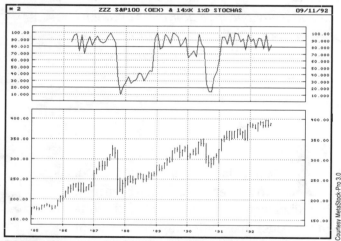

FIGURE 2: MONTHLY CHART OEX (S&P 100 INDEX) 14-BAR STOCHASTIC. *The 14-period stochastic turned up from 20 at opportunistic times.*

FIGURE 3: DAILY CHART OEX FROM MAY 1987 THROUGH JUNE 1988 AND THE 294-BAR STOCHASTIC SLOWED BY 21 BARS. *The long-term stochastic gave a sell signal several days before Black Monday in October 1987.*

extreme value simultaneously. That inspired me to overlay the stochastic plots.

Now, for more than a year, I have been overlaying multiple-length stochastic plots as a means of identifying low-risk trading opportunities in the OEX and in stocks. These low-risk times occur when each of the stochastic plots are at an extreme value (above 80 or below 20), similar to the strategies that use extreme readings of the CCI and RSI plots.

I decided empirically to use four stochastics — 150/5, 50/5, 13/5 and 5/5 — more or less at random; there is nothing magical about these numbers. I did not optimize the parameters. These four sets of numbers represent the long term, intermediate term, short term and very short term, and the two components of each set represent the %K and %D values of the stochastic. To minimize clutter in the charts, I didn't plot the slowed %D (sometimes used as a trigger). All stochastics were plotted with simple moving averages rather than with exponential averages because simple averages calculate faster than exponential averages. Although calculation speed is not an issue when using MetaStock Professional, it did become an issue when I screened the database of stocks using another program. With MetaStock, using simple moving averages for the stochastic calculations meant using 150/5/1/s (the formula setup) as the conditions for the long-term plot. I wrote several MetaStock macros to perform the charting procedure for two, three or four stochastic plots overlaid.

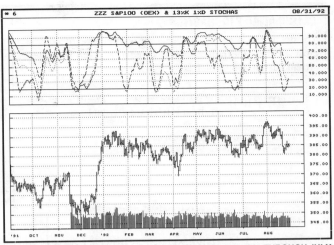

FIGURE 4: DAILY CHART FOR THE OEX FROM OCTOBER 1991 THROUGH JULY 1992 SHOWING THREE STOCHASTIC PLOTS: THE 150/5 (SOLID LINE), 50/5 (DOTTED LINE) AND 13/5 (DASHED LINE). *Important turns in the market occurred when all three indicators were either above 80 or below 20.*

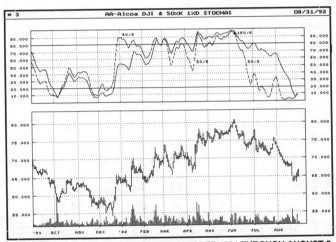

FIGURE 5: DAILY CHART ALCOA FROM OCTOBER 1991 THROUGH AUGUST 5, 1992, SHOWING THE 150/5 AND THE 50/5 STOCHASTIC PLOTS. *A successful buy signal appeared in December and a successful sell was indicated in June. As with most techniques, stop-loss orders can be used to help avoid large losses in case of false signals.*

SOME SPECIFICS

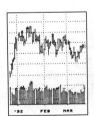

Figure 4 shows the OEX and the three longest stochastic plots overlaid; the dashed line corresponds to the 13/5 stochastic, the dotted line represents the 50/5 stochastic and the solid line is the 150/5 stochastic. In general, when all three stochastic plots are above 80 or below 20, profitable trading opportunities exist. The best (most likely profitable) trade was to sell an index option. Sell a call when the three plots are above 80 and sell a put when the three plots are below 20; other traders might prefer to buy the opposite option. The trigger to open the trade is when the 13/5 stochastic crosses either the 80 or the 20 line.

Does this method work every time? No, because no indicator does. Does this catch every top or bottom? Of course not! Some trading opportunities will be lost, but it is better to make errors of omission rather than errors of commission. And using stochastic multiple lengths could increase my trading success rate.

STOCK TRADING

Do the multiple stochastic plots help identify buy and sell opportunities for stocks? Yes. First, you must determine the time frame you expect your trade to run. For example, if you are an intermediate-term trader, you might choose to follow the 50/5 stochastic line for crossovers of the 80 or 20 line. The trade is taken (open or closed) when this crossover occurs, but only if the next-longer stochastic line is also above 80 (for a sell signal) or below 20 (for

a buy signal). This signal works best with cyclical price movement but it should be confirmed by one or more of your other favorite indicators. This trading tool does not appear to be successful either with utility stocks or interest rate-sensitive stocks because of the recent strong underlying trend. It works equally well with low-priced (above, say, $2-3) and high-priced stocks.

Figure 5 shows two stochastic plots (150/5 and 50/5) for Alcoa (AA). The 50/5 stochastic plot crossed down through the 80 line several times and yet only the last crossover was successful. Not all trades will work. This technique would not have allowed the trader to ride with the entire move from mid-December to the end of May, because the stochastics indicator is an oscillator and not a trend-following method. A short-term trader can see several opportunities for trading options each time both stochastic plots turn up or down.

CALCULATING STOCHASTICS

The stochastics indicator calculates the relative level of today's closing price to the trading range selected by the user. Two lines are calculated, %K, which is:

$$\%K = 100\left(\frac{\text{Current Close} - \text{Lowest Low}_n}{\text{Highest High}_n - \text{Lowest Low}_n}\right)$$

This is the raw value of the stochastics indicator. The *n* period is the number of lookback days selected by the user, such as 10 days.

$$\%D = 100\left(\frac{\displaystyle\sum_{j=1}^{3}\left(\text{Current Close} - \text{Lowest Low}_n\right)}{\displaystyle\sum_{j=1}^{3}\left(\text{Highest High}_n - \text{Lowest Low}_n\right)}\right)$$

%D is a smoothed %K. The above example smoothes the %K by calculating the ratio of the summed last three periods of the numerator of %K to the summed last three periods of the denominator of %K.

In Figure 1, a 10-period %K and a three-period %D are presented. Column E is the highest high in the last 10 days. The formula for cell E24 is:

=MAX(B15:B24)

Column F is the lowest low in the last 10 days. The formula for cell for F24 is:

=MIN(C15:C24)

The numerator for %K is Column G. The formula for cell for G24 is:

=D24-F24

The denominator for %K is Column H. The formula for cell for H24 is:

=E24-F24

%K is calculated in column I. The formula for cell I24 is:

=100*(G24/H24)

Finally, %D is calculated in column J. The formula for J24 is:

=100*(SUM(G22:G24)/SUM(H22:H24))

The slow version of the stochastics indicator takes these steps to calculate the value of %D and then relabels %D as slow %K, then smoothes the slow %K with a three-day moving average for the %D.

—*Thom Hartle, Editor*

	A	B	C	D	E	F	G	H	I	J
1	Date	High	Low	Close	Max H	Min L	Num	Den	%K	%D
2	920817	421.89	419.44	420.74					10	3
3	920818	421.40	419.78	421.34					Period	Period
4	920819	421.62	418.19	418.19						
5	920820	418.85	416.93	418.26						
6	920821	420.35	413.58	414.85						
7	920824	414.85	410.07	410.72						
8	920825	411.64	408.30	411.61						
9	920826	413.61	410.53	413.51						
10	920827	415.83	413.51	413.53						
11	920828	414.95	413.38	414.84	421.89	408.30	6.54	13.59	48.12	
12	920831	415.29	413.76	414.03	421.62	408.30	5.73	13.32	43.02	
13	920901	416.07	413.35	416.07	421.62	408.30	7.77	13.32	58.33	49.81
14	920902	418.28	415.31	417.98	420.35	408.30	9.68	12.05	80.33	59.91
15	920903	420.31	417.49	417.98	420.35	408.30	9.68	12.05	80.33	72.50
16	920904	418.62	416.76	417.08	420.31	408.30	8.78	12.01	73.11	77.93
17	920908	417.18	414.30	414.44	420.31	408.30	6.14	12.01	51.12	68.20
18	920909	416.44	414.44	416.36	420.31	410.53	5.83	9.78	59.61	61.39
19	920910	420.52	416.34	419.95	420.52	413.35	6.60	7.17	92.05	64.12
20	920911	420.58	419.13	419.58	420.58	413.35	6.23	7.23	86.17	77.17
21	920914	425.27	419.58	425.27	425.27	413.35	11.92	11.92	100.00	94.03
22	920915	425.22	419.54	419.77	425.27	413.35	6.42	11.92	53.86	79.08
23	920916	422.44	417.77	419.92	425.27	414.30	5.62	10.97	51.23	68.83
24	920917	421.43	419.62	419.93	425.27	414.30	5.63	10.97	51.32	52.19

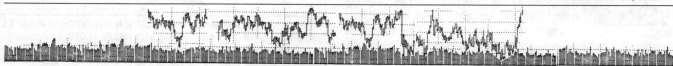

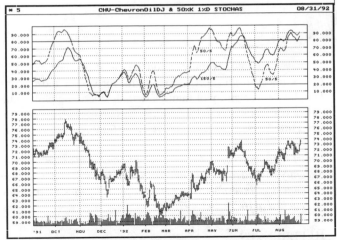

FIGURE 6: CHEVRON (CHV) DAILY (OCTOBER 1992-AUGUST 5, 1992) SHOWING THE 150/5 AND THE 50/5 STOCHASTIC PLOTS. *A good buy was indicated in March.*

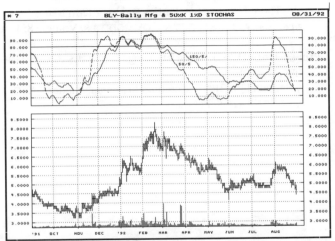

FIGURE 7: DAILY CHART BALLY FROM OCTOBER 1991 THROUGH AUGUST 5, 1992, SHOWING THE 150/5 AND THE 50/5 STOCHASTIC PLOTS. *The best signal happened with the downturn in late February.*

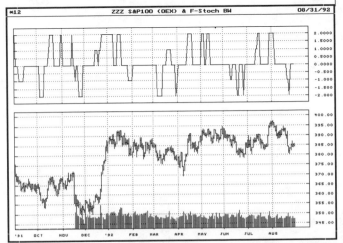

FIGURE 8: DAILY CHART OEX FROM AUGUST 1991 TO AUGUST 1992 SHOWING AS AN OSCILLATOR THE TIMES WHEN THE 10/5 AND THE 30/5 STOCHASTICS ARE ABOVE 80 OR BELOW 20 (+2 AND -2, RESPECTIVELY). *When the oscillator reads either +1 or -1, only the short stochastic is above 80 or below 20.*

Figure 6 shows similar data for Chevron (CHV). Three buy signals were given, in mid-December, early February and early March. Certainly, the signal in March would have been the most profitable. This is another reminder of the importance of using stop-loss orders to manage risk. If the trader was long a call purchased in March, then the first sell signal in mid-June should have caused the position to be closed. A short-term call buyer probably would have had a profitable trade in mid-December when both stochastics crossed the 20 line on the same day, but this signal was premature for the bottom.

> **Does this method work every time? No, because no indicator does. Some trading opportunities will be lost, but it is better to make errors of omission rather than errors of commission.**

An example of a low-priced stock is Bally (BLY), which is shown in Figure 7 with its two stochastic plots. Two sell signals were given, one in late January and one in late February. The late February signal would have been profitable. Both signals indicated that any long position must be closed. A buy signal was given shortly before the beginning of this chart. The crossover of the 20 line by the 50/5 stochastic in early June is not a valid buy signal because the 150/5 stochastic had not yet fallen below the 20 line. This only proves that this technique will miss some profitable opportunities.

I f a large number of stocks are followed, it is impractical to chart each one daily to find out if any have the desired stochastic pattern. Let the computer do that job. Several technical analysis screening programs exist that will determine if a security meets any desired stochastic pattern. I initially used TechniFilter Plus 6.0 from RTR Software but now have updated to version 7.0, which calculates much faster. Usually, only a very small number of securities — less than 1% of all the stocks in the database per day — display a desired stochastic pattern. On some days, no stocks exhibit the desired pattern. Once the program identifies a security with a desirable pattern, I subject it to a detailed technical analysis before making any buy or sell recommendation.

The formula in TechniFilter Plus for the 50/5 stochastic is:

$$((C-LN50)/(HM50-LN50))A5$$

where LN50 is the lowest low of the past 50 days, HM50 is the highest high for the past 50 days and A5 is a five-day simple average of the 50-day stochastic.

Using TechniFilter and MetaStock together, I have been successful in finding tradable stocks by using a stochastic-based filtering system.

Two short-term stochastics can be used to identify the best times to sell uncovered† OEX options. When both stochastics are above 80 or below 20, the OEX has reached short-term cyclical tops and bottoms during those times when the market is not in a strong up or down move. Such sideways movement occurs often, or at least it did during 1991 and 1992.

Figure 8 shows two stochastic lines, 10/3 and 30/3. A +2 or -2 indicates that both stochastics are above 80 or below 20, respectively. A value of +1 or -1 shows that only the short stochastic is beyond its extreme value. While another indicator is needed to determine the exact day to place the trade, these spikes in the stochastic lines, if they endure more than one day, clearly correspond to turning points. To be successful with this trading method, good money management techniques are necessary to control the occasional losses.

In MetaStock, the formula to produce the chart in Figure 8 is:
if(stoch(10,3),>,80,{AND}if(stoch(30,3),>,80,+2,+1),
    if(stoch(10,3),<,20,if(stoch(30,3),<,20,-2,-1),0))

I encourage the reader to experiment with values other than 10 or 30.

I have explored several ideas on the use of stochastic plots for timing trades from short to long term, for stocks and options. Despite the versatility of multiple-length stochastic plots, other indicators should be used to confirm the signals from the stochastics. Further research may improve on the findings presented here.

Stuart Meibuhr trades stocks and options for his own account. Recently moved to Scottsdale, AZ, he has lectured and taught on computerized investment topics for the past 10 years. He may now be reached at (602) 443-4926.

REFERENCES
Bressert, Walter [1991]. *The Power of Oscillator/Cycle Combinations*, Walter Bressert & Associates, Tucson, AZ.

Hartle, Thom [1990]. "Stochastics and long-term trends," *Technical Analysis of* STOCKS & COMMODITIES, Volume 8: January.

Pring, Martin [1992]. "Rate of change," STOCKS & COMMODITIES, August.

Star, Barbara [1992]. "The commodity channel index," STOCKS & COMMODITIES, February.

TA

DIANE BOSTWICK

Smart Stops

Setting stops is a fine art, whether you trade one contract or a thousand. The challenge in setting stops is to participate in long moves without getting shaken out of the trade by market volatility. A variable-index dynamic average (VIDYA) may be used to place trailing stops that adapt to market volatility, which combines enough sensitivity to price changes with flexibility to fit your trading needs. Using this combination may well provide an extremely profitable stop for the intermediate-term trader.

by Tushar S. Chande

nce a trade has been initiated, most traders will use the risk management technique of placing a stop order, which limits losses or captures profits. A stop order becomes a market order when trades occur at a predefined price, while a buy stop is placed above the current market price and a sell stop is placed below the current price. A trailing stop order will be adjusted by a trader as prices change, following the market up or down, while a fixed-stop order will stay put. A stop order may be good for the day or be an open order, which may be good until canceled. A trailing stop is simply a safety valve to protect your profits or limit your losses.

In practice, a trailing stop is a leaky safety valve. There is no assurance that your trade or fill will occur at or very close to the stop price. For example, the market may make a sharp move past your stop, thus triggering it. The first trade after your stop (which may not be your intended fill) may be well past the stop you ordered in rapidly changing markets. Though imperfect, the trailing stop should give your trade some protection in most markets.

Some traders argue that a trailing stop, far from being bulletproof, may be the fired bullet that kills a profitable trade by getting you out too soon. Skilled floor traders can sense where stops may be accumulating above or below the market; a favorite activity is apparently pushing the market around so as to set off stops, causing rapid price movement as the preset buy or sell orders burst forth into the trading pits. The underlying trend resumes a day or two later, leaving you in its wake. This is called *gunning* for stops. Traders can be found on both sides of this issue: some feel you cannot gun a liquid market, while others feel it happens routinely. Many big traders do not place actual stops, choosing instead to work with mental stops so as not to give away their plans. A mental stop requires great discipline to enforce. We mere mortals are better off placing the stop order with our brokers before trading begins.

SETTING STOPS

Your trading strategy should determine stop placement. As a short-term trader, you are looking for relatively small profits and would like to use tight stops, placed close to the market. As an intermediate- to long-term trend trader, you are looking for big market moves and would like to use loose stops placed far away from the current price to allow for random moves, giving the market room to breathe. There are no right stops or wrong stops. There are only stops you can live with.

Here are some examples of stop placement. As a short-term trader, if you are long the market, you may place a trailing stop a few ticks — say, one to five — below the most recent two- to five-day low (Figure 1). If short the market, you could place it above the most recent two- to five-day high. As an intermediate-term trader long the market, you could place your stop just below the most recent 14- to 30-day low (Figure 2). If short, you could place a stop just above the most recent 14- to 30-day high. Stops are often placed near a significant swing high or low in trending markets, while in trading markets, stops may be placed just above or below the current trading range. Traders could also place a stop at a fixed-dollar amount below the point of maximum profit. For example, you could set a stop $1,000 below the

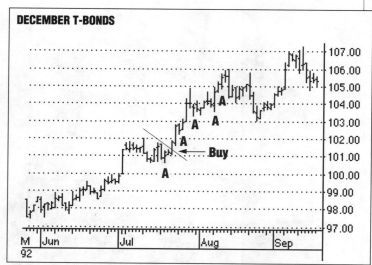

FIGURE 1: Trading short-term moves during a bull trend, stop-loss orders can be placed just a few ticks below the low of the last two to five trading days (A).

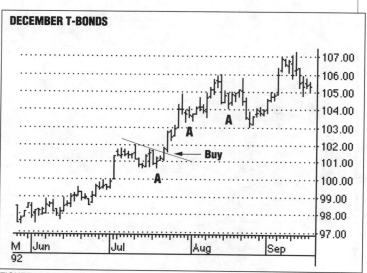

FIGURE 2: Trading intermediate-term moves during a bull trend requires taking more risk. A longer lookback period of 14 to 30 days can used to place stop-loss orders (A).

point of maximum profit.

As with trading in general, setting stops is a game of percentages. Any strategy you use will work well some percentage of the time. You will get some great exits as well as some lousy ones. So pick a strategy you like and stick with it.

THE IDEAL STOP

The ideal stop is unique. It is not placed so obviously that it can be gunned, while it is not so close that it gets you out of a trade too soon. It is not so far away as to be meaningless. Moreover, a smart stop has a mind of its own. Though no such ideal stop exists, I can come close using the variable index dynamic average (VIDYA) (discussed previously in March). VIDYA is an exponential moving average with a variable-index alpha that is tied to market volatility. The ratio of standard deviation of closing prices over a recent period to some historical norm is used to increase or decrease the variable weighting factor (alpha) and so, when volatility increases this factor increases, taking a greater chunk out of the most recent data to increment the moving average. Thus, the average takes large steps. When prices are quiet, this factor is smaller, using a smaller proportion of the most recent data to increment the moving average, and so the average moves more slowly. In effect, this moving average is more responsive to changing prices.

> **Setting stops is a game of percentages. You will get some great exits as well as some lousy ones. So pick a strategy you like and stick with it.**

To illustrate the use of VIDYA in setting stops, I will use the CSI Perpetual Contract data for the U.S. bond futures contract with data for November 25, 1991, to March 31, 1992. This covers the period of the Greenspan rally, powered by a 1% cut in the discount rate on December 20, 1991. The bond futures peaked in January 1992 and gave up all the gains since November over the first quarter.

I used 630 days of daily closing data starting January 2, 1990, to determine the maximum, minimum and average values of the 30-day standard deviation of the U.S. bond perpetual contract. The minimum value of the 30-day standard deviation was 0.39, the maximum was 2.03 and 1.02 was the average value. I picked a reference standard deviation value of 0.5 for VIDYA so that I would expect a maximum value approximately equal to 2/0.5 = 4. Hence, VIDYA would approximately simulate a 30-day to a seven-day moving average based on the value of the index. Hence, the value of VIDYA was as follows:

$$(1) \quad \text{VIDYA}_d = \left(\frac{\sigma}{0.5}0.065\right)C_d + \left(1 - \frac{\sigma}{0.5}0.065\right)\text{VIDYA}_{d-1}$$

In which

VIDYA$_d$ = VIDYA today
VIDYA$_{d-1}$ = VIDYA yesterday
C_d = Today's closing price
σ = 30-day standard deviation of closing prices

Note that 0.065 is the weighting factor for a 30-day exponential moving average (see sidebar, "Calculating VIDYA"). I could write similar expressions for VIDYA for the high or low by using the appropriate price in place of C_d.

I plotted the daily close along with the VIDYA (from Equation 1) and the 30-day exponential moving average in Figure 3. VIDYA's responsiveness to price changes is clearly superior to

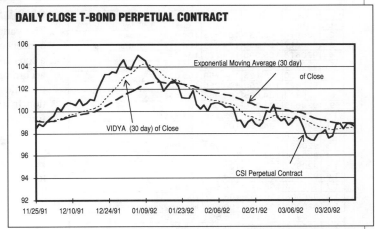

FIGURE 3: *The 30-day exponential moving average is compared with VIDYA. Note that as the daily close price rallied into January, VIDYA automatically adjusted while the 30-day exponential moving average lagged the market move.*

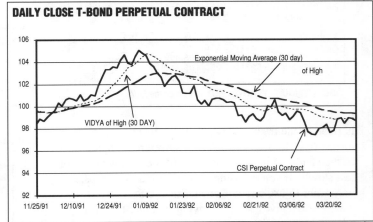

FIGURE 4: *VIDYA can use the daily high price instead of the closing price. A decision to liquidate a long position could be executed the morning after a close below the VIDYA of the high price.*

the equivalent exponential moving average. VIDYA values can be used as an intraday stop and in this case would have been triggered during the first dip in early January. An alternative approach is to sell at the open as of tomorrow if today's close was below the VIDYA level. The intraday stop is suitable for aggressive trading, while the closing basis allows a trader to participate in longer moves.

A second approach to setting stops with VIDYA is to use the daily high price for the calculations instead of the close and to act on the open tomorrow for a close above or below the average. As shown in Figure 4, this also allows the user to participate in longer moves, but with greater sensitivity than VIDYA based on closing prices.

A third alternative is to use VIDYA based on daily highs for short trades and one based on daily lows for long trades. As shown in Figure 5, this approach allows the user to participate in long moves, but the benefits are more pronounced with the standard exponential moving average than they are with VIDYA.

The stops using VIDYA thus meet many characteristics for an ideal stop. The choice of the combination depends on the time

	A	B	C	D	E	F
1	Date	High	Low	Close	30 day	VIDYA
2	920814	105.031	104.375	104.812	Standard	
3	920817	104.906	104.093	104.312	Deviation	
4	920818	105.000	104.281	104.843		
5	920819	104.937	104.500	104.906		
6	920820	105.125	104.750	105.093		
7	920821	105.750	104.250	104.500		
8	920824	104.656	103.468	103.531		
9	920825	103.906	103.062	103.218		
10	920826	103.625	103.156	103.625		
11	920827	104.062	103.625	103.812		
12	920828	104.156	103.687	103.843		
13	920831	104.031	103.687	103.968		
14	920901	104.593	103.843	104.562		
15	920902	105.000	104.468	104.718		
16	920903	104.906	104.562	104.812		
17	920904	106.343	104.843	105.937		
18	920908	106.968	106.187	106.906		
19	920909	106.906	106.500	106.562		
20	920910	106.812	106.093	106.750		
21	920911	107.062	105.781	105.937		
22	920914	107.250	106.000	106.281		
23	920915	106.375	105.218	105.500		
24	920916	105.875	104.812	105.343		
25	920917	105.781	105.218	105.375		
26	920918	105.750	104.968	105.781		
27	920921	105.562	104.906	105.313		
28	920922	105.375	104.156	104.250	30 day	VIDYA
29	920923	104.250	103.750	103.813	Standard	
30	920924	104.656	103.875	104.625	Deviation	
31	920925	105.593	104.468	105.500	0.969	105.500
32	920928	105.781	105.250	105.719	0.979	105.528
33	920929	105.750	105.375	105.469	0.974	105.520
34	920930	105.593	105.250	105.313	0.975	105.494
35	921001	106.343	105.187	106.250	0.999	105.592

SIDEBAR FIGURE 1: VIDYA. *VIDYA builds on the EMA.*

CALCULATING VIDYA

The variable index dynamic moving average (VIDYA) builds on the concept of the exponential moving average (EMA). While the EMA uses a constant (alpha) to smooth today's data, the VIDYA adjusts the alpha according to the data's volatility. The volatility is measured by taking the ratio of a 30-day standard deviation to a reference standard deviation. In sidebar Figure 1, column E is the 30-day standard deviation. The formula for cell E 35 is:

$$=STDEVP(D6:D35)$$

Here, the 30-day standard deviation of the last 30 days' closing price (column D) is measured. Column F is the VIDYA of the closing price. The formula for cell F35 is:

$$=(E35/0.5*0.065*D35)+((1-(E35/0.5*0.065))*F34)$$

To calculate the VIDYA of the high for each day, substitute values from column B into the formula in columns E and F:

$$=STDEVP(B6:B35)$$

$$=(E35/0.5*0.065*B35)+((1-(E35/0.5*0.065))*F34)$$

To calculate the VIDYA of the low for each day, substitute values from column C into the formula in columns E and F:

$$=STDEVP(C6:C35)$$

$$=(E35/0.5*0.065*C35)+((1-(E35/0.5*0.065))*F34)$$

—Editor

horizon of the trade and whether you want to set tight or loose stops. Because you can vary the reference factor (that is, the factor 0.5 in Equation 1), VIDYA can move more or less slowly. If you are using VIDYA for intraday stops, you may want to use a factor greater than 0.5 — say, 1.0 — which would give a slower moving average. The principal advantage in varying this factor is being able to set a unique stop, which cannot be gunned easily. VIDYA's greater sensitivity relative to the corresponding exponential moving average allows the user to capture a greater portion of potential profits. By design, VIDYA automatically tightens when the market makes a move and loosens when the market pauses for breath. Thus, it works as though it were a smart stop.

SHOP 'N STOP

Setting stops is a fine art because so many ways exist to strike a fine balance between risk and reward. VIDYA offers a new alternative that adapts automatically to market volatility with the flexibility to meet individual needs. VIDYA may end up being a handy addition to your trading tools when you shop for stops.

Tushar Chande, CTA, is a principal of Kroll, Chande, & Co., 1

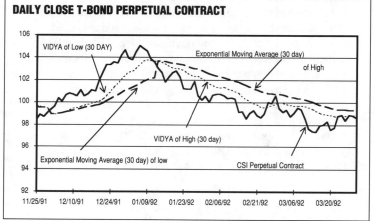

DAILY CLOSE T-BOND PERPETUAL CONTRACT

FIGURE 5: *Long trades can use VIDYA of the daily lows for a stop-loss price and short positions can use VIDYA of the daily highs for a stop-loss price.*

Todd Drive, Sands Point, NY 11050, (516) 627-0800.

REFERENCES

Chande, Tushar S. [1992]. "Adapting moving averages to market volatility," STOCKS & COMMODITIES, March.

Perpetual Contract, Commodity Systems Inc. (CSI), Boca Raton, FL.

MARAL SASSOUNI

Gold And The CRB Index

John Murphy, the leading proponent of intermarket analysis, closes the current circle of tradable interrelationships by examining how gold and the CRB index interact.

by John J. Murphy

T he gold market plays a key role in intermarket analysis. Last time, I discussed gold's tendency to trade in the opposite direction of the U.S. dollar. Falling U.S. interest rates, which are usually associated with a weak dollar, at some point begin to reawaken inflation pressures. One of the first places that inflation begins to manifest itself is in a rising gold

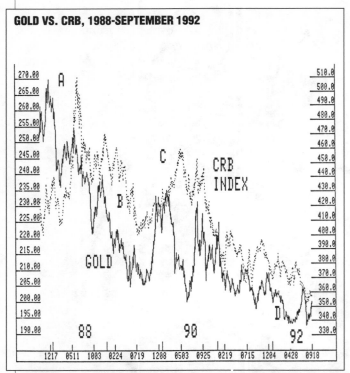

GOLD VS. CRB, 1988-SEPTEMBER 1992

FIGURE 1: *Gold's tendency (solid line) to lead turns in the CRB index (dotted line) can be seen at four different junctures from early 1988 to September 1992.*

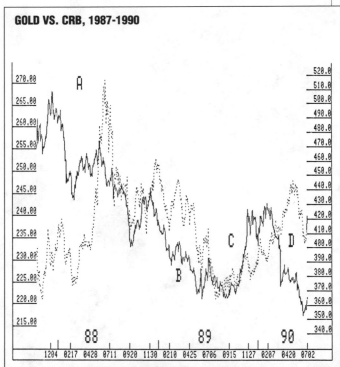

GOLD VS. CRB, 1987-1990

FIGURE 2: *During the period from the end of 1987 to mid-1990, gold (solid line) acted as an excellent leading indicator of the CRB index (dotted line).*

market. Because of gold's historical link to the dollar, a weak dollar will usually affect gold prices first. A rising gold market is an early signal that commodity prices in general may start to strengthen, due to gold's history as a leading indicator of the CRB index at important tops and bottoms.

During the past 12 years, the CRB Futures Price Index of 21 commodities has seen three major turns. The November 1980 peak in the CRB index marked the end of the inflationary spiral of the 1970s. Gold hit its all-time high in January 1980, peaking

> **Figure 1 compares gold (the solid line) to the CRB index (the dotted line) from the beginning of 1988 to September 1992. Letters A, B, C and D show gold leading the CRB index at four different points in time.**

10 months before the CRB index. The CRB troughed in mid-1986 and then rallied 35% during the ensuing two years. Gold hit its low point in February 1985, 16 months before the CRB index. Figure 1 shows the third major turn in the CRB index, which turned back down in mid-1988. Point A in Figure 1 shows that gold peaked in December 1987, leading the CRB peak by six months. Gold led those three major turns in the commodity price level with an average lead time of 10 months. That being the case, gold can provide some useful clues to the inflationary threat presented by the CRB index.

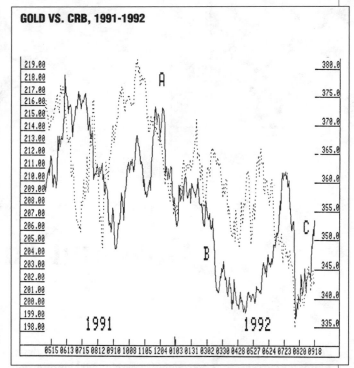

GOLD VS. CRB, 1991-1992

FIGURE 3: *Gold (solid line) led the CRB index (dotted line) lower from mid-1991 to September 1992, correctly signaling that inflation was not a threat. Gold, however, is beginning to outperform the CRB index for the first time in a long while.*

Figure 1 compares gold (the solid line) to the CRB index (the dotted line) from the beginning of 1988 to September 1992. Letters A, B, C and D show gold leading the CRB index at four different points in time. Points A and C show gold peaking well before the CRB index in early 1988 and early 1990, while points B and D show gold leading the CRB lower during 1989 and 1992. Figure 2 gives a closer view of the time span from late 1987 to mid-1990. The two earlier gold peaks in 1988 (A) and 1990 (D) can be seen more clearly. Point B in Figure 2 shows gold resuming its downtrend at the start of 1989, correctly anticipating the CRB breakdown several months later. Point C indicates a double bottom in gold during the autumn of 1989, providing an early warning of an upturn in the CRB index.

Figure 3 shows the period from mid-1991 to September 1992. Point A shows the relative underperformance by gold (solid line) in late 1991, calling into question the upside breakout in the CRB index (dotted line). Point B shows gold dropping to a new low in March 1992, which was four months before the CRB breakdown. Point C in mid-September 1992 shows a possible double bottom forming in gold combined with a weaker CRB index, which is similar to the September 1989 pattern shown in Figure 2.

The normal sequence of events has falling interest rates and a weak dollar pushing gold higher, which eventually pulls the CRB index higher. Rising gold mining shares, which usually lead the price of bullion higher, are an early warning that a bottom in commodities may not be far off. Gold and gold shares can also function as safe havens during currency upheavals and when stock market confidence is waning.

John Murphy is president of JJM Technical Advisors Inc. and publishes the monthly "Futures Trends and Intermarket Analysis." He is also the technical analyst for CNBC.

REFERENCES

JJM Technical Advisors Inc., 297-101 Kinderkamack Road Ste 148, Oradell, NJ 07649.

Murphy, John J. [1991]. *Intermarket Technical Analysis*, John Wiley & Sons.

_____ [1986]. *Technical Analysis of the Futures Markets*, New York Institute of Finance.

_____ [1992]. "Gold and the U.S. dollar," STOCKS & COMMODITIES, November.

_____ [1992]. "The CRB index/bond ratio," STOCKS & COMMODITIES, July.

Contrarian Thought

As a rule of thumb, the crowd is always wrong at the top or at the bottom, but how does one gain insight into what the crowd is doing*? John Blasic discusses some basics of measuring crowd psychology and using it in contrarian strategy.*

by John Blasic

C ontrary thinking is an art form that should be included in every technician's arsenal. It is a single concept that comprises many individual parts. Contrary analysis studies market extremes as a form of psychological analysis, emphasizing the principle that whenever the crowd agrees on *anything*, they must be wrong. How can traders profit from contrary opinion? How indeed? Remember: the facts themselves are unimportant. It is what they are *perceived* to be that determines the course of events.

Whether stocks or futures or just about any other market that involves human activity is being analyzed, crowd psychology becomes the dominant force behind price movement. While supply and demand affect price, price is also affected by trader or investor perception. At any given time, prices will accurately reflect the level at which a seller is willing to part with a given object and the price that a buyer is willing to pay. When an imbalance occurs between these factors, a price move results.

BIGGER FOOL WE

Such thinking encourages us to consider the *bigger fool theory*, which states that in any given stock transaction (or any other instrument that can be bought or sold, for that matter), the seller expects to sell the given instrument at a profit to a willing buyer, whom he or she regards as a fool for believing that the stock price (or relative worth of the object) will go up whereas the seller believes it will drop. Transaction participants buy and sell based on where they think prices are headed, whether or not the reasoning has any real world application. In sum, the seller believes that the issue is fully valued and sells the issue to someone whose reasons for buying are not relevant. Stated another way, the action of market participants

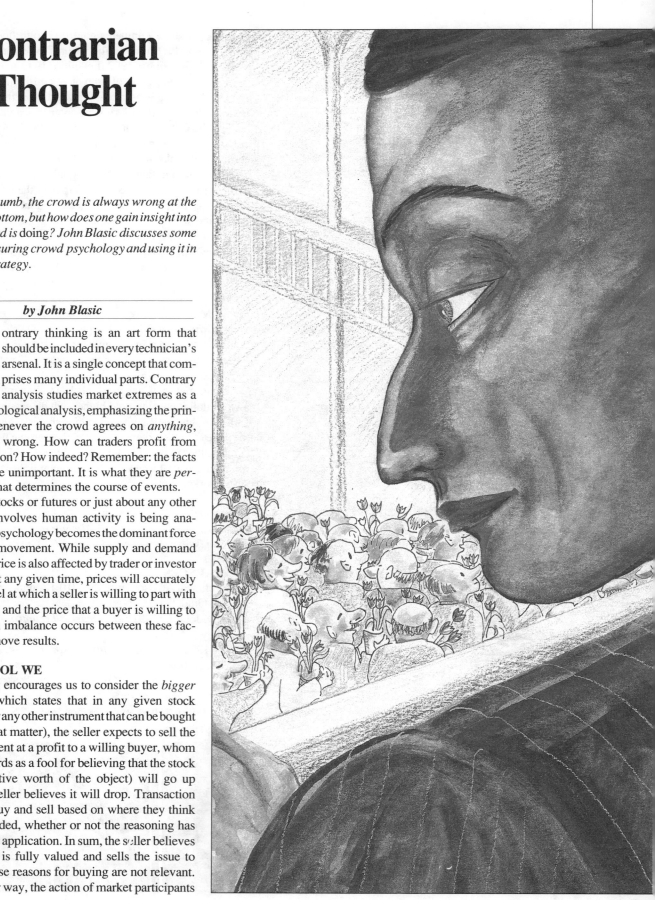

is the only reason prices move.

A well-known illustration of crowd psychology occurred in Tulipmania, the massive overspeculation of tulip bulbs that occurred in Holland in the 1600s. The prices of tulip bulbs skyrocketed to astounding and phenomenal levels, during the peak of which the price of a single tulip bulb was as much as $400 in current prices. Houses, property and personal belongings were sold to take part in the mass speculation. When bulb prices reached so high that sellers could no longer find buyers, the bottom abruptly fell out of the market. The same concept of crowd psychology could be seen in the 1973 price spike in the nifty 50 stocks, preceding the top in the stock market. The Dow Jones Industrial Average (DJIA) subsequently fell nearly 50%.

An exceptional analyst will always be well ahead of the crowd, and when the crowd follows, he or she will be off in another direction. Regardless of the apparent facts, market prices move as a result of the actions of market participants. In Tulipmania, all the market speculators were fully positioned until no one of the opposite mind was left. The lack of new market participants fails to drive prices further regardless of the technical or fundamental factors. In such instances, the herd instinct develops because weaker market participants are generally crowd followers who overreact to market news. It is only when stronger and larger participants decide to take profits that a mad rush occurs because the weaker players become fearful of losses and dash to sell.

Further, mass psychology can be defined by the emotions of fear and greed. Investors naturally tend to impulsively participate in the markets, believing that the easiest thing to do is turn a profit. Greed's counterpart is fear. These emotions define not the value of what is being traded, but why the trading seems to be occurring. Other fundamentals become secondary as the fear of loss dominates market action. Psychiatrists rank these motives with love and hate as a driving force behind the masses.

EVALUATING CONVENTIONAL WISDOM

It is not the markets that beat market participants; rather, market participants allow themselves to get beaten. Contrary opinion has become a widely accepted investment tool that is part of conventional wisdom. While this method was misunderstood and overlooked for many years, it is now recognized as a popular method by which to turn a profit. Simply, this method advocates seeking out those issues that are out of favor but still represent a solid value. The ability to profit from this philosophy occurs because when an investment is undervalued, the speculator has little or no interest in it. The contrarian speculator, in the purest form, attempts to evaluate the psychological climate through the use of various tools to make the investment decision more precise. Most of the time, this is the most difficult portion of the investment decision for the market participant to make for fear of being wrong. While it may take somewhat longer to see whether the trading decision was correct, it becomes an emotional test by forcing the market participant to wait out the trading storm. At times it may be difficult to fight these feelings, but the investor with experience has developed an intuitive sense of value.

Furthermore, contrarians are naturally attracted to markets and issues that have taken a significant beating. The art of timing may not be as precise as other methods, but independent thought is mainly utilized to become the leader instead of the follower. Such a scenario is easily painted when you walk into a broker's office. Anxious market participants quickly look for crowd acceptance and therefore accept the prevailing opinion.

The use of contrary opinion allows market participants using contrarian thought to profit in the markets by doing the opposite of what the crowd is doing; contrarian theory is based on the estimation of the prevailing crowd emotion and not in forecasting the future. When you try to forecast the future, more likely than not you will be at the mercy of the forecast because pride of opinion quickly becomes the dominating factor. By *not* following the crowd, there is a much better chance of being right.

> **The herd instinct develops because weaker market participants are generally crowd followers who over-react to market news. When stronger participants take profits, a rush occurs because weaker players become fearful of losses and sell.**

Putting aside your own feelings and evaluating the crowd enables the market participant to join in major moves by getting aboard at the right time. Contrary opinion is most effective at major turning points as predefined extremes of bullishness or bearishness are reached.

TOOLS FOR THE CONTRARIAN

Some of the more popular measures of market sentiment are advisors' sentiment, short interest, the put/call ratio, secondary offerings and the advance-decline line.

For almost 30 years, *Investors Intelligence* has compiled data on advisors' sentiment by tracking the opinions of market newsletter publishers. Newsletter writers are considered to be well-informed and therefore most likely to offer quality market advice. The findings of the data compiled show that the market newsletter publishers act in a manner indicating the majority opinion and therefore provide a good source for the contrarian thinker. When the four-week moving average of the bullish percentage of market newsletter publishers reaches 80%, a top in the market is at hand. When the four-week moving average of the bullish percentage of market newsletter publishers reaches 37%, a bottom in the market is near.

Market Vane publishes an indicator of similar construction. Each week, an assortment of market participants are sampled to determine bullish market participation. Many traders only register bullishness when they become long the market, which hence are used as short-term indications showing that little potential buying power is left. A unique feature of this indicator is its weighting formula, which is applied to various market letters. Those with the largest followings receive a greater weighing to determine its influence more accurately, and the same is true for the bearish side of the market. Again, a four-week moving average should be applied to smooth the data.

Of these market sentiment indicators, the put/call ratio is perhaps one of the most widely followed. To refresh your memory, a put gives an investor or trader the option to sell a specific issue at a predetermined price level and time frame, while a call gives the investor or trader the option to purchase an issue at a predetermined price level and time frame. By developing a ratio between the volume of the two, the indicator measures the market swings between bullishness and bearishness. When a low ratio is produced, the more bullish the crowd is perceived to be and the more likely the market is to decline. On the other hand, a high ratio indicates that a large number of traders are bearish and thus the more likely the market is to rise. This ratio is commonly used with a 10-day moving average to smooth the volatility of the day-to-day swings of this indicator.

Another indicator that a market participant should consider using to determine contrarian thought is secondary offerings, which has the ability to indicate how easily companies are able to issue new stock and how quickly the market can absorb them. The indicator is plotted next to the Dow Jones Industrial Average (DJIA) to visually spot the peaks and valleys. A high level of offerings can be seen at market tops, while a trickle of offerings signal important market bottoms. This occurs because investors are no longer interested in purchasing new stocks and prefer to hold cash during periods of uncertainty. Experimentation shows that an application of a moving average will smooth the erratic nature of this indicator and give fewer but more precise points.

The advance-decline line is somewhat removed from the traditional sense of a contrarian indicator but is widely followed because it shows the breadth of participation. Breadth of participation refers to the raw value of the number of stocks up minus the number of stocks down each day. This value is added (if positive) or subtracted (if negative) from the previous day's value. A rising line indicates wide participation in the market, leading a market observer to conclude that the current trend can be maintained. One of the best values that this indicator has is its ability to register market divergences, forewarning possible trend reversals.

IMPLEMENTING A GAME PLAN
One of the most important steps to take in contrary thinking is the implementation of a solid methodology. The value of contrary opinion lies in the ability for independent thought to challenge the generally accepted viewpoints, so it pays to be contrary once the accepted viewpoints are defined. Experience will show that the crowds are only right during the trends but wrong at both ends. Emotions swing widely on hopes, fears and passions, which is why monitoring market sentiment, options activity and the breadth of individual stock participation in the market trend can help you avoid being part of the crowd.

The investor or trader should use these methodologies and indicators as a reference for developing a complete strategy. The general premise behind contrarian thought is to discover values before they have been discounted in the markets. Use your common sense to purchase under favorable conditions and be aware of crowd psychology.

John J. Blasic is a New Jersey-based registered investment advisor using technical analysis for money management strategies. He has authored the Market Technicians Association's Index of Journal articles from its inception.

FURTHER READING
Colby, Robert W., and Thomas A. Meyers [1988]. *The Encyclopedia of Technical Market Indicators*, Dow Jones-Irwin.

Hadady, R. Earl [1983]. *Contrary Opinion*, Key Book Press, Pasadena, CA.

MacKay, Charles [1932]. *Extraordinary Popular Delusions and the Madness of Crowds,* now available through Fraser Publishing, Burlington, VT.

McGinley, John R. [1986]. "Sentiment: The bottom line," *MTA Journal*, November.

Trading The Santa Claus Rally

'Tis the season to be jolly and *make a profit. What could be finer? Michael Sheimo explores the whys and wherefores of this seasonal phenomenon.*

by Michael D. Sheimo

Holiday rallies in the stock market are a fact of life. Various theories abound as to why they occur: institutional traders don't want any loose cash sitting around for a long weekend, trading houses want to maintain optimism for the holiday, investors are in a buying mood, a culmination of technical influences come together near holidays. The cause of a holiday rally can be as simple as institutional portfolio managers leaving work early. Upon exiting, they leave instructions that are more likely to be made up of buys rather than sells.

Whatever the reason, the stock market tends to rally at holiday time and you can profit from that knowledge. Figure 1 shows all holiday markets going back more than three years. The holidays are designated by a vertical line rising from the baseline up to the graph line. Years are separated by full-length vertical lines. Most of the holidays show a rally that starts a few days earlier than the holiday and frequently continues after the holiday has passed. In fact, it is difficult to find a holiday without a rally of *some* kind.

WHAT DOES SANTA KNOW?

Through the years, the best-known holiday rally has been the Santa Claus rally, occurring between Thanksgiving Day and Christmas Day. Sometimes the rally stops at Christmas Eve and the market drops, with investors selling some holdings before the year-end. At other times, the rally continues into January.

Looking back through the last three years, however, the appearance of the Santa Claus rally is consistent. The rally can even appear in relatively slow or bad years. Christmas and New Year's Day are shown on Figure 1 by the two vertical lines that are very close together. The letter "C" signifies Christmas.

If we look at just the Santa Claus rally, we can observe the action better. Figure 2 looks at the daily closing levels of the Dow Jones Industrial Average (DJIA) from the day after Thanksgiving until the end of that year. The Christmas holiday can be found at the break in the graph, the empty space where no trading occurs. The gridlines are divided into blocks of 50 points.

TRADING THE RALLY

It appears that 1989 had the smallest Santa Claus rally. It had a good start but ran out of steam a week before Christmas. Even

JIM FRISINO

so, the DJIA did advance about a hundred points. The following year, 1990, had a more consistent rally, but it started from a level lower than 1989's rally. This rally followed the end of the short bear market of that year, which turned up in mid-October. The best year was obviously 1991. The first few days were not encouraging as the market drifted lower, but then the market gave us a strong rally for Christmas. These graphs clearly show a consistent recurrence of stock prices moving up during the period between Thanksgiving and Christmas. The real question: Can this rally be profitably traded?

> **The year 1991 was a great time for the Santa Claus rally, when the DJIA rose more than 274 points. As we saw in Figure 1, this was a rally that continued well into the 1992 trading year.**

OUR SANTA RALLY OBJECTIVE

Can we earn $10,000 or more by trading the DJIA at Christmas? To test this hypothesis, take a look at three consecutive Santa rallies — 1989, 1990 and 1991 — and see how our investment would have done. We will lock in the buy and sell for an automatic order execution to remove any advantage we might have gained from trading finesse. That way, any profits can be linked more directly to the rally. We will buy the closing price for the day after Thanksgiving and hold the stock until the end of the last trading day of the year. We will buy 500 shares of five different stock issues. Let's see what happens.

The following are five stocks that I believe participated in the Santa Claus rallies for 1989, 1990 and 1991. They were not actually selected at random, nor were they chosen because they were successful (previous performance was not taken into account). Again, we are not trying to select good stocks; rather, our aim is to select rally participants.

As stated earlier, we will precisely control times of purchase and sale for purposes of this illustration. As another method of control, all individual stock analysis will be ignored. We have removed all fundamental or technical study of the stocks involved and just pick five. Our strategy will allow us to partake of the Santa Claus rally as it occurs without using trading techniques that could confuse the results.

After the rally is observed, we will then turn back to some technical and fundamental factors to see if analysis might have helped us do a better job of selecting stocks.

OBJECTIVE PARAMETERS

We will buy 500 shares of five different stock issues. The period will be the closing price on the day after Thanksgiving (for the buy) until the closing price for the year (for the sell). Other parameters include figuring an extra $150 in commission costs

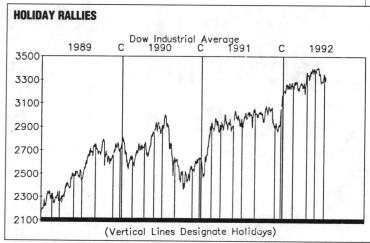

FIGURE 1: *The stock market has a strong tendency to rally just before a holiday.*

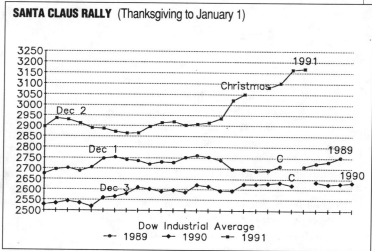

FIGURE 2: *The stock market has attempted some sort of a rally in the last three years during the holiday season.*

per transaction (actual commissions may differ). This takes $300 away from any individual stock profits, because both buys and sells are involved.

The stocks purchased on the day after Thanksgiving will be:

Buy 500 shares of:			
	1989	**1990**	**1991**
Coke at	$38.63	$45.88	$69.38
Disney at	130.50	95.13	104.75
Exxon at	46.75	50.75	58.63
GE at	61.25	53.75	64.75
IBM at	99.25	113.13	92.50

FIGURE 3: BUY STRATEGY. *Here are the chosen stocks and their purchase prices for 1989, 1990 and 1991.*

At this point in the exercise, we are flying blind. We have selected stocks based on personal preference (we just *think* they will do well) and technical association (we know that the DJIA rallied, and that these stocks are part of that average). Remember, we are intentionally avoiding trying to pick the best stocks or the most opportune timing. Although we are using stocks selected from the DJIA, in reality, any list of stocks can be used, as long as the group shows some history of a rally between Thanksgiving and Christmas.

One advantage in this example is diversification. We have five different companies in five disparate industries. We have also set an interesting pattern by selecting the same five stocks for all three years, which can give us some insight into any surprises.

1989 Santa Rally Results	
Sell 500 shares of:	
	Profit or loss
Coke for $38.63	$(300)
Disney for $112.00	(6,550)
Exxon for $50.00	1,325
GE for $64.50	1,325
IBM for $94.13	(2,860)
Total	$(7,060)

FIGURE 4: 1989 SANTA RALLY RESULTS. *The results from 1989 were poor.*

Our first year of trading the Santa Claus rally, 1989 (Figure 4), was a disappointment. A loss of $7,060 represents more than 3% of our investment, not a serious loss for most investors but also not much encouragement to try again. The surprise here is the stock market did well in 1989, rising from below 2200 to more than 2500, which is also factoring in the 190-point DJIA correction in October. We will try again in 1990 with the same stock and number of shares.

Success with the Santa Claus rally is selective with individual stocks. Coke (prices here are adjusted for a two-for-one stock split) and Disney were the obvious big losers, with Exxon and GE at almost a tie for largest winners, up $1,450 and $1,325, respectively, a gain of more than 7% in a one-month period.

 look back at more detailed information can help our understanding of what happened. Analysis of the data and information will show us the advantage of taking a closer look than just depending on Santa. Take a look at some earlier price movements on Disney (Figure 5). We bought Disney at one of its highest levels — in fact, we bought the stock at a strong resistance point. Remember, this market was still reeling from a harsh correction in October. Had we seen this graph before the selection, we most likely would have looked for a DJIA stock with a more favorable trend in 1989.

Now take a look at Coke (Figure 6). Our purchase of Coke stock was also at a fairly high level, and we sold the stock at the beginning of a correction. Observing the price action on graphs such as these can give us better understanding of the current situation and help us select more profitable stocks. It is actually the current *situation* we are buying, not the stock.

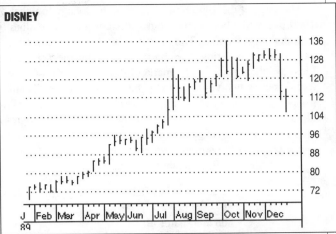

FIGURE 5: *Disney was in an uptrend but near important resistance established from a previous selloff.*

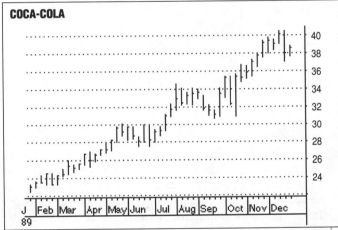

FIGURE 6: *Coke was also in an uptrend without any indication of resistance.*

We only plan to hold the stock for about a month. For the purposes of this speculative activity, we assume the stocks to be of acceptable quality.

We want to profit primarily from the influence of a market move, rather than an individual stock move, although if we are fortunate enough to partake of an individual stock move it will be welcomed.

The results for 1990 are shown in Figure 7.

1990 Santa Rally Results	
Sell 500 shares of:	
	Profit or loss
Coke at $46.50	$10
Disney at $101.50	2,885
Exxon at $51.75	200
GE at $57.38	1,475
IBM at $113.00	(365)
Total	$4,205

FIGURE 7: RESULTS FOR 1990. *The results for 1990 were much better than those for 1989.*

The DJIA of the 1990 holiday season dropped below that of 1989 due to the bear market but still showed a move slightly greater than 100 points. The 1990 bear market might have made us reconsider investing in a Santa Claus rally, but the fact is it was ideal technical timing. The market hit bottom in mid-October and was already on its way up by the time we reached Thanksgiving. The gain of more than $4,000 here represents going along for the ride on a market move that is already in progress.

Note the only losing position was IBM, with Exxon showing some weakness but still in positive territory.

The results for 1991 are shown in Figure 8.

1991 Santa Rally Results	
Sell 500 shares of:	
	Profit or loss
Coke at $80.25	$5,135
Disney at $114.50	4,575
Exxon at $60.88	825
GE at $76.50	5,575
IBM at $89.00	2,050
Total	$14,060

FIGURE 8: RESULTS FOR 1991. *1991 was another improvement over 1989.*

The year 1991 was a great time for the Santa Claus rally, when the DJIA rose more than 274 points. As we saw in Figure 1, this was a rally that continued well into the 1992 trading year. For the first time in three years, we would have exceeded our $10,000 objective in this, our third annual attempt. (We would have earned $14,060, an actual gain of 7.2% in just over a month.) Income investors are often happy to earn this return in a one-year period.

The year was a steady one, with only one sharp correction just after Thanksgiving (see Figure 1) that made the rally here one with some alarming connotations, but the market turned up as quickly as it corrected. The Santa Claus rally of 1991 was also selective. Coke, Disney and General Electric did exceptionally well, but IBM and Exxon fared poorly by comparison.

In three trading sessions, our profits show mixed results:

1989	$(7,060)
1990	4,245
1991	14,060

Our best Santa Claus rally experience also occurred in the best year for the market as a whole. Good market years will often be the best climates for solid holiday rallies. Holiday rallies can be selective, showing good gains with stocks that have been doing well throughout the year, due to technical or fundamental causes. If a stock has shown technical weakness or is at a technical point of strong resistance when we are ready to buy, we should probably let it go in favor of a stock with better technical strength and possibilities.

Our objective stated that we were looking to earn better than $10,000 in a period between the day following Thanksgiving to the end of the year. We intentionally picked stocks without performing analysis and kept the same stocks for all three years, purchasing 500 shares of each stock. This strategy allowed our portfolio to depend on the market move of the Santa Claus rally to pay our profits.

Buying the holiday rally can be a speculative yet profitable experience. Risk can be hedged by further analysis of individual stock trading patterns. Trading pattern information can be found in graphs available from such services as Trendline through Standard & Poor's. Often, further research can do wonders to improve the perspective on the strategy. Maintaining a clear perspective in investing can produce greater profits.

Michael D. Sheimo has been an investor, stockbroker and registered options principal in the Minneapolis area. He has just completed a book on stock selection for John Wiley & Sons, The Stock Selector System, *due out in February 1993.*

REFERENCES

Kaeppel, Jay [1990]. "The January barometer: Myth and reality," *Technical Analysis of* STOCKS & COMMODITIES, Volume 8: July.

Kargenian, Bob [1990]. "'Tis the season," *Technical Analysis of* STOCKS & COMMODITIES, Volume 8: July.

TA

STAN SHAW

Market Turns And Continuation Moves With The Tick Index

The tick index is a little-known indicator that can be used to indicate short-term stock market reversals and provide trend confirmation. Short-term traders should consider using the tick index, for though this indicator does not always tell you a story, it can help alert you to overbought and oversold situations.

by Tim Ord

 little over a year ago, I wrote an article in which I described a buy and sell method using the tick index on the New York Stock Exchange (NYSE). The tick index is the difference between the number of issues trading with the last trade higher (an uptick) from the previous price and the number of issues trading with the last trade lower (a downtick) from the previous price. For example, if exchange X has 500 issues trading on an uptick and 250 issues trading on a downtick, the tick index would be 500 - 250 = 250.

To summarize my method of using the tick index, a buy signal is generated when two intraday 600-plus downtick readings are recorded at approximately the same price level on the Dow Jones Industrial Average (DJIA). These 600-plus downticks should be at least one day apart but not more than 10 days apart. If the market makes a double bottom and the tick index has reached 600 or more downticks at both bottoms, then the *second* reading of 600 or more intraday downticks is a buy signal. For a sell signal, the reverse is true: When the market is making a double top and the tick index readings on both tops intraday exceed 600, then the second reading of 600 or more upticks is the sell signal.

The tick index is useful for a host of other market applications. After years of analyzing the tick index as a market indicator, I have discovered numerous trading rules that are useful in day-to-day trading. Familiarizing yourself with these rules will help you become more aware of market conditions leading to market turns.

TRADING RULES FOR THE TICK INDEX

Here are four trading rules that use the tick index and apply these rules to two recent market moves. The first rule is for a continuation move:

1 The New York tick index records high intraday tick readings (in excess of 600 up- or downticks) and the market closes near the high or low for the day. Further price movement can be inferred from these conditions.

The next three rules are to identify upcoming turning points in the market and confirm trend reversals:

2 When the difference between opening and closing prices become narrow and intraday tick readings exceed 600, a turn in the market is likely.

3 Closing tick index readings that exceed 600 is a sign that a market turn is fast approaching.

4 At breakaways from tops or bottoms, the tick index will usually record high intraday tick readings exceeding 500. This confirms that the trend has reversed and a new trend begun in the opposite direction of the previous trend.

Next, using these four rules, we'll analyze two recent market moves on the June Standard & Poor's futures contract: the December 19, 1991, low and the April 8, 1992, low.

On December 19, 1991 (Figure 1, using the candlestick technique), a downtick reading of 670 was recorded and an

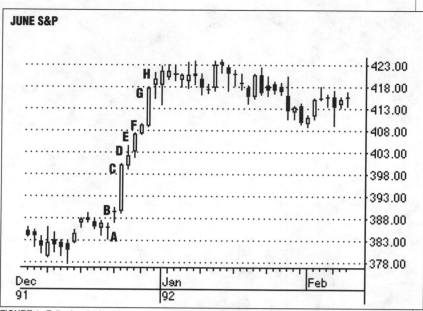

JUNE S&P

FIGURE 1: *Following the intraday and closing readings for the tick indicator can confirm market trends and forewarn of reversals.*

intraday buy signal (A) was generated based on rule 2. The next day (B), the market gapped up, 860 upticks were recorded and the opening and closing range narrowed. As mentioned in rule 4, high tick readings occur on breakouts from tops and bottoms, which turned out to be the case here. Also, the difference between the market's opening and closing range was narrow and

THE CANDLESTICK METHOD

The candlestick chart can be used to interpret the movement of markets from intraday out to a monthly chart format. The basic candlestick chart depicts the market open, high, low and close. The opening and close for the day define the basic body of the candlestick (called the "real body"), while the high and low are the thin lines that extend beyond the body and are known as the "shadows." If the market closes higher than the opening, then the body is empty or white. On those days that the market closes below the opening, then the body is black or filled in.

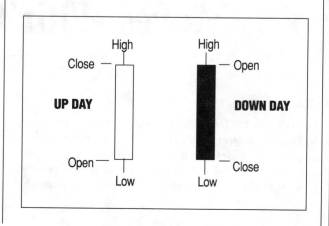

high tick readings were recorded (rule 2), implying a pending top. Here we have a conflict between rules 2 and 4. Experience has taught me that this conflict represents an important market point, so sell stops from the previous buy signal should be tightened and a trader should go with the market direction that follows that trading day.

On Monday, December 23 (C), the conflict is resolved: the June S&P impressively rallied more than 10 points, but only recording 610 upticks intraday and a closing tick reading of +230. Because the market moved up freely and held its gains with high upticks recorded, still higher prices could be expected in the near term, according to rule 1. On December 24 (D), the market kept its momentum but showed signs of stalling, as 710 upticks intraday were recorded but only a two-point gain was achieved. Again, stops should be tightened. The market was closed December 25, while on December 26 (E) the market picked up steam, gaining five points. The uptick reading intraday was only 620. From these conditions we can infer higher prices, because tick readings decreased from the day before while the gains doubled (rule 1).

On December 27 (F), the market gained another two points and the closing tick was 538 upticks. This reading can be considered normal and not a sign of a top. On December 30 (G),

the market made another impressive rally, gaining over eight points and closing on 660 upticks. Such high uptick readings at the close tip us off that a top is approaching (rule 3). The next day, December 31 (H), provides more evidence that a market top is occurring. On December 31, the market opened and closed in a 1-1/2 point range and a closing reading of 796 upticks was recorded (rules 2 and 3). Here, the market traded in a narrow range and closed on an extreme uptick reading exceeding 600, conditions that imply the market has run out of steam — an excellent time to sell positions.

For our second example (Figure 2), the April 8, 1992 (A), low, the tick index method indicated a reversal based on rule 2. The

> **Following and applying these rules using the tick index should help you be able to identify impending market turns and continuation moves.**

intraday reading was 1,000 downticks and the market had a fairly narrow range between the open and closing price. The buy signal method described above states that a buy signal is

"Does 'ho, ho, ho' mean yes or no?"

generated when two intraday 600-plus downtick readings are recorded at approximately the level of the DJIA. The next day, April 9, the market rallied, hitting 750 upticks intraday and closing up eight points on the June S&Ps. Even though high upticks were recorded, the market held its gain, so an impending top was not indicated (rule 1). In addition, at breakaways from tops or bottoms, the tick index will usually record high intraday tick readings exceeding 500 (rule 4).

O n Friday, April 10 (B), the market continued its rally, closing up about 1-1/2 points and hitting 920 upticks. This warned of a possible market top, because the June S&Ps traded in a narrower range than the previous day and on higher upticks (rule 2). On April 13, the June S&Ps were open only part of the day because the Chicago Exchange floor had flooded, precluding trading for that day. The day closed down about 1-1/2 points on 143,000 contracts. No meaningful analyses on market data can be made about the trading that day.

On April 14 (C), the market gapped higher and resumed its advance, closing up 8-1/2 points on the June S&P and hitting 1,000 upticks. Again, no top is indicated because the market held its gain, even though high upticks were recorded (rule 1). As a reminder, however, sell stops should be tightened as a protective measure. On April 15 (D), the market kept its momentum, closing up 3-1/2 points and hitting 450 upticks; again, trailing stops should be raised. On Thursday (E), action did not get into the intraday 600 range, nor did the market stay in a narrow range (rule 1). However, if a stop order had been placed at the previous day's low, the trader would have been stopped out on April 16 for a nice gain. The June S&Ps began to decline from this point. The intraday and closing tick method failed to alert me to a top

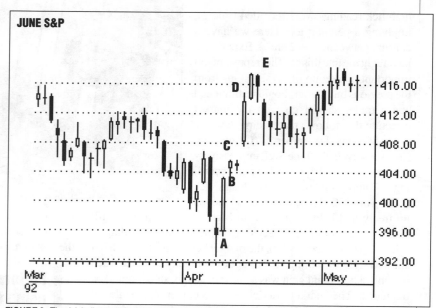

FIGURE 2: *The tick indicator helped identify the April bottom and confirmed the new trend but did not indicate the trend reversal. This is one example of the importance of using trailing stops.*

in the market, which is why stop orders should always be placed with positions.

Following and applying these rules using the tick index should help you be able to identify impending market turns and continuation moves, so that one day you will be able to read the market as you would a book.

Tim Ord, P.O. Box 45, Eagle NE 68347-0045, is president and editor of "The Ord Oracle," an advisory service for OEX options traders.

FURTHER READING

Ord, Tim [1991]. "Picking tops and bottoms with the tick index," *Technical Analysis of* STOCKS & COMMODITIES, Volume 9: June.

Appreciating The Risk Of Ruin

Traders focus on developing trading rules and systems that identify market entry and exit points. A factor that is often overlooked is the percentage of trading capital available that is risked on trades. STOCKS & COMMODITIES contributor and author Nauzer Balsara analyzes the risk of ruin by varying three parameters using a Monte Carlo simulation. The results can help you determine your chances of success.

by Nauzer J. Balsara

A trader is said to be ruined if his or her available capital falls below the minimum required to trade. The risk of ruin is a probability estimate ranging between zero and 1. A probability estimate of 0 suggests that ruin is impossible, whereas an estimate of 1 implies that ruin is assured. The risk of ruin is a function of:

- The probability of success
- The payoff ratio, or the ratio of the average win to the average loss on completed trades
- The fraction of capital exposed to trading.

In its most elementary form, the formula for computing the risk of ruin as defined by statistician William Feller makes two simplifying assumptions: that the payoff ratio is 1 and that the entire capital in the account is risked to trading. Under these assumptions, the risk of ruin (R) is defined as:

$$R = \frac{\left(\frac{q}{p}\right)^a - \left(\frac{q}{p}\right)^k}{\left(\frac{q}{p}\right)^a - 1}$$

where:

a = overall market capitalization
k = trader's capital exposed to trading
p = the probability of success
q = the complementary probability of failure
where:

$$q = (1-p)$$

Assuming the trader's opponent is personified by the market as a whole, a is a very large number compared with k, and hence the term

$$\left(\frac{q}{p}\right)^a$$

tends toward zero, reducing the probability of ruin to

$$\left(\frac{q}{p}\right)^k$$

Note that the risk of ruin in the above formula is directly proportional to the units of capital exposed to trading and inversely proportional to the probability of success. The lower the fraction of capital exposed to trading is, the lower the risk of ruin is. Conversely, the higher the probability of success is, the lower the risk of ruin is.

The formula above is silent regarding the payoff ratio, assuming that the average dollar win is exactly equal to the average dollar loss. When the average win does not equal the average loss, the risk of ruin calculations become more involved. In fact, when the average win is greater than twice the average loss, the differential equations associated with the risk of ruin calculations do not lend themselves to a precise or closed-form solution. Because of this mathematical difficulty, the next best alternative is to simulate the risk of ruin.

SIMULATING THE RISK OF RUIN

The risk of ruin is simulated as a function of three variables:

> p = the probability of success
> k = the percentage of capital exposed to trading
> W = the payoff ratio

For the purposes of the simulation, the probability of success ranges from 0.05 to 0.90 in increments of 0.05. Similarly, the payoff ratio ranges from 1 to 10 in increments of 1. The simulation is based on the premise that a trader risks $1 in each round of trading. This represents $(100/k)\%$ of the initial capital of k. For the present study, the percentage of capital exposed to trading (k) is set at 100%, 50%, 25% and 10%, respectively.

A fraction between zero and 1 is selected at random by a random number generator. If the fraction lies between zero and $(1-p)$, with p being the probability of success, the trade is said to result in a loss of $1. Alternatively, if the fraction is greater than $(1-p)$ but less than 1, then the trade is said to result in a win of W, with W being the payoff ratio, which is added to the capital at the beginning of that round of trading.

Trading continues in a given round until such time as the entire capital accumulated at the start of that round is lost or the initial capital increases 100 times to $100k$, at which stage the risk of ruin is presumed to be negligible. Exiting a trade for either reason marks the end of that round. The simulation is repeated 100,000 times to arrive at the most likely estimate of the risk of ruin for a given set of parameters. The risk of ruin is defined by the fraction of times the available trading capital at the start of a round is lost over the course of 100,000 trials. To simplify the analysis, we will assume that there is no withdrawal of profits from the account.

SIGNIFICANCE OF SIMULATION RESULTS

The simulation results are presented in Figures 1, 2, 3 and 4. As expected, the risk of ruin is directly proportional to the fraction of capital exposed to trading and inversely proportional to the probability of success and the payoff ratio. The risk of ruin is 1 for all payoff ratios less than or equal to 2, regardless of capital exposure, as long as the probability of success is less than or equal to 0.30 (Figures 1, 2, 3 and 4). The risk of ruin drops rapidly as either the probability of success or payoff ratio increases, the magnitude of the drop depending upon the fraction of capital at risk. The risk of ruin falls most rapidly to zero when only 10% of available capital is exposed (Figure 4).

> **As expected, the risk of ruin is directly proportional to the fraction of capital exposed to trading and inversely proportional to the probability of success and the payoff ratio.**

For example, when the probability of success is 0.65 and the payoff ratio is 0.50, the risk of ruin is 1.00 regardless of capital exposure (Figures 1, 2, 3 and 4). When 100% of available capital is exposed to trading, the risk of ruin diminishes to a steady level of 0.349 when the payoff ratio increases to 5 (Figure 1). When 50% of capital is exposed to trading, the risk of ruin dwindles to a constant level of 0.125 when the payoff ratio increases to 4 (Figure 2). With only 25% of capital exposed to trading, the risk of ruin levels off at 0.016 (Figure 3) when the payoff ratio is 3. And finally, when only 10% of capital is exposed to trading, the risk of ruin is reduced to 0.002 when the payoff ratio is just 1 (Figure 4).

PROBABILITY OF SUCCESS

A low probability of success of 0.15 can lead to assured ruin notwithstanding an exceptionally high payoff ratio of 5 and an exposure fraction as low as 10% (Figure 4). Similarly, a low payoff ratio of 0.50 results in assured ruin even if the probability of success is as high as 0.65 and the exposure fraction is a low 10% (Figure 4). What is needed is a reasonably high probability of success coupled with a payoff ratio greater than 1.

Figure 4 shows that the risk of ruin is 0.608 when the probability of success is 0.35, the payoff ratio is 2 and the capital exposed to trading is 10%. The risk of ruin drops dramatically to 0.033 when the probability of success increases to 0.45 (Figure 4)! Small wonder, then, that so much time and money is invested in enhancing the effectiveness of technical trading systems: the probability of success and the payoff ratio are variables that are exclusively trading-system dependent.

However, the capital exposed to trading is yet another critical factor influencing the risk of ruin that ought not to be overlooked. This is a money management consideration that is as important as, if not more important than, the system-dependent factors alluded to above. If the trader risks everything he or she has to a single trade (Figure 1) and the trade does not materialize as expected, there is a 40% probability of being ruined, notwithstanding an astronomical payoff ratio of 10 and a probability of success of 0.60! This should not be ignored by traders in their relentless quest for the ultimate trading system.

A trader can use the simulation results in one of two ways. The trader can assess the risk of ruin for a given exposure level. Alternatively, Figures 1, 2, 3 and 4 can be used to determine the exposure level that will translate into a prespecified risk of ruin. Assume that the probability of success is 0.55 and the payoff ratio is 2. Assume, furthermore, that the trader wishes to risk 50% of capital to open trades at any given time. Figure 2 shows that the associated risk of ruin is 0.289. Assume, then, that the trader is comfortable with a risk of ruin estimate not exceeding 0.10. By the trader working with the same probability of success and payoff ratio, Figure 3 implies that he or she should risk only 25% of available capital instead of the 50% contemplated earlier, giving the trader a more acceptable risk of ruin estimate of 0.082.

CONCLUDING REMARKS

The obsession with enhancing the performance measures of a technical trading system to the total exclusion of money management considerations, embodied in the fraction of capital exposed to trading, can lead to traders' ruin. Traders with superior trading systems may be tempted to discount this as a remote possibility. However, a trader who equates a remote possibility with a zero probability is unlikely to be prepared either financially or emotionally to deal with ruin should it occur.

PROBABILITY OF RUIN TABLES
AVAILABLE CAPITAL = $1; CAPITAL RISKED = $1 OR 100%

PROBABILITY OF SUCCESS				PAYOFF RATIO						
	0.50	0.75	1	2	3	4	5	6	8	10
0.05	1.000	1.000	1.000	1.000	1.000	1.000	1.000	1.000	1.000	1.000
0.10	1.000	1.000	1.000	1.000	1.000	1.000	0.999	0.979	0.923	0.978
0.15	1.000	1.000	1.000	1.000	1.000	0.990	0.926	0.886	0.844	0.894
0.20	1.000	1.000	1.000	1.000	1.000	0.990	0.926	0.886	0.844	0.822
0.25	1.000	1.000	1.000	1.000	0.990	0.887	0.834	0.804	0.775	0.761
0.30	1.000	1.000	1.000	1.000	0.881	0.794	0.756	0.736	0.715	0.705
0.35	1.000	1.000	1.000	0.951	0.778	0.713	0.687	0.671	0.659	0.653
0.40	1.000	1.000	1.000	0.825	0.691	0.647	0.621	0.611	0.602	0.599
0.45	1.000	1.000	1.000	0.714	0.615	0.579	0.565	0.558	0.551	0.550
0.50	1.000	1.000	0.989	0.618	0.541	0.518	0.508	0.505	0.499	0.498
0.55	1.000	1.000	0.819	0.534	0.478	0.463	0.453	0.453	0.453	0.453
0.60	1.000	0.857	0.667	0.457	0.419	0.406	0.402	0.402	0.400	0.400
0.65	1.000	0.648	0.537	0.388	0.363	0.356	0.349	0.349	0.349	0.347
0.70	0.798	0.493	0.430	0.322	0.306	0.300	0.300	0.300	0.300	0.300
0.75	0.557	0.366	0.335	0.266	0.252	0.252	0.252	0.252	0.249	0.249
0.80	0.375	0.263	0.251	0.205	0.201	0.201	0.198	0.198	0.198	0.198
0.85	0.242	0.181	0.175	0.153	0.151	0.151	0.150	0.150	0.150	0.150
0.90	0.135	0.111	0.110	0.101	0.101	0.101	0.101	0.101	0.100	0.100

FIGURE 1: *This table illustrates your chances of ruin if you risk 100% of your capital on each trade. If your probability of success is 0.60 and your expected payoff ratio is 10 times, you still have a 40% chance of ruin.*

PROBABILITY OF RUIN TABLES
AVAILABLE CAPITAL = $2; CAPITAL RISKED = $1 or 50%

PROBABILITY OF SUCCESS				PAYOFF RATIO						
	0.50	0.75	1	2	3	4	5	6	8	10
0.05	1.000	1.000	1.000	1.000	1.000	1.000	1.000	1.000	1.000	1.000
0.10	1.000	1.000	1.000	1.000	1.000	1.000	1.000	1.000	1.000	0.962
0.15	1.000	1.000	1.000	1.000	1.000	1.000	1.000	0.966	0.850	0.798
0.20	1.000	1.000	1.000	1.000	1.000	0.990	0.858	0.781	0.714	0.680
0.25	1.000	1.000	1.000	1.000	0.991	0.789	0.695	0.645	0.601	0.581
0.30	1.000	1.000	1.000	1.000	0.773	0.631	0.572	0.541	0.511	0.500
0.35	1.000	1.000	1.000	0.906	0.606	0.511	0.470	0.451	0.433	0.426
0.40	1.000	1.000	1.000	0.678	0.479	0.416	0.392	0.377	0.366	0.363
0.45	1.000	1.000	1.000	0.506	0.378	0.337	0.321	0.312	0.305	0.302
0.50	1.000	1.000	0.990	0.382	0.295	0.269	0.260	0.253	0.251	0.251
0.55	1.000	1.000	0.672	0.289	0.229	0.212	0.208	0.205	0.203	0.203
0.60	1.000	0.743	0.443	0.208	0.174	0.166	0.161	0.161	0.161	0.159
0.65	1.000	0.434	0.289	0.151	0.130	0.125	0.125	0.125	0.123	0.122
0.70	0.645	0.250	0.185	0.106	0.093	0.090	0.090	0.090	0.090	0.088
0.75	0.321	0.137	0.112	0.071	0.064	0.063	0.063	0.063	0.063	0.063
0.80	0.146	0.071	0.063	0.044	0.042	0.040	0.040	0.040	0.040	0.039
0.85	0.061	0.033	0.032	0.023	0.023	0.023	0.023	0.023	0.023	0.022
0.90	0.019	0.012	0.012	0.010	0.010	0.010	0.010	0.010	0.010	0.010

FIGURE 2: *This table illustrates your chances of ruin if you risk 50% of your capital on each trade. If your expected payoff ratio is twice and your probability of success is 0.60, you have a 20.8% chance of ruin.*

Nauzer Balsara, Ph.D., is a Commodities Trading Advisor and an associate professor of finance at Northeastern Illinois University, Chicago, IL. He is actively involved in futures and options trading. The BASIC/PASCAL programming code used to calculate the tables shown in this article is available upon request. Send $3.00 for postage and handling to Money Management Strategies, PO Box 59592, Chicago, IL 60659-0592.

PROBABILITY OF RUIN TABLES
AVAILABLE CAPITAL = $4; CAPITAL RISKED = $1 or 25%

PROBABILITY OF SUCCESS	PAYOFF RATIO									
	0.50	0.75	1	2	3	4	5	6	8	10
0.05	1.000	1.000	1.000	1.000	1.000	1.000	1.000	1.000	1.000	1.000
0.10	1.000	1.000	1.000	1.000	1.000	1.000	1.000	1.000	1.000	0.926
0.15	1.000	1.000	1.000	1.000	1.000	1.000	1.000	0.936	0.727	0.638
0.20	1.000	1.000	1.000	1.000	1.000	0.990	0.736	0.612	0.503	0.459
0.25	1.000	1.000	1.000	1.000	0.991	0.620	0.487	0.422	0.358	0.337
0.30	1.000	1.000	1.000	1.000	0.599	0.399	0.327	0.290	0.260	0.250
0.35	1.000	1.000	1.000	0.820	0.366	0.264	0.222	0.201	0.187	0.180
0.40	1.000	1.000	1.000	0.458	0.229	0.174	0.152	0.142	0.133	0.130
0.45	1.000	1.000	1.000	0.259	0.142	0.111	0.102	0.097	0.092	0.092
0.50	1.000	1.000	0.990	0.147	0.086	0.072	0.067	0.064	0.063	0.062
0.55	1.000	1.000	0.447	0.082	0.052	0.045	0.044	0.043	0.042	0.041
0.60	1.000	0.564	0.195	0.043	0.030	0.027	0.027	0.025	0.025	0.025
0.65	1.000	0.199	0.083	0.023	0.016	0.016	0.015	0.015	0.015	0.015
0.70	0.431	0.067	0.036	0.011	0.009	0.008	0.008	0.008	0.008	0.008
0.75	0.112	0.022	0.013	0.005	0.004	0.004	0.004	0.004	0.004	0.004
0.80	0.024	0.005	0.004	0.002	0.002	0.002	0.002	0.002	0.002	0.001
0.85	0.004	0.001	0.001	0.001	0.001	0.001	0.001	0.001	0.001	0.001
0.90	0.000	0.000	0.000	0.000	0.000	0.000	0.000	0.000	0.000	0.000

FIGURE 3: *This table illustrates your chances of ruin if you risk 25% of your capital on each trade. If your expected payoff ratio is 4 times and the probability of success is 0.60, you then have a 2.7% chance of ruin.*

REFERENCES
Balsara, Nauzer J. [1992]. *Money Management Strategies for Futures Traders*, John Wiley & Sons.

Feller, William [1950]. *An Introduction to Probability Theory and Its Applications*, Volume I, John Wiley & Sons.

PROBABILITY OF RUIN TABLES
AVAILABLE CAPITAL = $10; CAPITAL RISKED = $1 or 10%

PROBABILITY OF SUCCESS	PAYOFF RATIO									
	0.50	0.75	1	2	3	4	5	6	8	10
0.05	1.000	1.000	1.000	1.000	1.000	1.000	1.000	1.000	1.000	1.000
0.10	1.000	1.000	1.000	1.000	1.000	1.000	1.000	1.000	1.000	0.822
0.15	1.000	1.000	1.000	1.000	1.000	1.000	1.000	0.849	0.449	0.325
0.20	1.000	1.000	1.000	1.000	1.000	0.990	0.467	0.297	0.178	0.144
0.25	1.000	1.000	1.000	1.000	0.990	0.303	0.162	0.113	0.078	0.067
0.30	1.000	1.000	1.000	1.000	0.277	0.102	0.060	0.045	0.034	0.031
0.35	1.000	1.000	1.000	0.608	0.082	0.036	0.023	0.018	0.015	0.014
0.40	1.000	1.000	1.000	0.143	0.025	0.013	0.008	0.008	0.007	0.006
0.45	1.000	1.000	1.000	0.033	0.008	0.004	0.003	0.003	0.002	0.002
0.50	1.000	1.000	0.990	0.008	0.002	0.001	0.001	0.001	0.001	0.001
0.55	1.000	1.000	0.132	0.002	0.001	0.001	0.000	0.000	0.000	0.000
0.60	1.000	0.248	0.017	0.000	0.000	0.000	0.000	0.000	0.000	0.000
0.65	1.000	0.021	0.002	0.000	0.000	0.000	0.000	0.000	0.000	0.000
0.70	0.128	0.001	0.000	0.000	0.000	0.000	0.000	0.000	0.000	0.000
0.75	0.004	0.000	0.000	0.000	0.000	0.000	0.000	0.000	0.000	0.000
0.80	0.000	0.000	0.000	0.000	0.000	0.000	0.000	0.000	0.000	0.000
0.85	0.000	0.000	0.000	0.000	0.000	0.000	0.000	0.000	0.000	0.000
0.90	0.000	0.000	0.000	0.000	0.000	0.000	0.000	0.000	0.000	0.000

FIGURE 4: *This table illustrates your chances of ruin if you risk just 10% of your capital on each trade. If your probability of success is 0.45 and your expected payoff ratio is only twice, your chance of ruin drops to 3.3.*

CHRISTINE MORRISON

Bond Yield Diagnosis

Inflation is usually the first choice for analyzing the forces driving the direction of bond yields, but systems analyst and STOCKS & COMMODITIES *contributor John Kean illustrates that charting government borrowing can help determine the trend of interest rates.*

by John Kean

Bond yields are one financial factor that stands out from the rest in importance. They are a critical item in economic growth, have a particularly strong influence on stock prices and foreign exchange rates and are often used as a metaphor for a country's overall economic and political health. Although bond yields are acknowledged to be important, they are also considered to be hard to explain and even harder to predict. Breaking bond yields down into component parts can help us understand them. Of the factors often mentioned in connection with bond yields, three of the most substantial should be examined in detail: inflation, economic activity and government borrowing.

INFLATION, ECONOMICS, BORROWING
Inflation is most often cited in connection with long-term interest rates. Superficially, this makes good sense. In reality, however, the last 80 years have seen prolonged and sharp departures between U.S. bond yields and inflation rates, and in

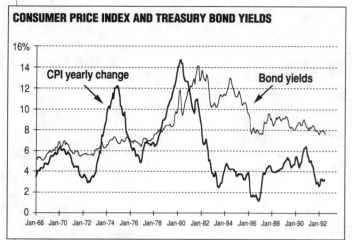

CONSUMER PRICE INDEX AND TREASURY BOND YIELDS

FIGURE 1: *In the last 10 years, the T-bond yields have stayed stubbornly high with low inflation.*

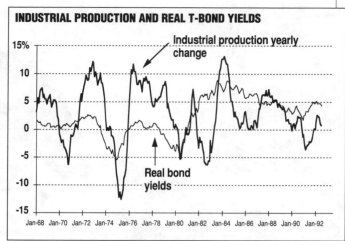

INDUSTRIAL PRODUCTION AND REAL T-BOND YIELDS

FIGURE 2: *Lagging the industrial production figures by six months and comparing to real T-bond yields indicates that the direction of bond yields precedes the direction of the economy by about six months.*

the last few years, the U.S. has been in one of the more pronounced divergences. As Figure 1 shows, inflation has offered only limited explanation, much less prediction, for bond rates over the last 24 years. Number-crunching reveals that highest-grade U.S. bond real yields (that is, yield minus inflation) averaged only 0.81% from 1914 through 1982 and 1.05% from 1950 through 1982. During the 1980s, average real Treasury bond yields expanded to 5.5% from 1983 on, a huge increase. Clearly, culprits other than inflation are at work in determining bond rates.

Because inflation can explain some but not nearly all the levels and permutations in bond rates, let us examine other possible factors that affect real bond yields. It is a common assumption that higher levels of economic activity lead to higher loan demand, in turn lifting interest rates independent of immediate inflation considerations. Figure 2 compares year-on-year changes in industrial production (lagged six months) with real Treasury bond yields. The relationship between them over the last two decades has been poor, to say the least. The closest

correlation indicates that if anything, real bond yield increases tend to precede economic upturns by around six months, rather than vice versa. Economic activity by itself is not much of a harbinger for bonds.

> **The last 80 years have seen prolonged departures between U.S. bond yields and inflation rates, and in the last few years, the U.S. has been in one of the more pronounced divergences. Inflation has offered only limited explanation.**

That brings us to the influence of government borrowing on long-term interest rates. Figure 3 shows a comparison of real bond rates and government deficits (both state and federal) as a percent of gross domestic product (GDP). Seldom in finance

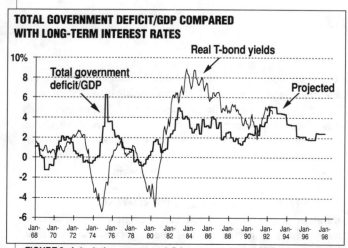

TOTAL GOVERNMENT DEFICIT/GDP COMPARED WITH LONG-TERM INTEREST RATES

FIGURE 3: *A rise in the government deficit as a percentage of GDP has been followed by a rise in interest rates.*

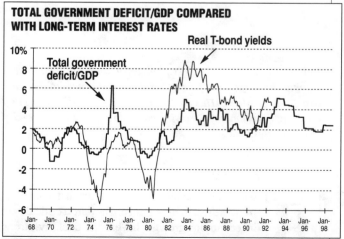

TOTAL GOVERNMENT DEFICIT/GDP COMPARED WITH LONG-TERM INTEREST RATES

FIGURE 4: *Shifting the deficit figures forward by 10 months increases the timeliness of expected changes in interest rates.*

does one get as clear and solid a relationship between two factors as that shown between real bond yields and government deficits. The solid connection between the two is unmistakable if you know what to look for, and yet the relationship between the two gets only muddled recognition. A runup in the deficit as a percent of GDP is an excellent forecaster of higher real bond rates. Likewise, when the ratio decreases, a real yield reversal is ahead.

OF BONDS AND DEFICITS

To further highlight this relationship, the deficit/GDP ratio is shifted forward 10 months in Figure 4. The variations, and to a lesser extent the levels, of real bond yields track quite well. As the government spends more than it takes in, it appropriates cash in the debt market to close the difference, which in turn forces bond yields up. The recent rise in real rates is clearly a product of a rise in the deficit/GDP ratio that began in mid-1989.

For playing the bond market, it appears to be best to keep at least two ideas in mind: deficits and inflation. The major trend in bond yields can be forecast by first looking at recent levels and shifts in the deficit/GDP ratio, lending an advantage to judging where real long-term rates will be heading in the 10-month period ahead. To be even further out in time, various government agencies and branches issue (sometimes politicized) estimates for future budget balances and GDP growth rates, which frequently show up in *The Wall Street Journal*. The second step involves more risk, making an estimate of the inflation trend ahead, which is then combined with that existing for the deficit/GDP ratio to arrive at an estimate for coming movements in nominal bond yields.

For the time ahead, at least, the continued borrowing needs of the federal government has set grounds for a reversal in the latest decline in real bond rates. In any case, as more traders become aware of the importance of government deficits, we should expect the bond market to become increasingly sensitive to news concerning taxes and spending, perhaps shortening the 10-month response time that has characterized the last two decades.

John Kean is a systems analyst and has been investing and trading for more than 10 years. He can be reached at (719) 282-2027 or P.O. Box 26463, Colorado Springs, CO 80932.

ADDITIONAL READING

Chande, Tushar [1992]. "Stocks yield to bonds," STOCKS & COMMODITIES, October.

A Spreadsheet For Time Ratio Analysis

Traders using ratio of time cycle analysis will find this spreadsheet version of determining future target dates of possible cyclical highs or lows helpful. STOCKS & COMMODITIES contributor Robert Miner discusses the use of projected target dates, along with an example of a trade.

by Robert Miner

A s W. D. Gann described more than 70 years ago, markets make swing highs or lows in proportion (relation) to past market cycles. My March 1991 STOCKS & COMMODITIES article, "Time as a trading tool," described the theory and methodology of projecting proportions of past cycles forward in time to determine future dates with the greatest probability of change in trend. Past cycles are proportioned by the most important geometric ratios, and these proportions of past cycles are in turn projected forward. Future changes in trend should coincide with clusters of target dates from proportions of past cycles. Any spreadsheet program, as I will demonstrate, can project the future dates.

Proportioning and projecting forward dates with a spreadsheet program is as easy as dividing a price cycle for retracements or projections. A time projection spreadsheet will simply treat the values as dates instead of prices. A time projection spreadsheet proportions various past cycles and projects the future dates of the proportioned past cycles.

CYCLES, RATIOS, DATES

Three important considerations must be addressed before we construct the time projection spreadsheet: which cycles to project from, what ratios to use and just how to use the projected dates to make a trading decision. First, we must decide which cycles are to be proportioned and projected forward in time. Five cycles are the most important. The symbol on the spreadsheet (Figure 1) to identify the cycle projected follows the name of the cycle (Figure 2):

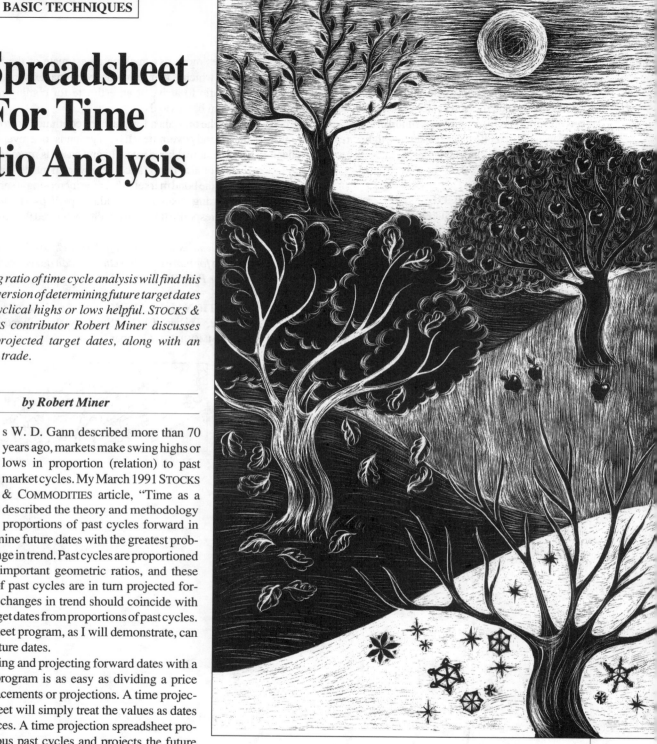

1 *Direct time retracements* (DR): The most recent cycle or the swing into the last pivot point. I call the forward dates from this cycle *direct time retracements*. In Figure 2, this would be the number of days from point 2 to point 1 and then projected forward from point 1.

2 *The prior two alternate cycles* (1st and 2nd alt): These are the prior two swings in the same direction of the current market direction from the last pivot point. The last two alternate cycles are proportioned and the projections made from the last swing point. In Figure 2, the first alternate cycle is the day

KRISTIN TROSTLE

	A	B	C	D	E	F
1		TIME			MARKET	Gold
2		PROJECTIONS			FROM:	9/11/91
3		(UNSORTED)				LOW
4						
5					PRICE	Swing Time
6	SWING	DATE	H/L	PRICE	RANGE	Range-CDs
7						
8	6	8/24/90	H	415.50	-	-
9	5	10/16/90	L	360.50	-55.00	53
10	4	1/16/91	H	406.90	46.40	92
11	3	4/29/91	L	352.60	-54.30	103
12	2	6/10/91	H	375.00	22.40	42
13	1	9/11/91	L	343.00	-32.00	93
14						
15	CYCLES				RATIOS	
17	DR	1-2->			0.382	1.618
18	1st Alt.	3-2 Fr. 1			0.5	1.732
19	2nd Alt.	5-4 Fr. 1			0.618	2
20	C	4-2->			0.707	2.618
21	DC	6-2->			1	3
22					1.414	
23	TARGET					
25	DATE	RATIO	CYCLE			
26						
27	10/16/91	0.382	DR			
28	10/27/91	0.5	DR			
29	11/7/91	0.618	DR			
30	11/15/91	0.707	DR			
31	12/13/91	1	DR			
32	1/20/92	1.414	DR			
33	2/8/92	1.618	DR			
34	2/19/92	1.732	DR			
35	3/15/92	2	DR			
36	5/11/92	2.618	DR			
37	6/16/92	3	DR			
38	9/27/91	0.382	1st Alt.			
39	10/2/91	0.5	1st Alt.			
40	10/6/91	0.618	1st Alt.			
41	10/10/91	0.707	1st Alt.			
42	10/23/91	1	1st Alt.			
43	11/9/91	1.414	1st Alt.			
44	11/17/91	1.618	1st Alt.			
45	11/22/91	1.732	1st Alt.			
46	12/4/91	2	1st Alt.			
47	12/29/91	2.618	1st Alt.			
48	1/15/92	3	1st Alt.			
49	10/16/91	0.382	2nd Alt.			
50	10/27/91	0.5	2nd Alt.			
51	11/6/91	0.618	2nd Alt.			
52	11/15/91	0.707	2nd Alt.			
53	10/16/91	1	2nd Alt.			
54	10/27/91	1.414	2nd Alt.			
55	2/6/92	1.618	2nd Alt.			
56	2/17/92	1.732	2nd Alt.			
57	3/13/92	2	2nd Alt.			
58	5/8/92	2.618	2nd Alt.			
59	6/13/92	3	2nd Alt.			
60	8/4/91	0.382	C			
61	8/21/91	0.5	C			
62	9/7/91	0.618	C			
63	9/20/91	0.707	C			
64	11/2/91	1	C			
65	1/1/92	1.414	C			
66	1/30/92	1.618	C			
67	2/16/92	1.732	C			
68	1/10/93	2	DC			
69	7/8/93	2.618	DC			
70	10/27/93	3	DC			
71	9/28/91	0.382	DC			
72	11/2/91	0.5	DC			
73	12/6/91	0.618	DC			
74	1/1/92	0.707	DC			
75	3/26/92	1	DC			
76	7/24/92	1.414	DC			
77	9/21/92	1.618	DC			
78	10/24/92	1.732	DC			
79	1/10/93	2	DC			
80	7/8/93	2.618	DC			
81	10/27/93	3	DC			

FIGURE 1: TARGET DATE SPREADSHEET.
Here is an example of the target date spreadsheet with the target dates unsorted.

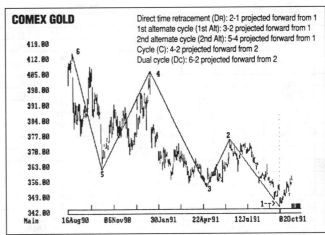

FIGURE 2: *The five cycles of intermediate degree going into gold's September 11, 1991, low.*

count from point 3 to point 2 and projected forward from point 1. The second alternate cycle is the day count from point 5 to point 4 and projected from point 1.

3 The prior cycle (C): If the last pivot point was a low, the prior cycle would be the last high - high. If the last pivot point was a high, the prior cycle would be the last low - low. In Figure 2, this would be the day counts between points 4 and 2 and projected from 2.

4 The prior dual cycle (Dc): If the last pivot point was a low, the prior dual cycle would be the period from the last high to the third high back or the dual or double cycle of similar degree. From a high pivot, the prior dual cycle would be the period from the last to the third prior low. In Figure 2, this would be the day count from point 6 to point 2 and projected from point 2.

These are the five most important cycles to consider from a swing high or low. While the time projection spreadsheet that I use includes a total of 10 different cycle relationships, first we must concentrate on the most important cycles. The time projection spreadsheet shown includes only the five cycles described.

Figure 2 is a chart of the five swings of intermediate degree going into the September 11, 1991, low in gold. These

are the cycle highs and lows that are projected forward to arrive at the target dates.

The second consideration is which ratios to use. Literally dozens of geometric ratios can be found in the time and price analysis of markets. If we used them all, we would have many target projections for every day in the following months. It is important to use only those ratios that are consistently reliable for time analysis. The Figure 1 spreadsheet includes those most important ratios. The ratios in bold (2.618, 1.618, 1, 0.618, 0.5) on the spreadsheet are of primary importance. A future cluster of dates should not be considered valid unless one or more of the bold ratios of past cycles are in the future time cluster. The ratio time projections not in bold should be considered to be confirming time factors.

The third consideration is how to use the projected periods of clusters of target dates. This time projection information is valid only if it can help us prepare to make a trading decision.

Two factors should be kept in mind:

1 Using the cycle relationships described in the first consideration, we should regard the future dates as a potential change in trend opposite to the last swing point. If the last swing point was a cycle low, the future dates are only valid as a potential cycle high. If the last swing point was a cycle high, the future dates are only valid as a potential cycle low.

2 The time projections must be used in the context of the price and pattern position of the market.

SPREADSHEET INSTRUCTIONS

Figure 1 is a spreadsheet that will project all the target dates by all the ratios and cycle relationships by simply entering the date and price of the prior six swing highs and lows. The target dates in this spreadsheet have not yet been sorted. The dates are then sorted chronologi-

	A	B	C	D	E	F
1		TIME			MARKET:	Gold
2		PROJECTIONS			FROM:	9/11/91
3						LOW
4						
5					PRICE	Swing Time
6	SWING	DATE	H/L	PRICE	RANGE	Range-CDs
7						
8	6	8/24/90	H	415.50	-	-
9	5	10/16/90	L	360.50	-55.00	53
10	4	1/16/91	H	406.90	46.40	92
11	3	4/29/91	L	352.60	-54.30	103
12	2	6/10/91	H	375.00	22.40	42
13	1	9/11/91	L	343.00	-32.00	93
14						
15	CYCLES			RATIOS		
16						
17	DR	1-2->		0.382	1.618	
18	1st Alt.	3-2 Fr. 1		0.5	1.732	
19	2nd Alt.	5-4 Fr. 1		0.618	2	
20	C	4-2->		0.707	2.618	
21	DC	6-2->		1	3	
22	Target			1.414		
23						
24	DATE	RATIO	CYCLE			
26	10/2/91	0.5	1st Alt.			
27	10/6/91	0.618	1st Alt.			
28	10/10/91	0.707	1st Alt.			
29	10/16/91	0.382	2nd Alt.			
30	10/16/91	0.382	DR			
31	10/23/91	1	1st Alt.	Oct. 23-27		
32	10/27/91	0.5	2nd Alt.			
33	10/27/91	0.5	DR			
34	11/2/91	1	C	Nov. 2-7		
35	11/2/91	0.5	DC			
36	11/6/91	0.618	2nd Alt.			
37	11/7/91	0.618	DR			
38	11/9/91	1.414	1st Alt.			
39	11/15/91	0.707	2nd Alt.			
40	11/15/91	0.707	DR			
41	11/17/91	1.618	1st Alt.			
42	11/22/91	1.732	1st Alt.			
43	12/4/91	2	1st Alt.	Dec. 4-13		
44	12/6/91	0.618	DC	Top made Dec. 9.		
45	12/12/91	1	2nd Alt.			
46	12/13/91	1	DR			
47	12/29/91	2.618	1st Alt.			
48	1/1/92	1.414	C			
49	1/1/92	0.707	DC			
50	1/15/92	3	1st Alt.			
51	1/19/92	1.414	2nd Alt.			
52	1/20/92	1.414	DR			
53	1/30/92	1.618	C			

FIGURE 3: TARGET DATE SPREADSHEET. *The target dates have been sorted chronologically by date. Look for clusters of dates that include the important concentrations.*

cally (Figure 3) and the trader may then quickly scan the target dates for clusters of dates that fall within narrow time periods. The formulas used in the spreadsheet are shown in Figure 4.

1 Enter the swing date, H or L symbol and the price of the current pivot and the prior five pivots. Choose the degree of swing desired: minor, intermediate or primary.

2 All the future target dates related to the ratios are projected under the target date heading.

3 Sort the target dates in chronological order. Delete any of the early or later dates that may not fall into the parameters of the typical period of the swings of the degree chosen.

4 Under the list of ratios used, those in bold tend to be the most reliable for all markets. They will also be shown in bold under the target dates for easy identification.

5 Scan the projected dates and note if there is a cluster of target dates in any month (particularly those in bold) that fall in a fairly narrow time zone. These will be the periods that have the highest probability of a change in trend of the degree of the swings chosen. The target dates must fall in an obvious cluster to be a valid potential change in trend period.

PROJECTIONS FROM 9/11/91 GOLD LOW

The target date clusters must not be used indiscriminately. As we are projecting from an intermediate-term low, ideally they will point to the next intermediate-term top. The target date clusters will only be relevant as a potential for trend change if the market is making a high. The position of the market relative to price and pattern will help qualify if the market is likely to make a trend reversal as it advances into a projected period.

> **By integrating ratio time analysis into your trading plan, you will have a much greater opportunity to make successful trades and understand the position of the market at any time.**

In the four and a half months from the September 11, 1991, low through February 1, 1992, only three time periods were indicated as a potential for a high: October 23-27, November 2-7 and December 4-13, 1991. Since none of the past five swings exceeded 103 days and historical analysis of the gold market shows that intermediate-term swings rarely last more than 110 days, an intermediate-term high would most likely be made prior to February 1, 1992, with the greatest probability occurring within one of the three time periods as indicated by the target date clusters on the spreadsheet.

The prior five intermediate-degree swings lasted from 42 to 103 days in length. After all the target dates were sorted, those dates before October 1 and after January 30 were deleted. The first cluster of bold dates falls in the period of October 23-27, just 42-46 days following the September 11th low, falling within the minimum parameters of past swings of similar degree. The market had made a high on October 21 and had begun to decline (Figure 5). The October 23-27th period would be ignored, as the market was not advancing into the period. The time projections are only valid as potential highs.

	A	B	C	D	E	F
1	TIME				MARKET:	Gold
2	PROJECTIONS				FROM:	32030
3	(FORMULAS)					LOW
4						
5					PRICE	Swing Time
6	SWING H/L	DATE		PRICE	RANGE	Range-CDs
8	6	31647	H	415.5	-	-
9	5	31700	L	360.5	=D9-D8	=B9-B8
10	4	31792	H	406.9	=D10-D9	=B10-B9
11	3	31895	L	352.6	=D11-D10	=B11-B10
12	2	31937	H	375	=D12-D11	=B12-B11
13	1	32030	L	343	=D13-D12	=B13-B12
15	CYCLES PROJECTED			RATIOS USED		
17	Dir.R	1-2->		0.382	1.618	
18	1st Alt.	3-2 Fr. 1		0.5	1.732	
19	2nd Alt.	5-4 Fr. 1		0.618	2	
20	C	4-2->		0.707	2.618	
21	DC	6-2->		1	3	
22				1.414		
25	TARGET DATE	RATIO	CYCLE			
27	=$D$17*$F$13+$B$13	=$D$17	=$A$17			
28	=$D$18*$F$13+$B$13	=$D$18	=$A$17			
29	=$D$19*$F$13+$B$13	=$D$19	=$A$17			
30	=$D$20*$F$13+$B$13	=$D$20	=$A$17			
31	=$D$21*$F$13+$B$13	=$D$21	=$A$17			
32	=$D$22*$F$13+$B$13	=$D$22	=$A$17			
33	=$E$17*$F$13+$B$13	=$E$17	=$A$17			
34	=$E$18*$F$13+$B$13	=$E$18	=$A$17			
35	=$E$19*$F$13+$B$13	=$E$19	=$A$17			
36	=$E$20*$F$13+$B$13	=$E$20	=$A$17			
37	=$E$21*$F$13+$B$13	=$E$21	=$A$17			
38	=$F$12*$D$17+$B$13	=$D$17	=$A$18			
39	=$F$12*$D$18+$B$13	=$D$18	=$A$18			
40	=$F$12*$D$19+$B$13	=$D$19	=$A$18			
41	=$F$12*$D$20+$B$13	=$D$20	=$A$18			
42	=$F$12*$D$21+$B$13	=$D$21	=$A$18			
43	=$F$12*$D$22+$B$13	=$D$22	=$A$18			
44	=$F$12*$E$17+$B$13	=$E$17	=$A$18			
45	=$F$12*$E$18+$B$13	=$E$18	=$A$18			
46	=$F$12*$E$19+$B$13	=$E$19	=$A$18			
47	=$F$12*$E$20+$B$13	=$E$20	=$A$18			
48	=$F$12*$E$21+$B$13	=$E$21	=$A$18			
49	=$F$10*$D$17+$B$13	=$D$17	=$A$19			
50	=$F$10*$D$18+$B$13	=$D$18	=$A$19			
51	=$F$10*$D$19+$B$13	=$D$19	=$A$19			
52	=$F$10*$D$20+$B$13	=$D$20	=$A$19			
53	=$F$10*$D$17+$B$13	=$D$21	=$A$19			
54	=$F$10*$D$18+$B$13	=$D$22	=$A$19			
55	=$F$10*$E$17+$B$13	=$E$17	=$A$19			
56	=$F$10*$E$18+$B$13	=$E$18	=$A$19			
57	=$F$10*$E$19+$B$13	=$E$19	=$A$19			
58	=$F$10*$E$20+$B$13	=$E$20	=$A$19			
59	=$F$10*$E$21+$B$13	=$E$21	=$A$19			
60	=($B$12-$B$10)*$D$17+$B$12	=$D$17	=$A$20			
61	=($B$12-$B$10)*$D$18+$B$12	=$D$18	=$A$20			
62	=($B$12-$B$10)*$D$19+$B$12	=$D$19	=$A$20			
63	=($B$12-$B$10)*$D$20+$B$12	=$D$20	=$A$20			
64	=($B$12-$B$10)*$D$21+$B$12	=$D$21	=$A$20			
65	=($B$12-$B$10)*$D$22+$B$12	=$D$22	=$A$20			
66	=($B$12-$B$10)*$E$17+$B$12	=$E$17	=$A$20			
67	=($B$12-$B$10)*$E$18+$B$12	=$E$18	=$A$20			
68	=($B$12-$B$8)*$E$19+$B$12	=$E$19	=$A$21			
69	=($B$12-$B$8)*$E$20+$B$12	=$E$20	=$A$21			
70	=($B$12-$B$8)*$E$21+$B$12	=$E$21	=$A$21			
71	=($B$12-$B$8)*$D$17+$B$12	=$D$17	=$A$21			
72	=($B$12-$B$8)*$D$18+$B$12	=$D$18	=$A$21			
73	=($B$12-$B$8)*$D$19+$B$12	=$D$19	=$A$21			
74	=($B$12-$B$8)*$D$20+$B$12	=$D$20	=$A$21			
75	=($B$12-$B$8)*$D$21+$B$12	=$D$21	=$A$21			
76	=($B$12-$B$8)*$D$22+$B$12	=$D$22	=$A$21			
77	=($B$12-$B$8)*$E$17+$B$12	=$E$17	=$A$21			
78	=($B$12-$B$8)*$E$18+$B$12	=$E$18	=$A$21			
79	=($B$12-$B$8)*$E$19+$B$12	=$E$19	=$A$21			
80	=($B$12-$B$8)*$E$20+$B$12	=$E$20	=$A$21			
81	=($B$12-$B$8)*$E$21+$B$12	=$E$21	=$A$21			

FIGURE 4: TARGET DATE SPREADSHEET FORMULAS. *Here are the formulas used in the spreadsheet for calculating the target dates.*

The next cluster of bold dates fell on November 2-7 (but the second and the third was a weekend). The market was declining into that period, so the projected time period was not relevant as an indication of the termination of the trend from September 11, 1991.

The next and final time zone that was an important period for the termination of the rally fell a month later on December 4-13. Of the three periods to date, this period would be the most important for a potential high. It included the 2X and 1X projections of the two prior alternate cycles, a 0.618 ratio of the prior dual cycle (H-H) and the 100% time retracement of the prior cycle. On Monday, December 9, gold made a reversal day for the final top of the advance from the September 11th low.

The reversal day of December 9 fell in the price resistance zone of a 62-67% retracement level, plus using Elliott wave analysis; this rally was the fifth wave of a C wave. All the pieces had come together in just one of the three periods in a time of four and a half months with the greatest probability of terminating the advance from the September 11th low. Time, price, pattern and daily reversal signals all indicated trend termination. It is very important to note that the only time signal that was valid in the period of four and a half months fell in the December 4-13th projected period. Of the three periods, that was the only period that the market was making a new high.

Another factor to note is that the market made a new high precisely at the 62% retracement level on November 11. Traders who only look at price relationships may have considered this the final high. However, this high was not made in a time projection for a top and the pattern was not complete. Termina-

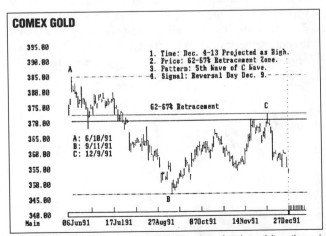

FIGURE 5: *Trends will not terminate until all dimensions of market activity — time, price and pattern — terminate. The gold market made a new high at the 62% retracement level on November 11, but this high was not made in a projected period for a high and the pattern was not complete. On December 9, all the pieces fell together to indicate termination of the advance. Time had terminated with an important price resistance zone with a completed pattern and reversal signal. This was the first set-up of time, price and pattern termination since the low of September 11.*

tion of trend will not occur unless *all* dimensions of market activity terminate, including time, price and pattern. Be wary of making a trading decision from the information of only one or two dimensions of market activity, because trend will simply not terminate until time is up.

A new time projection spreadsheet would be run as soon as the December 9th high was confirmed to project the periods after that high with the best probability of making an intermediate-term low.

FACTORS TO KEEP IN MIND

1 It is important to use a fairly small series of the most important ratios. If a large series of geometric ratios are used instead, there will be one or more target dates on just about every day of each month after the last swing pivot. It is easy to show multiple time ratio projections at every minor swing pivot when using a large number of ratios indiscriminately. For this time projection technique to be of practical value, the trader must have only a few well-defined periods that are determined well in advance. Anything else is analysis after the fact.

2 The projected time periods are primarily relevant for projecting the termination of the trend from the last swing point recorded. Do not fall into the trap of thinking every cluster of target dates will result in a change in trend, whether the market is making a high or low.

3 A thorough study of the cycle ratios at past swing points will reveal that individual markets have particular time ratios that are peculiar to that market. When you discover those ratios, you may easily add them to your spreadsheet. For our purposes, I have just included the ratios that are the most consistent throughout all markets.

4 The time projections may be performed from swings of various degrees including intraday periods. Just as Elliott wave analysis looks at smaller and smaller degrees of pattern to confirm the position of the market at any time from a larger degree, hourly charts of time ratio projections will confirm

the daily charts of intermediate-term degree. From the spreadsheet standpoint, the formulas are much more complex if entering less than daily periods, as you must take into consideration the intraday time period chosen, hours of trading, non-trading days and so forth. I have kept things simple for this example and stayed with daily bars and intermediate-term swings that usually last at least 30 days.

5 Last but most important: The time projection clusters must not be used out of context of the price and pattern position of the market. Do not blindly make a trade because the market is moving into a time projection. Price and pattern analysis, as well as a reversal signal, must also be present to indicate the termination of the trend.

By integrating ratio time analysis into your trading plan, you will have a much greater opportunity to make successful trades and understand the position of the market at any time. Remember, a trend change will not occur until *time is up*.

Robert Miner is a private trader and the author of the W. D. Gann Trading Techniques Home Study Course. *Miner also publishes the "Major Market Analysis Report," a monthly report of time and price analysis. Gann/Elliott Educators, 6336 N. Oracle, Suite 326-346, Tucson, AZ 85704, (602) 797-3668.*

ADDITIONAL READING

Gilmore, Bryce [1992]. *Geometry of Markets,* Gann/Elliott Educators, 2d edition.

Miner, Robert [1991]. "Form and pattern as a trading tool," *Technical Analysis of* STOCKS & COMMODITIES, Volume 9: May.

_____ [1991]. "Price as a trading tool," *Technical Analysis of* STOCKS & COMMODITIES, Volume 9: April.

_____ [1991]. "Time as a trading tool," *Technical Analysis of* STOCKS & COMMODITIES, Volume 9: March.

_____ [1989]. "Time, price, pattern," *Technical Analysis of* STOCKS & COMMODITIES, Volume 7: May.

_____ . *W.D. Gann Trading Techniques Home Study Course,* Gann/Elliott Educators.

TA

Looking At Momentum With TRIX

The TRIX oscillator has unique properties that make it ideal for identifying direction of trend as well as cyclical entry points. Last month, Ed Downs showed us how various oscillators can be tuned to the personality of an individual stock through optimization. This month, he'll explain the use of a derivative technique using the TRIX oscillator.

by Ed Downs

If you smooth an exponential moving average (EMA) of the closing price twice (taking the EMA of the EMA of the EMA) and then plot the percentage change per period on the *y*-axis, you'll have one version of the TRIX. The original TRIX is the one-day difference of the triple exponentially smoothed log of the closing prices. This value is then multiplied by 10,000 to aid in plotting the line. The two different methods will plot virtually identical curves.

The calculations for TRIX found in MetaStock Professional can be represented as:

$$E1 = \text{EMA}(d,p) \qquad d = \text{initial data array (that is, close)}$$
$$E2 = \text{EMA}(E1,p) \qquad p = \text{period of moving average}$$
$$E3 = \text{EMA}(E2,p)$$
$$\text{TRIX} = ((E3(\text{today})\text{-}E3(\text{yesterday}))/E3(\text{yesterday}))(100)$$

where EMA(d,p) represents the exponential moving average of data values *d* over *p* time periods.

To understand how TRIX works, we can look at a progressive development of the indicator. The first part of Figure 1 shows E1 (from the formulas above) for 14 days. The second part of Figure 1 plots E2 for 14 days, and the third part of Figure 1 depicts E3 for 14 days. Each time we take an exponentially smoothed moving average of the previous value, we get a smoother curve. That's what triple smoothing is supposed to do for us—filter out all the cycles that are less than the value of our exponential moving average period (in this case, 14 days).

If we take E3 and plot the daily percentage rate of change, we get TRIX as shown in Figure 2. Because TRIX represents the percentage change in the smoothed average, positive values indicate a rising trend and negative values indicate a falling one. Trades are placed when the TRIX indicator changes direction, which is normally detected using a moving average crossover system. We buy when TRIX goes above its moving average to the upside and sell when it goes below the moving average. Using MetaStock's system tester, we get the trades shown in Figure 2. (See sidebar, "TRIX momentum in MetaStock," for details on system testing.)

> ## We can define a system test in which trades are taken on peak reversals of TRIX momentum above and below an arbitrary signal level. The arrows in Figure 3 show the results of such a test.

We see the result. Not bad! The TRIX oscillator does a decent job of identifying significant turning points in the stock. However, quite a few of the trades are two to five days late. This lag is one of the problems inherent in moving average-based trading systems. Notice, though, how smoothly TRIX transits from up to down. The curve is smooth because TRIX is the rate of change of the triple-smoothed EMA. Consider what would happen if we plotted the rate of change or momentum of TRIX from one day to the next. We can define a simple TRIX momentum formula as:

$$\text{TRIX momentum} = \text{TRIX}_{today} - \text{TRIX}_{yesterday}$$

This formula is plotted in Figure 3. The peaks represent points where the day-to-day momentum reaches a maximum (plus or minus). In other words, these are the points at which the TRIX value is slowing down in its current direction. Trading these points will give us an early signal because we're catching the place where TRIX is running out of steam before it reverses. In mathematical terms, the TRIX momentum is the second derivative of the triple-smoothed moving average.

We can define a system test in which trades are taken on peak reversals of TRIX momentum above and below an arbitrary signal level. The arrows in Figure 3 show the results of such a test. Now compare the trades in Figures 2 and 3. In virtually every case, the trades generated by TRIX momentum are earlier — in some cases by as much as a week!

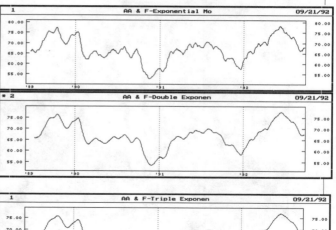

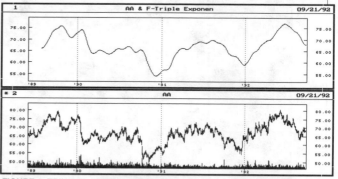

FIGURE 1: TRIX AND ALCOA. *The top plot shows E1, the 14-day exponential moving average of closing prices of Alcoa, followed by plots of E2 and E3. The stock itself is shown at the bottom.*

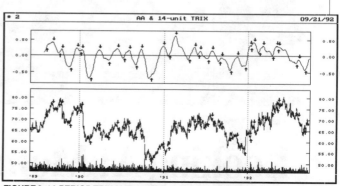

FIGURE 2: 14-PERIOD TRIX AND ALCOA. *Classic TRIX trading system using a 14-period TRIX and three-period moving average. The arrows illustrate buy and sell signals as determined by a crossover of the TRIX indicator and three-day moving average.*

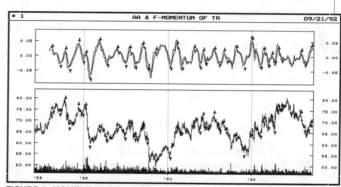

FIGURE 3: MOMENTUM OF 14-DAY TRIX. *Trading signals occur sooner using TRIX momentum.*

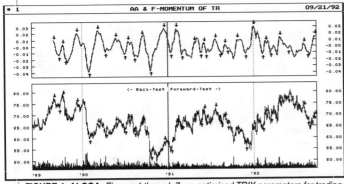

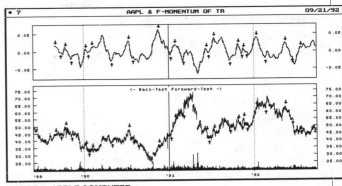

FIGURE 4: ALCOA. *Figures 4 through 7 are optimized TRIX parameters for trading.*

FIGURE 5: APPLE COMPUTER

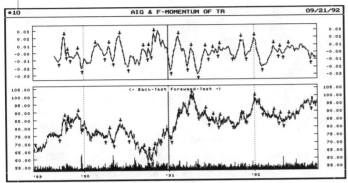

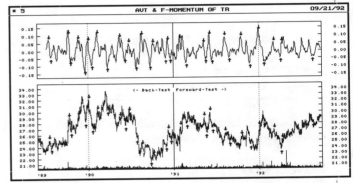

FIGURE 6: AMERICAN INTERNATIONAL GROUP

FIGURE 7: AVNET

TRIX MOMENTUM AND PRICE CYCLES

Last month, I explained that oscillator cycles can be determined using data from the immediate past to find high-probability trades in the immediate future. How does this apply to the period used in the TRIX calculation?

Figures 4 through 7 show four stocks (Alcoa, Apple Computer, American International Group and Avnet) that have been optimized in a back test and then forward tested. In studying these figures, two phenomena related to the stocks' personali-

ties surface. First, in each case, the forward test tends to correlate with the back test — that is, approximately the same quantity and quality of trades were generated in both time periods. This lends credence to the idea that a stock's personality persists over time.

Second, as with other oscillators, TRIX momentum works better on some stocks than others. Obviously, Alcoa (AA) was a superb candidate for this approach. On the other hand, Apple Computer (AAPL) tends to trend more, so the oscillator trading

TRIX MOMENTUM IN METASTOCK

MetaStock Professional users may find the following profit systems helpful. The basic TRIX trading system illustrated in Figure 2 is defined as follows:

Trix profit system with optimized period
Enter long:
    when(ref(trix(OPT1),-1),<,mov(trix(OPT1),3,E))
    AND when(trix(OPT1),>=,mov(trix(OPT1),3,E))

Enter short:
    when(ref(trix(OPT1),-1),>,mov(trix(OPT1),3,E))
    AND when(trix(OPT1),<=,mov(trix(OPT1),3,E))

(Note: All the information under "Enter long" and "Enter short" above fits on one line in MetaStock's System Tester.)

OPT1 : TRIX periods {5,21,4}
    Min = 5; Max = 21; Step = 4

The TRIX momentum profit system is considerably more complex, because the optimization parameters (OPT1) need to be included in the system definition. If you are entering this into MetaStock, be sure to copy it exactly.

Momentum of TRIX profit system with optimized period
Enter long:
    when(trix(OPT1)-ref(trix(OPT1),-1),<,0)
    AND when(mov(trix(OPT1)-ref(trix(OPT1),-1),3,S),<,trix(OPT1)-ref(trix(OPT1),-1))

Enter short:
    when(trix(OPT1)-ref(trix(OPT1),-1),>,0)
    AND when(mov(trix(OPT1)-ref(trix(OPT1),-1),3,S), >,trix(OPT1)-ref(trix(OPT1),-1))

OPT1 : TRIX periods {5,21,4}
Min = 5; Max = 21; Step = 4

---

signals were less reliable. Again, each stock's personality determines its propensity to trade successfully using the oscillator.

CONCLUSION

As an indicator, TRIX momentum can alert traders to an early trading opportunity. By optimizing TRIX over past time periods for each stock in our database and then screening for TRIX momentum trading signals, we can identify opportunities that can be verified for trend direction and for confirmation by other oscillators. As with all indicators, some stocks work better than others. Since stocks tend to repeat their behavior in the future, we are provided with an even greater degree of predictive value.

Ed Downs has been studying the stock market and trading for 12 years. He holds bachelor's and master's degrees in engineering from the University of Texas and is president of Nirvana Systems, Inc., which specializes in automation of trading technology for individual investors using MetaStock Professional and other software.

REFERENCES

Downs, Ed [1992]. "Fine-tuning oscillators," STOCKS & COMMODITIES, November.

Raff, Gilbert [1992]. "Exponentially smoothing the daily number of declines," STOCKS & COMMODITIES, January.

MIKE HORSWILL

On Index Funds

Do mutual funds underperform the market? Statistics would indicate so. Stephen Littauer suggests that index funds would better suit the investors' needs.

by Stephen Littauer

Most mutual funds underperform the market. Over the past 10 years, CDA/Wiesenberger Mutual Funds Update reports that 356 mutual funds with an investment objective of long-term growth had an average annual return of 15.8%. The equivalent annual return for the Standard & Poor's 500 index during the same period was 19.1%. Was the difference of 3.3% a fluke or statistical error? Let's look at figures from additional sources.

Morningstar Mutual Funds service reports that over the same 10-year period, 534 U.S. diversified equity mutual funds had an average annualized total return of 15.95%, compared with 19.1% for the S&P 500 and 18.2% for the Wilshire 5000 index, which is a measure of the total U.S. stock market. Returns for the one-, three- and five-year time frames also trailed both indices. In fact, according to the Vanguard Group, one of the largest mutual fund managers in the U.S., the S&P 500 outperformed

76% of all general equity mutual funds over the past five years as of March 31, 1992.

The evidence is compelling. Over time, the broad stock market indices have consistently outperformed the average general equity mutual fund. As can be seen in Figure 1 with data from Lipper Analytical Services, the total return (capital change plus income) of the Wilshire 5000 was +344.3% over the 10-year period ended December 31, 1991. During the same period, the average general equity fund had a total return of 286.1%.

TOTAL RETURN FOR 10 YEARS (12/31/91)		
	Cumulative	Annual rate
Wilshire 5000	+344.3%	+16.1%
Average General Equity Fund	+286.1	+14.5

FIGURE 1: *The broad stock market indices have outperformed the average general equity mutual fund.*

The failure to match or exceed the performance of the major indices extends to virtually all mutual fund groups regardless of investment objective. With three exceptions, Figure 2 shows that all fund groups underperformed the market over four different time periods, using data from CDA/Wiesenberger Mutual Funds Update.

PERFORMANCE RESULTS THROUGH JULY 31, 1992					
		Annualized Total Return (Years)			
# Funds	Fund groups	1	3	5	10
101	Maximum Capital Gain	10.8	7.9	6.3	12.9
58	Small Company Growth	10.5	10.1	8.5	14.6
142	International Equity	1.5	1.3	2.9	16.2
356	Long-Term Growth	11.2	9.2	7.9	15.
8	Growth & Current Income	12.1	8.6	8.2	15.9
55	Balanced	12.8	9.0	8.3	15.8
64	Equity Income	13.8	8.1	8.1	15.8
	S&P 500 Index	12.7	10.6	9.5	19.1
	Wilshire 5000	13.2	9.9	9.0	18.28

FIGURE 2: *Virtually all fund groups underperformed the market over four different time periods.*

Balanced funds, on average, slightly outperformed the S&P 500 but not the Wilshire 5000 for one year, and equity income funds outperformed both the S&P 500 and Wilshire 5000 for the same period. In the only other exception, small company growth funds outpaced the Wilshire 5000 but not the S&P 500 over the past three years.

MARKET MAJORITY

Why do the majority of mutual funds underperform the market? After all, they *are* run by professional investment managers with access to comprehensive investment and economic data on which to base their decisions. The major factor, besides general investment manager competence, relates to the expense ratio and transaction costs. Costs in the expense ratio include advisory fees, distribution charges and operating expenses. Transaction costs include brokerage and other trading costs.

Typical conventional stock mutual funds have average costs from these two sources of approximately 2% of investor assets. The average general equity fund has an annual expense ratio of 1.3% of investor assets. Traditionally, mutual fund managers have high portfolio activity. According to data from Lipper, the average fund's portfolio turnover rate is 90% per year. The trading costs implicit with this portfolio activity may be expected to subtract another 0.5% to 1% annually from a fund's total return. Funds that charge sales commissions use up even more of the returns. So conventional mutual fund investors have their total returns reduced by the expense ratio, transaction costs and, in many cases, sales charges.

> **Why do the majority of mutual funds underperform the market? After all, they are run by professional investment managers with access to comprehensive investment and economic data on which to base their decisions.**

INVESTORS VS MANAGERS: INDEXING

What if it were possible for an investor to buy the entire market? Suppose that an investor could buy and hold all the stocks in the S&P 500 or some other index of choice. If this could be done with low-enough transaction and administration costs, it should be theoretically possible to obtain a total return (capital change plus income) close to that of the index.

Attempting to parallel the investment returns of a specified stock or bond market index is known as "indexing," which is a passive approach emphasizing broad diversification and low portfolio trading activity. The investor attempts to duplicate the investment results of the target index by holding all (or in the case of very broad indices, a representative sample) of the securities in the index. Traditional active money management, using market timing techniques or identifying hot stock or industry sectors to outpace the indices is not attempted.

The case for indexing was first introduced in the early 1970s by academics who argued that securities markets were highly random and so efficient that it is in fact very difficult for professional managers to consistently outperform the broad market averages through individual stock selection. The problem is, the typical investor would find this impossible to do. To duplicate the results of the S&P 500, an investor would have to purchase and hold 500 individual stocks. Even using a discount broker, the transaction costs would be too much for the typical investor. The portfolio would have to be adjusted whenever a stock dividend or stock split occurred or if a company were added to or deleted from the index. If dividends are to be reinvested, that would have to be done at once and into the same stocks to keep the portfolio in proper balance — all of which would be an overwhelming set of tasks for the private investor.

As a group, it is impossible for all stock investors to outperform the overall stock market. According to Ibbotson Associates, the stock market index on a long-term historical basis has provided a compound total return of 10% per annum. But that figure is the gross return, before costs. Investors who pay typical costs for buying and holding individual securities may expect to have a net return significantly reduced by these costs and will earn significantly less than the market return.

Mutual fund companies have the same problem. Conventional stock mutual funds have average costs of approximately 2% of invested assets. Assuming a gross return of 10%, therefore, the investor in a conventional mutual fund might expect these costs of about 2% would reduce the net return to about 8%. To solve this problem, some mutual fund companies have introduced index funds. With this approach, they attempt to parallel the investment returns of specified stock or bond market indices. The Vanguard Group, which established the Vanguard Index Trust in 1976, was one of the first to do so, when they sought to mirror the S&P 500.

A key advantage of an index fund should be its low cost. An index fund should pay no advisory fees, reduce operating expenses to the lowest possible level and keep portfolio transaction costs at minimal levels. The total return of a properly run index fund should be as close as possible to the total return of the index it mirrors.

In any given year, hundreds of equity mutual funds provide returns in excess of market indices. However, as shown in Figure 3 below, in eight out of the 10 years since 1982, the Wilshire 5000, which was designed to represent the entire U.S. stock market, matched or surpassed the average performance of equity mutual funds. The index was never a poor performer and was rarely in the bottom third. Largely as a result of the broad diversification of the index and the year-by-year buildup of the cost advantage, the index surpassed 63% of general equity funds over the entire 10-year period.

GENERAL EQUITY MUTUAL FUNDS OUTPERFORMED BY WILSHIRE 5000 INDEX	
1982	29%
1983	64
1984	68
1985	77
1986	61
1987	54
1988	68
1989	73
1990	41
1991	56

FIGURE 3: The returns of the index have been reduced by 0.30% per year.

FUND PERFORMANCE

So how *have* the index funds performed? Most index funds are of recent origin and so do not have long-term track records. The performance of several funds with at least one full year of operation as of July 31, 1992, is indicated in Figure 4, with data from Morningstar. Figure 5 provides a partial list of index funds currently being offered.

There will always be actively managed mutual funds that outperform index funds over long periods. Some investment managers will provide exceptional returns over long winning streaks, whether by chance or even skill. There may be some investment managers with exceptional abilities who can earn superior returns over time. The problem is to identify, in advance, those that will be consistently superior.

For the investor who does not want to gamble more than he

FUND PERFORMANCE (IN PERCENTAGE)				
Years	**1**	**3**	**5**	**10**
Fidelity Market Index	12.47%			
Gateway Index Plus	10.81	13.42%	10.10%	12.60%
Vanguard Index Trust				
500 Portfolio	12.60	10.39	9.25	18.70
Extended Market Portfolio	14.62	7.72		
U.S. Equity Fund Average	11.98	9.37	8.34	16.03
S&P 500 Index	12.74	10.63	9.54	19.12

FIGURE 4: The performance of several funds is presented here.

CURRENT INDEX FUNDS		
Fund	**Index**	**Operating expenses**
Dreyfus Peoples Index Fund	S&P 500	0.88%
Dreyfus Peoples S&P Midcap		
Index Fund	S&P MidCap 400	2.50
Fidelity Market Index Fund	S&P 500	0.45
Gateway Index Plus Fund	S&P 100	1.22
Helmsman Equity Index Portfolio	S&P 500	0.89
Vanguard Index Trust		
500 Portfolio	S&P 500	0.20
Extended Market Portfolio	Wilshire 4500	0.19
Total Market Portfolio*	Wilshire 5000	0.22

FIGURE 5: The Helmsman Fund has a 5.5% sales load. The Vanguard Extended Market Portfolio assesses a 1% purchase fee and the Total Market Portfolio a 0.25% purchase fee.

or she must on a specific actively managed mutual fund, an index fund with low operating costs makes it possible to buy and hold an entire segment of the securities market and come close to matching its total return.

Stephen Littauer has been in the financial and investment business for more than 30 years. He is a former vice president of SouthTrust and Shearson Lehman Brothers and the author of How to Buy Mutual Funds the Smart Way, *published by Dearborn Publishing.*

ADDITIONAL READING

Data attributed to Lipper Analytical Services, Inc., and Ibbotson Associates were taken from *Some Plain Talk About Indexing*, a publication of The Vanguard Group.

Littauer, Stephen [1992]. *How to Buy Mutual Funds the Smart Way*, Dearborn Financial Publishing.

Morningstar Mutual Funds. 53 West Jackson Blvd. Chicago, IL 60604.

"Mutual Funds Update." CDA Investment Technologies, Inc., 1355 Piccard Drive, Rockville, MD 20850.

Vanguard Group, Vanguard Financial Center, PO Box 2600, Valley Forge, PA 19482.

Talking With "Turtle" Russell Sands

"Most people in life take the easy way out when they're faced with a difficult choice. Because of that, they don't wind up getting anywhere and they're not enormously successful. To buck the trend and become successful, you have to pay your dues and be willing to put in the time and effort necessary. That's hard. In terms of trading, doing the hard thing is probably most rewarding."

"Price is the best indicator. The fact that you have a profit tells you that your trade is right. If you have a loss, your trade is wrong."

None of Russell Sands' three degrees — two bachelors' degrees, one in business administration and one in economics, and a master's in business administration in finance — helped him in his trading career as much as his avid interest in backgammon, which led him to play in and win the 1980 backgammon world championship tournament in Las Vegas. From his winnings he bought a seat on the then-fledgling New York Futures Exchange, which, unfortunately, taught him nothing about the intricacies of trading. It was only when Sands inadvertently stumbled upon an advertisement from one of the world's top traders and answered it that led him to understand what it takes to be a successful trader. STOCKS & COMMODITIES Editor Thom Hartle interviewed Russell Sands via telephone on September 17, 1992, speaking about, among other things, the importance of risk management, following the trend and understanding crowd behavior.

How did you end up becoming one of the turtles?

Believe it or not, I was reading the help-wanted section in *The New York Times* and I saw this ad. I don't think it was very specific at all. It just said "prominent Chicago trading firm looking for people that they can train in their methods" and went on to say that they were willing to train and bankroll you. So I sent in a resume and they sent back this question and answer test. I understand they got about 1,500 or 2,000 resumes, and they asked about 50 people

to come to Chicago for interviews. I don't know why I was chosen, because I didn't do so well on the tests — like I said, I didn't know a lot — and so I got a lot of the test questions wrong.

So how did you manage?

Well, when I went out to Chicago for the interview, the three partners interviewed me and we talked about the commodities market for about five minutes or so, which exhausted my knowledge. Then we talked about backgammon and probabilities for about half an hour. We talked a lot about probabilities in blackjack and backgammon, and they said it was the same thing in commodities trading. I guess they thought that the combination of my MBA, education and my backgammon and blackjack successes was what they were looking for, with some mathematical aptitude, games playing type-oriented people. I fit the profile.

How long did you stay with the firm?

About a year, from the end of 1983 to the end of 1984. They taught us in a classroom for a couple of weeks; he and a couple of his partners lectured about their trading methods, a lot of chart patterns,

> **There's definitely a psychological aspect of trading. Markets respond to human behavior because they're made up of individuals who trade using mass psychology more than economics or supply and demand. Every major price move in history has had some psychological aspect to it.**

technical analysis, money management concepts. After about two weeks of classroom instruction, they put about a million dollars in each of our accounts, turned us loose and said, "Okay, go trade." For the first two weeks or so, we were only trading single lots just so we could get the mechanics down. Then they said, "Okay, trade full speed." And that's how I learned about trading.

What were some issues that had the biggest impact on you for trading?

I'd *like* to say that trading is real simple. They didn't teach us any complicated algorithms or whatever; they just taught us some basic rules of trend following and how to look at simple chart patterns and channel breakouts. The hard part was having the discipline to follow the rules all the time, because as a trend follower you tend to lose money 65-70% of the time. It's difficult to sit there when you're losing money and you want to second guess yourself or try something different. Discipline and consistency were a lot harder than knowing the rules of when to get in and out of positions.

What are some of the rules that you use, like money management rules?

We have a lot of different formulas, most of which are based on standard probability theory and risk of ruin calculations. It all boils down to setting your risk of ruin at a certain level, like 1% or 2% for an institutional trader or 5% for an individual trader. Those are the chances that you're going to bust out and lose all your money. In our case, "ruin" meant losing 50% of your money, because we were told that if you lose 50% of your account, you're fired! So our drawdown was 50%.

In that case, how do you measure the probability of losing all your money?

I'm not sure. You just hope it doesn't happen. They just had a bunch of algorithms they crunched through the computer that figured that if you trade this much based on the last thousand trades over 10 years this was how much an adverse sequence would cost you, and this was what a three-standard deviation, 99% probability, worst adverse sequence would look like. So you kept that in mind and you just traded small enough so that it didn't cost you.

So basically, you take a strategy, test it to find out what the profit and loss profile is and then draw your probability conclu-

sions from that?

You take that profit and loss profile and you work backward from that, figuring out how much or how little to trade. The stops or risk points are something along the lines of never losing more than 2% of your bankroll on any given trade. That's an absolute stop regardless of what the chart looks like or how sure you are. If you lose 2% of your money on a trade, that's enough to get out for survival purposes.

And that's it?

No, the next rule is never risk more than 10% of your bankroll on your open exposure of your total portfolio at any given time, whether that's three positions or 12. Just try and set your stops so that if everything goes against you in the worst possible way and all your stops get hit and you get blown out, it never costs more than 10% of your bankroll.

This is a fail-safe method so you'll always be around for the next trade?

Right! That's the most important goal. You *could* trade bigger, or you *could* set your stops tighter, or you *could* just use technical stops or be more technically efficient. But the 2% rule is a fail-safe method to keep you in business. The worst thing that could possibly happen is that you trade well just during an adverse period and then you lose money, maybe through no fault of your own, because the markets don't cooperate with your style or whatever. And you lose so much money that you go out of business before the market turns around for you.

I t's important for a trader to focus on doing the right thing and not so much what the markets are doing.
Absolutely. The first year we traded, all we cared about was doing the right thing. Doing the right thing meant following the rules. It had absolutely nothing to do with making or losing money, because if we followed the rules, eventually we *would* make money. So we were told not to worry about making money, just think about doing the right thing and following the rules, making the trades you're supposed to; getting in and out when you're supposed to.

The way I understand it, then, when you're put on a position, your confidence is focused on following the rules and not that you know what the market's going to do?

Yes. You have no idea what the market's going to do. If you've got a signal that's really got everything going for it, you've got *maybe* a 53% chance of being right. If I could predict the market, I wouldn't have to trade for a living. I don't believe these people who try to tell you how to pick tops and bottoms or whatever. But if we do the same thing every time and the numbers have been crunched up, there's a probability advantage in doing so — of 52-53% — so if you do it in the long run, you're going to make money.

But only in the long run.

The laws of probability only work in the long run; on any given trade you have no idea. We can't predict how the trade's going to work or where it's going to go; we like to *think* it's going to go our way. If it does, we stay with it as long as it goes our way, and if it doesn't, we have a stop to tell us when we're wrong. In the absence of a technical structure, it's just a hard money stop. It tells you when to get out.

Do you think the trading rules that you use are appropriate for everyone?

What do you mean by "everyone"? People with different account sizes?

Different personalities. Some people don't have the patience to stay with a trade for three or four months because of their impulse to cash in their profits prematurely.

In my opinion, they should try and force themselves, no matter what their immediate impulses are, to stay with that trade for three or four months if that's what they're supposed to do. If the price volatility is troublesome, then I'd say to just trade with smaller positions.

What would some specific rules be for initiating trades?

What we do is half technical and half psychological. The psychological part is hard to quantify. The technical part is basically looking at channel breakouts. A channel is defined as a horizontal channel as opposed to a slant or diagonal — a trending channel. A breakout is simply if the market goes higher than the last high in X number of days, that's a buy signal, and if the market goes lower than its lowest low in X days, in turn, that's a sell signal. If the market makes new highs or new lows for the last 50 days, that is a signal to initiate a trade, a liquidation signal on new lows or new highs since the last 20 days.

Do different markets have different lookback periods?

Absolutely not! Anybody who wants to get into optimizing different parameters for different markets is looking for trouble because they tend to change over time. You can't use nine days in beans, then 42 days in Standard & Poor's and 16 days in gold, because that was the best set of parameters over the last five or 10 years or whatever. Whatever worked best in the past probably won't work in the future because the parameters will change.

So can you look for a system that works reasonably well on all markets?

Well, you *have* to look for one, anyway. In fact, when we do testing we don't even know what markets we're looking at, because testing just consists of inputting prices, highs and lows and closes and looking for an algorithm. You can't tell a computer to look at bonds differently than it would beans, say. When I look at a chart, I like to say that I could cut off the part of the page with the name of the market and just look at the chart pattern.

So you don't use different lookbacks —

We don't use different lookback periods, we use a concept that suggests that maybe the larger the breakout the more significant it is. Going higher than the last high in the last 50 days is better than going higher than the highest high in the last 20, for example — three-month highs or contract highs or lows on a chart that's significant. So the more time that's passed, the better it is.

Let me get this clear. When you put on a trade, you have an automatic 2% maximum stop bought.

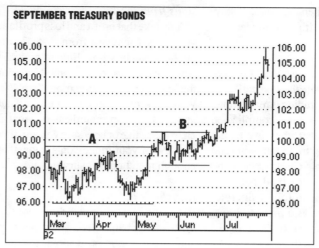

FIGURE 1: *Price channels are sideways trading patterns. Price channels can be tops or bottoms (A) or consolidation patterns (B).*

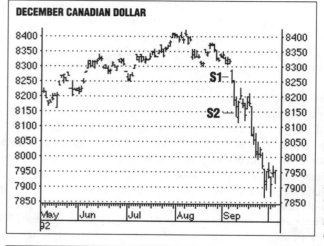

FIGURE 2: *A sell signal occurred at S1 when the Canadian dollar moved to a 20-day new low. The second sell (S2) occurred when the Canadian dollar moved to 50-day new lows.*

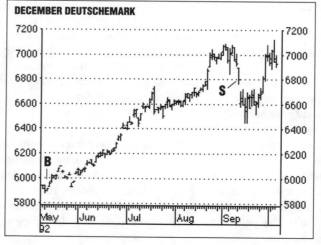

FIGURE 3: *The Deutschemark moved to new 50-day highs (B) at 6000 on May 13. A sell signal occurred on 10-day new lows (S) at 6800 on September 11.*

That's the money stop. And the technical stop, basically, is just the opposite if the position goes against you. If you buy something because it's made a higher high than it has been in the last X days, for example, as long as the market keeps going up you stay with it, whereas if it turns around and starts going back down, then your liquidation signal comes once the market breaks the lowest low of the past X days. Actually, that should be of the past Y days, because it's a different parameter.

You need more to get into a trade and less to knock you out.

Right. So maybe you get in when the market's gone above the highest high in the last 50 days and if it turns south and goes below the lowest low of the past 20, that's your liquidation signal.

Are the numbers themselves important?

No, because we've tested different things, and the fact is channel breakouts are a valid concept. Different parameters work equally well. You could buy something at 50 days higher and liquidate at 20 days lower or you could buy something at 30 days higher and liquidate at 12 days lower — all those things work.

Is that the best parameter? Is there such a thing?

I'm not going to say that, because even if it is, it's not going to be the best one in the future.

So what happens if you put on a position?

You hope that it'll go up enough so when it turns around and starts going down, by the time it breaks the 10-day or 20-day low, it's still above your initiation price. That's how you make a profit out of a trade. If it never goes up but starts going down after you buy it, you'll probably hit your hard-money stop before you hit any technical low on the chart.

Your focus is strictly price. You don't include any other technical indicators?

I do look at other indicators such as RSI, open interest, 50% retracements and others. I like to get as much information as possible. But you can run the risk of useless or contradictory information. In the final analysis, price is the most important indicator.

You said earlier that trading is half technical and half psychological.

Yes. There's definitely a psychological aspect of trading. *Everybody* can trade technically, but the psychology is the hard part. We take the attitude that the markets respond to human behavior — in fact, markets *are* human behavior because they're made up of individuals who tend to trade using mass psychology more than economics or supply and demand. You have to remember that. Every major price move in history has had some psychological aspect to it.

What are some examples?

The best example is Tulipmania, the tulip bulb craze in Holland in the 1600s, when one bulb went for what today would be the equivalent of $400 a flower. That had absolutely nothing to do with economics, obviously; it was just mass psychology. So you have to be aware of that. One of the things we try to do is be a contrarian and not go with the crowd because the crowd is always wrong.

That's a common axiom.

If the crowd is always wrong and most people lose money, you want to go in and trade like the few and not the many. Most people in life, and I say this in my seminar, take the easy way out when they're faced with a difficult choice. Because of that, they don't wind up getting anywhere and they're not enormously successful. To buck the trend and become successful, you have to pay your dues and be willing to put in the time and hours and effort necessary. That's hard. In terms of trading, again, doing the hard thing is probably most rewarding.

What's an example, in terms of trading?

Well, everybody loves to take profits, so you've got a nice trade with a big profit

in it. The temptation is to want to take that profit, and that's absolutely wrong because that violates the rule of letting your profits run. *You never want to take a profit.* So it's difficult to sit there with a big open equity profit and not worry about it. But that's absolutely the right thing to do; that's the only way that you're going to give it room to potentially turn into a home run. So that's an example of doing the hard thing.

The fact that you have a big profit tells you that you're on the right side of the market.

Yes. Price is the best indicator. The fact that you have a profit tells you that your trade is right. If you have a loss, your trade is wrong.

What if you have a big profit and you can clearly see that the market is in an uptrend, and the news is pretty positive. You sense the crowd is looking at the same thing. Does that tell you that you will start liquidating at some point based

> I think traders and would-be traders should read *Reminiscences of a Stock Operator* every year, repeatedly. I've owned the book 10 years and I've read it three times. If I'd read it every year instead, I probably would have saved myself a lot of money.

on price?

Not as long as the trend is still up. Maybe liquidating more quickly when the trend starts to turn. If there's a lot of bullish news and everybody's predicting how this market's going to go to the moon, *then* maybe when it does turn around, and it eventually will, then maybe you want to speed up your liquidation and get out at 10-day lows instead of 20-day lows.

specially if the market turns around.

Especially if the market turns around and goes lower for a couple of days and you start reading in the papers that analysts say they're confident that the market will resume new highs by the end of the week or whatever. Now that's *really* a warning sign that you want to think about getting out a little quicker. But as long as it's going up your way, though, you never want to get out. You want to wait till it turns against you.

Do you have some favorite books? On trading, I mean.

I have four. Edwin LeFèvre's *Reminiscences of a Stock Operator* is my all-time favorite book. I think traders and would-be traders should read it every year, repeatedly. I've owned this book 10 years and I've read it three times. If I'd read it every year instead of every three or four years, I probably would have saved myself a lot of money because I go in and read it and think, "Oh, yes! Why didn't I remember that three months ago on that stupid trade?" It's just wonderful. I think Jesse Livermore, who supposedly wrote the book under a pseudonym, is half the greatest trader that ever lived and half the worst money manager that ever lived. The way LeFèvre looks at the market is just great. He tells you about money management; if you've got a profit it means you're right, if you've got a loss it means you're wrong.

You know, most of our interviewees cite that book as one of their favorites, too. What are the others?

My other favorites are *The Commodity Futures Game—Who Wins? Who Loses? Why?*, by Teweles, Harlow and Stone, which teaches you fundamentals, technicals, money management, what to look for in a brokerage firm. It's got a good overview of the market. My favorite book for trading psychology is *Extraordinary Popular Delusions and the Madness of Crowds* by Charles MacKay, and my favorite book for statistics is *Theory of Gambling and Statistical Logic* by Richard Epstein, which has no words in it, just algebra. It took me about two years just to read the first 50 pages.

In that case, how do you know what you're reading or get anything out of it?

It's a tough book to read. If you're mathematically inclined, you could read it or if you're not mathematically inclined, you should only read it if you've made a stupid trade and you want to punish yourself.

What do you have planned now?

Well, my life has changed a lot. I had been planning on going to law school this year, but for a couple of reasons I've taken a year deferment. One reason is after being away from the markets for six months, I found that I missed trading, and the other reason is the recent hurricane [Hurricane Andrew] damaged the school campus.

Why did you stop trading for six months?

I had a bad year in 1991. The first 11 months of the year, the markets simply did not trend and because of that I suffered extended drawdowns. My customers did not stay with me. I was extremely disappointed and decided to stop trading completely. I decided to do something less frustrating. And then I was all set to go to law school, but I found that I missed the markets and I missed trading and so I committed myself to trading again. I'm currently trading my own account and looking forward to managing money again.

Is that it?

No, there's more. I'm going to start a newsletter called "Turtletalk" and just recap everything from my seminars, maybe go over a chapter a month, giving some examples, recapping the actual trading I'm doing in my own accounts so people can follow along. If anybody wants more information than that, you can put in my phone number at Raintree Futures and have them call me. I'd be happy to tell them what I'm doing.

Sounds like everything's going along well. Thanks, Russell.

You're welcome!

> What we do is half technical and half psychological. The psychological part is hard to quantify. The technical part is basically looking at channel breakouts.

REFERENCES

Epstein, Richard A. [1977]. *Theory of Gambling and Statistical Logic*, Academic Press.

LeFèvre, Edwin [1980]. *Reminiscences of a Stock Operator*, Books of Wall Street, Fraser Publishing. Originally published in 1923.

MacKay, Charles [1932]. *Extraordinary Popular Delusions and the Madness of Crowds*, now published by Fraser Publishing, Burlington, VT.

Raintree Futures, Inc., 1800 NE 114th St., Apt. 401, North Miami, FL 33181, (305) 892-2203.

Teweles, Richard J., Charles V. Harlow, Herbert L. Stone [1974]. *The Commodity Futures Game—Who Wins? Who Loses? Why?*, McGraw-Hill, 2nd ed.

TRADERS' TIPS

Do you have a custom formula, solution or user tip for your software that you would like to share? Have you ever pondered a trading question that you'd like to share with our readers? Have you ever contemplated a question for a while and come up with a solution that you'd like to share with others? Or are you still stuck without a solution? Send your formulas, solutions, tips and questions to Traders' Tips, STOCKS & COMMODITIES, 3517 SW Alaska St., Seattle, WA 98126-2700. Please send a hard copy and, if possible, the information on a disk in unformatted ASCII along with your name, address and phone number. Contributors whose material is selected for publication will receive a Technical Analysis of STOCKS & COMMODITIES T-shirt.

■ METASTOCK PROFESSIONAL AND CANDLESTICKS

Candlestick charts are still new to traders in the U.S. Here's a method to assist you in identifying specific candlestick patterns in MetaStock Professional.

Candlestick patterns use the open, high, low and closing prices, and so your data will need all four to correctly plot a candlestick pattern. The opening and close for the day define the body of the candlestick, while low and high are the thin lines that extend beyond the body. The thin lines are called the shadows. If the market closes above the opening, the body is empty or white. Closes below the opening will have a black or filled-in body. Three important candlestick patterns are the bullish engulfing line (large white body engulfing a small black body), the bearish engulfing line (large black body engulfing a small white body), and the doji (open and closing price are the same).

Pattern Recognition: Figure 1 lists the custom formulas that will plot a binary wave composite indicator of the engulfing lines. Formula 1 determines whether the candlestick is empty (the close is above the open), whereas formula 2 determines whether the candlestick is filled (the close is lower than the open). Formula 3 determines if the candlestick is a doji (the open and close are the same price). Plotted separately, each of these three formulas will plot a +1 whenever the particular pattern is detected.

Formula 4 searches for bearish engulfing lines (a pattern that occurs after a significant uptrend). When formula 4 is plotted and the pattern detected, the resulting indicator will plot a -1. Formula 5 searches for bullish engulfing lines (a pattern that occurs after a significant downtrend). When this pattern is detected, the resulting indicator will plot +1.

Composite Indicator: The binary wave composite indicator uses formula 6, which is the combination of formulas 4 and 5. The result is a binary wave that plots +1 when a bullish engulfing line is detected and plots a -1 when a bearish engulfing line is detected.

In this example, you would buy on +1 and sell on -1. However, a word of caution: While the bullish and bearish engulfing lines are useful indicators of price direction, you shouldn't place trades solely upon their signals.

If you already have some formulas stored in MetaStock, you will need to substitute the formula reference numbers used in Figure 1 (that is, fml(#1)) with numbers that match the locations available in your personal custom formula menu.

—Allan McNichol
Equis International

Formula 1, empty candlestick:
 if(c,>,o{then empty},+1,0)

Formula 2, filled candlestick:
 if(c,<,o{then filled},+1,0)

Formula 3, doji:
 if(c,=,o{then doji},+1,0)

Formula 4, bearish engulfing lines:
if(fml(#2),=,+1,if(ref(fml(#1),1),=,+1,
if(c,<=,ref(o,-1),if(o,>=,ref(c,-1),
-1,0),0),0),0)

Formula 5, bullish engulfing lines:
if(fml(#1),=,+1,if(ref(fml(#2),1),=,+1,
if(c,>=,ref(o,-1),if(o,<=,ref(c,-1),
+1,0),0),0),0)

Formula 6, engulfing line binary wave:
 fml(#4) + fml(#5)

FIGURE 1: CUSTOM FORMULAS. *Here are the formulas to plot the engulfing line binary wave indicator.*

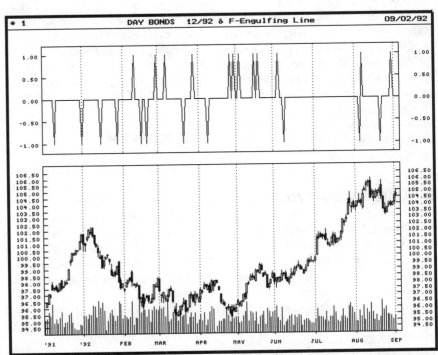

FIGURE 2: TREASURY BONDS. *A +1 reading indicates a bullish engulfing line and a -1 reading indicates a bearish engulfing line.*

GANN-DO ATTITUDE

Editor,

January's article, "The Gann Quarterly Chart," was the best article I have read in nine months. I can use it for buying and selling mutual funds for long-term investing.

I would appreciate more articles simply written with actual buy and sell dates for long and intermediate investing.

Could you explain the difference between a 50-day moving average and a 10-week moving average?

DAVID PORTNEY
Staten Island, NY

The moving average, a mathematical procedure to smooth or eliminate the fluctuations in data, emphasizes the direction of a trend and confirms trend reversals, thereby assisting the user in determining when to buy and sell.

The simple moving average is the arithmetic mean or average of a series of prices over a period of time. The longer the period of time studied (i.e., the larger the denominator of the average), the less impact an individual data point has on the average. To find a five-day average, take the sum of the prices from days 1 to 5 and divide by 5. Repeat and plot for a moving average.

The 50-day moving average uses 50 data items (the daily closes), whereas the 10-week moving average uses only 10 data items (the Friday closes). In effect, the 50-day average provides more information and may pick up on trend changes sooner, but the 10-week may filter out false breakouts and other misleading data spikes that may occur during the week. —Editor

SIMULATED OVERSTATEMENT?

Editor,

This letter refers to the article "Money management using simulation and chaos" in the April 1992 issue of STOCKS & COMMODITIES. I realize that the data in this article are simulated; still, one must be careful about overstating which models may be appropriate to the price data of any market.

A model is presented in which hog price data are detrended, then long cycles

are removed, and then seasonal trends are removed. The residual price time series or "irregulars" are equated with chaos: according to the article, these "represent chaos."

Irregular data are not necessarily chaos. Chaos is a particular kind of patterned noise defined by the exponential divergence over time of originally close points. On the other hand, "white noise" shows no relationship with time. The usual way of formally demonstrating chaos versus white noise is to calculate what is known as the Lyapunov exponent. Edgar Peters has done this for the S&P 500 and has demonstrated a positive Lyapunov exponent, which implies chaotic dynamics for stock indices.

Mr. Pelletier does not reference any work in which a Lyapunov exponent has been calculated for hog price data. Therefore, one cannot assume that the irregulars are chaos. It has been repeatedly shown that similar-looking data can result from different processes. For example, it has been shown that measles outbreaks conform to chaotic dynamics, while chicken pox outbreaks conform to annual cycles with added white noise.

Irregulars have to be assumed to be white noise unless the calculations needed for the demonstration of chaos have been done and a positive Lyapunov exponent is found. This also affects trading: while prices conforming to chaotic dynamics have short-term predictability, white noise has no predictability.

VICTOR KRYNICKI, Ph.D.
Bahama, NC

ASSET ALLOCATION

Editor,

I read with great interest Arthur Merrill's article in the June 1992 issue, "Selecting stocks." The article explained very clearly his method for ranking stocks. Please inquire of Mr. Merrill if his portfolio is 100% invested at all times or, if not, what factors he uses to determine the percent of the portfolio that should be invested at any given time.

CHARLENE M. DEHAVEN
Mesa, AZ

Arthur Merrill replies:
Your question is a good one. The prob-

lem of what percentage to invest in equities isn't dealt with in my stock selection routine. I have to look elsewhere.

In a roaring bull market, my percentage in equities rises to 100%. When the bull begins to get winded, I ease off. When prices rise to expensive levels, as measured by the price/dividends ratio of the DJIA, my percentage in equities drops to 25% or lower. My benchmark for expensiveness is a ratio above 28. It's currently 35!

For more on this, see my S&C articles "Price/dividends ratio" (October 1988) and "Price/dividends ratio revisited" (August 1991).

TIPS FROM THE STOCK SELECTOR HIMSELF

Editor,

June's "Selecting stocks" was one of the best articles I have read on this subject. There were, however, some important details in the article for which I need further clarification:

1. In calculating the relative strength (one of the technical factors), how many days of data should be used — one, 50 or 200? Should the relative strength be based on a fixed historical date, such as January 1, 1988?

2. The Mw wave (another technical factor) is not fully clear to me. Although I have read Arthur Merrill's November 1991 article "Merrill Mw waves," it doesn't explain which of the 16 "M" patterns are the most bullish and which of the 16 "W" patterns are the most bearish. And do Mw waves work equally well when they are limited to swings of 5% versus the 10% that you cite?

3. In determining the stocks with the fastest growth, you fit a regression line to the earnings per share (EPS). Which EPS, quarterly or yearly, do you use for this calculation and over what time period?

4. Similarly, in determining recent earnings trends (a fundamental factor), which EPS, quarterly or yearly, do you use and over what time period (for instance, quarterly over two years or yearly over five years)?

I'd appreciate your answers.

AKBER ZAIDI
Torrance, CA

LETTERS TO S&C

Arthur Merrill replies:
Your letter raises some good questions. I'll try to answer them in the same order.

1. For relative strength, I try to adjust for the difference in volatility of the S&P and that of an individual stock by calculating a regression line with logarithmic stock price as Y and log S&P as X, using data for the last 25 weeks. The current stock price is compared to the value to be expected (on the regression line) for the current value of S&P.

2. My discussion of the MW waves was an abbreviation due to space limitations. A more complete report is available from Technical Trends (Technical Trends, PO Box 792, Wilton, CT 06897-0229, 203-762-0229, 800-736-0229, $20 postpaid). The selection of 10% swings wasn't determined mathematically; it just seemed to work well with the average stock. Actually, a higher percentage could be used for the more volatile stocks. I use 5% swings for the DJIA.

3. To determine the trend of EPS, I use the yearly figures for at least four or five years; if I have earlier years they are also included. I include the most recent interim quarterly report plus the three preceding quarters.

4. In determining the most recent earnings trend, I note the earnings of the most recent four quarters. This total is compared with the earnings trend regression line determined according to the criteria listed in question 3 above. The percentage difference is noted: Are earnings slipping (a negative percent)? Or are they improving (positive)?

ADVICE FROM AN S&C AUTHOR
In an author survey conducted by S&C, one author, Clifford Creel, threw in some extra words of advice for novice traders that we thought we'd share.—Editor

1. Don't spend all your time trying to find the magic indicator to predict the market so that you never get around to trading.

2. The market is a lot like the weather: Short-term forecasts are much more reliable than longer-term forecasts.

3. Technical analysis is useful for providing insight into short-term changes, while fundamental analysis is more helpful for the longer term.

4. Many traders develop an instinct for predicting future market behavior by looking at charts on a daily basis and keeping close to the market. This kind of knowledge is generally independent of the information produced by the particular indicators used. Find indicators that are best for you.

5. Remember that most indicators are redundant. For a stock, there are three basic pieces of information: price, volume and relative strength. Most indicators just combine these data in various ways. I recommend that each trader find one indicator that measures price trend, one that measures volume activity and one that measures relative strength versus the market. A common mistake is to focus on several indicators, such as RSI, stochastics, MACD and so forth, that all give basically the same information.

6. A buy and sell signal are not necessarily opposites. There is no reason to expect that the same indicator used to enter a position is the best one for exiting the position. Think of a buy signal as representing a significant probability that the price will rise during the time frame of interest. A sell signal should be designed to capture as much of the price increase as possible.

7. Set realistic stops to exit a position before a small loss becomes a large one. Often, a stop of 10% off the highest price reached during a trade is a reasonable stop. You may want to tighten your stops as profits build.

8. When a stock has a profit of 20% or more, continually ask yourself if you would buy more. When the answer becomes no, consider selling it.

9. Begin your technical analysis each day by looking at the market (S&P 500, advance-decline line, interest rates and so on) and decide in what direction you think the market is headed. Then, when analyzing stocks, be very careful in taking a position against the market. That is, don't take long positions in a down market or short positions in an up market unless you have a good reason to think that the stock will go against the trend.

10. Be wary of anyone who offers the magic answer to guaranteed profits.

CLIFFORD L. CREEL, Ph.D.

STATISTICS: IT'S ELEMENTARY
Readers often tell us that our articles are too statistical for their level of understanding. Last month in my Opening Position, I suggested that readers who feel uncomfortable with statistics but who want to be able to analyze trading system results go to a college bookstore and look for a book on basic statistics. Our good friend Arthur Merrill, long-time STOCKS & COMMODITIES contributor and veteran technician, sent us these book recommendations.—Editor

Byrkit, Donald [1972]. *Elements of Statistics,* Van Nostrand.

Franzblau, Abraham [1958]. *A Primer of Statistics for Non-Statisticians,* Harcourt Brace.

Downie, N., and R. Heath [1959]. *Basic Statistical Methods,* Harper and Row.

Hultquist, Robert [1969]. *Introduction to Statistics,* Holt Rinehart Winston.

Lentner, Marvin [1972]. *Elementary Applied Statistics,* Bogden and Quigley.

Moroney, M.J. [1951]. *Facts from Figures,* Pelican, Penguin.

Naiman, Rosenfeld and Zirkel [1972]. *Understanding Statistics,* McGraw-Hill.

Reichard, Robert [1972]. *The Numbers Game,* McGraw-Hill.

CHARTERED MARKET TECHNICIAN
Editor,
I have enjoyed your magazine for some time now and have found many helpful trading techniques. I am interested in discovering what CMT certification represents. Many of the individuals whom you have interviewed hold this title, yet I have little idea who offers such a certification.

GARY ORDWAY
New York, NY

The CMT (Chartered Market Technician) designation is granted by the Accreditation Committee of the Market Technicians Association, Inc. (MTA), a non-profit professional organization. The CMT program is the MTA's effort to promote continuing education, raise the standards in the practice of technical analysis and further its professionalism. The CMT program consists of two exams and an original research paper accepted for publication in the "MTA Journal." While MTA affiliates and non-members may enroll in and successfully complete the CMT program, only regular members of the MTA and members of other International Federation of Technical Analysts, Inc. (IFTA) societies will be awarded the MTA designation. This limitation helps to ensure that the MTA can effectively uphold the CMT standards. For information about enrolling in the CMT program, contact the Market Technicians Association, 2nd Floor, 71 Broadway, New York, NY 10006, (212) 344-1266, fax (212) 673-9334.

The registration fee for the CMT program is $350. Annual dues in the MTA are $150 plus a $10 application fee for new members.—Editor

HANDOUT FOR METASTOCK USERS

Editor,

I found "Forecasting tomorrow's trading day" (STOCKS & COMMODITIES, May 1992) a very beneficial article, particularly with respect to Tushar S. Chande's use of %F, a regression forecast oscillator, and R^2, the coefficient of determination. The article is an excellent example of the application of linear regression in market forecasting.

I have adapted this method for Equis International's MetaStock-Pro 3.0 software. MetaStock-Pro users may find these formulas more efficient than a spreadsheet-type calculation.

R^2, the coefficient of determination, is a measure of the strength of the linear relationship between two variables. The regression forecast oscillator, %F, is defined by Chande as:

$$\%F = \left(\frac{Y - Y_{Forecast}}{Y}\right)100$$

An Excel spreadsheet example calculating these values was provided in the article's sidebar.

Users of Equis International's MetaStock-Pro 3.0 can calculate these values from the indicators and functions provided in MetaStock without needing to use a spreadsheet.

MetaStock's time series forecast (TSF) indicator calculates a linear regression trendline for a set of data. Rather than

FIGURE 1

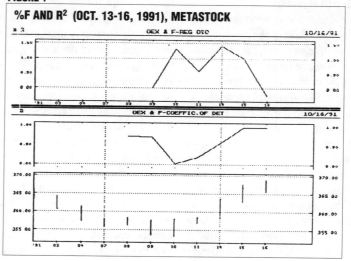

FIGURE 2

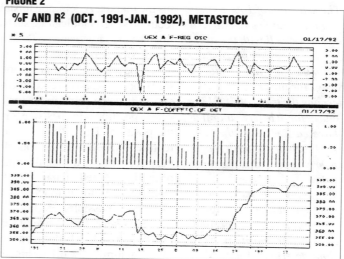

FIGURE 3

METASTOCK CUSTOM FORMULAS

%F Oscillator
((C-ref(tsf(C,5),-1))/C)*100

R-Squared
pwr(corr(cum(1),C,5,0),2)

Slope
((5*(sum(cum(1)*C,5)))-(sum(cum(1),5)*(sum(C,5))))/
((5*sum(pwr(cum(1),2),5))-pwr(sum(cum(1),5),2))

These custom formulas can be used in MetaStock Professional 3.0 software to find the regression forecast oscillator (%F), the regression coefficient of determination (R²) and slope of the linear regression line. The formula under "slope" is one line of text.

plotting a straight linear regression line, the TSF indicator plots the last point of multiple linear regression trendlines. In other words, the value displayed by TSF at data T is the forecast value for day $T+1$. Therefore, %F, the regression oscillator, can be calculated as follows:

$$\%F = ((C\text{-REF}(\text{TSF}(C,5),-1)) / C*100$$

where:

$\text{TSF}(C,5)$ = five-period time series forecast of the close

$\text{REF}(\text{TSF}(C,5),-1)$ = forecast value one day back

R^2, the regression coefficient of determination, can be calculated using the fact that R^2 equals the square of R, the correlation coefficient. Therefore,

$$R^2 = \text{PWR}(\text{CORR}(\text{cum}(1),c,5,0),2)$$

where:

$\text{CUM}(1)$ = an indicator that rises one point per day; that is, an ordinal series used as the independent variable in the analysis

$\text{CORR}(\text{cum}(1),c,5,0)$ = correlation between the close and the ordinal series over five days without any forward shift

$\text{PWR}(\ (\ )\ ,)$ squares the correlation coefficient

These formulas can be entered as "custom formulas" and displayed with the market being analyzed. Figures 1 and 2 show the MetaStock version of the OEX analysis presented in the article.

BRUCE C. KRAMER
Charlotte, NC

Equis International has provided a third formula, one to calculate the slope of the linear regression line (Figure 3).—Editor

THE PERILS OF PARAMETERS

Editor,

The article in the April 1992 issue by Bob Pelletier ("Money management using simulation and chaos") introduced some very interesting concepts and also raises some questions about the definition of a control parameter in a trading system. As Bob indicates, the overuse of control parameters can cause a trading system to be over-optimized, and he presents a model for degrading the system performance based on the number of parameters.

Let's look at a very simple system and see how this concept applies. The system is:

Entry: Close +/- Close(k)
Stop: -$1,000 stop loss from entry
Exit: +$2,000 profit target
where k is a constant.

This is a simple breakout system where your entry points are buy and sell stops that are placed each trading day depending on the previous day's close. The entry can also stop and reverse a position. You only go flat if a stop loss is hit (-$1,000) or a profit target is hit (+$2,000).

My question is, how many control parameters are in this system? While the initial answer to this question may seem simple, consider the following. The entry can both exit a position and start a new position but only in the opposite direction. The stop can only exit a position that has moved too far in an adverse direction. It can't initiate a new position. The profit target can only exit a position that moves into a profitable area, and it cannot initiate a new position. The stop and profit target can, in some cases, set the system up for new entry points that would not be hit if the entry was used alone. In other words, assume you had initiated a long position and exited at a $2,000 profit. The next entry signal is another long entry. Without the $2,000 profit target exit, the second long entry would not have been used since you would already be long from the first entry. The use of stops causes a system to go flat at certain times, which opens up the possibility for more entries. This would increase the number of trades over any given time length.

While this logic may sound like I'm making something simple into a complicated problem, what I'm driving at is whether all parameters carry the same weight in controlling a system. Is it possible for a parameter to have a fractal weight depending on how it affects the system timing? This question was prompted by the dialog between [S&C Technical Editor] John Sweeney and Bob Pelletier in the March 1992 issue (Letters to S&C) regarding the introduction of stops to a system. John took the position that the use of stops does not affect system timing, but as I've shown, stops can affect timing to a certain extent in that they can set up new entries that are independent from those that occur without stops. Bob and John, what are your thoughts on this?

MIKE STOCK
Kirkland, WA

Mr. Stock's illustration has three possibilities for parameter assignment, namely k, which is identified as a constant, the $1,000 stop loss value (s), which looks like a constant, and the $2,000 profit target (t), which also appears to be a constant. If, on the other hand, all the settings of k, s and t can take on parameter status, then they can be jointly varied and the group should be taken as three parameters. If k, s and t are, in fact, constants that will never change regardless of time period or market studied, then because no other parameters are present, I believe the group would pass as a single parameter. This would impose some hindsight penalty. It would be improper to accept any record without some degradation to qualify (penalize) the system's performance for seizing the opportunity to view the past.

I understand the concern expressed by Mr. Stock wherein each parameter's role is interdependent with one or more other parameters. My view is that whenever artificial control is introduced regardless of the nature, intensity or impact of the control, a freedom restricting parameter is consumed.

It may be tempting to contrive variable weights for parameters, such as in his fractal suggestion, but I don't know of any good mathematical basis for this. If he is wrong, he may be taking a chance.

The science of parameter counting introduced in the April 1992 S&C article "Money management using simulation and chaos" and applied in our Trader's Money Manager software, for example, has as its purpose the removal of hindsight bias in simulated trading. If one removes more bias than is present in the simulated trading exercise and the mathematical expectation goes negative, then you would have to ask yourself if backing off on fractional parameters to achieve a marginally positive mathematical expectation would qualify a system that is worthy of trading. My cautious opinion is that it would not!

Review Freebies!

by John Sweeney

People think reviewers have it made in the shade. "Freebies!" they think. Little do they know. In fact, being a reviewer is a large pain in the ass. Novice reviewers abound — until they do a few and decide they're tired of it. Professional reviewers learn to live with discomfort.

SHIPPING

First of all, just getting "all that free hardware and software" is a problem. Usually you are set up by the marketing department, which means you bypass the company's normal customer contact people who are experienced — even good at — delivering the goods and answering questions. Instead, someone's secretary gets the unenviable job of getting your equipment/software, mailing it to you and, in the case of data services, turning on our account or, more likely, not turning it on.

RECEIVING

On your end, you get the 300-page manual and materials and start reading at the installation page. A question comes up; you dial the number in the manual for service. The service department has never heard of you and suspects you of ripping off the company. It turns out that your account is a back-door access available only to insiders. Make another call to marketing to vouch for you to customer service. Wait for the company to make you visible to customer service. Ask customer service the original questions. *Then* see if the installation actually works. Don't let this uncertainty influence your review unduly.

SECURITY

Next, start using the product. Whoops! Your security device (password, key, account activation, whatever) seems to be keeping the product from running. Check with customer service. Naturally, you don't get the same person you got last time, and your account, though visible, isn't granted access to whatever it is you're supposed to be reviewing. The entire company staff is in Las Vegas at a seminar and there's no one at home except the shipping-room clerk, who, it turns out, is also a hacker and knows a back door into the program. I swear I am not making this up. Problem solved for a day or three. A week later, marketing calls back to ask how things are going and you mention you're waiting for access to the program's features. They ask if the review will make it into the next edition. Don't let this imbroglio affect your review unduly.

PAY UP, BUDDY!

Next you get a dunning letter from the payables people at the company. It seems that you haven't paid a damn dime on your account or the product, you deadbeat. You've got 10 days or *Technical Analysis of* STOCKS & COMMODITIES magazine's commercial credit record goes into the tubes and the product will stop working while you're using it. Check with marketing. Seems bypassing the normal delivery system by activating an account still stimulates nerves in the payables. Marketing will fight with payables for you but expect to continue to get dunning notices because "our system can't ignore a credit balance." Don't let this influence your review unduly.

VERSION WARS

Back at your desk, try the package. Read the manual and note that, by God, people are actually writing things that can be read these days. There's even a spark of originality or thoroughness in its preparation. Note also that it doesn't appear to be quite finished, referring to segments that don't appear on the screen or have different labels than promised. Check with marketing: "Oh, yeah, that's an earlier version. Do you have 2.04.B1?" (Honest, I didn't make up that version number.) Ask, "Did I get the version the customer gets?" Marketing: "Well, why don't you have 3.0? Let me get you that right away." Put away your work and shift to another project.

Next, receive latest version, reinstall, reactivate yourself with customer service (who now is very cautious when they hear your name), reactivate accounts with new passwords, promise to ignore the dunning notices and fire up the package. Hooray! Quotes, charts, indicators, systems, tests, profits and losses! We're in business.

BETA TESTING

Start writing. Note that just about everything works. There are a few small glitches but you can't even crash the program if you try. Call technical support about the glitches: "Which version did you say you have? That's in beta. Yeah, there's a bug there, you should have picked it up off the bulletin board. Fix is there, too. Any questions?"

Just one: "How did I get into the beta testing business?" Quoth marketing: "The version you have will be the current version by the time the magazine comes out!" Think dark thoughts about integrity — yours — and what the readers expect. Don't let this influence your review unduly.

REVIEWING...

Resolve to even things out by noting all glitches in the review, taking the stance that what you have is what you review. Leaven the entire affair with any levity possible. Sprinkle liberally with nonstandard English to break up the droning effect of covering the basics yet again. Take lots of screen shots to give readers some feel for the program's feel.

Complete testing. Submit to copyfolk, who remove nonstandard English to appease their copy peers, remove any humor to appease the publisher, and shrink screen shots to invisibility to appease the art department. The editor then strikes all critical comments to appease advertising and shoots the whole affair to the vendor for prepublication review for errors and omissions. Review now closely resembles pap in last review. Pray they don't run your byline on this mishmash.

HARD BALL

Walk in next day to rampant cognitive dissonance. Calm nervous editor: vendor is enraged, please call him, magazine's future is at stake as well as his job, our marketing department wants to know if we're deliberately trying to destroy our relationship with "these guys," he's certain publisher will be very concerned. Threaten to let the editor write his own reviews. Gloat over his hasty retreat.

Call marketing at the vendor. They don't trust themselves to speak calmly: "Please talk to our technical people. They'll explain everything." Call the technoids. Techie hops on phone: "Whassa problem? What review?"

Us: "You probably got it from marketing? From STOCKS & COMMODITIES?"

Them: "Oh, yeah. Looked okay to me. Whassa problem?"

Us: "Well, you know, glitch 1, glitch 2, glitch 3."

Them: "Yeah, they were there but we've got all but glitch 3 cleaned up and I think I've got a fix for that. Wanna hear about it? It's really weird, just unbelievable." Discussion degenerates into mutual disgust with operating systems and other incompetent techies in the world.

Back at the ranch you water down the language some more and tell editor: "We dealt with all their concerns." He asks if we have to mention glitches 1 through n. Agree to say they'll be fixed "by the time you read this." He rushes off to production department breathing heavily and thinking of more colorful, "positive" adjectives. You box up the package, stow it in the library and vengefully delete the entire affair from your disk drive.

FLASHBACKS

Three months later, an alert reader calls from Singapore: "Do you remember that review you did back when?" All you can remember is wanting to drop-kick the secretary into the next century. "You didn't say anything about [glitch 1] or [glitch 2], let alone [glitch n]. Did you get paid to do this review? By whom?"

About the same time, reprisal letter from vendor's president arrives in mail along with the corrections letter from their marketing people. Editor promises to run it in the letters to the editor column along with the letter from the competing vendor claiming we ignored a superior product he produces to give free publicity to the "bozos" from vendor 1.

Resolve never to do another review, even if someone does pay you. Open next box at the scent of money. Admit you have no shame.

John Sweeney is the Technical Editor of STOCKS & COMMODITIES.

CHAOS AND ORDER IN THE CAPITAL MARKETS

A New View of Cycles, Prices and Market Volatility
John Wiley & Sons
605 Third Avenue
New York, NY 10158-0012
Order Phone: (800) 982-BOOK
Author: Edgar E. Peters
Price: $45.00
1991, 240 pages
John Wiley Finance Edition

At last there is a credible treatment of the state of the issue for investments, fractal data structures and chaos. Edgar Peters has written a first-class summary suitable for any investment professional or skilled investor.

Over the years, STOCKS & COMMODITIES has presented much evidence that traditional statistical measures of correlation and dependence miss the point in analyzing price time series. Of course, we and our authors had little idea of the real nature of the phenomenon we studied. Now, there is at least some suggestion of the nature of the order before us, though I don't believe we've even scratched the surface of reality.

Not so widely known is that mathematician Benoit Mandelbrot started his work on fractal structures in the early 1960s while studying the non-Gaussian distribution of returns in the markets. This distribution showed extraordinary returns — negative and positive — in the tails of the distributions and a narrower body as well. This work was widely ignored in the enthusiasm for the simplifications of the capital asset pricing model and its follow-ons. This lemming-like behavior met its end in the portfolio insurance debacle of October 1987, when one of those extraordinary events (an extraordinary return that would show up in the fat tail of the non-Gaussian distribution) occurred. As thousands of large, efficient investors headed for the exits at the same time, the crowd effect overwhelmed the transactions capability of the market makers and prices went into free fall.

Fractals are the geometry of chaos. Fractals are objects in which the structure of the parts is related to, possibly identical to, the structure of the whole because a fractal is the limiting set of resulting values from a random generating rule. For example, the branches of a tree or the alveoli in our lungs repeat their structure as they become smaller. Peters calls this phenomenon "self-similarity" and brings it to our trading world, observing that where fractal shapes show self-similarity with respect to space, time series (of prices, for example) show statistical self-similarity with respect to time.

It is, to me, always amazing that orderly results can come from randomly generated input treated by consistent rules. Sometimes in the case of "random" fractals, the results may not look orderly but the order can be discerned statistically (though not with traditional statistics). Deterministic fractals, on the other hand, produce the intricate structures so often shown us. It goes without saying that in price series we are dealing with random fractals, which nevertheless have an order of their own.

I wish I were capable of explaining this in a short review but I'm not. Nevertheless, the number of ideas and applications to trading that I got from Peters turned a Quick-Scan into days of reading and re-reading.

In this book can be found a possible explanation for the nature of the autocorrelation in our time series. Here is why efficient market theory breaks down in extraordinary situations and how that may relate to crowd phenomena. Here is a workable explanation how you can estimate the order in your times series — or when you can't — via something called the Hurst exponent and, at the same time,

find the true average cycle length in your data. On the side, we get a suggestion as to why cycles fade in and out: They exist but they aren't periodic. (Unfortunately for cyclists, they are "nonlinear dynamic systems.") Here are good data on the cycle length in stocks (yes, it *is* four years) and economic data (five years).

In *Chaos and Order in the Capital Markets,* the reader gets Edgar Peters' cogent personal assessment of the blend of fundamental and technical analysis. Also included is an idea of why daily price data tend to show more mean reversion than monthly data and why selecting your time horizon may be critical to your analysis. In here is good stuff on where to look for Markovian dependence and why, as Peters puts it, "…We must let go of many of the statistical diagnostics that we have used in the past." How about a hot tip for trading options volatility? How about some practice equations you can pop into your spreadsheet to generate chaotic spaces you can explore easily (Figure 1)? How about you just buy the book and dig in? This is the first publication I've seen on these subjects that makes sense to someone with BA/MBA-level math and that I could recommend to practitioners and public alike.

Beyond the book, Peters himself is impressive. He's a practitioner, an analyst and an excellent writer. He's objective in assessing the worlds of quants, fundamentalists and technicians and he's obviously capable of effective synthesis. We at *S&C* hope to read much more from him in the future.

—*John Sweeney, Technical Editor*

FIGURE 1

TWO ORDERLY AND RELATED TIME SERIES

Most of us would love to determine whether these two series have an order we could exploit. By the way, you can generate series like this via your spreadsheet and explore exactly how they are ordered.

STOCK MARKET LOGIC
A sophisticated approach to profits on Wall Street
Dearborn Financial Publishing, Inc.
520 North Dearborn Street
Chicago, IL 60610-4354
(312) 836-4400
Author: Norman G. Fosback
Price: $30.00
384 pages, 1991 (19th printing)

Considered a classic by reviewers since its original publication, *Stock Market Logic* by Norman G. Fosback is an excellent book for beginners and experienced investors alike. Neophyte investors reading this book will receive an easy-to-understand presentation of numerous techniques and concepts, while experienced investors perusing this book will have a chance to reconsider ideas that are worthy of reconsideration.

Stock Market Logic was first published in 1976 and, according to the publishing information inside, it is in its 19th printing. Most of the studies, charts and tables conclude in the years between 1975 and 1984. This observation, at first glance, may imply that the ideas presented here will be out of date, but that is not the case; the ideas presented are by and large still applicable today. In fact, there is a 35-page section devoted to the newsletter "Market Logic" (edited by *Stock Market Logic* author Norman Fosback) that more than likely allows you to keep up to date on most of the material presented.

RUNDOWN ON COMMON
The first section is a rundown on the most commonly discussed indicators for the stock market. Each indicator is listed as a chapter and ranges in length from three to four pages. There are 48 indicators listed. For example, you will find subjects such as the Dow theory, "three steps and a stumble" (referring to Federal Reserve Bank policy) and most active stocks. The second section addresses the concept of selecting stock indicators for designing a forecasting model. Fosback's major trend model is presented but not revealed, while the third section is an overview of stock selection theories such as price/earnings ratios, on-balance volume and relative strength. Combining a select group of

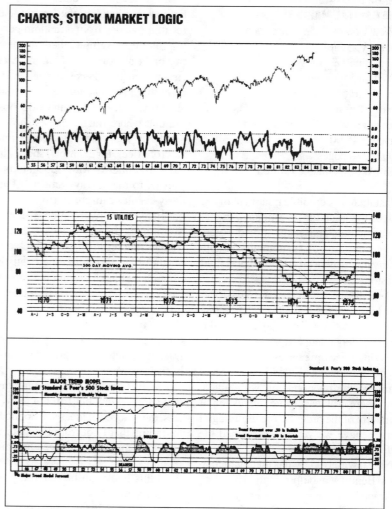

CHARTS, STOCK MARKET LOGIC

Some figures that can be found in Stock Market Logic. *Top: Ten-week exponential moving average of NYSE High Low Logic Index (versus Standard & Poor's 500 Index) with two horizontal dashed lines highlighting particularly bullish readings below 1% and extremely bearish readings above 5%; 1955-85. Middle: Dow Jones Utility Average, weekly price range and 200-day simple moving average; April 1970-July 1975. Bottom: Major trend model, monthly averages of weekly econometric estimates and Standard & Poor's Composite Index (monthly range of weekly average prices).*

indicators is discussed in section four. Author Fosback's favorite indicators for stock picking are also included. The basics of a financial management system, including compound interest and the two-edged sword of leveraged investing, are the topics of section five.

Each day on the news or in the newspaper, the current prices of various market indices such as the Dow Jones averages or the Standard & Poor's 500 are presented, but have you ever wondered what these indices are or how are they calculated? You will learn this and more in the sixth section, entitled "Evaluating market averages." Section seven is an introduction to "Market Logic," the

author's stock market newsletter. The final two sections cover mutual funds and the nature (nonrandom) of the stock market.

This book has two agendas: first is an agenda regarding an education about the stock market and a wide assortment of indicators and theories, while the second is the presentation and promotion of Norman Fosback's newsletter. All in all, this book has a lot of value and I recommend reading it.

—*Thom Hartle, Editor*

THE VOLATILITY HANDBOOK

*Charts of Volatility Zones for
the Advanced Options Trader*
Robert P. Krause
Box 873
Chicago, IL 60690
(312) 772-5734
Author: Robert P. Krause
Published 1992, 75 pages, $79

A handbook is for daily use, and that's exactly how often the practicing options trader will pull this reference work off the shelf. *The Volatility Handbook* is just the ticket for quick information on the historical and seasonal volatility of 32 futures contracts' options, with a separate breakout for each major trading delivery, for a total of 212 charts.

For example, suppose that it's January and you happen to run across an implicit volatility figure for September cocoa options of just 8%. Thinking this a tad low for cocoa, you whip out the handy *Handbook* and discover that not only is this figure low for implicit volatility in general, but it is *historically* low for September cocoa options in particular (Figure 1). At this time of year, the one standard deviation below normal expectancy for September cocoa options is perhaps 15%, and what's more, volatility normally rises into July. Buying volatility at this level

and time would not only bear out a high probability for profit but also would offer a very low-risk venture, given that September cocoa's typical volatility ranges from 20% to 30%.

Now, if you find the above paragraph incomprehensible, skip this book unless you're *really* ready to dig into exploiting options. Author Robert Krause, the Chicago Mercantile Exchange's maven of options (he designed its options & alternatives program and wrote the "CME futures and options strategy guide"), does show you "how to do it" in the manual, but you'd better have your option basics in place. He's taken no time to explain them — and why should he? Plenty of good primers on options trading can be found in the bookstores. *The Volatility Handbook* is for day-to-day use.

DATA DEPTH DEEP

Instead, options practitioners will love the depth of the data (from 1970 forward), the expertise of the discussion and the quick visual delivery of the information. Each chart shows the central tendency of each delivery's options by month. Above and below each chart are the log-normal first standard deviation values for volatility (Figure 1). Of this display, I can only say that I'd like to see three standard deviations plotted to get a sense of the full range

of values, because one standard deviation only covers the values expected to be seen just 68% of the time.

If Krause had simply published these data, *The Volatility Handbook* would still easily be worth $79. More value is added to this publication by the inclusion of an introductory discussion of volatility and the basic strategies that are used to exploit it, a discussion that would be of great value to novice traders though more examples would make up for the professionally terse, speedy coverage of the subjects. Thrown in are quick but cogent discussions of delta-neutral hedging with some great day-by-day examples, plus some practical wisdom on premium recovery and trading volatility skew.

On the downside, I do have to quibble with the author's decision to omit his formula for computing historical volatility. In addition, because he is a firm advocate of using bull and bear spreads over outright long or short options, the discussion of these two techniques could have been more complete. These are minor faults. *The Volatility Handbook* as it stands is well worth the money, and I hope that it will be updated with new data as time passes, becoming a handy standard for position traders using options.

—*John Sweeney, Technical Editor*

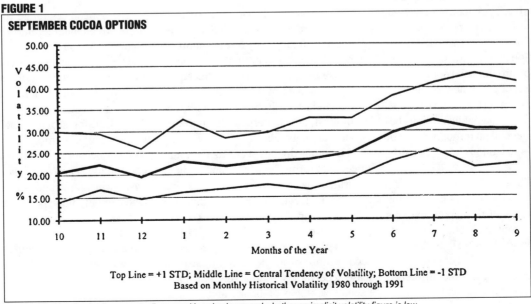

FIGURE 1

The Volatility Handbook *allows you to discover with a simple perusal whether an implicit volatility figure is low.*

THE NEW FINANCIAL INSTRUMENTS

John Wiley & Sons
605 Third Avenue
New York, NY 10158
(212) 850-6497
Author: Julian Walmsley
Published 1988, 454 pages, $35.00

Not sure what a heaven & hell bond is? *The New Financial Instruments* provides straightforward and succinct answers to this question and more as it leads the reader through the morass of new instruments. Since the author/tour guide, Julian Walmsley, is a London-based investment banker, it's not surprising that the book is especially thorough in its coverage of Euromarket innovations. But Walmsley doesn't ignore developments in the U.S. markets either, providing, among other things, a concise account of the development of the mortgage-backed securities market (replete with super sinkers, strips and REMICs).

Walmsley has organized the book in four sections: Origins, Basics, New Markets and New Instruments. In the origins section, Walmsley traces the history of financial innovation back to the 13th century and the hapless Ricciardi di Luca, who became an early victim of sovereign default after lending £400,000 to English kings who failed to repay him. The author categorizes financial innovations as either process or product and either aggressive or defensive. The pace of innovation, asserts Walmsley, has increased since the late 1970s for three main reasons: increasing competition among firms, the worldwide move toward financial deregulation and the impact of computer technology. He also notes that efforts to hedge risk have resulted in financial institutions becoming interdependent through chains of transactions — a tenuous house of cards.

THE BASICS

The second section of the book covers the basic instruments of the capital markets (equities, preferred stock, bonds, convertibles and warrants), as well as the concepts of value and risk. Although most readers will already know the difference between an equity and a bond, they may find this section useful for reviewing the formulas of basic financial ratios (price/earnings and payout ratios as well as dividend yield) and the formula for determining the price of a bond or the conversion premium of a convertible bond.

In the New Markets section, Walmsley discusses the major financial futures exchanges throughout the world, followed by a discussion of hedging strategies, basis risk and stock index futures. In the chapter on swaps, Walmsley explains cash flow, pricing and the factors that determine swap spreads and addresses the process of unwinding a swap. To show just how complicated swaps can be, Walmsley includes details of a series of deals done in 1986 that included three different borrowers and several interest rate and currency swaps. Finishing up the section is a discussion of options.

BEYOND BASICS

Having laid out the basics, Walmsley finally gets to the discussion of new instruments, starting with floating-rate notes (FRNs). He attributes the growth of floating-rate securities since the mid-1970s to the period of high interest rates, when issuers didn't want to lock themselves into paying high rates for the entire life of their issue. Other variations he discusses are bull, deferred coupon, step-up, partly paid, collateralized and currency convertible FRNs.

Next, it's on to zero coupons, perpetuals and other miscellaneous bond variants. Walmsley explains why a zero coupon is more volatile than other types of bonds. The discussion turns to the "receipts" securities that grew out of this market (TIGRs and so forth) and ends with medium-term notes, perpetuals, puttable bonds and tap bonds.

The author divides securitization into three main forms: loan sales and trading, securities that substitute for loans and asset-backed securities. He notes that loan sales have helped commercial banks compete against securities firms. The repackaging of receivables has led to the securitization of auto loan, credit card and lease receivables — markets that have become a staple of banks and finance companies eager to reduce risk.

Mortgage securitization rates its own chapter. Because thrift institutions were hurt by swings in interest rates during the 1970s, Walmsley explains that they were driven to find new ways to manage their balance sheets. Pass-through securities, mortgage-backed securities, collateralized mortgage obligations (CMOs) and stripped mortgage-backed securities are all discussed here.

HYBRIDS AND MORE

The final two chapters of the book are devoted to hybrids and option-related instruments. Floating-rate preferred was invented on the premise that adjustable rates would ensure that the stock would trade close to par even when interest rates rose. Puttable equity, issues that are convertible into shares of another company, non-voting shares and performance-linked shares are other equity innovations that Walmsley discusses.

Option-related instruments are securities that have had options embedded in their structure. Caps and floors, embedded call and put options and embedded currency options are all addressed in the final chapter, as are various types of warrant-linked bonds. Walmsley explains harmless, wedding, naked, income and money-back warrants and then finishes with details of a bond that has what *might* be called a synthetic warrant.

The appendices range from formulas for bond calculations and odd-period discounting to sample documents such as telexes inviting underwriters to join a Euro-note issuance facility and prospectuses for a synthetic bond issue.

If you need help finding your way through the forest of financial instruments with strange names and sometimes stranger behavior, Walmsley would be a good guide. *The New Financial Instruments* is insightful and global in its vision. One can only hope he is planning a new edition.

Anne Hall is on the editorial staff of a financial magazine in New York.

AGRICULTURAL MARKETING

A Business Manual Using Futures and Options as Marketing Tools
History of Major Grains 1970-1991
Aleris Consulting Inc.
3682 West 15th Ave.
Vancouver, BC Canada V6R 2Z5
(604) 222-2585
Author: Henry J. Van Kessel
272 pages, US$72, 1992

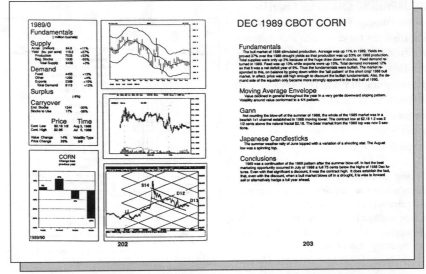

Van Kessel gives a rundown of major grains thoroughly — acreage harvested, yield, production, total supply, food and seed demand, exports and more.

A popular novelist would have a field day with this one: London School of Economics graduate quits the academic life to return to farming the land. Ah, romance. How about adding this twist: After farming the family homestead for a number of years, our LSE graduate decides to turn to trading commodities futures and rides soybeans to their peak in 1977.

Unfortunately — for this is a true story and the guiding hand of a novelist is absent — our hero also rides soybeans to the bottom, learning his first lesson in trading futures. *Agricultural Marketing* author Henry Van Kessel was ignorant but, as he observes, "Everyone is ignorant when they start out. ... There is no other way to ascend the learning curve ... but to learn from experience."

With this background, then, *Agricultural Marketing* makes sense. It's rare that one runs across someone who's been on both ends of the commodities game (growing and trading), and that makes author Van Kessel someone worth reading. Surely commodities trading takes on entirely new dimensions when the commodities in question are not far from personal experience.

So what exactly is "agricultural marketing," anyway? Pretty much what you'd assume it means: getting the best price for what you produce, the marketing of a given crop, a task that Van Kessel asserts is as important as the production of the crop itself. As Van Kessel observes: "We have entered a time when the farmer is not really different from the Harvard business school graduate. Survival demands the application of rigorous business and marketing principles in every field of enterprise married to long experience in the field married to a deep appreciation for the subjective limitations of the individual applying the strategies."

In *Agricultural Marketing*, Van Kessel explains that the science of farming can easily and logically be merged with the science of marketing. He points out that farming and marketing have much in common and also explains how using futures and options as a strategy in the marketing of farm produce can result in agreeable rewards — if you know what you're doing. From there, Van Kessel goes into concepts designed to help the reader to the possible rewards with minimal loss (always the goal), the time frames in which this can be achieved, the information that you need and don't need, as well as a few chapters covering familiar topics — moving average envelopes, the Gann technique and Japanese candlesticks. Author Van Kessel also covers the basics: greed and fear, cash, futures, options and his nine guidelines of strategy.

You may have noticed the second part of the title: *History of Major Grains 1970-1991*. Van Kessel wraps up *Agricultural Marketing* with exactly that — wheat, corn and soybeans and what each has done from 1970 to 1991. He gives a rundown of how to read the information given, acreage harvested, yield, production, total supply, food and seed demand, feed, exports, total demand, carryover — you get the idea. Van Kessel manages to go into detail and at the end even gives you a conclusion if you choose not to peruse each and every page.

In short, this is worth a quick read. This is worth a careful and detailed read. This is worth constant reference as a reference; it should be kept on hand as a invaluable tool.

—Elizabeth Flynn, Copy Editor

THE JAPANESE CHART OF CHARTS

Tokyo Futures Trading Publishing Co.
U.S. distributors: Probus Publishing, Windsor Books
P.O. Box 280
Brightwaters, NY 11718
Author: Seiki Shimizu, translated by Gregory S. Nicholson
Price: $50
210 pages, 1986

Buying and selling of stocks and commodities when one doesn't have a clear picture of price movements is the same as jumping a rope without looking at its movement. In other words, one should consult the chart before entering into a trading contract.

—*Seiki Shimizu*

Some things don't change across national boundaries, cultures, time or even trading method, whether you are a devotee of the candlestick method or Gann. With the current interest in candlestick charting, if you decide to do any research at all into the subject you can't help but run across at least a mention of this volume, whence much of the primary information about candlesticks available in the West (and in English) originates and to which Western candlestick proponent Steve Nison has referred.

First the reader may find *The Japanese Chart of Charts* something of a curiosity, especially if said reader is a native speaker of English and has little or no experience with any language other than English (not unusual in the U.S.). This volume was translated from Japanese with information the main goal, and as a consequence the idiomatic aspect of translation was overlooked. So this book may sound weird. This should not deter you, dear reader. If you have any amount of curiosity at all about candlestick technique and how it came about, *The Japanese Chart of Charts* is definitely worth a look-see.

DELVING INTO CONCEPT

Shimizu, a well-known figure in financial circles in Japan, is an excellent candidate to explain the technique to receptive candlestick neophytes. In *The Japanese Chart of Charts* he delves into the concept of charts in general purely from a Japanese point of view (with subtitles such as, "A chart is like a cat's whiskers" and

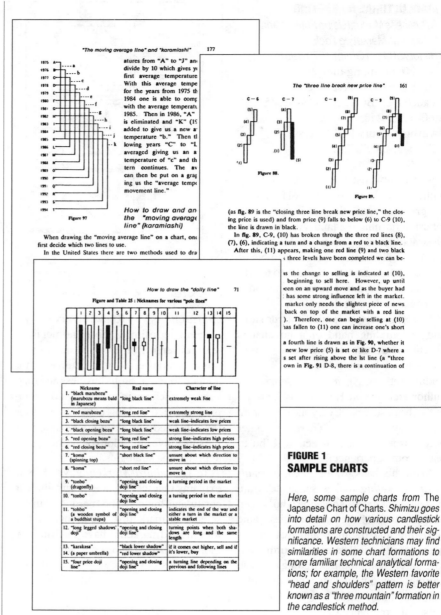

**FIGURE 1
SAMPLE CHARTS**

Here, some sample charts from The Japanese Chart of Charts. Shimizu *goes into detail on how various candlestick formations are constructed and their significance. Western technicians may find similarities in some chart formations to more familiar technical analytical formations; for example, the Western favorite "head and shoulders" pattern is better known as a "three mountain" formation in the candlestick method.*

"This is a sumo wrestling scoreboard. This is a chart!") — how they began, how to draw one, how to draw a "tome" line (pronounced "tomeh" and meaning to "stop"), the different kinds of candlestick charts. This volume is also interesting from an anthropological point of view; it reminds the Western reader that one's viewpoint too often tends to be purely ethnocentric, for at the end, in the section with the subtitle "Can imported graphs be called charts?" foreign, "imported" charts such as the Elliott wave theory, the 10% reversal method and the on-balance volume line get mentioned as possible, al-most incidental, forms of "charts" but winds up by concluding "Japanese charts [lead] others." Shimizu mentions, of all people, Joe Granville; Shimizu wonders if Granville "gained some insight from Japanese ideas."

So *The Japanese Chart of Charts* can be a valuable work on different levels. First information about candlestick technique, from the original language itself, unfiltered by Western culture; second sociological, on the ethnocentricity of mankind. —*E.M.S. Flynn, Copy Editor*

QUICK-SCANS

THE ALL-SEASON INVESTOR

Successful Strategies for Every Stage in the Business Cycle

John Wiley & Sons, publisher
Also available through
International Institute for
Technical Research
P.O. Box 329, Blackville Rd.
Washington Depot, CT 06794
(800) 221-7514
Author: Martin J. Pring
Published 1992, 337 pages, $29.95

Martin Pring, market analyst, publisher and author of numerous books including the classic *Technical Analysis Explained*, has brought together practical and straightforward methods for tracking the business cycle and choosing appropriate investments. *The All-Season Investor* is based on the philosophy that the business cycle or growth path of business activity has two dominant phases, the expansion phase and the contraction or recessionary phase. During these two phases, the course of three asset classes — bonds, stocks and commodities — are strongly influenced. In *The All-Season Investor*, Pring has reviewed years of financial market history and concluded that the chronological sequence of events is as follows: After the economy enters into a recession, there is a bottoming of bond prices (that is, a peak in interest rates), after which the stock market bottoms and begins to advance, and finally, the commodity markets turn up. As the business activity moves from contraction into expansion, the bond market peaks (while interest rates hit a trough), equities peak after bonds and then the commodity markets crest. To understand this rotation principle, to track the economic cycle and to select appropriate assets for each stage of the business cycle are the goals of this book. It succeeds magnificently.

ALLOCATING ASSETS

The introduction begins with a discussion of asset allocation. Asset allocation has three goals, we are told: to reduce risk through diversification; to allow for those periods when a specific asset is attractive and for those when it is not; and to reduce the emotional aspect of decision making by carefully and gradually shifting emphasis from one asset type to another. Chapter 1 introduces the reader to diversifying to manage risk. The issues of risk are broken down into unsystematic and systematic risk. The value of diversification is explained as a method to both manage risk and increase the chance for a larger gain. In chapter 2, the reader learns about the characteristics of bonds, stocks and publicly traded inflation hedge vehicles and cash (defined as debt instruments with a maturity of less than one year). Mutual funds are the subject of chapter 3. Chapters 2 and 3 provide the basic descriptions for understanding the assets that are selected for asset allocation.

The power of compounding is addressed in chapter 4. This topic is important for understanding the rewards of building consistent modest returns versus volatile returns. This chapter leads the way to looking at each asset from a risk/reward viewpoint. Chapter 5 outlines the risk/reward characteristics of each of the assets.

In chapter 6, outlined are the business cycle and how the markets fit in. The steps in the sequence of the rotation of each of the markets, stocks, bonds and commodities are detailed along with numerous charts to give the reader a clear understanding of the process. Tracking a typical cycle by utilizing a rate of change indicator of different measurements of the economy is demonstrated in chapter 7, which is one method for identifying what position the business cycle is in. Again, there are historical charts (close to 40 years) showing the cyclical nature of these indicators.

Chapter 8 brings together the asset allocation process based on the position of the business cycle, which is broken down into six stages. The characteristics of each stage is discussed along with why a particular stage favors a particular asset (Figure 1). Chapters 9 and 10 provide methods for pinpointing the various stages. In chapter 9, the individual markets (that is, U.S. Treasury bonds, Standard & Poor's Composite and the Commodity Research Bureau composite) are presented with technical indicators such as moving averages, rate of change and relative strength measurements to clarify which stage the

FIGURE 1

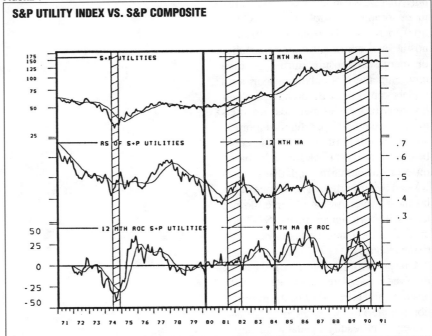

S&P UTILITY INDEX VS. S&P COMPOSITE

During stage 1 (shaded areas), interest rates are falling, and consequently, interest rate-sensitive stocks such as the S&P utility index (top chart) will outperform the S&P 500 as illustrated by the relative strength line of the S&P utility index (center graph). The bottom chart is the 12-month rate of change of the S&P utility index.

business cycle is in.

The second method of looking at the business cycle can be found in chapter 10. Business cycle barometers are explained here. A barometer is a composite indicator of economic, financial and technical indicators that on average have worked well to identfy bull and bear markets in bonds, stocks and commodities. Chapter 11 is a historical look at the relationship of gold and the business cycle. (Because gold pays neither interest nor a dividend, it was not previously addressed as an asset.)

The final chapter discusses designing an individual's portfolio and percentage allocation of assets based on his or her personal investment objectives and the stage of the business cycle. Two different styles, either conservative or aggressive approaches, are presented. In addition, there are four appendices, the first three of which detail the individual barometers (bond, stock and inflation) and the final one of which is a collection of 40-year charts. The charts of the S&P, bonds and the spot raw materials index are reviewed in each of the six stages.

UNIVERSALITY

Who can benefit from this book? *Everyone!* Investors can learn how to identify times to adjust portfolios (asset allocation) to reduce the negative impact of hostile environments for their portfolios or increase exposure during positive environments. Not only that, short-term traders can benefit by broadening their horizons for applying methods to markets that offer the best opportunities. For example, identifying the current stage could be used as a filter. Look for trades based on technical trading methods that are forewarned by the current or next stage of the business cycle. As an example, do not take sell-short signals in the S&P 500 until after the interest rates have started rising (stage 5).

One problem you may face is the work involved to completely duplicate the methods recommended. Most of the information required to follow the methods and strategies is readily available in larger libraries, but it would be time consuming to keep track of it all. I would recommend subscribing to Martin Pring's "Pring

Market Review," which is a 48-page monthly report that among other things will save you the trouble of tracking, calculating and interpreting the barometers and models and identifying the stages. Not only that, those who decide to try it out will have the benefit of Pring's current interpretations and recommendations.

As I was reading this book I felt as though I was seeing the results of Martin Pring's life work. I can highly recommend reading *The All-Season Investor*.

—*Thom Hartle, Editor*

MONEY MANAGEMENT STRATEGIES FOR FUTURES TRADERS

John Wiley & Sons, Inc.
605 Third Avenue
New York, NY 10158-0012
Order Phone: (800) 982-BOOK
Author: Nauzer J. Balsara
267 pages, $45, 1992
John Wiley Finance Edition

There exists a small — *very* small — set of books devoted to the subject of avoiding the loss of money, the first rule of investing. In futures trading, Fred Gehm and, more recently, Bob Pelletier have written on the subject. Regular STOCKS & COMMODITIES readers know that I expound on this topic monthly, perhaps *ad nauseum*. Now Nauzer Balsara, an associate professor of finance at Northeastern Illinois University and a futures trader as well, has taken a comprehensive look at the subject, summarizing both academic and practical thought in a book that hits all the essentials without an overly mathematical emphasis.

FROM THEORY TO PRACTICE

Unfortunately, trading, especially futures trading, is best described — at our state of knowledge — with statistical concepts. I say "unfortunately" because statistical education is even rarer than economics education and very few front-line traders can take something theoretical from a book and use it in practice. Author Balsara's book by itself can't be expected to solve this, but his approach is a beginning; nothing more than algebra is required and you'd gain if you did nothing but skimmed the text, because you'd at least become aware of the issues lurking in the background, issues that could bite you but of which you may not be aware.

Reducing ruin to probability of success, payoff ratio and percentage of capital risked per trade should be simplified things for those who choose to read *Money Management Strategies for Futures Traders*. In practice, probabilities are mind-numbing and difficult to estimate even if it does generate neat numbers academically. Moreover, they aren't very reassuring in the heat of the action.

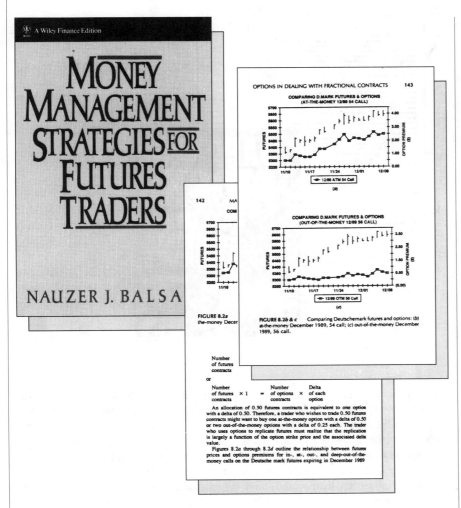

FIGURE 8.2a the-money Decer

FIGURE 8.2b & c Comparing Deutschemark futures and options: (b) at-the-money December 1989, 54 call; (c) out-of-the-money December 1989, 56 call.

Number of futures contracts

or

$$\text{Number of futures contracts} \times 1 = \text{Number of options contracts} \times \text{Delta of each option}$$

An allocation of 0.50 futures contracts is equivalent to one option with a delta of 0.50. Therefore, a trader who wishes to trade 0.50 futures contracts might want to buy one at-the-money option with a delta of 0.50 or two out-of-the-money options with a delta of 0.25 each. The trader who uses options to replicate futures must realize that the replication is largely a function of the option strike price and the associated delta value.

Figures 8.2a through 8.2d outline the relationship between futures prices and options premiums for in-, at-, out-, and deep-out-of-the-money calls on the Deutsche mark futures expiring in December 1989.

UNIQUE AND WILLING

Balsara goes about explaining the art of avoiding the loss of money in a unique mix of the practical (charts, trading indicators) and, for speculators, the arcane (diversification, ruin, capital allocation). What I admire is the willingness to address tough topics (estimating "reward," for example) using most of the tools practically available.

In an area I emphasize personally, an entire chapter is devoted to managing unrealized profits and losses, one of which is the unrealized loss patterns on profitable trades. This is a *very* fruitful area, and Balsara provides great examples of analyzing Swiss francs and Eurodollars for good stop points. He manages to do this with tables that anyone can understand with no exotic math or analysis involved. Along the same lines, he delves into avoiding bull and bear traps and even provides tables of opening price behavior for 24 commodities for use in setting stops.

Assuming you've picked the best tradeable, defined your risk/reward outlook, prepared a diversification plan and are prepared to cut losses quickly and rationally, there are still the issues of the size of the next trade or package of trades and then, if you are brave enough to specify risk and return, the portfolio to be traded. The first issue is handled well, including martingale† strategies for adjusting the size of your bet. The second, though handled as ably as our current knowledge permits, founders on all the limitations in estimating returns and risks when speculating. The discussion of pyramiding is similarly devoid of insight, advocating the trader to intuitively set a reinvestment fraction of profits rather than provide some quantitative guideline for that decision.

The chapter on evaluating mechanical trading systems deserves special mention because of a unique analysis of the impact of trading rules and market conditions on results. Sparing you the variance analysis — which is the heart of the presentation and a valuable technique of which I hope to see much more — the result is that for the systems tested, the results were dependent on market conditions rather than the rules used. This fits with the common trading wisdom that, for example, you need a trending market to make money with a trending system. This is a very substantial contribution to trading literature, and every quantitatively minded trader should review the book for these 10 pages if nothing else.

TO SUM THIS UP

This book is easily the most comprehensible of the money management genre. Though limited space prevents us from providing detailed worksheets of the techniques described, it may be more valuable for the effective presentation of techniques too often buried in statistical formulas and verbiage. Certainly, the overview of the entire process is valuable for novice and intermediate traders alike. A seasoned trader (say, 10 years or more) may well have developed responses to all the issues discussed here, but absent tutoring or mentoring, many issues will have been unclear or confusing to traders still developing competence. Fortunately, you may take a shortcut through the learning process somewhat by reading Balsara's *Money Management Strategies for Futures Traders*.

—*John Sweeney, Technical Editor*

REFLECTION OF CHANGES

Price movements are simply the reflection of changes in supply and demand. The technician does not care what the underlying forces of a shift in supply and demand are, rather he is interested in what occurs. If demand is greater than supply, prices will increase. On the other hand, if supply is greater than demand, prices will decline. The study of market prices is all that is necessary.

—Thomas A. Meyers
The Technical Analysis Course

JAPANESE STOCKS
Make Money on the Tokyo Stock Exchange
Kodansha International Ltd.
114 Fifth Avenue
18th floor
New York, NY 10011
(212) 727-6460
Author: Toru Matsumoto
Price: $12.95
216 pages, 1989; update published by
TAB Books, 1990

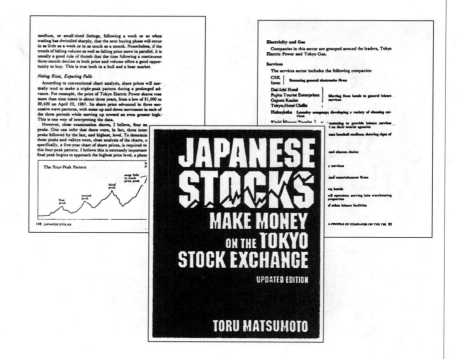

I n a recent STOCKS & COMMODITIES interview, technician John Murphy spoke of how all global markets in this day and age are interconnected and how intermarket analysis has been a reality for some time. How much more telling than to quote the first lines of *Japanese Stocks*, by Toru Matsumoto:

> Until recently, movement in the Japanese stock market has been firmly linked to trends in overseas markets. With few exceptions, Japanese investment decisions were made with an eye on what was happening on the New York Stock Exchange.

For those U.S. investors who rarely venture off their own shores for investment opportunities, this volume may inspire and incite them to explore other possibilities in other parts of the world. Why *not* the Japanese stock market?

Author Matsumoto, who is referred to on the back cover of *Japanese Stocks* as the president and editor-in-chief of *Nikkan Toshi Shimbun* ("Investment Daily"), a newspaper publishing company, and who has written a number of other books on Japanese investing (unfortunately but not unexpectedly not translated from the native Japanese), has here dissected and explained for the novice investor how the Japanese market works and how to profit from it. He obligingly (but briefly) gives us an overview of how the Japanese financial markets are structured and how it compares with U.S. markets. Matsumoto tells us about the large Japanese companies that are everyday names, even to us: Toyota, Matsushita, Sony, Nomura.

RULES OF THE GAME

In order to succeed, it is necessary to understand the infrastructure of the society on which the exchange and the market are based as well as the rules of the game. The rules of this game are more or less similar, but more often than not they have a twist; it's not your ballpark, no matter how much it may look like it, but much the same things may happen — *viz wit.*, a sharp stock market correction. The second chapter begins by explaining some of those differences between me and thee: Japanese culture, according to Matsumoto, "has long had an aversion to the making of profit from the trading of goods and money," an attitude that has only changed since the end of World War II, with drastic measures necessary to revitalize the economy that was destroyed through the war. It took years for the taint of profit to be lifted from the Japanese securities firms, but after it did — that is, after Westernization hit Tokyo's financial district — there was no stopping it. According to the author, Japan's securities industry has expanded more than a hundredfold — and that's only since 1968 or so. The third chapter, in a similar vein, gives us an overview of how the theme may be similar — the Japanese stock market also suffered from the October 1987 stock

market fall — but the story may not be the one you expect: the author points out that the stock of heretofore-unpopular companies rose dramatically, spearheading a wave of mergers and acquisitions, the likes of which had not been seen in Japan before then. The rest of the chapter blends familiar themes and unfamiliar ones — what speculators on the Japanese stock market look for and why.

Chapter 4 profiles companies that make up the Japanese stock market and all the different sections that make up the Tokyo Stock Exchange, the Osaka Securities Exchange, the OTC market, not to mention the smaller regional exchanges, and, of course, the barometer by which the rises and falls of the Japanese market are monitored — the Nikkei. Here you learn (but probably not for the first time) all the different industries that are emphasized in the Japanese markets. Also mentioned almost as an aside are how companies with similar names may have very different concentrations. One example is that of the different glass companies listed on the Tokyo Stock Exchange. Asahi Glass, Nippon Sheet Glass, Ishizuka Glass, Yamamura Glass, Sasaki Glass and Nippon Electric Glass all on first glance look alike, until your research shows that Sasaki Glass produces domestic glassware products and Nippon Electric is the primary producer of large cathode ray tubes for television sets, which just goes to prove once again that research *does* pay off.

> Japanese culture, according to Matsumoto, "has long had an aversion to the making of profit from the trading of goods and money," an attitude that has only changed since the end of World War II.

WINNERS AND LOSERS

The next chapter will be of particular interest, with industry forecasts, both winners and losers, suggested, and the reasons why each will prosper or suffer. Many of the factors that affect U.S. investors affect Japanese ones, too, you may discover. A wide variety of industries are covered: everything from foods and fishery, through textiles, all the way to banking and insurance. (Curious to know Matsumoto's predictions? Of course you are. Among companies with bio-pharmaceutical products, those with anti-cholesterol agents under development will likely prosper; mobile phone technology, Matsumoto predicts, will be streamlined and worked into the structure of the automobile, perhaps even into the steering wheel, making companies with a technological slant a good buy; companies with specialty glass development, with an eye beyond only its optical characteristics and on to its various other physical properties and uses are equally promising; high-definition television, which even now is making inroads; fifth-generation computer technology, developing neuro-computer systems, will also be something to keep an eye on; and companies with projects in high-temperature superconductivity.) Matsumoto also suggests current bets.

Chapters 6 through 10 covers changing investor attitudes toward the Japanese market, how investment strategies have shifted in recent years due to current events,

including a mention of who or what profits from the end of the Persian Gulf crisis, the "tools, timing and tricks" of dealing with the markets in general (which chapter also has a mention of technical analysis), riding the Japanese bull market through 1994 and the Japanese jinx that stocks that rise one year are not likely to do so the next.

The last chapter, "How to buy and sell Japanese stocks," gives the nuts and bolts of doing business in the Japanese stock market. It gives the caveats and the whys and wherefores. The volume ends with a three-part appendix of companies listed on the Tokyo Stock Exchange (first and second sections), original company name and romanization, industry performance both present and future, and a partial glossary.

MINDMELD

Toru Matsumoto, with his background in the Japanese financial press, is well-qualified to explain in detail the world of the Japanese financial markets, its past, its present, and even its future. Readers who are interested in the whole world market in general and in the Japanese financial markets in particular will find this book an intriguing way to enter the mindset of another country. Even after taking note of the wild fluctuations that the Japanese stock markets have experienced since this book was originally written and even since this particular update has been published, reading *Japanese Stocks* will be both an illuminating and intriguing insight into how the other hemisphere lives.

—*E.M.S. Flynn, Copy Editor*

CLIENTWATCH, VERSION 2.0
Austin Associates
1438 Dry Creek Circle
Derby, KS 67037
(316) 788-3255
Contacts: Ted Austin, Patty Austin
Price: $98

Besides a fancy trading system, most brokers would love to have a simple database that could track the information for individual clients and pump out lists of those interested in specific commodities. That way, when something is up in, say, corn, no one misses getting a call and more business is generated.

Clientwatch is a nicely done little dBase program that allows quick entry of client information and virtually immediate retrieval. The format is fixed so you can't add fields that aren't currently supported, but there *is* a good-sized comment field in which you can insert miscellaneous data.

This *isn't* a system that tracks client trading positions. Some other software would have to do that for you. The trouble with most systems that track the trades is that they don't provide information on which clients like to do what and when they like to be called. Clientwatch provides this sort of personalization.

The program occupies maybe 250,000 bytes on your hard disk and can run from floppy if you wish. This is a simple application, well done, that can run on virtually any DOS machine. Since it would easily cost you more than the price in time to do it yourself, it's a great buy.

—*John Sweeney, Technical Editor*

GLOBAL PORTFOLIOS

Quantitative Strategies for Maximum Performance

Business One Irwin
1818 Ridge Road
Homewood, IL 60430
(800) 841-8000
Editors: Robert Z. Aliber
and Brian R. Bruce
Price: $75
350 pages, 1991

From the smallest of small investors to the largest of institutional investors, the goal of all investors is to maximize returns while minimizing risks. Diversification is the standard strategy by which to achieve this. But for most U.S. investors, diversification just means buying a portfolio of domestic equities or fixed-income instruments. Robert Z. Aliber and Brian R. Bruce, who edited the compilation of articles in *Global Portfolios*, hold that such thinking is much too narrow; the sophisticated investor should look toward foreign investment possibilities to reap higher returns and reduce risk.

That returns are higher can be seen at a glance in any publication carrying information about foreign investments; many examples are cited throughout *Global Portfolios*. That risk reduction is less evident is explained in several articles in this book. The main argument is that risk is lessened mainly because there is little correlation between foreign fixed-income and equity issues and those in the U.S.

PORTFOLIO PREMISE

If an investor accepts the premise that global holdings mean higher returns at lower risks, then his or her natural desire is to acquire such holdings as soon as possible. But then the investor must build an international portfolio the way his or her domestic portfolio was built. It must be well-balanced, not only in the ratio between domestic and international instruments, but the investor must seek the best balance between fixed-income and equity assets within the international component. Finally, investors must protect themselves against currency fluctuation.

Part 1 deals with asset allocation: How much of a portfolio should be foreign assets and how should those assets be

FIGURE 1
EQUITIES, BONDS AND TRENDS

Here, from Global Portfolios: *If an investor accepts the premise that global holdings mean higher returns at lower risk, then the investor must build an international portfolio the way a domestic portfolio is built, seeking the best balance between fixed-income and equity assets within the international component.*

distributed across countries? Gary Brinson and Denis Karnofsky argue that the basic asset ratio should be based on global market capitalization, of which the U.S. controls about 33%, indicating a two-to-one international domestic asset ratio. Robert Arnott and Roy Hendriksson use a simpler methodology, measuring risk by comparing equity yields to cash or bond yields for each country and then weighting this information for their portfolio construction. Eric Sorenson and Joseph Mezrich add more complexity to their model by using a system developed by Salomon Brothers to analyze time series data to optimize their portfolio. Lee Thomas, answering the question of currency in most investors' minds, explains the use of a three-part process to build up their foreign assets, eliminating currency risk while allowing the investor latitude in asset selection.

Edgar Barksdale and William Green address the problem of who is to manage the new and improved portfolio. They suggest using either an unmanaged portfolio or an index by which to measure the relative success of the managed portfolio. If the manager consistently outperformed the index or the control, then he or she may be worth the premium demanded for the service. If not, investors could look for a manager who does better or leave their portfolios unmanaged.

In Part 2, international fixed-income assets (bonds) and their role in an investor's portfolio are discussed. Philippe Jorion writes that nondollar bonds make up 64% of the bonds issued around the world, although less than 1% of U.S. pension funds are invested in them. He reasserts that foreign fixed-income instruments are an excellent investment because they have little correlation with U.S. issues, thus decreasing overall risk due to diversification.

The other three articles in the fixed-income asset portion of the book deal with the merits of managed vs. unmanaged portfolios and the ways by which to measure success. Gifford Fong and Eric Tang, like Barksdale and Green, suggest using an unmanaged index as an overall guide as to how well a managed portfolio is performing, but they urge that the investor look at the returns from maturity, the returns from spread/equity and the returns from individual stocks for each country should be examined with closer attention than overall performance alone. Christopher Orndorff expands on this idea and lists certain performance areas where an unmanaged portfolio can be enhanced.

Peter Vann goes further about keeping one's portfolio unmanaged, arguing that a managed portfolio is inherently riskier than an unmanaged one. If an investor insists on active management, Vann suggests tools such as futures and options to effectively limit the downside risk of active management.

EQUITY EMPHASIS

Part 3 resembles Part 2, but emphasizing equity issues instead of fixed income. Roger Ibbotson, Laurence Siegel and Paul Kaplan look at the past, the present and the future for global portfolios and give an overview of the rest of Part 3. The look back examines equity issues of the major global markets over the past few years and notes the lack of correlation between those markets and the U.S. markets. Ibbotson *et al.* predict that economic bar-

riers to capital movement will disappear, a process apparent today; they also believe in a "one-world" vision in the not-so-distant future.

Brian Bruce, Heydon Traub and Larry Martin are also concerned with management strategy, noting that passive global indices have outperformed the median actively managed indices. They argue that the added costs of active management, such as fixed and transaction costs and other fees, are a large part of the problem.

Hans Erickson uses a more sophisticated method of weighting by proposing a quadratic programming algorithm based on portfolio characteristics instead of the stocks within the portfolio. His analysis is at once interesting and challenging.

Robert Aliber suggests weighting by economic performance (such as the rate of growth of manufactured goods), but his main concern is with hedging. He notes that such returns gave the investor 1.5% more per year more than holding U.S. issues during the past 30 years. Gary Bergstrom, Ronald Frashure and John Chisholm examine some of the problems of foreign equities, including poor statistical databases and higher transaction costs in the field. Dean LeBaron and Lawrence Speidell note the different accounting standards and the different definitions of corporations and equity rights in various countries, while Rex Sinquefield analyzes the promise of small-company global equities, which, like their U.S. cousins, typically outperform the rest of their markets.

Andrew Rudd looks at emerging markets, which represent about 7,000 companies and $600 billion; 60% of these markets are in South Korea and Taiwan — almost 10% of all global capitalization. Rudd notes the lack of correlation with the developed markets and each other, thus ensuring diversification and oppor-

tunities for profit.

EXCHANGE EXPOSURE

Part 4 concerns itself with the foreign exchange exposure decision. Fischer Black develops a universal hedging formula for equities and recommends 100% hedging for foreign bonds, while Lee Thomas writes of the currency risk of foreign equities, urging investors to hedge unless the investor is certain that the currency of the equity issuer will appreciate. He notes that, based on betas, foreign equity markets hold little risk and offer opportunities for diversification. David DeRosa, on the other hand, offers currency insurance, instead of hedging, as a way to avoid currency fluctuations by using a rebalancing algorithm, which adds to add appreciating currency exposure and reduce depreciating currency exposure.

Remi Browne ends the book by arguing for no hedging at all, noting that the benefits of diversification outweigh the cost of hedging.

This book is an excellent primer on global investing. It illustrates the lack of interest on the part of U.S. investors and the opportunities in global markets. After *Global Portfolios*, an investor should be convinced of the value of investing overseas and how to do so properly, utilizing the optimal ratio of international to domestic holding, the best mix of foreign bonds and equities and with the appropriate amount of managerial manipulation.

Gary Race, 144-30 Sanford Ave., #6P, Flushing, NY 11355, (718) 886-6781, has a master's from the School of International and Public Affairs of Columbia University with a concentration in international business.

RELATIVE DIVIDEND YIELD

Common stock investing for income and appreciation
John Wiley & Sons
605 Third Avenue
New York, NY 10158
(212) 850-6497
Author: Anthony E. Spare with Nancy C. Tengler
Price: $39.95
Published 1992, 276 pages

Technicians use a number of measurements to determine market optimism or pessimism to help identify possible market extremes, among which are ratios of call and put option volume and surveying the comments of various newsletter writers. The technician is studying crowd psychology for extreme bullishness or bearishness to trade *contrarily*. The fundamentalist, on the other hand, uses tools that are somewhat similar but typically will speak in terms of *value*. An overvalued stock has, in a sense, too much enthusiasm built into the price of the stock, while an undervalued stock has too much pessimism reflected in the price of the stock. Here, the technician and the fundamentalist are both trying to do the same thing — buy low, sell high. With *Relative Dividend Yield*, Anthony Spare presents a program with which to select stocks to buy or sell based on enthusiasm or despair, as can be discovered from reviewing the history of the stock's dividend.

Relative Dividend Yield can assist you in identifying stocks that are at the upper channel of their historical yield ranges for buying and selling those stocks that are at the lower side of *their* historical yield ranges. This approach helps relieve the emotional tension of concerning yourself with the overall direction of the stock market so that you will not be caught with the crowd during the broader market turns. This technique is a long-term style, which means less turnover and consequently lower commissions, thus maintaining a possible higher return.

Relative Dividend Yield is divided into two sections. The first section introduces the reader to relative dividend yield (RDY) investments; here, you will find numerous examples, including a study of 100 large companies from 1976 to 1986. The second section is the application of RDY to portfolios. In addition, topics such as portfolio construction and diversification are discussed. Three appendices follow up the end, the first being a study utilizing the 30 stocks that make up the Dow Jones Industrial Average using absolute dividend yield, while the second discusses addtional research that was published in the *Journal of Portfolio Management*. The third and final appendix is a presentation of 95 RDY charts (Figure 1).

Overall, I can recommend *Relative Dividend Yield* — the book, that is — for long-term investors, who will definitely find it worth their while and give them food for thought as well.

—Thom Hartle, Editor

STAYING WITH DOS

How to get the most from your computer without changing your operating system
Ventana Press, Inc.
P.O. Box 2468
Chapel Hill, NC 27515
(919) 942-0220
Author: Dan Gookin
Published 1990
293 pages, $22.95

If you have recently purchased a personal computer (PC), congratulations — but you may not have been prepared for the knowledge level required to use your new machine, no matter how simple the use. For some reason, the PC world just doesn't want to make it too easy for you to operate your computer. I don't know why. Before you made your purchase, you may not have been really interested in learning exactly how a disk operating system (DOS) runs. Did you really want to know how memory is allocated or even what a terminate-and-stay resident is? Well, the salesclerk at your computer store might offer the analogy that today's automobile has a lot of features that you need to understand, and so does the PC. Personally, I don't consider the mandatory knowledge of the workings of the PC to be a feature.

THERE IS HOPE

Fortunately, there is a good book on on the subject that will take you, step by step, through the exciting — and complex — world of DOS. *Staying with DOS* is clearly written in an easy-to-understand format. Author Dan Gookin combines explanatory text, question-and-answer formats and handy checklists to help assess your personal computer needs. Ultimately, this book will make you a more informed and hopefully less frustrated PC user.

The history of DOS and PCs make up the first five chapters, providing a framework of reference for the rest of the book. Newer operating systems are also evaluated.

Chapters 6 through 11 present current solutions to overcome memory limitations, boost software and hardware performance and produce better graphics. Two ways of handling memory limita-

FIGURE 1

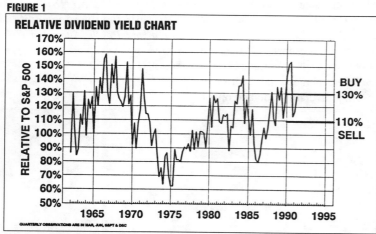

Here is a relative dividend yield chart for J.P. Morgan.

tions are presented. The first is virtual memory—memory added to your PC without plugging in a random access memory (RAM) chip. The second is with expanded memory specifications that are used in combination with utility programs. To make DOS work harder, the addition of shells and menu systems, maintenance programs and program switchers are presented here. An overview of hard disk management and speed-up techniques are covered for getting the most from your hard drive. Suggestions on improving the graphics is accomplished through a rundown of software that's currently available and a description of how they work.

The final chapter discusses the extended DOS environments available in Microsoft's Windows 3.0 and Quarterdeck's DESQview. The pros and cons of DOS, OS/2, UNIX and other operating systems are presented. The appendix provides a product index, list of product vendors, glossary and a bibliography.

Obviously, books on computers can become out of date quickly, but if you have a PC and are frustrated, then this book's style and content will certainly help you understand and find solutions.

—Thom Hartle, Editor

THE NEW STOCK MARKET

A Complete Guide to the Latest Research, Analysis and Performance
Probus Publishing
1925 N. Clybourn St.
Chicago, IL 60614
(800) PROBUS-1
Authors: Diana R. Harrington, Frank J. Fabozzi and H. Russell Fogler
Published 1990, 360 pages, $37.50

The New Stock Market is unique. This book examines the theories, strategies, trading systems and tools that are used by academics, technicians, cycle theorists and academics for selecting stocks. It does not advocate a particular trading system but describes various techniques and offers objective evaluations drawn from academic literature. The topics covered in *The New Stock Market* are quite diverse, ranging from the capital asset pricing model to a very brief description of the Elliott wave. Charts and tables are used extensively to demonstrate concepts and results. Not only that, at the end of each chapter are notes that elaborate briefly on any points made that may require further elucidation. The reference section provided at the end of each chapter ranges from two to eight pages, supplying the reader with plenty of additional reading material on any subject that strikes the reader's fancy. One item I especially appreciated was the use of sidebars to explain terminology, such as a particular statistical test, referred to in the chapter.

THOSE IMPORTANT BASICS

The first chapter of *The New Stock Market* answers the basic questions important to anyone even remotely involved with the stock market. How are equity prices set? What *is* a profit, anyway? How does a market participant determine an exploitable opportunity? The issues of studying the market's progress and direction are the subject of the second chapter. Harrington *et al.* examine cycle theory, long and short waves and the business cycle all briefly. Timing, whether time of year, month, week or day, is examined for investing strategies. Again, the reference

section proves to be an excellent source of additional information.

Chapters 3 through 5 look at theories for stock selection. Chapter 3 explores the more popular forms of technical analysis, covering moving averages, relative strength, price volume relationships, the Dow theory and odd-lot trading, among other methods. A model trading system called CRISMA (which stands for cumulative volume, relative strength and moving average), which was tested from 1976 to 1985, is also presented, while chapter 4 explains those strategies that utilize company earnings reports and earnings forecasts for profitable stock selection. Chapter 5 presents methods of identifying valuable stocks based on other fundamental valuation such as asset value, book value to market price, market capitalization and merger activity.

OF INCREASING COMPLEXITY

Chapters 6 through 8 examines the world of derivatives. Common stock options, stock index options and stock index futures and their descriptions, theories and the evidence of successful strategies are analyzed and summarized. Chapter 8 includes a discussion about "One way volatility—the cascade effect," which appears to be a polite — or perhaps prudent — way of referring to a market crash. This leads to an accounting of October 19, 1987, presented from numerous sources.

The New Stock Market concludes with thoughts about strategies for investing, including a collection of some common sense suggestions when studying any technique or investment strategy.

In conclusion, the reader should be forewarned that *The New Stock Market* is not an easy book, but the reader will certainly find it a worthwhile and intelligent book. If you want to understand investing using technical and fundamental analysis, if you want statistical evidence to support investment strategies and you appreciate an honest and candid appraisal of them, then this is the book for you.

—Thom Hartle, Editor

TECHNICAL TRADERS GUIDE TO COMPUTER ANALYSIS OF THE FUTURES MARKET

Business One Irwin
1818 Ridge Road
Home Road, IL 60430
(800) 841-8000
Authors: Charles Le Beau and David W. Lucas
234 pages, $65, 1992

My personal philosophy regarding the pursuit of successful trading requires research and understanding a vast array of analytical and trading methods. You need to understand everything from Elliott wave to mechanical trading systems. After you have gone through this learning process, you will be able to discern what methods and styles will work for you as a trader. One way of studying the field is to read everything about trading that you can get your hands on, but some books do an excellent job of presenting one method and are therefore worthy of special mention. *Computer Analysis of the Futures Market* is such a book.

HOW-TO

This is definitely a "how-to" book for developing a system approach to trading. The introduction begins with some down-to-earth questions that a trader developing a system needs to think about. The questions are aimed at understanding what your goals are. In addition, Le Beau and Lucas warn that trading isn't easy and that you can expect to devote a great deal of

time and effort to understanding and dealing with the markets. Chapter 1, which is entitled "System building," starts with some basic problems and possible solutions — for example, determining a trend and how to identify the direction of the trend are only two of the subjects looked at. Suggested uses of multiple moving averages, techniques for setting stop losses and developing exit strategies are covered. One key idea that is addressed is the issue of re-entering the market should the first exit be a bit premature. Finally, the last section covers system monitoring to identify a point where the system has gone bad by developing guidelines for monitoring the system.

The second chapter is a fairly in-depth look at numerous technical studies (otherwise known as indicators). Here, the book offers a solution to a problem that many new traders encounter. The manuals that accompany new software usually don't explain the indicators that the software plots in enough detail. This chapter goes a *long* way toward explaining basic uses of numerous indicators. The more popular indicators are profiled here, including directional movement, trading bands, envelopes and channels, the commodity channel index, moving average convergence/divergence and many more. You will receive insight into how these indicators function and their suggested uses in developing a trading system. In addition, at the end of the chapter is a suggested reading list for more information.

The third chapter delves into system

testing, looking at optimization and curve fitting. Typically, new traders explore optimizing a trading system, and Le Beau and Lucas present, with candor, the pitfalls in doing so. Data selection, testing periods, slippage and commissions are covered before numerous measurements of performance are discussed. Then Le Beau and Lucas walk you through testing entries, exits and stops using five markets from December 1986 through 1990 before creating a trading system based on the results of the testing. The cumulative net monthly performance of this system can be seen in Figure 1.

Chapter 4 is about day trading markets using technical analysis. Le Beau and Lucas state that it is their opinion that your chances of success are minimal, but that they also know that the interest in this subject is high, so they wanted to pass on the material that others have claimed to have had success with. There is also a short appendix presenting the mathematical formulas of some of the technical studies.

This book was written with an easy-to-read style so that authors Le Beau and Lucas are right there with you as you work on your trading system. Occasionally, they do move away from the subject (bashing other techniques that are attempting to forecast the markets), but nonetheless, you will gain insight into the work involved in building a trading system. I said it at the beginning: to become a successful trader, you need to have a working knowledge of a multitude of trading techniques, including how mechanical systems work. *Computer Analysis of the Futures Market* is a worthy choice for an education on developing a trading system. Now all you have to do is implement it.

—Thom Hartle, Editor

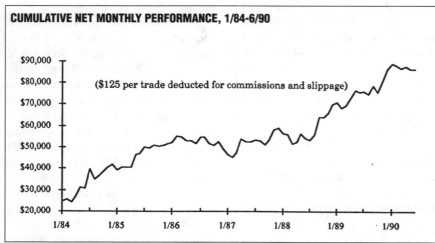

CUMULATIVE NET MONTHLY PERFORMANCE, 1/84-6/90

($125 per trade deducted for commissions and slippage)

FIGURE 1: *Presenting the results of the trading system profiled as a tutorial for designing a trading system.*

100 BEST STOCKS TO OWN IN AMERICA

Dearborn Trade Publishing
520 North Dearborn Street
Chicago, IL 60601-4354
(312) 836-4400
Author: Gene Walden
Price: $22.95
Second edition, 1991, 393 pages

I'm always suspicious when I come across anything that purports to have come up with a definitive list. Since investing in the stock market is a complex undertaking and every investor has different goals and acceptable levels of risk, it's hard to believe that one book could really come up with the 100 best stocks for *everyone*. Financial journalist Gene Walden, author of *100 Best Stocks to Own in America*, has not. What he *has* compiled is a sensible list of companies that are established industry leaders with consistent patterns of growth. You won't find the next Microsoft here; in fact, Microsoft, which comes in at 82 on the list, didn't even make the 1989 edition of the book.

To choose the companies featured, Walden has zeroed in on five, quite traditional, basic performance criteria: earnings growth, stock growth, dividend yield, dividend growth and consistency of performance. He then rates the companies in these areas on a scale of one to four stars. One less traditional category that he examines is shareholder perks. These include the small gifts and discounts that some companies offer shareholders, as well as automatic reinvestment of dividends and stock purchase plans. Walden admits that this category may be somewhat controversial but argues that he has noticed a correlation between scoring high in the perks category and achieving high overall performance. Point totals from all six categories are summed up (each star is worth a point) to determine a company's total score (24 points represent a perfect score). For those with a social conscience, Walden also touches on corporate responsibility, but only for companies that are particularly notable (for either good or bad reasons) in this respect. For those without a social conscience, however, the comments on corporate responsibil-

ity have no bearing on the ratings.

The companies that have made the team cover a broad spectrum of industries from advertising to telecommunications, although more than a quarter are in the relatively recession-proof business of producing food and consumer products. Coming out on top are widely diversified Philip Morris (no. 1, score: 21) and UST (no. 2, score: 20). Rounding out the top 10 are Rubbermaid (no. 3), Wm. Wrigley Jr. Co. (no. 4), Anheuser-Busch Cos. (no. 5), The Limited (no. 6), Giant Food (no. 7), Sara Lee Corp. (no. 8), Torchmark Corp. (no. 9) and H.J. Heinz Co. (no. 10). Each of the 100 companies gets a four-page entry summarizing strategy and business lines and explaining the reasons for the ratings in each category. A table at the end of each entry gives a five-year financial summary. Eighty-five of the top 100 trade on the New York Stock Exchange (NYSE), three on the American Stock Exchange (AMEX) and 12 on NASDAQ. Author Walden also breaks down the 100 best by state and by industry after the entries.

Even though Walden manages to choose companies with long and consistent track records, the two editions of his book provide dramatic proof that past performance is not necessarily an indicator of future performance. Fully one-third of the companies that made his list in 1989 failed to qualify for this edition. And the top 100 list contains no companies from volatile industries such as stock brokerage firms or computer hardware manufacturers.

If you're looking to invest in high-tech high-fliers, this book probably isn't for you. If you're a conservative investor, however, it would fill your requirements quite nicely.

Anne Hall is on the editorial staff of a financial magazine in New York.

WALL STREET WORDS

The Basics and Beyond
Probus Publishing
1925 N. Clybourn St.
Chicago, IL 60614
(800) PROBUS-1
Author: Richard J. Maturi
Published 1991
169 pages, $14.95

Who *is* the "average investor," anyway? The term has been bandied around to the extent that it's become a cliché, with nothing to indicate its origins or its intended meaning. This is a case of overcomplication, because the "average investor" is exactly that — not the novice investor, the beginner for whom the jargon of finance is a complete mystery, nor the experienced investor, for whom the jargon of finance may be a first language. No, the average investor perhaps has some investments already, probably has the number of a broker handy somewhere in his or her desk, but still has questions from time to time about the language of finance. And it is for the average investor that Richard J. Maturi, author of *Wall Street Words*, has written this book of definitions.

Wall Street Words is an easy-to-read handbook of definitions clarifying the jargon that today's investor is likely to encounter in the jungle of media today. The book is divided into two sections, with the first section simply an alphabetical list of tersely defined terms commonly found in Wall Street usage. Each definition is rarely more than one paragraph. The goal here is to provide a brief but concise explanation of the terms, thus providing the reader a quick overview of the topic. The terminology defined covers most common terms, from American depository receipts to zero-plus tick.

On the other hand, if it's further detail that you're after, the second half of *Wall Street Words* gives you exactly what you're looking for, because this section goes into greater detail of the most widely used terms. Here, you will find a much more in-depth explanation of the terms — but be forewarned, only of the most widely used terms. There are numerous examples and strategies that the average investor can use in his or her continuing research of the relevant terms. For example, under "put option," there are nearly three pages providing an explanation of what exactly a put option is, an example of listed quotations and not only that, even a few examples of the correct use of put options. Very handy indeed.

The "average investor" will find this book useful in many ways, not the least of which will be the combination of a handbook of quick references and easy-to-understand explanations of today's investment products, making this book an easy-to-justify purchase.

—Thom Hartle, Editor

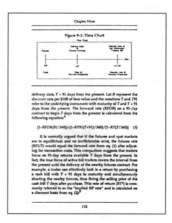

WALL STREET WORDS

108   Section II

Chart 4

HEAD AND SHOULDERS A stock or commodity chart pattern outlining the head and shoulders of a person.
The chart illustrates the top of the head around 27 1/2 and the shoulders peaking around 26.

Chart 5

Wall Street Words *is an easy-to-read handbook of definitions clarifying the jargon that today's investor is likely to encounter in the jungle of media today.*

FINANCIAL FUTURES AND OPTIONS

Managing Risk in the Interest Rate, Currency and Equity Markets
Probus Publishing
1925 N. Clybourn
Chicago, IL 60614
(800) 969-8878
Author: Ira G. Kawaller
Price: $65, 286 pages

The futures markets provide three things: price discovery, asset allocation and risk management. Most participants are aware of the value and opportunity of the first two attributes, but not all money managers may be fully comfortable with the use of futures to manage risk. Ira Kawaller, vice president and director of the New York office of the Chicago Mercantile Exchange, has put together a collection of articles he has written for a how-to book for users and potential users of financial futures and options to manage risk.

The book is divided into three sections, the first of which is interest rates. Among the topics are Eurodollar futures and options presented as a mechanism for improving the performance of a short-term funds manager; assessing conditions to decide whether to build a strip or stack Eurodollars for a particular hedge; and considering Euros as a substitute for an interest rate swap.

The second section concerns currency futures. Topics covered include currency futures arbitrage, futures contracts to manage foreign exchange rate exposure and using options on currency futures. The explanation and application of cross-currency futures spreads for trading cross-rates are discussed.

The third section is about stock indices. A brief chapter on speculative trading strategies leads into the chapter on determining the relevant fair value of the Standard & Poor's 500 futures contract, and then the importance of managing cash flow risk due to variation margin requirements from the use of S&P 500 futures is presented. The final chapter is on the use of Nikkei stock index futures and options to permit a money manager to increase exposure to the Japanese stock market while still managing the risk.

This book is not necessarily for the everyday trader; however, it would be useful for and is designed for the money manager who should be fully conversant in managing risk.

—Thom Hartle, Editor

PATIENCE IS A VIRTUE

Major advances require time to complete. Don't take profits during the first eight weeks of a move unless the stock gets into serious trouble or is having a two- or three-week "climax" rapid runup on a stock split. Stocks that show a 20% profit in less than eight weeks should be held through the eight weeks unless they are of poor quality without institutional sponsorship or strong group action. In certain cases, dramatic stocks advancing 20% or more in only four or five weeks are the most powerful stocks of all, capable of increases of 100%, 200%, or more. You can try for long-term moves in many of them, once your account shows a good profit and you are ahead for the year.

—William J. O'Neil
How to Make Money in Stocks

EURODOLLAR FUTURES AND OPTIONS
Controlling Money Market Risk
Probus Publishing Co., 1925 N. Clybourn Street, Chicago, IL 60614, (800) 776-2871, (312) 868-1100
Authors: Burghardt, Belton, Lane, Luce, McVey
Published 1991, 500 pages
$60.00 plus $3.50 for postage and handling

Eurodollars† are a very large component of the international financial market with deposits outstanding currently valued at about $3 trillion and futures and options at about $1.5 trillion. However, the role they play in international finance and economics *can* be confusing. *Eurodollar Futures and Options* clears up some misconceptions and takes the reader from an elementary explanation of Eurodollars to the exotic world of caps and collars, SLICs, GICs, FRAs and ARMs (savings and loan investment contracts, guaranteed investment contracts, forward rate agreements† and adjustable-rate mortgages, respectively).

Eurodollar Futures and Options is in three parts. The first part defines the concepts of the Eurodollar market and allows the reader to acquire the language and understanding needed to make use of the advanced information illustrated later on. The first chapter gives us a history of the

> One of the uncertainties of life, the general level of interest rates, can be either hedged away or traded away with Treasury bills. ... Unless one has a position on what the credit spread should be, swaps and strips can be a poor hedge for Treasury securities.

Eurodollar market, noting that that market has replaced the certificate of deposit (CD) market because of its greater flexibility and better credit. In the second chapter, the reader is introduced to some concepts of the Eurodollar market. Further definitions and explanations in this chapter include length of maturities, method of quotations, the importance of the London Interbank Offer Rate (LIBOR) and how interest is calculated.

In introducing Eurodollar futures, authors Burghardt, Belton *et al.* discuss the exchanges at which the futures are bought and sold, the standard contract, the daily cash basis settlement and, most important, how the contracts are priced. The rest of the second chapter is concerned with how to hedge with Eurodollar futures and an explanation of FRAs, which can also be hedged with Eurodollar futures.

Interest rate swaps and their Eurodollar near relatives, Eurodollar strips, are the subjects of the third chapter. The difference between them is that interest rate swaps are more expensive to trade and offer less flexibility than do futures. The timing, size and calculation of cash payments in swaps are illustrated, as are variations in swap agreements.

Burghardt and the others also carefully describe Eurodollar strips, going through rate calculations and defining how swaps and strips differ and why investors prefer the latter. Some reasons offered include better rates, lower transaction costs and the quality of the intermediaries.

Chapters 4 through 6 are more technical. Analysis and illustration are given via formulas and diagrams on what caps, collars, floors and Eurodollar options are and how they are used, and how swaps, Treasuries and caps are hedged.

The authors consider Eurodollar futures the best vehicle with which to hedge swaps. They explain the mechanics of such strategies as hedging against shifts in the yield curve and how to stack hedges instead of dealing with simple and complex strips, and also what to do with hedge mismatches.

One of the uncertainties of life, the general level of interest rates, can be either hedged away or traded away with Treasury bills, the authors explain, warning that unless one has a position on what the credit spread should be, swaps and strips can be a poor hedge for Treasury securities. With that caveat, they examine how good swaps and strips can be for the positioned investor, explaining how to measure the credit spread, its sensitivity to the yield curve slope, how to trade it and how to construct and measure the trade performance.

There are Eurodollar options, much like stock options. However, instead of puts and calls, in the Eurodollar market one finds caps, collars, floors and Eurodollar options (the exchange-place traded counterparts to caps, floors and collars). These options are very popular, amounting to about $500 billion worth of business in 1989. Caps and floors are introduced as being similar to Eurodollar puts and calls, while a collar is "much like a long Eurodollar put combined with a short Eurodollar call."

CAPS AND MORE CAPS
The authors analyze caps in detail, adding that their analysis is also appropriate for floors, collars and other options such as straddles, range forwards and corridors. After the basic features of interest rate caps are listed, the authors explain how caps are priced, how prices can be compared with Eurodollar puts, and about the four measures of sensitivity of cap prices — delta, the sensitivity to changes in underlying yield levels; gamma, the sensitivity of *deltas* to yield changes; zeta, the sensitivity to changes in volatility; and theta, the sensitivity to time.

With these variables to consider, hedging caps and other options alone is a huge business. The writers consider two approaches to cap hedging: dynamic hedging and option replication, with the first relying on offsetting the net delta of one's portfolio and the second the cap portfolio's owner offsetting not only delta but the other sensitivity indicators. Burghardt *et al.* explain the ins and outs of each method and how to go about each strategy.

To conclude the first part, the authors give examples of hedging strategies utilizing the knowledge presented up to this point and explain how to hedge long, medium, and short, what the typical hedge structure is like, how hedges can be combined, how they are managed over time and when to choose futures or options.

ADVANCED CONCEPTS

In chapters 7 through 10, the emphasis is on more advanced concepts and applications of the building blocks presented in the first six chapters. The first concept analyzed is bias in interest rate futures. The rest of the chapter is concerned with the source of the bias, its size, its sensitivity to rate correlations and yield levels, and finally, its implications for traders, hedgers and bankers.

Options on swaps (or "swaptions") are explained next. As of 1989, these variations were an $80 billion industry, with the popularity of these instruments due to the flexibility they offer, especially in changing callable debt into fixed-rate debt and vice versa. Four types of swaptions are available: call and put swaptions, and callable and putable swaps. The authors give some example of how such instruments are applied, how they are priced and their price sensitivity. Swaptions, like other options, can be readily hedged.

GICs, BICs and SLICs are dissected next. These contracts are attractive be- cause of their interest rate guarantees. They are negotiated term deposits, GICs being issued by insurance companies and the others by banks and savings and loan institutions (these are backed by federal deposit insurance). The differences between bullet GICs and window GICs are explained, as are the withdrawal and transfer provisions. Like swaptions, these contracts can be hedged with Eurodollar futures and options, and like other instruments examined here, their sensitivities to pricing and time are examined.

Adjustable-rate mortgages (ARMs) have been popular since the greatly volatile interest rates of the 1970s. There are $30 billion of ARM securities currently on the market via the Federal Home Loan Mortgage Corporation and the Federal National Mortgage Association. This chapter explains the components of ARMs, including pricing, why they are so volatile and how they can be hedged not only by Eurodollars but with Eurodollar options.

The last part of the book consists of appendices, including specifications of futures contracts and cash futures arbitrage transactions.

CHALLENGING REWARD

This is a difficult but rewarding book to read. The difficulty comes from the technical subject, while the reward comes from having a virtual encyclopedia of Eurodollar futures and options in a single volume. As expected when dealing with such a subject matter, formulas and diagrams are of great importance, and Burghardt, Belton *et al.* have provided the reader with copious charts, graphs, tables and glossaries to make the material as accessible as possible.

Gary Race, 144-30 Sanford Ave., #6P, Flushing, NY 11355, (718) 886-6781, has a master's from the School of International and Public Affairs of Columbia University with a concentration in international business.

TA

MARKETBASE, *Version 3.24*
MarketBase, Inc. (formerly MP Software, Inc.)
368 Hillside Avenue
P.O. Box 37
Needham Heights, MA 02194
Phone: (800) 735-0700, (617) 449-8460
Product: Fundamental database of NASDAQ-NMS, AMEX and NYSE stocks together with analysis and screening software.
Price: $59, introduction package
Equipment: IBM-PC AT, XT or higher; 256K RAM, hard drive
Data: $345 per year for quarterly data, $695 per year for monthly data, $2,300 per year for weekly data. Additional options available.

Care to whip through 4,500 stocks with eight different criteria and pick the winners in less than 20 seconds on your beater IBM-AT? Want to sort those hummers by one of, say, 52 criteria in less than five seconds? Want to change the criteria and resort in another five seconds? Want to look as though you've done all your homework in less than 15 minutes? How about defining your own ratios and scoring the companies by your standards? If you do, look no further. Guru, here's your toy: MarketBase.

DATADUMP

What MarketBase is really selling is data, as you can see from the pricing above, but the analytical software, though short on technical indicators (more specifically, it doesn't have any), is long on the fundamental screens that many like to use to home in on likely stocks. Since MarketBase accesses NASDAQ as well as the traditional AMEX/NYSE stocks, this makes sense even for individuals, given that many of the companies won't have the capitalization to support heavy institutional investment.

What both the individual and institutional analysts will appreciate, though, is MarketBase's speed and functionality. Running on just about any hard disk/IBM or better combination, MarketBase flies through the routines. You can jump from module to module with shift-F key combinations in split seconds. Selection and sorting are as effortless as a menu-ori-

FIGURE 1

```
THE BASICS

   Version 3.24
                        MARKET BASE MAIN MENU

                        1. DISPLAY COMPANIES

                        2. SELECT COMPANIES

                        3. SORT COMPANIES

                        4. REPORTS

                        5. USER VALUES

                        6. SCORE COMPANIES

                        7. PORTFOLIOS


                        Select Option 1

   Copyright(c)1986-1990 MP Software, Inc.   PO Box 37 Needham Hts., Ma  02194
                          1-800-735-0700
                                                        F10-HELP
```

MarketBase is a very fast program for selecting stocks by various criteria and developing reports on the selections.

FIGURE 2

```
SELECTION CRITERIA

                        SELECT ACTIVE COMPANIES
   Active Companies: Entire Data Base
   Number Active  : 4593    Sorted by NAME
                        Field   Rel   Value   Undefined   OR

                        MRK     >     20        N
                        MRK     <     100       N
                        ISH     <     15        Y
                        EPS     >     0         N
                        EPS1    >     0         N
                        EPS2    >     0         N
                        REV5    >     0         N
                        SIC     #     6*        N          OR
                        SIC     =     65*       N




   File #  6 - AAII SHADOW STOCK CRITERIA
   F1-Select  F2-Load  F3-Save  F4-All  F5-Fields  F6-Prior  F7-Insert   F10-HELP
```

Selection criteria can be very involved and include the capability of AND/OR logical operators. This selection is for the AAII shadow stock portfolio criteria.

FIGURE 3

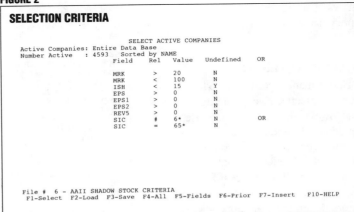

```
COMPANY DATA

   ═══ Active Companies: AAII SHADOW STOCK CRITERIA ═══

   BIM    AMEX        I C N BIOMEDICALS INC   Score 46    SIC 2831

   Recent Price $   6.13    TTM PE    11.40          Shares       11.9
       52   Hi $   9.25    Div Yld %  2.28          Market Cap   72.9
     Weeks Lo $   4.50    Pr/Sales   0.61          Inst Hold %   6.23
   Book Value  $   5.24    Pr/Book    1.17          Closely Held % 75.24


                            FYE Nov
   In Millions     2Q    TTM   1990    1989    1988    1987    1986
   SELECTED RELATIONS
   Earnings Yield %        8.77      Free Cash Flow $       0.41
   Dividend Payout %      24.14      FCF/Price %            6.63
   Return on Revenue %     5.36      LTD/Capitalization %  38.62
   Return on Equity %     10.27
   Value of ROE (ROE/PE)   0.90      Working Capital       28.6
   Return on Invest %      6.31      Current Ratio          1.49
   Return on Assets %      4.01      Quick Ratio            0.83
   Inventory Turns         3.11      Net CA per Sh / Pr   ( 0.15)
   ═══ Company # 11 of 190  Sorted by TICKER ═══
   PgDn/Up F1-Prev F2-Next F4-Mode F5-Find F6-Prnt F7-PrYr F8-Avg F9-Bus  F10-HELP
```

Once the universe you want is selected, you can page through the companies individually or pop up a specific company by ticker name.

ented interface can produce, and help plus the little tedious data often missing (abbreviations for fields, tickers and so forth) are always available.

Once past the selection-sort-report (Figures 2 through 4) mode, you're getting

into making your own fundamental indicators feeding from the 30-plus indicators MarketBase supplies as well as 15 financials (for example, earnings, inventories, deferred taxes, and so on). Operators include the basic four, plus the ability to specify previous periods.

The nifty thing about your own specifications is that they are then available on all the reporting, and you can use them for selection and sorting. Creating them is highly structured, so editing is easy for, I'd say, just about anyone.

In addition, you have the option of four different data formats for reports sent to disk: text, WKS, DIF or PRN.

Graphics are minimal (see Figure 5), and there's no question of working graphically with the data, but in truth, most technicians would only use MarketBase to focus in on a target or two before getting the data into a sophisticated technical analysis package. Since MarketBase is comprehensive, easy and fast, it's ideal.

MANUALLY TUTORING

MarketBase's manual comes in the form of a tutorial, a practice I've questioned in the past. However, in MarketBase's case, the program is solid enough and so easy to use that little need exists for the complications of a full-reference manual. Once you get through the 40-odd pages of tutoring, you're proficient. Should you want some more detail, there are appendices, but only the essentials are to be found. For example, the MarketBase scoring system is not explained, although it *is* available if you call for it.

SUMMARY

There's very little to complain about in MarketBase. I had no desire to burden the program with hordes of technical features. The only question is the value of the data. MarketBase can't read databases other than its own, and I saw no way to convert their price data to standard formats for use by any technical packages. That being the case, you're looking at buying a set of fundamental data and then price data for your technical package.

If you're a solid fundamentalist without a data source or with a source you want to lose, MarketBase is a beautiful screening package, one that can be easily recommended.

—*John Sweeney, Technical Editor*

FIGURE 4

MBASE SCORING SYSTEM

```
Active Companies: AAII SHADOW STOCK CRITERIA
MARKET BASE DATA UPDATED 09/21/91
COMPANY NAME                   PE      SCR       PB      CSH
----------------------------- ------- -------- -------- --------
BASIC PETROLEUM INTL           4.82    143      1.50     34.06
KAMENSTEIN INC (M)             9.50    123      1.93     55.04
TEKNEKRON COMM SYSTEMS        11.76    123     30.30     57.30
UNITED AMER HEALTHCARE        13.48    122      7.61     38.93
CENTURY MEDICORP              10.65    116      5.01     39.05
SEVENSON ENVIRONMENTL SRV      9.78    115      1.81     60.70
FIRST TEAM SPORTS             25.99    112      7.01     31.56
BIOMEDICAL DYNAMICS           38.28    112      7.29     30.96
MILLFELD TRADING CO           21.67    109      5.57     53.80
MICROS SYS INC                13.01    108      2.44     71.23
NOREX AMERICA                  4.74    107      1.40     56.90
SOFTWARE SPECTRUM             17.35    106      7.43     56.65
RAG SHOPS                     23.09    106      5.48     65.16
G M I S INC                   39.58    106       NM      31.81
R & B INC                     11.39    105      2.34     46.41
GROUP 1 SOFTWARE              21.26    105      4.70     82.55
ECOLOGY & ENVIRONMENT         12.69    104      1.94     81.45
AIRTRAN CORP                   7.55    102      2.14     15.86
AMERICAN BIODYNE              25.85     99     12.19     47.32
TENERA L P                     5.31     98      3.96     17.86
KOLL MGMT SERVICES            16.14     96     15.47     66.67
OUTLOOK GRAPHICS              17.46     96      2.92     19.15
RAINBOW TECHNOLOGIES          22.92     96      5.07     36.98
E M P I INC                   41.42     96      8.57     19.90
SELAS CORP OF AMERICA          6.51     95      1.09      3.59
RAMSAY HEALTH CARE            10.59     95      1.86     56.50
COMPUTER NETWORK TECH         34.23     94      8.43
BOSTON ACOUSTICS              18.56     93      3.97     46.46
BARNWELL INDUSTRIES            7.85     92      5.61     40.01
MACHINE TECHNOLOGY             8.81     92      4.27     57.82
MYLEX                         17.64     92      5.22     16.22
PONDER INDUSTRIES             20.45     92      2.68     33.52
ELECTRONIC TELE-COMM INC      22.00     92      3.81     66.33
HAWKINS CHEMICAL              12.45     91      1.86     54.85
COOKER RESTAURANT CORP        30.85     89      4.41     35.78
ARTISTIC GREETINGS            29.52     88      5.78     15.20
INTEGRATED WASTE SERVICES     31.91     88      2.19     47.09
MERIDIAN DIAGNOSTICS          32.01     88      3.13     78.19
BERTUCCIS                     40.38     88      3.34     42.09
MEDICUS SYSTEMS               41.03     88     21.88     80.70
VIDMARK                       11.06     87      1.19
REHABCARE CORP                18.00     87     10.72     49.19
MICHAEL ANTHONY JEWELERS       9.27     85      1.23
DIANON SYSTEMS                38.46     84      8.77     20.32
BENCHMARK ELECTRONICS         12.80     83      1.70     63.41
INTEGRATED CIRCUIT SYS        22.18     83     13.47     70.64
MARTECH USA                    9.11     82      2.21     56.25
I M C O RECYCLING             11.81     81      2.14
FUTURE NOW                    17.94     81      2.00     15.56
HENLEY INTL                   25.80     81      2.89     55.56
C E SOFTWARE HOLDINGS         36.93     81     12.61     65.02
JOHNSON PRODUCTS CO            7.03     80      1.37      0.16
GREAT NORTHERN IRON ORE       10.28     80      6.73      0.00
```

Here, the AAII shadow stocks have been sorted by the MBase scoring system and displayed with the P/E ratio, the price/book (P/B) ratio, and the percentage of stock closely held (CSH).

FIGURE 5

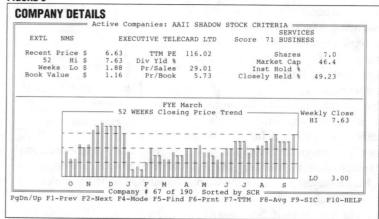

COMPANY DETAILS

```
============ Active Companies: AAII SHADOW STOCK CRITERIA ============
                                                          SERVICES
  EXTL    NMS          EXECUTIVE TELECARD LTD    Score  71 BUSINESS

Recent Price $   6.63    TTM PE   116.02              Shares       7.0
    52   Hi $   7.63    Div Yld %                  Market Cap    46.4
  Weeks Lo $   1.88    Pr/Sales  29.01            Inst Hold %
Book Value  $   1.16    Pr/Book    5.73          Closely Held %  49.23
```

Two keystrokes and a name away from the summary table is the detail on the company, including rudimentary price charts. Most of the data are like those in Figure 3.

THE DIRECTOR
WhatWorks, AutoStock, Systems!

Nirvana Systems, Inc.
3415 Greystone Drive, Suite 205
Austin, TX 78731
Phone: (800) 880-0338, (512) 345-2545
Product: Trading system testing and signal generation using MetaStock Professional. Includes 40 indicator-based trading systems.
Price data: MetaStock data files
Fundamental data: N/A
Price: AutoStock3, version 1.0, $49
WhatWorks3, version 1.0, $79
Systems!, version 1.0, $49
The Director, version 1.7, free
AutoStock3 & WhatWorks3, $89
AutoStock3, WhatWorks3,
  Systems!, $99
MetaStock Professional with
  all three, $390
Required equipment: 286 CPU or better, 650K of extended memory and DOS 3.0 or higher. For reasonable processing times, a 386 with a coprocessor and a hard disk with 2+ megabytes (MB) of free space is better.

The Director is a Terminate-and-Stay Resident (TSR) that, once loaded, preferably at startup, will stay in the background and run the utilities that Nirvana has created at the appointed times — or on command. This is handy, but you must have 650K of true extended memory (not extended memory configured as expanded memory) available to The Director. That's where it lives.

In turn, the utilities — AutoStock, WhatWorks and Systems! — total up to a dandy package for creating and testing trading systems. WhatWorks will find the best trading system for your tradeables and then AutoStock will give you the signals from your chosen system on a daily basis. To make life even easier, Systems! gives you a true host of 40 ready-to-run trading indicator-based trading systems you can use or use as models for developing your own system. System junkies' delight!

The Director is designed to run as an adjunct to MetaStock Professional version 3.0. The systems you design in MetaStock are the systems tested by WhatWorks. And if you believe in opti-

FIGURE 1
WHATWORKS3

WhatWorks will test all your MetaStock Pro-compatible systems against all your data, producing output that can be put on hard disk.

FIGURE 2
SORTING RESULTS

Fortunately, you can sort results by security or trading system and then by percentage profitability, raw profitability or percentage of wins and losses. Navistar with a +DI/-DI crossover topped our testing.

FIGURE 3
CHART OF TRADES

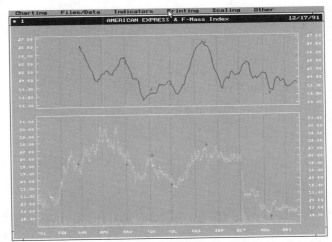

From WhatWorks, you go directly to MetaStock Professional to see the chart of the trades made for the system you selected.

mization, moreover, Valhalla has arrived! WhatWorks goes into your MetaStock data directory and applies *all* the systems you've specified to *all* the data you have. Naturally, this can't be done instantaneously, but it *is* done rapidly. You can watch the progress on your screen as the system flashes MetaStock through all its menus.

Just to see how this could go in extremis, I asked The Director to apply all 40 systems supplied with Systems! to all the data MetaStock had supplied: all the 1991 data for the Dow Jones 30. Our trusty 386 (with no disk cache) and its coprocessor were able to knock off a system test every 40 seconds or so. An entire tradeable — say, Bethlehem Steel — averaged 20 minutes for all 40 systems. Results were saved to disk for later perusal and printing.

The results were fascinating. A printed 3/8-inch stack of paper summarized the wins, in my case by percentage profitability (Figure 1). I could have sorted by number of long trades, number of short trades (though I don't know why), percentage of profitable long or short trades or on raw profit. Raw listings of abbreviated results are available for all securities and all systems (Figure 2). No sorting of any kind by risk/return measure was available, however.

Details of the system parameters are immediately available and so, the manual says, are MetaStock's profit reports. However, I got an error message when I tried it. It turned out I exceeded the amount of memory available for loading the output report. On the other hand, when I ran the option to see the trading chart (prices and arrows for trades), the program accessed MetaStock smoothly and ran the appropriate simulation to produce Figure 3.

Once you select the systems and tradeables you want, you can specify a list of them in AutoStock3, replete with the parameters for each system if needed. Once the day's action is recorded in the databanks, you release AutoStock3 and it generates a complete list of the signals for each tradeable.

SUMMARY

First, the caveats:

- Since everything is accomplished by feeding commands to MetaStock, things will never run as fast as with a dedicated program. They will run faster than you could ever run MetaStock!

- Just a suggestion, but things *could* go faster if MetaStock's screen redraw could be turned off.
- Since The Director is a TSR program, you may have to change your autoexec if you are already loading other TSRs when your machine powers up. Once The Director is in memory, other items can then be loaded. To run cleanly, be sure to start The Director from the DOS prompt.
- On-line help isn't finished yet, but it's due on the next release.
- There are some typo-cleanups to be performed in specifying directories, but it's minimal. The program gets rid of all that for you when it's running MetaStock.

Kudos next: *Wow!* Turning What-Works3 loose is just plain exciting, especially with all the fully disclosed systems included in the package. Just from the standpoint of buying trading systems, Systems! is a best buy, hands down. You could pick up MetaStock and the whole Director package for just $390. *What a deal!* Go for it!

—*John Sweeney, Technical Editor*

OPTION SIMULATOR & OTC OPTION SIMULATOR

Bay Options
1235 Walnut Street
Berkeley, CA 94709
Phone: (510) 845-6425,
fax (510) 704-0322
Product: Option simulator and evaluation capability for U.S. exchange-listed options, European/Asian options and over-the-counter options.
Price: $425
Equipment: DOS machine with 640K running Microsoft Windows 3.x or better with a mouse. Hard-disk drive with 3.1+ megabytes (MB).

The idea quite simply is to make both market movements and volatility movements work in the same direction. No matter what the market outlook, or the volatility outlook, there is always some option position which will simultaneously take advantage of both.
— Option Simulator

OpSim (for U.S. options) and OTC OpSim (for over-the-counter and European/Asian options) are handy programs for professionals to use in hedging and trading activities involving stocks, currencies, indices and futures. I say "professionals" because the typical retail speculator would probably find the level of expertise found here intimidating. Though the program is well-executed and the manual and textbook are brilliantly clear, you're still clearly working with output from top talent. Most people aren't exposed to this sort of intelligence every day. None of it is toned down, but there aren't any overwhelming mathematics — just very fast thinking.

On the other hand, retail traders could learn a lot from this package, and indeed, OpSim is pitched both as a tutorial and a trading tool. Equipped with variants of four good models (Figure 1), OpSim flips easily from the interbank currency market to stock options to futures.

OpSim provides all the graphics and analytics (Figure 2) to put in as compli-

FIGURE 1
EVALUATION MODELS

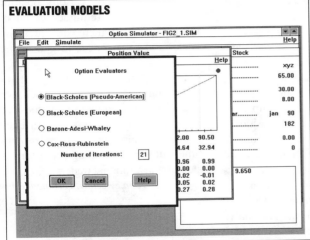

OpSim comes with four different evaluation models, including popular variants of Black-Scholes.

FIGURE 2
ANALYTICS

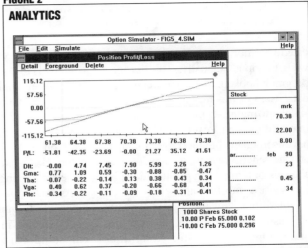

Analytics can handle any level of complexity, and graphics are fast and precise. Windows may be moved but not resized.

FIGURE 3
OPTION SIMULATOR VOLATILITIES

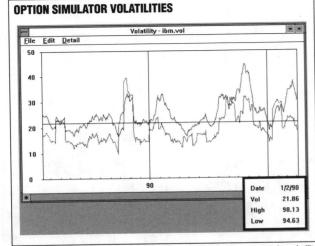

OpSim is an educational package as well as providing trading support. Its volatility analysis suggests trading opportunities as well.

FIGURE 4
OPTIONS

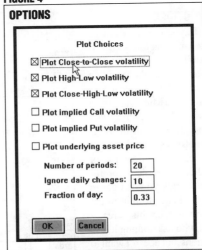

Volatility analysis options include just about every variant known to man.

FIGURE 5

OPSIM GRAPHICS

OpSim provides quick graphics with the choice of unlimited overlays plus time (theta) and volatility (vega) charting. Rate sensitivity is handled in the bottom line of the table (Rte).

options characteristics (that is, delta, theta and so on), you're ready to play (Figure 5) at much faster speeds and with faster menu-flipping than OpVue IV, plus you're not limited to three comparable positions. You're always encouraged here to try one more "What if?"

The book *Option Simulator* is simply great, the equivalent of an intense seminar and one that you may constantly reread. As a reference, I can only say it has no index, which I regard as a dire deficiency, but it does have a fair table of contents. As a practically oriented textbook, *Option Simulator* has no better that I know of. It constantly demonstrates the practical process of managing options positions as they evolve and also reminds you of the equivalency of various positions with the endless reminder to choose the position in which you are buying cheap and selling dear to gain advantage.

In sum, this package has great programming, great manual, super book, great analytics and super tutoring. It does need to be hooked up to a data source to relieve tedious updating and increase response time, but there is nothing better for self-study by institutional traders.

—*John Sweeney, Technical Editor*

cated a position as you wish as long as you wish to input manually. This is not a program hooked to a datastream or a database. For this reason, it may not be suitable to trading-desk work where speed may be important. Position traders should have no trouble exploiting OpSim, though, and the benefits of having a sophisticated analysis of a multi-leg position done instantly are substantial.

Volatilities, always a key concern, are easily studied with a separate program, Option Simulator Volatilities (Figure 3). The program can accept your data from any ASCII, comma-delimited file and gives you a variety of "slants" (Figure 4) to use in estimating volatility. Even when running under the Simulator, you can get the implied volatility for an individual option series, a group of options series and that of a given position. At least on a 386-33, both programs are extremely fast in calculations and graphics, even running under Windows.

As to daily usage, I found OpSim very amenable to mouse support. This is as good as it gets in Windows. The analytical setup isn't as easy as it is in OptionVue IV, but once you've typed in the position and calculated the

EXCEL FUNCTIONS

For $325, Bay Options will make available to you what looks to be its own series of Excel worksheets that allow you to make up daily trading sheets as shown here (sidebar Figure 1). You'll need Microsoft Excel for Windows and some facility with spreadsheets, but you can do everything from get dates to expiration to get all the options valuations for stocks, indices, currencies or futures. Most of this you can get in considerably slicker format in the Option Simulator, so this is really for the user who has nothing left to learn in options and doesn't want to buy the book.

SIDEBAR FIGURE 1

1100	1110										
intval	0.5		354		354.5		355		355.5		356
vol	Strike											Pos
0.16	345	18.71	0.69	19.05	0.70	19.41	0.71	19.76	0.71	20.12	0.72
		5.59	-0.30	5.44	-0.29	5.29	-0.29	5.15	-0.28	5.01	-0.28
0.14	350	14.28	0.64	14.60	0.65	14.93	0.66	15.26	0.66	15.59	0.67
		6.06	-0.35	5.89	-0.34	5.72	-0.34	5.55	-0.33	5.39	-0.32
0.12	355	10.07	0.57	10.35	0.58	10.65	0.59	10.94	0.60	11.24	0.61	-10
		6.75	-0.42	6.54	-0.41	6.34	-0.40	6.14	-0.39	5.94	-0.39	-10
0.14	360	8.98	0.48	9.23	0.49	9.47	0.50	9.73	0.51	9.98	0.52
		10.57	-0.51	10.32	-0.50	10.07	-0.49	9.82	-0.48	9.58	-0.48
0.16	365	8.28	0.42	8.49	0.43	8.71	0.44	8.92	0.44	9.15	0.45
		14.77	-0.57	14.48	-0.56	14.20	-0.56	13.93	-0.55	13.65	-0.54
			-1.49		-1.67		-1.86		-2.04		-2.22
yield	0.03										
irate	0.08										
prds	21										
days	62										

3D

John Ehlers
MESA
Box 1801
Goleta, CA 93116
(805) 969-6478
(800) 633-6372
Product: System-testing program with three-dimensional results display.
Equipment: IBM-PC compatibles with DOS 3.1 or better, one floppy, 640K RAM, CGA/EGA/VGA color graphics. Graphics printer and math coprocessors are very desirable.
Price: $199; demo disk available.

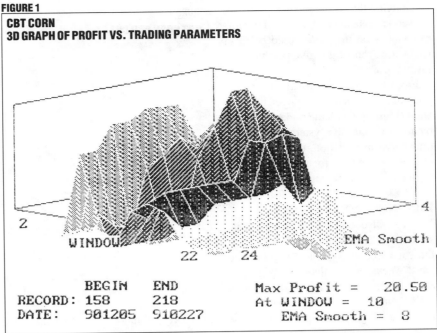

FIGURE 1

CBT CORN
3D GRAPH OF PROFIT VS. TRADING PARAMETERS

	BEGIN	END	Max Profit =	20.50
RECORD:	158	218	At WINDOW =	10
DATE:	901205	910227	EMA Smooth =	8

3D displays data, computing, testing and results all into a simple profit graph.

There's optimizing and then there's optimizing in style. 3D definitely has style and even elegance because it compresses a massive amount of data, computing, testing and results all into one elegant picture: a three-dimensional graph of profit vs. two trading parameters (Figure 1). It really makes things look too simple for its own good.

3D allows you to test one of five different trading systems on your data, which, in turn, can be in one of six formats (CSI, CompuTrac, ASCII, Technical Tools, Future Source, or N²), which can be located anywhere on your hard disk's directory structures.

A crossover double moving average, relative strength index (RSI), stochastic, moving average convergence/divergence (MACD) and parabolic trading systems are included. While you can't tweak the trading rules, you won't need to tweak the parameters because the program does it for you automatically in the process of testing most conceivable values. All the rules are fully disclosed in BASIC code in the manual, so there should be no confusion.

An additional note of sophistication: Ehlers's long experience in optimizing these indicators for cyclical content has been brought to bear. Where smoothing takes place, its amount is adjusted to the length of the averages being tested. The RSI, for example, is smoothed to create a "slow RSI," the crossover of which by RSI generates the trading signal.

Keeping all this in mind, program op-

eration is amazingly simple. Installation amounts to copying over all the files to a new directory. The program is copy-protected and the protection is hard core: the number of installations is counted and it won't run without the key disk or the program's signature installed on your hard disk. A couple of years ago, this technology caused many problems but now appears to be painless. You can un-install the copy protection to move it to another computer, but you won't be able to share the cost of the program with your buddies.

Once into the main program, you set the data path with defaults or by typing in your own unique path. All that's left is the selection of a trading system — I'm partial to double moving averages — and a 30- to 90-second wait for the grinding of a year's data. 3D goes out and tries every combination of the parameters in an "always in the market" mode, computes profitability at each setting and then draws a graph of the results. The process is too easy to get a lot of respect!

GETTING THE SPECIFICS

Once you see one of these charts, you inevitably want to dig deeper: "What's that point? How about that one?" The optimal profit point is calculated and shown by the program, but it may not be

the point at which you want to trade. It may be an outlier, a very steep peak with miserable values all around it. Point one is that you can probably see immediately what range of values in which you would like to trade. Getting the specifics may be tricky, though.

Even in full color, it's tough to track exactly what parameter value is assigned to which color. The colored bands may be hidden by others, but you can look at the picture from different angles to try to figure it out, though the top view is singularly uninformative because you lose all surface structure (use the down view instead). It would help if the colored surface appeared to be bounded by its axes. Sometimes it is, but usually it appears to be floating outside the axes, making the determination of where a particular point is a difficult or even impossible job. Sometimes the orientation of the surface when viewed from left or right isn't good and once in a while, part of it isn't even on the screen! This isn't a full computer-aided design (CAD) program that can move, expand, contract and twist your surface; usually, you can find a view that not only shows the area you want to see but also has delineated lines you can count to find the parameters. Neat additions would be a faint trace grid extending from the axes and making the whole picture bigger on the screen. Barring that, overlaid parameter values on the axes would be nice. Right now, you are just given the high and low values.

From the 3D display, for a reality check you can immediately pop over to a bar chart (Figure 2) with the trades indicated by arrows. Since the system provides no drawdown information, this will be the only way to get a feel for how badly things went en route to making your fortune.

PICKING AMONG SYSTEMS

You can also quickly determine what system works best with 3D. Think about that for a second. Typically, you'd spend days, weeks or months optimizing just *one* indicator or trading system. Here, we're going so fast we're going to be able to pick among systems probably in less than an hour or so.

After checking out, say, moving averages and looking at the bar chart, you may decide a parabolic would do a better job. No need to back out and restart the analysis. Punch "I" (for indicators) and select parabolic. A couple minutes later, the parabolic 3D results are in front of you ready for inspection, which in graphic format takes seconds, not counting twisting the image around for different views. *Bango!* You know in very short time if parabolics are good or not.

A thorough soul working at this speed might go ahead and check the trades for parabolics and repeat the entire process for the other three systems, just to avoid missing anything. It wouldn't take long. Using this program, pretty soon, I found myself doing this routinely and then doing it to the tradeables in different years just to see if there was any consistency.

FIGURE 2

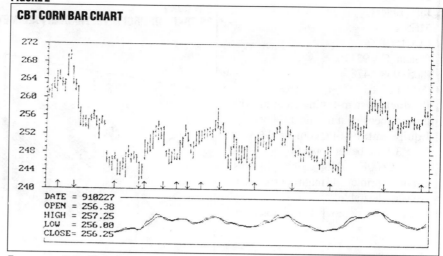

CBT CORN BAR CHART

```
DATE = 910227
OPEN = 256.38
HIGH = 257.25
LOW  = 256.00
CLOSE= 256.25
```

To compare with the 3D display, you can easily pop over to a bar chart with the trades indicated by arrows.

(Try a yen/10-day and 12-day dual moving average crossover system on any of the past five years.)

CHECKING STABILITY

Point three, you can check how much the parameters move around through a feature called "slide show." The program will take a two-month period and draw the profit surface, showing you the rough area where the parameters are best. Then it steps forward two weeks and does it again. As it repeats this process, you get a vivid impression of where stable parameters appear, all visually, very quickly.

SUMMARY

It's hard to appreciate how much work is done for you in 3D and how well it's done. The program is virtually effortless. It has its warts — the display problems described above, plus it crashed when it encountered a bad data file — but nothing

I know of can go through so much data with so many basic systems so fast and present the results so effortlessly.

An easy way to check this out is to order the demo disk. This is one demo disk worth getting. It's great! It will step you through using the entire family of Ehlers's cycle-based products, and it may be better than the manual for many purposes. There's also a three-hour video that I haven't seen but I would order were I starting fresh with these products.

I can hardly give an unbiased recommendation on Ehlers's products any more, sold as I was on MESA originally and all the follow-on products since. 3D is the cheapest of the pack and it's ideal for novice or pro alike, given its ease of use. If you'd like an easy but effective introduction to the best cycles work around, get the demo and then get 3D.

—John Sweeney, Technical Editor

FIGURE 1

REAL-TIME NEWS

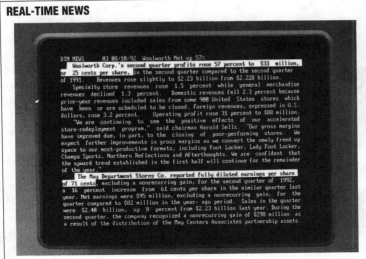

Unlike the quotes, the news you get from DTN is in real time.

DTN WALL STREET

Data Transmission Network Corp.
9110 West Dodge Road Ste 200
Omaha, NE 68114
Phone: (800) 475-4755
Product: Delayed datafeed for stocks, futures and news
Price: $37.95 per month

Perhaps the first thing a novice trader wants is a real-time datafeed to keep abreast of the market. This translates into staring at the CRT for a lot of extraneous information. It's probable that no novice should be trading off the floor on a real-time basis. It took me about nine months to get over this fixation, so let me spare *you* the expense!

There is a phenomenal alternative these days: delayed datafeeds. These offer data sent to you via satellite 10 to 30 minutes after it actually happens in the market. News is real time, though — no delay. The data can be downloaded and stored in a computer, building a superb database, and shuffled thence to your analytical programs. The price? How about $38 a month?

What was that? Did I say $38 a month? This compares to real-time services that start at $150 per month plus exchange fees, generating bills of $400 to $800 a month. Institutional users routinely pay thousands a month per station, often for something that sits ignored and unwatched on a senior officer's credenza, on the off-

chance that he might need to look up and instantly know the market's status.

I'm biased — I did a seminar for DTN — but I smell a revolution in data services.

Obviously, you wouldn't use DTN Wall Street for day-trading, but if you need reasonably current quotes and news — or even your guru's opinions — for next to nothing, this is your number, and already, 65,000 other DTN subscribers agree with you.

HOW IT WORKS

DTN has gone out of its way to make it easy for you to sign up. For no cash outlay, they will ship you the 30-inch satellite dish, the receiver, the data box and the cable to hook the system up. You take everything out and assemble it following the manual's instructions. Twiddle the antenna until you get a good signal and you're in business.

Is this easy process flawless? No. When I first got my unit, my handyman and I put it together and scrambled around the roof to set it up. We got a good signal but never got a signal sufficiently strong to avoid "framing errors" — as a result, quotes were erratic. Repeated calls to DTN brought much hand-holding and even a shipment of completely new components, no questions asked. However, the signal stayed weak. I even hired a local radio engineer to try setting things up — with no better luck.

Finally, and fortuitously, DTN switched to a new satellite, and a visiting DTN add-on vendor, RJT Systems, helped me get a rock-solid signal. My conclusion and DTN's: as many as 30% of initial DTN customers will make a call to the support service while setting up, while the other 70% will experience no problems at all.

As I say, they ship you all this for nothing. If you decide to sign up, they bill a $295 signup fee for the equipment lease. DTN owns and maintains the equipment. You pay the $37.95 in quarterly installments unless you'd like to get the bill down to $35 a month by paying for a year at a time. The minimum lease is for one year. This is truly a financially painless startup.

WHACHUGET

Once you turn the boxes on, you never turn them off. The screens are set up with five segments: news, financials, stocks, quote screens and futures screens. News is real time (Figure 1), while almost all equity quotes are delayed by 15 minutes. From New York futures exchanges, there is a 30-minute delay. The Chicago futures exchanges are on a 10-minute delay. The only options quotes — OEX quotes — are delayed 20 minutes.

You flip between the screens by means of two switches protruding from the DTN data box (Figure 2), a technique for which there is little on-screen guidance and which I found easy to lose myself in. Soon, depending on how often you use it, you'll learn how to toggle to the pages you want.

Once you're plugged into the world, you're going to be deluged with more information than you can possibly manage. All the economic releases are scheduled on the news page with their dates and times and estimated values as well as reported values. Corporate announcements, advertisements(!), technological reports, court decisions — you name it, it's constantly coming at you. The stuff streams in from just about every source except Dow Jones.

In the financial segment, numerous vendors compete to ship you information. Bear Stearns, for example, provides notes, bonds, yield curves, auction dates — you name it. DTN provides the current bond contract chart. American Investors Life

FIGURE 2

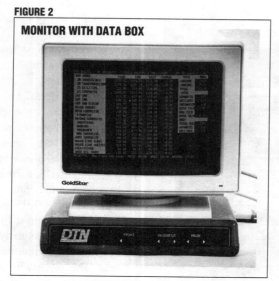

MONITOR WITH DATA BOX

It's easy to get lost in DTN's world using the data box.

Insurance advertises annuity rates, even. Currency, petroleum and metals prices summaries are available. If you want to add more data, that can be arranged. DTN is just a highway and the vendors can easily ship you custom data, opinions, instructions — in a word, information over that highway.

Similarly, the stock segment provides quotes from over-the-counter, American and New York exchanges plus foreign market summaries, more hour-by-hour commentary, earnings reports, company news and some more advertisements.

To home in on your personal problems, the quotes segment lets you set up quote pages that can handle stocks, futures, indices, New York-listed bonds, money market funds and mutual funds. All the popular market indicators such as A-D, tick and TRIN are computed and sent to you along with the major market indices. Programming — via toggle switches — is not easy and it's time consuming, so you will by necessity focus on those tradeables in which you are truly interested out of the 17,000-plus coming in on your datafeed.

The futures segment, my personal favorite, has all the markets I like to trade: financials, currencies, metals, petroleum, plus volume and open interest statistics. I dump a lot of this onto my computer, which brings up the subject of add-on services.

ADD-ONS

To get the most from this service, you should consider dedicating a cheap DOS machine to gathering and storing the data. Given the current price war, you can take the money you save from two or three months' real-time prices and buy yourself a completely equipped 486/33 for, say, $1,600 (in Seattle, anyway). The computer will take the information from DTN and put it on a hard disk where a number of vendors' packages will analyze it for you. I haven't had time to do a complete survey, but I know of one package — Quote Express — which will provide on-screen quotes and ship the data to virtually all the popular analytical packages. I'll review that capability next month.

SUMMARY

Correct me if I'm wrong, but the potential is here for a tremendous deal. First off, if you don't need real time, you're going to save thousands of dollars a year buying a delayed service. (Institutional accounts should love this!) Second, you can try it out for no cash outlay. Send it back free if you don't like it. Third, you get more pricing and news than you can possibly handle. Fourth, you can customize the service and get your particular market or guru added to your datafeed. Fifth, you can dump some or all the data to your computer to build a database for analytics and trading decisions.

Is it perfect? No. Setup may be a problem for you. Toggling switches are definitely very old news. The manual isn't much help, but the telephonic handholding is persuasive. Color isn't available (it's due out later on this year) but for $35-40 a month, what do you want? DTN got started selling to some very down-to-earth customers: farmers. These guys, notorious for their sense of value, turned DTN into a major player. My guess is that the financial community and traders will easily recognize similar value in DTN Wall Street.

—John Sweeney, Technical Editor

SIGNAL 3.0 WITH SIGNALREPORTS

Data Broadcasting Corp.
1900 South Norfolk Street
San Mateo, CA 94403-0979
Phone: (415) 571-1800, (800) 892-1697
Product: Real-time and end-of-day price quotes and news
Price: SignalPlus FM or cable receiver, $695; activation fee, $125; basic monthly subscription, $180. Plus, additional subscription and exchange fees.

Required equipment: IBM PC, XT, AT, Portable or Ps/2 or 100% compatible, hard disk, 640K RAM, communications serial port, DOS 3.3 or later. Data may be obtained via FM (radio), cable (TV) or satellite antenna reception.

Signal is certainly the Cadillac of quote delivery systems and serves the public well. Access to the FM/satellite/cable-fed data is smooth and, to say the least, voluminous. Signal 3.0 is a typically unruffled upgrade that provides text services as well as new data highlighting the intraday volume leaders and top percentage gainers/losers for the New York Stock Exchange (NYSE), American Stock Exchange (AMEX) and Over-The-Counter (OTC) stocks and options.

With the advent of truly cheap 10- or 15-minute delayed services*, Signal is under pressure to increase the value of its datafeed, and one way to do so is to add news to a service that already offers options — literally — that competing delayed services don't offer (Figure 1). I tried out the new package with a similarly new FM receiver, the SignalPlus FM Receiver.

The Plus receiver arrives with the usual well-produced manual, a power pack and an FM antenna. Plug in the receiver with the supplied cable to your serial port and turn on the power.

Next, you load the Signal 3.0 software. Installation will be generally smooth, but you can't install from B drive — the program looks for the disk in A drive, no matter what. Type "Signal" (without the quotes) and the program immediately downloads the operating system to the receiver, after which you enter two extremely long and tortuous passwords and *bingo!* you're in business. Plan on about 20 minutes and maybe 1.2 megabytes

FIGURE 1

OPTIONS QUOTATIONS

One of Signal's strong features is its extensive pallet of options quotations.

FIGURE 2

SIGNAL SUMMARY PAGE

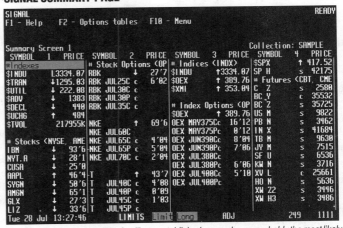

Signal's summary page will be familiar to established users who are probably the most likely market users of the new text services.

FIGURE 3

TEXT SERVICES

Five new text services are downloaded after hours to your receiver and hard disk, one of which is MarketLine. You may choose any combination of those offered.

(MB) on your hard disk. Plan, too, on leaving your system on 24 hours a day to run Signal — which will run in the background under DESQview 2.4 — because all the text files come in after the markets close and your machine must be ready for them.

Once set up, quotes (Figure 2) are instantaneous because the receiver keeps the last quote on everything it receives — no need to wait around for the datafeed to get to the issue about which you inquire.

DollarLink and AIQ/Potomac were the first analysis packages to link to the new SignalPlus receivers and they also offer the SignalReports feature. AIQ(EOD), Aspen Research, Bristol Financial, Equis International, International Pacific Trading, Montgomery Investment Group, Roberts-Slade, Omega Research, Savant Corporation, T.B.S.P., Townsend Analytics and Trendsetter Software are among those developers who have confirmed compatibility with the SignalPlus Receivers. Others are quickly coming online, so call for more details.

OPINIONS

Wouldn't you like to call on the opinions of top market experts (Figure 3)? Signal 3.0 offers access to Signal Reports. Reports currently offered are: the Future World News Summary Service (pre-market and post-market for $30 per month), MarketLine ($35), Comtex News Summary ($30), the Instant Advisor (equity and options trades, $20) and Downing & Associates Technical Analysis ($30). Not only that, effective August 1992, these reports became available: SGA Goldstar Research Market Report for $30 a month; SGA Goldstar Research Futures Report, $20 a month; Forex Report (for currency traders), $25 a month; IPO Spotlight Report (Bi-Weekly Report) for $30 a month; and an upcoming weather service report for traders, $20 a month. For four weeks they are free, after which you may turn them off or subscribe. Should your guru be on the air, this may be the slickest way of all to get his stuff. Even a fax service won't be this good. Heed well, though, the usual disclaimer.

More useful to me were the market summaries from overseas and those of all the economic data. Reading this download, which comes sometime in the night after the markets have closed, is like scanning the summary sections of *The Wall Street Journal* or *Investor's Business Daily* but loaded more toward hard facts than those publications at present.

The only drawback to this that I could see is that there is no intraday news available. The datafeed is too busy with numbers at that time to accommodate late-breaking news.

SUMMARY

Signal 3.0 is a worthwhile upgrade. New features include an instant quote window, a new leaders' page and tick trend. The text service is not for news junkies but for interday players who want seamless access to their news sources after hours, though "after hours" is getting harder and harder to define these days. The "four weeks free" offer is a generous chance to try them out. If your service is offered and you're moderately time-sensitive, SignalReports may be an effective, if costly, way to get it.

—*John Sweeney, Technical Editor*

*Editor's note: As STOCKS & COMMODITIES went to press, Data Broadcasting Corporation announced the release of Signal Delayed, a new service that provides continuous information with no dropped data and with the minimum delay allowed by the exchanges.

SIT TIGHT

After spending many years in Wall Street and after making and losing millions of dollars I want to tell you this: It never was my thinking that made the big money for me. It always was my sitting. Got that? My sitting tight!

—Edwin Lefevre
Reminiscences of a Stock Operator

PROSEARCH VERSION 2.0

Telescan, Inc.
10550 Richmond Suite 250
Houston, TX 77042
(800) 324-8246
Product: Stock research software
Equipment required: IBM-PC and compatibles with 512K memory minimum. *System:* MS-DOS version 2.1 or higher. *Monitor:* Hercules monochrome graphics, EGA or VGA. *Modem:* 1200 baud or higher Hayes Smartmodem or compatible. Also requires Telescan 2.5 or higher.
Price: ProSearch alone, $295; with Telescan Analyzer, $395. (These products have not been sold separately in the past two years.)

Telescan's ProSearch version 2.0 is a stock search program that can easily help investors find stocks that meet their fundamental and technical criteria. For each search, ProSearch uses a selected portion of the Telescan database of more than 11,000 issues. You may select stocks, optionable stocks, mutual funds, industry groups or stocks within specified industry groups. The database is accessed through Telescan Analyzer, an investment software and communications package that allows investors to access a database of news, company information, price and indicators. The database is updated every 20 minutes continuously on a 15-minute delay.

The auto-installation batch file allows you to install and set up ProSearch easily. After installation, you will need to enter your system's configuration, required password and phone number to access Telescan's database.

INTUITIVE AND SIMPLE

Using ProSearch in conjunction with Telescan Analyzer is intuitive and simple with their well-structured menus. The information that can be accessed with this Telescan package is impressive. News, quotes, charts, institutional holdings, insider trades and custom stock selection are just some features that this package has to offer. *And* the cost is reasonable. With a 1200-baud modem (which must be 100% Hayes compatible), a stock search using 30 criteria would take about one minute of on-line time. Cost estimates

TELESCAN PROSEARCH INDICATORS

ProSearch lets you select and weigh more than 100 criteria to define your search to meet your goals.

Fundamental Indicators
Valuation indicators
P/E ratio
Relative P/E ratio
Projected P/E ratio (next FY)
Price to book value ratio
Relative price to book value ratio
Price to cash flow ratio
Price to capital spending ratio
Price to sales ratio
Price to sales ratio
Growth ratios
    Company growth ratio
    Company/industry growth ratio
    Company/S&P growth ratio

Stock Market Performance Indicators
Stock price
Relative strength
    1-day relative strength
    1-week relative strength
    3-week relative strength
    6-week relative strength
    18-week relative strength
    26-week relative strength
    1-year relative strength
    3-year relative strength
    5-year relative strength
Percent yield
Dividend growth rate
    5-year dividend growth rate
Dividend consistency
    5-year dividend consistency
    10-year dividend consistency
Price growth rates (LSQ)
    Price growth rate (LSQ)
        3 years
        5 years
        10 years
        15 years
    LSQ deviation
        3 years
        5 years
        10 years
        15 years

Earnings Indicators
Earnings per share

Earnings growth rate
    1-year earnings growth rate
    3-year earnings growth rate
    5-year earnings growth rate
Projected earnings growth rate
    1-year (current fiscal year)
    2-year (next fiscal year)
    5-year (annualized)
    30-day change in 1-year projected EPS
    Growth rate
1-year sales growth rate
5-year cash flow growth rate
Earnings consistency
    5 years
    10 years
Return on sales
Return on assets
Return on stockholder's equity

Debt Risk Indicators
Current ratio
Debt to equity ratio
Interest coverage
Debt service/share ratio

Balance Sheet Indicators
5-year book value growth rate
5-year capital spending growth rate
Cash/share ratio
Inventory turnover
Receivables turnover
Asset turnover

Volume Indicators
Volume/no. of shares
30-day average volume
1-day to 30-day average volume ratio
5-day to 30-day average volume ratio
Short interest ratio

Technical Indicators
Moving averages
• 30-day moving average ratio
• 150-day moving average ratio
• 30-day moving average breakout
• 150-day moving average breakout
Moving average convergence/divergence
    MACD breakouts
        8-17-9 day
        12-25-9 day
        8-17-9 week
    MACD HST (histogram)

        8-17-9 day
        12-25-9 day
        8-17-9 week
MACD value
    8-17-9 day
    12-25-9 day
    8-17-9 week
MACD delta
    8-17-9 day
    12-25-9 day
    8-17-9 week
Stochastics
    Stochastics breakout
        9-3 day
        14-5 day
        30-15 day
    Stochastic value
        9-3 day
        14-5 day
        30-15 day
Wilder RSI
    Wilder RSI breakout
        9-day
        14-day
        9-week
    Wilder RSI value
        9-day
        14-day
        9-week
Daily range
    Daily range
    % daily range
    % daily range 5-day average
    Daily range gap
Beta
Volatility
McClellan oscillator

Background Indicators
Number of analysts making projections
    1 year
    2 years
    5 years
Institutional holdings
    Number of institutional holdings
    Percentage of institutional holdings
Number of outstanding shares
Market capitalization
Insider trading
    Insider trading
    Exercise of options

would be about $1 during non-prime time and $2 during prime time, or $15 for unlimited non-prime time usage. The user can retrieve up to 200 stocks per search.

Selecting your criteria to prepare your search is easy. But creating a trading strategy as well as determining desired stock selection criteria takes some thought and time, especially since ProSearch provides more than 100 fundamental and technical indicators to help define your investment goals in a search strategy. More than a third of ProSearch's 130 criteria are technical indicators, of which 11 are technical breakouts for various time periods. There are eight major indicator categories: valuation, performance, earnings, debt risk, balance sheet, volume, technical and background. (See sidebar, "Telescan Pro-Search indicators.")

Not only that, ProSearch has a dozen preset criteria to help you get started and oriented in creating criteria for a stock selection. Each search provides a report based on selected criteria. The maximum number of criteria possible in one request is 30. Generally, each search, whether there are five or 30 criteria, takes about 30 seconds. The criteria is user defined and can be a balance of absolute, relative and list-only rules.

The absolute search mode allows the user to define a specific level of any indicator. For example, criteria can be added to find stocks that meet technical and fundamental news and still be absolutely between $5 to $20 per share, or list stocks with a Relative Strength Indicator (RSI) reading over 70.

The relative search mode allows you to rate the significance or weigh the importance of any selected criteria. For example, when selection criteria isolate stocks in a trend, less importance is placed on stochastics and more on relative strength and moving averages.

The list-only search mode will list specified indicators and data to the final report of stocks that fit your absolute and relative search criteria. For example, stock price or daily range can be listed but not be part of the selection criteria; this will provide needed information to the final report and save you from having to backtrack and look up additional information separately.

IN SEARCH OF

With a search strategy, ProSearch will first eliminate all stocks that do not meet the specific "absolute search mode" requirements. Then the program looks for the highest scores for the "relative search mode" criteria. Finally, it adds up the combined scores and lists them in descending order. Thus, a report is generated based on the search criteria. Included in the report will be the list-only information that was selected on as many as 200 stocks.

The search can be made through the entire TeleScan database or within four segments: stocks with tradable options, mutual funds, industry groups or stocks within selected industry groups. You can choose between the New York Stock Exchange, American Stock Exchange or NASDAQ.

ProSearch and Telescan Analyzer is a powerful, easy-to-use investment software and data package. The combination gives investors access to an enormous amount of information, including stocks that fit their investment criteria, company information and news and price charts with popular indicators. This package is for any serious investor who needs to quickly and conveniently follow stock price and news information.

—*Michael Takano*

FIGURE 1

OUTPUT FROM STOCK SEARCH

```
                          P R O S E A R C H

           Criteria                      Criteria Values
       --------------------          --------------------
       DAILY RANGE GAP               -1.0          1.0
       PERCENT DAILY RANGE           60.0          100.0
       PERCENT DAILY RANGE           HIGH          100 %
       % DLY RNGE/5DY AVG            HIGH          100 %
       DAILY RANGE                            List Only
       REL STRENGTH  1-DY            HIGH          100 %


              ***************************
              Prosearch Top Stock Report
                       5/22/92
              ***************************


   1) HDS    HILLS DEPT STORES INC
      DRGap= 0.0   %Rnge= 100   %Rnge= 100   DRAvg= 80   Range= 25
      1-Dy = 120

   2) ASBI   AMERIANA SVGS BK F S B IND
      DRGap= 0.0   %Rnge= 100   %Rnge= 100   DRAvg= 90   Range= 200
      1-Dy = 110

   3) ARTG   ARTISTIC GREETINGS INC
      DRGap= 0.0   %Rnge= 100   %Rnge= 100   DRAvg= 82   Range= 100
      1-Dy = 113

   4) HENP   HENLEY PPTYS INC CL A
      DRGap= 0.0   %Rnge= 100   %Rnge= 100   DRAvg= 95   Range= 6.3
      1-Dy = 108

   5) ESIO   ELECTRO SCIENTIFIC INDS INC
      DRGap= 0.0   %Rnge= 100   %Rnge= 100   DRAvg= 80   Range= 37
      1-Dy = 111

   6) ENSO   ENVIROSOURCE INC
      DRGap= 0.0   %Rnge= 100   %Rnge= 100   DRAvg= 80   Range= 37
      1-Dy = 110

   7) IASG   INTERNATIONAL AIRL SUPPORT
      DRGap= 0.0   %Rnge= 100   %Rnge= 100   DRAvg= 77   Range= 62
      1-Dy = 111

   8) BELD   BELDEN & BLAKE CORP COM
      DRGap= 0.0   %Rnge= 100   %Rnge= 100   DRAvg= 76   Range= 50
      1-Dy = 112

   9) DUSAW  DEPRENYL USA INC *W EXP
      DRGap= 0.0   %Rnge= 100   %Rnge= 100   DRAvg= 96   Range= 62
      1-Dy = 107
```

Here is an abbreviated list of the output from a search for those stocks that closed at the top of their daily range and closed at their highs for the last five days. Today's low is above yesterday's close and the daily range listed.

UNIVERSAL
A Simple System for Trading All Markets
Futures Truth Company
815 Hillside Road
Hendersonville, NC 28739
(704) 697-0273
Product: Fully disclosed technical trading system
Price: $1,900 or $2,250 with software. For PC version: any IBM-compatible PC, 640K of memory, graphics CGA or higher.

Futures Truth has published its tabulations of trading systems' performances since 1986, serving as a reasonably calm arbiter of the incendiary subject. Though its founder, John Hill, has often tangled publicly with other system vendors (particularly Bruce Babcock), Futures Truth, which according to the introduction to the manual has been running at a net loss, has now decided to recoup its losses by becoming a vendor itself.

Well, who would know better how to put together a system? Futures Truth, headed by John Fisher, has seen the guts of many systems and monitored their performance for more than half a decade. From this work have emerged several strong possibilities, one of which is disclosed as the Universal system.

Though it *is* simple, it's not quite universal. Fisher and crew have come up with parameters for Treasury bonds, Eurodollars, Treasury bills, Treasury notes, Standard & Poor's 500 futures contracts, the U.S. Dollar Index, the British pound sterling, Deutschemarks, yen, Swiss francs, coffee, sugar, orange juice, copper, silver, crude, pork bellies and soybeans. They are working on others but so far admit defeat on New York Futures Exchange contracts, cotton, gold, cattle and lumber.

EASY SETUP
The Universal can easily be done by hand on worksheets provided in the package. Those in love with computers may pay $350 extra for IBM-PC compatible software that can speed things up and avoid mental errors.

To get started, read the 18 pages of explanation. It's well done, with excellent

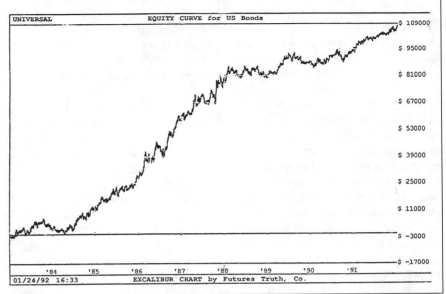

EQUITY CURVE FOR U.S. BONDS

FIGURE 1: *The Universal system on T-bonds in 1991 generated two wins for every loss. The system was profitable every year, ranging from 100% of $2,700 margin to 1,100% of margin.*

graphics. No one would have any questions about the trading rules when he or she is finished. You're looking at a modified breakout system with automatic reversal that is in the market 100% of the time. I would say the average trade runs five or six days and wins and losses run about 10 to 15 trading points, though this will vary by tradable and volatility.

The next 150 pages in the manual detail — and I *mean* detail — all the testing results from using the system on 18 markets with nine years (1983-91) of data. You get the nine-year summary and the trade-by-trade description for 1991, the year the system was first published. Even handier, the trade-by-trade data are laid out perfectly to be fed to Commodity Systems, Inc.'s Trader's Money Manager (TMM version 2.0 was reviewed in STOCKS & COMMODITIES, August 1992) for analysis. Good adverse price movement data are not listed, but Futures Truth must have set out to set a standard for system disclosure because this is absolutely the best trading system disclosure I have ever seen.

RESULTS
Unfortunately, when I ran some of the best equity curves (Figure 1 is bonds, for example) through Trader's Money Manager, TMM pronounced the likelihood of

profit too small to capture, even with $35,000 of trading capital per contract. TMM assesses trading system performance by degrading the system's results in proportion to the number of parameters required to get the trading decisions — in this case, five. TMM tends to be conservative. I've never seen it approve anything with more than two parameters!

I ran the Universal system through maximum adverse excursion (MAE) testing on T-bonds — one of the better equity results — and found an unusual result: the system's adverse price movement showed no difference between that of winning trades and losing trades. The system selected trades where, after entry, there appeared to be no difference in price movement. Indeed, the system on T-bonds in 1991 generated two wins for every loss. The Universal system was profitable every year, ranging from 100% of $2,700 margin to 1,100% of margin. I concluded that the automatic reversing feature was an effective stop-loss mechanism.

More conservatively, Futures Truth calculates a return on margin plus drawdown. For 1983-91, these ran from 107.8% for T-bonds down to 10.4% on the Swiss franc. Win/loss ratios ran from 2:1 with T-bonds to a low of 1.4:1 with the Swiss franc. Given that we are being offered the system, results for all 17 commodities across all nine years were uniformly in the black.

TRADERS

I was able to find two traders who were using the system intensively. As usual, everyone else had bought it, tinkered with it and been unable to find the trigger. The intensive users were pleased, however, and felt it was making them money, though neither had detailed records to support that — their accounts were just up and running. They both agreed that the system did well on some currencies — British pound, yen and the Canadian dollar — but not the Swiss franc or D-mark. Bonds, yen, T-notes, Eurodollars, bills — anything that pops around seemed to be fruitful. Not so good were sugar, bellies, copper and coffee. The S&P was rated acceptable on balance, and beans and crude were okay to slightly profitable.

Both intensive users felt you could get large equity drawdowns with the system, especially when the tradables went into a slow move in one direction or another.

Neither had any problems with installation of the software. One had never heard from the publisher again and wondered if there had been any updates or follow-ups. (No.) The other was in weekly contact with Futures Truth, tweaking the system.

SUMMARY

My limited testing confirms a sample of the numbers in the disclosure document. My testing also found that the sample tested showed no large equity drawdowns, but real-life traders had found large drawdowns were possible, even when trading the whole portfolio. Profitability, per the track record, was more than adequate.

Futures Truth has provided an exemplary product but I must question whether any trading system is worth $2,000. Back when I got started old systems were, and still are, a dime a dozen. Still, if you're content to lay out this kind of money, I'd start with the Universal system because it has a reliable vendor, full disclosure, good track records and solid, even enthusiastic, user recommendations.

—John Sweeney, Technical Editor

TA

MARKET MASTER VERSION 4.5

Ingenious Technologies Corp.
556 Roxbury Avenue NW
Massillon, OH 44646-3281
(216) 477-9900 or (800) 776-6488
Product: Price direction and target forecaster of stocks, commodities and indices
Price: $349 to $795, depending on the version ordered for use with daily data; $1,595 for the intraday trading version; $49 for a fully operational trial version that works with daily data.
Requirements: IBM PC or compatible with a minimum of 512K RAM, 950K of hard-drive space and MS or PC DOS 2.0 or higher. CGA/EGA/VGA monitor. Printers compatible with Epson FX or MX, IBM Proprinter or Hewlett-Packard Laserjet.
Discount: To readers who mention this Quick-Scan, Ingenious Technologies has offered to discount the retail price of any version ordered (except the trial version).

Sometimes, a trader purchases a system and finds it so impressive that he wants to acquire the sole rights to its distribution. That's precisely what Dr. Edward Lin did with Market Master, which was developed about three years ago by RMC (which still provides the technical support), but now it is distributed by Dr. Lin's company, Ingenious Technologies.

Composed of algorithms that create leading indicators of price action, Market Master forecasts both the direction and probable price objective of stocks, commodities and indices. Mutual fund and option traders can also gauge price direction and target by following the underlying index or security to which their investments are tied.

Market Master is sold in two-, four- and six-indicator versions that handle daily price data; the more indicators, the higher the software price. And for those who prefer to day trade, the company also offers a version that permits the manual entry of intraday prices.

The forecasting indicators in Market Master are proprietary — in other words, it's a black-box system, inherently disquieting to traders who like to know how

things work, even if they don't understand all the mathematical gyrations. The Market Master system has to be taken on faith (but for ye of little faith, it comes with a 60-day money-back guarantee). By way of rationale, the distributor points out that the benefits of aspirin are the same whether or not you know its chemical properties. To extend the analogy, the value of any black-box system depends on how well it relieves your financial headaches.

Theoretically, all versions of Market Master provide advance warning of price change and price objective through quantitative pattern analysis plus automatic learning that continually refines its analyses. The differences between the versions are threefold: first, the four- and six-indicator versions include volume in their analyses, whereas the two-indicator version works entirely from price data; second, each version adds indicators that approach or analyze the data differently; and third, the greater the number of indicators, the earlier the prediction.

DATA AND PROGRAM OPERATION

Market Master requires high, low, close and (in some versions) volume data for a minimum of 18 days to begin its forecast. The program refines its analysis as more data are added until it reaches a maximum of 62 days. No matter how extensive the database, it analyzes only the most recent 62 days. The first 12 days of data provide the initial basis for its computations and are not displayed. Therefore, the graphic display can exhibit, at most, the past 50 days of analyses (see Figure 1).

The program uses data in dBase format that may be entered manually or converted from MetaStock, CompuTrac, CSI or ASCII format via a converter disk (sold separately). Because it only uses the last 62 days of data at any given point, backtesting signals on a large database entails working backward by deleting recent data.

Installation is simple; the only quirk is the need to copy the DOS Command.com file to the Market Master subdirectory. Program options and commands are straightforward and easy to learn. All commands are listed across the bottom of the screen and can be accessed by a touch

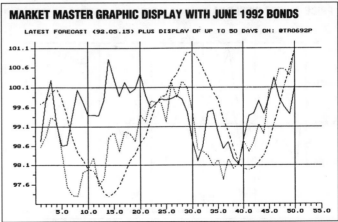

FIGURE 1: *Market Master displays up to 50 days of data on each screen. The solid line represents the leading indicator, the dotted line represents the closing price and the dashed line is the confirming indicator.*

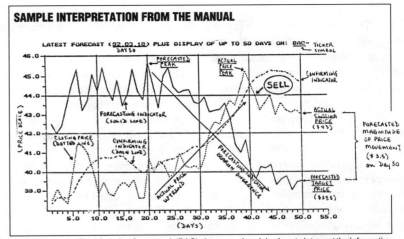

FIGURE 2: *Using BankAmerica Corp. stock (BAC), the manual explains how to interpret the information contained on the graphic display. The leading indicator (solid line) drops below the price several days before the actual price decline and price tends to zigzag its way toward the price target forecast instead of moving down directly.*

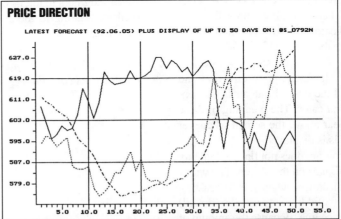

FIGURE 3: *Because the forecasting indicator often changes direction well in advance of the actual price change, it is best to wait until price closes above the confirming line. The ideal scenario seems to be when price is "sandwiched" between the forecasting indicator and the confirming indicator, as was the case with July 1992 soybeans from day 15 to day 34 (approximately mid-April to mid-May).*

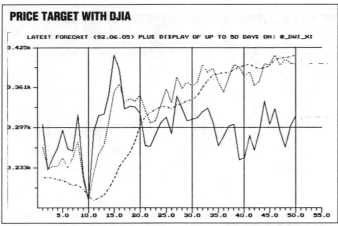

FIGURE 4: *Examining the magnitude or distance between the forecasting indicator and the closing price provides clues about the ultimate price objective.*

of a key. The software comes with several demonstration files that allow the new user to experiment with the various commands. Calculations for any indicator take less than five seconds, with no optimizing necessary. The program supports CGA/EGA/VGA monitors. The print drivers work with Epson FX, Epson MX, HP-Laserjet or IBM Proprinter-compatible printers.

The slim manual describes the program operation well and provides general rules plus a few examples of how to interpret the indicators (see Figure 2). It could, however, benefit from many more examples and specific explanations about ways to interpret and integrate the findings of the indicators.

INTERPRETING THE INDICATORS

Market Master displays three lines for each indicator chosen. The dotted line represents the actual closing price for the last 50 days or less, the solid line forecasts the probable future price direction and target and the dashed line acts as a confirming indicator. The meaning of these lines appear above the screen whenever an analysis is displayed.

The program does not flash actual buy and sell signals on the screen. The warning signal comes when the forecasting indicator (solid line) crosses the (dotted) closing price line. Because the amount of lead time between the forecasting signal and the actual change in price varies with each security, the program manual suggests waiting until the closing price is also above (to buy) or below (to sell) the

confirming indicator line before establishing a position (see Figure 3). In addition to the main forecasting indicators, the program offers a five- and 11-day moving average crossover selection to further confirm a trend change.

One difference between Market Master and many other programs or systems that forecast market direction is this program's ability to suggest price targets as well. Potential price targets for each signal are indicated by the magnitude of the solid indicator line in relation to the current closing price (see Figure 4), allowing the trader to determine whether the possible reward justifies the risk of taking a position.

Even though Market Master requires some user judgment to interpret, it might be worth comparing to the system you currently use.

Barbara Star, Ph.D., is a frequent STOCKS & COMMODITIES contributor.

Css: Statistica

STATSOFT
2325 East 13th Street
Tulsa, OK 74104
(918) 583-4149

Product: Integrated statistical data analysis, graphics and data management system.

Equipment: PC Dos (or Os/2 2.0) compatible computers with at least 640K; if expanded or extended memory is installed, it will automatically be detected and used by the system. The program fully supports math co-processors and graphics co-processors, although none is required. A hard disk is recommended (15 megabytes), but individual modules can also be run from high-density floppy disks.

Price: $795
Full package integrates Css/3, the Complete Statistical System ($595 separately); Css: Graphics ($495); Megafile Manager ($295). A subset of Css/3 is Quick Css ($295). Statistica/Mac lists for $495, and Quick Css/Mac for $295.

by Hugh Stokely

ophisticated quantitative analysis has always held its fascination for technical analysts and economists. It ranks with Fed watching and chart reading on the growing, overlapping list between those professions. Both require judgment about what's changed and what has not in the cause-and-effect patterns of the markets. In both, judgments need to be validated with proven statistical methods. It's better to learn what's wrong with your trading rule from your computer than from the marketplace.

But the tools of statistics are anything but user-friendly. To use them safely requires up-to-date understanding of statistical theory, backed by a software package organized to exploit the cheaper data and computing power now becoming available. For those willing to put forward significant time and effort, Css:Statistica is an excellent choice. It pulls together the general-purpose methodology that has been tested over time against real-world outcomes for medical, electoral, marketing and actuarial populations. Statistica's routines are fast and rigorous, accessible through a straightforward menu system that works on a 386 clone standing alone or with a mouse as a non-Windows application under Microsoft Windows 3.0. Organized that way, I can switch back and forth between Statistica, Xerox Ventura Publisher and a screen editor in true multitasking. Thus, I can perform statistical tests, graph the results, write them up and see how the finished document looks with pleasing integration and efficiency.

Particular strengths include Statistica's ability to handle many massive data files, each limited to 32,000 variables, 300 characteristics per variable and 8 megabytes of disk space. You can import data from most common formats quickly (Figure 1). An extensive menu allows you to apply a wide range of statistical tests with a minimum of keystrokes or mouse-clicks.

FIGURE 1

FILE FORMATS

Lotus 1-2-3 .WK1 and .WK3
Symphony
Microsoft Excel
dBASE III+ and IV
Spss
Sylk
.DIF
Ascii

Graphics files can be saved in various formats for use with desktop publishing and word processing programs, including:
  PostScript
  Cgm (Computer Graphics Metafile)
  Hpgl (Hewlett-Packard Plotter)

Statistica imports and exports in the above file formats.

At each point, as you work with the data, Statistica's spectacular graphics package is at your fingertips through a menu that accesses more than 80 prepackaged templates, extended with numerous options and variations, including the ability to embed one graph in another to present a complex concept. Statistica's capability for interactive, on-screen rotation of multiple charts, each portraying three dimensions of a data set that extends to four or more dimensions, enables hands-on visualization and statistical testing of approaches such as catastrophe analysis, entrainment or fractals.

On my first try, Statistica's graphics commands plotted a high-resolution chart successfully on my PostScript laser printer. First-try success was better than my experience with systems integration led me to expect. The software outputs graphics and text smoothly on desktop monitors and printers — at the sharpest resolution available on typesetters. Statistica sent Figure 3, which is reasonably complicated, to an Encapsulated PostScript (Eps) file in one minute 25 seconds, with Ventura and a screen editor running in the background. Then it took three minutes 36 seconds for a PostScript printer to turn that file into hard copy. As an alternative, Statistica produces Ascii standard Computer Graphics Metafiles with good resolution at a slightly faster speed.

StatSoft emphasizes its commitment to keeping the product at the state of the art as more advanced visual and print hardware becomes available. That commitment came across when I called Tulsa to ask for some of their free technical support. They were able to spot immediately what configuration statements needed changing to output a graph that Ventura could use.

The sophistication and commitment of the StatSoft customer service are the main reasons I'm willing to overlook the frustrations I occasionally encountered installing Statistica, and with menu idiosyncrasies. StatSoft is upgrading its user interface within the framework of Windows 3.1, which Microsoft expects to release in early 1992. That forthcoming Statistica version should be very user-friendly, although the inherently forbidding nature of statistics means that a user

FIGURE 2

FUNCTIONS	
Basic statistics (means, standard deviation, correlation, t-test)	Log-linear modeling
Multiway frequency tables and banners	Non-linear estimation including Logit/Probit analysis
Multiple regression methods	Canonical correlation
Time series analysis methods (including ARIMA, transformations, smoothing and modeling, Fourier decomposition and autocorrelations)	Survival/failure time analysis
	Quality control
	Experimental design and process analysis
Distributed lags analysis	
General ANOVA/ANCOVA/MANOVA/MANCOVA	***Statistical Advisor.*** Statistica includes an "expert system" to help you select the appropriate statistic to analyze your data. The Statistical Advisor prompts you to answer a series of questions about your data and the information you want to extract from it. The Statistical Advisor then suggests which techniques to use and where to find out more about them.
Stepwise discriminant function analysis	
Nonparametric statistics	
Distribution fitting	
Factor analysis and principal components	
Multidimensional scaling	
Reliability/item analysis	
Cluster analysis techniques	

Here is an abbreviated list of the numerous features of Statistica.

should regard any advanced package as presenting a degree of difficulty more like learning how to fly than how to drive.

WHY BOTHER?

The value-conscious reader may ask, "Why don't I simply use the regression package that I've already paid for in my spreadsheet program?" Indeed, a user who is expert in statistics, who works with only a few small data sets, and who is willing to carry out data transformations and chart design by hand may find bare-bones statistical capability sufficient.

But a user who is less experienced or more ambitious needs a comprehensive package, with separate routines tailored for the main statistical questions likely to come up and with documentation that shows how to apply the statistical technicalities and to carry them through to an accurate reading of the odds. It's danger-ous using recipes not remembered clearly from statistics class without reviewing and re-sharpening one's skills. Since the 1960s, disappointments among managers who made commitments on the basis of high R-squares only to see them go wrong have created widespread distrust for econometric forecasting. Many of the analyses that went astray were scarred by three specific errors:

■ If you correlate series that trend up or down together, without careful correction, you risk saying that a forecast has a 0.90 R-square in its favor, when the fit actually is 0.30 or less.

■ If you use the popular and powerful Almon lag approach without tightly constraining the degree of the polynomial, you can get a spuriously strong fit for past history that falls apart when you use it to forecast future activity.

■ If your understanding of a statistical technique is superficial, your conclusion about overall odds can be far off the mark. As one simple example, if your bottom-line outcome depends on five forecasts each carrying 80% probability, your odds are only 33% of being right.

To avoid these and other dangers requires significant analytic commitment. Statistica represents a thoroughly professional package for drawing on the tested body of statistical knowledge to establish reliable odds. For investors and analysts willing to invest the necessary learning time, it offers a potential edge against less systematic investment competitors who rely on catch-as-catch-can methods.

FEATURES AND PRICING

Calculating accurate odds on an outcome is complicated. Given degrees of freedom and number of observations, the CSS: Statistica probability calculator will handle data from F† and chi-squared† tests and normal distributions as well as differences between means, correlations and sample proportions. Statistica fits nine different frequency distributions and handles 16 different nonparametric statis-

FIGURE 3

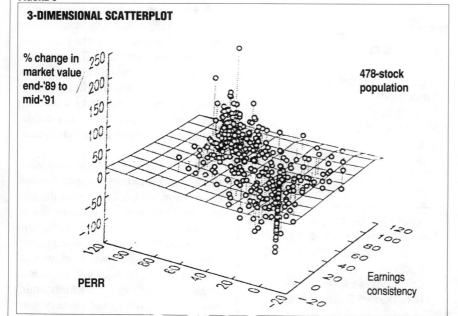

This three-dimensional scatterplot presents the market value change against the price/earnings ratio reliability and earnings consistency at year-end 1989 of 478 stocks.

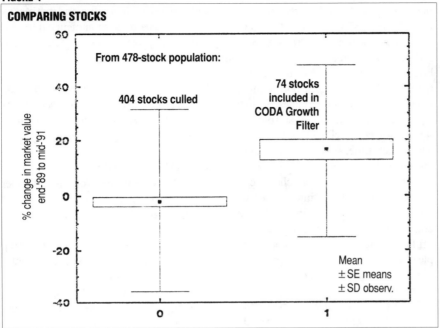

FIGURE 4

COMPARING STOCKS

From 478-stock population:

404 stocks culled

74 stocks included in CODA Growth Filter

Mean
± SE means
± SD observ.

Here's a comparison between the two groups of stocks screened by PERR using a box and whisker plot. The whiskers extend one standard deviation above and below the mean, while the boxes show standard error of mean.

tics. Documented examples take the user step by step through the more important options. The log-linear model necessary for realistic work with security prices gets a chapter and a menu heading of its own, as does nonlinear estimation, with coverage of Logit, Probit and penalty-loss functions. Comprehensive routines are provided for ANOVA and Multiple Analysis of Variance, plus separate routines and chapters spelling out how factor analysis, multidimensional scaling, stepwise discriminant analysis and several types of cluster analyses are related and how they differ.

In addition to the simple regression analysis that I walked through in the October STOCKS & COMMODITIES with Ken Stewart, Statistica provides multiple correlation routines that permit hands-on experiments with ridge regression and adjustment of tolerances. For time series, there's a full capability for handling autocorrelation, lagged variables, spectral analysis and ARIMA. Survival analysis, quality control and process analysis tools are in place to look at stock data as an actuarial life table and to detect significant divergences from the norm. (See Figure 2 for a list of features.)

In data handling, Statistica's data management and megafile manager modules are fast and convenient. Because of the ease with which Statistica accepts standard data transfer conventions, I find it preferable to shift key data into Statistica when detailed analysis or production-quality charts are needed. For particularly challenging data problems, StatSoft provides its own specialized data management language.

LIMITATIONS
In gauging the impact of government policy on financial markets, I develop models of several hundred equations, with large simultaneous-solution blocks. That requires the specialized capabilities of Data Resources' EPS simulation language, or the third-party clone that runs on my PC. While Statistica was not designed for production runs of large-scale simulation models, its graphics can be helpful in pinning down specific statistical results in such a model.

One recent advance in understanding the economy and financial markets is a sharpened perception of phase shift or structural change. There was a time when a move in the funds rate affected equity indices with a quarter's lag; starting in the mid-1980s, they began to move simultaneously. There was a time when a funds rate change moved money supply with a lag; in 1991, that linkage snapped. Analyzing such shifts requires state-space analysis, a newly emerging method provided neither in Statistica nor in competing PC products.

A STOCK MARKET APPLICATION
In the October STOCKS & COMMODITIES, Ken Stewart and I discussed price/earnings reliability (PERR), a statistic that measures the degree of correlation between a stock's earnings change and its stock price change. I've just put Statistica through its paces on a project to examine PERR, earnings growth trend, earnings consistency and change in market value for the 478 stocks that were present in the Standard & Poor's 500 from year-end 1989 through mid-1991. For these 478 stocks, Figure 3 shows market value change over that period in a three-dimensional scatterplot against the PERR and earnings consistency at year-end 1989. The observations for each stock are plotted in three-dimensional space, with a wire-frame outlining a surface fitted to their interaction.

Usually, an initial look at a complex system produces a messy, confused picture such as Figure 3, which some will find portrays the market as they know it. As you'd expect, the scatterplot shows only weak correlation—an R-bar-squared of 0.075, far below the confidence level that an investor should require. Some high-PERR stocks, where earnings matter to stock price, rose a lot, while others rose little and some dropped. Meanwhile, stocks with low PERR performed only slightly worse.

But PERR is designed as a filter variable —an on-off switch, rather than a rheostat. If you apply criteria that screen out stocks with low PERR, a five-year earnings growth trend less than 8% a year and showing earnings inconsistency, you can create an unmanaged, buy-and-hold portfolio as of year-end 1989 that screens out all but 74 stocks.

For the 18 months from year-end 1989 to mid-1991, growth in market value for those 74 stocks averaged 16.5%, compared with a negative 2% for the 404 stocks screened out. Figure 4 contrasts the two groups in a box and whisker plot.

■ The whiskers extend one standard deviation above and below the mean — 68% of future observations from the population sampled should fall within the whiskers.

■ The boxes show standard error of the mean — for future samples of the same size from the same population, 68% of the means should fall within the boxes. As Figure 4 suggests graphically, Statistica's probability calculator indicates odds well above 1,000 to 1 that average performance for this 74-stock portfolio will exceed the average for the 478-stock population.

Out of the real-world confusion evident in Figure 3, PERR has helped to isolate a group of stocks worth considering for above-average performance, identifying a good "fishing hole" for investors.

Despite the complexity of Figure 3,

Statistica did the calculations and popped the chart up on the color screen of my 20-mhz PC-386/387 in 25 seconds — and in about the same time on a 20-mhz 386SX/387 black-and-white notebook. In half an hour, I was able to cycle through more than 50 different charts portraying the interaction of market variables. Statistica zipped through calculations and plots with lightning speed, giving me a close look, in a very short time, at many aspects of how these data have been behaving.

This project barely scratches the surface of the probability interaction going on inside the financial markets. Statistica empowers the researcher to take the lid off the financial markets and other complex real-world systems, to probe with reliable statistical techniques and to pin down the odds on interesting results.

For an analyst or investor pondering a statistical question, I urge either deep immersion or abstention. Casual dabbling in statistics can be disastrous to your reputation and your portfolio. Statistica's combination of computerization and docu-

mentation is an excellent way to sharpen and apply statistical skills, and that makes available to a broader audience a toolkit that can improve the odds of being right about the future.

Hugh Stokely, CFA, is research director for CODA SmartLine. He has headed his own econometric strategy company since 1978.

FURTHER READING

Box, George E.P., and Norman R. Draper [1987]. *Empirical Model-Building and Response Surfaces*, John Wiley & Sons.

Stokely, Hugh, and Ken Stewart [1991]. "P/E ratio reliability," STOCKS & COMMODITIES, October.

Shumway, Robert H. [1988]. *Applied Statistical Time Series Analysis*, Prentice-Hall.

Omega TradeStation Version 2

OMEGA RESEARCH, INC.
3900 NW 79th Avenue, Suite 520
Miami, FL 33166
(800) 556-2022

Product: Real-time and historical technical analysis program with real-time custom trading system automation.
Equipment: IBM PC 286/386/486 or 100% compatible, two-megabyte minimum of installed RAM (four megs recommended), 15 megs of free hard disk space after installing Windows 3.0, EGA/VGA display, DOS version 3 or later, Microsoft-compatible mouse, FNN Signal receiver. TradeStation supports more than 200 printers via Windows. Optional equipment (at additional cost) includes support for up to four very high resolution (1024 x 768) color monitors with special video card and drivers and Dynamic Data Exchange (DDE) link, which feeds real-time quotes to Excel or any other Windows application.
Prices: TradeStation purchase price: $1,895. Or on the installment plan: startup of $395 plus 24 consecutive payments at $195 a month. Maintenance and phone support, new releases, BBS access and so on, $495 a year. Free TradeStation demo available. (Prices for FNN Signal vary according to usage. Call 1-800-S-MARKET for details.) A second data feed, S&P Comstock, is available. Call for details and prices.

---

by William Blau

T radeStation is one of a new genre of computer programs designed specifically for intraday traders to handle daily and other user-supplied historical data. As a Windows 3.0 application, it has much of what the current computer state of the art has to offer. As such, it has all the advantages of Windows-based programs.

INSTALLATION

There are three components of installation: installing the FNN receiver, installing Microsoft Windows 3.0, and finally, installing Omega TradeStation itself. My equipment included a 386-25 MHz DTK (IBM-compatible) computer with four megs of RAM, a math co-processor (not required but supported) and an MS-compatible mouse with an ATI VGA Wonder video board. Installing Windows 3.0 was straightforward but tedious, due to my unfamiliarity with the software. The FNN receiver installation was also uneventful. TradeStation was then installed from within Windows. This was also easy and direct, following instructions on the monitor screen.

As you boot up the computer and watch the Windows 3.0 logo zip by, a double click of the TradeStation Server icon puts you into the program. At this point, you may check out the interface with FNN or set up your intraday and daily portfolios for viewing quotes only or for collection of tick data to be stored on your hard disk.

TradeStation is subdivided into three major components, as shown in Figures 1 and 2. The server feeds the charting and editor components. Click over to the charts. Setting up the charts involves creating a new page (file) and as many windows on the page as you desire. We have chosen three windows: a 30-minute bar chart of the December S&P, the commodity channel index and stochastics (Figure 3).

Studies such as moving averages and oscillators are built-in functions (indicators), which are immediately clicked up on the five-minute screen. Fine tuning is simply performed, colors selected. We opt to have indicators and price ticks updated on a tick-by-tick basis so that in the event a decision must be made, it can be made before the bars are completed. We further click up candlestick chart mode (another built in) for a more visual graphic representation.

WHAT DO WE HAVE?

TradeStation gives a visually striking graphic display due to the wide range of color choices for background, price bars and study plots. I like the price bars (yellow against a black background) with overlays of the indicators both maximized to fill the screen. (The visual impact is a function of the video board employed in your computer and your display's resolution.) Using the mouse, it is a simple matter to click up all three windows, adjust them at will, or maximize any one window. For example, selecting the five-minute chart for the active window, we watch the screen and note a region of possible support developing. A support trendline is quickly drawn. Another trendline previously drawn slopes downward, defining a descending triangle. We are in oversold territory with our (red) oscillator. We observe that the 15-minute December S&P is in a clear uptrend and the hourly chart is at a solid support level. Waiting patiently, we are rewarded with the next bar, a reversal to the upside with increased tick volume. We put an order in to buy at the market.

Without the bells and whistles to be described later, TradeStation is a modern, user-friendly, professional-quality program designed for the serious day trader. For old-fashioned screen watchers, it also provides all tools that are necessary and then some. TradeStation also permits you to tailor your charts to your own liking, and includes a range of indicators ranging from trendlines (fast and easy), personal text messages, cycle lines and Fibonacci time to % retracement to zoom to enlarge selected chart portions, which I found to be very easy to use.

Charting studies involves only a few mouse-clicks from the 120 built-in functions (see Figure 4) that come with the package. These include most of the popular indicators and studies, plus a large group of functions unique to TradeStation. Any additional indicators that are needed can be built and implemented by the user. All built-in functions are completely disclosed in the excellent users' manual and in the function library of the program. Sources of information are given and authorship acknowledged. Additional indicators will be gradually made available

as new releases are made available.

TradeStation's Easy Language recognizes specific reserved words for use in the editor. For intraday, the words are date, time, open, high, low, close, uptick (volume), downtick (volume) and tick

(total tick volume). The offbeat capability to use up and down tick volume will open some avenues of trading for savvy day traders. For daily trading, the reserved words are date, open, high, low, close, volume, open interest. Indicators (func-

FIGURE 1

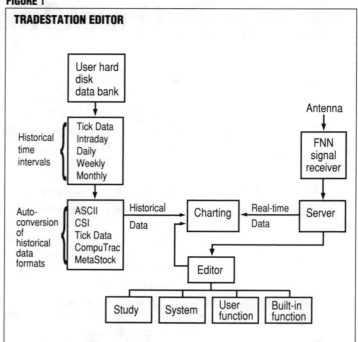

TradeStation is divided into three major components. The server receives data from the Signal receiver and feeds the data to the charting and editor components.

FIGURE 2

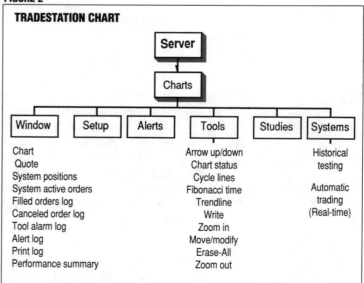

Here are some examples of the various pulldown menus in the charts' components.

FIGURE 3

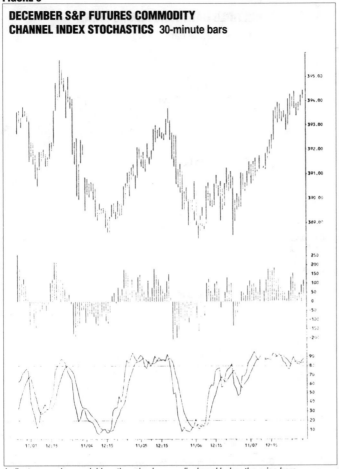

DECEMBER S&P FUTURES COMMODITY CHANNEL INDEX STOCHASTICS 30-minute bars

Indicators can be overlaid on the price bars or displayed below the price bars.

FIGURE 4

BUILT-IN FUNCTIONS

Studies and Indicators		Mathematical
AccumDist	TrueRange	AbsValue
Average	WAverage-Weighted	AvgList
CCI-Commodity Channel	Average	Cosine
Index	WeeklyCloseAverage	ExpValue
DMI-Directional	WeeklyHighAverage	FracPortion
Movement Index	WeeklyLowAverage	IntPortion
DMIMinus	WeeklyOpenAverage	Log
MNIPlus		MaxList#n
FastD-Stochastics	**Data Information**	MinList#n
FastK-Stochastics	Commission	Rndm
Highest#n	CommodityNumber	Rnd
LinearRegSlope	DailyLimitAmount	Sine
LinearRegValue	DeliveryMonth	Square
Lowest#n	DeliveryYear	SquareRoot
LowestBar#n	FirstCalcDate	StdDevList
Macd-Moving Average	LastCalcDate	SumList
Convergence-Divergence	Margin	
MacdAverage	MaxBarsBack	**Calendar**
Momentum	Slippage	DateToJulian
Most Recent Occurence		DayOfMonth
PercentR	**Trade Information**	DayOfWeek
Range	BarsSinceEntry	JulianToDate
RawK	BarsSinceExit	Month
RSI-Relative Strength	EntryDate	Year
Index	EntryPrice	
SlowD-Stochastics	EntryTime	**Performance Information**
SlowK-Stochastics	ExitDate	AvgBarsLosTrades
StdDev-Standard	ExitPrice	AvgBarsWinTrades
Deviation	ExitTime	GrossLoss
SwingHigh#n	Market Position	GrossProfit
SwingLow#n	NumContracts	LargestLosTrade
TLSlope-Trend Line Slope	TradeProfit	LargestWinTrade
TLValue-Trend Line Value	WeightedClose	NetProfit
TrueHigh		NumLosTrades
TrueHighest#n		NumWintrades
TrueLow		PercentProf
TrueLowest#n		TotalBarsLosTrades
		TotalBarsWinTrades
		TotalTrades

TradeStation has 120 built-in functions — most of the popular functions, plus a large group of functions unique to TradeStation.

tions) based on a single data stream are made accountable by the language. Thus, bar charts of price, bar charts of stock market "diaries" TICK, ADV, DEC, as well as others are all generated and indicators based on reserved words applied to these symbols are available. In addition, multiple data files implemented in version 2 permit functions (indicators) from up to 50 data streams to be cast together in the formation of indicators (McClellan oscillator, advance/decline indicators, and so forth). Comparison of symbols (data streams) permits comparison of different commodities with the same bar time spacing, with different time spacings (daily vs. weekly, for example), the same commodity at different time spacings, spreads or even fundamental outside data when adequately described.

Traders often employ multiple charts: a slow chart (monthly), an intermediate chart (weekly) and a trading chart (daily). In like manner, day traders often employ charts varying in length from hourly to 20 minutes to 10 minutes. Three such charts can be placed in subgraphs, one below the other, with the x-axis of the graph showing the common time for all. As time advances (or is shifted in historical testing), the bar charts, all of different time spacing, advance together in correct time relationship. Overlaid indicators are used to specify long-, intermediate- and short-term trends, all at a glance in a single window. Not bad at all!

TradeStation charts offer a variety of presentations, depending on trading style. If you trade with a few indicators, their overlay on the bar chart may be the presentation of choice. Indicators or moving averages are large, easy on the eyes, and closely identified with corresponding points on the bar chart. But if your trading style requires a large number of indicators, overlaying too many on a single chart (window) becomes confusing and difficult. TradeStation also gives you the option of using a chart window split in up to eight user-selectable subgraphs, excellent for displaying indicators below the bar chart. All subgraphs of a window split in this manner scroll together. In addition, each subgraph can contain additional data series (symbols), or studies. Up to 50 symbols (far more than I can anticipate

FIGURE 5

USER FUNCTION

```
{USER FUNCTION: DS_Stochastic                    }

{Double-smoothed Stochastic......by William Blau}
{Format: @DS_Stochastic(q,r,s)
     where  q = number of bars in highest high or lowest low
            r = number of bars in 1st exponential moving average
            s = number of bars in 2nd exponential moving average}

{  DS(q,r,s) = 100 * (DoubleEma of Close-LowestLow)/
                     (DoubleEma of HighestHigh-LowestLow)    }

{-----------------------------------------------------------}

Inputs:.q(NumericSimple), r(NumericSimple), s(NumericSimple);

Value1 = DXAverage(Close-Lowest(Low,q),r,s); {DoubleEma of Numerator}
Value2 = DXAverage(Highest(High,q)-Lowest(Low,q),r,s);
.....  (DoubleEma of Denominator)
If Value2 <>0 then
.Value3 = 100 * Value1/Value2
Else
.Value3 = 0;
DS_Stochastic = Value3;
```

Here's a user function in Easy Language, in this case double-smoothed stochastics. The indicator calculates the difference between today's close and the lowest low q bars back and is then smoothed twice using two exponential moving average of r and s lengths for the numerator. The denominator is the difference between tthe highest high and the lowest low q bars back and is then smoothed twice using two exponential moving averages of r and s lengths.

FIGURE 6

PLOTTING USER FUNCTIONS

```
{STUDY: DS_Stochastic....by Bill Blau                 }

Inputs: q(2), r(25), s(3), ma(3), BuyZone(30), SellZone(70);

Value1= @DS_Stochastic(q,r,s);
Value2= @Average(Value1,ma);        {simple moving average}

Plot1(Value1,"DS");
Plot2(Value2,"DS_s");
Plot3(BuyZone,"BuyZone");
Plot4(SellZone,"SellZon");
```

Here is an example of the instructions to plot double-smoothed stochastics. The input values are 2, 25, and 3 for the q, r, and s variables . The screen will also show oversold levels (Buyzone(30)) and overbought levels (Sellzone(70)).

FIGURE 7

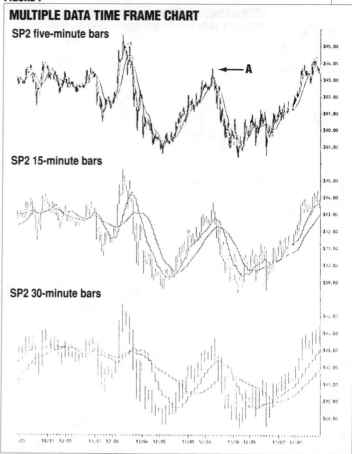

MULTIPLE DATA TIME FRAME CHART

SP2 five-minute bars

SP2 15-minute bars

SP2 30-minute bars

TradeStation allows you to test and automate systems that reference multiple time frames and/or different symbols. It displays a chart with bars synchronized on the time axis. The user can then scroll through the chart. TradeStation also overlays buy and sell arrows (A) to identify where the system bought or sold.

---

using) can be referenced within an alert, system or study of a chart window. If you wish to perform extensive historical testing or you use long-term moving averages, be advised that up to 16,000 price bars can be accommodated via scrolling into a chart window.

INDIVIDUALITY

TradeStation is an intraday trading program that permits traders individual leeway to devise indicators, studies and trading systems to suit his personal trading style.

The underpinnings of TradeStation reside in its libraries (files) of functions, studies and systems. Functions are mathematical relationships for indicators, data and trading information, performance information and so on. Functions may be groups of other functions; after all, functions are the mathematics that computers

use. Studies, on the other hand, relate functions to charts. Systems relate functions to actions (as in, "if this occurs, then..."). The ability to create new functions allows the computer program and the trader to be imaginative. There are built-in functions and user functions. The latter devised by the trader or your sources enlarge the overall function library.

Functions, studies and systems are expressed in terms of Omega's Easy Language. You do not have to be a programmer to be facile with the language. How-

TradeStation provides a framework and means for computer-directed trading according to preset criteria. A hierarchy of trading rules is incorporated into the system library with entry and exit conditions, order types, protective stops and trading strategies.

ever, it does take practice and perseverance; it may also not be for those lacking basic math skills. See Figure 5 for a user function in Easy Language for the double-smoothed stochastic. Because of my frequent use of double exponential smoothing, I designed a user function for it: DXAverage(Price, r, s), meaning take the double exponential moving average for r and s price bars. This function is now a permanent part of my function library. Take some time and you will recognize the general idea of Easy Language.

A study for the double-smoothed stochastic is shown in Figure 6. Essentially, the study plots the Ds-stochastic with default values of its parameters, q, r, s; it plots a simple moving average; it draws basis lines of overbought ("SellZone") and oversold ("BuyZone") regions. All this remains in the study file, waiting to be called up for placement on the selected chart window. No further redesign of the study is necessary. It may be pressed into service on another chart, intraday or daily, or a group of commodities with different parameters if so desired.

SYSTEM BELLS AND WHISTLES

TradeStation gives the user the choice of pulldown menus or almost universal control via your mouse. The latter has definite advantages in speed and in making more efficient use of the monitor screen. By placing mouse buttons on the perimeter of the monitor desktop, scrolling in all directions and increments is accomplished without the need for scroll bars. Changing windows, colors, charting and so on —all functions normally menu controlled — are efficiently activated by clicking the mouse. If you are mouse-oriented, you will love this feature, called Easy Icons, which is totally pictorial and user-customizable.

TradeStation provides a framework and means for computer-directed trading according to preset criteria. A hierarchy of trading rules is incorporated into the system library with entry and exit conditions, order types, protective stops and trading strategies. This is described in terms of functions, which, once created in the editor, reside in the library. A simple trading system is presented in Figures 7 and 8.

The package contains 20 built-in systems ready to trade after fine-tuning to your particular situation (Figure 9). However, one of the systems, trendline breakout, did not perform as I thought it should. This system depends on computer-generated trendlines, which very often turn out to be unlike those generated by a trader. Based on my results, I would be reluctant to use it.

The results for other systems were very satisfactory within the capabilities of the underlying indicators, however. I did have some difficulty getting consistent results with the divergence system, but this didn't bother me too much, since identification and use of divergence is not always clear. Once again, systems were fully disclosed in the excellent manual. You may create your own personal system using a group of indicators, for example, and incorporate it in the system library.

Historical system testing is performed on any selected chart window. Entry and exit points are shown and a performance summary is generated (Figures 10, parts a and b). TradeStation goes an additional step: When activated, it provides automatic order generation for your system in real time. Complete records of transactions and how they affect your portfolio are kept automatically. (Of course, you must call the broker to place your orders.)

"AT&T closed at 39 ... AWsts closed at 6 5/8 ...
AmWtr closed at 21 7/8 ..."

FIGURE 8

```
WRITING A SYSTEM IN EASY LANGUAGE
                            SYSTEM

Name        : Multiple Time Frame
Notes :

Last Update : 11/07/91 06:50pm
Printed on  : 11/07/91 06:51pm
Verified    : YES

//////////////////////////////////// CODE \\\\\\\\\\\\\\\\\\\\\\\\\\\\\\\\\\\\

{ Comment: Anything between { } is a comment.
Note: For this system the following data is used:
      Data1 is  5 minute SP 21
      Data2 is 15 minute SP 21
      Data3 is 30 minute SP 21
}

{ Check to see that 30 minute data above 18 bar moving average }
Condition1 = Close of Data3 > Average(Close,18) of Data3;

{ Check to see that close of 15 minute bar below 18 bar moving average }
Condition2 = Close of Data2 < Average(Close,18) of Data2;

{ Check to see that close of 15 minute bar below 18 bar moving average }
Condition3 = High of Data1 > High of 1 bar ago of Data1 and
             Low  of Data1 < Low of 1 bar ago of Data1;

{ If all conditions true then place buy/sell on breakout of 5 min bar }
If Condition1 and Condition2 and Condition3 then
  Buy at High + 1 point stop;

If Condition1 and Condition2 and Condition3 then
  Sell at Low - 1 point stop;
```

TradeStation's English-like language allows a user without any programming experience to write the rules of virtually any trading system. Once written, TradeStation will test trading systems historically and automate system orders on a real-time basis.

FIGURE 9

```
SYSTEM LIBRARY

First Bar Breakout
Channel Breakout Intrabar
Channel Breakout on Close
Channel Breakout on Weighted Close
Consecutive Closes
Divergence
EX1: First System
Key Reversal Major
MACD
Moving Average Crossover
Parabolic
Parabolic System
PercentR Oscillator
RangeLeader
RSI Oscillator
Stochastic Crossover
Three ma Crossover
Trendline Breakout
Weighted Avg Crossover
Exponential Avg Crossover
```

TradeStation comes with its own disclosed trading systems.

How well does historical testing and automation work in TradeStation? That question is best answered by the individual trader. If you use a system that is adequately described by functions in your library, then your trading, testing and automation will be adequately served. (This statement is applicable to all computer trading programs, not just to TradeStation.) I use support and resistance lines extensively as a part of my trading system. I employ trendlines, chart formations inclusive of channels, and triangles, among others. Opportunities to create these lines depend on market conditions and, of course, the user's skills to recognize them. Historical testing systems and real-time automation systems are inadequate for the way I trade at the moment. This view, obviously, may not be shared by others.

TESTING AND POSITION TRADING
TradeStation now permits historical testing of user-supplied data. The data must reside in directories of the user's hard disk. Updated daily data, for example, is accessed via a path command and provided the data have one of the five formats listed (ASCII, CSI, Tick Data, CompuTrac or MetaStock), it is automatically converted, producing daily charts. Overlays of indicators on the desktop page are then automatically calculated and displayed. CompuTrac and MetaStock files of daily,

weekly or monthly data may be charted on TradeStation. The powerful editor, with its associated libraries of functions and studies, is immediately applicable. Stock data obtained in ASCII format (from Prodigy, CompuServe, and so forth) can be graphed and analyzed by the program. Any historical operation that TradeStation performs on Signal-derived data can be performed on any directory-resident tick data, intraday OHLCV data, daily, weekly or monthly data. One program does it all.

SUMMING IT UP
There *are* a few things to pick about. Version 1 had an excellent manual. Version 2 was released with the manual to follow shortly, greatly enhanced, I have been informed. I *was* able to figure out the new features from the old manual — but wouldn't it have been nice if …? In addition, occasional crashes occur; this seems to be present in all Windows-based programs.

Also, although installation of Version 2 over Version 1 retains libraries of functions, studies and systems, the installation procedure does not retain pages that have settings for graphs.

TradeStation is recommended for the serious individual trader and professional traders. Many requirements of the day trader and position (daily) trader can be satisfied with TradeStation. It can satisfy the needs of those traders who wish to

design their own trading systems as well as those who enjoy the simplicity of picking and choosing from a list.

TradeStation is still expensive. This is a trading and historical program at a professional level. It is not designed for the novice trader.

To confirm my conclusions about this system, I invited a group of traders and would-be traders to a test trading session. TradeStation was indexed bar by bar throughout the previous market day. "Trading" decisions were made by group consensus the old-fashioned way—screen watching, indicators, trendline/chart patterns, support/resistance. Without exception, the program elicited positive responses from the trading group, veterans and novices alike.

For years, I have been searching for a product that allows me to devise new indicators and to help me make money trading. TradeStation currently is it. To put it mildly, I really like TradeStation. If I were asked to recommend an all-around intraday/daily trading system, it would be TradeStation, hands down.

William Blau, (407) 368-9095, is an independent futures trader.

FURTHER READING
Blau, William [1991]. "Double smoothed-stochastics," STOCKS & COMMODITIES, January.

FIGURE 10, PART A

HISTORICAL TEST RESULTS SCREENS

```
System:Multiple File System  Data:SP Z1-5 min   Range:10/24/91 - 11/07/91

                  Performance Summary:  All Trades

Total net profit         $   4325.00   Open position P/L       $   1775.00
Gross profit             $   5050.00   Gross loss              $   -725.00

Total # of trades                6     Percent profitable             83%
Number winning trades            5     Number losing trades            1

Largest winning trade    $   2475.00   Largest losing trade    $   -725.00
Average winning trade    $   1010.00   Average losing trade    $   -725.00
Ratio avg win/avg loss        1.39     Avg trade(win & loss)   $    720.83

Max consec. winners              3     Max consec. losers              1
Avg # bars in winners           57     Avg # bars in losers           13

Max intraday drawdown    $  -1050.00
Profit factor                 6.97     Max # contracts held            1
Account size required    $   4050.00   Return on account            107%

- - - - - - - - - - - - - - - - - - - - - - - - - - - - - - - - - - - - - -

                  Performance Summary:  Long Trades

Total net profit         $   1950.00   Open position P/L       $   1775.00
Gross profit             $   1950.00   Gross loss              $      0.00

Total # of trades                3     Percent profitable            100%
Number winning trades            3     Number losing trades            0

Largest winning trade    $   1575.00   Largest losing trade    $      0.00
Average winning trade    $    650.00   Average losing trade    $      0.00
Ratio avg win/avg loss        0.00     Avg trade(win & loss)   $    650.00

Max consec. winners              3     Max consec. losers              0
Avg # bars in winners           40     Avg # bars in losers            0

Max intraday drawdown    $   -450.00
Profit factor                 0.00     Max # contracts held            1
Account size required    $   3450.00   Return on account             57%

- - - - - - - - - - - - - - - - - - - - - - - - - - - - - - - - - - - - - -

                  Performance Summary:  Short Trades

Total net profit         $   2375.00   Open position P/L       $      0.00
Gross profit             $   3100.00   Gross loss              $   -725.00

Total # of trades                3     Percent profitable             67%
Number winning trades            2     Number losing trades            1

Largest winning trade    $   2475.00   Largest losing trade    $   -725.00
Average winning trade    $   1550.00   Average losing trade    $   -725.00
Ratio avg win/avg loss        2.14     Avg trade(win & loss)   $    791.67

Max consec. winners              1     Max consec. losers              1
Avg # bars in winners           84     Avg # bars in losers           13

Max intraday drawdown    $  -1000.00
Profit factor                 4.28     Max # contracts held            1
Account size required    $   4000.00   Return on account             59%
```

FIGURE 10, PART B

HISTORICAL TEST RESULTS SCREENS

```
System:Multiple File System  Data:SP Z1-5 min   Range:10/24/91 - 11/07/91
Date      Time    Type  Cnts  Price  Signal Name   Entry P/L  Cumulative
11/01/91 10:20am Buy    1     391.60
11/01/91  2:25pm LExit  1     394.75              $  1575.00 $  1575.00
11/01/91  2:25pm Sell   1     394.75
11/04/91  1:10pm SExit  1     389.80              $  2475.00 $  4050.00
11/04/91  1:10pm Buy    1     389.80
11/04/91  2:50pm LExit  1     390.45              $   325.00 $  4375.00
11/04/91  2:50pm Sell   1     390.45
11/05/91  9:35am SExit  1     391.90              $  -725.00 $  3650.00
11/05/91  9:35am Buy    1     391.90
11/05/91  1:55pm LExit  1     392.00              $    50.00 $  3700.00
11/05/91  1:55pm Sell   1     392.00
11/06/91  3:40pm SExit  1     390.75              $   625.00 $  4325.00
11/06/91  3:40pm Buy    1     390.75
```

Historical test results include a detailed performance summary, trade-by-trade report and arrows overlaid on the bar chart, showing exact entry and exit of every trade.

_____ [1991]. "Double-smoothed momenta," STOCKS & COMMODITIES, May.

EDITOR'S NOTE

William Blau, the author of this review, runs TradeStation on a 386-25 MHz IBM-compatible, which I had the opportunity to see work. Charts and indicators could be manipulated very quickly. The visual presentation was superb. I was impressed, and I looked forward to testing TradeStation in my office, where we have a 286 with one meg of RAM. Unfortunately, I was not able to duplicate the results that I had observed on Blau's 386. I had constant error data on my intraday charts that required me to manually enter into the data file and correct the data. I checked with another Signal data user and determined that the problem was not incorrect data coming in. Correcting the bad data was a very time-consuming process, because the Windows application on a 286 is extremely slow to respond to either quick key commands or mouse commands when multi-tasking is involved and a program like TradeStation is processing a lot of data in the background. Whenever I wanted to try something, I had to wait for the computer to give me my turn. Occasionally, the computer would crash, so I sent a printout of my CONFIG.SYS files to Omega customer support, which made some recommendations. After we made the adjustments that Omega customer support suggested, the computer only crashed one more time. Customer support at Omega Research were professional and helpful in their efforts, but I was never able to get TradeStation to run properly on my 286. Discussing the problems further with Omega indicated that our 286 may have some incompatibilities with Windows. Nonetheless, Omega Research stated that they had a number of customers who used 286 machines who were satisfied with the product. Omega recommends that you use a 386 with four megs of RAM. I have to agree with that recommendation.

—Thom Hartle, Editor

MINITAB

Release 8 for the Mac

MINITAB, INC.
3081 Enterprise Drive
State College, PA 16801-3008
(814) 238-3280

Product: Full-bore statistical analysis package for the Apple Macintosh. Includes ARIMA time series and non-parametric capabilities.

Requirements: Mac Plus or better with System 6.0.1 or later. Release 8 compatible with System 7. An accelerated version of Minitab can use the 68020 or 68030 processor with the 68881 or 68882 co-processors to dramatically speed things up. Hard disk with 3.7 megabytes (MB) available, just for the program itself — more for data files. Can be site-licensed. Discounts for volume purchasers available. Technical support included.

Price: $695

by John Sweeney

 nyone who's suffered through statistics classes in college or graduate school can remember MINITAB as a frightfully congested pile of opaque subroutines whose sole virtue was the awe that the reams of output inspired in our professors. We were, it seemed, graded by weight and I, for one, never failed to include a boxload of green-striped, full-sized computer paper with all my submissions.

Thankfully, all that is now past and I've been handed a shiny new Mac version of MINITAB. Can *anything* make statistical analysis fun and games? Actually, yes, MINITAB on the Mac can be fun. Not that MINITAB 8.01 doesn't have some minor blemishes, but it's now a great tool for exploration as though you had the helping hand of a senior statistician, a guy who'll do all the nitty-gritty number mashing.

It seems to take a jump in mindset for traders to think statistically. It's not normal — or maybe it's just not easy — for people to think in probabilistic terms. We'd like to have certainty, not "most of the time *this* and some of the time *that*" or worse, "a range of outcomes from here to there and you don't know where any one result will be."

To put it in practical terms, can we predict whether tomorrow's prices will ever be above (or below) today's close? What are the chances of that? What's the likelihood of profiting from betting on that information? Will buying a heavy-duty statistical package unearth things I wouldn't otherwise see?

Actually, probably not. Even the brush with statistics that your business-school types get isn't going to be enough to fully exploit a package like MINITAB. Let's face it. To use these packages, you are going to put in — or you've already put in — some serious work. That said, let's take a look at MINITAB on the Mac.

INSTALLATION

It's too easy to bother discussing. Next topic.

DATA ENTRY

Data can be loaded into MINITAB manually or via Excel (or some other spreadsheet program) into tab-delimited text files. It can also read any ASCII file. MINITAB was developed in the arcane world of academic statistics and is as a result incompatible with the more common data formats you may be familiar with: CSI, CompuTrac, Dow Jones, IDS, MJK — you name it, it won't work directly with it.

That said, the manual gives excellent instructions for transferring data along with — even better — examples with lots of screen dumps to show how things should look as they go along. (I don't want to miss the opportunity to say that

FIGURE 1

FUNCTIONAL GRAPHICS

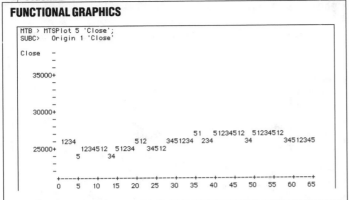

```
MTB > MTSPlot 5 'Close';
SUBC>    Origin 1 'Close'

Close  -

       -
35000+
       -
       -
       -
       -
30000+
       -
       -                                      51   51234512  51234512
       - 1234                       512     3451234   234          34          34512345
25000+        1234512  51234    34512
       -        5          34
       -
       +----+----+----+----+----+----+----+----+----+----+----+----+----+
       0    5   10   15   20   25   30   35   40   45   50   55   60   65
```

Minitab Mac's graphics suffer in comparison with the typical trading package but are extremely functional for statisticians who love to use numbers as much as possible. This is, believe it or not, a time series chart of just 60 days of closing prices.

FIGURE 2

WORKSHEET AND FORMAT

	C1	C2	C3	C4	C5	C6	C7
→	Date	High	Low	Close	SRES1	FITS1	Nscores
1	880104	25644	24708	25594	2.81449	25151.5	-1.73020
2	880105	26178	25594	25863	-0.14343	25885.7	-1.48982
3	880106	25979	25718	25889	0.12294	25869.6	-1.44812
4	880107	26132	25618	26107	1.44069	25879.3	-1.32081
5	880108	26107	24295	24340	-5.08415	25118.4	-2.70325
6	880111	24751	24107	24749	2.06647	24423.0	-2.34399
7	880112	24749	24046	24542	0.97966	24387.5	-2.60049
8	880113	24925	24141	24581	0.40104	24517.8	-2.51960
9	880114	24700	24397	24588	0.14381	24565.3	-2.45244
10	880115	25365	24588	25205	1.54009	24962.3	-2.01673
11	880118	25286	24998	25188	0.17426	25160.5	-2.04105
12	880119	25333	24875	24932	-1.13355	25111.1	-2.25742
13	880120	24932	24114	24263	-1.54058	24505.6	-3.10622

S&P 500D.MTW

All Minitab data are loaded into and manipulated in a worksheet whose familiar format invites inspection and tinkering.

the manuals that come with MINITAB are outstanding, especially for a novice, because they not only show the techniques but explain the conceptual thinking behind them.) I don't see any problem getting data from CompuTrac, Dow Jones, System Writer or Roberts Slade to MINITAB, and others should be just as easy.

GRAPHICS

Before you as a trader go ga-ga over the raw power that MINITAB offers, please realize that "graphics" to a statistician aren't the graphics you might expect. These guys love numbers so much they even use them as dots on their charts, as in Figure 1. The program can't compress a lot of data into one chart, either — it just prints many, many charts if you have lots and lots of data. In fact, for charting purposes this is pretty much what you get. Though there are high-resolution capabilities in MINITAB Mac 8.0, they aren't supported for the time series option.

It goes without saying that you cannot add a quick relative strength indicator (RSI) (or any other trading indicator), draw lines, poke at a point for its specific value or any of the other graphic analytics to which we've become accustomed. These things can be created, albeit tediously, in the worksheet's calculations, which offer everything you could dream up plus a number of things you never imagined, but the ease and sophistication of trading graphics isn't available.

MATHEMATICS

Like SystemWriter and SNAP, MINITAB uses the worksheet format to handle the raw data (Figure 2). This makes it easy — or at least familiar — to manipulate the data. As soon as you finish putting in a specification for a column, the results are there for quick inspection. Naturally, this is not a full spreadsheet with all the commercial gee-whiz features, but it does make time-series manipulation quick and fun. Its limitations are that you can't go in and find out how a cell was calculated or select a range of cells for actions. It's truly a worksheet.

One improvement would focus on the spreadsheet where you can easily create many columns of values — and then forget how you did it! A feature — perhaps the column heading — that you could click to get the formulation for a column's values would be really neat. In all fairness, though, MINITAB does have a feature called Journal that allows you to record the commands but not the output, so you have a record of what you did.

Arithmetic operators include a full list of algebraic operators, trigonometric functions, comparison operators (equal to, not equal to, less than, greater than, less than or equal to, greater than or equal to) for use in calculations, logical operators (and, or, not), normal scores, statistical functions (natch!), lags, differences, sorts and rankings.

Curiously, parenthetical expression is not supported. Parentheses are used instead for algebraic expression and subscripting, which does allow you to refer to a specific cell in your worksheet. However, you cannot refer to a cell in its relationship to another cell; for example, "subtract the cell three rows up and two columns over from this cell." This makes commonplace trading indicators like moving averages tedious to construct.

USABILITY

One nifty feature, easily available on the Mac, are the many windows available to you — a session window that captures all the input you've made and teaches you the command language in the process; a worksheet window to easily see the raw data; a history window; an information window that reminds you of all the variables you're working; a help window; a graphics window or windows — you could have 15 of them open at once.

Because you can do most everything in MINITAB from the menus while the program is writing out the equivalent instructions in the session window, MINITAB is constantly tutoring you on its commands. You'll soon find yourself flipping back and forth from keyboard to mouse, if you can type quickly, and just "telling" MINITAB what to do next. By then, you will have learned the structure and syntax of the program by observation. It's hard to overestimate the value of this function, since most traders are going to be relatively new to the sort of thinking that MINITAB encapsulates.

Of course, MINITAB isn't all roses. For one thing, it would be nice if every win-

FIGURE 3

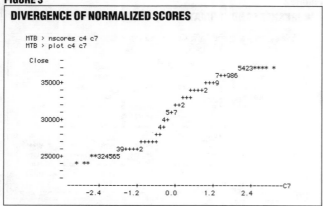

DIVERGENCE OF NORMALIZED SCORES

```
MTB > nscores c4 c7
MTB > plot c4 c7

Close -
                                                5423**** *
                                            7++986
     35000+                              +++9
          -                            +++2
          -                          +++
          -                        ++2
          -                      5+7
     30000+                     4+
          -                    4+
          -                   ++
          -                 +++++
          -           39++++2
     25000+      **324565
          -    * **
          -
          +-------+-------+-------+-------+-------+-------C7
              -2.4    -1.2     0.0     1.2     2.4
```

One simple indicator of trending activity is divergence of normalized "scores" of prices from a constant value. Here, the S&P 500 has moved.

FIGURE 4, PART A

BASIC SCATTERPLOT

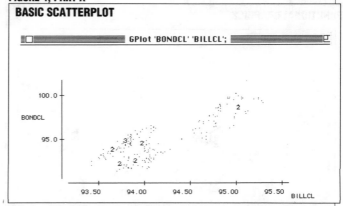

Minitab easily generates the scatterplots that most analysts use for associative data exploration. Here, a bifurcated relationship between the closes of bonds and bills is suggested by the two concentrations of dots. The numbers refer to points that occurred more than once.

FIGURE 4, PART B

HISTOGRAM

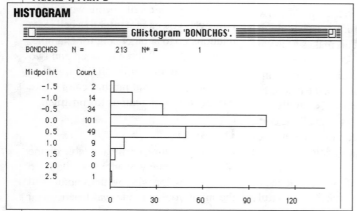

```
BONDCHGS   N =      213    N* =         1

Midpoint    Count
  -1.5         2
  -1.0        14
  -0.5        34
   0.0       101
   0.5        49
   1.0         9
   1.5         3
   2.0         0
   2.5         1

            0      30      60      90     120
```

FIGURE 4, PART C

HISTOGRAM

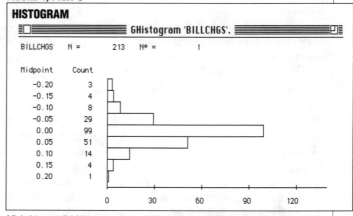

```
BILLCHGS   N =      213    N* =         1

Midpoint    Count
  -0.20        3
  -0.15        4
  -0.10        8
  -0.05       29
   0.00       99
   0.05       51
   0.10       14
   0.15        4
   0.20        1

            0      30      60      90     120
```

Minitab's two-click histograms can quickly show you the distribution of your data, in this case the similar distribution in changes of bond and bill prices.

dow had the name of the model you're working on and then an extension indicating the type of window. As it is, you can lose track of which model you're working with. Once you start generating perturbation #51 of your work, for example, you wonder if you're on 50, 51 or what. That's really the only complaint I can come up with, though. MINITAB's menu bar says it all for the workday world: calculations, statistics, and graphics. It's all easy to find. MINITAB will even remember exactly how you like the windows distributed about your screen. Just give it your preferences and, when MINITAB launches, that's the way they'll appear.

USEFULNESS

Putting a package like this to work for a trader is tough for two reasons. First, the learning curve is steep, and second, the tests provided are slanted toward those handy for use in conventional statistical analysis. Clifford Sherry has presented techniques in STOCKS & COMMODITIES suggesting that the traditional techniques relating to correlation, randomness and stationarity may be inappropriate when used in securities work. Suffice it to say that MINITAB's techniques fall squarely in the traditional mode.

Here, our pleasures must be more cerebral. We might, for instance, wonder if our data are distributed normally, theoretically random. We can easily normalize a huge pile of data and see if the normalized scores are flat. For example, I popped some 800 values from an Excel worksheet into the Standard & Poor's 500 index. Were there no "trend," we'd expect the normalized values in Figure 3 to be evenly distributed roughly in a flat line.

Here, however, we see there's some variation in the distribution of the scores. For quantitative verification, we ask if there's a significant correlation between the prices and the normalized scores. For 800 values, the correlation is naturally quite high — 0.967 — but not high enough at the 0.01, 0.05 or even 0.1 levels, where the values would need to be, respectively, 0.9983, 0.9980, and 0.9973 — in other words, the data not being normally distributed is evidence of trend.

So what? This sort of easy testing on shorter segments of data — probably the last 20 to 60 days — might indicate a change in the behavior of the market, and one discovered in an objective fashion.

In a powerhouse like MINITAB, this is all done with a few typed commands, if you prefer keyboard, or by menu selection that can invoke most of the program's

FIGURE 5

BOND PRICE CHANGE VS. BILLS

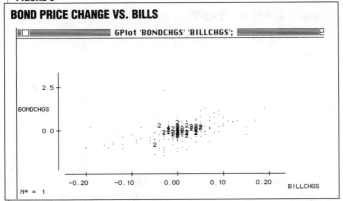

This quickie plot suggests a relationship of some sort between the two series as we'd expect. But how strong is it?

FIGURE 6

REGRESSING BONDS AGAINST BILLS

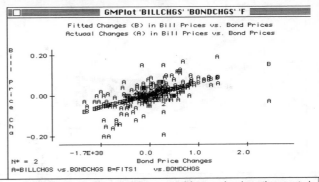

Suspecting the free market has more influence, a quick regression shows the expected values (B) and actual values (A) of bill price changes given bond price changes. The wide dispersion of the As suggests a weak relation.

FIGURE 7

REGRESSION RESULTS

```
MTB > Regress 'BILLCHGS' 1 'BONDCHGS' 'SRES1' 'FITS1'.

The regression equation is
BILLCHGS = 0.00523 + 0.0607 BONDCHGS

213 cases used 1 cases contain missing values

Predictor      Coef       Stdev     t-ratio        p
Constant    0.005226    0.003385      1.54     0.124
BONDCHGS    0.060712    0.006648      9.13     0.000

s = 0.04938      R-sq = 28.3%     R-sq(adj) = 28.0%

Analysis of Variance

SOURCE         DF        SS          MS          F         p
Regression      1     0.20333     0.20333     83.40     0.000
Error         211     0.51442     0.00244
Total         212     0.71774
```

The r-squared for this relationship is only 28.3%, evidence that roughly one fourth of the variation in bill prices is related somehow to the changes in bond prices.

FIGURE 8

BONDS VS. THE CRB

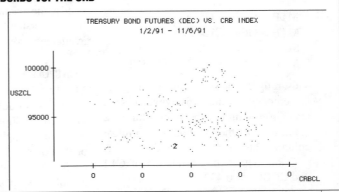

Much is made of the relationship between the two, but here the raw scatterplot suggests little correlation.

---

capabilities. I found that the typed commands are slightly faster than the menu commands, but there is more potential for minor typing errors. Though I type well, I ended up using the menus most of the time. Should even menus be too tedious, invoke the macro recorder and lead the program through a sample session. It will remember what you've done and then be able to rerun it for you at any time later.

DINKING AROUND

"Exploratory data analysis" — otherwise known as "dinking around" — really is the beginning of most statistical work. Here, we judge how convenient the package makes the trial-and-error process of poking and prodding the data. The easiest way to do this is graphically and I've mentioned the limitations of MINITAB's graphics before. Nevertheless, you can still get basic scatterplots like Figure 3, which suggest relationships worth exploring.

Figure 4a suggests that bonds and bills will be close in a reasonable relationship to each other, at least in two different yield curves. If you weren't already aware of it, this sort of graph forming a new cluster day after day might alert you to a shift in the curve.

Quick histograms of the two series (Figures 4b and 4c) suggest their changes are similarly distributed as well, but of more interest is whether the two change in concert consistently. MINITAB can difference the two time series within 30 seconds and then scatterplot them, as in Figure 5. Of course, this plot is suggestive but not definitive. A quick regression — four or five clicks' effort — and a replot of the fitted values in Figure 6 shows some relationship, but the quantitative measures in Figure 7 are not reassuring, r^2 being only 28%. The bottom line is you'd be unlikely to bet money on how bonds and bills affect each other, though there is

clearly a low-level relationship.

More likely, were you using MINITAB, you'd be poking at relationships between different tradeables such as bonds vs. the Commodity Research Bureau (CRB) index, stocks vs. interest rates or crude vs. heating oil. You'd either suspect a relationship or be curious about its current status. For example, I believe bonds and the CRB are roughly inversely related (see Jim Bianco's article in December 1991), but there are lags and leads in this relationships, and sometimes it hardly seems to hold at all!

Curious about 1991's situation while puzzling out the bond market's holding zone in the 98 - 100 area, I loaded up the CRB and December bonds in MINITAB and ordered up a quick scatterplot (Figure 8), which showed virtually no relationship. A check via correlation (less than 0.01) and regression (yes, 1%) confirmed the visual (Figure 9).

FIGURE 9

FITTED BONDS VS. THE CRB

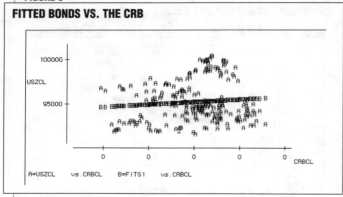

A=USZCL   vs.CRBCL   B=FITS1   vs.CRBCL

A quick regression of the coincident series confirms practically no relation.

FIGURE 10

LAGGED BONDS VS. THE CRB

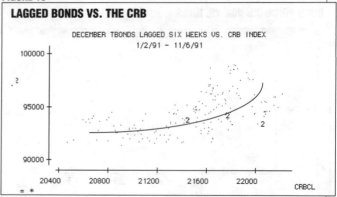

By trial and error, correlation between bonds lagged various periods and the CRB index peaked at 0.6 at just under six weeks of lag. The curved shape of the distribution suggests, via the hand-drawn line, a lag that changed over 1991.

Curious to see if lag were a factor, I issued the following via menu selection:

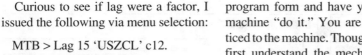

MTB > Lag 15 'USZCL' c12.
MTB > GPlot C12 'CRBCL';
SUBC> Symbol '.'.
MTB > Correlation C12 'CRBCL'.

This, roughly translated, means "Lag the December bond close 15 days and put the result in column 12. Then plot column 12 using a '.' as the symbol and correlate column 12 to the CRB's close."

Quoth MINITAB: Correlation of C12 and CRBCL = 0.432.

Setting the bond series back three weeks (15 days) vastly improved the correlation. Setting it back four weeks raised it to 0.498, five weeks got me to 0.516, and six weeks to 0.569, after which correlations started to decline rapidly. The resulting scatterplot, Figure 10, showed more order and even suggested a slightly curved relationship. Linear regression r^2 was on the order of 35% (I didn't bother fitting a curvilinear line). Although there are problems with cross-correlation, r^2 with Treasury bills and the CRB gets as high as 50%. The point of all this is that this exploration took me less than an hour and a half and most of that was exporting and importing data.

IS TUTORING AVAILABLE?

Can MINITAB be used as a tutor? Nope! Treating a program such as MINITAB as a teaching vehicle is unrealistic, though it is widely used as an adjunct to statistics classes. Still, it's possible that the practical, on-the-job approach these days is to hand you the process, properly encoded in program form and have you watch the machine "do it." You are now apprenticed to the machine. Though you don't at first understand the mechanism, that's available if you want to dig into it.

SUMMARY

MINITAB is definitely for someone already comfortable with statistical thinking — a discipline I recommend to everyone, even though I know that maybe 5% of the folks out there would follow my advice. MINITAB is quick and efficient, has all the basic bells and whistles and, on the Mac anyway, is very easy to use. The manual and examples are good enough for any BA/MBA to use. However, it doesn't exploit the Mac's graphics capability well and, as far as traders are concerned, doesn't easily create the indicators they are used to using. Nevertheless, if you'd like to put some numbers to your suspected relationships, this is an easy package to recommend.

REFERENCES

Bianco, Jim [1991]. "Comparing the CRB with bonds," STOCKS & COMMODITIES, December.
Sherry, Clifford [1985]. "Gambler's paradox," *Technical Analysis of* STOCKS & COMMODITIES, Volume 3: October.

‡TA‡

MINITAB BASICS

A package as massive as Minitab has become is nearly impossible to review thoroughly. The brochures go on for pages and the "cheat sheet" alone takes up 26 sections in 12 pages! Nevertheless, here are the basics:

- Basic statistics including descriptive statistics, correlation and chi-square testing
- Regression analysis including simple, polynomial, multiple, stepwise, and best subsets
- Statistical process control, including Shewhart control charts, Pareto charts, process capability, cusum charts and analysis of means
- Analysis of variance and covariance
- Multivariate analysis
- Crosstabulations
- Nonparametric methods (Wilcoxon, Mann-Whitney, Kruskal-Wallis, Mood median, and Friedman)
- Time series analysis including autocorrelation, partial autocorrelation, cross-correlation, difference lagging, ARIMA
- Exploratory data analysis including plots, boxplots, stem-and-leaf testing and data smoothing
- Simulation and distributions
- Design of experiments incorporating two-level full and fractional factorials and Plackett-Burman designs. Response surface modeling is available in versions after 8.0.

DollarLink

Version S4.2D

DollarLink Software
1407 Douglass Street
San Francisco, CA 94131
(415) 641-0721
Product: Real-time data retrieval, storage and analysis optimized for intraday trading.
Price: $1,300 or $100 a month rental. Our recommendation: buy it. One-month trial for $50!
Equipment: PC XT/AT or higher with 640K RAM (575K available) and 10 megabytes on a hard disk. Hercules, EGA/CGA/VGA, and a serial data port.
Datafeeds: Signal, Bonneville or PC Quote

by John Sweeney

ver since STOCKS & COMMODITIES signed up with Signal and vowed to review everything we had using Signal data, we've been falling behind. They're adding stuff faster than we can review. Plus, I found myself jaded with the online mode. Having abandoned it personally years ago, I rediscovered some of my antipathy to unending datastreams as I waded through different packages, liking some and disliking many.

I approached DollarLink with a little more optimism, having heard through the grapevine favorable comments and enjoying talking to the real people who own and run the company. Far from being a megacorporation with hundreds of overpaid programmers stepping on each others' code, DollarLink is a throwback to just a decade ago when one or two guys would hack together something exciting. Looks like it's still possible.

CRANKING UP

DollarLink's manual comes in a binder from Woolworth but is professionally produced inside. The table of contents is, for example, 14 pages long! The index is 19 pages of small type. I was impressed and these two features made finding things

a breeze. It's actually rare, in my experience, to find a good manual, though, admittedly, things are getting better. I found that reading the contents and index were interesting, a very quick way to scan the program's multitudinous abilities.

Installation is as straightforward as it gets in the DOS world. Check to make sure you have 6 megabytes (MB) on your hard disk with maybe another four MB free for day-to-day use. Make sure your hard disk is *fast*. Make sure your computer is fast — a 386 isn't too fast. Though DollarLink runs on an XT, a 486 with its built-in math co-processor and four to eight megabytes of RAM is best.

Back up your CONFIG.SYS and AUTOEXEC.BAT files (the installation program may modify them, though DollarLink will save or copy for you), type A:INSTALL and step back. Next, unload all your RAM-resident utilities to free up to 575K of RAM. (I snuck by with 540K but used small portfolios. If you have any DOS before 5.0, it's going to be just about impossible to get the full 575K; count on an occasional freeze.) Then run the program's setup utility to enter passwords for DollarLink and Signal. Set up channels, network speed, ports, all the DOS procedures, in the proper configuration. That done, you're ready to change to your newly created directory and type "$" to fire up DollarLink.

It's worth noting that DollarLink is smart. It will use any extended or expanded memory it finds on your machine and, if you have it, it can use a RAM disk or a disk cache to speed things up. Another nifty feature: you can have your PC drive two monitors, say one for quotes and one for graphics.

Keeping in mind that DollarLink is a huge program doing a lot of work all at once, you'll be delighted that there is a setup utility that will guide you through some 43 different ways the program can be run. Fortunately, the day you start, you need only answer some basics about your hardware. Everything else has default values that function well. Later, you fine-tune things.

DollarLink has two worlds built in, a text mode for the usual quote screen and a graphics mode for the real-time and interday graphs. Different things happen

in different modes depending on keystrokes, which confused me initially. Generally, this distinction is imperceptible to the user in today's packages. Here it allows a greater variety of commands, but also requires you to return to text mode before exiting.

As you load up the quotes and graphics pages with symbols, you find you need to know the symbols. A really nice touch would be to select from a menu of available symbols, particularly when loading graphics. Otherwise, you get to memorize the process necessary to call up the particular symbol you want, many of which were not familiar to me. Fortunately, there is a feature whereby you can type in an English-like description — for example, "JUN45C" for a June 45 call option — and the program will generate the more cryptic "A FI."

DollarLink is the sort of program that consumes an entire machine, in a manner of speaking. Once you're committed to real-time data, there can't be extended periods when it isn't being gathered. Hence, you'll need a dedicated machine unless you have Windows or Desqview.

RUNNING HARD

DollarLink is a keyboard-based program, though mouse use is occasionally supported, which means you'd better be friendly with your fingers and patient with your computer. On a 486, things really hum. On a 286 or XT, well, things are slower. Type, wait a while. Type, wait a while. Menus are even slower, taking up to a second to appear and the choices have no explanatory line of text, just a highlighted word or letter. Thus, the excellent manual is also an essential manual.

Screens (Figure 1) come in colorful glory in virtually all common formats, even CGA, and can be customized to a degree. You can specify how you want the screen laid out (Figures 2 and 3) and the graphics can be lines, bar or candlestick (Figure 10). However, the windows, once specified, aren't resizable but can zoom in and out on the data. Charts can be line or bar charts in periods from tick to daily and the individual charts can be scaled in every conceivable fashion. Rescaling can be manual or automatic — DollarLink calls it "repositioning."

Studies can be accessed immediately from the chart window. The usual assortment is available: relative strength index (RSI), averages, momentum, stochastics, and moving average convergence/divergence (MACD) plus a proprietary Trader's Balance. There are plenty of customization options, and all of them computed and displayed reliably except momentum, on which I occasionally generated DOS math error messages followed by a frozen machine.

DollarLink is keeping a *lot* of data from the stream flowing in. It tracks every tick of every symbol in your portfolios. Thus, if you save it all, you can reconstruct the intraday data from two months ago to compare it with other situations in other days. If you do, come prepared with a *huge* hard disk. If not, DollarLink will mercifully delete all the excess files it creates as it goes along.

Naturally, once all this is flowing, you're going to slow things up by printing out numbers and pictures. DollarLink shines here by supporting Epson and Hewlett-Packard (HP) originals and emulations. You can capture screens from within the program menus for later manipulation in publishing programs. You can even take a look at the captured screens with a slick utility called PCX that DollarLink sends along with the program. (DollarLink supplies a number of these handy utilities at no additional cost. Kudos to them!) PCX will do everything but your laundry: flash the picture on the screen, direct it to your printer, direct a series of pictures to your screen for, say, two minutes each to create a slide show, or do the show and then print everything.

This thoughtfulness extends to the program's day-to-day usage, which has the virtue of time-tested features; they have the comfortable fit of features worked out through actual usage day in and day out, rather than having been created with theoretical specifications by a systems analyst and handed to a programmer for implementation. The most obvious goody is the automatically selected default for every option. Although it's not unusual for DollarLink to present you with 20 choices, the one you want is almost always the default. It's so well done you start hitting the return or enter keys mind-

FIGURE 1

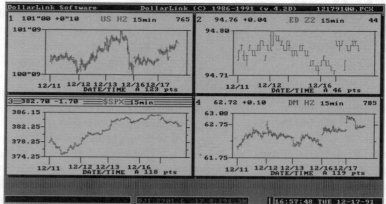

DollarLink has the pleasant ability to dump PCX screen captures, which can be easily put into drawing, painting or desktop publishing programs.

FIGURE 2

If the usual four screens are too small, any one of them can be blown up to full size.

FIGURE 3

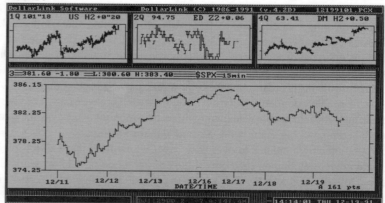

DollarLink offers a variety of standard layouts, of which I found this one most useful.

lessly! The best feature of all: the program is constantly saving information so that, should your machine go down or freeze, you usually lose only a minute or two of data.

For example, trend lines are invoked in the graphics section by pressing D for "data," then D for "draw lines" and click-

ing the beginning and ending points (mouse or cursor keys). An analyst wouldn't set things up that way because the invocation of the mouse or cursor is invisible to the user at the start. The upside is that once you do invoke the mechanism and draw the line, DollarLink offers some practical assistance: it asks if you want the trendline to alert you if it's violated. That's an easy way to put in an alert! DollarLink also remembers the last 26 lines you drew on the screen for later recall. You could conceivably draw and have active 3,744 trend lines all waiting to alert you if the price touches them! They could be Fibonacci retracement levels, parallel lines, Andrews pitchfork lines and so on. This is, suffice to say, an absolutely unique feature in itself and typical of the experience the developer has put in throughout the program.

You can find cycles (Figure 4), draw pitchforks (Figure 5), trendlines, circles (Figure 6), zigzags, Fibonacci retracements of small or large sizes, and even Gann lines (Figure 8). Suffice to say, most of the graphic hoopla in today's upper-level packages is cunningly available — "cunningly" because you invoke it via the keyboard and draw it via mouse or keyboard.

OPTIONS

Option data is a keystroke ("O") away on most tradeables. The program uses its own storage of data to calculate volatilities for you and generates the characteristics of the options — that is, delta, beta and so forth — of descriptive parameters virtually instantly. It keeps a detailed table of all the *active* options — the ones truly trading — for flashing up on your screen and it can also evaluate your proposed position, though this is wisely limited to outright longs or shorts, complexity being an overrated feature of options trading. Volatilities can be estimated at a keystroke for all but futures options. All this is tabular, text-based information. No graphics are used.

WHAT'S A "CHARTLINK"?

DollarLink comes with a solid band of tried-and-true indicators (Figure 7), all of which are updated constantly. In addition, you can do studies of studies, though the update of these must be invoked manually (or by macro). Studies, RSI, for example, are invoked via keyboard specification of parameters and can be cleaned out with a keystroke.

Studies can also serve as alarm-setting devices in DollarLink. Once specified, hit "control T" and enter the value at which

FIGURE 4

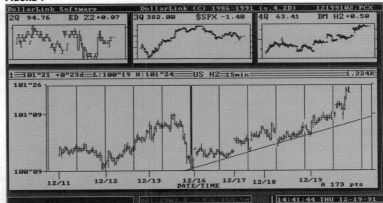

A cycle finder allows you to eyeball the fit of waves with lines that can be expanded, contracted or moved left and right.

FIGURE 5

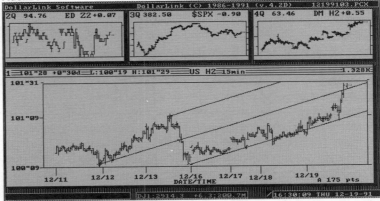

Pitchfork aficionados will find their technique still works even if the computer does the line-drawing.

FIGURE 6

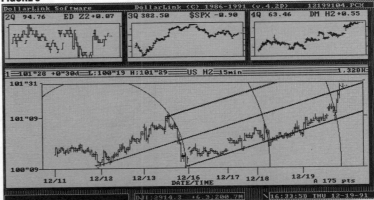

Circles combined with pitchforks still work neatly, here defining cyclical content without the trouble of wave analysis.

you wish to be notified. Once it hits that value, the alarm will be set off, at least in graphics mode. This handy feature won't operate when you're in text mode unless you have a Hercules graphics card, in which case you won't have color graphics.

Studies are routine in DollarLink. Cus-

tom indices and ChartLinks are also available, the first of which is the most convenient. Examples of custom indices are spreads or ratios between tradeables, your current portfolio, a breakout indicator, a continuous futures contract, an industry group index or an options spread. The format for calculation is somewhat limit-

FIGURE 7

STUDIES INCLUDED

Moving averages, arithmetic and exponential, with percent or Bollinger bands. Lead or lag using high, low or last

Rate of change and momentum

Stochastics

RSI

Directional movement indicator (DMI)

Williams' %R

CCI

OBV, money flow, NVI, PVI, market facilitation index, accumulation/distribution, Chaikin oscillator, price-volume plots

Price spectrum analysis

Fibonacci retracement and projection

Gann angles and squares

Cycle finders

Andrews pitchfork

Candlesticks

Point and figure

Oscillators and MACD

Random walk index (ChartLink)

Elder Ray (ChartLink)

FIGURE 8

For Gann work, you again select the point and specify the rate of change via mouse or keyboard. DollarLink handles the calculations and the drawing.

FIGURE 9

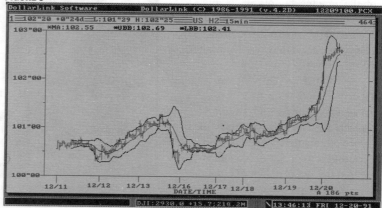

Bollinger Bands are a hot item among daytraders, and DollarLink provides them from one half to five standard deviations about your arithmetic average, in this case 10 15-minute periods.

FIGURE 10

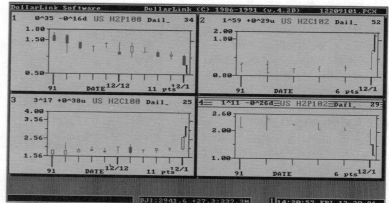

Even tried-and-true DollarLink offers candlesticks.

ing but allows you to add, subtract, multiply or divide, use some logic and call on a variety of math functions in a strict sequence. The manual provides many examples, thankfully. Once created, this little hummer can be plotted and analyzed like any other item in the portfolio.

WHAT STANDS OUT?

Quote pages? Easy. Charts? Takes a minute to switch but there they are, easily customizable, four windows with studies overlaying the charts. Custom formulations? You bet. Options? In spades, with a Bookbinder valuation available, as well as Black-Scholes.

It takes a page of nine-point type to list all the features in this beast, but I like DollarLink for its reliability and efficiency. It's complicated, the interface is old and the graphics aren't state of the DOS art, but the information, studies and formulations you need to trade or daytrade — especially for options — are there when you need them and, once you get proficient with the keyboard and upgrade to 386 or 486, it's there quickly. Add to that the

price or rent, either of which is a bargain, the efficient service developer Stan LeKach gives you, the monthly updates, the *free* upgrades and the newsletter and you have something that can be com-

pletely molded to your requirements.

John Sweeney is Technical Editor of STOCKS & COMMODITIES.

MetaStock Professional 3.0

EQUIS INTERNATIONAL
3950 South 700 East Suite 100
Salt Lake City, UT 84107
(801) 265-8886
Product: Advanced-level technical analysis and profitability testing.
Price: $349; DownLoader, $69-195.
Equipment required: IBM-AT or faster, MS-DOS 3.0 or higher. EGA or better monitor, hard disk with at least two MBs of available space. Optional and recommended, serial or bus mouse, math coprocessor and expanded or extended memory. Printer required for printing charts.
Equipment used: 386/33, math coprocessor, Microsoft bus mouse and Hewlett-Packard LaserJet with Adobe Postscript cartridge. VGA monitor. Also a 386/20 with a math coprocessor.

by Jack Karczewski

MetaStock Professional is one of the originals in the industry, something you can depend on. But the last time STOCKS & COMMODITIES reviewed it (July 1988), the reviewer mentioned how complicated the installation process was. Well, not any more. It's now a breeze! About all a user needs to do now is put the disks in at appropriate intervals when prompted. Especially since I've used versions 2.0 and 2.5, the installation process for this version was straightforward.

Windows 3.0 has been around for almost two years, and so those of us who are WIMPS (that is, proponents of windows, icons, menus and pointers) have anticipated with relish the arrival of programs that take advantage of these devices. We aren't there quite yet with this package, but the feel of Windows lies just beneath MetaStock Professional's surface. MetaStock Professional is really two programs: the charting package and the profitability testing package. Those of us who disdain mechanical systems will still have a very powerful and versatile program,

while those of us who are interested in trading systems and the testing of those systems will find the new MetaStock Professional to their liking, particularly if programming isn't their strong suit.

MetaStock Professional comes with sample data and directions about different methods by which to acquire data in the future. When I originally started using MetaStock Professional — that was back in version 2.0 — I was disappointed to find that I needed yet another software package to download prices. You will need software from either your data vendor, a third-party software company or Equis's DownLoader to collect price data and store them directly into MetaStock Professional's data files. This initially delayed my use of the program while I waited for DownLoader, the companion program. If you want to track a portfolio, an additional program from Equis is available, a portfolio management program called Pulse.

Printer support for this product has been beefed up, and while I use an HP, I have worked occasionally with a Panasonic 1124i (Epson-compatible) and the charts were quite acceptable. If there are any newsletter writers out there, the program allows the charts to be saved as PCX files and then be pasted into a word-processing program. There is also a crude but acceptable means of writing directly on the chart.

SUPPORT

I found the Equis technical support staff to be very helpful and knowledgeable, but unfortunately, it's going to be on your own dime: Equis offers no 800 number except for sales. The support staff is very friendly and seems eager to solve any problems that may pop up. For example, I found changing subdirectories from the menu painfully slow. The support staff pointed out the solution in the manual and explained to me how to specify the "top" directory that MetaStock Professional should use when searching for

subdirectories to list in the menu. The documentation for MetaStock Professional is complete and easy to peruse, with the explanations of various technical indicators concise and accurate. Equis publishes a newsletter that gives updates on various trading systems and information about their programs, so it pays to be a registered MetaStock Professional owner. There are also MetaStock Professional user groups around the country, and CompuServe also offers on-line help.

UPGRADE

This version has a new graphic user interface with dialog boxes (Figure 1) all over the place, making the learning process for new users a much less tricky one. Dialog boxes let you perform multiple functions within one window. The dialog boxes are concise and straightforward, and inputting the information is a breeze. For old MetaStock Professional hands, you can still use the familiar keystrokes, if you like. The upgrade is totally compatible with versions 2.0 and 2.5 — except for the charts. Unfortunately, only the data are compatible for versions before 2.0 and 2.5. Thus, you are required to redo all the charts in the program, but this isn't nearly as difficult as it sounds, because you can set the default charts to your own preferences.

DOCUMENTATION

As I mentioned before, the documentation for MetaStock Professional 3.0 is very good. With this edition, it is softcover bound reminiscent of a good-quality college text. If you're a hands-on user, there is a temptation to delve right into the program, but you are cautioned against doing so prior to reviewing chapter 5. This is good advice, but if you are upgrading and are Windows-literate, you can plunge straightaway into MetaStock Professional 3.0 without reviewing chapter 5. The information in the manual is thorough and easy to read, and as John Sweeney, the previous MetaStock Professional reviewer, commented about that version, the explanations of the various indicators are very good. This compendium of technical information would be useful even without the program. The index is now up to nine pages, but addi-

FIGURE 1
DIALOG BOXES

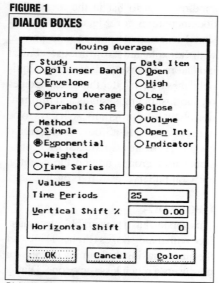

Dialog boxes are a major part of the graphic user interface enhancements.

FIGURE 2
ZOOM SCALING

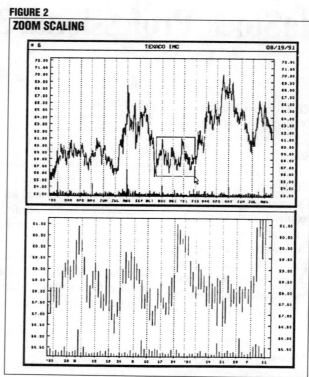

Zoom scaling is available. A section of a chart can be selected and then expanded for visual inspection.

tional material has been added, information about options, for one. The information is a good basic primer on technical analysis.

GRAPHIC ANALYSIS

The *real* strength of this program is the charting capabilities. The traditional chartist will be very comfortable with this program. It is a day-end, close-of-business sort of chart package. People who are using chart services such as Daily Graphs or Trendline will be very comfortable with this package.

Once you've acquired the data and are ready to plot the information, the program will hazard a guess at the type of chart that you want. Initially, however, it will be a bar chart and it will guess the scale on the Y-axis. It will also prompt you for the data that you want to plot — for example, if there are 600 days of information, the program will allow you to plot up to the entire 600 days or less. It is useful to load all the data and then use the zoom feature (Figure 2) to look at the most recent information. This is particularly important since long-term trendlines or other studies still remain on the chart, though the time frame has been compressed.

CHARTING

Producing charts with this package is easy. If you are satisfied with the default charts, you would never need to make any

adjustments. That's unlikely, but at least you are up and running at the beginning with relatively little confusion or pain. As you become more familiar with MetaStock Professional 3.0 and your demands for different kinds of information become more complex, you can progress to more sophisticated charting methods. The program has a macro program that allows you to automate routine procedures. The program also has a layout feature analogous to a workspace in a program such as Microsoft Excel, allowing you to recall a group of stocks with characteristics that you are studying and retrieve them with a single command. One feature that I find useful, particularly when trading low-priced and volatile stocks, is the ability to plot semi-log charts. Fans of Edwards and Magee's *Technical Analysis of Stock Trends* wouldn't be caught dead viewing an arithmetic chart, but semi-log charts give a different perspective on these vehicles.

The previous version of MetaStock Professional was somewhat clunky when certain procedures were called on. It wouldn't have been *too* bad, except it was those things that chartists like to do most

that the clunkiness prevented you from undertaking — you know, things like drawing trendlines, parallel lines and regression lines. This problem has been solved with the introduction of the mouse, which now makes quick work of drawing trendlines (Figure 3) and linear regressions. The ability to draw lines are so compelling that the MetaStock Professional user, too absorbed in trying it, can end up with lines all over the place.

The solution is to make the lines different colors, a fairly easy process — but you need hardware that lets you have color, of course. If you do, each added line is added sequentially, making it easier to keep tabs on which lines need editing. Lines can be extended as new data are added. Adding the mouse is a major improvement over the previous version and if no other improvements had been on this version, that alone would be worth the price of the upgrade.

Another new feature that is useful and improved in this version is the ability to use daily data to produce weekly charts. In previous versions, weekly or monthly charts were a compression of daily data such as five days of data compressed to

FIGURE 3
USING THE POINTER

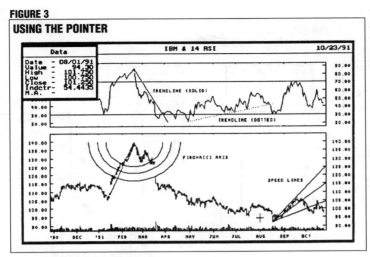

You can use the pointer to draw trendlines, which is a fast and easy method.

make a week. Sometimes the week's closing price would not be Friday's close but Monday's. Now they are true weekly, monthly and yearly charts. This is very handy when analyzing longer-term trends, as it also saves on downloading data in different formats.

MOUSE SUPPORT
Using the mouse is akin to drawing with a very intelligent pencil, and in fact the pointer looks like a little pencil on the screen. Be forewarned that the program requires a fairly recent mouse driver; I was using Microsoft mouse version 7.0 and it wasn't pointing exactly where I wanted it. When I asked the tech support staff over at Equis about this, I was advised that a newer version might solve the problem. So I installed version 8.1 and *poof!* the problem was solved, just like that. Using the mouse with this program increases productivity by a quantum leap over previous versions. I have used other charting and technical analysis programs without mouse support, and after having used MetaStock Professional with a mouse, I wouldn't even consider using the others as a primary package now.

INDICATORS
I didn't count all the indicators that are available with this package, but needless to say there are enough to satisfy even the most discriminating technician (see sidebar, "MetaStock Professional indicators"). The program lacks the ability to group more than two securities to form a group index. (Dow Jones's Market Analyzer has it, and I miss it here.)

In addition, version 2.5 was able to plot a linear regression based on a semi-log chart. The current version doesn't do this.

This program will grow with you as your technical proficiency grows. An extremely useful feature is the transparent chart, which allows the user to superimpose one chart over another or allow a series of charts to view the movements over the same period. This feature is very useful in visually measuring the performance of different vehicles. Actual relative strength numbers are available along with the lines on the chart.

Equis recognizes that some users will devise arcane methods of trading that even the most technically proficient minds haven't. For those inventive souls, there is, in addition to the predefined indicators available, a custom formulas feature that is the prelude to designing your own system.

You can start with a previously established technical indicator and modify it and incorporate it into your own indicator. There is a dialog box that allows you to modify an existing formula such as TRIX by redesigning it. Mind that this differs from changing the variables in the indicator — that is, a 14-day Relative Strength Indicator (RSI) vs. a nine-day RSI. You can actually get into the formula and change the composition and characteristics of the indicator itself. If you can think logically, no programming experience is required. For rocket scientists out there, this will be a piece of cake. If you make an error in creating a formula, the system will advise you of your error, but it will only clean up syntax errors, such as dividing by zero. The manual states "it is impossible to enter an invalid formula." Some of the formulas available are correlation, demand index, directional movement, Moving Average Convergence/Divergence (MACD) and most popular indicators that you can think of that are used in daily technical analysis.

SYSTEM TESTING

The system-testing portion of the program is probably the most powerful and useful feature. However, it is only useful to those who like to test systems. With MetaStock Professional 3.0, you can: Write trading systems using your own trading rules; test the systems; examine the results visually and with tabular reports; and automatically optimize parameters within your trading rules to improve the results. (See Figure 4.)

Before embarking on systems-testing, the manual strongly recommends that the system tutorial be read. This is sound advice, since it *is* your system and the tech support staff won't have the foggiest idea of what you are trying to accomplish. It behooves you to do your homework in this session. This is a complex part of the program, but if you are into trading strategies and mechanical systems and are not a computer programmer, the time will be well spent and reduce frustration later.

The system-testing tutorial should take only about 30 minutes to complete and it will be an informative and enjoyable time for you. The tutorial takes you through a simple trading strategy, always in the

FIGURE 4

SYSTEM TESTING

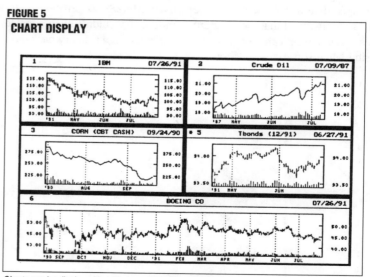

System testing involves the development of testing trading systems to determine the systems' historical profitability. This flow chart shows the system testing map.

FIGURE 5

CHART DISPLAY

Charts can be displayed in a tile format. The size of the charts depends on the number of charts in the memory.

market both long and short with a 25-day exponential moving average. The system goes through a series of dialog boxes that are easy to fill in and set up the trading system for you. It then asks some basic questions about entry and commissions and trade delay after the signal is generated. The equipment that I ran this with gave me results on 1,000 days of the OEX in less than a minute.

The results of the system test are presented in graphic and tabular form, and

METASTOCK PROFESSIONAL INDICATORS

Accumulation/distribution
Accumulation swing index
Andrews's pitchfork
Bollinger Bands
Candlestick charting
Chaikin oscillator
Chaikin's volatility
Commodity channel index
Commodity selection index
Correlation analysis
Demand index
Directional movement
Fibonacci studies
  Arcs
  Fans
  Time zones
Fourier transform
Herrick payoff index
Moving average convergence/
  divergence
Median price
Momentum
Moving averages
  Calculations
  Interpretations
  Envelopes
Negative volume index
On-balance index
Open interest
Option analysis
Put/call price
  Delta
  Gamma
  Option life

Theta
Vega
Volatility
Parabolic stop and reverse
Performance
Point & figure
Positive volume index
Price oscillator
Price rate of change
Price and volume trend
Relative strength, comparative
Relative strength index
Speed resistance lines
Spread
Standard deviation
Stochastics oscillator
Swing index
Time series forecast
Trendlines
  General
  Support and resistance levels
  Trendline angles
TRIX
Ultimate oscillator
Volatility, general
Volatility, option
Volatility, Wilder's
Volume
Volume oscillator
Volume rate of change
Weighted close
Williams's accumulation/distribution
Williams's %R
Zigzag

---

the graphic form presents the stock or commodity that was tested with small arrows at entry and exit points. If the signals are very sensitive, you will have arrows all over the chart. In the tabular form the results are presented in a test summary report, which contains information such as: total net profit, initial investment, days in test, average profit per trade and other useful data. Clearly, a considerable amount of thought went into this. It also appears that the brain behind this is someone who has traded stock and/or commodities and is not simply an academic or programmer. The system keeps track of thousands of test details and presents them in a usable format so changes in the system can be made intelligently.

After the initial tutorial is completed, a feature called optimization runs various moving averages in different increments and selects the optimum indicator. I can remember a major brokerage firm devoted considerable manpower to testing this type of system in the 1980s; now it can be done in just a few minutes with a personal computer.

SUMMING IT UP

I *do* have some peeves with MetaStock Professional, and the inability to use linear regression in semi-log format is one of them. The requirement to purchase additional software in order to download prices is a disappointment, although a smart business practice. Still, MetaStock Pro-

fessional is better than other products that only permit access to their own databases, which is not unlike giving away the razor to sell the blades. MetaStock Professional 3.0 converts data from many other formats but it isn't universal, so check it out first by calling Equis to see if your data can be converted if you are currently using another program. The MetaStock Professional tech support staff is courteous and helpful, and they'll call you back if they don't have the answer at their fingertips. The phone reps are backed by a supervisor who is thoroughly familiar with the programs and the concepts. But remember: They aren't going to help you debug your system and they shouldn't be expected to.

As mentioned earlier, I would like to see this as a full-fledged Windows product and not just close. I spoke recently with Equis, who said that it would have compromised its installed base of customers if they had made MetaStock Professional 3.0 a Windows program. If you get this program, a math coprocessor makes a considerable difference in performance.

I've been a MetaStock Professional user for more than two years, and I like it. Version 3.0 is a *big* improvement over the previous versions, and the changes are more than cosmetic. Equis has continued the overall feel of previous versions while breaking into new ground with a graphic user interface (GUI); as a result, newcomers to the software will be up and running and be productive in a much shorter time than ever before. For previous users of MetaStock Professional, if they choose they can still work with the old familiar keystrokes and not ever have to use the mouse, although that would be a waste.

Jack Karczewski is a Paine Webber broker residing in Scottsdale, AZ.

OptionVue IV

OPTIONVUE SYSTEMS INTERNATIONAL
175 East Hawthorn Parkway, Suite 180
Vernon Hills, IL 60061
(708) 816-6610 or (800) 733-6610
Fax: (708) 816-6647

Product: Real-time or off-line options analysis program for stocks, bonds, futures, indices and currencies, replete with trade selection ranking and portfolio management.
Price: $895 for base system plus $500 for the real-time option.
Hardware: 286 or better CPU, PC-DOS 2.1 or better, 640K RAM, one high-density floppy or a hard drive. Signal or Comstock datafeed and receiver (if online). As tested: 386-25 CPU with DOS 5.0. CGA, EGA, VGA or Hercules graphics. 80-column printer for tabular output. Graphics require HP LaserJet, Panasonic or Epson graphics-style printers. Can use 80287 or 80387 math coprocessor.

by John Sweeney

I initially reviewed OptionVue in 1988 and rated it the Cadillac of the retail options programs. It's now in version 1.28 (does that mean 28 updates?) and there's nothing to indicate it's ready to give up its lead.

I recently sought out the program for review again because I had heard that it now had a real-time (via Signal) capability that I wanted to see in action. The version I had looked at before required a daily input of recent underlying prices, which was tedious. Were things easier in the new version? I had to look.

BIG-TIME HELP

OpVue does a ton of work for you. It keeps track of all the options specifications. It figures all the expiration dates and calculates the number of days to expiration. It figures margin requirements for you. It generates the codes to send to the Signal receiver for quotes. As options expire, the program automatically deletes them and adds a new expiration month following the pattern you've set up. It evaluates — literally — every conceivable strategy at once and pops up a list of the best risk/return combinations based on your forecast of the underlying price movement and your personal emphasis on risk or return as the primary considerations, as well as the amount of money you want to sink into the proposed position. (See Figure 1.) There is little chance of running out of capacity: OpVue handles up to 14 strike prices, five months per strike, puts and calls for a total of 140 options on every underlying asset.

A true grace note is the valuation sheets the program puts out for intraday use. Another absolute essential is the "scripting" or macro facility, which can record what you do and rerun it later. Even the data downloading has been automated completely.

If you're a spreadsheet user, the OpVue keyboarding will be familiar: it's usually "slash-letter" to do anything. As a result, it's pretty fast to get from one part of the program to another, though not as fast as clicking on another window on an Apple Macintosh. As practical enhancements, there are a number of usage-generated keystroke combinations to speed things up — for example, Ctrl-D to repeat an entry, Ctrl-L to display format information, T to enter today's date, and T+n to enter the date *n* days from now. Up to 48 F-key combinations can be defined to whiz through the maze of menus that operate the program.

Since the program's interface is menus via keyboard, you may be more than usually dependent on the manual. It's thick but not easy to get around in. Though I read manuals for a living (what have I come to?), I missed the section on defining the receiver in the front of the manual, only to find it in the back of the manual (page 215). Don't get me wrong: everything I sought was *somewhere* in the 300-odd pages and there is a fair index to help, but count on reading the whole thing to understand how OpVue works.

The same goes for the menus, whose euphemisms I found hard to grasp. Some things are "defined," some are "modeled" and some things "viewed." *Definitely* stay away from the clear menu — I wiped out an entire transactions journal with a keystroke! In summary, the interface is old news to graphically oriented people, so count on a significant learning curve.

TYPICAL DAY

Hopefully, you've left your receiver on and it has been faithfully gathering quotes for your favorite tradeables. Thus, when you fire up OpVue, all it has to do to fill in the matrix is get fresh quotes from the receiver, a process that takes a few seconds. If you are using the Signal software, just be sure that it too is selecting data for the options you will be following with OpVue.

What OpVue doesn't do, however, is keep track of your past data, so you're not building a history or a quote page. Once you specify that you want to look at Ford, you can forget about the machine collecting data in the background on bonds. OpVue *will* update your bond matrix, for example, with current quotes when you do switch to bonds, though, and it is possible your receiver has been collecting current quotes on those symbols, provided you started the day by telling it what symbols to track.

The other thing about quotes via OpVue is that they are solely dependent on the refresh rate of Signal, anywhere from instantly to 12 minutes, depending on the activity of the item. Although OpVue will give you a six-item pop-up window to track current quotes, I definitely wouldn't want to use OpVue as *my* only quote system, which brings up an interesting question: Do you want to give up quotes to do options?

SPLITTING SIGNAL

I called the Signal folks to ask about this dilemma: one Signal signal and two uses. Do I pay for two receivers so I can run,

FIGURE 1

ANALYTICS AND POSSIBLE TRADES

```
                * * *  OPTIONVUE IV SELECTIONS  * * *
---------------------------------------------------------------------
 SYMBOL: OEX         TODAY'S DATE: APR 16 1992   VALUATION DATE: MAY 06 1992
 CAPITAL: $10,000          PRICE: 389.19         VLTY: Variable
 STRATEGY: Vertical Debit Spreads
 TG.PRICE: Bell curve centered around 400.00        INTRST:  3.8%
 RANKING BASIS: 50% Exp.Ret. / 50% 1st St.Dev.Downside Exp.Ret.
---------------------------------------------------------------------
    Recommended Trade                                 Exp.Ret.   St.Dev.
    ------------------                                 --------   -------
 1.  B 204 May405c @  3/4,    S 204 May410c @  5/16    +22,400   ~39,271
 2.  B  79 May400c @1 1/2,    S  79 May410c @  5/16    +20,564   ~31,837
 3.  B  39 May395c @2 3/4,    S  39 May410c @  5/16    +16,285   ~23,619
 4.  B 114 May400c @1 1/2,    S 114 May405c @ 11/16    +14,006   ~23,033
 5.  B  46 May395c @2 3/4,.   S  46 May405c @ 11/16    +12,792   ~18,868
 6.  B  20 May390c @5,        S  20 May410c @  5/16    +10,463   ~15,644
 7.  B  22 May390c @5,        S  22 May405c @ 11/16     +8,466   ~13,114
 8.  B  71 May395c @2 3/4,    S  71 May400c @1 7/16     +8,753   ~14,187
 9.  B  38 Jun400c @3 3/4,    S  38 Jun410c @1 5/16     +7,069   ~11,224
10.  B  12 May385c @8 1/8,    S  12 May410c @  5/16     +6,997   ~11,150
11.  B  21 Jun395c @5 3/4,    S  21 Jun410c @1 5/16     +5,854   ~9,254
12.  B  87 Jun405c @2 3/8,    S  87 Jun410c @1 5/16     +6,362   ~12,288


               [ END OF REPORT.  Press any key... ]
```

OpVue not only provides analytics, it tells you how the possible trades compare to each other so you can pick just the one you want. Here, with the OEX at about 390 and the trader looking for it to go higher in the next 20 days, OpVue is touting vertical debit spreads.

FIGURE 2

OPVUE MATRIX

```
OPTIONVUE IV        MATRIX      S&P 100 Index        12:13 THUR APR 16 1992
/ACTUALS===================================================================\
! !====== OEX Index ======! !------ SPX Index ------!
!     -0.92    OEX   12:13        -1.71    SPX   12:12
!    389.20  390.37  387.21      414.57  416.28  413.40
!FUTURES-------------------------------------------------------------------
! !-------JUN-(65)--------! !------SEP-(156)-------! !-------DEC-(247)------!
!   415.05    -2.40    +10      416.50   -2.20 _____      Last    Chg  Ex.Pos
!   12:13    57.9K _____       12:10    333  _____       Time    Vol  Trade
!OPTIONS-------------------------------------------------------------------
! !-------APR-(2)--------! !------MAY-(30)--------! !------JUN-(30)------!
!!
!CALLS>   5                   8       13.8% _____    11      14.0% _____
!385    4 3/8   83.3 _____  8 1/2    59.6 _____   11 3/4    58.4 _____
!CALLS    1/2    8.4%   -41   5 1/8   12.6%   -41    8 1/4    13.0%   -41
!390      3/4   36.7 _____  5 3/8    47.2    -4     8 3/4    50.0     -4
!!
!PUTS>   1/16                 4 5/8   14.1% _____   7 7/8    15.0% _____
!385     3/16  -12.1 _____  4 3/4  -40.3 _____    7 7/8   -41.9 _____
!PUTS   1 1/8    3.2% _____  6 3/4   13.4% _____     Last    MIV  Ex.Pos
!390    1 5/8  -65.3 _____  6 7/8  -52.8 _____      Th.Pr   Delta Trade
!SUMMARY===================================================================
! Orig.Reqmt:   $994,047  Commis: $1,072.81   Delta: -836.9  AvgMIV: 12.8%
!Maint.Reqmt: $1,415,850                       Gamma:   -708  Calls: 12.7%
! Cash Flow:   +$61,271   Theta: +$2,325/day   Vega: -5,370   Puts: 13.1%
\- [F1]=Help ----------------------------------------------------- 34K ----/
```

The heart of OpVue is its matrix. Here, the actuals, futures, options, margin requirements and volatility are summarized. The display can be extensively customized to show just what you want to see — and there's a pop-up field (lower right in each section) to help you remember it all.

say, TradeStation, at the same time or what? It turns out that Signal sells additional hardware and software at half the price, but the exchanges treat this as if there are two data users and charge for it.

Practically speaking, if you're a position player, to assemble the data for a decision, you'll need a chartbook or trading program with the interday data plus all your indicators, the *intra*day data for entry/exit information, and OpVue for analyzing trades with current pricing. (If you're just looking for mispricings, I'd advise you to give it up — OpVue does a great job of showing them, but you'll never get the execution to capture them.) That means you get to switch from one

program to OpVue and then wait for the matrix to refresh itself with fresh prices before you can do an on-line analysis.

The other option is to use OpVue's Access program, which can download the prices you want at any time for less money. Access, by the way, can get data automatically from Signal, Comstock, Dow Jones or an ASCII file you have generated. It has an unattended mode, which will allow you to start it and have it download the data at a specific time even if you're not there. This is handy if you don't need the on-line, real-time feature.

TRADE SELECTION
OpVue gets really exciting when you're

FIGURE 3

Purchase calls Purchase puts	Horizontal debit spread Horizontal credit spread
Sell naked calls Sell naked puts	Purchase straddle Sell straddle
Sell covered calls Sell covered puts	Diagonal debit spread Diagonal credit spread
Vertical debit spread Vertical credit spread	Roll covered calls

OpVue can evaluate a wide variety of options positions and then rank them by risk and return as you prefer. It can also evaluate any one position or all the positions, not including naked positions. Here are the positions included in version 1.28.

poking at different options positions. What was once tedious and slow becomes instantaneous and fascinating. Once you've got the matrix (Figure 2) on the screen, you can easily pop in different positions, existing or potential, and see the results immediately in terms of the parameters at the bottom of the screen or graphically via the series of commands to generate the graphics. This allows you to easily find delta-neutral positions or slant the positions in any direction your inclination specifies. Option prices, margin requirements, volatility, delta, gamma and so forth are always right on the screen. In fact, the program tracks far more than you can ever get on the screen — you'll have to pick out what's important to you.

Moreover, OptionVue has clearly upgraded the analytics in the program with new "real-world" sophistication; the theoretical prices are much closer to the actual pricing than in the previous version, and the computed market-implied volatilities are much more consistent. You have your choice of the Black-Scholes, Cox-Ross-Rubenstein or Yates models. Take the Yates model. It's an adjusted Black-Scholes model, very fast and, judging by the market's valuations, extremely accurate. The result is a high level of comfort that the information on which your analysis rides is solidly based.

FINDING THE BEST TRADE
Perhaps the neatest thing about OpVue is its ability to sort through the entire matrix of available positions (Figure 3) and rank their desirability by profit and loss, yield or annualized return while you're on-line.

To say this speeds things up is a vast understatement. It's an order-of-magnitude improvement in your trading capability and an education in itself. You'll soon be looking at trades you probably would never have considered before. Now, seeing the potential return, you'll have ample motivation to investigate. This may pay for the package all by itself.

To take an example, on March 31, 1992, I was sorting out the Treasury bond trading range in Figure 4 when I turned OpVue loose on the problem. From the matrix (Figure 5), which showed all the futures and options, all I had to do was go to the trade selection screen (Figure 6) and order up an evaluation of all strategies. About 30 seconds later, my 386, with coprocessor, had generated Figure 7, which focused on using the December puts with their relatively high market-implied volatility of 9.5%.

If you'd thought of actually putting on the recommended trade (short two actual, short two 96 puts), you'd have wondered if the pricing were really available, either in the futures contracts or the cash contracts. In fact, the top four recommendations all use the September and December contracts where there are bound to be wide bid-asked spreads. That's because I asked that the selections be ranked on pure expected return versus risk. To fix that, I asked for annualized return next and got Figure 8, which — ignoring recommendation 1's paltry return — brought up a June situation (choice 3), which looked promising.

The matrix showed a position delta of -61 and theta of $40.92 per day (not shown). Plopping that up on the screen (Figure 9) showed a 5.5-point range of profitability from 94.03 to 99.25 on the underlying June bond. Comparing this to the chart, I could see that I'd have long since covered my exposure by buying or selling the bonds before reaching either point. Thus, though the option position itself had a positive expectation, there would be a good opportunity to cover the expected breakout of the trading range and keep a large chunk of the premium.

OpVue made this inspection a less-than-five-minute process and popped up several alternatives I don't normally consider. For example, choice 2 I had already

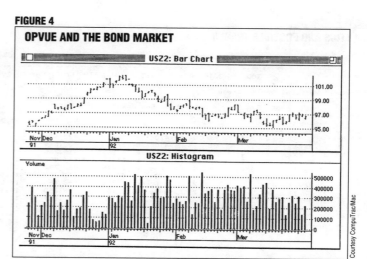
FIGURE 5

BOND MATRIX

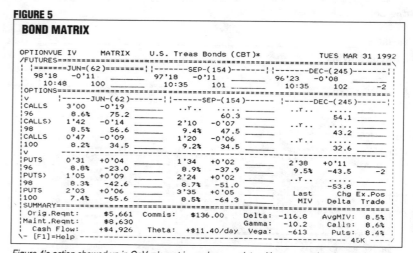

Figure 4's action showed up in OpVue's matrix as above, replete with a contemplated covered short in the December bonds. Before doing that, I asked the program what it thought the best approach was.

FIGURE 6

OPVUE SPECIFICATIONS

```
OPTIONVUE IV   DEF. SELECTION   U.S. Treas Bonds (CBT)*  10:49 TUES MAR 31 1992
-----------------------------------------------------------------------------

                 Valuation Date: JUN 1 1992
                    Target Type: [Bell]/Price/Range
                   Center Price: 98'00
                     Volatility:  8.3%
                       Strategy: [All strategies]/...
               Capital Provided: $12,000
               Comparison Basis: [Yield]/Ann.Yield/P/L
              Volatility Change: 0.0%
               Int.Rate Change: +0.20%

                           RANKING BASIS
                  Proportion Exp.Ret:  1
         Proportion Downside Exp.Ret:  1




-- [F1]=Help -------------------------------------------------------- 99K -----
```

In defining the situation for OpVue, I specified my expectation that bonds on June 1, 1992, would still be at 98, with a slight increase in the short-term interest rate but the same volatility as today. I gave the program $12,000 to commit.

rejected but 1, another strangle, was interesting. So was 5, a covered short. Figure 10 shows the comparison of projected outcomes for my favorite plus these two new alternatives, another two minutes' work.

RECORDING THE ACTION

Once you've mastered the intricacies of the program, there's only the actual trading left. OpVue helps this along with a transactions journal, which has automatic repricing ability. It even automates the entry of trades into the transactions journal by lifting them directly from the matrix (Figure 11) and posting all the details into the transactions journal (lower Figure 11) for you using the matrix prices. Later, you go back and modify the prices to reflect those actually received through your broker.

SETTING UP

Installing OptionVue IV is not painless. There's a hardware key that must go on the back of the machine (along with any other keys already there), and you then fire up the installation program to uncompress all the files sent you. In my case, the 1.44 MB disks that were sent to me had an unreadable install program, so I switched to the true floppies OptionVue had thoughtfully sent. These loaded fine, absorbing 2.7 MB on my trusty hard drive. As for random access memory (RAM), using MS-DOS 5.0, I was able to grant 596K, an amount that turned out to be adequate at all times except when I tried to

FIGURE 7

OPVUE RECOMMENDATIONS

```
              * * *  OPTIONVUE IV SELECTIONS  * * *
--------------------------------------------------------------
 SYMBOL: USM2        TODAY'S DATE: MAR 31 1992    VALUATION DATE: JUN 01 1992
 CAPITAL: $12,000           PRICE: 98'18                   VLTY: Variable
 STRATEGY: All Strategies
 TG.PRICE: Bell curve centered around 98               INTRST: 4.0%
 RANKING BASIS: 50% Exp.Ret. / 50% 1st St.Dev.Downside Exp.Ret.
--------------------------------------------------------------
      Recommended Trade                            % Exp.Ret.      St.Dev.
      -----------------                            ----------      -------
  1.  S  2 futures  @96'23,      S  2 Dec96p   @2'34       +5%         ~29%
  2.  S  2 Sep98c   @2'04,       S  2 Sep96p   @1'31       +1%         ~16%
  3.  S  2 futures  @97'18,      S  2 Sep98p   @2'20       +2%         ~25%
  4.  S  2 futures  @97'18,      S  2 Sep96p   @1'31       +5%         ~34%
  5.  S  2 Jun98c   @1'41,       S  2 Jun96p   @0'30       +4%         ~32%
  6.  S  3 futures  @96'23,      S  3 Dec100p  @4'43        0%         ~24%
  7.  S  2 futures  @98'18,      S  2 Jun98p   @1'04       +4%         ~33%
  8.  S  2 futures  @98'18,      S  2 Jun96p   @0'30       +7%         ~44%
  9.  S  5 Sep100c  @1'16                                  +9%         ~44%
 10.  B  2 Dec100p  @4'61,       S  2 Jun96p   @0'30       +1%         ~29%
 11.  S  2 Jun96c   @2'58,       S  2 Jun98p   @1'04       +2%         ~31%
 12.  S 10 Sep102c  @0'45                                 +12%         ~54%


              [ END OF REPORT.  Press any key... ]
```

OpVue came back with more than 12 recommendations, the top one of which was the sale of the December contracts and the December puts.

FIGURE 8

RANKING OUTCOME BY ANNUALIZED PERCENTAGE RETURN

```
              * * *  OPTIONVUE IV SELECTIONS  * * *
--------------------------------------------------------------
 SYMBOL: USM2        TODAY'S DATE: MAR 31 1992    VALUATION DATE: JUN 01 1992
 CAPITAL: $12,000           PRICE: 98'15                   VLTY: Variable
 STRATEGY: All Strategies
 TG.PRICE: Bell curve centered around 98               INTRST: 4.0%
 RANKING BASIS: 50% Exp.Ret. / 50% 1st St.Dev.Downside Exp.Ret.
--------------------------------------------------------------
      Recommended Trade                          Ann % Exp.Ret.     St.Dev.
      -----------------                          --------------     -------
  1.  S  2 Sep98c   @2'04,       S  2 Sep96p   @1'31      +2%         ~95%
  2.  S  2 futures  @96'23,      S  2 Dec96p   @2'34     +29%        ~173%
  3.  S  2 Jun98c   @1'39,       S  2 Jun96p   @0'31     +22%        ~186%
  4.  B  2 Dec100p  @4'61,       S  2 Jun96p   @0'31     +10%        ~173%
  5.  S  2 futures  @97'15,      S  2 Sep98p   @2'20      +6%        ~152%
  6.  S  2 Jun96c   @2'58,       S  2 Jun98p   @1'07     +15%        ~185%
  7.  S  2 futures  @98'15,      S  2 Jun98p   @1'07     +22%        ~192%
  8.  S  2 futures  @97'15,      S  2 Sep96p   @1'31     +19%        ~201%
  9.  S  5 Sep100c  @1'16                                +50%        ~262%
 10.  B  2 Dec100p  @4'61                                +16%        ~246%
 11.  S  2 futures  @98'15,      S  2 Jun96p   @0'31     +36%        ~260%
 12.  S  7 Jun102c  @0'16                                +18%        ~185%


              [ END OF REPORT.  Press any key... ]
```

Reconsidering the same situation but ranking outcomes by annualized percentage return rather than pure expected return generated a slightly different set of choices. Now June options (alternative 3) looked good.

FIGURE 9

SHOWING THE TRADE GRAPHICALLY

```
OPTIONVUE IV  GRAPHIC ANALYSIS  U.S. Treas Bonds (CBT) *      TUES MAR 31 1992
Account: Lind            Vlty: Variable                       Ex-Div:  n/a
Capital: $8,612                                               INTRST:  3.8%
```

Val. Date: 5/16/92
Short 2 Jun98 calls,
Short 2 Jun96 puts

B.E.: 94'03
B.E.: 99'25
T: $242 ±2820

```
Profit/Loss by change in Price
Pr   92.25  94.12  96.03  98.00  100.00 102.03 104.12
    -3608    48    2454   2454   -390   -4296  -8452
```

From the table, it's a short trip via a couple of menus to show the new trade graphically. OpVue is primarily text-based, though.

FIGURE 10

PROFITABILITY EXPECTATIONS

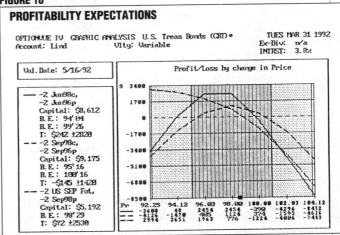

```
OPTIONVUE IV  GRAPHIC ANALYSIS  U.S. Treas Bonds (CBT) *      TUES MAR 31 1992
Account: Lind            Vlty: Variable                       Ex-Div:  n/a
Capital: $8,612                                               INTRST:  3.8%
```

Val. Date: 5/16/92

— -2 Jun98c,
    -2 Jun96p
    Capital: $8,612
    B.E.: 94'04
    B.E.: 99'26
    T: $242 ±2820
- - -2 Sep98c,
    -2 Sep96p
    Capital: $9,175
    B.E.: 95'16
    B.E.: 100'16
    T: -$145 ±1420
— — -2 US SEP Fut,
    -2 Sep98p
    Capital: $5,192
    B.E.: 98'29
    T: $72 ±2530

```
Profit/Loss by change in Price
Pr   92.25  94.12  96.03  98.00  100.00 102.03 104.12
    -3608    48    2454   2454   -390   -4296  -8452
    -4124  -1470   374   1124   -1595  -4611
    2994   2651   1963   776   -1224  -4006  -7443
```

OpVue places the profitability expectations for up to three positions on the graphs for easy comparison.

FIGURE 11

POSITION AND TRANSACTION JOURNAL

```
OPTIONVUE IV        MATRIX        S&P 100 Index          11:32 TUES APR 14 1992
/ACTUALS=====================================================================\
|     !====== OEX Index ======!   !------ SPX Index ------!                  |
|          +6.84    OEX   11:32      +6.94    SPX   11:32                     |
|         387.49  388.32 380.66     413.02  413.86 406.08                    |
|FUTURES=====================================================================|
|!------JUN-(67)------!  !------SEP-(158)------!  !------DEC-(249)------!     |
|   413.60   +8.50 _____  415.25   +9.05 _____    414.10   +6.55 _____       |
|   11:31    13.1K  +10   11:30      79  _____    11:22      15  _____       |
|OPTIONS=====================================================================|
|!   !------APR-(4)------!  !------MAY-(32)------!  !------JUN-(67)------!)   |
|!CALLS    3 7/8  15.1%        7 5/8  14.8% _____   11 1/4  15.0% _____       |
|385      3 7/8  64.8 _____    7 7/8  55.6 _____   11 1/4  55.6 _____        |
|CALLS)   1 1/8  13.3%         5      13.6% _____    8 1/4  13.9% _____       |
|390      1 1/8  32.0   -41    5      43.5   -41    8 3/8  47.4   -41        |
|!!                                                                          |
|PUTS)    3 3/8  12.2%         8 1/4  14.4% _____   10 5/8  14.6% _____       |
|390      3 3/4  -68.2 _____   8      -56.4 _____   10 3/4  -52.5 _____      |
|PUTS     7 1/2  16.1%        11 1/4  14.2% _____   15      14.2% _____       |
|395      7 3/4  -92.0 _____  11      -68.7 _____   13 1/2  -60.9 _____      |
|SUMMARY=====================================================================|
| Orig.Reqmt:  $925,722   Commis:  $956.35    Delta:   +1.28   AvgMIV: 14.4% |
|Maint.Reqmt: $1,416,030               Gamma:    -439   Calls: 14.2%         |
| Cash Flow:  +$55,675    Theta: +$1,939/day  Vega:  -5,140   Puts:  14.8%   |
\- [F1]=Help -----------------------------------------------------  34K ----/
```

```
OPTIONVUE IV        MATRIX        Boeing Co.            11:37 THUR APR 16 1992
/===========================================================================\
|                    TRANSACTION LOG FOR ACCOUNT Lind                        |
|---------------------------------------------------------------------------|
|Trans  Date     Time   Code   Qty  Symbol Type Price   Commis    Net     R  |
|-----  ----     ----   ----   ---  ------ ---- -----   ------    ---     -- |
|   5. 03/31/92 13:21  [Sel]    2  USU2P98  G  2'24     78.00   +4,672.00  ^ |
|   6. 04/09/92 11:02  [Buy]    1  USM2C98  G  2'45     39.00   -2,742.12    |
|   7. 04/09/92 11:02  [Buy]    1  USM2P98  G  0'27     39.00     -460.87    |
|   8. 04/09/92 11:03  [Buy]    1  USM2C98  G  2'45     39.00   -2,742.12    |
|   9. 04/09/92 11:03  [Buy]    1  USM2P98  G  0'27     39.00     -460.87    |
|  10. 04/14/92 08:17  [Sel]    1  DMK2C600 G  0.80     39.00     +961.00    |
|  11. 04/14/92 08:17  [Sel]    1  DMK2P600 G  0.58     39.00     +686.00    |
|  12. 04/14/92 08:54  [Buy]    1  EDM2     F  95.89    29.00      -29.00    |
|  13. 04/14/92 08:54  [Sel]    3  EDM2C9600 G 0.07    117.00     +408.00    |
|  14. 04/14/92 11:09  [Sel]    2  USM2C98  G  2'17      0.00   +4,531.25    |
|  15. 04/14/92 11:09  [Sel]    2  USM2P98  G  0'22      0.00     +687.50    |
|  16. 04/14/92 11:33  [Buy]   10  SPM2     F  413.80  290.00     -290.00    |
|  17. 04/14/92 11:33  [Sel]   41  OEXDR    O  1 1/16  145.65   +4,210.60    |
|  18. 04/14/92 11:33  [Sel]   41  OEXER    O  4 7/8   239.64  +19,747.86    |
|  19. 04/14/92 11:33  [Sel]   41  OEXFR    O  8       283.92  +32,516.08    |
|  20.                 [  ]                                                  |
|---------------------------------------------------------------------------|
|Press [Ctrl-F] to toggle display format                                    |
\===========================================================================/
```

From the matrix, OpVue will transfer this position (upper), long 10 June bonds, short 123 April, May and June calls, directly to the transactions journal (lower), sparing you typing. There's no break in your concentration to take care of your paperwork. Later, you can manually correct the prices to match your broker's fills.

FIGURE 12

TRACKING OPEN POSITIONS

```
            * * *  OPTIONVUE IV PORTFOLIO UNREALIZED G/L  * * *
-------------------------------------------------------------------------
ACCOUNT: Lind                                       TODAY'S DATE: 4/14/92
Posn                         Open      Open Cost   Current   Gain   Percent
Type  Symbol  Type  Posn     Date     (Proceeds)    Value   (Loss)   G/L
----  ------  ----  ----     ----     ----------   -------  ------  -------
STDL/ IBMDQ    O     -1    3/31/92  \
    \ IBMPQ    O     -1    3/31/92  / (    311) (      390) (    79)  -25%
STDL/ USU2C98  G     -2    3/31/92  \
    \ USU2P98  G     -2    3/31/92  / (  8,688) (    8,969) (   281)   -3%
STDL/ DMK2C600 G     -1    4/14/92  \
    \ DMK2P600 G     -1    4/14/92  / (  1,647) (    1,769) (   122)   -7%
CVWT/ EDM2     F     +1    4/14/92  \
    \ EDM2C9600 G    -3    4/14/92  / (    379) (      564) (   160)  -42%
COMB/ SPM2     F    +10    4/14/92  \
    ! OEXDR    O    -41    4/14/92  !
    ! OEXER    O    -41    4/14/92  !
    \ OEXFR    O    -41    4/14/92  / ( 56,185) (   57,815) ( 2,130)   -4%
                                                          =========
                              Total Gain/(Loss)  (         2,773)
-------------------------------------------------------------------------
```

OptionVue will also track your open positions, showing profit or loss in a special report that consolidates all positions entered at one time from the matrix. Here, the trade from Figure 11 is shown as a combination with a current outstanding loss of $2,130.

capture a screen. OpVue uses essentially all your 640K and doesn't use extended or expanded memory (that will come with the next update), so forget keeping your favorite terminate-and-stay residents (TSRs) around.

Next, I immediately started the program, only to be confronted with an error code, which, on calling the company, turned out to be a problem with the hardware lock. A new one was immediately promised and sent off to me.

Several days later, I arrived in the office to find a fresh set of disks and a new lock. After installing the lock and the program, I banged in OpVue and got "Error in program enablement code. Run setup and double-check it." Then the screen blanked and the machine froze. I repeated this twice to see if it was always going to happen, and it did. This is really irritating when you've got quotes being picked up on your machine by other programs and suddenly you're missing a segment of them. I'd have preferred a more graceful exit. Hence my advice: Don't install this thing during prime time.

I tried several configurations of keys and printer cables on the back and then called OptionVue again. An OptionVue representative promptly gave me a back-door code into the program. I'd have to say that the program's security is overdone, but the service representatives are very good, which mitigates the hassle.

The next day, I fired up the program with the back-door password and *voilà!* it worked. What's more, I stumbled across Appendix D in the 300-page manual on setting up OpVue. It told me how to get the Signal feed to automatically update the matrix, which is the heart of the OpVue system. That worked, too! After adjusting the strike prices in the sample program to those of current pricing, I was soon contentedly watching the OEX options market live. I had to admit: This is truly slick!

SUMMARY

OpVue remains my favorite options analysis program. In fact, for the retail trader and most institutional traders, there just aren't a lot of other choices. Also, OpVue comes in a number of different configurations and price levels to meet the needs of different traders, from market makers to occasional position players. The ordinary off-line version is fine for 90% of the people who don't need real-time access to options analysis, though this program would be great for thinking up trades for brokers' clients. For the on-line version, it would be nice if it could run in the background or under Windows. That way, you could use your machine for something besides just options analysis.

Looking back, I seem to have emphasized the program's warts in this review, but those are mostly of the security features and the manual. Once you've gone through the learning curve, you've got thorough, fast and accurate analytical capability at your fingertips, more than enough to get on top of the complicated options game and milk it for some decent money.

John Sweeney is Technical Editor of STOCKS & COMMODITIES.

QuoteMaster Pro 1.63

STRATEGIC PLANNING SYSTEMS, *distributor*
PO Box 4019
Simi Valley, CA 93093
(805) 522-8979 or (800) 488-5898
Developer: Donald L. Bell
Product: A real-time security monitoring system
Markets: All major stock and commodity exchanges, NASDAQ, options, mutual and money market funds
Price: $495
Price stream: Telemet America or Signal
Required equipment: Apple Macintosh Plus or higher with two megabytes (MB) of RAM or more when using Multifinder and System 6.0.5 or later; 3.5 MB with System 7. QuoteMaster Pro is System 7-compatible.

by John Sweeney

Macintosh users have been blessed of late with more and more packages of software that take advantage of the Mac's high-resolution screens, easy use and superb memory management. Nearly every analytical function can now be performed on your Mac, and Strategic Planning Systems has made second-to-second quote monitoring easy.

Here at STOCKS & COMMODITIES, we installed QuoteMaster 1.6 with the idea that it would be a convenient accessory to keep us up to date during the day. We had previously reviewed and used many of the systems that can access Signal on DOS machines, packages that came with every imaginable bell and whistle. Surprise! QuoteMaster 1.6 turned out to be one of those handy items that ends up being a constant favorite.

QuoteMaster Pro will truly run in the background. Given the superiority of MultiFinder or System 7 on the Mac, this wasn't an unheard-of achievement, but it *is* nice. Background applications I'd used on the DOS machines generally had some problems, though they are getting fewer. Given that you buy the memory to dedicate to QuoteMaster Pro to leave your computer on, you're going to have full charting and analytics instantly available while using your machine for workaday tasks.

BASICS

With QuoteMaster Pro, all you do is install the package (another "Install, click, drag" breeze on the Mac, and only 1.4 MB on your disk) and start up (QuoteMaster Pro wants 1 MB of RAM for itself, but I found I got no "out of memory" messages if I gave it 1.4 MB for my 60-odd tickers. You can always allocate more memory to QuoteMaster if you have it on your machine). You must select the signal you've plugged into your serial port, but that's just about the extent of the complexity of the setup. A few minutes later, you're setting up your first quote page.

QuoteMaster Pro provides complete support for color, so displays can be as vivid as your imagination. You may group securities in unlimited numbers in the windows and you can call up intraday and interday charts at any time. Historical price and volume data are saved automatically for you, and because it can truly run in the background, there will be no holes in your data if you leave your machine on. Tick or intraday data are not saved; if you quit the program during the day, you lose that day's action, retaining only the high-low-close historical data. Alarms are available when running in the background and data may be exported to spreadsheets or databases easily.

USAGE

QuoteMaster Pro handles most details with extensive setup options (Figure 1). You may specify just about everything from the color of the lines to the handling and display of fractions. There is supposed to be an on-line help system, but I couldn't find it with the key combination or under the Apple menu. Relations with the Signal receiver I used were perfect, which is to say, practically invisible to me.

Quote pages are truly Mac-like, which means you can cut and paste tickers the way you would with any other Mac object. No more must you delete in one place and recreate in another; just cut the ticker you want and paste it where you want it. Page setup is actually fun. It's also nice that QuoteMaster 1.6 remembers your screen layout so that when you come back to it, it will automatically create what you want.

Graphics (Figure 2) are three-click deals: click the tradeable, click the graph icon and click OK to the preferences window that you previously set up. Graphs can be resized and moved about the screen as you wish. There are also vertical or horizontal ticker tapes for those finding this display useful. Any window you've created can be closed, thankfully, and if you've selected "monitor," a closed window with tradeables in it will have its tradeables constantly updated.

Adding a ticker is the path to setting up most of the activity in your system. At this point (Figure 3), you specify the type of chart with just about any time frame from tick to 60 minutes with a 15-minute default. You specify sizing and colors as well as alarms and portfolio information. You cannot, unfortunately, indicate short positions, so from a trading standpoint, the portfolio box is 50% crippled. It's

FIGURE 1

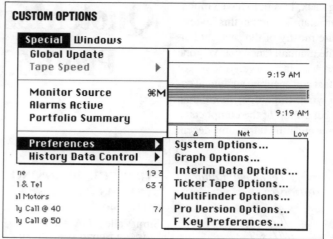

Host program options let you customize QuoteMaster to your heart's desire.

FIGURE 2

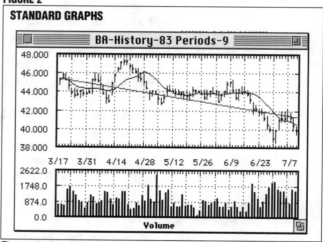

The standard graph may have four indicators, and the screen may be carved up in two charts of various sizes.

FIGURE 4

QUOTEMASTER DISPLAYS

By Symbol
By Name
By Price
By Bid
By Ask
By Volume
By Change
By Percent Change
By News Alerts

By Purchase Date
By Yield on Invest.
By Gain (Loss)
By Invest. CMU

Sorting the huge displays that QuoteMaster 1.6 can create is a breeze with the alternatives built into the program.

FIGURE 3

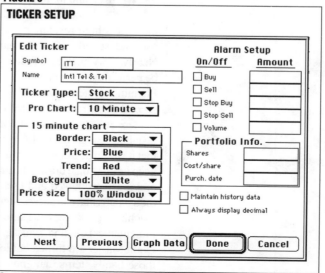

QuoteMaster's setup for the tickers allows you to specify just about everything that will control the display of that quote.

really not designed to keep track of anything but current positions anyway, but it can give you constant feedback on those through portfolio information columns in your quote windows.

To beat the bane of most intraday systems — creating correct ticker symbols —QuoteMaster 1.6 will guide you through the process with a series of windows that can create the symbols for you. Combinations of options and futures, indices, warrants, you name it — they can all be created by QuoteMaster 1.6. It will even create a whole raft of options symbols covering a range of strike prices for you, speeding things up immensely. Note that it doesn't automatically save the history for these new tickers — you must manually set up each ticker to assure that. Another startling feature (if you're using Signal) is the list of things you can put on a quote page (Figure 5). There's no way you can get all this on one screen!

Once you've created huge pages, they can be rapidly sorted with an option that can do it by name, by ticker, by percentage change, by purchase date or any of the other things listed in Figure 4. Since you could have 1200 ticker symbols loaded up in the window, this can rapidly get you what you want to know. Complementing this is the find function, which can instantly get you the ticker you want, no matter what window it's in.

One feature I particularly like is the import/export feature. This can actually spread the price quotes around your entire office by constantly exporting the data to a file, which can be accessed over your office network. No one needs to call you or look over your shoulder. They just mount your exported data file and look for themselves. Of course, you *could* go overboard here. QuoteMaster 1.6 will let you collect every tick if you wish, and since it has the most elaborate export capabilities I've ever seen, you may be tempted to fill all your spreadsheets and word processors with the data.

Importing is slick as well. The access window (Figure 6) lets you configure QuoteMaster to read just about anything that comes to you in tab or comma-delimited formats.

There is even an activity journal where you and the program may enter your notes on what's happening — sort of a built-in trader's notebook. This material is supposed to be stored in your system folder, further encouraging clutter. Fortunately, it didn't work in my test, but had I wanted it, putting it in the system folder would have been a demerit.

GRAPHICS

A host of indicators (Figure 7), the usual Mac flexibility in window-handling and a speedy processor (68030 at 16 megahertz or better) will make short work of 90% of your graphics needs (Figures 8 and 9 are examples). The graphics are great for 95% of daily monitoring. You can zoom in and out, draw trendlines semi-freehand and pull data values right off the chart — all high-end features. The only thing I didn't like was that you couldn't have one chart with both historical and intraday data on it. There is no live chart where the most recent bar is constantly updating, though there is tick-by-tick charting. I ran across only one minor bug in the candlestick charting.

ANALYTICS

QuoteMaster Pro comes with a solid suite of analytics (Figure 7). This isn't the package that will knock over Master Chartist for the Mac, but it's more than 90% of what most people need, comes with extensive defaults and customization, costs less and is extremely easy to access. Together with the chart specification window, you may use this to put together exactly the analytical presentation you want as a default, speeding up cycling through tradeables quite a bit. As a suggestion, being able to customize it by the tradeable — you may not want to use %R on everything, for instance — would be a nice addition.

NEXT STEPS...

QuoteMaster is so fun to use, you almost don't realize its limitations. On the other hand, I'm so comfortable with what's there, I wouldn't be shy about building on it. It would be nice to be able to compress data into weekly and monthly charts. The ability to define your own indicators would be neat to have someday. Defining new

tickers — say, the spread between Bank of America and Citicorp or the value of a portfolio — would be hot stuff. The portfolio should be able to show short positions. Some competing packages offer the ability to define a suite of charts and their indicators — a very nice idea.

QuoteMaster is ideal for the retail trader who wants on-line tracking and quick access to historical data. I easily imported data from CompuTrac to give me more history than I had picked up on-line. Because it runs so smoothly in the back-

FIGURE 5

SOME POSSIBLE QUOTEMASTER DATA

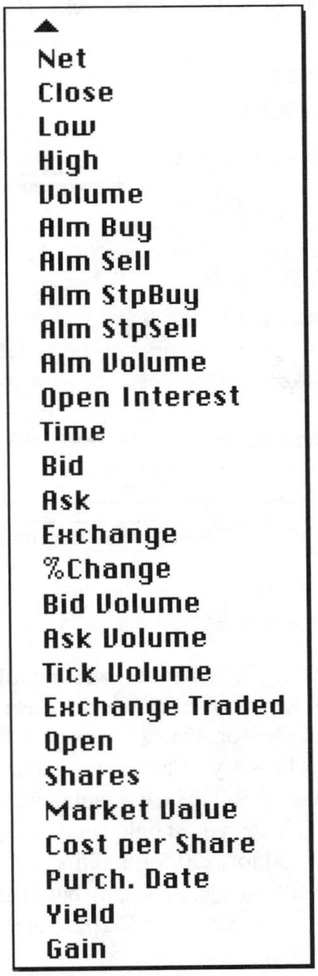

▲
Net
Close
Low
High
Volume
Alm Buy
Alm Sell
Alm StpBuy
Alm StpSell
Alm Volume
Open Interest
Time
Bid
Ask
Exchange
%Change
Bid Volume
Ask Volume
Tick Volume
Exchange Traded
Open
Shares
Market Value
Cost per Share
Purch. Date
Yield
Gain

Here's a partial listing of the various items of information that QuoteMaster 1.6 can display besides the standard price and change information. Any item can be displayed in any order in the window or deleted completely from the window's display.

FIGURE 6

DATA IMPORT AND EXPORT

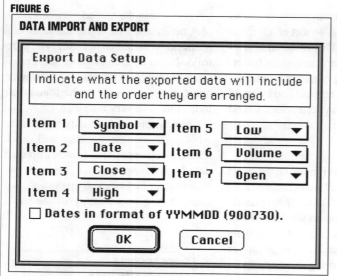

Import and export of data has exceptional flexibility; you can completely specify each column of data with this access window.

FIGURE 7

CUSTOMIZABLE INDICATORS

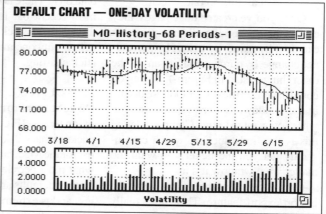

Twenty-three indicators, all customizable, give the user great flexibility of analysis.

FIGURE 8

CANDLESTICK CHARTS

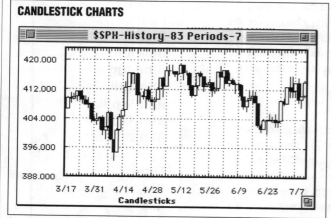

Candlestick charts are fast and beautifully done.

FIGURE 9

DEFAULT CHART — ONE-DAY VOLATILITY

A convenient default chart is the one-day volatility calculation. Other defaults include ease of movement and stochastics.

ground, QuoteMaster will rapidly assemble your own reliable database if you just leave it on. Quote screens are flexible and Mac-easy to arrange. Graphics and studies appear to be without fault. All for $495! True, you should count on spending $150 to $250 for additional RAM to dedicate to the program, but still, this baby's a great value and a pleasure to use.

John Sweeney is the Technical Editor of STOCKS & COMMODITIES.

The Equalizer 2.3

CHARLES SCHWAB & CO., INC.
The Schwab Building
101 Montgomery Street
San Francisco, CA 94104
(800) 334-4455 (6 a.m. - 8 p.m. PST)
Product: Investment information and trade submission software
Price data: Dow Jones, Charles Schwab & Co., Warner Computer
Fundamental data: Warner, Dow Jones, Standard & Poor's
Price: $69
Required equipment: IBM-PC compatible MDA, CGA/EGA/VGA adapter and monitor; floppy disk and hard disk drive; Hayes-compatible modem capable of 300-, 1200- or 2400-baud transmission; parallel or serial printer.

by John Sweeney

s a rule, editors are all for surprising you (pleasantly or not), so I felt my usual dutiful amazement when STOCKS & COMMODITIES honcho Thom Hartle laid The Equalizer on me. Being a futures trader, all I knew about Charles Schwab came from their ads in the financial press — "retail oriented," "stock oriented," "affordable" (that is, cheap), "computer-submitted trades" — since they don't deal in futures. I didn't anticipate a jolly time wading through everything in the 2.5-inch box planted squarely in the middle of my desk, especially to trade stocks, bonds, mutual funds or stock options.

Well, you're never too old to learn. There is, it turns out, a pleasant, easy way to get information, enter trades and monitor your portfolio, and it's The Equalizer.

Installation went swimmingly until the very last screen, when the program informed me it had modified my CONFIG.SYS file on its own. Being the nervous sort when dealing with the MS-DOS operating system, I suspiciously took a look at the modified file. It looked odd since the first two letters in seven of the 11 lines were missing. Two new files and buffer commands had been appended, one of which would have made it impos-

sible for another program to run on the machine without bombing.

I restored the mangled lines. This sort of error usually doesn't become apparent until much later when some other program starts misbehaving. I was grateful for the warning, but I'd rather have had the program ask for permission to modify these critical files, as most other programs do.

MENU-DRIVEN

The Equalizer is a menu-driven program covering the key areas (see Figure 1) that most retail traders need, but it is not a technical analysis program nor is there more than a smattering of the graphics that technical traders love so much. Here, you may discover the real-time market quotes (Figure 2), get a basic price/volume graph (Figure 3) and dig up a company profile before firing in an order. Market information is also available (Figures 4 and 5, S&P Marketscope and Market Indicators) to focus on the issues with movement potential.

This is all done effortlessly because all the communications with the data services, all the data handling and all the printing, storage, screen management and so on are done by the machine via The Equalizer. Though you don't work hard and The Equalizer seems flawless, the supporting data services sometimes have their traditional hangups. Warner Computer, for example, always fussy to access in my experience, could not be raised consistently for this review. The Equalizer can get hung up in the depths of the Dow Jones News Service's options (I counted 39 different databases you could access in all). As for day-to-day usage, The Equalizer does not use a mouse, but the menu system is as fast as your fingers. You may effectively escape the most tangled situation with the ESC key.

A much-ignored but vital function in these packages is the data maintenance and portfolio reporting. The Equalizer gets a B+ for the former, just below an A mostly because it won't let you change date fields in transactions once entered manually; you must delete and re-enter

the transaction. But if you use Schwab pricing, it's extremely fast getting the data and getting offline.

It gets an A from me for reporting. It's just a couple of keystrokes for the machine to go get the current prices from assorted databases and update your portfolio report for you (Figure 6). This sort of function has always been a nice idea, but usually freighted with obscure telecommunications and database problems. Here, it works like a charm. The Equalizer does all that for you.

Of course, the jazziest thing The Equalizer does is enter your trades for you. Given the security of the telecommunications capability, this is feasible and even trustworthy! Like everything else, you're guided through this process by detailed charts. When you've fully specified the order and accepted it, the program dials in to Schwab, checks your account status and margin and places the order.

SUMMARY

Really, what could go wrong here, to take a trader's view? Not the communications; that's solid. The Schwab account interface also appears bulletproof. You could go nuts with the research time and run up a fancy bill on Dow Jones, but you'd have only yourself to blame.

For stock and bond fundamentalists, the program itself is duck soup and very fast, at least on a 386. There's no Apple Macintosh version, unfortunately, so if you're a Mac addict, you are out of luck. Charting is nowhere close to state of the art, so don't throw away your analytical package or, for that matter, your data service subscription. Though you can export the data you download, getting it to an analytical package necessitates a detour through a spreadsheet, ASCII, or dBASE file format — an inconvenient sequence of which you'll soon tire.

The Equalizer is really a souped-up quotes, trading and portfolio tracking package; it focuses on the brokers' concerns about making your contact with the firm efficient, naturally enough. Given that, it still has great potential. It's handy as it is but hooked up with Dow Jones's analytical software, The Equalizer could be a real winner.

John Sweeney is the Technical Editor of STOCKS & COMMODITIES.

FIGURE 1

MAIN MENU

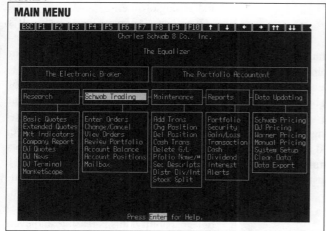

Research, trading and portfolio maintenance are the key parts of the Schwab package.

FIGURE 2

BASIC QUOTES

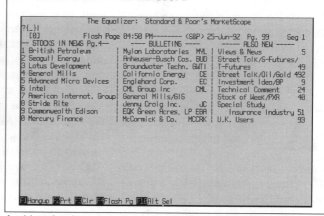

Basic quotes (shown here) and extended quotes are about 30 seconds away with The Equalizer.

FIGURE 3

TYPICAL CHART

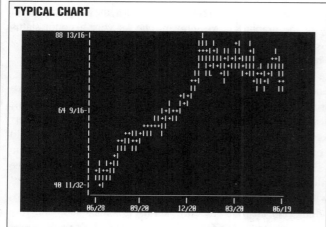

Unfortunately, graphics via The Equalizer are three or four years out of date.

FIGURE 4

STANDARD & POOR'S MARKETSCOPE

A quick read on the markets can be assembled via the Marketscope feature, which keeps you abreast of news and announcements. It also has a section of ideas and commentary that is an on-line education in itself.

FIGURE 5

MARKET INDICATORS

The Equalizer easily accesses up-to-the-minute market information for 42 different indicators. Top, left to right: DJIA, advance-declines, most active, greatest percentage up. Bottom: NASDAQ most active, the Arms index, S&P 500 Index, European currency unit index.

FIGURE 6

PORTFOLIO REPORT

The Equalizer is very fast at assembling a portfolio report with today's prices and dumping it to disk, printer or screen. Here, a Ford-GM spread.

Relevance III Advanced Market Analysis

Version 2.4

RELEVANCE III INC.
4741 Trousdale Drive, Suite 1
Nashville, TN 37220
(615) 333-2005
Product: Advanced-level technical analysis package for stocks, commodities, indices and mutual funds.
Price: $800
System Requirements:
IBM XT, AT, PS/2 or compatible hard-disk system. Cannot be run from floppies. Program uses approximately 1.4 megabytes of hard-drive space. The data disk included uses another 440K. PC/MS DOS 3.3 or higher. 512K minimum; 640K recommended.
Color card: EGA/VGA. Does not support Hercules card.
Monitor: CGA (black and white only), EGA, VGA.
Printer: Epson 9-pin MX/FX 80/100 or compatible; Epson 24-pin LQ 850, LQ 1050, LQ 2550, FX 1050 or compatible; Hewlett-Packard LaserJet series II (high-resolution charts and charts produced in the trading simulation mode may only be printed on Epson-compatible dot matrix printers).
Data formats: Supports CSI, CompuTrac and MetaStock. (Some functions such as converting daily data to weekly or monthly charts and the trading simulation mode only work with CSI data.)
Downloading: Built-in auto call program to permit modem downloading of CSI data.

---

by Barbara Star, Ph.D.

ccording to promotional literature, this version of Relevance III is eight times more powerful than earlier versions. And powerful it is, with such features as multiple-page creation, automerge of long- and short-term trend and indicator lines, automatic indicator updating of previous charts, Japanese candlesticks, a simulated trading mode and unattended chart printing (both 8-1/2 by 11-inch and 11 by 14-inch pages if your printer can accommodate it). The program boasts 32 technical indicators and a dozen other trading lines for the bar chart, called "studies," some of which cannot be found on other technical analysis programs. That's the good news.

The bad news is, with the exception of the main menu, everything is keyboard-driven with one, or sometimes many, keystrokes. This means learning several Alt, Ctrl and special-function keys — about on par with learning WordPerfect 5.1. There is no mouse support, not even pulldown menus from which to make selections. On the other hand, once portfolio and indicator files are created, the program moves quickly through its paces just by touching the space bar or arrow keys. I was told by someone who owns and uses Relevance III that some of the features he would like are not available on other software, so he was willing to put up with the time-consuming learning and typing required to run the program.

EASY INSTALLATION

Installation is relatively easy, but no autoinstall here. Installation requires making a directory on a hard drive and copying files from the program and data disks to the new directory. I encountered only one hitch. An error occurred partway through the copy process, but the problem resolved itself when I selected "retry" from the DOS prompt. The data disk is installed in its own directory using the same procedure.

Once the files have been transferred to the hard drive, the final step is to install the authorization file that copy protects the program and permits it to execute the program files. Unlike similar copy-protection systems that allow only one installation, this one allows up to three installations so you can use the program at work and at home without having to physically unload and reload the authorization file each time you want to run the program on a different computer.

THE OPERATING MANUAL

Relevance III comes with one of the best operating manuals I have seen. Not only does it describe each function and feature, it also provides several mini-tutorials that explains the keystrokes needed to access a particular feature. Mini-tutorials are a great way to take advantage of the full power the program offers. Unfortunately, as is often the case, the index does not completely cover the contents of the manual. For instance, when it came time to exit the program after my initial use, I searched the index and found no mention of how to leave the program.

My suggestion is to skim the manual once or twice before attempting to run the program. The program is complex and it's not easy to maneuver intuitively from one feature to another. Once a chart is displayed, however, pressing the forward slash key (/) provides easy access to a help menu that names the function or indicator and indicates which key to use.

Accompanying the manual is another really useful book written by program originator Maynard Holt called *Stocks and Commodities: Trading Methods and Strategies.* This book contains a wealth of information about ways to use the program features to perform Gann, Elliott and Andrews analyses and explains how to interpret the other indicators and studies contained in the program. These explanations even include chart illustrations, tutorials, and trading guidelines. Nice bonus.

GRAPHICS

The graphics on this program would make it a shame to use a monochrome monitor. The user can custom-define the colors or

FIGURE 1

PRICE CHART WITH MULTIPLE INDICATORS

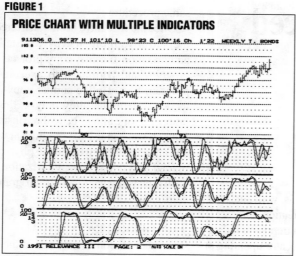

Depending on your graphics card and monitor, up to seven indicators can be tiled under the price chart.

FIGURE 2

DUAL SCREENS

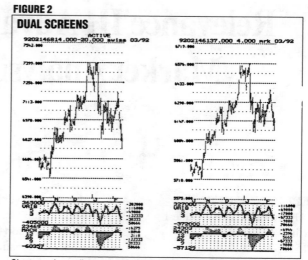

Charts can be easily compared with dual screens. Here, the Swiss franc and the Deutschemark are shown with the volatility range index and the MACD histogram.

stick with the default colors; there is a choice. One novel feature is the automatic color rotation of various moving averages to help differentiate them on the screen. Displayed across the top of each chart is the open, high, low, close and change from yesterday's close.

The maximum number of indicators that can be displayed under the chart depends on the type of graphics card and monitor used — two with CGA, five with EGA, and seven with VGA or S/VGA (Figure 1). The values of moving averages and indicators are placed along the right side of the chart in the same color as the indicator or moving average lines, which makes distinguishing between them very easy. There is even a dual-screen feature that permits chart comparisons (Figure 2).

FILES

With Relevance III, there is no need to load each chart. Creating a portfolio file makes chart watching a breeze. Build portfolios to include all your securities or divide them into categories, such as grains or biotech stocks. Once you have saved and named each portfolio, you can view each security one at a time simply by selecting the portfolio from the main menu. When a chart appears on the screen, just press the space bar to go to the next chart in that portfolio. The process is seamless and effortless.

All indicators and studies can be saved and are automatically updated each time new price information is added, which is a real time-saver. But there is a price to be paid for this, the use of hard drive or data disk memory space. Expect to use approximately 4K of memory for each study. Be forewarned, however, that it can mount up rapidly. The files created for this review took up about 50K of memory. Considering the convenience, though, it seems to be a small price to pay.

The data files that come with the program contain both ready-made portfolio and indicator files (Figure 3). Experiment with them first to familiarize yourself with the program and to stimulate ideas about how you might organize files and charts.

After developing portfolio and indicator files to your liking, create an autorun file and zip through your charts hunting for indicator/study setups that identify potential buy or sell candidates. Autorun files may be displayed on the screen or printed as hard copy.

The program permits easy toggling of price data between fixed parameters of 62, 124, 248 and 496 days. All user studies, trendlines and indicators selected in a longer time frame, such as 248 days, are automatically stored and displayed when zooming into a shorter-term price chart. This useful feature can help remind the trader of former support or resistance zones or Gann anniversary

dates. Traders who use CSI data may also compress daily data into a weekly or monthly format. Too bad it is not available for those who use other data vendors and program formats.

INDICATORS AND STUDIES

Indicators and studies compose the meat and potatoes of any technical analysis program, and Relevance III contains enough ingredients to satisfy even the hungriest trader (Figure 4).

Indicators: Users can select from among 31 technical analysis indicators and up to three moving averages. Choosing an indicator automatically calls up an indicator portfolio menu, where you can find many old standbys—relative strength index (RSI), stochastics, MACD — but you can also find some newer ones, such as the MACD histogram, Williams' ultimate oscillator, and Elder's bull and bear power oscillator. The indicators that intrigued me most were those with a unique twist, such as Relevance III's modified Commodity Channel Index (CCI) and RSI or the volatility range index. Not only that, have you ever seen indicators such as on-balance open interest or moving average convergence/divergence of *volume*? You will here (Figure 5).

In addition to the current numeric value of the indicator, Relevance III also shows the value for yesterday and the day before.

Even the mundane moving average assumes new glitter with options for shift-

FIGURE 3
DATA FILE STUDIES

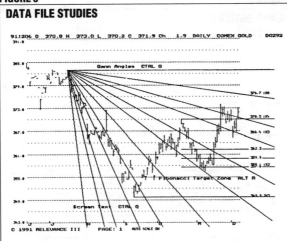

The data disk you receive with Relevance III contains ready-made portfolio and indicators files on which you can practice learning the program.

FIGURE 5
UNIQUE INDICATORS

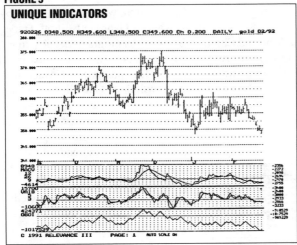

The MACD of volume, volatility range index, and on-balance open interest are some of the unique indicators built into the program.

FIGURE 4
INDICATOR AND STUDIES LIST

INDICATORS

MACD — Moving average convergence/divergence of price
MACV — Moving average convergence/divergence of volume
MACO — Moving average convergence/divergence of open interest
%R — Larry Williams' %R
%D — Stochastics
%DS — Slow stochastics
RSI — Wilder's relative strength index
RSIF — Relevance III modified RSI
TVOL — Total volume and open interest
OBV — On-balance volume
OBOI — On-balance open interest
MM — Single or dual momentum of open, high, low or close
MAMM — Moving average momentum with moving average
MMHH — Highest-high oscillator with moving average
MMLL — Lowest-low oscillator with moving average
UO — Larry Williams' ultimate oscillator
ADI — Williams' accumulation/distribution index
DM — Wilder's directional movement system
DI — Directional movement oscillator
ADX — Wilder's ADX and ADXR
CCI — Commodity Channel Index
CCI2 — Relevance III modified Commodity Channel Index
VRIB — Relevance III volatility range index — buy signals
VRIS — Relevance III volatility range index — sell signals
TI% — Trend index
OSC1 — Moving average oscillator
OSC2 — Moving average oscillator
OSC3 — Moving average oscillator
DRO — Daily range oscillator
MACH — MACD histogram
ERAY — Elder's bull and bear power oscillators

STUDIES

Andrews: Median and parallel lines for Andrews' pitchfork
Babson: Babson action-reaction lines
Bollinger: Bollinger Bands
Bands (fixed): Trading bands with fixed values
Bands (%): Trading bands using a percentage from the moving average
Channel: Divides trading channels into parts, for example, 1/4's
Cycles: Both fixed and Fibonacci (sequence, ratio, arithmetic) time lines
Elliott: 30, 50, 62% target price and/or retracements; channel lines; wave filters
Gann: Angles; swings divided into 1/8th's; percentage of high and low price; former tops and bottoms; anniversary dates
Percent high/low: Projects high or low price targets from a user-selected percentage
Time/price: A user-drawn swing chart
Trendlines: Single or parallel lines
Wilder parabolic: Parabolic stop and reverse
Relevance III modified parabolic

ing it forward or backward in time (good for cycle work) and choices that include (high + low + close) ÷ 3 or (high + low) ÷ 2. Additional moving averages can be selected while a chart is displayed.

Unfortunately, building an indicator portfolio forces the user to move through a series of steps beginning with the moving averages, whether you want them or not, and ending with typing out the abbreviations for each indicator selected. It's a cumbersome process that would progress much more rapidly and smoothly with a pulldown indicator menu and up or down arrow selection capability used on many other software. I hope this is targeted for change in upcoming versions.

Studies: Experiment to your heart's content with Gann lines, angles or retracements; Fibonacci price and/or time ratios; Elliott filters (based on Arthur Merrill's work); Andrews pitchfork; Babson action/reaction lines; Bollinger Bands; cycles; and price channels (Figure 6). Each bar chart retains the user's choice of bar chart studies, which are automatically updated when the user updates the data.

The studies are overlaid on the price chart and the program automatically selects different colors when more than one of the same type of study, for example, Gann angles, are being used. However,

FIGURE 6
STUDIES

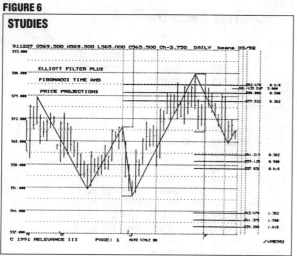

Three studies — Fibonacci time projections, Fibonacci price projections and an Elliott wave filter — were applied to March 1992 soybeans. The chart title was created with the write-on-screen feature.

FIGURE 7
CANDLESTICKS

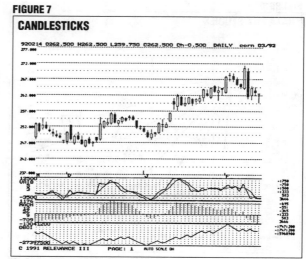

Convert any bar chart to Japanese candlesticks.

studies, moving averages and trendlines cannot be overlaid on the indicators tiled below the price chart.

The program includes an easy toggle that converts bar charts to Japanese candlesticks. The software does not label patterns, but any of the studies and indicators can be applied to the candlesticks (Figure 7).

Traders interested in Gann and Elliott work will find an impressive array of analytic tools. Although the program does not automatically locate Gann lines or label Elliott waves (as is done by the Advanced Gann and Elliott Trader and Stockmaster programs developed by Tom Joseph), it does permit user-selected high and/or low points from which the program will draw Gann lines, calculate Fibonacci ratios for Elliott wave projections, display time and price data and even project changes in price trend. Both time/price and change in trend data are exportable to a Lotus spreadsheet for further analysis. With these powerful features, users can advance their knowledge and skills well beyond the basics provided by most other technical analysis software.

Users may switch to the simulation mode to backtest indicator or study performance and make buy, sell or hold decisions as the price data and indicators are revealed one day at a time. But this highly desirable feature does have limitations. Time compressions, moving averages and some studies are not available in this version. In addition, it will only work with CSI data, and printouts can only be made on Epson-compatible dot matrix printers.

OTHER FEATURES
In keeping with his belief that consistently successful trading requires a well-thought-out plan, Relevance III's Maynard Holt designed several components of the program geared toward helping traders develop plans of action.

FIGURE 8, Part A
REPORTS

```
                    RELEVANCE III                 Copyright 1990
                    Daily Predictions             Portfolio: S2

Commodity      DATE    OPEN     HIGH     LOW      CLOSE    CHNG     PL-1      PL-2      PH-1      PH-2     RNGE 1 2 3 4  COMMENTS/ACTION
sugar 03/92    920214  7.990    8.050    7.980    8.020    0.000    7.983     7.947     8.053     8.087    0.070 0 + + -  _____
coffee 03/92   920214  68.900   69.750   68.900   69.100   -0.050   68.750    68.400    69.600    70.100   0.850 - - - +  _____
silver 03/92   920214  419.000  419.500  413.000  415.800  -4.500   412.433   409.067   419.733   423.667  7.300 - - - +  _____
bonds 03/92    920214  99.750   99.750   99.719   99.750   -0.063   99.708    99.667    99.802    99.855   0.094 - - - +  _____
mrk 03/92      920214  6132.000 6168.000 6075.000 6137.000 4.000    6085.333  6033.667  6178.333  6219.667 93.000 + - - -  _____
swiss 03/92    920214  6833.000 6865.000 6755.000 6814.000 -20.000  6757.667  6701.333  6867.667  6921.333 110.000 - - - -  _____
yen 03/92      920214  7821.000 7843.000 7802.000 7818.000 -7.000   7799.000  7780.000  7840.000  7862.000 41.000 - - - -  _____
wheat 03/92    920214  427.000  427.000  427.000  427.000  4.750    423.833   420.667   428.583   430.167  4.750 + - - -  _____
cattle 4/92    920214  77.150   77.570   77.050   77.300   -0.020   77.043    76.787    77.563    77.827   0.520 - - - -  _____
corn 03/92     920214  262.500  262.500  259.750  262.500  -0.500   260.500   258.500   263.750   265.000  3.250 - - + -  _____
beans 03/92    920214  568.500  568.500  566.000  568.500  -1.750   566.250   564.000   570.500   572.500  4.250 - + + -  _____
cocoa 03/92    920214  1070.000 1082.000 1070.000 1078.000 3.000    1071.333  1064.667  1083.333  1088.667 12.000 + - - +  _____
sp500 03/92    920214  413.500  414.900  411.300  412.250  -2.050   410.733   409.217   414.333   416.417  3.600 - - + +  _____
meal 03/92     920214  172.100  172.100  171.500  172.100  -0.700   171.467   170.833   172.767   173.433  1.300 - + - -  _____
gold 04/92     920214  357.200  357.500  354.400  355.100  -2.200   353.833   352.567   356.933   358.767  3.100 - - - +  _____
```

FIGURE 8, Part B

```
                    RELEVANCE III                 Copyright 1990
                    Pattern forecast              Portfolio: S2

Commodity      DATE    OPEN     HIGH     LOW      CLOSE    CHNG     RNGE 1 2 3 4  COMMENTS/ACTION
sugar 03/92    920214  7.990    8.050    7.980    8.020    0.000    0.070 0 + + -  _____
coffee 03/92   920214  68.900   69.750   68.900   69.100   -0.050   0.850 - - - +  _____
silver 03/92   920214  419.000  419.500  413.000  415.800  -4.500   7.300 - - - +  _____
bonds 03/92    920214  99.750   99.750   99.719   99.750   -0.063   0.094 - - - +  _____
mrk 03/92      920214  6132.000 6168.000 6075.000 6137.000 4.000    93.000 + - - -  _____
swiss 03/92    920214  6833.000 6865.000 6755.000 6814.000 -20.000  110.000 - - - -  _____
yen 03/92      920214  7821.000 7843.000 7802.000 7818.000 -7.000   41.000 - - - -  _____
wheat 03/92    920214  427.000  427.000  427.000  427.000  4.750    4.750 + - - -  _____
cattle 4/92    920214  77.150   77.570   77.050   77.300   -0.020   0.520 - - - -  _____
corn 03/92     920214  262.500  262.500  259.750  262.500  -0.500   3.250 - - + -  _____
beans 03/92    920214  568.500  568.500  566.000  568.500  -1.750   4.250 - + + -  _____
cocoa 03/92    920214  1070.000 1082.000 1070.000 1078.000 3.000    12.000 + - - +  _____
sp500 03/92    920214  413.500  414.900  411.300  412.250  -2.050   3.600 - - + +  _____
meal 03/92     920214  172.100  172.100  171.500  172.100  -0.700   1.300 - + - -  _____
gold 04/92     920214  357.200  357.500  354.400  355.100  -2.200   3.100 - - + +  _____
```

Relevance III generates pattern reports, price prediction reports and action reports.

One of those program components is the user's ability to create multiple "pages" — screens specifically designated for various types of analysis. For instance, you may reserve one page for weekly price charts plus indicators or studies that determine the intermediate- or long-term trend and support/resistance areas. Another page might contain only Gann analysis of daily data, while a third page might hold Elliott studies. Up to nine separate pages can be created, and by using the write-on-screen mode, the trader can label, leave arrows or make other notations as reminders. Each page has its own editor that allow deletions of indicator, study, moving average or trendlines. The goal is to create trading plans that enable the user to flip through his or her portfolio and quickly identify high-probability trades.

Some traders think only in terms of winning or losing, but experienced traders know that capital preservation is the real game. Relevance III has a risk/reward analysis function that helps traders make money management decisions before and after trading.

Let's say the risk/reward looks good and your indicators flash a "go." Should you enter the trade? First, check the Pattern Report, one of the highly original printouts that Relevance III generates. Based on the Nofri Congestion Phase model, the report uses a plus (+) or minus (-) pattern analysis of closing prices for the preceding four days. Holt suggests that two or three consecutive + signs means the market is overbought, so expect a short-term decline or congestion. If you were planning to buy, perhaps you should wait for a more favorable sign, but if you were planning to sell, this could be the time. Then consult the daily predictions report, which predicts tomorrow's potential high and low price using a formula developed by George Cole. When you are ready to enter the trade, print out an action report, which displays the open, high, low, close, change from yesterday's close, the true range and a space to write comments for each security in your portfolio (Figure 8).

SUMMING UP

Relevance III contains the basic components that traders need to develop a sound trading plan. While it does not present the array of indicators and studies available in some other technical analysis software packages or the ability to create and profit test your own formulas, it does offer a number of unique features that I have not seen in other programs. It possesses some outstanding features for traders interested in Gann, Fibonacci, Elliott, Andrews and cycle analyses. The daily charts are all updated automatically so the user can maximize the time spent on analysis.

Barbara Star, (818) 712-9020, is a university professor and leads a MetaStock users group. She is currently writing a book on candlestick analysis of stocks and commodities.

Trader's Money Manager

Version 2.0

COMMODITY SYSTEMS, INC. (CSI)
200 West Palmetto Park Road
Boca Raton, FL 33432
(407) 392-8663
Product: Software for statistical analysis of your trading results to figure the probability of making a given profit level.
Price: $499

Equipment required: IBM-PC or compatible computer. Coprocessor not necessary but strongly recommended. Requires hard disk drive. Minimum 640K memory required, 512K of which *must* be available to the software. CGA, EGA, VGA and Hercules monochrome graphics monitors are supported. Operating system must be MS-DOS or PC-DOS version 2.0 or higher. More than 190 different printers are supported for producing hard-copy tables and charts.

---

by John Sweeney

We'd better mention a few caveats before I get started on this one! I should say at the outset that CSI's Bob Pelletier is an old friend of STOCKS & COMMODITIES and an occasional author, not to mention a regular advertiser. I also have my own stake in the money management debate with my concept of maximum adverse excursion. All this flits by me when reviewing Commodity Systems, Inc.'s Trader's Money Manager (TMM).

First off, let me say that Bob is addressing the golden rule of trading, which is: don't *lose* money. For that he will get little gratitude and, I suspect, few sales, but he should at least get the highest professional respect. I have labored in this bailiwick since 1982 and it certainly hasn't made *me* wealthy or famous!

There's also another point for congratulation. This is a first in the industry, a professional analysis of a taboo subject: "Why trading systems go bad!" Bob's answer lies in the humdrum and careful thought of statistics, *not* a popular area for easy sales. However, Bob is the only data vendor who has realized — and brilliantly so — that his data customers will last longer if they don't wipe out trading easy-money schemes. Now all he has to do is entice people to study *why* trading systems go bad while charging them $500 for the privilege.

WHAT IS IT?

Trader's Money Manager is a program that takes the actual series of losses and wins you have experienced — or a simulated series — and through *simulation* computes the likelihood of you making a target profit level given the amount of money you're willing to commit to the campaign.

HOW IT WORKS

Trader's Money Manager develops an estimate of your chances by randomly sampling your profits and losses to simulate trading the system in question many, many times. However, it "degrades" your actual profits and increases your losses in doing so, so that the results will be worse than you experienced. The amount of degradation it inflicts depends mostly on the number of trading rules you are using to generate your trades.

WHAT IT GIVES YOU

Three things pop out of Trader's Money Manager: a chart (and table) showing the "probability" of reaching your profit goal at a range of capital stake levels (Figure 1), as well as a table (Figure 4) specifying how much money you should commit for any given probability of success; a "degree of merit" rating, which is the return on investment (Figure 2); and a "money management" graph (Figure 3) showing how you should change the number of contracts or lots you are trading as the campaign progresses.

For example, I ran the reversing system described in my June 1992 Settlement column through this little hummer, setting as my goal a profit of $35,000. Figure 1 informs me that it will take 413 trades to be 99.9% certain of making $35,000 from an initial $35,000 stake. To relate this to your more usual reporting, this is a system that generates 37 wins out of 50 trades — $29,230 in wins and $11,020 in losses over five years. Most traders would be intrigued with such results, but the Trader's Money Manager shows that while it's possible to gain 100% profitability from the system (that is, $35,000 in profit for $35,000 committed), it is likely to take 413 divided by 50 trades or eight years to do it!

Other capital commitments would produce equivocal results. In Figure 4, it turns out that the minimum capital needed to at least break even 95% of the time is roughly $2,000. In fact, Figure 2 rates the reversing system somewhere between good and excellent, though not "incredible" on an annualized return (ROI) basis. In Figure 1, committing only $10,000 (point A) to this system would give you a 72% chance (point B) of making $35,000 before wiping out. More conservatively (point C), you could be 95% confident that you'd have a 68% shot at making $35,000 before wiping out.

What you have to do here is pick the combination of stake and probability that you can live with. You can do it from the graph or from the detail in Figure 5, where I decided to go with a 99% probability requiring a commitment of $35,000. I could just as easily select another combination of capital and probability from Figure 5. This sets the parameters for my trading and is also used in the next round of analysis to determine how many con-

FIGURE 1

TRADER'S MONEY MANAGER

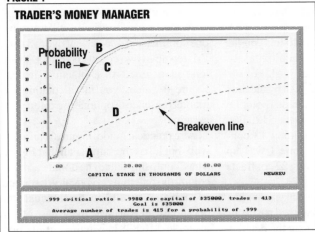

.999 critical ratio = .9980 for capital of $35000, trades = 413
Goal is $35000
Average number of trades is 415 for a probability of .999

To generate this graph, Technical Editor Sweeney specified that he would invest $35,000 and was shooting for a $35,000 return. The result of Trader's Money Manager's "cold shower" evaluation: a trading system that wins 74% of the time would be likely to take 413 trades to generate that level of return.

FIGURE 3

ADDING CONTRACTS

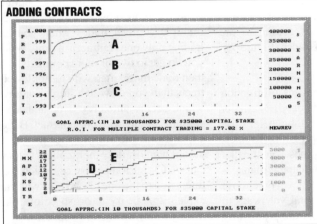

Trader's Money Manager shows you when to add additional contracts to your trading, based on your profitability to date. (Annotations are ours.)

FIGURE 5

USING A CAPITAL STAKE OF $35,000 TO MAKE $35,000 WITH A 99.9% PROBABILITY OF WINNING

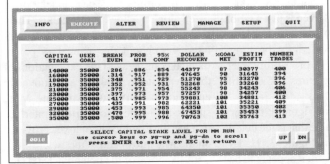

CAPITAL STAKE	USER GOAL	BREAK EVEN	PROB WIN	95% CONF	DOLLAR RECOVERY	%GOAL MET	ESTIM PROFIT	NUMBER TRADES
14000	35000	.286	.886	.854	44377	87	30377	400
16000	35000	.314	.917	.889	47645	90	31645	394
18000	35000	.340	.951	.929	51279	95	33270	396
19000	35000	.352	.952	.931	52268	95	33268	396
21000	35000	.375	.971	.954	55243	98	34243	406
23000	35000	.397	.973	.957	57257	98	34257	400
25000	35000	.417	.985	.973	59881	100	34881	412
27000	35000	.435	.991	.982	62221	101	35221	409
29000	35000	.453	.993	.985	64350	101	35350	402
32000	35000	.478	.995	.988	67453	101	35453	399
35000	35000	.500	.999	.996	70763	102	35763	413

SELECT CAPITAL STAKE LEVEL FOR MM RUN
use cursor keys or pg-up and pg-dn to scroll
press ENTER to select or ESC to return

If just $1,500 were committed to the task, we'd have only a 1.6% chance of getting both the $1,500 back and "winning" $35,000 (Figure 4). (Remember that breakeven is just a ratio, not a breakeven probability.) Technical Editor John Sweeney decided he'd be most comfortable at the 99.9% probability level of winning point E, which requires $35,000 of capital.

FIGURE 2

SAMPLE TRADING SYSTEM

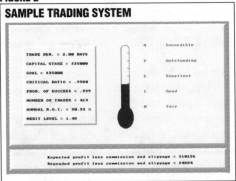

Expected profit less commission and slippage = $10126
Degraded profit less commission and slippage = $4004

Trader's Money Manager rated the trading system described in the July 1992 Settlement at somewhere between good and excellent based on its ROI.

FIGURE 4

CHOOSING COMBINATIONS OF PROBABILITY AND CAPITAL

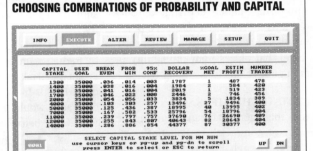

CAPITAL STAKE	USER GOAL	BREAK EVEN	PROB WIN	95% CONF	DOLLAR RECOVERY	%GOAL MET	ESTIM PROFIT	NUMBER TRADES
1300	35000	.036	.014	.003	1787	1	487	478
1400	35000	.038	.016	.004	1984	2	584	420
1500	35000	.041	.016	.004	2019	1	519	423
1700	35000	.046	.022	.008	2446	2	746	456
2000	35000	.054	.056	.033	3834	5	1034	389
4000	35000	.103	.303	.257	13496	27	9496	400
5000	35000	.125	.436	.387	18995	40	13995	402
7000	35000	.167	.582	.533	25796	54	18796	404
11000	35000	.239	.797	.757	37690	76	26690	409
12000	35000	.255	.843	.807	40643	82	28643	404
14000	35000	.286	.886	.854	44377	87	30377	400

SELECT CAPITAL STAKE LEVEL FOR MM RUN
use cursor keys or pg-up and pg-dn to scroll
press ENTER to select or ESC to return

The hard data behind Figure 1 is in a table you use to pick the combination of probability and capital you'd be comfortable committing to the system.

FIGURE 6

SPECIFYING CONTRACTS

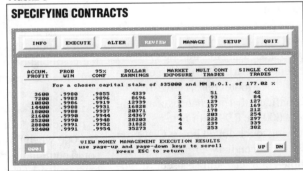

ACCUM. PROFIT	PROB WIN	95% CONF	DOLLAR EARNINGS	MARKET EXPOSURE	MULT CONT TRADES	SINGLE CONT TRADES
For a chosen capital stake of $35000 and MM R.O.I. of 177.02 %						
3600	.9980	.9855	4339	1	51	42
7200	.9986	.9896	8696	2	93	84
10800	.9986	.9919	12939	3	129	127
14400	.9988	.9931	16828	3	157	169
18000	.9988	.9937	20371	3	178	212
21600	.9988	.9944	24367	4	203	254
25200	.9990	.9948	28203	4	222	297
28800	.9991	.9952	31822	4	239	339
32400	.9991	.9964	35273	4	253	382

VIEW MONEY MANAGEMENT EXECUTION RESULTS
use page-up and page-down keys to scroll
press ESC to return

The detail behind Figure 3 guides you in specifying the number of contracts you trade at any one time.

FIGURE 7

MONEY MANAGEMENT EXECUTION

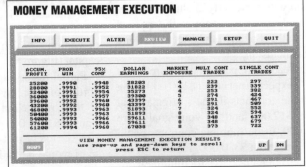

ACCUM. PROFIT	PROB WIN	95% CONF	DOLLAR EARNINGS	MARKET EXPOSURE	MULT CONT TRADES	SINGLE CONT TRADES
25200	.9990	.9948	28203	4	222	297
28800	.9991	.9952	31822	4	239	339
32400	.9991	.9954	35273	4	253	382
36000	.9992	.9957	39300	5	274	424
39600	.9992	.9960	43399	6	291	467
43200	.9992	.9960	43399	7	291	509
46000	.9993	.9963	51893	7	324	552
50400	.9993	.9963	51893	8	324	594
54000	.9993	.9966	59611	8	348	637
57600	.9993	.9966	59611	8	348	679
61200	.9994	.9968	67038	8	373	722

VIEW MONEY MANAGEMENT EXECUTION RESULTS
use page-up and page-down keys to scroll
press ESC to return

Accumulated profits of $61,200 with 373 multiple contract trades or 722 single contract trades.

tracts to trade.

In Figure 1 at point D, it turns out that

$$[\$10,000/(\$10,000+\$35,000)]=0.22$$

which is a result labeled in the manual as "the probability level required on the average to recover your capital stake." Actually, this line, the graphic depiction of the column of figures labeled "breakeven" on Figure 5, should not be on this graph, since it is not a simulated result like the other two lines but a simple calculated ratio of the stake to the stake plus the goal. This translates into an *a priori* probability reference, not an empirical probability as you might have anticipated. It should only be used as a breakeven reference point. You will need to select an operating capital level that places your probability of winning above this line.

GETTING THE MESSAGE

Money management means "figuring the number of contracts" in Pelletier's vocabulary. Though Figure 3 is tough to understand, the results are fascinating.

The top graph's horizontal scale is roughly 10 times your earnings goal, while on the left is the probability of staying solvent. Ignore the right scale for now and examine points A and B. If, for example, my goal had been to make $18,000 with a $35,000 stake using this trading system, I have better than a 0.9988 chance of making that. To be more conservative, I can be 95% confident that my chances of making the $18,000 are 0.9937 or better.

Turning to the dotted line at C, we run across an incendiary argument: when multiple-contract trading is used, "no additional resources are required and the probability of remaining solvent in the long run actually improves." That is, piling on with a properly evaluated system can make gobs of money with *less* risk! Bob will get plenty of chances to defend that conclusion.

To read the upper box of Figure 3, one could expect to net about $130,000 using multiple contracts if one's original goal were $12,000 and, if your goal were $35,000, using multiple contracts could generate about $380,000. Finally, the estimated annualized ROI for multiple-contract trading is 177.02%!

How this is achieved is explained in the lower part of Figure 3. The left scale — market exposure — refers to the step-function line and is meant to tell you the number of contracts you should trade as you progress toward your goal. For example, with a goal of $35,000, by the time I was up $80,000 I would trade (point D) 10 contracts. When I had made $120,000 (point E), I would start trading 13 contracts at a time. By the time I was up $320,000, I would be trading 22 contracts at a time.

What, you ask, about when you are just starting out and haven't zoomed past your goal? Check Figure 5, where the detail is shown for the lower levels of profitability.

Should you elect to be more cautious by trading a single contract, the estimate is that it will take you 722 trades for a goal of $61,200. In contrast, using multiple contracts would reduce getting to the $61,200 to below 373 trades (Figure 7).

RESULTS

I feel compelled to repeat this information so that you can think about what Pelletier is doing here. This time, though, let's use the tabular output the program provides, as in Figure 4, which comes from the first part of his analysis, the capital management section. This table lets you choose the combination of capital you want to sink into the system and the probability level of success with which you are comfortable.

I specified using Figure 4, making $35,000 when this analysis was run. If I could commit just $1,500 to the task, I'd have only a 1.6% chance of getting both the $1,500 back and "winning" $35,000. (Remember that breakeven is just a ratio, not a breakeven probability.) Looking over the table, I decided I'd be most comfortable at the 99.9% probability level of winning, which requires $35,000 of capital (Figure 5).

Partial results are in Figure 6, the top portion of a *lengthy* table that is the detail of the lower chart in Figure 3. Had I wanted $14,400 in profit, it appears to be 99.88% likely that I could achieve that and I would be trading one contract at a time for, on average, 169 trades. More conservatively, I could have a 95% confi-

dence level that there was a 99.31% chance of winning the $14,400.

At this level of profit, I'd still trade just one contract, but once I went over $3,600, I'd step up to two contracts (or 100-share lots) at a time. As a practical matter, Figure 6 guides you in calculating the market presence to optimally exploit your system.

As a practical guide, Figure 6 can work well, but it has the same snag that Figure 4 has, confusing data. The dollar earnings column is something cryptically described as "residual profit" in the manual but doesn't mean you have, in the case of our example, $16,828 in winnings in addition to your $14,400. It appears to mean that if you've gotten to the $14,400 level you most likely have $16,828. This could be dropped without loss of information.

In addition, in the multiple contract trades column, you appear to have 51 multiple contract trades when you are trading only one contract at a time. When you do get to two or more contracts, you then trade more often with multiple contracts than you do with a single contract, which seems unlikely — or at least a stimulus to stay with one contract. Better explanations and more logic in the calculations would reduce the number of phone calls to CSI customer service, which then refers you to the one or two reps who can explain this or try to do so before ultimately referring you to Pelletier.

HOW WELL IT WORKS

You install Trader's Money Manager with a lightning-fast install program. You'll be up and running in less than two minutes.

Things will slow down once you try to use it, unfortunately. The manual is organized along the lines of the menus. There is no tutorial, except that which is scattered throughout the manual as parenthetical comments to the explanations of the menu items. This is an innovative approach, but an unsuccessful one. More successful is the menu-driven interface that has the graphic alternatives provided on the Macintosh and Windows.

If, like 99% of the potential TMM customers, you are uncertain about the concepts involved, you should definitely pick up the TMM manual and read and ponder pages one through eight and 77-93 —

many times — pages that try to let you in on the program's purpose. I found the manual tantalizing but incomplete. I can also recommend Bob's article in the April 1992 S&C ("Money management using simulation and chaos").

Some pluses, briefly: beautiful color, nice graphic layouts. Fast on all the input and output, even data input. Easy, effective print drivers. Life-saving index will help you find the guidance you'll need in the manual, but this could be expanded even more. Some minuses: Deleting a line of data, should you have made entry errors, is not possible. Program occasionally locks up with an error message (for example, "Expected profit too small or capital too high"). Even a 386 needs a coprocessor to get the statistical work done in a few minutes.

KEY IDEAS

The key ideas are:
- We should degrade the trading results by a factor related to the number of rules we used to trade. The more rules, the more the degradation of the results.
- If things still look feasible, we should calculate the probability of achieving a specific monetary goal for various capital commitments to find the best combination for our personal situation.

- If, after trading, we find our profitability advancing, we should pile on additional contracts to maximally exploit our system with little or even less risk.

Underlying all these is the notion that trade results are independent of each other. There's good support for this assumption in traditional statistical testing, but it hasn't been examined with some techniques that more recent investigators such as Clifford Sherry employ. For now, it's the best premise available.

SUMMARY

There's no escaping getting smart about statistically evaluating your trading system if you want something back for the money you invest into TMM. The key thing will be to learn what a parameter is so that you can count them in your trading system and give the program the correct input. Remember, all it has are your results, which it just samples. All the statistical features of your system come from *you*. If you're not up to that, you've got some training to go through.

Even harder will be giving up some cherished system — accepting the evaluation that what you've got may not be safe to trade.

After you find something tradeable,

you must get comfortable sorting out capital stakes at different probability levels. This is real world, not the one-shot "how much money can you get into the account today?" stuff. Plus, you'll have to get comfortable taking on more lots as you go along.

Still, with TMM everything could hardly have been made easier for you. All you have to do is put in the wins and losses from your experience or testing and hit a few keystrokes to get a vital, realistic analysis in practically no time at all. If you're trading systems, you'd better pony up the $500 and give all your trading ideas a hard, realistic look with Trader's Money Manager.

John Sweeney is the Technical Editor of STOCKS & COMMODITIES.

FURTHER READING

Sherry, Clifford J. [1990]. "How random is random?" *Technical Analysis of* STOCKS & COMMODITIES, Volume 8: August.

Sweeney, John [1992]. "Reversing for dollars," STOCKS & COMMODITIES, June.

Market Center 4.0

BONNEVILLE MARKET INFORMATION
19 West South Temple
Salt Lake City, UT 84101
Phone: (800) 255-7374, (801) 532-3400
Product: 19,200 baud real-time futures and stock quotes, delayed futures and end-of-day stock quotes.
Price: Setup, satellite dish, receiver, controller, $597; FM reception setup and equipment, $397; datafeed starting at $197 per month for stocks *or* commodities. Exchange fees are extra and may be the bulk of your costs.
Required equipment: *Futures:* PC-XT or better with 640K RAM, CGA or monochrome display, RS232 serial port. *Futures and/or stocks:* Uses AT or PS/2 or better. Add one megabyte of memory for each additional 4,500 quotes capability.

When I first started trading in 1981 or 1982, I shopped real-time systems and settled on Bonneville Telecommunications. They were quite professional: a Bonneville rep had my den wired for pricing in less than a week. It was an FM feed and because I live on top of one of Seattle's higher hills, the reliability was perfect. It was only several years later, when I started reviewing things for STOCKS & COMMODITIES, that I discovered that all the world doesn't run that well.

Bonneville still does, though. The old reliables from Utah are still sending out the prices and news in a datafeed that has seen the emergence of major rivals but is still chugging along reliably. My general impression? Old interface but vast capability and good pricing.

INSTALLATION

This isn't too bad. We used the FM setup for the datafeed. Software installation is old news. Instead of typing INSTALL, you get to type "COPY A:*.* C:\MC1" — and that's it. You run it and the program latches on to the datafeed itself

before running you through setup questions, some of which are explained in the manual and some of which are not. Immediately, you're into the quote page setup mode, though you won't know if things are working until you feed it a quote symbol and wait for the datafeed to send it for display on the screen.

The manual is a mixed bag. I give it high marks for having a complete set of symbols for virtually everything (63 pages' worth!), mucho redundancy and clarity. But the absence of an index or tutorial, a minimal table of contents and being out of date or silent on some subjects are disappointing. The organization is, well, sporadic. Fortunately, a new one is in the works and telephone help is genuinely helpful.

Market Center makes good use of expanded memory and the more that is available, the more symbols you can follow. The basic core is 1,000 from the datastream's 100,000, but you can go up to 23,000, should you have the memory and the wish to do so. The program runs nicely under Windows 3.0 but would not collect data or update files while you're off doing something in some other window — at least for us. Bonneville says,

however, that customers can multitask under Windows, but that it recommends using Desqview.

QUOTES

The bane of on-line systems is setting up your screen. Here, most of the work is done for you, a real plus. There's really only one format (Figure 1) and you just decide what symbols you want. The rightmost two or three columns can be changed to show information on a particular investment, bid/asks, volumes, ranges and so forth.

The function keys are active — *extremely* active — but you'd never know it from this screen. Market Center has saved screen space by shipping you a template to fit on your keyboard to guide your use of function keys. For example, to set up an alert, hit F6. To get news, try F10. There are also market statistics, news, your personal notes — a ton of stuff can be accessed through these keys, and once you get the hang of it it's extremely fast because it's keyboard-based. Should you be keyboard-impaired, however, there is no mouse or menu support.

An especially neat screen setup feature is the use of "wild card" symbols, programmer-talk for the ability to specify all the variants of a particular symbol. For example, type "US*" and, over time, your screen will be filled with *all* the symbols coming in that have "US" in them. This reduces typing by an order of magnitude! Maybe *two* orders. I typed in "US" and waited a day. Every bond future and re-

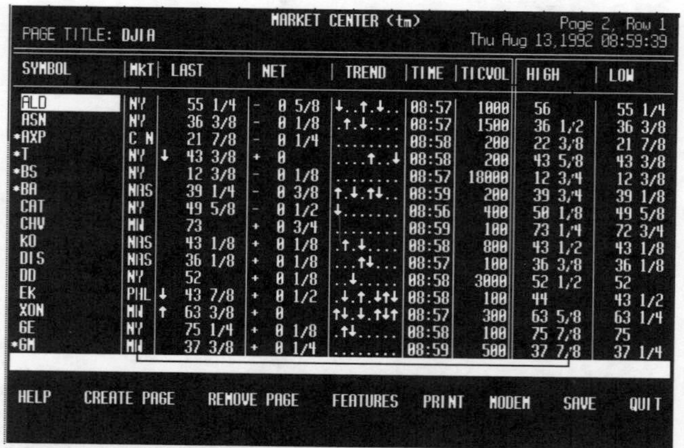

FIGURE 1: TEXT-BASED INTERFACE. *Market Center uses a text-based interface, the right two columns of which are reserved for goodies like statistics and alerts.*

SEPARATE ADD-ONS

Like many data feeds, Market Center is just the beginning of the offerings you can access. Software that can use the information from BMI include Ensign IV, Aspen Graphics, DollarLink, Echelon, First Alert!, MBC Software, Master Chartist, MetaStock Professional, Optionomics, Papyrus Technology and Windo Trader.

GOODIES

Bonneville exploits its high-speed data path in more ways than simply shipping numbers to you. Also available is a host of news and advisory services, some of which are listed here:

Service	Price/Month	Comment
Bonneville News	Free	Wide range of topics
Bullish Consensus	$10	
Cattlefax	$55	Members only
CBOT Liquidity Data Bank	$70	Overpriced
Computer Petroleum Corp.	Varies	Commercial users
Dow Jones alerts & headlines	$17	Okay if day-trading
Futures World News	$75	Pricey
IPO Spotlight	$40	Call your broker
Market News Service	$20	Okay if day-trading
Market News full stories	$350	Expensive but cheaper than Dow Jones
National Provisioner	$70	Trade news
Petroflash	$125	Pricey but good
Software Aided Market Investments (SAMI)	$15/area	Okay deal
SGA Goldstar Research	$60	Okay if you like their stuff

lated option was placed on my screen for me, neatly alphabetized. Then I deleted the ones I didn't want. It worked so well, I used it on every one of my tradables and it reduced the job to less than five minutes.

Of course, in setting up this way I also produced some pages with 300-plus lines on them before I thinned it down some. You could also increase manageability by splitting up your pages into smaller groups, perhaps an industry group or a personal portfolio, and you may also direct the computer to take you directly to a particular symbol or page. You can get a "snap quote" on an issue if you have thoughtfully instructed the machine beforehand to collect the information somewhere on some page. This contrasts to the capability of keeping the last quote on everything that comes in so you can get a quote — right *now* — on something you haven't been tracking.

Market Center itself provides no historical data other than the 52-week high and low for stocks, so if you immediately want to know past prices having seen the current price, count on buying an add-on package like Ensign IV or Master Chartist, to name only two of many (see sidebar, "Separate add-ons"). Market Center will save the data for you as an ASCII file that your "other" software will import.

NEWS

Pumping up the datafeed to 19,200 baud means there's lots of room to send you more than numbers. These real-time networks have the potential (once costs decline) to become pathways for all your trading information, custom-tailored to your demands. For now, you pay for each separate add-on (see sidebar), anywhere from $17 a month to $700, depending on how much you want. You could structure things to get your basic data, your guru's incantations and trading signals from your technical advisor, all instantly available via Bonneville Market Information (BMI) and your computer.

Access is fast via the keyboard: F10 to get news and a few keystrokes to highlight the story you want. It's worth noting that BMI provides an excellent *free* news service (Figure 2) with great depth. BMI even delivers weather and precipitation maps (Figure 3). I preferred Bonneville News to Dow Jones, as the full Dow Jones stories cost $600-700 per month when delivered real-time and you can get the Dow Jones headlines for just $17 per month. The add-on news section even includes trading advice and signals as in Figure 4 and you may save up to 2,000 stories at a time based on your memory or just "lock" the ones you want to keep. (See sidebar, "Goodies.")

DATA DOWNLOAD

To get the most out of Market Center, you'll want it to save data that your other analytical programs can access. In this way, you may be able to build up an extensive database at a reasonable price. It won't be cheap; this is real time and you must pay exchange fees, but if you're going to get real-time data you may as well get the most for your money by saving it.

Unfortunately, this process isn't really seamless. You can set it up to be automatic but what you get is an ASCII file that you and your analytical package must then access every day. Needless to say, if anything relies on you (or me) there are going to be holes in the data, destroying the utility of the whole affair. Much better is the ability I've seen in other programs to write data directly into the analytical program's data format periodically and/

or automatically. Ideally, this would be done in the background by a terminate and stay resident (TSR) and the only decision you would make would be to leave the machine on 'round the clock.

> **Do you need on-line service? Consider the price carefully. The costs of exchange fees are a considerable overhead on your trading. Take only those you really need.**

PORTFOLIO MANAGEMENT
Second-by-second updating of your trading positions is available, but only the basics. By setting up a page for each client or portfolio, you can keep track of that particular portfolio's total (Figure 5) and its individual components (Figure 6). No comprehensive tabular summary is available on screen or as a printout.

SUMMARY
Do you need on-line service? Consider the price carefully. The costs of exchange fees are a considerable overhead on your trading. Take only those you really need. Perhaps delayed data would be better, especially if you are not day-trading. Bonneville does provide a combination of both real-time and delayed data, so get what you want real time and you get access to delayed futures quotes.

Considering the technology, the price of the datafeed itself is very reasonable. If you can make it even more valuable by accumulating data you would subscribe to anyway, it might be even more worthwhile. However, Market Center's clumsy dump to other packages makes it unrealistic here. There's too much operator intervention and, thus, chance for error or omission. Perhaps it will be better with BMI's own package, Ensign IV. We'll know more about that next month.

Market Center is very competitive as a convenient quotes and news package. They practically give it to you. Given that the news via Bonneville Telecommuni-

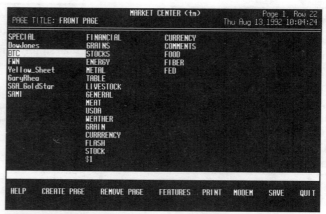

FIGURE 2: NEWS SERVICE. *The news service, here listed under its old name BTC for Bonneville Telecommunications, is free and covers a tremendous range of subjects.*

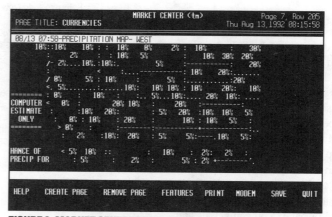

FIGURE 3: MARKET CENTER NEWS CATEGORY. *Yes, it is a map and it shows the precipitation probabilities for the western U.S., just one of 20 free categories of news available via Market Center.*

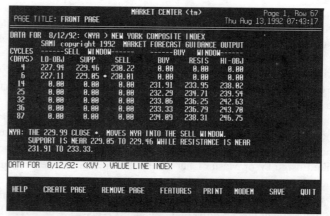

FIGURE 4: SAMI CYCLIC FORECASTER. *Gurus arrive via the 19,200-baud datafeed as well as prices. Here, a cyclic forecaster (Software Aided Market Investments) points out support and resistance levels.*

cations is free, that's quite a deal. Still, it's not a standalone best buy for a technical trader because most of the data go down the drain and can't easily be used later.

There aren't built-in graphics of historical or even intraday data and no analytics at all.

Finally, I couldn't run Market Center

in the background and use my machine for running the packages that *do* have graphics and analytics; I had to choose between collecting data and doing trade setup, not a fun choice while the markets are open. Bonneville did say that Market Center will run under Desqview, but there is no documentation provided on the subject; at this time, you will have to contact Bonneville to implement multitasking in Desqview. Market Center, it seems, needs to be paired with its powerful cousin Ensign IV to become a solid deal.

John Sweeney is Technical Editor of STOCKS & COMMODITIES.

FIGURE 5: PORTFOLIO SUMMARY. *Market Center's portfolio summary is terse, to say the least.*

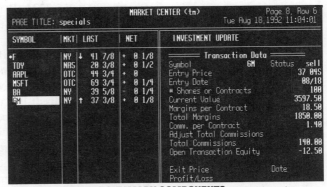

FIGURE 6: MARKET SUMMARY COMPONENTS. *To break out the components of a market summary, you must remember the items and call them up individually, as in this GM short.*

Ensign IV

ENSIGN SOFTWARE
2641 Shannon Court
Idaho Falls, ID 83404
(208) 524-0755
Phone: (800) 255-7374 (BMI)
Product: Full-featured real-time trading support system
Price: $695 plus $10 a month for the basic package, $1,295 plus $10 a month for the deluxe version. Free demo available.
Equipment required: IBM compatible, 286 or better, 16 MHz or better, 640K RAM, EGA or VGA, 20-MB hard disk (or more), serial and parallel ports, Epson or Hewlett-Packard Laserjet compatible printer, MS-DOS 3.0 or later. Financial data screen data feed from Bonneville Market Information via FM or satellite.

by John Sweeney

 nsign IV, which is fed by the Bonneville Market Information (BMI) service, is an impressive package, even for a DOS-based product. It's big, for one thing, with just about every feature I'd use in trading, but it's also fast and easy to use: a nimble giant. Even though this was developed by just one guy, Howard Arrington, it's as finished as products being turned out by the committees at Microsoft.

INSTALLATION

Truly slick. Type "Install" and the next thing you know, you're not only installed, you're running. Ensign IV has put itself on the drive, installed more than 200 data files and automatically gone into the tutorial to teach you about itself.

SETUP

The mouse works even though this is a menu-driven program! I mention this because it's a typical grace note in Ensign IV, which is really a keyboard-based, menu-driven program. As such, for the keyboard-enabled, this program is extremely fast: virtually instantaneous on a 386/33 machine.

The manual is large and well-organized along the lines of thought of the typical user: that is, (1) How do I get this to run? (2) Where are the prices? (3) Where are the charts? To help, should one have any patience at all, there is a truly outstanding self-playing tutorial to whisk you through the entire program while you watch. This is worth doing, if only to appreciate the immensity of what you face on the screen.

Another way to get started is to use the online version of the manual itself, a menu-driven vehicle for exploring the program. As you can see from Figure 1, Ensign IV presents you with just about every tool for day-to-day trading in a

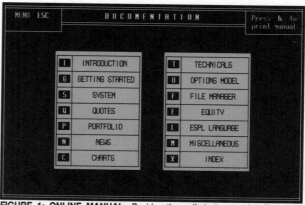

FIGURE 1: ONLINE MANUAL. *Besides the self-playing tutorial, Ensign IV features a comprehensive online manual to answer questions or use just to get started with the mammoth program.*

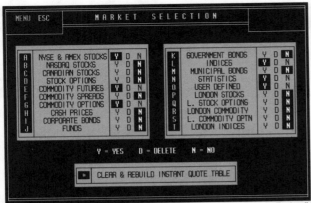

FIGURE 2: BMI. *Via BMI, you can track just about everything through Ensign IV including cash prices, rarely found in real time.*

FIGURE 3: ENSIGN QUOTE SCREEN. *A typical quote screen in Ensign IV is one of its rare points of inflexibility. There are nine different formats so one will likely be close to your favorite.*

well-integrated package. The "P" stands for the ability to flop a screenful of symbols up at once rather than ordering up quotes individually. Your personal portfolio management area is labeled "Equity" and the ability to do a little formulaic machination through ESPL programming is under "L."

We were able to run Ensign IV under Windows, but unfortunately, documentation was not provided. There is, however, documentation for running Ensign IV under Desqview.

MARKETS

Before drawing up screens, pick your markets. Choices are in Figure 2, a listing with which I could not cavil. With that you go to structuring a portfolio quote screen, of which you have 16 as in Figure 3. These arrive already filled in with items, most of which you will delete but which basically serve as ready examples. The screen format may be changed around to nine different versions but is really a rare point of inflexibility — I like to be able to see just the columns I want to see. You can select the colors you want for the quotes page.

Use a little cunning at this juncture: the sequence in which you set up the pages may help later because some screens may be condensed in sequence by F-key options. Thus, to get stocks, bonds and energy all on one screen from three successive pages, put these pages one right after the other. An instant quote function provides the open, high, low, last, bid and ask from anywhere in the program.

Being hooked up to Bonneville Market Information (BMI) also means news and weather information is available in spades, arriving at 19,200 baud. The information from Dow Jones is truncated to headlines but the BMI news service is there in full. Weather data are also constantly available via the news service or the once-a-day maps.

Alerts are set via the page setup function and will normally pop up in the top right-hand corner of your screen unless you're viewing a weather map, in which case all you get is the beep. Alerts set in either manner show up on all your graphics screens automatically as green lines. As far as I could tell, there's no way to instantly shift to the chart or the quote page with the alert on it. Alerts can also be set visually on the graphs with the cursor or mouse pointer and, because the intraday charts are live, you may see the alerts hit if you're in that chart.

CHARTS

What everyone *really* wants are charts. Here you get pro-level charting at extreme speed. From your basic intraday chart, single keystrokes take you to daily, weekly, candlesticks, Market Profile, point and figure and Equivolume (Figure 4).

The program never bombed on me. If I had a problem, I was always able to start fresh via the escape key and then get what I wanted by asking for it first thing.

At this point, you really must have a demo to play (and you can get theirs free): I simply can't show all the options available. (See sidebar, "Technical studies,"

for a listing of what's available.) My favorites — moving averages, on-balance volume (OBV) and relative strength index (RSI) — are always going to be available and you'd naturally check for yours. What I did appreciate, though, was the ability to change the cursor to large or small crosshairs (Figure 5), one keypress technical studies (Figures 6 and 7), putting several graphs on one screen in various configurations, annotating the charts and the noise feature.

Noise feature? Yes. Get this: you hit control N and the machine beeps higher with each rising tick and lower with each lower tick. You don't even watch the screen to feel the market's pulse; your subconscious monitors the frequency and tone of the ticks. At first it might be annoying, but after a while it's reassuring. A truly unique grace note!

You can easily bounce from window to window with the space bar and immediately edit the data, throw on technical studies for just that window, set up alerts, zoom to full screen and back or even completely respecify the window — *pop!* — just like that. It's easily the best graphic screen manipulation interface I've seen on a DOS-based technical analysis program.

It's not the best for selecting data, though. You don't make choices of what you want from lists; you must remember the symbols you want and the codes for how they are to be displayed — and then type it all in without errors. Even if the program is forgiving, this part of Ensign IV is old news.

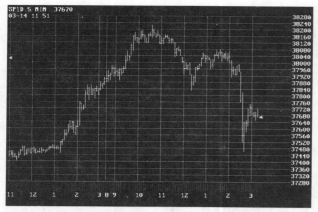

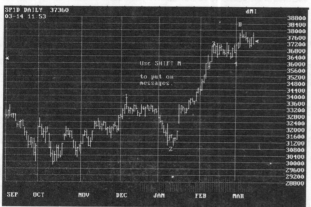

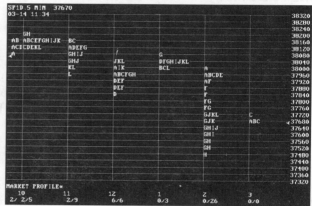

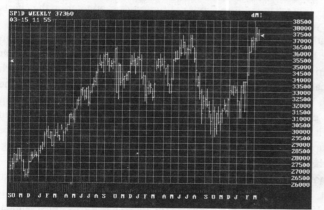

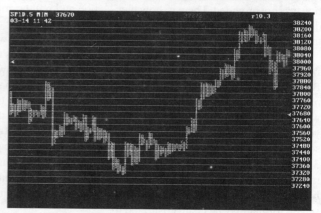

FIGURE 4: ENSIGN GRAPHICS. Ensign IV graphics go from tick to monthly in single keystrokes. For example, the chart at top left is a five-minute bar chart. Below that is the daily chart and below that is a weekly chart. Ensign IV will also make monthly charts (not shown). You can also produce candlestick charts, such as the five-minute candlestick (top right), Market Profile charts (next down), point and figure (second from bottom) or overlay charts, such as the Equivolume chart overlaid on a bar chart at bottom right.

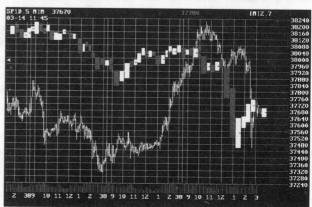

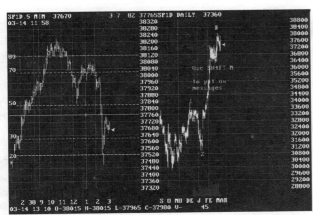

FIGURE 5: ENSIGN INDICATORS. *Indicators — a vast number of them — can overlay the price charts or go on separate charts. Up to four charts can be shown on a screen, each with its own indicators and annotations.*

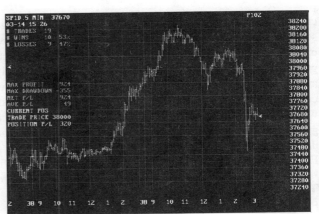

FIGURE 6: SYSTEM EVALUATION. *Ensign IV evaluates a parabolic trading system on live S&P five-minute data virtually instantly, showing all longs and shorts and totaling financial results.*

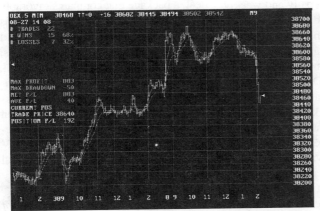

FIGURE 7: MOVING AVERAGE CROSSOVER. *A moving average crossover system catches a nice pop in the OEX.*

FIGURE 8: INDICATOR SPECIFICATIONS. *Not only are the usual indicators available in Ensign IV, but you can give each of them nine different sets of parameters via this specifications table.*

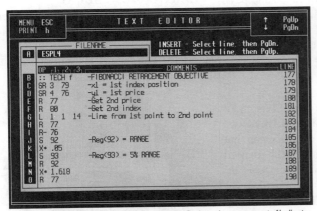

FIGURE 9: ESPL INDICATOR PROGRAMMING. *A moderate amount of indicator programming can be done through ESPL, the software's own programming language.*

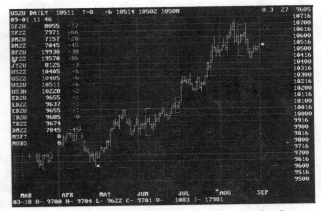

FIGURE 10: ENSIGN CYCLE FUNCTION. *Ensign IV's cycle function allows you to define the cycles (the arcs on the bottom) or let its built-in cycle function do the work (the brackets by the price bars).*

You can set up studies with *nine* different sets of parameters (Figure 8 shows three of these sets), modify the studies with three different constants, run studies on studies, set alerts on studies — you name it. I couldn't find anything I *couldn't* do.

PROGRAMMING

To provide even more capability, Ensign IV provides the Ensign Software Programming Language (ESPL), a capability that I regretfully predict will not take the world by storm, given the syntax it uses (Figure 9). ESPL will, however, let you create your own symbols to place on your screens — a spread or the crack value, for example. It can also do a fair amount of graphics work — drawing lines, boxes and so forth — on the chart for you, a capability for laymen I haven't seen anywhere else. Indeed, sample ESPL programs (Ensign IV calls them "toolkits") draw up Andrews pitchforks and even Fibonacci retracement lines.

TRADING SYSTEMS

Ensign IV provides easy testing of simple, indicator-based trading systems directly from the charts, provided you have thoughtfully set up your trading indicators and trading rules beforehand. It's not so easy to set up the parameters of the trading systems (as a mnemonic, what

---

TECHNICAL STUDIES

Accumulation/distribution volume
Andrews pitchforks
Bollinger bands
Candlesticks
Commodity channel index
Cycle arcs/forecasts
Derivative stop
Directional movement index
Envelopes
Equivolume
Exponential moving averages
Fibonacci lines
Fibonacci time ruler
Gann fan lines
Gann time ruler
Keltner channel
Market Profile
Momentum
On-balance volume
Oscillators
Parabolic stop
Point and figure charts
Prime lines
Relative strength index
Simple moving averages
Stochastics
Support and resistance
Swing lines
Uni-channel
Volatility stop
Volume and open interest
Williams' %R

---

does ",4X%" suggest to you? Me neither) and figure out how to invoke them. But once they are set, the test is virtually instantaneous and you may quickly shift to another chart, rerunning the same system, again instantly. It would be nice if Ensign IV would always put the tabular summary someplace where the price bars aren't, but this is a minor quibble. The testing system is fine for indicator-based systems without complex logic.

DATA

The bane of online systems is a hole in the datastream; you end up with a gap that fouls up all the indicators and your charts. Ensign beats this with daily and weekly refreshes. I just left the machine on for a week and sometime on Monday, it filled in all the three-month gaps in my data — every symbol on all my screens. That's quite a pile of data. Daily, weekly and monthly files are updated automatically each day after the markets close.

If that isn't sufficient, you can also get data from your ASCII, tick, CSI or CompuTrac data files via Ensign IV's file manager. Ensign IV will even automatically *update* your CSI and CompuTrac files, should you forget to call for your daily download. (That doesn't mean you can stop paying for CSI data, because it expires if you don't download and pay.) There's also a text editor to allow data editing and a "merge" function to facilitate handling splits or building perpetual contracts.

SUMMARY

It's hard to convey the size of Ensign IV — or its nimbleness and speed. I reviewed it on a 386/33 with a co-processor (but Ensign doesn't use it) and medium-speed hard disk; most of its reactions were instantaneous. It never froze and never bombed. It started itself, hooked itself up to the datastream and anticipated my needs from tutorial to quote page.

Remnants of early days remain: the tabular input format (smoothly overlaid by mouse control); the segregation of specifications for the quote pages, indicators and systems tests from the display pages or charts; and the need to remember lots of different keyboard inputs and symbols with no hints. These are seamless in

---

modern packages. There are funny conventions: Shift-letter gets you the *lowercase* letter. There are pleasant conveniences: point and click circle drawing and regression lines plus cycle data calculation (Figure 10). In return, you get speed, speed, speed and vast capabilities in programming and graphic data display.

Ensign's data refresh service is a tremendous plus because it constantly corrects and fills gaps in your data, solving a problem that all broadcast services have. BMI has a delayed-data service, reduced-cost option available, making this a service that every trader can afford.

For the money, Ensign IV is a good deal, a package that compares favorably to other online trading support systems and exceeds most in its power and customization. Quotes, news, graphics, indicators, trading systems, data refresh, hooks to CSI or CompuTrac, a programming language, options, portfolio tracking: What's missing? We'll find out when we see Ensign V, scheduled out in December 1992. Meanwhile, pair Ensign IV with a fast PC and you've got a real winner.

John Sweeney is Technical Editor of STOCKS & COMMODITIES.

ADDITIONAL READING

Sweeney, John [1992]. "Market Center 4.0" product review, STOCKS & COMMODITIES, November.

Viking 5.12

DELPHI ECONOMICS
8 Bonn Place
Weehawken, NJ 07087
(201) 867-4303
Product: Integrated charting, trading model builder, day-to-day trading signal monitor. Also has options calculations and portfolio maintenance functions.
Price: $495
Requirements: Not specified. Probably IBM compatible, 512K RAM or more, 20-megabyte (MB) hard disk.
Datafeeds: None, but can read data from I.P. Sharp, Telemet America, Data Broadcasting Corp., Warner Computer Systems, MetaStock, CompuTrac, CSI

iking? I think it's an in-house program that Delphi Economics whipped together. Looks like they built it up over time and then recast it some for commercial consumption.

"Not bad, but a little rough around the edges. Pretty fast, okay graphics, a handy but simple trading system module that does have some unique built-in functions. Options features are limited. Looks best for stocks — it even has a simple portfolio tracker. Some arcane terminology. The 'manual' is a tutorial — which is usually a good idea — but sometimes it switches to true manual mode. No index, small table of contents. No reference section. Data download isn't built in — a subprogram to access other databases is provided. Technical support was slow in coming, to be expected from a three-person company.

"Not really ready for prime time but might be handy for someone who had access to the innards and had the time to tweak it to the right comfort level."

WHY?

Why would anyone be interested in this package if you heard that description in a bar after a hard day in the market? Well, the vendor, Delphi Economics, has credibility, as a long-time European supplier of economic information and analysis. Plus, Delphi's hooked up in the U.S. with the respected Center for International Business Cycle Research at Columbia University, though exactly how this hookup works isn't clear.

Viking is keyboard-based and fast, even on a 286. Setup is as straightforward as it gets in DOS, except that you have to call Viking for an installation access code, and, once running, input is as fast as your fingers are. Output to printers can be controlled through a separate setup program that's mentioned toward the end of the manual — but not in the setup section. In this program, you will discover that Viking can seize additional RAM for running and that you can control that. You will not know how much RAM you need, minimum, but my experiments indicate it's more than 500K and less than 550K. This may mean unloading most of your resident utilities.

Before trying the bells and whistles, you'll need to update the database that Delphi sends you. This will be tricky, should you rely on your manual. I attempted to use our Warner account but couldn't get it to work. Page 80 of the manual assures us that simply telling the Viking Data Import program the name of the service, the location of the data to import and a Viking code is enough. Assuming you are already getting data from somewhere else and it is in the proper format (or you can convert it), this should not be a problem. However, it is subpar for a program in this genre to leave data collection off the list of features.

At this point, you're ready to dive into the tutorials, which have the virtue of thoroughly exploring the program's features. Appended to the tutorials are several appendices with details on, say, trading models and functions available (see sidebar, "Standard Viking studies"). The tutorials take you through the basic graphics (charts, trendlines and so forth), creat-

FIGURE 1

VIKING RSI

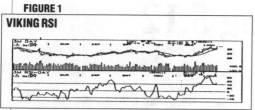

Viking's version of RSI, as shown here, has the unique ability to go below 0.

FIGURE 2

VIKING POINT AND FIGURE

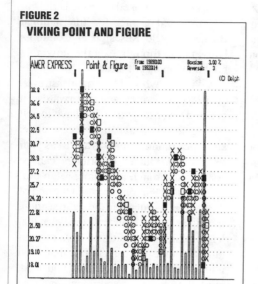

Another interesting innovation is Viking's point and figure chart, which has the volume data plotted right along with the Xs and Os.

FIGURE 3

VIKING SUPPORT AND RESISTANCE

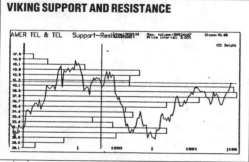

Support and resistance is shown graphically via volume levels and price levels.

ing sets of charts, creating sets of items (possibly, portfolios), creating trading models and checking profitability and optimal values and generating trading signals.

Figures 1-3 are typical graphics products, albeit in living color. Once you have the stuff on screen, there's little to do with it compared with, say, MetaStock or CompuTrac — no wands, line drawing is keyboard driven, no mouse poking or

prodding. The program can find tops and bottoms on its own, though — a good piece of work — and any trendlines you do draw serve as alert levels ("guards" in Viking vernacular), which can be sensitive to volume as well as price, a nice grace note. Another convenience feature is a "fast commands" mode that recognizes and deals with the tedium of flipping back and forth with menus constantly. I took that to mean that the person using Viking in-house at Delphi used it a lot!

Charts can be popped up in a variety of layouts, plus you can assemble groups of charts (called "suites" in some packages) in custom-configured layouts for later, regular recall (Figure 4). These can even be run off in a slideshow for a quick morning briefing without the keystrokes. Very handy.

The range of indicators that can be employed with the charts is extensive but not overwhelming. An especially interesting study, though, is the fast Fourier transform (FFT) "prognosis." I don't know how they do it, but this FFT model (Figure 5) runs on surprisingly little data and pops up with trend- and amplitude-adjusted forecasts, which often have the virtue of being on the money. *Very* nice.

Once past basic graphics and studies, you direct your attention to the profitability modules. Here, you specify the trading idea you have and allow the program to do the checking for profit and loss. The Viking specification does have a neat format: first seeing the buys and sells graphically (Figure 6), then specification of parameters, then full profitability testing. This follows the intuitive development path for most trading models. Plus, once a model is specified graphically, it can be imported into the parameter testing section where you specify ranges of values for up to six parameters to be checked — or you can start fresh, writing a whole new model.

Once you've targeted the range of values for your parameters, a more detailed profitability analysis is run in the formal

FIGURE 4

SCREEN LAYOUTS

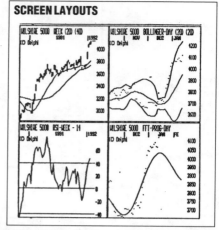

Viking offers a variety of screen layouts, one of which is shown here.

"Profitability" section. This section really does very little, comparing the results of the test to buy-and-hold and calculating some percentage gains or losses. There is no information on losses, equity drawdowns, maximum adverse movement or any standard risk/reward measure.

Viking's testing allows only a single buy and sell specification. You cannot have separate stops for buy and sells and separate exit rules for buy and sells. In fact, there are no stops at all. Add-on trades aren't covered, nor is pyramiding. Viking does have a logic checker to speed up the debugging process but there is no way to check the actual calculation of values to debug or verify trades.

Once you've built a model, Viking handily implements it on a day-to-day basis. A quick signal capability scans your database for current signals (that is, within the last *n* days or even just today). This can be automated via macro to provide you with a ranking of your database. Moreover, this scan may be connected with other signals in review of several models, which shows when several signals align with each other in the same or opposed directions. This, displayed graphically (Figure 7), is a nifty way to check whether your techniques work across a broad range of tradeables but does feed the mania for more confirming signals before you take action. Another nifty feature: computing the price levels necessary to trip signals tomorrow.

FIGURE 5

VIKING FAST FOURIER TRANSFORM

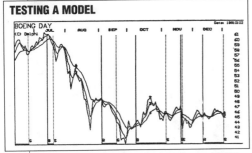

A fast Fourier transform is implemented innovatively with Viking, allowing good forecasts from a fairly small amount of data.

FIGURE 6

TESTING A MODEL

When you're ready to test a simple trading model, Viking will start the process graphically, indicating where your buys and sells came and speeding up the development process.

FIGURE 7

VIKING VIA DIRECTION

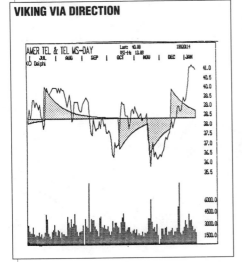

Once trading signals are defined, Viking can display whether one or more signals are positive or negative at the same time. The higher the shaded portion, the more the number of signals are headed in the same direction.

SUMMARY

Viking looks as though it was assembled in-house, over time, by a very talented, innovative, probably European programmer/analyst. However, there are clues that this person was not working primarily to create a commercial product: The manual is an efficient tutorial, but portions are out of date with the version of the program we got (for example, there's an instruction on page 32 telling you to avoid hiding a model when you would actually be deleting it). Much of the terminology is techspeak or arcane: "vectors," "courtage," percentages in decimal form — even r_x values, something only a BASIC programmer could love. Support and resistance receive a unique treatment and the distinction between vertical and horizontal isn't clear.

The flip side to this is that the program is a dream to work with if it does what you want. For instance, you can create both standard and proprietary market indices. The indices can be weighted based on individual components, plus the volume will be included, which is hard to find on most published stock group indices other than the prominent ones such as the DJIA. I loved the FFT module and this is the only program I've seen with a Coppock model. Many of the tools that a true technical hacker would want are here, but you should test to see if they do what you want because they were created to meet the needs of the creator, not you.

So, for $495, are you buying a package of technical ideas as well as the usual charting and some system building and testing capabilities? I'd say so. Viking's true virtue is its variety of insightful analytical techniques. Still, it's impossible to say these ideas (RSI, price strength, positioning, FFT forecasting, volatility and volatility signals, the trading models) have merit absent explanation or your testing. Viking gets kudos for innovation, but I recommend you buy this one on inspection.

John Sweeney is the Technical Editor for STOCKS & COMMODITIES.

STANDARD VIKING STUDIES

Momentum, point and figure, oscillator, spreads, ratios, a proprietary RSI, proprietary price strength, Equivolume, averages, parabolics, fast Fourier transform and fast Fourier forecast, support and resistance, volatility, Bollinger Bands, regression, positive and negative volume indicators, Coppock indicator, price/volume trend, Chaikin indicator, advance/decline volume, stochastics, moving average convergence/divergence (MACD).

Viking also comes with three trading indicators and some proprietary indicators: volatility studies, "V-signals," a trend model and something called "multi time," which appears to be a combination of monthly, weekly and daily charts. This material is explained only cryptically (no formulas) in the manual, but they are interesting to see on screen.

A Priori — Known ahead of time.

ABC—Elliott wave terminology for a three-wave countertrend price movement. Wave A is the first price wave against the trend of the market. Wave B is a corrective wave to Wave A. Wave C is the final price move to complete the countertrend price move. Elliott wave followers study A and C waves for price ratios based on numbers from the Fibonacci series.

Accumulation—An addition to a trader's original market position. The first of three distinct phases in a major trend in which investors are buying.

Accumulation/Distribution Line — *See* Chaikin Oscillator.

Actuals—Refers to actual physical commodities, as distinguished from futures.

ADA—Block-structured programming language developed under the guidance of the U.S. Department of Defense to provide a medium for writing real-time, concurrent applications, for facilitating program verification.

Adaptive Filter—Smoothing and/or forecasting prices with continuously updated weighting of past prices.

Advance-Decline Line—Each day's number of declining issues is subtracted from the number of advancing issues. The net difference is added to a running sum if the difference is positive or subtracted from the running sum if the difference is negative.

AKA—An acronym for "automated knowledge acquisition." Refers to the use of programs to create knowledge needed by other programs (usually expert systems).

American Depository Receipts (ADRs)— Certificates that are issued by a bank of U.S. origin and traded in the U.S. as domestic shares. The certificates represent the foreign securities that the bank holds in that security's country of origin.

Analysis of Variance (ANOVA) — The partitioning of total sum of squares into the sum of squares explained by the model and the remaining sum of squares unexplained.

Andrews Method—A technique whereby a technician will pick an extreme low or high to use as a pivot point and draw a line, called the median line, from this point that bisects a line drawn through the next corrective phase that occurs after the pivot point. Lines parallel to the median line are drawn through the high and low points of the corrective phase. The parallel lines define the resistance and support levels for the price channel.

Arbitrage—The simultaneous purchase and sale of two different, but closely related, securities to take advantage of a disparity in their prices.

ARIMA—*See* AutoRegressive Integrated Moving Average

ARMAX (Autoregressive Moving Average eXogenous variables model)— The combination of fundamental variables outside the particular market that correlates with the independent variable added with the ARMA modeling of the remaining residuals.

Arms Index—Also known as TRading INdex (TRIN):

$$= \frac{\dfrac{\text{No. of advancing issues}}{\text{No. of declining issues}}}{\dfrac{\text{Total up volume}}{\text{Total down volume}}}$$

An advance/decline stock market indicator. A reading of less than 1.0 indicates bullish demand, while greater than 1.0 is bearish. The index is often smoothed with a simple moving average.

Assign—To transfer to another to whom property is assigned.

Astrophysical Cycle—Any earthly cycle, such as a market cycle, that has been scientifically related to the physics of the planetary system.

At-the-Money—An option whose strike price is nearest the current price of the underlying deliverable.

Attenuation—The fractional part of reduced energy or lost power due to smoothing or filtering.

Autocorrelation—A technique used to detect cyclic activity.

AutoRegressive Integrated Moving Average (ARIMA)—A linear stochastic model forecasting methodology described by Box and Jenkins in their book *Time Series Analysis, Forecasting and Control.*

Autoregressive—Using previous data to predict future data.

Average Directional Movement Index (ADX) — Indicator developed by J. Welles Wilder to measure market trend intensity.

Back Month—The out, or *back*, contract month, as opposed to the current contract month; the expiration month farther in the future than the current, or *spot*, month.

Back-Testing — A strategy is tested or optimized on historical data and then the strategy is applied to new data to see if the results are consistent.

Balanced Mutual Fund—A mutual fund that seeks a return that is a combination of capital appreciation and current income, generally by building a portfolio of bonds, preferred stocks and common stocks.

Band Pass Filter—An oscillator that accentuates only the frequencies in an intermediate range and rejects high and low frequencies. Implemented by first applying a low pass filter to the data and then a high pass filter to the resulting data (e.g., two SMA crossover system).

Bank Investment Contracts (BICs)—A negotiated-term deposit issued by a commercial bank. See *Guaranteed Investment Contracts (GICs).*

Basis — The difference between spot (cash) prices and the futures contract price.

Basis Points—The measure of yields on bonds and notes; one basis point equals 0.01% of yield.

Basket Trades—Large transactions made up of a number of different stocks.

Beta—Higher sensitivity to market swings.

Beta —A regression of the estimated coefficient that belongs to a particular variable.

Beta (Coefficient)—A measure of the market or nondiversifiable risk associated with any given security in the market. A ratio of an individual's stock historical returns to the historical returns of the stock market. If a stock increased in value by 12% while the market increased by 10%, the stock's beta would be 1.2.

Bimodal Distribution — In which observations are displayed as having two distinct peaks.

Block Trades—Large transactions of a particular stock sold as a unit.

Blow-Off Top—A steep and rapid increase in price followed by a steep and rapid drop in price.

Boolean—Describes a variable that may have one of only two possible values: true or false. After George Boole, English logician, credited with the invention of "Boolean logic."

Box-Jenkins Linear Least Squares—The additive structure of Box-Jenkins models with a polynomial structure.

Box-Jenkins Nonlinear Least Squares— The multiplicative structure of Box-Jenkins models using the Gauss-Newton algorithm with numerical derivatives.

Box-Jenkins Method—From G.E.P. Box and G.M. Jenkins, who authored *Time Series Analysis: Forecasting and Control.* The method refers to the use of autoregressive integrated moving averages (ARIMA), which fit seasonal models and nonseasonal models to a time series.

Bracketing—A trading range market or a price region that is non-trending.

Breakout—The point when the market price moves out of the trend channel.

Broker's Deck—Orders physically held by the floor broker in the trading pit.

C Language—Widely used systems development language, also block-structured, but with more facilities to control the machine at the level of the hardware.

Call Option—An option that gives the buyer the right to buy the underlying contract at a specific price within a certain time and that obligates the seller to sell the contract for the premium received before expiration of the time limit.

Candlestick Charts—A charting method, originally from Japan, in which the high and low are plotted as a single line and are referred to as shadows. The price range between the open and the close is plotted as a narrow rectangle and is referred to as the body. If the close is above the open, the body is white. If the close is below the open, the body is black.

Capital Gains Distribution—A distribution to investment company shareholders from net long-term capital gains realized by a regulated investment company on the sale of portfolio securities.

Chaikin Oscillator—An oscillator created by subtracting a 10-day EMA from a three-day EMA of the accumulation/distribution line.

Channel—In charting, a price channel contains prices throughout a trend. There are three basic ways to draw channels: parallel, rounded and channels that connect lows (bear trend) or highs (bull trend).

Chaos Theory—Describes the behavior of nonlinear systems.

Chi Square—A statistical test to determine if the patterns exhibited by data could have been produced by chance. The chi-square test with Yates's correction using two-way statistics for decline vs. advance is:

$$\chi^2 = \sum_{j=1}^{k} \frac{\left(\left|o_j - e_j\right| - 0.5\right)^2}{e_j}$$

where:

o_j = actual observed frequency of test
e_j = expected or theoretical frequency of test.

Christmas Tree Spread—The simultaneous purchase and writing of options with either a different strike price or expiration date or combination of the two.

Coefficient—A constant used to multiply another quantity or series; as in $3x$ and ax, 3 and a are *coefficients* of x.

Coefficient of Determination — R-squared. The proportion of the variation in the data explained by the model.

Coincidence—In Gann theory, a projected reversal point.

Comparative Relative Strength—Compares the price movement of a stock with that of its competitors, industry group or the entire market. This is distinct from J. Welles Wilder's Relative Strength Index, which compares current price movement to previous price movement of the same instrument.

Confidence Factor—A measure of the degree of likelihood that a rule is correct, which may reflect the percentage of times that it has proven to be correct in the past or just a subjective measure of our confidence in its degree of reliability.

Confidence Level—The degree of assurance that a specified failure rate is not exceeded.

Congestion Area or Pattern—A series of trading days in which there is no visible progress in price.

Consolidation—Also known as a congestion period. A pause that allows participants in a market to reevaluate the market and sets the stage for the next price move.

Continuation Chart—A chart in which the price scale for the data for the end of a given contract and the data for the beginning of the next contract are merged in order to ease the transition of one contract to the next.

Convergence—When futures prices and spot prices come together at the futures expiration.

Conversion Arbitrage—Traders buy and sell two different securities (or synthetic securities), forcing equivalent prices for equivalent securities.

Correction Wave—A wave or cycle of waves moving against the current impulse trend's direction.

Correction—Any price reaction within the market leading to an adjustment by as much as one-third to two-thirds of the previous gain.

Correlation Coefficient—When two random variables X and Y tend to vary together. The measurement is given by the ratio of the covariance of X and T to the square root of the product of the variance of X and the variance of Y.

$$r = \frac{\sum XY - n\overline{XY}}{\sqrt{\left(\sum X^2 - n\overline{X}^2\right)\left(\sum Y^2 - n\overline{Y}^2\right)}}$$

Correlogram—A numerical and graphical display of the test statistics of an autocorrelation diagnostic routine.

Countermove—A price bar showing movement opposite to the direction of the prior time period; a retracement.

Covariance—Multiplies the deviation of each variable from its mean, adds those products and then divides by the number of observations.

Cover—Purchasing back a contract sold earlier.

Covered Write—Writing a call against a long position in the underlying stock. By receiving a premium, the writer intends to realize additional return on the underlying common stock or gain some element of protection (limited to the amount of the premium less transaction costs) from a decline in the value of that underlying stock.

Crack Spreads—The spread between crude oil and its products: heating oil and unleaded gasoline plays a major role in the trading process.

Credit Spread—The difference in value of two options, where the value of the one sold exceeds the value of the one purchased.

CTI2—Market Profile terminology for commercial clearing members, as opposed to CTI1, local floor traders.

Curve—The continuous image of the unit interval.

Curve-Fitting—Developing complicated rules that map known conditions.

Cutoff Frequency—A point where higher frequency cycles will not pass through a filter (e.g., a 10-day SMA will eliminate cycles of 20 days or less).

Cycle—A variation where a point of observation returns to its origin.

Daily Range—The difference between the high and low price during one trading day.

Debit Spread—The difference in value of two options, where the value of the long position exceeds the value of the short position.

Deep-in-the-Money — A deep-in-the-money call option has the strike price of the option well below the current price of the underlying instrument. A deep-in-the-money put option has the strike price of the option well above the current price of the underlying instrument.

Degrees of Freedom — The number of independent observations; the number of observations minus the number of parameters to be estimated.

Delay—The amount of time that elapses between a change in an input event and the resultant change in a related output event or time series.

Delta—The change in the price of the option divided by the change in the underlying instrument.

Delta-Hedged—An options strategy that protects an option against small price changes in the option's underlying instrument. These hedges are constructed by taking a position in the underlying instrument that is equal in magnitude but opposite in sign (+/-) to the option's delta.

Delta Neutral—This is an "options/options" or "options/underlying instrument" position constructed so that it is relatively insensitive to the price movement of the underlying instruments. This is arranged by selecting a calculated ratio of offsetting short and long positions.

Demand Index — An index that shows the buying and selling power of markets and stocks from mathematical calculations of volume and price ratios.

Density Function—For any measure m, a function that gives rise to m when integrated with respect to some other specified measure. A probability density function is a function whose integral over any set gives the probability that a random variable has values in this set.

Dependence—A relationship between two different experimental results in which the first result does not directly influence the chances of the second result occurring, but instead, the two results are indirectly related because they are subject to influences from a common outside factor.

Deterministic—Known in advance when the sum of one-step ahead forecast mean squared errors is zero.

Deterministic—The fundamental continuous effect of an exogenous variable such as money supply that can be determined to be explanatory.

Detrend—To remove the general drift, tendency, or bent of a set of statistical data as related to time.

Difference-in-Means Test — A statistical test that indicates the likelihood of observing the difference if the true difference were zero. A large value of this statistic leads to nonacceptance of the null hypothesis that the true difference is zero.

Differencing—Subtracting previous from current values to obtain a stationary (detrended) time series: $P_{stationary} = P_t - P_t - 1$.

Diffusion Equation—A partial differential equation, used in solving a random walk problem.

Distribution—Large monied interests use the current rally to liquidate old positions in the face of good news.

Divergence—When two or more averages or indices fail to show confirming trends.

Doji — A session in which the open and close are the same (or almost the same). Different varieties of doji lines (such as a gravestone or long-legged doji) depend on where the opening and close are in relation to the entire range. Doji lines are among the most important individual candlestick lines. They are also components of important candlestick patterns.

Double Bottom (Top)—The price action of a security or market average where it has declined (advanced) two times to the same approximate level, indicating the existence of a support (resistance) level and a possibility that the downward (upward) trend has ended.

Double-Smoothed—A price series that has been smoothed by a mathematical technique such as a moving average. This first series of smoothed price data is then smoothed a second time.

Double Top—*See* Double Bottom.

Drawdown—The reduction in account equity as a result of a trade or series of trades.

Durbin-Watson statistic — The probability that first order correlation exists. With a range between 0 and 4, the closer to 2.0, the lower the probability is.

Early Entry—A large price movement in one direction within the first 15 minutes after the open of the daily session.

Elasticity—The ability to recover an original configuration.

Elliott Wave Theory—A pattern-recognition technique published by Ralph Nelson Elliott in 1939, which holds that the stock market follows a rhythm or pattern of five waves up and three waves down to form a complete cycle of eight waves. The three waves down are referred to as a "correction" of the preceding five waves up.

EMA—*See* Exponential Moving Average.

Envelope — Lines surrounding an index or indicator — that is, trading bands.

Equilibrium Market—A price region that represents a balance between demand and supply.

Equivolume Chart—Created by Richard W. Arms, a chart in which the vertical axis is the high-low range for each day, while the horizontal axis represents the volume of shares of stock or the number of contracts traded for the day. The purpose of the chart is to highlight the relationship between price and volume.

Eurodollar—Dollars deposited in foreign banks, with the futures contract reflecting the rates offered between London branches of top U.S. banks and foreign banks.

Ex-Dividend Date—The day on or after which the right to receive a current dividend is not automatically transferred to a buyer.

Exercise—The process by which the holder of an option purchases or sells shares of the underlying security.

Expiration—The last day on which an option can be exercised.

Explained—The relative reduction in the variation of variable Y that can be attributed to a knowledge of variable X and its relationship to Y.

Exponential Moving Average—The EMA for day D is calculated as: $EMA_D = \alpha PR_D + (1-\alpha)EMA_{D-1}$ where PR is the price on day D and α (alpha) is a smoothing constant ($0<\alpha<1$). Alpha may be estimated as $2/(n+1)$, where n is the simple moving average length.

Exponential Smoothing—A mathematical-statistical method of forecasting that assumes future price action is a weighted average of past periods; a mathematic series in which greater weight is given to more recent price action.

Extreme—The highest or lowest price during any time period, a price extreme; in the CBOT Market Profile, the highest/lowest prices the market tests during a trading day.

F Statistics — The ratio of the variance explained by treatments to the unexpected variance.

Fade—Selling a rising price or buying a falling price. A trader fading an up opening would be short, for example.

Failure—In Elliott wave theory, a five-wave pattern of movement in which the fifth impulse wave fails to move above the end of the third, or in which the fifth wave does not contain the five subwaves.

Failure Swings—The inability of price to reaffirm a new high in an uptrend or a new low in a downtrend.

Fair Values—The theoretical prices generated by an option pricing model (i.e., the Black-Scholes option pricing model).

Fast Fourier Transform — A method by which to decompose data into a sum of sinusoids of varying cycle length, with each cycle being a fraction of a common fundamental cycle length.

Fast Market — A declaration that market conditions in the futures pit are so disorderly temporarily to the extent that floor brokers are not held responsible for the execution of orders.

Feedforward Computation—Neural network in which neurons receive information only from the previous layer and send outputs only to the following layer.

Fibonacci Ratio—The ratio between any two successive numbers in the Fibonacci sequence, known as phi (ϕ). The ratio of any number to the next higher number is approximately 0.618 (known as the Golden Mean or Golden Ratio), and to the lower number approximately 1.618 (the inverse of the Golden Mean), after the first four numbers of the series. The three important ratios the series provides are 0.618, 1.0 and 1.618.

Fibonacci Sequence—The sequence of numbers (0, 1, 2, 3, 5, 8, 13, 21, 34, 55, 89, 144, 233...), discovered by the Italian mathematician Leonardo de Pisa in the 13th century and the mathematical basis of the Elliott wave theory, where the first two terms of the sequence are 0 and 1 and each successive number in the sequence is the sum of the previous two numbers. Technically, it is a sequence and not a series.

Fill—An executed order; sometimes the term refers to the price at which an order is executed.

Fill Order—An order that must be filled immediately (or canceled).

Filter—A device or program that separates data, signal or information in accordance with specified criteria.

Filter Point—The time at which a portfolio insurance program makes an adjusting trade.

Fire—(verb) In expert system programming, ordinarily used to describe the "triggering" or "activation" of a rule. A rule is "fired," "triggered" or "activated" when its conditions have been met, and its "consequents" (resultant facts) are added to the knowledge base.

Fit Criterion—A quantitative comparable measure used to minimize model errors.

5% Confidence—Before conducting statistical tests, an analyst must select a confidence level that will be used to determine when to accept the null hypothesis. A 5% confidence level indicates that one is not willing to accept the null hypothesis when the average net return calculated from the sample could have occurred in only five of 100 samples if the null hypothesis were true.

Float—The number of shares currently available for trading.

Floor Traders—Employees of brokerage firms working on exchange trading floors.

Flyers — Speculative or high-risk trades.

Forward-Rate Agreements (FRAs) — Cash payments are made daily as the spot rate varies above or below an agreed-upon forward rate and can be hedged with Eurodollar futures.

Frequency—The number of complete cycles observed per time period (i.e., cycles per year).

Frequency Component—That part of a time series that may be represented as a cycle.

Frequency Distribution—A chart showing the number of times (or "frequency") an event occurs for each possible value of the event. The vertical or y-axis of the chart is the frequency axis and the horizontal or x-axis shows the different values the variable being measured can take.

Frequency Domain — Variation in a time series is accounted for by cyclical components at different frequencies.

Frequency Response—The transfer of the frequency of the underlying data, usually prices, to the frequency of its moving average.

Front-Loaded—Commission and fees taken out of investment capital before the money is put to work.

Front Month—The first expiration month in a series of months.

Fundamental Analysis —The analytical method by which only the sales, earnings and the value of a given tradable's assets may be considered.

Fundamentals — The theory that holds that stock market activity may be predicted by looking at the relative data and statistics of a stock as well as the management of the company in question and its earnings.

Future Volatility—A prediction of what volatility may be like in the future.

Gann's Square of 9—A trading tool that relates numbers, such as a stock price, to degrees on a circle.

Gap—A day in which the daily range is completely above or below the previous day's daily range.

Golden Mean or Golden Ratio—The ratio of any two consecutive numbers in the Fibonacci sequence, known as phi and equal to 0.618; a proportion that is an important phenomenon in music, art, architecture and biology.

Golden Section—Any length divided so that the ratio of the smaller to the larger part is equivalent to the ratio between the larger part and the whole and is always 0.618.

Growth Fund—A more speculative mutual fund made up primarily of the growth or performance stocks that are expected to appreciate in price more than the broad market over an extended time period.

Guaranteed Investment Contracts (GICs) — A single lump-sum deposit that earns a guaranteed interest until a known maturity date. GICs are issued by insurance companies.

Hanning Weight—

$$W_J = 1/2 \left[1 - \cos\left(\frac{2\pi J}{N-1}\right) \right]$$

where weight (W) at point J in window width of N points is determined by this formula.

Heuristic Method—Problem solving approached by trying out several different methods and comparing which provides the best solution.

Heuristics (computer science)—Computational rules of thumb. Distinct from algorithms, which are programs guaranteed to generate the correct result under all circumstances, heuristics may only turn out to be correct a certain percentage of time.

High Pass Frequency Filter—A detrending filter that lets pass the high frequency noise and rejects low frequency trend. Implemented by first applying a low pass filter to the data, then subtracting the filtered data from the original data.

Hines Ratio — A modified put/call ratio that refines traditional option ratio analysis by including the open interest figures in the equation and can be defined as (Total put volume/Total put open interest) divided by (Total call volume/Total call open interest)

Historic Volatility—How much contract price has fluctuated over a period of time in the past; usually calculated by taking a standard deviation of price changes over a time period.

Historical Data—A series of past daily, weekly or monthly market prices (open, high, low, close, volume, open interest).

Hook Day—A trading day in which the open is above/below the previous day's high/low and the close is below/above the previous day's close with narrow range.

Implied Alpha—The excess return expected from a stock to justify its current weighing in the portfolio.

Implied Volatility—The volatility computed using the actual market prices of an option contract and one of a number of pricing models. For example, if the market price of an option rises without a change in the price of the underlying stock or future, implied volatility will have risen.

Impulse—A sharply defined change in a series of input data being studied, such as market prices or volume.

Impulse Wave—A wave or cycle of waves that carries the current trend further in the same direction.

In Play—A stock that is the focus of a public bidding contest, as in a takeover or bear raid.

In-the-Money—A call option whose strike price is lower than the stock or future's price, or a put option whose strike price is higher than the underlying stock or future's price. For example, when a commodity price is $500, a call option with a strike price of $400 is considered in-the-money.

Income Dividends—Payments to mutual fund shareholders consisting of dividends, interest and short-term capital gains earned on the fund's portfolio securities after deduction of operating expenses.

Initial Balance—The first or first two half-hour trading periods in the CBOT Market Profile during which prices tend to converge; the initial auction of the trading day.

Inside Day—A day in which the daily price range is completely within the previous day's daily price range.

Interest Rate Swaps — An arrangement that requires both sides of the transaction to make payments to each other based on two different interest rates. The most commonly traded requires one side to pay a fixed rate and the other to pay a floating rate.

Intermarket Analysis — Observing the price movement of one market for the purpose of evaluating a different market.

Intrinsic Value—The portion of an option's premium that is represented when the cash market price is greater than the exercise price; a known constant equal to the difference between the strike price and underlying market price.

Irregular Flat—A type of Elliott wave correction that has a 3-3-5 wave pattern, where the B wave terminates beyond the start of wave A. A "flat" is in progress, implying that a larger pattern is developing. It will contain waves of one higher degree than the A-B-C waves just completed.

January Effect—The tendency for securities prices to recover in January after tax-related selling is completed before the year-end.

Knowledge Base— In artificial intelligence, a given inventory of knowledge specific to a set of rules.

KST — Indicator developed by Martin Pring. A weighted summed rate of change oscillator. Four different rates of change are calculated, smoothed, multiplied by weights and then summed to form one indicator.

Lag—The number of data points that a filter, such as a moving average, follows or trails the input price data.

Lead—The number of data points that a filter, much as a moving average, precedes the input price data.

Least Squares Method—A technique of fitting a curve close to some given points that minimizes the sum of the squares of the deviations of the given points from the curve.

Leg—One side of a spread.

Leg Out—In rolling forward in futures, a method that would result in liquidating a position.

Limit Move—A change in price that exceeds the limits set by the exchange on which the contract is traded.

Limit Order—An order to buy or sell when a trade in the market occurs at a pre-determined price.

Limit Up, Limit Down—Commodity exchange restrictions on the maximum upward or downward movements permitted in the price for a commodity during any trading session day.

LISP—A programming language based on predicate logic and is the one most commonly used in artificial intelligence applications.

Ljung-Box statistic—A chi-square test of significance of higher order correlation existence. The marginal significance level is the probability that a no more higher order correlation exists.

Load — Commission and fees taken out of investment capital; that is, the situation in which a front-loaded mutual fund takes commission and fees out of investment capital before the money is put to work.

Local—The trader in a pit of a commodity exchange who buys and sells for his or her account.

Locked Limit—A market that, if not restricted, would seek price equilibrium outside the limit but, instead, moves to the limit and ceases to trade.

Long—Establishing ownership of the responsibilities of a buyer of a tradeable; holding securities in anticipation of a price increase in that security.

Lookback Interval — The number of periods of historical data used for observation and calculation.

Low Pass Frequency Filter—A data smoother or filter that lets pass low frequency trend sinusoids and rejects high frequency noise (*see* SMA).

MACD—*See* Moving Average Convergence/Divergence.

Major Auction—The overall trend of the market such as might be observed on a bar chart.

Mandelbrot Set — Complex but structured pattern produced by an equation in which the result is fed back into the equation repeatedly; self-similarity.

Mapping—A function, or relation between values.

Margin—In stock trading, an account in which purchase of stock may be financed with borrowed money; in futures trading, the deposit placed with the clearinghouse to assure fulfillment of the contract. This amount varies daily and is settled in cash.

Marginal Significance Level of Test-Statistics—The probability distribution used to test the hypothesis that the beta coefficient does not equal zero. A T-statistic of approximately 1.65 reflects a 0.90 or 90% confidence and the marginal significance is 1-0.90 = 0.1 or 10%.

Marked to Market—At the end of each business day the open positions carried in an account held at a brokerage firm are credited or debited funds based on the settlement price of the open positions that day.

Market If Touched — Resting order with the floor broker that becomes a market order to be executed if the trigger price is traded.

Market Maker—A broker or bank continually prepared to make a two-way price to purchase or sell for a security or currency.

Market on Close—An order specification that requires the broker to get the best price available on the close of trading, usually during the last five minutes of trading.

Market Order — Instructions to the broker to immediately sell to the best available bid or to buy from the best available offer.

Market Risk—The uncertainty of returns attributable to fluctuation of the entire market.

Market Sentiment — Crowd psychology, typically a measurement of bullish or bearish attitudes among investors and traders.

Martingale—From roulette; a tactical system that requires doubling your bet after each loss, so that winning once you recoup the amount originally bet.

Maximum Adverse Excursion — A historical measurement of the closed losing trades versus the closed profitable trades of a trading system. Used to determine the stop-loss level that can be used that will allow winning trades to remain; the extreme unfavorable price level reached for both profitable and unprofitable trades.

Maximum Entropy Method—More flexible than Fourier analysis, the maximum entropy method is both a tool for spectrum analysis and a method of adaptive filtering and trend forecasting. As a tool for spectrum analysis, the MEM system can provide high resolution spectra for identifying the dominant data cycles within relatively short time series, such as open, high, low, close, volume and open interest,

or study results, such as RSI, TRIX, and so on. (Fourier analysis, in contrast, gives best results when applied to time series of six months or longer.) As a forecasting tool, MEM is used in conjunction with moving averages to forecast lower and upper trend channels in the data.

Maximum Entropy Spectrum Analysis— See Maximum Entropy Method.

Mean — When the sum of the values is divided by the number of observation.

Mean Reverting—The term adopted in academic literature for one possible state of a price series: that state when price is oscillating randomly about some (unknown) mean value. That is, it is not trending.

Median Line—The line that is drawn from an extreme that bisects a line drawn through the next corrective phase after the pivot point. *Cf.* Andrews Method.

MEM—See Maximum Entropy Method.

MESA—See Maximum Entropy Spectrum Analysis.

Minor Auction—The latest trend of the market, i.e., what it is doing now.

Mode — The most frequently occurring value.

Model—Equation.

Momentum—A time series representing change of today's price from some fixed number of days back in history.

Momentum Filter—A measure of change, derivative or slope of the underlying trend in a time series. Implemented by first applying a low pass filter to the data and then applying a differencing operation to the results.

Momentum Indicator—A market indicator utilizing price and volume statistics for predicting the strength or weakness of a current market and any overbought or oversold conditions, and to note turning points within the market.

Monowave—In Elliott wave theory, a single wave within a range of waves.

Moving Average—A mathematical procedure to smooth or eliminate the fluctuations in data and to assist in determining when to buy and sell. Moving averages emphasize the direction of a trend, confirm trend reversals and smooth out price and volume fluctuations or "noise" that can confuse interpretation of the market; the sum of a value plus a selected number of previous values divided by the total number of values.

Moving Average Crossovers—The point where the various moving average lines

intersect each other or the price line on a moving average price bar chart. Technicians use crossovers to signal price-based buy and sell opportunities.

Moving Average Model—A time series equation representing an observed value at time t as a linear combination of present and past random shocks ε_t (forecast errors). A moving-average process of order Q, MA(q), may be written: $P_t = \varepsilon_t - b_1\varepsilon_{t-1} - b_2\varepsilon_{t-2} \ldots b_q\varepsilon_{t-q}$.

Moving Average Convergence/ Divergence (MACD)—The crossing of two exponentially smoothed moving averages that are plotted above and below a zero line. The crossover, movement through the zero line, and divergences generate buy and sell signals.

Moving Window — Snapshot of a portion of a time series at an instant in time. The window is moved along the time series at a constant rate.

Multicolinearity—Two variables that have a correlation of greater than 0.70 or less than -0.70 in a regression model. The final result is the two variables explaining the same portion of variation where either variable would be sufficient.

Multiple Linear Regression—More than one independent variable is used to account for the variability in one dependent variable.

Narrow Range Day—A trading day with a smaller price range relative to the previous day's price range.

Near-Month Contract/Far-Month Contract—Contract whose expiration is near/far.

Near-the-Money—An option with a strike price close to the current price of the underlying tradable.

Neckline—A trendline drawn along the support or resistance points of various reversal and consolidation pattern (i.e., head and shoulder, double and triple top/bottom formations).

Negative Divergence—When two or more averages, indices or indicators fail to show confirming trends.

Net Asset Value—The total market value of all securities contained in a mutual fund; also known as price per share.

Neural Network — An artificial intelligence program that is capable of learning through a training process of trial and error.

No-Load—Without any sales charge. For mutual funds, shares sold at net asset value.

Noise—Price and volume fluctuations that can confuse interpretation of market direction.

Noisy Signal—A signal in which the effects of random influences cannot be dismissed.

Non-Seasonal Autocorrelation—Autocorrelation that shows up other than at 12-month lag intervals.

Non-Trend Day—A narrow range day lacking any discernible movement in either direction.

Normal Distribution — For the purposes of statistical testing, the simulated net returns are assumed to be drawn from a particular distribution. If net returns are drawn from a normal distribution, low and high returns are equally likely, and the most likely net return in a quarter is the average net return.

Normalized—Adjusting a time series so that the series lies in a prescribed normal, standard range.

Notice Day—The day that a notice of intent to deliver is issued to a futures contract holder.

Null Hypothesis—The hypothesis that there is no validity to the specific claim that two variations (treatments) of the same thing can be distinguished by a specific procedure.

Observer — A concept used in radar research, applicable to trading, in how often and what manner detection or radar contact is achieved.

OBV—See On-Balance Volume.

Odd Lot—An order to buy/sell fewer than 100 shares of stock.

On-Balance Volume—Plotted as a line representing the cumulative total of volume. The volume from a day's trading with a higher close when compared with the previous day is assigned a positive value, while volume on a lower close from the previous day is assigned a negative value. Traders look for a confirmation of a trend in OBV with the market or a divergence between the two as an indication of a potential reversal.

One-Tailed T-Test — A statistical test of significance for a distribution that changes its shape as N gets smaller; based on a variable *t* equal to the difference between the mean of the sample and the mean of the population divided by a result obtained by dividing the standard deviation of the sample by the square root of the number of individuals in the sample.

Opening Call—A period at the opening of a futures market in which the price for each contract is established by outcry.

Opening Range—The range of prices that occur during the first 30 seconds to five minutes of trading, depending on the preference of the individual analyst.

Opportunity Costs—Income foregone by the commitment of resources to another use.

Order—The number of days of past price history used to predict the following day's price.

Out-of-Sample—An item within the range of a sample that does not conform to the mean of the sample.

Out-of-the-Money—A call option whose exercise price is above the current market price of the underlying security or futures contract. For example, if a commodity price is $500, then a call option purchased for a strike price of $550 is considered out-of-the-money.

Outdata—The result (singular) stemming from a statistical test.

Outlier — A value removed from the other values to such an extreme that its presence cannot be attributed to the random combination of chance causes.

Outside Reversal Month—A month in which the recent monthly trading range exceeds the previous month's range and closes opposite (reverses) the previous month's close.

Overbought—Market prices that have risen too steeply and too fast.

Oversold—Market prices that have declined too steeply and too fast.

Overbought/Oversold Indicator—An indicator that attempts to define when prices have moved too far and too fast in either direction and thus are vulnerable to a reaction.

Par—The full principal amount of an investment instrument.

Parameter—A variable, set of data, or rule that establishes a precise format for a model.

Pareto's Law — A law that states that 80% of results come from 20% of the effort.

PASCAL—Block-structured programming language developed originally as an aid to instruction, now widely used for applications development.

Percentile — A value on a scale of one hundred that indicates the percent of a distribution that is equal to or below it.

Perceptron—A pattern-recognition machine, based on an analogy to the human nervous system, capable of learning by means of a feedback system that reinforces correct answers and discourages wrong ones.

Phase Delay—The time lag that a filter falls behind the pre-filtered data.

Point and Figure Chart—A price-only chart that plots up prices as Xs and down prices as Os. The minimum price recorded is called the *box size*. Typically, a three-box reversal indicates a change in the direction of prices.

Prewhitening—Removing the bulk of first, second and possibly third order autocorrelations using non-linear regression.

Premium—The price a buyer pays to an option writer for granting an option contract.

Probability Density Function—A graph showing the probability of occurrence of a particular data point (price).

Program Trading—Trades based on signals from computer programs, usually entered directly from the trader's computer to the market's computer system.

Put—An option to sell a specified amount of a stock or commodity at an agreed time at the stated exercise price.

Pyramid — To increase holdings that an investor has by using the most buying power available in a margin account with paper and real profits.

Quotron—A proprietary financial data service.

R-squared—The percentage of variation in the dependent variable that is explained by the regression equation. A relative measure of fit.

Rally Tops—A price level that concludes a short-term rally in an ongoing trend. A bull market will be made up of a series of rally tops.

Random Shock—The unexplained component of an equation that models a time series (ε forecast errors).

Random Walk—A theory that says there is no sequential correlation between prices from one day to the next, that prices will act unpredictably as they seek a level in response to supply and demand.

Range—The difference between the high and low price during a given period.

Range Extension—In the CBOT Market Profile, a price movement beyond the range set by the initial auction.

Rate of Change — In which today's closing price is divided by the closing price *n* days ago. Multiply by 100. Subtract 100 from this value. $((C_{today}/C_n) * 100) - 100$.

Ratio—The relation that one quantity bears to another of the same kind, with respect to magnitude or numerical value.

Reaction—A short-term decline in price.

RBAR-squared—The R-squared value adjusted for the number of degrees of freedom.

Recursive—A process that is repetitive and usually dependent upon the results of the previous repetition.

Relative Strength—A comparison of the price performance of a stock to a market index such as Standard & Poor's 500 stock index.

Relative Strength Index — An indicator invented by J. Welles Wilder and used to ascertain overbought/oversold and divergent situations.

Regression (simple)—A mathematical way of stating the statistical linear relationship between one independent and one dependent variable.

Residual Value—The standard deviation of the unexplained portion of the monthly return.

Resistance—A price level at which rising prices have stopped rising and either moved sideways or reversed direction; usually seen as a price chart pattern.

Response—The change in value of the average in response to the impulse.

Retracement—A price movement in the opposite direction of the previous trend.

Reversal Gap—A chart formation where the low of the last day is completely above the previous day's range with the close above midrange and above the open.

Reversal Stop—A stop that, when hit, is a signal to reverse the current trading position, i.e., from long to short. Also known as *stop and reverse*.

Rich—Price higher than expected.

Roll—Substituting a far option for a near option on the same underlying instrument at the same strike price; also to roll forward or roll over.

Rotation—Moving funds from one sector to another sector of the stock market as the business cycle unfolds.

Running Market—A market wherein prices are changing rapidly in one direction with very few or no price changes in the opposite direction.

Running Total — Each day's value is added to yesterday's total or subtracted if the value is negative.

Savings and Loan Investment Contracts (SLICs) — A negotiated-term deposit issued by a savings and loan.

Scalp—In commodities, purchasing and selling in equal amounts so there is no net position at the end of the trading day; a speculative attempt to make a quick profit by buying at the initial offering price in the hope the issue will increase and can be sold.

Schwarz-a-tron—A dedicated computer system for options calculations and simulations.

Seasonal Autocorrelation —Autocorrelation that shows up at 12-, 24-, 36- and 48-month lag intervals or at four, eight, 12 and 16 quarterly lags.

Seasonal Trend—A consistent but short-lived rise or drop in market activity that occurs due to predictable changes in climate or calendar.

Sector Fund—A mutual fund that concentrates on trading a range of securities within a broad industry group, such as technology, energy or financial services.

Secular Trend — Pertaining to a long indefinite period of time.

Self-Affine Transformation—A rescaling procedure used in fractal geometry and performed on a two-variable system. For example, in a system utilizing an x-axis and y-axis representing time and price, the x-axis could be rescaled by one ratio and/or procedure while the y-axis is rescaled by a different ratio and/or procedure.

Selling Short—Selling a security and then borrowing the security for delivery with the intent of replacing the security at a lower price. In futures trading, selling short is to assume the responsibility of the seller vs. the buyer in the establishment of the futures contract between parties.

Sensitivity—The rate of change of the moving average in response to the movement of the underlying data. The most sensitive period is that in which the rate of change of the moving average is fastest in response to changes in the sinewave.

Serial Correlation—The extent to which simulated net returns in adjacent quarters are correlated with one another. Simulated net returns are highly correlated if high net returns are followed by high net returns and low net returns are followed by low net returns. The autocorrelation coefficient takes values between -1 and +1 and measures the extent of serial correlation.

Serially Independent —A number that is unrelated to the previous number in a given series in any way.

Settlement—The price at which all outstanding positions in a stock or commodity are marked to market. Typically, the closing price.

Shapiro-Wilkes Test — A statistical test indicating the likelihood that the sample of simulated net returns was drawn from a normal distribution. A small value of this statistic leads to non-acceptance of the null hypothesis that the sample is drawn from a normal distribution.

Sharpe Ratio Method—(Also see *Sterling ratio method*) The Sharpe Ratio Method is the classic return/risk measure, given by:

$$\frac{E - I}{sd}$$

where:
E = Expected return
I = Risk-free interest rate
sd = Standard deviation of returns
Both the Sharpe and the Sterling ratio methods compare returns with variability of returns, as opposed to risk of loss of original investment.

Short Interest—Shares that have been sold short but not yet repurchased.

Short Interest Ratio—A ratio that indicates the number of trading days required to repurchase all of the shares that have been sold short. A short interest ratio of 2.50 would tell us that based on the current volume of trading, it will take two and a half days' volume to cover all shorts.

Signal—In the context of stock or commodity time series historical data, this is usually daily or weekly prices.

Signal Line—In artificial intelligence, a numeric variable that is prevalued in the knowledge base. In moving average jargon, the first moving average is smoothed by a second moving average. The second moving average is the signal line.

Significance—The probability of rejection on the basis of a statistical test and a hypothesis that there is no validity to the specific claim that two variations of the same thing can be distinguished by a specific procedure.

Simple Moving Average—The arithmetic mean or average of a series of prices over a period of time. The longer the period of time studied (that is, the larger the denominator of the average), the less impact an individual data point has on the average.

Simple Regression—A mathematical way of stating the statistical linear relationship between one independent and one dependent variable.

Sinewave—A wave whose amplitude varies as the sine of a linear function